The College Board
Scholarship
Handbook
2002

The College Board Scholarship Handbook

2002

Fifth Edition

Foreword by Joseph A. Russo
Director of Financial Aid
University of Notre Dame

The College Board
New York

The College Board is a national nonprofit membership association dedicated to preparing, inspiring, and connecting students to college and opportunity. Founded in 1900, the association is composed of more than 3,900 schools, colleges, universities, and other educational organizations. Each year, the College Board serves over three million students and their parents, 22,000 high schools, and 3,500 colleges, through major programs and services in college admission, guidance, assessment, financial aid, enrollment, and teaching and learning. Among its best-known programs are the SAT®, the PSAT/NMSQT™, the Advanced Placement Program® (AP®), and Pacesetter®. The College Board is committed to the principles of equity and excellence, and that commitment is embodied in all of its programs, services, activities, and concerns.

The scholarship descriptions in this book are based on information supplied by the program sponsors themselves in response to the College Board's Annual Survey of Financial Aid Programs 2001–2002. The survey was completed in the spring of 2001. Over 1,200 sponsoring organizations throughout the United States participated in this effort, and the information they provided was reviewed and verified by a staff of College Board editors. While every effort was made to ensure the completeness and accuracy of the information contained in this book, sponsors' policies and programs are subject to change without notice, and the College Board cannot take responsibility for changes made by sponsoring organizations after the information was submitted. If users of this book find that any of the descriptions are inaccurate, please contact the College Board Annual Survey of Financial Aid Programs, Attn: Guidance Services, by mail at 45 Columbus Avenue, New York, NY 10023-6992, or by telephone: 212 713-8000.

Copies of this book are available from your local bookseller or may be ordered from College Board Publications, Two College Way, Forrester Center, WV 25438. The book may also be ordered online through the College Board Store at www.collegeboard.com. The price is $25.95.

Library of Congress Catalog Number: 97-76451
International Standard Book Number: 0-87447-668-2

Printed in the United States of America

Contents

Dear Friend,

The College Board is dedicated to preparing, inspiring, and connecting students to college and opportunity, while emphasizing equity and excellence. With the College Board's publications, we hope to put an authoritative source of college information at your fingertips and help connect you to a college education.

College is a dream for many, a dream worth working hard to achieve. I've been a businessman, a governor, and now the president of the College Board, but nothing makes me prouder than to say that I graduated from college. With perseverance, anyone who desires a college education can attain one. College Board publications can help you get there.

My best wishes on your journey to success—

Gaston Caperton
President
The College Board

Foreword

A college education is understandably one of the more commonly sought-after goals of American families. The opportunities it provides are arguably the finest and most diverse in the world. Both access and wide choices are generally available to just about everyone who wants to pursue education beyond high school.

The benefits

The benefits that come with additional schooling are clearly evident to individuals as well as to our society. Most college graduates enjoy a significantly higher economic status than those without the same level of education. In addition to the obvious financial advantages, statistics show that college-educated people often live healthier and longer lives, are more involved in their communities, and raise children who are more likely to attend college and share in the same intellectually and economically richer lifestyle. Society as a whole benefits from a more involved citizenry, less crime and unemployment, and a strong tax base.

The cost factors

Steadily rising college costs have created much concern among students and parents about the affordability of this American dream. While it's true that the costs of college have been rising at a rate greater than the cost of living, media commentators have tended to exaggerate the impact of this escalation, making it appear much worse than it really is. The facts are that the vast majority (almost 75 percent) of students pay less than $8,000 a year for college tuition and fees, while only 7 percent pay more than $20,000. As Donald M. Stewart, former president of the College Board, pointed out in testimony before the U.S. Senate Hearing on Access and Costs, "the misinformation fosters public alarm and discourages many students and families from even considering the option of higher education and the chance of reaping the benefits enjoyed by those with a college degree."

The challenge

Nonetheless, paying for college is a concern for most American families. While traditional need-based financial aid programs continue to help students afford the costs of higher education, those resources are limited and more than ever include troublesome levels of student loans. Current government efforts to provide additional resources lean heavily toward further borrowing opportunities. Although such programs offer generous provisions in the form of low interest rates and deferred repayment over lengthy periods of time, they leave students and families with the prospect of long-term debt. Yet, even an individual's level of student debt upon graduation needs proper perspective, as the impact of such debt against a college graduate's starting salary is actually *less* today than it was 10 years ago, further reinforcing the value of a college degree. Nonetheless, the challenge is to find ways of achieving college and graduate school goals in the face of limited financial aid resources.

The options

The good news is that there are a number of things that families can do to position themselves to meet that challenge. The most basic step is finding out what their options are in order to make informed decisions about tailoring lifestyle choices to the needs of educational priorities.

Every family makes decisions regarding lifestyle on a regular basis. Food, housing, transportation, clothing, and entertainment are fundamental expenses, but there's considerable latitude in how much income is earmarked for any of those categories. Even if there hasn't been much advance planning, as the college-going years approach, parents have the choice of reordering some of their priorities—spending less on clothing and entertainment, for example, so they can increase the amount of money they allocate for savings and investments, or take advantage of the benefits of a tuition prepayment plan. Almost every state in the country now offers one or more programs intended to help families prepare for college costs through college savings plans or pre-paid tuition plans or both. Students have comparable choices—cutting back on what they spend for CDs, movies, or the latest fad in clothes; forgoing afternoons at the mall in favor of an after-school job; taking AP®

courses that could reduce overall college costs by a full year's tuition and fees.

Financial aid eligibility versus availability

Prior to the 1970s, before the federal government began to provide substantial aid to cover college costs, families had to depend almost entirely on their own resources. The need to save for college was paramount.

With the advent of financial aid and formulas for expected family contribution, it seemed to some that saving was counterproductive because it reduced student aid eligibility. If that point of view ever had validity, it certainly doesn't today. As families are discovering, often the hard way, *eligibility* does not automatically translate into *availability* of funds. And the funds that are available are more likely to be in the form of loans than gift aid so the results of not having saved are often a much more expensive set of options at best, or a very reduced set of college opportunities at worst. Recent legislation designed to help families through limited tax credits for tuition costs, although admirable, will fall far short of the resources needed by many families.

Incentives for saving

What is encouraging and very positive about some of the new tax legislation are the incentives to save for college. These incentives may not be of immediate help to families with students about to enter college, but they can have an impact on future years so parents should certainly investigate these avenues and begin to take advantage of them. It goes without saying that the earlier a saving program begins, the better. But the type of program and the amount of money to be set aside will depend on individual family circumstances such as income, nondiscretionary expenses, number of children, number of years remaining prior to college, and, of course, the choice of college and its actual cost when the time comes. There are simple ways of projecting costs, using an estimated inflation factor compounded by the number of years remaining before college.

Once you know the estimated costs, the next step is to develop a savings/investment plan that assumes a compounded rate of return and monthly amount to be saved. There are a number of educational and financial organizations that have developed methods for making those kinds of projections, among them the College Board and the National Association of Student Financial Aid Administrators (NASFAA). Information and guidelines are available on the Internet from those organizations as well as from a number of others, including most major investment companies.

Even with careful advance planning and saving, the majority of families need some financial aid, including loans, to help them cover the full annual costs of college. But that doesn't mean that the decision about where to apply should be based on cost of tuition and fees. Families should not be discouraged by the price tag, and should never rule out a college, no matter how expensive, before exploring every financial aid option available. All colleges and universities have a variety of programs to assist in paying the bill. Most of them include scholarship, grant, loan, and work opportunities, often combined in "packages" based on individual family circumstances. For families who do not receive financial aid or who, for whatever reason, may be concerned about meeting some remaining expenses even after financial aid has been considered, there are a number of alternatives. Some colleges offer other financial products and services as well, so it's important to find out what the "net cost" will be after all financial aid has been factored in before making a decision.

The role of private scholarships

The one additional source of funding that hasn't been addressed up to this point is private scholarship opportunities—and they can play a significant role in supplementing a family's personal resources. As this book demonstrates, there are substantial programs sponsored by foundations; civic, fraternal, veterans, and religious associations; corporations; the military; and other private and public sector organizations.

Eligibility for these programs often requires meeting some condition such as demonstrating special talents or skills; being a member of a particular organization or ethnic group; pursuing a specified major or career goal; or agreeing to fulfill some postgraduate obligation. Such programs can be very helpful, though their resources are not always adequate to meet the full demand. Applicants have to realize that they're competing for limited resources—so identifying potential programs and applying to them as early as possible offer the best chances for success.

A few words of caution—don't let your common sense be overwhelmed by the glowing claims of some commercial scholarship search companies that offer, for hefty fees, to tap into "untold millions of scholarship dollars" that go unused each year because no one applies. The general rule is that if it sounds too good to be true, it probably is. If scholarships are guaranteed for a fee, then beware. Rely on your own search efforts using resources such as this book or one of the annually updated scholarship search software programs that may be available free of charge in your local library or high school. The Internet is also an up-to-date, accurate source of free scholarship information. You can use the CD-ROM included with this book to access the College Board's online scholarship and college search programs at collegeboard.com.

There is also a growing number of other free scholarship search organizations and other enterprises on the Internet, advertising to assist in the college entrance process, that provide similar information. Some will require a "registration," which includes personal data about yourself and even your family. Those using such services should be aware of the terms and options that these registrations authorize, including the potential of sharing your personal information with other "organizations" and vendors. Again, the disclosure of your personal data to third parties should not occur without your authorized permission.

Students who want to explore scholarship prospects need to be especially diligent in their schoolwork and extracurricular activities because superior academic and personal credentials often are critical factors in awarding scholarships. Moreover, colleges tend to look favorably on the awarding of outside scholarships as an indication of students' initiative and sense of responsibility, often adjusting those students' financial aid packages to reduce the loan and work study components rather than the gift aid portion. Scholarship awards clearly enhance students' credentials and, all things being equal, make them stronger candidates from the colleges' perspective.

Meeting the challenge

Even with more than $68 billion in financial aid currently made available, paying for college is indeed a major challenge for most families. But with resources such as *The College Board Scholarship Handbook,* students and parents can expand their access to funding for college and move another step closer to their goals for the future.

Joseph A. Russo
Director of Financial Aid
University of Notre Dame

Important advice and information

How to use this book

General information

Searching for scholarships has often been described as looking for a needle in a haystack. There are thousands of award programs available, but the typical student can expect to qualify for only a small number of them. *The College Board Scholarship Handbook* with *Real Stuff* CD-ROM is designed to point you toward the specific award programs that match your own personal and academic qualifications.

What's included. Compiled within this book are detailed descriptions of national and state level award programs for undergraduates students. Most are available to all undergraduates, but some are restricted to entering freshmen, and others are only for continuing students—sophomores, juniors, or seniors. Local award programs that are restricted to a single community or school are not included; these are best located through your high school guidance office or local chamber of commerce. Also not included are award programs offered by the colleges themselves to their own students. For these "inside" awards, you should consult the financial aid offices at the colleges you are considering. Detailed financial aid information for almost 3,000 colleges can also be found in *The College Board College Cost & Financial Aid Handbook*.

The award program descriptions are based on information provided by the sponsors themselves, in response to the College Board's Annual Survey of Financial Aid Programs, conducted in the spring of 2001. A staff of editors, under the direction of Odette Blackwell, Project Manager, with the assistance of Susan Bailey and Simon Lawson, Administrative Associates, verified the facts for every award program to be certain that each description is as complete and accurate as possible. While every effort was made to ensure that the information is correct and up-to-date, we urge students to confirm facts, especially deadline information, with the programs themselves.

Getting started. The opening sections of *The College Board Scholarship Handbook* offer advice from financial aid experts, guidance on paying for college, tips for avoiding scholarship scams, answers to some of the most frequently asked questions about funding college or graduate studies, and a glossary of terms.

You may be tempted to go directly to the program descriptions and start browsing, but to get the most out of this book, start by reading the information and advice in the opening pages. They'll help you get a realistic perspective on financial aid and give you useful guidelines for understanding and taking advantage of your college funding options.

Your next step should be to complete the personal characteristics checklist on page xxiv. This will help you inventory all possible qualifications that can be used to match award program eligibility requirements. Check anything that applies to you or your family members. Even if you are undecided about a major or what career you want to pursue, check any that might be of interest. On a separate list, write down any organization, civic group, or industry that you or members of your immediate family are, or have been, involved with.

Match yourself to the programs. After your checklist is complete, use the eligibility indexes beginning on page 1 to find the award programs that correspond to your qualifications. If you have access to a Windows®-based PC with a CD-ROM drive and an Internet browser, use the *Real Stuff* CD-ROM found in the back of this book to go directly to the award-winning scholarship search program on collegeboard.com. This user-friendly program enables you to search with more criteria and with much greater speed than is possible with print indexes.

The eligibility indexes

- **Corporate/Employer:** Listed here are the many companies and businesses that offer scholarships to employees and/or their employees' dependents or relatives. You should check out any company that employs a member of your family.

- **Disabilities:** This category covers students with disabilities. Most awards in this category, as well as other categories, have additional eligibility requirements.

- **Field of Study/Intended Career:** This category, by far the longest, identifies broad major and career areas, so if you don't see your specific area of interest, look for the general area into which it might fit.

- **Gender:** Although the vast majority of awards are not gender-specific, there are over 100 awards in this book exclusively for females, and more than 20 for males.

- **International Students:** This category includes awards that are open to students from outside the United States.

- **Military Participation:** Many of the awards in this category are for the children, descendants, or spouses of members of the military, including the Reserves and National Guard, going back as far as the Civil War.

- **Minority Status:** There are seven groups within this category, representing a wide range of awards.

- **National/Ethnic Background:** The national/ethnic groups in this category are determined by the sponsoring organizations that responded to our annual survey.

- **Organization/Civic Affiliation:** Many membership organizations and civic associations have generous higher education funding programs that are available for their members and/or their members' dependents or relatives. Check to see if any apply to your family.

- **Religious Affiliation:** The 10 groups in this category represent a broad range but, like the national/ethnic category, are determined by the respondents to our annual survey.

- **Returning Adult:** This category includes awards for undergraduate, graduate, and nondegree study. The age qualification varies, but most often is for students 25 years or older.

- **State of Residence:** Each state has several award programs exclusively for state residents. Be sure to examine closely all those listed under your state.

- **Study Abroad:** While most award programs for study abroad are for graduate students, a few are geared for undergraduates, and you will find them listed here.

In addition to the eligibility indexes preceding the scholarship descriptions, there are two general indexes in the back of the book, following the descriptions, which list award programs by sponsor name and program name.

Ground rules for college planning

- When it comes to planning for college, the very first rule to remember is: *Time is money!*

Experts suggest that parents start saving for college somewhere between the time they decide on a name for the baby and the start of middle school.

- The second rule is: *It's never too early to begin saving and planning but it's never too late to develop strategies and options if your savings aren't sufficient.*

Virtually all colleges and graduate schools have financial aid professionals on staff to help you bridge the gap between your resources and the cost of attending those institutions. Last year, over $68 billion in financial aid enabled millions of students to continue their education beyond high school.

- The third rule is: *The responsibility of paying for college begins with you and your family.*

While help comes from colleges and universities as well as federal and state governments, you are a partner in the effort to cover the costs of your higher education. You are expected to contribute an amount calculated by the federal government and/or the institution you're attending as a fair share based on your family financial situation.

- The fourth rule is: *The cost of a college or graduate degree is an investment in the future.*

An investment is money spent to earn a financial return—and for most people, one of the benefits of a college education is higher lifetime earnings potential. When you add to that some of the more subjective benefits such as broadened perspectives and interests, expanded knowledge, and friendships, college begins to look like one of the best, most reliable, and high-yield investments you can make.

Advice to parents: The "five C's" of preparing for college and graduate school costs

1. **Collect** as much information as possible. Catalogs from colleges and graduate schools, federal government brochures, state education department publications, bank and credit union information, and, increasingly important, Web sites on the Internet, provide extensive information on college preparatory courses, college savings strategies, college costs, financial aid programs, and private sector scholarship opportunities.

2. **Coordinate** the information and develop a timetable for getting the most out of your own resources. Understand what colleges and graduate studies cost today, anticipate that those costs will continue to increase, and at least estimate what share of those costs you might be expected to pay. If you're starting the planning process several years before that first tuition bill is due, you have a number of options to consider in terms of savings and investment strategies. You also have time to explore need and non-need scholarship opportunities to get an idea of what supplemental funds may be available.

3. **Consider** all of your options and opportunities. Time can be your most important advantage if you have even modest resources to invest in the stock market, mutual funds, prepaid tuition plans, state-sponsored Section 529 college savings programs, or in "Education IRA" savings plans. Remember that, although 68 billion dollars of financial aid was available to students last year, an increasing percentage of that money is in the form of education loans. Making your money work for you enables you to earn interest now rather than pay interest later.

4. **Communicate** with college or graduate school financial aid offices and with private sector scholarship programs. Find out in advance what their requirements and application deadlines are; get a sense of what typical college financial aid packages or private scholarship awards may consist of and whether they're renewable. This book is a good place to either start or continue your efforts. The extensive listing of award programs illustrates the extent to which support is available to supplement what you are able to contribute toward college costs.

5. **Copy** all scholarship applications and financial aid documents you submit and keep them on file so that you can refer to them if any questions arise or duplicate them if necessary. No matter how reliable the

postal service and electronic communications systems are, sometimes things you've sent get lost in the mail, don't arrive by fax, or disappear on their way via e-mail. Don't risk having to start over from scratch if that should happen.

Take the time to collect, coordinate, consider, communicate, and copy—you'll find that it's a wise investment of your time and your money.

Jack Joyce
Director, Guidance Services and
Manager, Training and Special Projects
The College Board

What does college cost?
How much will you be expected to pay?

Some of the best things in life may be free, but college is not one of them. The purpose of this book is to help you:

- understand the components of college costs
- get a sense of what you'll be expected to contribute toward those costs
- learn from financial aid experts about ground rules and strategies for paying for college
- find additional resources to cover the costs of your college education

The components of college costs

Whether you're an undergraduate or graduate student, part-time or full-time, commuting or living on campus, your outlay is going to include both direct educational expenses and living expenses. Typically, they fall into the following five categories:

- tuition and fees
- books and supplies
- room and board
- personal expenses
- transportation

Tuition and fees

Tuition is the charge for instruction. Fees may be charged for services such as Internet access, student activities, or the health center. The amount of tuition and fees charged by a particular college varies considerably. Public colleges, because they're funded by tax dollars, are generally less expensive than private institutions, though out-of-state (or, in the case of community colleges, out-of-district) students usually pay higher tuition, which can make a public college as costly as a private one for nonresident students.

Books and supplies

The amount you spend for books, pens, pencils, paper, and other basic supplies isn't affected by the type of college you're attending, but will vary considerably based on the courses you're taking. Science, engineering, and art courses, for example, require specialized equipment and materials.

Room and board

Whether you live in a campus dorm or in a private apartment off-campus, you have to cover the basic living expenses of food and housing. Even students who live at home have to factor in meals and snacks at school, and their parents still have the expense of providing them with living quarters and food.

Personal expenses

You're probably used to paying for some of your personal expenses—clothes, toiletries, magazines, CDs, movies. But once you're at college, you're also going to be responsible for laundry and dry cleaning bills, phone bills, accessories and supplies for your living quarters, and a lot of other little incidentals, which can add up to anywhere from $600 to more than twice that.

Transportation

If you live on campus, you will need to consider the cost of travelling to get there at the beginning of the academic year and to return home at the end, and for as many times as you expect to go home during the year. For financial aid purposes, colleges often factor in two round-trips home per year by the lowest-cost means of transportation available. If you're a commuter student, you will need to figure the cost of your weekly commute, either by public transportation or by private car. These costs, too, are built into student expense budgets by colleges for financial aid purposes.

Estimating your expected family contribution

As Jack Joyce of the College Board's Guidance Services pointed out in the preceding section, the responsibility of paying for college begins with you and your parents. The amount that you as a family are expected to pay is the sum of what your parents can contribute from their income and assets plus what you can contribute from earnings and savings. If you're curious about what that means in terms of dollars, the table on page xvi gives you a sense of what parental contribution is expected at various income and asset levels. Pick the combination of annual income and asset figures that are closest to your family's, and you'll have a very rough idea of what your parents' share might be.

Don't panic!

Although the expense of going to college or graduate school may seem like a heavy burden, the fact is that the majority of students get financial aid that covers at least a portion of the cost. Of the four basic potential sources, this book deals with the first three listed below:

1. Much of the aid comes from the federal government in the form of grants, work-study programs, and subsidized loans.

2. State governments also dispense significant amounts of financial aid in various forms to state residents.

3. In addition, there are a number of private foundations and corporations that have established scholarship programs to help qualified students pay for college.

4. Financial aid awards sponsored and administered by colleges, universities, and graduate schools are another important resource. They include scholarships, fellowships, fee waivers, internships, and teaching and research assistantships. Because criteria and application procedures vary considerably, your best source of information is the institution's own catalog or financial aid bulletin.

In this book you'll find detailed descriptions of over 2,300 scholarship, internship, and loan programs representing over two million awards, with eligibility indexes to help you zero in on the awards for which you're likely to qualify.

Frequently asked questions

Q When should I start looking for scholarships?

A It's never too early to start finding out about what kinds of scholarships are available. If you're a high school student, it's a good idea to start research in your sophomore or junior year, even if you can't apply until you're a senior. If you're in college and need financial aid for graduate school, there's no time like the present to start exploring your options.

Q Will going to college part-time lessen my chances of receiving aid?

A Depending on your personal circumstances, you could be eligible for a Pell Grant and a number of other forms of federal aid. Many of the private sector scholarships in this book make no distinction between full-time and part-time study in awarding funds.

Q Are international students eligible for financial aid?

A If you're an international student (a noncitizen from abroad), you're generally not eligible for tax-supported aid such as federal or state grants, but there are private sector awards included in this book for which international students are eligible.

Q If I get a scholarship from a foundation or corporation, will the financial aid offered by the college be affected?

A Colleges' policies on outside scholarships vary a great deal, so you'd have to check with the financial aid officer at the college itself to find out.

Q Is it true that my college financial aid package could be reduced by as much as the full amount of any outside scholarship I receive?

A Probably yes if your financial aid package meets your full need (as measured by the college); probably no if your need has been only partially met. The other factor to take into consideration is that many colleges will reduce the loan or work-study component of your aid package rather than the gift aid portion.

Q Are there scholarships that cover the whole four years or are they only awarded for one year?

A That varies from sponsor to sponsor. Many undergraduate scholarships cover a single year of study but are renewable. Some graduate and postgraduate grants and fellowships cover the entire period required to earn the degree or complete a research project.

2001–2002 Estimated parents' contribution

Net assets	$25,000				$50,000			
Family size	**3**	**4**	**5**	**6**	**3**	**4**	**5**	**6**
2000 income before taxes								
$10,000	$0	$0	$0	$0	$0	$0	$0	$0
$15,000	$0	$0	$0	$0	$0	$0	$0	$0
$20,000	$0	$0	$0	$0	$0	$0	$0	$0
$25,000	$200	$0	$0	$0	$401	$0	$0	$0
$30,000	$963	$233	$0	$0	$1,164	$433	$0	$0
$35,000	$1,726	$996	$311	$0	$1,927	$1,196	$512	$0
$40,000	$2,489	$1,758	$1,074	$302	$2,714	$1,959	$1,275	$503
$45,000	$3,372	$2,523	$1,837	$1,065	$3,637	$2,751	$2,038	$1,265
$50,000	$4,430	$3,415	$2,612	$1,828	$4,740	$3,679	$2,840	$2,028
$55,000	$5,706	$4,480	$3,519	$2,602	$6,071	$4,790	$3,783	$2,830
$60,000	$7,221	$5,765	$4,602	$3,506	$7,650	$6,130	$4,912	$3,771
$65,000	$8,546	$7,156	$5,908	$4,587	$8,974	$7,585	$6,282	$4,897
$70,000	$9,870	$8,480	$7,190	$5,787	$10,298	$8,909	$7,618	$6,152
$75,000	$11,194	$9,805	$8,514	$7,035	$11,623	$10,233	$8,943	$7,464
$80,000	$12,629	$11,240	$9,949	$8,470	$13,058	$11,668	$10,378	$8,899
$85,000	$14,099	$12,710	$11,419	$9,940	$14,528	$13,138	$11,848	$10,369
$90,000	$15,569	$14,179	$12,889	$11,410	$15,997	$14,608	$13,318	$11,839
$95,000	$17,039	$15,649	$14,359	$12,880	$17,467	$16,078	$14,787	$13,309
$100,000	$18,509	$17,119	$15,829	$14,350	$18,937	$17,548	$16,257	$14,779

Net assets	$100,000				$150,000			
Family size	**3**	**4**	**5**	**6**	**3**	**4**	**5**	**6**
2000 income before taxes								
$10,000	$0	$0	$0	$0	$563	$0	$0	$0
$15,000	$170	$0	$0	$0	$1,490	$668	$0	$0
$20,000	$958	$228	$0	$0	$2,278	$1,548	$819	$0
$25,000	$1,721	$990	$306	$0	$3,114	$2,310	$1,626	$854
$30,000	$2,484	$1,753	$1,069	$297	$4,104	$3,150	$2,389	$1,617
$35,000	$3,366	$2,517	$1,832	$1,060	$5,323	$4,154	$3,241	$2,380
$40,000	$4,422	$3,408	$2,607	$1,823	$6,796	$5,382	$4,276	$3,229
$45,000	$5,697	$4,472	$3,512	$2,596	$8,425	$6,865	$5,525	$4,261
$50,000	$7,235	$5,756	$4,594	$3,500	$10,055	$8,495	$7,033	$5,508
$55,000	$8,865	$7,304	$5,899	$4,579	$11,685	$10,124	$8,663	$7,013
$60,000	$10,470	$8,934	$7,472	$5,882	$13,290	$11,754	$10,292	$8,643
$65,000	$11,794	$10,405	$9,102	$7,452	$14,614	$13,225	$11,922	$10,272
$70,000	$13,118	$11,729	$10,438	$8,960	$15,938	$14,549	$13,258	$11,780
$75,000	$14,443	$13,053	$11,763	$10,284	$17,263	$15,873	$14,583	$13,104
$80,000	$15,878	$14,488	$13,198	$11,719	$18,698	$17,308	$16,018	$14,539
$85,000	$17,348	$15,958	$14,668	$13,189	$20,168	$18,778	$17,488	$16,009
$90,000	$18,817	$17,428	$16,138	$14,659	$21,637	$20,248	$18,958	$17,479
$95,000	$20,287	$18,898	$17,607	$16,129	$23,107	$21,718	$20,427	$18,949
$100,000	$21,757	$20,368	$19,077	$17,599	$24,577	$23,188	$21,897	$20,419

Note: The figures shown are parents' contribution under Federal Methodology (FM), assuming the older parent is age 45; both parents are employed (equal wages); income is only from employment; no unusual circumstances; standard deductions on U.S. income tax; 1040 tax return filed; and one undergraduate child enrolled in college. Net assets exclude primary place of residence and family farms.

How to avoid scholarship scams

As college costs continue to rise, families have begun to look beyond government and college sources of funding, which has given rise to a growing industry of scholarship search services. Some do a responsible job for a modest fee, but many make unrealistic claims and charge substantial fees. Some are outright fraudulent in their tactics.

Buyer beware!

The Federal Trade Commission (FTC) developed Project $cholar$cam to alert consumers about potential scams and how to recognize them. Here are the FTC's six basic warning signs and advice:

"The scholarship is guaranteed or your money back."
> No one can guarantee that they'll get you a grant or a scholarship. Refund policies often have conditions or strings attached. Get refund policies in writing before you pay.

"You can't get this information anywhere else."
> Check with your school or library before you decide to pay someone to do the work for you.

"May I have your credit card or bank account number to hold this scholarship?"
> Don't give out your credit card or bank account number on the phone without getting information in writing first. It may be a setup for an unauthorized withdrawal.

"We'll do all the work for you."
> Don't be fooled. There's no way around it. You must apply for scholarships or grants yourself.

"The scholarship will cost some money."
> Don't pay anyone who claims to be "holding" a scholarship or grant for you. Free money shouldn't cost a thing.

"You've been selected by a national foundation to receive a scholarship" or "You're a finalist" in a contest you never entered.
> Before you send money to apply for a scholarship, check it out. Make sure the foundation or program is legitimate.

Sources of information about state grant programs

Alabama
Alabama Commission on Higher Education
P.O. Box 302000
Montgomery, AL 36130-2000
334 242-1998; www.ache.state.al.us

Alaska
Alaska Commission on Postsecondary Education
3030 Vintage Boulevard
Juneau, AK 99801-7109
907 465-6740; www.state.ak.us/acpe

Arizona
Department of Education
P.O. Box 6490
Phoenix, AZ 85005
602 542-4367; www.ade.state.az.us

Arkansas
Department of Higher Education
114 East Capitol
Little Rock, AR 72201
501 371-2000; www.adhe.arknet.edu

California
California Student Aid Commission
P.O. Box 419026
Rancho Cordova, CA 95741-9026
916 526-7590; www.edfund.org

Colorado
Department of Education
1300 Broadway
Denver, CO 80203
303 866-2723; www.state.co.us

Connecticut
Department of Higher Education
61 Woodland Street
Hartford, CT 06105
860 947-1800; www.ctdhe.org/dheweb

Delaware
Delaware Higher Education Commission
820 North French Street
Fourth Floor
Wilmington, DE 19801
302 577-3240; www.doe.state.de.us

Florida
Florida Department of Education, Office of Student Financial Assistance
325 West Gaines Street
Tallahassee, FL 32399-0400
850 488-4095; www.firn.edu/doe

Georgia
Georgia Student Finance Authority
2082 East Exchange Place
Suite 100
Tucker, GA 30084
770 724-9000; www.hope.gsfc.org

Hawaii
Hawaii Department of Education
244 Dole Street
Honolulu, HI 96822-2394
808 956-8213

Idaho
Office of the State Board of Education
P.O. Box 83720
Boise, ID 83720-0037
208 334-2270; www.sde.state.id.us

Illinois
Illinois Student Assistance Commission
1755 Lake Cook Road
Deerfield, IL 60015
800 899-4722; www.isac-online.org

Indiana
State Student Assistance Commission of Indiana
150 W. Market Street
Suite 500
Indianapolis, IN 46204
317 232-2350; www.ai.org/ssaci

Iowa

Iowa College Student Aid Commission
200 Tenth Street
Fourth Floor
Des Moines, IA 50309-3609
www.state.ia.us/collegeaid

Kansas

Board of Regents
700 SW Harrison
Suite 1410
Topeka, KS 66603-3760
785 296-3421; www.kansasregents.org

Kentucky

KHEAA Student Aid Branch
1050 U.S. 127 South
Frankfort, KY 40601
502 696-7345; www.kheaa.com

Louisiana

Office of Student Financial Assistance for Louisiana
Scholarship/Grant Division
P.O. Box 91202
Baton Rouge, LA 70821-9202
800 259-5626; www.osfa.state.la.us

Maine

Finance Authority of Maine
Maine Education Assistance Division
P.O. Box 949
83 Western Avenue
Augusta, ME 04333
207 623-3263; www.famemaine.com

Maryland

Maryland Higher Education Commission/
State Scholarship Administration
16 Francis Street
Annapolis, MD 21401-1781
410 974-5370; www.mhec.state.md.us

Massachusetts

Board of Higher Education,
Office of Student Financial Assistance
One Ashburton Place, Rm 1401
Boston, MA 02116
617 994-6950; www.mefa.org

Michigan

Michigan Higher Education Assistance Authority,
Office of Scholarships and Grants
P.O. Box 30462
Lansing, MI 48909
517 373-3394; www.treas.state.mi.us

Minnesota

Minnesota Higher Education Services Office
1450 Energy Park Drive
Suite 350
St. Paul, MN 55101
651 642-0533; www.mheso.state.mn.us

Mississippi

Mississippi Office of State Student Financial Aid
3825 Ridgewood Road
Jackson, MS 39211-6453
601 982-6663

Missouri

Missouri Coordinating Board for Higher Education
3515 Amazonas Drive
Jefferson City, MO 65109
573 751-3940; www.mocbhe.gov

Montana

Montana Board of Regents of Higher Education
P.O. Box 203101
Helena, MT 59620-3101
406 444-6570; www.montana.edu

Nebraska

Nebraska Department of Education
P.O. Box 95005
Lincoln, NE 68509
402 471-2847; www.ccpe.state.ne.us

Nevada

Nevada Department of Education, Financial Aid
700 East 5th Street
Capitol Complex
Carson City, NV 89701
775 687-9200; www.nde.state.nv.us

New Hampshire

New Hampshire Postsecondary Education Commission
2 Industrial Park Drive
Concord, NH 03301-8512
603 271-2555; www.state.nh.us

New Jersey
New Jersey Higher Education Student Assistance Authority
4 Quakerbridge Plaza
P.O. Box 540
Trenton, NJ 08625
800 792-8670; www.hesaa.org

New Mexico
Commission on Higher Education
1068 Cerillos Road
Santa Fe, NM 87501-4295
505 827-7383; www.nmche.org

New York
Higher Education Services Corporation,
Student Information
99 Washington Ave.
14th Floor
Albany, NY 12255
888 697-4372; www.hesc.state.ny.us

North Carolina
North Carolina State Education Assistance Authority
P.O. Box 13663
Research Triangle Park, NC 27709-3663
919 549-8614; www.nsceaa.edu

North Dakota
North Dakota University System
600 East Boulevard
Dept. 215
Bismarck, ND 58505
701 328-4114; www.ndus.nodak.edu

Ohio
Ohio Board of Regents
P.O. Box 1842452
Columbus, OH 43218-2452
614 466-7420; www.regents.state.oh.us

Oklahoma
Oklahoma State Regents for Higher Education,
Tuition Aid Grant Program
500 Education Bldg.
Oklahoma City, OK 73105-4500
405 524-9100; www.okhighered.org

Oregon
Oregon State Scholarship Commission,
Valley River Office Park
1500 Valley River Drive, Suite 100
Eugene, OR 97401
800 452-8807; www.ossc.state.or.us

Pennsylvania
Pennsylvania Higher Education Assistance Agency
1200 N. Seventh St.
Harrisburg, PA 17102
800 233-0557; www.pheaa.org

Puerto Rico
Departmento de Educacion
P.O. Box 190759
San Juan, PR 00919-0759
787 724-7100

Rhode Island
Rhode Island Higher Education Assistance Authority
560 Jefferson Boulevard
Warwick, RI 02886
401 736-1100; www.riheaa.org

South Carolina
South Carolina Tuition Grants Commission
1310 Lady Street
Suite 811
P.O. Box 12159
Columbia, SC 29211
803 737-2260; www.che400.state.sc.us

South Dakota
Department of Education and Cultural Affairs,
Office of the Secretary
700 Governors Drive
Pierre, SD 57501-2291
605 773-3134; www.state.sd.us/deca

Tennessee
Tennessee Student Assistance Corporation
Parkway Towers Suite 1950
404 James Robertson Parkway
Nashville, TN 37243-0820
615 741-3605; www.state.tn.us/thec

Texas
Texas Higher Education Coordinating Board
Division of Student Services
P.O. Box 12788, Capital Station
Austin, TX 78711
512 483-6101; www.thecb.state.tx.us

Utah
Utah Higher Education Assistance Authority
355 West North Temple
3 Triad Center, Suite 550
Salt Lake City, UT 84180
801 321-7200; www.uheaa.org

Vermont
Vermont Student Assistance Corporation
Champlain Mill, P.O. Box 2000
Winooski, VT 05404-2601
802 655-9602; www.vsac.org

Virginia
Virginia Council of Higher Education
James Monroe Building
101 North 14th Street
Richmond, VA 23219
804 225-2628; www.schev.edu

Washington
Washington State Higher Education Coordination Board
917 Lakeridge Way
P.O. Box 43430
Olympia, WA 98504-3430
360 753-7800; www.hecb.wa.gov

West Virginia
West Virginia State College and University Systems
Central Office, Higher Education Grant Program
1018 Kanawha Boulevard East
Suite 700
Charleston, WV 25301-2827
304 558-3264; www.usys.wvnet.edu

Wisconsin
Wisconsin Higher Educational Aids Board
131 West Wilson
P.O. Box 7885
Madison, WI 53707
608 267-2578; www.heab.state.wi.us

Wyoming
Wyoming State Department of Education
Hathaway Building
2300 Capitol Avenue
Cheyenne, WY 82002
307 777-6265; www.k12.wy.us

Guam
Student Financial Aid Office UOG Station, 40G Station
Mangilao, GU 96923
671 734-4469

Virgin Islands
Financial Aid Office, Virgin Islands Board of Education
P.O. Box 11900
St. Thomas, VI 00801
809 774-4546

What's in the program descriptions

The scholarship programs in this book are organized alphabetically by sponsor within three sections:

- **Scholarships:** This section covers public and private scholarships and research grants for undergraduates. To be included, a scholarship program must be granting a monetary award of at least $250 in the upcoming year for the purpose of financing some aspect of higher education: tuition and fees, research, study abroad, travel expenses, or other educational endeavors.

- **Internships:** This section covers public and private internships, providing opportunities to either earn money for education or to gain academic credit. To be included, paid internships must pay at least $100 per week and provide a viable path towards a future career. (The Sony Music internship is an example of this—the Oscar Mayer Wienermobile is not.)

- **Loans:** This section covers public and private educational loan programs. Many have loan forgiveness options, usually in exchange for public or community service for a certain period of time.

Each program description contains all of the information provided by the sponsor and verified for accuracy by a staff of editors at the College Board. A typical description includes:

Type of award: tells you whether the award is a scholarship, grant, internship, or loan; and whether it's renewable

Intended use: tells you the range and limitations of the award, such as level of study, full-time or part-time, at what kind of institution, whether in the United States or abroad

Eligibility: indicates the characteristics you must have to be considered for an award—for example, U.S. citizenship, specific state of residence, disability, membership in a particular organization, minority status

Basis for selection: may include major or career interest; personal qualities such as seriousness of purpose, high academic achievement, depth of character; financial need

Application requirements: outlines what you must provide in support of your application, such as recommendations, essay, transcript, interview, proof of eligibility, résumé, references

Additional information: gives you any facts or requirements not covered in the categories above—for example, which test scores to submit, GPA level required, whether a particular type of student is given special consideration, when application forms are available, etc.

Amount of award: a single figure generally means the standard amount, but may indicate the maximum of a range of amounts; two figures indicate the range of awards from lowest to highest amounts

Number of awards: tells you how many awards are granted by the sponsor

Number of applicants: tells you how many students applied the previous year

Application deadline: the date by which your application must be submitted; some scholarships have two deadlines for considering applications

Notification begins: the earliest date that an award notification is sent; in some cases, all go out on the same date, in others, notification is on a rolling basis; if there are two application deadlines, there are usually two notification dates

Total amount awarded: tells you how much money is disbursed in the current award year, including renewable awards

Contact name, address, phone, fax, and Web site: gives you all available information on where to get application forms and further information. Where the contact name and address are identical for several different scholarship programs sponsored by the same organization, this information will appear at the end of the last scholarship in that group.

While some descriptions don't include all these details because they were either not applicable or not supplied by the sponsor, in every case all essential information is provided.

Glossary

College Scholarship Service® (CSS®). A unit of the College Board's College and University Enrollment Services (CUES) that assists postsecondary institutions, state scholarship programs, and private scholarship organizations in the equitable and efficient distribution of student financial aid funds.

Credit by examination: Academic credit granted by a college to entering students who have demonstrated proficiency in college-level studies through examinations such as those sponsored by the College Board's AP and CLEP® programs. This is a means of cutting college costs by reducing the number of courses needed to earn a degree.

CSS/Financial Aid PROFILE®. A form and service offered by the College Board and used by some colleges, universities, and private scholarship programs to award their own private financial aid funds. Students pay a fee to register for PROFILE and send reports to institutions and programs that use it. Students register with CSS® by calling a toll-free telephone service or by connecting to the College Board Web site: collegeboard.com. CSS provides a customized application for each registrant, based on the individual's information and the requirements of the colleges and programs from which she or he is seeking aid. Students complete and submit the customized application and supplements, if required, to CSS for processing and reporting to institutions. CSS/Financial Aid PROFILE® is not a federal form and may not be used to apply for federal student aid.

Expected family contribution: The total amount that you and your family are expected to pay toward college costs from your income and assets. The amount is determined by a need analysis of your family's overall financial circumstances. A Federal Methodology is used to determine your eligibility for federal student aid. Colleges, state agencies, and private aid programs may use a different methodology in assessing eligibility for nonfederal sources of financial aid.

Federal Work-Study Program: A federally sponsored campus-based program. Participating colleges provide employment opportunities for students with demonstrated need who are enrolled at either the undergraduate or graduate level.

Fellowship: A form of graduate financial aid that usually requires service—often in the form of time devoted to a research project.

Financial aid package: The total financial aid award offered to you. It may be made up of a combination of aid that includes both gift aid (which doesn't have to be repaid) and self-help (work-study and/or loans). Many colleges try to meet a student's full financial need, but availability of funds, the institution's aid policies, and the number of students needing aid all affect the composition of a financial aid package.

Financial need: The difference between the cost of attending college and your expected family contribution.

Free Application for Federal Student Aid (FAFSA): A form you must complete to apply for federal student aid. In many states, completing the FAFSA is the way to establish your eligibility for state-sponsored aid programs. There is no charge to you for submitting this form, which is widely available in high schools and colleges, and may be filed any time after January 1 of the year for which you're seeking aid.

Internship: A short-term, supervised work experience, usually related to your major, for which you may earn either academic credit or a stipend.

Need analysis form: The starting point in applying for financial aid. All students must file the FAFSA to apply for federal financial aid programs. Some colleges will also require CSS/Financial Aid PROFILE to determine eligibility for nonfederal financial aid. To apply for state financial aid programs, the FAFSA may be all that you'll need to file, but check to be sure.

Research grants: Some scholarships are for research and require you to describe the project for which you're requesting funds. Although most research grants are for graduate students, some in this book are available for undergraduates.

SASE: Self-addressed stamped envelope.

Scholarship or grant: A type of financial aid that doesn't have to be repaid. Grants are often based on financial need. Scholarships may be based on need, on need combined with other criteria, or solely on other criteria such as academic achievement, artistic ability, talent in the performing arts, and the like.

Personal characteristics checklist

Disability:
- ☐ hearing
- ☐ learning
- ☐ physical
- ☐ visual

Field of study/intended career:
- ☐ Agricultural science, business, and natural resources conservation
- ☐ Architecture and design
- ☐ Area and ethnic studies
- ☐ Arts, visual and performing
- ☐ Biological and physical sciences
- ☐ Business, management, administration
- ☐ Communications
- ☐ Computer and information sciences
- ☐ Education
- ☐ Engineering and engineering technology
- ☐ English and literature
- ☐ Foreign languages
- ☐ Health professions and allied services
- ☐ Home economics
- ☐ Law
- ☐ Liberal arts and interdisciplinary studies
- ☐ Library science
- ☐ Mathematics
- ☐ Military science
- ☐ Mortuary science
- ☐ Protective services
- ☐ Philosophy, religion, and theology
- ☐ Social sciences and history
- ☐ Trade and industry

☐ Female   ☐ Male
☐ International student   ☐ Returning adult

Military participation/affiliation:
- ☐ Air Force
- ☐ Army
- ☐ Marines
- ☐ Coast Guard
- ☐ Navy
- ☐ Reserves/National Guard

Minority status:
- ☐ African American
- ☐ Alaskan Native
- ☐ American Indian
- ☐ Asian American
- ☐ Hispanic American
- ☐ Mexican American
- ☐ Puerto Rican

National/ethnic background:
- ☐ Armenian
- ☐ Chinese
- ☐ Danish
- ☐ Greek
- ☐ Italian
- ☐ Japanese
- ☐ Mongolian
- ☐ Polish
- ☐ Swiss
- ☐ Ukrainian
- ☐ Welsh

Religious affiliation:
- ☐ Christian
- ☐ Eastern Orthodox
- ☐ Episcopal
- ☐ Jewish
- ☐ Lutheran
- ☐ Presbyterian (USA)
- ☐ Protestant
- ☐ Roman Catholic
- ☐ Unitarian Universalist
- ☐ United Methodist

Want to study abroad: ☐

Eligibility Indexes

Corporate/Employer

Disabilities

Hearing impaired

Learning disabled

Physically challenged

Visually impaired

Field of Study/ Intended Career

Agricultural science, business, and natural resources conservation

Architecture and design

Area and ethnic studies

Arts, visual and performing

Biological and physical sciences

Eligibility Indexes

Business/management/administration

Communications

Computer and information sciences

Education

Engineering and engineering technology

Home economics

Law

ORISE Energy Research Undergraduate Laboratory Fellowships (DOE), 547
ORISE Fossil Energy Technology Internship, 547
ORISE Office of Civilian Radioactive Waste Management Scholarship, 379
ORISE Professional Internship Program at Federal Energy Technology Center, 548
ORISE Student Research - National Center for Toxicological Research, 549
ORISE U.S. Nuclear Regulatory Commission Historically Black Colleges and Universities Student Research Participation, 559
Pacific Gas and Electric Internships, 551
Payzer Scholarship, 212
Pearl I. Young Scholarship, 323
Plasma Physics National Undergraduate Fellowship Program, 552
ROTC/Air Force Four-Year Scholarship (Types 1, 2 and Targeted), 412
ROTC/Air Force Three-Year Scholarship (Types 2 and Targeted), 413
SEG Foundation Scholarship, 419
SGI (Silicon Graphics) Internship/ Co-op Program, 554
Siemens Awards for Advanced Placement, 422
Siemens Westinghouse Science & Technology Competition, 422
State Farm Companies Exceptional Student Fellowship, 449
UNCF/GTE Summer Science Program, 480
Undergraduate Scholarship Program, 491
Vermont Space Grant Consortium Undergraduate Scholarships, 484
Washington Gas Scholarships, 490
Willems Scholarship, 316

Military science

Center for Defense Information Internship, 515
Horizons Foundation Scholarship, 253
NROTC Scholarship Program, 469
United States Army Four-Year Nursing Scholarship, 413
United States Army Four-Year Scholarship, 413

Mortuary science

Mortuary Education Grant, 250

Philosophy, religion, and theology

Denver Rescue Mission Interns, 518

Institute for Humane Studies Fellowship, 262
Ira Page Wallace Bible Scholarship, 400
Juliette M. Atherton Scholarship, 244
Knights Templar Educational Foundation Loan, 570
Leonard M. Perryman Communications Scholarship for Ethnic Minority Students, 474
Marion MacCarrell Scott Scholarship, 245
Mellon Minority Undergraduate Fellowship Program, 152
National Federation of the Blind Humanities Scholarship, 336
United Methodist Bass Scholarship, 473

Protective services

Alphonso Deal Scholarship, 332
Developmental Disabilities and Mental Health Workforce Tuition Assistance Program, 294
Firefighter Exemption, 456
Floyd Boring Award, 284
Former Agents of the U.S. Secret Service Scholarship, 163
Honors Internship Program, 522
Law and Social Sciences Summer Research Fellowship for Minority Undergraduates, 510
Maryland Reimbursement of Firefighters, 298
National Technical Investigators' Captain James J. Regan Memorial Scholarship, 284
Police Corps Scholarship, 468
Sheryl A. Horak Law Enforcement Explorer Scholarship, 284

Social sciences and history

American Center of Oriental Research/Jennifer C. Groot Fellowship, 72
Anne U. White Fund, 162
ARRL Donald Riebhoff Memorial Scholarship, 135
Assunta Lucchetti Martino Scholarship for International Studies, 340
Behavioral Sciences Student Fellowship, 218
Bethesda Lutheran Homes and Services Cooperative Program Internship, 513
Bolla Wines Scholarship, 340
Business and Professional Women's Career Advancement Scholarship, 179
Center for Defense Information Internship, 515
CIA Undergraduate Scholarship, 189
The Cloisters Summer Internship Program, 534

Congressional Institute Internships, 516
Congressional Internship, 516
Congressman Alfred E. Santangelo and Betty Santangelo Scholarship, 341
Delaware Space Grant Undergraduate Summer Scholarship, 326
Delaware Space Grant Undergraduate Tuition Scholarship, 327
Denver Rescue Mission Interns, 518
Developmental Disabilities and Mental Health Workforce Tuition Assistance Program, 294
Developmental Disability Scholastic Achievement Scholarship, 171
Dr. Hans and Clara Zimmerman Foundation Health Scholarship, 242
Edward D. Stone, Jr., and Associates Minority Scholarship, 282
Federal Reserve Cooperative Education Program, 514
Federal Reserve Summer Internship, 522
Ford Motor Company Fellows Program, 539
Frank J. Corsaro Scholarship, 341
Franklin D. Roosevelt Library/Roosevelt Summer Internship, 524
Friends of Oregon Students Scholarship, 386
Geography Students Internship, 540
Harriett Barnhart Wimmer Scholarship, 282
Harry S. Truman Scholarship, 239
Horizons Foundation Scholarship, 253
House Member Internships, 560
Institute for Humane Studies Fellowship, 262
Karla Scherer Foundation Scholarship, 277
Kawasaki-McGaha Scholarship Fund, 244
Kennedy Library Archival Internship, 530
Knights Templar Educational Foundation Loan, 570
Law and Social Sciences Summer Research Fellowship for Minority Undergraduates, 510
Library of Congress Anvario Hispano Hispanic Division Fellowship, 532
Marion MacCarrell Scott Scholarship, 245
Mashantucket Pequot Public Policy Internship Program, 533
Mellon Minority Undergraduate Fellowship Program, 152
Michael and Marie Marucci Scholarship, 336
Mildred Towle Trust Fund Scholarship, 246
Mississippi Health Care Professional Loan/Scholarship, 574
Mississippi Psychology Apprenticeship Program, 535

Trade and industry

Gender

Female

Male

Eligibility Index

American Legion Missouri Lillie Lois Ford Boy's Scholarship, 106

American Legion National Eagle Scout of the Year, 108

American Legion New Hampshire Boys State Scholarship, 111

American Legion "Boy Scout of the Year" Award, 97

American Legion Wisconsin Eagle Scout of the Year Scholarship, 126

Arthur E. Copeland Scholarship for Males, 481

Boy Scouts of America/Eastern Orthodox Committee on Scouting Scholarship, 174

E. Urner Goodman Scholarship, 174

Eagle Scout of the Year Award, 122

Frank D. Visceglia Memorial Scholarship, 284

Frank L. Weil Memorial Eagle Scout Scholarship, 348

Frank W. McHale Memorial Scholarship, 96

Mooty Scholarship, 201

National Eagle Scout Scholarship, 174

Sigma Alpha Epsilon Resident Educational Advisor, 554

Sigma Alpha Epsilon Scholarships, 423

Sons of the American Revolution Eagle Scout Scholarship, 354

Spence Reese Scholarship, 175

Willems Scholarship, 316

International Student

Account for Your Future Scholarship, 403

Alaska Airlines Travel Industry Scholarship, 147

American Center of Oriental Research/Jennifer C. Groot Fellowship, 72

American Express Travel Scholarship, 148

American Heart Association Undergraduate Student Research Program, 82

ASM International Foundation Undergraduate Scholarship, 160

Barbara Carlson Scholarship, 167

BMI Student Composer Awards, 172

Cal Grant A Entitlement Award Program, 183

Cal Grant B Entitlement Award Program, 183

Cal Grant C Award Program, 183

Carl F. Dietz Memorial Scholarship, 167

Chevron Accounting Internship Program, 515

Competitive Cal Grant A and B Award Programs, 184

Daughters of Penelope Past Grand Presidents Award, 205

Dosatron International Scholarship, 167

Dr. Tom Anderson Memorial Scholarship, 356

Earl J. Small Growers Scholarship, 167

Ed Markham International Scholarship, 168

Emily Tamaras Memorial Award, 205

Enology and Viticulture Scholarship, 141

Eric and Bette Friedhiem Scholarship, 356

Federal Reserve Summer Internship, 522

Fight-For-Sight Student Research Fellowship, 220

Fran Johnson Non-Traditional Scholarship, 168

Genentech Internship Program, 525

Ginger and Fred Deines Canada Scholarship, 462

Ginger and Fred Deines Mexico Scholarship, 462

Guggenheim Museum Internship, 555

H. Neil Mecaskey Scholarship, 356

Hannaford Internships, 526

Harold Bettinger Memorial Scholarship, 168

Health Career Scholarship, 269

Healy Travel Industry Scholarship, 148

Holland America Line-Westours Travel Industry Scholarship, 149

Jacob Van Namen Marketing Scholarship, 169

Japanese American Music Scholarship Competition, 273

Jerry Baker Scholarship, 169

Jerry Wilmot Scholarship, 169

J.K. Rathmell, Jr., Memorial for Work/Study Abroad, 169

John H. Lyons, Sr. Scholarship, 267

Joseph R. Stone Travel Industry Scholarship, 149

Kappa Kappa Gamma Scholarship, 277

Kenneth Andrew Roe Mechanical Engineering Scholarship, 146

King Olav V Norwegian-American Heritage Fund, 443

Kottis Family Award, 206

Louise Dessureault Memorial Scholarship, 356

Louisiana Leveraging Educational Assistance Partnership, 287

Louisiana Rockefeller Wildlife Scholarship, 287

Mary M. Verges Award, 206

Maryland Delegate Scholarship, 294

Maryland HOPE Scholarship Program Science and Technology Scholarship, 297

Maryland Senatorial Scholarship, 298

Mildred Towle Trust Fund Scholarship, 246

Montana University System High School Honor Scholarship, 314

Monte R. Mitchell Global Scholarship, 64

Museum of Modern Art Internship, 538

National Society of Accountants Scholarship, 353

Nicaraguan and Haitian Scholarship Program, 224

Owens Corning Internships, 550

Paris Fracasso Production Floriculture Scholarship, 170

Past Grand Presidents' Memorial Award, 206

Paul Cole Scholarship, 215

Praxair International Scholarship, 152

SELECT Internship Program, 517

Serteen Scholarships, 420

Sertoma Communicative Disorders Scholarships, 420

Sertoma Scholarships for Hearing-Impaired Students, 420

Society of Automotive Engineers (SAE) Yanmar Scholarship, 426

Summer Internship for College Students, 534

Sun Microsystems Student Intern and Co-op Program, 558

Swiss Benevolent Society Medicus Student Exchange, 451

Texas Good Neighbor Scholarship, 458

Tourism Foundation Quebec Scholarship, 358

Tourism Foundation Yellow Ribbon Scholarship, 359

Treadway Inns, Hotels, and Resorts Scholarship, 359

United States Holocaust Memorial Museum Internship, 560

Universal Air Travel Plan (UATP) Travel Industry Scholarship, 150

USA Funds Scholarship, 483

Vocational Horticulture Scholarship, 170

Wolf Trap Foundation for the Performing Arts Internship, 563

Military Participation

Air Force

Air Force Aid Society Education Grant, 60

Arkansas Missing/Killed in Action Dependents Scholarship, 155

Chief Master Sergeants of the Air Force Scholarship, 65

Katherine F. Gruber Scholarship Program, 171

Minority Status

African American

Alaskan native

American Indian

Asian American

Hispanic American

National/ethnic background

Arab or Jewish

Armenian

Chinese

Danish

Greek

AHEPA Scholarship, 384
Alexandra A. Sonenfeld Award, 205
Daughters of Penelope Past Grand
Presidents Award, 205
Emily Tamaras Memorial Award, 205
Eos #1 Mother Lodge Chapter
Award, 205
Kottis Family Award, 206
Mary M. Verges Award, 206
Past Grand Presidents' Memorial
Award, 206

Italian

Agnes E. Vaghi-Cornaro
Scholarship, 338
Alex and Henry Recine
Scholarship, 339
Alyce M. Cafaro Scholarship, 339
Angela Scholarship, 339
Antonio and Felicia Marinelli
Scholarships, 339
Antonio F. Marinelli Founders
Scholarship, 339
Assunta Lucchetti Martino
Scholarship for International
Studies, 340
Bolla Wines Scholarship, 340
Capital Area Regional
Scholarship, 340
Communications Scholarship, 340
Congressman Alfred E. Santangelo
and Betty Santangelo
Scholarship, 341
Daniel Stella Scholarship, 341
Dr. William L. Amoroso Jr.
Scholarship, 341
F.D. Stella Scholarship, 341
Frank J. Corsaro Scholarship, 341
Gianni Versace Scholarship in Fashion
Design, 342
Greater New York Regional
Scholarship, 342
Henry Salvatori Scholarship, 442
Italian Catholic Federation
Scholarship, 271
Italian Cultural Society and NIAF
Matching Scholarship, 342
Italian Regional Scholarship, 342
John A. Volpe Scholarship, 342
Louis A. Caputo, Jr. Scholarship, 343
Lower Mid-Atlantic Regional
Scholarship, 343
Major Don S. Gentile
Scholarship, 471
Merrill Lynch Scholarship, 343
Mid-America Regional
Scholarship, 343
Mid-Pacific Regional Scholarship, 343
Nerone/NIAF Matching Art
Scholarship, 344
New England Regional
Scholarship, 344
NIAF Pavarotti Scholarship, 344
NIAF/NOIAW Cornaro
Scholarship, 344

NIAF/SACI Scholarships, 265
Nina Santavicca Scholarship, 345
North Central Regional
Scholarship, 345
Northwest Regional Scholarship, 345
Paragano Scholarship, 345
Piancone Family Agriculture
Scholarship, 345
Richard Perrone Scholarship, 346
Robert J. Di Pietro Scholarship, 346
Rose Basile Green Scholarship for
Literature, 346
Sergio Franchi Music Scholarship for
Voice Performance, 346
Silvio Conte Internship, 541
Sons of Italy National Leadership
Grant, 442
South Central Regional
Scholarship, 347
Southeast Regional Scholarship, 347
Southwest Regional Scholarship, 347
Study Abroad Scholarship, 347
Thomas Joseph "Willie" Ambrosole
Scholarship, 347
Vincente Minelli Scholarship, 348
West Virginia Italian Heritage Festival
Scholarship, 348
William C. Davini Scholarship, 472

Japanese

Japanese American General
Scholarship, 273
Japanese American Music Scholarship
Competition, 273

Polish

Kosciuszko Foundation Tuition
Scholarships, 279
Polish Culture Scholarship, 88
Sons of Poland Scholarship, 163

Swiss

Sonia Streuli Maguire Outstanding
Scholastic Achievement Award, 451
Swiss Benevolent Society Medicus
Student Exchange, 451
Swiss Benevolent Society Pellegrini
Scholarship, 452

Ukrainian

Eugene and Elinor Kotur
Scholarship, 470
Ukrainian Fraternal Association
Scholarship, 470

Welsh

Cymdeithas Gymreig (Welsh Society)
Philadelphia Scholarship, 202
Saint David's Society
Scholarship, 414
Welsh Heritage Scholarship, 493

Organization/civic affiliation

1199 National Benefit Fund

Joseph Tauber Scholarship, 53

25th Infantry Division Association

25th Infantry Division Educational
Memorial Scholarship, 53

Aid Association for Lutherans

All-College Scholarship Program, 59

Alpha Beta Gamma

Alpha Beta Gamma International
Scholarship, 69

Alpha Mu Gamma

Alpha Mu Gamma Scholarship, 69

American Academy of Physician Assistants

Physician's Assistants Scholarship, 70

American Association of Critical Care Nurses

Critical Care Nurses Education
Advancement Scholarship, 71
Critical Care Nurses Education
Advancement Scholarship
(BSN), 71

American Classical League

McKinlay Summer Award, 73
M.V. O'Donnell Memorial Teacher
Training Award, 73

American Congress of Surveying and Mapping

AAGS Joseph F. Dracup Scholarship
Award, 74
Allen Chelf Scholarship, 75
Berntsen International Scholarship in
Surveying, 75
Berntsen International Scholarship in
Surveying Technology, 75
Cady McDonnell Memorial
Scholarship, 75
CaGIS Scholarship Award, 76
Mary Feindt Forum for Women in
Surveying Scholarship, 76
Nettie Dracup Memorial
Scholarship, 76
NSPS Board of Governors
Scholarship, 76
NSPS Scholarships, 76

American School Food Service Foundation

ASFSA Lincoln Food Service Research Grant, 141

ASFSA Tony's Food Service Scholarship, 141

American Society of Civil Engineers

B. Charles Tiney Memorial ASCE Student Chapter Scholarship, 142

Freeman Fellowship, 142

Samuel Fletcher Tapman ASCE Student Chapter Scholarship, 143

American Society of Composers/Authors/ Publishers

Rudolf Nissim Composers Competition, 159

American Society of Mechanical Engineers

American Society of Mechanical Engineers Foundation Scholarship, 145

ASME Student Loan Program, 566

Frank William and Dorothy Given Miller Mechanical Engineering Scholarship, 145

F.W. "Beich" Beichley Scholarship, 145

Garland Duncan Mechanical Engineering Scholarship, 146

John and Elsa Gracik Mechanical Engineering Scholarship, 146

Kenneth Andrew Roe Mechanical Engineering Scholarship, 146

Melvin R. Green Scholarship, 146

W.J. and M.E. Adams, Jr., Mechanical Engineering Scholarship, 146

Appaloosa Horse Club

Appaloosa Youth Foundation Educational Scholarships, 153

ASM International

ASM International Foundation Undergraduate Scholarship, 160

Association for Library/ Information Science Education

ALISE Bodhan S. Wynar Research Paper Competition, 161

ALISE Research Grant Award, 161

Association of American Geographers

Anne U. White Fund, 162

ASTA Arizona Chapter

Arizona Dependent/Employee Membership Scholarship, 148

Boy Scouts of America

American Legion Illinois Boy Scout Scholarship, 94

Boy Scouts of America/Eastern Orthodox Committee on Scouting Scholarship, 174

E. Urner Goodman Scholarship, 174

Boy Scouts of America, Eagle Scouts

American Legion Eagle Scout of the Year, 123

American Legion National Eagle Scout of the Year, 108

American Legion "Boy Scout of the Year" Award, 97

Eagle Scout of the Year Award, 122

Frank D. Visceglia Memorial Scholarship, 284

Frank L. Weil Memorial Eagle Scout Scholarship, 348

National Eagle Scout Scholarship, 174

Sons of the American Revolution Eagle Scout Scholarship, 354

California Teachers Association

California Teachers Association Martin Luther King, Jr., Memorial Scholarship, 185

CTA Scholarship for Dependent Children, 185

CTA Scholarships for Members, 185

L. Gordon Bittle Memorial Scholarship for Student CTA, 186

Cashiers' Association of Wall Street

Cashiers' Association of Wall Street Scholarship, 188

Catholic Aid Association

Catholic Aid Association Scholarship, 189

Catholic Workman Fraternal Life Association

National Catholic Workman Scholarship, 189

Chicago Association of Spring Manufacturing

CASMI Scholarship, 192

Data Management Division of Wall Street

Data Management Division of Wall Street Scholarship Program, 204

Daughters of Penelope

Alexandra A. Sonenfeld Award, 205

Daughters of Penelope Past Grand Presidents Award, 205

Emily Tamaras Memorial Award, 205

Eos #1 Mother Lodge Chapter Award, 205

Kottis Family Award, 206

Mary M. Verges Award, 206

Past Grand Presidents' Memorial Award, 206

Delta Delta Delta Fraternity

Delta Delta Delta Undergraduate Scholarship, 208

Delta Gamma

Delta Gamma Scholarship, 208

Delta Gamma Student Loan, 568

Descendants of the Signers of the Declaration of Independence

Descendents of the Signers of the Declaration of Independence Scholarship, 209

Electrical Equipment Representatives Association

EERA Scholarship, 215

Elks

Elks National Foundation Legacy Awards, 216

Financial Management Division of SIA

Financial Management Division of SIA Scholarship, 220

Fraternal Grange

Doris Deaver Memorial Scholarship, 181

Grange Insurance Scholarship, 237

Peter Marinoff Memorial Scholarship, 182

Sehlmeyer Scholarship, 182

Futures Services Division of the Futures Industry Association

Futures Services Division Scholarship, 229

Girls Incorporated

Donna Brace Ogilvie-Zelda Gitlin
  Poetry Writing Award, 233
Girls Incorporated Scholars
  Program, 233

Golden Key National Honor Society

Art International, 234
Ford Motor Company/Golden Key
  Undergraduate Scholarships, 234
GEICO/Golden Key Adult Scholar
  Awards, 234
Literary Achievement Awards, 235
Performing Arts Showcase, 235
Research Travel Grants, 235
Student Scholastic Showcase, 235
Study Abroad Scholarships, 235

Golf Course Superintendents Association of America

GCSAA Footsteps on the Green
  Award, 236
GCSAA Legacy Awards, 236
GCSAA Scholars Competition, 236
GCSAA Student Essay Contest, 236

Harness Racing Industry

Harness Tracks of America
  Scholarship, 239

Hawaii Carpenter's Union Local 745

Walter H. Kupau Memorial Fund, 247

Hawaii Construction Industry Federal Credit Union

Frances S. Watanabe Memorial
  Scholarship, 243

Hawaii Pacific Tennis Association

Jean Fitzgerald Scholarship Fund, 243

IEEE Computer Society

Lance Stafford Larson Student
  Scholarship, 256
Richard E. Merwin Award, 256
Upsilon Pi Epsilon Award, 256

Institution of Mining and Metallurgy

Centenary Scholarship, 266

International Association of Fire Fighters

W.H. McClennan Scholarship, 267

International Brotherhood of Teamsters

Teamsters Council #37 Federal Credit
  Union Scholarship, 393
Teamsters Local 305 Scholarship, 393
Teamsters/Clyde C. Crosby/Joseph M.
  Edgar Memorial Scholarship, 393

International Buckskin Horse Association

Buckskin Horse Association
  Scholarship, 267

International Executive Housekeepers Association

IEHA Educational Foundation
  Scholarship, 268

International Order of Job's Daughters

Supreme Guardian Council,
  International Order of Job's
  Daughters Scholarship, 451

International Union of EESMF Workers, AFL-CIO

James B. Carey Scholarship, 266
Paul Jennings Scholarship, 266

Int'l Association Bridge/ Structural/Ornamental/ Reinforcing Iron Workers

John H. Lyons, Sr. Scholarship, 267

Jaycees

Charles R. Ford Scholarship, 273
Thomas Wood Baldridge
  Scholarship, 274

Kappa Kappa Gamma

Kappa Kappa Gamma
  Scholarship, 277

Knights of Columbus

Knights of Columbus Student
  Loan, 572
Matthews/Swift Educational Trust -
  Military Dependants, 279
Matthews/Swift Educational Trust -
  Police/Firefighters, 279
Pro Deo/Pro Patria Scholarship, 279

Lambda Alpha

National Dean's List Scholarship, 280
National Lambda Alpha Scholarship
  Award, 280

Learning for Life

Floyd Boring Award, 284
National Technical Investigators'
  Captain James J. Regan Memorial
  Scholarship, 284
Sheryl A. Horak Law Enforcement
  Explorer Scholarship, 284

Massachusetts Glass Dealers Association

Massachusetts Glass Dealers
  Association Scholarship, 301

National Achievers Society

National Achievers Society Scholars
  Award, 361

National Advisory Group

Convenience Stores/Petroleum
  Marketers Association Scholarship
  Program, 333

National Art Materials Trade Association

National Art Materials
  Scholarship, 329

National Association for Advancement of Colored People

Agnes Jones Jackson Scholarship, 315
Roy Wilkins Scholarship, 316
Sutton Education Scholarship, 316
Willems Scholarship, 316

National Association of Black Accountants

National Scholarship Program, 329

National Association of Letter Carriers

Costas G. Lemonopoulos
  Scholarship, 330
William C. Doherty Scholarship, 330

National Athletic Trainers Association

Athletic Trainers Curriculum
  Scholarship, 331
Athletic Trainers Student Writing
  Contest, 331
Athletic Trainers Undergraduate
  Scholarship, 331

National Black Nurses' Association

Black Nurses Scholarship, 332

Eligibility Indexes

Religious Affiliation

Eligibility Indexes

Cady McDonnell Memorial
Scholarship, 75
California-Hawaii Elks Major Project
Undergraduate Scholarship Program
for Students with Disabilities, 186
Castle & Cooke George W.Y. Yim
Scholarship Fund, 241
Cora Aguda Manayan Fund, 241
David T. Woolsey Scholarship, 281
Dolly Ching Scholarship Fund, 241
Dorice & Clarence Glick Classical
Music Scholarship, 241
Dr. Hans & Clara Zimmerman
Foundation Education
Scholarship, 242
Dr. Hans and Clara Zimmerman
Foundation Health Scholarship, 242
E.E. Black Scholarship, 242
Ellison Onizuka Memorial
Scholarship, 242
Frances S. Watanabe Memorial
Scholarship, 243
General Pool Scholarships, 247
Hawaii Student Incentive Grant, 248
Hawaii Tuition Waiver, 248
Henry and Dorothy Castle Memorial
Scholarship, 243
Jean Fitzgerald Scholarship Fund, 243
John Dawe Dental Education
Fund, 243
John Ross Foundation, 244
Juliette M. Atherton Scholarship, 244
Ka'iulani Home for Girls Trust
Scholarship, 244
Kawasaki-McGaha Scholarship
Fund, 244
K.M. Hatano Scholarship, 244
Koloa Scholarship, 245
Laura N. Dowsett Fund, 245
Margaret Jones Memorial Nursing
Scholarship, 245
Marion MacCarrell Scott
Scholarship, 245
Mid-Pacific Regional Scholarship, 343
Mildred Towle Trust Fund
Scholarship, 246
NASA Space Grant Hawaii
Undergraduate Fellowship, 319
NASA Space Grant Hawaii
Undergraduate Traineeship, 538
Pacific Printing and Imaging
Scholarship, 395
Scholarships for Specific Areas, 246
Scholarships for Specific Majors, 246
Scholarships with Special
Criteria, 247
Thz Fo Farm Fund, 247
Walter H. Kupau Memorial Fund, 247

Idaho

American Legion Idaho Auxiliary
Nursing Scholarship, 94
Cady McDonnell Memorial
Scholarship, 75
Grange Insurance Scholarship, 237
Idaho Education Incentive Loan
Forgiveness Program, 571

Idaho Minority and "At-Risk" Student
Scholarship, 255
Idaho Robert C. Byrd Honors
Scholarship, 255
Idaho state Scholarship Catergory
A, 255
Leveraging Educational Assistance
State Partnership Program
(LEAP), 255
Mary Lou Brown Scholarship, 138
Northwest Regional Scholarship, 345
Pacific Printing and Imaging
Scholarship, 395
Treacy Company Scholarship, 463

Illinois

Ada Mucklestone Memorial
Scholarship, 94
Alfred R. Chisholm Memorial
Scholarship, 475
Allstate Internships, 509
American Legion Illinois Auxiliary
Special Education Teaching
Scholarships, 95
American Legion Illinois Auxiliary
Student Nurse Scholarship, 95
American Legion Illinois Boy Scout
Scholarship, 94
American Legion Illinois Oratorical
Contest, 94
American Legion Illinois
Scholarship, 94
ARRL Earl I. Anderson
Scholarship, 135
Chicago FM Club Scholarship, 136
Congressional Black Caucus
Foundation Spouses
Scholarship, 197
Edmond A. Metzger Scholarship, 137
Ford Motor Company Fellows
Program, 539
Illinois D.A. DeBolt Teacher Shortage
Scholarship, 257
Illinois Incentive for Access, 257
Illinois Merit Recognition
Scholarship, 257
Illinois Minority Teachers
Scholarship, 257
Illinois Monetary Award, 258
Illinois National Guard Grant, 258
Illinois Robert C. Byrd Honors
Scholarship, 258
Illinois Student-to-Student Grant, 258
Illinois Veteran Grant, 259
Italian Catholic Federation
Scholarship, 271
Leo Burnett Scholarship Program, 478
Marie Sheehe Trade School
Scholarship, 95
Mildred R. Knoles Opportunity
Scholarship, 95
NASA Space Grant Illinois
Undergraduate Scholarship, 320
North Central Regional
Scholarship, 345
Shell Legislative Internship Program
(SLIP), 539

Six Meter Club of Chicago
Scholarship, 139
Youth Entertainment Summer, 563

Indiana

American Cancer Society
Scholarship, 72
American Legion Indiana Oratorical
Contest, 95
ARRL Earl I. Anderson
Scholarship, 135
Chicago FM Club Scholarship, 136
Congressional Black Caucus
Foundation Spouses
Scholarship, 197
Edmond A. Metzger Scholarship, 137
Edna M. Barcus Memorial
Scholarship, 96
Frank W. McHale Memorial
Scholarship, 96
Indiana Higher Education Grant, 260
Indiana Hoosier Scholar Program, 260
Indiana Minority Teacher
Scholarship, 260
Indiana Nursing Scholarship, 261
Indiana Robert C. Byrd Honors
Scholarship, 261
Indiana Special Education Services
Scholarship, 261
Indiana Twenty-First Century Scholars
Program, 261
Katharine M. Grosscup
Scholarship, 230
NASA Space Grant Indiana
Undergraduate Scholarship, 320
National Guard Supplemental
Grant, 261
North Central Regional
Scholarship, 345
Past President's Parley Nursing
Scholarship, 96

Iowa

American Legion Iowa Auxiliary
Mary Virginia Macrea Memorial
Nurses Scholarship, 97
American Legion Iowa Oratorical
Contest, 96
American Legion Iowa "Outstanding
Citizen of Boys State"
Scholarship, 96
American Legion Iowa "Outstanding
Senior Baseball Player"
Scholarship, 97
American Legion "Boy Scout of the
Year" Award, 97
Department of Iowa Scholarships, 97
Easter Seal Society of Iowa Disability
Scholarship, 213
E.L. Peterson Scholarship, 212
Harriet Hoffman Memorial
Scholarship, 97
Iowa Grant, 270
Iowa National Guard Educational
Assistance Program, 270
Iowa Robert C. Byrd Honor
Scholarship, 270

Developmental Disabilities and
Mental Health Workforce Tuition
Assistance Program, 294
Italian Cultural Society and NIAF
Matching Scholarship, 342
Maryland Child Care Provider
Scholarship, 294
Maryland Distinguished Scholar:
Achievement, 294
Maryland Distinguished Scholar:
National Merit and National
Achievement Finalists, 295
Maryland Distinguished Scholar:
Talent, 295
Maryland Distinguished Scholar:
Teacher Education Program, 572
Maryland Educational Assistance
Grant, 295
Maryland Edward T. Conroy
Memorial Scholarship
Program--Disabled Public Safety
Employees, 295
Maryland Guaranteed Access
Grant, 296
Maryland HOPE Scholarship Program
Community College Transfer
Student Hope Scholarship, 572
Maryland HOPE Scholarship Program
Hope Scholarship, 296
Maryland HOPE Scholarship Program
Maryland Teacher Scholarship, 296
Maryland HOPE Scholarship Program
Science and Technology
Scholarship, 297
Maryland Jack F. Tolbert Memorial
Grant, 297
Maryland Loan Assistance Repayment
Program, 573
Maryland Part-Time Grant
Program, 297
Maryland Physical/Occupational
Therapists and Assistants
Grant, 297
Maryland Professional School
Scholarship, 298
Maryland Reimbursement of
Firefighters, 298
Maryland Senatorial Scholarship, 298
Maryland Sharon Christa McAuliffe
Memorial Teacher Education
Award, 298
Maryland State Nursing Scholarship
and Living Expenses Grant, 299
Piancone Family Agriculture
Scholarship, 345

Massachusetts

American Legion Massachusetts
Auxiliary Past President's Parley
Scholarship, 103
American Legion Massachusetts
Auxiliary Scholarship, 103
American Legion Massachusetts
General and Nursing
Scholarships, 102

American Legion Massachusetts Past
County Commander's
Scholarship, 102
Biotechnology Scholars Program, 299
Department of Massachusetts
Oratorical Contest, 102
Dr. James L. Lawson Memorial
Scholarship, 137
EMC Summer Internship Program and
Co-ops, 521
Horticulture Research Institute
Timothy Bigelow Scholarship, 253
John A. Volpe Scholarship, 342
Lighthouse College-Bound Incentive
Award, 286
Lighthouse Undergraduate Incentive
Award I, 286
Lighthouse Undergraduate Incentive
Award II, 286
Massachusetts Christian A. Herter
Memorial Scholarship Program, 299
Massachusetts Gilbert Grant, 300
Massachusetts MASSgrant
Program, 300
Massachusetts No Interest Loan, 573
Massachusetts Public Service
Program, 300
Massachusetts Robert C. Byrd Honors
Scholarship, 300
Massachusetts Tuition Waiver, 300
NASA Space Grant Massachusetts
Summer Jobs for Students, 538
New England Board of Higher
Education's Regional Student
Program, 364
New England Femara
Scholarship, 138
New England Regional
Scholarship, 344
Paid Summer Internship: JFK
Scholars Award, 533
Piancone Family Agriculture
Scholarship, 345
Worcester County Horticultural
Society, 505

Michigan

Alfred R. Chisholm Memorial
Scholarship, 475
American Cancer Society
Scholarship, 72
American Legion Michigan Auxiliary
Memorial Scholarship, 104
American Legion Michigan Auxiliary
National President's
Scholarship, 104
American Legion Michigan Auxiliary
Scholarship for
Nurses/Therapists, 104
American Legion Michigan Guy M.
Wilson Scholarship, 103
American Legion Michigan Oratorical
Contest, 103
Congressional Black Caucus
Foundation Spouses
Scholarship, 197

Ford Motor Company Fellows
Program, 539
Katharine M. Grosscup
Scholarship, 230
Michigan Adult Part-Time Grant, 304
Michigan Competitive
Scholarship, 304
Michigan Educational Opportunity
Grant, 304
Michigan Robert C. Byrd Honors
Scholarship, 305
Michigan Society of Professional
Engineers Scholarships, 305
Michigan Tuition Grant, 305
Michigan Work-Study Program, 534
Midwest Student Exchange
Program, 307
NASA Space Grant Michigan
Undergraduate Fellowship, 321
North Central Regional
Scholarship, 345
Tourism Foundation Michigan
Scholarship, 357
William D. Brewer--Jewell W. Brewer
Scholarship Trusts, 103
Youth Entertainment Summer, 563

Minnesota

American Legion Minnesota Auxiliary
Department Scholarship, 105
American Legion Minnesota Auxiliary
Past President's Parley Nursing
Scholarship, 105
American Legion Minnesota
Legionnaire Insurance Trust
Scholarship, 104
American Legion Minnesota
Memorial Scholarship, 105
American Legion Minnesota
Oratorical Contest, 105
Burlington Northern Santa Fe
Foundation Scholarship, 84
Midwest Student Exchange
Program, 307
Minnesota Educational Assistance for
Veterans, 308
Minnesota Educational Assistance for
War Orphans, 308
Minnesota Post-Secondary Child Care
Grant, 308
Minnesota Safety Officers Survivors
Program, 308
Minnesota Service Scholarship
Matching Grant, 309
Minnesota State Grant Program, 309
Minnesota Student Educational Loan
Fund (SELF), 573
Minnesota Work-Study Program, 535
Mooty Scholarship, 201
NASA Space Grant Minnesota
Undergraduate Scholarship, 321
North Central Regional
Scholarship, 345
Scholarship for People with
Disabilities, 201

New Jersey

New Mexico

New York

Pennsylvania

Puerto Rico

Rhode Island

South Carolina

Eligibility Indexes

Wyoming

Study Abroad

Scholarships

1199 National Benefit Fund

Joseph Tauber Scholarship

Type of award: Scholarship, renewable.
Intended use: For full-time undergraduate or non-degree study at accredited vocational, 2-year or 4-year institution in or outside United States.
Eligibility: Applicant or parent must be member/participant of 1199 National Benefit Fund.
Basis for selection: Applicant must demonstrate financial need.
Application requirements: Transcript, proof of eligibility.
Additional information: High school graduates, postsecondary school students and previous awardees whose parents have been in Benefit Fund Wage Class One for one year at time of application are eligible.
  Amount of award: $750-$8,000
  Number of awards: 5,000
  Application deadline: February 1
Contact:
1199 National Benefit Fund
310 West 43 Street
New York, NY 10036

25th Infantry Division Association

25th Infantry Division Educational Memorial Scholarship

Type of award: Scholarship.
Intended use: For full-time freshman study at accredited 4-year institution in United States.
Eligibility: Applicant or parent must be member/participant of 25th Infantry Division Association. Applicant must be U.S. citizen. Applicant must be in military service, veteran or disabled while on active duty; or dependent of active service person, veteran, disabled veteran or deceased veteran who serves or served in the Army. Deceased member must have died on active duty with division or as a result thereof. Veterans must be association members. Applicant on active duty must be scheduled for release/retirement or discharged from division by December 31 of award year.
Basis for selection: Applicant must demonstrate financial need, high academic achievement, depth of character, leadership, seriousness of purpose and service orientation.
Application requirements: Recommendations, essay, transcript, proof of eligibility. SAT or ACT scores.
Additional information: Must be pursuing first bachelor's degree. May not be used at U.S. military academies.

  Amount of award: $1,000-$1,500
  Number of awards: 12
  Number of applicants: 35
  Application deadline: April 1
  Notification begins: June 1
Contact:
25th Infantry Division Association
c/o Lawrence Weist
3930 South Bridlewood Drive
Bountiful, UT 84010
Phone: 801-292-7354
Fax: 801-585-3350

A.F. and H.G. McNeely Foundation

A.F. and H.G. McNeely Scholarship

Type of award: Scholarship.
Intended use: For undergraduate or graduate study at accredited vocational, 2-year or 4-year institution.
Eligibility: Applicant or parent must be employed by Space Center Company.
Additional information: For further information or an application, contact Space Center Co./McNeely Foundation directly.
  Amount of award: $1,000-$2,600

A.M. Castle & Co.

John M. Simpson Memorial Scholarship

Type of award: Scholarship, renewable.
Intended use: For full-time undergraduate study.
Eligibility: Applicant or parent must be employed by A. M. Castle & Co. Applicant must be high school senior.
Application requirements: Recommendations, essay, transcript.
Additional information: For children of A.M. Castle & Co. employees only. Parent must be employed by A.M. Castle & Co. for minimum of three years.
  Amount of award: $2,500
  Number of awards: 2
  Total amount awarded: $5,000
Contact:
AMC & Company
3400 North Wolf Road
Franklin Park, IL 60131
Phone: 847-455-7111

Abbie Sargent Memorial Scholarship Fund

Abbie Sargent Memorial Scholarship

Type of award: Scholarship, renewable.
Intended use: For freshman, sophomore, junior, senior or graduate study at accredited 2-year or 4-year institution. Designated institutions: May be used for out-of-state institutions.
Eligibility: Applicant must be residing in New Hampshire.
Basis for selection: Major/career interest in agriculture or veterinary medicine. Applicant must demonstrate financial need, high academic achievement and depth of character.
Application requirements: Transcript.
Additional information: Only New Hampshire residents should apply. Recipient may attend out-of-state university. Send SASE for application. Award amount tentatively set at $400, but may vary from year to year depending on funding.

Amount of award:	$400
Number of awards:	2
Number of applicants:	35
Application deadline:	March 15
Notification begins:	May 1

Contact:
Abbie Sargent Memorial Fund
295 Sheep Davis Road
Concord, NH 03301
Phone: 603-224-1934

Academy of Motion Picture Arts and Sciences

Screenplay Writing Scholarship

Type of award: Scholarship.
Intended use: For undergraduate study.
Basis for selection: Competition/talent/interest in Writing/journalism. Major/career interest in playwriting/screen writing.
Additional information: For students majoring in Screenplay Writing.

Number of awards:	5
Application deadline:	June 1
Total amount awarded:	$20,000

Contact:
Academy of Motion Picture Arts and Sciences
8948 Wilshire Boulevard
Beverly Hills, CA 90211
Phone: 213-278-8990

Academy of Television Arts and Sciences Educational Programs and Services

College Television Award

Type of award: Scholarship.
Intended use: For full-time undergraduate or graduate study in United States.
Basis for selection: Competition/talent/interest in visual arts, based on excellence of submitted film/video. Major/career interest in radio/television/film.
Application requirements: Must submit 3/4 inch cassette of originial film/tape made for course credit within eligibility period. Must be student producer of record. Yearly updated official entry form must be submitted.
Additional information: Video and filmmakers award for student videos and films in categories of drama, comedy, music, documentary, news/sports/magazine shows, traditional and computer animation. Submissions must have been made for college credit course. First-place and second place winners chosen for their work on humanitarian concerns eligible for $2,000 Bricker Family College Award. First and second place winners also receive grants in film stock from Kodak. Foreign applicants must be pursuing degree at college or university in United States.

Amount of award:	$500-$2,000
Number of awards:	21
Number of applicants:	350
Application deadline:	December 15
Notification begins:	February 1
Total amount awarded:	$24,500

Contact:
Academy of Television Arts and Sciences
Educational Programs and Services
5220 Lankershim Boulevard
North Hollywood, CA 91601-3109
Phone: 818-754-2830
Fax: 818-761-8524
Web: www.emmys.org

Acrometal Management Corporation

Acrometal Family of Companies Scholarship Program

Type of award: Scholarship.
Intended use: For undergraduate study at vocational, 2-year or 4-year institution.
Eligibility: Applicant or parent must be employed by Acrometal Management Corporation. Applicant must be high school senior.
Additional information: For further information or an application, contact Acrometal Management Corporation directly.

Amount of award:	$1,000

Acterna Corporation

Acterna Corporation Scholarship Program

Type of award: Scholarship, renewable.
Intended use: For undergraduate study at vocational, 2-year or 4-year institution.
Eligibility: Applicant or parent must be employed by Acterna Corporation. Applicant must be high school senior.
Additional information: For futher information or application, contact Acterna Corporation directly.
    Amount of award: $5,000

Actuarial Education and Research Fund

Wooddy Scholarship

Type of award: Scholarship.
Intended use: For full-time senior study at 4-year institution in or outside United States or Canada.
Eligibility: Applicant must be U.S. citizen or permanent resident.
Basis for selection: Major/career interest in insurance/actuarial science. Applicant must demonstrate high academic achievement.
Application requirements: Recommendations, essay, transcript. Must be in top quartile of class.
Additional information: Applicant must have passed at least one actuarial examination. Recommendation must come from professor. Leadership judged in relation to extracurricular activities. Application is available on Website.
    Amount of award: $2,000
    Number of awards: 4
    Number of applicants: 33
    Application deadline: June 29
    Notification begins: August 31
    Total amount awarded: $8,000
Contact:
Actuarial Education and Research Fund
475 Martingale Road, Suite 800
Schaumburg, IL 60173-2226
Phone: 847-706-3500
Fax: 847-706-3599
Web: http://www.aerf.org/grants&competitions.html

ADA Endowment and Assistance Fund, Inc.

Allied Dental Health Scholarship for Dental Assisting Students

Type of award: Scholarship.
Intended use: For full-time freshman study in United States. Designated institutions: Must be accredited by Commission on Dental Accreditation.
Eligibility: Applicant must be U.S. citizen.
Basis for selection: Major/career interest in dental assistant. Applicant must demonstrate financial need and high academic achievement.
Application requirements: Completed application form, typed biographical questionnaire, two sealed references, copy of school's acceptance letter (if first year).
Additional information: Minimum 2.8 GPA, 12 credit hours enrollment. Applicants must be entering students enrolled in dental assisting program accredited by Commission on Dental Accreditation. Must demonstrate minimum financial need of $1,000. Contact school for application. Notification in fall.
    Amount of award: $1,000
    Application deadline: September 15
Contact:
The ADA Endowment and Assistance Fund, Inc.
Scholarship Coordinator
211 East Chicago Avenue
Chicago, IL 60611-2678
Phone: 312-440-2567

Allied Dental Health Scholarship for Dental Hygiene Students

Type of award: Scholarship.
Intended use: For full-time sophomore study in United States. Designated institutions: Must be accredited by Commission on Dental Accreditation.
Eligibility: Applicant must be U.S. citizen.
Basis for selection: Major/career interest in dental hygiene. Applicant must demonstrate financial need and high academic achievement.
Application requirements: Completed application form, typed biographical questionnaire, two sealed references, copy of school's acceptance letter (if first year).
Additional information: Minimum 3.0 GPA, 12 credit hours enrollment. Applicants must be entering second year students currently attending dental hygiene program accredited by Commission on Dental Accreditation. Must demonstrate minimum financial need of $1,000. Contact school for application. Notification in fall.
    Amount of award: $1,000
    Application deadline: August 15
Contact:
The ADA Endowment and Assistance Fund, Inc.
Scholarship Coordinator
211 East Chicago Avenue
Chicago, IL 60611-2678
Phone: 312-440-2567

Allied Dental Health Scholarship for Dental Laboratory Technology Students

Type of award: Scholarship, renewable.
Intended use: For full-time freshman or sophomore study in United States. Designated institutions: Must be accredited by Commission on Dental Accreditation.
Eligibility: Applicant must be U.S. citizen.
Basis for selection: Major/career interest in dental laboratory technology. Applicant must demonstrate financial need and high academic achievement.
Application requirements: Completed application form, typed biographical questionnaire, two sealed references, copy of school's acceptance letter (if first year).
Additional information: Minimum GPA 2.8, 12 credit hours enrollment. Applicants must be entering first or second year

students currently attending or enrolled in dental laboratory technology program accredited by Commission on Dental Accreditation. Must demonstrate minimum financial need of at least $1,000. Contact school for application. Notification in fall.

  Amount of award: $1,000
  Application deadline: August 15
Contact:
The ADA Endowment and Assistance Fund, Inc.
Scholarship Coordinator
211 East Chicago Avenue
Chicago, IL 60611-2678
Phone: 312-440-2567

Dental Student Scholarship

Type of award: Scholarship.
Intended use: For full-time sophomore study in United States. Designated institutions: Dental schools accredited by the Commission on Dental Accreditation.
Eligibility: Applicant must be U.S. citizen.
Basis for selection: Major/career interest in dentistry. Applicant must demonstrate financial need and high academic achievement.
Application requirements: Completed application form, typed biographical questionnaire, two sealed references.
Additional information: Minimum 3.0 GPA, 12 credit hours enrollment. Applicants must be entering second year students attending dental school accredited by Commission on Dental Accreditation. Must demonstrate a minimum financial need of $2,500. Contact school for application. Notification in fall.

  Amount of award: $2,500
  Application deadline: July 31
Contact:
The ADA Endowment and Assistance Fund, Inc.
Scholarship Director
211 East Chicago Avenue
Chicago, IL 60611
Phone: 312-440-2567

Minority Dental Student Scholarship

Type of award: Scholarship.
Intended use: For full-time sophomore study in United States. Designated institutions: Dental schools accredited by the Commission on Dental Accreditation.
Eligibility: Applicant must be African American, Mexican American, Hispanic American, Puerto Rican or American Indian. Applicant must be U.S. citizen.
Basis for selection: Major/career interest in dentistry. Applicant must demonstrate financial need and high academic achievement.
Application requirements: Completed application form, typed biographical questionnaire, two sealed references.
Additional information: Minimum 3.0 GPA, 12 credit hours enrollment. Applicants must be entering second year students attending dental school accredited by Commission on Dental Accreditation. Must demonstrate a minimum financial need of $2,500. Contact school for application. Notification in fall.

  Amount of award: $2,500
  Application deadline: July 31
Contact:
The ADA Endowment and Assistance Fund, Inc.
211 East Chicago Avenue
Chicago, IL 60611
Phone: 312-440-2567

Adaptec

Adaptec Scholarship

Type of award: Scholarship, renewable.
Intended use: For undergraduate study at accredited postsecondary institution.
Eligibility: Applicant or parent must be employed by Adaptec. Applicant must be high school senior.
Basis for selection: Applicant must demonstrate financial need.
Additional information: For further information or an application, contact Adaptec directly.

  Amount of award: $5,000
Contact:
Adaptec

ADHA Institute for Oral Health

ADHA Institute for Oral Health Minority Scholarship

Type of award: Scholarship, renewable.
Intended use: For full-time undergraduate certificate study at postsecondary institution in United States.
Eligibility: Applicant must be Asian American, African American, Mexican American, Hispanic American, Puerto Rican or American Indian. Men are considered a minority in this field and are encouraged to apply for this program.
Basis for selection: Major/career interest in dental hygiene; dentistry; dental assistant or dental laboratory technology. Applicant must demonstrate financial need, depth of character, leadership, seriousness of purpose and service orientation.
Application requirements: Recommendations, essay, transcript, proof of eligibility, research proposal. FAFSA.
Additional information: GPA of 3.0 required. Applicants must provide a statement of professional activities related to dental hygiene. Applicants must be working toward a certificate or Associate Degree. Evidence of dental hygiene licensure eligibility must be provided. Applicants must be eligible for licensure in academic year award is being made.

  Amount of award: $1,500
  Number of awards: 2
  Application deadline: June 1
Contact:
ADHA Institute of Oral Health
444 N. Michigan Ave., Suite 3400
Chicago, IL 60611
Phone: 800-735-4916
Fax: 312-440-8929

ADHA Institute for Oral Health Part-Time Scholarship

Type of award: Scholarship, renewable.
Intended use: For half-time undergraduate or master's study at 4-year or graduate institution in United States. Designated institutions: Accredited dental hygiene schools.
Basis for selection: Major/career interest in dental hygiene. Applicant must demonstrate financial need, depth of character, leadership, seriousness of purpose and service orientation.

Application requirements: Recommendations, essay, transcript, proof of eligibility, research proposal. FAFSA.
Additional information: Minimum GPA of 3.0. Awarded to applicants pursuing associate/certificate, baccalaureate or graduate degree enrolled part-time in accredited dental hygiene school.

Amount of award:	$1,500
Number of awards:	1
Application deadline:	June 1

Contact:
ADHA Institute for Oral Health
444 N. Michigan Ave., Suite 3400
Chicago, IL 60611
Phone: 800-735-4916
Fax: 312-440-8929

Colgate "Bright Smiles, Bright Futures" Minority Scholarships

Type of award: Scholarship, renewable.
Intended use: For full-time junior, senior, master's or doctoral study at 4-year or graduate institution in United States.
Eligibility: Applicant must be Asian American, African American, Mexican American, Hispanic American, Puerto Rican or American Indian. Men are considered a minority in this field and are encouraged to apply for this program.
Basis for selection: Major/career interest in dental hygiene. Applicant must demonstrate financial need, high academic achievement, depth of character, leadership, seriousness of purpose and service orientation.
Application requirements: Recommendations. FAFSA.
Additional information: Minimum GPA 3.0. Graduate applicants must provide a statement of professional activities related to dental hygiene. Evidence of dental hygiene licensure must be provided or applicant must be eligible for licensure in the academic year the award is being made. Graduate applicants must provide evidence of acceptance into a full-time master's or doctoral degree program.

Amount of award:	$1,250
Number of awards:	2
Application deadline:	June 1

Contact:
ADHA Institute for Oral Health
444 N. Michigan Ave., Suite 3400
Chicago, IL 60611
Phone: 800-735-4916
Fax: 312-440-8929

Dr. Alfred C. Fones Scholarship

Type of award: Scholarship, renewable.
Intended use: For full-time senior or master's study at 4-year or graduate institution in United States.
Basis for selection: Major/career interest in dental hygiene. Applicant must demonstrate financial need, high academic achievement, depth of character, leadership, seriousness of purpose and service orientation.
Application requirements: Recommendations, essay, transcript, proof of eligibility, research proposal. FAFSA.
Additional information: Minimum GPA 3.0. Evidence of dental hygiene license must be provided and applicant must hold the minimum of a baccalaureate degree or be granted such by the end of the current academic year. Undergraduate applicants must be eligible for licensure in the academic year the award is being made. Applicant must provide evidence of acceptance into a full-time master's or doctoral degree program.

Amount of award:	$1,500
Number of awards:	1
Application deadline:	June 1

Contact:
ADHA Institute for Oral Health
444 N. Michigan Ave., Suite 3400
Chicago, IL 60611
Phone: 800-735-4916
Fax: 312-440-8929

Dr. Harold Hillenbrand Scholarship

Type of award: Scholarship, renewable.
Intended use: For full-time undergraduate study at 4-year institution in United States.
Basis for selection: Major/career interest in dental hygiene. Applicant must demonstrate financial need, high academic achievement, depth of character, leadership, seriousness of purpose and service orientation.
Application requirements: Recommendations. FAFSA.
Additional information: Applicants must provide a statement of professional activities related to dental hygiene. Evidence of dental hygiene licensure eligibility must be provided. Applicants must be eligible for licensure in the academic year the award is being made. Minimum GPA 3.5.

Amount of award:	$1,500
Number of awards:	1
Application deadline:	June 1

Contact:
ADHA Institute for Oral Health
444 N. Michigan Ave., Suite 3400
Chicago, IL 60611
Phone: 800-735-4916
Fax: 312-440-8929

Irene E. Newman Scholarship

Type of award: Scholarship.
Intended use: For full-time undergraduate, master's or doctoral study at 4-year or graduate institution in United States.
Eligibility: Applicant or parent must be member/participant of Student American Dental Hygenists' Association.
Basis for selection: Major/career interest in dental hygiene. Applicant must demonstrate financial need, high academic achievement, depth of character, leadership, seriousness of purpose and service orientation.
Application requirements: Recommendations. FAFSA. Applicant must have SADHA or ADHA membership.
Additional information: Minimum GPA 3.0. Awarded to an applicant who demonstrates strong potential in public health or community dental health. Evidence of dental hygiene licensure must be provided and applicant must hold the minimum of a baccalaureate degree or be granted such by the end of the current academic year. Undergraduate applicants must be eligible for licensure in the academic year the award is being made. Applicant must provide evidence of acceptance into a full-time master's or doctoral degree program.

Amount of award:	$1,500
Number of awards:	1
Application deadline:	June 1

Contact:
ADHA Institute for Oral Health
444 N. Michigan Ave., Suite 3400
Chicago, IL 60611
Phone: 800-735-4916
Fax: 312-440-8929

Scholarships

Margaret E. Swanson Scholarship

Type of award: Scholarship.
Intended use: For full-time undergraduate or master's study at 4-year or graduate institution in United States. Designated institutions: Accredited dental hygiene schools.
Eligibility: Applicant or parent must be member/participant of Student American Dental Hygenists' Association.
Basis for selection: Major/career interest in dental hygiene. Applicant must demonstrate financial need, depth of character, leadership, seriousness of purpose and service orientation.
Application requirements: Recommendations. FAFSA. Applicant must have SADHA or ADHA membership.
Additional information: Minimum GPA 3.0. Awarded to an applicant who demonstrates exceptional organizational leadership potential and is pursuing an associate/certificate, baccalaureate or graduate degree while enrolled at an accredited dental hygiene school.

Amount of award:	$1,500
Number of awards:	1
Application deadline:	June 1

Contact:
ADHA Institute for Oral Health
444 N. Michigan Ave., Suite 3400
Chicago, IL 60611
Phone: 800-735-4916
Fax: 312-440-8929

Oral-B Laboratories Dental Hygiene Scholarship

Type of award: Scholarship.
Intended use: For full-time undergraduate study at 4-year institution in United States.
Eligibility: Applicant or parent must be member/participant of American Dental Hygenists' Association.
Basis for selection: Major/career interest in dental hygiene. Applicant must demonstrate financial need, high academic achievement, depth of character, leadership, seriousness of purpose and service orientation.
Application requirements: Recommendations. FAFSA.
Additional information: Minimum GPA 3.5. Evidence of dental hygiene licensure eligibility must be provided. Applicant must be eligible for licensure in the academic year the award is being made. Applicant must have ADHA membership or Student ADHA membership (SADHA).

Amount of award:	$1,000-$1,500
Number of awards:	2
Application deadline:	June 1

Contact:
ADHA Institute for Oral Health
444 N. Michigan Ave., Suite 3400
Chicago, IL 60611
Phone: 800-735-4916
Fax: 312-440-8929

Sigma Phi Alpha Graduate Scholarship

Type of award: Scholarship.
Intended use: For full-time senior, master's or doctoral study at 4-year or graduate institution in United States.
Eligibility: Applicant or parent must be member/participant of American Dental Hygenists' Association.
Basis for selection: Major/career interest in dental hygiene. Applicant must demonstrate financial need, high academic achievement, depth of character, leadership, seriousness of purpose and service orientation.
Application requirements: Recommendations. FAFSA, statement of research interest, career goal statement. Submission of final thesis or dissertation.
Additional information: Minimum GPA 3.0. Applicants must provide a statement of professional activities related to dental hygiene. Evidence of dental hygiene licensure must be provided, and applicant must hold the minimum of a baccalaureate degree or be granted such by the end of the current application year and also provide evidence of acceptance into a full-time master's or doctoral degree program. Applicants must be eligible for licensure in the academic year the award is being made.

Amount of award:	$1,000
Number of awards:	1
Application deadline:	June 1

Contact:
ADHA Institute for Oral Health
444 N. Michigan Ave., Suite 3400
Chicago, IL 60611
Phone: 800-735-4916
Fax: 312-440-8929

Sigma Phi Alpha Undergraduate Scholarship

Type of award: Scholarship.
Intended use: For full-time undergraduate study at 4-year institution in United States. Designated institutions: Accredited dental hygiene schools.
Eligibility: Applicant or parent must be member/participant of American Dental Hygenists' Association.
Basis for selection: Major/career interest in dental hygiene. Applicant must demonstrate high academic achievement, depth of character, leadership, seriousness of purpose and service orientation.
Application requirements: Recommendations, essay. FAFSA.
Additional information: Minimum GPA 3.0. Awarded to applicants pursuing associate/certificate or baccalaureate degree at accredited dental hygiene school with an active chapter of the Sigma Phi Alpha Dental Hygiene Honor Society. Applicant must have ADHA membership or Student ADHA membership (SADHA). Visit Website to download application.

Amount of award:	$1,000
Number of awards:	1
Application deadline:	June 1

Contact:
ADHA Institute for Oral Health
444 N. Michigan Ave.
Suite 3400
Chicago, IL 60611
Phone: 800-735-4916
Fax: 312-440-8929
Web: www.adha.org/institute

AGC of Maine Education Foundation

AGC of Maine Scholarship Program

Type of award: Scholarship, renewable.
Intended use: For sophomore, junior or senior study.

Eligibility: Applicant must be residing in Maine.
Basis for selection: Major/career interest in construction or engineering, civil. Applicant must demonstrate financial need and high academic achievement.
Application requirements: Interview, recommendations, essay, transcript.
Additional information: Full-time enrolled students preferred.

Amount of award:	$500-$3,000
Number of awards:	8
Number of applicants:	30
Application deadline:	March 15
Total amount awarded:	$12,500

Contact:
AGC of Maine
P.O. Box 5519
Augusta, ME 04332
Phone: 207-622-4741

AGL Resources Service Company

AGL Resources Inc. Scholarship

Type of award: Scholarship, renewable.
Intended use: For undergraduate study at vocational, 2-year or 4-year institution.
Eligibility: Applicant or parent must be employed by AGL Resources Service Company. Applicant must be high school senior.
Additional information: For further information or an application, contact AGL Resources Incorporated directly.

Amount of award:	$500-$1,000

Aid Association for Lutherans

All-College Scholarship Program

Type of award: Scholarship, renewable.
Intended use: For full-time undergraduate study at accredited postsecondary institution in United States.
Eligibility: Applicant or parent must be member/participant of Aid Association for Lutherans. Applicant must be high school senior. Applicant must be Lutheran. Applicant must be U.S. citizen.
Basis for selection: Applicant must demonstrate leadership and service orientation.
Application requirements: Proof of eligibility. Send SAT or ACT scores.
Additional information: Applicant must be AAL benefit member. Applications available November through January. Church/school/community involvement important. Visit Website for further information.

Amount of award:	$500
Number of awards:	1,600
Number of applicants:	6,000
Application deadline:	January 31
Total amount awarded:	$1,000,000

Contact:
Aid Association for Lutherans
4321 N. Ballard Road
Appleton, WI 54919-0001
Phone: 800-225-5225
Web: www.aal.org

Lutheran Campus Scholarship Program

Type of award: Scholarship, renewable.
Intended use: For undergraduate study at accredited postsecondary institution in United States. Designated institutions: Participating Lutheran postsecondary institutions. List available on Website.
Eligibility: Applicant must be high school senior. Applicant must be Lutheran. Applicant must be U.S. citizen.
Basis for selection: Applicant must demonstrate leadership and service orientation.
Application requirements: Proof of eligibility.
Additional information: Applicant must be AAL benefit member. Deadlines set by college. Contact college financial aid office for application. Church/community/school involvement important. Visit Website for additional information.

Amount of award:	$200-$1,000
Number of awards:	1,600
Application deadline:	January 31
Total amount awarded:	$1,000,000

Contact:
Aid Association for Lutherans
4321 N. Ballard Road
Appleton, WI 54919-0001
Phone: 800-225-5225
Web: www.aal.org

Vocational/Technical School Scholarship Program

Type of award: Scholarship, renewable.
Intended use: For undergraduate study at accredited vocational or 2-year institution in United States.
Eligibility: Applicant must be high school senior. Applicant must be Lutheran. Applicant must be U.S. citizen.
Basis for selection: Applicant must demonstrate service orientation.
Application requirements: Proof of eligibility.
Additional information: Applicant must be AAL benefit member. Applications available November through January. Church/community/school involvement important. Visit Website for additional information.

Amount of award:	$500
Number of awards:	100
Number of applicants:	400
Application deadline:	January 31
Total amount awarded:	$50,000

Contact:
Aid Association for Lutherans
4321 N. Ballard Road
Appleton, WI 54919-0001
Phone: 800-255-5225
Web: www.aal.org

Scholarships

Air Force Aid Society

Air Force Aid Society Education Grant

Type of award: Scholarship.
Intended use: For full-time undergraduate study at accredited vocational, 2-year or 4-year institution in or outside United States.
Eligibility: Applicant must be dependent of active service person, veteran or deceased veteran; or spouse of active service person, veteran or deceased veteran who serves or served in the Air Force.
Basis for selection: Applicant must demonstrate financial need.
Application requirements: Proof of eligibility.
Additional information: Minimum 2.0 GPA. Veteran status alone not eligible. Veteran must either be retired reserve over age 60 and collecting retired pay, or retired with at least 20 years service in active duty Air Force. Air Force Reserve and Air National Guard only eligible if on active duty (all other Guard and Reserve are not eligible).

Amount of award:	$1,500
Number of awards:	5,000
Number of applicants:	9,300
Application deadline:	March 16
Notification begins:	June 15
Total amount awarded:	$7,500,000

Contact:
Air Force Aid Society
Education Assistance Department
1745 Jefferson Davis Highway, Suite 202
Arlington, VA 22202
Phone: 800-429-9475
Web: www.afas.org

Air Liquide America Foundation, Inc.

Air Liquide America Foundation Scholarship

Type of award: Scholarship, renewable.
Intended use: For freshman, sophomore, junior or senior study at accredited vocational, 2-year or 4-year institution.
Eligibility: Applicant or parent must be employed by Air Liquide America Corporation.
Basis for selection: Applicant must demonstrate financial need.
Additional information: Must be child of employee of ALAC. For further information or an application, contact Air Liquide America Corporation directly.

Amount of award:	$500-$2,000

Air Traffic Control Association, Inc.

Air Traffic Control Children of Specialists Scholarship

Type of award: Scholarship.
Intended use: For full-time undergraduate or graduate study at accredited 4-year institution.
Eligibility: Applicant or parent must be employed by Aviation industry. Applicant must be U.S. citizen.
Basis for selection: Applicant must demonstrate financial need, depth of character and seriousness of purpose.
Application requirements: Recommendations, transcript.
Additional information: Must be natural or adopted child of air traffic control specialist. Applicant's course work must lead to a bachelor's degree or higher. Application and terms or reference can be downloaded from Website.

Amount of award:	$1,500-$2,500
Number of awards:	3
Number of applicants:	200
Application deadline:	May 1
Total amount awarded:	$4,500

Contact:
Air Traffic Control Association, Inc.
Scholarship Coordinator
2300 Clarendon Boulevard, Suite 711
Arlington, VA 22201
Phone: 703-522-5717
Web: www.atca.org

Air Traffic Control Full-Time Employee Student Scholarship

Type of award: Scholarship.
Intended use: For undergraduate, graduate or non-degree study at postsecondary institution.
Eligibility: Applicant or parent must be employed by Aviation industry. Applicant must be returning adult student. Applicant must be U.S. citizen.
Basis for selection: Major/career interest in aviation; aviation repair or computer/information sciences. Applicant must demonstrate financial need, depth of character and seriousness of purpose.
Application requirements: Recommendations, transcript, proof of eligibility.
Additional information: Available only to full-time aviation career professional doing part-time study to enhance job skills. Employee applicant must work full-time in aviation-related field, and course work must enhance aviation skills. Scholarship must be used within four years of date awarded. Application and terms of reference can be downloaded from Website.

Amount of award:	$400-$600
Number of awards:	4
Number of applicants:	45
Application deadline:	May 1
Total amount awarded:	$2,400

Contact:
Air Traffic Control Association, Inc.
Scholarship Coordinator
2300 Clarendon Boulevard, Suite 711
Arlington, VA 22201
Phone: 703-522-5717
Web: www.atca.org

Air Traffic Control Half/Full-Time Student Scholarship

Type of award: Scholarship.
Intended use: For freshman, sophomore, junior, senior, master's, doctoral or postgraduate study at accredited 4-year or graduate institution in United States.
Eligibility: Applicant must be U.S. citizen.
Basis for selection: Major/career interest in aviation or aerospace. Applicant must demonstrate financial need, depth of character and seriousness of purpose.
Application requirements: Essay, proof of eligibility. Two recommendations, a 400 word essay on "How My Education Efforts Will Enhance My Potential Contribution To Aviation" and college transcript (high school transcript if under 30 semester hours or 45 quarter hours completed).
Additional information: Minimum of 30 semester hours or 45 quarter hours still to be completed before graduation and attend at least half time (six hours). Applicants' coursework must lead to bachelor's degree or higher. Application and terms of reference can be downloaded from Website.

Amount of award:	$1,500-$2,500
Number of awards:	3
Number of applicants:	300
Application deadline:	May 1
Total amount awarded:	$4,500

Contact:
Air Traffic Control Association, Inc.
Scholarship Coordinator
2300 Clarendon Boulevard, Suite 711
Arlington, VA 22201
Phone: 703-522-5717
Web: www.atca.org

Aircraft Electronics Association Educational Foundation

Bendix/King Avionics Scholarship

Type of award: Scholarship, renewable.
Intended use: For full-time undergraduate study at accredited vocational, 2-year or 4-year institution. Designated institutions: Accredited schools with avionics or aircraft repair programs.
Basis for selection: Major/career interest in aviation; aviation repair or electronics.
Application requirements: Recommendations, transcript, proof of eligibility.
Additional information: Available to anyone attending or planning to attend an accredited school in an avionics or aircraft repair program. Awards are announced at AEA Annual Convention and Trade Show each spring.

Amount of award:	$1,000
Number of awards:	1
Application deadline:	February 15
Total amount awarded:	$1,000

Contact:
Aircraft Electronics Association Educational Foundation
4217 S. Hocker Drive
Independence, MO 64055
Phone: 816-373-6565
Web: www.aea.net/educationalfoundation

BFGoodrich Component Services Scholarship

Type of award: Scholarship, renewable.
Intended use: For full-time undergraduate study at accredited vocational, 2-year or 4-year institution. Designated institutions: Accredited colleges/universities with avionics or aircraft repair programs.
Basis for selection: Major/career interest in aviation; aviation repair or electronics. Applicant must demonstrate depth of character and seriousness of purpose.
Application requirements: Recommendations, transcript, proof of eligibility.
Additional information: Available to anyone attending or planning to attend an accredited school in an avionics or aircraft repair program. Awards are announced at AEA Annual Convention and Trade Show each spring.

Amount of award:	$2,500
Number of awards:	1
Application deadline:	February 15
Total amount awarded:	$2,500

Contact:
Aircraft Electronics Association Educational Foundation
4217 S. Hocker Drive
Independence, MO 64055
Phone: 816-373-6565
Web: www.aea.net/educationalfoundation

Bose Corporation Scholarship

Type of award: Scholarship, renewable.
Intended use: For full-time undergraduate study. Designated institutions: Embry-Riddle Aeronautical University.
Eligibility: Applicant must be high school senior.
Basis for selection: Major/career interest in aviation; aviation repair or electronics. Applicant must demonstrate depth of character and seriousness of purpose.
Application requirements: Recommendations, transcript, proof of eligibility.
Additional information: Scholarship only applies to individuals who are attending or planning to attend Embry-Riddle Aeronautical University's avionics program. Awards are announced at AEA Annual Convention and Trade Show each spring.

Amount of award:	$1,500
Number of awards:	1
Application deadline:	February 15
Total amount awarded:	$1,500

Contact:
Aircraft Electronics Association Educational Foundation
4217 S. Hocker Drive
Independence, MO 64055
Phone: 816-373-6565
Web: www.aea.net/educationalfoundation

Bud Glover Memorial Scholarship

Type of award: Scholarship, renewable.
Intended use: For full-time undergraduate study at accredited vocational, 2-year or 4-year institution. Designated institutions: Accredited schools with avionics or aircraft repair programs.
Basis for selection: Major/career interest in aviation; aviation repair or electronics. Applicant must demonstrate depth of character and seriousness of purpose.
Application requirements: Recommendations, transcript, proof of eligibility.

Additional information: Available to anyone attending or planning to attend an accredited school in an avionics or aircraft repair program. Awards are announced at AEA Annual Convention and Trade Show each spring.

Amount of award:	$1,000
Number of awards:	1
Application deadline:	February 15

Contact:
Aircraft Electronics Association Educational Foundation
4217 S. Hocker Drive
Independence, MO 64055
Phone: 816-373-6565
Web: www.aea.net/educationalfoundation

College of Aeronautics Scholarship

Type of award: Scholarship, renewable.
Intended use: For full-time undergraduate study at 2-year institution. Designated institutions: College of Aeronautics in Flushing, N.Y.
Basis for selection: Major/career interest in aviation; aviation repair or electronics. Applicant must demonstrate depth of character and seriousness of purpose.
Application requirements: Recommendations, transcript, proof of eligibility.
Additional information: Available to anyone attending or planning to attend College of Aeronautics in Flushing, N.Y. Scholarship is for duration of two-year program, at $750 per semester with maximum of $3,000 for four semesters. Awards are announced at AEA Annual Convention and Trade Show each spring.

Amount of award:	$750-$3,000
Number of awards:	1
Application deadline:	February 15

Contact:
Aircraft Electronics Association Educational Foundation
4217 S. Hocker Drive
Independence, MO 64055
Phone: 816-373-6565
Web: www.aea.net/educationalfoundation

David Arver Memorial Scholarship

Type of award: Scholarship, renewable.
Intended use: For full-time undergraduate study at accredited vocational or 2-year institution. Designated institutions: Accredited vocational/technical schools with avionics or aircraft repair programs, located in Illinois, Indiana, Iowa, Kansas, Michigan, Minnesota, Missouri, Nebraska, North Dakota, South Dakota or Wisconsin institutions.
Basis for selection: Major/career interest in aviation; aviation repair or electronics. Applicant must demonstrate depth of character and seriousness of purpose.
Application requirements: Recommendations, transcript, proof of eligibility.
Additional information: Available to anyone attending or planning to attend an accredited school located in AEA Region Three (listed states) in an avionics or aircraft repair program. Awards are announced at AEA Annual Convention and Trade Show each spring.

Amount of award:	$1,000
Number of awards:	1
Application deadline:	February 15
Total amount awarded:	$1,000

Contact:
Aircraft Electronics Association Educational Foundation
4217 S. Hocker Drive
Independence, MO 64055
Phone: 816-373-6565
Web: www.aea.net/educationalfoundation

Dutch and Ginger Arver Scholarship

Type of award: Scholarship, renewable.
Intended use: For full-time undergraduate study at accredited vocational, 2-year or 4-year institution. Designated institutions: Accredited schools with avionics or aircraft repair programs.
Basis for selection: Major/career interest in aviation; aviation repair or electronics. Applicant must demonstrate depth of character and seriousness of purpose.
Application requirements: Recommendations, transcript, proof of eligibility.
Additional information: Available to anyone attending or planning to attend an accredited school in an avionics or aircraft repair program. Awards are announced at AEA Annual Convention and Trade Show.

Amount of award:	$1,000
Number of awards:	1
Application deadline:	February 15
Total amount awarded:	$1,000

Contact:
Aircraft Electronics Association Educational Foundation
4217 S. Hocker Drive
Independence, MO 64055
Phone: 816-373-6565
Web: www.aea.net/educationalfoundation

Field Aviation Co., Inc. Scholarship

Type of award: Scholarship, renewable.
Intended use: For full-time undergraduate study at vocational, 2-year or 4-year institution. Designated institutions: Accredited schools with avionics or aircraft repair programs, located in Canada.
Basis for selection: Major/career interest in aviation; aviation repair or electronics. Applicant must demonstrate depth of character and seriousness of purpose.
Application requirements: Recommendations, transcript, proof of eligibility.
Additional information: Available to anyone attending or planning to attend accredited school in avionics or aircraft repair program in Canada. Awards are announced at AEA Annual Convention and Trade Show each spring.

Amount of award:	$1,000
Number of awards:	1
Application deadline:	February 15

Contact:
Aircraft Electronics Association Educational Foundation
4217 S. Hocker Drive
Independence, MO 64055
Phone: 816-373-6565
Web: www.aea.net/educationalfoundation

Garmin Scholarship

Type of award: Scholarship, renewable.
Intended use: For full-time undergraduate study at accredited vocational, 2-year or 4-year institution. Designated institutions: Accredited schools with avionics and aircraft repair programs.

Basis for selection: Major/career interest in aviation; aviation repair or electronics. Applicant must demonstrate depth of character and seriousness of purpose.
Application requirements: Recommendations, transcript, proof of eligibility.
Additional information: Available to anyone attending or planning to attend an accredited school in an avionics or aircraft repair program. Awards are announced at AEA Annual Convention and Trade Show each spring.

Amount of award:	$2,000
Number of awards:	1
Application deadline:	February 15
Total amount awarded:	$2,000

Contact:
Aircraft Electronics Association Educational Foundation
4217 S. Hocker Drive
Independence, MO 64055
Phone: 816-373-6565
Web: www.aea.net/educationalfoundation

Gulf Coast Avionics to Fox Valley Technical College Scholarship

Type of award: Scholarship, renewable.
Intended use: For full-time undergraduate study at vocational or 2-year institution. Designated institutions: Fox Valley Technical College in Oshkosh, Wisconsin.
Basis for selection: Major/career interest in aviation; aviation repair or electronics. Applicant must demonstrate depth of character and seriousness of purpose.
Application requirements: Recommendations, transcript, proof of eligibility.
Additional information: Available to anyone attending or planning to attend Fox Valley Technical College in Oshkosh, Wisconsin. Awards are announced at AEA Annual Convention and Trade Show each spring.

Amount of award:	$1,000
Number of awards:	1
Application deadline:	February 15
Total amount awarded:	$1,000

Contact:
Aircraft Electronics Association Educational Foundation
4217 S. Hocker Drive
Independence, MO 64055
Phone: 816-373-6565
Web: www.aea.net/educationalfoundation

Johnny Davis Memorial Scholarship

Type of award: Scholarship, renewable.
Intended use: For full-time undergraduate study at accredited vocational, 2-year or 4-year institution. Designated institutions: Accredited schools with avionic or aircraft repair programs.
Basis for selection: Major/career interest in aviation; aviation repair or electronics. Applicant must demonstrate depth of character and seriousness of purpose.
Application requirements: Recommendations, transcript, proof of eligibility.
Additional information: Available to anyone attending or planning to attend an accredited school in an avionics or aircraft repair program. Awards are announced at AEA Annual Convention and Trade Show each spring.

Amount of award:	$1,000
Number of awards:	1
Application deadline:	February 15
Total amount awarded:	$1,000

Contact:
Aircraft Electronics Association Educational Foundation
4217 S. Hocker Drive
Independence, MO 64055
Phone: 816-373-6565
Web: www.aea.net/educationalfoundation

Lee Tarbox Memorial Scholarship

Type of award: Scholarship, renewable.
Intended use: For full-time undergraduate study at accredited vocational, 2-year or 4-year institution. Designated institutions: Accredited schools with avionics or aircraft repair programs.
Basis for selection: Major/career interest in aviation; aviation repair or electronics. Applicant must demonstrate depth of character and seriousness of purpose.
Application requirements: Recommendations, transcript, proof of eligibility.
Additional information: Available to anyone attending or planning to attend an accredited school in an avionics or aircraft repair program. Scholarship given by Pacific Southwest Instruments. Awards are announced at AEA Annual Convention and Trade Show each spring.

Amount of award:	$2,500
Number of awards:	1
Application deadline:	February 15
Total amount awarded:	$2,500

Contact:
Aircraft Electronics Association Educational Foundation
4217 S. Hocker Drive
Independence, MO 64055
Phone: 816-373-6565
Web: www.aea.net/educationalfoundation

Leon Harris/Les Nichols Memorial to Spartan School of Aeronautics

Type of award: Scholarship, renewable.
Intended use: For full-time undergraduate study. Designated institutions: NEC Spartan School of Aeronautics in Tulsa, OK.
Basis for selection: Major/career interest in aviation; aviation repair or electronics. Applicant must demonstrate depth of character and seriousness of purpose.
Application requirements: Recommendations, transcript, proof of eligibility.
Additional information: Available to students who pursue Associate's Degree in Applied Science in Aviation Electronics (avionics) at NEC Spartan School of Aeronautics in Tulsa, OK. Applicant may not be currently enrolled in Avionics program at Spartan. Award will cover tuition expenses for eight quarters or until Associate's Degree is completed, whichever comes first. All other costs (tools, living expenses and fees) must be covered by student. Awards are announced at AEA Annual Convention and Trade Show each spring.

Amount of award:	Full tuition
Number of awards:	1
Application deadline:	February 15

Contact:
Aircraft Electronics Association Educational Foundation
4217 S. Hocker Drive
Independence, MO 64055
Phone: 816-373-6565
Web: www.aea.net/educationalfoundation

Scholarships

Lowell Gaylor Memorial Scholarship

Type of award: Scholarship, renewable.
Intended use: For full-time undergraduate study at accredited vocational, 2-year or 4-year institution. Designated institutions: Accredited schools with avionics or aircraft repair programs.
Basis for selection: Major/career interest in aviation; aviation repair or electronics. Applicant must demonstrate depth of character and seriousness of purpose.
Application requirements: Recommendations, transcript, proof of eligibility.
Additional information: Available to anyone attending or planning to attend an accredited school in an avionics or aircraft repair program. Awards are announced at AEA Annual Convention and Trade Show each year.

Amount of award:	$1,000
Number of awards:	1
Application deadline:	February 15

Contact:
Aircraft Electronics Association Educational Foundation
4217 S. Hocker Drive
Independence, MO 64055
Phone: 816-373-6565
Web: www.aea.net/educationalfoundation

Mid-Continent Instrument Scholarship

Type of award: Scholarship, renewable.
Intended use: For full-time undergraduate study at accredited vocational, 2-year or 4-year institution. Designated institutions: Accredited schools with avionics or aircraft repair programs.
Basis for selection: Major/career interest in aviation; aviation repair or electronics. Applicant must demonstrate depth of character and seriousness of purpose.
Application requirements: Recommendations, transcript, proof of eligibility.
Additional information: Available to anyone attending or planning to attend an accredited school in an avionics or aircraft repair program. Awards are announced at AEA Annual Convention and Trade Show each spring.

Amount of award:	$1,000
Number of awards:	1
Application deadline:	February 15
Total amount awarded:	$1,000

Contact:
Scholarship Coordinator
4217 S. Hocker Drive
Independence, MO 64055
Phone: 816-373-6565
Web: www.aea.net/educationalfoundation

Monte R. Mitchell Global Scholarship

Type of award: Scholarship, renewable.
Intended use: For full-time undergraduate study at accredited vocational or 2-year institution in or outside United States. Designated institutions: Accredited institutions with aviation maintenance technology, avionics or aircraft repair programs, located in Europe or the United States.
Eligibility: Applicant must be high school senior. Applicant must be international student or international or European student.

Basis for selection: Major/career interest in aviation; aviation repair or electronics. Applicant must demonstrate depth of character and seriousness of purpose.
Application requirements: Proof of eligibility.
Additional information: Available to European student pursuing degree in aviation maintenance technology, avionics or aircraft repair at accredited school in Europe or the United States. Scholarship given by Mid-Continent Instruments Co. Awards are announced at AEA Annual Convention and Trade Show each spring.

Amount of award:	$1,000
Number of awards:	1
Application deadline:	February 15
Total amount awarded:	$1,000

Contact:
Aircraft Electronics Association Educational Foundation
4217 S. Hocker Drive
Independence, MO 64055
Phone: 816-373-6565
Web: www.aea.net/educationalfoundation

Plane & Pilot Magazine/Garmin Scholarship

Type of award: Scholarship, renewable.
Intended use: For full-time undergraduate study at accredited vocational institution. Designated institutions: Accredited vocational/technical schools with avionics or aircraft repair programs.
Basis for selection: Major/career interest in aviation; aviation repair or electronics. Applicant must demonstrate depth of character and seriousness of purpose.
Application requirements: Recommendations, transcript, proof of eligibility.
Additional information: Available to anyone attending or planning to attend an accredited vocational/technical school in an avionics or aircraft program. Awards are announced at AEA Annual Convention and Trade Show each spring.

Amount of award:	$2,000
Number of awards:	1
Application deadline:	February 15
Total amount awarded:	$2,000

Contact:
Aircraft Electronic Association Educational Foundation
4217 S. Hocker Drive
Independence, MO 64055
Phone: 816-373-6565
Web: www.aea.net/educationalfoundation

Russell Leroy Jones Memorial Scholarship to Westwood College of Aviation Technology

Type of award: Scholarship, renewable.
Intended use: For full-time undergraduate study. Designated institutions: Westwood College of Aviation Technology in Broomfield, CO.
Basis for selection: Major/career interest in aviation; aviation repair or electronics. Applicant must demonstrate depth of character and seriousness of purpose.
Application requirements: Recommendations, transcript, proof of eligibility.
Additional information: Available to anyone planning to attend Westwood College of Aviation Technology in Broomfield, CO for electronics/avionics program. This award covers tuition only. Tools, fees, room and board must be paid

for by student. Applicant may not be currently enrolled at Westwood College of Aviation Technology. Awards are announced at AEA Annual Convention and Trade Show each spring.

Amount of award:	$6,000
Number of awards:	3
Application deadline:	February 15

Contact:
Aircraft Electronics Association Educational Foundation
4217 S. Hocker Drive
Independence, MO 64055
Phone: 816-373-6565
Web: www.aea.net/educationalfoundation

Aircraft Owners and Pilots Association

AOPA Air Safety Foundation/ McAllister Memorial Scholarship

Type of award: Scholarship.
Intended use: For full-time undergraduate study at accredited 4-year institution in United States. Designated institutions: Institutions with aviation programs.
Eligibility: Applicant must be U.S. citizen or permanent resident.
Basis for selection: Major/career interest in aviation or aviation repair. Applicant must demonstrate financial need and high academic achievement.
Application requirements: Essay, transcript, proof of eligibility.
Additional information: Applicant must be enrolled in an aviation program at a four-year institution. Application available online, and must be mailed to: Dr. David A. NewMyer, Chairperson; Aviation Management and Flight College of Applied Sciences and Arts; Southern Illinois University Carbondale; Carbondale, IL 62901-6623.

Amount of award:	$1,000
Number of awards:	1
Application deadline:	March 1
Notification begins:	July 1
Total amount awarded:	$1,000

Contact:
Aircraft Owners and Pilots Association Air Safety Foundation
McAllister Memorial Scholarship
421 Aviation Way
Frederick, MD 21701
Phone: 301-695-2000
Fax: 301-695-2375
Web: www.aopa.org

Airgas, Inc.

Airgas Scholarship

Type of award: Scholarship, renewable.
Intended use: For undergraduate study at accredited vocational, 2-year or 4-year institution.
Eligibility: Applicant or parent must be employed by Airgas, Inc.

Basis for selection: Applicant must demonstrate financial need.
Additional information: For further information or an application, contact Airgas, Inc. directly.

Amount of award:	$500-$2,000

Airmen Memorial Foundation

Chief Master Sergeants of the Air Force Scholarship

Type of award: Scholarship.
Intended use: For full-time undergraduate study at accredited vocational, 2-year or 4-year institution in or outside United States.
Eligibility: Applicant must be single, no older than 23. Applicant must be dependent of active service person or veteran in the Air Force or Reserves/National Guard. Must be child of active duty or retired enlisted member of U.S. Air Force, Air National Guard, or Air Force Reserves.
Basis for selection: Applicant must demonstrate high academic achievement, depth of character and leadership.
Application requirements: Recommendations, essay, transcript, proof of eligibility.
Additional information: Must be single dependent, including legally adopted child or stepchild, who will not reach 23rd birthday by September 1 of award year. Applications available November 1 to March 31. For application, send self-addressed, stamped ($0.78) envelope (size #10).

Amount of award:	$500-$3,000
Number of awards:	35
Number of applicants:	200
Application deadline:	April 15
Notification begins:	August 1

Contact:
Airmen Foundation Scholarships
P.O. Box 50
Temple Hills, MD 20757-0050
Phone: 800-638-0594

Alabama Commission on Higher Education

Alabama National Guard Educational Assistance Award

Type of award: Scholarship, renewable.
Intended use: For undergraduate or graduate study at postsecondary institution. Designated institutions: Alabama public institution.
Eligibility: Applicant must be U.S. citizen residing in Alabama. Applicant must be in military service in the Reserves/National Guard. Must be active members in good standing with federally recognized unit of Alabama National Guard.
Application requirements: Proof of eligibility.
Additional information: Award covers tuition, books, fees and supplies (minus any Federal Veterans' benefits) at Alabama public institution.

Amount of award:	$25-$1,000
Number of awards:	952
Number of applicants:	952
Total amount awarded:	$668,162

Contact:
Alabama National Guard Unit
Phone: 334-242-1998
Fax: 334-242-0270
Web: www.ache.state.al.us

Alabama Student Assistance Program

Type of award: Scholarship, renewable.
Intended use: For full-time undergraduate study at vocational, 2-year or 4-year institution. Designated institutions: Eligible Alabama postsecondary institutions. Nearly 80 institutions participate in program.
Eligibility: Applicant must be residing in Alabama.
Basis for selection: Applicant must demonstrate financial need.
Application requirements: Proof of eligibility. FAFSA.
Additional information: Students urged to apply early.

Amount of award:	$300-$2,500
Number of awards:	3,931
Total amount awarded:	$1,830,550

Contact:
Applications available at high school or college financial aid office.
Phone: 334-242-1998
Fax: 334-242-0270
Web: www.ache.state.al.us

Alabama Student Grant

Type of award: Scholarship, renewable.
Intended use: For undergraduate study at 2-year or 4-year institution. Designated institutions: Birmingham-Southern College, Concordia College, Faulkner University, Huntingdon College, Judson College, Miles College, Oakwood College, Samford University, Southeastern Bible College, Spring Hill College, Stillman College, University of Mobile.
Eligibility: Applicant must be residing in Alabama.
Additional information: Award is not need-based. Up to $1,200 per academic year. Deadlines printed on application form.

Amount of award:	$1,200
Number of awards:	9,513
Total amount awarded:	$5,613,888

Contact:
Contact financial aid office of institution for application.
Phone: 334-242-1998
Fax: 334-242-0270
Web: www.ache.state.al.us

Police/Firefighters' Survivors Educational Assistance Program

Type of award: Scholarship, renewable.
Intended use: For undergraduate study at vocational, 2-year or 4-year institution. Designated institutions: Public postsecondary institutions in Alabama.
Eligibility: Applicant must be residing in Alabama. Applicant's parent must have been killed or disabled in work-related accident as fire fighter or police officer.
Application requirements: Proof of eligibility.

Additional information: Grant covers full tuition, fees, books, and supplies at Alabama public institutions for dependents and eligible spouses of Alabama police officers and firefighters killed or disabled in line of duty.

Amount of award:	Full tuition
Number of awards:	17
Number of applicants:	17
Total amount awarded:	$42,079

Contact:
Alabama Commission on Higher Education
P.O. Box 302000
Montgomery, AL 36130-2000
Phone: 334-242-2274
Fax: 334-242-0270
Web: www.ache.state.al.us

Alabama Department of Education

Alabama Robert C. Byrd Honors Scholarship

Type of award: Scholarship, renewable.
Intended use: For full-time undergraduate study at 2-year or 4-year institution.
Eligibility: Applicant must be high school senior. Applicant must be U.S. citizen residing in Alabama.
Basis for selection: Applicant must demonstrate high academic achievement.
Application requirements: Nomination by high school guidance counselor.
Additional information: Contact high school guidance office or principal for application. Award continues through senior year if qualifications are met. There are 15 winners for each U.S. Congressional District, with seven districts in the state. 105 new winners, up to 315 renewals.

Amount of award:	$1,500
Number of awards:	105
Number of applicants:	800

Contact:
Local high school guidance counselor.
For additional information, contact:
Alabama Department of Education.
Phone: 334-242-8059

Alabama Scholarship for Dependents of Blind Parents

Type of award: Scholarship, renewable.
Intended use: For undergraduate study at vocational, 2-year or 4-year institution. Designated institutions: Alabama public postsecondary institutions.
Eligibility: Parent must be visually impaired. Applicant must be U.S. citizen or permanent resident residing in Alabama.
Basis for selection: Applicant must demonstrate financial need.
Application requirements: Proof of eligibility.
Additional information: Award covers instructional fees and tuition costs at Alabama public institutions of higher education. Students must apply for this award no later than two years after completing high school studies. Parent must be head of household and legally blind, and family must demonstrate financial need.

Amount of award: Full tuition
Number of awards: 15
Contact:
Alabama Department of Education
Special Educ. Services
P.O. Box 302101
Montgomery, AL 36130-2101
Phone: 334-242-8114
Web: www.ache.state.al.us

Alabama Department of Postsecondary Education

Alabama Junior/Community College Athletic Scholarship

Type of award: Scholarship, renewable.
Intended use: For full-time freshman or sophomore study at 2-year institution in United States. Designated institutions: Two-year public institutions in Alabama.
Eligibility: Applicant must be U.S. citizen or permanent resident residing in Alabama.
Basis for selection: Competition/talent/interest in athletics/sports.
Application requirements: Competitive tryout will be scheduled. Must be enrolled.
Additional information: Awards not need-based. Award covers tuition and books at Alabama two-year public institutions. Eligibility based on athletic ability determined through tryouts. Renewal dependent on continued athletic participation.
Amount of award: Full tuition
Contact:
Coach, Athletic Director or Financial Aid Officer at two-year Alabama public institution.
Web: www.ache.state.al.us

Institutional Scholarship Waivers

Type of award: Scholarship, renewable.
Intended use: For freshman or sophomore study at accredited postsecondary institution. Designated institutions: Two-year public institutions in Alabama.
Eligibility: Applicant must be U.S. citizen or permanent resident residing in Alabama.
Basis for selection: Applicant must demonstrate high academic achievement.
Application requirements: Transcript.
Additional information: Awards not need-based. Awards based on demonstrated merit. Focus of scholarship is determined by each institution. Application deadlines printed on application forms. Preference given to in-state residents. Award may be renewed if student demonstrates academic excellence.
Amount of award: Full tuition
Number of awards: 5,250
Total amount awarded: $19,350,000
Contact:
Two-year Alabama public institution for information and application.
Web: www.ache.state.al.us

Alabama Department of Veterans Affairs

Alabama GI Dependents Educational Benefit

Type of award: Scholarship, renewable.
Intended use: For undergraduate or graduate study at postsecondary institution. Designated institutions: State-supported institution.
Eligibility: Applicant must be dependent of disabled veteran, deceased veteran or POW/MIA; or spouse of disabled veteran, deceased veteran or POW/MIA. Veteran must have been involved in active military duties for at least 90 days on continuous active duty. Disabled veterans must be rated at least 20% disabled due to service connected disabilities.
Application requirements: Proof of eligibility.
Additional information: Veteran parent/spouse must have been resident of Alabama at least one year prior to enlistment. Children of veterans must submit application before their 26th birthday. Spouses of veterans have no age limit.
Amount of award: Full tuition
Number of awards: 967
Number of applicants: 1,014
Total amount awarded: $6,585,395
Contact:
Alabama Department of Veterans Affairs
P.O. Box 1509
Montgomery, AL 36102-1509
Phone: 334-242-5077
Fax: 334-242-5102

Alaska Space Grant Program

Alaska Student Rocket Project Scholarship

Type of award: Research grant, renewable.
Intended use: For undergraduate or graduate study in United States. Designated institutions: University of Alaska.
Eligibility: Applicant must be U.S. citizen.
Basis for selection: Major/career interest in aerospace; engineering or science, general.
Application requirements: Recommendations, transcript, research proposal by and sponsorship by University of Alaska faculty member. Resume, research proposal, cover letter describing career goals and space-related interests.
Additional information: Provides students with hands-on experience in all aspects of rocket and payload testing and launching. Internships awarded to students who assume leadership positions in interdisciplinary student team. Size of award commensurate with scope of proposed project, usually less than $5,000. More details and research proposal forms available on Website.
Application deadline: March 3
Notification begins: June 1

Contact:
Alaska Space Grant Program Office
Duckering Building, Room 225
Univ. of Alaska Fairbanks, P.O. Box 755919
Fairbanks, AK 99775-5919
Phone: 907-474-6833
Web: www.uaf.edu/asgp/

Student Research Scholarship

Type of award: Research grant, renewable.
Intended use: For full-time undergraduate or graduate study at accredited 4-year institution in United States. Designated institutions: University of Alaska at Fairbanks and Anchorage, University of Alaska Southeast, Alaska Pacific University.
Eligibility: Applicant must be U.S. citizen.
Basis for selection: Major/career interest in aerospace; astronomy; engineering or physics.
Application requirements: Recommendations, essay, transcript, research proposal, nomination by University of Alaska faculty member willing to supervise proposed aerospace research project. Resume, research proposal, cover letter describing career goals and space-related interests.
Additional information: Awardee receives support for working on a specific aerospace-related research project. Must be used at an Alaska Space Grant Consortium member institution. Number of scholarships and amount of funding varies; most awards $5,000 or less. Deadline usually in April or May. Contact sponsor for information.

Application deadline:	March 3
Notification begins:	June 1

Contact:
Alaska Space Grant Program Office
Duckering Building, Room 225
Univ. of Alaska Fairbanks, P.O. Box 755919
Fairbanks, AK 99775-5919
Phone: 907-474-6833
Web: www.uaf.edu/asgp/

Alcoa Foundation

Alcoa Foundation Sons and Daughters Scholarship Program

Type of award: Scholarship.
Intended use: For undergraduate study at accredited postsecondary institution.
Eligibility: Applicant or parent must be employed by Alcoa Inc. Applicant must be high school senior.
Basis for selection: Applicant must demonstrate high academic achievement, depth of character, leadership, seriousness of purpose and service orientation.
Application requirements: Interview, essay, transcript, proof of eligibility. Must be employed by Alcoa, Inc.
Additional information: Must have 2.3 GPA or better, or rank in upper half of class. SAT I required. Award is renewable for up to three years.

Amount of award:	$1,500
Number of awards:	150
Number of applicants:	557
Notification begins:	March 15

Contact:
Alcoa Foundation
201 Isabella Street
Pittsburgh, PA 15212-5858
Phone: 412-553-4786

Alexander Graham Bell Association for the Deaf and Hard of Hearing

AG Bell College Scholarship Awards

Type of award: Scholarship.
Intended use: For full-time undergraduate or graduate study at accredited 2-year, 4-year or graduate institution in or outside United States.
Eligibility: Applicant must be hearing impaired.
Basis for selection: Applicant must demonstrate financial need, high academic achievement and seriousness of purpose.
Application requirements: Recommendations, essay, transcript, proof of eligibility. Current audiogram.
Additional information: Must have had hearing loss since birth or before acquiring language with 60db or greater loss in the better ear in speech frequencies of 500, 1,000, and 2,000 Hz. Applicant must use speech and residual hearing and/or speechreading (lipreading) as preferred form of communication. Must be accepted or enrolled in college or university program that primarily enrolls students with normal hearing. Requests for applications must be received before December 1. Only first 500 requests will be accepted. Number of awards granted varies yearly. Write or send e-mail to attention of Dana Hughes, Financial Aid Coordinator (Financialaid@agbell.org).

Amount of award:	$200-$1,500
Application deadline:	January 1
Notification begins:	June 11

Contact:
Alexander Graham Bell Association for the Deaf and Hard of Hearing
Scholarship Awards Committee
3417 Volta Place, NW
Washington, DC 20007-2778
Phone: 202-337-5220
Web: www.agbell.org

Alliance Coal, LLC and Affiliates

Alliance Coal Scholars Program

Type of award: Scholarship, renewable.
Intended use: For freshman study at vocational, 2-year or 4-year institution.
Eligibility: Applicant or parent must be employed by MAPCO Coal Inc. and Affiliates. Applicant must be high school senior.
Additional information: For further information or an application, contact Mapco Coal Incorporated and Affiliates directly.

Amount of award:	$500-$1,000

Alliant Energy Foundation

Alliant Energy Foundation Scholarship

Type of award: Scholarship, renewable.
Intended use: For freshman study at accredited vocational, 2-year or 4-year institution.
Eligibility: Applicant or parent must be employed by Wisconsin Power & Light.
Additional information: For further information or an application, contact Wisconsin Power and Light Foundation directly.

    Amount of award: $1,000

Allstate Foundation

Allstate Foundation Scholarship

Type of award: Scholarship, renewable.
Intended use: For undergraduate study at accredited vocational, 2-year or 4-year institution.
Eligibility: Applicant or parent must be employed by Allstate Insurance Company. Applicant must be high school senior.
Basis for selection: Applicant must demonstrate financial need.
Additional information: For further information or an application, contact Allstate Foundation. Applicants may be high school seniors, recent graduates who plan to enroll in eligible institution, or students already enrolled. Applicants who do not demonstrate financial need or whose parents choose not to submit required financial documents may be eligible for a one-time award of $500.

    Amount of award: $500-$2,500

Alpha Beta Gamma International, Inc.

Alpha Beta Gamma International Scholarship

Type of award: Scholarship.
Intended use: For full-time junior or senior study at accredited 4-year institution.
Eligibility: Applicant or parent must be member/participant of Alpha Beta Gamma. Applicant must be U.S. citizen.
Basis for selection: Major/career interest in business; business, international; business/management/administration; accounting or computer/information sciences. Applicant must demonstrate high academic achievement and leadership.
Application requirements: Recommendations. Completed institutional financial forms.
Additional information: Awarded to enrollees of two year schools who have been accepted at four year schools to pursue baccalaureate degrees in business or related professions, including computer and information sciences.

    Amount of award:
    Number of awards:
    Number of applicants:
    Total amount awarded:
Contact:
Alpha Beta Gamma
Scholarship Committee
75 Grasslands Road
Valhalla, NY 10595
Web: www.abg.org

Alpha Mu Gamma National

Alpha Mu Gamma Scholarship

Type of award: Scholarship.
Intended use: For full-time sophomore, junior, senior, master's, doctoral, first professional or postgraduate study at 2-year, 4-year or graduate institution.
Eligibility: Applicant or parent must be member/participant of Alpha Mu Gamma.
Basis for selection: Major/career interest in foreign languages. Applicant must demonstrate high academic achievement and seriousness of purpose.
Application requirements: Recommendations, essay, transcript. Copy of full Alpha Mu Gamma membership certificate.
Additional information: Applicant must be a Alpha Mu Gamma member. Three $500 awards will be granted for the study of any foreign language; one $400 award for expenses towards a free, intensive one-month course of French at Laval University, Quebec, Canada; and one $200 award for the study of Esperanto or Spanish.

    Amount of award: $200-$500
    Number of awards: 5
    Application deadline: January 10
    Notification begins: April 1
    Total amount awarded: $2,100
Contact:
Sponsor/adviser of the Local Alpha Mu Gamma Chapter of your school.

Alumnae Panhellenic Association of Washington, DC

Alumnae Panhellenic Association Women's Scholarship

Type of award: Scholarship, renewable.
Intended use: For undergraduate or graduate study at 4-year or graduate institution.
Eligibility: Applicant must be female.
Basis for selection: Applicant must demonstrate high academic achievement, depth of character and service orientation.
Application requirements: Essay.
Additional information: Applicants must live or attend school in Washington, DC area and have a demonstrated interest in philanthropic activities.

...ard:	$500
...awards:	3
...n deadline:	March 15
...mount awarded:	$1,500

...:
...nae Panhellenic Association of Washington, DC
...Lisa Gordon
...0 N. Randolph St. # 702
Arlington, VA 22203

AMBUCS

AMBUCS Scholars-Scholarship for Therapists

Type of award: Scholarship.
Intended use: For junior, senior or master's study at accredited 4-year or graduate institution in United States.
Eligibility: Applicant must be U.S. citizen.
Basis for selection: Major/career interest in occupational therapy; physical therapy or speech pathology/audiology. Applicant must demonstrate financial need, high academic achievement, depth of character and service orientation.
Application requirements: Some documentation requested if named a semi-finalist.
Additional information: One additional 2-year award of $6,000 offered. Program must be accredited by appropriate health therapy association. Students must apply online. No paper applications accepted. Applicants may print enrollment certificate online. Students must send 1040 form from previous year and accompanying documents by mail if named a semi-finalist. Visit Website to apply online between January 15, and April 15, each year.

Amount of award:	$500-$1,500
Number of awards:	300
Number of applicants:	2,400
Application deadline:	April 15
Notification begins:	June 20
Total amount awarded:	$200,000

Contact:
AMBUCS Resouce Center
P.O. Box 5127
High Point, NC 27262
Phone: 336-869-2166
Web: www.ambucs.com

America's Junior Miss Pageant, Inc.

Junior Miss Scholarship

Type of award: Scholarship.
Intended use: For undergraduate study at 4-year institution.
Eligibility: Applicant must be single, female, high school junior or senior. Applicant must be U.S. citizen.
Basis for selection: Competition/talent/interest in poise/talent/fitness, based on scholastic evaluation, skill in creative and performing arts, physical fitness, presence and composure, and panel interview.

Additional information: Must compete in state of legal residence. State winners expected to compete at higher levels. Must never have been married. Only seniors can compete in finals but students are encouraged to begin application process during sophomore year. Vist Website for application deadline information, as it varies from state to state.

Amount of award:	$1,000-$40,000
Number of applicants:	6,000

Contact:
America's Junior Miss Pageant
Contestant Inquiry
P.O. Box 2786
Mobile, AL 36652-2786
Phone: 800-256-5435
Fax: 334-431-0063
Web: www.ajm.org

American Academy of Physician's Assistants

Physician's Assistants Scholarship

Type of award: Scholarship.
Intended use: For junior, senior or master's study at accredited 4-year institution in United States. Designated institutions: Any physician assistant program accredited by Committee on Allied Health Education and Accreditation/Commission on Accreditation of Allied Health Education Programs.
Eligibility: Applicant or parent must be member/participant of American Academy of Physician Assistants.
Basis for selection: Major/career interest in physician assistant. Applicant must demonstrate financial need, high academic achievement, seriousness of purpose and service orientation.
Application requirements: Transcript, proof of eligibility. Letter from financial aid office verifying aid if any. Passport-type photo.
Additional information: Must have at least one semester of P.A. program grades to apply. Must be student member of American Academy of Physician Assistants at time of application. Funding levels/number of awards may vary.

Amount of award:	$2,000-$5,000
Number of awards:	75
Number of applicants:	450
Application deadline:	February 1
Notification begins:	May 15

Contact:
Physician Assistant Foundation
American Academy of Physician Assistants
950 North Washington Street
Alexandria, VA 22314
Web: www.aapa.org/paf.html

American Alpine Club

Alpine Club A.K. Gilkey and Putnam/Bedayn Research Grant

Type of award: Research grant.
Intended use: For undergraduate or graduate study.
Eligibility: Applicant must be U.S. citizen.
Basis for selection: Major/career interest in science, general; biology; environmental science; forestry or atmospheric sciences/meteorology.
Application requirements: Recommendations, research proposal.
Additional information: Research proposals evaluated on scientific or technical quality and contribution to scientific endeavor germane to mountain regions. Grant applications available from Website. Most awards in the $200 to $500 range.

Amount of award:	$200-$1,000
Number of awards:	8
Number of applicants:	14
Application deadline:	March 1
Total amount awarded:	$4,476

Contact:
American Alpine Club
710 Tenth Street
Suite 100
Golden, CO 80401
Phone: 303-389-0110
Fax: 303-384-0111
Web: www.americanalpineclub.org

American Association of Airport Executives

AAAE Foundation Scholarship

Type of award: Scholarship.
Intended use: For full-time junior or senior study at accredited 4-year institution.
Basis for selection: Major/career interest in aviation. Applicant must demonstrate financial need and high academic achievement.
Application requirements: Recommendations, nomination by school or aviation management department. Must apply through school scholarship or aviation management department. Only one recommendation per school.
Additional information: Must have 3.0 GPA. Extracurricular and community activities important. Applicant must have reached junior year in an aviation/airport management program.

Amount of award:	$1,000
Number of awards:	10
Application deadline:	May 15
Notification begins:	July 15
Total amount awarded:	$10,000

Contact:
Scholarship Coordinator
American Association of Airport Executives
601 Madison Street, Suite 400
Alexandria, VA 22314-1756

American Association of Critical Care Nurses

Critical Care Nurses Education Advancement Scholarship

Type of award: Scholarship.
Intended use: For junior or senior study.
Eligibility: Applicant or parent must be member/participant of American Association of Critical Care Nurses. At least 20% of these awards will be allocated for ethnic minorities. Applicant must be U.S. citizen or permanent resident.
Basis for selection: Major/career interest in nursing or nurse practitioner. Applicant must demonstrate high academic achievement and seriousness of purpose.
Additional information: For students who do not hold RN license (applicants may hold degrees in other nursing fields). Must be currently enrolled in NLN-accredited BSN program and have cumulative GPA of 3.0 or better. National Student Nurses Association members eligible, or applicant must be member of American Association of Critical Care Nurses. Program administered by National Student Nurses Association. Application available online at www.nsna.org starting in August, through January 15, 2002. Send SASE (55 cents postage) with all inquiries.

Amount of award:	$1,500
Application deadline:	February 1
Notification begins:	March 30

Contact:
National Student Nurses Association
555 West 57 Street
New York, NY 10019
Phone: 212-581-2211
Web: www.aacn.org

Critical Care Nurses Education Advancement Scholarship (BSN)

Type of award: Scholarship, renewable.
Intended use: For junior or senior study at accredited 4-year institution in United States.
Eligibility: Applicant or parent must be member/participant of American Association of Critical Care Nurses. At least 20% of these awards will be allocated for ethnic minorities. Applicant must be U.S. citizen or permanent resident.
Basis for selection: Major/career interest in nursing.
Application requirements: Essay, transcript, proof of eligibility.
Additional information: Minimum 3.0 GPA required. Must be licensed nurse (RN) and American Association of Critical Care Nurses member working in critical care unit or one year's experience in last three years. Current enrollment in NLN-accredited nursing program. Recipients announced in early summer for the fall academic term.

Amount of award:	$1,500
Number of awards:	100
Application deadline:	April 1
Total amount awarded:	$150,000

Scholarships

Contact:
American Association of Critical Care Nurses
101 Columbia
Aliso Viejo, CA 92656-1491
Phone: 800-899-2226
Fax: 949-362-2020
Web: www.aacn.org

American Association of School Administrators/ Discover Card, Inc.

Discover Card Tribute Award Scholarships

Type of award: Scholarship.
Intended use: For undergraduate study at accredited postsecondary institution in United States or Canada.
Eligibility: Applicant must be high school junior. Applicant must be U.S. citizen.
Basis for selection: Applicant must demonstrate high academic achievement, leadership and service orientation.
Application requirements: Recommendations, essay, transcript. Essay must describe achievements in multiple areas including leadership, community service, special talents, obstacles overcome and future career plans.
Additional information: Minimum 2.75 GPA required. Deadline in January; paper and electronic applications available in September; more specific information on deadline dates and application materials on Website. Applicants compete first for multiple level state scholarships; state winners compete for nine national scholarships. State and national scholarships recognize career study in the following fields: trade and technical; arts and humanities; science, business and technology. Awards may be used for certification or licensing also.

Amount of award:	$2,500-$25,000
Number of awards:	468
Number of applicants:	7,500
Total amount awarded:	$1,500,000

Contact:
American Association of School Administrators
Discover Card Tribute Award Scholarships
P.O. Box 9338
Arlington, VA 22219
Phone: 703-875-0708
Web: www.aasa.org/discover.htm

American Cancer Society

American Cancer Society Scholarship

Type of award: Scholarship, renewable.
Intended use: For undergraduate study at accredited postsecondary institution in United States. Designated institutions: Accredited Michigan or Indiana university, college or community college.

Eligibility: Applicant must have been diagnosed with cancer before age 21. Applicant must be no older than 20. Applicant must be U.S. citizen residing in Indiana or Michigan.
Basis for selection: Applicant must demonstrate financial need, depth of character, leadership and service orientation.
Application requirements: Recommendations, proof of eligibility.
Additional information: The American Cancer Society's College Scholarships are Michigan and Indiana's first and only scholarship opportunities exclusively for students with a history of cancer.

Amount of award:	$1,000
Number of awards:	52
Number of applicants:	100
Application deadline:	April 16
Total amount awarded:	$52,000

Contact:
American Cancer Society Great Lakes Division
College Scholarship Program
1755 Abbey Road
East Lansing, MI 48823
Phone: 800-723-0360

American Center of Oriental Research

American Center of Oriental Research/Jennifer C. Groot Fellowship

Type of award: Research grant.
Intended use: For undergraduate or graduate study at 4-year or graduate institution outside United States.
Eligibility: Applicant must be U.S. citizen, international student or Canadian citizen.
Basis for selection: Competition/talent/interest in study abroad. Major/career interest in archaeology; Middle Eastern studies; ancient near eastern studies or ethnic/cultural studies.
Application requirements: Archaeological fieldwork in Jordan.
Additional information: Provides support for beginners in archaeological fieldwork who have been accepted as staff members on archaeological projects in Jordan with ASOR/CAP affiliation. Open to undergraduate and graduate students.

Amount of award:	$1,500
Number of awards:	2
Application deadline:	February 1

Contact:
American Center of Oriental Research
Reseach Grant Coordinator
656 Beacon Street
Boston, MA 02215-2010
Phone: 617-353-6571
Fax: 617-353-6575

American Chemical Society

American Chemical Society Scholars Program

Type of award: Scholarship.
Intended use: For full-time freshman, sophomore, junior or senior study at accredited 2-year or 4-year institution in United States.
Eligibility: Applicant must be Alaskan native, African American, Mexican American, Hispanic American, Puerto Rican or American Indian. Applicant must be U.S. citizen or permanent resident.
Basis for selection: Major/career interest in chemistry; biochemistry; engineering, chemical; materials science; environmental science or forensics. Applicant must demonstrate financial need, high academic achievement, seriousness of purpose and service orientation.
Application requirements: Recommendations, transcript. FAFSA.
Additional information: Applicant must intend to pursue career in chemistry, biochemistry, or chemical engineering. Other possible majors/careers interest are chemical sciences, organic chemistry, forensics. Student must have minimum 3.0 GPA. Award up to $3,000.

Number of awards:	100
Number of applicants:	1,000
Application deadline:	February 15
Notification begins:	June 1
Total amount awarded:	$700,000

Contact:
American Chemical Society
Scholars Program
1155 Sixteenth Street, NW
Washington, DC 20036
Phone: 800-227-5558 ext.6250
Web: www.acs.org/minorityaffairs/scholars.html

American Classical League/ National Junior Classical league

Latin Honor Society Scholarship

Type of award: Scholarship.
Intended use: For full-time freshman study at 2-year or 4-year institution.
Eligibility: Applicant or parent must be member/participant of National Junior Classical League. Applicant must be high school senior.
Basis for selection: Major/career interest in Classics.
Application requirements: Recommendations, essay, transcript. Application.
Additional information: Must have been member of National Junior Classics League for at least three years and must be enrolled in National Junior Classics League Latin Honor Society for current academic year and at least one preceding year. Must be planning to teach Latin or Classics. Application available online.

Amount of award:	$1,000-$1,500
Number of awards:	1
Application deadline:	May 1
Total amount awarded:	$1,000

Contact:
American Classical League
Miami University
Oxford, OH 45056
Phone: 513-529-7741
Fax: 513-529-7742
Web: www.aclclassics.org

M.V. O'Donnell Memorial Teacher Training Award

Type of award: Scholarship.
Intended use: For junior, senior or master's study at 4-year or graduate institution.
Eligibility: Applicant or parent must be member/participant of American Classical League.
Basis for selection: Major/career interest in education, teacher or Classics. Applicant must demonstrate financial need.
Application requirements: Recommendations, transcript.
Additional information: Must be training for certification to teach Latin and have completed a substantial part of these courses.

Amount of award:	$500
Number of awards:	5
Application deadline:	December 1, March 1
Total amount awarded:	$2,500

Contact:
American Classical League
Miami University
Oxford, OH 45056
Phone: 513-529-7741
Fax: 513-529-7742
Web: www.aclclassics.org

McKinlay Summer Award

Type of award: Scholarship.
Intended use: For non-degree study.
Eligibility: Applicant or parent must be member/participant of American Classical League.
Basis for selection: Major/career interest in Classics. Applicant must demonstrate financial need.
Application requirements: Recommendations.
Additional information: Must have been member of American Classical League for 3 years preceding application. Must be planning to teach Classics in elementary or secondary school in the coming school year. May apply for independent study program funding or support to attend American Classical League Institute for first time. Total amount awarded varies each year.

Amount of award:	$1,000
Application deadline:	January 15

Contact:
American Classical League
Miami University
Oxford, OH 45056
Phone: 513-529-7741
Fax: 513-529-7742
Web: www.aclclassics.org

National Junior Classical League Scholarship

Type of award: Scholarship.
Intended use: For full-time freshman study at 2-year or 4-year institution.
Eligibility: Applicant or parent must be member/participant of National Junior Classical League. Applicant must be high school senior.
Basis for selection: Major/career interest in Classics or humanities/liberal arts. Applicant must demonstrate financial need, high academic achievement, depth of character, leadership, patriotism, seriousness of purpose and service orientation.
Application requirements: Recommendations, transcript, proof of eligibility.
Additional information: Preference is given to applicants who intend to teach Latin, Greek, or classical humanities.

Amount of award:	$500-$1,000
Number of awards:	6
Application deadline:	May 1
Total amount awarded:	$4,000

Contact:
American Classical League
Miami University
Oxford, OH 45056
Phone: 513-529-7741
Fax: 513-529-7742
Web: www.aclclassics.org

American College of Musicians/National Guild of Piano Teachers

American College of Musicians $200 Scholarship

Type of award: Scholarship.
Intended use: For non-degree study.
Basis for selection: Major/career interest in music.
Application requirements: Nomination by piano teacher.
Additional information: Award to be used for piano study. Student must have been in National or International solo auditions for ten years, be Guild Paderewski winner, and be Guild High School Diploma recipient. Teacher must be member of National Guild of Piano Teachers.

Amount of award:	$200
Number of awards:	150
Application deadline:	September 15
Notification begins:	October 1

Contact:
American College of Musicians/National Guild of Piano Teachers
International Headquarters
P.O. Box 1807
Austin, TX 78767-1807
Phone: 512-478-5775

American College of Musicians Piano Composition Contest

Type of award: Scholarship.
Intended use: For non-degree study.
Basis for selection: Competition/talent/interest in music performance/composition, based on compositions for solo keyboard and keyboard ensemble considered. Compositions rated on imagination, originality, and skill. Major/career interest in music.
Application requirements: Manuscript of composition.
Additional information: Teacher must be member of National Guild of Piano Teachers. Entry fees vary according to classification of students and length of composition.

Amount of award:	$50-$150
Number of awards:	14
Application deadline:	November 15

Contact:
National Guild of Piano Teachers
International Headquarters
P.O. Box 2215
Austin, TX 78767-2215
Phone: 512-478-5775

Raissa Tselentis J. S. Bach Scholarship

Type of award: Scholarship.
Intended use: For non-degree study.
Basis for selection: Competition/talent/interest in music performance/composition, based on student's scores at Guild auditions. Major/career interest in music.
Application requirements: Audition, nomination by teacher.
Additional information: Competition in performance and literature of Bach. One award for early Bach, one for advanced Bach. Teacher must be member of National Guild of Piano Teachers. Entry fees vary according to classification of students.

Amount of award:	$100
Number of awards:	2
Total amount awarded:	$200

Contact:
National Guild of Piano Teachers
International Headquarters
P.O. Box 1807
Austin, TX 78767-1807
Phone: 512-478-5775

American Congress on Surveying and Mapping

AAGS Joseph F. Dracup Scholarship Award

Type of award: Scholarship, renewable.
Intended use: For undergraduate study at 4-year institution.
Eligibility: Applicant or parent must be member/participant of American Congress of Surveying and Mapping.
Basis for selection: Major/career interest in surveying/mapping. Applicant must demonstrate high academic achievement and seriousness of purpose.
Application requirements: Recommendations, essay, transcript, proof of eligibility. Completed application.

Additional information: Preference will be given to applicants with significant focus on geodetic surveying. Visit Website for additional information.

Amount of award:	$2,000
Number of awards:	1
Application deadline:	December 1
Total amount awarded:	$2,000

Contact:
American Congress on Surveying and Mapping
6 Montgomery Village Avenue
Suite 403
Gaithersburg, MD 20879
Phone: 240-632-9716 ext. 105
Fax: 240-632-1321
Web: www.acsm.net/scholar.html

Allen Chelf Scholarship

Type of award: Scholarship, renewable.
Intended use: For undergraduate study at 2-year or 4-year institution in United States.
Eligibility: Applicant or parent must be member/participant of American Congress of Surveying and Mapping.
Basis for selection: Major/career interest in surveying/mapping or cartography. Applicant must demonstrate high academic achievement and seriousness of purpose.
Application requirements: Recommendations, essay, transcript, proof of eligibility. Completed application.
Additional information: Visit Website for additional information.

Amount of award:	$500
Application deadline:	December 1

Contact:
American Congress on Surveying and Mapping
6 Montgomery Village Avenue
Suite 403
Gaithersburg, MD 20879
Phone: 240-632-9716 ext. 105
Fax: 240-632-1321
Web: www.acsm.net/scholarship.html

Berntsen International Scholarship in Surveying

Type of award: Scholarship, renewable.
Intended use: For undergraduate study at 4-year institution.
Eligibility: Applicant or parent must be member/participant of American Congress of Surveying and Mapping.
Basis for selection: Major/career interest in surveying/mapping. Applicant must demonstrate high academic achievement and seriousness of purpose.
Application requirements: Recommendations, essay, transcript, proof of eligibility. Completed application.
Additional information: Open to students in four-year degree program in surveying (or in closely related degree programs such as geomatics or surveying engineering). Awarded by Berntsen International Inc. of Madison, Wisconsin. Visit Website for additional information.

Amount of award:	$1,500
Application deadline:	December 1

Contact:
American Congress on Surveying and Mapping
6 Montgomery Village Avenue
Suite 403
Gaithersburg, MD 20879
Phone: 240-632-9716 ext. 105
Fax: 240-632-1321
Web: www.acsm.net/scholar.html

Berntsen International Scholarship in Surveying Technology

Type of award: Scholarship, renewable.
Intended use: For undergraduate certificate study at 2-year institution.
Eligibility: Applicant or parent must be member/participant of American Congress of Surveying and Mapping.
Basis for selection: Major/career interest in surveying/mapping or cartography. Applicant must demonstrate high academic achievement and seriousness of purpose.
Application requirements: Recommendations, essay, transcript, proof of eligibility. Completed application.
Additional information: Open to students in two-year degree program in surveying technology. Awarded by Berntsen International Inc. of Madison, Wisconsin. Visit Website for additional information.

Amount of award:	$500
Application deadline:	December 1

Contact:
American Congress on Surveying and Mapping
6 Montgomery Village Avenue
Suite 403
Gaithersburg, MD 20879
Phone: 240-632-9716 ext. 105
Fax: 240-632-1321
Web: www.acsm.net/scholar.html

Cady McDonnell Memorial Scholarship

Type of award: Scholarship, renewable.
Intended use: For undergraduate study at 2-year or 4-year institution.
Eligibility: Applicant or parent must be member/participant of American Congress of Surveying and Mapping. Applicant must be female. Applicant must be residing in New Mexico, Idaho, Montana, Nevada, Oregon, Alaska, Arizona, California, Utah, Washington, Colorado, Hawaii or Wyoming.
Basis for selection: Major/career interest in surveying/mapping or cartography. Applicant must demonstrate high academic achievement and seriousness of purpose.
Application requirements: Recommendations, essay, transcript, proof of eligibility. Completed application and proof of legal home residence.
Additional information: Intended to recognize woman student enrolled in field of surveying who is resident of one of listed western states. Visit Website for additional information.

Amount of award:	$1,000
Number of awards:	1
Application deadline:	December 1
Total amount awarded:	$1,000

Contact:
American Congress on Surveying and Mapping
6 Montgomery Village Avenue
Suite 403
Gaithersburg, MD 20879
Phone: 240-632-9716 ext. 105
Fax: 240-632-1321
Web: www.acsm.net/scholar.html

CaGIS Scholarship Award

Type of award: Scholarship, renewable.
Intended use: For full-time undergraduate or graduate study at 4-year or graduate institution.
Eligibility: Applicant or parent must be member/participant of American Congress of Surveying and Mapping.
Basis for selection: Major/career interest in cartography or surveying/mapping. Applicant must demonstrate high academic achievement and seriousness of purpose.
Application requirements: Recommendations, essay, transcript, proof of eligibility. Completed application.
Additional information: Open to students enrolled in four-year or graduate degree program in cartography, GIS or other mapping sciences. Preference will be given to undergraduates with junior or senior standing. Awarded by the Cartography and Geographic Information Society (CaGIS). Visit Website for additional information.

Amount of award:	$1,000
Number of awards:	1
Application deadline:	December 1
Total amount awarded:	$1,000

Contact:
American Congress on Surveying and Mapping
6 Montgomery Village Avenue
Suite 403
Gaithersburg, MD 20879
Phone: 240-632-9716 ext. 105
Fax: 240-632-1321
Web: www.acsm.net/scholar.html

Mary Feindt Forum for Women in Surveying Scholarship

Type of award: Scholarship, renewable.
Intended use: For undergraduate study at 4-year institution in United States.
Eligibility: Applicant or parent must be member/participant of American Congress of Surveying and Mapping. Applicant must be female.
Basis for selection: Major/career interest in surveying/mapping or cartography. Applicant must demonstrate high academic achievement and seriousness of purpose.
Application requirements: Recommendations, essay, transcript, proof of eligibility. Completed application.
Additional information: Visit Website for additional information.

Amount of award:	$1,000
Application deadline:	December 1

Contact:
American Congress on Surveying and Mapping
6 Montgomery Village Avenue
Suite 403
Gaithersburg, MD 20879
Phone: 240-632-9716 ext. 105
Fax: 240-632-1321
Web: www.acsm.net/scholar.html

Nettie Dracup Memorial Scholarship

Type of award: Scholarship, renewable.
Intended use: For undergraduate study at accredited 4-year institution.
Eligibility: Applicant or parent must be member/participant of American Congress of Surveying and Mapping. Applicant must be U.S. citizen.
Basis for selection: Major/career interest in surveying/mapping. Applicant must demonstrate high academic achievement and seriousness of purpose.
Application requirements: Recommendations, essay, transcript, proof of eligibility. Completed application.
Additional information: Intended to provide financial assistance to U.S. citizen who is undergraduate student enrolled in geodetic surveying. Visit Website for additional information.

Amount of award:	$2,000
Application deadline:	December 1

Contact:
American Congress on Surveying and Mapping
6 Montgomery Village Avenue
Suite 403
Gaithersburg, MD 20879
Phone: 240-632-9716 ext. 105
Fax: 240-632-1321
Web: www.acsm.net/scholar.html

NSPS Board of Governors Scholarship

Type of award: Scholarship, renewable.
Intended use: For junior study at 4-year institution.
Eligibility: Applicant or parent must be member/participant of American Congress of Surveying and Mapping.
Basis for selection: Major/career interest in surveying/mapping or cartography. Applicant must demonstrate high academic achievement and seriousness of purpose.
Application requirements: Recommendations, essay, transcript, proof of eligibility. Completed application, minimum 3.0 GPA.
Additional information: Visit Website for additional information.

Amount of award:	$1,000
Number of awards:	1
Application deadline:	December 1
Total amount awarded:	$1,000

Contact:
American Congress on Surveying and Mapping
6 Montgomery Village Avenue
Suite 403
Gaithersburg, MD 20879
Phone: 240-632-9716 ext. 105
Fax: 240-632-1321
Web: www.acsm.net/scholar.html

NSPS Scholarships

Type of award: Scholarship, renewable.
Intended use: For full-time undergraduate study at 4-year institution.
Eligibility: Applicant or parent must be member/participant of American Congress of Surveying and Mapping.
Basis for selection: Major/career interest in surveying/mapping. Applicant must demonstrate high academic achievement and seriousness of purpose.

Application requirements: Recommendations, essay, transcript, proof of eligibility. Completed application.
Additional information: Intended to recognize outstanding students enrolled full-time in undergraduate surveying programs. Awarded by National Society of Professional Surveyors. Visit Website for additional information.

Amount of award:	$1,000
Number of awards:	2
Application deadline:	December 1
Total amount awarded:	$2,000

Contact:
American Congress on Surveying and Mapping
6 Montgomery Village Avenue
Suite 403
Gaithersburg, MD 20879
Phone: 240-632-9716 ext. 105
Fax: 240-632-1321
Web: www.acsm.net/scholar.html

Schonstedt Scholarships in Surveying

Type of award: Scholarship, renewable.
Intended use: For undergraduate study at 4-year institution.
Eligibility: Applicant or parent must be member/participant of American Congress of Surveying and Mapping.
Basis for selection: Major/career interest in surveying/mapping. Applicant must demonstrate high academic achievement and seriousness of purpose.
Application requirements: Recommendations, essay, transcript, proof of eligibility. Completed application.
Additional information: Preference will be given to applicants with junior or senior standing. Awarded by Schonstedt Instrument Company of Kearneysville, West Virginia. Schonstedt donates magnetic locator to surveying program at each recipient's school. Visit Website for additional information.

Amount of award:	$1,500
Number of awards:	2
Application deadline:	December 1
Total amount awarded:	$3,000

Contact:
American Congress on Surveying and Mapping
6 Montgomery Village Avenue
Suite 403
Gaithersburg, MD 20879
Phone: 240-632-9716 ext. 105
Fax: 240-632-1321
Web: www.acsm.net/scholar.html

American Council of the Blind

Floyd Qualls Memorial Scholarship

Type of award: Scholarship, renewable.
Intended use: For full-time undergraduate or graduate study at postsecondary institution in United States.
Eligibility: Applicant must be visually impaired.
Basis for selection: Applicant must demonstrate high academic achievement, depth of character and leadership.
Application requirements: Interview, recommendations, essay, transcript, proof of eligibility. Proof of legal blindness.

Entering or transferring students must show proof of registration at accredited school.
Additional information: Applicant must be legally blind in both eyes. Must be in or currently under consideration for postsecondary program. Two awards for entering freshmen, two for other undergraduates, two for graduates, two for vocational students. Additional scholarships available: contact ACB for more information.

Amount of award:	$2,500
Application deadline:	March 1
Notification begins:	May 15

Contact:
American Council of the Blind Scholarships
Attn: Terry Pacheco
1155 15 Street NW, Suite 1004
Washington, DC 20005
Phone: 202-467-5081 or 800-424-8666
Fax: 202-467-5085
Web: www.acb.org

American Dental Assistants Association/Oral B Laboratories

Juliette A. Southard/Oral B Laboratories Scholarship

Type of award: Scholarship.
Intended use: For undergraduate study.
Eligibility: Applicant or parent must be member/participant of American Dental Assistants Association.
Basis for selection: Major/career interest in dental assistant. Applicant must demonstrate high academic achievement, depth of character and leadership.
Application requirements: Recommendations, transcript, proof of eligibility.
Additional information: Scholarship open to high school graduates and GED certificate holders. Must be American Dental Assistants Association member or American Dental Assistants Association student member. Applicants must be enrolled in dental assisting program or be taking courses applicable to furthering career in dental assisting.

Amount of award:	$500
Number of awards:	10
Application deadline:	January 31

Contact:
American Dental Assistants Association
Grace Shelton
203 North LaSalle Street, Suite 1320
Chicago, IL 60601
Phone: 312-541-1550

American Dietetic Association Foundation

Baccalaureate or Coordinated Program Scholarships

Type of award: Scholarship, renewable.
Intended use: For full-time junior, senior or graduate study at accredited 4-year institution. Designated institutions: CADE-accredited/approved dietetics education programs.
Eligibility: Applicant must be U.S. citizen or permanent resident.
Basis for selection: Major/career interest in dietetics/nutrition. Applicant must demonstrate financial need, high academic achievement and seriousness of purpose.
Application requirements: Recommendations, proof of eligibility. GPA documentation necessary, signed by academic advisor.
Additional information: Sponsor awarded 209 scholarships to graduates and undergraduates 2000-2001. Number and amount of awards vary. Some require ADA membership. Financial need and minority status considered. Must demonstrate or show promise of being a valuable, contributing member of the profession.

Amount of award:	$500-$5,000

Contact:
American Dietetic Association
Accreditation, Educ. Prog. & Stud. Operations
216 West Jackson Blvd.
Chicago, IL 60606
Phone: 800-877-1600 ext. 5400
Web: www.eatright.org/scholelig.html

American Dryer Corporation

American Dryer Scholarship

Type of award: Scholarship, renewable.
Intended use: For undergraduate or graduate study at accredited vocational, 2-year or 4-year institution.
Eligibility: Applicant or parent must be employed by American Dryer Corporation.
Additional information: For further information or an application, contact American Dryer Corporation directly.

American Electroplaters and Surface Finishers Society Scholarship Committee

American Electroplaters and Surface Finishers Society Scholarship

Type of award: Scholarship, renewable.
Intended use: For full-time junior, senior or graduate study.

Basis for selection: Major/career interest in engineering, materials; engineering, chemical; engineering, environmental or chemistry.
Application requirements: Recommendations, essay, transcript. Resume.
Additional information: May apply to any field of study or research related to plating and surface finishing technologies. Award notification occurs between late July and early August. Must re-apply for renewal.

Amount of award:	$1,500
Number of applicants:	75
Application deadline:	April 15
Total amount awarded:	$10,500

Contact:
AESF Scholarship Committee
12644 Research Parkway
Orlando, FL 32826-3298
Phone: 407-281-6441

American Express Foundation

American Express Scholarship Program

Type of award: Scholarship, renewable.
Intended use: For freshman study at 2-year or 4-year institution.
Eligibility: Applicant or parent must be employed by American Express Foundation. Applicant must be high school senior.
Additional information: For further information or an application, contact American Express Foundation directly.

Amount of award:	$500-$3,000

American Federation of State, County and Municipal Employees

State/County/Municipal Employees Family Scholarship

Type of award: Scholarship, renewable.
Intended use: For full-time undergraduate study at accredited 4-year institution.
Eligibility: Applicant or parent must be member/participant of American Fed. of State/County/Municipal Employees. Applicant must be high school senior.
Application requirements: Recommendations, essay, transcript, proof of eligibility. SAT or ACT scores. Essay on subject: "What ASME means to me."
Additional information: Minimum 3.0 GPA required. Scholarship open to children and grandchildren of ASME members. Application period opens August 1.

Amount of award:	$2,000
Number of awards:	10
Number of applicants:	900
Application deadline:	December 31
Notification begins:	March 31

Contact:
American Federation of State, County and Municipal
Employees
Education Department
1625 L Street NW
Washington, DC 20036
Web: www.afscme.org

State/County/Municipal Employees Jerry Clark Memorial Scholarship

Type of award: Scholarship.
Intended use: For full-time junior or senior study at accredited 4-year institution.
Eligibility: Applicant or parent must be member/participant of American Fed. of State/County/Municipal Employees.
Basis for selection: Major/career interest in political science/government. Applicant must demonstrate high academic achievement.
Application requirements: Proof of eligibility.
Additional information: Scholarship open to children and grandchildren of ASME members. Applicant must be a current college sophomore with a declared political science major. Winner given opportunity to intern at International Union Headquarters in Political Action department. Minimum 3.0 GPA required. Award renewable for senior year. Opens March 15th.

Amount of award:	$10,000
Number of awards:	1
Number of applicants:	30
Application deadline:	July 1
Notification begins:	August 1
Total amount awarded:	$10,000

Contact:
American Federation of State, County and Municipal
Employees
Education Department
1625 L Street NW
Washington, DC 20036
Web: www.afscme.org

American Foundation for Aging Research

American Foundation for Aging Research Fellowship

Type of award: Research grant, renewable.
Intended use: For full-time undergraduate, master's, doctoral or first professional study in United States.
Basis for selection: Major/career interest in gerontology; medical specialties/research; biology; chemistry or neuroscience. Applicant must demonstrate high academic achievement.
Application requirements: $3 application fee. Recommendations, transcript, proof of eligibility, research proposal.
Additional information: Must be actively involved or planning active involvement in a specific biomedical or biochemical research project in field of aging. Also applicable toward PhD, MD, DVM and DDS degrees. Number of awards varies. Call sponsor for information regarding deadline. SASE preferred.

Amount of award:	$500-$1,000
Number of applicants:	150
Total amount awarded:	$4,000

Contact:
American Foundation for Aging Research
North Carolina State University
Biochem.Dept., 128 Polk Hall, P.O. Box 7622
Raleigh, NC 27695-7622
Phone: 919-515-5679
Fax: 919-515-2047

American Foundation for Pharmaceutical Education

American Association of Pharmaceutical Scientists/AFPE Gateway Research Scholarship

Type of award: Research grant.
Intended use: For sophomore, junior or senior study at accredited 4-year or graduate institution.
Basis for selection: Major/career interest in pharmacy/pharmaceutics/pharmacology; biochemistry; chemistry or health sciences.
Application requirements: Recommendations, essay, transcript, research proposal. AFPE application, AFPE summary sheet, letter from faculty sponsor describing research.
Additional information: Awards intended to encourage undergraduates from any discipline to undertake mentored research experience and to consider pursuing Ph.D. in pharmaceutical science. U.S. citizenship or permanent resident status not required.

Amount of award:	$5,000
Number of awards:	6
Application deadline:	January 28
Notification begins:	April 15
Total amount awarded:	$30,000

Contact:
American Foundation for Pharmaceutical Education
AAPS-AFPE "Gateway" Scholarship Program
One Church Street, Suite 202
Rockville, MD 20850
Phone: 301-738-2160
Fax: 301-738-2161

Gateway Pharmaceutical Research Scholarship

Type of award: Research grant.
Intended use: For sophomore, junior or senior study at 4-year or graduate institution.
Eligibility: Applicant must be U.S. citizen.
Basis for selection: Major/career interest in pharmacy/pharmaceutics/pharmacology.
Application requirements: Recommendations, essay, transcript, proof of eligibility, research proposal. AFPE application, AFPE summary sheet, letter from faculty sponsor describing the research.

Additional information: To encourage students in last three years of B.S. or Pharm.D. program to undertake mentored research experience and to consider pursuing the Ph.D.in pharmaceutical science. Applicant must be enrolled in degree program for one more full academic year following award of scholarship. U.S. citizenship or permanent resident status not required.

Amount of award:	$5,000
Number of awards:	12
Application deadline:	January 28
Notification begins:	April 15
Total amount awarded:	$60,000

Contact:
American Foundation for Pharmaceutical Education
One Church Street
Suite 202
Rockville, MD 20850
Phone: 301-738-2160
Fax: 301-738-2161

American Foundation for the Blind

Delta Gamma Memorial Scholarship

Type of award: Scholarship.
Intended use: For undergraduate or graduate study at accredited postsecondary institution.
Eligibility: Applicant must be visually impaired. Applicant must be U.S. citizen.
Basis for selection: Major/career interest in health-related professions; rehabilitation/therapeutic services; education or education, special. Applicant must demonstrate high academic achievement, depth of character, seriousness of purpose and service orientation.
Application requirements: Recommendations, essay, transcript, proof of eligibility.
Additional information: Applicant must be legally blind and studying in the field of rehabilitation and/or education of blind or visually impaired persons.

Amount of award:	$1,000
Number of awards:	1
Application deadline:	April 30
Total amount awarded:	$1,000

Contact:
American Foundation for the Blind
Information Center
11 Penn Plaza, Suite 300
New York, NY 10001
Phone: 212-502-7600
Web: www.afb.org

Ferdinand Torres Scholarship

Type of award: Scholarship.
Intended use: For full-time undergraduate study at postsecondary institution.
Eligibility: Applicant must be visually impaired. Applicant must be U.S. citizen or permanent resident.
Basis for selection: Applicant must demonstrate financial need, leadership, patriotism and seriousness of purpose.

Application requirements: Recommendations, essay, transcript, proof of eligibility.
Additional information: Applicant must be legally blind. Preference given to residents of New York City metropolitan area and new immigrants to the USA.

Amount of award:	$1,000
Number of awards:	1
Application deadline:	April 30
Total amount awarded:	$1,000

Contact:
American Foundation for the Blind
Information Center
11 Penn Plaza, Suite 300
New York, NY 10001
Phone: 212-506-7600
Fax: 212-502-7777
Web: www.afb.org

Gladys C. Anderson Memorial Scholarship

Type of award: Scholarship.
Intended use: For undergraduate study at accredited postsecondary institution.
Eligibility: Applicant must be visually impaired. Applicant must be female. Applicant must be U.S. citizen.
Basis for selection: Major/career interest in music. Applicant must demonstrate depth of character and seriousness of purpose.
Application requirements: Recommendations, essay, transcript, proof of eligibility.
Additional information: Applicant must be legally blind. Provide sample performance tape under 30 minutes, voice or instrumental selection of religious or classical music.

Amount of award:	$1,000
Number of awards:	1
Application deadline:	April 30
Total amount awarded:	$1,000

Contact:
American Foundation for the Blind
Information Center
11 Penn Plaza, Suite 300
New York, NY 10001
Phone: 212-502-7600
Fax: 212-502-7777
Web: www.afb.org

Paul W. Ruckes Scholarship

Type of award: Scholarship.
Intended use: For undergraduate or graduate study at 2-year or 4-year institution.
Eligibility: Applicant must be visually impaired. Applicant must be U.S. citizen.
Basis for selection: Major/career interest in engineering; computer/information sciences or science, general.
Application requirements: Recommendations, essay, transcript, proof of eligibility.
Additional information: Applicant must be visually impaired, but may or may not be legally blind. Applicant must be pursuing degree in engineering or computer, physical, or life sciences.

Amount of award:	$2,500
Number of awards:	1
Application deadline:	April 30
Total amount awarded:	$2,500

Contact:
American Foundation for the Blind
Information Center
11 Penn Plaza, Suite 300
New York, NY 10001
Phone: 212-502-7600
Fax: 212-502-7771
Web: www.afb.org

R.L. Gillette Scholarship

Type of award: Scholarship, renewable.
Intended use: For full-time undergraduate study at 4-year institution.
Eligibility: Applicant must be visually impaired. Applicant must be female, high school senior. Applicant must be U.S. citizen.
Basis for selection: Major/career interest in literature or music.
Application requirements: Recommendations, essay, transcript, proof of eligibility, nomination. Evidence of admission to desired school and a performance tape not to exceed 30 minutes or a creative writing sample.
Additional information: Applicant must be female student who is legally blind and enrolled in undergraduate degree program in literature or music.

Amount of award:	$1,000
Number of awards:	2
Application deadline:	April 30
Total amount awarded:	$2,000

Contact:
American Foundation for the Blind
11 Pen Plaza Ste. 300
New York, NY 10001
Phone: 212-502-7661
Fax: 212-502-7771

Rudolph Dillman Memorial Scholarship

Type of award: Scholarship.
Intended use: For undergraduate or graduate study at accredited postsecondary institution in United States.
Eligibility: Applicant must be visually impaired. Applicant must be U.S. citizen.
Basis for selection: Major/career interest in health-related professions; rehabilitation/therapeutic services or education. Applicant must demonstrate depth of character, leadership, seriousness of purpose and service orientation.
Application requirements: Recommendations, essay, transcript, proof of eligibility.
Additional information: Applicant must be legally blind and studying in the field of rehabilitation and/or education of blind or visually impaired persons.

Amount of award:	$2,500
Number of awards:	3
Application deadline:	April 30
Total amount awarded:	$7,500

Contact:
American Foundation for the Blind
Information Center
11 Penn Plaza, Suite 300
New York, NY 10001
Phone: 212-502-7600
Fax: 212-502-7777
Web: www.afb.org

Rudolph Dillman Memorial Scholarship Based on Need

Type of award: Scholarship.
Intended use: For undergraduate or graduate study at accredited postsecondary institution in United States.
Eligibility: Applicant must be visually impaired. Applicant must be U.S. citizen.
Basis for selection: Major/career interest in health-related professions; rehabilitation/therapeutic services or education. Applicant must demonstrate financial need, depth of character, seriousness of purpose and service orientation.
Application requirements: Recommendations, essay, transcript, proof of eligibility.
Additional information: Applicant must be legally blind and studying in the field of rehabilitation and/or education of blind or visually impaired persons.

Amount of award:	$2,500
Number of awards:	1
Application deadline:	April 30
Total amount awarded:	$2,500

Contact:
American Foundation for the Blind
Information Center
11 Penn Plaza, Suite 300
New York, NY 10001
Phone: 212-502-7600
Web: www.afb.org

American General Scholarship

Scholarship for Students with Good Hearts

Type of award: Scholarship.
Intended use: For undergraduate study in United States.
Eligibility: Applicant must be high school senior. Applicant must be residing in Tennessee, Alabama, Virginia, Florida, Texas, Georgia, Ohio, Kentucky, California or Pennsylvania.
Basis for selection: Applicant must demonstrate high academic achievement, depth of character, leadership, seriousness of purpose and service orientation.
Application requirements: Present evidence of good character by participating in extracurricular activities at school, involvement in community affairs, after-school employment and demonstrate character traits such as kindness, respect and good citizenship.
Additional information: Established to recognize high school seniors who demonstrate positive character traits of kindness, respect and good citizenship. Write or call to request application.

Amount of award:	$500-$1,500
Number of awards:	220
Application deadline:	March 1
Total amount awarded:	$83,500

Contact:
American General Scholarship
c/o Scholarship Program
P.O. Box 22492
Nashville, TN 37202-2492
Phone: 615-320-3149

American Ground Water Trust

American Ground Water Trust Amtrol Award

Type of award: Scholarship.
Intended use: For freshman study at vocational, 2-year or 4-year institution.
Eligibility: Applicant must be high school senior. Applicant must be U.S. citizen or permanent resident.
Basis for selection: Major/career interest in engineering, environmental; geology/earth sciences; environmental science or natural resources/conservation. Applicant must demonstrate leadership, seriousness of purpose and service orientation.
Application requirements: Recommendations, essay, transcript. In addition to essay, students must provide description of previously completed high school science project involving ground water resources or of non-school work experience related to environment and natural resources.
Additional information: Must be entering field related to ground water, i.e. hydrology or hydrogeology. 3.0 GPA required. Write to American Ground Water Trust for application form and details of application procedure.

Amount of award:	$1,000-$2,000
Number of awards:	2
Number of applicants:	100
Application deadline:	June 1
Notification begins:	August 1
Total amount awarded:	$2,000

Contact:
American Ground Water Trust Scholarship
P.O. Box 1796
Concord, NH 03302
Phone: 603-228-5444
Web: www.agwt.org

Ben Everson Scholarship

Type of award: Scholarship.
Intended use: For full-time freshman study at 4-year institution.
Eligibility: Applicant must be U.S. citizen or permanent resident.
Basis for selection: Major/career interest in ecology; engineering, environmental; geology/earth sciences; hydrology; natural resources/conservation or environmental science. Applicant must demonstrate seriousness of purpose.
Application requirements: Recommendations, essay, proof of eligibility. Description of high school science/environmental project directly involving ground water, or of vacation/out-of-school work experience related to environment or natural resources. Letter establishing that one parent is employed in ground water industry.
Additional information: Applicant must intend to pursue career in ground water related field. Parent must be employed in ground water industry. Write to American Ground Water Trust for application form.

Amount of award:	$2,500
Number of awards:	1
Number of applicants:	20
Application deadline:	June 1
Notification begins:	August 31
Total amount awarded:	$2,500

Contact:
American Ground Water Trust
Ben Everson Scholarship Application
P.O. Box 1796
Concord, NH 03302
Phone: 603-228-5444
Web: www.agwt.org

American Health Information Management Association

FORE Undergraduate Scholarship

Type of award: Scholarship.
Intended use: For full-time undergraduate study. Designated institutions: Accredited Institutions with Health Information Management/Technology Programs, or AHIMA's Independent Study Programs.
Eligibility: Applicant or parent must be member/participant of American Health Information Management Association. Applicant must be U.S. citizen.
Basis for selection: Major/career interest in health services administration or information systems. Applicant must demonstrate high academic achievement.
Application requirements: Recommendations, transcript, proof of eligibility.
Additional information: Applicants must be members of AHIMA. Must be accepted for Independent Study Program of American Health Information Management Association, or accepted into accredited health information management or health information technology program with major career interest in Health Information Management. Must have 2.5 GPA (out of 4.0). Number of awards varies.

Amount of award:	$1,000-$5,000
Application deadline:	May 31

Contact:
American Health Information Management Association
Foundation of Research and Education
233 North Michigan Avenue, Suite 2150
Chicago, IL 60601-5800
Phone: 312-233-1100
Fax: 312-233-1090
Web: www.ahima.org

American Heart Association Western States Affiliate

American Heart Association Undergraduate Student Research Program

Type of award: Research grant.
Intended use: For full-time junior or senior study at 4-year institution. Designated institutions: Cardiovascular or cerebrovascular research laboratories in California, Nevada, Utah.

Eligibility: Applicant must be U.S. citizen, international student, foreign national holding student, exchange or or permanent resident visa. Applicant must be residing in Nevada, Utah or California.

Basis for selection: Major/career interest in biology; chemistry; physics or computer/information sciences. Applicant must demonstrate high academic achievement, depth of character, seriousness of purpose and service orientation.

Application requirements: Interview, recommendations, essay, transcript, proof of eligibility.

Additional information: Must have completed combined total of at least four semesters or six quarters of biological sciences, physics or chemistry. Must have completed at least one quarter of calculus, statistics, computational methods or computer science. Students are assigned to scientist-supervised laboratories to work for ten weeks during summer exploring careers in heart or stroke research. Must be attending institution in or be resident of California, Utah or Nevada. Women and minorities encouraged to apply. Must request application before December 15. Awardees required to participate in roundtable discussion meetings held during August to discuss research experience with supervisors and other students.

Amount of award:	$4,000
Application deadline:	January 16
Notification begins:	March 30

Contact:
American Heart Association, Western States Affiliate
Research Department
1710 Gilbreth Road
Burlingame, CA 94010-1317
Phone: 650-259-6700
Fax: 650-259-6891
Web: www.heartsource.org/research/

American Helicopter Society, Inc.

Vertical Flight Foundation Scholarship

Type of award: Scholarship.

Intended use: For full-time junior, senior or graduate study at accredited postsecondary institution.

Basis for selection: Major/career interest in engineering; aerospace or aviation. Applicant must demonstrate high academic achievement, depth of character and seriousness of purpose.

Application requirements: Recommendations, essay, transcript. Academic endorsement.

Additional information: Must major in helicopter or vertical flight engineering industry. Minimum 3.0 GPA required, 3.5 recommended.

Amount of award:	$1,000-$2,000
Number of awards:	14
Number of applicants:	300
Application deadline:	February 1

Contact:
Debbie Cochran, American Helicopter Society, Inc.
Vertical Flight Foundation
217 North Washington Street
Alexandria, VA 22314
Phone: 703-684-6777
Web: www.vtol.org

American Holistic Nurses' Association

Holistic Nursing Charlotte McGuire Scholarship

Type of award: Scholarship.

Intended use: For undergraduate or graduate study.

Eligibility: Applicant or parent must be member/participant of American Holistic Nurses' Association.

Basis for selection: Major/career interest in nursing. Applicant must demonstrate depth of character and seriousness of purpose.

Application requirements: Recommendations, essay, transcript, proof of eligibility. Two recommendations, financial statement required. One recommendation must be from AHNA member.

Additional information: 3.0 GPA required. Experience in holistic or alternative health care practices preferred. Graduates must be member of AHNA for one year, undergraduates for six months. Amount of award varies.

Number of awards:	2
Number of applicants:	6
Application deadline:	March 15
Notification begins:	May 15

Contact:
American Holistic Nurses' Association
Scholarships
P.O. Box 2130
Flagstaff, AZ 86003-2130
Phone: 800-278-2462
Fax: 520-526-2752

Holistic Nursing Research Grant

Type of award: Research grant.

Intended use: For non-degree study.

Eligibility: Applicant or parent must be member/participant of American Holistic Nurses' Association.

Basis for selection: Major/career interest in nursing; health-related professions; nurse practitioner; health sciences or health education. Applicant must demonstrate seriousness of purpose and service orientation.

Application requirements: Proof of eligibility, research proposal.

Additional information: Must be member of AHNA for at least one year and be conducting research on topics related to holistic nursing. Number of awards/applicants varies.

Amount of award:	$500-$5,000
Number of awards:	1
Number of applicants:	2
Application deadline:	April 15
Notification begins:	May 15
Total amount awarded:	$500

Contact:
American Holistic Nurses' Association
Research Grants
P.O. Box 2130
Flagstaff, AZ 86003-2130
Phone: 800-278-2462
Fax: 520-526-2752

Scholarships

American Hotel Foundation

American Express Scholarship Program

Type of award: Scholarship, renewable.
Intended use: For undergraduate study at 2-year or 4-year institution.
Basis for selection: Major/career interest in hotel/restaurant management or hospitality administration/management. Applicant must demonstrate financial need and high academic achievement.
Application requirements: Essay, transcript. Industry-related work experience; academic record/educational qualifications; professional, community and extracurricular activities; and personal attributes including career goals. Copy of course curriculum and copy of tax form 1040 or 1040EZ.
Additional information: Must work at hotel 20 hours a week and have 12 months experience. Hotel must be member of American Hotel & Motel Association. Dependents of hotel employees may also apply. Award must be used in hospitality management degree program.

Amount of award:	$500-$2,000
Number of awards:	8
Number of applicants:	24
Application deadline:	May 1
Notification begins:	June 15

Contact:
American Hotel Foundation
1201 New York Avenue NW 600
Washington, DC 20005-3931
Phone: 202-289-3181
Fax: 202-289-3199
Web: www.ahma.com/ahf.htm

Ecolab Scholarship Program

Type of award: Scholarship.
Intended use: For full-time undergraduate study at 2-year or 4-year institution in United States.
Basis for selection: Major/career interest in hotel/restaurant management. Applicant must demonstrate financial need and high academic achievement.
Application requirements: Essay, transcript. Industry-related work experience; academic record/educational qualifications; professional, community and extracurricular activities; and personal attributes including career goals. Copy of course curriculum and copy of tax form 1040 or 1040EZ.
Additional information: Applicant must maintain minimum of 12 credit hours. Must be used in hospitality management degree program. Industry-related work experience considered in making awards.

Amount of award:	$1,000
Number of awards:	16
Application deadline:	June 1
Notification begins:	July 15

Contact:
American Hotel Foundation
1201 New York Avenue, NW
Suite 600
Washington, DC 20005-3931
Phone: 202-289-3181
Fax: 202-289-3199
Web: www.ahma.com/ahf.htm

American Indian Science and Engineering Society

A.T. Anderson Memorial Scholarship

Type of award: Scholarship.
Intended use: For full-time undergraduate or graduate study at accredited 2-year or 4-year institution in United States or Canada.
Eligibility: Applicant or parent must be member/participant of American Indian Science & Engineering Society. Applicant must be Alaskan native or American Indian. Applicant must be member of American Indian tribe, be considered American Indian by tribe of claimed affiliation, be at least 1/4 American Indian blood or 1/4 Alaskan Native, or be considered Alaskan Native by Alaskan Native group of claimed affiliation.
Basis for selection: Major/career interest in science, general; engineering; medicine; natural resources/conservation; mathematics or physical sciences. Applicant must demonstrate financial need, high academic achievement, depth of character, leadership, seriousness of purpose and service orientation.
Application requirements: Recommendations, essay, transcript, proof of eligibility.
Additional information: Minimum 2.0 GPA. Applicant attending two-year college must be enrolled in program leading to academic degree. Undergraduate student award $1,000 per year; graduate student award $2,000. Membership and scholarship applications available on Website. Otherwise, send SASE with all information/application requests.

Amount of award:	$1,000-$2,000
Application deadline:	June 15

Contact:
AISES
Higher Ed. Coordinator
PO Box 9828
Albuquerque, NM 87119-9828
Phone: 505-765-1052
Web: www.aises.org

Burlington Northern Santa Fe Foundation Scholarship

Type of award: Scholarship, renewable.
Intended use: For full-time freshman, sophomore, junior or senior study at accredited postsecondary institution in United States or Canada.
Eligibility: Applicant or parent must be member/participant of American Indian Science & Engineering Society. Applicant must be Alaskan native or American Indian. Applicant must be member of American Indian tribe, otherwise be considered American Indian by tribe claimed affiliation, be at least 1/4 American blood or 1/4 Alaskan Native by Alaskan Native group of claimed affiliation. Applicant must be high school senior. Applicant must be U.S. citizen residing in New Mexico, Montana, Oklahoma, Oregon, North Dakota, South Dakota, Arizona, Kansas, California, Washington, Colorado or Minnesota.
Basis for selection: Major/career interest in science, general; engineering; mathematics; physical sciences; medicine or natural resources/conservation. Applicant must demonstrate financial need, high academic achievement, depth of character, leadership, seriousness of purpose and service orientation.

Application requirements: Recommendations, essay, transcript, proof of eligibility.
Additional information: Minimum 2.0 GPA. In California, only residents of San Bernardino County eligible. Award is renewable for four years (eight semesters) or until baccalaureate obtained, whichever comes first, assuming eligibility maintained. Membership and scholarship applications available on Website. Otherwise, include SASE with all application/information requests.

Amount of award:	$2,500
Number of awards:	5
Application deadline:	April 15

Contact:
AISES
Higher Ed. Coordinator
PO Box 9828
Albuquerque, NM 87119-9828
Phone: 505-765-1052
Web: www.aises.org

United States EPA Tribal Lands Environmental Science Scholarship

Type of award: Scholarship.
Intended use: For full-time junior, senior or graduate study at accredited 4-year or graduate institution in United States.
Eligibility: Applicant or parent must be member/participant of American Indian Science & Engineering Society. Applicant must be U.S. citizen.
Basis for selection: Major/career interest in environmental science or engineering, environmental. Applicant must demonstrate high academic achievement, depth of character, leadership, seriousness of purpose and service orientation.
Application requirements: Recommendations, essay, transcript, proof of eligibility.
Additional information: Minimum 2.7 GPA. Those studying environmental studies, biochemistry, environmental economics, or related environmental disciplines also eligible. Must show demonstrated commitment to environmental protection on tribal lands. Membership and scholarship applications available on Website. Otherwise, send SASE with all information/application requests. Summer employment at EPA facility and/or on Indian reservation also offered contingent upon availability of resources. Non-Indians may apply.

Amount of award:	$4,000
Application deadline:	June 15

Contact:
AISES
Higher Ed. Coordinator
PO Box 9828
Albuquerque, NM 87119-9828
Phone: 505-765-1052
Web: www.aises.org

American Institute for Foreign Study

Foreign Study/Minority Scholarship Strategic Studies Award

Type of award: Scholarship.
Intended use: For freshman, sophomore, junior or senior study in Argentina, Australia, Czech Republic, Russia, South Africa, Western Europe. Designated institutions: University of Belgrano, Buenos Aires; Macquarie University, Sydney; University of Salzburg, Austria; University of Economics, Prague; Charles University, Czech Republic; Richmond, The American International University in London; College International de Cannes, University of Grenoble, University of Paris IV (Sorbonne), France; Holland International Business School and Vrije Universiteit, Amsterdam; University of Limerick, Ireland; Richmond in Florence and Richmond in Rome, Italy; St. Petersburg State Polytechnic University, Russia; University of Stellenbosch, South Africa; University of Grenada and University of Salamanca, Spain.
Eligibility: Applicant must be Alaskan native, Asian American, African American, Mexican American, Hispanic American, Puerto Rican or American Indian.
Basis for selection: Competition/talent/interest in study abroad. Applicant must demonstrate financial need, high academic achievement, depth of character, leadership, seriousness of purpose and service orientation.
Application requirements: $50 application fee. Essay. Include letter of reference with application.
Additional information: Must have completed minimum 24 credits toward degree when program starts. Must be interested in multicultural/international issues and involved in multicultural/international activities. Six awards of $2,000, two full scholarships, $10,000 each, including round trip air fare, awarded each year. Award must be used for an AIFS program. Students who are unable to pay $50 application fee may submit fee waiver endorsed by their financial office or study abroad advisor.

Amount of award:	$2,000-$10,000
Number of awards:	8
Number of applicants:	70
Application deadline:	October 15, April 15
Total amount awarded:	$32,000

Contact:
AIFS College Division
River Plaza
9 West Broad Street
Stamford, CT 06902-3788
Phone: 800-727-2437
Fax: 203-399-5597
Web: www.aifsabroad.com

International Semester Scholarship

Type of award: Scholarship.
Intended use: For freshman, sophomore, junior or senior study at postsecondary institution in Argentina, Australia, Czech Republic, Russia, South Africa, Western Europe. Designated institutions: University of Belgrano, Buenos Aires; Macquarie University, Sydney; University of Salzburg, Austria; University of Economics, Prague; Charles University, Czech Republic; Richmond, The American International University in London; College International de Cannes; University of Grenoble; University of Paris IV (Sorbonne), France; Holland International Business School and Vrije Universiteit, Amsterdam; University of Limerick; Richmond, Florence, Italy; Richmond in Rome, Italy; St. Petersburg State Polytechnic University, Russia; University of Stellenbosch, South Africa; University of Grenada and University of Salamanca, Spain.
Basis for selection: Competition/talent/interest in study abroad. Applicant must demonstrate high academic achievement, leadership, seriousness of purpose and service orientation.
Application requirements: $50 application fee. Essay, transcript.

Additional information: Applicant must be currently enrolled college undergraduate with at least 3.0 cumulative GPA. Must be interested in multicultural/international issues and involved in multicultural/international activities. Minorities encouraged to apply. Award must be used in AIFS program. Preference given to those applying for full academic year.

Amount of award:	$1,000
Number of awards:	150
Number of applicants:	300
Application deadline:	April 15, October 15
Total amount awarded:	$150,000

Contact:
AIFS College Division
River Plaza
9 West Broad Street
Stamford, CT 06902-3788
Phone: 800-727-2437
Fax: 203-399-5597
Web: www.aifsabroad.com

International Summer Scholarship

Type of award: Scholarship.
Intended use: For freshman, sophomore, junior or senior study at postsecondary institution in Czech Republic, England, France, Italy, Poland, Russia, South Africa, Spain, traveling programs. Designated institutions: University of Economics, Prague; Richmond, The American International University in London, England; London Summer Art with Central St. Martins and Chelsea Colleges of Art and Design, London; College International de Cannes, University of Paris IV, France; Richmond in Florence, Italy; Jagiellonian University, Krakow, Poland; St. Petersburg State Polytechnic University, Russia; University of Stellenbosch, South Africa; University of Salamanca and University of Santiago de Compostela, Spain.
Eligibility: Applicant must be U.S. citizen.
Basis for selection: Competition/talent/interest in study abroad. Applicant must demonstrate high academic achievement, leadership and service orientation.
Application requirements: Essay. Must submit essay on benefits of study abroad.
Additional information: Applicant must be currently enrolled college undergraduate with at least 3.0 cumulative GPA. Should be interested in multicultural/international issues and involved in multicultural/international activities. Minorities strongly encouraged to apply. Award must be used on an AIFS program.

Amount of award:	$750
Number of awards:	50
Number of applicants:	200
Application deadline:	March 15
Total amount awarded:	$37,500

Contact:
AIFS College Division
River Plaza
9 West Broad Street
Stamford, CT 06902-3788
Phone: 800-727-2437
Fax: 203-399-5597
Web: www.aifsabroad.com

Moonves Scholarship

Type of award: Scholarship, renewable.
Intended use: For full-time undergraduate study at postsecondary institution. Designated institutions: Holland International Business School, The Vrije Universiteit in Amsterdam; Richmond College in Rome, Italy.

Basis for selection: Applicant must demonstrate depth of character and seriousness of purpose.
Application requirements: $50 application fee. Recommendations, essay, transcript. AIFS program application. Essay topic: benefits of study abroad.
Additional information: Awarded to students attending AIFS programs in Amsterdam and Rome (sites may change in future years). Students must meet all existing AIFS GPA requirements. Award is based on outstanding potential and innovative spirit, rather than past academic performance. Visit Website for additional information.

Amount of award:	$2,500
Number of awards:	2
Number of applicants:	50
Application deadline:	October 15, April 15
Notification begins:	November 15, May 15
Total amount awarded:	$5,000

Contact:
AIFS College Division
River Plaza
9 West Broad Street
Stamford, CT 06902-3788
Phone: 800-727-2437
Fax: 203-399-5597
Web: www.aifsabroad.com

Tcherepnine Scholarships

Type of award: Scholarship, renewable.
Intended use: For full-time undergraduate study at postsecondary institution. Designated institutions: St. Petersburg State Polytechnic University in St. Petersburg, Russia.
Basis for selection: Applicant must demonstrate high academic achievement.
Application requirements: $50 application fee. Recommendations, essay, transcript. AIFS program application. Essay topic: benefits of study abroad.
Additional information: Awarded to students attending the AIFS programs in St. Petersburg, Russia. Eligible students must have 3.0 GPA or better. Visit Website for additional information.

Amount of award:	$2,500
Number of awards:	4
Number of applicants:	25
Application deadline:	October 15, April 15
Notification begins:	November 15, May 15
Total amount awarded:	$10,000

Contact:
AIFS College Division
River Plaza
9 West Broad Street
Stamford, CT 06902-3788
Phone: 800-727-2437
Fax: 203-399-5597
Web: www.aifsabroad.com

American Institute of Aeronautics and Astronautics

Aeronautics and Astronautics Undergraduate Scholarship

Type of award: Scholarship, renewable.
Intended use: For full-time sophomore, junior or senior study at accredited 4-year institution.
Eligibility: Applicant must be U.S. citizen or permanent resident.
Basis for selection: Major/career interest in aerospace or engineering. Applicant must demonstrate high academic achievement.
Application requirements: Recommendations, essay, transcript, proof of eligibility. 500 to 1,000 word typewritten essay on how academic program supports career objectives.
Additional information: Institution must be accredited by Accreditation Board for Engineering and Technology. Must have completed at least two quarters or semesters of full-time college work. Minimum 3.0 GPA. Must join American Institute of Aeronautics and Astronautics before receiving award. Not open to members of any American Institute of Aeronautics and Astronautics national committees or subcommittees. Applications must be requested by January 15 if applying by mail. Applications may be downloaded up to January 31 deadline. Applicants must reapply for renewal.

Amount of award:	$2,000
Number of awards:	30
Application deadline:	January 31
Notification begins:	June 15
Total amount awarded:	$60,000

Contact:
AIAA Foundation Undergraduate Scholarship Program
1801 Alexander Bell Drive
Suite 500
Reston, VA 20191-4344
Phone: 703-264-7536
Web: www.aiaa.org

American Institute of Architects

AIA New Jersey Scholarship Foundation

Type of award: Scholarship, renewable.
Intended use: For full-time sophomore, junior, senior, master's or first professional study at accredited postsecondary institution. Designated institutions: Accredited architectural schools.
Eligibility: Applicant must be residing in New Jersey.
Basis for selection: Major/career interest in architecture. Applicant must demonstrate financial need, high academic achievement and seriousness of purpose.
Application requirements: $5 application fee. Portfolio, recommendations, essay, transcript, proof of eligibility. FAFSA.
Additional information: Applicant must be permanent resident of New Jersey.

Amount of award:	$1,000-$2,000
Number of awards:	7
Number of applicants:	12
Application deadline:	April 30
Notification begins:	July 15
Total amount awarded:	$7,000

Contact:
AIA New Jersey Scholarship Foundation Inc.
c/o Robert Zaccone
212 White Avenue
Old Tappan, NJ 07675

AIA/AAF Award for First Professional Degree Candidates

Type of award: Scholarship.
Intended use: For full-time junior, senior or master's study at accredited 4-year or graduate institution in United States. Designated institutions: Institution must be NAAB-accredited.
Basis for selection: Major/career interest in architecture.
Application requirements: Portfolio, recommendations, essay. Application, financial needs analysis, class ranking.
Additional information: Applicant must supply drawing along with application. Applicant must be in third year of a five year B. Arch. program or working toward M. Arch. Assists students in one of final two years of professional degree program in architecture. Applications only available from Department of Architecture at NAAB- or RAIC-accredited schools.

Amount of award:	$500-$2,500
Application deadline:	February 1
Notification begins:	April 1

Contact:
American Architectural Foundation
1735 New York Avenue, NW
Washington, DC 20006-5292
Web: www.e-architect.com

AIA/AAF Minority/Disadvantaged Scholarship

Type of award: Scholarship, renewable.
Intended use: For full-time freshman study in United States. Designated institutions: Institution must be NAAB accredited.
Eligibility: Applicant must be high school senior. Applicant must be U.S. citizen or permanent resident.
Basis for selection: Major/career interest in architecture. Applicant must demonstrate financial need.
Application requirements: Recommendations, essay, transcript, nomination by high school guidance counselor, AIA component, architect, or other individual who can speak to student's aptitude for architecture program. Statement of disadvantaged circumstances.
Additional information: Application sent to eligible students after nomination screening. Nomination form due early December. Request nomination form between September 15 and December 1 by calling 202-626-7511. Nomination form also available from Website. Open to high school seniors and college freshmen who plan to enter programs leading to a professional degree in architecture. Students who have completed full year of undergraduate course work not eligible. Renewable up to two years.

Amount of award:	$500-$3,000
Number of awards:	20
Application deadline:	January 15

Contact:
American Architectural Foundation
1735 New York Avenue, NW
Washington, DC 20006-5292
Web: www.e-architect.com/institute

AIA/AAF RTKL Traveling Fellowship

Type of award: Research grant.
Intended use: For full-time senior or master's study at accredited 4-year or graduate institution in United States. Designated institutions: Institution must be NAAB accredited.
Eligibility: Applicant must be U.S. citizen or permanent resident.
Basis for selection: Major/career interest in architecture.
Application requirements: Recommendations, transcript. Travel proposal budget outlining a foreign itinerary which is directly relevant to applicant's educational goals.
Additional information: Application form available from NAAB-accredited institutions or the AAF. Application also available from Website.

Amount of award:	$2,500
Number of awards:	1
Application deadline:	February 15

Contact:
American Architectural Foundation
1735 New York Ave, NW
Washington, DC 20006-5292
Web: www.e-architect.com/institute

American Institute of Certified Public Accountants

Certified Public Accountants Minorities Scholarship

Type of award: Scholarship, renewable.
Intended use: For full-time sophomore, junior, senior or master's study at accredited 4-year or graduate institution in United States.
Eligibility: Applicant must be Alaskan native, Asian American, African American, Mexican American, Hispanic American, Puerto Rican or American Indian. Applicant must be U.S. citizen.
Basis for selection: Major/career interest in accounting. Applicant must demonstrate financial need, high academic achievement and seriousness of purpose.
Application requirements: Essay, transcript. Applicant must be declared accounting major.
Additional information: For purposes of this program, AICPA defines minorities as those of Black, Native American/Alaskan Native, or Pacific Island races, or of Hispanic ethnic origin. Persons who are already CPAs not eligible. Minimum GPA 3.0 required. Must have completed thirty semester hours, or forty-five quarter hours, of college work, including the equivalent of six semester hours in accounting. Applications may be downloaded from Website listed below.

Amount of award:	$1,500-$5,000
Number of awards:	296
Number of applicants:	400
Application deadline:	June 1
Notification begins:	July 1
Total amount awarded:	$600,000

Contact:
American Institute of Certified Public Accountants
1211 Avenue of the Americas
New York, NY 10036-8775
Phone: 212-596-6270
Web: www.aicpa.org

American Institute of Polish Culture

Polish Culture Scholarship

Type of award: Scholarship.
Intended use: For full-time undergraduate study at 4-year institution.
Eligibility: Applicant must be Polish.
Basis for selection: Major/career interest in journalism; communications or public relations. Applicant must demonstrate high academic achievement.
Application requirements: $25 application fee. Recommendations, transcript. Three original, signed letters of recommendation on institution letterhead. Resume.
Additional information: Send SASE with application request. Must be full-time undergraduate by application deadline. High school seniors ineligible.

Amount of award:	$1,000
Number of awards:	10
Application deadline:	February 16
Notification begins:	April 16
Total amount awarded:	$10,000

Contact:
American Institute of Polish Culture
1440 79 Street Causeway, Suite 117
Miami, FL 33141

American Isuzu Motors, Inc.

AIMI/J. E. Reilly Scholarship

Type of award: Scholarship, renewable.
Intended use: For undergraduate study at accredited vocational, 2-year or 4-year institution.
Eligibility: Applicant or parent must be employed by American Isuzu Motors, Inc.
Basis for selection: Applicant must demonstrate financial need.
Additional information: For further information or an application, contact American Isuzu Motors, Inc. directly.

Amount of award:	$1,000-$5,000

American Legion Alabama

American Legion Alabama Oratorical Contest

Type of award: Scholarship.
Intended use: For undergraduate study at postsecondary institution.
Eligibility: Applicant must be enrolled in high school. Applicant must be U.S. citizen residing in Alabama.
Basis for selection: Competition/talent/interest in oratory/debate, based on breadth of knowledge, originality, application of knowledge of topic, skill in selecting examples and analogies, logic, voice, diction, style of language, and delivery. Applicant must demonstrate patriotism.
Application requirements: Proof of eligibility. State Oratorical Contest 1st, 2nd and 3rd place winners.
Additional information: Topic: U.S. Constitution and citizenship. State finals are held in March. 1st -$5,000, 2nd-$3,000, 3rd-$2,000.

Amount of award:	$2,000-$5,000
Number of awards:	3
Total amount awarded:	$10,000

Contact:
The American Legion
Department Adjutant
P.O. Box 1069
Montgomery, AL 36101-1069
Phone: 334-262-6638

American Legion Alabama Scholarship

Type of award: Scholarship, renewable.
Intended use: For undergraduate study at postsecondary institution. Designated institutions: Alabama postsecondary institutions.
Eligibility: Applicant must be U.S. citizen or permanent resident residing in Alabama. Applicant must be descendant of veteran; or dependent of veteran during Korean War, Persian Gulf War, WW I, WW II or Vietnam.
Additional information: Send business-size SASE. Four-year scholarships. Applicant may be grandchild of eligible veteran.

Amount of award:	$850
Number of awards:	130
Application deadline:	May 1
Total amount awarded:	$110,500

Contact:
The American Legion
Department Adjutant
P.O. Box 1069
Montgomery, AL 36101-1069
Phone: 334-262-6638
Fax: 334-262-6638

American Legion Alabama Auxiliary

American Legion Alabama Auxiliary Scholarship

Type of award: Scholarship, renewable.
Intended use: For undergraduate or graduate study at postsecondary institution. Designated institutions: Alabama state-supported institutions.
Eligibility: Applicant must be U.S. citizen or permanent resident residing in Alabama. Applicant must be descendant of veteran; or dependent of veteran during Grenada conflict, Korean War, Lebanon conflict, Panama conflict, Persian Gulf War, WW I, WW II or Vietnam.
Application requirements: Proof of eligibility.
Additional information: Annual scholarships. Send SASE with request for application. Grandchildren of veterans also eligible.

Amount of award:	$850
Number of awards:	40
Application deadline:	April 1
Total amount awarded:	$34,000

Contact:
American Legion Auxiliary, Department of Alabama
Department Headquarters
120 North Jackson Street
Montgomery, AL 36104
Phone: 334-262-1176

American Legion Alaska

American Legion Alaska Oratorical Contest

Type of award: Scholarship.
Intended use: For undergraduate study at postsecondary institution.
Eligibility: Applicant must be enrolled in high school. Applicant must be U.S. citizen or permanent resident residing in Alaska.
Basis for selection: Competition/talent/interest in oratory/debate, based on comprehensiveness of knowledge, originality, application of knowledge on topic, skill in selecting examples and analogies, logic, voice, diction, style of language and delivery.
Application requirements: Proof of eligibility.
Additional information: Topic: U.S. Constitution and citizenship. Must participate in local speech contests.

Amount of award:	$500-$1,000
Number of awards:	2
Total amount awarded:	$1,500

Contact:
American Legion, Department of Alaska
Department Adjutant
519 West 8 Avenue, Suite 208
Anchorage, AK 99501
Phone: 907-278-8598
Fax: 907-278-0041

Scholarships

American Legion Alaska Auxiliary

American Legion Alaska Auxiliary Scholarship

Type of award: Scholarship.
Intended use: For undergraduate study at postsecondary institution.
Eligibility: Applicant must be at least 17, no older than 24, high school senior. Applicant must be U.S. citizen or permanent resident residing in Alaska. Applicant must be dependent of veteran during Grenada conflict, Korean War, Lebanon conflict, Panama conflict, Persian Gulf War, WW I, WW II or Vietnam.
Basis for selection: Applicant must demonstrate high academic achievement.
Application requirements: Proof of eligibility.
Additional information: Scholarship funds apply toward tuition, matriculation, laboratory, or similar fees. Award paid half first semester, half second semester. High school graduate may not have attended institution of higher education.
    Amount of award: $1,000
    Application deadline: March 15
Contact:
American Legion Auxiliary, Department of Alaska
P.O. Box 220887
Anchorage, AK 99522-0887
Phone: 907-283-3222

American Legion Arizona Auxiliary

American Legion Arizona Auxiliary Health Occupation Scholarship

Type of award: Scholarship.
Intended use: For undergraduate study at accredited vocational, 2-year or 4-year institution. Designated institutions: Arizona institution offering certificate or degree in health occupations.
Eligibility: Applicant must be U.S. citizen residing in Arizona.
Basis for selection: Major/career interest in health-related professions or health sciences.
Additional information: Must be resident of Arizona at least one year. Preference given to immediate family members of veterans.
    Amount of award: $300
    Application deadline: May 15
Contact:
American Legion Auxiliary Department of Arizona
4701 North 19th Avenue, Suite 100
Phoenix, AZ 85015-3727
Phone: 602-241-1080

American Legion Arizona Auxiliary Nurses' Scholarship

Type of award: Scholarship.
Intended use: For sophomore study at accredited 2-year or 4-year institution.

Eligibility: Applicant must be U.S. citizen residing in Arizona.
Basis for selection: Major/career interest in nursing.
Additional information: For student nurses enrolled at institutions awarding Registered Nurse degrees. Must be Arizona resident for at least one year. Preference given to immediate family members of veterans.
    Amount of award: $400
    Application deadline: May 15
Contact:
American Legion Auxiliary Department of Arizona
4701 North 19th Avenue, Suite 100
Phoenix, AZ 85015-3727
Phone: 602-241-1080

American Legion Arkansas

American Legion Arkansas Oratorical Contest

Type of award: Scholarship.
Intended use: For undergraduate study at postsecondary institution.
Eligibility: Applicant must be residing in Arkansas.
Basis for selection: Competition/talent/interest in oratory/debate, based on breadth of knowledge, originality, application of knowledge of topic, skill in selecting examples and analogies, logic, voice, diction, style of language and delivery.
Application requirements: Proof of eligibility.
Additional information: Topic: U.S. Constitution and citizenship. Four awards in area division; four in state division.
    Amount of award: $100-$1,000
    Number of awards: 8
    Total amount awarded: $3,550
Contact:
American Legion Arkansas
Department Adjutant
Box 3280
Little Rock, AR 72203
Phone: 501-375-1104
Fax: 501-375-4236

American Legion Arkansas Scholarship

Type of award: Scholarship.
Intended use: For undergraduate study.
Eligibility: Applicant or parent must be member/participant of American Legion. Applicant must be residing in Arkansas. Applicant must be descendant of veteran.
Application requirements: Proof of eligibility. For child, grandchild, or great-grandchild of American Legion member.
    Amount of award: $500
    Number of awards: 4
    Total amount awarded: $2,000
Contact:
American Legion Arkansas
Department Adjutant
Box 3280
Little Rock, AR 72203
Phone: 501-375-1104
Fax: 501-375-4236

American Legion Arkansas Auxiliary

American Legion Arkansas Auxiliary Academic Scholarship

Type of award: Scholarship.
Intended use: For undergraduate study at postsecondary institution. Designated institutions: Arkansas postsecondary institutions.
Eligibility: Applicant must be high school senior. Applicant must be residing in Arkansas. Applicant must be dependent of veteran during Grenada conflict, Korean War, Lebanon conflict, Panama conflict, Persian Gulf War, WW I, WW II or Vietnam.
Application requirements: When writing to request application, include name of high school student attends.

Amount of award:	$1,000
Number of awards:	1
Application deadline:	March 1
Total amount awarded:	$1,000

Contact:
American Legion Auxiliary Department of Arkansas
1415 West 7th St.
Little Rock, AR 72201
Phone: 501-374-5836

American Legion Arkansas Auxiliary Nurse Scholarship

Type of award: Scholarship.
Intended use: For undergraduate study at postsecondary institution.
Eligibility: Applicant must be U.S. citizen residing in Arkansas. Applicant must be dependent of veteran during Grenada conflict, Korean War, Lebanon conflict, Panama conflict, Persian Gulf War, WW I, WW II or Vietnam.
Basis for selection: Major/career interest in nursing.
Application requirements: When writing to request application, include name of high school student attends.
Additional information: Academic scholarship at $1,000; nurse scholarship at $500. Scholarship is paid half in first semester, half in second semester.

Amount of award:	$500-$1,000
Number of awards:	2
Application deadline:	March 1
Total amount awarded:	$1,500

Contact:
American Legion Auxiliary Department of Arkansas
1415 West 7th St.
Little Rock, AR 72201
Phone: 501-374-5836

American Legion California

American Legion California Oratorical Contest

Type of award: Scholarship.
Intended use: For undergraduate study at postsecondary institution.

Eligibility: Applicant must be enrolled in high school. Applicant must be residing in California.
Basis for selection: Competition/talent/interest in oratory/debate, based on breadth of knowledge, originality, application of knowledge of topic, skill in selecting examples and analogies, logic, voice, diction, style of language and delivery. Applicant must demonstrate patriotism.
Application requirements: Proof of eligibility.
Additional information: Topic: U.S. Constitution and Citizenship. Students selected by schools and participation in district contests, followed by area and departmental finals.1st-$1,200, 2nd-$1,000, 3rd-$800, 4th-$600, 5th and 6th-$700 each.

Amount of award:	$700-$1,200
Number of awards:	6
Total amount awarded:	$4,600

Contact:
Local high school counseling office
Phone: 415-431-2400
Fax: 415-255-1571

American Legion Colorado Auxiliary

American Legion Colorado Auxiliary/Past President's Parley Nurse's Scholarship

Type of award: Scholarship.
Intended use: For undergraduate study. Designated institutions: Any school of nursing in Colorado.
Eligibility: Applicant must be residing in Colorado. Applicant must be veteran; or dependent of veteran; or spouse of veteran during Grenada conflict, Korean War, Lebanon conflict, Panama conflict, Persian Gulf War, WW I, WW II or Vietnam.
Basis for selection: Major/career interest in nursing.
Additional information: Number of awards and financial level of awards variable. Must live and attend school in Colorado.

Amount of award:	$250-$500
Number of awards:	5
Application deadline:	April 15

Contact:
American Legion Colorado Auxiliary
Department Headquarters
7465 East First Avenue, Suite D
Denver, CO 80230
Phone: 303-367-5388
Fax: 303-366-7618

Department President's Scholarship

Type of award: Scholarship.
Intended use: For undergraduate study. Designated institutions: Colorado colleges and institutions.
Eligibility: Applicant or parent must be member/participant of American Legion Auxiliary. Applicant must be residing in Colorado. Applicant must be descendant of veteran during Grenada conflict, Korean War, Lebanon conflict, Panama conflict, Persian Gulf War, WW I, WW II or Vietnam.
Additional information: Up to three awards given. Must live and attend school in Colorado.

Amount of award: $250-$500
Number of awards: 3
Application deadline: March 12
Total amount awarded: $750
Contact:
American Legion Colorado Auxiliary
Department Headquarters
7465 East First Avenue, Suite D
Denver, CO 80230
Phone: 303-367-5388
Fax: 303-366-7618

President's Scholarship for Junior Members

Type of award: Scholarship.
Intended use: For undergraduate study. Designated institutions: Colorado colleges and universities.
Eligibility: Applicant or parent must be member/participant of American Legion Auxiliary. Applicant must be residing in Colorado.
Application requirements: Must be junior auxiliary member.
Amount of award: $500
Number of awards: 1
Application deadline: March 12
Contact:
American Legion Colorado Auxiliary
Department Headquarters
7465 East First Avenue, Suite D
Denver, CO 80230
Phone: 303-367-5388
Fax: 303-367-7618

American Legion Connecticut Auxiliary

Memorial Educational Grant

Type of award: Scholarship.
Intended use: For undergraduate study at postsecondary institution.
Eligibility: Applicant or parent must be member/participant of American Legion Auxiliary. Applicant must be at least 16, no older than 23. Applicant must be residing in Connecticut. Applicant must be descendant of veteran; or dependent of veteran.
Basis for selection: Applicant must demonstrate financial need.
Application requirements: Proof of eligibility.
Additional information: Two awards for child or grandchild of member of American Legion/Auxiliary, two awards to child of veteran who is Connecticut resident. Apply in December.
Amount of award: $500
Number of awards: 4
Application deadline: March 1
Total amount awarded: $2,000
Contact:
American Legion Auxiliary, Department of Connecticut
Headquarters
P.O. Box 266
Rocky Hill, CT 06067
Phone: 860-721-5945

Past President's Parley Education Grant

Type of award: Scholarship, renewable.
Intended use: For undergraduate study at postsecondary institution.
Eligibility: Applicant or parent must be member/participant of American Legion Auxiliary. Applicant must be at least 16, no older than 23. Applicant must be residing in Connecticut. Applicant must be descendant of veteran; or dependent of veteran.
Basis for selection: Applicant must demonstrate financial need.
Application requirements: Proof of eligibility.
Additional information: Children and grandchildren of ex-servicewomen who have been American Legion Auxiliary members for five years given preference; children and grandchildren of members or children and grandchildren who themselves are members for five years given second preference.
Amount of award: $500
Number of awards: 4
Application deadline: March 1
Contact:
American Legion Auxiliary, Department of Connecticut
Headquarters
P.O. Box 266
Rocky Hill, CT 06067
Phone: 860-721-5945

American Legion Delaware Auxiliary

American Legion Delaware Auxiliary Past President's Parley Nursing Scholarship

Type of award: Scholarship.
Intended use: For undergraduate study.
Eligibility: Applicant must be residing in Delaware. Applicant must be dependent of veteran.
Basis for selection: Major/career interest in nursing.
Amount of award: $300
Number of awards: 1
Application deadline: February 28
Total amount awarded: $300
Contact:
American Legion Auxiliary
Executive Secretary
43 Blades Drive
Dover, DE 19901-5536

American Legion District of Columbia

National High School Oratorical Contest

Type of award: Scholarship.

Intended use: For undergraduate study at postsecondary institution.
Eligibility: Applicant must be enrolled in high school. Applicant must be U.S. citizen residing in District of Columbia.
Basis for selection: Competition/talent/interest in oratory/debate, based on breadth of knowledge, originality, application of knowledge of topic, skill in selecting examples and analogies, logic, voice, diction, style of language and delivery.
Application requirements: Proof of eligibility. Four department finalists, National High School Oratorical Contest.
Additional information: All awards in U.S. Savings Bonds. 1st-$200, 2nd-$100, 3rd-$75, 4th-$50. Topic: U.S. Constitution and citizenship.

Amount of award:	$50-$200
Number of awards:	4
Total amount awarded:	$425

Contact:
American Legion, Department of District of Columbia
3408 Wisconsin Avenue NW, Suite 212
Washington, DC 20016
Phone: 202-362-9151

American Legion Florida Auxiliary

American Legion Florida Auxiliary Memorial Scholarship

Type of award: Scholarship.
Intended use: For undergraduate study at vocational, 2-year or 4-year institution. Designated institutions: Florida colleges and universities.
Eligibility: Applicant or parent must be member/participant of American Legion Auxiliary. Applicant must be female. Applicant must be residing in Florida.
Application requirements: Members, daughters/granddaughters of members with memberships of at least 3 years. Request application by January 1.
Additional information: Junior college and technical school grants not to exceed $500. $1,000 for four-year university.

Amount of award:	$500-$1,000
Application deadline:	January 1

Contact:
American Legion Auxiliary, Department of Florida
Department Secretary
P.O. Box 547917
Orlando, FL 32854-7917
Fax: 407-299-6522

American Legion Florida Auxiliary Scholarship

Type of award: Scholarship.
Intended use: For undergraduate study at vocational, 2-year or 4-year institution.
Eligibility: Applicant must be residing in Florida. Applicant must be dependent of veteran.
Application requirements: Proof of eligibility. Must be sponsored by local auxiliary unit.
Additional information: $500 award for junior colleges and technical vocational school; $1,000 for four-year university.

Amount of award:	$500-$1,000
Application deadline:	January 1

Contact:
American Legion Auxiliary, Department of Florida
Department Secretary
P.O. Box 547917
Orlando, FL 32854-7917

American Legion Georgia Auxiliary

American Legion Georgia Auxiliary Scholarship

Type of award: Scholarship.
Intended use: For undergraduate study at postsecondary institution. Designated institutions: Georgia colleges and universities.
Eligibility: Applicant must be high school senior. Applicant must be residing in Georgia. Applicant must be dependent of veteran.
Basis for selection: Applicant must demonstrate high academic achievement.
Application requirements: Essay, transcript, proof of eligibility. Must be sponsored by local Auxiliary unit.
Additional information: Preference given to children of deceased veterans. Must be Georgia resident. Information and application materials available through local American Legion Auxiliary units. Send SASE with application request.

Amount of award:	$1,000
Number of awards:	2
Total amount awarded:	$2,000

Contact:
The American Legion Georgia Auxiliary
Dept. Headquarters
3035 Mt. Zion Road
Stockbridge, GA 30281

Past President's Parley Nursing Scholarship

Type of award: Scholarship.
Intended use: For undergraduate study at 2-year or 4-year institution.
Eligibility: Applicant must be female, high school senior. Applicant must be residing in Georgia. Applicant must be dependent of veteran.
Basis for selection: Major/career interest in nursing. Applicant must demonstrate high academic achievement.
Application requirements: Proof of eligibility.
Additional information: Amount of award and number of scholarships determined by available funds. Must be sponsored by local Auxiliary Unit. Daughter of deceased veteran preferred candidate.
Contact:
American Legion Georgia Auxiliary
Dept. Headquarters
3035 Mt. Zion Road
Stockbridge, GA 30281

Scholarships

93

American Legion Idaho Auxiliary

American Legion Idaho Auxiliary Nursing Scholarship

Type of award: Scholarship.
Intended use: For undergraduate study at 2-year or 4-year institution.
Eligibility: Applicant must be residing in Idaho. Applicant must be veteran; or dependent of veteran.
Basis for selection: Major/career interest in nursing.
Application requirements: Idaho resident for at least 5 years.

Amount of award:	$750
Application deadline:	March 15
Total amount awarded:	$750

Contact:
American Legion Auxiliary, Department of Idaho
Department Headquarters
905 Warren Street
Boise, ID 83706
Phone: 208-342-7066

American Legion Illinois

American Legion Illinois Boy Scout Scholarship

Type of award: Scholarship.
Intended use: For undergraduate study at postsecondary institution.
Eligibility: Applicant or parent must be member/participant of Boy Scouts of America. Applicant must be male, high school senior. Applicant must be residing in Illinois.
Basis for selection: Competition/talent/interest in writing/journalism.
Application requirements: Essay, proof of eligibility. Topic: Legion's Americanism and Boy Scout Programs. Essay must be 500 words. Explorers also eligible.
Additional information: Boy Scout Scholarship $1,000. Four runners-up receive $200 each.

Amount of award:	$200-$1,000
Number of awards:	5
Application deadline:	April 30
Total amount awarded:	$1,800

Contact:
The American Legion, Department of Illinois
P.O. Box 2910
Bloomington, Il 61702
Phone: 309-663-0361
Fax: 309-663-5783
Web: www.illegion.org

American Legion Illinois Oratorical Contest

Type of award: Scholarship.
Intended use: For undergraduate study at postsecondary institution.

Eligibility: Applicant must be enrolled in high school. Applicant must be U.S. citizen or permanent resident residing in Illinois.
Basis for selection: Competition/talent/interest in oratory/debate, based on breadth of knowledge, originality, application of knowledge of topic, skill in selecting examples and analogies, logic, voice, diction, style of language and delivery.
Application requirements: Proof of eligibility.
Additional information: Topic: U.S. Constitution and citizenship. Applications available in the fall. Contest begins in January. Oratorical Contest starts at the Post level, to District level, to Division level, to Department level, then to National Competition.

Amount of award:	$75-$1,600
Number of awards:	12
Total amount awarded:	$7,175

Contact:
American Legion Illinois
Department Headquarters
P.O. Box 2910
Bloomington, IL 61702
Phone: 309-663-0361
Fax: 309-663-5783

American Legion Illinois Scholarship

Type of award: Scholarship.
Intended use: For undergraduate study at accredited vocational, 2-year or 4-year institution.
Eligibility: Applicant or parent must be member/participant of American Legion. Applicant must be high school senior. Applicant must be residing in Illinois.
Basis for selection: Applicant must demonstrate financial need and high academic achievement.
Application requirements: Proof of eligibility.
Additional information: Applications available after September 15. Must be a graduating high school senior and children of American Legion Post members in IL.

Amount of award:	$1,000
Number of awards:	20
Application deadline:	March 15
Total amount awarded:	$20,000

Contact:
The American Legion, Department of Illinois
P.O. Box 2910
Bloomington, IL 61702
Phone: 309-663-0361
Fax: 309-663-5783
Web: www.illegion.org

American Legion Illinois Auxiliary

Ada Mucklestone Memorial Scholarship

Type of award: Scholarship.
Intended use: For undergraduate study at postsecondary institution.
Eligibility: Applicant must be high school senior. Applicant must be residing in Illinois. Applicant must be descendant of veteran; or dependent of veteran during Grenada conflict,

Korean War, Lebanon conflict, Panama conflict, Persian Gulf War, WW I, WW II or Vietnam.
Application requirements: Applications from Local Unit. Unit sponsorship required. Graduates of accredited high schools also eligible but may not have attended an institution of higher education.
Additional information: Prizes: First $1,200; second $1,000; several $800. Must be Illinois resident; children or grandchildren of veterans who served in eligibility dates of The American Legion. Must be in senior year of high school or graduate of accredited high school but may not have attended an institution of higher institution.

Amount of award:	$800-$1,200
Application deadline:	March 15

Contact:
American Legion Auxiliary Department of Illinois
P.O. Box 1426
Bloomington, IL 61702-1426
Phone: 309-663-9366

American Legion Illinois Auxiliary Special Education Teaching Scholarships

Type of award: Scholarship.
Intended use: For sophomore or junior study at 4-year institution.
Eligibility: Applicant must be U.S. citizen or permanent resident residing in Illinois.
Basis for selection: Major/career interest in education, special.
Application requirements: Proof of eligibility. Application from Local Unit. Unit sponsorship is required.

Amount of award:	$1,000
Application deadline:	March 15
Total amount awarded:	$1,000

Contact:
American Legion Auxiliary Department of Illinois
P.O. Box 1426
Bloomington, IL 61702-1426
Phone: 309-663-9366

American Legion Illinois Auxiliary Student Nurse Scholarship

Type of award: Scholarship.
Intended use: For undergraduate study at 2-year or 4-year institution.
Eligibility: Applicant must be U.S. citizen or permanent resident residing in Illinois.
Basis for selection: Major/career interest in nursing.
Application requirements: Proof of eligibility. Application from Local Unit. Unit sponsorship required.

Amount of award:	$1,000
Number of awards:	1
Total amount awarded:	$1,000

Contact:
American Legion Illinois Auxiliary
P.O. Box 1426
Bloomington, IL 61702-1426
Phone: 309-663-9366

Marie Sheehe Trade School Scholarship

Type of award: Scholarship.

Intended use: For undergraduate study at vocational institution. Designated institutions: Trade schools.
Eligibility: Applicant must be residing in Illinois. Applicant must be descendant of veteran; or dependent of veteran during Grenada conflict, Korean War, Lebanon conflict, Panama conflict, Persian Gulf War, WW I, WW II or Vietnam.
Application requirements: Applications from Local Unit. Unit sponsorship is required.

Amount of award:	$800
Number of awards:	1
Application deadline:	March 15
Total amount awarded:	$800

Contact:
American Legion Auxiliary Department of Illinois
P.O. Box 1426
Bloomington, IL 61702-1426
Phone: 309-663-9366

Mildred R. Knoles Opportunity Scholarship

Type of award: Scholarship.
Intended use: For undergraduate study at postsecondary institution.
Eligibility: Applicant must be residing in Illinois. Applicant must be veteran or descendant of veteran; or dependent of veteran during Grenada conflict, Korean War, Lebanon conflict, Panama conflict, Persian Gulf War, WW I, WW II or Vietnam.
Basis for selection: Applicant must demonstrate financial need.
Application requirements: Proof of eligibility. Applications from Local Unit. Unit sponsorship required.
Additional information: Awards: One $1,200; several $800. Must be college student matriculating in program specializing in teaching developmentally disabled or handicapped children.

Amount of award:	$800-$1,200
Application deadline:	March 15

Contact:
American Legion Auxiliary Department of Illinois
P.O. Box 1426
Bloomington, IL 61702-1426
Phone: 309-663-9366

American Legion Indiana

American Legion Indiana Oratorical Contest

Type of award: Scholarship.
Intended use: For undergraduate study at postsecondary institution.
Eligibility: Applicant must be enrolled in high school. Applicant must be residing in Indiana.
Basis for selection: Competition/talent/interest in oratory/debate, based on breadth of knowledge, originality, application of knowledge of topic, skill in selecting examples and analogies, logic, voice, diction, style of language, and delivery. Applicant must demonstrate patriotism.
Application requirements: Proof of eligibility. Must participate in local contests.
Additional information: Topic: U.S. Constitution and citizenship. State awards: 1st-$1,200, 2nd-$500, 3rd-$500, 4th-$500. Zone: 4-$350 each.

Amount of award: $350-$1,200
Number of awards: 8
Application deadline: December 1
Total amount awarded: $4,100
Contact:
American Legion Indiana
Americanism Office, Department Headquarters
777 North Meridian Street
Indianapolis, IN 46204
Phone: 317-630-1264
Fax: 317-237-9891

Frank W. McHale Memorial Scholarship

Type of award: Scholarship.
Intended use: For undergraduate study.
Eligibility: Applicant or parent must be member/participant of American Legion, Boys State. Applicant must be male, high school junior. Applicant must be residing in Indiana.
Application requirements: Only Hoosier Boys Staters are eligible the year they attend.
Additional information: Selected by staff at Hoosier Boys State.
Number of awards: 3
Contact:
The American Legion
Americanism Office, Department Headquarters
777 North Meridian Street
Indianapolis, IN 46204
Phone: 317-630-1263
Fax: 317-237-9891

American Legion Indiana Auxiliary

Edna M. Barcus Memorial Scholarship

Type of award: Scholarship.
Intended use: For undergraduate study at postsecondary institution. Designated institutions: Indiana postsecondary institutions.
Eligibility: Applicant must be residing in Indiana. Applicant must be dependent of veteran during Civil War, Grenada conflict, Korean War, Lebanon conflict, Panama conflict, Persian Gulf War, Spanish/American War, WW I, WW II or Vietnam.
Basis for selection: Applicant must demonstrate high academic achievement.
Application requirements: Send SASE to departmental secretary.
Amount of award: $500
Application deadline: April 1
Contact:
American Legion Auxiliary, Department of Indiana
Department Secretary
777 North Meridian Street, Room 107
Indianapolis, IN 46204
Phone: 317-630-1390
Fax: 317-630-1277

Past President's Parley Nursing Scholarship

Type of award: Scholarship.
Intended use: For undergraduate study.
Eligibility: Applicant or parent must be member/participant of American Legion Auxiliary. Applicant must be female. Applicant must be residing in Indiana.
Basis for selection: Major/career interest in nursing.
Application requirements: Must be daughter of member of Auxiliary or deceased member; must be member of ALA if eligible. Send SASE to departmental secretary.
Amount of award: $500
Number of awards: 1
Application deadline: April 1
Total amount awarded: $500
Contact:
American Legion Auxiliary, Department of Indiana
Department Secretary
777 North Meridian Street, Room 107
Indianapolis, IN 46204
Phone: 317-630-1390
Fax: 317-630-1277

American Legion Iowa

American Legion Iowa Oratorical Contest

Type of award: Scholarship.
Intended use: For undergraduate study at postsecondary institution.
Eligibility: Applicant must be enrolled in high school. Applicant must be U.S. citizen or permanent resident residing in Iowa.
Basis for selection: Competition/talent/interest in oratory/debate, based on breadth of knowledge, originality, application of knowledge of topic, skill in selecting examples and analogies, logic, voice, diction, style of language, and delivery.
Application requirements: Proof of eligibility.
Additional information: Topic: U.S. Constitution and citizenship. Awards: 1st-$2,000, 2nd-$600, 3rd-$400. Must enter Oratorical Contest at local level in September.
Amount of award: $400-$2,000
Number of awards: 3
Total amount awarded: $3,000
Contact:
American Legion Iowa
720 Lyon Street
Des Moines, IA 50309
Phone: 515-282-5068
Fax: 515-282-7583

American Legion Iowa "Outstanding Citizen of Boys State" Scholarship

Type of award: Scholarship.
Intended use: For undergraduate study at postsecondary institution. Designated institutions: Eligible colleges and universities in Iowa.

Eligibility: Applicant or parent must be member/participant of American Legion, Boys State. Applicant must be male, high school senior. Applicant must be residing in Iowa.
Application requirements: Recommendations.
Additional information: Must have completed junior year in high school to attend Boys State. Awarded on recommendation of Boys State.

Amount of award:	$2,500
Number of awards:	1

Contact:
American Legion Iowa
720 Lyon Street
Des Moines, IA 50309
Phone: 515-282-5068
Fax: 515-282-7583

American Legion Iowa "Outstanding Senior Baseball Player" Scholarship

Type of award: Scholarship.
Intended use: For undergraduate study at postsecondary institution.
Eligibility: Applicant must be high school senior. Applicant must be residing in Iowa.
Basis for selection: Competition/talent/interest in athletics/ sports. Applicant must demonstrate high academic achievement.
Application requirements: Recommendations. Participant in the Iowa American Legion Senior Baseball Program. Outstanding sportsmanship, team play, and athletic ability.
Additional information: Awarded on recommendation of State Baseball Committee.

Amount of award:	$1,500
Number of awards:	1
Total amount awarded:	$1,500

Contact:
American Legion Iowa
720 Lyon Street
Des Moines, IA 50309
Phone: 515-282-5068
Fax: 515-282-7583

American Legion "Boy Scout of the Year" Award

Type of award: Scholarship.
Intended use: For undergraduate study at postsecondary institution.
Eligibility: Applicant or parent must be member/participant of Boy Scouts of America, Eagle Scouts. Applicant must be male. Applicant must be residing in Iowa.
Basis for selection: Applicant must demonstrate service orientation.
Application requirements: Recommendations. Eagle Scout Award.
Additional information: Awards: First-$2,000; Second- $600; and Third-$400. Recommendation of Boy Scout Committee considers service to religious institution, school, and community.

Amount of award:	$400-$2,000
Number of awards:	3
Application deadline:	February 1
Total amount awarded:	$3,000

Contact:
American Legion Iowa
720 Lyon Street
Des Moines, IA 50309
Phone: 515-282-5068
Fax: 515-282-7583

American Legion Iowa Auxiliary

American Legion Iowa Auxiliary Mary Virginia Macrea Memorial Nurses Scholarship

Type of award: Scholarship.
Intended use: For undergraduate study at 2-year or 4-year institution. Designated institutions: Eligible Iowa postsecondary institutions.
Eligibility: Applicant must be residing in Iowa. Applicant must be descendant of veteran; or dependent of veteran; or spouse of veteran or deceased veteran.
Basis for selection: Major/career interest in nursing.
Additional information: Also eligible: mother, sister, grandchildren, great-grandchildren of veterans.

Amount of award:	$400
Number of awards:	1
Application deadline:	June 1
Total amount awarded:	$400

Contact:
American Legion Auxiliary, Department of Iowa
720 Lyon Street
Des Moines, IA 50309
Phone: 515-282-5068
Fax: 515-282-7583

Department of Iowa Scholarships

Type of award: Scholarship.
Intended use: For undergraduate study at postsecondary institution. Designated institutions: Eligible Iowa postsecondary institutions.
Eligibility: Applicant must be residing in Iowa. Applicant must be descendant of veteran; or dependent of veteran during Grenada conflict, Korean War, Lebanon conflict, Panama conflict, Persian Gulf War, WW I, WW II or Vietnam.
Application requirements: Child, grandchild, or great-grandchild of veteran.

Amount of award:	$300
Number of awards:	10
Application deadline:	June 1
Total amount awarded:	$3,000

Contact:
American Legion Auxiliary, Department of Iowa
720 Lyon Street
Des Moines, IA 50309
Phone: 515-282-7987
Fax: 515-282-7583

Harriet Hoffman Memorial Scholarship

Type of award: Scholarship.

Intended use: For undergraduate study at postsecondary institution. Designated institutions: Must attend Iowa school.
Eligibility: Applicant must be residing in Iowa. Applicant must be descendant of veteran; or dependent of veteran, disabled veteran or deceased veteran.
Basis for selection: Major/career interest in education or education, teacher.
Additional information: Teacher training scholarship. Also eligible: grandchild, great-grandchild of veteran. Preference given to descendent of disabled or deceased veteran.

Amount of award:	$400
Number of awards:	1
Application deadline:	June 1
Total amount awarded:	$400

Contact:
American Legion Auxiliary, Department of Iowa
720 Lyon Street
Des Moines, IA 50309
Phone: 515-282-5068
Fax: 515-282-7583
Web: info@iaamerlegaux.bostofiowal.com

American Legion Kansas

Albert M. Lappin Scholarship

Type of award: Scholarship.
Intended use: For freshman or sophomore study at accredited vocational, 2-year or 4-year institution. Designated institutions: Eligible colleges, universities, and trade schools in Kansas.
Eligibility: Applicant or parent must be member/participant of American Legion. Applicant must be residing in Kansas.
Additional information: Must be child of Legion or Auxiliary member.

Amount of award:	$1,000
Number of awards:	1
Application deadline:	February 15
Total amount awarded:	$1,000

Contact:
American Legion Kansas
1314 Southwest Topeka Boulevard
Topeka, KS 66612-1886
Phone: 913-232-9315
Fax: 913-232-1399

American Legion Music Scholarship

Type of award: Scholarship.
Intended use: For freshman or sophomore study at 2-year or 4-year institution. Designated institutions: Eligible Kansas colleges or universities.
Eligibility: Applicant must be residing in Kansas.
Basis for selection: Major/career interest in music.
Application requirements: Proof of eligibility.

Amount of award:	$1,000
Number of awards:	1
Application deadline:	February 15
Total amount awarded:	$1,000

Contact:
American Legion Kansas
1314 Southwest Topeka Boulevard
Topeka, KS 66612-1886
Phone: 913-232-9315
Fax: 913-232-1399

Dr. Click Cowger Scholarship

Type of award: Scholarship.
Intended use: For freshman or sophomore study at vocational, 2-year or 4-year institution. Designated institutions: Eligible Kansas colleges, universities and trade schools.
Eligibility: Applicant must be high school senior. Applicant must be residing in Kansas.
Basis for selection: Competition/talent/interest in athletics/sports.
Application requirements: Proof of eligibility. Must play or have played Kansas American Legion Baseball.
Additional information: College-level freshmen and sophomores also eligible.

Amount of award:	$500
Number of awards:	1
Application deadline:	July 15
Total amount awarded:	$500

Contact:
American Legion Kansas
1314 Southwest Topeka Boulevard
Topeka, KS 66612-1886
Phone: 913-232-9315
Fax: 913-232-1399

Hugh A. Smith Scholarship

Type of award: Scholarship.
Intended use: For freshman or sophomore study at vocational, 2-year or 4-year institution. Designated institutions: Eligible Kansas colleges, universities, and trade schools.
Eligibility: Applicant or parent must be member/participant of American Legion. Applicant must be residing in Kansas.
Application requirements: Children of Legion or Auxiliary members.
Additional information: High school seniors, college-level freshman and sophomores eligible.

Amount of award:	$500
Number of awards:	1
Application deadline:	February 15
Total amount awarded:	$500

Contact:
American Legion Kansas
1314 Southwest Topeka Boulevard
Topeka, KS 66612-1886
Phone: 913-232-9315
Fax: 913-232-1399

John and Geraldine Hobble Licensed Practical Nursing Scholarship

Type of award: Scholarship.
Intended use: For undergraduate study at accredited 2-year or 4-year institution. Designated institutions: Kansas school which awards LPN diploma.
Eligibility: Applicant must be at least 18. Applicant must be residing in Kansas.
Basis for selection: Major/career interest in nursing.
Application requirements: Proof of eligibility.
Additional information: Applicant must be age 18 prior to taking Kansas State Board Examination.

Amount of award:	$300
Number of awards:	1
Application deadline:	February 15
Total amount awarded:	$300

Contact:
American Legion Kansas
1314 Southwest Topeka Boulevard
Topeka, KS 66612-1886
Phone: 913-232-9315
Fax: 913-232-1399

Legion Oratorical Contest

Type of award: Scholarship.
Intended use: For undergraduate study at postsecondary institution.
Eligibility: Applicant must be enrolled in high school. Applicant must be residing in Kansas.
Basis for selection: Competition/talent/interest in oratory/debate, based on breadth of knowledge, originality, application of knowledge of topic, skill in selecting examples and analogies, logic, voice, diction, style of language, and delivery.
Additional information: Awards: $1,000 for winner provided by National Organization, 2nd-$500, 3rd-$250, 4th-$150. Topic: U.S. Constitution and citizenship.

Amount of award:	$150-$1,000
Number of awards:	4
Total amount awarded:	$1,900

Contact:
American Legion Kansas
1314 Southwest Topeka Boulevard
Topeka, KS 66612-1886
Phone: 913-232-9315
Fax: 913-232-1399

Ted and Nora Anderson Scholarship

Type of award: Scholarship.
Intended use: For freshman or sophomore study at vocational, 2-year or 4-year institution. Designated institutions: Eligible colleges, universities and trade schools in Kansas.
Eligibility: Applicant or parent must be member/participant of American Legion. Applicant must be residing in Kansas. Applicant must be dependent of veteran.
Application requirements: Proof of eligibility. Child of Legion or Auxiliary member.
Additional information: High school seniors, college-level freshmen and sophomores eligible.

Amount of award:	$500
Number of awards:	4
Application deadline:	July 15
Total amount awarded:	$2,000

Contact:
American Legion Kansas
1314 Southwest Topeka Boulevard
Topeka, KS 66612-1886
Phone: 913-232-9315
Fax: 913-232-1399

American Legion Kansas Auxiliary

American Legion of Kansas General Scholarship

Type of award: Scholarship.

Intended use: For freshman study at vocational, 2-year or 4-year institution. Designated institutions: Kansas institutions.
Eligibility: Applicant must be high school senior. Applicant must be residing in Kansas. Applicant must be dependent of veteran; or spouse of veteran or deceased veteran during Grenada conflict, Korean War, Lebanon conflict, Panama conflict, Persian Gulf War, WW I, WW II or Vietnam.
Additional information: $500 total, $250 per year for two years. Applicants must be entering college for the first time. Spouses of deceased veterans must not be remarried.

Amount of award:	$500
Number of awards:	8
Application deadline:	April 1
Total amount awarded:	$4,000

Contact:
American Legion Kansas Auxiliary
1314 SW Topeka Boulevard
Topeka, KS 66612-1886
Phone: 913-232-1396

American Legion Kentucky Auxiliary

American Legion Kentucky Auxiliary Mary Barrett Marshall Scholarship

Type of award: Scholarship.
Intended use: For undergraduate study at vocational, 2-year or 4-year institution. Designated institutions: Eligible postsecondary institutions in Kentucky.
Eligibility: Applicant must be female. Applicant must be residing in Kentucky. Applicant must be descendant of veteran; or dependent of veteran; or spouse of veteran or deceased veteran during Grenada conflict, Korean War, Lebanon conflict, Panama conflict, Persian Gulf War, WW I, WW II or Vietnam.
Application requirements: Proof of eligibility. Wife, sister, widow or descendant of veteran eligible for membership in American Legion.
Additional information: Include SASE with request for application.

Amount of award:	$500
Number of awards:	1
Application deadline:	April 1
Total amount awarded:	$500

Contact:
American Legion Auxiliary, Department of Kentucky
Chairman: Velma Greefleaf
1448 Leafdale Road
Hodgenville, KY 42748
Phone: 720-358-3341

Laura Blackburn Memorial Scholarship

Type of award: Scholarship.
Intended use: For undergraduate study.
Eligibility: Applicant must be high school senior. Applicant must be residing in Kentucky. Applicant must be descendant of veteran; or dependent of veteran during Grenada conflict, Korean War, Lebanon conflict, Panama conflict, Persian Gulf War, WW I, WW II or Vietnam.

Application requirements: Proof of eligibility.

Amount of award:	$1,000
Number of awards:	1
Number of applicants:	1
Application deadline:	March 31
Total amount awarded:	$1,000

Contact:
American Legion Auxiliary, Department of Kentucky
Ruth James, Education Chairman
7340 Lilydale Road
Byrdstown, TN 38549

American Legion Maine

Children and Youth Scholarship

Type of award: Scholarship.
Intended use: For undergraduate study at postsecondary institution.
Eligibility: Applicant or parent must be member/participant of American Legion. Applicant must be high school senior. Applicant must be residing in Maine.
Basis for selection: Applicant must demonstrate financial need, high academic achievement and depth of character.
Application requirements: Students must be in upper half of class.
Additional information: High school seniors, college students, and veterans all eligible. Parent must be Maine American Legion member.

Amount of award:	$500
Number of awards:	7
Number of applicants:	300
Application deadline:	April 15
Total amount awarded:	$3,500

Contact:
American Legion Maine
Department Adjutant, State Headquarters
P.O. Box 900
Waterville, ME 04903
Phone: 207-873-3229

Daniel E. Lambert Memorial Scholarship

Type of award: Scholarship.
Intended use: For undergraduate study at vocational, 2-year or 4-year institution.
Eligibility: Applicant must be high school senior. Applicant must be U.S. citizen residing in Maine. Applicant must be dependent of veteran.
Basis for selection: Applicant must demonstrate financial need and depth of character.

Amount of award:	$500
Number of awards:	1
Number of applicants:	300
Application deadline:	May 1
Total amount awarded:	$500

Contact:
American Legion Maine
Department Adjutant, State Headquarters
P.O. Box 900
Waterville, ME 04903
Phone: 207-873-3229

James V. Day Scholarship

Type of award: Scholarship.
Intended use: For freshman study at vocational, 2-year or 4-year institution.
Eligibility: Applicant or parent must be member/participant of American Legion. Applicant must be high school senior. Applicant must be residing in Maine.
Basis for selection: Applicant must demonstrate financial need, high academic achievement and depth of character.
Application requirements: Must be in top half of graduating class.
Additional information: Parent must be Maine American Legion member.

Amount of award:	$500
Number of awards:	1
Application deadline:	May 1
Total amount awarded:	$500

Contact:
American Legion Maine
Department Adjutant
P.O. Box 900
Waterville, ME 04903
Phone: 207-873-3229

American Legion Maine Auxiliary

American Legion Maine Auxiliary General Scholarship

Type of award: Scholarship.
Intended use: For undergraduate study at vocational, 2-year or 4-year institution.
Eligibility: Applicant must be high school senior. Applicant must be residing in Maine. Applicant must be dependent of veteran.
Basis for selection: Applicant must demonstrate financial need.
Additional information: Graduates from accredited high school also eligible. Only residents of Maine qualify. Send SASE with application request.

Amount of award:	$300
Number of awards:	2
Application deadline:	April 15
Total amount awarded:	$600

Contact:
American Legion Auxiliary, Department of Maine
Department Secretary
P.O. Box 887
Bucksport, ME 04416-0887

President's Parley Nursing Scholarship

Type of award: Scholarship.
Intended use: For undergraduate study.
Eligibility: Applicant must be residing in Maine. Applicant must be descendant of veteran; or dependent of veteran during WW I or WW II.
Basis for selection: Major/career interest in nursing.
Application requirements: Proof of eligibility.

Additional information: For training in accredited nursing school. Must be graduate of accredited high school.

Amount of award:	$300
Number of awards:	1
Application deadline:	April 15
Total amount awarded:	$300

Contact:
American Legion Auxiliary, Department of Maine
Department Secretary
P.O. Box 887
Bucksport, ME 04416

American Legion Maryland

Adler Science/Math Scholarship

Type of award: Scholarship.
Intended use: For undergraduate study at postsecondary institution.
Eligibility: Applicant must be at least 16, no older than 19. Applicant must be residing in Maryland. Applicant must be dependent of veteran.
Basis for selection: Major/career interest in science, general or mathematics.
Application requirements: Transcript.

Amount of award:	$500
Number of awards:	1
Application deadline:	March 31
Total amount awarded:	$500

Contact:
American Legion Maryland
Department Adjutant, War Memorial Building
101 North Gay Street
Baltimore, MD 21202-1405
Phone: 301-752-3104
Web: www.mdlegion.org

American Legion Maryland Boys State Scholarship

Type of award: Scholarship.
Intended use: For undergraduate study at postsecondary institution.
Eligibility: Applicant or parent must be member/participant of American Legion, Boys State. Applicant must be male, at least 16, no older than 19. Applicant must be residing in Maryland. Applicant must be dependent of veteran.
Application requirements: Must be Maryland Boys State graduate.

Amount of award:	$500
Number of awards:	5
Application deadline:	May 1
Total amount awarded:	$2,500

Contact:
American Legion Maryland
Department Adjutant, War Memorial Building
101 North Gay Street
Baltimore, MD 21202-1405
Phone: 301-752-3104
Web: www.mdlegion.org

American Legion Maryland General Scholarship

Type of award: Scholarship.
Intended use: For undergraduate study at postsecondary institution.
Eligibility: Applicant must be at least 16, no older than 19. Applicant must be residing in Maryland. Applicant must be dependent of veteran.
Application requirements: Transcript. Applicant must not have reached 20th birthday by January 1st of calendar year application is filed.

Amount of award:	$500
Number of awards:	11
Application deadline:	March 31
Total amount awarded:	$5,500

Contact:
American Legion Maryland
Department Adjutant, War Memorial Building
101 North Gay Street
Baltimore, MD 21202-1405
Phone: 301-752-3104
Web: www.mdlegion.org

American Legion Maryland Oratorical Contest

Type of award: Scholarship.
Intended use: For undergraduate study at postsecondary institution.
Eligibility: Applicant must be at least 16, no older than 19. Applicant must be residing in Maryland.
Basis for selection: Competition/talent/interest in oratory/debate, based on breadth of knowledge, originality, application of knowledge of topic, skill in selecting examples and analogies, logic, voice, diction, style of language and delivery.
Application requirements: Proof of eligibility. American Legion Oratorical Contest Department Winner.
Additional information: Awards: first-$2,500; second-$1,000; third through seventh-$500 each.

Amount of award:	$500-$2,500
Number of awards:	7
Application deadline:	October 1
Total amount awarded:	$6,000

Contact:
Local American Legion Post.
Phone: 410-752-1405
Fax: 410-752-3822
Web: www.mdlegion.org

American Legion Maryland Auxiliary

American Legion Maryland Auxiliary Nursing Scholarship

Type of award: Scholarship.
Intended use: For undergraduate study at 2-year or 4-year institution.
Eligibility: Applicant must be female, at least 16, no older than 22. Applicant must be residing in Maryland. Applicant must be dependent of veteran.

Basis for selection: Major/career interest in nursing. Applicant must demonstrate financial need.

Application requirements: Recommendations. For daughter of ex-servicewoman or ex-serviceman. Submit application for Department's Past President's Parley Scholarship.

Additional information: For the RN degree only.

Amount of award:	$1,000
Number of awards:	1
Application deadline:	May 1
Total amount awarded:	$1,000

Contact:
American Legion Maryland Auxiliary
Chairman, Past President's Parley Fund
5205 East Drive, Suite R-1
Baltimore, MD 21227
Phone: 410-242-9519

American Legion Maryland Auxiliary Scholarship

Type of award: Scholarship.

Intended use: For undergraduate study at 2-year or 4-year institution. Designated institutions: Mayland college or university.

Eligibility: Applicant must be female, high school senior. Applicant must be residing in Maryland. Applicant must be dependent of veteran.

Basis for selection: Major/career interest in arts, general; science, general; business; public administration/service or education, teacher.

Additional information: Additional field of study considered: medical sciences other than nursing.

Amount of award:	$2,000
Number of awards:	1
Application deadline:	May 1
Total amount awarded:	$2,000

Contact:
American Legion Auxiliary, Department of Maryland
Department Secretary
5205 East Drive, Suite R-1
Baltimore, MD 21227
Phone: 410-242-9519

American Legion Massachusetts

American Legion Massachusetts General and Nursing Scholarships

Type of award: Scholarship.

Intended use: For freshman study at 2-year or 4-year institution.

Eligibility: Applicant or parent must be member/participant of American Legion. Applicant must be residing in Massachusetts. Applicant must be descendant of veteran; or dependent of veteran.

Application requirements: Parent or grandparent must be member in good standing of Department of Massachusetts Legion.

Additional information: General Scholarships: eight-$1,000; ten-$500; Nursing Scholarship: One-$1,000.

Amount of award:	$500-$1,000
Number of awards:	19
Application deadline:	April 1
Total amount awarded:	$16,000

Contact:
American Legion Massachusetts
Department Scholarship Chair
State House, Room 546-2
Boston, MA 02133

American Legion Massachusetts Past County Commander's Scholarship

Type of award: Scholarship.

Intended use: For freshman study at 2-year or 4-year institution.

Eligibility: Applicant must be residing in Massachusetts. Applicant must be descendant of veteran; or dependent of veteran.

Application requirements: Child or grandchild of paid-up living or deceased member of Hampden County American Legion Post. May be adopted or under legal guardianship.

Additional information: Awards: one-$500; additional $250 awards contingent on availability of funds.

Amount of award:	$250-$500
Application deadline:	April 15

Contact:
American Legion Massachusetts
Chairman
46 Brickett Street
Springfield, MA 01119
Phone: 617-727-2966
Fax: 617-727-2969

Department of Massachusetts Oratorical Contest

Type of award: Scholarship.

Intended use: For undergraduate study at postsecondary institution.

Eligibility: Applicant must be no older than 19, high school junior or senior. Applicant must be residing in Massachusetts.

Basis for selection: Competition/talent/interest in oratory/debate, based on breadth of knowledge, originality, application of knowledge of topic, skill selecting examples and analogies, logic, voice, diction, style of language and delivery.

Application requirements: Proof of eligibility.

Additional information: Topic: U.S. Constitution and citizenship. Awards: 1st-$1,000, 2nd-$800.

Amount of award:	$600-$1,000
Number of awards:	4
Application deadline:	December 15
Total amount awarded:	$1,600

Contact:
American Legion Massachusetts
Department Oratorical Chair
State House, Room 546-2
Boston, MA 02133-1044
Phone: 617-727-2966
Fax: 617-727-2969

American Legion Massachusetts Auxiliary

American Legion Massachusetts Auxiliary Past President's Parley Scholarship

Type of award: Scholarship.
Intended use: For undergraduate study.
Eligibility: Applicant must be residing in Massachusetts. Applicant must be descendant of veteran; or dependent of veteran or deceased veteran.
Basis for selection: Major/career interest in nursing.
Application requirements: Child of living or deceased veteran not eligible for Federal or Commonwealth scholarships.

Amount of award:	$200
Number of awards:	1
Application deadline:	April 1
Total amount awarded:	$200

Contact:
American Legion Massachusetts Auxiliary
Department Secretary
Room 546-2, State House
Boston, MA 02133-1044
Phone: 617-727-2966

American Legion Massachusetts Auxiliary Scholarship

Type of award: Scholarship.
Intended use: For undergraduate study at vocational, 2-year or 4-year institution.
Eligibility: Applicant must be at least 16, no older than 22. Applicant must be residing in Massachusetts. Applicant must be descendant of veteran; or dependent of veteran, disabled veteran or deceased veteran during Grenada conflict, Korean War, Lebanon conflict, Panama conflict, Persian Gulf War, WW I, WW II or Vietnam.
Application requirements: Related to living or deceased veteran as designated by American Legion eligibility.
Additional information: Awards: one-$500 and ten-$100.

Amount of award:	$100-$500
Number of awards:	11
Application deadline:	April 1
Total amount awarded:	$1,500

Contact:
American Legion, Department of Massachusetts
Department Secretary
Room 546-2 State House
Boston, MA 02133-1044
Phone: 617-727-2966

American Legion Michigan

American Legion Michigan Guy M. Wilson Scholarship

Type of award: Scholarship.
Intended use: For undergraduate study at 2-year or 4-year institution. Designated institutions: Michigan junior colleges, colleges and universities.
Eligibility: Applicant must be residing in Michigan. Applicant must be dependent of veteran or deceased veteran.
Application requirements: Essay, transcript, proof of eligibility. Copy of living or deceased veteran's honorable discharge to be attached to application. Copy of parents' Federal Tax Form.
Additional information: Minimum 2.5 GPA. Application should be filed at local American Legion post.

Amount of award:	$500
Number of applicants:	500
Application deadline:	February 1

Contact:
American Legion Michigan
212 North Verlinden Avenue
Lansing, MI 48915
Phone: 517-371-4720
Fax: 517-371-2401
Web: www.michiganlegion.org

American Legion Michigan Oratorical Contest

Type of award: Scholarship.
Intended use: For undergraduate study at postsecondary institution.
Eligibility: Applicant must be enrolled in high school. Applicant must be residing in Michigan.
Basis for selection: Competition/talent/interest in oratory/debate, based on breadth of knowledge, originality, application of knowledge of topic, skill in selecting examples and analogies, logic, voice, diction, style of language and delivery.
Application requirements: Proof of eligibility. Finalists in Zone Oratorical Contest.
Additional information: Topic: U.S. Constitution and citizenship. Local contest early February. Awards: $1,000, $800, $600.

Amount of award:	$600-$1,000
Number of awards:	3
Application deadline:	February 1
Total amount awarded:	$2,400

Contact:
American Legion Michigan
212 North Verlinden Avenue
Lansing, MI 48915
Phone: 517-371-4720
Fax: 517-371-2401
Web: www.michiganlegion.org

William D. Brewer--Jewell W. Brewer Scholarship Trusts

Type of award: Scholarship.
Intended use: For undergraduate study at postsecondary institution.
Eligibility: Applicant must be residing in Michigan. Applicant must be dependent of veteran.
Application requirements: Essay, transcript, proof of eligibility. Copy of deceased or living veteran's honorable discharge. Copy of parents' Federal Tax Form.
Additional information: Minimum 2.5 GPA. Applications to be filed at local American Legion post. Number of awards varies.

Amount of award:	$500
Application deadline:	February 1

Contact:
American Legion Michigan
212 North Verlinden Avenue
Lansing, MI 48915
Phone: 517-371-4720
Fax: 517-371-2401
Web: www.michiganlegion.org

American Legion Michigan Auxiliary

American Legion Michigan Auxiliary Memorial Scholarship

Type of award: Scholarship, renewable.
Intended use: For undergraduate study at postsecondary institution. Designated institutions: Michigan educational institutions.
Eligibility: Applicant must be female, at least 16, no older than 21. Applicant must be residing in Michigan. Applicant must be descendant of veteran; or dependent of veteran during Grenada conflict, Korean War, Middle East War, Lebanon conflict, Panama conflict, Persian Gulf War, WW I, WW II or Vietnam.
Basis for selection: Applicant must demonstrate financial need and high academic achievement.
Application requirements: Proof of eligibility. Must have been Michigan resident for one year preceding date of award.
Additional information: Applicant may be daughter, granddaughter, or great-granddaughter of veteran of eligible combat service. Can apply for renewal for second year. Application available online.

Amount of award:	$500
Number of awards:	35
Number of applicants:	1,000
Application deadline:	March 15
Total amount awarded:	$20,000

Contact:
American Legion Auxiliary, Department of Michigan
212 North Verlinden Avenue
Lansing, MI 48915
Web: www.michalaux.org

American Legion Michigan Auxiliary National President's Scholarship

Type of award: Scholarship.
Intended use: For undergraduate study at postsecondary institution.
Eligibility: Applicant must be high school senior. Applicant must be residing in Michigan. Applicant must be dependent of veteran during Grenada conflict, Korean War, Lebanon conflict, Panama conflict, Persian Gulf War, WW I, WW II or Vietnam.

Amount of award:	$1,000-$2,500
Number of awards:	10
Application deadline:	March 10

Contact:
American Legion Auxiliary, Department of Michigan
212 North Verlinden Avenue
Lansing, MI 48915
Web: www.michalaux.org

American Legion Michigan Auxiliary Scholarship for Nurses/ Therapists

Type of award: Scholarship.
Intended use: For freshman study at vocational, 2-year or 4-year institution.
Eligibility: Applicant must be residing in Michigan. Applicant must be descendant of veteran; or dependent of veteran; or spouse of veteran or deceased veteran during Grenada conflict, Korean War, Lebanon conflict, Panama conflict, Persian Gulf War, WW I, WW II or Vietnam.
Basis for selection: Major/career interest in nursing; physical therapy or respiratory therapy. Applicant must demonstrate financial need and high academic achievement.
Application requirements: Proof of eligibility. Must be Michigan resident for one year preceding award.
Additional information: Applications available after November 15 from Website or by mail.

Amount of award:	$500
Number of awards:	15
Application deadline:	March 15
Total amount awarded:	$7,500

Contact:
American Legion Auxiliary, Department of Michigan
212 North Verlinden Avenue
Lansing, MI 48915
Web: www.michalaux.org

American Legion Minnesota

American Legion Minnesota Legionnaire Insurance Trust Scholarship

Type of award: Scholarship.
Intended use: For undergraduate study at postsecondary institution. Designated institutions: Minnesota institution or instutitions in neighboring states with reciprocity agreements.
Eligibility: Applicant or parent must be member/participant of American Legion. Applicant must be U.S. citizen residing in Minnesota. Applicant must be dependent of veteran. Also cligible: grandchildren, adopted children, stepchildren of American Legion member or children, adopted children, grandchildren, stepchildren of American Legion Auxiliary member.
Basis for selection: Applicant must demonstrate financial need, depth of character and patriotism.
Application requirements: Proof of eligibility, nomination by Minnesota American Legion post.
Additional information: Initiative, honesty, thrift and religious background expected of applicants.

Amount of award:	$500
Number of awards:	3
Application deadline:	April 1
Total amount awarded:	$1,500

Contact:
American Legion Minnesota
Education Committee
State Veterans Service Building
St. Paul, MN 55155-2069
Phone: 651-291-1800
Fax: 651-291-1057
Web: www.mnlegion.org

American Legion Minnesota Memorial Scholarship

Type of award: Scholarship.
Intended use: For undergraduate study at postsecondary institution. Designated institutions: Minnesota institution or institution in neighboring state with reciprocity agreement.
Eligibility: Applicant or parent must be member/participant of American Legion. Applicant must be U.S. citizen residing in Minnesota.
Basis for selection: Applicant must demonstrate financial need.
Application requirements: Child of American Legion or American Legion Auxiliary member.

Amount of award:	$500
Number of awards:	6
Application deadline:	April 1
Total amount awarded:	$3,000

Contact:
American Legion Minnesota
Education Committee
State Veterans Service Building
St. Paul, MN 55155-2069
Phone: 612-291-1800
Fax: 612-291-1057
Web: www.mnlegion.org

American Legion Minnesota Oratorical Contest

Type of award: Scholarship.
Intended use: For undergraduate study at postsecondary institution.
Eligibility: Applicant must be enrolled in high school. Applicant must be U.S. citizen residing in Minnesota.
Basis for selection: Competition/talent/interest in oratory/debate, based on breadth of knowledge, originality, application of knowledge of topic, skill in selecting examples and analogies, logic, voice, diction, style of language and delivery.
Application requirements: First, second, third and fourth place winners from Department of Minnesota Annual Oratorical Contest.
Additional information: Topic: U.S. Constitution and citizenship. Award amounts: $1,200, $900, $700, $500.

Amount of award:	$500-$1,200
Number of awards:	4
Application deadline:	December 15
Total amount awarded:	$3,300

Contact:
Department Oratorical Liaison
State Veterans Service Building
St. Paul, MN 55155-2069
Phone: 651-291-1800
Fax: 651-291-1057
Web: www.mnlegion.org

American Legion Minnesota Auxiliary

American Legion Minnesota Auxiliary Department Scholarship

Type of award: Scholarship.
Intended use: For undergraduate study at postsecondary institution. Designated institutions: Minnesota postsecondary instituions.
Eligibility: Applicant must be U.S. citizen residing in Minnesota. Applicant must be descendant of veteran; or dependent of veteran during Grenada conflict, Korean War, Middle East War, Lebanon conflict, Panama conflict, Persian Gulf War, Spanish/American War, WW I, WW II or Vietnam.

Amount of award:	$750
Number of awards:	7
Application deadline:	March 15
Total amount awarded:	$5,250

Contact:
American Legion Auxiliary, Department of Minnesota
State Veterans Service Building
St. Paul, MN 55155
Phone: 651-224-7634

American Legion Minnesota Auxiliary Past President's Parley Nursing Scholarship

Type of award: Scholarship.
Intended use: For undergraduate study at postsecondary institution. Designated institutions: Minnesota postsecondary institutions.
Eligibility: Applicant or parent must be member/participant of American Legion Auxiliary. Applicant must be U.S. citizen residing in Minnesota.
Basis for selection: Major/career interest in nursing; health-related professions; health sciences; medical assistant or midwifery.
Additional information: Up to three awards given. Applicable toward any educational phase of health care field.

Amount of award:	$750
Number of awards:	7
Application deadline:	March 15
Total amount awarded:	$5,250

Contact:
American Legion Auxiliary, Department of Minnesota
State Veterans Service Building
St. Paul, MN 55155-2069
Phone: 612-224-7634

American Legion Mississippi Auxiliary

American Legion Mississippi Auxiliary Scholarship

Type of award: Scholarship.
Intended use: For freshman study at postsecondary institution. Designated institutions: Mississippi postsecondary institutions.

Eligibility: Applicant must be residing in Mississippi. Applicant must be descendant of veteran; or dependent of veteran during Korean War, Lebanon conflict, Panama conflict, Persian Gulf War, WW I, WW II or Vietnam.
Basis for selection: Applicant must demonstrate financial need.

Amount of award:	$500
Number of awards:	1
Application deadline:	March 10
Total amount awarded:	$500

Contact:
American Legion Mississippi Auxiliary
Department Headquarters
P.O. Box 1382
Jackson, MS 39215-1382

American Legion Missouri

American Legion Missouri Charles L. Bacon Memorial Scholarship

Type of award: Scholarship.
Intended use: For full-time undergraduate study at accredited 2-year or 4-year institution.
Eligibility: Applicant or parent must be member/participant of American Legion. Applicant must be single, no older than 20. Applicant must be residing in Missouri.
Additional information: Applicants must be current member of The American Legion, American Legion Auxiliary or the Sons of the American Legion, or descendent of any member.

Number of awards:	1
Total amount awarded:	$500

Contact:
American Legion Missouri
P. O. Box 179
Jefferson City, MO 65102
Phone: 573-893-2353
Fax: 573-893-2980

American Legion Missouri Erman W. Taylor Memorial Scholarship

Type of award: Scholarship.
Intended use: For full-time undergraduate study at accredited 2-year or 4-year institution.
Eligibility: Applicant must be residing in Missouri. Applicant must be descendant of veteran; or dependent of veteran. Must be dependent of veteran who served 90 or more days of active duty in the Armed Forces and have an honorable discharge.
Application requirements: Essay, proof of eligibility. Copy of discharge certificate for veteran parent, grandparent; 500-word or less essay "What the American Flag Means to Me"; evaluation form.

Number of awards:	1
Total amount awarded:	$250

Contact:
American Legion Missouri
P.O. Box 179
Jefferson City, MO 65102
Phone: 573-893-2353
Fax: 573-893-2980

American Legion Missouri Lillie Lois Ford Boy's Scholarship

Type of award: Scholarship.
Intended use: For undergraduate study at postsecondary institution.
Eligibility: Applicant must be male. Applicant must be U.S. citizen residing in Missouri. Applicant must be descendant of veteran; or dependent of veteran.
Basis for selection: Applicant must demonstrate financial need.
Application requirements: Transcript, proof of eligibility. Must have attended complete session of Boy's State or Cadet Patrol Academy, be dependent child or grandchild of resident veteran, not be receiving any other scholarship.

Amount of award:	$900
Number of awards:	1
Total amount awarded:	$900

Contact:
American Legion Missouri
PO Box 179
Jefferson City, MO 65102
Phone: 573-893-2353
Fax: 573-893-2980

American Legion Missouri Lillie Lois Ford Girl's Scholarship

Type of award: Scholarship.
Intended use: For undergraduate study at postsecondary institution.
Eligibility: Applicant must be female. Applicant must be residing in Missouri. Applicant must be descendant of veteran; or dependent of veteran.
Basis for selection: Applicant must demonstrate financial need.
Application requirements: Must have attended complete session of Girl's State or Cadet Patrol Academy, be dependent child or grandchild of resident veteran, not be receiving any other scholarship. Missouri residents only.

Amount of award:	$900
Number of awards:	1
Total amount awarded:	$900

Contact:
American Legion Missouri
Department Adjutant
P.O. Box 179
Jefferson City, MO 65102
Phone: 573-893-2353
Fax: 573-893-2980

American Legion Missouri M.D. "Jack" Murphy Memorial Nursing Scholarship

Type of award: Scholarship, renewable.
Intended use: For full-time undergraduate study at 2-year or 4-year institution.
Eligibility: Applicant must be single. Applicant must be residing in Missouri.
Basis for selection: Major/career interest in nursing. Applicant must demonstrate financial need.
Additional information: Available to students training to be Registered Nurses. Applicants must have graduated in top 40% of high school class and have minimum 2.0 GPA in semester

prior to applying for award. Award payment: $300 per semester.
May reapply for two additional semesters.

Amount of award: $600
Number of awards: 1
Total amount awarded: $600
Contact:
American Legion Missouri
Department Adjutant
P.O. Box 179
Jefferson City, MO 65102
Phone: 573-893-2353
Fax: 573-893-2980

American Legion Missouri Oratorical Contest

Type of award: Scholarship.
Intended use: For undergraduate study at vocational, 2-year or 4-year institution.
Eligibility: Applicant must be enrolled in high school. Applicant must be residing in Missouri.
Basis for selection: Competition/talent/interest in oratory/debate, based on breadth of knowledge, originality, application of knowledge of topic, skill in selecting examples and analogies, logic, voice, diction, style of language and delivery.
Application requirements: Proof of eligibility. Must have won 1st, 2nd, 3rd, or 4th place at Department of Missouri Annual Oratorical Contest.
Additional information: Total of four awards are offered, for the amounts of $2,000, $1,800, $1,600, and $1,400. Awards to be used to defray expenses of higher education.

Amount of award: $1,400-$2,000
Number of awards: 4
Total amount awarded: $6,800
Contact:
American Legion Missouri
Department Adjutant
P.O. Box 179
Jefferson City, MO 65102
Phone: 573-893-2353
Fax: 573-893-2980

American Legion Missouri Auxiliary

American Legion Missouri Auxiliary Past President's Parley Scholarship

Type of award: Scholarship.
Intended use: For freshman study at vocational, 2-year or 4-year institution.
Eligibility: Applicant must be high school senior. Applicant must be residing in Missouri. Applicant must be descendant of veteran; or dependent of veteran.
Basis for selection: Major/career interest in nursing.
Additional information: Applicant must be dependent child or grandchild of veteran. Cannot have attended institution of higher learning.

Amount of award: $1,000
Number of awards: 1
Application deadline: March 15
Total amount awarded: $1,000
Contact:
American Legion Missouri Auxiliary
Department Secretary
600 Ellis Bvld.
Jefferson City, MO 65101-2204

American Legion Missouri Auxiliary Scholarship

Type of award: Scholarship.
Intended use: For freshman study at postsecondary institution.
Eligibility: Applicant must be high school senior. Applicant must be residing in Missouri. Applicant must be descendant of veteran; or dependent of veteran during Korean War, Lebanon conflict, Panama conflict, Persian Gulf War, WW I, WW II or Vietnam.
Additional information: Applicant cannot have attended institution of higher learning.

Amount of award: $500
Number of awards: 2
Application deadline: March 15
Total amount awarded: $1,000
Contact:
American Legion Missouri Auxiliary
Department Secretary
600 Ellis Blvd.
Jefferson City, MO 65101-2204

American Legion National Headquarters

American Legion Auxiliary Girl Scout Achievement Award

Type of award: Scholarship.
Intended use: For undergraduate study.
Eligibility: Applicant must be female, enrolled in high school.
Basis for selection: Applicant must demonstrate service orientation.
Application requirements: Gold Award recipient.
Additional information: Applicant must be active member of religious institution and have received religious emblem. Must have demonstrated practical citizenship in church, school, scouting and community. Applicant must demonstrate service orientation.

Application deadline: February 15
Total amount awarded: $1,000
Contact:
American Legion Auxiliary
777 North Meridan Street, 3rd Floor
Indianapolis, IN 46204-1189
Phone: 317-955-3845
Web: www.legion.org

American Legion Auxiliary National President's Scholarship

Type of award: Scholarship.

Intended use: For undergraduate study at postsecondary institution.
Eligibility: Applicant must be high school senior. Applicant must be dependent of veteran during Grenada conflict, Korean War, Lebanon conflict, Panama conflict, Persian Gulf War, WW I, WW II or Vietnam.
Basis for selection: Applicant must demonstrate financial need, high academic achievement, depth of character, leadership and patriotism.
Application requirements: Applications from Unit President of Auxiliary in one's own community, from Department Secretary, or Department Education Chairman.
Additional information: Five-$2,500 scholarships, five-$2,000 scholarships, and five-$1,500 scholarcips are awarded annually.

Amount of award:	$1,500-$2,500
Number of awards:	15
Application deadline:	March 15
Total amount awarded:	$30,000

Contact:
American Legion Auxiliary
777 North Meridan Street, 3rd Floor
Indianapolis, IN 46204-1189
Phone: 317-635-6291
Web: www.legion.org

American Legion Auxiliary Spirit of Youth Scholarship For Junior Members

Type of award: Scholarship.
Intended use: For undergraduate study at postsecondary institution.
Eligibility: Applicant or parent must be member/participant of American Legion Auxiliary. Applicant must be high school senior. Applicant must be U.S. citizen.
Basis for selection: Applicant must demonstrate financial need, high academic achievement, depth of character, leadership and patriotism.
Application requirements: Proof of eligibility. Junior member of 3 years standing, holding current membership card. Applications from Unit President of the Auxiliary in one's own community, Department Secretary, or Department Education Chairman.
Additional information: One scholarship available in each of five divisions.

Amount of award:	$1,000
Number of awards:	5
Application deadline:	March 10
Total amount awarded:	$5,000

Contact:
American Legion Auxiliary
777 North Meridan, 3rd Floor
Indianapolis, IN 46204-1189
Phone: 317-635-6291
Web: www.legion.org

American Legion National Eagle Scout of the Year

Type of award: Scholarship.
Intended use: For freshman, sophomore, junior or senior study at accredited postsecondary institution in United States.
Eligibility: Applicant or parent must be member/participant of Boy Scouts of America, Eagle Scouts. Applicant must be male, enrolled in high school. Applicant must be U.S. citizen.

Application requirements: Recommendations, nomination by group leaders of religious institution, school, community and scouting. Registered, active members of Boy Scout troop, Varsity Scout team, or Explorer Post sponsored by American Legion Post or Auxiliary Unit. Must be son or grandson of American Legion or Auxiliary member. Request application from state or national headquarters.
Additional information: Must have received Eagle Scout Award, be active member of religious institution, and must have received religious emblem. Scholarships available upon graduation from accredited high school and must be used within four years of graduation date. Awards: one-$10,000, three-$2,500.

Amount of award:	$2,500-$10,000
Number of awards:	4
Total amount awarded:	$17,500

Contact:
Eagle Scout of the Year
P. O. Box 1055
Indianapolis, IN 46206-1055
Phone: 317-630-1249
Web: www.legion.org

The American Legion National High School Oratorical Contest

Type of award: Scholarship.
Intended use: For undergraduate study at postsecondary institution.
Eligibility: Applicant must be no older than 20, enrolled in high school. Applicant must be U.S. citizen or permanent resident.
Basis for selection: Competition/talent/interest in oratory/debate, based on breadth of knowledge, originality, application of knowledge of topic, skill in selecting examples and analogies, logic, voice, diction, style of language and delivery.
Application requirements: Obtain oratorical contest rules from local legion post or state department headquarters.
Additional information: Scholarship awards: State winners participating in regional level win $1,500; second-round participants not advancing to national finals receive additional $1,500. Finalists win $18,000 (first place), $16,000 (runner-up), and $14,000 (third place).

Amount of award:	$1,500-$18,000
Number of awards:	54

Contact:
Local Legion post or state American Legion headquarters.
Web: www.legion.org/orarules.htm

Eight and Forty Lung and Respiratory Nursing Scholarship Fund

Type of award: Scholarship.
Intended use: For undergraduate, graduate or non-degree study.
Eligibility: Applicant must be returning adult student.
Basis for selection: Major/career interest in nursing or respiratory therapy.
Application requirements: Proof of eligibility. Contact Eight and Forty Scholarship Chairman or The American Legion Education Program.
Additional information: Applicant must be registered nurse. Program assists registered nurses with advanced preparation for positions in supervision, administration or teaching. On

completion of education, must have full-time employment prospects related to lung and respiratory control.

Amount of award:	$2,500
Application deadline:	May 15
Notification begins:	July 1

Contact:
American Legion Education Program
Eight and Forty Scholarships
P.O. Box 1055
Indianapolis, IN 46206-1055

The Memorial Scholarship of the Twenty and Four

Type of award: Scholarship.
Intended use: For undergraduate or graduate study.
Eligibility: Applicant or parent must be member/participant of American Legion Twenty and Four. Applicant must be female, at least 16, no older than 25. Applicant must be veteran or descendant of veteran; or dependent of veteran. Applicant must be veteran or descendant of female veteran.
Basis for selection: Applicant must demonstrate financial need and high academic achievement.
Application requirements: Involvement in school activities. Must be child, grandchild, or great-grandchild of living or deceased member in good standing.
Additional information: Memorial to women who served in armed forces during wartime. Age restrictions do not apply to current members of the Twenty and Four. Contact local chapter.

Amount of award:	$500

Contact:
Scholarship Aide
10300 West Bluemound Street #312
Milwaukee, WI 53226-4352
Web: www.legion.org

American Legion Nebraska

American Legion Nebraska Maynard Jensen Memorial Scholarship

Type of award: Scholarship.
Intended use: For undergraduate study at vocational, 2-year or 4-year institution. Designated institutions: Nebraska postsecondary institutions.
Eligibility: Applicant must be residing in Nebraska. Applicant must be descendant of veteran.
Basis for selection: Applicant must demonstrate financial need and high academic achievement.
Application requirements: Must be descendant, adopted, or stepchild of American Legion member, or of POW, MIA, KIA, or any deceased veteran.

Amount of award:	$500
Number of awards:	10
Application deadline:	March 1
Total amount awarded:	$5,000

Contact:
American Legion Nebraska
Department Headquarters
P.O. Box 5205
Lincoln, NE 68505-0205
Phone: 402-464-6338
Fax: 402-464-6330
Web: www.ne.legion.org

American Legion Nebraska Oratorical Contest

Type of award: Scholarship.
Intended use: For undergraduate study at postsecondary institution.
Eligibility: Applicant must be enrolled in high school. Applicant must be residing in Nebraska.
Basis for selection: Competition/talent/interest in oratory/debate, based on breadth of knowledge, originality, application of knowledge of topic, skill in selecting examples and analogies, logic, voice, diction, style of language and delivery.
Application requirements: Proof of eligibility. Participants in Nebraska Department Oratorical Contest.
Additional information: Topic: U.S. Constitution and citizenship. All awards given in U.S. Savings Bonds. 1st-$1,000, 2nd-$600, 3rd-$400, 4th-$200, plus one $100 award for 1st place in each District upon participation in area contest.

Amount of award:	$200-$1,000
Number of awards:	4

Contact:
American Legion Nebraska
Department Headquarters
P.O. Box 5205
Lincoln, NE 68505-0205
Phone: 402-464-6338
Fax: 402-464-6330
Web: www.ne.legion.org

American Legion Nebraska Auxiliary

American Legion Auxiliary Junior Member Scholarship

Type of award: Scholarship.
Intended use: For undergraduate study at postsecondary institution.
Eligibility: Applicant or parent must be member/participant of American Legion Auxiliary. Applicant must be residing in Nebraska.
Additional information: Given to Nebraska's entry for National President's Scholarship for Junior member, in event applicant does not win same. Award: 1st-$200, 2nd-$150, 3rd-$100.

Amount of award:	$100-$200
Number of awards:	3
Total amount awarded:	$450

Contact:
American Legion Nebraska Auxiliary
Department Education Chairman
P.O. Box 5227
Lincoln, NE 68505-0227
Phone: 402-466-1808
Web: www.ne.legion.org

American Legion Nebraska Auxiliary Nurse Gift Tuition Scholarship

Type of award: Scholarship.
Intended use: For undergraduate study at accredited vocational institution. Designated institutions: Hospital schools of nursing.
Eligibility: Applicant must be residing in Nebraska. Applicant must be descendant of veteran; or dependent of veteran; or spouse of veteran.
Basis for selection: Major/career interest in nursing. Applicant must demonstrate financial need.
Additional information: Awards given as funds permit. Must be Nebraska resident; must show financial need; be accepted at accredited hospital school of nursing; be veteran-connected.

Amount of award:	$400-$500
Application deadline:	April 16

Contact:
American Legion Nebraska Auxiliary
Department Headquarters
P.O. Box 5227
Lincoln, NE 68505-0227
Phone: 402-466-1808
Web: www.ne.legion.org

American Legion Nebraska Auxiliary Practical Nurse Scholarship

Type of award: Scholarship.
Intended use: For undergraduate study at vocational, 2-year or 4-year institution.
Eligibility: Applicant must be residing in Nebraska. Applicant must be veteran or descendant of veteran; or dependent of veteran; or spouse of veteran.
Basis for selection: Major/career interest in nursing. Applicant must demonstrate financial need.
Application requirements: State resident for three years. Must be accepted at school of practical nursing.

Amount of award:	$200-$400
Number of awards:	23
Number of applicants:	200
Application deadline:	April 16
Total amount awarded:	$3,300

Contact:
American Legion Nebraska Auxiliary
Department Headquarters
P.O. Box 5227
Lincoln, NE 68505-0205
Phone: 402-466-1808

American Legion Nebraska Auxiliary Roberta Marie Stretch Memorial Scholarship

Type of award: Scholarship.

Intended use: For undergraduate or master's study at 4-year or graduate institution.
Eligibility: Applicant must be female. Applicant must be residing in Nebraska. Applicant must be descendant of veteran; or dependent of veteran; or spouse of veteran.
Application requirements: Must be enrolled or accepted in undergraduate or master's program.
Additional information: Preference given to former Nebraska Girls State citizens.

Amount of award:	$400
Application deadline:	April 16

Contact:
American Legion Nebraska Auxiliary
Department Headquarters
P.O. Box 5227
Lincoln, NE 68505-0205
Phone: 402-466-1808

American Legion Nebraska Auxiliary Ruby Paul Campaign Fund Scholarship

Type of award: Scholarship.
Intended use: For freshman study at accredited 2-year or 4-year institution.
Eligibility: Applicant or parent must be member/participant of American Legion Auxiliary. Applicant must be high school senior. Applicant must be residing in Nebraska.
Basis for selection: Applicant must demonstrate high academic achievement.
Application requirements: State resident for three years. B average during last three years of high school and accepted for fall term at college or university. Cannot be nursing student. Must be Legion member, ALA member, Sons of the American Legion member of two years standing, or child or grandchild of Legion or ALA member of two years standing.
Additional information: Award varies with availability of funding.

Application deadline:	April 16

Contact:
American Legion Nebraska Auxiliary
Department Headquarters
P.O. Box 5227
Lincoln, NE 68505
Phone: 402-466-1808
Web: www.ne.legion.org

American Legion Nebraska Auxiliary Student Aid Grant or Vocational Technical Scholarship

Type of award: Scholarship.
Intended use: For undergraduate study at vocational or 2-year institution in United States.
Eligibility: Applicant must be residing in Nebraska. Applicant must be veteran; or dependent of veteran.
Basis for selection: Applicant must demonstrate financial need.
Application requirements: State resident for five years. Accepted at postsecondary institution.

Amount of award:	$200-$300
Application deadline:	April 16

Contact:
American Legion Nebraska Auxiliary
Department Headquarters
P.O. Box 5227
Lincoln, NE 68505-0227
Phone: 402-466-1808
Web: www.ne.legion.org

American Legion Nebraska President's Scholarship

Type of award: Scholarship.
Intended use: For undergraduate study at postsecondary institution.
Eligibility: Applicant must be residing in Nebraska.
Application requirements: State resident for five years.
> **Amount of award:** $150
Contact:
American Legion Nebraska Auxiliary
Department Headquarters
P. O. Box 5227
Lincoln, NE 68505-0227
Phone: 402-464-1808
Web: www.ne.legion.org

American Legion New Hampshire

American Legion New Hampshire Albert T. Marcoux Memorial Scholarship

Type of award: Scholarship.
Intended use: For undergraduate study at 4-year institution.
Eligibility: Applicant or parent must be member/participant of American Legion. Applicant must be U.S. citizen residing in New Hampshire.
Application requirements: Child of living or deceased Legion or Auxiliary member; graduate of New Hampshire high school and state resident of three years.
Additional information: Must be pursuing B.A. SASE required.
> **Amount of award:** $1,000
> **Number of awards:**   1
> **Application deadline:**   May 1
> **Total amount awarded:** $1,000
Contact:
American Legion New Hampshire
Department Adjutant/State House Annex
25 Capitol Street, Room 431
Concord, NH 03301-6312
Phone: 603-271-2211

American Legion New Hampshire Boys State Scholarship

Type of award: Scholarship.
Intended use: For undergraduate study at postsecondary institution.
Eligibility: Applicant or parent must be member/participant of American Legion, Boys State. Applicant must be male. Applicant must be U.S. citizen residing in New Hampshire.

Additional information: Award given to participants of Boys State during Boys State Session. Award amount varies. Recipient eligible for regional and national awards.
Contact:
American Legion New Hampshire
Department Adjutant/State House Annex
25 Capitol Street, Room 431
Concord, NH 03301-6312
Phone: 603-271-2211

American Legion New Hampshire Christa McAuliffe Scholarship

Type of award: Scholarship.
Intended use: For freshman study at 4-year institution.
Eligibility: Applicant must be U.S. citizen residing in New Hampshire.
Basis for selection: Major/career interest in education.
Application requirements: State resident for 3 years. Send SASE to "Contact" address.
Additional information: May be high school senior or recent graduate.
> **Amount of award:** $1,000
> **Number of awards:**   1
> **Application deadline:**   May 1
> **Total amount awarded:** $1,000
Contact:
American Legion New Hampshire
Department Adjutant/State House Annex
25 Capitol Street, Room 431
Concord, NH 03301-6312
Phone: 603-271-2211

American Legion New Hampshire Department Scholarship

Type of award: Scholarship.
Intended use: For freshman study at vocational, 2-year or 4-year institution.
Eligibility: Applicant must be enrolled in high school. Applicant must be U.S. citizen residing in New Hampshire.
Application requirements: Graduate from New Hampshire high school; state resident for three years.
Additional information: Must send SASE.
> **Amount of award:** $1,000
> **Number of awards:**   2
> **Application deadline:**   May 1
> **Total amount awarded:** $2,000
Contact:
American Legion New Hampshire Scholarship Coordinator
Department Adjutant/State House Annex
25 Capitol Street, Room 431
Concord, NH 03301-6312
Phone: 603-271-2211

American Legion New Hampshire Department Vocational Scholarship

Type of award: Scholarship.
Intended use: For freshman study at vocational institution.
Eligibility: Applicant must be enrolled in high school. Applicant must be U.S. citizen residing in New Hampshire.
Application requirements: Graduate from New Hampshire high school; state resident for three years.
Additional information: Must send SASE.

111

Amount of award:	$1,000
Application deadline:	May 1
Total amount awarded:	$1,000

Contact:
American Legion New Hampshire
Department Adjutant/State House Annex
25 Capitol Street, Room 431
Concord, NH 03301-6312
Phone: 603-271-2211

American Legion New Hampshire Oratorical Contest

Type of award: Scholarship.
Intended use: For undergraduate study at postsecondary institution.
Eligibility: Applicant must be enrolled in high school. Applicant must be residing in New Hampshire.
Basis for selection: Competition/talent/interest in oratory/debate, based on breadth of knowledge, originality, application of knowledge of topic, skill in selecting examples and analogies, logic, voice, diction, style of language and delivery.
Application requirements: Proof of eligibility. Finalist in Department Oratorical Contest.
Additional information: Subject: U.S. Constitution and citizenship. Awards: $1,000, $750, $500, $250, and four at $100.

Amount of award:	$100-$1,000
Number of awards:	8
Total amount awarded:	$2,900

Contact:
American Legion New Hampshire
Department Adjutant/State House Annex
25 Capitol Street, Room 431
Concord, NH 03301-6312
Phone: 603-271-2211
Fax: 603-271-2361

American Legion New Hampshire Auxiliary

American Legion New Hampshire Auxiliary Grace S. High Memorial Child Welfare Scholarship

Type of award: Scholarship.
Intended use: For undergraduate study at postsecondary institution.
Eligibility: Applicant or parent must be member/participant of American Legion Auxiliary. Applicant must be female. Applicant must be U.S. citizen residing in New Hampshire.
Basis for selection: Applicant must demonstrate financial need.
Additional information: Applicant must be high school graduate and daughter of Legion member or Auxiliary member. Send SASE.

Amount of award:	$300
Number of awards:	2
Application deadline:	April 15
Total amount awarded:	$600

Contact:
American Legion Auxiliary, Department of New Hampshire
Department Secretary/State House Annex
25 Capitol Street, Room 432
Concord, NH 03301-6312

American Legion New Hampshire Auxiliary Marion J. Bagley Scholarship

Type of award: Scholarship.
Intended use: For undergraduate study at postsecondary institution.
Eligibility: Applicant must be U.S. citizen residing in New Hampshire.
Additional information: Applicant must be high school graduate. SASE required.

Amount of award:	$1,000
Number of awards:	1
Application deadline:	May 1
Total amount awarded:	$1,000

Contact:
American Legion Auxiliary, Department of New Hampshire
Department Secretary/State House Annex
25 Capitol St., Room 432
Concord, NH 03301-6312

American Legion New Hampshire Auxiliary Past President's Parley Nursing Scholarship

Type of award: Scholarship.
Intended use: For undergraduate study at vocational, 2-year or 4-year institution.
Eligibility: Applicant must be U.S. citizen residing in New Hampshire.
Basis for selection: Major/career interest in nursing. Applicant must demonstrate financial need.
Application requirements: Must be high school graduate.
Additional information: Child of veteran given preference. One award to Registered Nurse study and one to Licensed Practical Nurse study. Award amount varies; contact sponsor for information. SASE required.

Number of awards:	2
Application deadline:	May 10

Contact:
American Legion Auxiliary, Department of New Hampshire
Department Secretary/State House Annex
25 Capitol Street, Room 432
Concord, NH 03301-6312

American Legion New Jersey

American Legion New Jersey David C. Goodwin Scholarship

Type of award: Scholarship.
Intended use: For undergraduate study at 4-year institution.
Eligibility: Applicant must be high school junior. Applicant must be residing in New Jersey.

Application requirements: Must be high school junior participating in New Jersey American Legion Baseball Program. Applications mailed to players.
Additional information: Awards: $4,000 ($1,000/year for four years); $2,000 ($500/year for four years).

Amount of award:	$2,000-$4,000
Number of awards:	2
Application deadline:	September 1
Total amount awarded:	$6,000

Contact:
American Legion New Jersey
Baseball Committee
135 West Hanover St.
Trenton, NJ 08618
Phone: 609-695-5418
Fax: 609-394-1532

American Legion New Jersey Lawrence Luterman Memorial Scholarship

Type of award: Scholarship.
Intended use: For freshman study at 4-year institution.
Eligibility: Applicant or parent must be member/participant of American Legion. Applicant must be high school senior. Applicant must be residing in New Jersey. Applicant must be descendant of veteran; or dependent of veteran.
Additional information: Awards: two-$4,000 scholarships ($1,000/yr.); two-$2,000; two-$1,000. Applicant must be natural or adopted descendant of member of American Legion, Department of New Jersey.

Amount of award:	$1,000-$4,000
Number of awards:	6
Application deadline:	February 15
Total amount awarded:	$14,000

Contact:
American Legion New Jersey
Department Adjutant
135 West Hanover Street
Trenton, NJ 08618
Phone: 609-695-5918

American Legion New Jersey Oratorical Contest

Type of award: Scholarship.
Intended use: For freshman study at postsecondary institution.
Eligibility: Applicant must be enrolled in high school. Applicant must be residing in New Jersey.
Basis for selection: Competition/talent/interest in oratory/ debate, based on breadth of knowledge, originality, application of knowledge of topic, skill in selecting examples and analogies, logic, voice, diction, style of language and delivery.
Application requirements: Proof of eligibility. Participants in New Jersey Department Oratorical contest.
Additional information: Subject: U.S. Constitution and citizenship. See high school counselor for additional information. Awards:1st-$4,000, 2nd-$2,000, 3rd-$1,000, 4th-$750, 5th-$500.

Amount of award:	$500-$4,000
Number of awards:	5
Total amount awarded:	$8,250

Contact:
American Legion New Jersey
135 West Hanover Street
Trenton, NJ 08618
Phone: 609-695-5418
Fax: 609-394-1532

American Legion New Jersey Stutz Memorial Scholarship

Type of award: Scholarship.
Intended use: For undergraduate study at vocational, 2-year or 4-year institution.
Eligibility: Applicant or parent must be member/participant of American Legion. Applicant must be high school senior. Applicant must be residing in New Jersey. Applicant must be dependent of veteran.
Application requirements: May be natural or adopted child of member of American Legion, Department of New Jersey.
Additional information: Award: $1,000 per year for four years.

Amount of award:	$4,000
Number of awards:	1
Application deadline:	February 15
Total amount awarded:	$4,000

Contact:
American Legion New Jersey
Department Adjutant
War Memorial Building
Trenton, NJ 08608
Phone: 609-695-5418

American Legion Press Club of New Jersey Scholarship

Type of award: Scholarship.
Intended use: For freshman study at accredited 4-year institution.
Eligibility: Applicant must be permanent resident residing in New Jersey. Applicant must be descendant of veteran; or dependent of veteran.
Basis for selection: Major/career interest in communications.
Application requirements: Send SASE to Education Chairman (see address under "Contact.").
Additional information: Applicant must be child or grandchild of veteran, or of current member of Legion or Auxiliary, including Sons of American Legion and Junior members. Graduates from Boys and Girls State programs also eligible. NJ resident only; must plan to study communications; child, grandchild entering freshman year in accredited four-year college, or current member of AL or ALA, member of SAL or ALA Juniors.

Amount of award:	$500
Number of awards:	1
Application deadline:	July 15
Total amount awarded:	$500

Contact:
Jack W. Keupfer, Education Chairman
American Legion Press Club of New Jersey
68 Merrill Road
Clifton, NJ 07012-1622
Phone: 201-473-5176

American Legion New Jersey Auxiliary

American Legion New Jersey Auxiliary Claire Oliphant Memorial Scholarship

Type of award: Scholarship.
Intended use: For freshman study at vocational, 2-year or 4-year institution.
Eligibility: Applicant must be high school senior. Applicant must be U.S. citizen residing in New Jersey. Applicant must be dependent of veteran.
Application requirements: State resident for two years.
Additional information: Information and application obtained from high school guidance department.

Amount of award:	$1,800
Number of awards:	1
Application deadline:	March 15
Total amount awarded:	$1,800

Contact:
American Legion Auxiliary, Department of New Jersey
Department Secretary
146 Route 130
Bordentown, NJ 08505-2226
Phone: 609-291-9338

American Legion New Jersey Auxiliary Department Scholarship

Type of award: Scholarship.
Intended use: For freshman study at vocational, 2-year or 4-year institution.
Eligibility: Applicant must be high school senior. Applicant must be U.S. citizen residing in New Jersey. Applicant must be descendant of veteran; or dependent of veteran.
Application requirements: State resident for two years.
Additional information: Several awards are offered. Award amounts and number of awards varies; contact sponsor for information.

Application deadline:	March 15

Contact:
American Legion Auxiliary, Department of New Jersey
Department Secretary
146 Route 130
Bordentown, NJ 08505-2226
Phone: 609-291-9338

American Legion New Jersey Auxiliary Past President's Parley Nursing Scholarship

Type of award: Scholarship.
Intended use: For freshman study at 2-year or 4-year institution.
Eligibility: Applicant must be high school senior. Applicant must be residing in New Jersey. Applicant must be descendant of veteran; or dependent of veteran.
Basis for selection: Major/career interest in nursing.
Application requirements: State resident for two years.
Additional information: Applicant must be enrolled in nursing program. Award amount varies. Contact sponsor for more information.

Application deadline:	March 15

Contact:
American Legion Auxiliary, Department of New Jersey
Department Secretary
146 Route 130
Bordentown, NJ 08505-2226
Phone: 609-291-9338

American Legion New Mexico Auxiliary

American Legion New Mexico Auxiliary Teachers of Exceptional Children Scholarship

Type of award: Scholarship.
Intended use: For undergraduate, graduate or non-degree study at postsecondary institution.
Eligibility: Applicant must be residing in New Mexico.
Basis for selection: Major/career interest in education, special or education.
Additional information: Covers actual cost of tuition plus $50 travel and miscellaneous expenses not to exceed $250. To teach exceptional children for one year.

Amount of award:	Full tuition
Number of awards:	1
Application deadline:	March 1

Contact:
American Legion Auxiliary, Department of New Mexico
Department Secretary
1215 Mountain Road, N.E.
Albuquerque, NM 87102

American Legion New York

American Legion New York Dr. Hannah K. Vuolo Memorial Scholarship

Type of award: Scholarship.
Intended use: For freshman study at accredited 2-year or 4-year institution.
Eligibility: Applicant or parent must be member/participant of American Legion. Applicant must be no older than 20, high school senior. Applicant must be descendant of veteran.
Basis for selection: Major/career interest in education, teacher. Applicant must demonstrate financial need and high academic achievement.
Additional information: Natural or adopted direct descendant of member or deceased member of American Legion, Department of New York. Must be high school senior or graduate. Preference given to state residents.

Amount of award:	$250
Number of awards:	1
Application deadline:	May 1
Total amount awarded:	$250

Scholarships

Contact:
American Legion New York
Department Adjutant
112 State Street, Suite 400
Albany, NY 12207
Phone: 518-463-2215
Fax: 518-427-8443
Web: www.ny.legion.org

American Legion New York James F. Mulholland Scholarship

Type of award: Scholarship.
Intended use: For freshman study at postsecondary institution.
Eligibility: Applicant or parent must be member/participant of American Legion. Applicant must be high school senior. Applicant must be residing in New York. Applicant must be dependent of veteran.
Basis for selection: Applicant must demonstrate financial need and high academic achievement.
Additional information: Applicant must be graduating from New York high school.

Amount of award:	$500
Number of awards:	2
Application deadline:	May 1
Total amount awarded:	$1,000

Contact:
American Legion New York
Department Adjutant
112 State Street, Suite 400
Albany, NY 12207
Phone: 518-463-2215
Fax: 518-427-8443
Web: www.ny.legion.org

American Legion New York Oratorical Contest

Type of award: Scholarship.
Intended use: For undergraduate study at postsecondary institution.
Eligibility: Applicant must be enrolled in high school. Applicant must be residing in New York.
Basis for selection: Competition/talent/interest in oratory/debate, based on breadth of knowledge, originality, application of knowledge of topic, skill in selecting examples and analogies, logic, voice, diction, style of language, and delivery.
Application requirements: Proof of eligibility. New York State Oratorical Contest finalist.
Additional information: Topic: U.S. Constitution and citizenship. Also open to junior high school students. 1st-$6,000, 2nd-$4,000, 3rd-$2,500, 4th-$2,000, 5th-$2,000.

Amount of award:	$2,000-$6,000
Number of awards:	5
Total amount awarded:	$16,500

Contact:
American Legion New York
Department Adjutant
112 State Street, Suite 400
Albany, NY 12207
Phone: 518-463-2215
Fax: 518-427-8443
Web: www.ny.legion.org

New York State Legion Press Association Scholarship

Type of award: Scholarship.
Intended use: For full-time undergraduate study at accredited 4-year institution.
Eligibility: Applicant or parent must be member/participant of American Legion. Applicant must be residing in New York.
Basis for selection: Major/career interest in communications.
Additional information: Applicant must be child of Legion or Auxiliary member; Junior member; Sons of American Legion member; or graduate of New York Boys State or Girls State.

Amount of award:	$1,000

Contact:
Scholarship Chairman
P.O. Box 1239
Syracuse, NY 13201-1239
Web: www.ny.legion.org

American Legion New York Auxiliary

American Legion New York Auxiliary Medical & Teaching Scholarship

Type of award: Scholarship.
Intended use: For full-time freshman study at postsecondary institution.
Eligibility: Applicant must be no older than 19. Applicant must be residing in New York. Applicant must be descendant of veteran; or dependent of veteran.
Basis for selection: Major/career interest in health-related professions or education, teacher. Applicant must demonstrate financial need.
Additional information: One scholarship in each of the ten New York judicial districts. Applicant must be high school senior or graduate.

Amount of award:	$1,000
Number of awards:	10
Application deadline:	March 25
Total amount awarded:	$10,000

Contact:
Local American Legion Auxiliary Unit

American Legion New York Auxiliary Past President's Parley Student Nurses Scholarship for Girls or Boys

Type of award: Scholarship.
Intended use: For freshman study at 2-year or 4-year institution.
Eligibility: Applicant must be no older than 19. Applicant must be residing in New York. Applicant must be descendant of veteran; or dependent of veteran during Korean War, WW I, WW II or Vietnam.
Basis for selection: Major/career interest in nursing. Applicant must demonstrate financial need.
Additional information: May be high school graduate if under age 20.

115

Amount of award: $500
Number of awards: 1
Application deadline: March 25
Total amount awarded: $500
Contact:
Local American Legion Auxiliary Unit

American Legion New York Auxiliary Scholarship

Type of award: Scholarship.
Intended use: For undergraduate study at postsecondary institution.
Eligibility: Applicant must be residing in New York. Applicant must be descendant of veteran; or dependent of veteran or deceased veteran.
Additional information: Must be high school graduate. May use other scholarships.
Amount of award: $1,000
Number of awards: 1
Application deadline: March 25
Total amount awarded: $1,000
Contact:
Local American Legion Auxiliary Unit

American Legion North Dakota

American Legion North Dakota Oratorical Contest

Type of award: Scholarship.
Intended use: For undergraduate study at postsecondary institution.
Eligibility: Applicant must be enrolled in high school. Applicant must be residing in North Dakota.
Basis for selection: Competition/talent/interest in oratory/debate, based on breadth of knowledge, originality, application of knowledge of topic, skill in selecting examples and analogies, logic, voice, diction, style of language and delivery.
Application requirements: Proof of eligibility.
Additional information: Topic: U.S. Constitution and citizenship. Top four contestants in North Dakota Oratorical Contest win $400, $300, $200, and $100. Awards also given to East and West Divisional and 10 District Contest winners. Contact local legion post or department headquarters after start of school year.
Amount of award: $100-$400
Number of awards: 4
Contact:
American Legion North Dakota
Department Headquarters
Box 2666
Fargo, ND 58108-2666
Phone: 701-293-3120
Fax: 701-293-9951

American Legion North Dakota Auxiliary

American Legion North Dakota Auxiliary Past President's Parley Scholarship

Type of award: Scholarship.
Intended use: For undergraduate study at 2-year or 4-year institution. Designated institutions: North Dakota hospital or school of nursing.
Eligibility: Applicant or parent must be member/participant of American Legion Auxiliary. Applicant must be residing in North Dakota.
Basis for selection: Major/career interest in nursing.
Additional information: Children, grandchildren or great-grandchildren of American Legion or Auxiliary member in good standing. Must be graduate of North Dakota high school. Apply to Local Auxiliary unit. Local unit addresses are available at "Contact" address.
Amount of award: $350
Application deadline: May 15
Contact:
American Legion Auxiliary, Department of North Dakota
Chair of Dept. Parley Scholarship Committee
P.O. Box 250
Beach, ND 58621
Phone: 701-872-3865

American Legion North Dakota Auxiliary Scholarship

Type of award: Scholarship.
Intended use: For undergraduate study at postsecondary institution. Designated institutions: North Dakota postsecondary institutions.
Eligibility: Applicant must be residing in North Dakota.
Additional information: Must be resident of North Dakota enrolled in university or college in state of North Dakota. Number of awards varies.
Amount of award: $350
Application deadline: January 10
Contact:
Local American Legion Auxiliary unit.

American Legion Ohio

American Legion Ohio Scholarship

Type of award: Scholarship.
Intended use: For undergraduate study.
Eligibility: Applicant or parent must be member/participant of American Legion. Applicant must be residing in Ohio. Applicant must be dependent of deceased veteran; or spouse of deceased veteran.
Additional information: Also eligible: direct descendants of Legionnaires in good standing; direct descendants of deceased Legionnaires; spouses, children of deceased U.S. military persons who died on active duty or of injuries received on active duty. Number and amount of awards vary: there were 17

at $2,000 and one $3,000 awards in 2000. Contact sponsor for further information.

Amount of award:	$1,500-$2,000
Number of awards:	17
Application deadline:	April 15

Contact:
American Legion Ohio
Department Scholarship Committee
4060 Indianola Avenue
Columbus, OH 43214
Phone: 614-268-7072
Fax: 614-268-3048

Department Oratorical Awards

Type of award: Scholarship.
Intended use: For undergraduate study.
Eligibility: Applicant must be enrolled in high school. Applicant must be residing in Ohio.
Basis for selection: Competition/talent/interest in oratory/debate, based on breadth of knowledge, originality, application of knowledge of topic, skill in selecting examples and analogies, logic, voice, diction, style of language and delivery.
Application requirements: Ohio Oratorical Contest finalist.
Additional information: Must be presently enrolled in high school (public, private, parochial or home schooled). Awards: 1st-$1,000; 2nd-$500; 3rd-$300; 4th-200.

Amount of award:	$200-$1,000
Number of awards:	4
Total amount awarded:	$2,000

Contact:
American Legion Ohio
Department of Ohio
P. O. Box 14348
Columbus, OH 43214
Phone: 614-268-7072
Fax: 614-268-3048

American Legion Ohio Auxiliary

American Legion Ohio Auxiliary Scholarship

Type of award: Scholarship.
Intended use: For freshman study at postsecondary institution.
Eligibility: Applicant must be high school senior. Applicant must be residing in Ohio. Applicant must be descendant of veteran; or dependent of veteran or deceased veteran during Grenada conflict, Korean War, Lebanon conflict, Persian Gulf War, WW I, WW II or Vietnam.
Additional information: Additional scholarship of $1,000 awarded to second place applicant.

Amount of award:	$1,000-$1,500
Number of awards:	2
Application deadline:	March 1
Total amount awarded:	$2,500

Contact:
American Legion Ohio Auxiliary
P.O. Box 2760
Zanesville, OH 43702-2760

American Legion Ohio Auxiliary Scholarship For Nurse's Training or Medical Field

Type of award: Scholarship.
Intended use: For undergraduate study at vocational, 2-year or 4-year institution.
Eligibility: Applicant must be residing in Ohio. Applicant must be descendant of veteran; or dependent of veteran; or spouse of veteran.
Basis for selection: Major/career interest in nursing; health-related professions; health sciences or medical assistant.
Additional information: Fifteen awards of $300 and two $500 awards are available. Adopted children and grandchildren of veteran also eligible. Must be sponsored by Legion Auxiliary Unit.

Amount of award:	$300-$500
Number of awards:	17
Application deadline:	June 1
Total amount awarded:	$5,500

Contact:
American Legion Ohio Auxiliary
P.O. Box 2760
Zanesville, OH 43702-2760

American Legion Oregon

American Legion Oratorical Contest

Type of award: Scholarship.
Intended use: For undergraduate study at postsecondary institution.
Eligibility: Applicant must be enrolled in high school. Applicant must be U.S. citizen residing in Oregon.
Basis for selection: Competition/talent/interest in oratory/debate, based on breadth of knowledge, originality, application of knowledge of topic, skill in selecting examples and analogies, logic, voice, diction, style of language and delivery.
Application requirements: Proof of eligibility. Participant in Oregon Oratorical Contest.
Additional information: Topic: U.S. Constitution and citizenship. Awards: 1st-$500, 2nd-$400, 3rd-$300, 4th-$200. December 1 deadline is for local American Legion post. Applications available at local high schools after October 1.

Amount of award:	$200-$500
Number of awards:	4
Application deadline:	December 1
Total amount awarded:	$1,400

Contact:
American Legion Department of Oregon
P.O. Box 1730
Wilsonville, OR 97070-1730
Phone: 503-685-5006
Fax: 503-685-5008

American Legion Oregon Auxiliary

American Legion Oregon Auxiliary National President's Scholarship

Type of award: Scholarship.
Intended use: For undergraduate study at postsecondary institution.
Eligibility: Applicant must be residing in Oregon. Applicant must be dependent of veteran during Grenada conflict, Korean War, Lebanon conflict, Panama conflict, Persian Gulf War, WW I, WW II or Vietnam.
Additional information: Two awards in each division: one at $2,000; and one at $1,500.

Amount of award:	$1,500-$2,000
Number of awards:	10
Application deadline:	March 15
Total amount awarded:	$3,500

Contact:
American Legion Auxiliary, Department of Oregon
Chairman of Education
P.O. Box 1730
Wilsonville, OR 97070-1730

American Legion Oregon Auxiliary Nurses Scholarship

Type of award: Scholarship.
Intended use: For undergraduate study at accredited 2-year or 4-year institution. Designated institutions: School of nursing (may be hospital school of nursing).
Eligibility: Applicant must be residing in Oregon. Applicant must be dependent of disabled veteran; or spouse of disabled veteran or deceased veteran.
Basis for selection: Major/career interest in nursing. Applicant must demonstrate financial need, depth of character, seriousness of purpose and service orientation.
Application requirements: Proof of eligibility.

Amount of award:	$1,500
Number of awards:	1
Application deadline:	June 1
Total amount awarded:	$1,500

Contact:
American Legion Auxiliary, Department of Oregon
Chairman of Education
P.O. Box 1730
Wilsonville, OR 97070-1730

American Legion Oregon Auxiliary Scholarship

Type of award: Scholarship.
Intended use: For undergraduate study at vocational, 2-year or 4-year institution.
Eligibility: Applicant must be residing in Oregon. Applicant must be dependent of veteran or disabled veteran; or spouse of veteran, disabled veteran or deceased veteran.
Additional information: One of three grants designated for vocational or business school.

Amount of award:	$1,000
Number of awards:	3
Application deadline:	March 15
Total amount awarded:	$3,000

Contact:
American Legion Auxiliary, Department of Oregon
Chairman of Education
P.O. Box 1730
Wilsonville, OR 97070-1730

American Legion Oregon Auxiliary Spirit of Youth Scholarship

Type of award: Scholarship.
Intended use: For undergraduate or graduate study at accredited postsecondary institution.
Eligibility: Applicant or parent must be member/participant of American Legion Auxiliary. Applicant must be residing in Oregon. Applicant must be dependent of veteran; or spouse of disabled veteran or deceased veteran.
Application requirements: Junior member of American Legion Auxiliary for past three years and hold current membership.
Additional information: One scholarship in each division.

Amount of award:	$1,000
Application deadline:	March 15
Total amount awarded:	$1,000

Contact:
American Legion Auxiliary, Department of Oregon
Chairman of Education
P.O. Box 1730
Wilsonville, OR 97070-1730

American Legion Pennsylvania

American Legion Pennsylvania Joseph P. Gavenonis Scholarship

Type of award: Scholarship, renewable.
Intended use: For full-time undergraduate study at 4-year institution. Designated institutions: Pennsylvania colleges and universities.
Eligibility: Applicant or parent must be member/participant of American Legion. Applicant must be high school senior. Applicant must be residing in Pennsylvania. Applicant must be dependent of deceased veteran or POW/MIA.
Application requirements: Proof of eligibility.
Additional information: Award is made each year for four years. Amount may vary, based on student's progress. Order of eligibility: child of deceased member of Pennsylvania American Legion Post, or person certified by U.S. Department of Defense as MIA or KIA; child of member in good standing in American Legion Post in Pennsylvania. Preference given to children of members with most continuous years of membership.

Amount of award:	$1,000
Application deadline:	May 1
Total amount awarded:	$1,000

Contact:
American Legion Pennsylvania
Dept. Adjutant Attn: Scholarship Secretary
P.O. Box 2324
Harrisburg, PA 17105-2324
Phone: 717-730-9100
Fax: 717-975-2836
Web: www.pa-legion.com

American Legion Pennsylvania Robert W. Valimont Endowment Fund Scholarship

Type of award: Scholarship, renewable.
Intended use: For full-time undergraduate certificate, freshman or sophomore study at vocational or 2-year institution. Designated institutions: Pennsylvania less-than-four year postsecondary schools, or career training programs.
Eligibility: Applicant must be high school senior. Applicant must be residing in Pennsylvania. Applicant must be dependent of veteran, deceased veteran or POW/MIA.
Application requirements: Proof of eligibility. Membership in Pennsylvania American Legion Post not required, but must be documented if claimed.
Additional information: Award: $600 for first year; must reapply for second year. Order of eligibility: children of members in good standing of American Legion Post in Pennsylvania; children of veterans; children of disabled veterans; children of deceased veterans.

Amount of award:	$600
Application deadline:	June 1
Total amount awarded:	$600

Contact:
American Legion Pennsylvania
Dept. Adjutant Attn: Scholarship Secretary
P.O. Box 2324
Harrisburg, PA 17105-2324
Phone: 717-730-9100
Fax: 717-975-2836
Web: www.pa-legion.com

American Legion Pennsylvania Auxiliary

American Legion Pennsylvania Auxiliary Scholarship

Type of award: Scholarship.
Intended use: For undergraduate study at postsecondary institution. Designated institutions: Pennsylvania postsecondary institutions.
Eligibility: Applicant must be high school senior. Applicant must be permanent resident residing in Pennsylvania. Applicant must be dependent of veteran.
Basis for selection: Applicant must demonstrate financial need.
Additional information: Award $600 per year for four years.

Amount of award:	$2,400
Number of awards:	1
Application deadline:	March 15
Total amount awarded:	$2,400

Contact:
American Legion Auxiliary, Department of Pennsylvania
Department Education Chairman
P.O. Box 2643
Harrisburg, PA 17105
Phone: 717-763-7545

American Legion Pennsylvania Auxiliary Scholarship for Children of Deceased/Disabled Veterans

Type of award: Scholarship.
Intended use: For undergraduate study at postsecondary institution. Designated institutions: Pennsylvania postsecondary institutions.
Eligibility: Applicant must be high school senior. Applicant must be residing in Pennsylvania. Applicant must be dependent of disabled veteran or deceased veteran.
Basis for selection: Applicant must demonstrate financial need.
Additional information: Award is $600 per year for four years. Disabled vet must be totally disabled.

Amount of award:	$2,400
Number of awards:	1
Application deadline:	March 15
Total amount awarded:	$2,400

Contact:
American Legion Auxiliary, Department of Pennsylvania
Department Education Chairman
P.O. Box 2643
Harrisburg, PA 17105-2643
Phone: 717-763-7545

American Legion Puerto Rico Auxiliary

American Legion Puerto Rico Auxiliary Nursing Scholarship

Type of award: Scholarship.
Intended use: For undergraduate study at 2-year or 4-year institution. Designated institutions: Eligible institutions in Puerto Rico.
Eligibility: Applicant must be residing in Puerto Rico.
Basis for selection: Major/career interest in nursing.
Application requirements: Interview. Must be in nurses' training program.
Additional information: Award distributed in two yearly installments of $250. Selected after filing application and attending personal interview.

Amount of award:	$500
Number of awards:	2
Application deadline:	March 15
Total amount awarded:	$1,000

Contact:
American Legion Auxiliary, Department of Puerto Rico
Education Chairman
P.O. Box 11424
Caparra Heights, PR 00922-1424

American Legion South Carolina

American Legion South Carolina Robert E. David Children's Scholarship

Type of award: Scholarship, renewable.
Intended use: For undergraduate study at 4-year institution.
Eligibility: Applicant must be residing in South Carolina. Applicant must be dependent of veteran during Grenada conflict, Korean War, Lebanon conflict, Panama conflict, Persian Gulf War, WW I, WW II or Vietnam.
Basis for selection: Applicant must demonstrate financial need and high academic achievement.
Additional information: Must have relative who is member of American Legion. Must reapply yearly for renewal.

Amount of award:	$500
Number of awards:	10
Application deadline:	May 1
Total amount awarded:	$5,000

Contact:
American Legion South Carolina, Department Adjutant
P.O. Box 11355
132 Pickens Street
Columbia, SC 29211
Phone: 803-799-1992

American Legion South Carolina Scholarship

Type of award: Scholarship.
Intended use: For undergraduate study.
Eligibility: Applicant must be enrolled in high school. Applicant must be residing in South Carolina.
Basis for selection: Competition/talent/interest in oratory/debate.
Application requirements: Zone winners of High School Oratorical Contest. Post level contests must be completed by February 1.
Additional information: Award totals: First-$1,600; second-$1,000; and third and fourth-$500. Distributed over four-year period.

Amount of award:	$500-$1,600
Number of awards:	4
Application deadline:	February 1
Total amount awarded:	$3,600

Contact:
American Legion South Carolina
P.O. Box 11355
132 Pickens St.
Columbia, SC 29211
Phone: 803-799-1992

American Legion South Carolina Auxiliary

American Legion South Carolina Auxiliary Gift Scholarship

Type of award: Scholarship.
Intended use: For undergraduate study at postsecondary institution.
Eligibility: Applicant or parent must be member/participant of American Legion Auxiliary. Applicant must be residing in South Carolina.
Application requirements: Junior member with three-year consecutive membership at application time.
Additional information: Applicant or parent must be member of American Legion Auxiliary.

Amount of award:	$1,000
Number of awards:	2
Total amount awarded:	$2,000

Contact:
American Legion Auxiliary, Department of South Carolina
Department Secretary
132 Pickens Street
Columbia, SC 29205
Phone: 803-799-6695
Fax: 803-799-7907

American Legion South Dakota

American Legion South Dakota Oratorical Contest

Type of award: Scholarship.
Intended use: For undergraduate study at postsecondary institution. Designated institutions: Postseconday institutions in South Dakota.
Eligibility: Applicant must be enrolled in high school. Applicant must be residing in South Dakota.
Basis for selection: Competition/talent/interest in oratory/debate, based on breadth of knowledge, originality, application of knowledge of topic, skill in selecting examples and analogies, logic, voice, diction, style of language and delivery.
Application requirements: Proof of eligibility.
Additional information: Topic: U.S. Constitution and citizenship. Awards: first-$600; second-$400; third-$300; fourth and fifth-$200. Redeemable within five years of date of award.

Amount of award:	$100-$600
Number of awards:	4
Total amount awarded:	$1,500

Contact:
American Legion South Dakota
Department Adjutant
P.O. Box 67
Watertown, SD 57201-0067
Phone: 605-886-3604
Fax: 605-886-2870

Thelma Foster Senior American Legion Auxiliary Member Scholarship

Type of award: Scholarship.
Intended use: For undergraduate study.
Eligibility: Applicant or parent must be member/participant of American Legion Auxiliary. Applicant must be residing in South Dakota.
Application requirements: Senior member for past three years plus current year.

Amount of award:	$300
Number of awards:	1
Application deadline:	March 1
Total amount awarded:	$300

Contact:
American Legion South Dakota Auxiliary
Patricia Coyle, Department Secretary
P.O. Box 117
Huron, SD 57350-0117
Phone: 605-353-1793

American Legion South Dakota Auxiliary

American Legion South Dakota Auxiliary College Scholarship

Type of award: Scholarship.
Intended use: For undergraduate study at vocational, 2-year or 4-year institution.
Eligibility: Applicant or parent must be member/participant of American Legion Auxiliary. Applicant must be at least 16, no older than 22. Applicant must be residing in South Dakota. Applicant must be dependent of veteran.
Application requirements: Child of either veteran or Auxiliary member.
Additional information: College scholarships: two at $500; Vocational scholarships: two at $500.

Amount of award:	$500
Number of awards:	4
Application deadline:	March 1
Total amount awarded:	$2,000

Contact:
American Legion South Dakota Auxiliary
Patricia Coyle, Department Secretary
P.O. Box 117
Huron, SD 57350-0117
Phone: 605-353-1793

American Legion South Dakota Auxiliary Nurse's Scholarship

Type of award: Scholarship.
Intended use: For undergraduate study at postsecondary institution.
Eligibility: Applicant or parent must be member/participant of American Legion Auxiliary. Applicant must be at least 16, no older than 22. Applicant must be residing in South Dakota. Applicant must be dependent of veteran.
Basis for selection: Major/career interest in nursing.

Additional information: Child of veteran or Auxiliary member.

Amount of award:	$500
Number of awards:	2
Application deadline:	March 1
Total amount awarded:	$1,000

Contact:
American Legion South Dakota Auxiliary
Patricia Coyle, Department Secretary
P.O. Box 117
Huron, SD 57350-0117
Phone: 605-353-1793

American Legion South Dakota Auxiliary Vocational Scholarship

Type of award: Scholarship.
Intended use: For undergraduate or non-degree study at postsecondary institution.
Eligibility: Applicant or parent must be member/participant of American Legion Auxiliary. Applicant must be residing in South Dakota.
Application requirements: Senior member; membership (Junior or Senior) at least three years.

Amount of award:	$500
Number of awards:	2
Application deadline:	March 1
Total amount awarded:	$1,000

Contact:
American Legion South Dakota Auxiliary
Patricia Coyle, Departmental Secretary
P.O. Box 117
Huron, SD 57350
Phone: 605-353-1793

Thelma Foster Junior American Legion Auxiliary Members Scholarship

Type of award: Scholarship.
Intended use: For freshman study.
Eligibility: Applicant or parent must be member/participant of American Legion Auxiliary. Applicant must be residing in South Dakota.
Application requirements: High school senior or graduate. Junior member for past three years plus current year.

Amount of award:	$300
Number of awards:	1
Application deadline:	March 1

Contact:
American Legion South Dakota Auxiliary
Patricia Coyle, Department Secretary
P.O. Box 117
Huron, SD 57350-0117
Phone: 605-353-1793

American Legion Tennessee

American Legion Tennessee Oratorical Contest

Type of award: Scholarship, renewable.

Intended use: For undergraduate study at postsecondary institution in United States.
Eligibility: Applicant must be enrolled in high school. Applicant must be residing in Tennessee.
Basis for selection: Competition/talent/interest in oratory/ debate, based on breadth of knowledge, originality, application of knowledge of topic, skill in selecting examples and analogies, logic, voice, diction, style of language, and delivery.
Application requirements: Proof of eligibility. Enter High School Oratorical Contest through local high school.
Additional information: Scholarship awarded to top three winners. Awards: 1st-$5,000, 2nd-$2,500, 3rd-$1,500. Includes savings bonds as well. First place winner eligible to enter national contest. National winner receives $18,000.

Amount of award:	$1,500-$5,000
Number of awards:	3
Application deadline:	January 1
Total amount awarded:	$9,000

Contact:
American Legion Tennessee
Department Adjutant
215 Eighth Avenue, North
Nashville, TN 37203-3583
Phone: 615-254-0568
Fax: 615-255-1551

Eagle Scout of the Year Award

Type of award: Scholarship.
Intended use: For undergraduate study at postsecondary institution in United States.
Eligibility: Applicant or parent must be member/participant of Boy Scouts of America, Eagle Scouts. Applicant must be male. Applicant must be residing in Tennessee.
Application requirements: Nomination by Tennessee Americal Legion; name of winner of state award is submitted to national organization.

Amount of award:	$1,500
Number of awards:	1
Application deadline:	January 1
Total amount awarded:	$1,500

Contact:
American Legion Tennessee
State Headquarters
215 Eighth Avenue, North
Nashville, TN 37203-3583
Phone: 615-254-0568
Fax: 615-255-1551

American Legion Tennessee Auxiliary

American Legion Tennessee Auxiliary Vara Gray Nursing Scholarship

Type of award: Scholarship.
Intended use: For freshman study at vocational, 2-year or 4-year institution.
Eligibility: Applicant must be high school senior. Applicant must be residing in Tennessee. Applicant must be dependent of veteran.
Basis for selection: Major/career interest in nursing.

Application requirements: Nomination by local American Legion Auxiliary unit.

Amount of award:	$500
Number of awards:	3
Application deadline:	March 1
Total amount awarded:	$1,500

Contact:
American Legion Auxiliary
Department Headquarters
4721 Trousdale Drive, Suite 131
Nashville, TN 37220
Phone: 615-781-1910
Fax: 615-781-1930

American Legion Texas

Texas Legion Oratorical Contest

Type of award: Scholarship.
Intended use: For undergraduate study at postsecondary institution.
Eligibility: Applicant must be no older than 18, enrolled in high school. Applicant must be residing in Texas.
Basis for selection: Competition/talent/interest in oratory/ debate, based on breadth of knowledge, originality, application of knowledge of topic, skill in selecting examples and analogies, logic, voice, diction, style of language, and delivery. Applicant must demonstrate patriotism.
Application requirements: Proof of eligibility.
Additional information: Topic: U.S. Constitution and citizenship. Awards: 1st-$1,000, 2nd-$750, 3rd-$500, 4th-$250. First place winner eligible to enter national contest.

Amount of award:	$250-$1,000
Number of awards:	4
Total amount awarded:	$2,500

Contact:
American Legion Texas
Oratorical Contest
P. O. Box 789
Austin, TX 78767
Phone: 512-472-4183
Fax: 512-472-0603
Web: www.txlegion.org

American Legion Texas Auxiliary

American Legion Texas Auxiliary General Scholarship

Type of award: Scholarship.
Intended use: For undergraduate study at postsecondary institution. Designated institutions: Texas postsecondary institutions.
Eligibility: Applicant must be residing in Texas. Applicant must be dependent of veteran.
Application requirements: Nomination by local units. Unit sponsorship.
Additional information: Applications must be obtained from local unit.

Amount of award:	$500
Application deadline:	February 1
Total amount awarded:	$500

Contact:
American Legion Texas Auxiliary
Department Headquarters
709 East 10 Street
Austin, TX 78701
Phone: 512-476-7278

American Legion Texas Auxiliary Nurses Scholarship

Type of award: Scholarship.
Intended use: For undergraduate study at postsecondary institution.
Eligibility: Applicant must be residing in Texas. Applicant must be dependent of veteran.
Basis for selection: Major/career interest in nursing; health sciences; health-related professions or medical assistant.
Application requirements: Nomination by local units. Unit sponsorship.
Additional information: Applications must be obtained from local unit.

Amount of award:	$500
Application deadline:	February 1
Total amount awarded:	$500

Contact:
American Legion Texas Auxiliary
Department Headquarters
709 East 10 Street
Austin, TX 78701
Phone: 512-476-7278

American Legion Utah Auxiliary

American Legion Auxiliary National President's Scholarship

Type of award: Scholarship.
Intended use: For undergraduate study.
Eligibility: Applicant must be high school senior. Applicant must be residing in Utah. Applicant must be dependent of veteran during Grenada conflict, Korean War, Lebanon conflict, Panama conflict, Persian Gulf War, WW I, WW II or Vietnam.

Amount of award:	$1,500-$2,000
Number of awards:	2
Application deadline:	February 15
Total amount awarded:	$3,500

Contact:
American Legion Utah Auxiliary
Department Headquarters
B-61 State Capitol Bldg.
Salt Lake City, UT 84114
Phone: 801-538-1014

American Legion Vermont

American Legion Eagle Scout of the Year

Type of award: Scholarship.
Intended use: For undergraduate study.
Eligibility: Applicant or parent must be member/participant of Boy Scouts of America, Eagle Scouts. Applicant must be male, high school senior. Applicant must be residing in Vermont.
Additional information: Awarded to Boy Scout chosen for outstanding service for his religious institution, school and community.

Amount of award:	$1,000
Number of awards:	1
Total amount awarded:	$1,000

Contact:
American Legion of Vermont
Education and Scholarship Committee
P.O. Box 396
Montpelier, VT 05601-0396
Phone: 802-223-7131

American Legion Vermont Scholarship

Type of award: Scholarship.
Intended use: For undergraduate study at vocational, 2-year or 4-year institution.
Eligibility: Applicant must be high school senior. Applicant must be residing in Vermont.
Application requirements: Seniors at Vermont secondary school, or seniors from adjacent state, whose parents are legal Vermont residents, or seniors from adjacent state attending Vermont schools.
Additional information: Awards: Five-$1,000 awards paid annually for four years ($250/year), five-$500 awards paid annually for two years ($250/year).

Amount of award:	$500-$1,000
Number of awards:	10
Total amount awarded:	$7,500

Contact:
American Legion of Vermont
Education and Scholarship Committee
P.O. Box 396
Montpelier, VT 05601-0396
Phone: 802-223-7131

American Legion Vermont Scholarship Program

Type of award: Scholarship.
Intended use: For undergraduate study.
Eligibility: Applicant must be high school senior. Applicant must be residing in Vermont.
Basis for selection: Applicant must demonstrate financial need.
Application requirements: Parents must be U.S. citizens.
Additional information: Amount and number of grants vary. Contact your local American Legion post or American Legion Auxiliary.

Scholarships

123

Scholarships

Contact:
American Legion of Vermont
Education and Scholarship Committee
P.O. Box 396
Montpelier, VT 05601-0396
Phone: 802-223-7131

National High School Oratorical Contest

Type of award: Scholarship.
Intended use: For undergraduate study.
Eligibility: Applicant must be enrolled in high school. Applicant must be U.S. citizen or permanent resident residing in Vermont.
Basis for selection: Competition/talent/interest in oratory/debate, based on breadth of knowledge, originality, application of knowledge of topic, skill in selecting examples and analogies, logic, voice, diction, style of language, and delivery.

Amount of award:	$2,000
Number of awards:	1
Total amount awarded:	$2,000

Contact:
American Legion of Vermont
Education and Scholarship Committee
P. O. Box 396
Montpelier, VT 05601-0396
Phone: 802-223-7131

American Legion Virginia

American Legion Virginia Oratorical Contest

Type of award: Scholarship.
Intended use: For undergraduate study at postsecondary institution.
Eligibility: Applicant must be enrolled in high school. Applicant must be residing in Virginia.
Basis for selection: Competition/talent/interest in oratory/debate, based on breadth of knowledge, originality, application of knowledge of topic, skill in selecting examples and analogies, logic, voice, diction, style of language and delivery.
Application requirements: Proof of eligibility. Speech winners of Virginia Department Oratorical Contest.
Additional information: Topic: U.S. Constitution and citizenship. Awards: 1st-$1,100; 2nd-$600; 3rd-$600.

Amount of award:	$600-$1,100
Number of awards:	3
Application deadline:	December 1
Total amount awarded:	$2,300

Contact:
American Legion Virginia
Department Adjutant
1805 Chantilly Street
Richmond, VA 23230
Phone: 804-353-6606
Fax: 804-358-1940
Web: www.erols.com/valeg

American Legion Virginia Auxiliary

American Legion Virginia Auxiliary Anna Gear Junior Scholarship

Type of award: Scholarship.
Intended use: For undergraduate study.
Eligibility: Applicant or parent must be member/participant of American Legion Auxiliary. Applicant must be high school senior. Applicant must be residing in Virginia.
Application requirements: Junior member of American Legion Auxiliary for three previous years.
Additional information: Must attend accredited Virginia high school.

Amount of award:	$1,000
Number of awards:	1
Application deadline:	April 1
Total amount awarded:	$1,000

Contact:
American Legion Auxiliary, Department of Virginia
Education Chairman
1805 Chantilly Street
Richmond, VA 23230
Phone: 804-355-6410

American Legion Virginia Auxiliary Dr. Kate Waller Barrett Grant

Type of award: Scholarship.
Intended use: For undergraduate study at accredited vocational, 2-year or 4-year institution.
Eligibility: Applicant or parent must be member/participant of American Legion Auxiliary. Applicant must be high school senior. Applicant must be residing in Virginia. Applicant must be dependent of veteran.
Basis for selection: Applicant must demonstrate financial need.
Additional information: Either child of veteran or child of Auxiliary member. Must be attending accredited Virginia high school.

Amount of award:	$1,000
Number of awards:	1
Application deadline:	March 15
Total amount awarded:	$1,000

Contact:
American Legion Auxiliary, Department of Virginia
Department Secretary-Treasurer
1805 Chantilly Street
Richmond, VA 23230
Phone: 804-355-6410

American Legion Washington

American Legion Department Oratorical Contest

Type of award: Scholarship.
Intended use: For undergraduate study.

Eligibility: Applicant must be enrolled in high school. Applicant must be residing in Washington.
Basis for selection: Competition/talent/interest in oratory/debate, based on breadth of knowledge, originality, application of knowledge of topic, skill in selecting examples and analogies, logic, voice, diction, style of language, and delivery.
Additional information: Student participates in Post, District, Area and Department contests.

Application deadline:	April 1
Total amount awarded:	$7,800

Contact:
American Legion Washington
Chairman, Department of Child Welfare
P.O. Box 3917
Lacey, WA 98509-3917
Web: www.walegion.org

American Legion Washington Scholarship

Type of award: Scholarship.
Intended use: For undergraduate study at accredited vocational, 2-year or 4-year institution. Designated institutions: Eligible institutions in Washington State.
Eligibility: Applicant or parent must be member/participant of American Legion. Applicant must be residing in Washington.
Basis for selection: Applicant must demonstrate financial need.
Additional information: Child of either Washington Legionnaire or Auxiliary member, living or deceased.

Amount of award:	$1,500-$2,500
Number of awards:	2
Application deadline:	April 1
Total amount awarded:	$4,000

Contact:
American Legion Washington
Chairman, Department of Child Welfare
P.O. Box 3917
Lacey, WA 98509-3917
Phone: 360-491-4373
Web: www.walegion.org

American Legion Washington Auxiliary

American Legion Washington Auxiliary Education Scholarship

Type of award: Scholarship.
Intended use: For undergraduate study at postsecondary institution.
Eligibility: Applicant must be residing in Washington. Applicant must be dependent of disabled veteran or deceased veteran.

Amount of award:	$300
Number of awards:	3
Application deadline:	March 11
Total amount awarded:	$900

Contact:
American Legion Washington Auxiliary
Education Scholarships
P.O. Box 5867
Lacey, WA 98509-5867
Phone: 360-491-4373

American Legion Washington Auxiliary Florence Lemcke Fine Arts Scholarship

Type of award: Scholarship.
Intended use: For undergraduate study at 2-year or 4-year institution.
Eligibility: Applicant must be residing in Washington. Applicant must be dependent of veteran.
Basis for selection: Major/career interest in arts, general or art/art history.
Additional information: For use in field of fine arts.

Amount of award:	$500
Number of awards:	1
Application deadline:	March 11
Total amount awarded:	$500

Contact:
American Legion Washington Auxiliary
Education Scholarships
P.O. Box 5867
Lacey, WA 98509-5867

American Legion Washington Auxiliary Margarite McAlpin Nurse's Scholarship

Type of award: Scholarship.
Intended use: For undergraduate study.
Eligibility: Applicant must be residing in Washington. Applicant must be veteran or descendant of veteran; or dependent of veteran.
Basis for selection: Major/career interest in nursing.

Amount of award:	$700
Number of awards:	1
Application deadline:	March 11
Total amount awarded:	$700

Contact:
American Legion Washington Auxiliary
Education Scholarships
P.O. Box 5867
Lacey, WA 98509-5867

American Legion Washington Auxiliary Susan Burdett Scholarship

Type of award: Scholarship.
Intended use: For undergraduate study at postsecondary institution.
Eligibility: Applicant must be female. Applicant must be residing in Washington.
Application requirements: Former Evergreen Girls State Citizen (WA).

Amount of award:	$400
Number of awards:	1
Application deadline:	March 11
Total amount awarded:	$400

Contact:
American Legion Washington Auxiliary
Education Scholarships
P.O. Box 5867
Lacey, WA 98509-5867

American Legion West Virginia

American Legion West Virginia Oratorical Contest

Type of award: Scholarship.
Intended use: For freshman study.
Eligibility: Applicant must be enrolled in high school. Applicant must be residing in West Virginia.
Basis for selection: Competition/talent/interest in oratory/ debate, based on breadth of knowledge, originality, application of knowledge of topic, skill in selecting examples and analogies, logic, voice, diction, style of language, and delivery.
Application requirements: District Oratorical Contest winners.
Additional information: Nine district awards of $200 and three section awards of $300. State winner receives $500 and 4-year scholarship to WV University or state college under control of Board of Regents. Contest is held in January and February. Information may be obtained from local high school or American Legion post.
Contact:
American Legion West Virginia
State Adjutant
2016 Kanawha Blvd. E., Box 3191
Charleston, WV 25332-3191
Phone: 304-343-7591

American Legion West Virginia Auxiliary

American Legion West Virginia Auxiliary Scholarship

Type of award: Scholarship, renewable.
Intended use: For undergraduate study at postsecondary institution. Designated institutions: Colleges and universities in West Virginia.
Eligibility: Applicant must be no older than 22. Applicant must be residing in West Virginia. Applicant must be dependent of veteran.
Application requirements: Proof of eligibility. Must be high school senior or high school graduate.
Additional information: Must be renewed annually, not to exceed total of four years.

Number of awards:	4
Application deadline:	March 1

Contact:
American Legion West Virginia Auxiliary
Secretary/Treasurer Mary Rose Yoho
RR 1 Box 144A
Proctor, WV 26055-9616
Phone: 304-455-3449

American Legion Wisconsin

American Legion Wisconsin Baseball Player of the Year Scholarship

Type of award: Scholarship.
Intended use: For undergraduate study.
Eligibility: Applicant must be residing in Wisconsin.
Basis for selection: Competition/talent/interest in Athletics/ sports.
Application requirements: Nomination by Board of Directors for Baseball Program. Current member of Wisconsin American Legion baseball team.

Amount of award:	$500
Number of awards:	1
Total amount awarded:	$500

Contact:
American Legion Wisconsin
812 East State Street
Milwaukee, WI 53202
Phone: 414-271-1940

American Legion Wisconsin Eagle Scout of the Year Scholarship

Type of award: Scholarship.
Intended use: For undergraduate study.
Eligibility: Applicant or parent must be member/participant of American Legion/Boys Scouts of America. Applicant must be male, high school senior. Applicant must be residing in Wisconsin.
Basis for selection: Applicant must demonstrate high academic achievement.
Application requirements: Boy Scout, Varsity Scout, or Explorer whose group is sponsored by Legion or Auxiliary post, or whose father or grandfather is Legion or Auxiliary member.
Additional information: National American Legion Eagle Scout of the Year: first place: $8,000 scholarship; three second place: $2,000 scholarships.

Amount of award:	$1,000
Number of awards:	1
Application deadline:	March 1
Total amount awarded:	$1,000

Contact:
American Legion Wisconsin
Department Headquarters
812 East State Street
Milwaukee, WI 53202
Phone: 414-271-1940

Oratorical Contest Scholarships

Type of award: Scholarship.
Intended use: For undergraduate study.

Eligibility: Applicant must be enrolled in high school. Applicant must be residing in Wisconsin.
Basis for selection: Competition/talent/interest in oratory/ debate.
Application requirements: Winners of Wisconsin high school Legion Oratorical Contests.
Additional information: Oratorical Contest Scholarships: 1st place, State-$2,000. Note: three regional contests, three regional awards $1,000 each. State Winner: $2,000, regional participants $600 each.

Amount of award:	$600-$2,000

Contact:
American Legion Wisconsin
Department Headquarters
812 East State Street
Milwaukee, WI 53202
Phone: 414-271-1940

American Legion Wisconsin Auxiliary

American Legion Wisconsin Auxiliary Della Van Deuren Memorial

Type of award: Scholarship.
Intended use: For undergraduate study.
Eligibility: Applicant must be residing in Wisconsin. Applicant must be descendant of veteran; or dependent of veteran; or spouse of veteran or deceased veteran.
Basis for selection: Applicant must demonstrate financial need and high academic achievement.
Additional information: Applicant must have minimum 3.2 GPA. Applicant's school need not be in Wisconsin. Grandchildren and great-children of veterans are eligible if they are members of American Legion Auxiliary. Applicant's mother or applicant must be member of American Legion Auxiliary.

Amount of award:	$1,000
Number of awards:	2
Application deadline:	March 15

Contact:
American Legion Wisconsin Auxiliary
Department Headquarters
812 East State Street
Milwaukee, WI 53202-3493
Phone: 414-271-0124

American Legion Wisconsin Auxiliary H.S. and Angeline Lewis Scholarship

Type of award: Scholarship.
Intended use: For undergraduate, master's or doctoral study at accredited postsecondary institution.
Eligibility: Applicant must be residing in Wisconsin. Applicant must be descendant of veteran; or dependent of veteran; or spouse of veteran or deceased veteran.
Basis for selection: Applicant must demonstrate financial need and high academic achievement.
Additional information: Minimum GPA 3.2. Grandchildren and great-grandchildren of veterans are eligible if members of

Auxiliary. One award for graduate study; five awards for undergraduate study. School selected needs to be in Wisconsin.

Amount of award:	$1,000
Number of awards:	6
Application deadline:	March 15
Total amount awarded:	$6,000

Contact:
American Legion Wisconsin Auxiliary
Department Headquarters
812 East State Street
Milwaukee, WI 53202-3493
Phone: 414-271-0124

American Legion Wisconsin Auxiliary Health Careers Award

Type of award: Scholarship.
Intended use: For undergraduate study at accredited postsecondary institution. Designated institutions: Hospital, university or technical school. Does not need to be four-year program.
Eligibility: Applicant or parent must be member/participant of American Legion Auxiliary. Applicant must be residing in Wisconsin. Applicant must be descendant of veteran; or dependent of veteran or deceased veteran; or spouse of veteran or deceased veteran.
Basis for selection: Major/career interest in health sciences or health-related professions. Applicant must demonstrate financial need and high academic achievement.
Application requirements: Transcript.
Additional information: Minimum GPA 3.2. Grandchildren and great-grandchildren of veterans are eligible if Auxiliary members. School selected does not have to be in Wisconsin.

Amount of award:	$750
Number of awards:	2
Application deadline:	March 15
Total amount awarded:	$1,500

Contact:
American Legion Wisconsin Auxiliary
Department Headquarters
812 East State Street, Second Floor
Milwaukee, WI 53202-3493
Phone: 414-271-0124
Fax: 414-217-9355

American Legion Wisconsin Auxiliary Merit and Memorial Scholarship

Type of award: Scholarship.
Intended use: For undergraduate study.
Eligibility: Applicant must be residing in Wisconsin. Applicant must be spouse of veteran or deceased veteran.
Basis for selection: Applicant must demonstrate financial need and high academic achievement.
Application requirements: Transcript.
Additional information: 3.2 GPA required. School selected need not be in Wisconsin.

Amount of award:	$1,000
Number of awards:	6
Application deadline:	March 15
Total amount awarded:	$6,000

Contact:
American Legion Wisconsin Auxiliary
Department Headquarters
812 East State Street
Milwaukee, WI 53202-3493
Phone: 414-271-0124
Fax: 414-271-9355

American Legion Wisconsin Auxiliary Registered Nurse Degree Award

Type of award: Scholarship.
Intended use: For undergraduate study at accredited postsecondary institution.
Eligibility: Applicant must be residing in Wisconsin. Applicant must be descendant of veteran; or dependent of veteran or deceased veteran; or spouse of veteran or deceased veteran.
Basis for selection: Major/career interest in nursing. Applicant must demonstrate financial need and high academic achievement.
Application requirements: Must be in nursing school or have positive acceptance to accredited school of nursing.
Additional information: Minimum GPA 3.2. Grandchild or great-grandchild of veteran must be Auxiliary member. May be used at accredited hospital nursing program.

Amount of award:	$750
Number of awards:	2
Application deadline:	March 15
Total amount awarded:	$1,500

Contact:
American Legion Wisconsin Auxiliary
Department Headquarters
812 East State Street, Second Floor
Milwaukee, WI 53202-3493
Phone: 414-271-0124
Fax: 414-271-9355

American Legion Wisconsin Auxiliary State President's Scholarship

Type of award: Scholarship.
Intended use: For undergraduate study at accredited postsecondary institution.
Eligibility: Applicant or parent must be member/participant of American Legion Auxiliary. Applicant must be residing in Wisconsin. Applicant must be descendant of veteran; or dependent of veteran; or spouse of veteran or deceased veteran.
Basis for selection: Applicant must demonstrate financial need and high academic achievement.
Application requirements: Transcript.
Additional information: Minimum 3.2 GPA. Mother of applicant or applicant must be Auxiliary member. Grandchildren and great-grandchildren of veterans eligible if Auxiliary members.

Amount of award:	$1,000
Number of awards:	3
Application deadline:	March 15
Total amount awarded:	$3,000

Contact:
American Legion Wisconsin Auxiliary
Department Headquarters
812 East State Street, Second Floor
Milwaukee, WI 53202-3493
Phone: 414-271-0124
Fax: 414-271-9355

Badger Girls State Scholarship

Type of award: Scholarship.
Intended use: For undergraduate study.
Eligibility: Applicant must be residing in Wisconsin. Applicant must be descendant of veteran; or dependent of veteran; or spouse of veteran or deceased veteran.
Basis for selection: Applicant must demonstrate financial need and high academic achievement.
Application requirements: WALA Badger Girls State Citizen of previous year.
Additional information: Applications automatically mailed to eligible students each year. Minimum 3.2 GPA. Awards: Badger Girls State Scholarship two at $500; King-Hahn Scholarship one at $500.

Amount of award:	$500
Number of awards:	3
Application deadline:	March 15
Total amount awarded:	$1,500

Contact:
American Legion Wisconsin Auxiliary
Department Headquarters
812 East State Street, Second Floor
Milwaukee, WI 53202-3493
Phone: 414-271-0124

American Legion Wyoming

American Legion Wyoming E.B. Blackmore Memorial Scholarship

Type of award: Scholarship.
Intended use: For undergraduate study at postsecondary institution.
Eligibility: Applicant or parent must be member/participant of American Legion. Applicant must be residing in Wyoming. Applicant must be veteran or descendant of veteran; or dependent of veteran.
Application requirements: Legionnaire/children or grandchildren of legionnaire.

Amount of award:	$700
Number of awards:	1
Application deadline:	May 1
Total amount awarded:	$700

Contact:
American Legion Wyoming
Department Adjutant
P.O. Box 545
Cheyenne, WY 82003
Phone: 307-634-3035

American Legion Wyoming Oratorical Contest

Type of award: Scholarship.

Intended use: For undergraduate study at postsecondary institution.
Eligibility: Applicant must be enrolled in high school. Applicant must be residing in Wyoming.
Basis for selection: Competition/talent/interest in oratory/ debate, based on breadth of knowledge, originality, application of knowledge of topic, skill in selecting examples and analogies, logic, voice, diction, style of language and delivery.
Application requirements: Proof of eligibility. Winner of state high school Oratorical Contest.
Additional information: Topic: U.S. Constitution and citizenship.

Amount of award:	$500
Number of awards:	1
Total amount awarded:	$500

Contact:
American Legion Wyoming
Department Adjutant
P.O. Box 545
Cheyenne, WY 82003
Phone: 307-634-3035
Fax: 307-635-7093

American Legion Wyoming Auxiliary

American Legion Wyoming Auxiliary Past Presidents' Parley Scholarship

Type of award: Scholarship.
Intended use: For undergraduate study at 2-year or 4-year institution.
Eligibility: Applicant must be residing in Wyoming.
Basis for selection: Major/career interest in nursing or health-related professions. Applicant must demonstrate high academic achievement.
Application requirements: Must be in 3rd quarter of training and have 3.0 GPA.
Additional information: Preference given to nursing students who are children of veterans.

Amount of award:	$300
Number of awards:	2
Total amount awarded:	$600

Contact:
American Legion Wyoming Auxiliary
Department Secretary
301 A Rockpile Blvd.
Gillette, WY 82716
Phone: 307-686-7137

American Medical Technologists

Medical Technologists Scholarship

Type of award: Scholarship.
Intended use: For full-time undergraduate or graduate study at accredited postsecondary institution in United States.

Eligibility: Applicant must be U.S. citizen or permanent resident.
Basis for selection: Major/career interest in medical assistant; dental assistant; dental laboratory technology or medical specialties/research. Applicant must demonstrate financial need, high academic achievement, seriousness of purpose and service orientation.
Application requirements: Recommendations, essay, transcript, proof of eligibility. Evidence of financial need and career goals. Application must be typed to be considered. All applications and supporting documents become the property of American Medical Technologists and can not be returned.
Additional information: Applicant must be high school senior, graduate or GED recipient. Applicant must be enrolled in school accredited by agency recognized by U.S. Department of Education, and course of study must lead to career in one of disciplines certified by American Medical Technologists. Applicants pursuing careers other than those certified will not be accepted. Late applications will not be considered. AMT Scholarship Committee, whose decision will be final, will determine scholarship recipients, and only recipients will be notified. Award may be used for tuition only and will be sent directly to school of recipient's choice. Winners will be notified thereafter and must furnish proof of being either student in good standing or enrolled for entrance into fall program of accredited school.

Amount of award:	$500
Number of awards:	5
Application deadline:	April 15
Total amount awarded:	$2,500

Contact:
American Medical Technologists
710 Higgins Road
Park Ridge, IL 60068
Phone: 847-823-5169

American Meteorological Society

American Meteorological Society Undergraduate Scholarships

Type of award: Scholarship.
Intended use: For full-time senior study at accredited 4-year institution in United States.
Eligibility: Applicant must be U.S. citizen or permanent resident.
Basis for selection: Major/career interest in atmospheric sciences/meteorology; oceanography/marine studies; hydrology or environmental science. Applicant must demonstrate high academic achievement and seriousness of purpose.
Application requirements: Recommendations, essay, transcript, proof of eligibility. No more than two students from any one institution may enter papers in any one contest.
Additional information: To obtain fellowship or scholarship application, visit Website. Please specify which application is being requested for which year of academic study. AMS encourages applications from women, minorities, and disabled students who are traditionally underrepresented in atmospheric and related oceanic and hydrologic sciences. Scholarships will be awarded to students entering final year of undergraduate study. Applicants must be majoring in atmospheric or related oceanic or hydrologic sciences, and/or must show clear intent to

129

pursue careers in atmospheric or related sciences. Marine biology majors not eligible. Number and amount of scholarships vary for different awards in this category.

Amount of award:	$2,000
Application deadline:	February 23

Contact:
American Meteorological Society
Scholarship Coordinator
45 Beacon Street
Boston, MA 2108-3693
Phone: 617-227-2426
Fax: 617-742-8718
Web: www.ametsoc.org/ams

American Meteorological Society/ Industry Minority Scholarship

Type of award: Scholarship.
Intended use: For full-time freshman or sophomore study at accredited 4-year institution in United States.
Eligibility: Applicant must be Alaskan native, Asian American, African American, Mexican American, Hispanic American, Puerto Rican or American Indian. Applicant must be high school senior. Applicant must be U.S. citizen or permanent resident.
Basis for selection: Major/career interest in atmospheric sciences/meteorology; oceanography/marine studies; hydrology or environmental science. Applicant must demonstrate high academic achievement.
Application requirements: Recommendations, essay, transcript, proof of eligibility. SAT scores.
Additional information: To obtain fellowship or scholarship application, visit Website. Please specify which application is being requested for which year of academic study. Award for minority students who have traditionally been underrepresented in sciences, especially Hispanic, Native American, and Black/African American students who intend to pursue careers in atmospheric or related oceanic and hydrologic sciences. Applicants must be entering freshman year. Marine biology majors ineligible. Two-year scholarships are $3,000 per year.

Amount of award:	$6,000
Application deadline:	February 23
Notification begins:	May 1

Contact:
American Meteorological Society
Fellowship Coordinator
45 Beacon Street
Boston, MA 2108-3693
Phone: 617-227-2426
Fax: 617-742-8718
Web: www.ametsoc.org/ams

American Meteorological Society/ Industry Undergraduate Scholarship

Type of award: Scholarship, renewable.
Intended use: For full-time junior or senior study at accredited 4-year institution in United States.
Eligibility: Applicant must be U.S. citizen or permanent resident.
Basis for selection: Major/career interest in atmospheric sciences/meteorology; oceanography/marine studies; hydrology; chemistry; computer/information sciences; mathematics; engineering; physics; environmental science or engineering, environmental. Applicant must demonstrate high academic achievement.

Application requirements: Recommendations, essay, transcript, proof of eligibility.
Additional information: To obtain fellowship or scholarship application, visit Website. Must have minimum 3.0 GPA. Intention to pursue career in atmospheric, oceanic and/or hydrologic sciences. Applicants must be entering junior year. Marine biology majors ineligible. Two-year scholarships are $2,000 per year. Second year funding dependent upon academic performance and faculty adviser recommendation.

Amount of award:	$4,000
Number of awards:	13
Number of applicants:	60
Application deadline:	February 23
Notification begins:	May 1

Contact:
American Meteorological Society
Scholarship Coordinator
45 Beacon Street
Boston, MA 2108-3693
Phone: 617-227-2426
Fax: 617-742-8718
Web: www.ametsoc.org/ams

Meteorological Society Father James B. MacElwane Annual Award

Type of award: Scholarship.
Intended use: For undergraduate study.
Eligibility: Applicant must be U.S. citizen or permanent resident.
Basis for selection: Competition/talent/interest in writing/journalism. Major/career interest in atmospheric sciences/meteorology.
Application requirements: Essay, transcript, proof of eligibility. Students must submit an original paper plus four photocopies; a letter, an application including contact information.
Additional information: Award intended to stimulate interest in meteorology among college students through encouragement of original student papers concerned with some phase of atmospheric sciences. Student must be enrolled as undergraduate when paper is written. Submissions from women, minorities, and disabled students who are traditionally underrepresented in atmospheric and related oceanic and hydrologic sciences encouraged. No more than two students from any one institution may enter papers in any one contest. Visit Website for application and information.

Amount of award:	$300
Number of awards:	1
Number of applicants:	10
Application deadline:	June 15
Total amount awarded:	$300

Contact:
American Meteorological Society
Scholarship Coordinator
45 Beacon Street
Boston, MA 02108-3693
Phone: 617-227-2426
Fax: 617-742-8718
Web: www.ametsoc.org/ams

American Morgan Horse Institute

AMHI Educational Scholarships

Type of award: Scholarship.
Intended use: For non-degree study.
Basis for selection: Applicant must demonstrate financial need, high academic achievement, depth of character, leadership, seriousness of purpose and service orientation.
Application requirements: Recommendations, essay, transcript. Achievement with Morgan horses.
Additional information: Send SASE for application or download from fastweb.com.

Amount of award:	$3,000
Number of awards:	5
Number of applicants:	200
Application deadline:	March 1
Notification begins:	June 1
Total amount awarded:	$15,000

Contact:
AMHI Scholarships
P.O. Box 837
Shelburne, VT 05482-0519
Web: www.morganhorse.com

AMHI Van Schaik Dressage Scholarship

Type of award: Scholarship, renewable.
Intended use: For non-degree study.
Basis for selection: Major/career interest in dressage. Applicant must demonstrate seriousness of purpose.
Application requirements: Recommendations, essay.
Additional information: Must be dressage rider using Morgan horse. For anyone competing in and interested in advancing through levels of dressage to Fourth level and above. Send SASE for application or download from fastweb.com.

Amount of award:	$1,000
Number of awards:	1
Number of applicants:	50
Application deadline:	November 30
Notification begins:	January 10
Total amount awarded:	$1,000

Contact:
AMHI Scholarships
P.O. Box 837
Shelburne, VT 05482-0960
Web: www.morganhorse.com

American Nuclear Society

American Nuclear Society Environmental Sciences Division Scholarship

Type of award: Scholarship, renewable.
Intended use: For full-time junior or senior study at accredited 4-year institution.
Eligibility: Applicant must be U.S. citizen or permanent resident.
Basis for selection: Major/career interest in environmental science; engineering, environmental or ecology. Applicant must demonstrate high academic achievement, depth of character, leadership, seriousness of purpose and service orientation.
Application requirements: Recommendations, transcript, proof of eligibility.
Additional information: Applicant must be at least an entering junior enrolled in program leading to degree related to environmental sciences field. Application available online.

Amount of award:	$2,000-$3,500
Number of awards:	1
Application deadline:	February 1
Notification begins:	May 9

Contact:
American Nuclear Society
555 North Kensington Avenue
La Grange Park, IL 60526
Phone: 708-352-6611
Fax: 708-352-0499
Web: www.ans.org

Angelo S. Biseti Scholarship

Type of award: Scholarship, renewable.
Intended use: For full-time junior or senior study at accredited 4-year institution.
Eligibility: Applicant must be U.S. citizen or permanent resident.
Basis for selection: Major/career interest in nuclear science; engineering, nuclear; chemistry or physics. Applicant must demonstrate financial need, high academic achievement, depth of character, leadership, seriousness of purpose and service orientation.
Application requirements: Recommendations, transcript, proof of eligibility.
Additional information: Applicant must be at least entering junior enrolled in program leading to degree in nuclear science, nuclear engineering or nuclear-related field. Application available online.

Amount of award:	$2,000
Number of awards:	1
Application deadline:	February 1
Notification begins:	May 9

Contact:
American Nuclear Society
555 North Kensington Avenue
La Grange Park, IL 60526
Phone: 708-352-6611
Fax: 708-352-0499
Web: www.ans.org/honors/scholarships/

ANS Undergraduate Scholarships

Type of award: Scholarship.
Intended use: For sophomore, junior or senior study at accredited 4-year institution in United States.
Eligibility: Applicant must be U.S. citizen or permanent resident.
Basis for selection: Major/career interest in nuclear science; engineering, nuclear; chemistry or physics. Applicant must demonstrate seriousness of purpose.
Application requirements: Recommendations, transcript.
Additional information: Maximum of four scholarships for students in course of study leading to degree in nuclear science, nuclear engineering, or nuclear-related field who will be entering sophomore year, and maximum of 21 scholarships for students who will be entering junior or senior year.

Scholarships

Amount of award: $2,000
Number of awards: 25
Application deadline: February 1
Contact:
American Nuclear Society
555 North Kensington Avenue
La Grange Park, IL 60526
Phone: 708-352-6611
Fax: 708-352-0499
Web: www.ans.org/honors/scholarships/

Decommissioning, Decontamination and Reutilization Scholarship

Type of award: Scholarship.
Intended use: For undergraduate study at accredited 4-year institution in United States.
Eligibility: Applicant must be U.S. citizen.
Basis for selection: Major/career interest in engineering, nuclear; environmental science or engineering, environmental. Applicant must demonstrate patriotism and seriousness of purpose.
Application requirements: Recommendations, transcript. Must join ANS.
Additional information: Applicants must be enrolled in curriculum of engineering or science associated with decommissioning/decontamination of nuclear facilities, management/characterization of nuclear waste, or restoration of environment. If awarded scholarship, student must join ANS and designate DDR Division as one professional division. Awardee must also provide student support to DDR Division at next ANS meeting after receiving award (funding provided for travel to meeting but does not include food and lodging).
Amount of award: $2,000
Application deadline: February 1
Contact:
American Nuclear Society
555 North Kensington Avenue
La Grange Park, IL 60526
Phone: 708-352-6611
Fax: 708-352-0499
Web: www.ans.org/honors/scholarships/

Delayed Education Scholarship for Women

Type of award: Scholarship, renewable.
Intended use: For undergraduate study at accredited 4-year institution.
Eligibility: Applicant must be female, returning adult student. Applicant must be U.S. citizen or permanent resident.
Basis for selection: Major/career interest in nuclear science; engineering, nuclear; chemistry or physics. Applicant must demonstrate financial need and high academic achievement.
Application requirements: Interview, transcript, proof of eligibility.
Additional information: Award for mature women who have had delay in their education in field of Nuclear Science and Engineering. One request and one application cover D.E.W.S. Award and John and Muriel Landis Award. Applicants must check appropriate box on Landis Scholarship form. Application available online.
Amount of award: $3,500
Number of awards: 1
Application deadline: February 1
Notification begins: May 9

Contact:
American Nuclear Society
555 North Kensington Avenue
La Grange Park, IL 60526
Phone: 708-352-6611
Fax: 708-352-0499
Web: www.ans.org

James R. Vogt Pittsburgh Local Section Scholarship

Type of award: Scholarship.
Intended use: For full-time sophomore, junior, senior, master's or doctoral study at accredited 4-year or graduate institution.
Eligibility: Applicant must be U.S. citizen or permanent resident residing in Pennsylvania.
Basis for selection: Major/career interest in chemistry or nuclear science. Applicant must demonstrate financial need, high academic achievement, depth of character, leadership, seriousness of purpose and service orientation.
Application requirements: Recommendations, transcript, proof of eligibility.
Additional information: Applicants must live in western Pennsylvania and be enrolled or have proposed to enroll in radio-analytical chemistry, or analytical chemistry or analytical applications of nuclear science program. Application available online.
Amount of award: $2,000-$3,000
Number of awards: 1
Number of applicants: 1
Application deadline: February 1
Notification begins: May 9
Contact:
American Nuclear Society
555 North Kensington Avenue
La Grange Park, IL 60526
Phone: 708-352-6611
Fax: 708-352-0499
Web: www.ans.org

James R. Vogt Scholarship

Type of award: Scholarship.
Intended use: For full-time undergraduate or graduate study at accredited 4-year or graduate institution.
Eligibility: Applicant must be U.S. citizen or permanent resident.
Basis for selection: Major/career interest in chemistry or nuclear science. Applicant must demonstrate financial need, high academic achievement, depth of character, leadership, seriousness of purpose and service orientation.
Application requirements: Recommendations, transcript, proof of eligibility.
Additional information: Applicants must be enrolled or proposing to enroll in radio-analytical, analytical chemistry or analytical applications of nuclear science. Applications available online.
Amount of award: $2,000-$3,000
Number of awards: 1
Application deadline: February 1
Notification begins: May 9

Contact:
American Nuclear Society
555 North Kensington Avenue
La Grange Park, IL 60526
Phone: 708-352-6611
Fax: 708-352-0499
Web: www.ans.org

John and Muriel Landis Scholarship

Type of award: Scholarship.
Intended use: For undergraduate or graduate study at accredited 4-year or graduate institution in United States.
Eligibility: Applicant must be U.S. citizen or permanent resident.
Basis for selection: Major/career interest in nuclear science; engineering, nuclear; chemistry or physics. Applicant must demonstrate financial need, high academic achievement, depth of character, leadership, seriousness of purpose and service orientation.
Application requirements: Recommendations, transcript, proof of eligibility.
Additional information: Awarded to students with greater than average financial need. Consideration given to conditions or experiences that render student disadvantaged (poor high school/undergraduate preparation, etc.). Applicants should be planning career in nuclear science, nuclear engineering or nuclear-related field. Qualified high school seniors eligible to apply. Application available online.

Amount of award:	$3,500
Number of awards:	8
Application deadline:	February 1
Notification begins:	May 9

Contact:
American Nuclear Society
555 North Kensington Avenue
La Grange Park, IL 60526
Phone: 708-352-6611
Fax: 708-352-0499
Web: www.ans.org

John R. Lamarsh Scholarship

Type of award: Scholarship, renewable.
Intended use: For full-time junior or senior study at accredited 4-year institution.
Eligibility: Applicant must be U.S. citizen or permanent resident.
Basis for selection: Major/career interest in nuclear science; engineering, nuclear; chemistry or physics. Applicant must demonstrate financial need, high academic achievement, depth of character, leadership, seriousness of purpose and service orientation.
Application requirements: Recommendations, transcript, proof of eligibility.
Additional information: Applicant must be at least an entering junior enrolled in program leading to degree in nuclear science, nuclear engineering, or nuclear-related field. Application available online.

Amount of award:	$2,000
Number of awards:	1
Application deadline:	February 1
Notification begins:	May 9

Contact:
American Nuclear Society
555 North Kensington Avenue
La Grange Park, IL 60526
Phone: 708-352-6611
Fax: 708-352-0499
Web: www.ans.org

Joseph R. Dietrich Scholarship

Type of award: Scholarship, renewable.
Intended use: For full-time junior or senior study at accredited 4-year institution.
Eligibility: Applicant must be U.S. citizen or permanent resident.
Basis for selection: Major/career interest in nuclear science; engineering, nuclear; chemistry or physics. Applicant must demonstrate financial need, high academic achievement, depth of character, leadership, seriousness of purpose and service orientation.
Application requirements: Recommendations, transcript, proof of eligibility.
Additional information: Applicant must be at least an entering junior enrolled in program leading to degree in nuclear science, nuclear engineering or nuclear-related field. Application available online.

Amount of award:	$2,000
Number of awards:	1
Application deadline:	February 1
Notification begins:	May 9
Total amount awarded:	$2,000

Contact:
American Nuclear Society
555 North Kensington Avenue
La Grange Park, IL 60526
Phone: 708-352-6611
Fax: 708-352-0499
Web: www.ans.org

Nuclear Operations and Power Division Scholarship

Type of award: Scholarship, renewable.
Intended use: For full-time sophomore, junior or senior study at accredited 4-year institution.
Eligibility: Applicant must be U.S. citizen or permanent resident.
Basis for selection: Major/career interest in nuclear science; engineering, nuclear; chemistry or physics. Applicant must demonstrate financial need, high academic achievement, depth of character, leadership, seriousness of purpose and service orientation.
Application requirements: Recommendations, transcript, proof of eligibility.
Additional information: Applicant must be at least an entering junior enrolled in program leading to degree in nuclear science, nuclear engineering or nuclear-related field. Application available online.

Amount of award:	$2,500
Number of awards:	1
Application deadline:	February 1
Notification begins:	May 9

Contact:
American Nuclear Society
555 North Kensington Avenue
La Grange Park, IL 60526
Phone: 708-352-6611
Fax: 708-352-0499
Web: www.ans.org

Raymond DiSalvo Scholarship

Type of award: Scholarship, renewable.
Intended use: For full-time junior or senior study at accredited 4-year institution.
Eligibility: Applicant must be U.S. citizen or permanent resident.
Basis for selection: Major/career interest in nuclear science; engineering, nuclear; chemistry or physics. Applicant must demonstrate financial need, high academic achievement, depth of character, leadership, seriousness of purpose and service orientation.
Application requirements: Recommendations, transcript, proof of eligibility.
Additional information: Applicant must be at least an entering junior enrolled in program leading to degree in nuclear science, nuclear engineering or nuclear related field. Application available online.

Amount of award:	$2,000
Number of awards:	1
Application deadline:	February 1
Notification begins:	May 9

Contact:
American Nuclear Society
555 North Kensington Avenue
La Grange Park, IL 60526
Phone: 708-352-6611
Fax: 708-352-0499
Web: www.ans.org

Robert G. Lacy Scholarship

Type of award: Scholarship, renewable.
Intended use: For full-time junior or senior study at accredited 4-year institution.
Eligibility: Applicant must be U.S. citizen or permanent resident.
Basis for selection: Major/career interest in nuclear science; engineering, nuclear; chemistry or physics. Applicant must demonstrate financial need, high academic achievement, depth of character, leadership, seriousness of purpose and service orientation.
Application requirements: Recommendations, transcript, proof of eligibility.
Additional information: Applicant must be at least an entering junior enrolled in program leading to degree in nuclear science, nuclear engineering or nuclear-related field. Application available online.

Amount of award:	$2,000
Number of awards:	1
Application deadline:	February 1
Notification begins:	May 9

Contact:
American Nuclear Society
555 North Kensington Avenue
La Grange Park, IL 60526
Phone: 708-352-6611
Fax: 708-352-0499
Web: www.ans.org

Robert T. (Bob) Liner Scholarship

Type of award: Scholarship, renewable.
Intended use: For full-time junior, senior or post-bachelor's certificate study at accredited 4-year institution.
Eligibility: Applicant must be U.S. citizen or permanent resident.
Basis for selection: Major/career interest in nuclear science; engineering, nuclear; chemistry or physics. Applicant must demonstrate financial need, high academic achievement, depth of character, leadership, seriousness of purpose and service orientation.
Application requirements: Recommendations, transcript, proof of eligibility.
Additional information: Applicant must be at least an entering junior enrolled in program leading to degree in nuclear science, nuclear engineering or nuclear-related field. Application available online.

Amount of award:	$2,000
Number of awards:	1
Application deadline:	February 1
Notification begins:	May 9

Contact:
American Nuclear Society
555 North Kensington Avenue
La Grange Park, IL 60526
Phone: 708-352-6611
Fax: 708-352-0499
Web: www.ans.org

American Physical Society

Minorities Scholarship Program

Type of award: Scholarship, renewable.
Intended use: For full-time freshman, sophomore or junior study at 2-year or 4-year institution in United States.
Designated institutions: Eligible institutions must have physics department or provide for procurement of physics degree.
Eligibility: Applicant must be African American, Mexican American, Hispanic American, Puerto Rican or American Indian. Applicant must be U.S. citizen.
Basis for selection: Major/career interest in physics. Applicant must demonstrate high academic achievement.
Application requirements: Recommendations, essay, transcript, proof of eligibility. ACT/SAT scores. Applications available early November and due first Friday in February.
Additional information: Must be high school senior, college freshman or sophomore to apply. Additional $500 awarded to physics department at eligible institution. Visit Website for additional information.

Amount of award:	$2,000-$3,000
Number of awards:	25
Number of applicants:	100
Notification begins:	May 15
Total amount awarded:	$70,000

Contact:
American Physical Society
Minorities Scholarship Program
One Physics Ellipse
College Park, MD 20740
Phone: 301-209-3232
Fax: 301-209-0865
Web: www.aps.org/educ

American Quarter Horse Youth Association

American Quarter Horse Foundation Scholarships

Type of award: Scholarship, renewable.
Intended use: For full-time undergraduate or non-degree study in United States.
Eligibility: Applicant or parent must be member/participant of American Quarter Horse Youth Association. Applicant must be at least 17, no older than 21, high school senior.
Basis for selection: Applicant must demonstrate financial need and high academic achievement.
Application requirements: Recommendations, essay, transcript, proof of eligibility. Essay must be 500 words explaining applicant's desire to pursue related career or topic listed in application. Minimum 2.5 GPA. 3x5 color photograph, tax forms, and three reference letters.
Additional information: Must have been member of American Quarter Horse Youth Association for at least three years.

Number of awards:	133
Number of applicants:	170
Application deadline:	May 15
Notification begins:	July 15

Contact:
American Junior Quarter Horse Youth Association
Laura Owens
2601 I-40 East
Amarillo, TX 79104
Phone: 806-376-4888 ext. 342
Web: www.aqha.com

American Radio Relay League Foundation, Inc.

ARRL Albuquerque Amateur Radio Club Scholarship

Type of award: Scholarship.
Intended use: For undergraduate study at accredited postsecondary institution in United States.
Eligibility: Applicant must be residing in New Mexico.
Basis for selection: Competition/talent/interest in amateur radio. Applicant must demonstrate financial need.
Application requirements: Recommendations, essay, transcript, proof of eligibility. One-page essay on role amateur radio has played in their life.
Additional information: Must be amateur radio operator holding any class license. Number of awards varies. Application may be obtained on Website.

Amount of award:	$500
Application deadline:	February 1

Contact:
ARRL Foundation Inc./Scholarship Program
225 Main Street
Newington, CT 06111
Phone: 860-594-0200
Fax: 860-594-0259
Web: www.arrl.org/arrlf/scholgen.html

ARRL Donald Riebhoff Memorial Scholarship

Type of award: Scholarship.
Intended use: For undergraduate or graduate study at accredited postsecondary institution in United States.
Eligibility: Applicant or parent must be member/participant of American Radio Relay League.
Basis for selection: Competition/talent/interest in amateur radio. Major/career interest in international relations. Applicant must demonstrate financial need.
Application requirements: Recommendations, transcript, proof of eligibility.
Additional information: Must be amateur radio operator with technician class license. Application may be obtained on Website.

Amount of award:	$1,000
Number of awards:	1
Application deadline:	February 1

Contact:
ARRL Foundation Inc./Scholarship Program
225 Main Street
Newington, CT 06111
Phone: 860-594-0200
Fax: 860-594-0259
Web: www.arrl.org/arrlf/scholgen.html

ARRL Earl I. Anderson Scholarship

Type of award: Scholarship.
Intended use: For undergraduate or graduate study at accredited postsecondary institution. Designated institutions: Postsecondary institutions in Wisconsin, Illinois, Indiana or Florida.
Eligibility: Applicant or parent must be member/participant of American Radio Relay League. Applicant must be residing in Illinois, Indiana or Wisconsin.
Basis for selection: Competition/talent/interest in amateur radio. Major/career interest in engineering, electrical/electronic. Applicant must demonstrate financial need.
Application requirements: Recommendations, transcript, proof of eligibility.
Additional information: Must be amateur radio operator holding any class license. Application may be obtained on Website.

Amount of award:	$1,250
Number of awards:	3
Application deadline:	February 1

Contact:
ARRL Foundation, Inc./Scholarship Program
225 Main Street
Newington, CT 06111
Phone: 860-594-0200
Fax: 860-594-0259
Web: www.arrl.org/arrlf/scholgen.html

ARRL Eugene "Gene" Sallee, W4YFR Memorial Scholarship

Type of award: Scholarship.
Intended use: For undergraduate or graduate study at accredited postsecondary institution in United States.
Eligibility: Applicant must be residing in Georgia.
Basis for selection: Competition/talent/interest in amateur radio. Applicant must demonstrate financial need and high academic achievement.

Scholarships

135

Application requirements: Recommendations, transcript, proof of eligibility.
Additional information: Must be amateur radio operator with technician plus class license. Minimum 3.0 GPA. Application may be obtained on Website.

Amount of award:	$500
Number of awards:	1
Application deadline:	February 1
Total amount awarded:	$500

Contact:
ARRL Foundation Inc./Scholarship Program
225 Main Street
Newington, CT 06111
Phone: 860-594-0200
Fax: 860-594-0259
Web: www.arrl.org/arrlf/scholgen.html

ARRL Henry Broughton, K2AE Memorial Scholarship

Type of award: Scholarship.
Intended use: For undergraduate study at accredited 4-year institution in United States.
Eligibility: Applicant must be residing in New York.
Basis for selection: Competition/talent/interest in amateur radio. Major/career interest in engineering or science, general. Applicant must demonstrate financial need.
Application requirements: Recommendations, transcript, proof of eligibility.
Additional information: Applicant must live within 70-mile radius of Schenectady, New York. Must be amateur radio operator with general class license. May offer additional awards if funding permits. Application may be obtained on Website.

Amount of award:	$1,000
Number of awards:	1
Application deadline:	February 1

Contact:
ARRL Foundation, Inc./Scholarship Program
225 Main Street
Newington, CT 06111
Phone: 860-594-0200
Fax: 860-594-0259
Web: www.arrl.org/arrlf/scholgen.html

ARRL Scholarship Honoring Senator Barry Goldwater, K7UGA

Type of award: Scholarship.
Intended use: For undergraduate or graduate study at accredited postsecondary institution in United States.
Basis for selection: Competition/talent/interest in amateur radio. Applicant must demonstrate financial need.
Application requirements: Recommendations, transcript.
Additional information: Must be amateur radio operator with novice license. Application may be obtained on Website.

Amount of award:	$5,000
Number of awards:	1
Application deadline:	February 1
Total amount awarded:	$5,000

Contact:
ARRL Foundation Inc./Scholarship Program
225 Main Street
Newington, CT 06111
Phone: 860-594-0200
Fax: 860-594-0259
Web: www.arrl.org/arrlf/scholgen.html

Charles Clarke Cordle Memorial Scholarship

Type of award: Scholarship.
Intended use: For undergraduate or graduate study at accredited postsecondary institution. Designated institutions: Georgia or Alabama postsecondary institutions.
Eligibility: Applicant must be residing in Alabama or Georgia.
Basis for selection: Competition/talent/interest in amateur radio. Applicant must demonstrate financial need.
Application requirements: Recommendations, transcript.
Additional information: Must have at least 2.5 GPA. Must be amateur radio operator holding any class license. Application may be obtained from Website.

Amount of award:	$1,000
Number of awards:	1
Application deadline:	February 1
Total amount awarded:	$1,000

Contact:
ARRL Foundation Inc./Scholarship Program
225 Main Street
Newington, CT 06111
Phone: 860-594-0200
Fax: 860-594-0259
Web: www.arrl.org/aarlf/scholgen.html

Charles N. Fisher Memorial Scholarship

Type of award: Scholarship.
Intended use: For undergraduate or graduate study at accredited postsecondary institution in United States.
Eligibility: Applicant must be residing in Arizona or California.
Basis for selection: Competition/talent/interest in amateur radio. Major/career interest in communications; electronics or engineering, electrical/electronic. Applicant must demonstrate financial need.
Application requirements: Recommendations, transcript.
Additional information: Must be amateur radio operator holding any class license. California candidates must reside in Los Angeles, Orange, San Diego, and Santa Barbara areas. Application may be obtained on Website.

Amount of award:	$1,000
Number of awards:	1
Application deadline:	February 1
Total amount awarded:	$1,000

Contact:
ARRL Foundation Inc./Scholarship Program
225 Main Street
Newington, CT 06111
Phone: 860-594-0200
Fax: 860-594-0259
Web: www.arrl.org/arrlf/scholgen.html

Chicago FM Club Scholarship

Type of award: Scholarship.
Intended use: For undergraduate study at accredited vocational, 2-year or 4-year institution in United States.
Eligibility: Applicant must be U.S. citizen residing in Illinois, Indiana or Wisconsin.
Basis for selection: Competition/talent/interest in amateur radio. Applicant must demonstrate financial need.
Application requirements: Recommendations, transcript.

Additional information: Student must be U.S. citizen or within three months of becoming U.S. citizen. Must be amateur radio operator with technician license. Number of awards varies. Application may be obtained on Website.

　Amount of award:　$500
　Application deadline:　February 1
Contact:
ARRL Foundation Inc./Scholarship Program
225 Main Street
Newington, CT 06111
Phone: 860-594-0200
Fax: 860-594-0259
Web: www.arrl.org/arrlf/scholgen.html

Dr. James L. Lawson Memorial Scholarship

Type of award: Scholarship.
Intended use: For undergraduate or graduate study at accredited postsecondary institution. Designated institutions: New England and New York postsecondary institutions.
Eligibility: Applicant must be residing in Connecticut, Massachusetts, Maine, New Hampshire, Rhode Island, New York or Vermont.
Basis for selection: Competition/talent/interest in amateur radio. Major/career interest in communications or electronics. Applicant must demonstrate financial need.
Application requirements: Recommendations, transcript.
Additional information: Must be amateur radio operator holding general license. Application may be obtained on Website.

　Amount of award:　$500
　Number of awards:　1
　Application deadline:　February 1
　Total amount awarded:　$500
Contact:
ARRL Foundation Inc./Scholarship Program
225 Main Street
Newington, CT 06111
Phone: 860-594-0200
Fax: 860-594-0259
Web: www.arrl.org/arrlf/scholgen.html

Edmond A. Metzger Scholarship

Type of award: Scholarship.
Intended use: For undergraduate, graduate or non-degree study at accredited postsecondary institution. Designated institutions: Illinois, Indiana, Wisconsin postsecondary institutions.
Eligibility: Applicant or parent must be member/participant of American Radio Relay League. Applicant must be residing in Illinois, Indiana or Wisconsin.
Basis for selection: Competition/talent/interest in amateur radio. Major/career interest in engineering, electrical/electronic. Applicant must demonstrate financial need.
Application requirements: Recommendations, transcript, proof of eligibility.
Additional information: Must be amateur radio operator with novice license. Application may be obtained on Website.

　Amount of award:　$500
　Number of awards:　1
　Application deadline:　February 1
　Total amount awarded:　$500

Contact:
ARRL Foundation Inc./Scholarship Program
225 Main Street
Newington, CT 06111
Phone: 860-594-0200
Fax: 860-594-0259
Web: www.arrl.org/arrlf/scholgen.html

Fred R. McDaniel Memorial Scholarship

Type of award: Scholarship.
Intended use: For undergraduate or graduate study at accredited postsecondary institution in United States. Designated institutions: Institutions in Arkansas, Louisiana, Mississippi, New Mexico, Oklahoma, and Texas.
Eligibility: Applicant must be residing in New Mexico, Oklahoma, Texas, Louisiana, Mississippi or Arkansas.
Basis for selection: Competition/talent/interest in amateur radio. Major/career interest in electronics; communications or engineering, electrical/electronic. Applicant must demonstrate financial need.
Application requirements: Recommendations, transcript.
Additional information: Preference to students with 3.0 GPA. Must be amateur radio operator holding general license. Application may be obtained on Website.

　Amount of award:　$500
　Number of awards:　1
　Application deadline:　February 1
　Total amount awarded:　$500
Contact:
ARRL Foundation Inc./Scholarship Program
225 Main Street
Newington, CT 06111
Phone: 860-594-0200
Fax: 860-594-0259
Web: www.arrl.org/arrlf/scholgen.html

The General Fund Scholarships

Type of award: Scholarship.
Intended use: For undergraduate or graduate study at accredited postsecondary institution in United States.
Basis for selection: Competition/talent/interest in amateur radio. Applicant must demonstrate financial need.
Application requirements: Recommendations, transcript.
Additional information: Must be amateur radio operator holding any class license. Number of awards varies. Application may be obtained on Website.

　Amount of award:　$1,000
　Application deadline:　February 1
Contact:
ARRL Foundation Inc./Scholarship Program
225 Main Street
Newington, CT 06111
Phone: 860-594-0200
Fax: 860-594-0259
Web: www.arrl.org/arrlf/scholgen.html

Irving W. Cook WAOCGS Scholarship

Type of award: Scholarship.
Intended use: For undergraduate or graduate study at accredited postsecondary institution in United States.
Eligibility: Applicant must be residing in Kansas.

Basis for selection: Competition/talent/interest in amateur radio. Major/career interest in communications; electronics or engineering, electrical/electronic. Applicant must demonstrate financial need.

Application requirements: Recommendations, transcript.

Additional information: Must be amateur radio operator holding any class license. Application may be obtained on Website.

Amount of award:	$1,000
Number of awards:	1
Application deadline:	February 1
Total amount awarded:	$1,000

Contact:
ARRL Foundation Inc./Scholarship Program
225 Main Street
Newington, CT 06111
Phone: 860-594-0200
Fax: 860-594-0259
Web: www.arrl.org/arrlf/scholgen.html

K2TEO Martin J. Green, Sr. Memorial Scholarship

Type of award: Scholarship.

Intended use: For undergraduate or graduate study at accredited postsecondary institution in United States.

Basis for selection: Competition/talent/interest in amateur radio. Applicant must demonstrate financial need.

Application requirements: Recommendations, transcript.

Additional information: Must be amateur radio operator with general license. Preference given to student ham from family of ham operators. Application may be obtained on Website.

Amount of award:	$1,000
Number of awards:	1
Application deadline:	February 1
Total amount awarded:	$1,000

Contact:
ARRL Foundation Inc./Scholarship Program
225 Main Street
Newington, CT 06111
Phone: 860-594-0200
Fax: 860-594-0259
Web: www.arrl.org/arrlf/scholgen.html

L. Phil Wicker Scholarship

Type of award: Scholarship.

Intended use: For undergraduate, graduate or non-degree study at accredited postsecondary institution. Designated institutions: Institutions in North Carolina, South Carolina, Virginia, West Virginia.

Eligibility: Applicant must be residing in Virginia, West Virginia, North Carolina or South Carolina.

Basis for selection: Competition/talent/interest in amateur radio. Major/career interest in communications; electronics or engineering, electrical/electronic. Applicant must demonstrate financial need.

Application requirements: Recommendations, transcript.

Additional information: Must be amateur radio operator holding general license. Preference to bachelor's or higher degree. Application may be obtained on Website.

Amount of award:	$1,000
Number of awards:	1
Application deadline:	February 1
Total amount awarded:	$1,000

Contact:
ARRL Foundation Inc./Scholarship Program
225 Main Street
Newington, CT 06111
Phone: 860-594-0200
Fax: 860-594-0259
Web: www.arrl.org/arrlf/scholgen.html

Mary Lou Brown Scholarship

Type of award: Scholarship.

Intended use: For undergraduate or graduate study at accredited postsecondary institution in United States.

Eligibility: Applicant must be residing in Idaho, Montana, Alaska, Oregon or Washington.

Basis for selection: Competition/talent/interest in amateur radio. Applicant must demonstrate financial need.

Application requirements: Recommendations, transcript.

Additional information: Minimum 3.0 GPA. Must be amateur radio operator with general license. Application may be obtained on Website.

Amount of award:	$2,500
Application deadline:	February 1

Contact:
ARRL Foundation Inc./Scholarship Program
225 Main Street
Newington, CT 06111
Phone: 860-594-0200
Fax: 860-594-0259
Web: www.arrl.org/arrlf/scholgen.html

The Mississippi Scholarship

Type of award: Scholarship.

Intended use: For undergraduate or graduate study at accredited 4-year or graduate institution. Designated institutions: Postseconday institutions in Mississippi.

Eligibility: Applicant must be no older than 30. Applicant must be residing in Mississippi.

Basis for selection: Competition/talent/interest in amateur radio. Major/career interest in communications; electronics or engineering, electrical/electronic. Applicant must demonstrate financial need.

Application requirements: Recommendations, transcript, proof of eligibility.

Additional information: Must be amateur radio operator with any class license. Application may be obtained on Website.

Amount of award:	$500
Number of awards:	1
Application deadline:	February 1
Total amount awarded:	$500

Contact:
ARRL Foundation Inc./Scholarship Program
225 Main Street
Newington, CT 06111
Phone: 860-594-0200
Fax: 860-594-0259
Web: www.arrl.org/arrlf/scholgen.html

New England Femara Scholarship

Type of award: Scholarship.

Intended use: For undergraduate, graduate or non-degree study at accredited postsecondary institution in United States.

Eligibility: Applicant must be residing in Connecticut, Massachusetts, Maine, New Hampshire, Rhode Island or Vermont.

Basis for selection: Competition/talent/interest in amateur radio. Applicant must demonstrate financial need.
Application requirements: Recommendations, transcript.
Additional information: Must be amateur radio operator holding technician license. Number of awards varies. Application may be obtained on Website.

Amount of award:	$600
Number of awards:	8
Application deadline:	February 1

Contact:
ARRL Foundation Inc./Scholarship Program
225 Main Street
Newington, CT 06111
Phone: 860-594-0200
Fax: 860-594-0259
Web: www.arrl.org/arrlf/scholgen.html

Paul and Helen L. Grauer Scholarship

Type of award: Scholarship.
Intended use: For undergraduate or graduate study at accredited postsecondary institution in United States. Designated institutions: Postsecondary institutions in Iowa, Kansas, Missouri and Nebraska.
Eligibility: Applicant must be residing in Missouri, Nebraska, Iowa or Kansas.
Basis for selection: Competition/talent/interest in amateur radio. Major/career interest in communications or electronics. Applicant must demonstrate financial need.
Application requirements: Recommendations, transcript.
Additional information: Must be amateur radio operator with novice license. Application may be obtained on Website.

Amount of award:	$1,000
Number of awards:	1
Application deadline:	February 1
Total amount awarded:	$1,000

Contact:
ARRL Foundation Inc./Scholarship Program
225 Main Street
Newington, CT 06111
Phone: 860-594-0200
Fax: 860-594-0259
Web: www.arrl.org/arrlf/scholgen.html

The PHD ARA Scholarship

Type of award: Scholarship.
Intended use: For undergraduate, graduate or non-degree study at accredited postsecondary institution in United States.
Eligibility: Applicant must be residing in Missouri, Nebraska, Iowa or Kansas.
Basis for selection: Competition/talent/interest in amateur radio. Major/career interest in journalism; computer/information sciences or engineering, electrical/electronic. Applicant must demonstrate financial need.
Application requirements: Recommendations, transcript.
Additional information: Must be amateur radio operator holding any class license. May be child of deceased radio amateur. Application may be obtained on Website.

Amount of award:	$1,000
Number of awards:	1
Application deadline:	February 1
Total amount awarded:	$1,000

Contact:
ARRL Foundation Inc./Scholarship Program
225 Main Street
Newington, CT 06111
Phone: 860-594-0200
Fax: 860-594-0259
Web: www.arrl.org/arrlf/scholgen.html

Six Meter Club of Chicago Scholarship

Type of award: Scholarship.
Intended use: For undergraduate study at accredited vocational, 2-year or 4-year institution in United States. Designated institutions: Postsecondary institutions in Illinois.
Eligibility: Applicant must be residing in Illinois.
Basis for selection: Competition/talent/interest in amateur radio. Applicant must demonstrate financial need.
Application requirements: Recommendations, transcript.
Additional information: Must be amateur radio operator holding any class license. Award open to remaining ARRL Central Division (Indiana, Wisconsin) if no qualified Illinois student identified. Application may be obtained on Website.

Amount of award:	$500
Number of awards:	1
Application deadline:	February 1
Total amount awarded:	$500

Contact:
ARRL Foundation Inc./Scholarship Program
225 Main Street
Newington, CT 06111
Phone: 860-594-0200
Fax: 860-594-0259
Web: www.arrl.org/arrlf/scholgen.html

Tom and Judith Comstock Scholarship

Type of award: Scholarship.
Intended use: For undergraduate study at accredited 2-year or 4-year institution in United States.
Eligibility: Applicant must be high school senior. Applicant must be residing in Oklahoma or Texas.
Basis for selection: Competition/talent/interest in amateur radio. Applicant must demonstrate financial need.
Application requirements: Recommendations, transcript.
Additional information: Must be amateur radio operator holding any class license. Application may be obtained on Website.

Amount of award:	$1,000
Number of awards:	1
Application deadline:	February 1
Total amount awarded:	$1,000

Contact:
ARRL Foundation Inc./Scholarship Program
225 Main Street
Newington, CT 06111
Phone: 860-594-0200
Fax: 860-594-0259
Web: www.arrl.org/arrlf/scholgen.html

"You've Got a Friend in Pennsylvania" Scholarship

Type of award: Scholarship.

Intended use: For undergraduate, graduate or non-degree study at accredited postsecondary institution. Designated institutions: Pennsylvania postsecondary institutions.
Eligibility: Applicant or parent must be member/participant of American Radio Relay League.
Basis for selection: Competition/talent/interest in amateur radio. Applicant must demonstrate financial need.
Application requirements: Recommendations, transcript, proof of eligibility.
Additional information: Must be amateur radio operator with general license. Application may be obtained from Website.

Amount of award:	$1,000
Number of awards:	1
Application deadline:	February 1
Total amount awarded:	$1,000

Contact:
ARRL Foundation Inc./Scholarship Program
225 Main Street
Newington, CT 06111
Phone: 860-594-0200
Fax: 860-594-0259
Web: www.arrl.org/arrlf/scholgen.html

American Respiratory Care Foundation

J.A. Young Memorial Education Recognition Award

Type of award: Scholarship, renewable.
Intended use: For sophomore, junior or senior study at accredited vocational, 2-year or 4-year institution.
Eligibility: Applicant must be Alaskan native, Asian American, African American, Mexican American, Hispanic American, Puerto Rican or American Indian.
Basis for selection: Major/career interest in respiratory therapy. Applicant must demonstrate high academic achievement, seriousness of purpose and service orientation.
Application requirements: Recommendations, essay, transcript, proof of eligibility by school or program representative. Minimum 3.0 GPA required.
Additional information: Must have completed at least one semester in accredited respiratory care program. Preference will be given to minority applicants. If nomination cannot be obtained, student may request foundation sponsorship. Foundation prefers nominations made by representative of applicant's school or accredited respiratory training program; however, any student may initiate application.

Amount of award:	$1,000
Number of awards:	1
Number of applicants:	50
Application deadline:	May 31
Notification begins:	August 1
Total amount awarded:	$1,000

Contact:
American Respiratory Care Foundation
11030 Ables Lane
Dallas, TX 75229-4593
Phone: 972-243-2272
Web: www.aarc.org

M.B. Duggan, Jr., Memorial Education Recognition Award

Type of award: Scholarship, renewable.
Intended use: For sophomore, junior or senior study at accredited 2-year or 4-year institution in United States.
Basis for selection: Major/career interest in respiratory therapy. Applicant must demonstrate high academic achievement, depth of character, seriousness of purpose and service orientation.
Application requirements: Recommendations, essay, transcript, proof of eligibility. Minimum 3.0 GPA required.
Additional information: Preference given to Georgia and South Carolina applicants. Must have at least one semester in Commission on Accreditation of Allied Health Education Programs-approved respiratory care program.

Amount of award:	$1,000
Number of awards:	1
Number of applicants:	50
Application deadline:	May 31
Notification begins:	August 1

Contact:
American Respiratory Care Foundation
11030 Ables Lane
Dallas, TX 75229-4593
Phone: 972-243-2272
Web: www.aarc.org

R.M. Lawrence Education Recognition Award

Type of award: Scholarship.
Intended use: For full-time junior or senior study at accredited 4-year institution in United States.
Basis for selection: Major/career interest in respiratory therapy. Applicant must demonstrate high academic achievement.
Application requirements: Recommendations, essay, transcript, proof of eligibility. Minimum 3.0 GPA required.
Additional information: Must provide letter verifying enrollment in Commission on Accreditation of Allied Health Education Programs-approved respiratory care program leading to Baccalaureate degree.

Amount of award:	$2,500
Number of awards:	1
Number of applicants:	50
Application deadline:	May 31
Notification begins:	August 1

Contact:
American Respiratory Care Foundation
11030 Ables Lane
Dallas, TX 75229-4593
Phone: 972-243-2272
Web: www.aarc.org

W.M. Burgin, Jr., Scholarship

Type of award: Scholarship.
Intended use: For full-time sophomore study at accredited 2-year institution in United States.
Basis for selection: Major/career interest in respiratory therapy. Applicant must demonstrate high academic achievement.
Application requirements: Recommendations, essay, transcript, proof of eligibility by school or educational program. Minimum 3.0 GPA required.

Scholarships

Additional information: Letter verifying enrollment in a Commission on Accreditation of Allied Health Education Programs-accredited program required. Applicants unable to obtain nomination may apply directly.

Amount of award:	$2,500
Number of awards:	1
Number of applicants:	10
Application deadline:	May 31
Notification begins:	August 1

Contact:
American Respiratory Care Foundation
11030 Ables Lane
Dallas, TX 75229-4593
Phone: 972-243-2272
Web: www.aarc.org

American School Food Service Foundation

ASFSA Lincoln Food Service Research Grant

Type of award: Research grant.
Intended use: For non-degree study at postsecondary institution.
Eligibility: Applicant or parent must be member/participant of American School Food Service Foundation.
Basis for selection: Major/career interest in dietetics/nutrition or food production/management/services. Applicant must demonstrate high academic achievement and seriousness of purpose.
Application requirements: Proof of eligibility, research proposal. Letter of support.
Additional information: Must be active member of ASFSA or be supervised on grant by active ASFSA member. Level of study is nonacademic research (no need to be enrolled in master's program). Research must be applicable to child nutrition and must support ASFSA grant program mission.

Amount of award:	$2,500
Number of awards:	1
Application deadline:	April 30
Notification begins:	August 15
Total amount awarded:	$2,500

Contact:
ASFSA Grant Coordinator
700 S. Washington St.
Suite 300
Alexandria, VA 22314
Phone: 800-877-8822 ext. 146

ASFSA Tony's Food Service Scholarship

Type of award: Scholarship, renewable.
Intended use: For undergraduate or graduate study at accredited postsecondary institution.
Eligibility: Applicant or parent must be member/participant of American School Food Service Foundation.
Basis for selection: Major/career interest in food production/management/services; dietetics/nutrition; food science/technology or culinary arts. Applicant must demonstrate high academic achievement, leadership, seriousness of purpose and service orientation.

Application requirements: Essay, transcript, proof of eligibility. Course description, two recommendations.
Additional information: Distance learning is accepted for correspondence courses. Must major or intend to pursue career in school food service or child nutrition. Applicant or parent must be current, active ASFSA member for at least one year. Scholarships are primarily for undergraduates; occasionally awarded to graduate students. Vocational and junior colleges accepted.

Amount of award:	$100-$1,000
Number of awards:	80
Application deadline:	April 15
Notification begins:	May 30
Total amount awarded:	$79,000

Contact:
ASFSA Scholarship Coordinator
700 S. Washington St.
Suite 300
Alexandria, VA 22314
Phone: 800-877-8822 ext. 146.

American Society for Enology and Viticulture

Enology and Viticulture Scholarship

Type of award: Scholarship, renewable.
Intended use: For full-time junior, senior, master's or doctoral study at accredited 4-year or graduate institution.
Eligibility: Applicant must be U.S. citizen, permanent resident, international student or Canadian or Mexican citizen.
Basis for selection: Major/career interest in agriculture; chemistry; food science/technology or horticulture. Applicant must demonstrate financial need and high academic achievement.
Application requirements: Recommendations, essay, transcript, proof of eligibility. Minimum 3.0 GPA for undergraduate, 3.2 GPA for graduate students. Applications will be considered complete upon receipt of following items by March 1 deadline: completed student questionnaire, written statement of intent relating to future career in wine or grape industry, interests in wine or grape industry or in related research.
Additional information: All completed forms, letters, and transcripts must be received by Scholarship Committee by March 1 for consideration for award for following scholastic year. All information (application, transcripts, and letters of recommendation) must be received together: do not have transcripts and letters sent separately. Incomplete application packets will not be considered. Applicants must be enrolled in a major or in graduate group emphasizing enology or viticulture or in curriculum emphasizing science basic to wine and grape industry. Student's financial needs and income will be considered. Awards may vary from year to year. Previous applicants and recipients eligible to reapply each year in open competition with new applicants.

Amount of award:	$500-$3,000
Number of awards:	36
Application deadline:	March 1
Notification begins:	May 31
Total amount awarded:	$45,000

Contact:
American Society for Enology and Viticulture
P.O. Box 1855
Davis, CA 95617-1855
Web: www.asev.org

American Society for Microbiology

ASM Minority Undergraduate Research Fellowship

Type of award: Research grant.
Intended use: For undergraduate study at 4-year institution.
Eligibility: Applicant must be Alaskan native, African American, Mexican American, Puerto Rican or American Indian. Applicant must be U.S. citizen or permanent resident.
Basis for selection: Major/career interest in microbiology or biology. Applicant must demonstrate high academic achievement, leadership and seriousness of purpose.
Application requirements: Recommendations, transcript. Six collated, stapled copies of application. Transcipt and recommendations must be sealed.
Additional information: Pacific Islanders also eligible. Fellowship lasts two to three months with stipend of $2,500. In addition to stipend, award covers travel and housing expenses and one-year membership in American Society for Microbiology. Student will pursue project directed by scientist in research lab. Must be majoring in fields of study indicated. Application available on Website.

Amount of award:	$2,500
Number of awards:	6
Application deadline:	February 1

Contact:
American Society for Microbiology Minority Undergraduate Fellowship
Education Department
1752 N Street NW
Washington, DC 20036
Phone: 202-942-9283
Fax: 202-942-9329
Web: www.asmusa.org/edusrc/edu23a.htm

ASM/Undergraduate Research Fellowship

Type of award: Research grant.
Intended use: For full-time undergraduate study at 4-year institution.
Eligibility: Applicant must be U.S. citizen or permanent resident.
Basis for selection: Major/career interest in microbiology. Applicant must demonstrate high academic achievement and seriousness of purpose.
Application requirements: Nomination by faculty member who is ASM member. Program requires joint application from both student applicant and nominating faculty member.
Additional information: Award for three to six months. Students conduct research in summer (or longer) and present results at ASM General Meeting following year. Funding for supplies and travel support to ASM General Meeting available. Must have ASM member at institution willing to serve as mentor. Student may not be receiving financial support from any other scientific organization during fellowship. Must have successful achievement in previous research experience. Project must be endorsed by faculty member's department head or dean.

Amount of award:	$2,500
Number of awards:	20
Application deadline:	February 1

Contact:
American Society for Microbiology, URF Program
Education Department
1752 N Street NW
Washington, DC 20036
Phone: 202-942-9283
Fax: 202-942-9329
Web: www.asmusa.org/edusrc/edu23a.htm

American Society of Civil Engineers

B. Charles Tiney Memorial ASCE Student Chapter Scholarship

Type of award: Scholarship, renewable.
Intended use: For undergraduate study at accredited postsecondary institution.
Eligibility: Applicant or parent must be member/participant of American Society of Civil Engineers.
Basis for selection: Major/career interest in engineering, civil. Applicant must demonstrate financial need, high academic achievement, depth of character and leadership.
Application requirements: Recommendations, essay, transcript, proof of eligibility. Completed application form. One-page resume. Detailed financial statement indicating how scholarship will finance applicant's education.
Additional information: Any undergraduate who is ASCE National Student Member may apply for this scholarship but must be member in good standing at time of application. Membership applications may be submitted with scholarship application. It is anticipated scholarship funds will be used for tuition expenses. Visit Website for additional information and to download application.

Amount of award:	$2,000
Number of awards:	12
Application deadline:	February 9

Contact:
American Society of Civil Engineers
Attention: Student Services
1801 Alexander Bell Drive
Reston, VA 20191-4440
Phone: 800-548-ASCE
Web: www.asce.org/students

Freeman Fellowship

Type of award: Research grant.
Intended use: For undergraduate or graduate study in or outside United States or Canada.
Eligibility: Applicant or parent must be member/participant of American Society of Civil Engineers.
Basis for selection: Major/career interest in engineering, civil.
Application requirements: Recommendations, essay, transcript, research proposal. One-two page resume. Detailed financial statement indicating how fellowship will finance

applicant's research. Statement from institution where research will be conducted.

Additional information: Grants are made toward expenses for experiments, observations and compilations to discover new and accurate data that will be useful in engineering. Grant may be in form of prize for most useful paper relating to science/art of hydraulic construction. Travel scholarships available to ASCE members under 45, in recognition of achievement or promise. Award is to be used for expenses for research and experiments. Visit Website for additional information and to download application.

Amount of award:	$2,000-$5,000
Application deadline:	February 9

Contact:
American Society of Engineers
Attention: Student Services
1801 Alexander Bell Drive
Reston, VA 20191-4400
Phone: 800-548-ASCE
Web: www.asce.org

Samuel Fletcher Tapman ASCE Student Chapter Scholarship

Type of award: Scholarship, renewable.
Intended use: For undergraduate study at accredited postsecondary institution.
Eligibility: Applicant or parent must be member/participant of American Society of Civil Engineers.
Basis for selection: Major/career interest in engineering, civil. Applicant must demonstrate financial need, high academic achievement, depth of character and leadership.
Application requirements: Recommendations, essay, transcript, proof of eligibility. One-page resume. Detailed financial statement indicating how scholarship will finance applicant's education.
Additional information: Any undergraduate who is ASCE National Student Member may apply for this scholarship but must be member in good standing at time of application. Membership applications may be submitted with scholarship application. It is anticipated scholarship funds will be used for tuition expenses. Visit Website for additional information and to download application.

Amount of award:	$2,000
Number of awards:	12
Application deadline:	February 9

Contact:
American Society of Civil Engineers
Attention: Student Services
1801 Alexander Bell Drive
Reston, VA 20191-4440
Phone: 800-548-ASCE
Web: www.asce.org/students

American Society of Heating/Refrigeration/Air-Conditioning Engineers, Inc.

A.S.H.R.A.E. Reuben Trane Scholarship

Type of award: Scholarship.
Intended use: For junior or senior study at accredited 4-year institution. Designated institutions: ABET-accredited schools with engineering technology program.
Basis for selection: Major/career interest in engineering or air conditioning/heating/refrigeration technology. Applicant must demonstrate financial need, high academic achievement, depth of character and leadership.
Application requirements: Recommendations, transcript.
Additional information: Minimum 3.0 GPA. Curriculum must be accredited by Accreditation Board for Engineering and Technology. Award is per year for two years, for students with two years of undergraduate studies remaining.

Amount of award:	$10,000
Number of awards:	4
Application deadline:	December 1
Total amount awarded:	$40,000

Contact:
Amer. Soc. of Heating/Refrigeration/Air-Conditioning Engineers, Inc.
1791 Tullie Circle NE
Atlanta, GA 30329
Phone: 404-636-8400
Fax: 404-321-5478
Web: www.ashrae.org

A.S.H.R.A.E. Undergraduate Scholarships

Type of award: Scholarship, renewable.
Intended use: For full-time junior or senior study. Designated institutions: ABET-accredited schools with engineering technology program.
Basis for selection: Major/career interest in air conditioning/heating/refrigeration technology or engineering. Applicant must demonstrate financial need, high academic achievement, depth of character and leadership.
Application requirements: Recommendations, transcript.
Additional information: Must have at least 3.0 GPA. Curriculum must be accredited by Accreditation Board for Engineering and Technology. Must be currently enrolled full-time with at least one full year of studies remaining. Must pursue career in Heating/Ventilation/Air Conditioning (HVAC) and refrigeration.

Amount of award:	$3,000
Number of awards:	6
Application deadline:	December 1
Total amount awarded:	$18,000

Scholarships

Contact:
Amer. Soc. of Heating/Refrigeration/Air-Conditioning
Engineers, Inc.
1791 Tullie Circle NE
Atlanta, GA 30329
Phone: 404-636-8400
Fax: 404-321-5478
Web: www.ashrae.org

Heating/Refrigeration/Air-Conditioning Engineering Technology Scholarship

Type of award: Scholarship, renewable.
Intended use: For full-time undergraduate study at accredited
2-year or 4-year institution.
Basis for selection: Major/career interest in engineering or air
conditioning/heating/refrigeration technology. Applicant must
demonstrate financial need, high academic achievement, depth
of character and leadership.
Application requirements: Recommendations, transcript.
Minimum 3.0 GPA.
Additional information: For those seeking associate's degree
in engineering technology. Curriculum must be accredited by
Accreditation Board for Engineering and Technology and
student must be working toward four-year bachelor's degree in
Engineering Technology. Must intend to pursue career in
Heating/Ventilation/Air Conditioning (HVAC) and/or
Refrigeration fields.

Amount of award:	$3,000
Number of awards:	2
Application deadline:	May 1
Total amount awarded:	$6,000

Contact:
Amer. Soc. of Heating/Refrigeration/Air-Conditioning
Engineers, Inc.
Scholarship Program
1791 Tullie Circle NE
Atlanta, GA 30329
Phone: 404-942-8400
Fax: 404-321-5478
Web: www.ashrae.org

American Society of Interior Designers Educational Foundation

Joel Polsky Academic Acheivement Award

Type of award: Scholarship.
Intended use: For undergraduate or graduate study.
Basis for selection: Competition/talent/interest in writing/
journalism, based on graphic presentation, content,
comprehensive coverage of topic, innovative subject matter,
bibliography, and references. Major/career interest in interior
design or architecture. Applicant must demonstrate high
academic achievement.
Additional information: Mainly for upperclassmen/women
and graduate students. Award to recognize outstanding interior
design research or thesis project. Papers should address such

topics as Educational Research, Behavioral Sciences, Business
Practices, Design Process, Theory, or other technical subjects.

Amount of award:	$1,000
Number of awards:	1
Application deadline:	March 9
Total amount awarded:	$1,000

Contact:
American Society of Interior Designers Educational Foundation
608 Massachusetts Avenue, NE
Washington, DC 20002-6006
Phone: 202-546-3480
Fax: 202-546-3240
Web: www.asid.org

Joel Polsky Prize

Type of award: Scholarship.
Intended use: For non-degree study.
Basis for selection: Competition/talent/interest in engineering/
architecture, based on graphic presentation, content,
comprehensive coverage of topic, innovative subject matter,
bibliography, and references. Major/career interest in interior
design.
Additional information: Award to recognize outstanding
contributions to the discipline of interior design through
literature or visual communication. Entries should address need
of public designers and students on such topics as Educational
Research, Behavioral Sciences, Business Practice, Design
Process, Theory, or other technical subjects.

Amount of award:	$1,000
Number of awards:	1
Application deadline:	March 9
Total amount awarded:	$1,000

Contact:
American Society of Interior Designers Educational Foundation
608 Massachusetts Avenue, NE
Washington, DC 20002-6006
Phone: 202-546-3480
Fax: 202-546-3240
Web: www.asid.org

S. Harris Memorial Interior Design Scholarship

Type of award: Scholarship.
Intended use: For sophomore, junior or senior study.
Basis for selection: Major/career interest in interior design.
Applicant must demonstrate financial need and high academic
achievement.
Application requirements: Recommendations, essay,
transcript. SASE.
Additional information: Notification begins in Spring.

Amount of award:	$1,500
Number of awards:	1
Application deadline:	March 9
Total amount awarded:	$1,500

Contact:
American Society of Interior Designers Educational Foundation
608 Massachusetts Avenue, NE
Washington, DC 20002-6006
Web: www.asid.org

Yale R. Burge Interior Design Competition

Type of award: Scholarship.
Intended use: For senior study.

Basis for selection: Competition/talent/interest in visual arts, based on quality of portfolio: presentation, design and planning, conceptual creativity. Major/career interest in interior design or architecture.

Application requirements: $10 application fee. Portfolio. Portfolio components submitted on slides.

Additional information: Entries must be postmarked by March 10. Award amounts varies; please contact sponsor for slide submission guidelines and application form.

Amount of award:	$250-$500
Application deadline:	March 10

Contact:
American Society of Interior Designers Educational Foundation
608 Massachusetts Avenue, NE
Washington, DC 20002-6006
Phone: 202-546-3480
Web: www.asid.org

American Society of Mechanical Engineers

American Society of Mechanical Engineers Foundation Scholarship

Type of award: Scholarship.

Intended use: For full-time undergraduate study at accredited 4-year or graduate institution.

Eligibility: Applicant or parent must be member/participant of American Society of Mechanical Engineers.

Basis for selection: Major/career interest in engineering, mechanical. Applicant must demonstrate high academic achievement, depth of character and leadership.

Application requirements: Recommendations, essay, transcript. Application must be endorsed by department head.

Additional information: Applicant must be student member of ASME, enrolled in mechanical engineering or related field.

Amount of award:	$1,500
Number of awards:	17
Application deadline:	March 15
Notification begins:	June 15
Total amount awarded:	$25,500

Contact:
American Society of Mechanical Engineers
Three Park Avenue
New York, NY 10016-5990
Phone: 212-591-8131
Fax: 212-591-7143
Web: www.asme.org/educate/aid/

ASME/FIRST Scholarship

Type of award: Scholarship.

Intended use: For full-time freshman study at accredited 4-year institution. Designated institutions: Schools with ABET-accredited program.

Eligibility: Applicant must be high school senior. Applicant must be U.S. citizen.

Basis for selection: Major/career interest in engineering, mechanical. Applicant must demonstrate financial need, high academic achievement and leadership.

Application requirements: Transcript, proof of eligibility, nomination by ASME member or student member active with FIRST. Completed nomination materials.

Additional information: Applicant must be active on FIRST team. Students on same team must be nominated by separate ASME members. Applicant may also enroll in mechanical engineering technology program. Recipient announced at FIRST National Championship. Visit Website for more information and to download forms.

Amount of award:	$5,000
Number of awards:	1
Application deadline:	March 1
Total amount awarded:	$5,000

Contact:
American Society of Mechanical Engineers
Three Park Avenue
New York, NY 10016-5990
Phone: 212-591-8131
Fax: 212-591-7143
Web: www.asme.org/educate/aid

F.W. "Beich" Beichley Scholarship

Type of award: Scholarship.

Intended use: For full-time undergraduate study.

Eligibility: Applicant or parent must be member/participant of American Society of Mechanical Engineers.

Basis for selection: Major/career interest in engineering, mechanical. Applicant must demonstrate financial need, high academic achievement, depth of character and leadership.

Application requirements: Recommendations, essay, transcript. Application must be endorsed by department head.

Additional information: Applicant must be member of ASME.

Amount of award:	$2,000
Number of awards:	1
Application deadline:	March 15
Notification begins:	June 15
Total amount awarded:	$2,000

Contact:
American Society of Mechanical Engineers
Three Park Avenue
New York, NY 10016-5990
Phone: 212-591-8131
Fax: 212-591-7143
Web: www.asme.org/educate/aid

Frank William and Dorothy Given Miller Mechanical Engineering Scholarship

Type of award: Scholarship.

Intended use: For full-time junior or senior study at accredited 4-year institution. Designated institutions: Designated institutions: schools with ABET-accredited program.

Eligibility: Applicant or parent must be member/participant of American Society of Mechanical Engineers. Applicant must be U.S. citizen.

Basis for selection: Major/career interest in engineering, mechanical. Applicant must demonstrate high academic achievement, depth of character and leadership.

Application requirements: Recommendations, essay, transcript. Application must be endorsed by department head. Applicant must be North American resident.

Additional information: Applicant must be member of ASME.

Amount of award: $2,000
Number of awards: 2
Application deadline: March 15
Notification begins: June 15
Total amount awarded: $4,000
Contact:
American Society of Mechanical Engineers
Three Park Avenue
New York, NY 10016-5990
Phone: 212-591-8131
Fax: 212-591-7143
Web: www.asme.org/educate/aid

Garland Duncan Mechanical Engineering Scholarship

Type of award: Scholarship.
Intended use: For full-time junior or senior study at accredited 4-year institution. Designated institutions: Schools with ABET-accredited program.
Eligibility: Applicant or parent must be member/participant of American Society of Mechanical Engineers.
Basis for selection: Major/career interest in engineering, mechanical. Applicant must demonstrate financial need, high academic achievement, depth of character and leadership.
Application requirements: Recommendations, essay, transcript. Application must be endorsed by department head.
Additional information: Applicant must be member of ASME.

Amount of award: $3,000
Number of awards: 3
Application deadline: March 15
Notification begins: June 15
Total amount awarded: $9,000
Contact:
American Society of Mechanical Engineers
Attn: Theresa Oluwanifise
Three Park Avenue
New York, NY 10016-5990
Phone: 212-591-8131
Fax: 212-591-7143
Web: www.asme.org/educate/aid

John and Elsa Gracik Mechanical Engineering Scholarship

Type of award: Scholarship.
Intended use: For full-time undergraduate study at accredited 4-year institution. Designated institutions: Schools with ABET-accredited program.
Eligibility: Applicant or parent must be member/participant of American Society of Mechanical Engineers. Applicant must be U.S. citizen.
Basis for selection: Major/career interest in engineering, mechanical. Applicant must demonstrate financial need, high academic achievement, depth of character and leadership.
Application requirements: Recommendations, essay, transcript, nomination by by department head.
Additional information: Applicant must be member of ASME.

Amount of award: $1,500
Number of awards: 17
Application deadline: March 15
Notification begins: June 15
Total amount awarded: $25,500

Contact:
American Society of Mechanical Engineers
Attn: Theresa Oluwanifise
Three Park Avenue
New York, NY 10016-5990
Phone: 212-591-8131
Fax: 212-591-7143
Web: www.asme.org/educate/aid

Kenneth Andrew Roe Mechanical Engineering Scholarship

Type of award: Scholarship.
Intended use: For full-time junior or senior study at accredited 4-year institution. Designated institutions: Schools with ABET-accredited program or one that is substantially equivalent.
Eligibility: Applicant or parent must be member/participant of American Society of Mechanical Engineers. Applicant must be U.S. citizen, permanent resident, international student, other North American (Canada or Mexico) resident.
Basis for selection: Major/career interest in engineering, mechanical. Applicant must demonstrate financial need, high academic achievement, depth of character and leadership.
Application requirements: Recommendations, essay, transcript. Application must be endorsed by department head.
Additional information: Applicant must be member of ASME.

Amount of award: $9,000
Number of awards: 1
Application deadline: March 15
Notification begins: June 15
Total amount awarded: $9,000
Contact:
American Society of Mechanical Engineers
Three Park Avenue
New York, NY 10016-5990
Phone: 212-591-8131
Fax: 212-591-7143
Web: www.asme.org/educate/aid

Melvin R. Green Scholarship

Type of award: Scholarship.
Intended use: For full-time junior or senior study at accredited 4-year institution. Designated institutions: Schools with ABET-accredited program.
Eligibility: Applicant or parent must be member/participant of American Society of Mechanical Engineers.
Basis for selection: Major/career interest in engineering, mechanical. Applicant must demonstrate high academic achievement, depth of character and leadership.
Application requirements: Recommendations, essay, transcript. Application must be endorsed by department head.
Additional information: Applicant must be student member of ASME.

Amount of award: $3,500
Number of awards: 2
Application deadline: March 15
Notification begins: June 15
Total amount awarded: $7,000
Contact:
American Society of Mechanical Engineers
Three Park Avenue
New York, NY 10016-5990
Phone: 212-591-8131
Fax: 212-591-7143
Web: www.asme.org/educate/aid

W.J. and M.E. Adams, Jr., Mechanical Engineering Scholarship

Type of award: Scholarship.
Intended use: For full-time undergraduate study in United States. Designated institutions: Schools in ASME region IX (California, Nevada, Hawaii).
Eligibility: Applicant or parent must be member/participant of American Society of Mechanical Engineers.
Basis for selection: Major/career interest in engineering, mechanical. Applicant must demonstrate financial need, high academic achievement, depth of character and leadership.
Application requirements: Recommendations, essay, transcript. Minimum 2.5 GPA. Application must be endorsed by department head.
Additional information: Applicant must be member of ASME. Award designated for student with special interest in product development and design.

Amount of award:	$2,000
Number of awards:	1
Application deadline:	March 15
Notification begins:	June 15
Total amount awarded:	$2,000

Contact:
American Society of Mechanical Engineers
Three Park Avenue
New York, NY 10016-5990
Phone: 212-591-8131
Fax: 212-591-7143
Web: www.asme.org/educate/aid

American Society of Naval Engineers

Naval Engineers Scholarship

Type of award: Scholarship.
Intended use: For full-time senior or master's study at accredited 4-year or graduate institution.
Eligibility: Applicant must be U.S. citizen.
Basis for selection: Major/career interest in engineering, marine; engineering, mechanical; engineering, electrical/ electronic; physical sciences or engineering, civil. Applicant must demonstrate high academic achievement.
Application requirements: Recommendations, essay, transcript.
Additional information: Award for last year of undergraduate study or one year of graduate study. Additional major/career interest: naval architecture, aeronautical engineering, ocean engineering, as well as other programs leading to careers with both military and civilian organizations requiring these educational backgrounds. Financial need may be considered.

Amount of award:	$2,500-$3,500
Number of awards:	22
Number of applicants:	90
Application deadline:	February 15
Notification begins:	May 15
Total amount awarded:	$64,000

Contact:
American Society of Naval Engineers
1452 Duke Street
Alexandria, VA 22314
Phone: 703-836-6727
Fax: 703-836-7491
Web: www.navalengineers.org

American Society of Travel Agents Foundation

A.J. "Andy" Spielman Travel Agents Scholarship

Type of award: Scholarship, renewable.
Intended use: For undergraduate certificate or non-degree study at accredited vocational institution in United States or Canada. Designated institutions: Recognized proprietary travel schools.
Eligibility: Applicant must be returning adult student.
Basis for selection: Major/career interest in tourism/travel. Applicant must demonstrate high academic achievement and service orientation.
Application requirements: Recommendations, transcript, proof of eligibility. 500-word essay entitled "Why I Have Chosen the Travel Profession for My Reentry into the Work Force."
Additional information: Send SASE or visit Website for requirements and application.

Amount of award:	$2,500
Number of awards:	2
Application deadline:	July 28

Contact:
American Society of Travel Agents Foundation
1101 King Street
Alexandria, VA 22314-2944
Phone: 703-739-2782
Web: www.astanet.com

Alaska Airlines Travel Industry Scholarship

Type of award: Scholarship, renewable.
Intended use: For sophomore, junior or senior study at accredited 4-year institution in United States or Canada.
Eligibility: Applicant must be U.S. citizen, permanent resident, international student or Canadian citizen/resident.
Basis for selection: Major/career interest in tourism/travel. Applicant must demonstrate high academic achievement.
Application requirements: Recommendations, transcript, proof of eligibility. Minimum 2.5 GPA. 500-word essay on travel and tourism. Include two career goals and reasons for pursuing career in travel and tourism.
Additional information: Send SASE or visit Website for requirements and application.

Amount of award:	$2,000
Number of awards:	1
Application deadline:	July 28
Notification begins:	December 1
Total amount awarded:	$2,000

Contact:
American Society of Travel Agents Foundation
1101 King Street
Alexandria, VA 22314
Phone: 703-739-2782
Fax: 703-684-8319
Web: www.astanet.com

American Express Travel Scholarship

Type of award: Scholarship, renewable.
Intended use: For undergraduate study at accredited vocational, 2-year or 4-year institution in United States or Canada.
Eligibility: Applicant must be U.S. citizen, permanent resident, international student or Canadian citizen/resident.
Basis for selection: Major/career interest in tourism/travel.
Application requirements: Recommendations, essay, transcript, proof of eligibility. Must be enrolled in travel and tourism program.
Additional information: Send SASE or visit Website for requirements and application.

Amount of award:	$2,500
Number of awards:	1
Application deadline:	July 28
Notification begins:	December 1
Total amount awarded:	$2,500

Contact:
American Society of Travel Agents Foundation
1101 King Street
Alexandria, VA 22314-2944
Phone: 703-739-2782
Fax: 703-684-8319
Web: www.astanet.com

Arizona Chapter Gold Travel Industry Scholarship

Type of award: Scholarship, renewable.
Intended use: For sophomore, junior or senior study at accredited 4-year institution in United States.
Eligibility: Applicant must be U.S. citizen or permanent resident residing in Arizona.
Basis for selection: Major/career interest in tourism/travel. Applicant must demonstrate high academic achievement, seriousness of purpose and service orientation.
Application requirements: Recommendations, transcript, proof of eligibility. Minimum 2.5 GPA. 500-word essay detailing applicant's plans in travel industry and interest in business of travel and tourism. Letter of recommendation must be from educator or employer regarding applicant's credentials.
Additional information: Send SASE or visit Website for requirements and application.

Amount of award:	$3,000
Number of awards:	1
Application deadline:	July 28
Notification begins:	December 1
Total amount awarded:	$3,000

Contact:
American Society of Travel Agents Foundation
1101 King Street
Alexandria, VA 22314-2944
Phone: 703-739-2782
Fax: 703-684-8319
Web: www.astanet.com

Arizona Dependent/Employee Membership Scholarship

Type of award: Scholarship, renewable.
Intended use: For sophomore, junior or senior study at accredited 2-year or 4-year institution. Designated institutions: Postsecondary institutions in Arizona.
Eligibility: Applicant or parent must be member/participant of ASTA Arizona Chapter. Applicant must be U.S. citizen or permanent resident.
Basis for selection: Applicant must demonstrate high academic achievement.
Application requirements: Recommendations, transcript, proof of eligibility. Minimum 2.5 GPA. 500-word essay entitled "My Career Goals." Application is open to any field of study.
Additional information: Applicant must be dependent of official representative of ASTA Arizona chapter, or Active Associate member, or employee of Arizona ASTA Active member travel agency. Open to applicants of all majors and fields of study; major in travel and tourism not required. Must be enrolled either in final year in two-year college or junior or senior year in four-year university. Send SASE or visit Website for requirements and application.

Amount of award:	$1,500
Number of awards:	1
Application deadline:	July 28
Notification begins:	December 1
Total amount awarded:	$1,500

Contact:
American Society of Travel Agents Foundation
1101 King Street
Alexandria, VA 22314-2944
Phone: 703-739-2782
Fax: 703-684-8319
Web: www.astanet.com

George Reinke Travel Agents Scholarship

Type of award: Scholarship, renewable.
Intended use: For undergraduate certificate, freshman, sophomore or non-degree study at accredited vocational or 2-year institution in United States or Canada.
Eligibility: Applicant must be U.S. citizen.
Basis for selection: Major/career interest in tourism/travel. Applicant must demonstrate financial need, high academic achievement, seriousness of purpose and service orientation.
Application requirements: Recommendations, transcript, proof of eligibility. Minimum 2.5 GPA. 500-word essay entitled "My Objectives in the Travel Agency Industry." Applicant should also address need for scholarship.
Additional information: For travel agent training. Send SASE or visit Website for requirements and application.

Amount of award:	$2,000
Number of awards:	17
Application deadline:	July 28, December 22
Notification begins:	December 1, March 1
Total amount awarded:	$6,000

Contact:
American Society of Travel Agents Foundation
1101 King Street
Alexandria, VA 22314-2944
Web: www.astanet.com

Healy Travel Industry Scholarship

Type of award: Scholarship, renewable.

Intended use: For freshman, sophomore, junior or senior study at accredited 4-year institution in United States or Canada.

Eligibility: Applicant must be U.S. citizen, permanent resident, international student or Canadian citizen/resident.

Basis for selection: Major/career interest in tourism/travel. Applicant must demonstrate high academic achievement and service orientation.

Application requirements: Recommendations, transcript, proof of eligibility. Minimum 2.5 GPA. 500-word essay suggesting improvements in travel industry.

Additional information: Must submit Send SASE or visit Website for requirements and application.

Amount of award:	$2,000
Number of awards:	1
Number of applicants:	6
Application deadline:	July 28
Notification begins:	December 1

Contact:
American Society of Travel Agents Foundation
1101 King Street
Alexandria, VA 22314-2944
Phone: 703-739-2782
Fax: 703-684-8319
Web: www.astanet.com

Holland America Line-Westours Travel Industry Scholarship

Type of award: Scholarship, renewable.

Intended use: For undergraduate study at accredited vocational, 2-year or 4-year institution in United States or Canada.

Eligibility: Applicant must be U.S. citizen, permanent resident, international student or Canadian citizen/resident.

Basis for selection: Major/career interest in tourism/travel. Applicant must demonstrate high academic achievement, seriousness of purpose and service orientation.

Application requirements: Recommendations, transcript, proof of eligibility. 500-word essay on future of cruise industry. Minimum 2.5 GPA.

Additional information: Send SASE or visit Website for requirements and application.

Amount of award:	$3,000
Number of awards:	2
Number of applicants:	23
Application deadline:	July 28
Notification begins:	December 1
Total amount awarded:	$6,000

Contact:
American Society of Travel Agents Foundation
1101 King Street
Alexandria, VA 22314-2944
Phone: 703-739-2782
Fax: 703-684-8319
Web: www.astanet.com

Joseph R. Stone Travel Industry Scholarship

Type of award: Scholarship, renewable.

Intended use: For freshman, sophomore, junior or senior study at accredited 2-year or 4-year institution in United States or Canada.

Eligibility: Applicant must be U.S. citizen, permanent resident, international student or Canadian citizen/resident.

Basis for selection: Major/career interest in tourism/travel. Applicant must demonstrate high academic achievement.

Application requirements: Recommendations, transcript, proof of eligibility. 500-word essay on applicant's goals in travel industry. Minimum 2.5 GPA.

Additional information: One parent must be employed by some aspect of travel industry. Send SASE or visit Website for requirements and application.

Amount of award:	$2,400
Number of awards:	3
Number of applicants:	5
Application deadline:	July 28
Notification begins:	December 1
Total amount awarded:	$7,200

Contact:
American Society of Travel Agents Foundation
1101 King Street
Alexandria, VA 22314-2944
Phone: 703-739-2782
Fax: 703-684-8319
Web: www.astanet.com

Northern California/Epping Travel Industry Scholarship

Type of award: Scholarship, renewable.

Intended use: For undergraduate study at accredited vocational, 2-year or 4-year institution in United States. Designated institutions: Colleges, universities and recognized proprietary travel and tourism schools in California or Northern Nevada.

Eligibility: Applicant must be U.S. citizen or permanent resident residing in Nevada or California.

Basis for selection: Major/career interest in tourism/travel. Applicant must demonstrate high academic achievement, depth of character, seriousness of purpose and service orientation.

Application requirements: Recommendations, transcript, proof of eligibility. Minimum 2.5 GPA. 500-word essay entitled "Why I Desire a Profession in the Travel and Tourism Industry."

Additional information: Applicants must be residents of Northern California or Northern Nevada. Application deadlines and notification dates vary. Recipient must make presentation at NorCal ASTA chapter meeting within six months of receiving scholarship. Send SASE or visit Website for requirements and application.

Amount of award:	$2,000
Number of awards:	1
Number of applicants:	5
Total amount awarded:	$2,000

Contact:
American Society of Travel Agents Foundation
1101 King Street
Alexandria, VA 22314-2944
Phone: 703-739-2782
Fax: 703-684-8319
Web: www.astanet.com

Princess Cruises and Tours Travel Industry Scholarship

Type of award: Scholarship, renewable.

Intended use: For undergraduate study at accredited vocational, 2-year or 4-year institution in United States or Canada.

Basis for selection: Major/career interest in tourism/travel. Applicant must demonstrate high academic achievement, seriousness of purpose and service orientation.
Application requirements: Recommendations, transcript, proof of eligibility. Minimum 2.5 GPA. 300-word essay on two features cruise ships will need to offer passengers in next ten years.
Additional information: Send SASE or visit Website for requirements and application.

Amount of award:	$2,000
Number of awards:	2
Number of applicants:	17
Application deadline:	July 28
Notification begins:	December 11
Total amount awarded:	$4,000

Contact:
American Society of Travel Agents Foundation
1101 King Street
Alexandria, VA 22314-2944
Phone: 703-739-2782
Fax: 703-684-8319
Web: www.astanet.com

Southern California/Pleasant Hawaiian Holidays Travel Industry Scholarship

Type of award: Scholarship, renewable.
Intended use: For freshman, sophomore, junior or senior study at accredited 2-year or 4-year institution in United States.
Eligibility: Applicant must be U.S. citizen.
Basis for selection: Major/career interest in tourism/travel. Applicant must demonstrate high academic achievement, seriousness of purpose and service orientation.
Application requirements: Recommendations, transcript, proof of eligibility. 1,000-word essay entitled "My Goals in the Travel Industry" and statement why applicant should receive award.
Additional information: Two awards: one for student from Southern California region; other award for anywhere in the United States. Send SASE or visit Website for requirements and application.

Amount of award:	$2,500
Number of awards:	2
Number of applicants:	9
Application deadline:	July 28
Notification begins:	December 1
Total amount awarded:	$5,000

Contact:
American Society of Travel Agents Foundation
1101 King Street
Alexandria, VA 22314-2944
Phone: 703-739-2782
Fax: 703-684-8319
Web: www.astanet.com

Stan and Leone Pollard Travel Industry Scholarship

Type of award: Scholarship, renewable.
Intended use: For undergraduate certificate, freshman, sophomore or non-degree study at accredited vocational or 2-year institution in United States or Canada.
Eligibility: Applicant must be returning adult student.
Basis for selection: Major/career interest in tourism/travel. Applicant must demonstrate high academic achievement.

Application requirements: Recommendations, transcript, proof of eligibility. Minimum 2.5 GPA. 500-word essay on objectives in travel and tourism industry.
Additional information: Must be reentering job market or changing careers by enrolling in travel and tourism program. Send SASE or visit Website for requirements and application.

Amount of award:	$2,000
Number of awards:	2
Number of applicants:	42
Application deadline:	July 28, December 22
Notification begins:	December 11, March 11
Total amount awarded:	$4,000

Contact:
American Society of Travel Agents Foundation
1101 King Street
Alexandria, VA 22314-2944
Phone: 703-739-2782
Fax: 703-684-8319
Web: www.astanet.com

Universal Air Travel Plan (UATP) Travel Industry Scholarship

Type of award: Scholarship, renewable.
Intended use: For undergraduate study at accredited 2-year or 4-year institution in United States or Canada.
Eligibility: Applicant must be U.S. citizen, permanent resident, international student or U.S. or Canadian citizen or international student.
Basis for selection: Major/career interest in tourism/travel. Applicant must demonstrate high academic achievement.
Application requirements: Recommendations, transcript, proof of eligibility. Minimum 2.5 GPA. 500-word essay defining importance and challenges of managing business travel. Must also include brief description of career goals and why career in travel and tourism is desired. Must currently be enrolled in travel curriculum.
Additional information: Send SASE or visit Website for requirements and application.

Amount of award:	$1,500-$3,000
Number of awards:	1
Application deadline:	July 28
Total amount awarded:	$3,000

Contact:
American Society of Travel Agents Foundation
1101 King Street
Alexandria, VA 22314-2944
Phone: 703-739-2782
Fax: 703-739-8319
Web: www.astanet.com

American Welding Society Foundation, Inc.

American Welding Society District Scholarship

Type of award: Scholarship.
Intended use: For undergraduate study at accredited vocational, 2-year or 4-year institution in United States.
Eligibility: Applicant must be U.S. citizen.
Basis for selection: Major/career interest in welding. Applicant must demonstrate financial need, high academic

achievement, depth of character, leadership and seriousness of purpose.

Application requirements: Recommendations, transcript, proof of eligibility.

Amount of award:	$250-$3,000
Number of awards:	150
Application deadline:	March 1
Notification begins:	July 1
Total amount awarded:	$110,000

Contact:
American Welding Society Foundation, Inc.
Attn: Scholarships
550 Northwest LeJeune Road
Miami, FL 33126
Phone: 800-443-9353

Donald F. Hastings Scholarship

Type of award: Scholarship, renewable.
Intended use: For sophomore, junior or senior study at 4-year institution in United States.
Eligibility: Applicant must be U.S. citizen.
Basis for selection: Major/career interest in welding. Applicant must demonstrate financial need and seriousness of purpose.
Application requirements: Recommendations, transcript, proof of eligibility. Minimum of 2.5 GPA. Interest in pursuing minimum 4 year degree in welding engineering or welding engineering technology.
Additional information: Priority given to residents of Ohio and California.

Amount of award:	$3,000
Number of awards:	1
Number of applicants:	14
Application deadline:	January 15
Notification begins:	March 15

Contact:
American Welding Society Foundation, Inc.
Attn: Scholarships
550 Northwest LeJeune Road
Miami, FL 33126
Phone: 800-443-9353

Edward J. Brady Scholarship

Type of award: Scholarship, renewable.
Intended use: For sophomore, junior or senior study at 4-year institution.
Eligibility: Applicant must be U.S. citizen.
Basis for selection: Major/career interest in welding or engineering. Applicant must demonstrate financial need and seriousness of purpose.
Application requirements: Recommendations, essay, transcript, proof of eligibility. Minimum GPA of 2.5. Proposed curriculum, brief biography, verification of hands-on welding experience. Interest in pursuing minimum 4 year degree in welding engineering or welding engineering technology.
Additional information: Must have proof of hands-on welding experience.

Amount of award:	$2,500
Number of awards:	1
Number of applicants:	9
Application deadline:	January 15
Notification begins:	March 15

Contact:
American Welding Society Foundation, Inc.
Attn: Scholarships
550 Northwest LeJeune Road
Miami, FL 33126
Phone: 800-443-9353

Howard E. Adkins Memorial Scholarship

Type of award: Scholarship, renewable.
Intended use: For full-time junior or senior study at 4-year institution.
Eligibility: Applicant must be U.S. citizen.
Basis for selection: Major/career interest in welding. Applicant must demonstrate high academic achievement and seriousness of purpose.
Application requirements: Recommendations, transcript, proof of eligibility. Minimum GPA of 3.2 in engineering scientific and technical subjects and 2.8 overall GPA. Interest in pursuing minimum 4 year degree in welding engineering or welding engineering technology.
Additional information: Priority given to residents of Kentucky and Wisconsin.

Amount of award:	$2,500
Number of awards:	1
Number of applicants:	11
Application deadline:	January 15
Notification begins:	March 15

Contact:
American Welding Society Foundation Inc.
Attn: Scholarships
550 Northwest LeJeune Road
Miami, FL 33126
Phone: 800-443-9353

James A. Turner, Jr. Scholarship

Type of award: Scholarship, renewable.
Intended use: For full-time sophomore, junior or senior study at accredited 4-year institution.
Eligibility: Applicant must be U.S. citizen.
Basis for selection: Major/career interest in welding or business/management/administration. Applicant must demonstrate financial need and seriousness of purpose.
Application requirements: Recommendations, transcript, proof of eligibility. Minimum GPA of 2.5. Verification of employment, brief biography, financial aid report, proposed curriculum. Interest in pursuing management career in welding.
Additional information: Must work minimum of ten hours per week at welding store.

Amount of award:	$3,000
Number of awards:	1
Number of applicants:	3
Application deadline:	January 15
Notification begins:	March 15

Contact:
American Welding Society Foundation, Inc.
Attn: Scholarships
550 Northwest LeJeune Road
Miami, FL 33126
Phone: 800-443-9353

John C. Lincoln Memorial Scholarship

Type of award: Scholarship, renewable.

Intended use: For sophomore, junior or senior study at 4-year institution.
Eligibility: Applicant must be U.S. citizen.
Basis for selection: Major/career interest in welding. Applicant must demonstrate financial need and seriousness of purpose.
Application requirements: Recommendations, transcript, proof of eligibility. Minimum GPA of 2.5. Interest in pursuing minimum 4 year degree in welding engineering or welding engineering technology.

Amount of award:	$2,500
Number of awards:	1
Number of applicants:	13
Application deadline:	January 15
Notification begins:	March 15

Contact:
American Welding Society Foundation, Inc.
Attn: Scholarships
550 Northwest LeJeune Road
Miami, FL 33126
Phone: 800-443-9553

Miller Electric Manufacturing Company Ivic Scholarship

Type of award: Scholarship.
Intended use: For undergraduate study at accredited vocational, 2-year or 4-year institution in United States.
Eligibility: Applicant must be U.S. citizen.
Basis for selection: Competition/talent/interest in engineering/architecture, based on AWS National Welding Trials. Major/career interest in welding. Applicant must demonstrate depth of character, leadership and seriousness of purpose.
Application requirements: Minimum GPA of 2.5.

Amount of award:	$40,000
Number of awards:	1

Contact:
American Welding Society Foundation, Inc.
Attn: Scholarships
550 Northwest LeJeune Road
Miami, FL 33126
Phone: 800-443-9353

Praxair International Scholarship

Type of award: Scholarship, renewable.
Intended use: For full-time sophomore, junior or senior study at 4-year institution.
Eligibility: Applicant must be U.S. citizen, international student or Canadian citizen/resident.
Basis for selection: Major/career interest in welding. Applicant must demonstrate financial need, leadership and service orientation.
Application requirements: Recommendations, transcript, proof of eligibility. Minimum GPA of 2.5. Interest in pursuing minimum 4 year degree in welding engineering or welding engineering technology.

Amount of award:	$2,500
Number of awards:	1
Number of applicants:	16
Application deadline:	January 15
Notification begins:	March 15

Contact:
American Welding Society Foundation Inc.
Praxair Scholarship
550 Northwest LeJeune Road
Miami, FL 33126
Phone: 800-443-9353

An Uncommon Legacy Foundation, Inc.

Lesbian Leadership Scholarship

Type of award: Scholarship, renewable.
Intended use: For full-time undergraduate or graduate study at accredited 4-year or graduate institution in United States.
Eligibility: Must be lesbian, bisexual or transgender. Applicant must be female.
Basis for selection: Applicant must demonstrate financial need, high academic achievement, depth of character, leadership, seriousness of purpose and service orientation.
Application requirements: Recommendations, essay, transcript, proof of eligibility. Minimum GPA of 3.0.
Additional information: Applicants must be "out" lesbian college students who show potential for leadership and demonstrate commitment or contribution to lesbian, gay, bisexual and transgender community; bisexual and transgender students who show leadership in the l/g/b/t community also eligible. Write to Foundation or visit Website for application.

Amount of award:	$2,500
Number of awards:	17
Number of applicants:	50
Application deadline:	July 1
Notification begins:	December 15
Total amount awarded:	$17,000

Contact:
An Uncommon Legacy Foundation, Inc.
Legacy Scholarship Committee
P.O. Box 33727
Washington, DC 20033
Phone: 202-265-1926
Fax: 202-265-1927
Web: www.uncommonlegacy.org

The Andrew W. Mellon Foundation

Mellon Minority Undergraduate Fellowship Program

Type of award: Scholarship.
Intended use: For full-time junior, senior or graduate study at accredited 4-year or graduate institution in United States. Designated institutions: 32 postsecondary institutions plus 17 member institutions of United Negro College Fund.
Eligibility: Applicant must be Alaskan native, African American, Mexican American, Hispanic American, Puerto Rican or American Indian. Applicant must be U.S. citizen or permanent resident.
Basis for selection: Major/career interest in literature; anthropology; geology/earth sciences; mathematics; foreign

languages; history; philosophy; religion/theology; art/art history or anthropology. Applicant must demonstrate high academic achievement.

Application requirements: Recommendations, essay, transcript, research proposal, nomination by by faculty member at eligible institution.

Additional information: Students indentified in sophomore year who have potential and interest in pursuing doctorate. Students receive faculty mentoring, modest term-time financial support, stipend for summer research, and loan repayment assistance if doctorate is pursued. Additional fields of study include Classics, musicology, ecology and physics. Goal is to increase number of minority faculty at U.S. colleges and universities.

    Total amount awarded: $22,000,000

Contact:
Lydia L. English, Director, The Andrew W. Mellon Foundation
Mellon Minority Undergrad. Fellowship Program
140 East 62nd Street
New York, NY 10021
Phone: 212-838-8400
Fax: 212-223-2778
Web: www.mmuf.org

Anglogold North America, Inc.

Anglogold North America, Inc. Scholarship

Type of award: Scholarship, renewable.
Intended use: For undergraduate study at vocational, 2-year or 4-year institution.
Eligibility: Applicant or parent must be employed by Independence Mining Co. Inc. (IMC). Applicant must be high school senior.
Additional information: For further information or an application, contact Independence Mining Company Incorporated directly.
    Amount of award: $500-$3,000

Annie's Homegrown, Inc.

Annie's Environmental Studies Scholarships

Type of award: Scholarship.
Intended use: For full-time undergraduate or graduate study at accredited vocational, 2-year, 4-year or graduate institution in United States.
Basis for selection: Major/career interest in environmental science or ecology. Applicant must demonstrate high academic achievement, depth of character and seriousness of purpose.
Application requirements: Recommendations, essay, transcript.
Additional information: Applicants must be focused on environmental studies. Criteria for selection place more emphasis on commitment to preserving and protecting the environment than on grades/GPA. Application and more information available on Website.

Amount of award:	$1,000
Number of awards:	25
Total amount awarded:	$25,000

Contact:
Annie's Scholarship Program
P. O. Box 128
Hampton, CT 06247
Phone: 781-224-9639
Web: www.annies.com

AOPA Air Safety Foundation

McAllister and Burnside Scholarships

Type of award: Scholarship.
Intended use: For junior or senior study at 4-year institution. Designated institutions: Must be described in section 170-C of the Internal Revenue Service Code of 1954.
Eligibility: Applicant must be U.S. citizen.
Basis for selection: Major/career interest in aviation. Applicant must demonstrate financial need, high academic achievement and seriousness of purpose.
Application requirements: Essay, transcript. Must be enrolled in a non-engineering aviation degree program.
Additional information: Send SASE. Minimum 3.25 GPA required.

Amount of award:	$1,000
Number of awards:	2
Number of applicants:	300
Application deadline:	March 31
Notification begins:	June 1
Total amount awarded:	$2,000

Contact:
AOPA Air Safety Foundation
421 Aviation Way
Frederick, MD 21701
Phone: 301-695-2170
Fax: 301-695-2343
Web: www.aopa.org/asf

Appaloosa Youth Foundation

Appaloosa Youth Foundation Educational Scholarships

Type of award: Scholarship, renewable.
Intended use: For full-time undergraduate or graduate study at accredited postsecondary institution in United States.
Eligibility: Applicant or parent must be member/participant of Appaloosa Horse Club. Applicant must be U.S. citizen or permanent resident.
Basis for selection: Based on participation in the Appaloosa industry. Applicant must demonstrate financial need, high academic achievement, depth of character, leadership, seriousness of purpose and service orientation.

Application requirements: Portfolio, recommendations, essay, transcript, proof of eligibility. Photo, SAT or ACT scores. GPA of 3.5 for one scholarship, GPA of 2.5 for other scholarships.

Additional information: Must be member of Appaloosa Horse Club or Appaloosa Youth Association. Certain awards require intent to pursue equine-related studies.

Amount of award:	$1,000
Number of awards:	8
Number of applicants:	30
Application deadline:	June 10
Notification begins:	July 15
Total amount awarded:	$8,000

Contact:
Appaloosa Youth Foundation Scholarship Committee
2720 Pullman Road
Moscow, ID 83843
Phone: 208-882-5578
Fax: 208-882-8150
Web: www.appaloosa.com

AptarGroup Charitable Foundation

Ervin J. LeCoque Leadership Scholars Program

Type of award: Scholarship, renewable.
Intended use: For undergraduate study at accredited vocational, 2-year or 4-year institution.
Eligibility: Applicant or parent must be employed by AptarGroup Charitable Foundation. Applicant must be high school senior.
Basis for selection: Applicant must demonstrate financial need.
Additional information: For further information or an application, contact AptarGroup Charitable Foundation.

Amount of award:	$2,500

Contact:
AptarGroup Chartitable Foundation

Arby Construction, Inc.

The Klumb Family Scholarship Program

Type of award: Scholarship.
Intended use: For undergraduate or graduate study at vocational, 2-year, 4-year or graduate institution.
Eligibility: Applicant or parent must be employed by Arby Construction. Applicant must be high school senior.
Additional information: For futher information or an application, contact Arby Construction, Inc. directly.

Amount of award:	$1,500

Arizona Board of Regents

Arizona Tuition Waiver for Non-Residents

Type of award: Scholarship, renewable.
Intended use: For full-time undergraduate or graduate study. Designated institutions: Arizona State University, Northern Arizona University, University of Arizona.
Basis for selection: Major/career interest in arts, general; music or performing arts. Applicant must demonstrate high academic achievement.
Application requirements: Students seeking need-based waiver must file FAFSA. Merit waiver requirements vary. Graduate students seeking merit waivers apply to graduate academic department. Must contact designated institution for application process.
Additional information: Waives all or part of out-of-state tuition (non-resident waivers do not cover resident tuition). Waivers generally used to recruit non-resident students with strong academic backgrounds or special talents. Financial need and academic achievement/talent considered separately. Award may be based on either or both criteria. Must maintain academic progress and complete community service requirement to renew. Additional Websites: NAU: www.nau.edu; UA: www.Arizona.edu. Selection process and application requirements may vary by institution.
Contact:
Financial aid office or academic department of designated institution.
Web: www.asu.edu

Arizona Tuition Waivers for Children/Spouses of Slain Public Servants

Type of award: Scholarship, renewable.
Intended use: For undergraduate study at accredited postsecondary institution. Designated institutions: Arizona State University, Northern Arizona University, University of Arizona.
Eligibility: Applicant must be U.S. citizen or permanent resident residing in Arizona. Applicant's parent must have been killed or disabled in work-related accident as fire fighter, police officer or public safety officer.
Application requirements: Proof of eligibility. Documentation of eligibility by Arizona Peace Officers, Arizona Fire Fighters, or Arizona Emergency Paramedics.
Additional information: Eligible public safety categories include Emergency Medical Service. Students must meet university admissions criteria and maintain satisfactory academic progress to renew. Waiver may also cover summer courses. Apply at financial aid office of University of Arizona, Arizona State University, or Northern Arizona University.
Contact:
Arizona Board of Regents
2020 North Central Avenue
Suite 230
Phoenix, AZ 85004-4593
Phone: 603-229-2500
Fax: 603-229-2555

Arizona Tuition Waivers for Residents

Type of award: Scholarship, renewable.
Intended use: For undergraduate or graduate study at postsecondary institution. Designated institutions: Arizona State University, Northern Arizona University, University of Arizona.
Eligibility: Applicant must be residing in Arizona.
Application requirements: Nomination by Arizona high schools or Arizona home-schooling families. Students seeking need-based waiver must file FAFSA. Graduate students seeking merit waivers apply to graduate academic department. Evidence for merit awards includes test scores, grades, and special talent.
Additional information: Waivers awarded to students who demonstrate financial need, merit or both. Eligibility for waivers generally established one year prior to enrollment. Must meet university admissions criteria and maintain satisfactory academic progress to renew. Additional Websites: NAU: www.nau.edu; UA: www.arizona.edu. Selection process and requirements may vary by institution.

Amount of award:	Full tuition

Contact:
Arizona high school counselor or admissions office of designated institution.
Web: www.asu.edu

Arkansas Department of Higher Education

Academic Challenge Scholarship

Type of award: Scholarship, renewable.
Intended use: For full-time undergraduate study at postsecondary institution. Designated institutions: Approved Arkansas college or university.
Eligibility: Applicant must be high school senior. Applicant must be U.S. citizen or permanent resident residing in Arkansas.
Basis for selection: Applicant must demonstrate financial need and high academic achievement.
Application requirements: Transcript. Completed application ACT and family federal income tax forms for two years preceding high school graduation.
Additional information: Applications available from high school counselor's office. Award is renewable annually up to four years, provided minimum cumulative GPA of 2.5 and at least 24 semester credit hours or equivalent are maintained per academic year. Need-qualified students who have not completed Pre-Collegiate Core Curriculum will be classified as conditionally eligible and have at least 12 months after high school graduation to satisfy core curriculum requirement and enroll in college. Students will not receive scholarship funds until academic requirements have been fully met. Visit Website for more information.

Amount of award:	$2,500
Application deadline:	October 1

Contact:
Arkansas Department of Higher Education
114 East Capitol Street
Little Rock, AR 72201-3818
Phone: 800-547-8839
Web: www.arkansashighered.com

Arkansas Freshman/Sophomore Minority Grant

Type of award: Scholarship, renewable.
Intended use: For full-time freshman or sophomore study at accredited postsecondary institution.
Eligibility: Applicant must be Asian American, African American, Mexican American, Hispanic American, Puerto Rican or American Indian. Applicant must be U.S. citizen or permanent resident residing in Arkansas.
Basis for selection: Major/career interest in education, teacher. Applicant must demonstrate high academic achievement.
Additional information: Deadline set by participating institutions.

Amount of award:	$1,000
Number of awards:	300
Total amount awarded:	$300,000

Contact:
Education department of institution you plan to attend.
Web: www.arkansashighered.com

Arkansas Law Enforcement Officers' Dependents Scholarship

Type of award: Scholarship, renewable.
Intended use: For undergraduate study at accredited vocational, 2-year or 4-year institution. Designated institutions: Arkansas public institutions.
Eligibility: Applicant must be U.S. citizen or permanent resident residing in Arkansas. Applicant's parent must have been killed or disabled in work-related accident as fire fighter, police officer or public safety officer.
Application requirements: Proof of eligibility. Documentation of eligibility.
Additional information: All eligible applicants will receive tuition waver. Children/spouses of Highway and Transportation Department employees disabled or killed in work-related accident also eligible. Applicant must be Arkansas resident for at least six months. Dependent child applicant may be no older than 23; no age restriction for spouse. Application deadlines May 1 and July 1 for summer study.

Amount of award:	Full tuition
Application deadline:	August 1, December 1
Total amount awarded:	$47,613

Contact:
Arkansas Department of Higher Education
114 East Capitol Street
Little Rock, AR 72201-3818
Phone: 800-371-2050
Web: www.arkansashighered.com

Arkansas Missing/Killed in Action Dependents Scholarship

Type of award: Scholarship, renewable.
Intended use: For undergraduate, master's or non-degree study at accredited vocational, 2-year, 4-year or graduate institution.
Eligibility: Applicant must be U.S. citizen or permanent resident residing in Arkansas. Applicant must be dependent of deceased veteran or POW/MIA; or spouse of deceased veteran or POW/MIA who served in the Army, Air Force, Marines, Navy, Coast Guard or Reserves/National Guard during Persian Gulf War or Vietnam. Parent/spouse must have been Arkansas resident prior to enlistment.

Application requirements: Proof of eligibility. Minimum 2.0 GPA.

Additional information: Child/spouse of person killed in action or missing in action. Applicant must be Arkansas resident for at least six months. Application deadlines for summer May 1 and July 1.

    Amount of award: $4,674
    Application deadline: August 1, December 1

Contact:
Arkansas Department of Higher Education
114 East Capitol Street
Little Rock, AR 72201-3818
Phone: 800-547-8839
Web: www.arkansashighered.com

Governor's Scholars Program

Type of award: Scholarship, renewable.

Intended use: For full-time undergraduate study at postsecondary institution. Designated institutions: Approved Arkansas college or university.

Eligibility: Applicant must be high school senior. Applicant must be U.S. citizen or permanent resident residing in Arkansas.

Basis for selection: Applicant must demonstrate high academic achievement and leadership.

Application requirements: Completed application. Applicants must have at least 3.60 grade point average or score at least 27 on ACT or at least combined score of 1100 on SAT to qualify.

Additional information: Chosen applicants receive award of $4,000 per year. Award is renewable annually up to four years, provided minimum cumulative GPA of 3.0 and at least 24 semester credit hours or equivalent are maintained per academic year. Applications available from high school counselor's office. Visit Website for more information.

    Amount of award: $4,000
    Number of awards: 100
    Application deadline: March 1
    Total amount awarded: $400,000

Contact:
Arkansas Department of Higher Education
114 East Capitol Street
Little Rock, AR 72201-3818
Phone: 800-547-8839
Web: www.arkansashighered.com

Second Effort Scholarship

Type of award: Scholarship, renewable.

Intended use: For undergraduate study at postsecondary institution. Designated institutions: Arkansas college or university.

Eligibility: Applicant must be returning adult student. Applicant must be U.S. citizen or permanent resident residing in Arkansas.

Basis for selection: Applicant must demonstrate high academic achievement.

Application requirements: Applicant must not have graduated from high school. Students do not apply for this award. Those scholars who achieved one of ten best scores on Arkansas High School Diploma test during previous calendar year are contacted directly by Arkansas Department of Higher Education.

Additional information: Second Effort Scholarship was established to recognize importance of Arkansas High School Diploma (GED) Program and to encourage those students who successfully pass the Arkansas High School test to enroll in Arkansas Postsecondary institutions. Award is renewable

annually up to four years (or equivalent if student enrolled part-time), provided minimum cumulative GPA of 2.50 is maintained. Visit Website for more information.

    Amount of award: $1,000

Contact:
Arkansas Department of Higher Education
114 East Capitol Street
Little Rock, AR 72201-3818
Phone: 800-547-8839
Web: www.arkansashighered.com

Armed Forces Communications and Electronics Association

AFCEA Copernicus Foundation Scholarship For Computer Graphic Design

Type of award: Scholarship.

Intended use: For full-time sophomore or junior study at accredited 4-year institution in United States.

Eligibility: Applicant must be U.S. citizen.

Basis for selection: Major/career interest in computer graphics.

Application requirements: Recommendations, essay, transcript. Must send single sample of original, digital artwork along with 100-word essay describing image and how it was created.

Additional information: Applicant must send single sample of digital artwork which must be original design created solely by applicant, not group effort or improvement on existing site. Graphic can be submitted in .JPEG or .GIF format on CD, zip disk or diskette or, if URL is provided, it can be viewed at Website. Artistic creativity as well as mastery of web technology is important. If Websites are submitted, one graphic from site must be identified for consideration; entire sites not eligible.

    Amount of award: $2,000
    Number of awards: 1
    Application deadline: October 15
    Total amount awarded: $2,000

Contact:
Armed Forces Communications and Electronics Association
Educational Foundation
4400 Fair Lakes Court
Fairfax, VA 22033-3899
Phone: 703-631-6149
Fax: 703-631-4693
Web: www.afcea.org

AFCEA General Emmett Paige Scholarship

Type of award: Scholarship.

Intended use: For full-time freshman, sophomore or junior study at accredited 4-year institution in United States.

Eligibility: Applicant must be U.S. citizen. Applicant must be in military service or veteran; or dependent of active service person, veteran or POW/MIA; or spouse of active service person, veteran or POW/MIA.

Basis for selection: Major/career interest in aerospace; computer/information sciences; engineering, computer; physics; mathematics or engineering, electrical/electronic. Applicant must demonstrate high academic achievement, depth of character, leadership, patriotism, seriousness of purpose and service orientation.

Application requirements: Recommendations, transcript, proof of eligibility. Freshman students must also have letters from employer or supervisor or copy of performance evaluation, fitness report or similar document. Proof of eligibility can be copy of discharge form DD214, certificate of service, facsimile of applicants current DOD or Coast Guard identification card.

Additional information: Send SASE or visit Website for application (available after November 1). Must have minimum 3.4 GPA. Graduating high school seniors not eligible, but veterans enrolled as freshmen are eligible to apply; spouses or dependents must be enrolled as sophomores or juniors at time of application.

Amount of award:	$2,000
Number of awards:	15
Number of applicants:	88
Application deadline:	March 1
Notification begins:	June 1
Total amount awarded:	$30,000

Contact:
Armed Forces Communications and Electronics Association
Educational Foundation
4400 Fair Lakes Court
Fairfax, VA 22033-3899
Phone: 703-631-6149
Fax: 703-631-4693
Web: www.afcea.org

AFCEA General John A. Wickham Scholarship

Type of award: Scholarship.
Intended use: For full-time sophomore or junior study at accredited 4-year institution in United States.
Eligibility: Applicant must be U.S. citizen.
Basis for selection: Major/career interest in aerospace; electronics; computer/information sciences; physics; mathematics or engineering, electrical/electronic. Applicant must demonstrate high academic achievement, depth of character, leadership, patriotism, seriousness of purpose and service orientation.

Application requirements: Recommendations, transcript. Minimum GPA 3.5. Two letters of recommendation from faculty member having personal knowledge of candidate's program, achievements and potential.

Additional information: Send SASE or visit Website for application. Student must be enrolled full-time as sophomore or junior at time of application.

Amount of award:	$2,000
Number of awards:	15
Number of applicants:	253
Application deadline:	May 1
Notification begins:	June 1
Total amount awarded:	$30,000

Contact:
Armed Forces Communications and Electronics Association
Educational Foundation
4400 Fair Lakes Court
Fairfax, VA 22033-3899
Phone: 703-631-6149
Fax: 703-631-4693
Web: www.afcea.org

AFCEA ROTC Scholarships

Type of award: Scholarship.
Intended use: For full-time sophomore or junior study at accredited 4-year institution in United States.
Eligibility: Applicant or parent must be member/participant of Reserve Officers Training Corps (ROTC). Applicant must be U.S. citizen.
Basis for selection: Major/career interest in aerospace; engineering, electrical/electronic; computer/information sciences; engineering, computer; physics; mathematics; science, general or electronics. Applicant must demonstrate high academic achievement, depth of character, leadership, patriotism, seriousness of purpose and service orientation.

Application requirements: Transcript, nomination by professor of military science, naval science or aerospace studies. Recommendations from ROTC commander and professor in stated major.

Additional information: Applicant must be in ROTC. For application information, contact commander of ROTC unit. Candidates must be enrolled as sophomores or juniors at time of application.

Amount of award:	$2,000
Number of awards:	60
Number of applicants:	188
Application deadline:	April 1
Notification begins:	June 1
Total amount awarded:	$120,000

Contact:
Armed Forces Communications and Electronics Association
Educational Foundation
4400 Fair Lakes Court
Fairfax, VA 22033-3899
Phone: 703-631-6149
Fax: 703-631-4693
Web: www.afcea.org

AFCEA/Orincon IT Scholarship

Type of award: Scholarship.
Intended use: For full-time sophomore or junior study at accredited 4-year institution in United States. Designated institutions: Postsecondary institutions in greater San Diego, CA geographical area.
Basis for selection: Major/career interest in aerospace; electronics; computer/information sciences; physics or mathematics. Applicant must demonstrate high academic achievement, depth of character, leadership, patriotism, seriousness of purpose and service orientation.

Application requirements: Transcript. Two letters of recommendation.

Additional information: Minimum 3.5 GPA required.

Amount of award:	$2,000
Number of awards:	1
Application deadline:	May 1
Notification begins:	June 1

Scholarships

Contact:
Armed Forces Communications and Electronics Association
Educational Foundation
4400 Fair Lakes Court
Fairfax, VA 22033-3899
Phone: 703-631-6149
Fax: 703-631-4693
Web: www.afcea.org

Vice Admiral Jerry O. Tuttle, USN (Ret.) and Mrs. Barbara A. Tuttle Science and Technology Scholarship

Type of award: Scholarship.
Intended use: For full-time sophomore or junior study at accredited 4-year institution in United States.
Eligibility: Applicant must be U.S. citizen.
Basis for selection: Major/career interest in computer/information sciences; engineering, computer or electronics. Applicant must demonstrate high academic achievement.
Application requirements: Recommendations, transcript. Priority consideration will be given to military enlisted candidate.
Additional information: Student must enrolled full-time as sophomore or junior at time of application.

Amount of award:	$2,000
Number of awards:	1
Number of applicants:	30
Application deadline:	November 1
Notification begins:	December 1

Contact:
Armed Forces Communications and Electronics Association
Educational Foundation
4400 Fair Lakes Court
Fairfax, VA 22033-3899
Phone: 703-631-6149
Fax: 703-631-4693
Web: www.afcea.org

Armenian General Benevolent Union

Armenian General Benevolent Union International Scholarship Program

Type of award: Scholarship, renewable.
Intended use: For full-time undergraduate or graduate study in countries outside of U.S.
Eligibility: Applicant must be Armenian. Applicant must be U.S. citizen or permanent resident.
Basis for selection: Competition/talent/interest in Study abroad. Applicant must demonstrate financial need, high academic achievement, depth of character, leadership, seriousness of purpose and service orientation.
Application requirements: Recommendations, transcript, proof of eligibility.
Additional information: Students must provide verification of enrollment. Must be of Armenian descent.

Amount of award:	$300-$1,200
Number of awards:	400
Number of applicants:	450
Application deadline:	May 15
Notification begins:	September 15
Total amount awarded:	$475,000

Contact:
Armenian General Benevolent Union
Mrs. Maral Achian
55 E. 59th Street
New York, NY 10022-1112
Phone: 212-319-6383
Fax: 212-319-6507
Web: www.agbu.org

ARMY Emergency Relief

MG James Ursano Scholarship Fund

Type of award: Scholarship, renewable.
Intended use: For full-time freshman, sophomore, junior or senior study at accredited vocational, 2-year or 4-year institution.
Eligibility: Applicant must be single, at least 16, no older than 22. Applicant must be U.S. citizen or permanent resident. Applicant must be dependent of active service person, veteran or deceased veteran who serves or served in the Army.
Basis for selection: Applicant must demonstrate financial need, high academic achievement and leadership.
Application requirements: Transcript, proof of eligibility.
Additional information: Applicants must be enrolled, accepted, or pending acceptance as full time dependent students for entire academic year in post-secondary institutions approved by Department of Education for Title IV funds. Applicants must maintain at least 2.0 GPA. Application may be downloaded from Website.

Amount of award:	$700-$1,800
Number of awards:	1,600
Number of applicants:	3,100
Application deadline:	March 1
Notification begins:	June 1
Total amount awarded:	$1,833,300

Contact:
ARMY Emergency Relief
200 Stovall Street
Alexandria, VA 22332-0600
Web: www.aerhq.org

Arrow Electronics, Inc.

Tony Winger, Jr., Scholarship

Type of award: Scholarship.
Intended use: For undergraduate study at accredited 4-year institution.
Eligibility: Applicant or parent must be employed by Arrow Electronics, Inc.
Basis for selection: Applicant must demonstrate financial need.
Additional information: For further information or an application, contact Arrow Electronics, Inc. directly.

Amount of award:	$1,000-$6,000

The Art Institutes

Culinary Scholarship Cook-off Competition

Type of award: Scholarship.
Intended use: For undergraduate study at vocational, 2-year or 4-year institution in United States.
Eligibility: Applicant must be enrolled in high school.
Basis for selection: Competition/talent/interest in culinary arts, based on ability and originality in meal preparation. Major/career interest in culinary arts or hotel/restaurant management.
Application requirements: Recommendations, essay, transcript. Resume; notebook of information, including a two-course meal menu, recipes, cost analysis, photographs of each course.
Additional information: Contest awards two full tuition waivers and other scholarships. Semifinalists notified prior to April 1. Top prizewinners decided in cook-off in May. Contact nearest Art Institutes campus for application or call sponsor.

Amount of award:	$29,000
Number of awards:	3
Application deadline:	February 9
Notification begins:	March 1

Contact:
The Art Institutes
Education Management Corporation
300 6th Avenue
Pittsburgh, PA 15222
Phone: 888-328-7900
Fax: 412-562-1732
Web: www.edumgt.com

Arthur and Doreen Parrett Scholarship Trust Fund

Arthur and Doreen Parrett Scholarship

Type of award: Scholarship, renewable.
Intended use: For full-time sophomore, junior, senior, master's, doctoral or first professional study.
Eligibility: Applicant must be residing in Washington.
Basis for selection: Major/career interest in science, general; engineering; dentistry or medicine. Applicant must demonstrate financial need and high academic achievement.
Application requirements: Recommendations, essay, transcript.
Additional information: Applicants must have completed first year of college. Include SASE with inquiries and information will be forwarded.

Amount of award:	$2,000-$4,000
Number of awards:	15
Number of applicants:	200
Application deadline:	July 31
Notification begins:	September 1
Total amount awarded:	$50,000

Contact:
Arthur and Doreen Parrett Scholarship Trust Fund
P.O. Box 720
Seattle, WA 98111-7206

ASCAP Foundation

ASCAP Morton Gould Young Composers Award

Type of award: Scholarship, renewable.
Intended use: For non-degree study.
Eligibility: Applicant must be U.S. citizen or permanent resident.
Basis for selection: Competition/talent/interest in music performance/composition. Major/career interest in music.
Application requirements: Must submit score or manuscript of one musical work, biographical information, list of compositions to date, and, if available, tape of submitted composition along with application.
Additional information: Number and amounts of awards given out varies.

Amount of award:	$250-$3,580
Number of applicants:	600
Application deadline:	March 15
Notification begins:	June 1
Total amount awarded:	$30,000

Contact:
ASCAP Foundation Morton Gould Young Composers Awards
c/o Fran Richard
One Lincoln Plaza
New York, NY 10023
Phone: 212-621-6219
Web: www.ASCAPFoundation.org

Rudolf Nissim Composers Competition

Type of award: Scholarship.
Intended use: For non-degree study.
Eligibility: Applicant or parent must be member/participant of American Society of Composers/Authors/Publishers.
Basis for selection: Competition/talent/interest in music performance/composition.
Application requirements: Proof of eligibility. Must submit an original music composition for a large ensemble which requires a conductor and has not been professionally performed, along with application.
Additional information: Applicant must be an ASCAP member.

Amount of award:	$5,000
Number of awards:	1
Number of applicants:	260
Application deadline:	November 15
Notification begins:	January 15
Total amount awarded:	$5,000

Contact:
Fran Richard
The ASCAP Foundation
One Lincoln Plaza
New York, NY 10023

Ashland, Inc.

Ashland Scholars Program

Type of award: Scholarship, renewable.

Intended use: For freshman study at accredited 2-year or 4-year institution.
Eligibility: Applicant or parent must be employed by Ashland Coal, Inc.
Additional information: For further information or an application, contact Ashland, Inc. directly.

>   **Amount of award:** $2,000

ASM International Foundation

ASM International Foundation Undergraduate Scholarship

Type of award: Scholarship, renewable.
Intended use: For full-time sophomore, junior or senior study at vocational, 2-year or 4-year institution in or outside United States.
Eligibility: Applicant or parent must be member/participant of ASM International. Applicant must be U.S. citizen or international student.
Basis for selection: Major/career interest in engineering, materials; engineering, mechanical; engineering, ceramic; engineering or materials science. Applicant must demonstrate high academic achievement, depth of character, leadership, seriousness of purpose and service orientation.
Application requirements: Recommendations, essay, transcript, proof of eligibility.
Additional information: Also open to those in polymer, metallurgical, industrial and aeronautical engineering. Applicant must be a member of ASM International. International students are eligible to apply for all awards except need-based scholarships. Visit Website for full details.

>   **Amount of award:** $500-$5,000
>   **Number of awards:**   34
>   **Number of applicants:**   93
>   **Application deadline:**   May 1
>   **Notification begins:**   July 15
>   **Total amount awarded:** $47,000

Contact:
ASM International Foundation
Scholarship Program
Materials Park, OH 44073-0002
Phone: 440-338-5151
Fax: 440-338-4634
Web: www.asminternational.org/foundation

Associated Builders and Contractors, CEF

Associated Builders and Contractors' Scholarship

Type of award: Scholarship, renewable.
Intended use: For sophomore, junior or senior study at 4-year institution.
Basis for selection: Major/career interest in construction management or construction. Applicant must demonstrate financial need and high academic achievement.

Application requirements: Recommendations, transcript. Academic evaluation, completed by student's academic advisor. Copy of Student Aid Report (first page of FAFSA). Application may not be faxed.
Additional information: Minimum 3.0 GPA required. Must be active member of Associated Builders and Contractors (ABC) Student Chapter, if there is one at applicant's school. Must have completed at least one year of Associate or Baccalaureate degree program and have one full year remaining. Construction-related employment history considered.

>   **Amount of award:** $500-$2,000
>   **Application deadline:**   June 1

Contact:
Scholarship Coordinator
Associated Builders and Contractors, CEF
1300 North Seventeenth Street
Rosslyn, VA 22209
Phone: 703-812-2010

Associated General Contractors Education and Research Foundation

AGC Education and Research Undergraduate Scholarship

Type of award: Scholarship, renewable.
Intended use: For full-time freshman, sophomore or junior study at accredited 4-year institution. Designated institutions: Must be enrolled in an ABET or ACCE accredited program to be eligible.
Eligibility: Applicant must be U.S. citizen or permanent resident.
Basis for selection: Major/career interest in engineering, civil; engineering, construction or construction. Applicant must demonstrate financial need and high academic achievement.
Application requirements: Recommendations, transcript. Application form.
Additional information: Must be enrolled in or planning to enroll in a full-time, four- or five-year university program of construction or civil engineering. Applications are available September 1 from AGC office or Website. Seniors with one full academic year of course work remaining are eligible.

>   **Amount of award:** $2,000-$8,000
>   **Application deadline:**   November 1

Contact:
Association of General Contractors Education and Research Foundation
Attn: Director of Programs
333 John Carlyle Street, Suite 200
Alexandria, VA 22314
Phone: 703-548-3118
Fax: 703-837-5402
Web: www.agc.org

Associated General Contractors James L. Allhands Essay Competition

Type of award: Scholarship.

Intended use: For full-time senior study at accredited 4-year institution. Designated institutions: ABET- or ACCE-accredited universities.

Basis for selection: Competition/talent/interest in writing/ journalism, based on essay concerning construction/contracting, which must have a management orientation and demonstrate clarity of thought, completeness, specific examples supporting opinions, grammar, neatness, adherence to contest rules. Major/ career interest in engineering, civil; engineering, construction or construction.

Application requirements: Essay.

Additional information: First prize is $1,000 and all expenses-paid trip to AGC convention. Second prize is $500. Third prize is $300. Competition is management oriented, not technical.

Amount of award:	$300-$1,000
Number of awards:	3
Number of applicants:	50
Application deadline:	November 1

Contact:
Association of General Contractors Education and Research Foundation
Attn: Director of Programs
333 John Carlyle Street, Suite 200
Alexandria, VA 22314
Phone: 703-548-3118
Fax: 703-837-5402
Web: www.agc.org

Associated Press

Associated Press/APTRA-CLETE Roberts Memorial Journalism Scholarship

Type of award: Scholarship.
Intended use: For undergraduate or graduate study at 4-year or graduate institution in United States. Designated institutions: Students must be enrolled in a California or Nevada college or university.

Basis for selection: Major/career interest in journalism or radio/television/film.

Application requirements: Recommendations, essay. May submit examples of broadcast-related work.

Additional information: For study in broadcast journalism. Applications due mid-December.

Amount of award:	$1,500
Number of awards:	4
Notification begins:	September 10
Total amount awarded:	$6,000

Contact:
Rachel Ambrose
The Associated Press
221 South Figueroa St. #300
Los Angeles, CA 90012
Phone: 213-626-1200

Association for Library and Information Science Foundation

ALISE Bodhan S. Wynar Research Paper Competition

Type of award: Scholarship.
Intended use: For non-degree study.
Eligibility: Applicant or parent must be member/participant of Association for Library/Information Science Education.

Basis for selection: Competition/talent/interest in research paper, based on any aspect of librarianship or information studies. Major/career interest in library science.

Application requirements: Proof of eligibility. Must send seven copies of research paper at time of application.

Additional information: Up to two awards given. Visit ALISE Website for detailed explanation of requirements. Research papers prepared by joint investigators are eligible; at least one author must be personal member of ALISE by deadline date. Winners expected to present papers at ALISE annual meeting.

Amount of award:	$2,500
Number of awards:	2
Application deadline:	September 14
Total amount awarded:	$5,000

Contact:
ALISE National Office
Attn: ALISE Awards
11250 Roger Bacon Drive, Suite 8
Reston, VA 20190
Web: www.alise.org

ALISE Methodology Paper Competition

Type of award: Scholarship.
Intended use: For non-degree study.
Basis for selection: Competition/talent/interest in research paper, based on description of methodology or technique, relevance of methodology or technique to library and information science, practical applications of technique towards library and information science research, and clarity and organization of presentation. Major/career interest in library science.

Additional information: Papers completed in pursuit of master's or doctoral degrees are eligible, as are papers generated as result of research grant or other source of funding. Must be personal member of ALISE. Papers prepared by joint authors are eligible; at least one author must be member of ALISE.

Amount of award:	$500
Number of awards:	1
Application deadline:	September 14
Total amount awarded:	$500

Contact:
ALISE National Office
Attn: ALISE Awards
11250 Roger Bacon Drive, Suite 8
Reston, VA 20190
Web: www.alise.org

Scholarships

161

ALISE Research Grant Award

Type of award: Research grant.
Intended use: For non-degree study.
Eligibility: Applicant or parent must be member/participant of Association for Library/Information Science Education.
Basis for selection: Major/career interest in library science. Applicant must demonstrate high academic achievement.
Application requirements: Proof of eligibility, research proposal. Proposal of not more than 20 double-spaced pages. Must send seven copies of proposal at time of application.
Additional information: Visit ALISE Website for detailed explanation of requirements. Must be personal member of ALISE as of deadline date. More than one grant may be awarded; however, total amount of funding for all grants not to exceed $5,000. Research grant award cannot be used to support doctoral dissertation.

Amount of award:	$5,000
Number of awards:	1
Application deadline:	September 14
Total amount awarded:	$5,000

Contact:
ALISE National Office
Attn: ALISE Awards
11250 Roger Bacon Drive, Suite 8
Reston, VA 20190
Web: www.alise.org

Association for Women in Architecture Foundation

Women in Architecture Scholarship

Type of award: Scholarship, renewable.
Intended use: For full-time junior, senior, master's, doctoral or first professional study at 4-year or graduate institution.
Eligibility: Applicant must be female. Applicant must be residing in California.
Basis for selection: Major/career interest in architecture; interior design; engineering; landscape architecture or urban planning. Applicant must demonstrate financial need, high academic achievement and seriousness of purpose.
Application requirements: Interview, portfolio, recommendations, essay, transcript. Student must have completed at least one year in architecture or related program leading to degree.
Additional information: Must be either California resident or attend California school to qualify. Applications may be downloaded from Website.

Amount of award:	$1,000-$2,500
Number of awards:	3
Number of applicants:	60
Application deadline:	April 26
Notification begins:	February 1
Total amount awarded:	$5,000

Contact:
Association for Women in Architecture Foundation
2550 Beverly Boulevard
Los Angeles, CA 90057
Phone: 213-389-6490
Web: www.awa-la.org

Association for Women in Communications

Association for Women in Communications Scholarship

Type of award: Scholarship.
Intended use: For full-time junior, senior or graduate study at accredited 4-year or graduate institution. Designated institutions: Must attend schools in Washington state.
Eligibility: Applicant must be residing in Washington.
Basis for selection: Major/career interest in communications; journalism; radio/television/film; film/video or graphic arts/design. Applicant must demonstrate financial need, high academic achievement, depth of character and service orientation.
Application requirements: Recommendations, essay, transcript. Writing sample.

Amount of award:	$1,000-$1,500
Number of awards:	3
Application deadline:	February 15

Contact:
Association for Women in Communications
1412 SW 102 Street
PMB 224
Seattle, WA 98146
Phone: 206-298-4966

Association of American Geographers

Anne U. White Fund

Type of award: Research grant, renewable.
Intended use: For undergraduate, graduate or non-degree study at postsecondary institution.
Eligibility: Applicant or parent must be member/participant of Association of American Geographers. Applicant must be U.S. citizen.
Basis for selection: Major/career interest in geography.
Application requirements: Research proposal. Both spouses must complete background information forms.
Additional information: Intention of Fund is to encourage field research conducted by member of AAG jointly with his/her spouse. Must have been member for at least two years at time of application. Report summarizing results and documenting expenses underwritten by grant must be submitted to Executive Director within 12 months after receiving award.

Amount of award:	$200-$1,000
Number of awards:	15
Number of applicants:	25
Application deadline:	December 31
Notification begins:	March 1

Contact:
Association of American Geographers
1710 16 Street, NW
Washington, DC 20009-3198
Phone: 202-234-1450
Web: www.aag.org

Association of Energy Service Companies

Energy Service Scholarship

Type of award: Scholarship, renewable.
Intended use: For full-time undergraduate or non-degree study at accredited vocational, 2-year or 4-year institution.
Eligibility: Applicant or parent must be employed by Association of Energy Service Companies.
Basis for selection: Applicant must demonstrate financial need, high academic achievement, depth of character, leadership and service orientation.
Application requirements: Essay, transcript. ACT or SAT scores.
Additional information: Student or parent must be employed by a member company of the Association of Energy Service Companies.

Amount of award:	$1,000
Number of awards:	39
Number of applicants:	100
Application deadline:	April 15
Notification begins:	May 28
Total amount awarded:	$39,000

Contact:
Association of Energy Service Companies
Jim Yancy
10200 Richmond Avenue
Houston, TX 77642
Phone: 800-692-0771
Fax: 713-781-7542
Web: www.aesc.net

Association of Former Agents of the U.S. Secret Service

Former Agents of the U.S. Secret Service Scholarship

Type of award: Scholarship.
Intended use: For full-time sophomore, junior, senior, master's or postgraduate study at accredited 2-year, 4-year or graduate institution in United States.
Eligibility: Applicant must be U.S. citizen.
Basis for selection: Major/career interest in criminal justice/law enforcement. Applicant must demonstrate financial need, high academic achievement, depth of character, leadership, patriotism, seriousness of purpose and service orientation.
Application requirements: Recommendations, essay, transcript.
Additional information: Send SASE with application request. Applications accepted from September through April 30. Unsigned documents will not be accepted.

Amount of award:	$1,000-$3,000
Number of awards:	5
Number of applicants:	120
Application deadline:	May 1
Total amount awarded:	$12,000

Contact:
Scholarship Coordinator
P.O. Box 848
Annandale, VA 22003-0848

Association of State Dam Safety Officials

Dam Safety Officials Scholarship

Type of award: Scholarship, renewable.
Intended use: For junior or senior study in United States.
Eligibility: Applicant must be U.S. citizen.
Basis for selection: Major/career interest in engineering, civil. Applicant must demonstrate financial need, high academic achievement, depth of character, leadership, seriousness of purpose and service orientation.
Application requirements: Recommendations, essay, transcript.
Additional information: Decisions based on grades, career goals, and extracurricular activities.

Amount of award:	$2,500
Number of awards:	2
Number of applicants:	50
Application deadline:	February 15
Notification begins:	May 11
Total amount awarded:	$5,000

Contact:
Association of State Dam Safety Officials
450 Old Vine Street, 2nd Floor
Lexington, KY 40507
Phone: 859-257-5140
Fax: 859-328-1958
Web: www.damsafety.org

Association of the Sons of Poland

Sons of Poland Scholarship

Type of award: Scholarship.
Intended use: For full-time freshman study at accredited 2-year or 4-year institution in United States.
Eligibility: Applicant or parent must be member/participant of Sons of Poland. Applicant must be high school senior. Applicant must be Polish. Applicant must be U.S. citizen or permanent resident.
Basis for selection: Applicant must demonstrate high academic achievement.
Application requirements: Essay, transcript, proof of eligibility. Must be a member for two years. Applicant must be a high school senior.
Additional information: Must be an insured member of the Association. High GPA and SAT I scores needed.

Amount of award:	$50-$500
Number of awards:	11
Number of applicants:	11
Application deadline:	May 14
Notification begins:	February 1
Total amount awarded:	$2,900

Contact:
Association of the Sons of Poland
Achievement Scholarship
333 Hackensack Street
Carlstadt, NJ 07072
Phone: 201-935-2807

Astra Zeneca

Astra Zeneca Scholarship Program

Type of award: Scholarship, renewable.
Intended use: For undergraduate study at 2-year or 4-year institution.
Eligibility: Applicant or parent must be employed by Astra Zeneca. Applicant must be high school senior.
Additional information: For further information or an application, contact Astra Zeneca directly.

Amount of award:	$3,000

Atlanta Association of Black Journalists

AABJ Xernona Clayton Scholarship

Type of award: Scholarship.
Intended use: For freshman, sophomore or junior study in United States.
Eligibility: Applicant must be African American. Applicant must be U.S. citizen residing in Georgia.
Basis for selection: Based on academic achievement. Major/career interest in communications; English or public relations.
Application requirements: Essay. Minimum GPA required is 2.5.
Additional information: For more information, please send a SASE with request. Topic of essay changes every year. Information should be available from university's financial aid office.

Amount of award:	$500-$1,000
Number of awards:	3

Contact:
Atlanta Association of Black Journalism
P.O. Box 54128
Atlanta, GA 30308
Phone: 770-593-5837
Web: www.aabj.org

Atlas Pacific Engineering Company

Atlas Pacific Scholarship Program

Type of award: Scholarship, renewable.
Intended use: For freshman study at vocational, 2-year or 4-year institution.

Eligibility: Applicant or parent must be employed by Atlas Pacific Engineering Company. Applicant must be high school senior.
Additional information: For further information or an application, contact Atlas Pacific Engineering Company directly.

Amount of award:	$2,500

Automotive Hall of Fame

Automotive Educational Fund Scholarship

Type of award: Scholarship, renewable.
Intended use: For full-time undergraduate study at accredited 2-year, 4-year or graduate institution in United States.
Basis for selection: Major/career interest in automotive technology; engineering, mechanical; engineering, chemical or engineering, electrical/electronic.
Application requirements: Recommendations, transcript, proof of eligibility. High school seniors must have proof of acceptance to postsecondary institution.
Additional information: Students with major/career interest in aftermarket engineering also eligible to apply. Applicant must have interest in pursuing automotive career upon graduation. SASE must be received in order to get scholarship application. All required materials must be submitted with application to be considered. Only award recipients will be notified.

Amount of award:	$250-$2,000
Number of awards:	12
Application deadline:	May 30

Contact:
Automotive Hall of Fame
21400 Oakwood Blvd.
Dearborn, MI 48124-4078
Phone: 313-240-4000
Fax: 313-240-8641
Web: www.automotivehalloffame.org

Aventis Pharmaceuticals

Aventis Pharmaceuticals Scholarship Program

Type of award: Scholarship, renewable.
Intended use: For undergraduate study at accredited vocational, 2-year or 4-year institution.
Eligibility: Applicant or parent must be employed by Aventis Pharmaceuticals.
Basis for selection: Applicant must demonstrate financial need.
Additional information: For further information or an application, contact Aventis Pharmaceuticals directly.

Amount of award:	$1,000-$4,000

Avery Dennison

Avery Dennison Scholars Program

Type of award: Scholarship, renewable.
Intended use: For freshman study at accredited vocational, 2-year or 4-year institution.
Eligibility: Applicant or parent must be employed by Avery Dennison.
Basis for selection: Applicant must demonstrate financial need.
Additional information: For further information or an application, contact Avery Dennison directly.
  Amount of award: $500-$2,500

Avnet, Inc.

Avnet Scholarship Program

Type of award: Scholarship, renewable.
Intended use: For undergraduate study at vocational, 2-year or 4-year institution.
Eligibility: Applicant or parent must be employed by Avnet, Inc. Applicant must be high school senior.
Additional information: For futher information or an application, contact Avnet Incorporated directly.
  Amount of award: $500-$2,000

Baker Manufacturing Company

Baker Scholarship Program

Type of award: Scholarship.
Intended use: For undergraduate study at accredited vocational, 2-year or 4-year institution.
Eligibility: Applicant or parent must be employed by Baker Manufacturing Company.
Additional information: For further information or an application, contact Baker Manufacturing Company directly.
  Amount of award: $1,000

Bandag, Inc.

Bandag Scholarship

Type of award: Scholarship, renewable.
Intended use: For freshman study at vocational, 2-year or 4-year institution.
Eligibility: Applicant or parent must be employed by Bandag, Incorporated. Applicant must be high school senior.
Additional information: For futher information or an application, contact Bandag Incorporated directly.
  Amount of award: $500-$1,250

Banta Corporation Foundation, Inc.

Banta Scholarship Program

Type of award: Scholarship, renewable.
Intended use: For freshman study at 2-year or 4-year institution.
Eligibility: Applicant or parent must be employed by Banta Corporation Foundation, Inc. Applicant must be high school senior.
Additional information: For futher information or an application, contact Banta Corporation Foundation Incorporated directly.
  Amount of award: $2,500

The Bardes Fund

Bardes Fund Scholarship

Type of award: Scholarship, renewable.
Intended use: For undergraduate study at accredited vocational, 2-year or 4-year institution.
Eligibility: Applicant or parent must be employed by Bardes Company.
Additional information: For further information or an application, contact Bardes Company directly.
  Amount of award: $500-$3,500

Barnes Group Foundation, Inc.

Barnes Group Foundation Scholarship

Type of award: Scholarship, renewable.
Intended use: For undergraduate study at accredited vocational, 2-year or 4-year institution.
Eligibility: Applicant or parent must be employed by Barnes Group.
Basis for selection: Applicant must demonstrate financial need.
Additional information: For further information or an application, contact Barnes Group Foundation, Inc. directly.
  Amount of award: $500-$3,500

Barry M. Goldwater Scholarship and Excellence In Education Foundation

Barry M. Goldwater Scholarship

Type of award: Scholarship, renewable.

Intended use: For full-time junior or senior study at accredited 4-year institution in United States. Designated institutions: Those listed in Directory of Postsecondary Institutions published by US Deparment of Education.

Eligibility: Applicant must be U.S. citizen or permanent resident.

Basis for selection: Major/career interest in engineering; mathematics; natural sciences; science, general; computer/ information sciences; medical specialties/research; astronomy or geology/earth sciences. Applicant must demonstrate high academic achievement, depth of character, leadership and seriousness of purpose.

Application requirements: Recommendations, transcript, proof of eligibility, nomination by college faculty representative. Minimum 3.0 GPA required. Essay (600 words or less) relating to student's chosen career. Nominations of resident aliens must include letter of nominee's intent to obtain U.S. citizenship and photocopy of Alien Registration Card.

Additional information: Bulletin of information, nomination materials, application and list of faculty representatives available on Website. Students must be nominated by university's Goldwater Scholarship faculty representative. Applicant must be legal resident of state from which he or she is candidate. Residents of District of Columbia, Puerto Rico, Guam, American Samoa, Virgin Islands, and Commonwealth of North Mariana Islands also eligible.

Amount of award:	$7,500
Number of awards:	300
Number of applicants:	12,000
Application deadline:	February 1
Notification begins:	April 1

Contact:
Barry M. Goldwater/Excellence In Education Foundation
6225 Brandon Avenue, Suite 315
Springfield, VA 22150-2519
Phone: 703-756-6012
Fax: 703-756-6015
Web: www.act.org/goldwater

Bartley Corporation

Marcia Doyle Bartley Scholarship

Type of award: Scholarship, renewable.

Intended use: For undergraduate study at accredited vocational, 2-year or 4-year institution.

Eligibility: Applicant or parent must be employed by Bartley Corporation.

Basis for selection: Applicant must demonstrate financial need.

Additional information: For further information or an application, contact Bartley Corporation directly.

Amount of award:	$5,000

Bashinsky Foundation, Inc.

Golden Enterprises Scholarship

Type of award: Scholarship, renewable.

Intended use: For undergraduate or graduate study at accredited vocational, 2-year or 4-year institution.

Eligibility: Applicant or parent must be employed by Golden Enterprises, Inc.

Additional information: For further information or an application, contact Golden Enterprises, Inc., or Golden Flake.

Amount of award:	$2,500

Bass Hotels & Resorts

Bass Hotels & Resorts Scholarship

Type of award: Scholarship, renewable.

Intended use: For undergraduate study at vocational, 2-year or 4-year institution.

Eligibility: Applicant or parent must be employed by Holiday Hospitality, Corporation. Applicant must be high school senior.

Additional information: For further information or an application, contact Holiday Hospitality Corporation directly.

Amount of award:	$3,000

The Baxter Allegiance Foundation

Baxter Allegiance Foundation Scholarship

Type of award: Scholarship, renewable.

Intended use: For undergraduate study at accredited vocational, 2-year or 4-year institution.

Eligibility: Applicant or parent must be employed by Baxter International, Inc.

Application requirements: Proof of eligibility.

Additional information: For further information or an application, contact Baxter Allegiance Foundation directly.

Amount of award:	$1,000

Bay State Gas Company

Bay State Gas Company Scholarship

Type of award: Scholarship.

Intended use: For full-time undergraduate or non-degree study at vocational, 2-year or 4-year institution in or outside United States.

Eligibility: Applicant or parent must be employed by Bay State Gas Company.

Basis for selection: Applicant must demonstrate financial need, high academic achievement, depth of character, leadership, seriousness of purpose and service orientation.

Application requirements: Recommendations, transcript, proof of eligibility.

Additional information: For further information or an application, contact Bay State Gas Company directly.

Amount of award:	$1,000
Number of awards:	10
Application deadline:	April 1

Contact:
Bay State Gas Company
Human Resource Department
300 Friberg Parkway
Westboro, MA 1581-5039
Phone: 508-836-7155

Beacon Capital Partners

Robert Leventhal Scholars Program

Type of award: Scholarship.
Intended use: For undergraduate study at accredited vocational, 2-year or 4-year institution.
Eligibility: Applicant or parent must be employed by Beacon Companies.
Basis for selection: Applicant must demonstrate financial need.
Additional information: For further information or an application, contact Beacon Capital Partners directly.

Amount of award:	$500-$2,000

Bedding Plants Foundation, Inc.

Barbara Carlson Scholarship

Type of award: Scholarship.
Intended use: For sophomore, junior, senior or graduate study at accredited vocational, 2-year, 4-year or graduate institution in United States or Canada.
Eligibility: Applicant must be U.S. citizen, permanent resident, international student or Canadian citizen.
Basis for selection: Major/career interest in horticulture. Applicant must demonstrate financial need and high academic achievement.
Application requirements: Recommendations, transcript. Statement of academic and professional intentions. Minimum 3.0 GPA.
Additional information: Study of horticulture or career interest in horticulture required. To be eligible for this scholarship, applicant must intern with or work for public gardens. Number of scholarships and dollar amount awarded varies. Applications are available from January 1 to May 1. Current info and applications can be obtained at BPFI Website. Send SASE for application and/or acknowledgement of receipt of application.

Amount of award:	$500-$2,000
Number of awards:	1
Application deadline:	May 1

Contact:
Bedding Plants Foundation, Inc.
Scholarship Applications
P.O. Box 280
East Lansing, MI 48826-0280
Phone: 517-333-4617
Fax: 517-333-4494
Web: www.bpfi.org

Carl F. Dietz Memorial Scholarship

Type of award: Scholarship.
Intended use: For full-time sophomore, junior or senior study at accredited 2-year or 4-year institution in United States or Canada.
Eligibility: Applicant must be U.S. citizen, permanent resident, international student or Canadian citizen.
Basis for selection: Major/career interest in horticulture. Applicant must demonstrate financial need and high academic achievement.
Application requirements: Recommendations, transcript. Statement of academic and professional intent. Minimum 3.0 GPA.
Additional information: Study of horticulture or career interest in horticulture required. To apply for this scholarship, applicant's interest must lie in horticultural allied trades (i.e., supply sales, trade press, greenhouse equipment, etc.). Number of scholarships and dollar amount awarded varies. Applications are available from January 1 to May 1. Current info and applications can be obtained at BPFI Website. Send SASE for application and/or acknowledgement of receipt of application.

Amount of award:	$500-$1,000
Number of awards:	1
Application deadline:	May 1

Contact:
Bedding Plants Foundation, Inc.
P.O. Box 280
East Lansing, MI 4882-0280
Phone: 517-333-4617
Fax: 517-333-4494
Web: www.bpfi.org

Dosatron International Scholarship

Type of award: Scholarship.
Intended use: For junior, senior or graduate study at accredited 4-year or graduate institution in United States or Canada.
Eligibility: Applicant must be U.S. citizen, permanent resident, international student or Canadian citizen.
Basis for selection: Major/career interest in horticulture. Applicant must demonstrate financial need and high academic achievement.
Application requirements: Recommendations, transcript. Statement of academic and professional intent. Minimum 3.0 GPA.
Additional information: Study of horticulture or career interest in horticulture required. To apply for this scholarship, applicant's interest must lie in floriculture production, with career goal to work in a greenhouse environment. Number of scholarships and dollar amount awarded varies. Applications are available from January 1 to May 1. Current info and applications can be obtained at BPFI Website. Send SASE for application and/or acknowledgement of receipt of application.

Amount of award:	$500-$2,000
Application deadline:	May 1

Contact:
Bedding Plants Foundation, Inc.
Scholarship Applications
P.O. Box 280
East Lansing, MI 48826-0280
Phone: 517-333-4617
Fax: 517-333-4494
Web: www.bpfi.org

Earl J. Small Growers Scholarship

Type of award: Scholarship.
Intended use: For full-time sophomore, junior or senior study at accredited 4-year institution in United States or Canada.
Eligibility: Applicant must be U.S. citizen, permanent resident, international student or Canadian citizen.
Basis for selection: Major/career interest in horticulture.
Application requirements: Recommendations, transcript. Statement of academic and professional intent. Minimum 3.0 GPA.
Additional information: Study of horticulture or career interest in horticulture required. To apply for this scholarship, applicant's interest must lie in greenhouse production with a main interest in potted plants. Number of scholarships and dollar amount awarded varies. Applications are available from January 1 to May 1. Current info and applications can be obtained at BPFI Website. Send SASE for application and/or acknowledgement of receipt of application.

Amount of award:	$500-$1,000
Number of awards:	1
Application deadline:	May 1

Contact:
Bedding Plants Foundation, Inc.
Scholarship Spplications
P.O. Box 280
East Lansing, MI 48826-0280
Phone: 517-333-4617
Fax: 517-333-4494
Web: www.bpfi.org

Ed Markham International Scholarship

Type of award: Scholarship.
Intended use: For sophomore, junior, senior or graduate study at accredited 2-year, 4-year or graduate institution in United States or Canada.
Eligibility: Applicant must be U.S. citizen, permanent resident, international student or Canadian citizen.
Basis for selection: Major/career interest in horticulture or marketing. Applicant must demonstrate financial need and high academic achievement.
Application requirements: Recommendations, transcript. Statement of academic and professional intent. Minimum 3.0 GPA.
Additional information: For students in pursuit of a career in horticulture who wish to further their understanding of horticulture marketing through international travel. Number of scholarships and dollar amount awarded varies. Applications are available from January 1 to May 1. Current info and applications can be obtained at BPFI Website. Send SASE for application and/or acknowledgement of receipt of application.

Amount of award:	$500-$2,000
Application deadline:	May 1

Contact:
Bedding Plants Foundation Inc.
Scholarship Applications
P.O. Box 280
East Lansing, MI 48826-0280
Phone: 517-333-4617
Fax: 517-333-4494
Web: www.bpfi.org

Fran Johnson Non-Traditional Scholarship

Type of award: Scholarship.
Intended use: For full-time undergraduate study at accredited 4-year or graduate institution in United States or Canada.
Eligibility: Applicant must be returning adult student. Applicant must be U.S. citizen, permanent resident, international student or Canadian citizen.
Basis for selection: Major/career interest in horticulture. Applicant must demonstrate financial need and high academic achievement.
Application requirements: Recommendations, transcript. Statement of academic and professional intent.
Additional information: Must have been out of academic setting for at least five years and reentering school. Study of horticulture or career interest in horticulture required. Specific interest in bedding plants and/or floral crops required. Number of scholarships and dollar amount awarded varies. Applications are available from January 1 to May 1. Current info and applications can be obtained at BPFI Website. Send SASE for application and/or acknowledgement of receipt of application.

Amount of award:	$500-$1,000
Number of awards:	1
Application deadline:	May 1

Contact:
Bedding Plants Foundation, Inc.
Scholarship Applications
P.O. Box 280
East Lansing, MI 48826-0280
Phone: 517-333-4617
Fax: 517-333-4494
Web: www.bpfi.org

Harold Bettinger Memorial Scholarship

Type of award: Scholarship.
Intended use: For full-time sophomore, junior or senior study at accredited 4-year or graduate institution in United States or Canada.
Eligibility: Applicant must be U.S. citizen, permanent resident, international student or Canadian citizen.
Basis for selection: Major/career interest in horticulture; business or marketing. Applicant must demonstrate financial need and high academic achievement.
Application requirements: Recommendations, transcript. Statement of academic and professional intent. Minimum 3.0 GPA.
Additional information: Study of horticulture or career interest in horticulture required. To apply for this scholarship, applicant's major or minor must be in business and/or marketing with intent to apply it to a horticulture-related business. Number of scholarships and dollar amount awarded varies. Applications are available from January 1 to May 1. Current info and applications can be obtained at BPFI Website. Send SASE for application and/or acknowledgement of receipt of application.

Amount of award:	$500-$2,000
Number of awards:	1
Application deadline:	May 1

Contact:
Bedding Plants Foundation, Inc.
Scholarship Applications
P.O. Box 280
East Lansing, MI 48909-0280
Phone: 517-333-4617
Fax: 517-333-4494
Web: www.bpfi.org

J.K. Rathmell, Jr., Memorial for Work/Study Abroad

Type of award: Scholarship.
Intended use: For full-time junior, senior or graduate study at accredited 4-year or graduate institution in or outside United States or Canada.
Eligibility: Applicant must be U.S. citizen, permanent resident, international student or Canadian citizen.
Basis for selection: Competition/talent/interest in Study abroad. Major/career interest in horticulture or landscape architecture. Applicant must demonstrate financial need, high academic achievement, depth of character and seriousness of purpose.
Application requirements: Recommendations, transcript. Statement of academic and professional intent. Minimum 3.0 GPA.
Additional information: Study of horticulture or career interest in horticulture required. Applicants must plan work/study abroad and submit specific plan for such. Preference given to those planning to work or study for six months or longer. Must have interest in floriculture, ornamental horticulture, or landscape architecture. Must include letter of invitation from host institution abroad. Number of scholarships and dollar amount awarded varies. Applications are available from January 1 to May 1. Current info and applications can be obtained at BPFI Website. Send SASE for application and/or acknowledgement of receipt of application.

Amount of award:	$2,000
Number of awards:	1
Application deadline:	May 1
Total amount awarded:	$2,000

Contact:
Bedding Plants Foundation, Inc.
Scholarship Applications
P.O. Box 280
East Lansing, MI 48826-0280
Phone: 517-333-4617
Fax: 517-333-4494
Web: www.bpfi.org

Jacob Van Namen Marketing Scholarship

Type of award: Scholarship.
Intended use: For sophomore, junior or senior study at accredited 2-year or 4-year institution in United States or Canada.
Eligibility: Applicant must be U.S. citizen, permanent resident, international student or Canadian citizen.
Basis for selection: Major/career interest in horticulture; agribusiness; marketing; botany or agriculture. Applicant must demonstrate financial need and high academic achievement.
Application requirements: Recommendations, transcript. Statement of academic and professional intent. Minimum 3.0 GPA.
Additional information: Study of horticulture or career interest in horticulture required. To apply for this scholarship,

applicant's interest must lie in agribusiness marketing and distribution of floral products. Number of scholarships and dollar amount awarded varies. Applications are available from January 1 to May 1. Current info and applications can be obtained at BPFI Website. Send SASE for application and/or acknowledgement of receipt of application.

Amount of award:	$500-$2,000
Number of awards:	1
Application deadline:	May 1

Contact:
Bedding Plants Foundation, Inc.
Scholarship Applications
P.O. Box 280
East Lansing, MI 48826-0280
Phone: 517-333-4617
Fax: 517-333-4494
Web: www.bpfi.org

Jerry Baker Scholarship

Type of award: Scholarship.
Intended use: For full-time freshman study at accredited 4-year institution in United States or Canada.
Eligibility: Applicant must be high school senior. Applicant must be U.S. citizen, permanent resident, international student or Canadian citizen/permanent resident.
Basis for selection: Major/career interest in horticulture or landscape architecture. Applicant must demonstrate financial need and high academic achievement.
Application requirements: Recommendations, transcript. Statement of academic and professional intent.
Additional information: Study of horticulture or career interest in horticulture, landscaping, and/or gardening required. Number of scholarships and dollar amount awarded varies. Applications are available from January 1 to May 1. Current info and applications can be obtained at BPFI Website. Send SASE for application and/or acknowledgement of receipt of application.

Amount of award:	$500-$2,000
Application deadline:	May 1

Contact:
Bedding Plants Foundation, Inc.
Scholarship Applications
P.O. Box 280
East Lansing, MI 48826-0280
Phone: 517-333-4617
Fax: 517-333-4494
Web: www.bpfi.org

Jerry Wilmot Scholarship

Type of award: Scholarship.
Intended use: For full-time sophomore, junior or senior study at accredited 2-year or 4-year institution in United States or Canada.
Eligibility: Applicant must be U.S. citizen, permanent resident, international student or Canadian citizen.
Basis for selection: Major/career interest in horticulture; business; finance/banking or business/management/administration. Applicant must demonstrate financial need and high academic achievement.
Application requirements: Recommendations, transcript. Essay stating academic and professional intent. Minimum 3.0 GPA.
Additional information: Study of horticulture or career interest in horticulture required. To apply for this scholarship, applicant must major or minor in business or finance with intent to apply it to garden center management. Number of

scholarships and dollar amount awarded varies. Applications are available from January 1 to May 1. Current info and applications can be obtained at BPFI Website. Send SASE for application and/or acknowledgement of receipt of application.

Amount of award:	$500-$2,000
Number of awards:	1
Application deadline:	May 1

Contact:
Bedding Plants Foundation, Inc.
Scholarship Applications
P.O. Box 280
East Lansing, MI 48826-0280
Phone: 517-333-4617
Fax: 517-333-4494
Web: www.bpfi.org

Paris Fracasso Production Floriculture Scholarship

Type of award: Scholarship.
Intended use: For junior or senior study at accredited 4-year institution in United States or Canada.
Eligibility: Applicant must be U.S. citizen, permanent resident, international student or Canadian citizen.
Basis for selection: Major/career interest in botany or horticulture. Applicant must demonstrate financial need and high academic achievement.
Application requirements: Recommendations, transcript. Statement of academic and professional intent. Minimum 3.0 GPA.
Additional information: Study of horticulture or career interest in horticulture required. To apply for this scholarship, applicant's interest must lie in floriculture production. Number of scholarships and dollar amount awarded varies. Applications are available from January 1 to May 1. Current info and applications can be obtained at BPFI Website. Send SASE for application and/or acknowledgement of receipt of application.

Amount of award:	$500-$2,000
Number of awards:	1
Application deadline:	May 1

Contact:
Bedding Plants Foundation, Inc.
Scholarship Applications
P.O. Box 280
East Lansing, MI 48826-0280
Phone: 517-333-4617
Fax: 517-333-4494
Web: www.bpfi.org

Vocational Horticulture Scholarship

Type of award: Scholarship.
Intended use: For full-time undergraduate certificate, freshman, sophomore or non-degree study at accredited vocational or 2-year institution in United States or Canada.
Eligibility: Applicant must be U.S. citizen, permanent resident, international student or Canadian citizen.
Basis for selection: Major/career interest in horticulture. Applicant must demonstrate financial need and high academic achievement.
Application requirements: Recommendations, transcript. Essay stating academic and professional intent. Minimum 3.0 GPA.
Additional information: Must have intention of becoming floriculture plant producer and/or operations manager. Number of scholarships and dollar amount awarded varies. Applications are available from January 1 to May 1. Current info and

applications can be obtained at BPFI Website. Send SASE for application and/or acknowledgement of receipt of application.

Amount of award:	$500-$2,000
Number of awards:	1
Application deadline:	May 1

Contact:
Bedding Plants Foundation, Inc.
Scholarship Applications
P.O. Box 280
East Lansing, MI 48826-0280
Phone: 517-333-4617
Fax: 517-333-4494
Web: www.bpfi.org

Bemis Company Foundation

Bemis Company Foundation Scholarship

Type of award: Scholarship, renewable.
Intended use: For undergraduate study at accredited vocational, 2-year or 4-year institution.
Eligibility: Applicant or parent must be employed by Bemis Company.
Basis for selection: Applicant must demonstrate financial need, high academic achievement, depth of character, leadership, seriousness of purpose and service orientation.
Application requirements: Transcript, proof of eligibility.
Additional information: Award may be renewed up to three times if attending a four-year school.

Amount of award:	$1,000-$5,000
Number of awards:	36
Number of applicants:	204
Total amount awarded:	$400,000

Contact:
Bemis Company Foundation
222 South Ninth Street
Suite 2300
Minneapolis, MN 55402-4099
Phone: 612-376-3093

Bethesda Lutheran Homes and Services, Inc.

Developmental Disabilities Nursing Scholastic Achievement Scholarship

Type of award: Scholarship.
Intended use: For full-time junior, senior, master's or doctoral study at accredited 2-year, 4-year or graduate institution.
Eligibility: Applicant must be Lutheran.
Basis for selection: Major/career interest in nursing. Applicant must demonstrate high academic achievement, seriousness of purpose and service orientation.
Application requirements: Recommendations, essay, transcript, proof of eligibility.
Additional information: Must have 3.0 GPA. Must be working toward registered nurse (R.N.) degree. Preference given to those interested in working with developmentally disabled persons.

Amount of award:	$1,000
Number of awards:	1
Application deadline:	March 15
Notification begins:	May 1
Total amount awarded:	$1,000

Contact:
Bethesda Lutheran Homes and Services, Inc.
Coordinator/Outreach Programs
700 Hoffmann Drive
Watertown, WI 53094
Phone: 800-369-4636 ext. 416
Fax: 920-262-6513
Web: www.blhs.org

Developmental Disability Scholastic Achievement Scholarship

Type of award: Scholarship.
Intended use: For full-time junior, senior or graduate study at accredited 4-year or graduate institution in United States.
Eligibility: Applicant must be Lutheran.
Basis for selection: Major/career interest in social work; education; psychology; mental health/therapy; education, special; education, early childhood; education, teacher; speech pathology/audiology; occupational therapy or health-related professions. Applicant must demonstrate financial need, high academic achievement, seriousness of purpose and service orientation.
Application requirements: Recommendations, essay, transcript, proof of eligibility.
Additional information: Preference to those interested in working with persons with mental retardation. Minimum 3.0 GPA. Also available for students of Lutheran Theology.

Amount of award:	$1,000
Number of awards:	2
Application deadline:	March 15
Notification begins:	May 1
Total amount awarded:	$2,000

Contact:
Bethesda Lutheran Homes and Services, Inc.
Coordinator, Outreach Programs
700 Hoffmann Drive
Watertown, WI 53094
Phone: 800-369-4636 ext. 416
Fax: 920-262-6513
Web: www.blhs.org

Bethlehem Steel Foundation

Bethlehem Steel Scholars

Type of award: Scholarship.
Intended use: For undergraduate study at vocational, 2-year or 4-year institution.
Eligibility: Applicant or parent must be employed by Bethlehem Steel Foundation. Applicant must be high school senior.
Additional information: For further information or an application, contact Bethlem Steel Foundation directly.

Amount of award:	$1,000

birthright israel

birthright israel gift

Type of award: Scholarship.
Intended use: For undergraduate study.
Eligibility: Applicant must be at least 18, no older than 26. Applicant must be Jewish.
Application requirements: Proof of eligibility.
Additional information: All eligible applicants receive free trip to Israel under the auspices of Aish HaTorah, Hillel and other organizations. Round-trip airfare and 10 days of program activity funded. Must not have visited Israel previously on an educational peer-group trip. International program seeks to "make Israel accessible to every Jewish youth regardless of his or her affiliation, nationality or economic status." Visit Website or contact sponsor for current offerings.
Contact:
Email: information@birthrightisrael.com
Phone: 888-99-ISRAEL
Web: www.birthrightisrael.com

Blinded Veteran's Association

Katherine F. Gruber Scholarship Program

Type of award: Scholarship, renewable.
Intended use: For full-time freshman, sophomore, junior, senior or graduate study at accredited postsecondary institution in United States.
Eligibility: Parent must be visually impaired. Applicant must be U.S. citizen. Applicant must be dependent of disabled veteran; or spouse of disabled veteran who served in the Army, Air Force, Marines, Navy or Coast Guard.
Application requirements: Recommendations, essay, transcript.
Additional information: Blinded veteran must meet definition of blindness used by Blinded Vererans Association. Veteran's blindness may be either service-connected or non-service-connected. Applicants may not be on probation during their study.

Amount of award:	$1,000-$2,000
Number of awards:	16
Number of applicants:	40
Application deadline:	April 13
Notification begins:	January 1
Total amount awarded:	$24,000

Contact:
Blinded Veteran's Association Katherine F. Gruber Scholarship
477 H Street NW
Washington, DC 20001-2694
Phone: 202-371-8880
Fax: 202-371-8258

Blue Bell Foundation

Blue Bell Scholarship

Type of award: Scholarship, renewable.
Intended use: For undergraduate study at accredited vocational, 2-year or 4-year institution.
Eligibility: Applicant or parent must be employed by Blue Bell Foundation.
Basis for selection: Applicant must demonstrate financial need.
Additional information: For further information or an application, contact Blue Bell Foundation directly.
   Amount of award: $1,000-$2,000

Blue Circle America Inc.

Blue Circle America Scholarship Program

Type of award: Scholarship, renewable.
Intended use: For undergraduate study at vocational, 2-year or 4-year institution.
Eligibility: Applicant or parent must be employed by Blue Circle America Inc. Applicant must be high school senior.
Additional information: For further information or an application, contact Blue Circle America Incorporated directly.
   Amount of award: $1,000-$2,000

BMI Foundation, Inc.

BMI Student Composer Awards

Type of award: Scholarship.
Intended use: For undergraduate study at accredited 4-year institution.
Eligibility: Applicant must be no older than 25. Applicant must be U.S. citizen, permanent resident, international student or citizen of a Western Hemisphere country.
Basis for selection: Competition/talent/interest in Music performance/composition, based on composition of classical concert music. Major/career interest in music. Applicant must demonstrate seriousness of purpose.
Application requirements: Completed official application form.
Additional information: Applicant must be under age of 26 on December 31 of year prior to deadline. Applicant must be enrolled in accredited public, private or parochial secondary schools; in accredited colleges or conservatories of music; or engaged in private study of music with recognized and established teachers. Applications usually available in November; send full mailing address to sponsor to receive official form.
   Amount of award: $500-$5,000
   Application deadline: February 12

Contact:
Ralph N. Jackson
BMI
320 W. 57th Street
New York, NY 10019
Web: www.bmi.com/bmifoundation/student.asp

John Lennon Scholarship

Type of award: Scholarship.
Intended use: For undergraduate study.
Eligibility: Applicant must be at least 15, no older than 24.
Basis for selection: Competition/talent/interest in Music performance/composition, based on best song of any genre with original music and lyrics. Major/career interest in music or performing arts. Applicant must demonstrate seriousness of purpose.
Application requirements: Nomination by participating school, college, community music organization, or youth orchestra.
Additional information: Each participating organization may submit one entry from a current student or alumnus/alumna who meets eligibility requirements. Students interested in applying should check with school or group to see if it is participant or whether it wishes to apply for inclusion.
   Amount of award: $2,500-$10,000
   Number of awards: 1
Contact:
BMI Foundation, Inc.
320 W. 57th Street
New York, NY 10019
Web: www.bmi.com/bmifoundation/index.asp

BNI Coal, Ltd.

BNI Coal, Ltd. Scholarship Program

Type of award: Scholarship.
Intended use: For undergraduate study at accredited vocational, 2-year or 4-year institution.
Eligibility: Applicant or parent must be employed by BNI Coal, Ltd.
Additional information: For further information or an application, contact BNI Coal, Ltd. directly.
   Amount of award: $500

Boart Longyear Inc. - Canada

The Boart Longyear Inc. Scholarship Program

Type of award: Scholarship.
Intended use: For undergraduate study at vocational, 2-year or 4-year institution.
Eligibility: Applicant or parent must be employed by Boart Longyear Inc.- Canada. Applicant must be high school senior.
Additional information: For further information or an application, contact Boart Longyear Incorporated - Canada directly.

Amount of award: $2,500

Bobst Group, Inc.

Jacques Bobst Scholarship

Type of award: Scholarship, renewable.
Intended use: For freshman study at accredited vocational, 2-year or 4-year institution.
Eligibility: Applicant or parent must be employed by Bobst Group Inc.
Additional information: For further information or an application, contact Bobst Group Inc. directly.
   Amount of award: $2,000-$4,000

Boddie-Noell Enterprises, Inc.

James H. Waters Scholarship

Type of award: Scholarship.
Intended use: For undergraduate study at accredited vocational, 2-year or 4-year institution.
Eligibility: Applicant or parent must be employed by Boddie-Noell Enterprises, Inc.
Basis for selection: Applicant must demonstrate financial need.
Additional information: Scholarship open to employees, as well as children of employees, of Boddie-Noell Enterprises. For more information or an application, contact Boddie-Noell Enterprises directly.
   Amount of award: $500-$1,000

Boehringer Ingelheim Corporation

Boehringer Ingelheim Scholarship

Type of award: Scholarship, renewable.
Intended use: For freshman study at accredited vocational, 2-year or 4-year institution.
Eligibility: Applicant or parent must be employed by Boehringer Ingelheim Corporation.
Basis for selection: Applicant must demonstrate financial need.
Additional information: For further information or an application, contact Boehringer Ingelheim Corporation directly.
   Amount of award: $1,500

The Boeing Company

Historically Black Colleges and Minority Institutions Scholarships

Type of award: Scholarship.
Intended use: For undergraduate study at 4-year institution in United States.
Eligibility: Applicant must be African American.
Additional information: Scholarships are awarded to students who attend these colleges: Atlanta Consortium (Morehouse, Spelman, Morris Brown colleges and Clark Atlanta University), North Carolina A&T State University, Alabama A&M University, Florida A&M University, Howard University, Tuskegee University, University of Texas-El Paso, Prairie View A&M University, Southern University, University of Hawaii. Contact your college advisor for more information and application materials.
Contact:
The Boeing Company
P.O. Box 3703, M/C 10-06
Seattle, WA 98124
Phone: 206-655-1131
Web: www.boeing.com

Undergraduate Scholarships

Type of award: Scholarship.
Intended use: For undergraduate study at 4-year institution in United States.
Additional information: These scholarships are based upon merit and are made by the college with cooperation from Boeing. They are available to students who attend one of the colleges and universities with whom Boeing partners. Contact your school advisor for more information.
   Amount of award: $3,000
   Number of awards: 1
   Total amount awarded: $3,000
Contact:
The Boeing Company
P.O. Box 3707, M/C 10-06
Seattle, WA 98124-2207
Phone: 206-655-1131
Web: www.boeing.com

Boston Society of Architects

Gabriel Prize

Type of award: Research grant.
Intended use: For non-degree study.
Eligibility: Applicant must be U.S. citizen.
Basis for selection: Major/career interest in architecture. Applicant must demonstrate seriousness of purpose.
Application requirements: Portfolio, recommendations, research proposal.
Additional information: Must use stipend for travel and study. To encourage personal investigative and critical studies of French architectural compositions completed between 1630 and 1830. Must submit a written request for an application by December first.

Amount of award:	$15,000
Number of awards:	1
Number of applicants:	24
Application deadline:	December 1
Total amount awarded:	$15,000

Contact:
Boston Society of Architects
BSA Gabriel Prize
52 Broad Street
Boston, MA 2109

Rotch Traveling Scholarship

Type of award: Scholarship.
Intended use: For non-degree study.
Basis for selection: Competition/talent/interest in engineering/ architecture, based on overall excellence in solving 2-stage design problem. Major/career interest in architecture.
Application requirements: Either degree or work experience must have taken place in Massachusetts.
Additional information: Must have degree from accredited school of architecture and one year of work experience in a Massachusetts architectural firm. Award for travel in foreign country for nine to twelve months. Must travel alone unless married or with dependent. Recipient must not work or study while traveling. Awards are announced in April.

Amount of award:	$35,000
Number of awards:	1
Application deadline:	January 1
Total amount awarded:	$35,000

Contact:
Boston Society of Architects
Rotch Traveling Scholarship
52 Broad Street
Boston, MA 2109

Boy Scouts of America

Boy Scouts of America/Eastern Orthodox Committee on Scouting Scholarship

Type of award: Scholarship.
Intended use: For full-time freshman study at accredited 4-year institution in United States.
Eligibility: Applicant or parent must be member/participant of Boy Scouts of America. Applicant must be male, high school senior. Applicant must be Eastern Orthodox. Applicant must be U.S. citizen.
Basis for selection: Applicant must demonstrate depth of character and service orientation.
Application requirements: Applicant must submit four letters of recommendation with application, one from each of following groups: religious institution, school, community leader, and head of Scouting unit.
Additional information: Offers one $1,000 scholarship and one $500 scholarship upon acceptance to four-year accredited college or university. Eligible applicant must be registered member of Boy Scouts unit; Eagle Scout; active member of Eastern Orthodox Church; have received Alpha Omega Religious Award; have demonstrated practical citizenship in his church, school, Scouting unit, and community.

Amount of award:	$500-$1,000
Number of awards:	2
Application deadline:	April 15
Total amount awarded:	$1,500

Contact:
EOCS Scholarship Committee
862 Guy Lombardo Avenue
Freeport, NY 11520
Phone: 516-868-4050
Fax: 516-868-4052
Web: www.eocs.org

E. Urner Goodman Scholarship

Type of award: Scholarship.
Intended use: For full-time undergraduate or graduate study.
Eligibility: Applicant or parent must be member/participant of Boy Scouts of America. Applicant must be male. Applicant must be U.S. citizen or permanent resident.
Additional information: Open to Arrowmen planning career in professional service of Boy Scouts. Amounts of individual scholarships vary each year. Send SASE with notation on lower left corner, "Order of the Arrow Scholarship Application."

Application deadline:	December 15
Notification begins:	March 1
Total amount awarded:	$20,000

Contact:
Boy Scouts of America National Order of the Arrow S214
1325 West Walnut Hill Lane
P.O. Box 152079
Irving, TX 75015-2079
Phone: 972-580-2032
Fax: 972-580-2502
Web: www.bsa.scouting.org

National Eagle Scout Scholarship

Type of award: Scholarship.
Intended use: For undergraduate study at accredited 2-year or 4-year institution.
Eligibility: Applicant or parent must be member/participant of Boy Scouts of America, Eagle Scouts. Applicant must be male, high school senior. Applicant must be U.S. citizen or permanent resident.
Basis for selection: Applicant must demonstrate financial need, high academic achievement and leadership.
Application requirements: Recommendations, transcript. Must have SAT of at least 1090 or ACT of 26.
Additional information: Applicant must be Eagle Scout. First contact should be at local council office for form 58-702. Must be endorsed by professional or volunteer scout leader. Applicants considered for five kinds of awards: one non-renewable $3,000 award, four awards of $1,000 per year for four years, four awards of $2,000 per year for four years, one Mabel and Lawrence S. Cooke scholarship of up to $12,000 per year for four years, and four $20,000 scholarships ($5,000 a year for four years) given annually. Award may not be used at military institution.

Amount of award:	$3,000-$48,000
Number of applicants:	2,500
Application deadline:	February 28
Notification begins:	June 1
Total amount awarded:	$212,000

Contact:
Boy Scouts of America
1325 West Walnut Hill Lane
Irving, TX 75015-2079
Phone: 972-580-2032
Web: www.bsa.scouting.org

Boys and Girls Clubs of San Diego

Spence Reese Scholarship

Type of award: Scholarship, renewable.
Intended use: For full-time freshman, sophomore, junior or senior study at accredited 4-year institution in United States.
Eligibility: Applicant must be male, high school senior.
Basis for selection: Major/career interest in law; political science/government; engineering or medicine. Applicant must demonstrate high academic achievement.
Application requirements: $10 application fee. Recommendations, essay, transcript. SAT. Must live in United States.
Additional information: Include SASE with application request. Finalists interview in San Diego. Travel expenses will be reimbursed.

Amount of award:	$8,000
Number of awards:	16
Number of applicants:	200
Application deadline:	May 15
Notification begins:	June 1
Total amount awarded:	$32,000

Contact:
Boys and Girls Clubs of San Diego
1761 Hotel Circle South, 123
San Diego, CA 92108

Bremer Financial Corporation

Bremer Employee Dependents' Scholarship Program

Type of award: Scholarship, renewable.
Intended use: For undergraduate or graduate study at accredited vocational, 2-year or 4-year institution.
Eligibility: Applicant or parent must be employed by Bremer Financial Corporation.
Basis for selection: Applicant must demonstrate financial need.
Additional information: For further information or an application, contact Bremer Financial Corporation directly.

Amount of award:	$700-$2,100

Bristol-Myers Squibb Foundation, Inc.

Bristol-Myers Squibb Career Education Awards

Type of award: Scholarship, renewable.
Intended use: For freshman study at accredited vocational or 2-year institution.
Eligibility: Applicant or parent must be employed by Bristol-Myers Squibb Foundation.
Basis for selection: Applicant must demonstrate financial need.
Additional information: For further information or an application, contact Bristol-Myers Squibb Foundation, Inc. directly.

Amount of award:	$500-$2,000

British Government

Marshall Scholarships

Type of award: Scholarship.
Intended use: For full-time undergraduate or master's study at 4-year or graduate institution in United Kingdom.
Eligibility: Applicant must be U.S. citizen.
Basis for selection: Competition/talent/interest in study abroad. Applicant must demonstrate high academic achievement, depth of character, leadership, seriousness of purpose and service orientation.
Application requirements: Interview, recommendations, essay, transcript. Endorsement by President or Dean of educational institution, or employer if no longer in school; description of proposed plan of study.
Additional information: Must pursue British first (bachelor's) or higher degree. Must have bachelor's from accredited U.S. institution by start of award year; may not have graduated more than two years previous. Must have minimum 3.7 GPA in academic courses. Award distributed in two yearly installments. Award period is two academic years, but in exceptional case may be extended a year. Americans already studying for or holding British degree or degree-equivalent qualification not eligible. Applications available after June 1. Applications submitted regionally; visit British Council Website for addresses. Application available on Website.

Amount of award:	$50,000
Number of awards:	40
Number of applicants:	1,000
Application deadline:	October 10

Contact:
The British Council Marshall Scholarships
3100 Massachusetts Avenue NW
Washington, DC 20008-3600
Phone: 202-588-7854
Web: www.marshallscholarship.org

Broadcast Education Association

Abe Voron Scholarship

Type of award: Scholarship.
Intended use: For full-time junior, senior or graduate study at 4-year or graduate institution. Designated institutions: BEA member institution.
Basis for selection: Major/career interest in radio/television/film; communications or journalism. Applicant must demonstrate high academic achievement, depth of character and seriousness of purpose.
Application requirements: Recommendations, essay, transcript. Completed application, waiver form. Should be able to evidence of potential.
Additional information: All scholarships must be applied to study at campus where at least one department is BEA institutional member. Obtain official application forms from your campus faculty or visit Website to download forms and for additional information. Deadline for requesting mailed application is September 1. Awards for tuition and fees. Current scholarship holders are not eligible for reappointment in year following award.

Amount of award:	$5,000
Number of awards:	1
Application deadline:	September 15

Contact:
Broadcast Education Association
1771 N Street, N.W.
Washington, DC 20036-2891
Phone: 202-429-5354
Web: www.beaweb.org

Alexander M. Tanger Scholarship

Type of award: Scholarship.
Intended use: For full-time junior, senior or graduate study at 4-year or graduate institution in United States. Designated institutions: BEA member institution.
Basis for selection: Major/career interest in radio/television/film; communications; journalism; film/video or computer/information sciences. Applicant must demonstrate high academic achievement, depth of character and seriousness of purpose.
Application requirements: Recommendations, essay, transcript. Completed application, waiver form. Should be able to show evidence of potential in electronic media.
Additional information: All scholarships must be applied to study at campus where at least one department is BEA institutional member. Obtain official application forms from your campus faculty or visit Website to download forms and for additional information. Deadline for requesting mailed application is September 1. Awards for tuition and fees. Current scholarship holders are not eligible for reappointment in year following award.

Amount of award:	$2,500
Number of awards:	2
Application deadline:	September 15
Total amount awarded:	$5,000

Contact:
Broadcast Education Association
1771 N Street, N.W.
Washington, DC 20036-2891
Phone: 202-429-5354
Web: www.beaweb.org

Andrew M. Economos Scholarship

Type of award: Scholarship.
Intended use: For full-time junior, senior or graduate study at 4-year or graduate institution. Designated institutions: BEA member institution.
Basis for selection: Major/career interest in communications; radio/television/film or journalism. Applicant must demonstrate high academic achievement, depth of character and seriousness of purpose.
Application requirements: Recommendations, essay, transcript. Completed application, waiver sheet. Should be able to show evidence of potential.
Additional information: All scholarships must be applied to study at campus where at least one department is BEA institutional member. Obtain official application forms from your campus faculty or visit Website to download forms and for additional information. Deadline for requesting mailed application is September 1. Awards for tuition and fees. Current scholarship holders are not eligible for reappointment in year following award.

Amount of award:	Full tuition
Number of awards:	1
Application deadline:	September 15
Total amount awarded:	$5,000

Contact:
Broadcast Education Association
1771 N Street, N.W.
Washington, DC 20036-2891
Phone: 202-429-5354
Web: www.beaweb.org

Broadcast Education Association Scholarship

Type of award: Scholarship.
Intended use: For full-time junior, senior or graduate study in or outside United States. Designated institutions: BEA institutional member campuses only.
Basis for selection: Major/career interest in radio/television/film. Applicant must demonstrate high academic achievement, depth of character, leadership and seriousness of purpose.
Application requirements: Recommendations, transcript. Completion of multi-page application form.
Additional information: Media experience a plus. Send SASE.

Amount of award:	$1,250-$5,000
Number of awards:	14
Number of applicants:	100
Application deadline:	January 15
Notification begins:	April 20
Total amount awarded:	$30,500

Contact:
Scholarship Coordinator
1771 N Street, N.W.
Washington, DC 20036
Phone: 202-429-5354

The Broadcasters' Foundation Helen J. Sioussat

Type of award: Scholarship.
Intended use: For full-time junior, senior or graduate study at 4-year or graduate institution. Designated institutions: BEA Member universities.
Basis for selection: Major/career interest in radio/television/film; communications; journalism; film/video or computer/information sciences. Applicant must demonstrate high academic achievement, depth of character and seriousness of purpose.
Application requirements: Recommendations, essay, transcript. Completed application, waiver sheet. Should be able to show evidence of potential in electronic media.
Additional information: All scholarships must be applied to study at campus where at least one department is BEA institutional member. Obtain official application forms from your campus faculty or visit Website to download forms and for additional information. Deadline for requesting mailed application is September 1. Awards for tuition and fees. Current scholarship holders are not eligible for reappointment in year following award.

Amount of award:	$1,250
Number of awards:	2
Application deadline:	September 15
Total amount awarded:	$2,500

Contact:
Broadcast Education Association
1771 N Street, N.W.
Washington, DC 20036-2891
Phone: 202-429-5354
Web: www.beaweb.org

Country Radio Broadcasters, Inc Scholarships

Type of award: Scholarship.
Intended use: For full-time junior, senior or graduate study at 4-year or graduate institution. Designated institutions: BEA member institutions.
Basis for selection: Major/career interest in radio/television/film; communications or journalism. Applicant must demonstrate high academic achievement, depth of character and seriousness of purpose.
Application requirements: Recommendations, essay, transcript. Completed application, waiver form. Should be able to show evidence of potential in media.
Additional information: All scholarships must be applied to study at campus where at least one department is BEA institutional member. Obtain official application forms from your campus faculty or visit Website to download forms and for additional information. Deadline for requesting mailed application is September 1. Awards for tuition and fees. Current scholarship holders are not eligible for reappointment in year following award.

Amount of award:	$3,000
Number of awards:	13
Application deadline:	September 15
Total amount awarded:	$39,000

Contact:
Broadcast Education Association
1771 N Street, N.W.
Washington, DC 20036-2891
Phone: 202-429-5354
Web: www.beaweb.org

Harold E. Fellows Scholarship

Type of award: Scholarship.
Intended use: For full-time junior, senior or graduate study at 4-year or graduate institution. Designated institutions: BEA member institutions.
Basis for selection: Major/career interest in radio/television/film; communications; journalism; film/video or computer/information sciences. Applicant must demonstrate high academic achievement, depth of character and seriousness of purpose.
Application requirements: Recommendations, essay, transcript. Completed application, waiver sheet, NAB station employment/internship affidavit. Should be able to show evidence of potential in electronic media.
Additional information: All scholarships must be applied to study at campus where at least one department is BEA institutional member. Obtain official application forms from your campus faculty or visit Website to download forms and for additional information. Deadline for requesting mailed application is September 1. Awards for tuition and fees. Current scholarship holders are not eligible for reappointment in year following award.

Amount of award:	$1,250
Number of awards:	4
Application deadline:	September 15
Total amount awarded:	$5,000

Contact:
Broadcast Education Association
1771 N Street, N.W.
Washington, DC 20036-2891
Phone: 202-429-5354
Web: www.beaweb.org

Philo T. Farnsworth Scholarship

Type of award: Scholarship.
Intended use: For full-time junior, senior or graduate study at 4-year or graduate institution. Designated institutions: BEA member institutions.
Basis for selection: Major/career interest in radio/television/film; communications; journalism; film/video or computer/information sciences. Applicant must demonstrate high academic achievement, depth of character and seriousness of purpose.
Application requirements: Recommendations, essay, transcript. Completed application, waiver sheet. Should be able to show evidence of potential in electronic media.
Additional information: All scholarships must be applied to study at campus where at least one department is BEA institutional member. Obtain official application forms from your campus faculty or visit Website to download forms and for additional information. Deadline for requesting mailed application is September 1. Awards for tuition and fees. Current scholarship holders are not eligible for reappointment in year following award.

Amount of award:	$1,500
Number of awards:	1
Application deadline:	September 15

Contact:
Broadcast Education Association
1771 N Street, N.W.
Washington, DC 20036-2891
Phone: 202-429-5354
Web: www.beaweb.org

Shane Media Scholarship

Type of award: Scholarship.
Intended use: For full-time junior, senior or graduate study at 4-year or graduate institution. Designated institutions: BEA member institutions.
Basis for selection: Major/career interest in radio/television/film; communications or journalism. Applicant must demonstrate high academic achievement, depth of character and seriousness of purpose.
Application requirements: Recommendations, essay, transcript. Completed application, waiver form. Should be able to show evidence of potential electronic media.
Additional information: All scholarships must be applied to study at campus where at least one department is BEA institutional member. Obtain official application forms from your campus faculty or visit Website to download forms and for additional information. Deadline for requesting mailed application is September 1. Awards for tuition and fees. Current scholarship holders are not eligible for reappointment in year following award.

Amount of award:	$3,000
Number of awards:	1
Application deadline:	September 15

Contact:
Broadcast Education Association
1771 N. Street, N.W.
Washington, DC 20036-2891
Phone: 202-429-5354
Web: www.beaweb.org

Two Year Community College BEA Award

Type of award: Scholarship.
Intended use: For full-time freshman or sophomore study at 2-year institution. Designated institutions: BEA 2-year/community college.
Basis for selection: Major/career interest in radio/television/film; communications; journalism; film/video or computer/information sciences. Applicant must demonstrate high academic achievement, depth of character and seriousness of purpose.
Application requirements: Recommendations, essay, transcript. Completed application, waiver form. Should be able to show evidence of potential in electronic media.
Additional information: All scholarships must be applied to study at campus where at least one department is BEA institutional member. Obtain official application forms from your campus faculty or visit Website to download forms and for additional information. Deadline for requesting mailed application is September 1. Awards for tuition and fees. Current scholarship holders are not eligible for reappointment in year following award.

Amount of award:	$1,500
Number of awards:	2
Application deadline:	September 15
Total amount awarded:	$3,000

Contact:
Broadcast Education Association
1771 N Street, N.W.
Washington, DC 20036-2891
Phone: 202-429-5354
Web: www.beaweb.org

Walter S. Patterson Scholarship

Type of award: Scholarship.
Intended use: For full-time junior, senior or graduate study at 4-year or graduate institution. Designated institutions: BEA member institution.
Basis for selection: Major/career interest in radio/television/film; communications or journalism. Applicant must demonstrate high academic achievement, depth of character and seriousness of purpose.
Application requirements: Recommendations, essay, transcript. Completed application, waiver sheet. Should be able to show evidence of potential.
Additional information: All scholarships must be applied to study at campus where at least one department is BEA institutional member. Obtain official application forms from your campus faculty or visit Website to download forms and for additional information. Deadline for requesting mailed application is September 1. Awards for tuition and fees. Current scholarship holders are not eligible for reappointment in year following award.

Amount of award:	$1,250
Number of awards:	2
Application deadline:	September 15
Total amount awarded:	$2,500

Contact:
Broadcast Education Association
1771 N Street, N.W.
Washington, DC 20036-2891
Phone: 202-429-5354
Web: www.beaweb.org

Brooklyn Hospital Center Employees' Activities Committee

The Brooklyn Hospital Center Employees' Activities Committee Scholarship

Type of award: Scholarship.
Intended use: For undergraduate study at accredited postsecondary institution.
Eligibility: Applicant or parent must be employed by Brooklyn Hospital Center.
Additional information: For further information or an application, contact The Brooklyn Hospital Center Employees' Activities Committee directly.

Amount of award:	$1,000

Contact:
Brooklyn Hospital Center Employees' Activities Committee

Bureau of Indian Affairs

Higher Education Grant Program

Type of award: Scholarship, renewable.
Intended use: For full-time undergraduate study at accredited 2-year or 4-year institution in United States.

Eligibility: Applicant must be American Indian. Member of or at least one-quarter degree descendant of member of federally recognized tribe.
Basis for selection: Applicant must demonstrate financial need.
Application requirements: Proof of eligibility. Proof of Native American Tribal Affiliation.
Additional information: Student must be accepted at/enrolled in nationally accredited higher education institution for study toward associate or bachelor's degree. Student should contact tribe of which he or she is member, nearest Bureau of Indian Affairs, or address below.

Amount of award:	$500-$2,500
Number of awards:	12,000
Number of applicants:	16,000

Contact:
Office of Indian Education Programs
1849 C. ST. NW
MS 3512-MIB
Washington 20240

Bureau of Indian Affairs-Oklahoma Area Education Office

Bureau of Indian Affairs-Oklahoma Area Quapaw Tribe Scholarship Grant

Type of award: Scholarship.
Intended use: For undergraduate study.
Eligibility: Applicant must be American Indian. Must be enrolled member of the Quapaw Tribe.
Application requirements: Recommendations, essay, transcript, proof of eligibility.
Additional information: Must maintain 2.0 GPA. Contact Bureau of Indian Affairs-Oklahoma Area Education Office for application and additional information.

Application deadline:	June 15, October 15
Notification begins:	June 30, October 30

Contact:
Bureau of Indian Affairs-Oklahoma Area Education Office
4149 Highline Blvd., Suite 380
Oklahoma City, OK 73108

Bureau of Indian Affairs-Osage Tribal Education Committee Award

Type of award: Scholarship.
Intended use: For undergraduate or graduate study at postsecondary institution in United States.
Eligibility: Applicant must be American Indian. Must be enrolled member of Osage Tribe. Applicant must be U.S. citizen.
Application requirements: Recommendations, transcript, proof of eligibility.
Additional information: Minimum 2.0 GPA. Contact Bureau of Indian Affairs-Oklahoma Area Education Office for application and additional information. Deadline for summer study applications is May 1, and notification begins May 15.

Application deadline:	July 1, December 31
Notification begins:	July 15, January 15

Contact:
Burea of Indian Affairs-Oklahoma Area Education Office
4149 Highline Blvd., Suite 380
Oklahoma City, OK 73108
Phone: 405-605-6051 ext.303

Burmah Castrol Holdings, Inc.

Burmah Castrol Scholarship

Type of award: Scholarship, renewable.
Intended use: For undergraduate study at accredited 2-year or 4-year institution.
Eligibility: Applicant or parent must be employed by Castrol North America.
Additional information: For further information or an application, contact Castrol North America directly.

Amount of award:	$2,500

Business and Professional Women's Foundation

Business and Professional Women's Career Advancement Scholarship

Type of award: Scholarship, renewable.
Intended use: For junior, senior, master's or first professional study at accredited 2-year, 4-year or graduate institution in United States.
Eligibility: Applicant must be female, at least 25. Applicant must be U.S. citizen.
Basis for selection: Major/career interest in science, general; education, teacher; engineering; law; computer/information sciences; humanities/liberal arts; social/behavioral sciences or business/management/administration. Applicant must demonstrate financial need.
Application requirements: Recommendations, essay, transcript, proof of eligibility. Tax forms.
Additional information: Also for applicants in the fields of paralegal studies and science or professional degrees (J.D., D.D.S., M.D.) Must be within 24 months of receiving degree, demonstrate critical financial need and have definite career plan. Must be accepted into an accredited program. Application available January 1 through April 1. Send business-size double-stamped SASE.

Amount of award:	$500-$2,000
Number of awards:	200
Number of applicants:	2,000
Application deadline:	January 1, April 1
Notification begins:	July 31

Contact:
Business and Professional Women's Foundation
Scholarship and Loan Programs
2012 Massachusetts Avenue NW
Washington, DC 20036
Phone: 202-293-1200 ext. 169
Fax: 202-861-0298

Business Men's Assurance Company of America

BMA Scholarship for Children of Employees

Type of award: Scholarship, renewable.
Intended use: For undergraduate study at vocational, 2-year or 4-year institution.
Eligibility: Applicant or parent must be employed by Business Men's Assurance Company of America. Applicant must be high school senior.
Additional information: For further information or an application, contact Business Men's Assurance Company of America directly.

Amount of award:	$2,000

Butler Manufacturing Company Foundation

Butler Manufacturing Company Foundation Scholarship

Type of award: Scholarship, renewable.
Intended use: For full-time freshman, sophomore, junior or senior study at accredited 4-year institution.
Eligibility: Applicant or parent must be employed by Butler Manufacturing Co. & subsidiaries. Applicant must be high school senior.
Basis for selection: Applicant must demonstrate financial need, high academic achievement, depth of character, leadership and service orientation.
Application requirements: Recommendations, essay, transcript. SAT 1 or ACT required.
Additional information: Applicant or parent must be employed by Butler Mfg. Co. or wholly owned subsidiary. Contact human resources office at workplace for information and application. Application deadline is mid February. Subsidiaries are: Bucon, Lester Building Systems, Vistawall, and Butler International.

Amount of award:	$2,500
Number of awards:	8
Number of applicants:	48
Notification begins:	April 15
Total amount awarded:	$80,000

Contact:
Butler Manufacturing Company Foundation
Foundation Administrator
P.O. Box 419917
Kansas City, MO 64141-0917

C.G. Fuller Foundation

C.G. Fuller Foundation Scholarship

Type of award: Scholarship, renewable.
Intended use: For full-time undergraduate study at 4-year institution. Designated institutions: Institutions in South Carolina.
Eligibility: Applicant must be enrolled in high school. Applicant must be residing in South Carolina.
Basis for selection: Applicant must demonstrate financial need and high academic achievement.
Application requirements: Interview, recommendations, transcript. SAT scores must meet or exceed 1100.
Additional information: Apply through financial aid office of university. Applications distributed between end of October and end of November. Minimum 3.0 GPA. Recipient must attend college in South Carolina. Total amount awarded and number of awards varies with changes in funding.

Amount of award:	$2,000
Number of awards:	15
Number of applicants:	200
Application deadline:	April 15
Notification begins:	August 1

Contact:
C.G. Fuller Foundation
c/o NationsBank of South Carolina
P.O. Box 448
Columbia, SC 29202-0448

Calgon

Take Me Away to College Scholarship

Type of award: Scholarship.
Intended use: For full-time freshman study at 2-year or 4-year institution in United States.
Eligibility: Applicant must be high school senior. Applicant must be U.S. citizen.
Additional information: Scholarship is open to those who will be starting college full-time in fall or who are already enrolled at accredited two-year or four-year school. Interested parties may apply online by visiting Website. Applicants will be required to respond to three questions posted on Website. Responses to each question should not be more than 450 character, about 100 words. Visit Website for deadline dates and complete rules and regulations.

Amount of award:	$500-$2,500
Number of awards:	8

Contact:
Calgon
Web: www.takemeaway.com

California Association of Realtors Scholarship Foundation

California Association of Realtors Scholarship

Type of award: Scholarship.

Intended use: For undergraduate or graduate study at 2-year or 4-year institution. Designated institutions: California colleges or universities.
Eligibility: Applicant must be U.S. citizen residing in California.
Basis for selection: Major/career interest in real estate. Applicant must demonstrate financial need.
Application requirements: Interview, recommendations, essay, transcript, proof of eligibility. Minimum 2.6 GPA. Must have completed minimum of 12 college level course units within last four years. At least two courses must be in real estate related.
Additional information: Students attending two-year colleges eligible for $1,000 award; four-year college/university students eligible for $2,000 award. Renewable one time only. Deadlines are rolling. Application and information available at Website: click on "about us".

Amount of award:	$1,000-$2,000
Number of awards:	2

Contact:
California Association of Realtors Scholarship Foundation
525 South Virgil Avenue
Los Angeles, CA 90020
Phone: 213-739-8243
Fax: 213-739-7202
Web: www.car.org

California Chicano News Media Association

Joel Garcia Memorial Scholarship

Type of award: Scholarship, renewable.
Intended use: For full-time undergraduate or graduate study at accredited postsecondary institution. Designated institutions: Out-of-state residents restricted to California schools.
Eligibility: Applicant must be Mexican American, Hispanic American or Puerto Rican. Applicant must be U.S. citizen or permanent resident.
Basis for selection: Competition/talent/interest in Writing/ journalism. Major/career interest in journalism. Applicant must demonstrate financial need, high academic achievement, seriousness of purpose and service orientation.
Application requirements: Interview, recommendations, essay, transcript, proof of eligibility. Applicant must include samples of work: newspaper clips, photographs, audio or television tapes.
Additional information: Applicant must be Latino. Can be resident of California attending school in or out of state or non-residents attending school in California. Must provide proof of full-time enrollment.

Amount of award:	$500-$2,000
Number of awards:	25
Number of applicants:	150
Application deadline:	April 6
Notification begins:	May 1
Total amount awarded:	$20,000

Contact:
California Chicano News Media Association
3502 Watt Way, ASC
Los Angeles, CA 90089-0281
Phone: 213-740-5263
Fax: 213-740-8524
Web: www.ccnma.org

California Farm Bureau

California Farm Bureau Scholarship

Type of award: Scholarship, renewable.
Intended use: For full-time freshman, sophomore, junior or senior study at accredited 4-year institution.
Eligibility: Applicant must be U.S. citizen.
Basis for selection: Major/career interest in agriculture; agribusiness; veterinary medicine or engineering, agricultural.
Application requirements: Recommendations, essay, transcript.
Additional information: Applications may be obtained from local County Farm Bureau office. Applicant must be preparing for career in agricultural industry. Award must be used at California four-year school.

Amount of award:	$2,000-$2,750
Number of applicants:	157
Application deadline:	March 1
Notification begins:	May 30
Total amount awarded:	$67,000

Contact:
California Farm Bureau Scholarship Foundation
2300 River Plaza Drive
Sacramento, CA 95833
Phone: 916-561-5520

California Grange Foundation

Deaf Activities Scholarship

Type of award: Scholarship.
Intended use: For undergraduate or graduate study at accredited vocational, 2-year or 4-year institution in United States.
Basis for selection: Major/career interest in deafness studies. Applicant must demonstrate depth of character, seriousness of purpose and service orientation.
Additional information: For students who are entering, continuing or returning to college to pursue studies that will be of benefit to deaf communities. Award amounts vary. Applications and additional information available after February 1.

Application deadline:	April 1

Contact:
California Grange Foundation
Scholarship Committee
2101 Stockton Blvd.
Sacramento, CA 95817
Phone: 916-454-5805
Fax: 916-739-8189

Doris Deaver Memorial Scholarship

Type of award: Scholarship.
Intended use: For freshman study at accredited vocational, 2-year or 4-year institution in United States.
Eligibility: Applicant or parent must be member/participant of Fraternal Grange. Applicant must be high school senior. Applicant must be residing in California.
Basis for selection: Applicant must demonstrate service orientation.

Additional information: Award amounts vary. Applicant must be member of California Fraternal Grange and must demonstrate Grange service orientation. Applications and additional information available after February 1.

Application deadline: April 1
Contact:
California Grange Foundation
Scholarship Committee
2101 Stockton Blvd.
Sacramento, CA 95817

Peter Marinoff Memorial Scholarship

Type of award: Scholarship.
Intended use: For undergraduate study at accredited vocational, 2-year or 4-year institution in United States.
Eligibility: Applicant or parent must be member/participant of Fraternal Grange. Applicant must be residing in California.
Basis for selection: Applicant must demonstrate service orientation.
Additional information: Award amounts vary. Applicant must be member of California Fraternal Grange and must demonstrate Grange service orientation. Available to graduating high school seniors and enrolled undergraduate students. Applications and additional information available after February 1.

Application deadline: April 1
Contact:
California Grange Foundation
Scholarship Committee
2101 Stockton Blvd.
Sacramento, CA 95817

Sehlmeyer Scholarship

Type of award: Scholarship.
Intended use: For full-time sophomore, junior or senior study at accredited vocational, 2-year or 4-year institution in United States.
Eligibility: Applicant or parent must be member/participant of Fraternal Grange. Applicant must be residing in California.
Basis for selection: Applicant must demonstrate service orientation.
Additional information: Applicant must be member of California Fraternal Grange. Service criterion limited to Grange activities. Award amounts vary. Applications and additional information available after February 1.

Amount of award:	$250-$2,000
Number of awards:	10
Number of applicants:	17
Application deadline:	April 1

Contact:
California Grange Foundation
Scholarship Committee
2101 Stockton Bvld.
Sacramento, CA 95817

California Junior Miss Program

California Junior Miss Competition

Type of award: Scholarship.
Intended use: For undergraduate study at accredited 2-year or 4-year institution in United States.
Eligibility: Applicant must be single, female, high school junior. Applicant must be U.S. citizen residing in California.
Basis for selection: Competition/talent/interest in poise/talent/fitness, based on interview, scholastics, poise, talent, and fitness. Applicant must demonstrate high academic achievement.
Application requirements: Interview. Minimum 3.0 GPA required.
Additional information: Initial inquiry should be made by December 31 of junior year in high school. Awards not limited to state Junior Miss finalists; winners of various judged categories also eligible.

Amount of award:	$300-$10,000
Number of awards:	20
Number of applicants:	60
Application deadline:	January 1
Notification begins:	August 18
Total amount awarded:	$30,000

Contact:
California Junior Miss Program
P.O. Box 729
Windsor, CA 95429
Phone: 707-837-1900
Fax: 707-837-9410
Web: www.ajm.org/california

California Masonic Foundation

California Masonic Foundation Scholarship

Type of award: Scholarship, renewable.
Intended use: For full-time undergraduate study at accredited 2-year or 4-year institution.
Eligibility: Applicant must be high school senior. Applicant must be U.S. citizen residing in California.
Basis for selection: Applicant must demonstrate financial need and high academic achievement.
Application requirements: Recommendations, essay, transcript, proof of eligibility. 1040 tax return, FAFSA, and Student Aid Report.
Additional information: Minimum 3.0 cumulative GPA. Requests for application forms accepted September 1 through January 31. Application forms sent out October 1 through February 1. Completed applications accepted until March 15. Dates are subject to change anually. Most awards are renewable. While not required, some preference is given to applicants with Masonic relationships and/or Masonic Youth Group membership. Application information and/or requests are not accepted or responded to February 1 through September 1.

Amount of award: $500-$10,000
Number of awards: 266
Number of applicants: 1,400
Application deadline: March 15
Total amount awarded: $918,316
Contact:
California Masonic Foundation
1111 California Street
San Francisco, CA 94108-2284
Phone: 415-292-9196
Web: www.californiamasons.org

California Physicians' Service Foundation

Blue Shield of California Scholarship

Type of award: Scholarship.
Intended use: For freshman, sophomore, junior or senior study at accredited vocational, 2-year or 4-year institution.
Eligibility: Applicant or parent must be employed by Blue Shield of California.
Additional information: For further information or an application, contact Blue Shield of California directly.
Amount of award: $2,000-$4,000

California Student Aid Commission

Cal Grant A Entitlement Award Program

Type of award: Scholarship, renewable.
Intended use: For undergraduate study at postsecondary institution. Designated institutions: Qualifying California postsecondary schools.
Eligibility: Applicant must be high school senior. Applicant must be U.S. citizen, permanent resident, international student or eligible non-citizens as defined by criteria for federal financial aid programs. Applicant must be residing in California.
Basis for selection: Applicant must demonstrate financial need and high academic achievement.
Application requirements: Continuing college students must submit FAFSA to federal processor and GPA Verification Form to CSAC.
Additional information: Awards given to all eligible applicants. Applicants must have income and assets below certain established levels. Applicants must also meet high school academic achievement standards. Awards to help pay tuition/fees. If attending a California community college, award can be reserved for up to two years until transfer to tuition/fee charging college, provided qualifications are still met. Students with no available GPA can submit SAT I, ACT or GED scores. Visit Website or contact CSAC for more details.

Amount of award: $700-$11,259
Number of applicants: 150,000
Application deadline: March 2
Notification begins: April 15
Total amount awarded: $221,100,000
Contact:
California Student Aid Commission
Grant Services Division
P.O. Box 419026
Rancho Cordova, CA 95741-9026
Phone: 888-CA-GRANT (888-224-7268)
Web: www.csac.ca.gov

Cal Grant B Entitlement Award Program

Type of award: Scholarship, renewable.
Intended use: For undergraduate study at postsecondary institution. Designated institutions: Qualifying California postsecondary schools.
Eligibility: Applicant must be high school senior. Applicant must be U.S. citizen, permanent resident, international student or eligible non-citizens as defined by criteria for federal financial aid programs. Applicant must be residing in California.
Basis for selection: Applicant must demonstrate financial need.
Application requirements: Continuing college students must submit FAFSA to federal processor and GPA Verification Form to CSAC.
Additional information: Awards given to all eligible applicants. Applicants must have income and assets below certain established levels. Applicants must also meet high school academic achievement standards. Awards up to $1,551 toward living expenses and costs for transportation, supplies and books. Can also help pay tuition costs for qualifying awardees receiving Cal Grant B for second year. Students with no available GPA can submit SAT I, ACT or GED scores. Visit Website or contact CSAC for more details.
Amount of award: $1,551
Application deadline: March 2
Notification begins: April 15
Contact:
California Student Aid Commission
Grant Services Division
P.O. Box 419026
Rancho Cordova, CA 95741-9026
Phone: 888-CA-GRANT (888-224-7268)
Web: www.csac.ca.gov

Cal Grant C Award Program

Type of award: Scholarship, renewable.
Intended use: For undergraduate study at postsecondary institution. Designated institutions: Qualifying California postsecondary and vocational institutions.
Eligibility: Applicant must be U.S. citizen, permanent resident, international student or eligible non-citizens as defined by criteria for federal financial aid programs. Applicant must be residing in California.
Basis for selection: Applicant must demonstrate financial need.
Application requirements: Students must submit FAFSA to federal processor and GPA Verification Form to CSAC.
Additional information: Applicants must have income and assets below certain established levels. Applicants must plan to enroll in a vocational/occupational program of at least four months. Students with no available GPA can submit SAT I,

ACT or GED scores. Visit Website or contact CSAC for more details.

Amount of award:	$288-$3,168
Number of awards:	7,761
Number of applicants:	23,000
Application deadline:	March 2
Notification begins:	May 15
Total amount awarded:	$19,000,000

Contact:
California Student Aid Commission
Grant Services Division
P.O. Box 419026
Rancho Cordova, CA 95741-9026
Phone: 888-CA-GRANT (888-224-7268)
Web: www.csac.ca.gov

California Child Development Teacher and Supervisor Grant Program

Type of award: Scholarship.
Intended use: For undergraduate study at accredited 2-year or 4-year institution. Designated institutions: California public or private postsecondary institutions with approved child development classes.
Eligibility: Applicant must be U.S. citizen or permanent resident residing in California.
Basis for selection: Major/career interest in education, early childhood or education, teacher. Applicant must demonstrate financial need and seriousness of purpose.
Application requirements: Recommendations. Recommendation from institution faculty. Points based on GPA, income and EFC. Applicant must be pursuing permit to teach/supervise in field of child care and development.
Additional information: Recipients attending two-year postsecondary institutions will receive up to $1,000 annually for up to two years. Recipients attending four year institutions will receive up to $2,000 annually for up to two years. Applicants continuing beyond two years may reapply but cannot cumulatively receive more than $6,000 through the program. Recipients must maintain at least half-time enrollment in Commission of Teaching Creditialing approved course of study leading to Child Development Permit; maintain satisfactory academic progress; meet federal Selective Service filing requirements; and commit to one year of full-time employment in a licensed child care center for every year they receive the grant. The commission can award up to 100 new recipients each year.

Amount of award:	$1,000-$2,000
Application deadline:	June 1, February 23
Notification begins:	August 1, March 1

Contact:
California Student Aid Commission
Specialized Programs
P.O. Box 419029
Rancho Cordova, CA 95741-9029
Phone: 888-224-7599
Fax: 916-526-7998
Web: www.csac.ca.gov

California Law Enforcement Personnel Dependents Scholarship

Type of award: Scholarship, renewable.
Intended use: For undergraduate study at accredited 2-year or 4-year institution. Designated institutions: California post-secondary institutions accredited by Western Association of Schools and Colleges (WASC).
Eligibility: Applicant must be U.S. citizen residing in California. Applicant's parent must have been killed or disabled in work-related accident as fire fighter, police officer or public safety officer.
Basis for selection: Applicant must demonstrate financial need.
Application requirements: Proof of eligibility. Application, copy of current Student Aid Report, birth certificate (not required for spouse). Applicant must be natural/adopted child or spouse, at time of death/injury, of CA peace/law enforcement officer, officer/employee of Dept. Corrections/Youth Authority, or firefighter.
Additional information: Additional application requirements: dependent/spouse of A) peace/law enforcement officers: death certificate of parent/spouse and coroner's report (if appropriate), police report, and any other necessary documentation; B) officers/employees of Dept. of Corrections/Youth Authority: death certificate of parent/spouse, coroner's report (if appropriate), and documentation showing death/total disability direct result of inmate; C) firefighters: death certificate of parent/spouse, coroner's report (if appropriate), and any other necessary documentation. All must include findings of Worker's Compensation Appeals Board or other evidence that fatality/disabling accident/injury compensable under Division 4.0 and 4.5 of the Labor Code.

Amount of award:	$100-$11,256
Number of awards:	14
Total amount awarded:	$52,000

Contact:
California Student Aid Commision
Specialized Programs
P.O. Box 419029
Rancho Cordova, CA 95741-9029
Phone: 888-224-7268
Fax: 916-526-7998
Web: www.csac.ca.gov

California Robert C. Byrd Honors Scholarship

Type of award: Scholarship, renewable.
Intended use: For full-time undergraduate study at accredited 2-year or 4-year institution in United States.
Eligibility: Applicant must be high school senior. Applicant must be U.S. citizen residing in California.
Basis for selection: Applicant must demonstrate high academic achievement.
Application requirements: Nomination by high school.
Additional information: Selection process begins at individual high schools. Contact guidance office for information. GED students may apply directly. Renewable up to four years.

Amount of award:	$1,500
Number of awards:	800
Number of applicants:	1,539
Notification begins:	May 1
Total amount awarded:	$4,938,000

Contact:
California Student Aid Commission
Robert C. Byrd Honors Scholarship Program
P.O. Box 419029
Rancho Cordova, CA 95741-9029
Phone: 888-224-7288
Fax: 916-526-7998
Web: www.csac.ca.gov

Competitive Cal Grant A and B Award Programs

Type of award: Scholarship, renewable.
Intended use: For undergraduate study at postsecondary institution. Designated institutions: Qualifying California postsecondary schools.
Eligibility: Applicant must be U.S. citizen, international student or eligible non-citizens as defined by criteria for federal financial aid programs. Applicant must be residing in California.
Basis for selection: Applicant must demonstrate financial need and high academic achievement.
Application requirements: Continuing college students must submit FAFSA to federal processor and GPA Verification Form to CSAC.
Additional information: Applicants must have income and assets below certain established levels. Competitive grant program awards used for same purpose as entitlement grants but not guaranteed to all applicants. Cal Grant A awards intended to help low- and middle-income families pay tuition/fees. Cal Grant B awards up to $1,551 to disadvantaged and low-income families toward living expenses and costs for transportation, supplies and books. Students with no available GPA can submit SAT I, ACT or GED scores. Visit Website or contact CSAC for more details.

Amount of award:	$700-$11,259
Number of awards:	22,500
Number of applicants:	300,000
Application deadline:	March 2
Notification begins:	May 1
Total amount awarded:	$43,300,000

Contact:
California Student Aid Commission
Grant Services Division
P.O. Box 419026
Rancho Cordova, CA 95741-9026
Phone: 888-CA-GRANT (888-224-7268)
Web: www.csac.ca.gov

California Teachers Association

California Teachers Association Martin Luther King, Jr., Memorial Scholarship

Type of award: Scholarship.
Intended use: For undergraduate or graduate study at accredited postsecondary institution.
Eligibility: Applicant or parent must be member/participant of California Teachers Association. Applicant must be Alaskan native, Asian American, African American, Mexican American, Hispanic American, Puerto Rican or American Indian.
Basis for selection: Major/career interest in education; education, teacher or education, special. Applicant must demonstrate financial need.
Application requirements: Proof of eligibility.
Additional information: Must be active CTA or Student CTA member, or dependent child of active, deceased, or retired life member. Must be ethnic minority. Information may also be obtained from chapter presidents or any Regional Resource Center Office. High school seniors are eligible.

Amount of award:	$2,000-$5,000
Number of applicants:	150
Application deadline:	March 15
Notification begins:	May 1

Contact:
California Teachers Association Human Rights Department
P.O. Box 921
Burlingame, CA 94011-0921
Phone: 650-697-1400
Web: www.cta.org

CTA Scholarship for Dependent Children

Type of award: Scholarship, renewable.
Intended use: For full-time undergraduate, master's or doctoral study at accredited postsecondary institution.
Eligibility: Applicant or parent must be member/participant of California Teachers Association.
Basis for selection: Major/career interest in education. Applicant must demonstrate high academic achievement, depth of character, leadership, seriousness of purpose and service orientation.
Application requirements: Transcript, proof of eligibility. Completed application, proof of registration from institution. Applicant must be dependent child of active, retired or deceased member of California Teachers Association. Scholarships are awarded based overall achievement in four categories: 1)involvement in and sensitivity to human, social and civic issues; 2)characteristics such as responsibility, reliability and integrity; 3)academic and vocational potential; and 4)special and personal achievements.
Additional information: Graduating high school seniors, undergraduate or graduate students are eligible. Applicant must be claimed as a dependent on current year's IRS tax forms. Information may also be obtained from chapter presidents, any Regional Resource Center Office or the CTA Website.

Amount of award:	$2,000
Number of awards:	25
Number of applicants:	900
Application deadline:	February 15
Notification begins:	May 1

Contact:
California Teachers Association Human Rights Department
P.O. Box 921
Burlingame, CA 94011-0921
Phone: 650-697-1400
Web: www.cta.org

CTA Scholarships for Members

Type of award: Scholarship, renewable.
Intended use: For undergraduate or graduate study at accredited postsecondary institution.
Eligibility: Applicant or parent must be member/participant of California Teachers Association.
Basis for selection: Applicant must demonstrate high academic achievement, depth of character, leadership, seriousness of purpose and service orientation.
Application requirements: Transcript. Completed application. Scholarships are awarded based on overall achievement in four categories: 1)involvement in and sensitivity to human, social and civic issues; 2)characteristics such as responsibility, reliability and integrity; 3)academic and vocational potential; and 4)special and personal achievements.
Additional information: Applicant must be current "active" member of California Teachers Association (including members

working on emergency credential). Further information may be obtained from chapter presidents, any Regional Resource Center Office or the CTA Website, or by contacting via e-mail (scholarships@cta.org).

Amount of award:	$2,000
Number of awards:	5
Number of applicants:	150
Application deadline:	February 15
Notification begins:	May 1
Total amount awarded:	$10,000

Contact:
California Teachers Association Human Rights Department
P.O. Box 921
Burlingame, CA 94011-0921
Phone: 650-697-1400 or 650-552-5346
Web: www.cta.org

L. Gordon Bittle Memorial Scholarship for Student CTA

Type of award: Scholarship, renewable.
Intended use: For full-time undergraduate or graduate study at accredited postsecondary institution. Designated institutions: Can be teacher credential program at accredited postsecondary institution.
Eligibility: Applicant or parent must be member/participant of California Teachers Association. Applicant must be residing in California.
Basis for selection: Major/career interest in education; education, teacher or education, special. Applicant must demonstrate high academic achievement, depth of character and service orientation.
Application requirements: Transcript. Application. Scholarships are awarded based on overall achievement in four categories: 1)involvement in and sensitivity to human, social and civic issues; 2)characteristics such as responsibility, reliability, and integrity; 3)academic and vocational potential; and 4)special and personal achievements.
Additional information: Not available to CTA members currently working in public schools. Must be current active member of Student CTA. Information may also be obtained from chapter presidents or any Regional Resource Center Office, or the CTA Website.

Amount of award:	$2,000
Number of awards:	3
Number of applicants:	20
Application deadline:	February 15
Notification begins:	May 1
Total amount awarded:	$6,000

Contact:
California Teachers Association Human Rights Department
P.O. Box 921
Burlingame, CA 94011-0921
Phone: 650-697-1400
Web: www.cta.org

California-Hawaii Elks Major Project, Inc.

California-Hawaii Elks Major Project Undergraduate Scholarship Program for Students with Disabilities

Type of award: Scholarship, renewable.
Intended use: For undergraduate study at accredited vocational, 2-year or 4-year institution.
Eligibility: Applicant must be visually impaired, hearing impaired or physically challenged. Applicant must be returning adult student. Applicant must be U.S. citizen residing in California or Hawaii.
Basis for selection: Applicant must demonstrate financial need, high academic achievement, depth of character, leadership, seriousness of purpose and service orientation.
Application requirements: Interview, recommendations, essay, transcript, proof of eligibility. Return application packets along with sealed official transcript, IRS tax returns, and recommendation completed by MD or Doctor of Osteopathy to California-Hawaii Elks Major Project, Inc. office.
Additional information: Scholarship open to high school seniors, high school graduates or applicants who have passed the GED Exam or California High School Proficiency Exam (CHSPE). Severity of disability, including neurological impairment or speech/language disorder considered in applicant selection. Funds to cover academic expenses, including tuition, books, and lab fees. Not for remedial skill development. Applicant must be interviewed by Scholarship Chairman or Exalted Ruler for Elks sponsorship. If not available, applicant should make appointment with elected Lodge officer. Application packet including personal information, recommendation, and financial analysis forms available after November 15, from any Elk Lodge in California or Hawaii.

Amount of award:	$1,000-$2,000
Number of awards:	35
Number of applicants:	100
Application deadline:	March 15
Notification begins:	June 1

Contact:
An Elk Lodge within the state of California or Hawaii or California-Hawaii Elks Major Project, Inc.
5450 East Lamona Ave.
Fresno, CA 93727-2224

Callaway Golf Company Foundation

Callaway Golf Scholarship Program

Type of award: Scholarship, renewable.
Intended use: For undergraduate study at vocational, 2-year or 4-year institution.
Eligibility: Applicant or parent must be employed by Callaway Golf Company Foundation. Applicant must be high school senior.

Additional information: For further information or an application, contact Callaway Golf Company Foundation directly.

Amount of award: $500-$2,000

Cambrex Corporation

Arthur I. Mendolia Scholarship Program

Type of award: Scholarship, renewable.
Intended use: For undergraduate study at accredited vocational, 2-year or 4-year institution.
Eligibility: Applicant or parent must be employed by Cambrex Corporation.
Additional information: For additional information or an application, contact Cambrex Corporation directly.

Amount of award: $1,500

Canned Foods, Inc.

Canned Foods Employees' Children Scholarship

Type of award: Scholarship.
Intended use: For undergraduate study at accredited vocational, 2-year or 4-year institution.
Eligibility: Applicant or parent must be employed by Canned Foods, Inc.
Basis for selection: Applicant must demonstrate financial need.
Additional information: For further information or an application, contact Canned Foods, Inc. directly.

Amount of award: $1,000-$5,000

The Capital Group Companies, Inc.

Capital Group Companies Scholarship Program

Type of award: Scholarship, renewable.
Intended use: For undergraduate study at accredited vocational, 2-year or 4-year institution.
Eligibility: Applicant or parent must be employed by Capital Group, Inc.
Basis for selection: Applicant must demonstrate financial need.
Additional information: For additional information or an application, contact The Capital Group Companies, Inc. directly.

Amount of award: $1,500-$5,000

Caremark Therapeutic Services

Eric Delson Memorial Scholarship

Type of award: Scholarship, renewable.
Intended use: For freshman, sophomore, junior or senior study at accredited vocational, 2-year or 4-year institution.
Basis for selection: Major/career interest in health-related professions.
Additional information: For further information or application, contact Caremark Therapeutic Services directly or request information at hemophilia treatment centers.

Amount of award: $1,500

Carl's Jr. Restaurants

Donald F. Karcher Scholarships

Type of award: Scholarship.
Intended use: For full-time undergraduate study at 2-year or 4-year institution.
Eligibility: Applicant or parent must be employed by Carl's Jr. Restaurants.
Basis for selection: Major/career interest in food production/management/services or food science/technology.
Application requirements: Must have a major in the food service industry.
Additional information: Apply at the Carl's Jr. Restaurant where you work.

Amount of award: $2,500
Number of awards: 2
Total amount awarded: $5,000
Contact:
CKE Restaurants
1200 North Harbor Blvd.
Anaheim, CA 92803
Web: www.ckr.com

Carolina Triangle Section of A.S.H.E.

American Society of Highway Engineers Scholarship

Type of award: Scholarship.
Intended use: For undergraduate study at accredited 4-year institution in United States.
Eligibility: Applicant must be U.S. citizen residing in North Carolina.
Basis for selection: Major/career interest in engineering, civil or transportation. Applicant must demonstrate high academic achievement, leadership and seriousness of purpose.
Application requirements: Interview, transcript. Must be U.S. citizen and permanent resident of North Carolina. Applicant must have completed at least one semester. If requested by review committee, applicant will be interviewed.

Additional information: North Carolina residents may be enrolled in any college or university, without restriction of location.

Amount of award:	$1,000
Number of awards:	3
Number of applicants:	9
Application deadline:	March 31
Notification begins:	May 1
Total amount awarded:	$3,000

Contact:
Carolina Triangle Section, American Society of Highway Engineers
5800 Faringdon Place, Suite 105
Raleigh, NC 27609
Phone: 919-878-9560

Case Western Reserve University

Marc A. Klein Playwriting Award

Type of award: Scholarship.
Intended use: For undergraduate or graduate study at 2-year or 4-year institution in United States.
Basis for selection: Competition/talent/interest in performing arts, based on creativity, originality. Major/career interest in theater arts.
Application requirements: Send a stage manuscript or screenplay.
Additional information: Manuscripts must be endorsed by faculty member of university theater or drama department. Only plays that have not been professionally produced can be entered. Musicals and children's plays will not be accepted. May submit only one script accompanied by endorsed Klein application form.

Amount of award:	$1,000
Number of awards:	1
Number of applicants:	40
Application deadline:	May 15
Notification begins:	August 1

Contact:
Marc A. Klein Playwriting Award
CWRU Department of Theater Arts
10900 Euclid Ave.
Cleveland, OH 44106-7077
Phone: 216-368-4868
Fax: 216-368-5184
Web: www.cwru.edu/artsci/thtr/website/theahome.htm

Cashiers' Association of Wall Street

Cashiers' Association of Wall Street Scholarship

Type of award: Scholarship.
Intended use: For undergraduate study at accredited vocational, 2-year or 4-year institution.
Eligibility: Applicant or parent must be member/participant of Cashiers' Association of Wall Street.

Additional information: For further information or an application, contact Cashiers' Association of Wall Street directly.

Amount of award:	$2,000

Casual Male Corporation

Casual Male Corporation Scholarship Program

Type of award: Scholarship.
Intended use: For undergraduate study at accredited vocational, 2-year or 4-year institution.
Eligibility: Applicant or parent must be employed by Casual Male Corporation.
Basis for selection: Applicant must demonstrate financial need.
Additional information: For further information or an application, contact Casual Male Corporation directly.

Amount of award:	$1,000

Catching the Dream

MESBEC Scholarships

Type of award: Scholarship, renewable.
Intended use: For full-time undergraduate or graduate study at accredited postsecondary institution in United States.
Eligibility: Applicant must be Alaskan native or American Indian. Must be an enrolled member of a tribe. Must be one-quarter Native American. Applicant must be U.S. citizen or permanent resident.
Basis for selection: Major/career interest in mathematics; engineering; science, general; business; education or computer/information sciences. Applicant must demonstrate high academic achievement, depth of character, leadership, seriousness of purpose and service orientation.
Application requirements: Recommendations, essay, transcript, proof of eligibility.
Additional information: Additional deadline: March 15 for summer funding, April deadline is for fall semester, September deadline for spring semester funding.

Amount of award:	$500-$5,000
Number of awards:	180
Number of applicants:	200
Application deadline:	April 15, September 15
Total amount awarded:	$300,000

Contact:
Catching the Dream
8200 Mountain Road NE
Suite 203
Alburquerque, NM 87110
Phone: 505-262-2351
Fax: 505-262-0534

Native American Leadership in Education Scholarship

Type of award: Scholarship, renewable.
Intended use: For full-time undergraduate or graduate study at accredited postsecondary institution in United States.

Eligibility: Applicant must be Alaskan native or American Indian. Must be an enrolled member of a tribe. Must be one-quarter Native American. Applicant must be U.S. citizen or permanent resident.
Basis for selection: Major/career interest in education. Applicant must demonstrate high academic achievement, depth of character, leadership, seriousness of purpose and service orientation.
Application requirements: Recommendations, essay, transcript, proof of eligibility.
Additional information: Additional deadline: March 15 for summer funding, April deadline is for fall semester, September deadline for spring semester funding.

Amount of award:	$500-$5,000
Number of awards:	30
Number of applicants:	40
Application deadline:	April 15, September 15
Total amount awarded:	$100,000

Contact:
Catching the Dream
8200 Mountain Road
Suite 203
Albuquerque, NM 87110
Phone: 505-262-2351
Fax: 505-262-0534

Catholic Aid Association

Catholic Aid Association Scholarship

Type of award: Scholarship.
Intended use: For full-time undergraduate study at vocational, 2-year or 4-year institution in United States.
Eligibility: Applicant or parent must be member/participant of Catholic Aid Association.
Basis for selection: Applicant must demonstrate financial need, high academic achievement, depth of character, leadership, seriousness of purpose and service orientation.
Application requirements: Portfolio, recommendations, transcript, proof of eligibility. Application form. Photo of applicant required.
Additional information: Open to college freshmen and high school seniors. Must have been member of Catholic Aid Association for two years. Application forms change every year.

Amount of award:	$300-$500
Application deadline:	January 15
Notification begins:	May 15

Contact:
Catholic Aid Association
3499 North Lexington Avenue
St. Paul, MN 55126
Phone: 651-490-0170
Fax: 651-490-0170

Catholic Workman Fraternal Benefit Society

National Catholic Workman Scholarship

Type of award: Scholarship, renewable.
Intended use: For full-time undergraduate or non-degree study at accredited postsecondary institution in or outside United States or Canada.
Eligibility: Applicant or parent must be member/participant of Catholic Workman Fraternal Life Association.
Basis for selection: Applicant must demonstrate high academic achievement, leadership and service orientation.
Application requirements: Recommendations, essay, transcript, proof of eligibility. SAT or ACT scores. Minimum 2.5 GPA. Must have volunteer backround.
Additional information: Applicant must be member of Catholic Workman Fraternal Life Association.

Amount of award:	$500-$1,000
Number of awards:	20
Number of applicants:	75
Application deadline:	July 1
Notification begins:	August 25
Total amount awarded:	$16,000

Contact:
Catholic Workman Fraternal Life Association
Scholarship Program
P.O. Box 47
New Prague, MN 56071
Phone: 800-346-6231

Central Intelligence Agency

CIA Undergraduate Scholarship

Type of award: Scholarship, renewable.
Intended use: For full-time freshman, sophomore, junior or senior study at accredited 4-year institution in United States.
Eligibility: Applicant must be high school senior. Applicant must be U.S. citizen.
Basis for selection: Major/career interest in engineering; computer/information sciences or economics. Applicant must demonstrate financial need, high academic achievement, depth of character, leadership, patriotism, seriousness of purpose and service orientation.
Application requirements: Transcript. SAT scores, resume.
Additional information: Minority or disabled applicants preferred, but others not excluded. Service commitment to CIA must be fulfilled or recipient must repay award. 3.0 GPA required. Applicants with family income over $70,000 not eligible. Applicants with family income between $60,000 and $70,000 accepted only if family has four or more dependents.

Amount of award:	$15,000
Number of awards:	2
Number of applicants:	300
Application deadline:	November 1
Notification begins:	June 30
Total amount awarded:	$30,000

Contact:
Central Intelligence Agency
Recruitment Center
P.O. Box 4090
Reston, VA 20195

Ceridian Corporation

Ceridian Scholarship Program

Type of award: Scholarship, renewable.
Intended use: For freshman, sophomore, junior or senior study at accredited vocational, 2-year or 4-year institution.
Eligibility: Applicant or parent must be employed by Ceridian Corporation.
Basis for selection: Applicant must demonstrate financial need.
Additional information: For further information or an application, contact Ceridian Corporation directly.
>   Amount of award: $500-$2,500

Chairscholars Foundation, Inc.

Chairscholars Scholarship

Type of award: Scholarship, renewable.
Intended use: For full-time freshman study at postsecondary institution.
Eligibility: Applicant must be physically challenged. Applicant must be single, high school senior. Applicant must be U.S. citizen.
Basis for selection: Applicant must demonstrate financial need, depth of character, leadership, seriousness of purpose and service orientation.
Application requirements: Recommendations, essay, transcript, proof of eligibility. Photograph.
Additional information: Eight awardees for this scholarship receive four $5,000 awards, given yearly.

Amount of award:	$5,000
Number of awards:	8
Number of applicants:	150
Application deadline:	March 15
Total amount awarded:	$40,000

Contact:
Chairscholars Foundation, Inc.
16101 Carencia Ln.
Odessa, FL 33556
Web: chairscholars.org

Champion International Corporation

Champion International Corporation Scholarship

Type of award: Scholarship, renewable.

Intended use: For freshman study at accredited vocational, 2-year or 4-year institution.
Eligibility: Applicant or parent must be employed by Champion International Corporation. Applicant must be high school senior.
Basis for selection: Applicant must demonstrate financial need.
Additional information: Must be child of employee of CIC. For further information or an application, contact Champion International Corporation directly.
>   Amount of award: $500-$2,500

Charles A. and Anne Morrow Lindbergh Foundation

Lindbergh Foundation Grant

Type of award: Research grant.
Intended use: For non-degree study.
Basis for selection: Major/career interest in environmental science; aviation; natural resources/conservation; education or health sciences.
Application requirements: Research proposal.
Additional information: Applicant research or educational project should address balance between technological advancement and environmental preservation.

Amount of award:	$1,000-$10,580
Number of awards:	10
Number of applicants:	200
Application deadline:	June 15
Notification begins:	April 15

Contact:
The Charles A. and Anne Morrow Lindbergh Foundation
2150 Third Avenue North
Suite 310
Anoka, MN 55303-2200
Phone: 763-576-1596
Fax: 763-576-1664
Web: www.lindberghfoundation.org

Charter Fund

Charter Fund Scholarship

Type of award: Scholarship.
Intended use: For full-time freshman study.
Eligibility: Applicant must be high school senior. Applicant must be U.S. citizen residing in Colorado.
Basis for selection: Applicant must demonstrate financial need.
Application requirements: Interview.

Amount of award:	$100-$5,000
Number of awards:	92
Application deadline:	May 11
Notification begins:	July 15
Total amount awarded:	$100,000

Scholarships

Contact:
Charter Fund- Jeanette Montoya
370 17th Street, Suite 5300
Denver, CO 80202
Phone: 303-572-1727

Chas. Levy Company

Chas. Levy Company's Harry Harrington Scholarship

Type of award: Scholarship.
Intended use: For undergraduate study at accredited 2-year or 4-year institution.
Eligibility: Applicant or parent must be employed by Chas. Levy Company.
Basis for selection: Applicant must demonstrate financial need.
Additional information: For further information or an application, contact Chas. Levy Company directly.
    Amount of award: $1,000

Chesapeake Corporation Foundation

Chesapeake Corporation Scholarship

Type of award: Scholarship, renewable.
Intended use: For full-time freshman, sophomore, junior or senior study.
Eligibility: Applicant or parent must be employed by Chesapeake Corporation. Applicant must be high school senior.
Basis for selection: Applicant must demonstrate high academic achievement.
Application requirements: SAT I or ACT scores required.

Amount of award:	$3,500
Number of applicants:	20
Application deadline:	November 15
Total amount awarded:	$15,000

Contact:
Chesapeake Corporation Foundation
James Center II
1021 East Cary Street, Box 2350
Richmond, VA 23218-2350

Chesterfield Film Company

Chesterfield Writers Film Project

Type of award: Scholarship.
Intended use: For non-degree study.
Basis for selection: Competition/talent/interest in writing/journalism, based on writing samples in any genre (film, fiction, theater); no specific format required. Major/career interest in film/video.

Application requirements: $40 application fee. Writing samples.
Additional information: Selection based solely on the basis of demonstrated writing ability. Fellowships last one year and fellows receive a $20,000 stipend. Up to five awards each year, but sponsor reserves the right to grant fewer or no awards in any given year. Successful submissions also considered for professional production, with additional remuneration if produced. No specific eligibility criteria; fiction, theater and film writers may apply. Several thousand applications received each year.

Amount of award:	$20,000
Number of awards:	5
Application deadline:	April 10

Contact:
Chesterfield Film Company
1158 26th Street
Box 544
Santa Monica, CA 90408
Phone: 213-683-3977
Web: www.chesterfield-co.com

Cheyenne-Arapaho Tribes of Oklahoma-Concho Agency

Cheyenne-Arapaho Federal Aid Grants

Type of award: Scholarship, renewable.
Intended use: For undergraduate or graduate study at accredited 2-year, 4-year or graduate institution in United States.
Eligibility: Applicant must be American Indian. Must be enrolled member of Cheyenne-Arapaho Tribe of OK, certified by Concho Agency to be 1/4 or more degree Cheyenne-Arapaho.
Basis for selection: Applicant must demonstrate financial need and high academic achievement.
Application requirements: Transcript, proof of eligibility. FAFSA, Cheyenne-Arapaho FNA. GED certificate accepted. Complete application including letter explaining educational plans.
Additional information: Applicant must be entering degree-granting program. Student receives $1,000 per semester for full-time enrollment; part-time enrollment 3 credit hours $250; 6 credit hours $500; 9 credit hours $750. Summer and part-time applicants considered. Summer application deadline is April 1.

Amount of award:	$1,000
Number of awards:	130
Number of applicants:	150
Application deadline:	June 1, November 1

Contact:
Cheyenne-Arapaho Tribe of Oklahoma-Concho Agency
Department of Education
P.O. Box 38
Concho, OK 73022
Phone: 405-262-0345 or 800-247-4612
Fax: 405-262-0745

Chicago Association of Spring Manufacturers

CASMI Scholarship

Type of award: Scholarship.
Intended use: For undergraduate study at accredited vocational, 2-year or 4-year institution.
Eligibility: Applicant or parent must be member/participant of Chicago Association of Spring Manufacturing.
Additional information: Must be child of member of CASMI. For further information or an application, contact Chicago Association of Spring Manufacturers directly.

Amount of award:	$1,000

Choctaw Nation of Oklahoma

Choctaw Nation Higher Eduation Grant

Type of award: Scholarship, renewable.
Intended use: For undergraduate or graduate study at accredited 2-year, 4-year or graduate institution in United States.
Eligibility: Applicant must be American Indian. Must be enrolled member of Choctaw Tribe and have Certificate Documenting Indian Blood (CDIB) and tribal membership card.
Basis for selection: Applicant must demonstrate financial need.
Application requirements: Transcript, proof of eligibility. FAFSA.
Additional information: Must first apply for federal financial assistance. Grant will assist with any unmet need. Must reapply for renewal. Also, $1,000 scholarship program now in effect for those with minimum 2.5 GPA; financial need not required, but FAFSA must be completed.

Amount of award:	$1,600
Number of awards:	1,600
Number of applicants:	3,200
Application deadline:	March 15
Notification begins:	July 15

Contact:
Choctaw Nation of Oklahoma
Higher Education Department
P.O. Drawer 1210
Durant, OK 74702-1210
Phone: 800-522-6170

Christian Record Services

Christian Record Services Scholarship

Type of award: Scholarship, renewable.
Intended use: For full-time undergraduate study in United States.
Eligibility: Applicant must be visually impaired.

Basis for selection: Applicant must demonstrate financial need and high academic achievement.
Application requirements: Recommendations. Picture, bio.
Additional information: Applicants must be legally blind or blind. Awardees must reapply yearly. Applications accepted beginning November 1.

Amount of award:	$500
Number of awards:	10
Number of applicants:	67
Application deadline:	April 1
Notification begins:	May 15
Total amount awarded:	$5,000

Contact:
Christian Record Services
4444 South 52 Street
Lincoln, NE 68516
Phone: 402-488-0981
Fax: 402-488-7582

Citizens State Bank of Roseau

Citizens State Bank of Roseau Scholarship Fund

Type of award: Scholarship.
Intended use: For freshman study at accredited 2-year or 4-year institution.
Eligibility: Applicant or parent must be employed by Citizen's State Bank of Roseau. Applicant must be high school senior.
Additional information: Must be child of employee of Citizens State Bank of Roseau. For further information and an application, contact Citizens State Bank directly.

Amount of award:	$1,000

Clara Abbott Foundation

Clara Abbott Foundation Educational Grant

Type of award: Scholarship, renewable.
Intended use: For full-time undergraduate study at accredited vocational, 2-year or 4-year institution in or outside United States.
Eligibility: Applicant or parent must be employed by Abbott Laboratories. Applicant must be high school senior.
Basis for selection: Applicant must demonstrate financial need.
Application requirements: Transcript, proof of eligibility. Applicant must provide tax forms (W-2 wage form).
Additional information: Applicant must be a child or dependent of an Abbott Laboratories employee or retiree. Applicant may reapply each year, for a maximum of five years.

Amount of award:	$1,100-$13,000
Number of awards:	3,500
Number of applicants:	4,100
Application deadline:	March 13
Notification begins:	June 1
Total amount awarded:	$10,000,000

Contact:
Clara Abbott Foundation
200 Abbott Park Road
D-579 J37
Abbott Park, IL 60064-3537

Contact:
The Coca-Cola Foundation
P. O. Drawer 1734
Atlanta, GA 30301
Web: www.thecocacolacompany.com

The Clorox Company Foundation

The Clorox Company Foundation Scholarship

Type of award: Scholarship, renewable.
Intended use: For freshman study at 2-year or 4-year institution.
Eligibility: Applicant or parent must be employed by The Clorox Company Foundation. Applicant must be high school senior.
Additional information: For further information or an application, contact Clorox Company Foundation directly.

Amount of award:	$2,500

CNF, Inc.

CNF Companies Scholarship

Type of award: Scholarship, renewable.
Intended use: For undergraduate study at accredited vocational, 2-year or 4-year institution.
Eligibility: Applicant or parent must be employed by CNF, Inc.
Basis for selection: Applicant must demonstrate financial need.
Additional information: For further information or an application, contact CNF, Inc. directly.

Amount of award:	$500-$2,500

The Coca-Cola Foundation

First Generation Scholarship Program

Type of award: Scholarship, renewable.
Intended use: For full-time undergraduate study at accredited 2-year or 4-year institution in United States. Designated institutions: 170 eligible institutions.
Eligibility: Applicant must be high school senior.
Basis for selection: Applicant must demonstrate high academic achievement.
Application requirements: Proof of eligibility.
Additional information: Applicant must be first in immediate family to seek college education. Must maintain 3.0 GPA and full-time status to renew.

Amount of award:	$5,000

Coca-Cola Scholars Foundation

Coca-Cola Scholars Program

Type of award: Scholarship, renewable.
Intended use: For full-time undergraduate study at accredited 2-year or 4-year institution in United States.
Eligibility: Applicant must be high school senior. Applicant must be U.S. citizen or permanent resident.
Basis for selection: Applicant must demonstrate high academic achievement, depth of character, leadership, seriousness of purpose and service orientation.
Additional information: Must be attending high school in U.S. or territories. Award per year is $1,000 to $5,000. Notification begins December 31 for semifinalists; end of February for finalists.

Amount of award:	$4,000-$20,000
Number of awards:	250
Number of applicants:	117,000
Application deadline:	October 31
Notification begins:	December 31
Total amount awarded:	$1,800,000

Contact:
Coca-Cola Scholars Foundation
P.O. Box 442
Atlanta, GA 30301-0442
Phone: 800-306-COKE

Coca-Cola Two-Year Colleges Scholarship

Type of award: Scholarship.
Intended use: For undergraduate study at 2-year institution in United States. Designated institutions: Two-year degree granting institution.
Eligibility: Applicant must be U.S. citizen or permanent resident.
Basis for selection: Applicant must demonstrate high academic achievement, depth of character and service orientation.
Application requirements: Nomination by college in which student is enrolled or planning to enroll. College will submit nomination/application.
Additional information: Applicant/nominee must have completed 100 hours community service within past 12 months. Minimum 2.5 GPA. Must be planning to enroll in at least two courses during next term. Children of Coca-Cola employees not eligible. Up to two nominations from each campus.

Amount of award:	$1,000
Number of awards:	400
Application deadline:	May 31
Notification begins:	July 15
Total amount awarded:	$400,000

193

Contact:
Coca-Cola Two-Year Colleges Scholarship Program
P.O. Box 1615
Atlanta, GA 30301-1615
Phone: 800-306-2653
Web: www.thecoca-colacompany.com/scholars/index.html

Contact:
College Foundation, Inc.
P.O. Box 12100
Raleigh, NC 27605-2100
Phone: 888-234-6400
Web: www.cfi.org

COLAGE (Children of Lesbians and Gays Everywhere) and the Family Pride Coalition

Lee Dubin Scholarship

Type of award: Scholarship, renewable.
Intended use: For undergraduate study at accredited postsecondary institution.
Eligibility: Applicant must have at least one lesbian, gay, bisexual, or transgender parent.
Basis for selection: Applicant must demonstrate financial need, depth of character, leadership and service orientation.
Application requirements: Essay, transcript. Proof of enrollment, financial aid information.
Additional information: Students working to combat homophobia and increase positive awareness of LGBT families encouraged to apply. Previous applicants or awardees encouraged to re-apply. Applicants encouraged to be willing to be named publicly in association with Family Pride Coalition, COLAGE and the Lee Dubin Scholarship. Awardees announced during Pride Month (June).

Amount of award:	$500-$1,000
Number of awards:	4
Total amount awarded:	$4,000

Contact:
COLAGE Scholarship Committee
3543 18th Street, #1
San Francisco, CA 94110
Phone: 415-861-KIDS (5437)
Web: www.colage.org

College Foundation, Inc.

North Carolina Student Incentive Grant

Type of award: Scholarship, renewable.
Intended use: For full-time undergraduate study at vocational, 2-year or 4-year institution. Designated institutions: Approved institutions in North Carolina.
Eligibility: Applicant must be residing in North Carolina.
Basis for selection: Applicant must demonstrate financial need.

Amount of award:	$200-$1,500
Number of awards:	3,900
Number of applicants:	60,500
Application deadline:	March 15
Notification begins:	August 1
Total amount awarded:	$2,300,000

Colorado Commission on Higher Education

Colorado Leveraging Education Assistance Program

Type of award: Scholarship.
Intended use: For undergraduate study at accredited postsecondary institution. Designated institutions: Eligible postsecondary institutions in Colorado.
Eligibility: Applicant must be residing in Colorado.
Basis for selection: Applicant must demonstrate financial need.
Application requirements: Completed FAFSA.
Additional information: Must demonstrate substantial financial need. Contact college financial aid office for information, deadlines and application. Maximum award is $5,000. Award is not renewable, must apply each year.
Contact:
Colorado Commission on Higher Education
1380 Lawrence Street
Suite 1200
Denver, CO 80204
Phone: 303-866-2723
Web: www.state.co.us

Colorado Nursing Scholarship

Type of award: Scholarship.
Intended use: For undergraduate or post-bachelor's certificate study at vocational, 2-year or 4-year institution. Designated institutions: Eligible postsecondary institution in Colorado participating in state programs that offer nursing degrees or certificates.
Eligibility: Applicant must be U.S. citizen residing in Colorado.
Basis for selection: Major/career interest in nursing; nurse practitioner or midwifery. Applicant must demonstrate financial need.
Application requirements: Completed FAFSA.
Additional information: Minimum of 6 credit hours. Must re-apply each year. Visit Website for additional information.

Amount of award:	Full tuition
Application deadline:	April 1

Contact:
Colorado Commission on Higher Education
1380 Lawrence Street
Suite 1200
Denver, CO 80204
Phone: 303-866-2723
Web: www.state.co.us

Colorado Student Grant

Type of award: Scholarship.

Intended use: For full-time undergraduate study at postsecondary institution. Designated institutions: Eligible postsecondary institutions in Colorado.
Eligibility: Applicant must be residing in Colorado.
Basis for selection: Applicant must demonstrate financial need.
Additional information: Contact college financial aid office or visit Website for additional information, deadline and application.

Amount of award: $5,000

Contact:
Colorado Commission on Higher Education
1380 Lawrence Street
Suite 1200
Denver, CO 80204
Phone: 303-866-2723
Web: www.state.co.us

Colorado Undergraduate Merit Award

Type of award: Scholarship, renewable.
Intended use: For undergraduate study at accredited postsecondary institution. Designated institutions: Eligible postsecondary institutions in Colorado.
Eligibility: Applicant must be residing in Colorado.
Basis for selection: Applicant must demonstrate high academic achievement.
Application requirements: Student must maintain 3.0 G.P.A. to be considered for renewal.
Additional information: Amount of award varies but cannot exceed tuition. Institutions may make awards for academic excellence or special talents, including music and athletics. Contact college financial aid office or visit Website for information and application.
Contact:
Colorado Commission on Higher Education
1380 Lawrence
Suite 1200
Denver, CO 80204
Phone: 303-866-2723
Web: www.state.co.us

Colorado Work-Study Program

Type of award: Scholarship.
Intended use: For undergraduate study at postsecondary institution. Designated institutions: Designated postsecondary institutions in Colorado.
Eligibility: Applicant must be residing in Colorado.
Basis for selection: Applicant must demonstrate financial need.
Application requirements: Applicant must demonstrate financial need and/or need to work.
Additional information: This is a part-time employment program designed to assist students with financial need or work experience. Amount of award cannot exceed need. Contact college financial aid office or visit Website for additional information, deadlines and application. Award is not renewable.
Contact:
Colorado Commission on Higher Education
1380 Lawrence Street
Suite 1200
Denver, CO 80204
Phone: 303-866-2723
Web: www.state.co.us

Colorado Masons Benevolent Fund Association

Colorado Masons Scholarship

Type of award: Scholarship, renewable.
Intended use: For full-time undergraduate study at accredited vocational, 2-year or 4-year institution in United States. Designated institutions: Can only be used at Colorado institutions.
Eligibility: Applicant must be high school senior. Applicant must be residing in Colorado.
Basis for selection: Applicant must demonstrate financial need, high academic achievement and depth of character.
Additional information: Applicant must be attending public high school. Contact high school college counselor for application details. Do not contact Association directly.

Amount of award: $5,000
Number of awards: 53
Application deadline: March 15
Total amount awarded: $265,000

Contact:
Contact public high school college counselor.

Colorado Society of CPAs Educational Foundation

Colorado CPAs Ethnic-College and University Scholarship

Type of award: Scholarship, renewable.
Intended use: For undergraduate or graduate study at accredited 2-year, 4-year or graduate institution in United States. Designated institutions: Colorado colleges and universities with accredited accounting programs.
Eligibility: Applicant must be Alaskan native, Asian American, African American, Mexican American, Hispanic American, Puerto Rican or American Indian. Applicant must be U.S. citizen residing in Colorado.
Basis for selection: Major/career interest in accounting. Applicant must demonstrate financial need and high academic achievement.
Application requirements: Transcript, proof of eligibility.
Additional information: Must have completed eight semester hours of accounting courses to be eligible to apply. Minimum 3.0 GPA required. Visit Website to download application.

Amount of award: $1,000
Number of awards: 2
Application deadline: June 30

Contact:
Colorado Society of CPAs Educational Foundation
7979 East Tufts Avenue Suite 500
Denver, CO 80237-2843
Phone: 800-523-9082
Web: www.cocpa.org

Scholarships

195

Colorado CPAs Gordon Scheer Scholarship

Type of award: Scholarship, renewable.
Intended use: For junior, senior or graduate study at accredited 4-year or graduate institution in United States. Designated institutions: Colorado colleges and universities with accredited accounting programs.
Eligibility: Applicant must be U.S. citizen residing in Colorado.
Basis for selection: Major/career interest in accounting. Applicant must demonstrate high academic achievement.
Application requirements: Interview, recommendations, transcript, proof of eligibility. Letter of reference from accounting faculty member.
Additional information: Minimum 3.5 GPA necessary to qualify. No financial information required. Visit Website to download application.

Amount of award:	$1,250
Number of awards:	1
Application deadline:	June 30
Total amount awarded:	$1,250

Contact:
Colorado Society of CPAs Educational Foundation
7979 East Tufts Avenue, Suite 500
Denver, CO 80237-2843
Phone: 800-523-9082
Web: www.cocpa.org

Colorado Society of CPAs General Scholarship

Type of award: Scholarship, renewable.
Intended use: For junior, senior or graduate study at accredited 4-year or graduate institution in United States. Designated institutions: Colorado colleges and universities with an accredited accounting program.
Eligibility: Applicant must be U.S. citizen residing in Colorado.
Basis for selection: Major/career interest in accounting. Applicant must demonstrate financial need and high academic achievement.
Application requirements: Transcript, proof of eligibility.
Additional information: Must have completed eight semester hours in accounting to be eligible to apply. Minimum 3.0 GPA required. Visit Website to download application.

Amount of award:	$1,000
Number of awards:	20
Number of applicants:	50
Application deadline:	June 30, November 30
Total amount awarded:	$20,000

Contact:
Colorado Society of CPAs Educational Foundation
7979 East Tufts Avenue, Suite 500
Denver, CO 80237-2843
Phone: 800-523-9082
Web: www.cocpa.org

The Comer Foundation

The Comer Foundation Scholarship Fund

Type of award: Scholarship, renewable.
Intended use: For undergraduate study at accredited postsecondary institution.
Eligibility: Applicant or parent must be employed by Lands' End. Applicant must be high school senior.
Basis for selection: Applicant must demonstrate financial need.
Additional information: For further information or an application, contact The Comer Foundation directly.

Amount of award:	$500-$2,500

Contact:
The Comer Foundation

ConAgra Foundation, Inc.

Mike Harper Leadership Scholars Program

Type of award: Scholarship, renewable.
Intended use: For freshman study at accredited vocational, 2-year or 4-year institution.
Eligibility: Applicant or parent must be employed by ConAgra, Inc. Applicant must be high school senior.
Basis for selection: Applicant must demonstrate financial need.
Additional information: For additional information or an application, contact ConAgra Foundation directly.

Amount of award:	$1,000-$2,500

Cone Mills Corporation

Cone Mills Scholarship Program

Type of award: Scholarship, renewable.
Intended use: For full-time undergraduate study at accredited vocational, 2-year or 4-year institution in United States.
Eligibility: Applicant or parent must be employed by Cone Mills Corporation. Applicant must be high school senior. Applicant must be U.S. citizen.
Basis for selection: Applicant must demonstrate high academic achievement.
Application requirements: Essay, transcript, proof of eligibility. CSS PROFILE Application required.

Amount of award:	$750-$2,500
Number of awards:	14
Number of applicants:	58
Application deadline:	November 30
Notification begins:	April 30
Total amount awarded:	$40,000

Contact:
Cone Mills Corporation
Scholarship Program
3101 North Elm Street
Greensboro, NC 27415-6540
Phone: 910-379-6252
Fax: 910-379-6930

Congressional Black Caucus Foundation, Inc.

Congressional Black Caucus Foundation Spouses Scholarship

Type of award: Scholarship, renewable.
Intended use: For full-time undergraduate or graduate study at accredited 4-year institution.
Eligibility: Applicant must be U.S. citizen or permanent resident residing in Missouri, Texas, Virgin Islands, New Jersey, New York, South Carolina, Pennsylvania, Virginia, Florida, District of Columbia, Maryland, Illinois, Georgia, Indiana, Ohio, Louisiana, California, Mississippi, Michigan or North Carolina.
Basis for selection: Applicant must demonstrate financial need.
Application requirements: Transcript. Minimum 2.5 GPA. Must reside or attend school in Congressional Black Caucus Members' District.
Additional information: Must reside or attend school in congressional district represented by Black Caucus member. Selection made at district level. List of eligible districts and members' addresses provided by national office. Award amounts vary. Employees and/or relatives of CBC Members, CBC Spouses, CBCF and/or General Mills are not eligible for this program. To obtain local contact information, see Website. Contact the Congressional Black Caucus member representing the Congressional District you attend, school or place of residence.
   Application deadline: May 15, January 15
Contact:
Phone: 202-675-6730
Fax: 202-547-3806
Web: www.cbcfonline.org

Congressional Hispanic Caucus Institute

CHCI Scholarship Award

Type of award: Scholarship.
Intended use: For full-time undergraduate or graduate study at accredited 2-year or 4-year institution in United States.
Eligibility: Applicant must be Mexican American, Hispanic American or Puerto Rican. Applicant must be U.S. citizen or permanent resident.
Basis for selection: Applicant must demonstrate financial need, depth of character, leadership and service orientation.
Application requirements: Recommendations, essay, transcript, proof of eligibility. Applicant must submit SAT, ACT, GMAT, LSAT scores if available.

Additional information: Student must be of Hispanic/Latino background.
   Amount of award: $2,000-$5,000
   Number of awards: 40
   Number of applicants: 40
   Application deadline: April 1
   Total amount awarded: $155,000
Contact:
Congressional Hispanic Caucus Institute
504 C Street, NE
Washington, DC 20002
Phone: 202-543-1771
Fax: 202-546-2143
Web: www.chci.org

Connecticut Building Congress Scholarship Fund

Connecticut Building Congress Scholarship

Type of award: Scholarship, renewable.
Intended use: For undergraduate study at 2-year or 4-year institution in United States.
Eligibility: Applicant must be residing in Connecticut.
Basis for selection: Major/career interest in engineering, construction; architecture or construction management. Applicant must demonstrate financial need and high academic achievement.
Application requirements: Recommendations, transcript. State applicant must reside in Connecticut.
   Amount of award: $500-$2,000
   Number of awards: 5
   Number of applicants: 85
   Application deadline: March 1, June 1
   Total amount awarded: $10,000
Contact:
Connecticut Building Congress Scholarship Fund
2600 Dixwell Ave.
Hamden, CT 06514

Connecticut Department of Higher Education

Connecticut Aid for Public College Students

Type of award: Scholarship, renewable.
Intended use: For undergraduate study. Designated institutions: Public institutions in Connecticut.
Eligibility: Applicant must be U.S. citizen residing in Connecticut.
Basis for selection: Applicant must demonstrate financial need.
Additional information: Awards up to amount of unmet financial need. Apply at financial aid office at Connecticut public college.

Amount of award:	$400-$1,900
Number of awards:	6,516
Total amount awarded:	$5,492,653

Contact:
Financial aid office of Connecticut public colleges.
Phone: 203-566-2618
Fax: 203-566-7865

Connecticut Aid to Dependents of Deceased/Disabled/MIA Veterans

Type of award: Scholarship.
Intended use: For undergraduate or graduate study.
Eligibility: Applicant must be U.S. citizen residing in Connecticut. Applicant must be dependent of disabled veteran, deceased veteran or POW/MIA; or spouse of disabled veteran, deceased veteran or POW/MIA. Death or disability must be service related.
Basis for selection: Applicant must demonstrate financial need.
Application requirements: Proof of eligibility.
Additional information: Parent/spouse must have been Connecticut resident prior to enlistment.

Amount of award:	$400
Number of awards:	6
Number of applicants:	6
Total amount awarded:	$2,400

Contact:
Connecticut Department of Higher Education
61 Woodland Street
Hartford, CT 06105-2391
Phone: 203-566-2618
Fax: 203-566-7865

Connecticut Capitol Scholarship Program

Type of award: Scholarship, renewable.
Intended use: For undergraduate study.
Eligibility: Applicant must be high school senior. Applicant must be U.S. citizen or permanent resident residing in Connecticut.
Basis for selection: Applicant must demonstrate financial need and high academic achievement.
Additional information: Must rank in top fifth of class or have SAT score of at least 1200. May be used at institutions in Connecticut or at institutions that have reciprocity agreements with Connecticut.

Amount of award:	$2,000
Number of awards:	4,500
Number of applicants:	7,500
Application deadline:	February 15
Notification begins:	June 30
Total amount awarded:	$5,500,000

Contact:
High school guidance office for application.
Phone: 860-947-1855
Fax: 860-947-1311
Web: www.ctdhe.commnet.edu

Connecticut Independent College Student Grant

Type of award: Scholarship, renewable.

Intended use: For undergraduate study at 4-year institution in United States. Designated institutions: Private institutions in Connecticut.
Eligibility: Applicant must be U.S. citizen residing in Connecticut.
Basis for selection: Applicant must demonstrate financial need.
Additional information: Applications can be obtained at college financial aid office.

Amount of award:	$7,777
Number of awards:	3,714
Total amount awarded:	$28,883,778

Contact:
Connecticut Independent College financial aid office.

Connecticut Robert C. Byrd Honors Scholarship

Type of award: Scholarship, renewable.
Intended use: For freshman, sophomore, junior or senior study.
Eligibility: Applicant must be high school senior. Applicant must be U.S. citizen residing in Connecticut.
Basis for selection: Applicant must demonstrate high academic achievement.
Additional information: Must rank in top two percent of high school graduating class.

Amount of award:	$1,500
Number of awards:	206
Number of applicants:	700
Total amount awarded:	$306,060

Contact:
Connecticut Department of Higher Education
61 Woodland Street
Hartford, CT 06105-2391
Phone: 860-947-1855
Fax: 860-947-1311
Web: www.ctdhe.commnet.edu

Connecticut Tuition Set Aside Aid

Type of award: Scholarship, renewable.
Intended use: For undergraduate study at 2-year or 4-year institution in United States. Designated institutions: Public institutions in Connecticut.
Eligibility: Applicant must be U.S. citizen residing in Connecticut.
Basis for selection: Applicant must demonstrate financial need.
Additional information: Awards up to unmet financial need. Apply at financial aid office of institution. Scholarship awarded through Connecticut public colleges.

Number of awards:	936
Total amount awarded:	$412,143

Contact:
Apply at Connecticut public colleges

Connecticut Tuition Waiver for Senior Citizens

Type of award: Scholarship.
Intended use: For undergraduate study at 2-year institution. Designated institutions: Public two-year intitutions in Connecticut.
Eligibility: Applicant must be returning adult student. Applicant must be U.S. citizen residing in Connecticut.
Application requirements: Proof of eligibility.

Additional information: Waivers approved on space available basis. Apply through financial aid office of institution.

Amount of award:	Full tuition
Number of awards:	1,949
Number of applicants:	1,949
Total amount awarded:	$448,292

Contact:
Financial aid office of Connecticut public colleges.
Phone: 203-566-2618
Fax: 203-566-7865

Connecticut Tuition Waiver for Veterans

Type of award: Scholarship, renewable.
Intended use: For undergraduate study. Designated institutions: Connecticut public institution.
Eligibility: Applicant must be U.S. citizen residing in Connecticut. Applicant must be veteran. Must have served during time of conflict.
Application requirements: Proof of eligibility.
Additional information: Must have been Connecticut resident at time of enlistment.

Amount of award:	Full tuition
Number of awards:	4,213
Number of applicants:	4,213
Total amount awarded:	$3,134,146

Contact:
Apply at Connecticut public colleges.
Phone: 203-566-2618
Fax: 203-566-7865

Connecticut Tuition Waiver for Vietnam MIA/POW Dependents

Type of award: Scholarship.
Intended use: For undergraduate study. Designated institutions: Connecticut public institutions.
Eligibility: Applicant must be U.S. citizen residing in Connecticut. Applicant must be dependent of POW/MIA; or spouse of POW/MIA during Vietnam.
Application requirements: Proof of eligibility.
Additional information: Apply at financial aid office of institution. Awarded through Connecticut public colleges.
Contact:
Connecticut public colleges
Phone: 203-566-2618
Fax: 203-566-7865

Connecticut League for Nursing

Connecticut Nursing Scholarship

Type of award: Scholarship.
Intended use: For senior or graduate study at accredited postsecondary institution. Designated institutions: Must be attending a Connecticut nursing school accredited by the National League of Nursing.
Eligibility: Applicant must be U.S. citizen residing in Connecticut.

Basis for selection: Major/career interest in nursing. Applicant must demonstrate financial need, high academic achievement, leadership and seriousness of purpose.
Application requirements: Recommendations, essay, transcript, proof of eligibility.
Additional information: One undergraduate and one graduate award given. Applicants must have 20 credit hours in nursing courses to be eligible to apply for graduate scholarship; Undergraduates must have completed one year of a two-year program or three years of a four-year program; RN students must be entering the senior year in upper division BSN program.

Amount of award:	$1,000
Number of awards:	2
Number of applicants:	15
Application deadline:	October 15
Notification begins:	November 15
Total amount awarded:	$2,000

Contact:
Connecticut League for Nursing
P.O. Box 365
Wallingford, CT 06492
Phone: 203-265-4248

Consolidated Freightways Corporation

Consolidated Freightways Corporation Scholarship Program

Type of award: Scholarship, renewable.
Intended use: For undergraduate study at vocational, 2-year or 4-year institution.
Eligibility: Applicant must be high school senior.
Additional information: For further information or an application, contact Consolidated Freightways Corporation directly.

Amount of award:	$500-$2,500

Corporate Actions Division, Inc. of the Securities Industry

Corporate Actions Division, Inc. Scholarship Program

Type of award: Scholarship, renewable.
Intended use: For undergraduate study at accredited 2-year or 4-year institution.
Eligibility: Applicant or parent must be member/participant of Reorganization Division of Securities Industry.
Additional information: Must be child of member. For further information or an application, contact the Corporate Actions Division of The Securities Industry directly.

Amount of award:	$750

Corporate Express

Corporate Express Scholarship

Type of award: Scholarship.
Intended use: For full-time undergraduate study at accredited vocational, 2-year or 4-year institution.
Eligibility: Applicant or parent must be employed by Corporate Express. Applicant must be no older than 24.
Basis for selection: Applicant must be a child of a full-time Express employee. Applicant must demonstrate high academic achievement and leadership.
Application requirements: Recommendations, essay, transcript, proof of eligibility. Must be 24 years old or less at time of deadline date. Statement of educational and career goals, work experience and community activities.
Additional information: Must be child or ward of full-time employee of Corporate Express who has worked for company for over one year at time of application. For further information or an application, contact Corporate Express Scholarship Program directly.

Amount of award:	$3,000
Number of awards:	45
Number of applicants:	50
Application deadline:	March 15
Total amount awarded:	$135,000

Contact:
Corporate Express Scholarship Program
Scholarship Management Services, CSFA
1505 Riverview Road, P.O. Box 297
St. Peter, MN 56082
Phone: 507-931-1682

Corporation for National Service

President's Student Service Scholarships

Type of award: Scholarship.
Intended use: For freshman study at accredited 2-year or 4-year institution in United States.
Eligibility: Applicant must be high school junior or senior. Applicant must be U.S. citizen or permanent resident.
Application requirements: Nomination by high school. Student should have performed outstanding service in his or her community.
Additional information: Each high school in United States may select two students who have performed outstanding service to their community.

Amount of award:	$1,000
Number of awards:	10,000
Application deadline:	April 1, June 30
Notification begins:	May 1
Total amount awarded:	$5,000,000

Contact:
Corporation for National Service
1150 Connecticut Avenue, N.W.
Suite 1100
Washington, DC 20036
Phone: 866-291-7700 (toll-free)
Web: www.nationalservice.org/scholarships/

Council on International Educational Exchange

Bowman Travel Grants

Type of award: Scholarship.
Intended use: For full-time undergraduate study at accredited 4-year institution in Africa, Asia, Latin America, the Middle East, and select European countries.
Eligibility: Applicant must be enrolled in high school. Applicant must be U.S. citizen or permanent resident.
Basis for selection: Applicant must demonstrate financial need, depth of character, seriousness of purpose and service orientation.
Application requirements: Recommendations, essay, transcript, proof of eligibility. Financial aid information.
Additional information: Grant provides voucher for round trip tickets to non-traditional study destinations. Applicants must be an undergraduate participating in study, work, or volunteer program in Council ISP Centers or institutions that are Official International Student Identity Card (ISIC) issuing offices in approved countries, or must be enrolled at a Council Member Institution or Official ISIC issuing office in U.S. Students with limited education abroad experience encouraged to apply. High school students also eligible. Application available on Website.

Number of awards:	18
Application deadline:	April 1, October 26
Notification begins:	May 13, December 7

Contact:
Council on International Educational Exchange
Bowman Travel Grant Committee
633 Third Ave., 20th Floor
New York, NY 10017
Phone: 800-40-STUDY
Web: www.ciee.org/study/scholarships/

Department of Education Scholarship for Programs in China

Type of award: Scholarship.
Intended use: For junior, senior, master's, doctoral or postgraduate study at 4-year or graduate institution in China. Designated institutions: Council on International Educational Exchange Study Centers at Peking University or Nanjing University.
Eligibility: Applicant must be U.S. citizen or permanent resident.
Basis for selection: Competition/talent/interest in study abroad. Major/career interest in foreign languages; education or asian studies. Applicant must demonstrate financial need and seriousness of purpose.
Application requirements: Transcript, proof of eligibility.
Additional information: Must have two years college-level Mandarin Chinese and intend to teach language or area studies. Additional fields of study include ethnic and cultural studies, Asian studies, Chinese language and literature. Application available on Website.

Amount of award:	$500-$7,000
Number of awards:	15
Number of applicants:	20
Application deadline:	April 1, October 26
Notification begins:	May 13, December 7
Total amount awarded:	$40,000

Contact:
Council-International Study Progams
Attn: Daniel Olds, Program Officer - Asia
205 E. 42nd Street
New York, NY 10017
Phone: 800-40-STUDY ext 2756
Web: www.ciee.org/study/scholarships/index.htm

International Study Programs (ISP) Scholarship

Type of award: Scholarship.
Intended use: For full-time undergraduate or graduate study at accredited 4-year or graduate institution. Designated institutions: Applicants must be from Academic Consortium member institutions (a complete list of member institutions is on Website).
Basis for selection: Applicant must demonstrate financial need, high academic achievement, depth of character and seriousness of purpose.
Application requirements: Recommendations, essay, transcript, proof of eligibility. Copy of FAFSA Student Aid Report or CSS/Financial Aid Profile and all other required financial aid information, additional photocopy of all materials.
Additional information: Available to Council Study Center applicants only. Applicants must be from Academic Consortium member institutions. Visit Website for list of member institutions. Applicants should demonstrate preparation for program through course work, volunteer work, or internships. The same application package may be used for the Bailey and ISP scholarship. Application available on Website.

Amount of award:	$500-$1,000
Number of awards:	42
Application deadline:	April 1, October 26
Notification begins:	May 13, December 7

Contact:
Council International Study Programs
Scholarship Committee
633 Third Ave., 20th Floor
New York, NY 10017
Phone: 800-40-STUDY
Web: www.ciee.org/study/scholarships/

Robert B. Bailey III Minority Scholarship

Type of award: Scholarship.
Intended use: For full-time undergraduate, master's, doctoral or postgraduate study at 2-year, 4-year or graduate institution. Designated institutions: Council-ISP Africa, Asia, Australia/New Zealand, Europe, Latin America, and Middle East study centers.
Eligibility: Applicant must be Alaskan native, Asian American, African American, Mexican American, Hispanic American, Puerto Rican or American Indian. Must be self-identified member of under-represented group to study abroad. Applicant must be U.S. citizen.
Basis for selection: Major/career interest in humanities/liberal arts. Applicant must demonstrate financial need.
Application requirements: Recommendations, essay. Copy of FAFSA Student Aid Report or CSS/Financial Aid Profile and all other required financial aid information, additional photocopy of all materials.
Additional information: Applicant must be applying to Council Study Center program or University Direct Enrollment Service institution for academic year, semester or summer session. Applicants should demonstrate preparation for program through course work, volunteer work or internships. Same

application package may be used for Bailey and ISP scholarship. Application available on Website.

Amount of award:	$500
Number of awards:	20
Number of applicants:	150
Application deadline:	April 1, October 26
Notification begins:	May 13, December 7
Total amount awarded:	$50,000

Contact:
Council-International Study Progams
Attn: Scholarship Coordinator
633 Third Avenue, 20th Floor
New York, NY 10017
Phone: 800-40-STUDY
Web: www.ciee.org/study/scholarships/index.htm

Courage Center Vocational Services-United Way Organization

Mooty Scholarship

Type of award: Scholarship, renewable.
Intended use: For full-time undergraduate study at accredited vocational, 2-year or 4-year institution in United States.
Eligibility: Applicant must be visually impaired, hearing impaired or physically challenged. Applicant must be male. Applicant must be U.S. citizen residing in Minnesota.
Basis for selection: Applicant must demonstrate financial need, high academic achievement, depth of character and seriousness of purpose.
Application requirements: Interview, essay. Include GPA information.
Additional information: Non-Minnesota resident must be participant in Courage Center Services. Awardee must reapply to receive award in succeeding years. Interview for finalists. Notification in July.

Amount of award:	$1,000
Number of awards:	10
Application deadline:	May 31

Contact:
Courage Center (United Way Organization), Vocational Services Dept.
Leanne Jackson-Butala
3915 Golden Valley Rd.
Golden Valley, MN 55422-4298

Scholarship for People with Disabilities

Type of award: Scholarship.
Intended use: For undergraduate study at accredited vocational, 2-year or 4-year institution.
Eligibility: Applicant must be visually impaired, hearing impaired or physically challenged. Applicant must be residing in Minnesota.
Basis for selection: Applicant must demonstrate financial need, depth of character, leadership and seriousness of purpose.
Application requirements: Interview, essay, proof of eligibility.
Additional information: If not a Minnesota resident, student must be U.S. citizen participating in Courage Center services. Student must have a sensory impairment or physical disability.

201

Selection emphasis is placed on the applicant's intentions and achievements.

Amount of award:	$500-$1,000
Number of awards:	12
Number of applicants:	24
Application deadline:	May 31
Total amount awarded:	$9,000

Contact:
Courage Center (United Way Organization), Vocational Services Dept.
Leanne Jackson-Butala
3915 Golden Valley Rd.
Golden Valley, MN 55422-4298

Crompton Corporation

Crompton Corporation Scholarship Program

Type of award: Scholarship, renewable.
Intended use: For undergraduate study at vocational, 2-year or 4-year institution.
Eligibility: Applicant or parent must be employed by Crompton Corporation. Applicant must be high school senior.
Additional information: For further information or an application, contact Crompton Corporation directly.

Amount of award:	$2,500

Cushion Cut, Inc.

Lester F. Kuzmick Memorial Scholarship

Type of award: Scholarship.
Intended use: For undergraduate study at accredited vocational, 2-year or 4-year institution.
Eligibility: Applicant or parent must be employed by Cushion Cut Inc.
Additional information: For further information or an application, contact Cushion Cut Inc. directly.

Amount of award:	$2,000

Cymdeithas Gymreig/ Philadelphia

Cymdeithas Gymreig (Welsh Society) Philadelphia Scholarship

Type of award: Scholarship.
Intended use: For full-time freshman, sophomore or junior study at accredited 2-year or 4-year institution in United States. Designated institutions: Must attend institutions in Delaware, Maryland, New Jersey or Pennsylvania.
Eligibility: Applicant must be Welsh. Applicant must be residing in Delaware, Maryland, New Jersey or Pennsylvania.

Basis for selection: Applicant must demonstrate high academic achievement, leadership, seriousness of purpose and service orientation.
Application requirements: Recommendations, essay, transcript, proof of eligibility. Proof of Welsh descent. Proof of participation in Welsh activities. SASE is required or sponsor will not respond.
Additional information: Applicant or parent must be member of or be active in Welsh organization, church, or activities. If inquiry does not have proof of Welsh descent and evidence of participation in Welsh activities, sponsor will not reply. Applicant may study in Wales if primary residence is within 150 miles of Philadelphia. Must rank in top third of class. Five to seven awards totalling $5,000 to $7,000 are given annually.

Amount of award:	$500-$1,000
Number of awards:	5
Number of applicants:	500
Application deadline:	March 1
Notification begins:	June 1
Total amount awarded:	$5,000

Contact:
Cymdeithas Gymreig/Philadelphia
Hen Dy Hapus 367 South River Street
Wilkes-Barre, PA 18702
Phone: 570-822-4871

Cystic Fibrosis Foundation

Cystic Fibrosis Student Traineeship

Type of award: Research grant, renewable.
Intended use: For full-time senior, master's or doctoral study at accredited 4-year or graduate institution in United States.
Basis for selection: Major/career interest in medical specialties/research.
Application requirements: Recommendations, research proposal.
Additional information: Trainees must work with faculty sponsor on research project related to cystic fibrosis. Applications accepted throughout the year, but should be submitted at least two months prior to projected start date of project.

Amount of award:	$1,500
Number of awards:	15

Contact:
Cystic Fibrosis Foundation
Office of Grants Management
6931 Arlington Road
Bethesda, MD 20814
Phone: 301-951-4422
Fax: 301-951-6378

Daimler Chrysler Corporation

Daimler Chrysler Corporation Fund Scholarship

Type of award: Scholarship, renewable.

Intended use: For undergraduate study at accredited vocational, 2-year or 4-year institution.
Eligibility: Applicant or parent must be employed by Daimler Chrysler Corporation.
Basis for selection: Applicant must demonstrate financial need.
Additional information: May also be used for nursing or secretarial/business schools. Must be child of employee of Daimler Chrysler Corporation or its U.S.-based subsidiaries. For further information or an application, contact administrator of fund, Citizens' Scholarship Foundation of America.

    Amount of award: $1,000-$5,000
Contact:
Citizens' Scholarship Foundation of America, Inc.
The Chrysler Corporation Fund
P.O. Box 297
St. Peter, MN 56082

Dairy Management, Inc.

Dairy Product Marketing Scholarship

Type of award: Scholarship.
Intended use: For full-time sophomore, junior or senior study at accredited 4-year institution.
Eligibility: Applicant must be U.S. citizen.
Basis for selection: Major/career interest in advertising; marketing; food production/management/services or food science/technology. Applicant must demonstrate high academic achievement, leadership and seriousness of purpose.
Application requirements: Recommendations, transcript. Student must have commitment to career in dairy.
Additional information: Applications available through Food Science Department Chairperson or financial aid officer of applicant's institution as well as online at Website listed below. Top-rated applicant will receive $2,500, while 19 other winners receive $1,500.

    Amount of award: $1,500-$2,500
    Number of awards: 20
    Number of applicants: 43
    Application deadline: March 31
    Notification begins: June 1
    Total amount awarded: $31,000
Contact:
Dairy Management Inc.
10255 West Higgins Road
Suite 900
Rosemont, IL 60018
Web: www.dairyinfo.com

Dairy Management, Inc. and the National Dairy Shrine

NDS/DMI Milk Marketing Scholarship

Type of award: Scholarship, renewable.

Intended use: For full-time sophomore, junior or senior study at 4-year institution.
Basis for selection: Major/career interest in dairy; marketing; food production/management/services; food science/technology; agricultural education; agricultural economics or animal sciences. Applicant must demonstrate high academic achievement.
Application requirements: Proof of eligibility. Two letters of recommendation required: one must be from faculty member in applicant's major department.
Additional information: Applications available through Food Science Department Chairperson or financial aid officer of applicant's institution as well as online at Website listed below. Must have commitment to career in dairy-food related disciplines. Top-rated applicant will receive $1,000, while 7 to 9 other winners receive $500 each.

    Amount of award: $500-$1,000
    Number of applicants: 25
    Application deadline: March 15
    Total amount awarded: $6,000
Contact:
National Dairy Shrine
1224 Alton Darby Creek Road
Columbus, OH 43228-9792
Web: www.dairyshrine.org

Dana Brake & Chassis

Dana Brake & Chassis Scholarship

Type of award: Scholarship, renewable.
Intended use: For undergraduate study at accredited postsecondary institution.
Eligibility: Applicant must be high school senior.
Basis for selection: Applicant must demonstrate financial need.
Additional information: For further information or an application, contact Dana Brake & Chassis directly.

    Amount of award: $500-$1,000
Contact:
Dana Brake & Chassis

Daniel E. O'Sullivan Memorial Scholarship Foundation

Daniel E. O'Sullivan Memorial Scholarship

Type of award: Scholarship.
Intended use: For undergraduate study at accredited vocational, 2-year or 4-year institution.
Eligibility: Applicant or parent must be employed by ULLICO, Inc.
Basis for selection: Applicant must demonstrate financial need.
Additional information: For further information or an application, contact Daniel E. O'Sullivan Foundation/Union Labor Life Insurance Company directly.

    Amount of award: $5,000

Data Management Division of Wall Street

Data Management Division of Wall Street Scholarship Program

Type of award: Scholarship.
Intended use: For undergraduate study at accredited vocational, 2-year or 4-year institution.
Eligibility: Applicant or parent must be member/participant of Data Management Division of Wall Street.
Additional information: For further information or an application, contact Data Management Division of Wall Street directly.

Amount of award:	$1,500

Datatel Scholars Foundation

Angelfire Scholarship

Type of award: Scholarship, renewable.
Intended use: For undergraduate, graduate or non-degree study at accredited postsecondary institution. Designated institutions: Must be a Datatel client institution.
Eligibility: If not Vietnam veteran, must be refugee from Cambodia, Laos or spouse/child of same. Applicant must be veteran; or dependent of veteran; or spouse of veteran during Vietnam.
Basis for selection: Applicant must demonstrate high academic achievement, depth of character and seriousness of purpose.
Application requirements: Nomination by eligible school's financial office. Criteria for selection: mix of academic merit, personal motivation and achievements including employment and extracurricular activities.
Additional information: Intended for Vietnam veterans or refugees from Cambodia, Laos or Vietnam (or spouse or child of same) during 1964-1975 time frame.

Amount of award:	$700-$2,000
Number of awards:	8
Number of applicants:	46
Application deadline:	February 15
Notification begins:	May 1
Total amount awarded:	$8,600

Contact:
Datatel Scholars Foundation
4375 Fair Lakes Court
Fairfax, VA 22033
Phone: 800-486-4332
Fax: 703-968-4573
Web: www.datatel.com

Datatel Scholars Foundation Scholarship

Type of award: Scholarship.
Intended use: For undergraduate, graduate or non-degree study at accredited postsecondary institution. Designated institutions: Must be a Datatel client institution.
Basis for selection: Applicant must demonstrate high academic achievement, depth of character and seriousness of purpose.

Application requirements: Recommendations, essay, transcript, proof of eligibility, nomination by eligible school's financial aid office. Criteria for selection: mix of academic merit, personal motivation and achievements including employment and extracurricular activities.
Additional information: Limited to institutions that are Datatel clients. When requesting application include institution name for determination of qualification. Apply through school's financial aid office, which may nominate up to two students per year. Client listing is available on Website.

Amount of award:	$700-$2,000
Number of awards:	225
Number of applicants:	351
Application deadline:	February 15
Notification begins:	May 1
Total amount awarded:	$300,000

Contact:
Datatel Scholars Foundation
4375 Fair Lakes Court
Fairfax, VA 22033
Phone: 800-486-4332
Fax: 703-968-4573
Web: www.datatel.com

Nancy Goodhue Lynch Scholarship

Type of award: Scholarship, renewable.
Intended use: For undergraduate, graduate or non-degree study at accredited postsecondary institution. Designated institutions: Must be a Datatel client institution.
Basis for selection: Major/career interest in computer/information sciences; engineering, computer; engineering, electrical/electronic; information systems; electronics; computer graphics or robotics. Applicant must demonstrate high academic achievement, depth of character and seriousness of purpose.
Application requirements: Nomination by eligible school's financial office. Criteria for selection: mix of academic merit, personal motivation and achievements including employment and extracurricular activities.
Additional information: Intended for students enrolled in technology-related curriculum program.

Amount of award:	$5,000
Number of awards:	1
Application deadline:	February 15
Notification begins:	May 1
Total amount awarded:	$5,000

Contact:
Datatel Scholars Foundation
4375 Fair Lakes Court
Fairfax, VA 22033
Phone: 800-486-4322
Fax: 703-968-4573
Web: www.datatel.com

Returning Student Scholarship

Type of award: Scholarship, renewable.
Intended use: For undergraduate, graduate or non-degree study at accredited postsecondary institution. Designated institutions: Must be a Datatel client institution.
Eligibility: Applicant must be returning adult student.
Basis for selection: Applicant must demonstrate depth of character and seriousness of purpose.
Application requirements: Nomination by eligible school's financial office. Criteria for selection: mix of academic merit, personal motivation and achievements including employment and extracurricular activities.

Additional information: Intended for any student returning to school after a five-year or more absence.

Amount of award:	$1,000
Number of awards:	25
Application deadline:	February 15
Notification begins:	May 1
Total amount awarded:	$25,000

Contact:
Datatel Scholars Foundation
4375 Fair Lakes Court
Fairfax, VA 22033
Phone: 800-486-4322
Fax: 703-968-4573
Web: www.datatel.com

Daughters of Penelope

Alexandra A. Sonenfeld Award

Type of award: Scholarship.
Intended use: For undergraduate study at accredited vocational, 2-year or 4-year institution in United States.
Eligibility: Applicant or parent must be member/participant of Daughters of Penelope. Applicant must be female. Applicant must be Greek. Applicant must be U.S. citizen.
Basis for selection: Applicant must demonstrate financial need, high academic achievement and depth of character.
Application requirements: Recommendations, essay, transcript, proof of eligibility. Also include Parents' IRS forms, Federal Aid Forms, SAT or ACT scores.
Additional information: Applicant must be a high school senior or recent graduate and have member of immediate family or legal guardian (court appointed) in the Daughters of Penelope, Order of AHEPA, or Maids of Athena and in good standing for at least two years. Applicant must not be a past recipient of any undergraduate award from the Daughters of Penelope National Scholarship program.

Amount of award:	$1,500
Number of awards:	1
Application deadline:	June 1
Total amount awarded:	$1,500

Contact:
Daughters of Penelope
1909 Q Street, NW
Suite 500
Washington, DC 20009
Phone: 202-234-9741
Fax: 202-483-6983

Daughters of Penelope Past Grand Presidents Award

Type of award: Scholarship.
Intended use: For freshman study at vocational, 2-year or 4-year institution.
Eligibility: Applicant or parent must be member/participant of Daughters of Penelope. Applicant must be female. Applicant must be Greek. Applicant must be U.S. citizen, permanent resident, international student or Canadian citizen.
Basis for selection: Applicant must demonstrate financial need and high academic achievement.
Application requirements: Recommendations, essay, transcript, proof of eligibility. Include SAT or ACT scores, copy of parents' IRS forms, federal aid forms.

Additional information: Applicant must be high school senior or recent graduate and have member of immediate family or legal guardian (court appointed) in the Daughters of Penelope, Order of AHEPA, or Maids of Athena in good standing for minimum of two years. Applicant must not be a past recipient of any undergraduate award from the Daughters of Penelope National Scholarship program.

Amount of award:	$1,500
Number of awards:	1
Application deadline:	June 1

Contact:
Daughters of Penelope
1909 Q Street NW
Suite 500
Washington, DC 20009
Phone: 202-234-9741
Fax: 202-483-6983

Emily Tamaras Memorial Award

Type of award: Scholarship.
Intended use: For freshman study at vocational, 2-year or 4-year institution.
Eligibility: Applicant or parent must be member/participant of Daughters of Penelope. Applicant must be female. Applicant must be Greek. Applicant must be U.S. citizen, permanent resident, international student or Canadian citizen.
Basis for selection: Applicant must demonstrate high academic achievement.
Application requirements: Recommendations, essay, transcript, proof of eligibility. Include SAT or ACT scores.
Additional information: Applicant must be high school senior or recent graduate and have member of immediate family or legal guardian (court appointed) in the Daughters of Penelope, Order of AHEPA, or Maids of Athena and in good standing for minimum of two years. Applicant must not be a past recipient of any undergraduate award from the Daughters of Penelope National Scholarship program.

Amount of award:	$1,000
Number of awards:	1
Application deadline:	June 1

Contact:
Daughters of Penelope
1909 Q Street, NW
Suite 500
Washington, DC 20009
Phone: 202-234-9741
Fax: 202-483-6983

Eos #1 Mother Lodge Chapter Award

Type of award: Scholarship.
Intended use: For undergraduate study at accredited vocational, 2-year or 4-year institution in United States.
Eligibility: Applicant or parent must be member/participant of Daughters of Penelope. Applicant must be female. Applicant must be Greek. Applicant must be U.S. citizen.
Basis for selection: Applicant must demonstrate high academic achievement and depth of character.
Application requirements: Recommendations, essay, transcript, proof of eligibility. Also include Parents' IRS forms, Federal Aid Forms, SAT or ACT scores.
Additional information: Applicant must be a high school senior or recent graduate and have member of immediate family or legal guardian (court appointed) in the Daughters of Penelope, Order of AHEPA, or Maids of Athena and in good

standing for at least two years. Applicant must not be a past recipient of any undergraduate award from the Daughters of Penelope National Scholarship program.

Amount of award:	$1,000
Number of awards:	1
Application deadline:	June 1
Total amount awarded:	$1,000

Contact:
Daughters of Penelope
1909 Q Street, NW
Suite 500
Washington, DC 20009
Phone: 202-234-9741
Fax: 202-483-6983

Kottis Family Award

Type of award: Scholarship.
Intended use: For freshman study at vocational, 2-year or 4-year institution.
Eligibility: Applicant or parent must be member/participant of Daughters of Penelope. Applicant must be female. Applicant must be Greek. Applicant must be U.S. citizen, permanent resident, international student or Canadian citizen.
Basis for selection: Applicant must demonstrate high academic achievement.
Application requirements: Recommendations, essay, transcript, proof of eligibility. Include SAT or ACT scores.
Additional information: Applicant must be high school senior or recent graduate and have member of immediate family or legal guardian (court appointed) in the Daughters of Penelope, Order of AHEPA or Maids of Athena in good standing for minimum of two years. Applicant must not be a past recipient of any undergraduate award from the Daughters of Penelope National Scholarship program.

Amount of award:	$1,000
Number of awards:	1
Application deadline:	June 1

Contact:
Daughters of Penelope
1909 Q Street, NW
Suite 500
Washington, DC 20009
Phone: 202-234-9741
Fax: 202-483-6983

Mary M. Verges Award

Type of award: Scholarship.
Intended use: For freshman study at vocational, 2-year or 4-year institution.
Eligibility: Applicant or parent must be member/participant of Daughters of Penelope. Applicant must be female. Applicant must be Greek. Applicant must be U.S. citizen, permanent resident, international student or Canadian citizen.
Basis for selection: Applicant must demonstrate high academic achievement.
Application requirements: Recommendations, essay, transcript, proof of eligibility. Include SAT or ACT scores.
Additional information: Applicant must be high school senior or recent graduate and have member of immediate family in the Daughters of Penelope, Order of AHEPA, or Maids of Athena in good standing for minimum of two years. Applicant must not be a past recipient of any undergraduate award from the Daughters of Penelope National Scholarship program.

Amount of award:	$1,000
Number of awards:	1
Application deadline:	June 1

Contact:
Daughters of Penelope
1909 Q Street, NW
Suite 500
Washington, DC 20009
Phone: 202-234-9741
Fax: 202-483-6983

Past Grand Presidents' Memorial Award

Type of award: Scholarship.
Intended use: For freshman study at vocational, 2-year or 4-year institution.
Eligibility: Applicant or parent must be member/participant of Daughters of Penelope. Applicant must be female. Applicant must be Greek. Applicant must be U.S. citizen, permanent resident, international student or Canadian citizen.
Basis for selection: Applicant must demonstrate high academic achievement.
Application requirements: Recommendations, essay, transcript, proof of eligibility. Include SAT or ACT scores.
Additional information: Applicant must be high school senior or recent graduate and have member of immediate family or legal guardian (court appointed) in the Daughters of Penelope, Order of AHEPA, or Maids of Athena and in good standing for minimum of two years. Applicant must not be a past recipient of any undergraduate award from the Daughters of Penelope National Scholarship program.

Amount of award:	$1,000
Number of awards:	1
Application deadline:	June 1

Contact:
Daughters of Penelope
1909 Q Street NW
Suite 500
Washington, DC 20009
Phone: 202-234-9741
Fax: 202-483-6983

Daughters of Union Veterans of the Civil War 1861-1865, Inc.

Grand Army of the Republic Living Memorial Scholarship

Type of award: Scholarship.
Intended use: For full-time junior, senior or graduate study at accredited 4-year institution in United States.
Eligibility: Applicant must be U.S. citizen. Applicant must be descendant of veteran during Civil War.
Basis for selection: Applicant must demonstrate high academic achievement, depth of character, leadership, patriotism, seriousness of purpose and service orientation.
Application requirements: Recommendations, transcript. Must be lineal descendant of a Union veteran. Ancestor's military record required. Must send stamped, self-addressed envelope when requesting information.
Additional information: Must be lineal descendant of Union Veteran of Civil War. Minimum 3.75 GPA required. Request for information, application honored only with SASE. Applications

available between October 1 and February 1 only. Number of awards granted may vary.

Amount of award:	$200
Number of awards:	3
Application deadline:	April 30
Notification begins:	September 30

Contact:
Daughters of Union Veterans of the Civil War 1861-1865, Inc.
503 South Walnut Street
Springfield, IL 62704-1932

Davis-Roberts Scholarship Fund

Davis-Roberts Scholarship

Type of award: Scholarship, renewable.
Intended use: For full-time undergraduate study at 2-year or 4-year institution.
Eligibility: Applicant or parent must be member/participant of Wyoming Job's Daughters/DeMolay. Applicant must be U.S. citizen residing in Wyoming.
Basis for selection: Applicant must demonstrate financial need.
Application requirements: Recommendations, essay, transcript. Applicant's photograph.
Additional information: Applicant must be member of Wyoming Job's Daughters/DeMolay.

Amount of award:	$350-$500
Number of awards:	10
Number of applicants:	15
Application deadline:	June 15
Notification begins:	July 1
Total amount awarded:	$3,500

Contact:
Davis-Roberts Scholarship Fund
c/o Gary D. Skillern
P.O. Box 20645
Cheyenne, WY 82003

Delaware Higher Education Commission

Delaware B. Bradford Barnes Scholarship

Type of award: Scholarship, renewable.
Intended use: For full-time freshman, sophomore, junior or senior study. Designated institutions: University of Delaware.
Eligibility: Applicant must be high school senior. Applicant must be permanent resident residing in Delaware.
Basis for selection: Applicant must demonstrate high academic achievement.
Application requirements: Essay, transcript, proof of eligibility. Must be Delaware resident.
Additional information: Must rank in top 25 percent of high school class. Minimum SAT score of 1200 (27 on ACT) required. Awards full tuition, fees, room and board at the University of Delaware.

Amount of award:	Full tuition
Number of awards:	1
Number of applicants:	100
Application deadline:	February 4
Notification begins:	March 1

Contact:
Delaware Higher Education Commission
820 North French Street
Wilmington, DE 19801
Phone: 302-577-3240
Fax: 302-577-6765

Delaware Diamond State Scholarship

Type of award: Scholarship, renewable.
Intended use: For full-time freshman, sophomore, junior or senior study at accredited vocational, 2-year or 4-year institution in United States.
Eligibility: Applicant must be high school senior. Applicant must be permanent resident residing in Delaware.
Basis for selection: Applicant must demonstrate high academic achievement.
Application requirements: Essay, transcript. Delaware Residency.
Additional information: Must rank in top 25 percent of high school class. Minimum SAT I score of 1200 (27 on ACT) required.

Amount of award:	$1,250
Number of awards:	50
Number of applicants:	250
Application deadline:	March 31
Notification begins:	May 1
Total amount awarded:	$62,500

Contact:
Delaware Higher Education Commission
820 North French Street
Wilmington, DE 19801
Phone: 302-577-3240
Fax: 302-577-6765

Delaware Education Fund for Children of Deceased Military Personnel/State Police

Type of award: Scholarship, renewable.
Intended use: For undergraduate study. Designated institutions: Public institutions in Delaware.
Eligibility: Applicant must be at least 16, no older than 24. Applicant must be permanent resident residing in Delaware. Applicant must be dependent of deceased veteran. Applicant's parent must have been killed or disabled in work-related accident as police officer.
Application requirements: Proof of eligibility. Must be Delaware resident.
Additional information: Parent must have been Delaware State Police officer killed in line of duty or veteran residing in Delaware at time of death. Awards full tuition and fees for four years at a Delaware public institution or reduced award for out-of-state school.

Amount of award:	Full tuition

Contact:
Delaware Higher Education Commission
820 North French Street
Wilmington, DE 19801
Phone: 302-577-3240
Fax: 302-577-6765

Delaware Herman M. Holloway, Sr. Memorial Scholarship

Type of award: Scholarship, renewable.
Intended use: For full-time freshman, sophomore, junior or senior study. Designated institutions: Delaware State University.
Eligibility: Applicant must be high school senior. Applicant must be U.S. citizen residing in Delaware.
Basis for selection: Applicant must demonstrate high academic achievement.
Application requirements: Proof of eligibility.
Additional information: Minimum 3.25 GPA and minimum SAT score of 850 required. Awards full tuition, fees, room and board at Delaware State University.

Amount of award:	Full tuition
Number of awards:	1
Number of applicants:	10
Application deadline:	March 10
Notification begins:	May 1
Total amount awarded:	$30,000

Contact:
Delaware Higher Education Commission
820 North French Street
Wilmington, DE 19801

Delaware Scholarship Incentive Program (SCIP)

Type of award: Scholarship.
Intended use: For full-time freshman, sophomore, junior, senior, master's, doctoral or first professional study at accredited 2-year, 4-year or graduate institution. Designated institutions: Delaware or Pennsylvania postsecondary institutions.
Eligibility: Applicant must be residing in Delaware.
Basis for selection: Applicant must demonstrate financial need.
Application requirements: Transcript. Must be Delaware resident.
Additional information: May be used outside of Delaware and Pennsylvania if program of study is not offered at tax-supported institution in Delaware.

Amount of award:	$700-$2,200
Number of awards:	1,100
Number of applicants:	11,000
Application deadline:	April 15
Notification begins:	July 1
Total amount awarded:	$1,300,000

Contact:
Delaware Higher Education Commission
820 North French Street
Wilmington, DE 19801
Phone: 302-577-3240
Fax: 302-577-3240

Delta Delta Delta Foundation

Delta Delta Delta Undergraduate Scholarship

Type of award: Scholarship.
Intended use: For sophomore, junior or senior study at 4-year institution.
Eligibility: Applicant or parent must be member/participant of Delta Delta Delta Fraternity.
Basis for selection: Applicant must demonstrate financial need, high academic achievement and service orientation.
Additional information: Campus, chapter, and community involvement important. Applicants must be initiated members of Delta Delta Delta and in good standing with chapter.

Amount of award:	$500-$1,500
Number of awards:	47
Number of applicants:	200
Application deadline:	March 1
Total amount awarded:	$50,000

Contact:
Delta Delta Delta Foundation
P.O. Box 5987
Arlington, TX 76005
Phone: 817-633-8001
Web: www.tridelta.org

Delta Gamma Foundation

Delta Gamma Scholarship

Type of award: Scholarship.
Intended use: For sophomore, junior or senior study at accredited 4-year institution in or outside United States.
Eligibility: Applicant or parent must be member/participant of Delta Gamma. Applicant must be female.
Basis for selection: Applicant must demonstrate high academic achievement.
Application requirements: Recommendations, essay, transcript.
Additional information: Student must be a member of Delta Gamma.

Amount of award:	$1,000
Number of awards:	182
Application deadline:	February 1
Notification begins:	June 1
Total amount awarded:	$182,000

Contact:
Delta Gamma Foundation
3250 Riverside Drive
P.O. Box 21397
Columbus, OH 43221-0397
Phone: 614-481-8169

Department of Rehabilitative Services

Virginia Assistance for the Visually Handicapped

Type of award: Scholarship.
Intended use: For full-time undergraduate study at postsecondary institution.
Eligibility: Applicant must be visually impaired. Applicant must be residing in Virginia.
Application requirements: FAFSA.
Additional information: Available only when need exists after federal, state and private funding have been used.
Contact:
Virginia Department for the Visually Handicapped.
Phone: 800-622-2155
Web: www.vadrs.org

Virginia Rehabilitative Services College Program

Type of award: Scholarship.
Intended use: For undergraduate study at postsecondary institution.
Eligibility: Applicant must be visually impaired, hearing impaired, physically challenged or learning disabled. Applicant must be residing in Virginia.
Basis for selection: Applicant must demonstrate financial need.
Application requirements: Proof of eligibility.
Additional information: Funding available only if need remains after federal, state and private sources are used. Award amounts and deadlines vary. Program provides vocational rehabilitation and related services to Virginians with disabilities. Goal is to provide individuals with skills necessary to achieve greater self-sufficiency, independence and employment. Contact nearest Department of Rehabilitative Services office: Central Region: 397 Azalea Ave. Richmond, VA 23227, 804-367-3786/ Fax 804-367-3783; Northern Region: 7411 Alban Station Court, B255, Springfield, VA 22150-2292, 703-313-4400/ Fax 703-569-3578; Southwest Region: 3433 Brambleton Ave., SW, Roanoke, VA 24018, 540-776-2720 / Fax 540-776-2722 Tidewater Region: Bristol Square 307 County Street, Suite 220, Portsmouth, VA 23704, 757-396-6730/Fax 757-396-6736.
Contact:
Web: www.vadrs.org

Descendents of the Signers of the Declaration of Independence, Inc.

Descendents of the Signers of the Declaration of Independence Scholarship

Type of award: Scholarship, renewable.

Intended use: For full-time freshman, sophomore, junior or senior study at accredited 4-year or graduate institution in United States.
Eligibility: Applicant or parent must be member/participant of Descendants of the Signers of the Declaration of Independence.
Basis for selection: Applicant must demonstrate high academic achievement, depth of character, leadership, patriotism, seriousness of purpose and service orientation.
Application requirements: Recommendations, transcript, proof of eligibility. Submit membership number and ancestor's name with request for application and information with SASE.
Additional information: Applicant must be a direct lineal descendant of a signer of the Declaration of Independence. Preference given to persons involved in community, school activities and volunteer work. Applicant must reapply for renewal.

Amount of award:	$1,100-$1,500
Number of awards:	10
Number of applicants:	26
Application deadline:	March 15
Notification begins:	May 1
Total amount awarded:	$12,000

Contact:
Descendents of the Signers of the Declaration of Independence, Inc.
c/o Richard H. Stromberg
Box 710
Deale, MD 20751
Phone: 301-261-5238

DeZurik

AL Kremers Scholarship Program

Type of award: Scholarship.
Intended use: For freshman study at vocational, 2-year or 4-year institution.
Eligibility: Applicant or parent must be employed by DeZurik. Applicant must be high school senior.
Additional information: For further information or an application, contact DeZurik directly.

Amount of award:	$1,000

Discover Financial Services, Inc. & the American Assoc. of School Administrators

Discover Card Tribute Award Scholarship Program

Type of award: Scholarship.
Intended use: For undergraduate study at accredited vocational, 2-year or 4-year institution.
Eligibility: Applicant must be high school junior. Applicant must be U.S. citizen or permanent resident.
Basis for selection: Applicant must demonstrate depth of character, leadership, seriousness of purpose and service orientation.
Application requirements: Statement of future goals.

Additional information: Applicant must be enrolled in public or accredited private high school in U.S. Minimum 2.75 GPA. Must demonstrate achievement in three of the four following areas: special talents, leadership, community service, obstacles overcome.

Amount of award:	$2,500-$25,000
Number of awards:	468
Number of applicants:	9,515
Application deadline:	January 1
Total amount awarded:	$1,372,500

Contact:
Discover Card Tribute Awards
AASA
P.O. Box 9338
Arlington, VA 22219
Web: www.aasa.org/discover.htm or www.discovercard.com/tribute.htm

District of Columbia Office of Postsecondary Education

District of Columbia Leveraging Educational Assistance Partnership Program

Type of award: Scholarship, renewable.
Intended use: For undergraduate study at 2-year or 4-year institution in United States.
Eligibility: Applicant must be U.S. citizen or permanent resident residing in District of Columbia.
Basis for selection: Applicant must demonstrate financial need.
Application requirements: Proof of eligibility. Must have substantial financial need and be in good academic standing. Student Aid Report generated by FAFSA.
Additional information: Must be enrolled or accepted for enrollment in an undergraduate program in a college or university certified as eligible by U.S. Department of Education. Must be resident of D.C. for 18 months prior to application. Considered on "first come, first served" basis for as long as funds are available.

Amount of award:	$1,000
Application deadline:	June 25

Contact:
District of Columbia Office of Postsecondary Ed./Rsrch/Assistance
2100 Martin Luther King, Jr. Avenue SE
Suite 401
Washington, DC 20020
Phone: 202-698-2400

Diversified Diemakers, Inc.

Diversified Diemakers Scholarship Program

Type of award: Scholarship, renewable.
Intended use: For undergraduate or graduate study at vocational, 2-year, 4-year or graduate institution.

Eligibility: Applicant or parent must be employed by Diversified Diemakers, Inc. Applicant must be high school senior.
Additional information: For further information or an application, contact Diversified Diemakers directly.

Amount of award:	$1,000

Dolphin Scholarship Foundation

Dolphin Scholarship

Type of award: Scholarship, renewable.
Intended use: For full-time undergraduate study at accredited 4-year institution.
Eligibility: Applicant must be single, no older than 24. Applicant must be U.S. citizen. Applicant must be dependent of active service person or veteran in the Navy. Must be child or stepchild of: (1) member/former member of Submarine Force who has qualified in submarines and has served at least eight years or died while on active duty; or (2) Navy member who served minimum of ten years active duty in submarine support activities.
Basis for selection: Applicant must demonstrate financial need, high academic achievement, depth of character, leadership, patriotism, seriousness of purpose and service orientation.
Application requirements: Recommendations, essay, transcript, proof of eligibility.
Additional information: The scholarship is open only to high school or undergraduate college children/stepchildren of Naval personnel under the age of 24 at time of deadline.

Amount of award:	$3,000
Number of awards:	127
Number of applicants:	215
Application deadline:	March 15
Notification begins:	April 25
Total amount awarded:	$381,000

Contact:
Dolphin Scholarship Foundation
5040 Virginia Beach Blvd., Suite 104A
Virginia Beach, VA 23462
Phone: 757-671-3200
Fax: 757-671-3330
Web: www.dolphinscholarship.org

U.S. Submarine Veterans of World War II Scholarship

Type of award: Scholarship, renewable.
Intended use: For full-time undergraduate study at accredited vocational, 2-year or 4-year institution outside United States.
Eligibility: Applicant or parent must be member/participant of U.S. Submarine Veterans of World War II. Applicant must be single, no older than 24, high school senior. Applicant must be U.S. citizen. Applicant must be dependent of veteran, disabled veteran or deceased veteran who served in the Navy during WW II. Parent must be paid-up, regular member of U.S. Submarine Veterans of World War II. Applicant must be child or stepchild of veteran, disabled veteran, or deceased veteran who served in Navy submarine service.

Basis for selection: Applicant must demonstrate financial need, high academic achievement, depth of character, leadership and seriousness of purpose.

Application requirements: Recommendations, essay, transcript, proof of eligibility.

Additional information: Address application requests to U.S. Submarine Veterans of World War II Scholarship Program. Applicant must be high school senior or have graduated from high school not more than four years prior to application, and must be under the age of 24 at application deadline. Requests for applications should include sponsor's U.S. Submarine Veterans of World War II membership number.

Amount of award:	$3,000
Number of awards:	9
Number of applicants:	11
Application deadline:	April 15
Notification begins:	May 31
Total amount awarded:	$27,000

Contact:
US Submairne Veterans of World War II
5040 Virginia Beach Blvd., Suite 104-A
Virginia Beach, VA 23462
Phone: 757-671-3200
Fax: 757-671-3330
Web: www.dolphinscholarship.org

Donaldson Foundation

Donaldson Company, Inc. Scholarship Program

Type of award: Scholarship, renewable.

Intended use: For undergraduate study at accredited vocational, 2-year or 4-year institution.

Eligibility: Applicant or parent must be employed by Donaldson Company, Inc.

Basis for selection: Applicant must demonstrate financial need.

Additional information: For further information or an application, contact Donaldson Foundation directly.

Amount of award:	$1,000-$2,000

Dunkin' Donuts Charitable Trust

Allied Domecq QSR Scholarship Program

Type of award: Scholarship.

Intended use: For undergraduate study at vocational, 2-year or 4-year institution.

Eligibility: Applicant or parent must be employed by Dunkin' Donuts Charitable Trust. Applicant must be high school senior.

Additional information: For further information or an application, contact Dunkin' Donuts Charitable Trust directly.

Amount of award:	$1,000

E. Stewart Mitchell, Inc.

E. Stewart Mitchell, Inc. Scholarship Program

Type of award: Scholarship, renewable.

Intended use: For undergraduate study at vocational, 2-year or 4-year institution.

Eligibility: Applicant or parent must be employed by E. Stewart Mitchell, Inc. Applicant must be high school senior.

Additional information: For futher information or an application, contact E.Stewart Mitchell Incorporated directly.

Amount of award:	$1,500

E.C. Styberg Engineering Company, Inc.

The E.C. Styberg Engineering Company Scholars

Type of award: Scholarship, renewable.

Intended use: For undergraduate study at accredited vocational, 2-year or 4-year institution.

Eligibility: Applicant or parent must be employed by E. C. Styberg Engineering Co. Inc.

Additional information: For further information or an application, contact E.C. Styberg Engineering Company, Inc. directly.

Amount of award:	$1,200

EAA Aviation Foundation, Inc.

EAA Aviation Achievement Scholarship

Type of award: Scholarship.

Intended use: For undergraduate, graduate or non-degree study at postsecondary institution.

Basis for selection: Major/career interest in aviation; aviation repair or engineering, mechanical. Applicant must demonstrate financial need, depth of character, leadership, patriotism, seriousness of purpose and service orientation.

Application requirements: $5 application fee. Recommendations, transcript, proof of eligibility. Must submitt completed application form, one page letter of application describing yourself and a copy of FAA Medical Certificate and Pilots license.

Additional information: Designed to encourage, recognize and support excellence in students pursuing the knowledge, technologies and skills of aviation. Applicants should be versatile, involved in school and community activities as well as aviation.

Amount of award:	$500
Number of awards:	2
Number of applicants:	300
Application deadline:	April 1
Notification begins:	September 1
Total amount awarded:	$1,000

Contact:
EAA Aviation Foundation,INC.
P.O. Box 3065
Oshkosh, WI 54903-3065
Phone: 920-426-6815
Fax: 920-426-6765
Web: www.eaa.org/education/scholarship/index.html

Payzer Scholarship

Type of award: Scholarship.
Intended use: For undergraduate study at accredited postsecondary institution.
Basis for selection: Major/career interest in engineering; mathematics; physical sciences or biology.
Application requirements: $5 application fee. Recommendations, transcript. Completed application form, one page letter of application.
Additional information: Applicant's post-secondary school choice should emphasize technical information.

Amount of award:	$5,000
Number of awards:	1
Number of applicants:	500
Application deadline:	April 1
Notification begins:	September 1
Total amount awarded:	$5,000

Contact:
EAA Aviation Foundation, Inc.
P.O. Box 3065
Oshkosh, WI 54903-3065
Phone: 920-426-6815
Web: www.eaa.org/education/scholarships/index.html

Richard Lee Vernon Aviation Scholarship

Type of award: Scholarship.
Intended use: For undergraduate or graduate study at vocational, 2-year or 4-year institution. Designated institutions: Aviation technical school. Higher Learning institution with recognized professional aviation training program.
Basis for selection: Major/career interest in aviation. Applicant must demonstrate financial need.
Application requirements: $5 application fee. Recommendations, transcript. Completed application form, one page letter of application.

Amount of award:	$500
Number of awards:	1
Number of applicants:	300
Application deadline:	April 1
Notification begins:	September 1
Total amount awarded:	$500

Contact:
EAA Aviation Foundation, Inc.
P. O. Box 3065
Oshkosh, WI 54903-3065
Phone: 920-426-6815
Web: www.eaa.org/education/scholarships/index.html

EAB

EAB/News 12 Scholar Athlete Program

Type of award: Scholarship.
Intended use: For undergraduate study at 2-year or 4-year institution.
Eligibility: Applicant must be high school senior. Applicant must be U.S. citizen or permanent resident residing in New York.
Basis for selection: Applicant must demonstrate high academic achievement, leadership and service orientation.
Application requirements: Nomination by high school guidance counselor and/or athletic director. Evidence of athletic achievements, community service record.
Additional information: Applicant must reside in Nassau or Suffolk County on Long Island. One recipient selected weekly during school year by panel of sports journalists and others. High school juniors may also be eligible.

Amount of award:	$1,000-$5,000
Number of awards:	30
Total amount awarded:	$40,000

Contact:
Phone: 516-296-5000
Web: www.eab.com www.eab.com

EAB/NY 1 Scholar Athlete Program

Type of award: Scholarship.
Intended use: For undergraduate study at 2-year or 4-year institution.
Eligibility: Applicant must be high school senior. Applicant must be U.S. citizen or permanent resident residing in New York.
Basis for selection: Applicant must demonstrate high academic achievement, leadership and service orientation.
Application requirements: Nomination by high school guidance counselor and/or athletic director. Evidence of athletic achievements, community service record.
Additional information: Applicant must reside in New York metropolitan area. One recipient selected weekly during school year by panel of sports journalists and others. High school juniors may also be eligible.

Amount of award:	$1,000-$5,000
Number of awards:	30
Total amount awarded:	$40,000

Contact:
Phone: 516-296-5000
Web: www.eab.com

Easter Seal Society of Iowa, Inc.

E.L. Peterson Scholarship

Type of award: Scholarship.
Intended use: For full-time sophomore, junior, senior or master's study at accredited 4-year or graduate institution in United States.
Eligibility: Applicant must be U.S. citizen or permanent resident residing in Iowa.

Basis for selection: Major/career interest in medical specialties/research; nursing; mental health/therapy or physical therapy. Applicant must demonstrate financial need and high academic achievement.
Application requirements: Recommendations, transcript. Completed application.
Additional information: Curriculum must be either physical or psychological rehabilitation-oriented. Student in nursing field must be accepted or participating in four-year program. Minimum GPA 2.8. Award letters and recommendation forms due no later than March 15th. Strictly limited to Iowa residents.

    Amount of award: $1,000
    Application deadline: March 15
Contact:
The Easter Seal Society of Iowa, Inc.
P.O. Box 4002
Des Moines, IA 50333
Phone: 515-289-1933
Fax: 515-289-1281

Easter Seal Society of Iowa Disability Scholarship

Type of award: Scholarship.
Intended use: For full-time freshman study at accredited 4-year institution in United States.
Eligibility: Applicant must be physically challenged or learning disabled. Applicant must be high school senior. Applicant must be U.S. citizen or permanent resident residing in Iowa.
Basis for selection: Applicant must demonstrate financial need and high academic achievement.
Application requirements: Recommendations, transcript by Completed application.
Additional information: Applicants must have a permanent disability. Minimum GPA 2.8. Award letters and recommendation forms due no later than March 15. Strictly limited to Iowa residents.

    Amount of award: $750
    Number of awards: 1
    Application deadline: March 15
Contact:
The Easter Seal Society of Iowa, Inc.
P.O. Box 4002
Des Moines, IA 50333
Phone: 515-289-1933
Fax: 515-289-4069

James L. & Lavon Maddon Mallory Disability Scholarship

Type of award: Scholarship.
Intended use: For full-time freshman study at accredited 4-year institution in United States.
Eligibility: Applicant must be physically challenged or learning disabled. Applicant must be U.S. citizen or permanent resident residing in Iowa.
Basis for selection: Applicant must demonstrate financial need and high academic achievement.
Application requirements: Recommendations, transcript, proof of eligibility, research proposal. Completed application.
Additional information: Applicant must have permanent disability. Minimum GPA 2.8. Award letters and recommendation forms due no later than March 15. Strictly limited to Iowa residents.

    Amount of award: $1,000
    Number of awards: 1
    Application deadline: March 15
Contact:
The Easter Seal Society of Iowa, Inc.
P.O. Box 4002
Des Moines, IA 50333
Phone: 515-289-1933
Fax: 515-289-1281

Lynn Marie Vogel Scholarship

Type of award: Scholarship.
Intended use: For full-time sophomore, junior, senior or master's study at accredited 4-year or graduate institution in United States.
Eligibility: Applicant must be U.S. citizen or permanent resident residing in Iowa.
Basis for selection: Major/career interest in nursing; medical specialties/research; mental health/therapy or physical therapy. Applicant must demonstrate financial need and high academic achievement.
Application requirements: Recommendations, transcript. Completed application.
Additional information: Curriculum must be either physical or psychological rehabilitation-oriented. Student in nursing field must be accepted or participating in four year program. Minimum GPA 2.8. Award letters, and recommendation forms due no later than March 15. Strictly limited to Iowa residents.

    Amount of award: $1,000
    Application deadline: March 15
Contact:
The Easter Seal Society of Iowa, Inc.
P.O. Box 4002
Des Moines, IA 50333
Phone: 515-289-1933
Fax: 515-289-1281

Rolfe B. Karlsson Scholarship

Type of award: Scholarship.
Intended use: For full-time sophomore, junior, senior or master's study at accredited 4-year or graduate institution in United States.
Eligibility: Applicant must be U.S. citizen or permanent resident residing in Iowa.
Basis for selection: Major/career interest in physical therapy; nursing; medical specialties/research or mental health/therapy. Applicant must demonstrate financial need and high academic achievement.
Application requirements: Recommendations, transcript by Completed application.
Additional information: Curriculum must be either physical or psychological rehabilitation-oriented. Student in nursing field must be accepted or participating in four year program. Minimum GPA 2.8. Award letters and recommendation forms due no later than March 15. Strictly limited to Iowa residents.

    Amount of award: $1,000
    Application deadline: March 14
Contact:
The Easter Seal Society of Iowa, Inc.
P.O. Box 4002
Des Moines, IA 50333
Phone: 515-289-1933
Fax: 515-289-1281

Scholarships

213

Eaton Corporation

Eaton Minority Engineering Scholars Program

Type of award: Scholarship, renewable.
Intended use: For full-time sophomore, junior or senior study at accredited 4-year institution in United States. Designated institutions: Targeted institutions across the United States.
Eligibility: Applicant must be Alaskan native, Asian American, African American, Mexican American, Hispanic American, Puerto Rican or American Indian. Applicant must be U.S. citizen or permanent resident.
Basis for selection: Major/career interest in engineering; engineering, computer; engineering, mechanical; engineering, electrical/electronic; computer/information sciences; manufacturing; electronics or engineering, materials. Applicant must demonstrate high academic achievement.
Application requirements: Recommendations, essay, transcript. Also send application, ACT or SAT scores, SAR and school's financial aid letter.
Additional information: Provides $3,000 annual scholarship in addition to paid summer internships, mentoring and other benefits. Visit Website for application and list of target schools. Must be engineering major. Must have completed one year in an accredited engineering program, maintain 2.8 GPA, and have three remaining years of course work to complete before earning a B.A. All applications are reviewed by Inroads.

Amount of award:	$3,000
Application deadline:	February 1
Notification begins:	April 1

Contact:
EMESP c/o Inroads
The Lorenzo Carter Building
1360 West. Ninth St., Suite 330
Cleveland, OH 44113
Phone: 800-386-1911
Web: www.eaton.com/careers

ECM Publishers, Inc.

ECM Publishers, Inc. Scholarship Program

Type of award: Scholarship.
Intended use: For undergraduate study at accredited postsecondary institution.
Eligibility: Applicant or parent must be employed by ECM Publishers, Inc. Applicant must be high school senior.
Additional information: For further information or an application, contact ECM Publishers, Inc. directly.

Amount of award:	$1,000

Contact:
ECM Publisher's Inc.

Edison International

Edison International Employees' Children College Scholarship Program

Type of award: Scholarship, renewable.
Intended use: For freshman study at accredited vocational, 2-year or 4-year institution.
Eligibility: Applicant or parent must be employed by Southern California Edison. Applicant must be high school senior.
Additional information: For further information or an application, contact Edison International directly.

Amount of award:	$2,000-$5,000

Edmund F. Maxwell Foundation

Edmund F. Maxwell Foundation Scholarship

Type of award: Scholarship, renewable.
Intended use: For full-time freshman study.
Eligibility: Applicant must be U.S. citizen or permanent resident residing in Washington.
Basis for selection: Applicant must demonstrate financial need, high academic achievement, depth of character, leadership, seriousness of purpose and service orientation.
Application requirements: Essay, transcript.
Additional information: Combined SAT I must be greater than 1200. College or university must be independent. Must submit financial need assessment with application. Only residents of Western Washington are eligible.

Amount of award:	$3,500
Number of awards:	102
Number of applicants:	250
Application deadline:	April 30
Notification begins:	June 1
Total amount awarded:	$388,700

Contact:
Edmund F. Maxwell Foundation
P.O. Box 22537
Seattle, WA 98122-0537
Web: www.maxwell.org

Education and Research Foundation, Society of Nuclear Medicine

Nuclear Medicine Student Fellowship Award

Type of award: Research grant.
Intended use: For undergraduate, master's, doctoral or first professional study at postsecondary institution.
Basis for selection: Major/career interest in nuclear medicine.

Application requirements: Recommendations, research proposal. Curriculum vitae. Preceptor for project: either nuclear medicine physician or nuclear medicine scientist.

Additional information: For summer research internship. Competence in physical and/or biological aspects of radioactivity essential. Will assist in clinical and basic research activities in nuclear medicine. Total amount awarded varies.

Amount of award:	$2,000-$3,000
Number of awards:	8
Number of applicants:	25
Application deadline:	November 15
Notification begins:	February 30

Contact:
Susan C. Weiss,
CNMT: Children's Memorial Hospital
1060 Arbor Lane
Northfield, IL 60614
Phone: 847-446-4176
Web: www.snmerf.org

Paul Cole Scholarship

Type of award: Scholarship.
Intended use: For full-time undergraduate study at accredited 2-year or 4-year institution.
Eligibility: Applicant must be international student or international student.
Basis for selection: Major/career interest in nuclear medicine. Applicant must demonstrate financial need and high academic achievement.
Application requirements: Recommendations, essay, transcript. Proof of acceptance or enrollment in nuclear medicine technology program.
Additional information: Major/career interest in nuclear medicine technology. Application must be submitted by director of nuclear medicine technology program on behalf of student. Though financial need is not a prerequisite, special consideration is given to students who demonstrate such need. Applicant must be international student.

Amount of award:	$1,000
Number of awards:	12
Number of applicants:	125
Application deadline:	October 15
Notification begins:	October 15
Total amount awarded:	$12,000

Contact:
Susan C. Weiss, Executive
1060 Arbor Lane
Northfield, IL 60093
Phone: 847-446-4176
Web: www.snmerf.org

Educational Communications Scholarship Foundation

Educational Communications Scholarship

Type of award: Scholarship.
Intended use: For undergraduate study at accredited postsecondary institution.

Eligibility: Applicant must be enrolled in high school. Applicant must be U.S. citizen or permanent resident.
Basis for selection: Based on grade point average, achievement test scores, leadership qualifications, work experience, evaluation of an essay and with some consideration for financial need. Awards are to be applied toward educational costs at an accredited college or university. Payments will be issued directly to the institution's financial aid office and applied to the student's account. Applicant must demonstrate high academic achievement and leadership.
Application requirements: Must have taken the ACT or SAT.
Additional information: Recipients selected by independent committee of professional educators on basis of GPA, achievement test scores, work experience, financial need. Request application by March 15. Requests must include student's name, permanent home address, city, state, zip code, name of school, approximate GPA and year in school.

Amount of award:	$1,000
Number of awards:	200
Application deadline:	May 15
Notification begins:	June 15, August 5
Total amount awarded:	$200,000

Contact:
Educational Communications Scholarship Foundation
P.O. Box 5012
Lake Forest, IL 60045
Phone: 847-295-6650
Fax: 847-295-3972

Electrical Equipment Representatives Association

EERA Scholarship

Type of award: Scholarship.
Intended use: For undergraduate study at accredited 4-year institution.
Eligibility: Applicant or parent must be member/participant of Electrical Equipment Representatives Association.
Additional information: Must be child of member of Electrical Equipment Representatives Association or of members' employees of Electrical Equipment Representatives Association. For further information or an application, contact Electrical Equipment Representatives Association directly.

Amount of award:	$1,500

Elie Wiesel Foundation for Humanity

Elie Wiesel Prize in Ethics

Type of award: Scholarship.
Intended use: For full-time junior or senior study at 4 year institution in United States.
Basis for selection: Competition/talent/interest in writing/journalism, based on essay on ethical dilemma, issue or question related to the contest's annual topic.
Application requirements: Essay. Letter of support verifying full-time junior or senior status from college or university

registrar. Sponsorship by faculty member. Students must request updated guidelines and application form.
Additional information: Application deadline early January. Send SASE after August 1 for application materials. Application and all information available on Website.

Amount of award:	$500-$5,000
Number of awards:	5
Notification begins:	May 31
Total amount awarded:	$10,000

Contact:
Elie Wiesel Prize In Ethics
The Elie Wiesel Foundation for Humanity
529 Firth Avenue, Suite 1802
New York, NY 10017
Phone: 212-490-7777
Web: www.eliewieselfoundation.org

Elizabeth Glaser Pediatric AIDS Foundation

Elizabeth Glaser Pediatric AIDS Foundation Short-Term Scientific Awards

Type of award: Research grant.
Intended use: For non-degree study in United States.
Basis for selection: Major/career interest in medical specialties/research or medicine. Applicant must demonstrate seriousness of purpose.
Application requirements: Research proposal.
Additional information: Major/career interest in pediatric research. Program provides funding for travel and short-term study to initiate critical research project, obtain preliminary data, learn new techniques or sponsor workshop.

Amount of award:	$5,000

Contact:
Program Manager Short-term Scientific Awards
2950 31st Street
Suite 125
Santa Monica, CA 90405
Phone: 310-314-1459
Fax: 310-314-1469
Web: www.pedaids.org

Elizabeth Greenshields Foundation

Elizabeth Greenshields Grant

Type of award: Scholarship, renewable.
Intended use: For undergraduate, graduate or non-degree study.
Basis for selection: Major/career interest in arts, general.
Application requirements: Slides.
Additional information: For artists (fine arts) in the early stages of careers creating representational or figurative works through painting, drawing, printmaking or sculpture. Must make a commitment to making art a lifetime career. Applications are

welcome throughout the year. All amounts are in Canadian dollars. Funds may be used for any art-related purpose.

Amount of award:	$10,000
Number of awards:	49
Number of applicants:	1,500
Total amount awarded:	$490,000

Contact:
Elizabeth Greenshields Foundation
1814 Sherbrooke Street West, Suite 1
Montreal
Quebec, Canada, H3H 1E4
Phone: 514-937-9225
Fax: 514-937-0141

Elks National Foundation

Elks Most Valuable Student Scholarship

Type of award: Scholarship, renewable.
Intended use: For full-time freshman, sophomore, junior or senior study at accredited 4-year institution in United States.
Eligibility: Applicant must be high school senior. Applicant must be U.S. citizen.
Basis for selection: Applicant must demonstrate financial need, high academic achievement and leadership.
Application requirements: Recommendations, essay, transcript. SAT I, ACT.
Additional information: Applications are not available until after Nov. 1, from local Benevolent and Protective Order of Elks Lodge or Website, or send SASE to the Foundation. Application deadline is technically mid-January. Membership in Elks not required. Applications submitted to local Elks Lodge for entry into competition. Judging occurs at Lodge, district, and state level before reaching national competion.

Amount of award:	$1,000-$14,000
Number of awards:	500
Application deadline:	January 15
Notification begins:	May 15
Total amount awarded:	$2,216,000

Contact:
Elks National Foundation
2750 North Lakeview Avenue
Chicago, IL 60614-1889
Web: www.elks.org; Keyword: mvs

Elks National Foundation Legacy Awards

Type of award: Scholarship.
Intended use: For freshman study at accredited postsecondary institution in or outside United States. Designated institutions: Institutions in Guam, Panama, Puerto Rico and the Phillipines for eligible applicants who are residents of those countries.
Eligibility: Applicant or parent must be member/participant of Elks. Applicant must be high school senior.
Basis for selection: Based on leadership and scholarship.
Application requirements: Recommendations, transcript. SAT or ACT scores, biographical questionnaire, Legacy Award application.
Additional information: Applicant must be child or step-child of Elk who is paid-up member in good standing for two years. Application available after August 1 from local Lodge's

Scholarship Chairman, on web site or by sending a SASE to the Foundation.

Amount of award:	$1,000
Number of awards:	500
Application deadline:	November 1
Total amount awarded:	$500,000

Contact:
Elks National Foundation
2750 North Lakeview Ave
Chicago, IL 60614
Web: www.elks.org

EMI Music Foundation, Inc.

EMI Scholars Program

Type of award: Scholarship.
Intended use: For undergraduate study at 2-year or 4-year institution.
Eligibility: Applicant or parent must be employed by EMI Music Foundation, Inc. Applicant must be high school senior.
Additional information: For further information or an application, contact EMI Music Foundation, Inc. directly.

Amount of award:	$2,500

Empire HealthChoice

Edwin R. Werner Scholarship

Type of award: Scholarship, renewable.
Intended use: For freshman study at accredited 4-year institution.
Eligibility: Applicant or parent must be employed by Empire HealthChoice.
Basis for selection: Applicant must demonstrate financial need.
Additional information: For further information or an application, contact Empire HealthChoice directly.

Enesco Corporation

Enesco Scholarship

Type of award: Scholarship.
Intended use: For full-time undergraduate or graduate study at accredited 2-year, 4-year or graduate institution.
Eligibility: Applicant or parent must be employed by Enesco Corporation.
Basis for selection: Applicant must demonstrate high academic achievement, leadership, seriousness of purpose and service orientation.
Application requirements: Recommendations, essay, transcript. SAT, PSAT or ACT scores.
Additional information: For children of full-time or regular part-time associates of Enesco Corporation only. Pre-application must be submitted in early September. The Entry Form must then be submitted to high school counselor by November 1. Number and amount of awards vary.

Contact:
Scholarship Coordinator
Enesco Corporation
225 Windsor Drive
Itasca, IL 60143
Phone: 800-4-ENESCO
Web: www.enesco.com

Engineers' Society of Western Pennsylvania

Joseph Levendusky Memorial Scholarship

Type of award: Scholarship.
Intended use: For undergraduate study at accredited 4-year institution.
Basis for selection: Major/career interest in engineering, chemical.
Application requirements: Essay, transcript.
Additional information: Must have been employed in the field of water technology for at least one year prior to selection (environmental wastewater, water pollution control and water resource management not included).

Amount of award:	$7,000
Number of awards:	1
Number of applicants:	4
Application deadline:	May 1
Notification begins:	August 15

Contact:
Engineers' Society of Western Pennsylvania
Pittsburgh Engineers' Building
337 Fourth Avenue
Pittsburgh, PA 15222
Phone: 412-261-0710 x12
Fax: 412-261-1606
Web: www.eswp.com

Student Paper Competition

Type of award: Scholarship.
Intended use: For undergraduate or graduate study at 4-year or graduate institution in United States.
Basis for selection: Competition/talent/interest in engineering/architecture, based on paper on bridge-related topic. Major/career interest in engineering. Applicant must demonstrate seriousness of purpose.
Additional information: Winning graduate paper receives $1,000. Winning undergraduate paper receives $250. One graduate and undergraduate paper per institution. Papers limited to ten pages, single spaced. Papers prepared for other purposes (e.g., thesis, project) are acceptable.

Amount of award:	$250-$1,000
Number of applicants:	2
Application deadline:	April 30
Notification begins:	May 14

Contact:
Engineers' Society of Western Pennsylvania
Pittsburgh Engineers' Building
Pittsburgh, PA 15222
Phone: 412-261-0710 x12
Fax: 412-261-1606
Web: www.eswp.com

Scholarships

217

Engineers Foundation of Ohio

Engineers Foundation of Ohio Scholarship

Type of award: Scholarship.
Intended use: For freshman study at accredited 4-year institution in United States. Designated institutions: Must be used at ABET-accredited school in Ohio or at Notre Dame University.
Eligibility: Applicant must be high school senior. Applicant must be U.S. citizen residing in Ohio.
Basis for selection: Major/career interest in engineering or engineering, civil. Applicant must demonstrate high academic achievement, leadership, seriousness of purpose and service orientation.
Application requirements: Transcript. SAT/ACT scores. Minimum 3.0 GPA.
Additional information: Award may be renewable in some circumstances.

Amount of award:	$500-$2,500
Number of awards:	27
Number of applicants:	375
Application deadline:	December 15

Contact:
Engineers Foundation of Ohio
236 E. Town Street
Suite 210
Columbus, OH 43215
Phone: 614-228-8606
Fax: 614-228-8611

Entomological Society of America

Entomological Society Undergraduate Scholarship

Type of award: Scholarship.
Intended use: For full-time sophomore, junior or senior study at 4-year institution in United States in Mexico and Canada.
Basis for selection: Competition/talent/interest in study abroad. Major/career interest in entomology; zoology; biology or science, general.
Application requirements: Recommendations, essay, transcript. Application packet: biographical information; student's statement of interest, financial need, and qualifications; recommendations; application form. Submit as e-mail to undergrad.scholarship@entsoc.org. All files must be in Adobe pdf format or MS Word-compatible.
Additional information: Applicants must have completed at least one course or project in entomology. Must have accumulated 30 semester hours by time award is given. Preference given to students demonstrating financial need. Transcript may be sent separately. Applicants without capacity to construct electronic packet may obtain support at local business provider. One $2,000 award sponsored by BioQuip Products. Visit Website for further details. Paper applications not accepted.

Amount of award:	$1,500-$2,000
Number of awards:	4
Number of applicants:	72
Application deadline:	May 31
Notification begins:	September 30
Total amount awarded:	$6,500

Contact:
Entomological Society of America
Undergraduate Scholarship Application Request
9301 Annapolis Road, Suite 300
Lanham, MD 20706-3115
Phone: 301-731-4535 ext. 3029
Fax: 301-731-4538
Web: www.entsoc.org/foundation/award_undergrad.html

Epilepsy Foundation of America

Behavioral Sciences Student Fellowship

Type of award: Research grant.
Intended use: For undergraduate or graduate study in United States.
Basis for selection: Major/career interest in social/behavioral sciences; sociology; social work; psychology; anthropology; nursing or economics.
Application requirements: Research proposal.
Additional information: Three-month fellowship for work on an epilepsy study project. The fellowship is awarded to a student of vocational rehabilitation counseling. A professor or advisor must accept responsibility for supervision of student and project. Women and minorities are especially encouraged to apply. Other appropriate fields include vocational rehabilitation, counseling, political science, and others relevant to epilepsy research or practice.

Amount of award:	$3,000
Application deadline:	March 1

Contact:
Epilepsy Foundation of America - Programs and Research
Cathy Morris, Administrative Coordinator
4351 Garden City Drive
Landover, MD 20785-2267
Phone: 301-459-3700
Fax: 301-577-2684
Web: www.efa.org

Executive Women International

Executive Women International Scholarship

Type of award: Scholarship, renewable.
Intended use: For full-time freshman study at accredited 4-year institution in United States.
Eligibility: Applicant must be female, high school junior.

Basis for selection: Applicant must demonstrate high academic achievement, depth of character, leadership, seriousness of purpose and service orientation.
Application requirements: Interview, recommendations, essay. Applicants must have sponsoring teacher at their school. Must have a major/career interest in a professional field.
Additional information: Applicant must reside within boundaries of participating EWI chapter. Scholarship awarded each academic year, for up to five consecutive years, until student completes degree.

Amount of award:	$250-$2,500
Number of awards:	50
Application deadline:	January 31
Notification begins:	April 15
Total amount awarded:	$140,000

Contact:
Executive Women International
515 South 700 East
Suite 2A
Salt Lake City, UT 84102

Explorers Club

Explorers Club Youth Activity Fund

Type of award: Research grant.
Intended use: For undergraduate or graduate study.
Eligibility: Applicant must be U.S. citizen.
Basis for selection: Based on scientific and practical merit of proposal, competence of the investigator, and appropriateness of budget. Major/career interest in natural sciences. Applicant must demonstrate financial need and seriousness of purpose.
Application requirements: Recommendations, essay, research proposal. Request application form from club. Two letters of recommendation must be submitted with application. Physical Release must accompany completed application.
Additional information: Applications will not be considered if they do not include two letters of recommendation. Recipients of grants must provide a one to two-page report on their exploration or research within the year of receiving the grant. Photographs are encouraged. Grants are made primarily to graduate students, but undergraduates are eligible. Send SASE when requesting application.

Amount of award:	$300-$1,200
Number of awards:	20
Number of applicants:	200
Application deadline:	January 15, April 1

Contact:
Explorers Club
The Exploration Fund Committee
46 East 70 Street
New York, NY 10021
Phone: 212-628-8383
Fax: 212-288-4449

Fannie Mae Foundation

David O. Maxwell Scholarship

Type of award: Scholarship, renewable.
Intended use: For undergraduate study at accredited 2-year or 4-year institution.

Eligibility: Applicant or parent must be employed by Archibald Candy Corporation.
Basis for selection: Applicant must demonstrate financial need.
Additional information: For further information or an application, contact Fannie Mae directly.

Amount of award:	$500-$2,000

Federal Employee Education and Assistance Fund

Federal Employee Education and Assistance Fund Scholarship

Type of award: Scholarship, renewable.
Intended use: For undergraduate, master's or doctoral study at accredited 2-year, 4-year or graduate institution.
Eligibility: Applicant or parent must be employed by Federal/U.S. Government.
Basis for selection: Applicant must demonstrate high academic achievement.
Application requirements: Recommendations, essay, transcript.
Additional information: Current civilian federal and postal employees with minimum three years service and their dependents are eligible. Must have 3.0 GPA. Employee applicants eligible for part-time study; dependents must enroll full-time. Send SASE for application materials.

Amount of award:	$300-$1,500
Number of awards:	401
Number of applicants:	4,788
Application deadline:	March 30
Notification begins:	August 31

Contact:
Federal Employee Education and Assistance Fund
8441 West Bowles Avenue
Suite 200
Littleton, CO 80123-9501
Phone: 800-323-4140
Web: www.feea.org

Federal Signal Corporation

Karl F. Hoenecke Memorial Scholarship

Type of award: Scholarship, renewable.
Intended use: For freshman study at accredited 4-year institution.
Eligibility: Applicant or parent must be employed by Federal Signal.
Additional information: For further information or an application, contact Federal Signal Corporation directly.

Amount of award:	$1,500

Fight-For-Sight

Fight-For-Sight Student Research Fellowship

Type of award: Research grant.
Intended use: For undergraduate, master's, doctoral or first professional study. Designated institutions: In United States or Canada.
Eligibility: Applicant must be U.S. citizen, international student or Canadian resident.
Basis for selection: Major/career interest in medicine or optometry/ophthalmology.
Application requirements: Research proposal.
Additional information: For students interested in eye-related clinical or basic research. Fellowships last 60 to 90 days, usually during the summer months.

Amount of award:	$700-$2,100
Number of awards:	20
Application deadline:	March 1
Notification begins:	May 15

Contact:
Program Coordinator Fight-For-Sight The Research Division of
500 East Remington Road
Prevent Blindness America, Program Coord
Schaumburg, IL 60173
Phone: 847-843-2020
Fax: 847-843-8458
Web: www.preventblindness.org

Finance Authority of Maine

Maine Robert C. Byrd Honors Scholarship

Type of award: Scholarship, renewable.
Intended use: For full-time undergraduate study at 2-year or 4-year institution.
Eligibility: Applicant must be high school senior. Applicant must be U.S. citizen or permanent resident residing in Maine.
Basis for selection: Applicant must demonstrate high academic achievement.
Application requirements: Essay, transcript. High school profile from guidance office; SAT scores, class rank, list of scholastic achievements, awards and honors.
Additional information: Information available through Maine high school guidance offices and Finance Authority of Maine. Applicants do not need to complete FAFSA. See Website for further details.

Amount of award:	$1,500
Application deadline:	April 15

Contact:
Finance Authority of Maine
Maine Education Assistance Division
P.O. Box 949
Augusta, ME 04332-0949
Phone: 207-623-3263 or 800-228-3734
Fax: 207-623-0095
Web: www.famemaine.com

Financial Management Division of SIA

Financial Management Division of SIA Scholarship

Type of award: Scholarship.
Intended use: For undergraduate study at accredited 2-year or 4-year institution.
Eligibility: Applicant or parent must be member/participant of Financial Management Division of SIA.
Additional information: For further information or an application, contact Financial Management Division of SIA directly.

Amount of award:	$1,000

First Data Corporation

First Data Corporation Scholarship

Type of award: Scholarship, renewable.
Intended use: For undergraduate study at accredited 2-year or 4-year institution.
Eligibility: Applicant or parent must be employed by First Data Corporation. Applicant must be high school senior.
Basis for selection: Applicant must demonstrate financial need.
Additional information: For further information or an application, contact First Data Corporation directly.

Amount of award:	$500-$3,000

Contact:
First Data Corporation

First Marine Division Association, Inc.

First Marine Division Association Scholarship

Type of award: Scholarship, renewable.
Intended use: For full-time undergraduate study at accredited vocational, 2-year or 4-year institution in United States.
Eligibility: Applicant must be high school senior. Applicant must be U.S. citizen. Applicant must be dependent of disabled veteran or deceased veteran who served in the Marines. Applicant must be dependent of disabled veteran or deceased veteran who served with 1st Marine Division, or was in a unit assigned to, attached to, or in support of the 1st Marine Division.
Basis for selection: Applicant must demonstrate depth of character and seriousness of purpose.
Application requirements: Essay, proof of eligibility.
Additional information: This program is to assist dependents of deceased or 100 percent permanently disabled veterans of service with the First Marine Division in furthering education towards a bachelor's degree. Contact office by phone, fax or mail for additional information and application deadlines.

Amount of award:	$1,500
Number of awards:	58
Number of applicants:	250
Total amount awarded:	$74,750

Contact:
First Marine Division Association, Inc.
14325 Willard Road
Suite 107
Chantilly, VA 20151-2110
Phone: 703-803-3195
Fax: 703-803-7114
Web: www.erols.com/oldbreed

Fisher Broadcasting Inc.

Fisher Broadcasting Scholarship for Minorities

Type of award: Scholarship.
Intended use: For full-time sophomore, junior or senior study at accredited vocational, 2-year or 4-year institution in United States.
Eligibility: Applicant must be Alaskan native, Asian American, African American, Mexican American, Hispanic American, Puerto Rican or American Indian. Applicant must be U.S. citizen.
Basis for selection: Major/career interest in radio/television/film; journalism; communications or marketing. Applicant must demonstrate financial need, depth of character, seriousness of purpose and service orientation.
Application requirements: Interview, recommendations, essay, transcript, proof of eligibility.
Additional information: Award totals vary each year. Minimum 2.5 GPA. Must have career interest in broadcast communications, broadcast journalism. Washington, Oregon, Idaho, Montana, and Georgia state residents may attend school in any state. Also open to applicants from other states attending school in Washington, Oregon, Idaho, Montana, and Georgia. Successful applicants may also be offered summer employment with Fisher Broadcasting at appropriate pay for position being filled. Only finalists will be interviewed.

Application deadline:	April 30
Notification begins:	July 1

Contact:
Sherry Johnston, Senior Vice President
Fisher Broadcasting Inc.
2001 6th Avenue, Suite 3425
Seattle, WA 98121
Phone: 206-404-6048

Fiskars, Inc.

Ed Nielson Scholarship

Type of award: Scholarship.
Intended use: For freshman study at accredited 4-year institution.
Eligibility: Applicant or parent must be employed by Fiskars, Inc.
Additional information: For further information or an application, contact Fiskars, Inc. directly.

Amount of award:	$500-$2,000

Florida Department of Education

Children of Deceased or Disabled Veterans or Children of Servicemen Classified as Prisoners of War or Missing in Action Scholarship Program

Type of award: Scholarship, renewable.
Intended use: For full-time undergraduate study at postsecondary institution. Designated institutions: Eligible Florida postsecondary institutions.
Eligibility: Applicant must be at least 16, no older than 22. Applicant must be U.S. citizen or permanent resident residing in Florida. Applicant must be dependent of disabled veteran, deceased veteran or POW/MIA during Grenada conflict, Korean War, Middle East War, Lebanon conflict, Panama conflict, Persian Gulf War, WW I, WW II or Vietnam.
Basis for selection: Applicant must demonstrate financial need.
Application requirements: Proof of eligibility. Military and residency status of parent must be verified by Florida Department of Veterans' Affairs. Must meet eligibility requirements for receipt of state aid.Consult Bureau of Student Financial Assistance for additional details regarding specific conflicts and additional residency requirements.
Additional information: Award amount cover tuition/fees for one academic year at eligible Florida public postsecondary institution; renewable up to four years (eight semesters). Award for eligible private schools based on Florida public tuition/fees costs. Initial applicant must be at least 16, no older than 22 years old. Renewal applicant must maintain minimum 2.0 GPA.

Amount of award:	Full tuition
Application deadline:	April 1

Contact:
Florida Department of Veterans Affairs
Executive Director
P.O. Box 31003
St. Petersburg, FL 33731-8903
Phone: 727-319-7400
Web: www.firn.edu/doe

Critical Occupational Therapist or Physical Therapist Shortage Tuition Reimbursement Program

Type of award: Scholarship, renewable.
Intended use: For non-degree study.
Eligibility: Applicant must be U.S. citizen or permanent resident residing in Florida.
Basis for selection: Major/career interest in occupational therapy or physical therapy.
Application requirements: Minimum of 3.0 GPA on all approved courses. Must be licensed or have valid temporary permit as therapist from Florida Department of Business and Professional Regulation and provide proof of same. Must be currently employed as full-time therapist in Florida public school or developmental research minimum of three years.

Additional information: Provides assistance to licensed therapists who take courses to improve their skills and knowledge and who have been employed as full-time therapists in Florida public schools for at least three years. Recipients receive up to $78 per credit hour for maximum of nine semester hours per academic year (or equivalent).

   Amount of award: $702
   Application deadline: September 15
Contact:
Florida Department of Education
Bureau of Student Financial Assistance
1940 North Monroe Street, Suite 70
Tallahassee, FL 32303-4759
Phone: 888-827-2004
Web: www.firn.edu/doe

Ethics in Business Scholarship

Type of award: Scholarship.
Intended use: For undergraduate study at 2-year or 4-year institution. Designated institutions: Florida community colleges and eligible private colleges and universities.
Basis for selection: Major/career interest in business.
Additional information: Scholarships funded by private and state contributions. Awards dependent on private matching funds. Contact financial aid office at participating institutions for more information.
Contact:
Phone: 888-827-2004
Web: www.firn.edu/doe

Florida Academic Scholars Award

Type of award: Scholarship, renewable.
Intended use: For undergraduate study at postsecondary institution. Designated institutions: Eligible Florida postsecondary institutions.
Eligibility: Applicant must be high school senior. Applicant must be U.S. citizen or permanent resident residing in Florida.
Basis for selection: Applicant must demonstrate high academic achievement and service orientation.
Application requirements: Send ACT or SAT scores. Applicant should have 75 hours of community service experience. Must 1) be National Merit Scholarship finalist/Achievement Scholar/Finalist or National Hispanic Scholar; 2) be International Baccalaureate (IB) Diploma recipient or have completed IB curriculum with at least 1270/SAT or 28/ACT; or 3) have earned 3.5 GPA. Two years of foreign language study necessary. Application must be completed before high school graduation.
Additional information: Part of Bright Futures Scholarship Program. Public institution: scholarship covers full tuition and fees with up to $600 stipend; private institution: covers equivalent amount. In addition, high school senior with highest academic ranking in each county, based on GPA and SAT/ACT score, will receive annual Top Scholars Award of $1,500. Applications available from high school guidance office, Office of Financial Assistance or online. Check Website for additional information and requirements.

   Amount of award: Full tuition
Contact:
Florida Department of Education
Bright Futures Scholarship Program
124 Collins, 325 West Gaines Street
Tallahassee, FL 32399-0400
Phone: 888-827-2004
Web: www.firn.edu/doe

Florida Gold Seal Vocational Scholars Award

Type of award: Scholarship, renewable.
Intended use: For undergraduate study at vocational, 2-year or 4-year institution. Designated institutions: Eligible Florida postsecondary institutions.
Eligibility: Applicant must be high school senior. Applicant must be U.S. citizen or permanent resident residing in Florida.
Basis for selection: Applicant must demonstrate high academic achievement.
Application requirements: CPT, SAT or ACT. Application must be completed before high school graduation.
Additional information: Part of Bright Futures Program. Public institution: scholarship covers 75 per cent of tuition and fees; private institution: covers equivalent amount. Applications available from high school guidance office, Office of Financial Assistance or online. Check Website for additional information and requirements.
Contact:
Florida Department of Education
Bright Futures Scholarship Program
124 Collins, 325 West Gaines Street
Tallahassee, FL 32303-4759
Phone: 888-827-2004
Web: www.firn.edu/doe

Florida Merit Scholars Award

Type of award: Scholarship.
Intended use: For undergraduate study at 2-year or 4-year institution. Designated institutions: Eligible Florida postsecondary institutions.
Eligibility: Applicant must be high school senior. Applicant must be U.S. citizen or permanent resident residing in Florida.
Basis for selection: Applicant must demonstrate high academic achievement.
Application requirements: Send ACT/SAT scores. Applicant must 1) be National Merit Scholarship finalist, Achievement Scholar/Finalist or National Hispanic Scholar; 2) have completed International Baccalaureate IB curriculum/home education program/GED/Early Admissions with at least 970/SAT or 20/ACT; or 3)have earned 3.0 GPA with SAT/ACT scores as stated. Two years of foreign language study necessary. Application must be completed before high school graduation.
Additional information: Part of Bright Futures Program. Public institution: scholarship covers 75 percent of tuition and fees; private institution: covers equivalent amount. Applications available from high school guidance office, Office of Financial Assistance or online. Check Website for additional information and requirements.
Contact:
Florida Department of Education
Bright Futures Scholarship Program
124 Collins, 325 West Gaines Street
Tallahassee, FL 32399-0400
Phone: 888-827-2004
Web: www.firn.edu/doe

Florida Robert C. Byrd Honors Scholarship

Type of award: Scholarship, renewable.
Intended use: For full-time undergraduate study at 2-year, 4-year or graduate institution in United States. Designated

institutions: Eligible Florida or non-Florida public or private non-profit postsecondary institution.
Eligibility: Applicant must be high school senior. Applicant must be U.S. citizen or permanent resident residing in Florida.
Basis for selection: Applicant must demonstrate high academic achievement.
Application requirements: Nomination by high school principal or Adult Education Director. Send ACT or SAT scores. Applicant must meet registration requirements of Selective Service System.
Additional information: Application requires unweighted cumulative GPA and SAT or ACT scores. Applicants are ranked with members of designated geographical region. Total amounts awarded determined annually.
   Number of awards: 1,400
   Application deadline: April 15
Contact:
Florida Department of Education
Bureau of Student Financial Assistance
1940 North Monroe Street, Suite 70
Tallahassee, FL 32303-4759
Phone: 888-827-2004
Web: www.firn.edu/doe

Florida Seminole and Miccosukee Indian Scholarship

Type of award: Scholarship, renewable.
Intended use: For undergraduate or graduate study at vocational, 2-year, 4-year or graduate institution in United States. Designated institutions: Eligible Florida postsecondary institutions.
Eligibility: Applicant must be American Indian. Must be member of or eligible for membership in Seminole or Miccosukee Tribes in Florida. Applicant must be U.S. citizen or permanent resident residing in Florida.
Basis for selection: Applicant must demonstrate financial need.
Application requirements: Proof of eligibility.
Additional information: Must be member or eligible for membership in either Seminole Indian Tribe of Florida or Miccosukee Indian Tribe of Florida. Award amount and deadline is determined by tribe. Must be enrolled at eligible institution. Applications can be obtained from either of the following addresses: Miccosukee Tribe of Florida, c/o Higher Education Committee, P.O. Box 440021 Tamiami Station, Miami, FL 33144, ph: 305-223-8380; or Seminole Tribe of Florida, c/o Higher Education Committee, 6300 Stirling Road, Hollywood, FL 33024, ph: 954-966-6300. For further information, contact address below.
   Number of awards: 23
Contact:
Florida Department of Education
Bureau of Student Financial Assistance
1940 North Monroe Street, Suite 70
Tallahassee, FL 32303-4759
Phone: 888-827-2004
Web: www.firn.edu/doe

Florida Student Assistance Grant Program

Type of award: Scholarship, renewable.
Intended use: For full-time undergraduate study at 2-year or 4-year institution. Designated institutions: Eligible Florida postsecondary institutions.

Eligibility: Applicant must be U.S. citizen or permanent resident residing in Florida.
Basis for selection: Applicant must demonstrate financial need.
Application requirements: Proof of eligibility. FAFSA. Minimum 2.0 cumulative GPA for renewal applicants.
Additional information: Full award covers tuition and fees at public institutions (based on previous year's costs), or dollar equivalent plus $1,000 at eligible private schools. Applicant must not have previously received a bachelor's degree. Applications available from high school guidance offices and at participating university's financial aid offices. FAFSA deadline established by each participating institution.
   Amount of award: $200-$1,000
   Number of awards: 94,452
Contact:
Florida Department of Education
Bureau of Student Financial Assistance
1940 North Monroe Street, Suite 70
Tallahassee, FL 32303-4759
Phone: 888-827-2004
Web: www.firn.edu/doe

Florida Teacher Scholarship and Forgivable Loan Program (Freshmen/Sophomores)

Type of award: Scholarship, renewable.
Intended use: For full-time freshman or sophomore study at accredited 4-year institution. Designated institutions: Eligible Florida postsecondary institutions.
Eligibility: Applicant must be high school senior. Applicant must be U.S. citizen or permanent resident residing in Florida.
Basis for selection: Major/career interest in education, teacher; education or education, special. Applicant must demonstrate high academic achievement and seriousness of purpose.
Application requirements: Proof of eligibility, nomination by high school. Submit SAT or ACT scores. Principal or Dean must review application before submitting to Office of Student Financial Assistance by April 1.
Additional information: Applicant must be member of future teaching organization (if high school has one), be in top 25 percent of class during seventh semester of the senior class, have 3.0 unweighted cumulative GPA, intend to teach in Florida. Renewal applicant must have minimum cumulative GPA of 2.5. Fifteen percent of scholarships reserved for minorities. Awards: one recipient from each public high school and proportionate number from all private high schools.
   Amount of award: $1,500-$3,000
   Application deadline: March 1
Contact:
Florida Department of Education
Bureau of Student Financial Assistance
1940 North Monroe Street, Suite 70
Tallahassee, FL 32303-4759
Phone: 888-827-2004
Web: www.firn.edu/doe

Jose Marti Scholarship Challenge Grant

Type of award: Scholarship, renewable.
Intended use: For full-time undergraduate or graduate study at 2-year, 4-year or graduate institution. Designated institutions: Eligible Florida postsecondary institutions.

Eligibility: Applicant must be Mexican American, Hispanic American or Puerto Rican. Applicant must be high school senior. Applicant must be U.S. citizen or permanent resident residing in Florida.
Basis for selection: Applicant must demonstrate financial need and high academic achievement.
Application requirements: Submit FAFSA by may 15.
Additional information: Seniors in high school or undergraduates applying to graduate school must have 3.0 cumulative, unweighted GPA and file Free Application for Federal Student Aid (FAFSA). Must be of Spanish culture and born in Mexico or Spain or a Hispanic country of the Caribbean, Central America or South America, or child of same. Must meet Florida eligibility criteria for state student aid. Award number is limited to the amount of available funds and renewals take priority over new awards. Applications available from high school guidance office or college office of financial aid.

Amount of award:	$2,000
Number of awards:	107
Number of applicants:	1,385
Application deadline:	April 1

Contact:
Florida Department of Education
Bureau of Student Financial Assistance
1940 North Monroe Street, Suite 70
Tallahassee, FL 32303-4759
Phone: 888-827-2004
Web: www.firn.edu/doe

Limited Access Competitive Grant

Type of award: Scholarship.
Intended use: For full-time junior or senior study at 4-year institution in United States. Designated institutions: Eligible Florida private college or university.
Eligibility: Applicant must be U.S. citizen or permanent resident residing in Florida.
Application requirements: Applicant must be graduate of Florida community college or transfer student from Florida state university. Applicant must not have previous B.A. Minimum cumulative GPA of 2.0 for renewal applicants.
Additional information: Provides enrollment opportunities for community college graduates or transfer students from state universities. Must plan to enroll in limited access programs available at private institutions in Florida. Limited access programs are defined as high priority employment fields requiring baccalaureate for which state universities have insufficient capacity to serve all qualified applicants. Award is 50 percent of tuition/fees. Applications and deadline dates are available from financial aid offices of designated institutions.

Number of awards:	362

Contact:
Florida Department of Education
Bureau of Student Financial Assistance
1940 North Monroe Street, Suite 70
Tallahassee, FL 32303-4759
Phone: 888-827-2004
Web: www.firn.edu/doe

Mary McLeod Bethune Scholarship

Type of award: Scholarship, renewable.
Intended use: For full-time undergraduate study at 4-year institution. Designated institutions: Bethune-Cookman College, Edward Waters College, Florida A&M University or Florida Memorial College.

Eligibility: Applicant must be high school senior. Applicant must be residing in Florida.
Basis for selection: Applicant must demonstrate financial need and high academic achievement.
Application requirements: Minimum 3.0 cumulative GPA for renewal applicants.
Additional information: Minimum 3.0 high school GPA required. Deadlines are established by participating institutions. Award is $3,000 per academic year, renewable for up to eight semesters or 12 quarters. General award availability contingent on matching funds raised by the eligible institutions. Must be enrolled full-time in eligible institution. Applications can be obtained from any of four designated institution's financial aid offices.

Amount of award:	$3,000
Number of awards:	148

Contact:
Florida Department of Education
Bureau of Student Financial Assistance
1940 North Monroe Street, Suite 70
Tallahassee, FL 32303-4759
Phone: 888-827-2004
Web: www.firn.edu/doe

Nicaraguan and Haitian Scholarship Program

Type of award: Scholarship.
Intended use: For full-time undergraduate or graduate study at 4-year institution. Designated institutions: Florida State University System affiliates.
Eligibility: Applicant must be permanent resident, international student or Nicaraguan or Haitian citizen or have been born in Haiti or Nicaragua. Applicant must be residing in Florida.
Basis for selection: Applicant must demonstrate financial need, high academic achievement and service orientation.
Application requirements: Proof of eligibility. Submit written documentation of service to community.
Additional information: Award given to one Nicaraguan and one Haitian student per year. Applicant must meet State of Florida's requirements for receipt of state aid. Minimum 3.0 GPA. Awardee may reapply in succeeding years.

Amount of award:	$5,000
Number of awards:	2
Application deadline:	July 1

Contact:
Florida Department of Education
Bureau of Student Financial Assistance
1940 North Monroe Street, Suite 70
Tallahassee, FL 32303-4759
Phone: 888-827-2004
Web: www.firn.edu/doe

Rosewood Family Scholarship Program

Type of award: Scholarship, renewable.
Intended use: For full-time undergraduate study at vocational, 2-year or 4-year institution in United States. Designated institutions: State university, public community college or public postsecondary vocational-technical school in Florida. Certificate programs must be minimum 900 clock hours.
Eligibility: Applicant must be Alaskan native, Asian American, African American, Mexican American, Hispanic American, Puerto Rican or American Indian. Applicant must be U.S. citizen or permanent resident residing in Florida.

Basis for selection: Applicant must demonstrate financial need.
Application requirements: FAFSA. If not Florida resident, copy of Student Aid Report (SAR) must be postmarked to Florida Bureau of Student Financial Assistance by May 15th (along with FAFSA).
Additional information: Descendants of African-American Rosewood families affected by the incidents of January 1923 given priority over other applicants. Award covers annual cost of tuition and fees up to $4,000 per semester for up to eight semesters. FAFSA applications available via internet at http:\\www.fafsa.ed.gov.

Amount of award:	$4,000
Number of awards:	25
Application deadline:	April 1
Total amount awarded:	$100,000

Contact:
Florida Department of Education
Bureau of Student Financial Assistance
1940 North Monroe Street, 70
Tallahassee, FL 32303-4759
Phone: 888-827-2004
Web: www.firn.edu/doe

William L. Boyd, IV, Florida Resident Access Grant

Type of award: Scholarship, renewable.
Intended use: For full-time undergraduate study at accredited 4-year institution. Designated institutions: Eligible private, non-profit Florida colleges and universities.
Eligibility: Applicant must be U.S. citizen or permanent resident residing in Florida.
Application requirements: Proof of eligibility. Applicant must not have prior B.A. Renewal applicant must have minimum 2.0 cumulative GPA.
Additional information: Applicant must not have previously received a bachelor's degree and may not use award for study of divinity or theology. Applications available from eligible institutions financial aid offices. Award amount determined by Florida Legislature on yearly basis.

Amount of award:	Full tuition

Contact:
Florida Department of Education
Bureau of Student Financial Assistance
1940 North Monroe Street, Suite 70
Tallahassee, FL 32303-4759
Phone: 888-827-2004
Web: www.firn.edu/doe

Florida Division of Blind Services

Florida Educational Assistance for the Blind

Type of award: Scholarship, renewable.
Intended use: For full-time undergraduate, graduate or non-degree study at vocational, 2-year, 4-year or graduate institution in United States.
Eligibility: Applicant must be visually impaired. Applicant must be U.S. citizen or permanent resident residing in Florida.

Basis for selection: Applicant must demonstrate financial need and seriousness of purpose.
Application requirements: Transcript, proof of eligibility. Must be a client of State of Florida Division of Blind Services and eligible for vocational rehabilitation. Applicant must first secure federal or state scholarships/grants/loans.
Additional information: In Florida, phone: 800-342-1828; out of state: 850-488-1330. Tuition, books, reader's service fees, and maintenance awarded for out-of-state institutions. Only tuition paid for in-state institutions. Deadline dates vary.

Amount of award:	Full tuition

Contact:
Florida State Division of Blind Services
2551 Executive Center Circle
Room 200
Tallahassee, FL 32399
Phone: 800-342-1828

Florida Education Fund

Florida Education Fund Minority Pre-law Scholarships

Type of award: Scholarship, renewable.
Intended use: For full-time undergraduate study at accredited 4-year institution in United States. Designated institutions: Florida postsecondary institutions.
Eligibility: Applicant must be Alaskan native, African American, Mexican American, Hispanic American, Puerto Rican or American Indian. Applicant must be U.S. citizen residing in Florida.
Basis for selection: Major/career interest in law. Applicant must demonstrate financial need and high academic achievement.
Application requirements: Recommendations, essay, transcript, proof of eligibility. Must submit application by deadline set by the MPLE office.
Additional information: Deadline varies; contact sponsor for information. Must submit official report of GPA. Must reside in Florida. Recipients required to enroll in a Florida law school after graduation.

Amount of award:	$7,750
Number of awards:	136

Contact:
The Florida Education Fund
15485 Eagle Nest Lane
Suite 200
Miami Lakes, FL 33014
Web: www.fl-educ-fd.org

Florida Rock Industries, Inc.

Florida Rock Industries Scholarship

Type of award: Scholarship, renewable.
Intended use: For undergraduate study at accredited vocational, 2-year or 4-year institution.
Eligibility: Applicant or parent must be employed by Florida Rock Industries, Inc.
Basis for selection: Applicant must demonstrate financial need.

Additional information: For further information or an application, contact Florida Rock Industries, Inc. directly.

Amount of award:	$500-$1,500

Florida Space Grant Consortium

NASA Space Grant Florida Summer Undergraduate Scholarships

Type of award: Scholarship, renewable.
Intended use: For undergraduate study at accredited 2-year or 4-year institution in United States. Designated institutions: Florida Institute of Technology, University of Central Florida, and University of Florida.
Eligibility: Applicant must be U.S. citizen residing in Florida.
Basis for selection: Major/career interest in aerospace; astronomy; atmospheric sciences/meteorology; biology; computer/information sciences; education; engineering; geology/earth sciences; medical specialties/research or physics.
Application requirements: Recommendations, essay, transcript, research proposal, nomination by mentor at consortium member institution.
Additional information: Scholarship recipients will receive up to $3,000 for ten week full-time research project alongside faculty researcher. Applicants must submit proposal for review. The Consortium actively encourages women, minority, and physically challenged students to apply. Four stipends for internships at Kennedy Space Center ($5,000) may be available, as well as one stipend for study at a designated NASA Academy. Contact sponsor or visit Website for full details.

Amount of award:	$3,000
Number of awards:	14
Application deadline:	February 15, March 2
Notification begins:	March 31

Contact:
Florida Space Grant Consortium
Mail Stop: FSGC
Kennedy Space Center, FL 32899
Phone: 321-452-4301
Fax: 321-449-0739
Web: fsgc.engr.ucf.edu

Foremost Farms USA Charitable Foundation, Inc.

Cow-lege Cash Scholarship Fund

Type of award: Scholarship.
Intended use: For undergraduate study at vocational, 2-year or 4-year institution.
Eligibility: Applicant or parent must be employed by Foremost Farms USA Employees. Applicant must be high school senior.
Additional information: For further information or an application, contact Foremost Farms USA Charitable Foundation, Inc. directly.

Amount of award:	$500

Foss Maritime Co.

Foss Maritime Scholarship

Type of award: Scholarship, renewable.
Intended use: For undergraduate study at accredited vocational, 2-year or 4-year institution.
Eligibility: Applicant or parent must be employed by Foss Maritime Co.
Basis for selection: Applicant must demonstrate financial need.
Additional information: For further information or an application, contact Foss Maritime Company directly.

Amount of award:	$500-$2,000

Foundation for Exceptional Children

Stanley Edward Jackson Award for Gifted/ Talented Students with Disabilities

Type of award: Scholarship.
Intended use: For full-time freshman study at postsecondary institution in United States.
Eligibility: Applicant must be physically challenged or learning disabled. Applicant must be high school senior. Applicant must be U.S. citizen.
Application requirements: Recommendations, essay, transcript, proof of eligibility.
Additional information: Statement verifying disability from physician or school counselor, three letters of recommendation and completed application required. Applicant must have demonstrated talented abilities in any one of the following categories: general intellect, high academic aptitude, creativity, leadership or visual/performing arts.

Amount of award:	$500
Number of awards:	8
Number of applicants:	500
Application deadline:	February 1
Total amount awarded:	$4,000

Contact:
Stanley E. Jackson Award for Gifted/Talented Students w/ Disabilities
Foundation for Exceptional Children
1110 North Glebe Rd. Suite 300
Arlington, VA 22201
Phone: 703-245-0607

Stanley Edward Jackson Scholarship Award for Ethnic Minority Students

Type of award: Scholarship.
Intended use: For full-time undergraduate study at vocational or 2-year institution in United States.
Eligibility: Applicant must be physically challenged or learning disabled. Applicant must be Alaskan native, Asian American, African American, Mexican American, Hispanic American, Puerto Rican or American Indian. Applicant must be high school senior.

Basis for selection: Applicant must demonstrate financial need, depth of character and leadership.
Application requirements: Recommendations, essay, transcript, proof of eligibility.
Additional information: Statement verifying disability from physician or school counselor.

Amount of award:	$500
Number of awards:	8
Number of applicants:	200
Application deadline:	February 1
Total amount awarded:	$4,000

Contact:
Stanley Edward Jackson Scholarship Award for Ethnic Minority Students
Foundation for Exceptional Children
1110 North Glebe Rd. Suite 300
Arlington, VA 22201
Phone: 703-245-0607

Stanley Edward Jackson Scholarship Award for Gifted/Talented Minorities with Disabilities

Type of award: Scholarship.
Intended use: For full-time freshman study at postsecondary institution in United States.
Eligibility: Applicant must be physically challenged or learning disabled. Applicant must be Alaskan native, Asian American, African American, Mexican American, Hispanic American, Puerto Rican or American Indian. Applicant must be high school senior. Applicant must be U.S. citizen or permanent resident.
Basis for selection: Applicant must demonstrate financial need and high academic achievement.
Application requirements: Recommendations, essay, transcript, proof of eligibility. Application.
Additional information: Statement verifying disability from physician or school counselor, three letters of recommendation and completed application required. Applicant must have demonstrated talented abilities in any one of the following categories: general intellect, high academic aptitude, creativity, leadership or visual/performing arts.

Amount of award:	$500
Number of awards:	8
Number of applicants:	200
Application deadline:	February 1
Total amount awarded:	$4,000

Contact:
Stanley E. Jackson Award for Gifted/Talented Minorities w/ Disabilites
Foundation for Exceptional Children
1110 North Glebe Rd. Suite 300
Arlington, VA 22201
Phone: 703-245-0607

Foundation for Seacoast Health

Foundation for Seacoast Health Scholarship Program

Type of award: Scholarship.

Intended use: For full-time undergraduate, graduate or non-degree study at accredited vocational, 2-year, 4-year or graduate institution.
Eligibility: Applicant must be residing in Maine or New Hampshire.
Basis for selection: Major/career interest in epidemiology; health sciences; health-related professions; medicine; nursing; physical therapy; public health; respiratory therapy or mental health/therapy. Applicant must demonstrate seriousness of purpose and service orientation.
Application requirements: Recommendations, essay, transcript, proof of eligibility. Application, FAFSA, community service record, affidavit of residency, class rank, SAT or ACT.
Additional information: Award for pursing degree program in health-related field, based on academics, educational goals, written communication skills and "unusual family or personal circumstances." Number of awards varies. Must be two-year or longer resident of designated New Hampshire/Maine coastal towns; visit Website for list. Applicants returning to school after absence of five years or more contact sponsor for additional information.

Amount of award:	$1,000-$10,000
Application deadline:	February 1

Contact:
Foundation for Seacoast Health
100 Campus Drive Suite One
Portsmouth, NH 03802-4606
Phone: 603-422-8200
Fax: 603-422-8207
Web: www.ffsh.org

Foundation for Surgical Technology

Foundation for Surgical Technology Scholarship Fund

Type of award: Scholarship.
Intended use: For undergraduate, post-bachelor's certificate or non-degree study at accredited vocational or 2-year institution in United States.
Basis for selection: Major/career interest in surgical technology. Applicant must demonstrate financial need or high academic achievement. Major/career interest in surgical technology. Applicant must demonstrate financial need and high academic achievement.
Application requirements: Recommendations, transcript, proof of eligibility. Must be recommended by CAAHEP instructor.
Additional information: Four scholarships totaling $5,000 will be awarded each year. Applicant must be currently enrolled in surgical technology program approved by CAAHEP.

Amount of award:	$500-$2,000
Number of applicants:	50
Application deadline:	March 1
Notification begins:	July 1
Total amount awarded:	$5,000

Contact:
Foundation for Surgical Technology
Scholarship Administrator
7108-C South Alton Way, Suite 200
Englewood, CO 80112-2106
Web: www.ffst.org

Foundation of the National Student Nurses Association, Inc.

National Student Nurses Association Scholarship

Type of award: Scholarship.
Intended use: For full-time undergraduate study at accredited 2-year or 4-year institution. Designated institutions: Stse-approved schools of nursing or pre-nursing.
Eligibility: Applicant must be U.S. citizen or permanent resident.
Basis for selection: Major/career interest in nursing or nurse practitioner. Applicant must demonstrate financial need, high academic achievement and service orientation.
Application requirements: $10 application fee. Recommendations, essay, transcript, proof of eligibility. Must be currently enrolled in nursing or pre-nursing program. National Student Nurses Association members must submit proof of membership.
Additional information: All applicants considered for the following scholarships: General Scholarships, Career Mobility Scholarships, Breakthrough to Nursing Scholarships for Ethnic People of Color, and Specialty Scholarships. Awards granted in spring for use in summer and following academic year. Include business-sized SASE with $.55 postage when requesting application. Applications available from August through January 15. Visit Website to download application.

Amount of award:	$1,000-$2,000
Application deadline:	February 1
Notification begins:	March 31
Total amount awarded:	$55,000

Contact:
Foundation of the National Student Nurses Association, Inc.
Suite 1327
555 West 57 Street
New York, NY 10019
Phone: 212-581-2215
Web: www.nsna.org

Francis Ouimet Scholarship Fund

Francis Ouimet Scholarship

Type of award: Scholarship, renewable.
Intended use: For full-time undergraduate study.
Basis for selection: Competition/talent/interest in athletics/sports. Applicant must demonstrate financial need, high academic achievement and service orientation.
Application requirements: Interview, recommendations, essay, transcript, proof of eligibility. Student must work for three years at a Massachusetts golf course.
Additional information: High school seniors may apply if they meet golf course criterion.

Amount of award:	$500-$4,000
Number of awards:	285
Application deadline:	December 1
Notification begins:	August 15

Contact:
Francis Ouimet Scholarship Fund
190 Park Road
Weston, MA 02493
Phone: 781-891-6400
Web: www.ouimet.org

Fred G. Zahn Foundation

Fred G. Zahn Foundation Scholarship

Type of award: Scholarship, renewable.
Intended use: For undergraduate study at accredited 2-year, 4-year or graduate institution in United States. Designated institutions: Washington state colleges and universities.
Eligibility: Applicant must be residing in Washington.
Basis for selection: Applicant must demonstrate financial need and high academic achievement.
Application requirements: Transcript. Letter detailing the cost of student's course of study and extracurricular activities, other financial resources available including part-time employment, career plans and work experience. Student Aid Report. Transcripts from all schools student has attended including high school.
Additional information: Must have graduated from Washington state high school. Minimum 3.75 GPA. May obtain additional information and/or application at eligible Washington state institution. Do not contact foundation.

Amount of award:	$1,500
Number of awards:	8
Number of applicants:	400
Application deadline:	April 15
Notification begins:	June 1

Contact:
Financial aid department of eligible Washington college or university

Freedom from Religion Foundation

Blanche Fearn Memorial Award

Type of award: Scholarship.
Intended use: For undergraduate study.
Eligibility: Applicant must be high school senior. Applicant must be U.S. citizen.
Basis for selection: Competition/talent/interest in writing/journalism, based on essay on why student is freethinker; essay most suitable for atheistic and agnostic student.
Application requirements: Essay, proof of eligibility. Submit 3-4 typed, double-spaced pages with standard margins, Include autobiographical paragraph giving permanent address, phone numbers and email. Identify high school and college/university to be attended. Include intended major and other interests.
Additional information: Applicant must be college-bound high school senior. Essay topics change annually and are announced in February. Students are requested not to inquire before then. Awards are $1,000 first place, $500 second place, $250 third place. Send SASE or visit Website for additional

information and current list in spring of contest year. Special award Web page: www.ffrf.org/essay.html.

Amount of award:	$250-$1,000
Number of applicants:	121
Application deadline:	July 1
Notification begins:	September 1
Total amount awarded:	$1,750

Contact:
Freedom from Religion Foundation
High School Essay Competition
P.O. Box 750
Madison, WI 53701
Phone: 608-250-8900
Web: www.ffrf.org

Phyllis Stevenson Grams Memorial Award

Type of award: Scholarship.
Intended use: For full-time undergraduate or graduate study at postsecondary institution.
Eligibility: Applicant must be U.S. citizen.
Basis for selection: Competition/talent/interest in writing/journalism, based on essay on free thought concerning religion; essay most suitable for atheistic and agnostic student.
Application requirements: Essay. Submit 5-6 typed, double-spaced pages with standard margins, Include autobiographical paragraph giving both campus and permanent addresses, phone numbers and email. Identify college/university, major and interests.
Additional information: Applicant must be currently enrolled college student. Essay topics change annually and are announced in February. Students are requested not to inquire before then. Awards are $1,000 first place, $500 second place, $250 third place. Send SASE or visit Website for additional information and current list in spring of contest year. Special award Web page: www.ffrf.org/essay.html.

Amount of award:	$250-$1,000
Number of applicants:	116
Application deadline:	July 1
Notification begins:	September 1
Total amount awarded:	$1,750

Contact:
Freedom from Religion Foundation
College Essay Competition
P.O. Box 750
Madison, WI 53701
Phone: 608-256-8900
Web: www.ffrf.org

Freightliner LLC

The Freightliner Fund Scholarship Program

Type of award: Scholarship, renewable.
Intended use: For undergraduate study at accredited vocational, 2-year or 4-year institution.
Eligibility: Applicant or parent must be employed by Freightliner LLC. Applicant must be high school senior.
Additional information: For further information or an application, contact Freightliner LLC directly.

Amount of award:	$1,000-$5,000

Contact:
Freightliner LLC

Frontier Insurance Group, Inc.

Frontier Scholarship Program for Children of Employees

Type of award: Scholarship, renewable.
Intended use: For undergraduate study at vocational, 2-year or 4-year institution.
Eligibility: Applicant or parent must be employed by Frontier Insurance Group, Inc. Applicant must be high school senior.
Additional information: For further information or an application, contact Frontier Insurance Group Incorporated directly.

Amount of award:	$2,000

Frost National Bank

Tom Frost Scholarship Program for Dependents of Frost National Bank

Type of award: Scholarship, renewable.
Intended use: For undergraduate study at 2-year or 4-year institution.
Eligibility: Applicant or parent must be employed by Frost National Bank. Applicant must be high school senior.
Additional information: For further information or an application, contact Frost National Bank directly.

Amount of award:	$5,000

Futures Services Division of the Futures Industry Association

Futures Services Division Scholarship

Type of award: Scholarship.
Intended use: For freshman, sophomore, junior or senior study at accredited 2-year or 4-year institution.
Eligibility: Applicant or parent must be member/participant of Futures Services Division of the Futures Industry Association.
Application requirements: Proof of eligibility.
Additional information: For further information and an application, contact Futures Services Division of the Futures Industry Association directly, or visit Website.

Amount of award:	$1,000

Contact:
Web: www.afcea.org

Scholarships

Garden Club of America

F.M. Peacock Native Bird Habitat Scholarship

Type of award: Scholarship.
Intended use: For senior or graduate study at graduate institution.
Basis for selection: Major/career interest in ornithology.
Additional information: Grant for advanced study of U.S. winter/summer habitat of threatened or endangered native birds. Awarded in cooperation with the Cornell Lab of ornithology. No phone calls. For further information, send SASE.

Amount of award:	$4,000
Number of awards:	1
Application deadline:	January 15
Total amount awarded:	$4,000

Contact:
Garden Club of America, Peacock Fellowship
Scholarship Committee
14 East 60th. Street
New York, NY 10022
Phone: 212-753-8287
Fax: 212-753-0134
Web: www.gcamerica.org

Garden Club of America Summer Environmental Awards

Type of award: Scholarship.
Intended use: For freshman, sophomore or junior study at 4-year institution.
Basis for selection: Major/career interest in environmental science or ecology.
Application requirements: Must send business-size SASE.
Additional information: Two or more awards for summer study in field of ecology and environmental studies.

Amount of award:	$1,500
Number of awards:	2
Application deadline:	February 10

Contact:
Garden Club of America
Attn: Scholarship Committee Summer Studies
14 East 60th Street
New York, NY 10022
Phone: 212-753-8287
Fax: 212-753-0134
Web: www.gcamerica.org

Katharine M. Grosscup Scholarship

Type of award: Scholarship.
Intended use: For junior, senior or graduate study at accredited 4-year or graduate institution in United States.
Eligibility: Applicant must be residing in Ohio, Indiana, Kentucky, West Virginia, Michigan or Pennsylvania.
Basis for selection: Major/career interest in horticulture. Applicant must demonstrate financial need and high academic achievement.
Application requirements: Interview, recommendations, transcript.
Additional information: Several scholarships available. Preference given to residents of Pennsylvania, Ohio, West Virginia, Michigan, Indiana and Kentucky. Please do not contact by phone. Application on GCA Website.

Amount of award:	$3,000
Application deadline:	February 1

Contact:
Grosscup Scholarship Committee/Cleveland Botanical Garden
11030 East Blvd, Attn: Mrs. Nancy Stevenson
Cleveland, OH 44106
Web: www.gcamerica.org

The Loy McCandless Marks Scholarship

Type of award: Scholarship.
Intended use: For junior, senior or graduate study in or outside United States.
Eligibility: Applicant must be U.S. citizen.
Basis for selection: Major/career interest in horticulture or botany.
Additional information: Complementary funding for science student to assist with tropical ornamental horticulture project that has been accepted by accredited American university. For graduate or advanced undergraduate students to study and do research at appropriate foreign institution specializing in study of tropical plants.

Amount of award:	$2,000
Number of awards:	1
Application deadline:	January 15

Contact:
Garden Club of america
Attn: Scholarship Committee Summer Studies
14 East 60th Street
New York, NY 10022
Phone: 212-753-8287
Fax: 212-753-0134
Web: www.gcamerica.org

GEICO Corporation

GEICO Family Scholars

Type of award: Scholarship, renewable.
Intended use: For undergraduate or graduate study at vocational, 2-year, 4-year or graduate institution.
Eligibility: Applicant or parent must be employed by GEICO Corporation. Applicant must be high school senior.
Additional information: For further information or an application, contact Geico Corporation directly.

Amount of award:	$500-$1,000

General Mills

General Mills Foundation Post-High School Scholarship

Type of award: Scholarship, renewable.
Intended use: For undergraduate study at accredited vocational, 2-year or 4-year institution.
Eligibility: Applicant or parent must be employed by General Mills, Inc.
Basis for selection: Applicant must demonstrate financial need.

Additional information: For further information or an application, contact General Mills directly.

Amount of award:	$500-$2,500

Georgia Space Grant Consortium

NASA Space Grant Georgia Fellowship Program

Type of award: Scholarship, renewable.
Intended use: For full-time junior, senior, master's or doctoral study at accredited postsecondary institution in United States. Designated institutions: Clark Atlanta University, Columbus State University, Georgia Institute of Technology, Kennesaw State University, Mercer University, Morehouse College, Spelman College, State University of West Georgia, University of Georgia.
Eligibility: Applicant must be U.S. citizen.
Basis for selection: Major/career interest in engineering; science, general; aerospace; physics; atmospheric sciences/meteorology; computer/information sciences; education or chemistry. Applicant must demonstrate seriousness of purpose and service orientation.
Application requirements: Interview, portfolio, recommendations, essay, transcript.
Additional information: Funding available for students in all areas of engineering and science, and many areas of social science.

Amount of award:	$550-$1,100

Contact:
Georgia Space Grant Consortium
Georgia Tech-Aerospace and Engineering
Space Science and Technology Bldg., Room 210
Atlanta, GA 30332-0150
Phone: 404-894-0521
Fax: 404-894-9313
Web: www.ae.gatech.edu/research/gsgc/

Georgia Student Finance Commission

Georgia Governor's Scholarship

Type of award: Scholarship, renewable.
Intended use: For full-time undergraduate study at accredited 2-year or 4-year institution. Designated institutions: Public or private colleges and universities in Georgia.
Eligibility: Applicant must be high school senior. Applicant must be U.S. citizen or permanent resident residing in Georgia.
Basis for selection: Applicant must demonstrate high academic achievement, depth of character, leadership, patriotism, seriousness of purpose and service orientation.
Application requirements: Completed Governor's Scholarship application.
Additional information: Must be valedictorian, salutatorian, STAR Student, or designated Georgia Scholar. Must enroll at eligible Georgia postsecondary school within seven months of high school graduation. Must maintain 3.0 GPA with 30 semester hours earned each year to renew.

Amount of award:	$1,575
Number of awards:	3,063
Number of applicants:	3,500
Total amount awarded:	$4,580,369

Contact:
Scholarship Committee
2082 East Exchange Place
Suite 100
Tucker, GA 30084
Phone: 800-776-6878
Fax: 770-724-9031

Georgia Hope Scholarship - GED Recipient

Type of award: Scholarship.
Intended use: For undergraduate study at accredited vocational, 2-year or 4-year institution. Designated institutions: Any branch of University System of Georgia, Georgia Department of Technical and Adult Education, or a HOPE-eligible private college or university in Georgia.
Eligibility: Applicant must be U.S. citizen or permanent resident residing in Georgia.
Application requirements: Proof of eligibility.
Additional information: Must have received GED from Georgia Department of Technical and Adult Education (DTAE) after June 30, 1993. Submit HOPE voucher upon enrollment. Students receiving GED from DTAE receive voucher automatically.

Amount of award:	$500
Number of awards:	3,771
Total amount awarded:	$1,881,237

Contact:
Hope Scholarship Program
Georgia Student Finance Commission
2082 East Exchange Place, Suite 100
Tucker, GA 30084
Phone: 800-546-HOPE
Fax: 770-724-9031

Georgia Hope Scholarship - Private Institution

Type of award: Scholarship, renewable.
Intended use: For full-time undergraduate study at accredited 2-year or 4-year institution. Designated institutions: Georgia private colleges or universities.
Eligibility: Applicant must be U.S. citizen or permanent resident residing in Georgia.
Basis for selection: Applicant must demonstrate high academic achievement.
Application requirements: Must complete Georgia Tuition Equalization Grant (TEG) Application.
Additional information: Award designed to help academically outstanding pupils. Must be attending eligible college or university in Georgia. To qualify, minimum 3.0 GPA required.

Amount of award:	$1,500-$3,000
Number of awards:	13,527
Total amount awarded:	$35,369,524

Scholarships

231

Contact:
Hope Scholarship Program
Georgia Student Finance Commission
2082 East Exchange Place, Suite 100
Tucker, GA 30084
Phone: 800-546-HOPE
Fax: 770-724-9031

Georgia Hope Scholarship - Public College or University

Type of award: Scholarship, renewable.
Intended use: For undergraduate study at accredited 2-year or 4-year institution. Designated institutions: Any eligible Georgia public college or university.
Eligibility: Applicant must be U.S. citizen or permanent resident residing in Georgia.
Basis for selection: Applicant must demonstrate high academic achievement.
Application requirements: Proof of eligibility. Submit FAFSA or HOPE application.
Additional information: Minimum GPA of 3.0. First-year HOPE assistance includes any tuition, mandatory fees. Also includes book allowance for up to $150 per semester. Applicant must have graduated high school after 1993. Must be designated HOPE scholar.

Amount of award:	Full tuition
Number of awards:	70,648
Total amount awarded:	$133,301,759

Contact:
Scholarship Committee
2082 East Exchange Place
Suite 100
Tucker, GA 30084
Phone: 800-546-HOPE
Fax: 770-724-9031

Georgia Hope Scholarship - Public Technical Institution

Type of award: Scholarship, renewable.
Intended use: For undergraduate certificate study at accredited vocational, 2-year or 4-year institution. Designated institutions: Must attend a branch or affiliate of the Georgia Department of Technical and Adult Education or a branch of the University System of Georgia.
Eligibility: Applicant must be U.S. citizen or permanent resident residing in Georgia.
Application requirements: FAFSA or HOPE appplication.
Additional information: Scholarship covers tuition, mandatory fees plus book allowance up to $150 per semester for full-time students. Must be enrolled, matriculated certificate or diploma student.

Amount of award:	Full tuition
Number of awards:	68,957
Total amount awarded:	$40,492,271

Contact:
Scholarship Committee
2082 East Exchange Place
Suite 100
Tucker, GA 30084
Phone: 800-546-HOPE
Fax: 770-724-9052

Georgia Law Enforcement Personnel Dependents Grant

Type of award: Scholarship, renewable.
Intended use: For full-time undergraduate study at accredited vocational, 2-year or 4-year institution. Designated institutions: Georgia's private or public colleges or public technical institutes.
Eligibility: Applicant must be U.S. citizen or permanent resident residing in Georgia. Applicant's parent must have been killed or disabled in work-related accident as fire fighter, police officer or public safety officer.
Application requirements: Proof of eligibility. LEPD Grant application.
Additional information: Must complete preliminary document that verifies claim with parent's former employer and doctors. Application deadline is last day of registration for the school term. Parent must have been permanently disabled or killed in the line of duty as Georgia police officer, firefighter or correction officer.

Amount of award:	$2,000
Number of awards:	35
Total amount awarded:	$63,997

Contact:
Scholarship Committee
2082 East Exchange Place
Suite 100
Tucker, GA 30084
Phone: 800-776-6878
Fax: 770-724-9031

Georgia Robert C. Byrd Scholarship

Type of award: Scholarship, renewable.
Intended use: For full-time undergraduate study at accredited 2-year or 4-year institution in United States.
Eligibility: Applicant must be high school senior. Applicant must be U.S. citizen or permanent resident residing in Georgia.
Basis for selection: Applicant must demonstrate high academic achievement, depth of character, leadership, seriousness of purpose and service orientation.
Application requirements: Recommendations, essay, transcript, proof of eligibility. Obtain application from high school guidance office.
Additional information: Application submitted to the Georgia Department of Education.

Amount of award:	$1,500
Number of awards:	655
Total amount awarded:	$939,500

Contact:
Georgia Student Finance Commission
Grants and Scholarships Section
2082 East Exchange Place, Suite 100
Tucker, GA 30084
Phone: 800-776-6878
Fax: 770-724-9031

Georgia Tuition Equalization Grant

Type of award: Scholarship, renewable.
Intended use: For full-time undergraduate study at accredited 4-year institution. Designated institutions: Agnes Scott College, American Intercontinental University, Andrew College, Atlanta Christian College, Atlanta College of Art, Art Institute of Atlanta, Berry College, Brenau College, Brewton-Parker College, Clark Atlanta University, Covenant College, DeVry Institute, Emmanuel College, Emory University, Georgia

Military College, Ga. Baptist College of Nursing, LaGrange College, Life College, Mercer University, Morehouse College, Morris Brown College, Oglethorpe University, Oxford College, Paine College, Piedmont College, Reinhardt College, Savannah College of Art, Shorter College, Spelman College, South College, Thomas College, Toccoa Falls College, Truett-McConnell College, Wesleyan College, Young Harris College. Also Clemson University, Florida A&M University, Florida State University, Troy State University at Dothan, University of Tennessee/Chattanooga.

Eligibility: Applicant must be U.S. citizen or permanent resident residing in Georgia.

Application requirements: Proof of eligibility. Mileage affidavit (out-of-state schools only).

Additional information: Must be enrolled full-time at eligible private college or university in Georgia, or be a junior or senior with no Georgia public college within 50 miles of home and enrolled at eligible public college outside Georgia. Application deadlines set by schools.

Amount of award:	$1,050
Number of awards:	30,350
Total amount awarded:	$26,427,613

Contact:
Grant Committee
2082 East Exchange Place
Suite 100
Tucker, GA 30084
Phone: 800-776-6878
Fax: 770-724-9031

Gerber Foundation

Gerber Scholarship

Type of award: Scholarship, renewable.
Intended use: For full-time undergraduate or graduate study at postsecondary institution.
Eligibility: Applicant or parent must be employed by Gerber Products Company.
Basis for selection: Applicant must demonstrate depth of character, leadership and service orientation.
Application requirements: Recommendations, essay, transcript. Application and SAT or PSAT scores and counselor's report. Must be at least high school senior.
Additional information: Applicant should demonstrate involvement in diverse curricular, extracurricular, and community activities. Applicant must be dependent child of full time associate or regular retiree of: Gerber Products Co., specific locations at Fremont, Fort Smith, Reedsburg, and Puerto Rico; Gerber (Canada); Gerber Sales Force; Gerber Life Insurance.

Amount of award:	$1,500
Number of awards:	220
Application deadline:	February 28
Notification begins:	May 15
Total amount awarded:	$330,000

Contact:
Catherine Obits
The Gerber Foundation
4747 W. 48th Steet, Suite 153
Fremont, MI 49412

Gerber Scientific, Inc.

H. Joseph Gerber Vision Scholarship Program

Type of award: Scholarship, renewable.
Intended use: For freshman study at vocational, 2-year or 4-year institution.
Eligibility: Applicant or parent must be employed by Gerber Scientific, Inc. Applicant must be high school senior.
Additional information: For further information or an application, contact Gerber Scientific Incorporated directly.

Amount of award:	$2,000

Girls Incorporated, National Resource Center

Donna Brace Ogilvie-Zelda Gitlin Poetry Writing Award

Type of award: Scholarship.
Intended use: For undergraduate study at 2-year or 4-year institution in or outside United States.
Eligibility: Applicant or parent must be member/participant of Girls Incorporated. Applicant must be female, at least 14, no older than 18, high school sophomore, junior or senior.
Basis for selection: Competition/talent/interest in Writing/journalism, based on poetry contest. Major/career interest in publishing; English literature or arts, general.

Amount of award:	$500
Number of awards:	2
Application deadline:	December 15
Notification begins:	March 8
Total amount awarded:	$1,000

Contact:
Girls Incorporated, National Resource Center
441 W. Michigan Street
Indianapolis, IN 46202

Girls Incorporated Scholars Program

Type of award: Scholarship.
Intended use: For undergraduate study at 2-year or 4-year institution in or outside United States.
Eligibility: Applicant or parent must be member/participant of Girls Incorporated. Applicant must be high school sophomore, junior or senior.
Basis for selection: Applicant must demonstrate depth of character, leadership, seriousness of purpose and service orientation.
Application requirements: Recommendations, essay, proof of eligibility.
Additional information: Must maintain minimum "C" average.

Amount of award:	$2,500-$10,000
Application deadline:	December 15
Notification begins:	February 15
Total amount awarded:	$180,000

Contact:
Girls Incorporated, National Resource Center
441 West Michigan Street
Indianapolis, IN 46202

Glamour Magazine

Top Ten College Women Competition

Type of award: Scholarship.
Intended use: For full-time junior study at accredited 4-year institution.
Eligibility: Applicant must be female.
Basis for selection: Applicant must demonstrate high academic achievement, depth of character, leadership, seriousness of purpose and service orientation.
Application requirements: Recommendations, essay, transcript. List of activities and organizations; black-and-white or color photograph.
Additional information: Must be goal-oriented female and full-time junior. Selection based on meritorious attributes. Applications available October 1. Award includes trip to New York City.

Amount of award:	$1,000
Number of awards:	10
Number of applicants:	800
Application deadline:	January 31
Notification begins:	June 1
Total amount awarded:	$10,000

Contact:
Glamour Magazine
4 Times Square
New York, NY 10036-6593
Phone: 800-244-4526 or 212-286-6667
Fax: 212-286-6922

Glaxo Wellcome Inc.

Glaxo Wellcome Employees' Dependents Scholarship

Type of award: Scholarship, renewable.
Intended use: For freshman study at accredited vocational, 2-year or 4-year institution.
Eligibility: Applicant or parent must be employed by Glaxo Wellcome Inc.
Basis for selection: Applicant must demonstrate financial need.
Additional information: For further information or an application, contact Glaxo Wellcome Inc. directly.

Amount of award:	$2,000

Contact:
Phone: 712-556-909

Golden Key National Honor Society

Art International

Type of award: Scholarship, renewable.
Intended use: For undergraduate or graduate study at accredited postsecondary institution.
Eligibility: Applicant or parent must be member/participant of Golden Key National Honor Society.
Application requirements: Application and slides. Basis for selection is artistic merit.
Additional information: Must be lifetime member of Golden Key National Honor Society. One entry per member per category. Applicants generally notified in June.

Amount of award:	$100-$1,000
Number of awards:	88
Number of applicants:	600
Application deadline:	April 1
Total amount awarded:	$16,000

Contact:
Golden Key National Honor Society
1189 Ponce de Leon Avenue
Atlanta, GA 30306-4624
Phone: 800-377-2401 or 404-373-2400
Fax: 404-373-7033
Web: goldenkey.gsu.edu

Ford Motor Company/Golden Key Undergraduate Scholarships

Type of award: Scholarship.
Intended use: For undergraduate study at accredited postsecondary institution.
Eligibility: Applicant or parent must be member/participant of Golden Key National Honor Society.
Basis for selection: Applicant must demonstrate high academic achievement, leadership and service orientation.
Application requirements: New member profile. Applicant must be new member of Golden Key National Honor Society.
Additional information: Must be new member of the Golden Key Honor Society. Application deadline same as chapter's membership deadline and varies with school chapters. Two applicants per chapter per school. Amount of award varies by university. Minimum amount of award $500.

Number of awards:	600
Total amount awarded:	$300,000

Contact:
Golden Key National Honor Society
1189 Ponce de Leon Avenue
Atlanta, GA 30306-4624
Phone: 800-377-2401 or 404-377-2400
Fax: 404-373-7033
Web: goldenkey.gsu.edu

GEICO/Golden Key Adult Scholar Awards

Type of award: Scholarship, renewable.
Intended use: For undergraduate study at accredited postsecondary institution.
Eligibility: Applicant or parent must be member/participant of Golden Key National Honor Society. Applicant must be at least 26, returning adult student.
Basis for selection: Applicant must demonstrate financial need, high academic achievement and depth of character.
Application requirements: Recommendations, essay, transcript.
Additional information: GEICO Adult Scholar Awards recognize outstanding adult students for high academic achievement while juggling multiple responsibilities. Funded by GEICO for Golden Key National Honor Society. Applicant must be lifetime member of Golden Key National Honor Society. Applicants generally notified in June.

Amount of award: $1,000
Number of awards: 5
Number of applicants: 100
Application deadline: April 1
Total amount awarded: $5,000
Contact:
Golden Key National Honor Society
1189 Ponce de Leon Avenue
Atlanta, GA 30306-4624
Phone: 800-377-2401 or 404-377-2400
Fax: 404-373-7033
Web: goldenkey.gsu.edu

Literary Achievement Awards

Type of award: Scholarship, renewable.
Intended use: For undergraduate or graduate study at accredited postsecondary institution.
Eligibility: Applicant or parent must be member/participant of Golden Key National Honor Society.
Basis for selection: Competition/talent/interest in writing/journalism. Major/career interest in journalism or literature.
Application requirements: Application form and entry.
Additional information: Applicant must be lifetime member of Golden Key National Honor Society. Only one entry per member per category. Applicants generally notified in June.
Amount of award: $1,000
Number of awards: 4
Application deadline: April 1
Total amount awarded: $4,000
Contact:
Golden Key National Honor Society
1189 Ponce de Leon Avenue
Atlanta, GA 30306-4624
Phone: 800-377-2401 or 404-377-2400
Fax: 404-373-7033
Web: goldenkey.gsu.edu

Performing Arts Showcase

Type of award: Scholarship, renewable.
Intended use: For undergraduate or graduate study at 4-year or graduate institution.
Eligibility: Applicant or parent must be member/participant of Golden Key National Honor Society.
Basis for selection: Competition/talent/interest in Performing arts, submitted video cassette entry (not to exceed ten minutes in length). Major/career interest in performing arts or music.
Application requirements: Application and videotaped performance of dance, drama, film, vocal performance, instrumental performance or original musical composition.
Additional information: Applicant must be lifetime member of Golden Key National Honor Society. Applicants generally notified in June. Winners receive free trip to Golden Key International Convention, where they perform before more than 1,000 delegates.
Amount of award: $1,000
Number of awards: 6
Number of applicants: 300
Application deadline: March 1
Total amount awarded: $6,000

Contact:
Golden Key National Honor Society
1189 Ponce de Leon Avenue
Atlanta, GA 30306-4624
Phone: 800-377-2401 or 404-377-2400
Fax: 404-373-7033
Web: goldenkey.gsu.edu

Research Travel Grants

Type of award: Research grant, renewable.
Intended use: For undergraduate study.
Eligibility: Applicant or parent must be member/participant of Golden Key National Honor Society.
Basis for selection: Applicant must demonstrate high academic achievement.
Application requirements: Recommendations, essay, transcript.
Additional information: Applicant must be lifetime member of Golden Key National Honor Society. Pays for members to travel to professional conferences and research symposia where they have been invited to present. Applicants are generally notified in June and December.
Amount of award: $500
Number of awards: 10
Number of applicants: 75
Application deadline: April 15, October 15
Total amount awarded: $5,000
Contact:
Golden Key National Honor Society
1189 Ponce de Leon Avenue
Atlanta, GA 30306-4624
Phone: 800-377-2401 or 404-377-2400
Fax: 404-373-7033
Web: goldenkey.gsu.edu

Student Scholastic Showcase

Type of award: Scholarship, renewable.
Intended use: For undergraduate or graduate study at accredited postsecondary institution.
Eligibility: Applicant or parent must be member/participant of Golden Key National Honor Society.
Application requirements: Research paper, abstract and faculty letter of support. Basis for selection is quality of undergraduate research.
Additional information: Must be member of Golden Key National Honor Society. Only one submission per member will be accepted.
Amount of award: $1,000
Number of awards: 4
Number of applicants: 100
Application deadline: March 1
Notification begins: June 15
Total amount awarded: $4,000
Contact:
Golden Key National Honor Society
1189 Ponce de Leon Avenue
Atlanta, GA 30306-4624
Phone: 800-377-2401 or 404-377-2400
Fax: 404 373 7033
Web: goldenkey.gsu.edu

Study Abroad Scholarships

Type of award: Scholarship, renewable.
Intended use: For undergraduate study.

Scholarships

Eligibility: Applicant or parent must be member/participant of Golden Key National Honor Society.
Basis for selection: Competition/talent/interest in Study abroad. Applicant must demonstrate high academic achievement.
Application requirements: Recommendations, essay, transcript. Involvement in Golden Key activities.
Additional information: Applicant must be lifetime member of Golden Key National Honor Society. Applicants generally notified in June and December.

Amount of award:	$2,000
Number of awards:	10
Number of applicants:	200
Application deadline:	April 15, October 15
Total amount awarded:	$20,000

Contact:
Golden Key National Honor Society
1189 Ponce de Leon Avenue
Atlanta, GA 30306-4624
Phone: 800-377-2401 or 404-377-2400
Fax: 404-373-7033
Web: goldenkey.gsu.edu

Golf Course Superintendents Association of America

GCSAA Footsteps on the Green Award

Type of award: Scholarship.
Intended use: For full-time undergraduate study at accredited 2-year or 4-year institution.
Eligibility: Applicant or parent must be member/participant of Golf Course Superintendents Association of America.
Basis for selection: Major/career interest in turf management.
Application requirements: Applicant and parent must be members of GCSAA.
Additional information: Awarded to children and grandchildren of GCSAA members. Applicant must be pursuing career in turf grass management and must have completed 12 hours in major field of study. Visit Website or contact via e-mail (psmith@gcsaa.org) for additional information.

Amount of award:	$500-$3,500
Number of awards:	4

Contact:
Scholarship Coordinator, Pam Smith
1421 Research Park Drive
Lawrence, KS 66049-3859
Phone: 785-841-2240
Fax: 785-832-3678
Web: www.gcsaa.org

GCSAA Legacy Awards

Type of award: Scholarship.
Intended use: For full-time undergraduate study at accredited 2-year, 4-year or graduate institution.
Eligibility: Applicant or parent must be member/participant of Golf Course Superintendents Association of America.
Application requirements: Recommendations, transcript. Applicant must be child or grandchild of GCSAA member.

Additional information: Applicants must be child or grandchild of GCSAA members who have been active for at least five years. Must be enrolled full-time at accredited postsecondary institution or, if high school senior, must be accepted for following academic year. Must be studying field unrelated to golf course management. Award is funded by Syngenta Professional Products. Visit Website or contact via e-mail (psmith@gcsaa.org) for additional information.

Amount of award:	$1,500
Number of awards:	10
Application deadline:	April 15
Total amount awarded:	$15,000

Contact:
Scholarships Coordinator Pam Smith
1421 Research Park Drive
Lawrence, KS 66049
Phone: 800-472-7878 ext. 678
Web: www.gcsaa.org

GCSAA Scholars Competition

Type of award: Scholarship.
Intended use: For sophomore, junior or senior study at accredited 2-year or 4-year institution.
Eligibility: Applicant or parent must be member/participant of Golf Course Superintendents Association of America.
Basis for selection: Major/career interest in turf management. Applicant must demonstrate high academic achievement.
Application requirements: Recommendations, transcript.
Additional information: Must be planning career as a golf course superintendent and have successfully completed at least 24 credit hours or the equivalent of one year of full-time study. Applicant must be a GCSAA member. Visit Website or contact via e-mail address (psmith@gcsaa.org) for additional information.

Amount of award:	$500-$3,500
Number of awards:	32
Application deadline:	June 1

Contact:
Scholarship Coordinator Pam Smith
1421 Research Park Drive
Lawrence, KS 66049-3859
Phone: 800-472-7878 ext. 678
Web: www.gcsaa.org

GCSAA Student Essay Contest

Type of award: Scholarship.
Intended use: For undergraduate or graduate study at accredited 2-year, 4-year or graduate institution.
Eligibility: Applicant or parent must be member/participant of Golf Course Superintendents Association of America.
Basis for selection: Competition/talent/interest in writing/journalism, based on seven to 12 page essay focusing on golf course management. Major/career interest in turf management.
Additional information: Applicant must be member of GCSAA. Applicant must be pursuing degrees in turfgrass science, agronomy or any field related to golf course management. First, $2,000; 2nd, $1,500; 3rd, $1,000. Visit Website or contact via e-mail (psmith@gcsaa.org) for additional information.

Amount of award:	$1,000-$2,000
Number of awards:	3
Number of applicants:	12
Application deadline:	March 31
Total amount awarded:	$4,500

Contact:
Scholarship Coordinator, Pam Smith
1421 Research Park Drive
Lawrence, KS 66049
Phone: 800-472-7878 ext. 678
Web: www.gcsaa.org

Scotts Company Scholars Program

Type of award: Scholarship.
Intended use: For freshman, sophomore or junior study at accredited 2-year or 4-year institution.
Basis for selection: Major/career interest in turf management.
Application requirements: Recommendations, transcript.
Additional information: Five finalists are selected for summer internships, receive a $500 award and an opportunity to compete for two $2,500 scholarships. Applicants must be pursuing a career in the green industry. Women, minorities, and persons with disabilities encouraged to apply. Visit Website or contact via e-mail (psmith@gcsaa.org) for additional information.

Amount of award:	$500-$2,500
Number of awards:	7
Application deadline:	March 1
Total amount awarded:	$7,500

Contact:
Scholarship Coordinator, Pam Smith
1421 Research Park Drive
Lawrence, KS 66049
Phone: 800-472-7878 ext. 678
Web: www.gcsaa.org

Graco Foundation

Graco Scholarship

Type of award: Scholarship, renewable.
Intended use: For undergraduate or graduate study at accredited vocational, 2-year or 4-year institution.
Eligibility: Applicant or parent must be employed by Graco.
Basis for selection: Applicant must demonstrate financial need.
Additional information: For further information or an application, contact Graco Foundation directly.

Amount of award:	$1,000-$5,000

Grange Insurance Association

Grange Insurance Scholarship

Type of award: Scholarship.
Intended use: For full-time undergraduate or graduate study at accredited vocational, 2-year, 4-year or graduate institution.
Eligibility: Applicant or parent must be member/participant of Fraternal Grange. Applicant must be U.S. citizen or permanent resident residing in Idaho, Montana, Oregon, California, Washington, Colorado or Wyoming.
Basis for selection: Applicant must demonstrate financial need, high academic achievement, depth of character, leadership, patriotism, seriousness of purpose and service orientation.
Application requirements: Recommendations, essay, transcript.
Additional information: Applicant or parents must be permanent residents of the designated state and members of The Grange in that state. Applicant or parents need not have insurance with The Grange.

Amount of award:	$750-$1,000
Number of awards:	25
Number of applicants:	117
Application deadline:	March 1
Notification begins:	May 15
Total amount awarded:	$19,500

Contact:
Grange Insurance Association
Scholarship Coordinator
P.O. Box 21089
Seattle, WA 98111-3089
Phone: 800-247-2643 ext. 2200

Greater Kanawha Valley Foundation

Greater Kanawha Valley Scholarship Program

Type of award: Scholarship, renewable.
Intended use: For full-time undergraduate or graduate study at postsecondary institution.
Eligibility: Applicant must be residing in West Virginia.
Basis for selection: Applicant must demonstrate financial need, high academic achievement, depth of character and leadership.
Application requirements: Recommendations, essay, transcript.

Amount of award:	$1,000-$4,400
Number of awards:	420
Number of applicants:	1,300
Application deadline:	February 15
Notification begins:	May 1
Total amount awarded:	$665,000

Contact:
Greater Kanawha Valley Foundation
P.O. Box 3041
Charleston, WV 25331
Phone: 304-346-3620

GreenPoint Foundation

GreenPoint Scholarship

Type of award: Scholarship, renewable.
Intended use: For undergraduate study at accredited postsecondary institution.
Eligibility: Applicant or parent must be employed by Greenpoint Foundation. Applicant must be high school senior.
Basis for selection: Applicant must demonstrate financial need.

Additional information: For further information or an application, contact GreenPoint Foundation directly.

    Amount of award: $5,000

Gregory Poole Equipment Company

Gregory Poole Scholarship

Type of award: Scholarship.
Intended use: For undergraduate study at accredited vocational, 2-year or 4-year institution.
Eligibility: Applicant or parent must be employed by Gregory Poole Equipment Company.
Additional information: For further information or an application, contact Gregory Poole Company directly.

    Amount of award: $500-$1,000

Guideposts

Norman Vincent Peale Scholarship Program

Type of award: Scholarship.
Intended use: For undergraduate study at vocational, 2-year or 4-year institution.
Eligibility: Applicant or parent must be employed by Guideposts. Applicant must be high school senior.
Additional information: For further information or an application, contact Guideposts directly.

    Amount of award: $1,000-$3,500

Young Writers Contest

Type of award: Scholarship.
Intended use: For undergraduate study at accredited vocational, 2-year or 4-year institution.
Eligibility: Applicant must be high school junior or senior.
Basis for selection: Competition/talent/interest in writing/journalism, based on nonfiction article (maximum 1,200 words), must be in first-person, written in style of Guideposts magazine, and demonstrating writer's faith in God.
Application requirements: Essay.
Additional information: Prizes must be used within five years after high school. Only high school juniors and seniors may compete. Submission of a true, first-person story in which the applicant writes of a significant experience.

    Amount of award: $250-$10,000
    Number of awards: 20
    Number of applicants: 5,000
    Application deadline: November 26
    Notification begins: January 4
    Total amount awarded: $38,500
Contact:
Youth Writing Contest/ Guideposts
16 East 34 Street
New York, NY 10016

Gulf States Paper Corporation

Jack & Elizabeth Warner College Scholarship Fund

Type of award: Scholarship, renewable.
Intended use: For undergraduate study at 4-year institution.
Eligibility: Applicant or parent must be employed by Gulf States Paper Corporation. Applicant must be high school senior.
Additional information: For further information or an application, contact Gulf States Paper Corporation directly.

    Amount of award: $500-$2,500

H&R Block Foundation

H&R Block Scholarship

Type of award: Scholarship.
Intended use: For undergraduate study at accredited vocational, 2-year or 4-year institution.
Eligibility: Applicant or parent must be employed by H&R Block Foundation. Applicant must be high school senior.
Basis for selection: Applicant must demonstrate financial need.
Additional information: For further information or an application, contact H&R Block Foundation directly.

    Amount of award: $500-$2,500

H.B. Fuller Company & It's International Locations

Elmer and Eleanor Andersen Global Scholarship Program

Type of award: Scholarship.
Intended use: For undergraduate study at vocational, 2-year or 4-year institution.
Eligibility: Applicant or parent must be employed by H.B. Fuller Company and its International Locations. Applicant must be high school senior.
Additional information: For further information or an application, contact H.B. Fuller Company and it's International Locations directly.

    Amount of award: $500-$10,000

Hannaford Charitable Foundation

Hannaford Scholarship

Type of award: Scholarship.
Intended use: For undergraduate or graduate study at accredited postsecondary institution.

Eligibility: Applicant or parent must be employed by Hannaford Charitable Foundation. Applicant must be high school senior.
Basis for selection: Applicant must demonstrate financial need.
Additional information: For further information or an application, contact Hannaford Charitable Foundation directly.

Amount of award:	$2,000-$5,000

Contact:
Hannaford Charitable Foundation

Harness Horse Youth Foundation

Harness Horse Youth Scholarship

Type of award: Scholarship, renewable.
Intended use: For full-time undergraduate or non-degree study at vocational, 2-year or 4-year institution.
Basis for selection: Major/career interest in animal sciences or veterinary medicine. Applicant must demonstrate financial need and high academic achievement.
Application requirements: Recommendations, essay, transcript. Foundation application form.
Additional information: Must pursue horse-related career. Experience in harness racing prefered. Preference given to applicants under 24 years of age.

Amount of award:	$1,000-$3,500
Number of applicants:	700
Application deadline:	April 30
Notification begins:	July 1
Total amount awarded:	$16,000

Contact:
Harness Horse Youth Foundation
14950 Greyhound Court
Suite 210
Carmel, IN 46032
Phone: 317-848-5132
Web: www.hhyf.org

Harness Tracks of America

Harness Tracks of America Scholarship

Type of award: Scholarship.
Intended use: For full-time undergraduate or graduate study at accredited postsecondary institution.
Eligibility: Applicant or parent must be member/participant of Harness Racing Industry.
Basis for selection: Applicant must demonstrate financial need and high academic achievement.
Application requirements: Essay, transcript, proof of eligibility. Submit FAFSA, U.S. or Canadian tax return.
Additional information: Must be child of licensed driver, trainer, breeder, owner or caretaker of harness horses or be personally active in harness racing industry. Children of deceased industry members also eligible. Recommendations not required but considered if included with application.

Scholarship awards based on financial need, academic excellence and active harness racing involvement.

Amount of award:	$5,000
Number of awards:	7
Number of applicants:	121
Application deadline:	June 15
Notification begins:	September 15
Total amount awarded:	$35,000

Contact:
Harness Tracks of America
4640 East Sunrise Road
Suite 200
Tucson, AZ 85718
Phone: 520-529-2525
Fax: 520-529-3235

Harry S. Truman Scholarship Foundation

Harry S. Truman Scholarship

Type of award: Scholarship.
Intended use: For full-time senior or graduate study at 4-year or graduate institution.
Eligibility: Applicant must be U.S. citizen.
Basis for selection: Major/career interest in public administration/service; governmental public relations; political science/government or education. Applicant must demonstrate high academic achievement, leadership and service orientation.
Application requirements: Recommendations, essay, transcript, nomination by participating institutions. Must have a signed Institution Nomination Form, a signed Nominee Information Form, and analysis of public policy issue.
Additional information: Applicants must participate in Truman Scholars Leadership Week, Awards Ceremony at Harry S. Truman Library, and Truman Scholars Washington Summer Institute. Awardees receive up to $3,000 for senior year and up to $27,000 for graduate study. Open to all fields of study as long as candidate plans to use degree in public service. Must be in top 25 percent of class.

Number of awards:	78
Application deadline:	January 28

Contact:
Harry Truman Scholarship Foundation
712 Jackson Place NW
Washington, DC 20006
Web: www.truman.gov

Hasbro, Inc.

Hasbro Scholarship

Type of award: Scholarship, renewable.
Intended use: For undergraduate study at accredited postsecondary institution.
Eligibility: Applicant or parent must be employed by Hasbro, Inc. Applicant must be high school senior.
Basis for selection: Applicant must demonstrate financial need.
Additional information: For further information or an application, contact Hasbro, Inc. directly.

Amount of award: $2,000

Hatfield, Inc.

Hatfield Quality Meats Scholarship

Type of award: Scholarship.
Intended use: For undergraduate study at accredited postsecondary institution.
Eligibility: Applicant or parent must be employed by Hatfield Quality Meats, Inc.
Additional information: For further information or an application, contact Hatfield Quality Meats, Inc. directly.
    Amount of award: $1,000

Havana National Bank

McFarland Charitable Foundation Scholarship

Type of award: Scholarship, renewable.
Intended use: For full-time undergraduate study at accredited vocational, 2-year or 4-year institution in United States.
Basis for selection: Major/career interest in nursing. Applicant must demonstrate seriousness of purpose.
Application requirements: $5 application fee. Interview, recommendations, transcript, proof of eligibility. Letter of acceptance to the RN program.
Additional information: Award recipients must contractually obligate themselves to return to Havana, IL and work as registered nurses for two years for each year of funding. Co-signer is required. To fund RN programs only.

Amount of award:	$1,000-$14,000
Number of awards:	6
Number of applicants:	30
Application deadline:	May 1
Notification begins:	June 15
Total amount awarded:	$75,000

Contact:
Havana National Bank
112 South Orange
P.O. Box 200
Havana, IL 62644-0200
Phone: 309-543-3361

Hawaii Community Foundation

Aiea General Hospital Association Scholarship

Type of award: Scholarship, renewable.
Intended use: For full-time undergraduate or graduate study at accredited 2-year, 4-year or graduate institution in United States.
Eligibility: Applicant must be U.S. citizen or permanent resident residing in Hawaii.

Basis for selection: Major/career interest in health-related professions. Applicant must demonstrate financial need, high academic achievement and depth of character.
Application requirements: Recommendations, essay, transcript.
Additional information: New applicants must be undergraduates. Applicant must be resident of Leeward Oahu zip codes: 96701, 96706, 96707, 96782, 96792, or 98797. Amount of award varies. Notifications mailed between April and July.

Amount of award:	$1,000
Number of awards:	23
Application deadline:	March 1

Contact:
Hawaii Community Foundation
900 Fort Street Mall
Suite 1300
Honolulu, HI 96813
Phone: 808-566-5570
Fax: 808-521-6286
Web: www.hcf-hawaii.org

Alma White--Delta Chapter, Delta Kappa Gamma Scholarship

Type of award: Scholarship.
Intended use: For full-time junior, senior or graduate study at accredited postsecondary institution in United States.
Eligibility: Applicant must be U.S. citizen or permanent resident residing in Hawaii.
Basis for selection: Major/career interest in education. Applicant must demonstrate high academic achievement and depth of character.
Application requirements: Recommendations, essay, transcript.
Additional information: Applicants must have permanent address in Hawaii. Applicants who take up mainland residency must have relatives living in Hawaii. Other former Hawaii residents considered on case by case basis. Notifications mailed between April and July.

Amount of award:	$1,000
Number of awards:	12
Application deadline:	March 1

Contact:
Hawaii Community Foundation
900 Fort Street Mall
Suite 1300
Honolulu, HI 96813
Phone: 808-566-5570
Fax: 808-521-6286
Web: www.hcf-hawaii.org

Blossom Kalama Evans Memorial Scholarship

Type of award: Scholarship, renewable.
Intended use: For full-time junior, senior or graduate study at accredited 4-year or graduate institution in United States.
Eligibility: Applicant must be U.S. citizen or permanent resident residing in Hawaii.
Basis for selection: Major/career interest in hawaiian studies. Applicant must demonstrate financial need, high academic achievement and depth of character.
Application requirements: Recommendations, essay, transcript.
Additional information: Hawaiian language students also eligible. Preference given to students of Hawaiian ancestry.

Award amount varies. Applicants must have permanent address in Hawaii. Applicants who take up mainland residency must have relatives living in Hawaii. Other former Hawaii residents considered on case by case basis. Notifications mailed between April and July. Members of the Hawaiian Girls Golf Association not eligible.

Amount of award:	$1,500
Number of awards:	5
Application deadline:	March 1

Contact:
Hawaii Community Foundation
900 Fort Street Mall, Suite 1300
Honolulu, HI 96813
Phone: 808-566-5570
Fax: 808-521-6286
Web: www.hcf-hawaii.org

Castle & Cooke George W.Y. Yim Scholarship Fund

Type of award: Scholarship.
Intended use: For full-time freshman study at accredited vocational, 2-year or 4-year institution in United States.
Eligibility: Applicant must be high school senior. Applicant must be U.S. citizen or permanent resident residing in Hawaii.
Basis for selection: Major/career interest in science, general; engineering or computer/information sciences. Applicant must demonstrate financial need, high academic achievement and depth of character.
Application requirements: Recommendations, essay, transcript.
Additional information: Applicants must be graduating senior from Leilehua, Mililani or Waialua high schools. Preference given to majors in high technology fields. Applicants must have permanent address in Hawaii. Applicants who take up mainland residency must have relatives living in Hawaii. Other former Hawaii residents considered on case by case basis. Notifications mailed between April and July.

Amount of award:	$1,000
Number of awards:	5
Application deadline:	March 1

Contact:
Bonnie Freitas, Human Resources
900 Fort Street Mall
Suite 1300
Honolulu, HI 96813
Phone: 808-548-3777
Web: www.hcf-hawaii.org

Cora Aguda Manayan Fund

Type of award: Scholarship, renewable.
Intended use: For full-time undergraduate or graduate study at accredited postsecondary institution in United States.
Eligibility: Applicant must be Asian American. Preference given to students of Filipino ancestry studying in Hawaii. Applicant must be U.S. citizen or permanent resident residing in Hawaii.
Basis for selection: Major/career interest in health-related professions. Applicant must demonstrate financial need, high academic achievement and depth of character.
Application requirements: Recommendations, essay, transcript.
Additional information: Amount of award varies. Applicants must have permanent address in Hawaii. Applicants who take up mainland residency must have relatives living in Hawaii. Other former Hawaii residents considered on a case by case

basis. Notifications mailed between April and July. Minimum 3.0 GPA.

Amount of award:	$550
Number of awards:	17
Application deadline:	March 1

Contact:
Hawaii Community Foundation
900 Fort Street Mall
Suite 1300
Honolulu, HI 96813
Phone: 808-566-5570
Fax: 808-521-6286
Web: www.hcf-hawaii.org

Dolly Ching Scholarship Fund

Type of award: Scholarship.
Intended use: For full-time undergraduate study at accredited postsecondary institution in United States. Designated institutions: Any institution in University of Hawaii system, including community colleges.
Eligibility: Applicant must be U.S. citizen or permanent resident residing in Hawaii.
Basis for selection: Applicant must demonstrate financial need, high academic achievement, depth of character and service orientation.
Application requirements: Recommendations, essay, transcript.
Additional information: Preference given to applicants demonstrating greatest financial need and greatest community service. Applicants must have permanent address in Hawaii. Applicants who take up mainland residency must have relatives living in Hawaii. Other former Hawaii residents considered on a case by case basis. Minimum 3.0 GPA.

Amount of award:	$1,400
Number of awards:	6
Application deadline:	March 1

Contact:
Hawaii Community Foundation
900 Fort Street Mall
Suite 1300
Honolulu, HI 96813
Phone: 808-566-5570
Fax: 808-521-6286
Web: www.hcf-hawaii.org

Dorice & Clarence Glick Classical Music Scholarship

Type of award: Scholarship.
Intended use: For full-time undergraduate or graduate study at accredited postsecondary institution in United States.
Eligibility: Applicant must be residing in Hawaii.
Basis for selection: Major/career interest in music. Applicant must demonstrate financial need, high academic achievement and depth of character.
Application requirements: Recommendations, essay, transcript. Personal statement describing how program of study relates to classical music.
Additional information: Applicants must have permanent address in Hawaii. Applicants who take up mainland residency must have relatives living in Hawaii. Other former Hawaii residents considered on case by case basis. Notifications mailed between April and July. Must be majoring in classical music.

Amount of award:	$750
Number of awards:	9
Application deadline:	March 1

Contact:
Hawaii Community Foundation
900 Fort Street Mall
Suite 1300
Honolulu, HI 96813
Phone: 808-566-5570
Fax: 808-521-6286
Web: www.hcf-hawaii.org

Dr. Hans & Clara Zimmerman Foundation Education Scholarship

Type of award: Scholarship, renewable.
Intended use: For undergraduate or graduate study at 2-year, 4-year or graduate institution in United States.
Eligibility: Applicant must be U.S. citizen or permanent resident residing in Hawaii.
Basis for selection: Major/career interest in education or education, teacher. Applicant must demonstrate financial need, high academic achievement, depth of character, leadership, seriousness of purpose and service orientation.
Additional information: Applicant must be a non-traditonal student who has worked for at least 2 years and is returning to school in the United States. Preference is given to students of Hawaiian acestry and students from the neighbor islands who plan on teaching in Hawaii. Preference is also given to students with some teaching experience. Applicants must have permanent address in Hawaii. Applicants who take up mainland residency must have relatives living in Hawaii. Other former Hawaii residents considered on a case by case basis. Notifications mailed between April and July.

Amount of award:	$1,650
Number of awards:	43
Application deadline:	March 1

Contact:
Hawaii Community Foundation, Scholarships
900 Fort Street Mall
Suite 1300
Honolulu, HI 96813
Phone: 808-566-5570
Fax: 808-521-6286
Web: www.hcf-hawaii.org

Dr. Hans and Clara Zimmerman Foundation Health Scholarship

Type of award: Scholarship, renewable.
Intended use: For full-time junior, senior or graduate study at accredited postsecondary institution in United States.
Eligibility: Applicant must be returning adult student. Applicant must be U.S. citizen or permanent resident residing in Hawaii.
Basis for selection: Major/career interest in health-related professions; health education; medical assistant; nursing; pharmacy/pharmaceutics/pharmacology; dental assistant; respiratory therapy; occupational therapy; physical therapy or psychology. Applicant must demonstrate financial need, high academic achievement and depth of character.
Application requirements: Recommendations, essay, transcript, proof of eligibility. Must be nontraditional student who has worked for at least two years.
Additional information: Award amount varies. Sports medicine, non-clinical psychology, and social work majors not eligible. Applicants must have permanent address in Hawaii. Applicants who take up mainland residency must have relatives living in Hawaii. Other former Hawaii residents considered on a case by case basis. Notifications mailed between April and July. Minimum 3.0 GPA.

Amount of award:	$2,700
Number of awards:	241
Application deadline:	March 1

Contact:
Hawaii Community Foundation
900 Fort Street Mall
Suite 1300
Honolulu, HI 96813
Phone: 808-566-5570
Fax: 808-521-6286
Web: www.hcf-hawaii.org

E.E. Black Scholarship

Type of award: Scholarship, renewable.
Intended use: For full-time undergraduate study at accredited postsecondary institution in United States.
Eligibility: Applicant or parent must be employed by Tesoro Petroleum Companies, Inc. Applicant must be U.S. citizen or permanent resident residing in Hawaii.
Basis for selection: Applicant must demonstrate financial need, high academic achievement and depth of character.
Application requirements: Recommendations, essay, transcript.
Additional information: Minimum 3.0 GPA. Award amount varies. Applicants must have permanent address in Hawaii. Applicants who take up mainland residency must have relatives living in Hawaii. Other former Hawaii residents considered on a case by case basis. Notifications mailed between April and July.

Amount of award:	$1,125
Number of awards:	8
Application deadline:	March 1

Contact:
Hawaii Community Foundation
900 Fort Street Mall, Suite 1300
Honolulu, HI 96813
Phone: 808-566-5570
Web: www.hcf-hawaii.org

Ellison Onizuka Memorial Scholarship

Type of award: Scholarship.
Intended use: For full-time freshman study at accredited 2-year or 4-year institution in United States.
Eligibility: Applicant must be high school senior. Applicant must be U.S. citizen or permanent resident residing in Hawaii.
Basis for selection: Major/career interest in aerospace. Applicant must demonstrate financial need and depth of character.
Application requirements: Recommendations, transcript, nomination by high school principal.
Additional information: Award amount varies. Applicants must have permanent address in Hawaii. Applicants who take up mainland residency must have relatives living in Hawaii. Other former Hawaii residents considered on case by case basis. Contact high school principal.

Application deadline:	March 1

Contact:
Hawaii Community Foundation
900 Fort Street Mall, Suite 1300
Honolulu, HI 96813
Phone: 808-566-5570
Fax: 808-521-6286
Web: www.hcf-hawaii.org

Frances S. Watanabe Memorial Scholarship

Type of award: Scholarship, renewable.
Intended use: For undergraduate or graduate study at accredited postsecondary institution in United States.
Eligibility: Applicant or parent must be member/participant of Hawaii Construction Industry Federal Credit Union. Applicant must be U.S. citizen or permanent resident residing in Hawaii.
Basis for selection: Applicant must demonstrate financial need, high academic achievement and depth of character.
Application requirements: Recommendations, essay, transcript.
Additional information: Award amount varies. Applicants must have permanent address in Hawaii. Applicants who take up mainland residency must have relatives living in Hawaii. Other former Hawaii residents considered on case by case basis. Credit union members must belong to Amana Street location. Notifications mailed between April and May.

Amount of award:	$750
Number of awards:	3
Application deadline:	March 1

Contact:
Hawaii Community Foundation
900 Fort Street Mall, Suite 1300
Honolulu, HI 96813
Phone: 808-566-5570
Web: www.hcf-hawaii.org

Henry and Dorothy Castle Memorial Scholarship

Type of award: Scholarship, renewable.
Intended use: For full-time undergraduate or graduate study at accredited postsecondary institution in United States.
Eligibility: Applicant must be U.S. citizen or permanent resident residing in Hawaii.
Basis for selection: Major/career interest in education, early childhood or education, teacher. Applicant must demonstrate financial need, high academic achievement, depth of character, leadership, seriousness of purpose and service orientation.
Application requirements: Recommendations, essay, transcript. Additional essay stating interests and goals in early childhood education, and plans to contribute to field.
Additional information: Award amount varies. Applicants must have permanent address in Hawaii. Applicants who take up mainland residency must have relatives living in Hawaii. Other former Hawaii residents considered on a case by case basis. Notifications mailed between April and May. (This scholarship is funded by the Samuel N. & Mary Castle Foundation.)

Amount of award:	$1,300
Number of awards:	15
Application deadline:	March 1

Contact:
Hawaii Community Foundation
900 Fort Street Mall, Suite 1300
Honolulu, HI 96813
Phone: 808-566-5570
Fax: 808-521-6286
Web: www.hcf-hawaii.org

Jean Fitzgerald Scholarship Fund

Type of award: Scholarship, renewable.
Intended use: For full-time freshman study at accredited 2-year or 4-year institution in United States.
Eligibility: Applicant or parent must be member/participant of Hawaii Pacific Tennis Association. Applicant must be female, high school senior. Applicant must be U.S. citizen or permanent resident residing in Hawaii.
Basis for selection: Applicant must demonstrate depth of character.
Application requirements: Recommendations, essay, transcript.
Additional information: Amount of award varies. Applicant must be active member of Hawaii Pacific Tennis Association for last four years. Applicants must have permanent address in Hawaii. Applicants who take up mainland residency must have relatives living in Hawaii. Other former Hawaii residents considered on case by case basis. Notifications mailed between April and July.

Amount of award:	$65
Number of awards:	1
Application deadline:	March 1

Contact:
Hawaii Pacific Tennis Association
2619 8 King Street, Suite 2A
Honolulu, HI 96826
Phone: 808-566-5570
Fax: 808-521-6286
Web: www.hcf-hawaii.org

John Dawe Dental Education Fund

Type of award: Scholarship, renewable.
Intended use: For full-time undergraduate or graduate study at accredited postsecondary institution in United States.
Eligibility: Applicant must be U.S. citizen or permanent resident residing in Hawaii.
Basis for selection: Major/career interest in dentistry; dental hygiene; dental assistant or dental laboratory technology. Applicant must demonstrate financial need, high academic achievement and depth of character.
Application requirements: Recommendations, essay, transcript, proof of eligibility. Dawe Supplemental Financial Form (obtain from Hawaii Community Foundation).
Additional information: Applicants must submit a letter from their school confirming enrollment in the dental hygiene program. Students in dental technology also eligible. Award amount varies. Applicants must have permanent address in Hawaii. Applicants who take up mainland residency must have relatives living in Hawaii. Other former Hawaii residents considered on a case by case basis. Award amount varies. Notifications mailed between April and July.

Amount of award:	$1,050
Number of awards:	10
Application deadline:	March 1

Contact:
Hawaii Dental Association
1000 Bishop Street
Suite 805
Honolulu, HI 96813
Phone: 808-566-5570
Fax: 808-521-6286
Web: www.hcf-hawaii.org

John Ross Foundation

Type of award: Scholarship, renewable.
Intended use: For full-time undergraduate or graduate study at accredited postsecondary institution in United States.
Eligibility: Applicant must be U.S. citizen or permanent resident residing in Hawaii.
Basis for selection: Applicant must demonstrate financial need, high academic achievement and depth of character.
Application requirements: Recommendations, essay, transcript. Essay should discuss applicant's relationship the the Big Island.
Additional information: Amount of award varies. Preference given to undergraduates born on, having ancestors from, and planning to reside on the Big Island. Preference also given to undergraduates. Applicants must have permanent address in Hawaii. Applicants who take up mainland residency must have relatives living in Hawaii. Other former Hawaii residents considered on a case by case basis. Notifications mailed between April and July.

Amount of award:	$1,000
Number of awards:	19
Application deadline:	March 1

Contact:
Hawaii Community Foundation
900 Fort Street Mall
Suite 1300
Honolulu, HI 96813
Phone: 808-566-5570
Fax: 808-521-6286
Web: www.hcf-hawaii.org

Juliette M. Atherton Scholarship

Type of award: Scholarship, renewable.
Intended use: For full-time undergraduate, graduate or non-degree study at accredited postsecondary institution in United States.
Eligibility: Applicant must be Protestant. Applicant must be U.S. citizen or permanent resident residing in Hawaii.
Basis for selection: Major/career interest in religion/theology. Applicant must demonstrate financial need, high academic achievement, depth of character, leadership, seriousness of purpose and service orientation.
Application requirements: Recommendations, essay, transcript, proof of eligibility. Children of ministers must provide in their personal statement: parent's current position, church/parish name, denomination, place and date of ordination, and name of seminary attended.
Additional information: Applicant must meet one of the following criteria: (1) be a dependant child of an active, ordained Protestant minister in an established denomination in Hawaii; (2) be planning to attend an accredited graduate school of theology with goal of ordination as Protestant minister; (3) be an ordained Protestant minister planning to pursue either an advanced degree related to profession or education in a field related to ministry through coursework, workshops, or seminars. Award amount varies. Applicants must have permanent address in Hawaii. Applicants who take up mainland residency must

have relatives living in Hawaii. Other former Hawaii residents considered on case by case basis.

Amount of award:	$2,100
Number of awards:	62
Application deadline:	March 1

Contact:
Hawaii Community Foundation
900 Fort Street Mall, Suite 1300
Honolulu, HI 96813
Phone: 808-566-5570
Fax: 808-521-6286
Web: www.hcf-hawaii.org

K.M. Hatano Scholarship

Type of award: Scholarship, renewable.
Intended use: For full-time undergraduate study at accredited 4-year institution in United States.
Eligibility: Applicant must be high school senior. Applicant must be U.S. citizen or permanent resident residing in Hawaii.
Basis for selection: Applicant must demonstrate depth of character.
Application requirements: Recommendations, essay, transcript.
Additional information: Amount of award varies. Applicant must be resident of Maui county, including Lanai and Molokai. Contact Hyatt Regency Maui address for more information.

Application deadline:	March 1

Contact:
Hyatt Regency Maui Human Resources Office
200 Nohea Kai Drive
Lahaina, HI 96761
Phone: 808-566-5570
Fax: 808-521-6286
Web: www.hcf-hawaii.org

Ka'iulani Home for Girls Trust Scholarship

Type of award: Scholarship, renewable.
Intended use: For full-time undergraduate or graduate study at accredited postsecondary institution in United States.
Eligibility: Applicant must be female. Applicant must be U.S. citizen or permanent resident residing in Hawaii.
Basis for selection: Applicant must demonstrate financial need, high academic achievement and depth of character.
Application requirements: Recommendations, essay, transcript, proof of eligibility. Include birth certificate to verify ancestry.
Additional information: Preference given to those of Hawaiian ancestry. Applicants must have permanent address in Hawaii. Applicants who take up mainland residency must have relatives living in Hawaii. Other former Hawaii residents considered on case by case basis. Notifications mailed between April and July.

Amount of award:	$750
Number of awards:	227
Application deadline:	March 1

Contact:
Hawaii Community Foundation
900 Fort Street Mall, Suite 1300
Honolulu, HI 96813
Phone: 808-566-5570
Fax: 808-521-6286
Web: www.hcf-hawaii.org

Kawasaki-McGaha Scholarship Fund

Type of award: Scholarship.
Intended use: For full-time undergraduate or graduate study at accredited postsecondary institution in United States.
Eligibility: Applicant must be permanent resident residing in Hawaii.
Basis for selection: Major/career interest in computer/information sciences or international studies. Applicant must demonstrate financial need, high academic achievement and depth of character.
Application requirements: Recommendations, essay, transcript.
Additional information: Preference given to Hawaii Pacific University students. Applicants must have permanent address in Hawaii. Applicants who take up mainland residency must have relatives living in Hawaii. Other former Hawaii residents considered on case by case basis. Notifications mailed between April and July.

Amount of award:	$1,000
Number of awards:	6
Application deadline:	March 1

Contact:
Hawaii Community Foundation
900 Fort Street Mall
Suite 1300
Honolulu, HI 96813
Phone: 808-566-5570
Fax: 808-521-6286
Web: www.hcf-hawaii.org

Koloa Scholarship

Type of award: Scholarship, renewable.
Intended use: For full-time undergraduate or graduate study at accredited vocational, 2-year or 4-year institution in United States.
Eligibility: Applicant must be U.S. citizen or permanent resident residing in Hawaii.
Basis for selection: Applicant must demonstrate depth of character.
Application requirements: Recommendations, essay, transcript. Essay must contain personal understanding of the meaning of "aloha."
Additional information: Applicant must be resident of one of the following Kauai areas in Hawaii: Koloa, including Omao and Poipu (96756), Lawai (96765) or Kalaheo (96741). Amount of award varies.

Amount of award:	$1,000
Number of awards:	5
Application deadline:	March 1

Contact:
Hawaii Community Foundation
900 Fort Street Mall
Suite 1300
Honolulu, HI 96813
Phone: 808-566-5570
Fax: 808-521-6286
Web: www.hcf-hawaii.org

Laura N. Dowsett Fund

Type of award: Scholarship.
Intended use: For full-time sophomore, junior, senior or graduate study at accredited 2-year or 4-year institution in United States.

Eligibility: Applicant must be U.S. citizen or permanent resident residing in Hawaii.
Basis for selection: Major/career interest in occupational therapy. Applicant must demonstrate financial need, high academic achievement and depth of character.
Application requirements: Recommendations, essay, transcript. Include at least one letter of recommendation should be from someone in the occupational therapy field.
Additional information: Applicants must have permanent address in Hawaii. Applicants who take up mainland residency must have relatives living in Hawaii. Other former Hawaii residents considered on a case by case basis. Notifications mailed in July.

Amount of award:	$750
Number of awards:	4
Application deadline:	March 1

Contact:
Hawaii Community Foundation
900 Fort Street Mall
Suite 1300
Honolulu, HI 96813
Phone: 808-566-5570
Fax: 808-521-6286
Web: www.hcf-hawaii.org

Margaret Jones Memorial Nursing Scholarship

Type of award: Scholarship, renewable.
Intended use: For full-time junior, senior or graduate study at accredited 4-year or graduate institution in United States.
Eligibility: Applicant must be U.S. citizen or permanent resident residing in Hawaii.
Basis for selection: Major/career interest in nursing. Applicant must demonstrate financial need, high academic achievement and depth of character.
Application requirements: Recommendations, essay, transcript.
Additional information: Applicants must be enrolled in BSN, MSN, or doctoral nursing program in Hawaii. Preference may be given to members of Hawaii Nurses Association. Minimum 3.0 GPA. Award amount varies. Applicants must have permanent address in Hawaii. Applicants who take up mainland residency must have relatives living in Hawaii. Other former Hawaii residents considered on a case by case basis. Notifications mailed between April and July.

Amount of award:	$500
Number of awards:	20
Application deadline:	March 1

Contact:
Hawaii Community Foundation
900 Fort Street Mall, Suite 1300
Honolulu, HI 96813
Phone: 808-566-5570
Fax: 808-521-6286
Web: www.hcf-hawaii.org

Marion MacCarrell Scott Scholarship

Type of award: Scholarship, renewable.
Intended use: For full-time undergraduate or graduate study at accredited postsecondary institution in United States.
Designated institutions: Institutions on U.S. Mainland.
Eligibility: Applicant must be U.S. citizen or permanent resident residing in Hawaii.

Basis for selection: Major/career interest in international relations; history; economics; sociology; political science/government; anthropology; geography; law; psychology or philosophy. Applicant must demonstrate financial need, high academic achievement, depth of character, leadership, seriousness of purpose and service orientation.

Application requirements: Recommendations, essay, transcript.

Additional information: Must be public high school graduate and pursue studies in fields listed on U.S. Mainland. Essay must demonstrate commitment to international understanding and world peace. Award amount varies. Minimum GPA 2.8. Applicants must have permanent address in Hawaii. Applicants who take up mainland residency must have relatives living in Hawaii. Other former Hawaii residents considered on case by case basis. Notifications mailed between April and July.

Amount of award:	$1,250
Number of awards:	212
Application deadline:	March 1

Contact:
Hawaii Community Foundation
900 Fort Street Mall
Suite 1300
Honolulu, HI 96813
Phone: 808-566-5570
Fax: 808-521-6286
Web: www.hcf-hawaii.org

Mildred Towle Trust Fund Scholarship

Type of award: Scholarship, renewable.

Intended use: For full-time undergraduate or graduate study at accredited postsecondary institution in or outside United States.

Eligibility: Applicant must be U.S. citizen, international student or foreign student with type F or J visa studying in Hawaii. Applicant must be residing in Hawaii.

Basis for selection: Major/career interest in social/behavioral sciences or international relations. Applicant must demonstrate financial need, high academic achievement and depth of character.

Application requirements: Recommendations, essay, transcript.

Additional information: Award for Hawaii residents studying either in foreign country or at Boston University. African-Americans or foreign students studying in Hawaii also eligible. Award amount varies. Minimum GPA 2.7.

Amount of award:	$650
Number of awards:	48
Application deadline:	March 1

Contact:
Hawaii Community Foundation
900 Fort Street Mall, Suite 1300
Honolulu, HI 96813
Phone: 808-566-5570
Fax: 808-521-6286
Web: www.hcf-hawaii.org

Scholarships for Specific Areas

Type of award: Scholarship, renewable.

Intended use: For undergraduate study at 2-year or 4-year institution in United States.

Eligibility: Applicant must be U.S. citizen or permanent resident residing in Hawaii.

Basis for selection: Applicant must demonstrate depth of character, leadership and seriousness of purpose.

Application requirements: Recommendations, essay, transcript.

Additional information: These scholarships are designed for candidates living in specific areas of Hawaii. The scholarship program is made up of many different scholarship funds established by generous individuals, firms or organizations wanting to assist Hawaii residents in obtaining a college education. The following scholarships are available: Fletcher & Fritza Hoffman Education Fund, Ka'a'awa Community Fund, Nick Van Pernis Scholarship Fund, Tommy Lee Memorial Scholarship. Some of the funds are part of Hawaii Community Foundation and some are private foundations that have asked Hawaii Community Foundation to adminster their scholarships. Students apply to the program and, if eligible, can be awarded from one or more of these different funds. Applicants must have permanent address in Hawaii. Applicants who take up mainland residency must have relatives living in Hawaii. Other former Hawaii residents considered on a case by case basis. Write or visit Website for application.

Amount of award:	$500-$1,500
Number of awards:	14
Application deadline:	March 1

Contact:
Hawaii Community Foundation, Scholarships
900 Fort Street
Suite 1300
Honolulu, HI 96813
Phone: 808-566-5570
Fax: 808-521-6286
Web: www.hcf-hawaii.org

Scholarships for Specific Majors

Type of award: Scholarship, renewable.

Intended use: For undergraduate study at 2-year, 4-year or graduate institution.

Eligibility: Applicant must be U.S. citizen or permanent resident residing in Hawaii.

Basis for selection: Major/career interest in arts, general; architecture; education; humanities/liberal arts; hawaiian studies; business; journalism; communications; computer/information sciences or physical sciences. Applicant must demonstrate financial need, high academic achievement, depth of character, leadership and seriousness of purpose.

Application requirements: Recommendations, essay, transcript.

Additional information: The Scholarship program is made up of many scholarship funds established by generious individuals, firms or organizations wanting to assist Hawaii residents in obtaining a college education. The following scholarships are available: Community Scholarship Fund, Oscar and Rosetta Fish Fund, and Edward Payson and Bernice Pi'ilani Irwin Scholarship Trust Fund, in addition to others listed elsewhere in this book. Some of the funds are part of Hawaii Community Foundation and some are private foundations that have asked Hawaii Community Foundation to administer their scholarships. Students apply to the program and, if eligible, can be awarded from one or more of these different funds. Applicants must have permanent address in Hawaii. Applicants who take up mainland residency must have relatives living in Hawaii. Other former Hawaii residents considered on a case by case basis. Write or visit Website for application.

Amount of award:	$600-$1,500
Number of awards:	235
Application deadline:	March 1

Contact:
Hawaii Community Foundation, Scholarships
900 Fort Street
Suite 1300
Honolulu, HI 96813
Phone: 808-566-5570
Fax: 808-521-6286
Web: www.hcf-hawaii.org

Scholarships with Special Criteria

Type of award: Scholarship, renewable.
Intended use: For full-time undergraduate or graduate study at accredited 2-year or 4-year institution in United States.
Eligibility: Applicant must be U.S. citizen or permanent resident residing in Hawaii.
Basis for selection: Applicant must demonstrate depth of character, leadership and seriousness of purpose.
Application requirements: Recommendations, essay.
Additional information: The Scholarship program is made up of many different scholarship funds established by generous individiauls, firms or organizations wanting to assist Hawaii residents in obtaining a college education. The following scholarships are available with special criteria: Ambassador Minerva Jean Falcon Hawaii Scholarship, Friends of Hawaii Public Housing Scholarship, and Victoria S. & Bradlley L. Geist Foundation, in addition to others listed elsewhere in this book. Some of the funds are part of Hawaii Community Foundation and some are private foundations that have asked Hawaii Community Foundation to administer their scholarships. Students apply to the program and, if eligible, can be awarded from one or more of these different funds. Applicants must have permanent address in Hawaii. Applicants who take up mainland residency must have relatives living in Hawaii. Other former Hawaii residents considered on a case by case basis. Write or visit Website for application.

Amount of award:	$600-$2,400
Number of awards:	60
Application deadline:	March 1

Contact:
Hawaii Community Foundation, Scholarships
900 Fort Street Mall
Suite 1300
Honolulu, HI 96813
Phone: 808-566-5570
Fax: 808-521-6286
Web: www.hcf-hawaii.org

Thz Fo Farm Fund

Type of award: Scholarship.
Intended use: For full-time undergraduate or graduate study at accredited postsecondary institution in United States.
Eligibility: Applicant must be Chinese. Applicant must be U.S. citizen or permanent resident residing in Hawaii.
Basis for selection: Major/career interest in gerontology. Applicant must demonstrate financial need, high academic achievement and depth of character.
Application requirements: Recommendations, essay, transcript.
Additional information: Applicants must have permanent address in Hawaii. Applicants who take up mainland residency must have relatives living in Hawaii. Other former Hawaii residents considered on case by case basis. Notifications mailed out between April and July.

Amount of award:	$1,000
Number of awards:	6
Application deadline:	March 1

Contact:
Hawaii Community Foundation
900 Fort Street Mall
Suite 1300
Honolulu, HI 96813
Phone: 808-566-5570
Fax: 808-521-6286
Web: www.hcf-hawaii.org

Hawaii Community Foundation, Scholarships

General Pool Scholarships

Type of award: Scholarship, renewable.
Intended use: For full-time undergraduate or graduate study at accredited 2-year, 4-year or graduate institution in United States.
Eligibility: Applicant must be U.S. citizen or permanent resident residing in Hawaii.
Basis for selection: Applicant must demonstrate financial need, high academic achievement and depth of character.
Application requirements: Recommendations, essay.
Additional information: Foundation pulls eligible students from the overall pool of applicants. Applicants will hear from these particular scholarships only if awarded. The scholarship program is made up of many different scholarship funds established by generous individuals, firms or organizations wanting to assist Hawaii residents in obtaining a college education. Some of the funds are part of Hawaii Community Foundation and some are private foundations that have asked Hawaii Community Foundation to administer their scholarships. Students apply to the program and, if eligible, can be awarded from one or more of these different funds. Applicants must generally have minimum 2.7 GPA.

Amount of award:	$500-$1,250
Number of awards:	40
Application deadline:	March 1

Contact:
Hawaii Community Foundation, Scholarships
900 Fort Street Mall
Suite 1300
Honolulu, HI 96813
Phone: 808-566-5570
Fax: 808-521-6286
Web: www.hcf-hawaii.org

Walter H. Kupau Memorial Fund

Type of award: Scholarship, renewable.
Intended use: For full-time undergraduate study at 2-year, 4-year or graduate institution.
Eligibility: Applicant or parent must be member/participant of Hawaii Carpenter's Union Local 745. Applicant must be U.S. citizen or permanent resident residing in Hawaii.
Basis for selection: Applicant must demonstrate financial need, high academic achievement, depth of character, leadership and seriousness of purpose.
Application requirements: Recommendations, essay, transcript.
Additional information: Scholarship open to descendants of Union Local 745 members, with preference given to descendants of retired members. Applicants must have permanent address in Hawaii. Applicants who take up mainland

residency must have relatives living in Hawaii. Other former Hawaii residents considered on a case by case basis. Notifications mailed between April and July.

Application deadline: March 1
Contact:
Hawaii Community Foundation, Scholarships
900 Fort Street Mall
Suite 1300
Honolulu, HI 96813
Phone: 808-566-5570
Fax: 808-521-6286
Web: www.hcf-hawaii.org

Hawaii Electric Industries Charitable Foundation

HEI Scholarship

Type of award: Scholarship, renewable.
Intended use: For undergraduate study at 4-year institution.
Eligibility: Applicant or parent must be employed by Hawaii Electric Industries, Inc.
Additional information: For further information or an application, contact Hawaii Electric Industries Charitable Foundation directly.
Amount of award: $1,200

Hawaii Postsecondary Education Commission

Hawaii Student Incentive Grant

Type of award: Scholarship, renewable.
Intended use: For undergraduate or graduate study at accredited postsecondary institution. Designated institutions: Participating institutions in the Hawaii system.
Eligibility: Applicant must be U.S. citizen residing in Hawaii.
Basis for selection: Applicant must demonstrate financial need.
Application requirements: Applicant must be eligible for a Pell grant.
Additional information: Deadlines vary by campus. Contact school's financial aid office. Maximum award determined annually by federal government.
Number of awards: 600
Number of applicants: 600
Application deadline: March 1, October 1
Notification begins: July 1, November 1
Contact:
Financial Aid Office of University of Hawaii campus
Phone: 808-956-8213
Fax: 808-956-5156
Web: www.hawaii.edu

Hawaii Tuition Waiver

Type of award: Scholarship, renewable.
Intended use: For undergraduate or graduate study at accredited postsecondary institution. Designated institutions: University of Hawaii campuses.

Eligibility: Applicant must be U.S. citizen or permanent resident residing in Hawaii.
Basis for selection: Applicant must demonstrate financial need and high academic achievement.
Additional information: Tuition waver. Applicant may demonstrate either financial need or high academic achievement. Deadline varies by campus.
Amount of award: Full tuition
Number of awards: 7,500
Total amount awarded: $10,000,000
Contact:
Contact financial aid office of University of Hawaii campus.
Phone: 808-956-8213
Fax: 808-956-5156
Web: www.hawaii.edu

Healthcare Convention & Ehxibitors Association

Return on Investment Research Grant Program

Type of award: Research grant.
Intended use: For undergraduate or graduate study at 2-year or 4-year institution.
Basis for selection: Major/career interest in marketing; health-related professions or health services administration.
Application requirements: Recommendations, transcript, research proposal.
Additional information: Grant to fund research of quantitative, or possibly qualitative, measure of healthcare exhibit marketing's effectiveness. Recipients may also receive credit hours through their college or university. Eligibility also determined by topic the candidate proposes to study. Visit Website for more information and to download application form.
Amount of award: $2,000
Application deadline: April 15
Contact:
Charlotte Arnemann, HCEA Communications Specialist
Phone: 404-252-3663
Fax: 404-252-0774
Web: www.hcea.org

Helicopter Association International

Helicopter Mechanic Technician Scholarship

Type of award: Scholarship.
Intended use: For non-degree study. Designated institutions: U.S. helicopter manufacturers or engine manufacturers.
Basis for selection: Major/career interest in aviation repair. Applicant must demonstrate high academic achievement.
Application requirements: Recommendations, nomination by FAA-approved Airframe and Powerplant (A&P) school.
Additional information: For students who wish to study helicopter maintenance who within next year will graduate from

FAA-approved Airframe and Powerplant (A&P) school, or recent graduates of same. Award includes free tuition.

Amount of award: $500-$1,500
Number of awards: 4
Number of applicants: 50
Application deadline: October 1
Notification begins: December 1
Total amount awarded: $3,750
Contact:
Helicopter Association International
1635 Prince Street
Alexandria, VA 22314-2818
Phone: 703-683-4646
Web: www.rotor.com

Helzberg Diamonds

Helzberg Diamonds Scholarship

Type of award: Scholarship, renewable.
Intended use: For undergraduate study at accredited vocational, 2-year or 4-year institution.
Eligibility: Applicant or parent must be employed by Helzberg Diamonds.
Basis for selection: Applicant must demonstrate financial need.
Additional information: For further information or an application, contact Helzberg Diamonds directly.
Amount of award: $500-$2,500

Henkel Corporation

Henkel Corporation Scholarship

Type of award: Scholarship, renewable.
Intended use: For undergraduate study at accredited vocational, 2-year or 4-year institution.
Eligibility: Applicant or parent must be employed by Henkel Corporation.
Basis for selection: Applicant must demonstrate financial need.
Additional information: For further information or an application, contact Henkel Corporation directly.
Amount of award: $500-$2,000

Herman Miller Inc.

Scholarship Fund for Children of Herman Miller Employees

Type of award: Scholarship, renewable.
Intended use: For undergraduate study at vocational, 2 year or 4-year institution.
Eligibility: Applicant or parent must be employed by Herman Miller Inc. Applicant must be high school senior.
Additional information: For further information or an application, contact Herman Miller Incorporated directly.
Amount of award: $2,500

Herschel C. Price Educational Foundation

Herschel C. Price Educational Scholarship

Type of award: Scholarship, renewable.
Intended use: For undergraduate or graduate study in United States. Designated institutions: Any West Virginia College.
Eligibility: Applicant must be U.S. citizen residing in West Virginia.
Basis for selection: Applicant must demonstrate financial need and high academic achievement.
Application requirements: Interview, transcript.
Additional information: Achievement in community activities also considered. Preference shown to undergraduates. A limited number of applications are released.

Amount of award: $250-$2,500
Number of awards: 170
Number of applicants: 400
Application deadline: April 1, October 1
Notification begins: May 15, November 15
Total amount awarded: $155,000
Contact:
Herschel C. Price Educational Foundation
P.O. Box 412
Huntington, WV 25708-0412
Phone: 304-529-3852

Hershey Foods Corporation

Hershey Foods Corporation Scholars Program

Type of award: Scholarship, renewable.
Intended use: For undergraduate study at accredited 4-year institution.
Eligibility: Applicant or parent must be employed by Hershey Foods Corporation.
Basis for selection: Applicant must demonstrate financial need.
Additional information: For further information or an application, contact Hershey Foods Corporation directly.
Amount of award: $500-$3,000

Hexcel Corporation

Hexcel Scholarship Program

Type of award: Scholarship, renewable.
Intended use: For undergraduate study at vocational, 2-year or 4-year institution.
Eligibility: Applicant or parent must be employed by Hexcel Corporation. Applicant must be high school senior.
Additional information: For further information or an application, contact Hexcel Corporation directly.
Amount of award: $1,000-$1,500

Scholarships

249

HickoryTech Corporation Foundation

Hickory Tech Employees' Daughter & Son Scholarship Program

Type of award: Scholarship, renewable.
Intended use: For undergraduate study at accredited postsecondary institution.
Eligibility: Applicant or parent must be employed by Hickory Tech Corporation. Applicant must be high school senior.
Additional information: For further information or an application, contact HickoryTech Corporation Foundation directly.

Amount of award: $1,000

Highway Ag Services

Highway Ag Services Scholarship

Type of award: Scholarship.
Intended use: For freshman study at accredited vocational, 2-year or 4-year institution.
Eligibility: Applicant or parent must be employed by Highway Ag Services. Applicant must be high school senior.
Additional information: Must be child of employee of HAS. For further information and an application, contact Highway Ag Services directly.

Amount of award: $500

Hilgenfeld Foundation for Mortuary Education c/o ABFSE

Mortuary Education Grant

Type of award: Scholarship.
Intended use: For undergraduate, graduate or non-degree study at postsecondary institution.
Eligibility: Applicant must be U.S. citizen.
Basis for selection: Major/career interest in mortuary science. Applicant must demonstrate financial need, high academic achievement, depth of character, leadership and seriousness of purpose.
Application requirements: Transcript and application form required.
Additional information: For individuals pursuing careers in Funeral Service Industry, including licensure and higher degrees. Applicants must be enrolled in funeral service program.

Amount of award: $250-$500
Number of awards: 60
Number of applicants: 120
Total amount awarded: $25,000
Contact:
American Board of Funeral Service Education
38 Florida Avenue
Portland, ME 04103

Hispanic Heritage Awards Foundation

Hispanic Heritage Youth Awards

Type of award: Scholarship.
Intended use: For undergraduate study at postsecondary institution.
Eligibility: Applicant must be Mexican American, Hispanic American or Puerto Rican. Applicant must be enrolled in high school. Applicant must be U.S. citizen or permanent resident.
Basis for selection: Applicant must demonstrate high academic achievement, depth of character, leadership and service orientation.
Application requirements: Recommendations, transcript, proof of eligibility.
Additional information: Contact corporate sponsor listed on internet site for application or download directly from site. Also available from high school guidance office. Students evaluated between December 15 and March 15 by sponsors and nominated in following areas: Academic Achievement, Leadership, Community Service, Science and Technology, the Arts, Literature/Journalism, and Sports. In June seven national winners will be selected from the regional winners and will attend an awards ceremony at the Kennedy Center for Performing Arts with parent or guardian in Washington, D.C. in September. Awards also include personal computer and $1,000 donation to nonprofit community organization of awardee's choice.

Amount of award: $1,000
Number of awards: 7
Total amount awarded: $7,000
Contact:
Phone: 202-861-9797
Web: www.hispanicawards.org/app_form.htm

Hispanic Scholarship Fund

Community College Transfer Scholarship

Type of award: Scholarship.
Intended use: For full-time undergraduate study at accredited 4-year institution in United States.
Eligibility: Applicant must be Mexican American, Hispanic American or Puerto Rican. One parent must be fully Hispanic, or both parents half Hispanic. Applicant must be U.S. citizen or permanent resident.
Basis for selection: Applicant must demonstrate financial need and high academic achievement.
Application requirements: Recommendations, essay, transcript, proof of eligibility. Completed and signed application, letter of recommendation from school administrator or teacher, Student Aid Report (if available) and copy of permanent resident card (if applicable).
Additional information: Designed to assist Latinos making transition from community college to four-year accredited postsecondary institutions. Number of awards granted varies. Visit Website for more information and for tips on how to apply.

Amount of award: $1,500-$2,500

Contact:
Community College Transfer Program
Hispanic Scholarship Fund
One Sansome Street, Suite 1000
San Francisco, CA 94104
Phone: 877-473-4636
Fax: 415-445-9942
Web: www.hsf.net

General Program

Type of award: Scholarship.
Intended use: For full-time sophomore, junior, senior or graduate study at postsecondary institution in United States. Designated institutions: Colleges in United States or Puerto Rico.
Eligibility: Applicant must be Mexican American, Hispanic American or Puerto Rican. Applicant must be U.S. citizen or permanent resident.
Basis for selection: Applicant must demonstrate financial need, high academic achievement, seriousness of purpose and service orientation.
Application requirements: Recommendations, essay, transcript, proof of eligibility. Minimum 2.70 GPA.
Additional information: Freshmen who have earned at least 15 undergraduate credits are eligible. Visit Website or contact via e-mail (info@hsf.net) for more information and tips on how to apply.

    Amount of award: $1,000-$3,000
    Application deadline: October 15
    Total amount awarded: $9,000,000
Contact:
General Selection Committee
Hispanic Scholarship Fund
One Sansome Street, Suite 1000
San Francisco, CA 94104
Phone: 888-473-4636
Fax: 415-445-9942
Web: www.hsf.net

National High School Program

Type of award: Scholarship.
Intended use: For full-time freshman study at accredited postsecondary institution in United States. Designated institutions: Accredited postsecondary institution in United states or Puerto Rico.
Eligibility: Applicant must be Mexican American, Hispanic American or Puerto Rican. Must be of at least half Hispanic background with one parent fully Hispanic, or both parents half Hispanic. Applicant must be high school senior. Applicant must be U.S. citizen or permanent resident.
Basis for selection: Applicant must demonstrate financial need, high academic achievement and seriousness of purpose.
Application requirements: Recommendations, essay, transcript, proof of eligibility. Completed application, ACT/SAT scores, Student Aid Report (if available), copy of permanent resident card (if applicable). Minimum 3.0 GPA.
Additional information: Designed to assist Latinos making transition from high school to four-year insitution. Seniors should have minimum GPA of 3.0 and have been accepted to attend college in fall. Number of awards granted and application deadlines varies. Send business-size SASE with application request or download from Website.

    Amount of award: $1,000-$3,000

Contact:
Hispanic Scholarship Fund High School Program
One Sansome Street
Suite 1000
San Francisco, CA 94104
Phone: 877-473-4636
Fax: 414-445-9942
Web: www.hsf.net

Hitachi America, Ltd.

USA Scholarship

Type of award: Scholarship.
Intended use: For undergraduate study at accredited 2-year or 4-year institution.
Eligibility: Applicant or parent must be employed by Hitachi America, Ltd.
Basis for selection: Applicant must demonstrate financial need.
Additional information: For further information or an application, contact Hitachi America, Ltd. directly.

    Amount of award: $500-$5,000

HMSHost-San Francisco International Airport

HMSHost Marriott Scholarship

Type of award: Scholarship.
Intended use: For undergraduate study at accredited vocational, 2-year or 4-year institution.
Eligibility: Applicant or parent must be employed by HMSHost-San Francisco International Airport. Applicant must be high school senior.
Additional information: For further information or application, contact them directly.

    Amount of award: $1,000
Contact:
Host Marriott-San Francisco International Airport

The Hoover Carden Scholarship Fund

The Hoover Carden Scholarship

Type of award: Scholarship, renewable.
Intended use: For senior study.
Eligibility: Applicant must be high school senior. Applicant must be U.S. citizen or permanent resident residing in Texas.
Basis for selection: Major/career interest in animal sciences or agriculture. Applicant must demonstrate leadership and service orientation.
Application requirements: Interview.
Additional information: Applicant must have earned a high school diploma with a minimum 2.70 GPA. Priority consideration given to students of Prairie View A&M

University and applicants with former 4-H membership experience.

Amount of award:	$1,500
Application deadline:	February 28

Contact:
The Hoover Carden Scholarship Fund
P.O. Box 2425
Prairie View, TX 77446
Phone: 936-857-3430

Hopi Tribe Grants and Scholarship Program

Hopi BIA Higher Education Grant

Type of award: Scholarship, renewable.
Intended use: For undergraduate or graduate study at accredited 2-year, 4-year or graduate institution.
Eligibility: Applicant must be American Indian. Must be an enrolled member of the Hopi Tribe.
Basis for selection: Applicant must demonstrate financial need.
Additional information: Entering freshmen must have 2.0 GPA for high school course work or minimum composite score of 45% on GED Exam. Continuing students must have 2.0 GPA for all graduate course work.

Amount of award:	$2,500
Application deadline:	July 31, November 30

Contact:
Hopi Tribe Grants and Scholarship Program
P.O. Box 123
Kykotsmovi, AZ 86039
Phone: 800-762-9630

Hopi Scholarship

Type of award: Scholarship, renewable.
Intended use: For full-time undergraduate or graduate study at accredited 4-year or graduate institution.
Eligibility: Applicant must be American Indian. Must be an enrolled member of the Hopi Tribe.
Basis for selection: Applicant must demonstrate high academic achievement.
Additional information: Entering freshmen must be in upper 10% of graduating class or have minimum of 21 on the ACT or 930 on the SAT. Undergraduate students must have and maintain a 3.0 CGPA, and graduate, postgraduate, and professional students must have a 3.25 CGPA for all graduate course work. $1,000 award given each semester. Number of awards varies.

Amount of award:	$1,000
Number of awards:	3
Application deadline:	July 31, November 30

Contact:
Hopi Tribe Grants and Scholarship Program
P.O. Box 123
Kykotsmovi, AZ 86039
Phone: 800-762-9630

Hopi Supplemental Grant

Type of award: Scholarship, renewable.
Intended use: For undergraduate or graduate study at accredited 2-year, 4-year or graduate institution.

Eligibility: Applicant must be American Indian. Must be an enrolled member of the Hopi Tribe.
Basis for selection: Applicant must demonstrate financial need.
Additional information: Entering freshmen must have 2.0 GPA for high school course work or minimum composite score of 45 percent on the GED Exam. Continuing students must have 2.0 GPA for all college work. $1,500 is awarded each semester.

Amount of award:	$1,500
Application deadline:	July 31, November 30

Contact:
Hopi Tribe Grants and Scholarship Program
P.O. Box 123
Kykotsmovi, AZ 86039
Phone: 800-762-9630

Hopi Tribal Priority Scholarship

Type of award: Scholarship, renewable.
Intended use: For full-time junior, senior or graduate study at accredited 4-year or graduate institution.
Eligibility: Applicant must be American Indian. Must be an enrolled member of the Hopi Tribe.
Basis for selection: Major/career interest in law; natural resources/conservation; education; business; engineering; health-related professions or medical specialties/research. Applicant must demonstrate financial need, high academic achievement, depth of character, leadership and seriousness of purpose.
Application requirements: Recommendations, transcript.
Additional information: Applicant must show certification of Indian blood. Award is based on amount of college cost. Applicant must have college submit a "financial needs analysis" to determine amount of award. Room and board, books and tuition are covered until graduation.

Amount of award:	Full tuition
Number of awards:	3
Application deadline:	July 31

Contact:
Hopi Tribe Grants and Scholarship Program
P.O. Box 123
Kykotsmovi, AZ 86039
Phone: 800-762-9630

Horace Mann Companies

Horace Mann Scholarship Program

Type of award: Scholarship, renewable.
Intended use: For full-time undergraduate study at accredited 2-year or 4-year institution.
Eligibility: Applicant or parent must be employed by U.S. public school district or public college/university. Applicant must be high school senior.
Basis for selection: Applicant must demonstrate high academic achievement, depth of character, leadership and service orientation.
Application requirements: Recommendations, essay, transcript, proof of eligibility. List of activities and honors.
Additional information: Student must have minimum 3.0 GPA, and score at least a 23 on the ACT or 1100 on the SAT. Parent must be employed by U.S. public school district or public college/university. Major award of $20,000 given over four years; ten $4,000 awards given over four years; 20 $1,000 one-time awards. Application available online.

Amount of award:	$1,000-$20,000
Number of awards:	16
Number of applicants:	10,000
Application deadline:	February 12
Notification begins:	March 31
Total amount awarded:	$50,000

Contact:
Horace Mann Scholarship Program
P.O. Box 20490
Springfield, IL 62708
Web: www.horacemann.com

Horizons Foundation

Horizons Foundation Scholarship

Type of award: Scholarship, renewable.
Intended use: For junior, senior or graduate study at 4-year or graduate institution in United States.
Eligibility: Applicant must be female. Applicant must be U.S. citizen.
Basis for selection: Must aim to to work in national defense or national security. Major/career interest in military science; computer/information sciences; physics; mathematics; business; law; international relations; political science/government; economics or engineering. Applicant must demonstrate financial need and high academic achievement.
Application requirements: Recommendations, essay, transcript. Application.
Additional information: For women employed or planning career in defense or national security areas. Minimum GPA 3.25. Requests for information must include a SASE or will not be answered. Information can also be obtained at Website.

Amount of award:	$500-$750
Number of awards:	4
Number of applicants:	60
Application deadline:	July 1, November 1
Total amount awarded:	$4,000

Contact:
Horizons Foundation
Women In Defense - c/o NDIA
2111 Wilson Blvd., Suite 400
Arlington, VA 22201-3061
Phone: 703-247-2552
Fax: 703-522-1820
Web: http://wid.ndia.org

Horticulture Research Institute

Horticulture Research Institute Timothy Bigelow Scholarship

Type of award: Scholarship.
Intended use: For full-time undergraduate or graduate study at accredited 2-year, 4-year or graduate institution.
Eligibility: Applicant must be residing in Connecticut, Massachusetts, Maine, New Hampshire, Rhode Island or Vermont.

Basis for selection: Major/career interest in landscape architecture or horticulture. Applicant must demonstrate financial need, high academic achievement, depth of character and seriousness of purpose.
Application requirements: Recommendations, transcript. Applicant must submit a one-page resume of background, employment history, and education; also two-page cover-letter.
Additional information: Must have at least 2.25 GPA for undergraduates and a 3.0 GPA for graduate students. Must be enrolled in accredited landscape/horticulture program. Applicant must have senior standing in two-year program, junior standing in four-year program, or graduate standing.

Amount of award:	$2,500
Number of awards:	3
Application deadline:	May 15
Notification begins:	June 1

Contact:
Director of Horticultural Research
Horticulture Research Institute
1250 I Street NW Suite 500
Washington, DC 20005-3922
Phone: 202-789-2900 ext. 3014
Fax: 202-789-1893
Web: www.anla.org

Household International (HFC)

Household Scholar Awards

Type of award: Scholarship.
Intended use: For full-time undergraduate study at accredited 2-year or 4-year institution.
Eligibility: Applicant or parent must be employed by Household International (HFC). Applicant must be high school senior.
Application requirements: Proof of eligibility.
Additional information: Household offers scholar awards and financial aid grants to college-bound children of Household employees. Contact employer for details.
Contact:
Household International Household Scholar Awards
2700 Sanders Road
Prospect Heights, IL 60070
Phone: 847-564-7968

Houston Livestock Show and Rodeo

Go Texan Scholarships

Type of award: Scholarship.
Intended use: For undergraduate study at 2-year or 4-year institution in United States. Designated institutions: Texas public and private schools.
Eligibility: Applicant must be high school senior. Applicant must be U.S. citizen or permanent resident residing in Texas.
Basis for selection: Applicant must demonstrate financial need, high academic achievement, depth of character, leadership and service orientation.

Application requirements: Recommendations, essay, transcript, proof of eligibility. SAT/ACT scores.
Additional information: Visit internet site or contact sponsor or high school guidance counselor for application information and deadlines. Must be enrolled in Texas institution.

Amount of award:	$2,500-$10,000
Number of awards:	60
Total amount awarded:	$312,500

Contact:
Houston Livestock Show and Rodeo Office of Education Programs
Astrohall, East Wing
2000 South Loop West
Houston, TX 77054
Phone: 713-794-9544
Web: www.hlsr.com

Opportunity Scholarship

Type of award: Scholarship.
Intended use: For undergraduate study at accredited 2-year or 4-year institution. Designated institutions: Texas postsecondary institutions.
Eligibility: Applicant must be high school senior. Applicant must be U.S. citizen residing in Texas.
Basis for selection: Applicant must demonstrate financial need, high academic achievement, depth of character, leadership and service orientation.
Application requirements: Recommendations, essay, transcript, proof of eligibility. SAT/ACT scores, class standing, photograph.
Additional information: Scholarship evaluation based 50% on financial need, 30% on academics, and 15% on leadership and community involvement. Must reside in the greater Houston metropolitan area including Brazoria, Chambers, Fort Bend, Galveston, Harris, Liberty, Montgomery and Waller counties. Visit internet site or contact sponsor for application information and deadlines. Applications also available at Fiesta Mart locations and from high school guidance counselors. Must be enrolled in Texas institution. Must pass TAAS Exit Level exam at time of application.

Amount of award:	$10,000
Number of awards:	100
Total amount awarded:	$1,000,000

Contact:
Houston Livestock Show and Rodeo Office of Education Programs
Astrohall, East Wing
2000 South Loop West
Houston, TX 77054
Phone: 713-794-9544
Web: www.hlsr.com

Hubbard ISA LLC

Hubbard Farms/B.U.T.A. Scholarship

Type of award: Scholarship, renewable.
Intended use: For undergraduate study at accredited vocational, 2-year or 4-year institution.
Eligibility: Applicant or parent must be employed by Hubbard Farms Inc.

Basis for selection: Applicant must demonstrate financial need.
Additional information: For further information or an application, contact Hubbard Farms Inc. directly.

Amount of award:	$500-$1,500

Hugo Neu Corporation

Hugo Neu Corporation Employees Scholarship Plan

Type of award: Scholarship, renewable.
Intended use: For undergraduate study at accredited vocational, 2-year or 4-year institution.
Eligibility: Applicant or parent must be employed by Hugo Neu and Sons, Inc.
Basis for selection: Applicant must demonstrate financial need.
Additional information: For further information or an application, contact Hugo Neu Corporation directly.

Amount of award:	$500-$7,000

The Humana Foundation

Humana Foundation Scholarship Program

Type of award: Scholarship, renewable.
Intended use: For undergraduate study at accredited 2-year or 4-year institution in United States.
Eligibility: Applicant or parent must be employed by The Humana Foundation. Applicant must be no older than 25. Applicant must be residing in Puerto Rico.
Basis for selection: Applicant must demonstrate high academic achievement, leadership and service orientation.
Application requirements: Extracurricular activities are a plus.
Additional information: Parent must be employed as Humana Associate in the United States or Puerto Rico. Award renews for maximum three years. Visit Website for additional information.

Amount of award:	$1,250-$2,500
Number of awards:	75
Application deadline:	February 1
Notification begins:	April 1

Contact:
The Humana Foundation Attn: Scholarship Program
500 W. Main Street
Louisville, KY 40202
Phone: 502-580-1245 or 800-537-4180
Web: www.humanafoundation.org/scholarship.html

Scholarships

Hydrite Chemical Co.

Richard C. Honkamp Scholarship Award

Type of award: Scholarship.
Intended use: For undergraduate study at vocational, 2-year or 4-year institution.
Eligibility: Applicant or parent must be employed by Hydrite Chemical Co. Applicant must be high school senior.
Additional information: For further information or an application, contact Hydrite Chemical Company directly.
  Amount of award: $2,500

Ida C. Koran Trust

Ida C. Koran Student Aid Program

Type of award: Scholarship, renewable.
Intended use: For undergraduate study at accredited vocational, 2-year or 4-year institution.
Eligibility: Applicant or parent must be employed by Ecolab Inc.
Basis for selection: Applicant must demonstrate financial need.
Additional information: For further information and an application, contact Ida C. Koran directly.
  Amount of award: $2,000-$10,000

Idaho State Board of Education

Idaho Minority and "At-Risk" Student Scholarship

Type of award: Scholarship.
Intended use: For full-time undergraduate study. Designated institutions: Boise State University, Idaho State University, North Idaho College, Eastern Idaho Technical College, Lewis-Clark State College, University of Idaho, College of Southern Idaho, Albertson College.
Eligibility: Applicant must be physically challenged. Applicant must be Alaskan native, Asian American, African American, Mexican American, Hispanic American, Puerto Rican or American Indian. Applicant must be U.S. citizen residing in Idaho.
Application requirements: Must be a graduate of an Idaho high school.
Additional information: Must be talented student at risk of failing to realize ambitions due to cultural, economic, or physical circumstances. Migrant farm workers, migrant farm worker dependents, and first-generation college students given special consideration. Contact high school counselor or financial aid office of participating postsecondary institutions designated above for specific eligibility requirements and application.
  Amount of award: $2,750
  Number of awards: 42
  Total amount awarded: $108,000

Contact:
High school counselor or financial aid office
Phone: 208-334-2270

Idaho state Scholarship Catergory A

Type of award: Scholarship, renewable.
Intended use: For full-time undergraduate study at accredited vocational, 2-year or 4-year institution in United States. Designated institutions: Idaho public institutions.
Eligibility: Applicant must be high school senior. Applicant must be U.S. citizen residing in Idaho.
Basis for selection: Applicant must demonstrate high academic achievement.
Application requirements: Recommendations. Academic applicants must submit ACT scores and class rank. Professional-technical applicants must take the COMPASS test.
Additional information: Contact high school guidance counselor or Idaho State Board of Education for information and application materials. Must be in top ten percent of class. Twenty-five percent of scholarships given to vocational students.
  Amount of award: $2,750
  Number of awards: 22
  Number of applicants: 600
  Application deadline: December 31
  Total amount awarded: $301,700
Contact:
Idaho State Board of Education
P.O. Box 83720
Boise, ID 83720-0037

Leveraging Educational Assistance State Partnership Program (LEAP)

Type of award: Scholarship, renewable.
Intended use: For freshman, sophomore, junior, senior, master's or doctoral study at vocational, 2-year, 4-year or graduate institution. Designated institutions: Idaho public or private colleges and universities.
Eligibility: Applicant must be U.S. citizen or permanent resident residing in Idaho.
Basis for selection: Applicant must demonstrate financial need.
Application requirements: FAFSA.
Additional information: Formerly Idaho Student Incentive Grant. Institution makes recommendations to Idaho State Board of Education. Awards of up to $5,000 for full-time students. Contact financial aid office of Idaho public colleges and universities for materials or additional information.
  Amount of award: $5,000
  Number of awards: 1,578
  Total amount awarded: $644,543
Contact:
Financial aid offices at Idaho colleges

Idaho State Department of Education

Idaho Robert C. Byrd Honors Scholarship

Type of award: Scholarship, renewable.

Intended use: For full-time freshman study at 2-year or 4-year institution.
Eligibility: Applicant must be high school senior. Applicant must be U.S. citizen or permanent resident residing in Idaho.
Basis for selection: Applicant must demonstrate high academic achievement.
Application requirements: Recommendations, transcript, proof of eligibility.
Additional information: Application and information available through high school guidance office after February 15.

    Amount of award: $1,500
    Application deadline: April 20
Contact:
Idaho State Department of Education
P.O. Box 83720
Boise, ID 83720-0027
Phone: 208-332-6946

Ideal Electric Company

Ideal Electric Scholarship

Type of award: Scholarship, renewable.
Intended use: For freshman study at accredited vocational, 2-year or 4-year institution.
Eligibility: Applicant or parent must be employed by Ideal Electric Company.
Additional information: For further information or an application, contact Ideal Electric Company directly.

    Amount of award: $1,000

IEEE Computer Society

Lance Stafford Larson Student Scholarship

Type of award: Scholarship.
Intended use: For full-time undergraduate study at postsecondary institution.
Eligibility: Applicant or parent must be member/participant of IEEE Computer Society.
Basis for selection: Competition/talent/interest in research paper, based on technical content, writing skills and overall presentation considered. Major/career interest in computer/information sciences.
Application requirements: Essay, proof of eligibility.
Additional information: Applicant must be a student member of IEEE Computer Society.

    Application deadline: October 31
    Total amount awarded: $500
Contact:
IEEE Computer Society
1730 Massachusetts Ave., NW
Washington, DC 20036-1992
Web: www.computer.org

Richard E. Merwin Award

Type of award: Scholarship.
Intended use: For full-time junior, senior or graduate study at accredited 4-year or graduate institution.

Eligibility: Applicant or parent must be member/participant of IEEE Computer Society.
Basis for selection: Major/career interest in computer/information sciences; engineering, computer or science, general. Applicant must demonstrate seriousness of purpose.
Application requirements: Recommendations, proof of eligibility.
Additional information: Minimum GPA of 2.5 required. Applicant must participate in IEEE Computer Society's student branch chapter. Student winners for previous year are not eligible.

    Amount of award: $2,000-$5,000
    Application deadline: September 15
Contact:
IEEE Computer Society
1730 Massachusetts Ave., NW
Washington, DC 20036-1992
Web: www.computer.org

Upsilon Pi Epsilon Award

Type of award: Scholarship.
Intended use: For full-time undergraduate or graduate study.
Eligibility: Applicant or parent must be member/participant of IEEE Computer Society.
Basis for selection: Major/career interest in computer/information sciences. Applicant must demonstrate high academic achievement and seriousness of purpose.
Application requirements: Recommendations, transcript, proof of eligibility. Three letters of recommendation on organization letterhead required.
Additional information: Applicant must be member of IEEE Computer Society. Student winners of computer society's Richard Merwin or UPE/CS Award for previous year not eligible.

    Amount of award: $500
    Application deadline: October 31
Contact:
IEEE Computer Society
1730 Massachusetts Ave., NW
Washington, DC 20036-1992
Web: www.computer.org

IHOP Corporation

Richard K. Herzer Scholarship for the Study of Entrepreneurial Business

Type of award: Scholarship.
Intended use: For undergraduate or graduate study at vocational, 2-year, 4-year or graduate institution.
Eligibility: Applicant or parent must be employed by IHOP Corp. Applicant must be high school senior.
Additional information: For further information or an application, contact IHOP Corporation directly.

    Amount of award: $4,000

Illinois Student Assistance Commission

Illinois D.A. DeBolt Teacher Shortage Scholarship

Type of award: Scholarship, renewable.
Intended use: For sophomore, junior, senior or graduate study at accredited 2-year or 4-year institution. Designated institutions: ISAC-approved institutions in Illinois.
Eligibility: Applicant must be U.S. citizen or permanent resident residing in Illinois.
Basis for selection: Major/career interest in education or education, teacher. Applicant must demonstrate financial need and high academic achievement.
Application requirements: Submit FAFSA and Teacher Education Program Application.
Additional information: Must major in teacher shortage discipline. Recipients must agree to teach at approved Illinois institution in approved field for one year for each year of assistance received. Failure to complete requirement turns scholarship into loan. Non-U.S. citizen who is resident of Illinois may be eligible. Contact ISAC or visit Website for additional information.

Amount of award:	$5,000
Number of awards:	291
Number of applicants:	1,200
Application deadline:	May 1
Total amount awarded:	$1,373,878

Contact:
Illinois Student Assistance Commission
Client Relations
1755 Lake Cook Road
Deerfield, IL 60015
Phone: 800-899-ISAC
Web: www.isac-online.org

Illinois Grant Program for Dependents of Police/Fire/Correctional Officers

Type of award: Scholarship, renewable.
Intended use: For undergraduate study at 2-year, 4-year or graduate institution. Designated institutions: ISAC-approved institutions in Illinois.
Eligibility: Applicant must be U.S. citizen or permanent resident. Applicant's parent must have been killed or disabled in work-related accident as fire fighter, police officer or public safety officer.
Application requirements: Proof of eligibility.
Additional information: Grant for tuition and fees for spouse and children of Illinois policemen, firemen or corrections officers over 90 percent disabled or killed in line of duty. Award amount adjusted annually. Applicant need not be Illinois resident at time of enrollment. Beneficiaries may receive the equivalent of 8 semesters or 12 quarters of assistance. Contact ISAC or visit Website for additional information.

Amount of award:	Full tuition
Number of awards:	47
Total amount awarded:	$148,894

Contact:
Illinois Student Assistance Commission
Client Relations
1755 Lake Cook Road
Deerfield, IL 60015
Phone: 800-899-ISAC
Web: www.isac-online.org

Illinois Incentive for Access

Type of award: Scholarship.
Intended use: For freshman study at postsecondary institution. Designated institutions: ISAC-approved institutions.
Eligibility: Applicant must be high school senior. Applicant must be U.S. citizen or permanent resident residing in Illinois.
Basis for selection: Applicant must demonstrate financial need.
Application requirements: FAFSA.
Additional information: Applicant must have been determined by federal needs calculation to have no family resources. Must meet Monetary Award Program eligibility requirements. Non-U.S. citizen who is Illinois resident may be eligible. Contact ISAC or visit Website for additional information.

Amount of award:	$500
Number of awards:	17,749
Number of applicants:	45,000
Total amount awarded:	$7,054,550

Contact:
Illinois Student Assistance Commission
Client Relations
1755 Lake Cook Road
Deerfield, IL 60015
Phone: 800-899-ISAC
Web: www.isac-online.org

Illinois Merit Recognition Scholarship

Type of award: Scholarship.
Intended use: For freshman study at postsecondary institution. Designated institutions: ISAC-approved institutions in Illinois or United States Service academies.
Eligibility: Applicant must be high school senior. Applicant must be U.S. citizen or permanent resident residing in Illinois.
Basis for selection: Applicant must demonstrate high academic achievement.
Application requirements: Proof of eligibility.
Additional information: Must rank in top five percent of class by class rank or standardized test score. Contact high school guidance counselor to certify eligibility and request applications. Non-U.S. citizen who is resident of Illinois may be eligible. Contact ISAC or high school counselor or visit Website for additional information.

Amount of award:	$1,000
Number of awards:	3,845
Total amount awarded:	$3,792,334

Contact:
Illinois Student Assistance Commission
Client Relations
1755 Lake Cook Road
Deerfield, IL 60015
Phone: 800-899-ISAC
Web: www.isac-online.org

Illinois Minority Teachers Scholarship

Type of award: Scholarship, renewable.
Intended use: For full-time sophomore, junior or senior study at postsecondary institution. Designated institutions: ISAC-approved institutions in Illinois.
Eligibility: Applicant must be Alaskan native, Asian American, African American, Mexican American, Hispanic American, Puerto Rican or American Indian. Applicant must be U.S. citizen or permanent resident residing in Illinois.
Basis for selection: Major/career interest in education, teacher or education.
Application requirements: Proof of eligibility.
Additional information: Applicants must submit Teacher Education Scholarship Application. Recipients must maintain 2.5 GPA (4.0 scale). Recipients agree to teach at approved Illinois institution in approved field for one year for each year of grant assistance received. Failure to complete requirement turns scholarship into loan. Non-U.S. citizens who are residents of Illinois may be eligible. Contact ISAC or visit Website for additional information.

Amount of award:	$5,000
Number of awards:	442
Number of applicants:	1,200
Application deadline:	May 1
Total amount awarded:	$2,063,956

Contact:
Illinois Student Assistance Commission
Client Relations
1755 Lake Cook Road
Deerfield, IL 60015
Phone: 800-899-ISAC
Web: www.isac-online.org

Illinois Monetary Award

Type of award: Scholarship, renewable.
Intended use: For undergraduate study at 2-year or 4-year institution. Designated institutions: ISAC/MAP approved institutions in Illinois.
Eligibility: Applicant must be U.S. citizen or permanent resident residing in Illinois.
Basis for selection: Applicant must demonstrate financial need.
Application requirements: Must submit FAFSA. Must reapply every year.
Additional information: Non-U.S. citizens who are residents of Illinois may be eligible. Contact ISAC or visit Website for application, deadline and additional information.

Amount of award:	$300-$4,530
Number of awards:	136,697
Number of applicants:	400,000
Total amount awarded:	$328,095,977

Contact:
Illinois Student Assistance Commission
Client Relations
1755 Lake Cook Road
Deerfield, IL 60015
Phone: 800-899-ISAC
Web: www.isac-online.org

Illinois National Guard Grant

Type of award: Scholarship, renewable.
Intended use: For undergraduate or graduate study at 2-year or 4-year institution. Designated institutions: Illinois public institutions only.
Eligibility: Applicant must be residing in Illinois. Applicant must be in military service in the Reserves/National Guard. Must have served at least one year of active duty in Illinois National Guard or Naval Militia.
Application requirements: Proof of eligibility. Only enlisted personnel or officers up to rank of captain currently serving with Guard are eligible.
Additional information: Award amounts vary; covers tuition and some fees. Recipients may use awards for eight semesters or 12 quarters (or the equivalent). Applications available from Illinois Student Assistance Commission or National Guard Units. Contact ISAC, National Guard Units or visit Website for additional information.

Amount of award:	Full tuition
Number of awards:	2,427
Number of applicants:	2,800
Total amount awarded:	$4,046,830

Contact:
Illinois Student Assistance Commission
Client Relations
1755 Lake Cook Road
Deerfield, IL 60015
Phone: 800-899-ISAC
Web: www.isac-online.org

Illinois Robert C. Byrd Honors Scholarship

Type of award: Scholarship, renewable.
Intended use: For full-time undergraduate study at accredited postsecondary institution in United States.
Eligibility: Applicant must be U.S. citizen or permanent resident residing in Illinois.
Basis for selection: Applicant must demonstrate high academic achievement.
Additional information: Must rank in top five percent of United States high school graduates. Obtain application from ISAC or high school guidance counselor. Contact ISAC, high school guidance counselor or visit Website for additional information.

Amount of award:	$1,500
Number of awards:	1,095
Application deadline:	January 15
Total amount awarded:	$1,611,939

Contact:
Illinois Student Assistance Commission
Client Relations
1755 Lake Cook Road
Deerfiled, IL 60015
Phone: 800-899-ISAC
Web: www.isac-online.org

Illinois Student-to-Student Grant

Type of award: Scholarship, renewable.
Intended use: For undergraduate study at postsecondary institution. Designated institutions: Participating institutions in Illinois.
Eligibility: Applicant or parent must be employed by Illinois Tool Works Foundation. Applicant must be U.S. citizen or permanent resident residing in Illinois.
Basis for selection: Applicant must demonstrate financial need.
Application requirements: Must reapply if renewing.

Additional information: Contact ISAC, high school guidance counselor or visit Website for additional information.

Amount of award:	$1,000
Number of awards:	3,049
Number of applicants:	3,306
Total amount awarded:	$908,247

Contact:
Illinois Student Assistance Commission
Client Relations
1755 Lake Cook Road
Deerfield, IL 60015
Phone: 800-899-ISAC
Web: www.isac-online.org

Illinois Veteran Grant

Type of award: Scholarship, renewable.
Intended use: For undergraduate or graduate study at postsecondary institution. Designated institutions: Public institutions in Illinois.
Eligibility: Applicant must be U.S. citizen or permanent resident residing in Illinois. Applicant must be veteran.
Application requirements: Proof of eligibility.
Additional information: Contact field office of Illinois Department of Veterans Affairs, financial aid office of institution, or ISAC, or visit Website, for additional information.

Amount of award:	Full tuition
Number of awards:	12,574
Number of applicants:	15,000
Total amount awarded:	$18,792,083

Contact:
Illinois Student Assistance Commission
Client Relations
1755 Lake Cook Road
Deerfield, IL 60015
Phone: 800-899-ISAC
Web: www.isac-online.org

Illinois Tool Works Foundation

ITW Foundation Scholarship

Type of award: Scholarship, renewable.
Intended use: For undergraduate study at accredited vocational, 2-year or 4-year institution.
Eligibility: Applicant or parent must be employed by Illinois Tool Works Foundation.
Basis for selection: Applicant must demonstrate financial need.
Additional information: For further information or an application, contact Illinois Tool Works Foundation directly.

Amount of award:	$1,000-$2,500

Immune Deficiency Foundation

Novartis Scholarship Program

Type of award: Scholarship, renewable.
Intended use: For undergraduate study at accredited vocational, 2-year or 4-year institution.
Eligibility: Applicant must be U.S. citizen or permanent resident.
Basis for selection: Applicant must demonstrate financial need, high academic achievement, depth of character and leadership.
Application requirements: Documentation of diagnosis.
Additional information: Applicants must have documented diagnosis of a Primary Immune Deficiency disease.

Amount of award:	$500-$2,000
Application deadline:	March 31
Total amount awarded:	$25,000

Contact:
Immune Deficiency Foundation Scholarship
40 West Chesapeake Ave.
Suite 308
Towson, MD 21204
Phone: 410-321-6647 or 800-296-4433
Fax: 410-321-9165

Independent Colleges of Southern California

Edison International

Type of award: Scholarship.
Intended use: For full-time undergraduate study at accredited 4-year institution in United States. Designated institutions: California Lutheran University, Claremont McKenna College, Loyola Marymount University, Mount St. Mary's College, Occidental College, Scripps College, University of Redlands, Whittier College, Chapman University, Harvey Mudd College, Pepperdine University, Pitzer College, Pomona College, Univerity of La Verne, University of San Diego, Westmont College.
Eligibility: Applicant must be Alaskan native, Asian American, African American, Mexican American, Hispanic American, Puerto Rican or American Indian. Applicant must be high school senior. Applicant must be U.S. citizen or permanent resident residing in California.
Basis for selection: Applicant must demonstrate high academic achievement.
Application requirements: Recommendations, essay, transcript, proof of eligibility. SAT/ACT scores.
Additional information: Must be from underrepresented ethnic group and first generation of immediate family to attend college. Award distributed over four years. Applicant must be accepted at designated institution as incoming freshman and must live or attend school in area served by Southern California Edison. Visit Website to obtain application, write to sponsor address or obtain through institution.

Amount of award:	$20,000
Number of awards:	2
Total amount awarded:	$40,000

Contact:
Independent Colleges of Southern California
555 S. Flower Street
Los Angeles, CA 90071
Phone: 213-553-9380
Fax: 213-553-9346
Web: www.cal-colleges.org

Macerich Scholarship

Type of award: Scholarship, renewable.
Intended use: For full-time undergraduate study at accredited 4-year institution in United States. Designated institutions: California Lutheran University, Claremont McKenna College, Loyola Marymount University, Mount St. Mary's College, Occidental College, Scripps College, University of Redlands, Whittier College, Chapman University, Harvey Mudd College, Pepperdine University, Pitzer College, Pomona College, Univerity of La Verne, University of San Diego, Westmont College.
Eligibility: Applicant must be high school senior. Applicant must be residing in California.
Basis for selection: Applicant must demonstrate high academic achievement and service orientation.
Application requirements: Recommendations, essay, transcript, proof of eligibility. List of extra curricular activities along with FA release and completed application.
Additional information: Must attend designated high schools near one of three Macerich shopping centers: Lakewood Shopping Center, Cerritos Shopping Center, Stonewood Shopping Center. Award distributed over four years.

Amount of award:	$10,000
Number of awards:	3
Application deadline:	May 15
Total amount awarded:	$30,000

Contact:
Independent Colleges of Southern California
555 S. Flower Street, Suite 610
Los Angeles, CA 90071
Phone: 213-553-9380
Fax: 213-553-9346
Web: www.cal-colleges.org

Ralph M. Parsons Memorial Scholarship

Type of award: Scholarship.
Intended use: For full-time undergraduate study at accredited 4-year institution in United States. Designated institutions: California Lutheran University, Claremont McKenna College, Loyola Marymount University, Mount St. Mary's College, Occidental College, Scripps College, University of Redlands, Whittier College, Chapman University, Harvey Mudd College, Pepperdine University, Pitzer College, Pomona College, Univerity of La Verne, University of San Diego, Westmont College, The Claremont Graduate Univerity.
Eligibility: Applicant or parent must be employed by The Parsons Corporation.
Application requirements: Recommendations, essay, transcript, proof of eligibility. SAT/ACT scores.
Additional information: Open to high school seniors or currently enrolled students who are relatives of employees of The Parsons Corporation or its subsidiaries. Visit Website to obtain application, write to sponsor address or obtain through institution.

Application deadline:	April 1

Contact:
Independent Colleges of Southern California
555 S. Flower Street
Los Angeles, CA 90071
Phone: 213-553-9380
Web: www.cal-colleges.org

Indiana Student Assistance Commission

Indiana Higher Education Grant

Type of award: Scholarship, renewable.
Intended use: For full-time undergraduate study at 2-year or 4-year institution. Designated institutions: Eligible Indiana schools.
Eligibility: Applicant must be U.S. citizen or permanent resident residing in Indiana.
Basis for selection: Applicant must demonstrate financial need.
Application requirements: FAFSA.
Additional information: Renewal recipients must maintain satisfactory academic progress. Summer work-study program available to recipients.

Amount of award:	$200-$8,518
Number of awards:	36,595
Number of applicants:	150,000
Application deadline:	March 1
Notification begins:	July 1
Total amount awarded:	$91,707,429

Contact:
Indiana Student Assistance Commission
150 West Market Street, Suite 500
Indianapolis, IN 46204
Web: www.state.in.us/ssaci

Indiana Hoosier Scholar Program

Type of award: Scholarship.
Intended use: For full-time freshman study at accredited vocational, 2-year or 4-year institution. Designated institutions: Eligible Indiana postsecondary schools (list provided to applicants).
Eligibility: Applicant must be high school senior. Applicant must be U.S. citizen or permanent resident residing in Indiana.
Basis for selection: Applicant must demonstrate high academic achievement.
Application requirements: Proof of eligibility, nomination by high school guidance counselor. Nomination forms must be submitted by March 1.
Additional information: List of eligible Indiana colleges provided with application. Applicant must be in top 20 percent of high school class.

Amount of award:	$500
Number of awards:	787
Number of applicants:	787
Application deadline:	March 1
Notification begins:	April 15
Total amount awarded:	$393,500

Contact:
Contact high school guidance counselor for further information.
Web: www.state.in.us/ssaci

Indiana Minority Teacher Scholarship

Type of award: Scholarship, renewable.
Intended use: For full-time undergraduate or graduate study at accredited 4-year or graduate institution. Designated institutions: Indiana schools.
Eligibility: Applicant must be African American, Mexican American, Hispanic American or Puerto Rican. Applicant must be U.S. citizen or permanent resident residing in Indiana.
Basis for selection: Major/career interest in education. Applicant must demonstrate high academic achievement.
Application requirements: Proof of eligibility.
Additional information: 2.0 GPA required.

Amount of award:	$1,000-$4,000
Number of awards:	252
Number of applicants:	252
Total amount awarded:	$311,340

Contact:
Contact financial aid office of applicant's chosen college.
Web: www.state.in.us/ssaci

Indiana Nursing Scholarship

Type of award: Scholarship, renewable.
Intended use: For undergraduate study at accredited vocational, 2-year or 4-year institution. Designated institutions: Eligible Indiana schools (list provided to applicants).
Eligibility: Applicant must be U.S. citizen residing in Indiana.
Basis for selection: Major/career interest in nursing. Applicant must demonstrate financial need and high academic achievement.
Application requirements: Proof of eligibility. FASFA.
Additional information: 2.0 GPA required. Must be admitted to eligible Indiana school. Deadline varies by institution. Contact financial aid office of institution for application or e-mail Student Assistance Commission: grants@ssaci.state.in.us. Commitment to work two years as nurse in any Indiana health care setting required.

Amount of award:	$50-$5,000
Number of awards:	637
Number of applicants:	637
Total amount awarded:	$322,286

Contact:
Contact financial aid office of chosen institution
Web: www.state.in.us/ssaci

Indiana Robert C. Byrd Honors Scholarship

Type of award: Scholarship, renewable.
Intended use: For full-time freshman, sophomore, junior or senior study at accredited 2-year or 4-year institution in United States.
Eligibility: Applicant must be high school senior. Applicant must be U.S. citizen residing in Indiana.
Basis for selection: Applicant must demonstrate high academic achievement.
Application requirements: Transcript, proof of eligibility.
Additional information: Must have minimum 1300 SAT I, 29 ACT, or 65 GED. Cannot be in debt default to Federal Government or been sentenced for drug offense. Award total cannot exceed $6,000 over four years.

Amount of award:	$1,500
Number of awards:	564
Number of applicants:	564
Application deadline:	April 24
Notification begins:	June 1
Total amount awarded:	$846,500

Contact:
Contact high school guidance counselor for information
Web: www.ai.org/ssaci/

Indiana Special Education Services Scholarship

Type of award: Scholarship, renewable.
Intended use: For full-time undergraduate study at accredited 4-year institution in United States. Designated institutions: Eligible Indiana schools (list provided to applicants).
Eligibility: Applicant must be U.S. citizen residing in Indiana.
Basis for selection: Major/career interest in education, special. Applicant must demonstrate high academic achievement.
Application requirements: Proof of eligibility.
Additional information: Scholarship selection made by individual schools. Minimum 2.0 GPA required to renew scholarship. Applicants must pursue or intend to pursue course of study that would enable student upon graduation to teach in accredited elementary or secondary school in Indiana. Must fulfill teaching requirements following graduation or reimburse.

Amount of award:	$1,000
Number of awards:	95
Number of applicants:	95
Total amount awarded:	$88,699

Contact:
Financial aid office of chosen institution
Web: www.ai.org/ssaci/

Indiana Twenty-First Century Scholars Program

Type of award: Scholarship.
Intended use: For full-time undergraduate study at accredited 2-year or 4-year institution. Designated institutions: Participating two- or four-year schools in Indiana.
Eligibility: Applicant must be high school senior. Applicant must be U.S. citizen or permanent resident residing in Indiana.
Basis for selection: Applicant must demonstrate financial need.
Application requirements: Proof of eligibility. FAFSA.
Additional information: Must have minimum 2.0 high school GPA. Must enroll in 8th grade by taking pledge to remain drug, alcohol and crime free. Must file affirmation that pledge was fulfilled in high school senior year. Full tuition waiver up to $8,518 after other financial aid applied.

Amount of award:	Full tuition
Application deadline:	March 1
Notification begins:	July 1
Total amount awarded:	$7,627,156

Contact:
Indiana Student Assistance Commission
150 West Market Street, Suite 500
Indianapolis, IN 46204
Phone: 317-232-2350
Fax: 317-232-3260

Scholarships

National Guard Supplemental Grant

Type of award: Scholarship, renewable.
Intended use: For undergraduate study at accredited 2-year or 4-year institution in United States. Designated institutions: Indiana public institutions only.
Eligibility: Applicant must be U.S. citizen or permanent resident residing in Indiana.
Application requirements: FAFSA and NG Certification. Must be member of Indiana National Guard.
Additional information: For undergraduates in Indiana Air or Army National Guard.

Amount of award:	$200-$4,600
Number of awards:	570
Number of applicants:	630
Application deadline:	March 1
Total amount awarded:	$1,400,000

Contact:
Indiana Student Assistance Commission
150 West Market Street, Suite 500
Indianapolis, IN 46204
Phone: 317-232-2350
Fax: 317-232-3260

Industrial Electric Wire and Cable Inc.

Ted Krzynski and Harlan Murray Scholarship Program

Type of award: Scholarship, renewable.
Intended use: For undergraduate study at vocational, 2-year or 4-year institution.
Eligibility: Applicant or parent must be employed by Industrial Electric Wire and Cable Inc. Applicant must be high school senior.
Additional information: For further information or an application, contact Industrial Electric Wire and Cable Incorporated directly.

Amount of award:	$1,000-$5,000

Innovex, Inc.

Innovex, Inc. Scholarship

Type of award: Scholarship, renewable.
Intended use: For freshman study at vocational, 2-year or 4-year institution.
Eligibility: Applicant or parent must be employed by Innovex, Inc. Applicant must be high school senior.
Additional information: For further information or an application, contact Innovex Incorporated directly.

Institute for Humane Studies

Institute for Humane Studies Fellowship

Type of award: Scholarship.
Intended use: For full-time junior, senior, master's, doctoral or first professional study at accredited 4-year or graduate institution.
Basis for selection: Major/career interest in humanities/liberal arts; social/behavioral sciences; communications; law; anthropology; economics; history; linguistics; literature or philosophy. Applicant must demonstrate high academic achievement, depth of character and seriousness of purpose.
Application requirements: $25 application fee. Recommendations, essay, transcript. Sibmit GRE scores if applicable.
Additional information: Fellowships last one year and provide stipend of up to $18,000. Other fields of study also considered: political science, sociology, journalism. Applicants should have clearly demonstrated interest in classical liberal/libertarian ideas and intend to pursue intellectual or scholarly career. Complete information and applications available in October.

Amount of award:	$18,000
Number of awards:	80
Application deadline:	December 31
Notification begins:	April 23

Contact:
Institute for Humane Studies at George Mason University
3401 N. Fairfax Drive
Suite 440
Arlington, VA 22201-4432
Phone: 800-697-8799
Web: www.theihs.org

Institute of Food Technologists

Institute of Food Technologists Freshman Scholarship

Type of award: Scholarship, renewable.
Intended use: For full-time freshman study at 4-year institution in United States or Canada. Designated institutions: Educational institutions with approved program in food science/technology.
Eligibility: Applicant must be high school senior.
Basis for selection: Major/career interest in food science/technology. Applicant must demonstrate high academic achievement.
Application requirements: Recommendations, essay, transcript. Minimum 2.5 GPA required. Previous scholarship recipients must be IFT members to reapply.
Additional information: Applicant must be high school senior or previous H.S. graduate entering college for first time. Must enroll in IFT approved program. Program description and application available through Website or via fax. All other inquiries and completed applications should be directed to the department head of the approved school.

Amount of award:	$1,000-$1,500
Number of awards:	25
Application deadline:	February 15
Notification begins:	April 15
Total amount awarded:	$25,500

Contact:
Institute of Food Technologists
Scholarship Department
221 North LaSalle Street
Chicago, IL 60601-1291
Fax: 800-234-0270, outside US/Canada 630-556-9176
Web: www.ift.org

Institute of Food Technologists Junior/Senior Scholarship

Type of award: Scholarship, renewable.
Intended use: For full-time junior or senior study at 4-year institution in United States or Canada. Designated institutions: Educational institutions with approved program in food science/technology.
Basis for selection: Major/career interest in food science/technology. Applicant must demonstrate high academic achievement.
Application requirements: Recommendations, essay, transcript, proof of eligibility. Minimum 2.5 GPA required. Previous scholarship recipients must be IFT members to reapply.
Additional information: Must be enrolled in IFT approved program. Programs description and application available through Website or via fax. All other inquiries and completed applications should be directed to the department head of the approved school.

Amount of award:	$1,000-$2,250
Number of awards:	60
Application deadline:	February 1
Notification begins:	April 15
Total amount awarded:	$68,250

Contact:
Scholarship Department
Institute of Food Technoligists
221 North LaSalle Street
Chicago, IL 60601
Fax: 800-234-0270, outside US/Canada 630-556-9176
Web: www.ift.org

Institute of Food Technologists Sophomore Scholarship

Type of award: Scholarship, renewable.
Intended use: For full-time sophomore study at 4-year institution in United States or Canada. Designated institutions: Educational institutions with approved program in food science/technology.
Basis for selection: Major/career interest in food science/technology. Applicant must demonstrate high academic achievement.
Application requirements: Recommendations, essay, transcript, proof of eligibility. Minimum 2.5 GPA required. Previous scholarship recipients must be IFT members to reapply.
Additional information: Applicant must be college freshman. Must be enrolled in or plan to enroll in IFT approved program. Program descriptions and application available through Website or via fax. All other inquiries and completed applications should be directed to the department head of the approved school.

Amount of award:	$1,000
Number of awards:	23
Application deadline:	March 1
Notification begins:	April 15
Total amount awarded:	$23,000

Contact:
Institute of Food Technologists
Scholarship Department
221 North LaSalle Street
Chicago, IL 60601-1291
Fax: 800-234-0270, outside US/Canada 630-556-9176
Web: www.ift.org

Quality Assurance Division Junior/Senior Scholarship

Type of award: Scholarship, renewable.
Intended use: For full-time junior or senior study at 4-year institution in United States or Canada. Designated institutions: Educational institutions with approved program in food science/technology.
Basis for selection: Major/career interest in food science/technology. Applicant must demonstrate high academic achievement.
Application requirements: Recommendations, essay, transcript, proof of eligibility. Minimum 2.5 GPA required. Previous scholarship recipients must be IFT members to reapply.
Additional information: Must be enrolled in IFT approved program. Preference given to applicants who are taking or have taken at least one course in quality assurance and demonstrate definite interest. Program descriptions and application available through Website or via fax. All other inquires and completed applications should be directed to the department head of the approved school.

Amount of award:	$2,000
Number of awards:	2
Application deadline:	February 1
Notification begins:	April 15
Total amount awarded:	$4,000

Contact:
Institute of Food Technologists
Scholarship Department
221 North LaSalle Street
Chicago, IL 60601-1291
Fax: 800-234-0270, outside US/Canada 630-556-9176
Web: www.ift.org

Institute of International Education

Anna K. Meredith Fund Scholarship

Type of award: Scholarship.
Intended use: For undergraduate study in Florence, Italy. Designated institutions: Studio Art Centers International (SACI).
Basis for selection: Competition/talent/interest in study abroad. Major/career interest in arts, general or art/art history. Applicant must demonstrate financial need.
Application requirements: Portfolio. Submit portfolio of 20 labeled slides of own work, student aid report from home school, or recent tax return if not currently enrolled.

Additional information: Number of awards offered varies according to budget.

Amount of award:	$500-$2,000
Application deadline:	March 31, October 1

Contact:
Institute of International Education
809 United Nations Plaza
U.S. Student Programs, SACI Coordinator
New York, NY 10017-3580
Phone: 212-984-5548
Fax: 212-984-5325

Asia-Pacific Undergraduate Scholarship

Type of award: Scholarship.
Intended use: For sophomore, junior or senior study in Australia, New Zealand, or Pacific Island nations. Designated institutions: An IIE West Coast region member college or university.
Eligibility: Applicant must be U.S. citizen or permanent resident.
Basis for selection: Competition/talent/interest in study abroad. Major/career interest in asian studies or humanities/liberal arts.
Application requirements: Proof of eligibility. Applicant must be currently enrolled in an IIE West Coast Region Associate college of university.
Additional information: Supports unique, innovative approaches to study abroad. Accepted fields of study include area, ethnic, and cultural studies and Pacific area studies. Must be currently enrolled in an IIE West Coast Region Education Associate college or university. Award amount varies and includes travel costs.

Amount of award:	$1,000
Number of awards:	10
Number of applicants:	35
Application deadline:	March 19
Notification begins:	May 1

Contact:
Institute of International Education- West Coast
41 Sutter Street, Suite 510
San Francisco, CA 94104
Phone: 415-362-6520
Fax: 415-392-4667
Web: www.iie.org/wcoast

Clare Brett Smith Scholarship

Type of award: Scholarship.
Intended use: For undergraduate or graduate study in Florence, Italy. Designated institutions: Studio Art Centers International (SACI).
Basis for selection: Competition/talent/interest in study abroad. Major/career interest in arts, general.
Application requirements: Portfolio. Must submit portfolio of 20 labeled slides of own work, student aid report from home school, or recent tax return if not currently enrolled.
Additional information: Applicant must be studying photography. Number of awards offered varies yearly according to budget.

Amount of award:	$1,000
Application deadline:	March 31, October 1

Contact:
Institute of International Education
809 United Nations Plaza
U.S. Student Programs, SACI Coordinator
New York, NY 10017-3580
Phone: 212-984-5548
Fax: 212-984-5325

Freeman Award for Study in Asia (Freeman-ASIA)

Type of award: Scholarship.
Intended use: For full-time undergraduate study at 2-year or 4-year institution in Cambodia, China, Hong Kong, Indonesia, Japan, Korea, Laos, Macao, Malaysia, Mongolia, Philippines, Singapore, Taiwan, Thailand, Vietnam.
Eligibility: Applicant must be U.S. citizen or permanent resident.
Basis for selection: Applicant must demonstrate financial need, depth of character and service orientation.
Application requirements: Proof of eligibility. Applicants must receive endorsement of campus study abroad advisor and complete application on Website.
Additional information: Applicants must perform community service upon return to U.S. Students with no experience in Asia encouraged to apply. Award amounts: $5,000 for fall or spring semester, $7,000 for academic year, $3,000 for summer. Deadlines: April 1 for fall/academic year, November 1 for spring, March 1 for summer. Hard copies of application received through mail not accepted.

Amount of award:	$3,000-$7,000

Contact:
Phone: 212-984-5542
Fax: 212-984-5325
Web: www.iie.org/pgms/Freeman-ASIA

IIE/Cora Faye Williamson Scholarship

Type of award: Scholarship.
Intended use: For undergraduate or graduate study in Florence, Italy. Designated institutions: Studio Art Centers International (SACI).
Basis for selection: Competition/talent/interest in Study abroad. Major/career interest in arts, general or art/art history.
Application requirements: Portfolio.
Additional information: Offered to assist undergraduate or graduate student meet academic objectives. May be used to offset any costs associated with significant study abroad experience. Preferences given to students from east Texas, especially from Beaumont area, or from Lamar University in particular.

Application deadline:	March 31, October 1

Contact:
Institute of International Education
809 United Nations Plaza
U.S. Student Programs, SACI Coordinator
New York, NY 10017-3580
Phone: 212-984-5548
Fax: 212-984-5235

International Incentive Awards

Type of award: Scholarship.
Intended use: For sophomore, junior or senior study in Florence, Italy. Designated institutions: Studio Art Centers International (SACI).

Basis for selection: Competition/talent/interest in study abroad. Major/career interest in arts, general or art/art history. Applicant must demonstrate financial need and high academic achievement.

Application requirements: Portfolio. Must submit portfolio of 20 labeled slides of own work, student aid report from home school, or recent tax return if not currently enrolled.

Additional information: Must be at least sophomore with minimum 3.0 GPA. Studio arts accepted fields of study. Special efforts are made to encourage applications from minorities and underrepresented groups. Up to two awards offered each semester.

Amount of award:	$1,500
Number of awards:	2
Application deadline:	March 31, October 1

Contact:
Institute of International Education
809 United Nations Plaza
U.S. Student Programs, SACI Coordinator
New York, NY 10017-3580
Phone: 212-984-5548
Fax: 212-984-5328

Jules Maidoff Scholarship

Type of award: Scholarship.

Intended use: For undergraduate or graduate study in Florence, Italy. Designated institutions: Studio Art Centers International (SACI).

Basis for selection: Competition/talent/interest in Study abroad. Major/career interest in arts, general or art/art history. Applicant must demonstrate financial need.

Application requirements: Portfolio.

Additional information: Awarded to students exhibiting both exceptional artistic talent and financial need.

Amount of award:	Full tuition
Application deadline:	March 31, October 1

Contact:
Institute of International Education
809 United Nations Plaza
U.S. Student Programs, SACI Coordinator
New York, NY 10017-3580
Phone: 212-984-5548
Fax: 212-984-5325

Lele Cassin Scholarship

Type of award: Scholarship.

Intended use: For undergraduate or graduate study in Florence, Italy. Designated institutions: Studio Art Centers International (SACI).

Basis for selection: Competition/talent/interest in Study abroad. Major/career interest in film/video.

Application requirements: Submit video, no longer than 15 minutes, of own work.

Additional information: For video filmmaking student. Number of awards offered varies yearly according to budget.

Amount of award:	$1,000
Application deadline:	March 31, October 1

Contact:
Institute of International Education
809 United Nations Plaza
U.S. Students Programs, SACI Coordinator
New York, NY 10017-3580
Phone: 212-984-5548
Fax: 212-984-5325

NIAF/SACI Scholarships

Type of award: Scholarship.

Intended use: For undergraduate or graduate study in Florency, Italy. Designated institutions: Studio Art Centers International (SACI).

Eligibility: Applicant must be Italian.

Basis for selection: Competition/talent/interest in Study abroad. Major/career interest in arts, general or art/art history.

Application requirements: Portfolio. Applicant must be currently enrolled in U.S. college.

Additional information: Made possible by SACI and National Italian American Foundation (NIAF). Award of $2,500 is given for Fall term and for Spring term.

Amount of award:	$2,500
Application deadline:	March 31, October 1

Contact:
Institute of International Education
809 United Nations Plaza
U.S. Student Programs, SACI Coordinator
New York, NY 10017-3580
Phone: 212-984-5548
Fax: 212-984-5325

SACI Consortium Scholarship

Type of award: Scholarship.

Intended use: For undergraduate or graduate study in Florence, Italy. Designated institutions: Studio Art Centers International (SACI).

Basis for selection: Competition/talent/interest in Study abroad. Major/career interest in arts, general or art/art history.

Application requirements: Portfolio, nomination by SACI consortium school.

Additional information: Each consortium school may submit one nominee for this award.

Amount of award:	Full tuition
Application deadline:	March 31, October 1

Contact:
Institute of International Education
809 United Nations Plaza
U.S. Student Programs, SACI Coordinator
New York, NY 10017-3580
Phone: 212-984-5548
Fax: 212-984-5325

Institute of Real Estate Management Foundation

George M. Brooker Collegiate Scholarship for Minorities

Type of award: Scholarship.

Intended use: For full-time junior, senior, master's or doctoral study at accredited 4-year or graduate institution.

Eligibility: Applicant must be Alaskan native, Asian American, African American, Mexican American, Hispanic American, Puerto Rican or American Indian. Applicant must be U.S. citizen.

Basis for selection: Major/career interest in real estate; business or business/management/administration. Applicant must demonstrate high academic achievement, depth of character, leadership and seriousness of purpose.

Application requirements: Interview, recommendations, essay, transcript.

Additional information: Must have 3.0 GPA in major. Must intend to enter the field of real estate management. Undergraduate scholarships $1,000; graduate $2,500.

Amount of award:	$1,000-$2,500
Number of awards:	3
Application deadline:	March 1
Notification begins:	July 1
Total amount awarded:	$4,500

Contact:
Institute of Real Estate Management Foundation
Foundation Coordinator
430 North Michigan Avenue
Chicago, IL 60611
Phone: 312-329-6008
Web: www.irem.org

Institution of Mining and Metallurgy

Centenary Scholarship

Type of award: Scholarship.

Intended use: For freshman or sophomore study in or outside United States.

Eligibility: Applicant or parent must be member/participant of Institution of Mining and Metallurgy.

Basis for selection: Major/career interest in geology/earth sciences. Applicant must demonstrate high academic achievement.

Application requirements: Application.

Additional information: Amount of Scholarship is 500 pounds sterling. Award is for projects, visits, etc., in furtherance of applicant's career development. Applicant must be student-member of Institution of Mining and Metallurgy. Application forms available from IMM. Recipients of award expected to produce reports on their use of the award for publication in International Mining and Minerals.

Application deadline:	March 15

Contact:
Institute of Mining and Metallurgy
Hallam Court
77 Hallam Street
London W1W 5BS
Phone: 44-207-580-3802
Fax: 44-207-436-5388
Web: www.imm.org.uk

Int'l Union of Electr., Salaried, Machine, and Furn. Wrkrs Dept. of Education

James B. Carey Scholarship

Type of award: Scholarship.

Intended use: For full-time undergraduate study in United States.

Eligibility: Applicant or parent must be member/participant of International Union of EESMF Workers, AFL-CIO. Applicant must be enrolled in high school.

Basis for selection: Applicant must demonstrate depth of character and service orientation.

Application requirements: Recommendations, essay, transcript, proof of eligibility. Local Union Seal.

Amount of award:	$1,000
Number of awards:	9
Number of applicants:	300
Application deadline:	April 15
Notification begins:	February 1
Total amount awarded:	$9,000

Contact:
Trudy Humphrey, IUE Department of Education
Int'l Union of EESMF Workers, AFL-CIO
1275 K Street, N.W.
Washington, DC 20005-4064

Paul Jennings Scholarship

Type of award: Scholarship.

Intended use: For full-time undergraduate study in United States.

Eligibility: Applicant or parent must be member/participant of International Union of EESMF Workers, AFL-CIO. Applicant must be high school senior.

Basis for selection: Applicant must demonstrate depth of character, leadership and service orientation.

Application requirements: Recommendations, essay, transcript, proof of eligibility. Evidence of family financial status. Short statement of interests and goals including career objectives, civic commitment and activities and extracurricular activities. Also include Local Union Seal.

Additional information: Applicants must be sons or daughters of I.U.E. local union elected officials.

Amount of award:	$3,000
Number of awards:	1
Number of applicants:	100
Application deadline:	April 15
Notification begins:	February 1
Total amount awarded:	$3,000

Contact:
Trudy Humphrey, Department of Educatoin
Int'l Union of EESMF Workers, AFL-CIO
1275 K Street, N.W.
Washington, DC 20000-4064

Intel Corporation

Intel Science Talent Search

Type of award: Scholarship.

Intended use: For undergraduate study.

Eligibility: Applicant must be enrolled in high school. Applicant must be U.S. citizen.

Basis for selection: Competition/talent/interest in science project, based on individual research reports, scientific originality and creative thinking. Major/career interest in biology; science, general; physics or mathematics.

Application requirements: Interview, transcript, proof of eligibility.

Amount of award:	$3,000-$100,000
Number of awards:	40
Number of applicants:	1,600
Application deadline:	December 2
Total amount awarded:	$1,100,000

Contact:
Science Service
1127 NW Connecticut Ave
Washington, DC 20036
Phone: 202-463-0512
Web: www.intel.com/education

Intermec Technologies Corporation, Norand Mobile Systems Division

George Chadima Memorial Scholarship

Type of award: Scholarship.
Intended use: For undergraduate study at accredited 4-year institution.
Eligibility: Applicant or parent must be employed by Intermec Technologies Corporation.
Additional information: For further information or an application, contact Intermec Technologies Corporation directly.

Amount of award:	$4,000

International Assoc of Bridge, Structural, Ornamental, Reinforcing Iron Workers

John H. Lyons, Sr. Scholarship

Type of award: Scholarship, renewable.
Intended use: For full-time undergraduate study at accredited 4-year institution. Designated institutions: In United States or Canada.
Eligibility: Applicant or parent must be member/participant of Int'l Association Bridge/Structural/Ornamental/Reinforcing Iron Workers. Applicant must be high school senior. Applicant must be U.S. citizen, permanent resident, international student or Canadian citizen.
Basis for selection: Applicant must demonstrate high academic achievement, depth of character and leadership.
Application requirements: Recommendations, essay, transcript, proof of eligibility. SAT I/ACT scores required. Canadian students must submit equivalent information.
Additional information: Applicant must rank in top third of graduating class. Applicant must be child/ stepchild of a member of International Association with at least five years membership at time of application. No other applicants with be considered. Sibling of previous recipient not eligible. Applications may be obtained between January 15 and March 31.

Amount of award:	$2,500
Number of awards:	2
Number of applicants:	225
Application deadline:	March 31
Notification begins:	June 1
Total amount awarded:	$5,000

Contact:
Intl. Assoc. of Bridge, Struct., Orn. and Reinforcing Iron Wrkrs
John H. Lyons, Sr. Scholarship Committee
1750 New York Avenue, NW Suite 400
Washington, DC 20006
Phone: 800-368-0105

International Association of Fire Fighters

W.H. McClennan Scholarship

Type of award: Scholarship, renewable.
Intended use: For full-time undergraduate or graduate study.
Eligibility: Applicant or parent must be member/participant of International Association of Fire Fighters. Applicant's parent must have been killed or disabled in work-related accident as fire fighter.
Basis for selection: Applicant must demonstrate financial need, high academic achievement, depth of character, seriousness of purpose and service orientation.
Application requirements: Essay, transcript, proof of eligibility. Two recommendations.
Additional information: Applicants must be children of firefighters who were killed in the line of duty and were members in good standing of the IAFF at the time of their deaths.

Amount of award:	$2,500
Number of awards:	20
Number of applicants:	20
Application deadline:	February 1
Notification begins:	April 1
Total amount awarded:	$50,000

Contact:
International Association of Fire Fighters
1750 New York Avenue, NW
Washington, DC 20006

International Buckskin Horse Association, Inc.

Buckskin Horse Association Scholarship

Type of award: Scholarship, renewable.
Intended use: For full-time undergraduate study at accredited postsecondary institution in United States.
Eligibility: Applicant or parent must be member/participant of International Buckskin Horse Association. Applicant must be high school senior. Applicant must be U.S. citizen.
Basis for selection: Applicant must demonstrate financial need, high academic achievement, depth of character, leadership and seriousness of purpose.

Application requirements: Portfolio, recommendations, proof of eligibility.
Additional information: Applicant must be association member for at least two years.

Amount of award:	$500-$1,500
Number of awards:	13
Number of applicants:	15
Application deadline:	February 1
Notification begins:	September 15
Total amount awarded:	$10,750

Contact:
International Buckskin Horse Association, Inc.
P.O. Box 268
Shelby, IN 46377

International Executive Housekeepers Association

IEHA Educational Foundation Scholarship

Type of award: Scholarship.
Intended use: For undergraduate, graduate or non-degree study at accredited postsecondary institution.
Eligibility: Applicant or parent must be member/participant of International Executive Housekeepers Association.
Basis for selection: Major/career interest in hospitality administration/management.
Application requirements: Essay, transcript.
Additional information: Applicant must be member of International Executive Housekeepers Association (IEHA). Other major/career interest: facilities management. Can be used for IEHA Certification program. No set limit on number of awards granted.

Amount of award:	$200-$1,000
Number of awards:	1
Application deadline:	January 15
Notification begins:	September 1
Total amount awarded:	$2,500

Contact:
International Executive Housekeepers Association
Educational Foundation Scholarships
1001 Eastwind Drive, Suite 301
Westerville, OH 43081-3361
Phone: 800-200-6342
Fax: 614-895-1248
Web: www.ieha.org

International Foodservice Editorial Council

Foodservice Communicators Scholarship

Type of award: Scholarship.
Intended use: For full-time undergraduate or master's study at accredited postsecondary institution in United States.
Basis for selection: Major/career interest in food science/technology; food production/management/services; culinary arts or communications. Applicant must demonstrate financial need, high academic achievement, depth of character, leadership, seriousness of purpose and service orientation.
Application requirements: Recommendations, transcript, proof of eligibility.
Additional information: Applicant must work or pursue academic study in both culinary arts and communications. Applications may be requested by e-mail: ifec@aol.com. Four to six awards granted each year for total of $6,000 to $10,000.

Amount of award:	$1,000-$2,500
Number of awards:	4
Number of applicants:	350
Application deadline:	March 15
Notification begins:	July 1
Total amount awarded:	$10,000

Contact:
International Foodservice Editorial Council (IFEC)
P.O. Box 491
Hyde Park, NY 12538

International Furnishings and Design Association Educational Foundation

International Furnishings and Design Student Scholarships

Type of award: Scholarship.
Intended use: For full-time undergraduate or graduate study at accredited postsecondary institution in or outside United States.
Basis for selection: Major/career interest in design; marketing; arts, general; graphic arts/design or education. Applicant must demonstrate high academic achievement, depth of character, seriousness of purpose and service orientation.
Application requirements: Recommendations, essay, transcript.
Additional information: Some scholarships require membership in IFDA. Membership fee is $45. Number and award amounts vary.

Amount of award:	$1,000-$2,500
Application deadline:	October 15
Notification begins:	November 1

Contact:
Jennifer Lewis
IFDA Educational Foundation
1200 19 Street, NW Number 300
Washington, DC 20036-2422
Phone: 202-857-1897

International Multifoods Corporation

International Multifoods Scholarship

Type of award: Scholarship.
Intended use: For undergraduate study at accredited vocational, 2-year or 4-year institution.

Eligibility: Applicant or parent must be employed by International Multifoods Corporation.
Additional information: For further information or an application, contact International Multifoods Corporation directly.

Amount of award:	$2,000

International Order of the King's Daughters and Sons

Health Career Scholarship

Type of award: Scholarship, renewable.
Intended use: For full-time junior, senior, master's or first professional study at accredited 4-year or graduate institution in United States or Canada.
Eligibility: Applicant must be U.S. citizen, international student or Canadian.
Basis for selection: Major/career interest in medicine; dentistry; pharmacy/pharmaceutics/pharmacology; nursing; health sciences or health-related professions. Applicant must demonstrate financial need, high academic achievement, depth of character, leadership, seriousness of purpose and service orientation.
Application requirements: Recommendations, essay, transcript, proof of eligibility. Resume, statement of professional intent. Recent photograph. Itemized budget of student expenses approved by Financial Aid Officer. Include two SASE.
Additional information: Physical/occupational therapy or other health-related majors also eligible, except pre-med. Inquiries must include SASE. To request application, state field and present level of study and enclose SASE. RN students must have completed first year of schooling; others must be at least college juniors.

Amount of award:	$500-$1,000
Number of awards:	50
Number of applicants:	350
Application deadline:	April 1
Total amount awarded:	$58,000

Contact:
International Order of the King's Daughters and Sons
Judith Isenhour
PO Box 9237
Savannah, GA 31412

North American Indian Scholarship

Type of award: Scholarship, renewable.
Intended use: For full-time undergraduate study at accredited 2-year or 4-year institution in United States.
Eligibility: Applicant must be Alaskan native or American Indian. Proof of Native American heritage. Applicant must be U.S. citizen.
Basis for selection: Applicant must demonstrate financial need, depth of character, leadership, seriousness of purpose and service orientation.
Application requirements: Recommendations, essay, transcript, proof of eligibility. Photograph, reservation registration number.
Additional information: Only one award per year to a family. Must request application between October 1 and March 1. Include SASE.

Amount of award:	$500-$650
Number of awards:	54
Application deadline:	April 15
Notification begins:	July 1

Contact:
Mrs. T.R. McConchie
Director of North American Indian Department
4831 Kempsville Green Pkwy.
Virginia Beach, VA 23462

Interstate Brands Corporation

Interstate Brands Post-High School Scholarship

Type of award: Scholarship, renewable.
Intended use: For undergraduate study at accredited vocational, 2-year or 4-year institution.
Eligibility: Applicant or parent must be employed by Interstate Brands Corporation.
Basis for selection: Applicant must demonstrate financial need.
Additional information: For further information or an application, contact Interstate Brands Corporation directly.

Amount of award:	$300-$2,000

Intertribal Timber Council

Truman D. Picard Scholarship

Type of award: Scholarship, renewable.
Intended use: For full-time undergraduate or graduate study at accredited 2-year, 4-year or graduate institution in United States.
Eligibility: Applicant must be Alaskan native or American Indian. Must be enrolled member of a federally recognized tribe. Applicant must be U.S. citizen.
Basis for selection: Major/career interest in natural resources/conservation; forestry; wildlife/fisheries or agriculture. Applicant must demonstrate financial need, high academic achievement, depth of character, leadership, seriousness of purpose and service orientation.
Application requirements: Recommendations, transcript. Resume.

Amount of award:	$1,200-$1,800
Number of awards:	14
Number of applicants:	70
Notification begins:	November 1
Total amount awarded:	$22,800

Contact:
Intertribal Timber Council
Education Committee
1112 NE 21st Avenue
Portland, OR 97232-2114
Web: www.itcnet.org

Intuit Scholarship Foundation

Intuit Scholarship

Type of award: Scholarship, renewable.
Intended use: For freshman study at vocational, 2-year or 4-year institution.
Eligibility: Applicant or parent must be employed by Intuit Scholarship Foundation. Applicant must be high school senior.
Additional information: For further information or an application, contact Intuit Scholarship Foundation directly.

Amount of award:	$500-$5,000

Iowa College Student Aid Commission

Iowa Grant

Type of award: Scholarship, renewable.
Intended use: For freshman, sophomore, junior or senior study at vocational, 2-year or 4-year institution. Designated institutions: Iowa colleges.
Eligibility: Applicant must be U.S. citizen residing in Iowa.
Basis for selection: Applicant must demonstrate financial need.
Application requirements: Proof of eligibility. Financial aid forms.
Additional information: The award amount may be adjusted (downward) for less than full-time study.

Amount of award:	$1,000
Number of awards:	2,250
Number of applicants:	2,300
Total amount awarded:	$1,429,437

Contact:
Iowa College Student Aid Commission
200 Tenth Street, Fourth Floor
Des Moines, IA 50309-3609
Web: www.iowacollegeaid.org

Iowa National Guard Educational Assistance Program

Type of award: Scholarship, renewable.
Intended use: For undergraduate study.
Eligibility: Applicant must be U.S. citizen residing in Iowa. Applicant must be in military service in the Reserves/National Guard.
Basis for selection: Based on National Guard designation.
Application requirements: National Guard application.
Additional information: Applicant must be in military service in the Iowa Reserves/National Guard.

Number of awards:	744
Total amount awarded:	$892,608

Contact:
Iowa College Student Aid Commission
200 Tenth Street, Fourth Floor
Des Moines, IA 50309-3609
Phone: 515-242-3380
Web: www.iowacollegeaid.org

Iowa Robert C. Byrd Honor Scholarship

Type of award: Scholarship.
Intended use: For full-time undergraduate study at accredited 2-year or 4-year institution in United States.
Eligibility: Applicant must be high school senior. Applicant must be U.S. citizen or permanent resident residing in Iowa.
Basis for selection: Applicant must demonstrate high academic achievement.
Application requirements: Recommendations, essay, transcript, proof of eligibility.

Amount of award:	$1,500
Number of awards:	68
Number of applicants:	357
Application deadline:	February 1
Notification begins:	May 1
Total amount awarded:	$321,727

Contact:
Iowa College Student Aid Commission
200 Tenth Street, Fourth Floor
Des Moines, IA 50309-3609
Phone: 515-242-6716
Fax: 515-242-3388
Web: www.iowacollegeaid.org

Iowa Tuition Grant

Type of award: Scholarship, renewable.
Intended use: For undergraduate study at accredited 2-year or 4-year institution. Designated institutions: Private colleges in Iowa.
Eligibility: Applicant must be U.S. citizen or permanent resident residing in Iowa.
Basis for selection: Applicant must demonstrate financial need.
Application requirements: Proof of eligibility. Financial aid forms.

Number of awards:	14,667
Number of applicants:	23,961
Application deadline:	July 1
Notification begins:	May 30
Total amount awarded:	$47,583,660

Contact:
Iowa College Student Aid Commission
200 Tenth Street, Fourth Floor
Des Moines, IA 50309-3609
Phone: 515-242-6716
Fax: 515-242-3388
Web: www.iowacollegeaid.org

Iowa Vocational-Technical Tuition Grant

Type of award: Scholarship, renewable.
Intended use: For undergraduate study at vocational institution. Designated institutions: Iowa community colleges.
Eligibility: Applicant must be U.S. citizen or permanent resident residing in Iowa.
Basis for selection: Applicant must demonstrate financial need.
Application requirements: Proof of eligibility. Financial aid forms.
Additional information: Only vocational-technical career majors considered.

Scholarships

Amount of award:	$150-$650
Number of awards:	5,129
Number of applicants:	20,261
Application deadline:	July 1
Total amount awarded:	$2,337,786

Contact:
Iowa College Student Aid Commission
200 Tenth Street, Fourth Floor
Des Moines, IA 50309-3609
Web: www.iowacollegeaid.org

State of Iowa Scholarship

Type of award: Scholarship.
Intended use: For full-time freshman study at accredited vocational, 2-year or 4-year institution. Designated institutions: Iowa schools.
Eligibility: Applicant must be high school senior. Applicant must be U.S. citizen or permanent resident residing in Iowa.
Basis for selection: Applicant must demonstrate high academic achievement.
Application requirements: Proof of eligibility.
Additional information: Must rank in top 15 percent of class and have taken ACT or SAT test. For class ranking and other criteria for selection, consult with high school guidance counselor.

Amount of award:	$400
Number of awards:	1,700
Number of applicants:	4,306
Application deadline:	November 1
Notification begins:	March 20
Total amount awarded:	$492,000

Contact:
Iowa College Student Aid Commission
200 Tenth Street, Fourth Floor
Des Moines, IA 50309-3609
Phone: 515-242-6716
Fax: 515-242-3388
Web: www.state.ia.us/collegeaid

Ispat Inland, Inc.

Ispat Inland Foundation Scholarship Program

Type of award: Scholarship, renewable.
Intended use: For full-time undergraduate study at accredited 4-year institution.
Eligibility: Applicant or parent must be employed by Inland Steel Industries, Inc. Applicant must be high school senior.
Basis for selection: Applicant must demonstrate high academic achievement, depth of character and leadership.
Application requirements: Recommendations, transcript, proof of eligibility. SAT scores, involvement in extracurricular and community activities. Applicant must demonstrate potential for achievement.
Additional information: Numbers do not include National Merit or National Achievement recipients. Student should be the child or legal ward of active, retired or deceased employee of Ispat Inland, Inc.

Amount of award:	$2,000-$3,000
Application deadline:	March 15

Contact:
Ispat Inland Foundation Scholarship Program
3210 Watling Street
East Chicago, IN 46312-8152

Italian Catholic Federation

Italian Catholic Federation Scholarship

Type of award: Scholarship, renewable.
Intended use: For full-time freshman study at accredited vocational, 2-year or 4-year institution.
Eligibility: Applicant must be high school senior. Applicant must be Italian. Applicant must be Roman Catholic. Applicant must be U.S. citizen residing in Illinois, Nevada or California.
Basis for selection: Applicant must demonstrate financial need and high academic achievement.
Application requirements: Recommendations, essay, transcript. Tax returns of family.
Additional information: Applicants must submit a copy of the first two pages of their parent's most recent federal tax return. Minimum GPA 3.2. Also open to non-Italian students whose parents or grandparents are members of the Italian Catholic Federation. First year's scholarship award is $400. Larger amounts available for advanced scholarships.

Amount of award:	$400-$1,000
Number of awards:	200
Number of applicants:	600
Application deadline:	March 15
Notification begins:	May 1
Total amount awarded:	$70,000

Contact:
Italian Catholic Federation
675 Hegenberger Road, #110 #110
Oakland, CA 94621
Phone: 510-633-9058

J.W. Pepper & Son, Inc.

Pepper Employees' Children Scholarship Fund

Type of award: Scholarship.
Intended use: For undergraduate study at vocational, 2-year or 4-year institution.
Eligibility: Applicant or parent must be employed by J.W. Pepper & Sons, Inc. Applicant must be high school senior.
Additional information: For further information or an application, contact J.W. Pepper & Son Incorporated directly.

Amount of award:	$250-$5,000

J.W. Saxe Memorial Fund

J.W. Saxe Memorial Prize

Type of award: Scholarship.
Intended use: For non-degree study.

Basis for selection: Major/career interest in public administration/service. Applicant must demonstrate financial need, depth of character, leadership, seriousness of purpose and service orientation.

Application requirements: Recommendations, essay. Resume and letter of support from faculty member. Three recommendations required and essay on short and long-term goals.

Additional information: Award enables public service-minded students to gain practical experience working no-pay or low-pay public service job or internship during summer or other term. Preference given to applicants who have already found a public-service oriented position, but who require additional funds.

Amount of award:	$1,500
Number of applicants:	200
Application deadline:	March 15
Notification begins:	May 1
Total amount awarded:	$10,000

Contact:
J.W. Saxe Memorial Fund
1524 31 St. N.W.
Washington, DC 20007
Web: www.jwsaxefund.org

Jackie Robinson Foundation

Jackie Robinson Scholarship

Type of award: Scholarship, renewable.

Intended use: For full-time undergraduate study at accredited 4-year institution in United States.

Eligibility: Applicant must be Alaskan native, Asian American, African American, Mexican American, Hispanic American, Puerto Rican or American Indian. Applicant must be high school senior. Applicant must be U.S. citizen.

Basis for selection: Applicant must demonstrate financial need, high academic achievement and leadership.

Application requirements: Interview, recommendations, essay, transcript. Applicant must have been accepted to accredited 4-year college or university.

Additional information: Applications sent November 1 through March 1 upon receipt of written request. Award amount varies up to $6,000. Applications may be reproduced.

Amount of award:	$6,000
Number of awards:	68
Number of applicants:	3,500
Application deadline:	April 2
Notification begins:	September 1
Total amount awarded:	$1,000,000

Contact:
Jackie Robinson Foundation
Attn: Scholarship Programs
3 West 35 Street, 11th Floor
New York, NY 10001-2204
Phone: 212-290-8600
Web: www.jackierobinson.org

James Beard Foundation

Friends of James Beard Scholarships

Type of award: Scholarship.

Intended use: For undergraduate, graduate or non-degree study in or outside United States or Canada. Designated institutions: Institution with approved program in Culinary arts or culinary institute.

Basis for selection: Major/career interest in culinary arts.

Application requirements: Recommendations, transcript. Essay, proof of residency may be required as well.

Additional information: Applications are available online in December. Visit Website for additional information.

Application deadline:	March 15

Contact:
Director of Scholarship Program via email:
jamesbeardfound@hotmail.com.
Web: www.jamesbeard.org

James F. Byrnes Foundation

James F. Byrnes Scholarship

Type of award: Scholarship.

Intended use: For full-time undergraduate study at accredited 4-year institution.

Eligibility: Applicant must be high school senior. Applicant must be U.S. citizen residing in South Carolina.

Basis for selection: Applicant must demonstrate financial need, high academic achievement, depth of character, leadership, patriotism, seriousness of purpose and service orientation.

Application requirements: Interview, recommendations, essay, transcript.

Additional information: Applicant must be high school senior, college freshman or sophomore. Applicant must have 2.5 GPA. One or both parents of applicant must be deceased. Visit Website for additional information.

Amount of award:	$2,750
Number of applicants:	200
Application deadline:	February 15
Notification begins:	April 20
Total amount awarded:	$177,000

Contact:
James F. Byrnes Foundation
P.O. Box 6781
Columbia, SC 29260-6781
Phone: 803-254-9325
Fax: 803-254-9354
Web: www.byrnesscholars.org

James S. Kemper Foundation

Kemper Scholars Grant Program

Type of award: Scholarship, renewable.

Intended use: For freshman study at 4-year institution in United States. Designated institutions: Beloit College, Brigham

Young University, Drake University, Howard University, Illinois State University, Lake Forest College, La Salle University, Loyola University, Millikin University, Northern Illinois University, Rochester Inst. of Technology, University of the Pacific, University Wisconsin - Whitewater, Valparaiso University, Wake Forest University, Washington and Lee University, Washington University - St. Louis.
Basis for selection: Major/career interest in business. Applicant must demonstrate financial need, high academic achievement, depth of character, leadership, seriousness of purpose and service orientation.
Application requirements: Interview, recommendations, essay, transcript. 3.0 GPA. Must apply during freshman year while attending participating institution.
Additional information: Deadlines vary by institution; apply early. Recipient must complete internship with Kemper Insurance Companies each summer to receive annual scholarship.

Amount of award:	$1,500-$8,000
Number of awards:	88
Total amount awarded:	$465,540

Contact:
James S. Kemper Foundation
1 Kemper Drive
Long Grove, IL 60049

Japanese American Association of New York

Japanese American General Scholarship

Type of award: Scholarship.
Intended use: For full-time freshman study at accredited 2-year or 4-year institution in United States.
Eligibility: Applicant must be Asian American. Applicant must be high school senior. Applicant must be Japanese. Applicant must be U.S. citizen or permanent resident residing in Connecticut, New Jersey or New York.
Basis for selection: Applicant must demonstrate financial need, high academic achievement and service orientation.
Application requirements: Recommendations, essay, transcript. SAT scores, photograph.
Additional information: Two awards given are need-based.

Amount of award:	$1,000-$5,000
Number of awards:	12
Number of applicants:	32
Application deadline:	May 10
Total amount awarded:	$25,500

Contact:
Japanese American Association of New York
15 West 44 Street
New York, NY 10036
Web: www.jaany.org

Japanese American Music Scholarship Competition

Type of award: Scholarship.
Intended use: For undergraduate or graduate study at postsecondary institution.
Eligibility: Applicant must be Asian American. Applicant must be Japanese. Applicant must be U.S. citizen, permanent resident, international student or Japanese.
Basis for selection: Competition/talent/interest in music performance/composition, based on piano or string performance. Major/career interest in music.
Additional information: Competition occurs in odd-numbered years. 2001 competition: piano.

Amount of award:	$1,500
Number of awards:	4
Number of applicants:	30
Total amount awarded:	$6,000

Contact:
Japanese American Association of New York
15 West 44 Street
New York, NY 10036
Web: www.jaany.org

Jaycee War Memorial Fund

Charles R. Ford Scholarship

Type of award: Scholarship.
Intended use: For undergraduate study at postsecondary institution.
Eligibility: Applicant or parent must be member/participant of Jaycees. Applicant must be returning adult student. Applicant must be U.S. citizen.
Basis for selection: Applicant must demonstrate financial need, high academic achievement and leadership.
Application requirements: $5 application fee. Nomination by applicant's state Junior Chamber organization. Send SASE and application fee between July 1 and February 1 to obtain application. Check or money order payable to The War Memorial Fund.
Additional information: Intended for active member who wishes to return to college or university to complete his or her education. Applicants must send applications to their Junior Chamber State President (address provided with application) postmarked no later than March 1. State President selects semi-finalist and forwards application to U.S. Junior Chamber of Commerce by March 15. Any descendant of Jaycee is eligible. Visit Website for additional information and to request application.

Amount of award:	$2,500
Application deadline:	March 1
Notification begins:	May 15

Contact:
Jaycee War Memorial Fund
Ford Scholarship
4 West 21st Street
Tulsa, OK 74114-1116
Phone: 918-584-2481 exts. 405 or 511
Web: www.usjaycees.org

Jaycee War Memorial Scholarship

Type of award: Scholarship.
Intended use: For full-time undergraduate study at accredited 2-year or 4-year institution.
Eligibility: Applicant must be high school senior. Applicant must be U.S. citizen.
Basis for selection: Applicant must demonstrate financial need, high academic achievement and leadership.

Application requirements: $5 application fee. Nomination by applicant's state Junior Chamber organization. Send SASE and application fee between July 1 and February 1 to obtain application. Check or money order payable to The War Memorial Fund.

Additional information: Twenty-five $1,000 scholarships offered. Applicant must send applications to their Junior Chamber State President (address provided with application) postmarked no later than March 1. State presidents select semi-finalists and forward applications to U.S. Junior Chamber of Commerce by March 15. Visit Website for additional information and to request application.

Amount of award:	$1,000
Number of awards:	25
Application deadline:	March 1
Notification begins:	May 15
Total amount awarded:	$25,000

Contact:
Jaycee War Memorial Fund
Jaycee War Memorial Scholarship
Department 94922
Tulsa, OK 74194-0001
Phone: 918-584-2481 ext. 405 or 511
Web: www.usjaycees.org

Thomas Wood Baldridge Scholarship

Type of award: Scholarship.
Intended use: For full-time undergraduate study at accredited 2-year or 4-year institution.
Eligibility: Applicant or parent must be member/participant of Jaycees. Applicant must be U.S. citizen.
Basis for selection: Applicant must demonstrate financial need, high academic achievement and leadership.
Application requirements: $5 application fee. Nomination by applicant's state Junior Chamber organization. Send SASE and application fee between July 1 and February 1 to obtain application. Check or money order payable to The War Memorial Fund.
Additional information: Applicants must send applications to their Junior Chamber State President (address provided with application) postmarked no later than March 1. State presidents select semi-finalists and forward applications to U.S. Junior Chamber of Commerce by March 15. Any descendant of Jaycee is eligible. Visit Website for additional information and to request application.

Amount of award:	$3,000
Number of awards:	1
Application deadline:	March 1
Notification begins:	May 15
Total amount awarded:	$3,000

Contact:
Jaycee War Memorial Fund
Baldridge Scholarship
4 West 21st Street
Tulsa, OK 74114-1116
Phone: 918-584-2481 ext. 405 or 511
Web: www.usjaycees.org

Jeannette Rankin Foundation

Women's Education Fund

Type of award: Scholarship.
Intended use: For undergraduate study at accredited vocational, 2-year or 4-year institution in United States.
Eligibility: Applicant must be female, at least 35, returning adult student. Applicant must be U.S. citizen.
Basis for selection: Applicant must demonstrate financial need, depth of character, leadership, seriousness of purpose and service orientation.
Application requirements: Recommendations, essay. Applicant must be 35+ as of April 1 of the award year.
Additional information: Application may be downloaded from Website during the months of November, December and January.

Amount of award:	$1,500
Number of awards:	25
Number of applicants:	700
Application deadline:	March 1
Notification begins:	June 30
Total amount awarded:	$35,000

Contact:
Jeannette Rankin Foundation
P.O. Box 6653
Athens, GA 30604
Web: www.rankinfoundation.org

The Jerold B. Katz Foundation

Jerold B. Katz Services Scholarship

Type of award: Scholarship, renewable.
Intended use: For freshman study at accredited 2-year or 4-year institution.
Eligibility: Applicant or parent must be employed by GC Services.
Basis for selection: Applicant must demonstrate financial need.
Additional information: For further information or an application, contact The Jerold B. Katz Foundation directly.

Amount of award:	$2,500

Johnson International, Inc.

Johnson International, Inc. Scholarship

Type of award: Scholarship.
Intended use: For undergraduate study at accredited vocational, 2-year or 4-year institution.
Eligibility: Applicant or parent must be employed by Johnson International, Inc.
Basis for selection: Applicant must demonstrate financial need.

Additional information: For further information or an application, contact Johnson International, Inc. directly.

    Amount of award: $250-$1,000

Johnson Outdoors Inc.

Johnson Outdoors Sons and Daughters Scholarship

Type of award: Scholarship, renewable.
Intended use: For undergraduate study at accredited postsecondary institution.
Eligibility: Applicant or parent must be employed by Johnson Outdoors, Inc. Applicant must be high school senior.
Basis for selection: Applicant must demonstrate financial need.
Additional information: For further information or an application, contact Johnson Outdoors, Inc. directly.

    Amount of award: $500-$2,500
Contact:
Johnson Worldwide Associates, Inc.

Junior Achievement of Maine

Junior Achievement of Maine Scholarship

Type of award: Scholarship.
Intended use: For freshman study at accredited 2-year or 4-year institution in United States.
Eligibility: Applicant must be high school senior. Applicant must be residing in Maine.
Basis for selection: Major/career interest in business. Applicant must demonstrate high academic achievement.
Application requirements: Recommendations, essay, proof of eligibility.
Additional information: Must have participated in Junior Achievement programs during high school or volunteered to teach a junior achievement class.

Amount of award:	$1,000
Number of awards:	1
Number of applicants:	10
Application deadline:	March 15
Notification begins:	May 1
Total amount awarded:	$1,000

Contact:
Scholarship Coordinator
Junior Achievement of Maine
185 Lancaster St. Suite 204
Portland, ME 04101
Web: www.ja.org

Juvenile Products Manufacturers Association

JPMA Scholarship

Type of award: Scholarship.
Intended use: For undergraduate study at accredited vocational, 2-year or 4-year institution.
Eligibility: Applicant or parent must be employed by Juvenile Products Manufacturers Assoc. Applicant must be high school senior.
Basis for selection: Applicant must demonstrate financial need.
Additional information: For further information or an application, contact Juvenile Products Manufacturers Association members directly.

    Amount of award: $2,000
Contact:
Juvenile Products Manufacturers Association

JVS Community Scholarship Fund

JVS Jewish Community Scholarship

Type of award: Scholarship, renewable.
Intended use: For full-time undergraduate or graduate study at accredited postsecondary institution in United States.
Eligibility: Applicant must be Jewish. Applicant must be U.S. citizen or permanent resident residing in California.
Basis for selection: Applicant must demonstrate financial need, seriousness of purpose and service orientation.
Application requirements: Recommendations, essay, transcript, proof of eligibility.
Additional information: Minimum 2.5 GPA required. Must be a Jewish, legal permanent resident of Los Angeles County. Call, write, or e-mail jgaynor@jvsla to request application.

Amount of award:	$500-$5,000
Number of awards:	156
Number of applicants:	600
Application deadline:	April 15
Total amount awarded:	$334,000

Contact:
JVS Jewish Community Scholarship Fund
6505 Wilshire Blvd., Suite 200
Los Angeles, CA 90048
Phone: 323-761-8888 ext. 8868
Fax: 323-761-8577
Web: www.jvsla.org

Kansas Board of Regents

Kansas Comprehensive Grant

Type of award: Scholarship, renewable.
Intended use: For full-time undergraduate study at accredited 4-year institution in United States. Designated institutions: Kansas private colleges and universities, the six public universities in Kansas; also Washburn University.

Eligibility: Applicant must be U.S. citizen or permanent resident residing in Kansas.
Basis for selection: Applicant must demonstrate financial need.
Application requirements: Proof of eligibility. FAFSA.
Additional information: State funding level allows for roughly one in three of eligible applicants to receive award. Award amount ranges from $100 to $1,100 for those attending public institutions, $200 to $3,000 for those attending private institutions. Although deadline is April 1, mail FAFSA by March 15.

Amount of award:	$100-$3,000
Number of awards:	7,114
Number of applicants:	21,235
Application deadline:	April 1
Notification begins:	May 1
Total amount awarded:	$10,505,504

Contact:
Kansas Board of Regents
700 SW Harrison
Suite 1410
Topeka, KS 66603-3760
Phone: 785-296-3517
Fax: 785-296-0983
Web: www.kansasregents.com

Kansas Ethnic Minority Scholarship

Type of award: Scholarship, renewable.
Intended use: For full-time undergraduate study at 2-year or 4-year institution. Designated institutions: Kansas postsecondary institutions.
Eligibility: Applicant must be Alaskan native, Asian American, African American, Mexican American, Hispanic American, Puerto Rican or American Indian. Applicant must be U.S. citizen or permanent resident residing in Kansas.
Basis for selection: Applicant must demonstrate financial need.
Application requirements: $10 application fee. Proof of eligibility. Complete State of Kansas Student Aid Application, FAFSA.
Additional information: Must be recognized in National Merit Scholarship competition, or be designated Hispanic scholar, or have at least 3.0 GPA, ACT score of 21, SAT I score minimum 816, or rank in upper-third of high school graduating class. One-time $10 processing fee for any or all programs listed on application form.

Amount of award:	$1,850
Number of awards:	242
Number of applicants:	623
Application deadline:	April 1
Notification begins:	May 20
Total amount awarded:	$338,671

Contact:
Kansas Board of Regents
700 SW Harrison
Suite 1410
Topeka, KS 66603-3760
Phone: 785-296-3517
Web: www.kansasregents.com

Kansas State Scholarship

Type of award: Scholarship, renewable.
Intended use: For full-time undergraduate study at postsecondary institution. Designated institutions: Kansas schools.

Eligibility: Applicant must be high school senior. Applicant must be residing in Kansas.
Basis for selection: Applicant must demonstrate financial need and high academic achievement.
Application requirements: $10 application fee. Proof of eligibility. Complete State of Kansas Student Aid Application, FAFSA.
Additional information: Must be designated by high school as Kansas State Scholar based on ACT/SAT scores, GPA, and completion of the Regents Recommended Curriculum. One-time $10 processing fee. Number of awards depends on state funding. Priority given to renewals. Must maintain minimum 3.0 GPA to renew.

Amount of award:	$50-$1,000
Number of awards:	1,496
Number of applicants:	2,105
Application deadline:	May 15
Total amount awarded:	$1,419,801

Contact:
Kansas Board of Regents
Student Assistance Section
700 SW Harrison, Suite 1410
Topeka, KS 66603-3760
Phone: 785-296-3517
Fax: 785-296-0983
Web: www.kansasregents.com

Kansas Teacher Scholarship

Type of award: Scholarship, renewable.
Intended use: For full-time freshman, sophomore, junior, senior, post-bachelor's certificate or first professional study at 4-year or graduate institution. Designated institutions: Kansas schools.
Eligibility: Applicant must be residing in Kansas.
Basis for selection: Major/career interest in education, teacher or education, special.
Application requirements: $10 application fee. Recommendations, transcript, proof of eligibility. ACT or SAT scores; class rank. Complete State of Kansas Student Aid Application, FAFSA.
Additional information: Must attend Kansas institution that offers education degree. Loan forgiveness for teaching in designated "hard-to-fill" subject areas in Kansas: one year for each year of financial assistance. Current shortage areas are Special Education, Vocational/Practical Arts, and Foreign Language. $10 processing fee for required state financial assistance application. Scholarship is not need based, but FAFSA required to process application. Minority applicants given special consideration. Priority to renewals (may be renewed for full 4 or five-year course of study). Reverts to loan if service requirement not fulfilled.

Amount of award:	$5,000
Number of awards:	87
Number of applicants:	234
Application deadline:	April 1
Total amount awarded:	$412,000

Contact:
Kansas Board of Regents
700 SW Harrison
Suite 1410
Topeka, KS 66603-3760
Phone: 785-296-3517
Fax: 785-296-0983
Web: www.kansasregents.com

Kansas Vocational Scholarship

Type of award: Scholarship, renewable.
Intended use: For full-time undergraduate study at vocational, 2-year or 4-year institution. Designated institutions: Kansas community or technical colleges, designated four-year programs.
Eligibility: Applicant must be U.S. citizen or permanent resident residing in Kansas.
Basis for selection: Based on vocational examination.
Application requirements: $10 application fee. Proof of eligibility. Must take Kansas vocational examination, offered in November and March.
Additional information: Must be among top 250 scorers on vocational examination. Funding for maximum two years of study in approved vocational program. Register by mid-October for November examination; by mid-February for March examination. Award notification in May. One-time $10 processing fee for any or all programs listed on application form. See your high school or college advisor (or financial aid office) for applications or contact Board of Regents. Approximately one in two applicants funded.

Amount of award:	$500
Number of awards:	244
Number of applicants:	529

Contact:
Kansas Board of Regents
700 SW Harrison
Suite 1410
Topeka, KS 66603-3760
Phone: 785-296-3517
Fax: 785-296-0983
Web: www.kansasregents.com

Kaplan, Inc.

Kaplan/Newsweek "My Turn" Essay Contest

Type of award: Scholarship.
Intended use: For full-time freshman or sophomore study at 2-year or 4-year institution.
Eligibility: Applicant must be enrolled in high school.
Basis for selection: Competition/talent/interest in writing/journalism, based on personal opinion or experience essay on topic chosen by student.
Application requirements: Essay. Applicant must be high school senior or college freshman.
Additional information: Winning essays may be published by Newsweek. Call number listed below for entry form including official rules. Entries may be sent to address listed. Essays must be original and factually accurate and are judged on effectiveness, creativity, insight, organization and development, consistent use of language, variety in sentence structure and vocabulary, use of proper grammar, spelling and punctuation.

Amount of award:	$1,000
Number of awards:	10
Application deadline:	March 1
Notification begins:	April 17
Total amount awarded:	$10,000

Contact:
Kaplan, Inc.
Community Outreach Director
888 7th Ave.
New York, NY 10106
Phone: 800-KAP-TEST
Web: www.kaplan.com

Kappa Kappa Gamma Foundation

Kappa Kappa Gamma Scholarship

Type of award: Scholarship, renewable.
Intended use: For full-time undergraduate or graduate study at 4-year or graduate institution in United States.
Eligibility: Applicant or parent must be member/participant of Kappa Kappa Gamma. Applicant must be female. Applicant must be U.S. citizen, permanent resident, international student or from Canada.
Basis for selection: Applicant must demonstrate high academic achievement.
Application requirements: Recommendations, essay, transcript.
Additional information: Applicant must be a member of Kappa Kappa Gamma fraternity. Applicant must be U.S. citizen or permanent resident from Canada.

Amount of award:	$3,000
Application deadline:	February 1

Contact:
Kappa Kappa Gamma Foundation
P.O. Box 38
Columbus, OH 43216-0038
Web: www.kappakappagamma.org

Karla Scherer Foundation

Karla Scherer Foundation Scholarship

Type of award: Scholarship, renewable.
Intended use: For full-time undergraduate, master's or doctoral study at accredited 4-year or graduate institution in United States.
Eligibility: Applicant must be female.
Basis for selection: Major/career interest in finance/banking; economics; business, international or business/management/administration. Applicant must demonstrate financial need, high academic achievement, depth of character, leadership, seriousness of purpose and service orientation.
Application requirements: Recommendations, essay, transcript, proof of eligibility.
Additional information: International students must have a U.S. study visa. Must have proof of enrollment in qualified U.S. institution. SASE must accompany application request by March 1 for the following academic year. Include identity of school to be attended, course of study, explanation of career plans and other reasons for granting application request. Only majors in finance and economics with plans for a corporate business career in the private manufacturing sector need apply.

Number of awards: 25
Number of applicants: 25,000
Application deadline: March 1
Contact:
The Karla Scherer Foundation
737 N. Michigan Ave., Suite 2330
Chicago, IL 60611
Web: www.comnet.org/kschererf

Keane, Inc.

Keane Educational Scholarship

Type of award: Scholarship.
Intended use: For undergraduate study at accredited 4-year institution.
Eligibility: Applicant or parent must be employed by Keane, Inc. Applicant must be high school senior.
Additional information: Must be child of employee of Keane, Inc. For further information or application, contact Keane, Inc. directly.
  Amount of award: $2,500

Kentucky Higher Education Assistance Authority (KHEAA)

Kentucky College Access Program Grant (KCAPG)

Type of award: Scholarship, renewable.
Intended use: For undergraduate study at 2-year or 4-year institution. Designated institutions: Postsecondary institutions in Kentucky.
Eligibility: Applicant must be U.S. citizen or permanent resident residing in Kentucky.
Basis for selection: Applicant must demonstrate financial need.
Application requirements: Proof of eligibility. FAFSA; applicant ineligible if family contribution exceeds $3100.
Additional information: May be used at eligible technical or proprietary schools. Visit Website for additional information.
  Amount of award: $50-$1,200
  Number of awards: 33,820
  Number of applicants: 194,300
  Notification begins: April 15
  Total amount awarded: $28,057,900
Contact:
Kentucky Higher Education Assistance Authority (KHEAA)
Grant Programs
1050 U.S. 127 South
Frankfort, KY 40601-4323
Phone: 800-928-8926
Fax: 502-695-7345
Web: www.kheaa.com

Kentucky Educational Excellence Scholarship (KEES)

Type of award: Scholarship, renewable.
Intended use: For undergraduate study at accredited vocational, 2-year or 4-year institution. Designated institutions: Participating public and private postsecondary institutions in Kentucky and selected out-of-state institutions if program of study not offered in Kentucky.
Eligibility: Applicant must be enrolled in high school. Applicant must be U.S. citizen or permanent resident residing in Kentucky.
Basis for selection: Applicant must demonstrate high academic achievement.
Application requirements: Minimum annual High School GPA of 2.50. Supplemental award is given for highest ACT or equivalent SAT score achieved by HS graduation, based on minimum ACT score of 15. High School districts routinely report annual year-end grades to Kentucky Department of Education.
Additional information: Applicant must be enrolled in postsecondary program at least half-time. Scholarship is earned each year of high school. Visit Website or contact via e-mail (tphelps@kheaa.com) for additional information.
  Amount of award: $125-$500
Contact:
Kentucky Higher Education Assistance Authority (KHEAA)
1050 U.S. 127 South
Frankfort, KY 40601-4323
Phone: 800-928-8926
Fax: 502-696-7345
Web: www.kheaa.com

Kentucky Tuition Grant

Type of award: Scholarship, renewable.
Intended use: For full-time undergraduate study at 2-year or 4-year institution. Designated institutions: Eligible private institutions in Kentucky.
Eligibility: Applicant must be U.S. citizen residing in Kentucky.
Basis for selection: Applicant must demonstrate financial need.
Application requirements: Interview, proof of eligibility. FAFSA.
Additional information: Visit Website for additional information.
  Amount of award: $200-$1,600
  Number of awards: 9,160
  Number of applicants: 15,110
  Notification begins: April 15
  Total amount awarded: $12,046,300
Contact:
Kentucky Higher Education Assistance Authority
Grant Programs
1050 U.S. 127 South
Frankfort, KY 40601-4323
Phone: 800-928-8926
Fax: 502-695-7345
Web: www.kheaa.com

Knights of Columbus

Matthews/Swift Educational Trust - Military Dependants

Type of award: Scholarship, renewable.
Intended use: For full-time undergraduate study at 4-year institution in United States. Designated institutions: Catholic colleges and universities.
Eligibility: Applicant or parent must be member/participant of Knights of Columbus. Applicant must be Roman Catholic. Applicant must be dependent of disabled veteran or deceased veteran during Korean War, Persian Gulf War, WW II or Vietnam. Parent must have been Knights of Columbus member when killed in action or died as result of service-connected disability. Parent disabled as result of military conflict must have kept Knights of Columbus membership active.
Application requirements: Proof of eligibility.
Additional information: Award pays tuition, room, board, books and incidental fees at a Catholic college. No application deadline. Applicant's parent must be a member.

Amount of award:	Full tuition
Number of awards:	10
Number of applicants:	10

Contact:
Knights of Columbus
Director of Scholarship Aid
P.O. Box 1670
New Haven, CT 06507-0901
Phone: 203-772-2130

Matthews/Swift Educational Trust - Police/Firefighters

Type of award: Scholarship, renewable.
Intended use: For full-time undergraduate study at 4-year institution in United States. Designated institutions: Catholic colleges and universities.
Eligibility: Applicant or parent must be member/participant of Knights of Columbus. Applicant must be Roman Catholic. Applicant's parent must have been killed or disabled in work-related accident as fire fighter or police officer.
Application requirements: Proof of eligibility. Applicant's father must have been killed or permanently and totally disabled as the result of criminal violence while performing his duties as a full-time fire fighter or law enforcement officer.
Additional information: Applicant's parent must be a member. Award pays tuition, room, board, books and incidental fees at a Catholic college. No application deadline.

Amount of award:	Full tuition
Number of awards:	10
Number of applicants:	10

Contact:
Knights of Columbus
Director of Scholarship Aid
P.O. Box 1670
New Haven, CT 06507-0901
Phone: 203-772-2130

Pro Deo/Pro Patria Scholarship

Type of award: Scholarship, renewable.
Intended use: For full-time undergraduate study at 4-year institution in United States. Designated institutions: Catholic colleges and universities.
Eligibility: Applicant or parent must be member/participant of Knights of Columbus. Applicant must be high school senior. Applicant must be Roman Catholic. Applicant must be U.S. citizen.
Basis for selection: Applicant must demonstrate high academic achievement, depth of character, leadership and seriousness of purpose.
Application requirements: Recommendations, essay, transcript, proof of eligibility.
Additional information: Must be Knights of Columbus member in good standing, or son or daughter of such a member or deceased member, or member in good standing of Columbian Squires. 12 scholarships designated for students at the Catholic University in Washington, DC; 50 are available to students entering other Catholic colleges in the United States. Scholarship applications must be filed by March 1 and are available from Director of Scholarship Aid, Knights of Columbus, in New Haven, CT.

Amount of award:	$1,500
Number of awards:	62
Number of applicants:	500
Application deadline:	March 1
Notification begins:	May 15
Total amount awarded:	$357,750

Contact:
Knights of Columbus
Director of Scholarship Aid
P.O. Box 1670
New Haven, CT 06510-0901
Phone: 203-772-2130

Kohler Co.

Kohler Co. College Scholarship Program

Type of award: Scholarship, renewable.
Intended use: For freshman study at 4-year institution.
Eligibility: Applicant or parent must be employed by Kohler Co.
Basis for selection: Applicant must demonstrate financial need.
Additional information: For further information or an application, contact Kohler Co. directly.

Amount of award:	$1,200-$1,500

Kosciuszko Foundation

Kosciuszko Foundation Tuition Scholarships

Type of award: Scholarship, renewable.
Intended use: For full-time junior, senior or graduate study at 4-year or graduate institution in United States.
Eligibility: Applicant must be Polish. Applicant must be U.S. citizen or permanent resident.
Basis for selection: Major/career interest in polish language/studies. Applicant must demonstrate financial need, high academic achievement, seriousness of purpose and service orientation.

Application requirements: $25 application fee.
Recommendations, essay, transcript. Proof of Polish descent.
Additional information: Minimum GPA 3.0. Applicant must
be entering upper level postsecondary or graduate program.
Limit of two tuition scholarships per individual during period of
his/her studies. Only one member of immediate family awarded
at a time. Eligible applicants must be either U.S. citizens of
Polish descent, Polish citizens with permanent residentcy status
in U.S., or U.S. citizens pursuing Polish studies as a major.
Students of other nationalities doing work in Polish studies
considered. Student must reapply for renewal of award. Visit
Website or call for application. Applications available from
August to December.

Amount of award:	$1,000-$5,000
Application deadline:	January 16
Notification begins:	May 15
Total amount awarded:	$330,000

Contact:
Kosciuszko Foundation
15 East 65 Street
New York, NY 10021-6595
Phone: 212-734-2130
Web: www.kosciuszkofoundation.org

Kosciuszko Foundation Year Abroad Program

Type of award: Scholarship, renewable.
Intended use: For full-time junior, senior or master's study at
4-year institution in Poland. Designated institutions:
Jagiellonian University, Polonia Institute in Poland.
Eligibility: Applicant must be U.S. citizen or permanent
resident.
Basis for selection: Competition/talent/interest in study
abroad. Major/career interest in polish language/studies.
Applicant must demonstrate high academic achievement.
Application requirements: $50 application fee. Essay. Essay
must explain motivation for pursuing studies in Poland.
Additional information: Must have interest in Polish subjects
and/or involvement in Polish-American community. Scholarship
covers tuition, housing monthly stipend for living expenses for
one academic year or semester. Travel costs not covered.
Minimum 3.0 GPA. Interview may be required. Previous
recipients and candidates may reapply. All applicants will be
notified in late spring. See Website for more details and
application. Applications available from August to December.
Faxed applications are not accepted. Student must reapply for
renewal.

Amount of award:	Full tuition
Application deadline:	January 16

Contact:
Kosciuszko Foundation
Year Abroad Program
15 East 65th Street
New York, NY 10021
Web: www.kosciuszkofoundation.org

Krause Publications, Inc.

Partners in Publishing Sons and Daughters Scholarship

Type of award: Scholarship.

Intended use: For undergraduate study at accredited
vocational, 2-year or 4-year institution.
Eligibility: Applicant or parent must be employed by Krause
Publications, Inc. Applicant must be high school senior.
Basis for selection: Applicant must demonstrate financial
need.
Additional information: For further information or
application, contact Krause Publication, Inc. directly.

Amount of award:	$1,500-$2,000

Laidlaw, Inc.

Laidlaw Scholarship

Type of award: Scholarship.
Intended use: For undergraduate study at vocational, 2-year or
4-year institution.
Eligibility: Applicant or parent must be employed by Laidlaw,
Inc. Applicant must be high school senior.
Additional information: For further information or an
application, contact Laidlaw Incorporated directly.

Amount of award:	$2,000-$3,000

Lambda Alpha

National Dean's List Scholarship

Type of award: Scholarship.
Intended use: For senior study at accredited 4-year or
graduate institution in United States in U.S. territories.
Eligibility: Applicant or parent must be member/participant of
Lambda Alpha. Applicant must be U.S. citizen or permanent
resident.
Basis for selection: Major/career interest in anthropology.
Applicant must demonstrate high academic achievement and
seriousness of purpose.
Application requirements: Recommendations, transcript,
nomination by faculty sponsor from department of
anthropology. Send a curriculum vitae.
Additional information: Institution must have chartered
Lambda Alpha chapter. Applicant must be member of Lambda
Alpha. Apply in junior year.

Amount of award:	$1,000
Number of awards:	1
Number of applicants:	7
Application deadline:	March 1
Notification begins:	April 1
Total amount awarded:	$1,000

Contact:
Lambda Alpha
Department of Anthropology
Ball State University
Muncie, IN 47306-1099
Phone: 765-285-1577
Web: www.lambdaalphahonorary.homestead.com

National Lambda Alpha Scholarship Award

Type of award: Scholarship.

Intended use: For undergraduate or graduate study. Designated institutions: Institution must have chartered Lambda Alpha chapter.
Eligibility: Applicant or parent must be member/participant of Lambda Alpha. Applicant must be U.S. citizen.
Basis for selection: Major/career interest in anthropology. Applicant must demonstrate seriousness of purpose.
Application requirements: Transcript by faculty sponsor from department of anthropology. Include curriculum vitae, statement of future plans and sample of professional writing.
Additional information: Applicant must be life member of Lambda Alpha. Apply in junior year.

Amount of award:	$5,000
Number of awards:	1
Number of applicants:	17
Application deadline:	March 1
Notification begins:	April 1
Total amount awarded:	$5,000

Contact:
Lambda Alpha
Department of Anthropology
Ball State University
Muncie, IN 47306-1099
Phone: 765-285-1577
Web: www.lambdaalphahonorary.homestead.com

Landscape Architecture Foundation

CLASS (California Landscape Architectural Student Scholarship) University Program

Type of award: Scholarship.
Intended use: For junior or senior study at accredited postsecondary institution in United States. Designated institutions: University of California Davis, California Polytechnic at Pomona and San Luis Obispo.
Eligibility: Applicant must be residing in California.
Basis for selection: Major/career interest in landscape architecture. Applicant must demonstrate financial need.
Application requirements: Recommendations, essay. Academic, community and professional involvement background 300-word statement on the profession. 100-word statement on intended use of funds. Two faculty recommendation letters.
Additional information: Open to students at University of California Davis, California Polytechnic at Pomona and San Luis Obispo. Two scholarships are awarded per institution. Contact Melissa Sippel for further information.

Amount of award:	$1,500
Number of awards:	6
Application deadline:	March 31
Total amount awarded:	$9,000

Contact:
Landscape Architecture Foundation
636 Eye Street, NW
Washington, DC 20001
Phone: 202-898-2444
Web: www.asla.org

CLASS Fund Scholarship Ornamental Horticulture Program

Type of award: Scholarship.
Intended use: For junior or senior study at accredited postsecondary institution in United States. Designated institutions: California Polytechnic at Pomona, San Luis Obispo, or University of California at Davis.
Eligibility: Applicant must be residing in California.
Basis for selection: Major/career interest in horticulture.
Application requirements: Recommendations, essay. Academic, community and professional involvement background. 300-word statement on the profession. 100-word statement indicating intended use of funds. Two faculty recommendation letters.
Additional information: For juniors or seniors enrolled in ornamental horticulture curriculum at California Polytechnic at Pomona, San Luis Obispo, or University of California at Davis. One award per institution. Contact Melinda Sippel for further information.

Amount of award:	$1,000
Number of awards:	3
Application deadline:	March 31
Total amount awarded:	$3,000

Contact:
Landscape Architecture Foundation
636 Eye Street
Washington, DC 20001-3736
Phone: 202-898-2444
Web: www.asla.org

CLASS Landscape Architecture Program

Type of award: Scholarship.
Intended use: For full-time undergraduate study. Designated institutions: University of California, Berkeley; University of California, Los Angeles; University of California, Davis; Cal Poly Pomona; Cal Poly San Luis Obispo.
Eligibility: Applicant must be residing in California.
Basis for selection: Major/career interest in landscape architecture. Applicant must demonstrate financial need and service orientation.
Application requirements: Recommendations, essay, transcript. Academic, community and professional involvement background. 300-word statement on the profession. 100-word statement on intended use of funds. Two faculty recommendation letters. One confidential department head recommendation.
Additional information: For use at designated insitutions only. Two awards per institution.

Amount of award:	$500
Number of awards:	10
Application deadline:	March 31
Total amount awarded:	$5,000

Contact:
Landscape Architecture Foundation
636 Eye Street NW
Washington, DC 20001
Phone: 202-898-2444
Web: www.asla.org

David T. Woolsey Scholarship

Type of award: Scholarship.

Intended use: For full-time junior, senior, master's or doctoral study at accredited 4-year or graduate institution.
Eligibility: Applicant must be residing in Hawaii.
Basis for selection: Major/career interest in landscape architecture. Applicant must demonstrate service orientation.
Application requirements: Portfolio, recommendations, essay, proof of eligibility. Autobiographical statement of personal and professional goals (500 word maximum). Sample of design work. Three eight-by-ten color and/or black and white photographs. Also include two letters of recommendation and proof of Hawaiian residency.
Additional information: Applicant must be enrolled in a landscape architecture program at an accredited college/ university to qualify.

Amount of award:	$1,000
Number of awards:	1
Number of applicants:	4
Application deadline:	March 31
Total amount awarded:	$1,000

Contact:
Landscape Architecture Foundation
636 Eye St. NW
Washington, DC 20001-3736
Phone: 202-216-9034
Web: www.asla.org

Edith H. Henderson Scholarship

Type of award: Scholarship.
Intended use: For undergraduate study at postsecondary institution.
Basis for selection: Major/career interest in landscape architecture.
Application requirements: Include a 200 to 400 word typewritten essay reviewing Edith Henderson's Home Landscape Companion. Also, participation in public speaking and creative writing classes welcomed.
Additional information: Applicant must be committed to developing practical communication skills in their role as a landscape architect. Scholarship under review for restructuring. Contact Melinda Sippel for more information.

Amount of award:	$1,000
Number of awards:	1
Application deadline:	March 31

Contact:
Landscape Architecture Foundation
636 Eye Street, NW
Washington, DC 20001
Phone: 202-898-2444
Web: www.asla.org

Edward D. Stone, Jr., and Associates Minority Scholarship

Type of award: Scholarship.
Intended use: For full-time junior or senior study at 4-year institution.
Eligibility: Applicant must be Alaskan native, Asian American, African American, Mexican American, Hispanic American, Puerto Rican or American Indian.
Basis for selection: Major/career interest in landscape architecture; horticulture; construction or urban planning. Applicant must demonstrate financial need and service orientation.
Application requirements: Portfolio, recommendations, essay, proof of eligibility, research proposal. 500-word essay describing a design or research effort you plan to pursue and

explain how it will contribute to the advancement of the profession and your ethnic heritage. Four to eight 35mm color slides arranged in a plastic folder or three to five 8x10 photos of work. Two letters of recommendation. Financial aid forms.
Additional information: Contact Melinda Sippel for further information. For more information, click on LAF at opening page of ASLA Website. Applicant must be enrolled in a landscape architecture program at an accredited college/ university.

Amount of award:	$1,000
Number of awards:	1
Number of applicants:	6
Application deadline:	March 31
Total amount awarded:	$1,000

Contact:
The Landscape Architecture Foundation
636 Eye St. NW
Washington, DC 20001-3736
Phone: 202-216-9034
Web: www.asla.org

Harriett Barnhart Wimmer Scholarship

Type of award: Scholarship.
Intended use: For full-time senior study at accredited 4-year institution.
Eligibility: Applicant must be female.
Basis for selection: Major/career interest in landscape architecture; horticulture; construction or urban planning. Applicant must demonstrate service orientation.
Application requirements: Portfolio, recommendations, essay, research proposal. 500-word essay. Letter of recommendation from a design instructor. Samples of solo work in the form of six eight-by-ten photographs and brief written descriptions of design. Financial aid forms.
Additional information: Contact Foundation for further information. Or click on LAF at opening page of Website.

Amount of award:	$1,000
Number of awards:	1
Number of applicants:	14
Application deadline:	March 31
Total amount awarded:	$1,000

Contact:
The Landscape Architecture Foundation
636 Eye St. NW
Washington, DC 20001-3736
Phone: 202-216-9034
Web: www.asla.org

Rain Bird Company Scholarship

Type of award: Scholarship.
Intended use: For full-time junior, senior or post-bachelor's certificate study at accredited 4-year institution.
Basis for selection: Major/career interest in landscape architecture; horticulture; construction or urban planning. Applicant must demonstrate financial need and high academic achievement.
Application requirements: Essay. Submission of 300-word essay stating career goals and expected contribution to landscape architecture. Completed financial aid forms.
Additional information: Fifth year undergraduates eligible. Award under review. Contact Foundation for latest information. Or click on "LAF" at opening page of Website.

Amount of award: $1,000
Number of awards: 1
Number of applicants: 30
Application deadline: March 31
Total amount awarded: $1,000
Contact:
Landscape Architecture Foundation
636 Eye St. NW
Washington, DC 20001-3637
Phone: 202-216-2356
Web: www.asla.com

Raymond E. Page Scholarship

Type of award: Scholarship.
Intended use: For full-time sophomore, junior or senior study at accredited 4-year institution.
Basis for selection: Major/career interest in landscape architecture; horticulture; urban planning or construction. Applicant must demonstrate financial need and seriousness of purpose.
Application requirements: Recommendations, essay. A two-page essay detailing financial need and how award will be used and a recommendation from a current professor who is familiar with that applicant's character and intent to pursue an education in landscape architecture.
Additional information: For students committed to directing the profession of landscape architecture by answering the challenges of tomorrow. Contact Foundation for further information or click on LAF at opening page of Website.
Amount of award: $1,000
Number of awards: 1
Application deadline: March 31
Total amount awarded: $1,000
Contact:
Landscape Architecture Foundation
636 Eye St. NW
Washington, DC 20001-3736
Phone: 202-216-9034
Web: www.asla.org

Thomas P. Papandrew Scholarship

Type of award: Scholarship, renewable.
Intended use: For full-time undergraduate study at accredited postsecondary institution in United States. Designated institutions: Arizona State University.
Eligibility: Applicant must be Alaskan native, Asian American, African American, Mexican American, Hispanic American, Puerto Rican or American Indian. Applicant must be residing in Arizona.
Basis for selection: Major/career interest in landscape architecture. Applicant must demonstrate financial need and high academic achievement.
Application requirements: Recommendations, essay, transcript. Letter summarizing need, career plans and background. Academic budget for coming year. Letter of reference attesting to career potential.
Additional information: Must be Arizona resident accepted or enrolled at Arizona State University in the College of Architecture and Environmental Design. Contact Melinda Sippel for further information.
Amount of award: $1,000
Application deadline: March 31

Contact:
School of Planning and Landscape Architecture at ASU
Phone: 202-898-2444
Web: www.asla.org

William J. Locklin Scholarship

Type of award: Scholarship.
Intended use: For full-time sophomore, junior or senior study at accredited 4-year or graduate institution.
Basis for selection: Major/career interest in landscape architecture; horticulture; urban planning or construction.
Application requirements: Recommendations, essay, research proposal. 300-word essay highlighting design project and anticipated results. Visual samples reduced to letter-size paper, in the form of schematics, sketches, or renderings. Letter of reccommendation relevant to the proposed project and applicant, preferably from a current professor.
Additional information: Proposal must be on lighting design project, emphasizing 24-hour lighting in landscape designs. Preference given to projects designed to see effect, not source. Contact Melinda Sippel for further information.
Amount of award: $1,000
Number of awards: 1
Number of applicants: 30
Application deadline: March 31
Total amount awarded: $1,000
Contact:
Scholarship Coordinator
636 Eye St. NW
Washington, DC 20001-3736
Phone: 202-216-9034
Web: www.asla.org

Latin American Educational Foundation

Latin American Educational Scholarship

Type of award: Scholarship, renewable.
Intended use: For full-time undergraduate, graduate or non-degree study at accredited postsecondary institution in United States.
Eligibility: Applicant must be Mexican American, Hispanic American or Puerto Rican. Must have Hispanic heritage or be actively involved in Hispanic community. Applicant must be residing in Colorado.
Basis for selection: Applicant must demonstrate financial need and high academic achievement.
Application requirements: Recommendations, essay, transcript, proof of eligibility.
Additional information: Minimum GPA 2.5 required. SATor ACTscores required for high school seniors. Recipients must fulfill ten hours of community service during the award year.
Amount of award: $500-$3,000
Number of awards: 200
Number of applicants: 350
Application deadline: February 15
Notification begins: May 31

Contact:
Executive Director
930 West 7th Avenue
Denver, CO 80204
Phone: 303-446-0541
Fax: 303-446-0526
Web: www.laef.org

Learning for Life

Floyd Boring Award

Type of award: Scholarship.
Intended use: For undergraduate study at accredited 2-year or 4-year institution.
Eligibility: Applicant or parent must be member/participant of Learning for Life. Applicant must be U.S. citizen or permanent resident.
Basis for selection: Major/career interest in criminal justice/ law enforcement. Applicant must demonstrate depth of character, leadership, seriousness of purpose and service orientation.
Additional information: Candidates must have performed "an act which assisted in the prevention or solution of a serious crime or an act which assisted in leading to the apprehension of a felony suspect wanted by a law enforcement agency." Applicant or parent must be member of Explorers. Visit Website for more information and to download application.

Amount of award:	$2,000
Number of awards:	2
Application deadline:	March 31
Total amount awarded:	$4,000

Contact:
Website.
Phone: 972-580-2003
Web: www.learning-for-life.org

Frank D. Visceglia Memorial Scholarship

Type of award: Scholarship, renewable.
Intended use: For full-time freshman study at accredited 4-year institution.
Eligibility: Applicant or parent must be member/participant of Boy Scouts of America, Eagle Scouts. Applicant must be male, high school senior. Applicant must be U.S. citizen or permanent resident residing in New Jersey.
Additional information: Must be an Eagle Scout. Preference given to applicants whose service projects relate to environment and/or economy.

Amount of award:	$1,000
Number of awards:	1
Number of applicants:	12
Application deadline:	September 30
Total amount awarded:	$1,000

Contact:
Frank D. Visceglia Memorial Scholarship Program
Dennis Kohl, Scout Executive
1170 R722W
Mountainside, NJ 07092

National Technical Investigators' Captain James J. Regan Memorial Scholarship

Type of award: Scholarship.
Intended use: For full-time undergraduate study.
Eligibility: Applicant or parent must be member/participant of Learning for Life. Applicant must be high school senior. Applicant must be U.S. citizen or permanent resident.
Basis for selection: Major/career interest in criminal justice/ law enforcement. Applicant must demonstrate high academic achievement, leadership and seriousness of purpose.
Application requirements: Recommendations, essay, transcript. Extracurricular activities. Subject of personal essay must be "what significance I place on a technical background in law enforcement." A black-and-white glossy photograph in uniform.
Additional information: Program open to law enforcement Explorers. Visit Website for more information and to download application.

Amount of award:	$500
Number of awards:	2
Application deadline:	March 31
Total amount awarded:	$1,000

Contact:
Website.
Phone: 972-580-2003
Fax: 972-580-2502
Web: www.learning-for-life.org

Sheryl A. Horak Law Enforcement Explorer Scholarship

Type of award: Scholarship.
Intended use: For full-time undergraduate study at accredited 2-year or 4-year institution.
Eligibility: Applicant or parent must be member/participant of Learning for Life. Applicant must be high school senior. Applicant must be U.S. citizen or permanent resident.
Basis for selection: Major/career interest in criminal justice/ law enforcement. Applicant must demonstrate high academic achievement, leadership and service orientation.
Application requirements: Recommendations, essay, transcript. Participation in extracurricular activities. Applicant must be a member of Explorers. Essay must be "Why I want to pursue a career in law enforcement."
Additional information: Vistit Website for more information and to download application. Must send two copies and original of both application and all support materials.

Amount of award:	$1,000
Number of awards:	1
Application deadline:	March 31

Contact:
Website.
Phone: 972-580-2003
Fax: 972-580-2502
Web: www.learning-for-life.org

Leggett & Platt Scholarship Foundation

Leggett & Platt Scholarship Program for Children of Employees

Type of award: Scholarship, renewable.
Intended use: For undergraduate study at vocational, 2-year or 4-year institution.
Eligibility: Applicant or parent must be employed by Leggett & Platt Scholarship Foundation. Applicant must be high school senior.
Additional information: For further information or an application, contact Leggett & Platt Scholarship Foundation directly.

Amount of award:	$1,000-$2,000

Leroy E. Dettman Foundation, Inc.

Leroy E. Dettman Foundation Scholarship

Type of award: Scholarship.
Intended use: For full-time undergraduate or graduate study at accredited postsecondary institution in United States.
Eligibility: Applicant or parent must be employed by Interim Services. Applicant must be U.S. citizen.
Basis for selection: Applicant must demonstrate financial need and high academic achievement.
Application requirements: Transcript, proof of eligibility. SAT/ACT scores.
Additional information: Employees of Interim Services given preference, but anyone can apply.Copy of parent's most recent year's income taxes required; copy of own return is required if applicant is financially independent.

Amount of award:	$500-$2,500
Number of awards:	76
Number of applicants:	365
Application deadline:	March 15
Notification begins:	June 15
Total amount awarded:	$75,000

Contact:
Leroy E. Dettman Foundation, Inc.
1615 South Federal Highway
Suite 300
Boca Raton, FL 33432
Phone: 561-367-9811

Levi Strauss Foundation

Levi Strauss Foundation Scholarship

Type of award: Scholarship, renewable.
Intended use: For undergraduate study at accredited vocational, 2-year or 4-year institution.

Eligibility: Applicant or parent must be employed by Levi Strauss & Co.
Basis for selection: Applicant must demonstrate financial need.
Additional information: For further information or an application, contact Levi Strauss & Co. directly.

Amount of award:	$750-$2,000

Lew Wasserman Scholarship Foundation

Lew Wasserman College Scholarship

Type of award: Scholarship.
Intended use: For undergraduate study at accredited 4-year institution.
Eligibility: Applicant or parent must be employed by Universal Studios - Southern California. Applicant must be high school senior.
Basis for selection: Applicant must demonstrate financial need.
Additional information: For further information or application, contact Lew Wasserman Scholarship Foundation-MCA Universal directly.

Amount of award:	$500-$4,000

Contact:
Lew Wasserman Scholarship Foundation

LifeScan Inc.

LifeScan Scholarship Program/Dana Pettengill Scholarship Fund

Type of award: Scholarship, renewable.
Intended use: For freshman study at 2-year or 4-year institution.
Eligibility: Applicant or parent must be employed by Lifescan Inc.
Additional information: For further information or an application, contact LifeScan Inc. directly.

Amount of award:	$1,250

Lifetouch

Richard P. Erickson Scholarship Program

Type of award: Scholarship.
Intended use: For undergraduate study at vocational, 2-year or 4-year institution.
Eligibility: Applicant or parent must be employed by Lifetouch. Applicant must be high school senior.
Additional information: For further information or an application, contact Lifetouch directly.

Amount of award:	$2,000

Lighthouse International

Lighthouse College-Bound Incentive Award

Type of award: Scholarship.
Intended use: For full-time freshman study at accredited 2-year or 4-year institution. Designated institutions: Schools in New York, New Jersey, Pennsylvania, Connecticut, Massachusetts, Maine, Vermont, New Hampshire, Rhode Island.
Eligibility: Applicant must be visually impaired. Applicant must be high school senior. Applicant must be U.S. citizen residing in Connecticut, Massachusetts, Maine, New Jersey, New Hampshire, New York, Rhode Island, Pennsylvania or Vermont.
Basis for selection: Applicant must demonstrate high academic achievement.
Application requirements: Recommendations, essay, transcript, proof of eligibility. Documentation of legal blindness from State Commission for the Blind. Recommendations required: one personal, one academic. Personal essay should be at least 500 words. Transcript must be official. Letter of acceptance to college.

Amount of award:	$5,000
Number of awards:	1
Application deadline:	March 29
Total amount awarded:	$5,000

Contact:
Lighthouse International
Career Incentive Awards Program
111 East 59 Street
New York, NY 10022
Phone: 212-821-9428
Fax: 212-821-9703
Web: www.lighthouse.org

Lighthouse Undergraduate Incentive Award I

Type of award: Scholarship.
Intended use: For full-time undergraduate study at postsecondary institution. Designated institutions: Schools in New Jersey, New York, Pennsylvania, Connecticut, Massachusetts, Maine, New Hampshire, Rhode Island, Vermont.
Eligibility: Applicant must be visually impaired. Applicant must be U.S. citizen residing in Connecticut, Massachusetts, Maine, New Jersey, New Hampshire, New York, Rhode Island, Pennsylvania or Vermont.
Basis for selection: Applicant must demonstrate high academic achievement.
Application requirements: Recommendations, essay, transcript, proof of eligibility. Documentation of legal blindness from State Commission for the Blind. Recommendations required: one personal, one academic. Personal essay should be at least 500 words. Transcript must be official.

Amount of award:	$5,000
Number of awards:	1
Application deadline:	March 29
Total amount awarded:	$5,000

Contact:
Lighthouse International
Career Incentive Awards Program
111 East 59 Street
New York, NY 10022
Phone: 212-821-9428
Fax: 212-821-9703
Web: www.lighthouse.org

Lighthouse Undergraduate Incentive Award II

Type of award: Scholarship.
Intended use: For full-time undergraduate study. Designated institutions: Schools in New York, New Jersey, Pennsylvania, Connecticut, Massachusetts, Rohde Island, Vermont, New Hampshire, Maine.
Eligibility: Applicant must be visually impaired. Applicant must be returning adult student. Applicant must be U.S. citizen residing in Connecticut, Massachusetts, Maine, New Jersey, New Hampshire, New York, Rhode Island, Pennsylvania or Vermont.
Basis for selection: Applicant must demonstrate high academic achievement.
Application requirements: Recommendations, essay, transcript, proof of eligibility. Documentation of legal blindness from State Commission for the Blind. Recommendations required: one personal, one academic. Personal essay should be at least 500 words. Transcript must be official.
Additional information: This award is for adults in any year of undergraduate study.

Amount of award:	$5,000
Number of awards:	1
Application deadline:	March 29
Total amount awarded:	$5,000

Contact:
Lighthouse International
Career Incentive Awards Program
111 East 59 Street
New York, NY 10022
Phone: 212-821-9428
Fax: 212-821-9703
Web: www.lighthouse.org

Link-Belt Construction Equipment Company

Link-Belt Scholarship

Type of award: Scholarship, renewable.
Intended use: For undergraduate study at vocational, 2-year or 4-year institution.
Eligibility: Applicant or parent must be employed by Link-Belt Construction Equipment Company. Applicant must be high school senior.
Additional information: For further information or an application, contact Link-Belt Constuction Equipment Company directly.

Amount of award:	$750-$1,500

Louisiana Department of Social Services

Louisiana Social Services Rehabilitation/Vocational Aid For Disabled Persons

Type of award: Scholarship, renewable.
Intended use: For undergraduate, graduate or non-degree study.
Eligibility: Applicant must be visually impaired, hearing impaired, physically challenged or learning disabled. Applicant must be residing in Louisiana.
Basis for selection: Applicant must demonstrate financial need.
Application requirements: Proof of eligibility. Must satisfy federal eligibility requirements relating to physical and/or mental disabilities.
Additional information: Must have significant, medically verifiable physical, mental or emotional disability which constitutes substantial impedement to employment. Provides monetary assistance for education leading to development of employable skill.
Contact:
Louisiana Rehabilitation Services
8225 Florida Boulevard
Baton Rouge, LA 70806
Phone: 225-925-4131

Louisiana Department of Veterans Affairs

Louisiana Veterans Affairs Educational Assistance for Dependent Children

Type of award: Scholarship, renewable.
Intended use: For full-time undergraduate, graduate or non-degree study at vocational, 2-year, 4-year or graduate institution. Designated institutions: Louisiana public institutions.
Eligibility: Applicant must be at least 16, no older than 25. Applicant must be residing in Louisiana. Applicant must be dependent of veteran, disabled veteran or deceased veteran.
Application requirements: Proof of eligibility. Must obtain certification of eligibility and application from parish veterans assistance counselor.
Additional information: Disability must be at least 90 percent as rated by U.S. Department of Veterans Affairs to qualify. Applicant also eligible if disability rating is 60 percent or more but employability rating is 100 percent unemployable. Award amounts vary and may be applied only toward state public schools.
  Amount of award: Full tuition
Contact:
Louisiana Department of Veterans Affairs
P.O. Box 94095, Capitol Station
Baton Rouge, LA 70804-9095

Louisiana Veterans Affairs Educational Assistance for Surviving Spouse

Type of award: Scholarship, renewable.
Intended use: For full-time undergraduate, graduate or non-degree study at postsecondary institution. Designated institutions: Louisiana public institutions.
Eligibility: Applicant must be single. Applicant must be residing in Louisiana. Applicant must be spouse of deceased veteran.
Application requirements: Proof of eligibility. Must obtain certification of eligibility and application from parish veterans assistance counselor.
Additional information: Veteran must have been a Lousiana resident at least 12 month prior to disability or death. Contact local Parish Veterans Service office for more information and application.
  Amount of award: Full tuition
Contact:
Louisiana Department of Veterans Affairs
P.O. Box 94095, Capitol Station
Baton Rouge, LA 70804-9095

Louisiana Office of Student Financial Assistance

Louisiana Leveraging Educational Assistance Partnership

Type of award: Scholarship, renewable.
Intended use: For full-time freshman, sophomore, junior or senior study at vocational, 2-year or 4-year institution. Designated institutions: Louisiana postsecondary institutions.
Eligibility: Applicant must be U.S. citizen, international student or eligible non-U.S. citizen. Applicant must be residing in Louisiana.
Basis for selection: Applicant must demonstrate financial need.
Additional information: Applicant must have been living in Louisiana 12 months before applying. Must have minimum of 45 on GED, 20 on ACT, or high school or postsecondary GPA minimum of 2.00. May not be in default on any student loan or grant. May be used at state technical institutions or proprietary schools. Must be registered with Selective Service if required. Contact financial aid office of institution. Must reapply for award annually.
  Amount of award: $200-$2,000
  Number of awards: 2,800
  Total amount awarded: $1,388,343
Contact:
Louisiana Office of Student Financial Assistance
P.O. Box 91202
Baton Rouge, LA 70821-9202
Phone: 800-259-5626
Web: www.osfa.state.la.us

Louisiana Rockefeller Wildlife Scholarship

Type of award: Scholarship, renewable.

Intended use: For full-time undergraduate or graduate study at 4-year or graduate institution. Designated institutions: Louisiana public institutions.
Eligibility: Applicant must be U.S. citizen, international student or eligible non-U.S. citizen. Applicant must be residing in Louisiana.
Basis for selection: Major/career interest in wildlife/fisheries; forestry or oceanography/marine studies. Applicant must demonstrate high academic achievement.
Application requirements: FAFSA. Rockefeller State Wildlife Scholarship application.
Additional information: Minimum 2.5 GPA required. May not be in default on any educational loan or grant. Must be registered with Selective Service if required. Must attain degree in eligible field at Louisiana public college or university or repay funds received, plus interest. Must achieve cumulative GPA of at least 2.5 at end of each spring semester and have earned at least 24 hours total credit by end of academic year (fall and spring). Recipients receive $500 for each semester. Cumulative amount of $7,000 will be awarded for up to five years of undergraduate and two years of graduate study.

Amount of award:	$1,000
Number of awards:	70
Number of applicants:	150
Application deadline:	July 1
Total amount awarded:	$60,000

Contact:
Louisiana Office of Student Financial Assistance
P.O. Box 91202
Baton Rouge, LA 70821-9202
Phone: 800-259-5626 ext. 1012
Web: www.osfa.state.la.us

Louisiana Tuition Opportunity Program for Students Honors Award

Type of award: Scholarship, renewable.
Intended use: For full-time undergraduate study. Designated institutions: Eligible Louisiana postsecondary schools.
Eligibility: Applicant must be U.S. citizen residing in Louisiana.
Basis for selection: Applicant must demonstrate high academic achievement.
Application requirements: FAFSA.
Additional information: All eligible students funded. Minimum 3.5 high school GPA required. Must be Louisiana resident for at least two years prior to graduation. ACT score of 27 or better required. Must have no criminal record; must be registered with Selective Service if required. Award includes annual stipend of $800 (for student), with remainder paid to educational institution. Beginning with graduating class of 2003, GPA to be calculated based on core curriculum courses only.

Amount of award:	$1,056-$2,708
Application deadline:	July 1

Contact:
Louisiana Office of Student Financial Assistance
P.O. Box 91202
Baton Rouge, LA 70821-9202
Phone: 800-259-5626 ext. 1012
Fax: 225-922-0790
Web: www.osfa.state.la.us

Louisiana Tuition Opportunity Program for Students Opportunity Award

Type of award: Scholarship, renewable.
Intended use: For full-time undergraduate study at 4-year institution. Designated institutions: Eligible four-year postsecondary institutions in Louisiana.
Eligibility: Applicant must be U.S. citizen residing in Louisiana.
Basis for selection: Applicant must demonstrate high academic achievement.
Application requirements: FAFSA.
Additional information: All eligible students funded. Applicant must be Louisiana resident for at least two years prior to high school graduation. Must have minimum high school cumulative GPA of 2.50 (beginning with graduating class of 2003, qualifying GPA will be calculated only using grades achieved on core curriculum course only). Minimum ACT score equal or greater than the state average for the prior year. Must enroll as first-time undergraduate by semester following the first anniversary of high school graduation. Must not be in default on any student loan. Must not have criminal record. Awards vary by school depending upon tuition. Must be registered with Selective Service if required. Submit FAFSA by April 15 for priority consideration and for receipt no later than final deadline of July 1.

Amount of award:	Full tuition
Application deadline:	July 1
Total amount awarded:	$7,422,479

Contact:
Louisiana Office of Student Financial Assistance
P.O. Box 91202
Baton Rouge, LA 70821-9202
Phone: 800-259-5626 ext. 1012
Fax: 225-922-0790
Web: www.osfa.state.la.us

Louisiana Tuition Opportunity Program for Students Performance Award

Type of award: Scholarship, renewable.
Intended use: For full-time undergraduate study at 4-year institution. Designated institutions: Louisiana public or LAICU-approved private institutions.
Eligibility: Applicant must be high school senior. Applicant must be U.S. citizen residing in Louisiana.
Basis for selection: Applicant must demonstrate high academic achievement.
Application requirements: FAFSA. Applicants should file by April 15 for priority consideration. Final deadline July 1.
Additional information: All eligible students funded. Amount of award varies. Applicant must be Louisiana resident at least two years prior to high school graduation. Must have minimum 3.5 GPA in high school (beginng with graduating class of 2003, qualifiying GPA will be calculated using grades achieved on core curriculum courses only). Must score minimum 23 on ACT. As first time freshman, must accept award by first semester following first anniversary of high school graduation. Must maintain 3.0 GPA and earn 24 credits to renew. Award recipients receive an additional $400 for books and supplies. Recipients usually receive notification by August 15.

Scholarships

Amount of award: Full tuition
Application deadline: July 1
Notification begins: June 15
Contact:
Louisiana Office of Student Financial Assistance
P.O. Box 91202
Baton Rouge, LA 70821-9202
Phone: 800-259-5626 ext. 1012
Fax: 225-922-0790
Web: www.osfa.state.la.us

Louisiana Tuition Opportunity Program for Students Tech Award

Type of award: Scholarship, renewable.
Intended use: For full-time undergraduate study at postsecondary institution. Designated institutions: Louisiana public postsecondary vocational or technical institutions.
Eligibility: Applicant must be U.S. citizen residing in Louisiana.
Basis for selection: Applicant must demonstrate high academic achievement.
Application requirements: FAFSA.
Additional information: Tuition waiver, up to two years. Must live in Louisana 24 months prior to high school graduation. For eligible high school graduates who choose to pursue occupational training. Must have high school GPA of 2.50 and minimum ACT score of 19. Must have no criminal record. Must be registered with the Selective Service if required.
Amount of award: Full tuition
Application deadline: July 1
Contact:
Louisiana Office of Student Financial Assistance
P.O. Box 91202
Baton Rouge, LA 70821-9202
Phone: 800-259-5626 ext. 1012
Fax: 255-922-0790
Web: www.osfa.state.la.us

Louisiana Space Consortium

LaSPACE Undergraduate Research Assistantship

Type of award: Research grant, renewable.
Intended use: For full-time undergraduate study at accredited 2-year or 4-year institution. Designated institutions: Dillard University, Grambling State University, LSU Agricultural Center, LSU and A&M College, Louisiana Tech University, Loyola University, McNeese State University, Nicholls State University, Northwestern State University of Louisiana, Southeastern Louisiana University, Southern University and A&M College, Southern University at New Orleans, Southern University at Shreveport, Tulane University, University of Louisiana at Lafayette, University of Louisiana at Monroe, University of New Orleans, Xavier University of Louisiana.
Eligibility: Applicant must be U.S. citizen residing in Louisiana.
Basis for selection: Major/career interest in aerospace; science, general; mathematics or engineering. Applicant must

demonstrate high academic achievement, depth of character, leadership and seriousness of purpose.
Application requirements: Recommendations, essay, transcript, proof of eligibility. Send ACT or SAT scores.
Additional information: LaSPACE Undergraduate Research Assistantship (LURA) is a research program that pairs award recipients with faculty-mentors to work on space-related projects. Applicant must be currently enrolled undergraduate attending a Louisiana Space Grant Consortium member university. Undergraduate researcher and faculty mentor to submit a joint application. Applicants must demonstrate capacity to conduct serious scientific research. Visit Website for latest information and deadlines or send e-mail to wefel@phunds.phys.lsu.edu.
Contact:
Louisiana Space Consortium (LaSPACE)
277 Nicholson Hall
Louisiana State University
Baton Rouge, LA 70803-4001
Web: phacts.phys.lsu.edu

Luck Stone Corporation

Luck Stone Corporation Scholarship

Type of award: Scholarship.
Intended use: For undergraduate study at accredited vocational, 2-year or 4-year institution.
Eligibility: Applicant or parent must be employed by Luck Stone Corporation.
Basis for selection: Applicant must demonstrate financial need.
Additional information: For further information or an application, contact Luck Stone Corporation directly.
Amount of award: $1,000-$3,000

Lund Food Holdings, Inc.

Russell T. Lund Scholarship Program

Type of award: Scholarship.
Intended use: For undergraduate study at vocational, 2-year or 4-year institution.
Eligibility: Applicant or parent must be employed by Lund Food Holdings, Inc. Applicant must be high school senior.
Additional information: For further information or an application, contact Lund Food Holdings Incoporated directly.
Amount of award: $2,000

Lyden Memorial Scholarship Fund

Lynden Memorial Scholarship Program

Type of award: Scholarship.

Intended use: For undergraduate or graduate study at 4-year or graduate institution.
Eligibility: Applicant or parent must be employed by Lynden. Applicant must be high school senior.
Additional information: For further information or application, contact Lyden Memorial Scholarship Fund directly.
   Amount of award: $1,000

MacDermid Graphic Arts, Inc.

MacDermid Graphic Arts, Inc. Scholarship Program

Type of award: Scholarship.
Intended use: For undergraduate study at vocational, 2-year or 4-year institution.
Eligibility: Applicant or parent must be employed by MacDermid Graphic Arts, Inc. Applicant must be high school senior.
Additional information: For further information or an application, contact MacDermid Graphic Arts, Inc. directly.
   Amount of award: $2,000

MagneTek, Inc.

MagneTek Scholarship Plan

Type of award: Scholarship, renewable.
Intended use: For freshman study at vocational, 2-year or 4-year institution.
Eligibility: Applicant or parent must be employed by MagneTek, Inc. Applicant must be high school senior.
Additional information: For further information or an application, contact Magnetek Incorporated directly.
   Amount of award: $1,000-$3,000

Maine Division of Veterans Services

Maine Veterans Services Dependents Educational Benefits

Type of award: Scholarship.
Intended use: For undergraduate or graduate study at vocational, 2-year or 4-year institution. Designated institutions: State of Maine-supported institutions.
Eligibility: Applicant must be at least 16, no older than 21. Applicant must be residing in Maine. Applicant must be dependent of disabled veteran, deceased veteran or POW/MIA; or spouse of disabled veteran or deceased veteran. Must apply for program prior to 22nd birthday or before 26th birthday if applicant was enrolled in the U.S. Armed Forces. Age limits apply to child applicants only, not spouses.
Application requirements: Proof of eligibility.

Additional information: Parent or spouse must have been resident of Maine prior to enlistment or a resident of Maine for five years preceding application for aid. Provides tuition at all branches of the University of Maine system, all State of Maine vocational-technical colleges, and Maine Maritime Academy for eight semesters to be used within six years.
   Amount of award: Full tuition
   Number of awards: 460
Contact:
Maine Division of Veterans Services
State House Station 117
Augusta, ME 04333-0117

Maine Innkeepers Association

Maine Innkeepers Association Scholarship

Type of award: Scholarship.
Intended use: For full-time undergraduate study at accredited vocational or 4-year institution in United States. Designated institutions: Institutions with fully accredited programs in Hotel Administration or Culinary Arts.
Eligibility: Applicant must be U.S. citizen or permanent resident residing in Maine.
Basis for selection: Major/career interest in culinary arts; hotel/restaurant management or hospitality administration/management. Applicant must demonstrate financial need and high academic achievement.
Application requirements: Recommendations, essay, transcript.
Additional information: Applicant must be a Maine resident who is a high school senior or currently in college. A minimum GPA of 2.5 is required.
   Amount of award: $250-$1,500
   Number of awards: 4
   Number of applicants: 35
   Application deadline: May 1
Contact:
Maine Innkeepers Association
Scholarship Chairperson
305 Commercial Street
Portland, ME 04101

Maine Lesbian/Gay Political Alliance

Maine Lesbian/Gay Political Alliance Scholarship

Type of award: Scholarship.
Intended use: For undergraduate study at postsecondary institution.
Eligibility: Applicant must be high school senior. Applicant must be U.S. citizen or permanent resident residing in Maine.
Basis for selection: Applicant must demonstrate depth of character and service orientation.

Application requirements: Recommendations, essay, proof of eligibility.
Additional information: Open to any senior regardless of sexual orientation. Applicant must have proof of college acceptance.

Amount of award:	$500-$750
Number of awards:	2
Number of applicants:	50
Application deadline:	April 15
Notification begins:	May 15
Total amount awarded:	$1,500

Contact:
Scholarship Coordinator MLGPA/MDA
P.O. Box 1951
Portland, ME 04104

Maine Metal Products Association

Maine Metal Products Scholarship

Type of award: Scholarship.
Intended use: For undergraduate study. Designated institutions: University of Maine and Maine Technical College System institutions.
Eligibility: Applicant must be permanent resident residing in Maine.
Basis for selection: Major/career interest in engineering. Applicant must demonstrate high academic achievement, depth of character, leadership, seriousness of purpose and service orientation.
Application requirements: Interview, recommendations, essay, transcript, proof of eligibility, nomination by Maine Metal Products Association member.
Additional information: Applicant must have career interest in metals industry and/or related academic majors. Amount of award varies from $500 to full scholarship.

Amount of award:	$500-$2,500
Number of awards:	5
Number of applicants:	22
Application deadline:	June 1
Notification begins:	June 7
Total amount awarded:	$10,000

Contact:
Catherine A. Rowe, Director of Operations
Maine Metal Products Association
87 Winthrop Street, Suite 400
Augusta, ME 04330
Phone: 207-629-5220
Fax: 207-629-5219

Maine Recreation and Parks Association

Maine Recreation and Parks Association Scholarship

Type of award: Scholarship.

Intended use: For full-time undergraduate study. Designated institutions: Institutions with Parks & Recreation or Leisure Studies programs.
Eligibility: Applicant must be U.S. citizen.
Basis for selection: Major/career interest in parks/recreation. Applicant must demonstrate high academic achievement.
Application requirements: Recommendations, transcript. Must send SASE to receive application form.
Additional information: For parks, recreation and leisure studies majors only. Students who intend to study physical education, wildlife management, natural resources or law enforcement are not eligible. Out-of-state applicant must attend college in Maine; Maine residents may attend out-of-state college. One $500 award reserved for high school seniors; remaining awards are for enrolled undergraduates.

Amount of award:	$500-$750
Number of awards:	3
Number of applicants:	40
Application deadline:	April 1
Total amount awarded:	$2,000

Contact:
Maine Recreation and Parks Association
c/o Gorham Recreation Department
270 Main St.
Gorham, ME 04038

Maine Restaurant Association

Russ Casey Scholarship

Type of award: Scholarship.
Intended use: For undergraduate or graduate study at accredited 2-year, 4-year or graduate institution. Designated institutions: New England colleges or universities.
Eligibility: Applicant must be U.S. citizen residing in Maine.
Basis for selection: Major/career interest in hotel/restaurant management; food production/management/services or culinary arts. Applicant must demonstrate high academic achievement.
Application requirements: Transcript. Two recommendations from high school or college teachers, one from restaurant owner/manager or allied member of Maine restaurant Association. Cover letter detailing applicant's interest in and connection to food service industry in 300 words or less.

Amount of award:	$1,000
Number of awards:	3
Number of applicants:	20
Application deadline:	April 1
Total amount awarded:	$3,000

Contact:
Maine Restaurant Association
P.O. Box 5060
5 Wade St.
Augusta, ME 04332

Maine Society of Professional Engineers

Maine Society of Professional Engineers Scholarship Program

Type of award: Scholarship.
Intended use: For freshman study at 2-year or 4-year institution in United States.
Eligibility: Applicant must be high school senior. Applicant must be permanent resident residing in Maine.
Basis for selection: Major/career interest in engineering or engineering, civil.
Application requirements: Recommendations, essay, transcript. Must submit SAT or ACT scores.
Additional information: Applicant must intend to earn a degree in engineering and to enter the practice of engineering after graduation. One or more scholarships awarded each year.

Amount of award:	$1,500
Number of awards:	1
Application deadline:	March 1
Notification begins:	May 30

Contact:
Robert G. Martin, PE Chairman, Scholarship Committee
Maine Society of Professional Engineers
RR #1, Box 70
Belgrade, ME 04917

Maine Space Grant Consortium

NASA Space Grant Research Scholarships and Fellowships

Type of award: Research grant, renewable.
Intended use: For full-time undergraduate study at accredited 4-year or graduate institution. Designated institutions: University of Maine (Orono), University of Southern Maine, University of New England, Maine Maritime Academy.
Eligibility: Applicant must be U.S. citizen.
Basis for selection: Major/career interest in astronomy; geology/earth sciences; geophysics; engineering; aerospace; biology or medicine.
Application requirements: Research proposal.
Additional information: For space or space-related research studies at Maine Space Grant Consortium member institution. Undergraduate program varies from campus to campus. Contact campus Maine Space Grant Consortium representative for application information, deadlines and awards requirements, or call toll-free information number. The Maine Space Grant Consortium actively encourages applications from women and minority students. Visit Website for additional details.

Amount of award:	$2,500-$15,000
Application deadline:	March 30
Notification begins:	April 16

Contact:
Maine Space Grant Consortium
87 Winthrop Street, Suite 200
Augusta, ME 04330
Phone: 877-397-7223
Web: www.msgc.org

Maine State Society of Washington, DC

Maine State Society of Washington, DC, Foundation Scholarship Program

Type of award: Scholarship.
Intended use: For full-time undergraduate study at accredited 4-year institution. Designated institutions: Postsecondary public or private undergraduate colleges or universities in Maine.
Eligibility: Applicant must be no older than 25. Applicant must be U.S. citizen residing in Maine.
Basis for selection: Applicant must demonstrate high academic achievement and seriousness of purpose.
Application requirements: Portfolio, essay, transcript, proof of eligibility. Must have completed one semester/quarter with a 3.0 GPA.
Additional information: Must have been born in Maine or have been legal resident of Maine for at least four years or have at least one parent who was born in or who has been a legal resident of Maine for at least four years. Applicant must currently attend college in Maine, with a minimum GPA of 3.0 for latest semester and not have reached his/her 25th birthday by next April 1. Requests for applications must include SASE.

Amount of award:	$1,000
Number of awards:	4
Application deadline:	April 1
Total amount awarded:	$4,000

Contact:
Maine State Society Scholarship Foundation
3508 Wilson Street
Fairfax, VA 22030
Phone: 703-352-0846

Maine Technical College System

Maine PIC/MH/VR/TDC Technical Scholarship

Type of award: Scholarship, renewable.
Intended use: For undergraduate study. Designated institutions: Maine Technical College System institutions.
Eligibility: Applicant must be physically challenged or learning disabled. Applicant must be residing in Maine.
Basis for selection: Applicant must demonstrate financial need.
Application requirements: Proof of eligibility.
Additional information: Applicants must have a recognized mental or physical disability. Award supplements cost of additional services required for disabled student to successfully complete educational goal. Funds disbursed by one of four co-sponsoring agencies: the 16-county job training system, Training and Development Corporation, Vocational Rehabilitation, and Bureau of Mental Health.

Number of awards:	46
Number of applicants:	46
Total amount awarded:	$20,000

Contact:
Maine Technical College System
Division of State and Federal Programs
323 State Street
Augusta, ME 04330
Phone: 207-287-1070
Web: www.mtcs.net

Making It Count

Chevrolet Making College Count Scholarships

Type of award: Scholarship.
Intended use: For full-time freshman study at accredited 2-year or 4-year institution.
Eligibility: Applicant must be high school senior. Applicant must be U.S. citizen or permanent resident.
Basis for selection: Applicant must demonstrate high academic achievement, seriousness of purpose and service orientation.
Application requirements: Recommendations, essay, transcript.
Additional information: Download application from Website. See site for further details concerning awards. Selection criteria include work experience, extracurricular activities and community volunteer work. A minimum GPA of 3.2 is necessary.

Amount of award:	$1,000
Number of awards:	25
Application deadline:	May 31
Notification begins:	August 31
Total amount awarded:	$25,000

Contact:
GM Scholarship Administration Center
702 West 5th Avenue
Naperville, IL 60563
Phone: 888-377-5233
Web: www.makingitcount.com

Manomet Center for Conservation Sciences

Kathleen S. Anderson Award

Type of award: Research grant.
Intended use: For junior, senior or graduate study in or outside United States. Designated institutions: Institutions in Western Hemisphere.
Basis for selection: Major/career interest in ornithology. Applicant must demonstrate leadership and seriousness of purpose.
Application requirements: Recommendations, research proposal.
Additional information: Either one $1,000 award or two $500 awards are given. Kathleen Anderson is asked to choose winner from five finalists submitted by Manomet staff.

Amount of award:	$500-$1,000
Number of awards:	2
Number of applicants:	25
Application deadline:	December 1
Notification begins:	February 1
Total amount awarded:	$1,000

Contact:
Manomet Center For Conservation Sciences
Kathleen Anderson Award
81 Stage Point Road, P.O. Box 1770
Manomet, MA 02345
Phone: 508-224-6521

Marine Corps Scholarship Foundation

Marine Corps Scholarship

Type of award: Scholarship, renewable.
Intended use: For undergraduate study at accredited vocational, 2-year or 4-year institution in United States.
Eligibility: Applicant must be high school senior. Applicant must be U.S. citizen. Applicant must be dependent of active service person or veteran in the Marines. Must be child of Marine, Marine reservist, or honorably discharged from the Marine Corps.
Basis for selection: Applicant must demonstrate financial need.
Application requirements: Transcript, proof of eligibility. FAFSA is also required.
Additional information: Gross family income must not exceed $47,000. Must be dependant of marine or former marine with honorable record. Undergraduates attending post-high school vocational/technical institutions also eligible.

Amount of award:	$500-$2,500
Number of awards:	1,080
Number of applicants:	1,600
Application deadline:	April 1
Total amount awarded:	$1,500,000

Contact:
Marine Corps Scholarship Foundation
P.O. Box 3008
Princeton, NJ 08543-3008
Phone: 609-921-3534
Fax: 609-452-2259
Web: www.marine-scholars.org

Marten Transport, Ltd.

Randolph L. Marten Scholarship Program

Type of award: Scholarship.
Intended use: For undergraduate study at vocational, 2-year or 4-year institution.
Eligibility: Applicant or parent must be employed by Marten Transport, Ltd. Applicant must be high school senior.
Additional information: For further information or an application, contact Marten Transport Ltd. Directly.

Amount of award:	$1,000

Marvin Lumber and Cedar Company

Marvin Lumber and Cedar/Marvin Windows Scholarship

Type of award: Scholarship.
Intended use: For undergraduate study at accredited vocational, 2-year or 4-year institution.
Eligibility: Applicant or parent must be employed by Marvin Lumber & Cedar Co.
Basis for selection: Applicant must demonstrate financial need.
Additional information: For further information or an application, contact Marvin Lumber and Cedar Co. directly.

Amount of award:	$500-$1,000

Maryland Higher Education Commission State Scholarship Administration

Developmental Disabilities and Mental Health Workforce Tuition Assistance Program

Type of award: Scholarship, renewable.
Intended use: For undergraduate or graduate study at 2-year or 4-year institution. Designated institutions: Maryland schools.
Eligibility: Applicant must be U.S. citizen or permanent resident residing in Maryland.
Basis for selection: Major/career interest in health-related professions; psychology; social/behavioral sciences; social work or criminal justice/law enforcement.
Application requirements: Transcript, proof of eligibility.
Additional information: Awardees agree to work in developmental disabilities or mental health field in Maryland. Must work one year for each year, or portion thereof, award held. Priority given to applicants currently employed at eligible institutions.

Amount of award:	$1,000-$3,000
Number of awards:	79
Application deadline:	October 1
Total amount awarded:	$123,000

Contact:
Maryland Higher Education Commission State Scholarship Administration
16 Francis Street
Annapolis, MD 24101-1781
Phone: 410-260-4565
Web: www.mhec.state.md.us

Maryland Child Care Provider Scholarship

Type of award: Scholarship, renewable.
Intended use: For undergraduate study at accredited 2-year or 4-year institution in United States. Designated institutions: Maryland schools.

Eligibility: Applicant must be U.S. citizen or permanent resident residing in Maryland.
Basis for selection: Major/career interest in education or education, early childhood.
Application requirements: Must complete CCP application.
Additional information: Minimum 2.0 GPA. Must be enrolled in program leading to degree in child development or early childhood education. Awardees agree to work as child care provider in Maryland. Must work one year for each year, or portion thereof, award held, beginning within six months of graduation.

Amount of award:	$500-$2,000
Number of awards:	72
Application deadline:	June 15
Notification begins:	August 15
Total amount awarded:	$78,750

Contact:
Maryland Higher Education Commission State Scholarship Administration
Child Care Provider Scholarship Program
16 Francis Street
Annapolis, MD 21401-1781
Phone: 410-260-4565
Web: www.mhec.state.md.us

Maryland Delegate Scholarship

Type of award: Scholarship, renewable.
Intended use: For undergraduate or graduate study at vocational, 2-year, 4-year or graduate institution. Designated institutions: Maryland institutions.
Eligibility: Applicant must be U.S. citizen, international student or eligible non-U.S. citizen.
Application requirements: Proof of eligibility, nomination by local state delegate. FAFSA also required.
Additional information: Rolling application deadline. Certain vocational programs eligible. Out-of-state institutions eligible only if major not offered in Maryland. Each State Delegate makes awards to students. Non-U.S. citizens living in Maryland may be eligible. Applicants must reapply yearly for renewal.

Amount of award:	$200-$9,774
Number of awards:	3,238
Notification begins:	July 1
Total amount awarded:	$2,211,924

Contact:
Maryland Higher Education Commission State Scholarship Administration
Delegate Scholarship
16 Francis Street
Annapolis, MD 21401-1781
Phone: 410-260-4565
Web: www.mhec.state.md.us

Maryland Distinguished Scholar: Achievement

Type of award: Scholarship, renewable.
Intended use: For full-time undergraduate study at 2-year or 4-year institution. Designated institutions: Eligible institutions in Maryland.
Eligibility: Applicant must be high school junior. Applicant must be U.S. citizen or permanent resident residing in Maryland.
Basis for selection: Applicant must demonstrate high academic achievement.

Application requirements: Transcript, nomination by high school guidance counselor at end of first semester of junior year. PSAT, ACT or SAT scores.

Additional information: Minimum 3.7 GPA.

Amount of award:	$3,000
Number of awards:	1,436
Notification begins:	June 30
Total amount awarded:	$4,210,250

Contact:
Maryland Higher Education Commission State Scholarship
Administration
Distinguished Scholar Program
16 Francis Street
Annapolis, MD 21401-1781
Phone: 410-260-4565
Web: www.mhec.state.md.us

Maryland Distinguished Scholar: National Merit and National Achievement Finalists

Type of award: Scholarship, renewable.

Intended use: For full-time undergraduate study at 2-year or 4-year institution in United States. Designated institutions: Eligible institutions in Maryland.

Eligibility: Applicant must be high school junior. Applicant must be U.S. citizen or permanent resident residing in Maryland.

Basis for selection: Based on national achievement.

Application requirements: Applicant must be National Merit Finalist or National Achievement Finalist.

Amount of award:	$3,000

Contact:
Maryland Higher Education Commission State Scholarship
Administration
Distinguished Scholar Program
16 Francis Street
Annapolis, MD 21401-1718
Phone: 410-260-4565
Web: www.mhec.state.md.us

Maryland Distinguished Scholar: Talent

Type of award: Scholarship, renewable.

Intended use: For full-time undergraduate study at 2-year or 4-year institution. Designated institutions: Eligible 2-year or 4-year institution in Maryland.

Eligibility: Applicant must be high school junior. Applicant must be U.S. citizen or permanent resident residing in Maryland.

Basis for selection: Competition/talent/interest in performing arts. Major/career interest in performing arts; theater arts or music.

Application requirements: Audition, nomination by high school in spring of junior year.

Additional information: Awards for dance, drama, visual arts, and vocal and instrumental music. Winners determined by panel of judges.

Amount of award:	$3,000

Contact:
Maryland Higher Education Commission State Scholarship
Administration
Distinguished Scholar Program
16 Francis Street
Annapolis, MD 21401-1781
Phone: 410-260-4565
Web: www.mhec.state.md.us

Maryland Educational Assistance Grant

Type of award: Scholarship, renewable.

Intended use: For full-time undergraduate study at 2-year or 4-year institution. Designated institutions: Maryland postsecondary schools.

Eligibility: Applicant must be residing in Maryland.

Basis for selection: Applicant must demonstrate financial need.

Application requirements: Proof of eligibility. Must file FAFSA before March 1.

Amount of award:	$400-$3,000
Number of awards:	20,297
Application deadline:	March 1
Notification begins:	April 15
Total amount awarded:	$30,537,538

Contact:
Maryland Higher Education Commission State Scholarship
Administration
Educational Assistance Grant
16 Francis Street
Annapolis, MD 21401-1781
Phone: 410-260-4565
Web: www.mhec.state.md.us

Maryland Edward T. Conroy Memorial Scholarship Program

Type of award: Scholarship, renewable.

Intended use: For undergraduate or graduate study. Designated institutions: Eligible Maryland institutions.

Eligibility: Applicant must be U.S. citizen. Applicant must be dependent of disabled veteran or deceased veteran; or spouse of disabled veteran, deceased veteran or POW/MIA. Must be disabled former POW from Vietnam War. Death or disablement must have come as direct result of military service and while a resident of Maryland. Disability must be declared 100 percent.

Application requirements: Must file Conroy application.

Additional information: Also open to sons and daughters of any U.S. military personnel disabled or killed as direct result of military duty after December 7, 1941.

Contact:
Maryland Higher Education Commission State
Edward T. Conroy Memorial Grant Program
Edward T. Conroy Memorial Grant Program
Annapolis, MD 21401-1781
Phone: 410-260-4565
Web: www.mhec.state.md.us

Maryland Edward T. Conroy Memorial Scholarship Program-- Disabled Public Safety Employees

Type of award: Scholarship, renewable.

Intended use: For undergraduate or graduate study. Designated institutions: Maryland colleges and universities.

Eligibility: Applicant must be U.S. citizen or permanent resident residing in Maryland. Applicant's parent must have been killed or disabled in work-related accident as fire fighter, police officer or public safety officer.

Application requirements: Must file Conroy application.

Additional information: Applicant's parent or spouse must have been killed in line of duty as fire fighter, police officer or public safety officer. If spouse, applicant must not be remarried. Applicant may also have been 100 percent disabled in line of duty as fire fighter, police officer or public safety officer. Amount of awards equal to tuition but may not exceed equivalent of tuition and mandatory fees for resident undergraduate at University of Maryland - College Park. Awards renewable provided applicant maintains eligibility.

Amount of award:	$200-$4,500
Number of awards:	59
Application deadline:	July 15
Notification begins:	July 31
Total amount awarded:	$184,571

Contact:
Maryland Higher Education Commission State Scholarship Administration
Edward T. Conroy Memorial Grant Program
Edward T. Conroy Memorial Grant Program
Annapolis, MD 21401-1781
Phone: 410-260-4565
Web: www.mhec.state.md.us

Maryland Guaranteed Access Grant

Type of award: Scholarship, renewable.

Intended use: For full-time undergraduate study at accredited postsecondary institution. Designated institutions: Degree-granting institution in Maryland.

Eligibility: Applicant must be U.S. citizen or permanent resident residing in Maryland.

Basis for selection: Applicant must demonstrate financial need.

Application requirements: Proof of eligibility. File FAFSA and G. A. Grant application by March 1 each award year.

Additional information: Applicant must have completed college preparatory program or vocational/technical program and begin college within one year of completing high school. GPA 2.5. Must have total family income no greater than 130 percent of federal poverty level.

Amount of award:	$400-$9,600
Number of awards:	622
Application deadline:	March 1
Total amount awarded:	$3,557,018

Contact:
Maryland Higher Education Commission State Scholarship Administration
Maryland Guaranteed Access Grant
16 Francis Street
Annapolis, MD 21401-1781
Phone: 410-260-4565
Web: www.mhec.state.md.us

Maryland HOPE Scholarship Program Hope Scholarship

Type of award: Scholarship, renewable.

Intended use: For full-time undergraduate study at 2-year or 4-year institution. Designated institutions: Allegany College of Maryland; Anne Arundel Community College; Baltimore City Community College; Baltimore Hebrew University; Baltimore International College; Binah Institute of Advanced Judaic Study; Bowie State University; Capitol College; Carroll Community College; Cecil Community College; Chesapeake College; Columbia Union College; Community College of Baltimore County at Catonsville, Dundalk, and Essex; Coppin State College; Frederick Community College; Frostburg State University; Garrett Community College; Goucher College; Hagerstown Community College; Hagerstown Business College; Harford Community College; Hood College; Howard Community College; The Johns Hopkins University; Loyola College; Maryland College of Art and Design; Maryland Institute College of Art; Montgomery College at Germantown, Rockville, and Takoma Park; Morgan State University; Mount St. Mary's College; National Labor College; College of Notre Dame; Prince George's Community College; Salisbury State University; Sojourner-Douglass College; College of Southern Maryland; St. Mary's College of Maryland; Towson University; University of Baltimore; University of Maryland - Baltimore, Baltimore County, and College Park; University of Maryland Eastern Shore; Villa Julie College; Washington College; Western Maryland College; and Wor-Wic Community College.

Eligibility: Applicant must be high school senior. Applicant must be U.S. citizen or permanent resident residing in Maryland.

Application requirements: Transcript, proof of eligibility. FAFSA and completed HOPE Scholarship Program application form.

Additional information: Applicant must enroll in eligible program at designated institution; visit Website or contact Scholarship Administration for complete list. Minimum 3.0 GPA. Applicant must have combined annual family income of $80,000 or less. Awardees agree to work full-time in Maryland one year for every year award held.

Amount of award:	$1,000-$3,000
Application deadline:	March 1

Contact:
Maryland Higher Education Commission State Scholarship Administration
16 Francis Street
Annapolis, MD 24101-1781
Phone: 410-260-4565
Web: www.mhec.state.md.us

Maryland HOPE Scholarship Program Maryland Teacher Scholarship

Type of award: Scholarship, renewable.

Intended use: For full-time undergraduate or graduate study at 2-year or 4-year institution.

Eligibility: Applicant must be residing in Maryland.

Basis for selection: Major/career interest in education; education, early childhood or education, teacher.

Application requirements: Transcript. Completed HOPE Scholarship Program application form.

Additional information: Applicant must be enrolled in program leading to professional teacher certification. Minimum 3.0 GPA. Applicant may not be certified teacher or student holding bachelor's degree. Awardees agree to teach full-time in Maryland public school one year for every year award held.

Amount of award:	$2,000-$5,000
Number of awards:	653
Application deadline:	March 1
Total amount awarded:	$1,695,500

Contact:
Maryland Higher Education Commission State Scholarship
Administration
16 Francis Street
Annapolis, MD 24101-1781
Phone: 410-260-4565
Web: www.mhec.state.md.us

Maryland HOPE Scholarship Program Science and Technology Scholarship

Type of award: Scholarship, renewable.
Intended use: For full-time undergraduate study at accredited 2-year or 4-year institution. Designated institutions: Allegany College of Maryland; Anne Arundel Community College; Baltimore City Community College; Bowie State University; Capitol College; Carroll Community College; Cecil Community College; Chesapeake College; Columbia Union College; Community College of Baltimore County at Catonsville, Dundalk, and Essex; Coppin State College; Frederick Community College; Frostburg State University; Goucher College; Hagerstown Community College; Harford Community College; Harry Lundeberg School of Seamanship; Hood College; Howard Community College; Johns Hopkins University; Loyola College; Montgomery College at Germantown, Rockville, and Takoma Park; Morgan State University; Mount St. Mary's College; College of Notre Dame of Maryland; Prince George's Community College; Salisbury State University; College of Southern Maryland; St. Mary's College of Maryland; Towson University; University of Baltimore; University of Maryland - Baltimore County, College Park, and Eastern Shore; Villa Julie College; Washington College; Western Maryland College; and Wor-Wic Community College.
Eligibility: Applicant must be high school senior. Applicant must be U.S. citizen, international student or eligible non-citizen. Applicant must be residing in Maryland.
Basis for selection: Major/career interest in computer/information sciences; engineering; biology; chemistry; physical sciences; mathematics or physics.
Application requirements: Transcript. Completed HOPE Scholarship Program application form.
Additional information: 3.0 GPA at completion of first semester, senior year of high school. Must begin college within two years of completion of high school. Must maintain 3.0 GPA in college enrolled in eligible program at designated institutions. Service obligation: recipient required to work one year for each year of tuition assistance in an occupation directly related to program of study. Otherwise, scholarship reverts to loan. Associate degree candidates eligible for up to $1,000/year for two years; bachelor's degree candidates, $3,000/year for four years.

Amount of award:	$1,000-$3,000
Number of awards:	743
Application deadline:	March 1
Notification begins:	May 1
Total amount awarded:	$2,084,000

Contact:
Maryland Higher Education Commission State Scholarship
Administration
Science and Technology Scholarship Program
16 Francis Street
Annapolis, MD 21401-1781
Phone: 410-260-4565
Web: www.mhec.state.md.us

Maryland Jack F. Tolbert Memorial Grant

Type of award: Scholarship, renewable.
Intended use: For full-time undergraduate study at vocational institution. Designated institutions: Private career schools in Maryland.
Eligibility: Applicant must be residing in Maryland.
Basis for selection: Applicant must demonstrate financial need.
Application requirements: Nomination by financial aid counselor at private career school. Must submit FAFSA.
Additional information: Award can only be held for one semester per academic year, for two years (two awards in all).

Amount of award:	$200
Number of awards:	1,000
Total amount awarded:	$200,000

Contact:
Maryland Higher Education Commission State Scholarship
Administration
Jack F. Tolbert Memorial Grant
16 Francis Street
Annapolis, MD 21401-1781
Phone: 410-260-4565
Web: www.mhec.state.md.us

Maryland Part-Time Grant Program

Type of award: Scholarship, renewable.
Intended use: For half-time freshman, sophomore, junior or senior study.
Eligibility: Applicant must be residing in Maryland.
Basis for selection: Applicant must demonstrate financial need.
Additional information: Must be taking 6 to 11 semester credit hours. Apply through financial aid office of Maryland institution.

Amount of award:	$200-$1,000
Number of awards:	2,400
Total amount awarded:	$800,000

Contact:
Maryland Higher Education Commission State Scholarship
Administration
Part-Time Grant Program
16 Francis Street
Annapolis, MD 21401-1781
Phone: 410-260-4565
Web: www.mhec.state.md.us

Maryland Physical/Occupational Therapists and Assistants Grant

Type of award: Scholarship, renewable.
Intended use: For full-time undergraduate study at 2-year or 4-year institution. Designated institutions: Maryland institutions with professional program leading to licensure in physical/occupational therapy.
Eligibility: Applicant must be U.S. citizen or permanent resident residing in Maryland.
Basis for selection: Major/career interest in physical therapy or occupational therapy. Applicant must demonstrate high academic achievement.
Application requirements: Transcript. File SSA application.
Additional information: Awardees agree to work in facility that provides service to handicapped children. Must work one year for each year, or portion thereof, award held.

Amount of award:	$200-$2,000
Number of awards:	11
Application deadline:	July 1
Notification begins:	August 1
Total amount awarded:	$22,000

Contact:
Maryland Higher Education Commission State Scholarship
Administration
Physical and Occupational Therapy Program
16 Francis Street
Annapolis, MD 21401-1781
Phone: 410-260-4565
Web: www.mhec.state.md.us

Maryland Professional School Scholarship

Type of award: Scholarship, renewable.
Intended use: For full-time undergraduate study. Designated institutions: Maryland schools offering Associate, Bachelors or Masters degree in Nursing. Also the University of Maryland - Baltimore Schools of Medicine, Dentistry, Law, Social Work or Pharmacy; University of Baltimore Law School; Johns Hopkins School of Medicine.
Eligibility: Applicant must be U.S. citizen or permanent resident residing in Maryland.
Basis for selection: Major/career interest in pharmacy/ pharmaceutics/pharmacology or nursing. Applicant must demonstrate financial need.
Application requirements: File FAFSA and SSA application by March 1.
Additional information: Also for graduate study in Law, medicine, dentistry and social work.

Amount of award:	$200-$1,000
Number of awards:	449
Application deadline:	March 1
Notification begins:	May 31
Total amount awarded:	$443,700

Contact:
Maryland Higher Education Commission State Scholarship
Administration
Professional School Scholarship Program
16 Francis Street
Annapolis, MD 21401-1781
Phone: 410-260-4565
Web: www.mhec.state.md.us

Maryland Reimbursement of Firefighters

Type of award: Scholarship, renewable.
Intended use: For undergraduate study. Designated institutions: Degree-granting Maryland institutions.
Eligibility: Applicant must be U.S. citizen or permanent resident residing in Maryland.
Basis for selection: Major/career interest in fire science/ technology or medical emergency.
Application requirements: Transcript, proof of eligibility.
Additional information: Applicant must be active career or volunteer firefighter, ambulance or rescue squad member serving the Maryland community while taking courses. Amount of award equal to tuition but may not exceed equivalent of tuition and mandatory fees for resident undergraduate at University of Maryland - College Park. Payment is made one year after completion of study if the recipient remains career or active volunteer firefighter/ambulance/rescue squad member

during the intervening year. Career interest in emergency medical technology eligible.

Amount of award:	$200-$4,600
Number of awards:	141
Application deadline:	July 1
Total amount awarded:	$315,743

Contact:
Maryland Higher Education Commission State Scholarship
Administration
Reimbursement of Firefighters
16 Francis Street
Annapolis, MD 21401-1781
Phone: 410-260-4565
Web: www.mhec.state.md.us

Maryland Senatorial Scholarship

Type of award: Scholarship, renewable.
Intended use: For freshman, sophomore, junior, senior, master's or doctoral study at postsecondary institution. Designated institutions: Maryland schools.
Eligibility: Applicant must be U.S. citizen, permanent resident, international student or eligible non-US citizens only. Applicant must be residing in Maryland.
Basis for selection: Applicant must demonstrate financial need.
Application requirements: Nomination by local state senator. File FAFSA by March 1.
Additional information: SAT I or ACT required for freshmen at four-year institutions unless applicant graduated from high school five years prior to aid application. Only certain vocational programs and certain vocational institutions eligible. Out-of-state institutions eligible with approved unique major status only if major not offered in Maryland. Each State Senator makes awards to students in his or her election district. Contact State Senator's office for further information and requirements.

Amount of award:	$400-$2,000
Number of awards:	6,268
Application deadline:	March 1
Total amount awarded:	$6,049,000

Contact:
Maryland Higher Education Commission State Scholarship
Administration
Senatorial Scholarship Program
16 Francis Street
Annapolis, MD 21401-1781
Phone: 410-260-4565
Web: www.mhec.state.mc.us

Maryland Sharon Christa McAuliffe Memorial Teacher Education Award

Type of award: Scholarship, renewable.
Intended use: For undergraduate or graduate study at 4-year or graduate institution. Designated institutions: Eligible Maryland institutions.
Eligibility: Applicant must be U.S. citizen or permanent resident residing in Maryland.
Basis for selection: Major/career interest in education, teacher or education, special. Applicant must demonstrate high academic achievement.
Application requirements: Essay, transcript. Submit McAuliffe Award application, and resume.
Additional information: Applicants must be certified teacher changing to critical shortage area, or undergraduate with at least 60 credits or college graduate wishing to be certified and teach in critical shortage area. Must have 3.0 GPA. Must have major/

career interest in critical shortage field identified by the Maryland State Department of Education. Awardees agree to work in Maryland public school teaching in critical shortage field for which student became certified. Must work one year for each year, or portion thereof, award held.

Amount of award:	$200-$12,600
Number of awards:	66
Total amount awarded:	$362,650

Contact:
Maryland Higher Education Commission State Scholarship Administration
S.C. McAuliffe Mem. Teacher Education Award
16 Francis Street
Annapolis, MD 21401-1781
Phone: 410-260-4565
Web: www.mhec.state.md.us

Maryland State Nursing Scholarship and Living Expenses Grant

Type of award: Scholarship, renewable.
Intended use: For undergraduate or graduate study at accredited 2-year or 4-year institution. Designated institutions: Maryland schools.
Eligibility: Applicant must be U.S. citizen or permanent resident residing in Maryland.
Basis for selection: Major/career interest in nursing. Applicant must demonstrate financial need.
Application requirements: FAFSA filed by March 1, SSA filed by June 30.
Additional information: Awardees agree to work full-time in Maryland nursing service. Must work one year for each year, or portion thereof, award held. Service must be at an eligible Maryland organization, including licensed hospitals, public health agencies, nursing homes, home health agencies or authorized adult day care centers. Must have 3.0 GPA. Grant provides additional $2,400 for living expenses; applicants must demonstrate financial need to receive grant.

Amount of award:	$200-$2,400
Number of awards:	327
Application deadline:	June 30
Notification begins:	July 31
Total amount awarded:	$711,623

Contact:
Maryland Higher Education Commission State Scholarship Administration
State Nursing Scholarship
16 Francis Street
Annapolis, MD 21401-1781
Phone: 410-260-4565
Web: www.mhec.state.md.us

Maryland Tuition Reduction for Out-of-State Nursing Students

Type of award: Scholarship, renewable.
Intended use: For half-time undergraduate study at postsecondary institution. Designated institutions: Maryland public institutions with degree-granting nursing program.
Eligibility: Applicant must be U.S. citizen.
Basis for selection: Major/career interest in nursing.
Additional information: Must be resident of state other than Maryland and accepted into Maryland degree-granting nursing program at four-year public institution or community college. Must take 6-11 credits per semester. Awardees agree to work as nurse in state of Maryland following graduation; two-years

service required if attending community college, four years if attending four-year public institution. Award amount varies.
Contact:
Maryland Higher Education Commission State Scholarship Administration
16 Francis Street
Annapolis, MD 21401-1781
Phone: 410-260-4565
Web: www.mhec.state.md.us

Massachusetts Biotechnology Council, Inc.

Biotechnology Scholars Program

Type of award: Scholarship.
Intended use: For freshman study at accredited 4-year institution.
Eligibility: Applicant must be high school senior. Applicant must be residing in Massachusetts.
Basis for selection: Major/career interest in science, general.
Additional information: Information is sent to counselors at participatory high schools in Massachusetts in Andover, Bedford, Beverly, Boston, Cambridge, Canton, Charlestown, Hopkinton, Framingham, Lexington, Marlborough, Medfield, Needham, Newton, Northboro, Norwell, Norwood, Randolph, Shrewsbury, Walpole, Waltham, Wellesley, West Bridgewater, Woburn and Worcester. See your guidance counselor for further information.

Amount of award:	$2,500

Massachusetts Board of Higher Education

Massachusetts Christian A. Herter Memorial Scholarship Program

Type of award: Scholarship, renewable.
Intended use: For full-time undergraduate study at accredited vocational, 2-year or 4-year institution.
Eligibility: Applicant must be high school sophomore or junior. Applicant must be U.S. citizen or permanent resident residing in Massachusetts.
Basis for selection: Applicant must demonstrate financial need, depth of character and seriousness of purpose.
Application requirements: Interview, recommendations, essay, transcript, nomination by high school principal, counselor, teacher, or social service agency.
Additional information: Program provides grant assistance for students from low income or disadvantaged backgrounds who have had to overcome adverse circumstances. Selection made during sophomore and junior years in high school. Average award $5,000.

Number of awards:	100
Number of applicants:	211
Application deadline:	April 15
Notification begins:	June 1
Total amount awarded:	$900,000

Contact:
Office of Student Financial Assistance
Massachusetts Board of Higher Education.
454 Broadway, Suite 200
Revere, MA 02151
Phone: 617-727-9420

Massachusetts Gilbert Grant

Type of award: Scholarship, renewable.
Intended use: For full-time undergraduate study at accredited 2-year or 4-year institution. Designated institutions: Private institutions only or hospital schools of nursing.
Eligibility: Applicant must be residing in Massachusetts.
Basis for selection: Applicant must demonstrate financial need.

Amount of award:	$250-$2,500
Number of awards:	7,000
Total amount awarded:	$20,000,000

Contact:
Apply to college financial aid office.

Massachusetts MASSgrant Program

Type of award: Scholarship, renewable.
Intended use: For full-time undergraduate study at accredited vocational, 2-year or 4-year institution. Designated institutions: Schools in Massachusetts, Connecticut, Maine, New Hampshire, Vermont, Rhode Island, Pennsylvania, Maryland, or DC.
Eligibility: Applicant must be U.S. citizen or permanent resident residing in Massachusetts.
Basis for selection: Applicant must demonstrate financial need.

Amount of award:	$250-$3,100
Number of awards:	32,000
Number of applicants:	250,000
Application deadline:	May 1
Notification begins:	June 15
Total amount awarded:	$33,000,000

Contact:
Office of Student Financial Assistance
Massachusetts Board of Higher Education
454 Broadway, Suite 200
Revere, MA 02151
Phone: 617-727-9420

Massachusetts Public Service Program

Type of award: Scholarship, renewable.
Intended use: For full-time undergraduate study at accredited 2-year or 4-year institution. Designated institutions: Massachusetts institutions.
Eligibility: Applicant must be U.S. citizen or permanent resident residing in Massachusetts. Applicant must be dependent of deceased veteran or POW/MIA. Applicant's parent must have been killed or disabled in work-related accident as fire fighter, police officer or public safety officer.
Application requirements: Proof of eligibility.
Additional information: Award in form of entitlement grant. Death of veteran or POW/MIA parent must have been service related for applicant to be eligible for this program. Applicant must be a resident of Massachusetts at least one year prior to start of school.

Amount of award:	$800-$2,500
Number of awards:	50
Number of applicants:	50
Application deadline:	May 1
Notification begins:	June 1
Total amount awarded:	$60,000

Contact:
Office of Student Financial Assistance
Massachusetts Board of Higher Education
454 Broadway, Suite 200
Revere, MA 02151
Phone: 617-727-9420

Massachusetts Tuition Waiver

Type of award: Scholarship.
Intended use: For undergraduate study at 2-year or 4-year institution. Designated institutions: Massachusetts public institutions.
Eligibility: Applicant must be residing in Massachusetts.
Basis for selection: Applicant must demonstrate financial need.
Additional information: Amount of award varies depending on tuition.

Amount of award:	Full tuition
Number of awards:	20,000
Total amount awarded:	$18,000,000

Contact:
Apply to financial aid office at public college.

Massachusetts Department of Education

Massachusetts Robert C. Byrd Honors Scholarship

Type of award: Scholarship, renewable.
Intended use: For full-time undergraduate study at postsecondary institution.
Eligibility: Applicant must be high school senior. Applicant must be residing in Massachusetts.
Basis for selection: Applicant must demonstrate high academic achievement, leadership and service orientation.
Application requirements: Nomination.
Additional information: Minimum 3.5 GPA required. Students are nominated by high school. See guidance officer for additional information and application procedure.

Amount of award:	$1,500
Number of awards:	514
Number of applicants:	700
Application deadline:	June 1
Total amount awarded:	$771,000

Contact:
Massachusetts Department of Education
Sally Teixeira
350 Main Street
Malden, MA 02148-5023
Phone: 781-338-6304

Scholarships

Massachusetts Glass Dealers Association

Massachusetts Glass Dealers Association Scholarship

Type of award: Scholarship.
Intended use: For undergraduate study at accredited vocational, 2-year or 4-year institution.
Eligibility: Applicant or parent must be member/participant of Massachusetts Glass Dealers Association.
Basis for selection: Applicant must demonstrate financial need.
Additional information: For further information or application, contact Massachusetts Glass Dealers Association directly.

Amount of award: $500

Material Sciences Corporation

Material Sciences Corporation Dependent Scholarship

Type of award: Scholarship.
Intended use: For freshman, sophomore, junior or senior study at accredited vocational, 2-year or 4-year institution.
Eligibility: Applicant or parent must be employed by Material Sciences Corporation.
Additional information: For further information and an application, contact Material Sciences Corporation directly.

Amount of award: $3,000

Mattel Children's Foundation

Mattel Children's Foundation Scholarship

Type of award: Scholarship, renewable.
Intended use: For undergraduate study at accredited vocational, 2-year or 4-year institution.
Eligibility: Applicant or parent must be employed by Mattel, Inc.
Basis for selection: Applicant must demonstrate financial need.
Additional information: For further information or an application, contact Mattel, Inc. directly.

Amount of award: $500-$2,500

MBNA Corporation

MBNA Cleveland Scholars Program

Type of award: Scholarship, renewable.
Intended use: For full-time senior study at accredited 4-year institution in United States. Designated institutions: Ohio colleges and universities.
Eligibility: Applicant must be high school senior. Applicant must be U.S. citizen or permanent resident residing in Ohio.
Basis for selection: Applicant must demonstrate financial need, high academic achievement, depth of character, leadership, seriousness of purpose and service orientation.
Application requirements: Interview, recommendations, essay, transcript, proof of eligibility. Applicants must provide SAT or ACT scores, MBNA Financial Aid Summary, high school academic records, Candidate Recommendation Forms with application.
Additional information: Applicant must live with parents or legal guardians in greater Cleveland area. SAT I or ACT must be taken no later than December of senior year. Minimum qualifying scores are 900 on SAT and 19 on ACT. Minimum 2.5 GPA required. Request application packets through school guidance counselors or via phone. Number of scholarships awarded varies. Award includes assigned advisors and paid summer internship eligibility. Renewable for a maximum of four years. Children of MBNA employees are not eligible for this program. Visit Website for more information and application deadline.

Amount of award: $500-$7,500
Contact:
MBNA Scholars Programs Educational Testing Service
Scholarship and Recognition Programs
P.O. Box 6730
Princeton, NJ 08541-6730
Phone: 800-441-7048 ext. 25155
Web: www.mbnainternational.com

MBNA Delaware Scholars Program

Type of award: Scholarship, renewable.
Intended use: For full-time undergraduate study at accredited 4-year institution. Designated institutions: Delaware colleges and universities.
Eligibility: Applicant must be high school senior. Applicant must be U.S. citizen or permanent resident residing in Delaware.
Basis for selection: Applicant must demonstrate financial need, high academic achievement, depth of character, leadership, seriousness of purpose and service orientation.
Application requirements: Interview, recommendations, essay, transcript, proof of eligibility. Applicants must provide SAT or ACT scores, MBNA Financial Aid Summary, high school academic records, Candidate Recommendation Forms with application.
Additional information: Open to students enrolling in Delaware institutions or in the University of Delaware's Parallel Program. SAT I or ACT must be taken no later than December of senior year. Minimum qualifying scores are 900 on SAT and 19 on ACT. Minimum 2.5 GPA required. Request MBNA Scholarship Program information/packets through school guidance counselors or via phone. Number of scholarships awarded varies. Award includes assigned advisors and paid summer internship eligibility. Renewable for a maximum of four years--eight consecutive semesters. Children of MNBA

employees not eligible for this program. Visit Websie for more information and application deadline.

Amount of award: $500-$7,500
Contact:
MBNA Scholars Programs Educational Testing Service
Scholarship and Recognition Programs
P.O. Box 6730
Princeton, NJ 08541-6730
Phone: 800-410-6262 ext. 25155
Web: www.mbnainternational.com

MBNA Maine Scholars Program

Type of award: Scholarship, renewable.
Intended use: For full-time undergraduate study at 4-year institution in United States or Canada.
Eligibility: Applicant must be high school senior. Applicant must be U.S. citizen or permanent resident residing in Maine.
Basis for selection: Applicant must demonstrate financial need, high academic achievement, depth of character, leadership, seriousness of purpose and service orientation.
Application requirements: Interview, recommendations, essay, transcript, proof of eligibility. Applicant must provide SAT or ACT scores, MBNA Financial Aid Summary, high school academic records, Candidate Recommendation Forms with application.
Additional information: Open to graduating high school seniors who live in Knox or Waldo Counties or one of the following Maine school districts: 1, 9, 27, and Chebeague, Cliff Island, Long Island, Peaks Island, Frenchboro, Islesford, Cranberry Isle, Swans Island, and Monhegan. Applicant must be enrolling in full-time, four-year, accredited college or university in Maine, and live with parents or legal guardians in their home state. SAT I or ACT must be taken no later than December of senior year. Minimum qualifying scores are 900 on SAT and 19 on ACT. Minimum 2.5 GPA required. Request MBNA Scholarship Program information/packets through school guidance counselors or sponsor contact. Number of scholarships awarded varies. Award includes assigned advisors and paid summer internship eligibility, but attendance is not mandatory. Renewable each year for a maximum of four years-- eight consecutive semesters. Children of MNBA employees are not eligible for this program. Visit Website for more information and application deadline.

Amount of award: $500-$6,500
Contact:
MBNA Scholars Programs Educational Testing Service
Scholarship and Recognition Programs
P.O. Box 6730
Princeton, NJ 08541-6730
Phone: 800-441-7048 ext. 25155
Web: www.mbnainternational.com

McKesson HBOC Foundation, Inc.

McKesson HBOC Pharmacy Scholarship

Type of award: Scholarship, renewable.
Intended use: For full-time junior, senior or first professional study.

Eligibility: Applicant or parent must be employed by McKesson Corporation. Applicant must be U.S. citizen or permanent resident.
Basis for selection: Major/career interest in pharmacy/ pharmaceutics/pharmacology.
Application requirements: Recommendations, essay, transcript.
Additional information: For further information or an application, contact Mckesson Foundation directly.

Amount of award: $1,000
Contact:
Citizens' Scholarship Foundation of America
McKesson Family Pharmacy Scholarship
P.O. Box 297
St. Peter, MN 56082

McKesson HBOC Scholarship Program

Type of award: Scholarship.
Intended use: For undergraduate study at accredited vocational, 2-year or 4-year institution.
Eligibility: Applicant or parent must be employed by McKesson Corporation.
Basis for selection: Applicant must demonstrate financial need.
Additional information: For further information or an application, contact McKesson HBOC Foundation, Inc. directly.

Amount of award: $1,000-$2,500

MDU Resources Foundation

MDU Resources Group Employees' Scholarship Program

Type of award: Scholarship.
Intended use: For undergraduate or graduate study at accredited vocational, 2-year or 4-year institution.
Eligibility: Applicant or parent must be employed by MDU Resources Group, Inc.
Additional information: For further information or an application, contact MDU Resources Foundation directly.

Amount of award: $1,200

Medical Arts Press, Inc.

MAP Scholarship

Type of award: Scholarship, renewable.
Intended use: For undergraduate study at vocational, 2-year or 4-year institution.
Eligibility: Applicant or parent must be employed by Medical Arts Press, Inc. Applicant must be high school senior.
Additional information: For further information or an application, contact Medical Arts Press Incorporated directly.

Amount of award: $2,500

Medtronic, Inc. and Medtronic Foundation

Medtronic Scholarship Program

Type of award: Scholarship, renewable.
Intended use: For undergraduate study at vocational, 2-year or 4-year institution.
Eligibility: Applicant or parent must be employed by Medtronic, Inc. Applicant must be high school senior.
Additional information: For further information or an application, contact Medtronic Inc. and Medtronic Foundation directly.
    Amount of award: $500-$4,000

Menominee Indian Tribe of Wisconsin

Menominee Adult Vocational Training Grant

Type of award: Scholarship, renewable.
Intended use: For undergraduate or non-degree study at accredited vocational or 2-year institution in United States.
Eligibility: Applicant must be American Indian. Applicant must be tribally enrolled and 1/4 Menominee Indian.
Basis for selection: Applicant must demonstrate financial need.
Application requirements: Submit completed FAFSA.
Additional information: Award also applicable toward Associate Degree. Must apply through college financial aid office and complete the FAFSA.
    Amount of award: $100-$2,200
    Number of awards: 35
    Number of applicants: 35
    Application deadline: October 30, March 1
Contact:
Menominee Indian Tribe of Wisconsin
P.O. Box 910
Keshena, WI 54135
Phone: 715-799-5118/5110

Menominee Higher Education Scholarship

Type of award: Scholarship, renewable.
Intended use: For full-time undergraduate study at accredited 2-year or 4-year institution in United States.
Eligibility: Applicant must be American Indian. Applicant must be tribally enrolled and 1/4 Menominee Indian.
Basis for selection: Applicant must demonstrate financial need.
Application requirements: Submit completed FAFSA.
Additional information: Applications and deadline dates available through college financial aid office.
    Amount of award: $100-$2,200
    Number of awards: 97
    Number of applicants: 97

Contact:
Menominee Indian Tribe of Wisconsin
P.O. Box 910
Keshena, WI 54135
Phone: 715-799-5118/5110

Merging Business & Academics

Quality of Life Research Competition

Type of award: Scholarship.
Intended use: For undergraduate study.
Eligibility: Applicant must be high school sophomore, junior or senior. Applicant must be U.S. citizen or permanent resident residing in New York.
Basis for selection: Competition/talent/interest in research paper, based on practicality, likely benefit to community, clarity of expression and breadth of vision.
Additional information: Obtain application from New York City high schools. Grades 10-12 eligible. Students research, write and present scholarly proposals suggesting practical ways to improve the quality of life in their community, then work with participating adult in editing paper. Proposals are due in March. Semifinalists notified starting in April; prize winners notified week of May.
    Amount of award: $1,000-$10,000
    Number of applicants: 1,000
Contact:
Merging Business & Academics
Quality of Life Research Competition
227 E. 56th. Street Suite 201
New York, NY 10022
Phone: 212-980-5054
Web: www.g/competition.org

Merrill Corporation

Kenneth F. Merrill Scholarship

Type of award: Scholarship.
Intended use: For undergraduate study at accredited postsecondary institution.
Eligibility: Applicant or parent must be employed by Merrill Corporation. Applicant must be high school senior.
Additional information: For further information or an application, contact Merrill Corporation directly.
    Amount of award: $1,500

Metal-Matic, Inc.

Jerome J. Bliss Memorial Fund

Type of award: Scholarship.
Intended use: For undergraduate study at accredited vocational, 2-year or 4-year institution.

Eligibility: Applicant or parent must be employed by Metal-Matic, Inc.
Basis for selection: Applicant must demonstrate financial need.
Additional information: For further information or an application, contact Metal-Matic, Inc. directly.

    Amount of award: $600-$1,500

Metropolitan Life Foundation

Metropolitan Life Foundation Pathways Scholarship

Type of award: Scholarship, renewable.
Intended use: For full-time undergraduate study at accredited vocational, 2-year or 4-year institution in United States.
Eligibility: Applicant or parent must be employed by Metropolitan Life Insurance Co. Applicant must be no older than 25.
Basis for selection: Applicant must demonstrate financial need.
Additional information: Award is renewed at same level for up to three years or until bachelor's degree or certificate earned, whichever happens first. Applicant must be dependent child of active, full-time U.S. employee of Metropolitan Life Insurance Company or Metropolitan Casualty and Property Co. Children of company officers not eligible. Award varies according to financial need. Those without financial need may apply for one-time honorarium of $500. MetLife Website contains no scholarship information.

    Amount of award: $500-$3,000
Contact:
Metropolitan Life Foundation
Attn: Deb Johnson
1505 Riverview Road
P.O. Box 297, MN 56082
Phone: 212-578-2519

Mexican American Grocers Association Foundation

Mexican American Grocers Association Scholarship

Type of award: Scholarship.
Intended use: For full-time sophomore, junior or senior study at accredited 4-year institution in United States.
Eligibility: Applicant must be Mexican American, Hispanic American or Puerto Rican.
Basis for selection: Major/career interest in business or business/management/administration. Applicant must demonstrate financial need and high academic achievement.
Application requirements: Interview, essay, transcript.
Additional information: Minimum 2.5 GPA. Send SASE for further information and application. Application must be postmarked between April 1 and July 31. Awards presented in October or November.

Amount of award:	$500-$1,500
Number of awards:	25
Number of applicants:	7,000
Application deadline:	July 31
Notification begins:	August 15

Contact:
Mexican-American Grocers Association Foundation
Attn: Jackie Solis
405 North San Fernando Road
Los Angeles, CA 90031
Phone: 323-227-1565

Michigan Higher Education Assistance Authority

Michigan Adult Part-Time Grant

Type of award: Scholarship, renewable.
Intended use: For half-time undergraduate study at 2-year or 4-year institution.
Eligibility: Applicant must be U.S. citizen or permanent resident residing in Michigan.
Basis for selection: Applicant must demonstrate financial need.
Application requirements: Proof of eligibility.
Additional information: Number of awards given varies. Apply to college financial aid office. Applications may be made at any time.

Amount of award:	$600
Number of applicants:	7,064

Contact:
Michigan Higher Education Assistance Authority
PO Box 30466
Lansing, MI 48909-7966
Phone: 517-241-3537

Michigan Competitive Scholarship

Type of award: Scholarship, renewable.
Intended use: For freshman, sophomore, junior or senior study at 2-year or 4-year institution. Designated institutions: Michigan public or private nonprofit educational institutions.
Eligibility: Applicant must be U.S. citizen or permanent resident residing in Michigan.
Basis for selection: Applicant must demonstrate financial need and high academic achievement.
Application requirements: FAFSA and qualifying ACT score.

Amount of award:	$100-$1,250
Number of awards:	28,463
Application deadline:	February 21, March 21
Total amount awarded:	$40,751,958

Contact:
Michigan Higher Education Assistance Authority
Office of Scholarships and Grants
P.O. Box 30462
Lansing, MI 48909-7962

Michigan Educational Opportunity Grant

Type of award: Scholarship, renewable.

Intended use: For undergraduate study at postsecondary institution. Designated institutions: Michigan public institutions.
Eligibility: Applicant must be U.S. citizen or permanent resident residing in Michigan.
Basis for selection: Applicant must demonstrate financial need.
Application requirements: Proof of eligibility.
Additional information: Applicant must be enrolled at least part-time.

   Amount of award: $1,000
   Number of awards: 5,564
   Total amount awarded: $2,119,663
Contact:
College financial aid office
P.O. Box 30462
Lansing, MI 48909-7966
Phone: 517-241-3537

Michigan Robert C. Byrd Honors Scholarship

Type of award: Scholarship, renewable.
Intended use: For full-time freshman study in United States.
Eligibility: Applicant must be high school senior. Applicant must be U.S. citizen or permanent resident residing in Michigan.
Basis for selection: Applicant must demonstrate high academic achievement.
Application requirements: Nomination by high school guidance counselor.

   Amount of award: $1,500
   Total amount awarded: $375,000
Contact:
Michigan Higher Education Assistance Authority
Office of Scholarships and Grants
P.O. Box 30462
Lansing, MI 48909-7966

Michigan Tuition Grant

Type of award: Scholarship, renewable.
Intended use: For freshman, sophomore, junior, senior, master's or doctoral study at 2-year, 4-year or graduate institution. Designated institutions: Michigan private nonprofit educational institutions.
Eligibility: Applicant must be U.S. citizen or permanent resident residing in Michigan.
Basis for selection: Applicant must demonstrate financial need.

   Amount of award: $100-$2,700
   Number of awards: 28,442
   Application deadline: February 21, March 21
   Total amount awarded: $50,147,198
Contact:
Michigan Higher Education Assistance Authority
Office of Scholarships and Grants
P.O. Box 30462
Lansing, MI 48909-7962

Michigan Mutual Insurance Company

Amerisure Scholarship

Type of award: Scholarship, renewable.
Intended use: For undergraduate study at accredited vocational, 2-year or 4-year institution.
Eligibility: Applicant or parent must be employed by Michigan Mutual Insurance Company.
Additional information: For further information or an application, contact Michigan Mutual Insurance Company directly.

   Amount of award: $1,000

Michigan Petroleum Association/Michigan Association of Convenience Stores

Michigan Petroleum Association/ Michigan Association of Convenience Stores Scholarship

Type of award: Scholarship.
Intended use: For undergraduate study at vocational, 2-year or 4-year institution.
Eligibility: Applicant or parent must be employed by Mich. Petrol. Assoc./Mich. Assoc. Convenience Stores. Applicant must be high school senior.
Additional information: For further information or an application, contact Michigan Petroleum Association/Michigan Association of Convenience Stores directly.

   Amount of award: $500-$1,000

Michigan Society of Professional Engineers

Michigan Society of Professional Engineers Scholarships

Type of award: Scholarship.
Intended use: For undergraduate study at accredited 4-year institution. Designated institutions: Must be an ABET accredited school in Michigan.
Eligibility: Applicant must be U.S. citizen residing in Michigan.
Basis for selection: Major/career interest in engineering. Applicant must demonstrate high academic achievement, depth of character and leadership.
Application requirements: Recommendations, essay, transcript. 3.0 GPA, evidence of involvement in extra-curricular activities, minimum score of 26 on ACT.
Additional information: State applicant must attend college in Michigan. Some scholarships for graduating high school

seniors and some for undergraduates; majority of awards are for high school seniors. January deadline for high school seniors; April deadline for undergraduates. Undergraduates must be members of MSPE. Contact guidance counselor or local MSPE chapter for application and specific eligibility requirements.

Amount of award:	$1,000-$3,000
Number of awards:	42
Application deadline:	January 1, April 2
Notification begins:	April 1

Contact:
Scholarship Coordinator Michigan Society of Professional Engineers
P.O. Box 15276
Lansing, MI 48901-5276
Phone: 517-487-9388
Fax: 517-487-0635
Web: www.voyager.net/mspe

Microfibres, Inc.

Microfibres Scholarship Program

Type of award: Scholarship, renewable.
Intended use: For undergraduate study at vocational, 2-year or 4-year institution.
Eligibility: Applicant or parent must be employed by Microfibres, Inc. Applicant must be high school senior.
Additional information: For further information or an application, contact Microfibres Incorporated directly.

Amount of award:	$1,500

Microscopy Society of America

Microscopy Presidential Student Award

Type of award: Scholarship.
Intended use: For undergraduate or graduate study.
Basis for selection: Competition/talent/interest in research paper, based on the quality of the paper submitted for presentation at the Annual Microscopy and Microanalysis meeting. Applicant must be the first author of the submitted paper. Major/career interest in science, general; biology; chemistry; physics or natural sciences. Applicant must demonstrate seriousness of purpose.
Additional information: Award consists of free registration for Microscopy and Microanalysis meeting, copy of proceedings, reimbursement for round trip travel. See Website "Call for Abstracts" section under Microscopy and Microanalysis.

Amount of award:	$1,200
Number of awards:	10
Number of applicants:	15
Application deadline:	February 15
Notification begins:	April 1

Contact:
Microscopy Society of America
230 East Ohio Street
Suite 400
Chicago, IL 60611
Phone: 800-538-3672
Web: www.msa.microscopy.com

Microscopy Society of America Undergraduate Research Scholarship

Type of award: Research grant.
Intended use: For full-time undergraduate study.
Basis for selection: Major/career interest in science, general; biology; physics; chemistry or natural sciences. Applicant must demonstrate seriousness of purpose.
Application requirements: Recommendations, research proposal. Letter from supervisor of lab where work will be done confirming project, applicant's curriculum vitae, and letter indicating how budget will be expended.
Additional information: Award for students interested in pursuing microscopy as career or major research tool. Must supply abstract of research project. Funds must be spent within a year of award date, but in special cases may be extended to cover additional research during summer semester following graduation.

Amount of award:	$3,000
Number of awards:	6
Number of applicants:	20
Application deadline:	December 31
Notification begins:	April 1
Total amount awarded:	$16,000

Contact:
Microscopy Society of America
230 East Ohio Street
Suite 400
Chicago, IL 60611
Phone: 800-538-3672
Web: www.msa.microscopy.com

Midrex Direct Reduction Corporation

The Donald Beggs Scholarship

Type of award: Scholarship.
Intended use: For undergraduate study at accredited 4-year institution.
Eligibility: Applicant or parent must be employed by Midrex Direct Reduction Corporation.
Additional information: For further information or an application, contact Midrex Direct Reduction Corporation directly.

Amount of award:	$3,000

Midwest Express Airlines

Flying Higher Scholarship Program

Type of award: Scholarship, renewable.
Intended use: For undergraduate study at vocational, 2-year or 4-year institution.
Eligibility: Applicant or parent must be employed by Midwest Express Airlines. Applicant must be high school senior.
Additional information: For further information or an application, contact Midwest Express Arilines directly.

   Amount of award: $2,000

Midwestern Higher Education Commission

Midwest Student Exchange Program

Type of award: Scholarship, renewable.
Intended use: For full-time undergraduate, master's, doctoral or first professional study at accredited 2-year, 4-year or graduate institution in United States. Designated institutions: Participating institutions in Kansas, Michigan, Minnesota, Missouri and Nebraska.
Eligibility: Applicant must be residing in Missouri, Nebraska, Kansas, Michigan or Minnesota.
Application requirements: Proof of eligibility.
Additional information: Reduced tuition rate for Kansas, Michigan, Minnesota, Missouri and Nebraska residents attending participating out-of-state institutions in one of the four other states in designated programs of study. For information, contact high school counselor or college admissions officer. For a list of participating institutions and programs contact either: (Kansas) Kansas Board of Regents, 700 SW Harrison, Suite 1410, Topeka, KS 66603, Phone: 785-296-3422; (Michigan) Michigan Department of Education, Hannah Building, Second Floor, 608 West Allegan Street, Lansing, MI 48909, Phone: 517-373-3360, Fax: 517-373-2759; or Presidents Council, State Universities of Michigan, 230 North Washington Square 302, Lansing, MI 48933, Phone: 517-482-1563, Fax: 517-482-1241; (Minnesota) Minnesota Higher Education Services Office, 1450 Energy Park Dr., Suite 350, St. Paul, MN 55108, Phone: 651-642-0567, Fax: 651-642-0675; (Missouri) Coordinating Board for Higher Education, 3515 Amazonas Drive, Jefferson City, MO 65109-5717, Phone: 573-751-2361, Fax: 573-751-6635; (Nebraska) Coordinating Commission for Postsecondary Education, 140 North Eighth Street, Suite 300, P.O. Box 95005, Lincoln, NE 68509-5005, Phone: 402-471-0022, Fax: 402-471-2886; or Midwestern Higher Education Commission, 1300 South Second Street, Suite 130, Minneapolis, MN 55454-1015, Phone: 612-626-8288.

   Amount of award: Full tuition
   Number of awards: 2,533
   Total amount awarded: $9,340,000
Contact:
Midwestern Higher Education Commission - MSEP Program Officer
1300 South 2nd Street
Suite 130
Minneapolis, MN 55454-1015
Phone: 612-626-8288
Fax: 612-626-8290
Web: www.mhec.org

Military Order of the Purple Heart

Military Order of the Purple Heart Scholarship

Type of award: Scholarship.
Intended use: For full-time undergraduate study at vocational, 2-year or 4-year institution.
Eligibility: Applicant must be U.S. citizen. Applicant must be descendant of veteran; or dependent of veteran. Must be son, daughter or grandchild of member of Military Order of the Purple Heart.
Basis for selection: Applicant must demonstrate financial need and high academic achievement.
Application requirements: $5 application fee. Recommendations, essay, transcript, proof of eligibility. SAT/ACT scores.
Additional information: Contact the Military Order of the Purple Heart for applications, deadline information, award amounts and other details. E-mail address: info@purpleheart.org. Applications available October 1.
Contact:
Military Order of the Purple Heart
Scholarship Coordinator
5413-B Blacklick Road
Springfield, VA 22151
Phone: 703-642-5360
Fax: 703-642-2054

The Millennium Society

UWC/MILLENIUM SCHOLARSHIP

Type of award: Scholarship.
Intended use: For full-time undergraduate study in or outside United States.
Eligibility: Applicant must be at least 17, no older than 25. Applicant must be U.S. citizen.
Basis for selection: Applicant must demonstrate depth of character, leadership and seriousness of purpose.
Application requirements: Recommendations, essay, transcript, proof of eligibility. Please submit a personal statement that addresses: your personal career goals and how studying internationlly will prepare you to accomplish them; your vision for the future and how you believe you will impact society in the next millennium; why you should be selected as a Millenium/ UWC Scholar; your definition of leadership and what type of leader you will be. copy of the acceptance letters from Send the UWC institutions to which you have applied.
Additional information: To apply to be a UWC/Millennium Scholar, complete the application on the Website. Applications are accepted throughout the year, and scholarship decisions are generally made by The Millennium Society's Scholarship Review Committee between May and July of each year. Applicants will be notified, in writing, of decisions as soon as possible following the meeting of the committee. Scholarships are awards for one academic year. Applicants seeking a scholarship for multiple years are required to reapply each academic year.

Contact:
The Millennium Society
195 North Harbor Drive
Suite 1802
Chicago, IL 60601
Phone: 312-729-1000
Fax: 312-540-6699
Web: http://millenniumsociety.org/scholars_program.html

Millipore Foundation

Millipore Foundation Scholarship Program

Type of award: Scholarship, renewable.
Intended use: For freshman study at accredited vocational, 2-year or 4-year institution.
Eligibility: Applicant or parent must be employed by Millipore Corporation.
Additional information: For further information or an application, contact Millipore Corporation directly.
    Amount of award: $5,000

Minnesota Department of Veteran's Affairs

Minnesota Educational Assistance for Veterans

Type of award: Scholarship.
Intended use: For undergraduate or graduate study at postsecondary institution. Designated institutions: All Minnesota institutions except the University of Minnesota.
Eligibility: Applicant must be residing in Minnesota. Applicant must be veteran.
Application requirements: Proof of eligibility.
Additional information: Must have exhausted eligible federal educational benefits. Information also available from institution or county veterans service officer.
    Amount of award: $350
Contact:
Minnesota Department of Veterans Affairs
Veterans Service Building, 2nd Floor
20 West 12 Street
St. Paul, MN 55155

Minnesota Educational Assistance for War Orphans

Type of award: Scholarship, renewable.
Intended use: For full-time undergraduate study at accredited vocational, 2-year or 4-year institution. Designated institutions: Approved Minnesota schools.
Eligibility: Applicant must be residing in Minnesota. Applicant must be dependent of deceased veteran. Veteran's death must have been on active duty or service connected.
Application requirements: Proof of eligibility.
Additional information: All recipients receive stipend and tuition waiver. Program not accepted at University of

Minnesota. Information also available from institution or county veterans service officer. Applicant must be a resident of Minnesota for 2 years prior to application. Available until recipients obtains bachelors degree or equvalent.
    Amount of award: $350
Contact:
Minnesota Department of Veterans Affairs
Veterans Service Building, 2nd Floor
20 West 12 Street
St. Paul, MN 55155-2079

Minnesota Higher Education Services Office

Minnesota Post-Secondary Child Care Grant

Type of award: Scholarship, renewable.
Intended use: For freshman, sophomore, junior or senior study at accredited vocational, 2-year or 4-year institution. Designated institutions: All Minnesota baccalaureate degree-granting institutions or public, non-profit vocational institutions.
Eligibility: Applicant must be U.S. citizen or permanent resident residing in Minnesota.
Basis for selection: Applicant must demonstrate financial need.
Additional information: Apply at college financial aid office. Eligibility limited to applicants with children twelve years or younger. Award amount prorated upon enrollment. Maximum of $2,200 per eligible child per academic year. Applicant cannot receive Aid to Families with Dependent Children, Minnesota Family Investment Program, tuition reciprocity, or be in default of loan. Those with bachelor's degree or eight semesters or twelve quarters of credit, or equivalent, are not eligible. Applicant must be enrolled at least half-time in nonsectarian program and must be in good academic standing. Award based on family income and size. Application available at financial aid office of Minnesota institution. Deadlines established by individual institution.
    Amount of award: $2,200
    Number of awards: 2,659
    Number of applicants: 2,659
Contact:
Financial Aid Office or
MHESO
1450 Energy Park Drive, Suite 350
St. Paul, MN 55108-5227
Phone: 651-642-0576 or 800-657-3866
Web: www.mheso.state.mn.us

Minnesota Safety Officers Survivors Program

Type of award: Scholarship.
Intended use: For undergraduate or non-degree study at accredited postsecondary institution.
Eligibility: Applicant must be residing in Minnesota. Applicant's parent must have been killed or disabled in work-related accident as fire fighter, police officer or public safety officer.
Application requirements: Proof of eligibility. Eligibility certificate.

Additional information: Must be enrolled in degree or certificate program at institution participating in State Grant Program. Also eligible if parent or spouse, not officially employed in public safety, was killed while assisting public safety officer or offering emergency medical assistance. Obtain eligibility certificate from Department of Public Safety, 211 Transportation Building, St. Paul, MN 55155. Apply through financial aid office.

Number of awards:	13
Number of applicants:	13
Total amount awarded:	$36,000

Contact:
Financial Aid Office or
MHESO
1450 Energy Park Drive, Suite 350
St. Paul, MN 55108-5227
Phone: 651-642-0567 or 800-657-3866
Web: www.mheso.state.mn.us

Minnesota Service Scholarship Matching Grant

Type of award: Scholarship.
Intended use: For undergraduate certificate or freshman study at accredited vocational, 2-year or 4-year institution. Designated institutions: Minnesota post-secondary institutions.
Eligibility: Applicant must be high school junior or senior. Applicant must be U.S. citizen or permanent resident residing in Minnesota.
Basis for selection: Applicant must demonstrate service orientation.
Application requirements: Nomination by high school principal. Applicant must be Minnesota high school graduate. State match is automatically awarded to those selected for federal scholarship: no separate state application is required.
Additional information: $500 state matching scholarship for Minnesota residents selected for $500 President's Service Scholarship.

Amount of award:	$500
Number of awards:	156
Application deadline:	April 1, June 30
Total amount awarded:	$250,000

Contact:
MHESO
1450 Energy Park Drive
Suite 350
St. Paul, MN 55108-5227
Phone: 651-642-0567 or 800-657-3866
Web: www.mheso.state.mn.us

Minnesota State Grant Program

Type of award: Scholarship, renewable.
Intended use: For undergraduate study at accredited vocational, 2-year or 4-year institution. Designated institutions: Minnesota institutions only.
Eligibility: Applicant must be U.S. citizen or permanent resident residing in Minnesota.
Basis for selection: Applicant must demonstrate financial need.
Application requirements: Proof of eligibility.
Additional information: Must not have completed four years of college. If not Minnesota high school graduate and parents not residents of Minnesota, applicant must be resident of Minnesota for at least one year. Can not be in default on loans or delinquent on child support payments. FAFSA used as application for Minnesota State Grant.

Amount of award:	$100-$7,725
Number of awards:	58,699
Number of applicants:	133,000
Application deadline:	June 30
Total amount awarded:	$96,280,731

Contact:
MHESO
1450 Energy Park Drive, Suite 350
St. Paul, MN 55108-5227
Phone: 651-642-0567 or 800-657-3866
Web: www.mheso.state.mn.us

Minnesota Mutual Life

Minnesota Mutual Life Presidents' Scholarship Fund

Type of award: Scholarship, renewable.
Intended use: For freshman study at accredited 4-year institution.
Eligibility: Applicant or parent must be employed by Minnesota Mutual Life.
Basis for selection: Applicant must demonstrate financial need.
Additional information: For further information or an application, contact Minnesota Mutual Life directly.

Amount of award:	$1,000

Minolta Corporation

Minolta Five-Plus Club Scholarship

Type of award: Scholarship.
Intended use: For freshman study at accredited 2-year or 4-year institution.
Eligibility: Applicant or parent must be employed by Minolta Corporation.
Additional information: For further information or application, contact Minolta Corporation directly.

Amount of award:	$3,000-$5,000

Miss America Organization

Miss America Competition Awards

Type of award: Scholarship.
Intended use: For undergraduate, graduate or non-degree study at accredited postsecondary institution.
Eligibility: Applicant must be single, female, at least 17, no older than 24. Applicant must be U.S. citizen.
Basis for selection: Competition/talent/interest in poise/talent/fitness. Applicant must demonstrate depth of character, leadership, patriotism, seriousness of purpose and service orientation.
Application requirements: Proof of eligibility.
Additional information: Contestants compete first at local level. Local winners go on to compete at state level and all state winners compete for Miss America. Contestants will apply

Scholarships

their talents, intelligence, speaking abilities and exercise their commitment to community service. Cash and tuition-based scholarships available at every level of competition. Some of the scholarships awarded at the National Level are as follows: first runner-up receives $40,000; second runner-up receives $30,000; third runner-up receives $25,000; fourth runner-up receives $5,000; and Miss America receives $50,000 in scholarship monies. Deadlines for local competitions vary. Contact the Miss America Organization for more information or visit Website.

Amount of award:	$100-$50,000
Number of awards:	30,000
Total amount awarded:	$40,000,000

Contact:
Miss America Organization
Two Ocean Way
Suite 1000
Atlantic City, NJ 08404
Phone: 609-345-7571 ext. 27
Fax: 609-345-2716
Web: www.missamerica.org

Mississippi Office of State Student Financial Aid

Gulf Coast Research Laboratory Minority Summer Grant

Type of award: Research grant.
Intended use: For undergraduate study at accredited 4-year institution in United States. Designated institutions: Gulf Coast Research Laboratory.
Eligibility: Applicant must be Alaskan native, Asian American, African American, Mexican American, Hispanic American, Puerto Rican or American Indian. Applicant must be U.S. citizen or permanent resident residing in Mississippi.
Basis for selection: Major/career interest in oceanography/ marine studies or environmental science.
Additional information: College credit possible, depending on grant-holder's educational institution. Grant provides $1,800 to Gulf Coast Research Laboratory Summer Academic Institute, plus $250 (total) for grant holder. Four- to ten-week program. Provides summer grants for minority students to attend classes or conduct independent study at Gulf Coast Research Laboratory in Gulf Coast Research Laboratory Summer Academic Institute. Number of awards and recipients are dependent upon availability of funds. Awards made on first-come, first-served basis.

Amount of award:	$250
Application deadline:	March 31

Contact:
Mississippi Office of State Student Financial Aid
3825 Ridgewood Road
Jackson, MS 39211-6453
Phone: 601-432-6997

Leveraging Educational Assistance Partnership Program (LEAP)

Type of award: Scholarship, renewable.
Intended use: For full-time freshman, sophomore, junior or senior study at accredited 2-year or 4-year institution. Designated institutions: Mississippi schools.

Eligibility: Applicant must be U.S. citizen residing in Mississippi.
Basis for selection: Applicant must demonstrate financial need and high academic achievement.
Application requirements: Recommendations, proof of eligibility.
Additional information: Must meet general requirements for participation in federal student aid program. Apply to college financial aid office.

Amount of award:	$200-$1,500
Total amount awarded:	$1,069,678

Contact:
Miss. Office of State Student Financial Aid
3825 Ridgewood Road
Jackson, MS 39211-6453
Phone: 601-432-6997

Mississippi Eminent Scholars Grant

Type of award: Scholarship, renewable.
Intended use: For full-time undergraduate certificate or freshman study at accredited 2-year, 4-year or graduate institution. Designated institutions: Public and nonprofit Mississippi institutions.
Eligibility: Applicant must be residing in Mississippi.
Basis for selection: Applicant must demonstrate high academic achievement.
Additional information: Must be resident of Mississippi for one year. Must be recognized as a semifinalist or finalist by the National Merit Scholarship Corporation or the National Achievement Scholarship Program. Must have 3.5 GPA or ACT of 29 or SAT combined score of 1280.

Amount of award:	$2,500
Application deadline:	September 15

Contact:
Mississippi Office of State Student Financial Aid
3825 Ridgewood Road
Jackson, MS 39211-6453
Phone: 601-432-6997

Mississippi Higher Education Legislative Plan for Needy Students

Type of award: Scholarship.
Intended use: For full-time freshman or sophomore study at accredited 2-year or 4-year institution. Designated institutions: Mississippi schools.
Eligibility: Applicant must be U.S. citizen residing in Mississippi.
Additional information: Minimum GPA 2.5 and 20 on ACT. Must be legal resident of Mississippi for at least two years. No criminal record. Student's family must have one child under age 21 and a two-year annual adjusted gross income of less than $36,500; or the family has two-year average annual adjusted gross income of less than $30,000 plus $5,000 for each additional child under 21. Award amounts vary. The number of awards and recipients are dependent upon availability of funds, and awards will be made on a first-come, first-serve basis.

Application deadline:	March 31

Contact:
Miss. Office of State Student Financial Aid
3825 Ridgewood Road
Jackson, MS 39211-6453
Phone: 601-432-6997

Mississippi Law Enforcement Officers/Firemen Scholarship

Type of award: Scholarship, renewable.
Intended use: For full-time undergraduate study at 2-year or 4-year institution.
Eligibility: Applicant must be residing in Mississippi. Applicant's parent must have been killed or disabled in work-related accident as fire fighter, police officer or public safety officer.
Application requirements: Proof of eligibility.
Additional information: Award covers tuition, room, and lab fees and may be used only at Mississippi public institution. Children entitled to award until age of 23. Spouses also eligible.

Amount of award:	Full tuition
Number of awards:	13
Total amount awarded:	$43,171

Contact:
Mississippi Office of State Student Financial Aid
3825 Ridgewood Road
Jackson, MS 39211-6453
Phone: 601-982-6663

Mississippi Resident Tuition Assistance Grant

Type of award: Scholarship, renewable.
Intended use: For full-time freshman, sophomore, junior or senior study at accredited 2-year or 4-year institution. Designated institutions: Mississippi schools.
Eligibility: Applicant must be U.S. citizen residing in Mississippi.
Application requirements: Submit FAFSA.
Additional information: Must be resident of Mississippi for no less than one year. Must be receiving less than full Federal Pell Grant. 2.5 high school GPA and ACT score of 15 required. Must not be in default on an educational loan.

Amount of award:	$500-$1,000
Application deadline:	September 15

Contact:
Mississippi Office of State Student Financial Aid
Grant Coordinator
3825 Ridgewood Road
Jackson, MS 39211-6453
Phone: 601-432-6997

Mississippi Southeast Asia POW/ MIA Scholarship

Type of award: Scholarship, renewable.
Intended use: For full-time undergraduate study at 2-year or 4-year institution. Designated institutions: Mississippi public institutions.
Eligibility: Applicant must be U.S. citizen or permanent resident residing in Mississippi. Applicant must be dependent of POW/MIA who served in the Army, Air Force, Marines or Navy during Vietnam.
Application requirements: Proof of eligibility.
Additional information: Award covers cost of tuition, room, and lab fees and must be used at a Mississippi public institution. Notification upon receipt of required documents.

Amount of award:	Full tuition

Contact:
Miss. Office of State Student Financial Aid
Student Financial Aid
3825 Ridgewood Road
Jackson, MS 39211-6453
Phone: 601-432-6997

Missouri Coordinating Board for Higher Education

Charles Gallagher Student Financial Assistance Program

Type of award: Scholarship, renewable.
Intended use: For full-time undergraduate study at accredited vocational, 2-year or 4-year institution in United States. Designated institutions: Missouri institutions.
Eligibility: Applicant must be U.S. citizen or permanent resident residing in Missouri.
Basis for selection: Applicant must demonstrate financial need.
Application requirements: Proof of eligibility. FAFSA must be received by central processor by April 1.
Additional information: May be used only toward first postsecondary degree, and may not be used for theology or divinity studies. Awards vary, depending on cost of school.

Amount of award:	$100-$1,500
Number of awards:	11,099
Number of applicants:	108,000
Application deadline:	April 1
Notification begins:	July 1
Total amount awarded:	$14,368,003

Contact:
Missouri Coordinating Board for Higher Education
3515 Amazonas Drive
Jefferson City, MO 65109
Phone: 800-473-6757
Web: www.cbhe.state.mo.us

Missouri Higher Education Academic Scholarship

Type of award: Scholarship, renewable.
Intended use: For full-time undergraduate study at accredited vocational, 2-year or 4-year institution in United States. Designated institutions: Approved Missouri institutions.
Eligibility: Applicant must be U.S. citizen or permanent resident residing in Missouri.
Basis for selection: Applicant must demonstrate high academic achievement.
Application requirements: Proof of eligibility. Academic progress important.
Additional information: Program also known as "Bright Flight." May not be used for theology or divinity studies. SAT or ACT test required for determining academic achievement, scores must be in top 3% of state students. Check with high school counselor or financial aid administrator for application and additional information. Also see Website.

Amount of award:	$2,000
Number of awards:	7,538
Application deadline:	July 31
Total amount awarded:	$14,308,835

Contact:
Missouri Coordinating Board for Higher Education
3515 Amazonas Drive
Jefferson City, MO 65109
Phone: 800-473-6757
Web: www.cbhe.state.mo.us

Missouri Public Service Survivor Grant

Type of award: Scholarship, renewable.
Intended use: For full-time undergraduate study at accredited vocational, 2-year or 4-year institution in United States. Designated institutions: Missouri-based institution must be approved.
Eligibility: Applicant must be U.S. citizen or permanent resident residing in Missouri. Applicant's parent must have been killed or disabled in work-related accident as fire fighter, police officer or public safety officer.
Basis for selection: Applicant must demonstrate depth of character.
Application requirements: Proof of eligibility.
Additional information: For spouses or children of Missouri public safety officers, including law enforcement, firefighters, corrections, water safety, and conservation, killed or totally and permanently disabled in the line of duty. Children or spouses of Missouri Deptartment of Highway and Transportation employees also eligible if parent died during performance of job. May not be used for theology or divinity studies. Award amounts vary; contact sponsor for information. The scholarship is based on demonstrated financial need as well as high school and college academic achievement. Minimum high school GPA must be 2.5 or higher; ACT score of 20 or higher; and SAT score of 950 or higher. FAFSA must be filed and received by central processor by April 1. No separate application.

Amount of award:	$2,014
Number of awards:	1,953
Total amount awarded:	$3,933,342

Contact:
Missouri Coordinating Board for Higher Education
3515 Amazonas Drive
Jefferson City, MO 65109
Phone: 800-473-6757
Web: www.cbhe.state.mo.us

Missouri Department of Elementary and Secondary Education

Missouri Minority Teaching Scholarship

Type of award: Scholarship, renewable.
Intended use: For full-time undergraduate certificate, freshman, sophomore, junior, senior or master's study at accredited 2-year or 4-year institution in United States. Designated institutions: Missouri institutions.
Eligibility: Applicant must be Alaskan native, Asian American, African American, Mexican American, Hispanic American, Puerto Rican or American Indian. Applicant must be high school senior. Applicant must be residing in Missouri.

Basis for selection: Major/career interest in education. Applicant must demonstrate high academic achievement.
Application requirements: Recommendations, transcript, proof of eligibility.
Additional information: Must rank in top 25 percent of class. Must score in top 25 percent on ACT or SAT. Must teach for five years in Missouri Public Schools or scholarship becomes loan. If in college, may have 3.0 GPA at 30 hours to qualify. If college graduate, may receive award if returning to a masters level math or science education program.

Amount of award:	$3,000
Number of awards:	100
Application deadline:	February 15
Notification begins:	April 15

Contact:
Missouri Department of Elementary and Secondary Education
Teacher Recruitment and Retention
P.O. Box 480
Jefferson City, MO 65102
Phone: 573-751-1668

Missouri Robert C. Byrd Honors Scholarship

Type of award: Scholarship, renewable.
Intended use: For freshman, sophomore, junior or senior study at accredited 4-year institution in United States.
Eligibility: Applicant must be high school senior. Applicant must be U.S. citizen or permanent resident residing in Missouri.
Basis for selection: Applicant must demonstrate high academic achievement.
Application requirements: Transcript.
Additional information: Must be completing high school or GED in year of application. Must be in top 10 percent of class or have GED score at or above national 90th percentile. Final selection at each congressional district level based on SAT or ACT scores and GPA. High school guidance counselor must sign application. Award amount varies, contact sponsor for more information. The applicants high school guidance counselor must sign and verify the application form.

Amount of award:	$1,500
Application deadline:	April 15
Notification begins:	October 1
Total amount awarded:	$355,500

Contact:
Missouri Department of Elementary and Secondary Education
Robert C. Byrd Honors Scholarship
P.O. Box 480
Jefferson City, MO 65102
Phone: 573-751-1668

Missouri Teacher Education Scholarship

Type of award: Scholarship.
Intended use: For full-time freshman or sophomore study at accredited 4-year institution.
Eligibility: Fifteen percent of awards set aside for minorities. Applicant must be high school senior. Applicant must be U.S. citizen residing in Missouri.
Basis for selection: Major/career interest in education. Applicant must demonstrate high academic achievement.
Application requirements: Recommendations, transcript, proof of eligibility. ACT/SAT and class rank.
Additional information: Must rank in top 15 percent of graduating class or score in top 15 percent on ACT, SAT I or

other standardized tests. Must teach in Missouri Public School for five years after graduation or scholarship becomes a loan.

Amount of award:	$2,000
Number of awards:	240
Number of applicants:	500
Application deadline:	February 15
Notification begins:	April 15
Total amount awarded:	$240,000

Contact:
Missouri Department of Elementary and Secondary Education
Teacher Recruitment and Retention
P.O. Box 480
Jefferson City, MO 65102
Phone: 573-751-1668

Missouri League for Nursing

Missouri Nursing Scholarship

Type of award: Scholarship, renewable.
Intended use: For full-time sophomore, junior, senior, master's or non-degree study in United States.
Eligibility: Applicant must be U.S. citizen residing in Missouri.
Basis for selection: Major/career interest in nursing. Applicant must demonstrate financial need and high academic achievement.
Additional information: Applications can be obtained from dean of National League for Nursing-accredited school of Nursing.

Number of awards:	4
Number of applicants:	60
Application deadline:	November 1
Notification begins:	December 30

Contact:
Contact Dean of school nursing program
Phone: 573-635-5355

Mitsui USA Foundation

Mitsui USA's Sons' & Daughters' Scholarship Program

Type of award: Scholarship, renewable.
Intended use: For undergraduate study at vocational, 2-year or 4-year institution.
Eligibility: Applicant or parent must be employed by The Mitsui USA Foundation. Applicant must be high school senior.
Additional information: For further information or an application, contact Mitsui USA Foundation directly.

Amount of award:	$2,000

Mobile Gas Service Corporation

Blue Flame Scholarship

Type of award: Scholarship, renewable.
Intended use: For freshman, sophomore, junior or senior study at accredited vocational, 2-year or 4-year institution.
Eligibility: Applicant or parent must be employed by Mobil Gas Service Corporation.
Basis for selection: Applicant must demonstrate financial need.
Additional information: Must be child of employee of Mobile Gas Service Corporation. For further information and an application, contact Mobile Gas Service Corporation directly.

Amount of award:	$500-$2,000

Moen Incorporated

Bill O'Neill Memorial Scholarship

Type of award: Scholarship.
Intended use: For freshman study at accredited 2-year or 4-year institution.
Eligibility: Applicant or parent must be employed by Moen.
Additional information: For further information or an application, contact Moen directly.

Amount of award:	$3,000

Montana Board of Regents of Higher Education

Leveraging Educational Assistance Partnership Program

Type of award: Scholarship.
Intended use: For undergraduate study. Designated institutions: Montana postsecondary institutions.
Eligibility: Applicant must be residing in Montana.
Basis for selection: Applicant must demonstrate financial need.

Amount of award:	$200-$600
Number of awards:	800
Total amount awarded:	$370,000

Contact:
Contact college financial aid office for application information.

Montana Tuition Fee Waiver for Dependents of POW/MIA

Type of award: Scholarship.
Intended use: For undergraduate or graduate study at accredited postsecondary institution. Designated institutions: Montana University system institutions.
Eligibility: Applicant must be residing in Montana. Applicant must be dependent of POW/MIA; or spouse of POW/MIA.
Application requirements: In order to approve for this fee waiver, the following information must be provided: 1) Proof

that your parent or spouse was declared by the Secretary of Defense to be a prisoner of war or missing or captured in connection with the conflict in Southeast Asia after January 1, 1961. 2) Proof that you are the spouse or child and dependent of the prisoner of war. 3) Proof that the prisoner of war was a Montana resident at the time he or she became a prisoner of war. Eligibility for waiver continues until completion of BA or certification of completion, as long as eligibility requirements continue to be met.

Additional information: Contact college financial aid office for application information.

Amount of award: Full tuition

Contact:
Montana Board of Regents of Higher Eduaction
PO Box 203101
Helena, MT 59620-3101

Montana Tuition Fee Waiver for Veterans

Type of award: Scholarship.

Intended use: For undergraduate or graduate study. Designated institutions: Montana University system institutions.

Eligibility: Applicant must be permanent resident residing in Montana. Applicant must be veteran. Must have been honorably discharged person who served with the United States forces during wartime.

Application requirements: Proof of eligibility. Vetrens who have served in the armed forces subsequent to the conflict in Vietnam are eligible for a fee waiver if the following conditions are met: 1) The veteran has been awarded an Armed Forces Expeditionary Medal for service in Lebanon, Grenada, or Panama or the veteran served ina combat theater in the Persian Gulf between August 2, 1990 and April 11, 1991 and received the Southwest Asia Service Medal. 2) The veteran is pursuing his or her initial undergraduate degree.

Additional information: Must have used up all federal veterans educational assistance benefits. Contact college financial aid office.

Amount of award: Full tuition

Contact:
Montana University System
PO Box 203101
Helena, MT 59620-3101
Web: www.mgslp.state.mt.us

Montana University System Community College Honor Scholarship

Type of award: Scholarship.

Intended use: For junior study at 4-year institution. Designated institutions: Montana University system institutions.

Eligibility: Applicant must be residing in Montana.

Basis for selection: Applicant must demonstrate high academic achievement.

Application requirements: Recommendations, proof of eligibility. Must be graduate with associate degree from and be recommended by president/faculty of accredited Montana community college.

Additional information: Holder of scholarship must enter Montana University System within nine months after receiving associate degree. Award provides for tuition/fee waiver in any unit of Montana University System. The waiver will be valid through the completion of the first academic year (two semesters) of enrollment, exclusive of any credits earned prior to high school or community college graduation.

Amount of award: Full tuition

Contact:
Financial aid office of community college.
Web: www.mgslp.state.mt.us

Montana University System High School Honor Scholarship

Type of award: Scholarship.

Intended use: For freshman study at 4-year institution. Designated institutions: Montana University system campus or Dawson, Flathead Valley, and Miles community colleges.

Eligibility: Applicant must be high school senior. Applicant must be U.S. citizen, international student or foreign student who has been exchange student. Applicant must be residing in Montana.

Basis for selection: Applicant must demonstrate high academic achievement.

Application requirements: Recommendations, transcript, proof of eligibility.

Additional information: Obtain information from high school guidance counselor who completes application for recommended students. Must have 3.0 GPA. Terms of award and which fees are covered specified at time scholarship is awarded. The scholarship must be utilized within nine months after high school graduation. The waiver will be valid through the completion of the first academic year, exclusive of any credit earned prior to high school graduation. Eligibility will continue for no more than three years after the date of issuance, provided satisfactory academic progress is maintained.

Amount of award: Full tuition

Application deadline: March 31

Contact:
Montana Board of Regents of Higher Education
PO Box 203101
Helena, MT 59620-3101
Web: www.mgslp.state.mt.us

Moyer Packing Company

Moyer Packing Company Sons and Daughters Scholarship Program

Type of award: Scholarship, renewable.

Intended use: For undergraduate study at vocational, 2-year or 4-year institution.

Eligibility: Applicant or parent must be employed by Moyer Packing Company. Applicant must be high school senior.

Additional information: For further information or an application, contact Moyer Packing Company Sons and Daughters Scholarship Program directly.

Amount of award: $1,000

Myasthenia Gravis Foundation

Myasthenia Gravis Foundation Nursing Research Fellowship

Type of award: Research grant.
Intended use: For full-time undergraduate or graduate study at accredited 4-year or graduate institution in United States.
Eligibility: Applicant must be U.S. citizen or permanent resident.
Basis for selection: Major/career interest in nursing.
Application requirements: Recommendations, transcript, research proposal.
Additional information: For nursing students or professionals interested in studying problems encountered by patients with Myasthenia Gravis or related neuromuscular conditions.

Amount of award:	$1,500

Contact:
Research Grant Committee
Myasthenia Gravis Foundation
5841 Cedar Lake Road, Suite 204
Minneapolis, MN 55416
Phone: 800-541-5454
Fax: 952-545-6073
Web: www.myasthenia.org

Viets Premedical/Medical Student Fellowship

Type of award: Research grant.
Intended use: For full-time junior, senior or first professional study at accredited 4-year or graduate institution in United States.
Eligibility: Applicant must be U.S. citizen or permanent resident.
Basis for selection: Major/career interest in medicine.
Application requirements: Recommendations, transcript, proof of eligibility, research proposal.
Additional information: Focus of research must be myasthenia gravis or related field.

Amount of award:	$3,000
Number of awards:	3
Number of applicants:	10
Application deadline:	March 15
Total amount awarded:	$9,000

Contact:
Research Grant Committee
Myasthenia Gravis Foundation
5841 Cedar Lake Road, Suite 204
Minneapolis, MN 55416
Phone: 800-541-5454
Fax: 952-545-6073
Web: www.myasthenia.org

NAACP Legal Defense and Education Fund, Inc.

Herbert Lehman Scholarship for African American Students

Type of award: Scholarship, renewable.
Intended use: For full-time freshman study at accredited 4-year institution in United States.
Eligibility: Applicant must be African American. Applicant must be high school senior. Applicant must be U.S. citizen.
Basis for selection: Applicant must demonstrate financial need, high academic achievement, depth of character, leadership, seriousness of purpose and service orientation.
Application requirements: Recommendations, essay, transcript. Send completed application.
Additional information: For initial application, must be entering first year of college where African Americans are substantially underrepresented. Application request should be made in writing between November 15 and March 15 with statement of career and educational goals, reason why assistance is needed, and name of college to be attended.

Amount of award:	$2,000
Number of awards:	20
Number of applicants:	2,500
Application deadline:	April 30
Notification begins:	July 1
Total amount awarded:	$150,000

Contact:
The Herbert Lehman Fund
NAACP Legal Defense and Educational Fund, Inc
99 Hudson Street Suite 1600
New York, NY 10013

NAACP Special Contribution Fund

Agnes Jones Jackson Scholarship

Type of award: Scholarship, renewable.
Intended use: For full-time undergraduate or graduate study at 2-year, 4-year or graduate institution.
Eligibility: Applicant or parent must be member/participant of National Association for Advancement of Colored People. Applicant must be no older than 25.
Application requirements: Recommendations, transcript, proof of eligibility. Inlcude financial aid forms or copies of parents latest income tax forms. Send one personal reference, one academic reference and one NAACP reference (from an officer).
Additional information: Must be current regular member of NAACP for at least one year or fully paid life member. Minimum 2.5 GPA for undergraduates, 3.0 for graduate students. Award amounts: $1,500 undergraduate, $2,500 graduate. Graduate students can be full-time or part-time. Applications may be requested after January 1; include business-sized SASE.

Amount of award:	$1,500-$2,500
Application deadline:	April 30
Notification begins:	July 31

Scholarships

315

Contact:
NAACP Special Contribution Fund
Education Department
4805 Mount Hope Drive
Baltimore, MD 21215-3297

Earl G. Graves/NAACP Scholarship Award

Type of award: Scholarship.
Intended use: For full-time junior, senior, master's or doctoral study at accredited 4-year or graduate institution in United States.
Basis for selection: Major/career interest in business. Applicant must demonstrate high academic achievement.
Application requirements: Recommendations, transcript, proof of eligibility.
Additional information: Applicant must be in top 20% of their class. May apply during sophomore year.
    Amount of award: $5,000
    Application deadline: April 30
    Notification begins: July 31
Contact:
NAACP Special Contribution Fund
4805 Mount Hope Drive
Baltimore, MD 21215
Web: www.naacp.org

NAACP/NASA Louis Stokes Science & Technology Award

Type of award: Scholarship.
Intended use: For full-time freshman study at accredited 4-year institution in United States. Designated institutions: Historically Black college or university.
Eligibility: Applicant must be U.S. citizen.
Basis for selection: Major/career interest in engineering; chemistry; biology or physics. Applicant must demonstrate financial need and high academic achievement.
Application requirements: Recommendations, transcript. Letter of recommendation from NAACP officer and two from teachers or professors in field of study.
Additional information: Minimum 2.5 required. NAACP membership and participation is highly desirable.
    Amount of award: $2,000
    Application deadline: April 30
    Notification begins: July 31
Contact:
NAACP Special Contribution Fund
405 Mount Hope Drive
Baltimore, MD 21215
Web: www.naacp.org

Roy Wilkins Scholarship

Type of award: Scholarship.
Intended use: For full-time freshman study at accredited 2-year or 4-year institution in United States.
Eligibility: Applicant or parent must be member/participant of National Association for Advancement of Colored People. Applicant must be high school senior. Applicant must be U.S. citizen.
Application requirements: Recommendations, transcript, proof of eligibility. One recommendation should be from NAACP officer. Send financial aid forms along with copy of letter of acceptance from college or university.

Additional information: Minimum 2.5 GPA. Applications may be requested after January 1. Include business-sized SASE.
    Amount of award: $1,000
    Application deadline: April 30
    Notification begins: July 31
Contact:
NAACP Special Contribution Fund
Education Department
4805 Mount Hope Drive
Baltimore, MD 21215-3297

Sutton Education Scholarship

Type of award: Scholarship, renewable.
Intended use: For full-time undergraduate or graduate study at accredited 2-year, 4-year or graduate institution in United States.
Eligibility: Applicant or parent must be member/participant of National Association for Advancement of Colored People. Applicant must be U.S. citizen.
Basis for selection: Major/career interest in education. Applicant must demonstrate high academic achievement and leadership.
Application requirements: Recommendations, transcript, proof of eligibility. One recommendation should be from NAACP officer. Financial aid forms. Also include recent transcript of grades, and acceptance letter from college or university and two letters of recommendation from teachers or professors in the major field of study.
Additional information: For students majoring in field with teacher certification. Undergraduates must have minimum 2.5 GPA, graduate students must have minimum 3.0 GPA. Applications available in January. Include business-sized SASE. Graduate students may be enrolled part-time.
    Amount of award: $1,000-$2,000
    Application deadline: April 30
    Notification begins: July 31
Contact:
NAACP Special Contribution Fund
Education Department
4805 Mount Hope Drive
Baltimore, MD 21215-3297

Willems Scholarship

Type of award: Scholarship, renewable.
Intended use: For full-time undergraduate or graduate study at accredited 2-year, 4-year or graduate institution in United States.
Eligibility: Applicant or parent must be member/participant of National Association for Advancement of Colored People. Applicant must be male. Applicant must be U.S. citizen.
Basis for selection: Major/career interest in engineering; chemistry; physics or mathematics. Applicant must demonstrate financial need and high academic achievement.
Application requirements: Recommendations, transcript, proof of eligibility. One recommendation should be from NAACP officer and two from teachers or professors in the field of study. Financial aid forms.
Additional information: Applications may be requested after January 1. Send 9- by 12-inch SASE. Minimum 2.0 GPA for undergraduates and 3.0 GPA for graduate students. Award is $2,000 for undergraduates, $3,000 for graduate students. Graduate students may be enrolled part-time.
    Amount of award: $2,000-$3,000
    Application deadline: April 30
    Notification begins: July 31

Contact:
NAACP Special Contribution Fund
Education Department
4805 Mount Hope Drive
Baltimore, MD 21215-3297

NASA District of Columbia Space Grant Consortium

NASA District of Columbia Undergraduate Scholarship

Type of award: Scholarship, renewable.
Intended use: For undergraduate or graduate study. Designated institutions: The American University, Gallaudet University, George Washington University, Howard University, University of District of Columbia.
Eligibility: Applicant must be U.S. citizen.
Basis for selection: Major/career interest in science, general; mathematics; engineering; aerospace; physical education; political science/government or engineering. Applicant must demonstrate high academic achievement.
Application requirements: Recommendations, transcript, proof of eligibility.
Additional information: Number of grants, amounts of funding, deadlines, and application requirements vary by year and by institutions. Contact sponsor for more information.
Contact:
District of Columbia Space Grant Consortium,
American University Department of Physics
McKinley Building Room 106
Washington, DC 20016-8058
Phone: 202-885-2780
Fax: 202-885-2723

NASA Nebraska Space Grant Consortium

NASA Space Grant Nebraska EPSCoR Undergraduate Scholarships

Type of award: Scholarship, renewable.
Intended use: For undergraduate study at accredited 4-year institution in United States. Designated institutions: Nebraska Space Grant Consortium member institution. Member institutions include: Chadron State College, College of St. Mary, Creighton University, Grace University, Metro Community College, Nebraska Indian Community College, University of Nebraska - Lincoln, University of Nebraska at Kearney, University of Nebraska at Omaha, University of Nebraska Medical Center, Western Nebraska Community College, Hastings College and Little Priest Tribal College.
Eligibility: Applicant must be U.S. citizen residing in Nebraska.
Basis for selection: Major/career interest in aerospace; aviation; energy research; engineering or science, general.
Application requirements: Essay, transcript.

Additional information: Awards amounts vary up to $750. Fellowships for course-work that does not entail research are available, but award amounts are not as substantial. View Website to download application.
    Application deadline: November 1
Contact:
NASA Nebraska Space Grant Consortium
Aviation Institute, Allwine Hall 422
6001 Dodge St.
Omaha, NE 68182
Web: www.unomaha.edu/~nasa

NASA Ohio Space Grant Consortium

NASA Space Grant Ohio Junior/ Senior Scholarship Program

Type of award: Scholarship, renewable.
Intended use: For full-time junior or senior study at accredited 4-year institution. Designated institutions: Ohio Space Grant Consortium members include: Air Force Institute of Technology, Case Western Reserve University, Cedarville College, Central State University, Cleveland State University, Marietta College, Ohio Northern University, Ohio University, Ohio State University, University of Akron, University of Cincinnati, University of Dayton, University of Toledo, Wilberforce University, Wright State University, Miami University, and Youngstown State University.
Eligibility: Applicant must be U.S. citizen residing in Ohio.
Basis for selection: Major/career interest in aerospace or engineering.
Application requirements: Recommendations, essay, transcript.
Additional information: Awards are $2,000 for juniors, $3,000 for seniors. Must attend a Consortium member institution.

Amount of award:	$2,000-$3,000
Number of awards:	50
Number of applicants:	150
Application deadline:	January 31
Notification begins:	April 30
Total amount awarded:	$130,000

Contact:
NASA Ohio Space Grant Consortium
Ohio Aerospace Institute
22800 Cedar Point Road
Cleveland, OH 44142
Web: www.osgc.org

NASA South Carolina Space Grant Consortium

Kathryn D. Sullivan Science and Engineering Undergraduate Fellowship

Type of award: Scholarship, renewable.

317

Intended use: For full-time senior study at accredited 4-year institution in United States. Designated institutions: South Carolina institutions.

Eligibility: Applicant must be U.S. citizen residing in South Carolina.

Basis for selection: Major/career interest in science, general; engineering or mathematics.

Application requirements: Recommendations, essay, transcript, nomination by faculty advisor.

Additional information: Applicants must attend a South Carolina institution. Applicants must have sponsorship from a faculty advisor. Awards are $3,500 per semester. The Consortium actively encourages women, minority, and disabled students to apply.

Amount of award:	$7,000
Number of awards:	1
Application deadline:	February 1

Contact:
NASA South Carolina Space Grant Consortium
Tara M. Baughman, MPA
College of Charleston Department of Geology
Charleston, SC 29424
Phone: 843-953-5463
Fax: 843-953-5446
Web: www.cofc.edu/~scsgrant/

NASA Space Grant South Carolina Undergraduate Academic Year Research Program

Type of award: Research grant, renewable.

Intended use: For full-time junior or senior study at accredited 4-year institution in United States. Designated institutions: Benedict College, The Citadel, Clemson University, Coastal Carolina University, Furman University, South Carolina State University, University of Charleston, University of South Carolina, Medical University of South Carolina, University of the Virgin Islands, and Wofford College.

Eligibility: Applicant must be U.S. citizen residing in South Carolina.

Basis for selection: Major/career interest in mathematics; science, general; astronomy; aerospace; engineering, mechanical; geophysics; geology/earth sciences or atmospheric sciences/meteorology.

Application requirements: Recommendations, essay, transcript, research proposal, nomination by faculty advisor.

Additional information: Applicants must attend a South Carolina Space Grant Consortium member institution. Applicants must have sponsorship from a faculty advisor. Applicants may have a field of study or interest related to any NASA enterprise. The Consortium actively encourages women, minority, and disabled students to apply.

Amount of award:	$3,000
Application deadline:	February 28

Contact:
NASA South Carolina Space Grant Consortium
Tara Baughman, MPA
College of Charleston Department of Geology
Charleston, SC 29424
Phone: 843-953-5463
Fax: 843-953-5446
Web: www.cofc.edu/~scsgrant/

NASA Space Grant Alabama Space Grant Consortium

NASA Space Grant Alabama Undergraduate Scholarship

Type of award: Scholarship, renewable.

Intended use: For full-time junior or senior study at accredited 4-year institution. Designated institutions: Alabama Space Grant member universities: University of Alabama Huntsville, Alabama A&M, University of Alabama, University of Alabarma Birmingham, University of South Alabama, Auburn University, Tuskegee University.

Eligibility: Applicant must be U.S. citizen.

Basis for selection: Major/career interest in aerospace; engineering or science, general. Applicant must demonstrate high academic achievement.

Application requirements: Recommendations, essay, transcript, nomination by faculty advisor at Alabama consortium member institution. Include resume.

Additional information: Applicants must have 3.0 or greater GPA. Must be in final term of sophomore year or later when applying. The Consortium actively encourages women, minority, and physically challenged students to apply, but others are not excluded.

Amount of award:	$1,000
Number of awards:	35
Application deadline:	March 1

Contact:
NASA Space Grant Alabama Space Grant Consortium
University of Alabama in Huntsville
Materials Science Building, 205
Huntsville, AL 35899
Phone: 256-824-6800
Fax: 256-824-6061
Web: www.uah.edu/ASGC/

NASA Space Grant Arkansas Space Grant Consortium

NASA Space Grant Arkansas Undergraduate Scholarship

Type of award: Scholarship.

Intended use: For full-time undergraduate study in United States. Designated institutions: Arkansas Space Grant Consortium members: University of Arkansas at Little Rock, Arkansas State University, Arkansas Tech University, Harding University, Henderson State University, Hendrix College, Lyon College, Ouachita Baptist University, University of Arkansas at Fayetteville, University of Arkansas at Pine Bluff, University of Arkansas for Medical Sciences, University of Central Arkansas, University of the Ozarks, and University of Arkansas at Monticello.

Eligibility: Applicant must be U.S. citizen residing in Arkansas.

Basis for selection: Major/career interest in aerospace; astronomy; chemistry; engineering; physics or medicine. Applicant must demonstrate high academic achievement.
Application requirements: Research proposal.
Additional information: Awards must be used at Consortium Member institutions. For any space-related research. Applications usually accepted September through November; contact program office at your campus. GPA of at least 3.0 preferred.

Amount of award:	$250-$5,000
Number of awards:	60
Application deadline:	November 30
Total amount awarded:	$109,089

Contact:
Visit web site and contact local campus Space Grant representative.
Phone: 501-569-8211 501-569-8212
Fax: 501-569-8039
Web: www.ualr.edu/~spacegrant/index.html

NASA Space Grant Connecticut Space Grant Consortium

NASA Space Grant Connecticut Undergraduate Fellowship

Type of award: Research grant, renewable.
Intended use: For full-time undergraduate study at accredited 4-year institution in United States. Designated institutions: Connecticut Space Grant Consortium member institutions including University of Connecticut, University of Hartford, University of New Haven, Trinity College.
Eligibility: Applicant must be U.S. citizen.
Basis for selection: Major/career interest in aerospace; engineering or science, general.
Application requirements: Recommendations, transcript, proof of eligibility. Resume.
Additional information: Must be used at a Connecticut Consortium member institution. Consortium actively encourages women, minority, and disabled students to apply.

Amount of award:	$2,500
Number of awards:	10
Application deadline:	April 14
Total amount awarded:	$25,000

Contact:
NASA Space Grant Connecticut Space Grant Consortium
University of Hartford
200 Bloomfield Ave.
West Hartford, CT 06117
Phone: 860-768-4813
Fax: 860-768-5220
Web: uhavax.hartford.edu/~ctspgrant

NASA Space Grant Hawaii Space Grant Consortium

NASA Space Grant Hawaii Undergraduate Fellowship

Type of award: Scholarship.
Intended use: For full-time junior or senior study in United States. Designated institutions: Consortium member schools.
Eligibility: Applicant must be U.S. citizen residing in Hawaii.
Basis for selection: Major/career interest in astronomy; geology/earth sciences; oceanography/marine studies; physics; zoology; law or geography.
Application requirements: Applicants must be sponsored by a faculty member willing to act as the student's mentor during the award period.
Additional information: Additional fields include math, physics, engineering, computer sciences, life sciences that are concerned with understanding, utilization, or exploration of space with investigation of Earth from space. Applicants must be U.S. citizens. Must be sponsored by faculty member who acts as student's advisor during period of award. Full-time undergraduates at Manoa, Hilo with major declared can apply for two-semester fellowships. Stipend of $3,000 per semester. Also up to $500 for supplies or travel. Recipients expected to work 10-15 hours per week on projects. Recipients must attend Consortium member institutions. Consortium members are: University of Hawaii at Manoa and Hilo, Honolulu, Kapiolani, Leeward, Maui, and Windward Community Colleges. Women, under-represented minorities (specifically Native Hawaiians, Filipinos, other Pacific Islanders, Native Americans, Blacks, Hispanics), physically challenged students who have interest in space-related fields are particularly encouraged to apply. Freshmen, sophomores may also apply in astrophysics.

Amount of award:	$3,000
Number of awards:	20
Application deadline:	June 15, December 1

Contact:
Hawaii Space Grant College
2525 Correa Road
Honolulu, HI 96822
Phone: 808-956-3138
Web: www.soest.hawaii.edu/SPACEGRANT

NASA Space Grant Idaho Space Grant Consortium

NASA Idaho Space Grant Undergraduate Scholarship

Type of award: Scholarship, renewable.
Intended use: For full-time undergraduate study at accredited 4-year institution. Designated institutions: Albertson College of Idaho, Boise State University, College of Southern Idaho, Idaho State University, Lewis Clark State College, North Idaho College, Northwest Nazarene University, BYU-Idaho, and the University of Idaho.
Eligibility: Applicant must be U.S. citizen.
Basis for selection: Major/career interest in engineering; mathematics; science, general or education.

Application requirements: Recommendations, essay, transcript. Include high school and college transcripts.
Additional information: Applicants must attend Idaho Space Grant Consortium member institution in the state of Idaho, and maintain a 3.0 GPA. Application should include ACT/SAT scores, if available. Consortium actively encourages women, minority, disabled students to apply. Application essay should not exceed 500 words. Applications may be downloaded from Website.

Amount of award:	$500-$1,000
Application deadline:	March 1
Notification begins:	May 1
Total amount awarded:	$22,000

Contact:
NASA Space Grant Idaho Space Grant Consortium
University of Idaho
P.O. Box 441011
Moscow, ID 83844-1011
Web: www.uidaho.edu/nasa_isgc

NASA Space Grant Illinois Space Grant Consortium

NASA Space Grant Illinois Undergraduate Scholarship

Type of award: Scholarship, renewable.
Intended use: For full-time undergraduate study.
Eligibility: Applicant must be U.S. citizen residing in Illinois.
Basis for selection: Major/career interest in engineering or aerospace.
Application requirements: Transcript.
Additional information: Must be used at Illinois Space Grant Consortium member institution. Contact sponsor for deadline information. Recipient required to work on research or design project.

Amount of award:	$500-$1,000

Contact:
Associate Director/ Illinois Space Grant Consortium
U of Illinois-Urbana, 306 Talbot
104 S. Wright St.
Urbana, IL 61801-2935
Phone: 217-244-8048
Fax: 217-244-0720
Web: www.aae.uiuc.edu

NASA Space Grant Indiana Space Grant Consortium

NASA Space Grant Indiana Undergraduate Scholarship

Type of award: Scholarship, renewable.
Intended use: For undergraduate study. Designated institutions: Indiana Space Grant Consortium member institutions: Purdue University at West Lafayette, Purdue University at Hammond, University of Notre Dame in South Bend, Indiana University in Bloomington, Ball State University, Taylor University, Valparaiso University.

Eligibility: Applicant must be U.S. citizen residing in Indiana.
Basis for selection: Major/career interest in science, general; mathematics; engineering or aerospace. Applicant must demonstrate high academic achievement.
Additional information: Number of grants, amounts of funding, deadlines, and application requirements vary by institution; contact sponsor for more information. Must be used at Indiana Space Grant Consortium member institution.

Amount of award:	$4,000
Number of awards:	4

Contact:
NASA Space Grant-Indiana Space Grant Consortium
Purdue U, Sch. of Aeronautics and Astronautic
1282 Grissom Hall, Room 338
West Lafayette, IN 47907-1282
Phone: 765-494-5873
Web: roger.ecn.purdue.edu/~isgc/consort.htm

NASA Space Grant Kansas Space Grant Consortium

NASA Space Grant Kansas Undergraduate Scholarship

Type of award: Scholarship.
Intended use: For undergraduate study at accredited postsecondary institution in United States. Designated institutions: Kansas Space Grant Consortium member institutions, including: Emporia State University, Fort Hayes State University, Haskell Indian Nations University, Kansas State University, Kansas University, Pittsburgh State University, Wichita State University.
Eligibility: Applicant must be U.S. citizen residing in Kansas.
Basis for selection: Major/career interest in mathematics; science, general or engineering.
Additional information: Contact sponsor for all deadline, scholarship and research participation application criteria information, and award amounts; these are determined locally by member institution. Applicant must attend Consortium member institution. Preference given to women and minorities.

Contact:
NASA KANSAS
Kansas Space Grant Consortium
135 Nichols Hall, 2335 Irving Hill Road
Lawrence, KS 66044-7612
Phone: 785-864-7401
Fax: 785-864-3361
Web: www.ksgc.org

NASA Space Grant Kentucky Space Grant Consortium

NASA Space Grant Kentucky Undergraduate Scholarship

Type of award: Scholarship, renewable.

Intended use: For full-time undergraduate study at accredited 4-year institution in United States. Designated institutions: Consortium member instituion: Centre College, Eastern Kentucky University, Kentucky Center for Space Enterprise, Kentucky State University, Morehead State University, Murray State University, Northern Kentucky University, Thomas More College, Transylvania University, University of Kentucky, University of Louisville, Western Kentucky University.
Eligibility: Applicant must be U.S. citizen residing in Kentucky.
Basis for selection: Major/career interest in aerospace; astronomy; education; engineering or physics.
Application requirements: Interview, recommendations, essay, transcript, research proposal, nomination by professor/ mentor at participating institution. Research proposal, written with mentor.
Additional information: Preference given to schools that waive tuition for recipient. Consortium actively encourages women, minority, and physically challenged students to apply. Application deadline in April. Visit Website for exact date. Applicants doing work related to space exploration may qualify for funding, whatever their field of study may be.

Amount of award:	$3,000
Number of awards:	2
Number of applicants:	4

Contact:
NASA Space Grant Kentucky Space Grant Consortium
Western Kentucky University
Dept. of Phys., TCCW 246, One Big Red Way
Bowling Green, KY 42101-3576
Phone: 270-745-4156
Web: www.wku.edu/KSGC

NASA Space Grant Michigan Space Grant Consortium

NASA Space Grant Michigan Undergraduate Fellowship

Type of award: Scholarship, renewable.
Intended use: For undergraduate study at accredited 4-year or graduate institution. Designated institutions: Michigan Space Grant Consortium member institutions.
Eligibility: Applicant must be U.S. citizen residing in Michigan.
Basis for selection: Major/career interest in aerospace; engineering; science, general or mathematics. Applicant must demonstrate high academic achievement.
Application requirements: Recommendations, essay, transcript.
Additional information: Award may include tuition and fees waiver. Fall applicants notified in February; spring applicants notified in May. For deadlines, e-mail sponsor (blbryant@umich.edu). Teaching opportunities also available for undergraduates and graduates through Michigan Space Grant Consortium Pre-College Outreach Program. Graduate fellowships also available.

Contact:
NASA Space Grant Michigan Space Grant Consortium
U of Michigan, 2106 Space Physics Rsrch Lab
2455 Hayward
Ann Arbor, MI 98109-2143

NASA Space Grant Minnesota Space Grant Consortium

NASA Space Grant Minnesota Undergraduate Scholarship

Type of award: Scholarship, renewable.
Intended use: For full-time undergraduate study at accredited 4-year institution in United States. Designated institutions: Augsburg College, Bethel College, Bemidji State University, Carleton College, College of St. Catherine, Fond du Lac Community College, Leech Lake Tribal College, Macalaster College, Normandale Community College, University of Minnesota - Duluth, University of Minnesota - Twin Cities, University of St. Thomas.
Eligibility: Applicant must be U.S. citizen residing in Minnesota.
Basis for selection: Major/career interest in aerospace; astronomy; atmospheric sciences/meteorology; biology; botany; chemistry; engineering; engineering, biomedical; engineering, chemical; engineering, civil or engineering, computer.
Application requirements: Recommendations, transcript.
Additional information: Applicants must include letter of intent and show 3.2 or greater GPA. Awardees must attend a Minnesota Space Grant Consortium member institution. The Consortium actively encourages women, minority, and physically challenged students to apply.

Amount of award:	$1,000-$2,500
Number of awards:	12
Number of applicants:	40
Application deadline:	March 1
Notification begins:	May 15

Contact:
NASA Space Grant Minnesota Space Grant Consortium
University of Minnesota
Dept. of Aerospace Engineering & Mechanics
Minneapolis, MN 55455
Web: www.aem.umn.edu/other/msgc

NASA Space Grant Mississippi Space Grant Consortium

NASA Space Grant Mississippi Space Grant

Type of award: Scholarship, renewable.
Intended use: For full-time undergraduate or graduate study in United States. Designated institutions: University of Mississippi, Jackson State University, University of Southern Mississippi, Mississippi State University, Alcorn State University, Delta

State University, Mississippi University for Women, Mississippi Valley State University, Coahoma Community College, Hinds Community College-Utica Campus, Itawamba Community College, Meridian Community College, Mississippi Delta Community College, Mississippi Gulf Coast Community College, Northeast Mississippi Community College, and Pearl River Community College.

Eligibility: Applicant must be U.S. citizen residing in Mississippi.

Basis for selection: Major/career interest in engineering; mathematics; science, general or aerospace. Applicant must demonstrate high academic achievement, leadership and seriousness of purpose.

Application requirements: Nomination by faculty mentor at participating Mississippi Space Grant consortium member institution.

Additional information: Award amounts/term vary; contact sponsor. Awardees must attend Mississippi Space Grant Consortium member institution. Selection criteria vary by institution; most institutions consider grade point average, major and written essay. Most awards require research or public service activity. List of campus contacts available online. Applicants from groups traditionally underrepresented in space-related fields encouraged.

Number of awards: 78
Contact:
NASA Space Grant Mississippi Space Grant Consortium
217 Vardaman Hall
P.O. Box 1848
University, MS 38677-1848
Phone: 662-915-1187
Fax: 662-915-3927
Web: www.olemiss.edu/programs/nasa/spacegrant.html

NASA Space Grant Montana Space Grant Consortium

NASA Space Grant Montana Undergraduate Scholarship Program

Type of award: Scholarship, renewable.
Intended use: For full-time undergraduate study at accredited 2-year or 4-year institution in United States. Designated institutions: Montana Space Grant Consortium member institutions include: Blackfeet Community College, Dull Knife Memorial College, Fort Belknap College, Fort Peck Community College, Little Big Horn College, Montana State University - Billings, Montana State University - Bozeman, Montana Tech, Rocky Mountain College, Salish Kootenai College, Stone Child College, University of Montana and Western Montana College.
Eligibility: Applicant must be U.S. citizen.
Basis for selection: Major/career interest in aerospace; biology; chemistry; geology/earth sciences; physics; astronomy; computer/information sciences; engineering, chemical; engineering, civil or engineering, electrical/electronic. Applicant must demonstrate depth of character and leadership.
Application requirements: In-state applicants must indicate name of Montana Consortium campus where they will be enrolled.
Additional information: Awards for one year, renewable on a competitive basis. Visit Website for more information.

Amount of award: $1,000
Application deadline: March 24
Contact:
NASA Space Grant Montana Space Grant Consortium
261 EPS Building, Montana State University
P.O. Box 173835
Bozeman, MT 59717-3835
Phone: 406-994-4223
Fax: 406-994-4452
Web: www.montana.edu/msgc

NASA Space Grant Nevada Space Grant Consortium

NASA Space Grant Nevada Undergraduate Scholarship

Type of award: Scholarship.
Intended use: For full-time undergraduate study at accredited postsecondary institution in United States. Designated institutions: University of Nevada, Las Vegas; University of Nevada, Reno; Community College of Southern Nevada, Las Vegas; Great Basin Community College, Elko; Truckee Meadows Community College, Reno; Western Nevada Community College, Carson City.
Eligibility: Applicant must be U.S. citizen residing in Nevada.
Basis for selection: Major/career interest in science, general; engineering; education; economics; business; social/behavioral sciences; computer/information sciences; communications; law or public administration/service.
Additional information: Liberal arts or majors in any relevant field eligible to apply. Applications also available on Website. Contact institution of interest for more detailed information, deadlines, award amounts and application requirements.
Contact:
NASA Space Grant Nevada Space Grant Consortium
James V. Taranik, PhD; or Lori M. Rountree
University of Nevada, Reno
Reno, NV 89557-0138
Phone: 775-784-6261
Fax: 775-327-2235
Web: www.unr.edu/spacegrant

NASA Space Grant New Mexico Space Grant Consortium

NASA Space Grant New Mexico Undergraduate Scholarship

Type of award: Research grant, renewable.
Intended use: For full-time sophomore, junior or senior study at accredited 4-year institution in United States. Designated institutions: New Mexico Space Grant Consortium member institute. Consortium members include: New Mexico Highlands University, University of New Mexico, New Mexico Institute of Mining and Technology and New Mexico State University.

Eligibility: Applicant must be U.S. citizen residing in New Mexico.

Basis for selection: Major/career interest in astronomy; biology; chemistry; computer/information sciences; engineering, chemical; engineering, civil; engineering, electrical/electronic; engineering, mechanical; geology/earth sciences or mathematics.

Application requirements: Recommendations, research proposal, nomination by faculty-mentor. Transcript with evidence of declared undergraduate major.

Additional information: Applicants must have 60 semester hours and a minimum GPA of 3.0. Preference given to applicants who can show non-federal matching funds. The Consortium actively encourages women, minority, and physically challenged students to apply. Applications may be obtained on Website.

Amount of award:	$2,000
Number of awards:	5
Application deadline:	April 3
Notification begins:	November 1
Total amount awarded:	$10,500

Contact:
NASA Space Grant New Mexico Space Grant Consortium
Program Office, New Mexico State University
Wells Hall, Bay 4, at Wells & Locust St.
Las Cruces, NM 88003-0001
Phone: 505-646-6414
Web: spacegrant.nmsu.edu

NASA Space Grant North Carolina Consortium

NASA North Carolina Space Grant Consortium Undergraduate Scholarship

Type of award: Scholarship.

Intended use: For full-time sophomore, junior or senior study. Designated institutions: North Carolina Space Grant Consortium member institution. Consortium members include: North Carolina State University, North Carolina Central University, Duke University, North Carolina A&T State University, Winston-Salem State University, University of North Carolina at Charlotte, University of North Carolina at Chapel Hill, University of North Carolina at Pembroke.

Eligibility: Applicant must be returning adult student. Applicant must be U.S. citizen residing in North Carolina.

Basis for selection: Major/career interest in science, general; engineering or aerospace. Applicant must demonstrate high academic achievement.

Application requirements: Recommendations, transcript, research proposal, nomination by faculty member.

Amount of award:	$4,000
Number of awards:	5
Number of applicants:	12
Application deadline:	January 31
Total amount awarded:	$20,000

Contact:
NASA Space Grant North Carolina Space Grant Consortium
Box 7515
Raleigh, NC 27511
Phone: 919-515-5937
Web: www.mae.ncsu.edu/spacegrant

NASA Space Grant North Dakota Space Grant Consortium

NASA Space Grant North Dakota Undergraduate Scholarship

Type of award: Scholarship, renewable.

Intended use: For full-time undergraduate study. Designated institutions: All community colleges, public colleges and universities, and tribal colleges in North Dakota.

Eligibility: Applicant must be U.S. citizen residing in North Dakota.

Basis for selection: Major/career interest in biology; chemistry; engineering; geology/earth sciences; computer/information sciences or mathematics.

Application requirements: Recommendations, transcript, nomination by sponsoring North Dakota Space Grant Consortium member-institution.

Additional information: Three awards of $500 are available at each of the two-year public and tribal colleges; three $750 scholarships are provided to four-year public state universities. Awardees must attend North Dakota Space Grant Consortium member institution. Consortium actively encourages women, minority, and physically challenged students to apply. Deadlines vary. Contact Consortium member institutions directly.

Amount of award:	$500-$750
Number of awards:	42

Contact:
NASA Space Grant North Dakota Space Grant Consortium
U of North Dakota, Space Studies Dept.
P.O. Box 9008
Grand Forks, ND 58202-9008
Phone: 701-777-4856
Web: www.space.edu/spacegrant/fellowships.html

Pearl I. Young Scholarship

Type of award: Scholarship.

Intended use: For full-time undergraduate study in United States. Designated institutions: University of North Dakota.

Eligibility: Applicant must be female. Applicant must be U.S. citizen or permanent resident residing in North Dakota.

Basis for selection: Major/career interest in biology; chemistry; engineering; geology/earth sciences; computer/information sciences or mathematics.

Application requirements: Nomination by chairs of science departments at University of North Dakota.

Additional information: Awarded to female science student. Must attend University of North Dakota. Must be North Dakota native. Scholarship only applies to those born, raised, and educated in North Dakota. Contact the coordinator for deadline information.

Amount of award:	$5,000
Number of awards:	1

Contact:
NASA Space Grant North Dakota Space Grant Consortium
U of North Dakota, Space Studies Dept.
P.O. Box 9008
Grand Forks, ND 58202-9008
Phone: 701-777-4856
Web: www.space.edu/spacegrant/fellowships.html

Scholarships

NASA Space Grant Oregon Space Grant Consortium

NASA Space Grant Oregon Community College Scholarship

Type of award: Scholarship.
Intended use: For full-time freshman or sophomore study at accredited 2-year institution in United States. Designated institutions: Lane Community College, Central Oregon Community College, Portland Community College.
Eligibility: Applicant must be U.S. citizen residing in Oregon.
Basis for selection: Major/career interest in aerospace; science, general or engineering.
Application requirements: Recommendations, essay, transcript.
Additional information: Contact one of three eligible community colleges for application, deadline and additional information. Also open to out-of-state residents attending one of these schools.

Amount of award:	$1,000
Number of awards:	10
Total amount awarded:	$10,000

Contact:
NASA Space Grant Oregon Space Grant Consortium
Oregon State University
130 Radiation Center
Corvalis, OR 97331-5902
Phone: 541-737-2414
Web: www.ne.orst.edu/spcgrant

NASA Space Grant Oregon Undergraduate Scholarship

Type of award: Scholarship.
Intended use: For full-time undergraduate study at accredited 2-year or 4-year institution in United States. Designated institutions: Oregon State University, University of Oregon, Portland State University, Eastern Oregon University, Southern Oregon University, Oregon Institute of Technology, Linfield College, Hatfield Marine Science Center, Pine Mountain Observatory.
Eligibility: Applicant must be U.S. citizen residing in Oregon.
Basis for selection: Major/career interest in science, general; engineering or aerospace. Applicant must demonstrate high academic achievement.
Application requirements: Recommendations, essay, transcript.
Additional information: Must attend one of the designated institutions. Contact Space Grant Consortium representative on campus for additional information.

Amount of award:	$1,000
Number of awards:	20
Application deadline:	April 30
Total amount awarded:	$20,000

Contact:
NASA Space Grant Oregon Space Grant Consortium
Oregon State University
130 Radiation Center
Corvalis, OR 97331-5902
Phone: 541-737-2414
Web: www.ne.orst.edu/spcgrant

NASA Space Grant Pennsylvania Space Grant Consortium

NASA Pennsylvania Space Grant Undergraduate Scholarship

Type of award: Scholarship.
Intended use: For full-time junior or senior study at accredited 4-year institution in United States. Designated institutions: Pennsylvania State University, Carnegie Mellon University, Lincoln University, Abington College, Altoona's Science and Technology Research Academy (ASTRA), Susquehanna University, Temple University, West Chester University, University of Pittsburgh.
Eligibility: Applicant must be U.S. citizen residing in Pennsylvania.
Basis for selection: Major/career interest in science, general; mathematics or engineering.
Application requirements: Interview, recommendations, essay, transcript. Must be sophomore to apply.
Additional information: Competitive scholarships are provided for undergraduates at Pennsylvania Space Grant Consortium member institutions. Sylvia Stein Memorial Space Grant Scholarship at Penn State University (two one year scholarships for $4,000 per year) are awarded to outstanding undergraduate with extensive community service. Other awards and eligibility requirements vary with institution. Contact campus Space Grant Consortium representative for details. Consortium actively encourages women, minority, and physically challenged students to apply.
Contact:
NASA Space Grant Pennsylvania Space Grant Consortium
Penn State, University Park
101 S. Frear Laboratory
University Park, PA 16802
Web: www.psu.edu/spacegrant/

NASA Space Grant Rhode Island Space Grant Consortium

NASA Space Grant Rhode Island Summer Undergraduate Scholarship

Type of award: Scholarship.
Intended use: For sophomore, junior or senior study at postsecondary institution. Designated institutions: Rhode Island Space Grant Consortium member institutions: Brown University, Bryant College, Community College of Rhode Island, Roger Williams University, Rhode Island College, Rhode Island School of Design, Salve Regina University, University of Rhode Island, Wheaton College.
Eligibility: Applicant must be U.S. citizen residing in Rhode Island.
Basis for selection: Major/career interest in physics; engineering; biology; geology/earth sciences or aerospace. Applicant must demonstrate high academic achievement.

Application requirements: Interview, recommendations, essay, transcript.

Additional information: Deadline in April; call sponsor for exact date. Topics of study in the space sciences funded. Number of awards may vary. Students should contact their campus representative or Rhode Island Space Grant office regarding program availability.

Amount of award:	$4,000
Number of awards:	2
Number of applicants:	6

Contact:
NASA Space Grant Rhode Island Space Grant Consortium
Brown University
Box 1846
Providence, RI 02912
Phone: 401-863-2889
Web: www.spacegrant.brown.edu/RI_Space_Grant

NASA Space Grant Rhode Island Undergraduate Academic Year Scholarship

Type of award: Scholarship, renewable.

Intended use: For sophomore, junior or senior study at postsecondary institution. Designated institutions: Rhode Island Space Grant Consortium member institutions: Brown University, Bryant College, Community College of Rhode Island, Roger Williams University, Rhode Island College, Rhode Island School of Design, Salve Regina University, University of Rhode Island, Wheaton College.

Eligibility: Applicant must be U.S. citizen residing in Rhode Island.

Basis for selection: Major/career interest in physics; engineering; biology; geology/earth sciences or aerospace. Applicant must demonstrate high academic achievement.

Application requirements: Interview, recommendations, essay, transcript, research proposal.

Additional information: Deadline in April; call sponsor for exact date. Topics of study in space sciences also funded. Number of awards may vary. Students should contact their campus representative or the Rhode Island Space Grant office.

Amount of award:	$4,000
Number of awards:	3
Number of applicants:	6

Contact:
NASA Space Grant Rhode Island Space Grant Consortium
Brown University
Box 1846
Providence, RI 02912
Phone: 401-863-2889
Web: www.spacegrant.brown.edu/RI_Space_Grant

NASA Space Grant Texas Space Grant Consortium

NASA Space Grant Texas Undergraduate Scholarship Program

Type of award: Scholarship.

Intended use: For full-time senior study at accredited 4-year institution in United States. Designated institutions: Baylor University, Lamar University, Prairie View A&M University, Rice University, Southern Methodist University, Sul Ross State University, Texas A&M University, Texas A&M University - Kingsville, Texas Christian University, Texas Southern University, Texas Tech University, University of Houston, University of Houston - Clear Lake, University of Houston - Downtown, University of Texas - Pan American, University of Texas at Arlington, University of Texas at Austin, University of Texas at Dallas, University of Texas at El Paso, University of Texas Houston State College - Houston, University of Texas at San Antonio, University of Texas Medical Branch - Galveston, University of Texas Southwestern Medical Center, West Texas A&M University.

Eligibility: Applicant must be U.S. citizen residing in Texas.

Basis for selection: Major/career interest in aerospace or education.

Application requirements: Recommendations, essay, transcript, proof of eligibility.

Additional information: Awardees must be juniors at time of application and must attend Texas Space Grant Consortium member institution.

Amount of award:	$1,000
Number of awards:	15
Number of applicants:	40
Application deadline:	April 16
Total amount awarded:	$15,000

Contact:
NASA Space Grant Texas Space Grant Consortium
University of Texas at Austin
Cntr for Space Rsrch., 3925 W. Braker Ln.
Austin, TX 78749-5321
Web: www.tsgc.utexas.edu/tsgc

NASA Space Grant West Virginia Consortium

NASA Space Grant West Virginia Undergraduate Fellowship Scholarship

Type of award: Scholarship, renewable.

Intended use: For full-time undergraduate study at accredited 4-year institution in United States. Designated institutions: West Virginia University, Bethany College, Fairmont State College, Marshall University, Salem International University, Shepherd College, West Virginia University Institute of Technology, West Virginia State College, Wheeling-Jesuit University, West Liberty State College, and West Virginia Wesleyan College.

Eligibility: Applicant must be U.S. citizen residing in West Virginia.

Basis for selection: Major/career interest in aerospace; science, general or engineering. Applicant must demonstrate high academic achievement and seriousness of purpose.

Application requirements: Research proposal.

Additional information: Awards provide full tuition, fees, and room and board for four years. 3.0 GPA preferred. During four-year tenure as Fellows, students work with a Consortium professor and a NASA advisor on an aerospace project, and spend three summers working at a NASA Center on a project. Some students gain experience working with researchers at their respective colleges during the three summers. Application deadline usually falls in mid- to late-September.

Amount of award:	Full tuition

Contact:
NASA Space Grant West Virginia Space Grant Consortium
West Virginia U, NASA Space Grant Prog.
P.O. Box 6070
Morgantown, WV 26506-6070
Phone: 304-293-4099
Fax: 304-293-4970
Web: www.cemr.wvu.edu/~wwwnasa/

NASA Space Grant Wisconsin Space Grant Consortium

NASA Space Grant Wisconsin Undergraduate Research Awards

Type of award: Research grant, renewable.
Intended use: For full-time undergraduate study at accredited 4-year institution in United States. Designated institutions: Alverno College, Carroll College, College of the Menominee Nation, Lawrence University, Marquette University, Medical College of Wisconsin, Milwaukee School of Engineering, Ripon College, St. Norbert College, and University of Wisconsin Green Bay, La Crosse, Madison, Milwaukee, Oshkosh, Parkside, and Whitewater.
Eligibility: Applicant must be U.S. citizen residing in Wisconsin.
Basis for selection: Major/career interest in aerospace; astronomy; engineering; physics; science, general or aviation. Applicant must demonstrate high academic achievement.
Application requirements: Recommendations, transcript, research proposal. Proposal and budget for project related to aerospace, space science or other space-related studies. SAT/ACT scores.
Additional information: Applicant must attend Wisconsin Space Grant Consortium member institution. Minimum 3.0 GPA. Qualified students may apply for summer session Undergraduate Research Award and academic year Undergraduate Scholarship. Consortium actively encourages women, minority, and disabled students to apply. See Website for application and complete list of eligible institutions.

Amount of award:	$3,500
Application deadline:	March 9
Notification begins:	April 10

Contact:
NASA Space Grant Wisconsin Space Grant Consortium
Office of Research Infrastructure, SSEC/CIMSS
Room 231, U Wisconsin Madison
Madison, WI 53706-1380
Phone: 414-229-3878
Web: www.uwm.edu/dept/WSGC

NASA Space Grant Wyoming Space Grant Consortium

NASA Space Grant Wyoming Undergraduate Research Fellowships

Type of award: Research grant.
Intended use: For undergraduate study at accredited postsecondary institution in United States. Designated institutions: University of Wyoming, Laramie County Community College, Sheridan College, Embry-Riddle Aeronautic University, other Wyoming community colleges.
Eligibility: Applicant must be U.S. citizen.
Basis for selection: Major/career interest in aerospace; engineering; science, general or energy research. Applicant must demonstrate high academic achievement.
Application requirements: Transcript, proof of eligibility, research proposal.
Additional information: Funding for research projects available through Wyoming Space Grant program. Contact Project Coordinator at the University of Wyoming. Proposals that cannot be funded from other sources given priority. Research expected to result in refereed publication. Underrepresented groups encouraged to apply. Visit Website for more details. Contact sponsor for complete list of eligible institutions.

Application deadline:	February 19

Contact:
NASA Space Grant Wyoming Space Grant Consortium
P.O. Box 3905
University of Wyoming
Laramie, WY 82071-3905
Phone: 307-766-2862
Web: wyoskies.uwyo.edu/spacegrant

NASA/Delaware Space Grant Consortium

Delaware Space Grant Undergraduate Summer Scholarship

Type of award: Scholarship, renewable.
Intended use: For full-time undergraduate study. Designated institutions: University of Delaware, Delaware Technical and Community College, Franklin and Marshall College, Gettysburg College, Lehigh University, Lincoln University, Swathmore College, Delaware State University at Dover, University of Pennsylvania, Villanova University Wilmington College.
Eligibility: Applicant must be U.S. citizen.
Basis for selection: Major/career interest in aerospace; astronomy; engineering; physics; engineering, materials; oceanography/marine studies; geography or geology/earth sciences.
Application requirements: Recommendations, transcript.
Additional information: Awardees must attend a Delaware Space Grant Consortium member institution.

Amount of award:	$3,000-$3,500
Number of awards:	8
Number of applicants:	8
Application deadline:	March 1
Notification begins:	March 15
Total amount awarded:	$19,400

Contact:
Delaware Space Grant Consortium Program Office
University of Delaware
104 Central Mall, # 217
Newark, DE 19716
Phone: 302-831-1094
Fax: 302-831-1843
Web: www.delspace.org

Delaware Space Grant Undergraduate Tuition Scholarship

Type of award: Scholarship, renewable.
Intended use: For full-time undergraduate study. Designated institutions: University of Delaware, Delaware Technical and Community College, Franklin and Marshall College, Gettysburg College, Lehigh University, Lincoln University, Swathmore College, Delaware State University at Dover, University of Pennsylvania, Villanova University, Wilmington College.
Eligibility: Applicant must be U.S. citizen.
Basis for selection: Major/career interest in aerospace; astronomy; communications; engineering; geography; geology/earth sciences; geophysics; physics or oceanography/marine studies.
Additional information: Awardees must attend Delaware Space Grant Consortium member institution.

Amount of award:	$4,000
Number of awards:	7
Number of applicants:	7
Application deadline:	March 1
Notification begins:	March 15
Total amount awarded:	$20,500

Contact:
Delaware Space Grant Consortium Program Office
University of Delaware
104 Central Mall, # 217
Newark, DE 19716
Phone: 302-831-1094
Fax: 302-831-1843
Web: www.delspace.org

Nash Finch Company

Nash Finch Company Scholarship Plan

Type of award: Scholarship, renewable.
Intended use: For freshman study at accredited vocational, 2-year or 4-year institution.
Eligibility: Applicant or parent must be employed by Nash Finch Company. Applicant must be African American.
Basis for selection: Applicant must demonstrate financial need.
Additional information: For further information or an application, contact Nash Finch Company directly.

Amount of award:	$200-$2,500

National Academy for Nuclear Training

Nuclear Training Educational Assistance Program

Type of award: Scholarship, renewable.
Intended use: For full-time sophomore, junior or senior study at accredited 4-year or graduate institution in United States. Designated institutions: Institution with accredited programs in relevant fields of study.
Eligibility: Applicant must be U.S. citizen.
Basis for selection: Major/career interest in engineering, chemical; engineering, mechanical; engineering, electrical/electronic or engineering, nuclear. Applicant must demonstrate high academic achievement, depth of character, leadership, seriousness of purpose and service orientation.
Application requirements: Recommendations, essay, transcript, proof of eligibility, nomination by department head.
Additional information: Renewal up to three years for eligible students. Minimum 3.0 GPA. Additional field of study: power generation health physics. Engineering field of study must include nuclear or power option. Applicant should be considering career in nuclear utility industry. For additional information, contact by e-mail: nanteap@inpo.org.

Amount of award:	$2,500
Number of awards:	150
Application deadline:	February 1
Total amount awarded:	$375,000

Contact:
Educational Assistance Program
National Academy for Nuclear Training
700 Galleria Parkway, SE, Suite 100
Atlanta, GA 30339-5957
Phone: 800-828-5489

National Alliance for Excellence, Inc.

Lucent Global Science Scholars Program

Type of award: Scholarship.
Intended use: For full-time freshman study at accredited 4-year institution in United States.
Eligibility: Applicant must be high school senior. Applicant must be U.S. citizen.
Basis for selection: Major/career interest in science, general; computer/information sciences or engineering. Applicant must demonstrate high academic achievement.
Application requirements: Recommendations, transcript, proof of eligibility. Minimum GPA 3.7 and minimum SAT scores 1400.
Additional information: Contact National Alliance for Excellence for application and details, or visit Website.

Amount of award:	$5,000
Number of awards:	50

Contact:
Lucent Global Science Scholars Program
c/o National Alliance for Excellence
63 Riverside Avenue
Red Bank, NJ 07701
Phone: 732-747-0028
Web: www.excellence.org

National Alliance for Excellence Honored Scholars and Artists Program: Academics

Type of award: Scholarship.
Intended use: For full-time undergraduate or graduate study at accredited 2-year, 4-year or graduate institution in or outside United States.
Eligibility: Applicant must be U.S. citizen.
Basis for selection: Competition/talent/interest in academics. Applicant must demonstrate high academic achievement.
Application requirements: $5 application fee. Recommendations, transcript. Entrance exam scores (SAT, GRE, LSAT, GMAT, etc.). Must have 3.7 GPA and combined SAT I score of 1300 or ACT composite of 30. Include list of all awards received; list of Advanced Placement or Honors courses with grades.
Additional information: Competitions year-round. Highly competitive award to country's best and brightest. Governors, senators, and congressional representatives present the awards. Send SASE with application request. Additional information and application is available on the Website.

Amount of award:	$1,000-$5,000
Number of awards:	60
Number of applicants:	7,000

Contact:
National Alliance for Excellence, Inc.
63 Riverside Ave.
Red Bank, NJ 07701
Phone: 732-747-0028
Web: www.excellence.org

National Alliance for Excellence Honored Scholars and Artists Program: Technological Innovation

Type of award: Scholarship.
Intended use: For full-time undergraduate certificate or graduate study at accredited 2-year, 4-year or graduate institution in or outside United States.
Eligibility: Applicant must be U.S. citizen.
Basis for selection: Competition/talent/interest in engineering/ architecture. Major/career interest in engineering; architecture or robotics.
Application requirements: $5 application fee. Recommendations. Evidence of expertise via architectural plans, designs for inventions, mechanisms, structures, etc. Include documentation/evaluation of design solutions.
Additional information: For students who excel in design engineering, robotics, architecture or other area that requires design or invention of new technology. Competitions year-round. Awards granted throughout year. Highly competitive. AutoCAD and 3D studio software, as well as computers given to awardees. Send SASE with application request. Additional information and application is available on Website.

Amount of award:	$1,000-$5,000
Number of awards:	10
Number of applicants:	500

Contact:
National Alliance for Excellence, Inc.
63 Riverside Avenue
Red Bank, NJ 07701
Phone: 732-747-0028
Web: www.excellence.org

National Alliance for Excellence Honored Scholars and Artists Program: Visual Arts

Type of award: Scholarship.
Intended use: For full-time undergraduate or graduate study at accredited 2-year, 4-year or graduate institution in or outside United States.
Eligibility: Applicant must be U.S. citizen.
Basis for selection: Competition/talent/interest in visual arts.
Application requirements: $5 application fee. Recommendations. 20 slides or photos, VHS video (up to 10 minutes long), computer disk or other evidence of work in visual arts.
Additional information: Competitions year-round. Awards granted throughout year. Highly competitive. Send SASE with application request. Additional information and application available on Website.

Amount of award:	$1,000-$5,000
Number of awards:	10
Number of applicants:	1,000

Contact:
National Alliance for Excellence, Inc.
63 Riverside Avenue
Red Bank, NJ 07701
Phone: 732-747-0028
Web: www.excellence.org

National Alliance for Excellence Honored Scholars and Artists: Performing Arts

Type of award: Scholarship.
Intended use: For full-time undergraduate or graduate study at accredited 2-year, 4-year or graduate institution in or outside United States.
Eligibility: Applicant must be U.S. citizen.
Basis for selection: Competition/talent/interest in performing arts. Major/career interest in performing arts; theater arts or music.
Application requirements: $5 application fee. Recommendations. VHS videotape (up to 10 minutes long) or other evidence of work in performing arts. May include clips from previous performances, must also include monologue/solo performance. May demonstrate more than one discipline by sending separate videos for each (e.g. dance, acting, vocal, musical instrument, etc.). Mark video(s) with name, state of residence and grade level.
Additional information: Competitions year-round. Awards granted throughout year. Highly competitive. Send SASE with application request. Additional information and application available on Website.

Amount of award:	$1,000-$5,000
Number of awards:	15
Number of applicants:	1,500

Contact:
National Alliance for Excellence, Inc.
63 Riverside Avenue
Red Bank, NJ 07701
Phone: 732-747-0028
Web: www.excellence.org

National Amateur Baseball Federation

Ronald and Irene McMinn Scholarship

Type of award: Scholarship, renewable.
Intended use: For freshman, sophomore, junior or senior study in or outside United States or Canada. Designated institutions: U.S. or Canadian Institutions.
Basis for selection: Competition/talent/interest in athletics/sports. Applicant must demonstrate financial need and high academic achievement.
Application requirements: Recommendations, proof of eligibility. Previous awards to candidates from sponsoring association.
Additional information: Must have participated in a National Amateur Baseball Federation event and be sponsored by National Amateur Baseball Federation-member association. Send SASE for application packet.

Amount of award:	$500-$1,000
Number of awards:	10
Number of applicants:	12
Total amount awarded:	$9,000

Contact:
National Amateur Baseball Federation
Attn: Chairman Awards Committee
P.O. Box 705
Bowie, MD 20718

National Art Materials Trade Association

National Art Materials Scholarship

Type of award: Scholarship.
Intended use: For undergraduate or graduate study at accredited postsecondary institution in or outside United States.
Eligibility: Applicant or parent must be member/participant of National Art Materials Trade Association.
Basis for selection: Applicant must demonstrate financial need, high academic achievement, depth of character, seriousness of purpose and service orientation.
Application requirements: Recommendations, essay, transcript, proof of eligibility.
Additional information: Applicant may also be an employee or relative of a National Art Materials Trade Association (NAMTA) member firm.

Amount of award:	$1,500
Number of awards:	3
Number of applicants:	83
Application deadline:	April 1
Notification begins:	June 1
Total amount awarded:	$4,500

Contact:
Katharine D. Coffey National Art Materials Trade Association
10115 Kincey Avenue
Suite 260
Huntersville, NC 28078
Phone: 800-746-2682
Fax: 704-948-5658

National Association of Black Accountants, Inc.

National Scholarship Program

Type of award: Scholarship.
Intended use: For full-time sophomore, junior, senior or master's study at 4-year or graduate institution.
Eligibility: Applicant or parent must be member/participant of National Association of Black Accountants. Applicant must be Alaskan native, Asian American, African American, Mexican American, Hispanic American, Puerto Rican or American Indian.
Basis for selection: Major/career interest in accounting or business. Applicant must demonstrate depth of character, leadership and service orientation.
Application requirements: Essay, transcript, proof of eligibility. Personal biography, student aid report.
Additional information: Applicants must have GPA 2.5 or better. Applicants may join association upon submission of scholarship application.

Amount of award:	$500-$6,000
Number of awards:	45
Number of applicants:	120
Application deadline:	December 31
Notification begins:	April 15
Total amount awarded:	$100,000

Contact:
National Association of Black Accountants, Inc.
National Scholarship Program
7249-A Hanover Parkway
Greenbelt, MD 20770
Phone: 301-474-6222
Fax: 301-474-3114
Web: www.nabainc.org

National Association of Black Journalists

NABJ Non-Sustaining Scholarship

Type of award: Scholarship.
Intended use: For undergraduate, master's, doctoral, first professional or postgraduate study at accredited 4-year or graduate institution.

Eligibility: Applicant must be African American. Applicant must be U.S. citizen.

Basis for selection: Major/career interest in journalism or radio/television/film.

Application requirements: Recommendations, essay, transcript, nomination. Applicant must maintain a minimum grade point average of 2.5, and attend NABJ convention to work on the convention student project.

Additional information: Must become member of National Association of Black Journalists before award is given and participate in the NABJ Mentor Program. Applicants of African descent from countries outside the United States, are also eligible.

Amount of award:	$2,500
Number of awards:	1
Number of applicants:	75
Application deadline:	April 30

Contact:
NABJ--Scholarship Programs
8701 Adelphi Road
Adelphi, MD 20783-1716
Phone: 301-445-7100
Fax: 301-445-7101
Web: www.nabj.org

National Association of Letter Carriers

Costas G. Lemonopoulos Scholarship

Type of award: Scholarship, renewable.

Intended use: For full-time freshman, sophomore, junior or senior study at 4-year institution. Designated institutions: St. Petersburg Junior College or any four-year public Florida university (no private schools).

Eligibility: Applicant or parent must be member/participant of National Association of Letter Carriers.

Basis for selection: Applicant must demonstrate high academic achievement.

Application requirements: Transcript. Include SAT I scores and NALC form.

Additional information: Awards are for Spring semester only. Open only to children of National Association of Letter Carriers members. High school seniors and college students may apply. Limit two awards. Must apply through NALC only. Winners notified in late September. Awards paid in December by the Pinellas County Community Foundation, Clearwater, Florida. Complete information published each April, with coupon, in the NALC Postal Record.

Amount of award:	$400-$1,000
Number of awards:	20
Number of applicants:	75
Application deadline:	June 1

Contact:
National Association of Letter Carriers
100 Indiana Avenue NW
Washington, DC 20001-2144

William C. Doherty Scholarship

Type of award: Scholarship, renewable.

Intended use: For full-time freshman, sophomore, junior or senior study at accredited 4-year institution.

Eligibility: Applicant or parent must be member/participant of National Association of Letter Carriers. Applicant must be high school senior.

Basis for selection: Applicant must demonstrate financial need and high academic achievement.

Application requirements: Recommendations, essay, transcript, proof of eligibility. SAT/ACT scores.

Additional information: For children of active, retired, or deceased letter carriers. Parent must be National Association of Letter Carriers member in good standing at least one year prior to candidate's application. Students will be notified through newsletter between July and November.

Amount of award:	$800
Number of awards:	15
Number of applicants:	1,600

Contact:
National Association of Letter Carriers
100 Indiana Avenue NW
Washington, DC 20001
Web: www.nalc.org

National Association of Water Companies (NJ Chapter)

Water Companies (NJ Chapter) Scholarship

Type of award: Scholarship.

Intended use: For sophomore, junior, senior or graduate study at accredited 2-year, 4-year or graduate institution in United States. Designated institutions: Institutions in New Jersey.

Eligibility: Applicant must be U.S. citizen residing in New Jersey.

Basis for selection: Major/career interest in hydrology; natural resources/conservation; science, general; engineering, environmental; finance/banking; communications; accounting; business; computer/information sciences or law. Applicant must demonstrate financial need, high academic achievement, depth of character, leadership, seriousness of purpose and service orientation.

Application requirements: Recommendations, essay, transcript. Essay must illustrate interest in investor-owned water utility field.

Additional information: Applicant must have interest in relating fields of study to water industry. Acceptable fields of study also include consumer affairs and human resources. At least five years residence in New Jersey required. Minimum 3.0 GPA.

Amount of award:	$2,500
Number of awards:	2
Number of applicants:	25
Application deadline:	April 1
Notification begins:	June 1
Total amount awarded:	$5,000

Contact:
National Association of Water Companies (NJ Chapter) Attn:
W.J.Brady
c/o Middlesex Water Company
1500 Ronson Road
Iselin, NJ 08830
Phone: 732-634-1502 ext. 213

National Association of Women in Construction

Women in Construction: Founders' Scholarship

Type of award: Scholarship.
Intended use: For full-time undergraduate study at accredited postsecondary institution in United States.
Eligibility: Applicant must be U.S. citizen.
Basis for selection: Major/career interest in construction; construction management or engineering, construction. Applicant must demonstrate financial need and high academic achievement.
Application requirements: Interview, recommendations, transcript.
Additional information: Number and amount of awards varies. Interest in construction, extracurricular activities and employment experience also taken into consideration. Applicants must have completed one term of study in construction-related field. Must have current GPA of 3.0 or higher. Only semi-finalists will be interviewed. Visit Website for additional information and to download application.

Application deadline:	February 1
Notification begins:	April 1

Contact:
National Association of Women in Construction
327 South Adams Street
Fort Worth, TX 76104
Phone: 800-552-3506
Web: www.nawic.org

National Athletic Trainers Association

Athletic Trainers Curriculum Scholarship

Type of award: Scholarship.
Intended use: For full-time undergraduate or master's study at accredited 4-year or graduate institution. Designated institutions: Contact Association for list of institutions.
Eligibility: Applicant or parent must be member/participant of National Athletic Trainers Association
Basis for selection: Major/career interest in athletic training. Applicant must demonstrate high academic achievement.
Application requirements: Recommendations, essay, transcript, proof of eligibility.
Additional information: Minimum 3.0 GPA required. Must be planning a career in athletic training.

Amount of award:	$2,000
Application deadline:	February 1
Notification begins:	April 15

Contact:
National Athletic Trainers Association
2952 Stemmons Freeway
Dallas, TX 75247
Web: www.nata.org

Athletic Trainers Student Writing Contest

Type of award: Scholarship.
Intended use: For undergraduate or graduate study at 2-year, 4-year or graduate institution.
Eligibility: Applicant or parent must be member/participant of National Athletic Trainers Association.
Basis for selection: Competition/talent/interest in writing/journalism, based on paper related to the athletic training profession. Major/career interest in athletic training. Applicant must demonstrate high academic achievement.
Application requirements: Essay, proof of eligibility.
Additional information: Entrants must submit one original and two copies. Topic may be case report, literature review, experimental report, analysis of training room techniques, etc. Must not have been published, or be under consideration for publication.

Amount of award:	$800
Number of awards:	1
Application deadline:	March 1
Notification begins:	April 15

Contact:
National Athletic Trainers Association Student Writing Contest
Life University, 1269 Barclay Circle
Marietta, GA 30060
Web: www.nata.org

Athletic Trainers Undergraduate Scholarship

Type of award: Scholarship.
Intended use: For full-time junior or senior study at 4-year institution.
Eligibility: Applicant or parent must be member/participant of National Athletic Trainers Association.
Basis for selection: Applicant must demonstrate high academic achievement.
Application requirements: Recommendations, essay, transcript, proof of eligibility.
Additional information: Minimum 3.0 GPA required. Intention to pursue the profession of athletic training as career required. Must be sponsored by a certified athletic trainer.

Amount of award:	$2,000
Number of awards:	50
Application deadline:	February 1
Notification begins:	April 15
Total amount awarded:	$100,000

Contact:
National Athletic Trainers Association
Research and Education Foundation
2952 Stemmons Freeway
Dallas, TX 75247
Web: www.nata.org

National Black Nurses Association

Black Nurses Scholarship

Type of award: Scholarship.
Intended use: For undergraduate or graduate study.
Eligibility: Applicant or parent must be member/participant of National Black Nurses' Association. Applicant must be African American.
Basis for selection: Major/career interest in nursing or nurse practitioner. Applicant must demonstrate seriousness of purpose and service orientation.
Application requirements: Recommendations, essay, transcript. Evidence of participation in both student nursing activities and the African-American community.
Additional information: Applicants must be currently enrolled in nursing program and have at least one full year of school left. Call association for current information on program.

Amount of award:	$500-$2,000
Number of awards:	5
Number of applicants:	500
Application deadline:	April 15
Notification begins:	July 1

Contact:
National Black Nurses Association
8630 Fenton Street
Silver Spring, MD 20910
Phone: 301-589-3200
Fax: 301-589-3223

National Black Police Association

Alphonso Deal Scholarship

Type of award: Scholarship.
Intended use: For freshman study at 2-year institution in United States.
Eligibility: Applicant must be enrolled in high school. Applicant must be U.S. citizen.
Basis for selection: Major/career interest in law or criminal justice/law enforcement. Applicant must demonstrate high academic achievement, depth of character, seriousness of purpose and service orientation.
Application requirements: Recommendations, essay, transcript. Applicant must be accepted by a college or university prior to date of award.
Additional information: Award provides higher education training for the betterment of the criminal justice system.

Amount of award:	$500
Number of awards:	5
Number of applicants:	2,500
Application deadline:	June 1
Total amount awarded:	$2,500

Contact:
National Black Police Association Scholarship Award
3251 Mount Pleasant Street, NW
Washington, DC 20010-2103
Phone: 202-986-2070
Fax: 202-986-0410

National Collegiate Athletic Association

Freedom Forum/NCAA Foundation Sports Journalism Scholarship

Type of award: Scholarship.
Intended use: For senior study. Designated institutions: National Collegiate Athletic Association member institutions.
Basis for selection: Competition/talent/interest in Writing/journalism, based on quality of three examples of sports journalism work such as newspaper articles, program copy, published photgraphs, editorials, television and/or radio scripts. VHS tapes and cassettes accepted. College transcript. Major/career interest in journalism.
Application requirements: Portfolio, recommendations, transcript. Request application form and information from Chief Executive Officer of Faculty Athletics Repressentatives or Chairperson of Journalism School/Department of NCAA meember instituions. Application also printable from Website. All materials, including transcripts, essay question statement, writing samples and recommendation letters, should be mailed with completed application.
Additional information: Students must apply during junior year of college. Eight scholarships awarded at National Collegiate Athletic Association member institutions. Winners invited to special programs, National Collegiate Athletic Association office. Expenses paid by Freedom Forum grant. Applications available in November.

Amount of award:	$3,000
Number of awards:	8
Application deadline:	December 15

Contact:
National Collegiate Athletic Association
P.O. Box 6222
Indianapolis, IN 46207-6222
Phone: 317-917-6222
Web: www.ncaa.org/ncaa_foundation/index.html

NCAA Degree Completion Award

Type of award: Scholarship.
Intended use: For senior study at 4-year institution. Designated institutions: Colleges in Division I of the NCAA.
Basis for selection: Competition/talent/interest in athletics/sports. Applicant must demonstrate financial need, depth of character, leadership and service orientation.
Application requirements: Recommendations, proof of eligibility.
Additional information: Must have received athletics-related grant-in-aid at National Collegiate Athletic Association Division I institution. Must be entering at least sixth year after initial collegiate enrollment. Must have less than 30 semester hours to finish degree. Application materials are also available at Director of Athletics office on member school campuses. Forty percent of applicants are awarded aid.

Number of awards:	125
Number of applicants:	313
Application deadline:	October 1, May 1
Total amount awarded:	$950,000

Contact:
National Collegiate Athletic Association
P.O. Box 6222
Indianapolis, IN 46206-6222
Web: www.ncaa.org

National Computer Systems

National Computer Systems Scholarship

Type of award: Scholarship, renewable.
Intended use: For undergraduate study at accredited vocational, 2-year or 4-year institution.
Eligibility: Applicant or parent must be employed by National Computer Systems.
Basis for selection: Applicant must demonstrate financial need.
Additional information: For further information or an application, contact National Computer Systems directly.
    Amount of award: $500-$3,000

National Convenience Store Advisory Group

Convenience Stores/Petroleum Marketers Association Scholarship Program

Type of award: Scholarship, renewable.
Intended use: For undergraduate study at vocational, 2-year or 4-year institution.
Eligibility: Applicant or parent must be employed by National Advisory Group. Applicant or parent must be member/participant of National Advisory Group. Applicant must be high school senior.
Additional information: For further information or application, contact National Convenience Store Advisory Group directly.
    Amount of award: $500

National Dairy Shrine

Dairy Student Recognition Program

Type of award: Scholarship.
Intended use: For senior study.
Basis for selection: Competition/talent/interest in writing/journalism. Major/career interest in dairy; food production/management/services or food science/technology. Applicant must demonstrate leadership.
Application requirements: Recommendations, essay, nomination by college or university dairy science departments.
Additional information: Only for graduating seniors planning career in dairy cattle. Two candidates eligible per institution. First place winner recieves $1,500, second place $1,000, third through fifth, $500. National Dairy Shrine chooses final winner. Students who placed in top five in previous years not eligible for further competition.

Amount of award: $500-$1,500
Number of awards: 7
Number of applicants: 20
Application deadline: March 15
Notification begins: June 10
Total amount awarded: $6,000
Contact:
National Dairy Shrine
1224 Alton Darby Creek Road
Columbus, OH 43228-9792

Marshall E. McCullough Undergraduate Scholarship

Type of award: Scholarship.
Intended use: For full-time senior study at accredited 4-year institution in United States.
Eligibility: Applicant must be high school senior. Applicant must be U.S. citizen.
Basis for selection: Major/career interest in animal sciences; dairy; communications or journalism.
Application requirements: Recommendations, essay.
Additional information: Two awards: one for $2,500; one for $1,000. Must major in dairy/animal science with communications emphasis or agricultural journalism with dairy/animal science emphasis.
Amount of award: $1,000-$2,500
Number of awards: 2
Application deadline: March 15
Notification begins: July 1
Contact:
National Dairy Shrine
1224 Alton Darby Creek Road
Columbus, OH 43228-9792
Phone: 614-878-5333
Fax: 614-870-9792
Web: www.dairyshrine.org

National Environmental Health Association

American Academy of Sanitarians Scholarship

Type of award: Scholarship.
Intended use: For full-time junior, senior or graduate study at accredited 4-year or graduate institution.
Basis for selection: Major/career interest in environmental science or public health. Applicant must demonstrate financial need, high academic achievement and seriousness of purpose.
Application requirements: Recommendations, transcript, proof of eligibility.
Additional information: Undergraduates must be enrolled in an Environmental Health Accreditation Council accredited school or National Environmental Health Association Institutional/Educational or sustaining member school (List available at sponsor Website). Graduates must be enrolled in a graduate program of studies in environmental health science and/or public health.

Amount of award:	$1,000-$2,000
Number of awards:	4
Application deadline:	February 1
Notification begins:	June 30
Total amount awarded:	$4,000

Contact:
National Environmental Health Association
NEHA/AAS Scholarship
720 South Colorado Blvd South Tower, 970
Denver, CO 80246-1925
Phone: 303-756-9090
Web: www.neha.org

National Federation of the Blind

Computer Science Scholarship

Type of award: Scholarship, renewable.
Intended use: For full-time undergraduate or graduate study at postsecondary institution.
Eligibility: Applicant must be visually impaired.
Basis for selection: Major/career interest in computer/information sciences; engineering, computer or computer graphics. Applicant must demonstrate financial need, high academic achievement and service orientation.
Application requirements: Recommendations, transcript. Personal letter from applicant, letter from state officer of National Federation of the Blind.
Additional information: Applicant must be legally blind. Recipients of Federation scholarships need not be members of National Federation of the Blind.

Amount of award:	$3,000
Number of awards:	1
Application deadline:	March 31
Notification begins:	June 1
Total amount awarded:	$3,000

Contact:
National Federation of the Blind Scholarship Committee
Mrs. Peggy Elliott, Chairman
805 Fifth Avenue
Grinnell, IA 50112
Phone: 641-236-3366
Web: www.nfb.org

E.U. Parker Memorial Scholarship

Type of award: Scholarship, renewable.
Intended use: For full-time undergraduate or graduate study at postsecondary institution.
Eligibility: Applicant must be visually impaired.
Basis for selection: Applicant must demonstrate financial need, high academic achievement and service orientation.
Application requirements: Recommendations, transcript. Personal letter from applicant, letter from state officer of National Federation of the Blind.
Additional information: Applicant must be legally blind. Recipients of Federation scholarships need not be members of National Federation of the Blind.

Amount of award:	$3,000
Number of awards:	1
Application deadline:	March 31
Notification begins:	June 1
Total amount awarded:	$3,000

Contact:
National Federation of the Blind Scholarship Committee
Mrs. Peggy Elliott, Chairman
805 Fifth Avenue
Grinnell, IA 50112
Phone: 641-236-3366
Web: www.nfb.org

Frank Walton Horn Memorial Scholarship

Type of award: Scholarship, renewable.
Intended use: For full-time undergraduate or graduate study at postsecondary institution.
Eligibility: Applicant must be visually impaired.
Basis for selection: Major/career interest in architecture or engineering. Applicant must demonstrate financial need, high academic achievement and service orientation.
Application requirements: Recommendations, transcript. Personal letter from applicant, letter from state officer of National Federation of the Blind.
Additional information: Applicant must be legally blind. Preference given to students studying architecture or engineering. Recipients of Federation scholarships need not be members of National Federation of the Blind.

Amount of award:	$3,000
Number of awards:	1
Application deadline:	March 31
Notification begins:	June 1
Total amount awarded:	$3,000

Contact:
National Federation of the Blind Scholarship Committee
Mrs. Peggy Elliott, Chairman
805 Fifth Avenue
Grinnell, IA 50112
Phone: 641-236-3366
Web: www.nfb.org

Hermione Grant Calhoun Scholarship

Type of award: Scholarship, renewable.
Intended use: For full-time undergraduate or graduate study at postsecondary institution.
Eligibility: Applicant must be visually impaired. Applicant must be female.
Basis for selection: Applicant must demonstrate financial need, high academic achievement and service orientation.
Application requirements: Recommendations, transcript. Personal letter from applicant, letter from state officer of National Federation of the Blind.
Additional information: Applicant must be legally blind. Recipients of Federation scholarships need not be members of National Federation of the Blind.

Amount of award:	$3,000
Number of awards:	1
Application deadline:	March 31
Notification begins:	June 1
Total amount awarded:	$3,000

Contact:
National Federation of the Blind Scholarship Committee
Mrs. Peggy Elliott, Chairman
805 Fifth Avenue
Grinnell, IA 50112
Phone: 641-236-3366
Web: www.nfb.org

Howard Brown Rickard Scholarship

Type of award: Scholarship, renewable.
Intended use: For full-time undergraduate or graduate study at postsecondary institution.
Eligibility: Applicant must be visually impaired.
Basis for selection: Major/career interest in law; medicine; engineering; architecture or natural sciences. Applicant must demonstrate financial need, high academic achievement and service orientation.
Application requirements: Recommendations, transcript. Personal letter from applicant, letter from state office of National Federation of the Blind.
Additional information: Applicant must be legally blind. Recipients of Federation scholarships need not be memebers of National Federation of the Blind.

Amount of award:	$3,000
Number of awards:	1
Application deadline:	March 31
Notification begins:	June 1
Total amount awarded:	$3,000

Contact:
National Federation of the Blind Scholarship Committee
Mrs. Peggy Elliott, Chairman
805 Fifth Avenue
Grinnell, IA 50112
Phone: 621-236-3366
Web: www.nfb.org

Jennica Ferguson Memorial Scholarship

Type of award: Scholarship, renewable.
Intended use: For full-time undergraduate or graduate study at postsecondary institution.
Eligibility: Applicant must be visually impaired.
Basis for selection: Applicant must demonstrate financial need, high academic achievement and service orientation.
Application requirements: Recommendations, transcript. Personal letter from applicant, letter from state officer of National Federation of the Blind.
Additional information: Applicant must be legally blind. Recipients of Federation scholarships need not be members of National Federation of the Blind.

Amount of award:	$5,000
Number of awards:	4
Application deadline:	March 31
Notification begins:	June 1
Total amount awarded:	$20,000

Contact:
National Federation of the Blind Scholarship Committee
Mrs. Peggy Elliott, Chairman
805 Fifth Avenue
Grinnell, IA 50112
Phone: 641-236-3366
Web: www.nfb.org

Kenneth Jernigan Memorial Scholarship

Type of award: Scholarship, renewable.
Intended use: For full-time undergraduate or graduate study.
Eligibility: Applicant must be visually impaired.
Basis for selection: Applicant must demonstrate financial need, high academic achievement and service orientation.

Application requirements: Recommendations, transcript. Personal letter from applicant, letter from state officer of National Federation of the Blind.
Additional information: Applicant must be legally blind. Recipients of Federation scholarships need not be members of National Federation of the Blind.

Amount of award:	$10,000
Number of awards:	1
Application deadline:	March 31
Notification begins:	June 1
Total amount awarded:	$10,000

Contact:
National Federation of the Blind Scholarship Committee
Mrs. Peggy Elliott, Chairman
805 Fifth Avenue
Grinnell, IA 50112
Phone: 641-236-3366
Web: www.nfb.org

Kucher-Killian Memorial Scholarship

Type of award: Scholarship, renewable.
Intended use: For full-time undergraduate or graduate study at postsecondary institution.
Eligibility: Applicant must be visually impaired.
Basis for selection: Applicant must demonstrate financial need, high academic achievement and service orientation.
Application requirements: Recommendations, transcript. Personal letter from applicant, letter from state officer of National Federation of the Blind.
Additional information: Applicant must be legally blind. Recipients of Federation scholarships need not be members of National Federation of the Blind.

Amount of award:	$3,000
Number of awards:	1
Application deadline:	March 31
Notification begins:	June 1
Total amount awarded:	$3,000

Contact:
National Federation of the Blind Scholarship Committee
Mrs. Peggy Elliott, Chairman
805 Fifth Avenue
Grinnell, IA 50112
Phone: 641-236-3366
Web: www.nfb.org

Lora E. Dunetz Scholarship

Type of award: Scholarship, renewable.
Intended use: For full-time undergraduate or graduate study at postsecondary institution.
Eligibility: Applicant must be visually impaired.
Basis for selection: Applicant must demonstrate financial need, high academic achievement and seriousness of purpose.
Application requirements: Recommendations, transcript. Personal letter from applicant, letter from state officer of National Federation of the Blind.
Additional information: Applicant must be legally blind. Preference given to those studying to enter medical field. Recipients of Federation scholarships need not be members of National Federation of the Blind.

Amount of award:	$3,000
Number of awards:	1
Application deadline:	March 31
Notification begins:	June 1
Total amount awarded:	$3,000

Contact:
National Federation of the Blind Scholarship Committee
Mrs. Peggy Elliott, Chairman
805 Fifth Avenue
Grinnell, IA 50112
Phone: 641-236-3366
Web: www.nfb.org

Melva T. Owen Memorial Scholarship

Type of award: Scholarship, renewable.
Intended use: For full-time undergraduate or graduate study at postsecondary institution.
Eligibility: Applicant must be visually impaired.
Basis for selection: Applicant must demonstrate financial need, high academic achievement and service orientation.
Application requirements: Recommendations, transcript. Personal letter from applicant, letter from state officer of National Federation of the Blind.
Additional information: Applicant must be legally blind. Field of study should be directed toward attaining financial independence. Excludes study of religion and those seeking only to further general or cultural education. Recipients of Federation scholarships need not be members of National Federation of the Blind.

Amount of award:	$7,000
Number of awards:	3
Application deadline:	March 31
Notification begins:	June 1
Total amount awarded:	$21,000

Contact:
National Federation of the Blind Scholarship Committee
Mrs. Peggy Elliott, Chairman
805 Fifth Avenue
Grinnell, IA 50112
Phone: 641-236-3366
Web: www.nfb.org

Michael and Marie Marucci Scholarship

Type of award: Scholarship, renewable.
Intended use: For full-time undergraduate or graduate study at postsecondary institution.
Eligibility: Applicant must be visually impaired.
Basis for selection: Major/career interest in foreign languages; literature; history; geography; political science/government; international studies or international relations. Applicant must demonstrate financial need, high academic achievement and service orientation.
Application requirements: Recommendations, transcript. Personal letter from applicant, letter from state officer of National Federation of the Blind.
Additional information: Applicant must be legally blind. Applicant must be studying foreign language or comparative literature; pursuing degree in history, geography or political science with concentration in international studies; or majoring in any other discipline that involves study abroad. Must also show evidence of competence in foreign language. Recipients of Federation scholarships need not be members of National Federation of the Blind.

Amount of award:	$3,000
Number of awards:	22
Application deadline:	March 31
Notification begins:	June 1

Contact:
National Federation of the Blind Scholarship Committee
Mrs. Peggy Elliott, Chairman
805 Fifth Avenue
Grinnell, IA 50112
Phone: 641-236-3366
Web: www.nfb.org

National Federation of the Blind Educator of Tomorrow Award

Type of award: Scholarship, renewable.
Intended use: For full-time undergraduate or graduate study at postsecondary institution.
Eligibility: Applicant must be visually impaired.
Basis for selection: Major/career interest in education, teacher or education. Applicant must demonstrate financial need, high academic achievement and service orientation.
Application requirements: Recommendations, transcript. Personal letter, from applicant, letter from state officer of National Federation of the Blind.
Additional information: Applicant must be legally blind. Must be planning career in elementary, secondary, or postsecondary teaching. Recipients of Federation scholarships need not be memebers of National Federation of the Blind.

Amount of award:	$3,000
Number of awards:	1
Application deadline:	March 31
Notification begins:	June 1
Total amount awarded:	$3,000

Contact:
National Federation of the Blind Scholarship Committee
Mrs. Peggy Elliott, Chairman
805 Fifth Avenue
Grinnell, IA 50112
Phone: 641-236-3366
Web: www.nfb.org

National Federation of the Blind Humanities Scholarship

Type of award: Scholarship, renewable.
Intended use: For full-time undergraduate or graduate study at postsecondary institution.
Eligibility: Applicant must be visually impaired.
Basis for selection: Major/career interest in humanities/liberal arts; art/art history; English; English literature; foreign languages; history; philosophy; religion/theology; arts, general or literature. Applicant must demonstrate financial need, high academic achievement and service orientation.
Application requirements: Recommendations, transcript. Personal letter from applicant, letter from state officer of National Federation of the Blind.
Additional information: Applicant must be legally blind. Applicant must be studying in traditional humanities such as art, English, foreign languages, history, philosophy or religion. Recipients of Federation scholarships need not be members of National Federation of the Blind.

Amount of award:	$3,000
Number of awards:	1
Application deadline:	March 31
Notification begins:	June 1
Total amount awarded:	$3,000

Contact:
National Federation of the Blind Scholarship Committee
Mrs. Peggy Elliott, Chairman
805 Fifth Avenue
Grinnell, IA 50112
Phone: 641-236-3366
Web: www.nfb.org

National Federation of the Blind Scholarships

Type of award: Scholarship, renewable.
Intended use: For full-time undergraduate or graduate study at postsecondary institution.
Eligibility: Applicant must be visually impaired.
Basis for selection: Major/career interest in humanities/liberal arts. Applicant must demonstrate financial need, high academic achievement and service orientation.
Application requirements: Recommendations, transcript. Personal letter from applicant, letter from state officer of National Federation of the Blind.
Additional information: Applicant must be legally blind. One $3,000 scholarship may be given to person working full-time and attending (or planning to attend) part-time course of study which will result in new degree and broader opportunities in present/future work. Recipients of Federation scholarships need not be members of National Federation of the Blind.

Amount of award:	$3,000-$7,000
Number of awards:	17
Application deadline:	March 31
Notification begins:	June 1
Total amount awarded:	$62,000

Contact:
National Federation of the Blind Scholarship Committee
Mrs. Peggy Elliott, Chairman
805 Fifth Avenue
Grinnell, IA 50112
Phone: 641-236-3366
Web: www.nfb.org

National Future Farmers of America

National Future Farmers of America Scholarship Program

Type of award: Scholarship.
Intended use: For undergraduate study.
Basis for selection: Major/career interest in agribusiness; agriculture; agricultural economics or agricultural education.
Additional information: Sponsors over 180 scholarships for members. Eligibility and deadlines vary. Contact FFA for further information. Scholarships held for full year beyond student's graduation date . If scholarship not requested within one year after graduation from high school, scholarship will be forfeited. Our purpose is to protect the scholarship for a reasonable period of time without accumulating unused scholarships.

Amount of award:	$250-$1,000
Application deadline:	February 15
Notification begins:	June 15

Contact:
National Future Farmers of America
Attn. Scholarship Office
P.O. Box 68960
Indianapolis, IN 46268-0960
Web: www.ffa.org

National Ground Water Association

Ground Water Association Auxiliary Scholarship

Type of award: Scholarship.
Intended use: For full-time undergraduate study at accredited 2-year or 4-year institution.
Eligibility: Applicant or parent must be member/participant of National Ground Water Association.
Basis for selection: Applicant must demonstrate financial need, high academic achievement, depth of character, leadership, patriotism, seriousness of purpose and service orientation.
Application requirements: Essay, transcript, proof of eligibility. Essay should be one page biography. Applicant or relative must be member/participant of National Ground Water Association.
Additional information: Application also open to extended relatives of National Ground Water Association. Minimum 2.5 GPA. Number of awards and amount varies annually.

Amount of award:	$500
Number of applicants:	14
Application deadline:	April 1

Contact:
National Ground Water Association
Julie Bullock
601 Dempsey Road
Westerville, OH 43081
Phone: 800-551-7379
Web: www.ngwa.org

National Guild of Community Schools of the Arts and the Hartt School

Young Composers Award

Type of award: Scholarship.
Intended use: For freshman study.
Eligibility: Applicant must be at least 13, no older than 18, enrolled in high school. Applicant must be U.S. citizen.
Basis for selection: Competition/talent/interest in music performance/composition, based on original musical composition. Major/career interest in music.
Application requirements: $5 application fee. Proof of eligibility. Original musical composition written by the applicant. Certification of composition by music teacher.
Additional information: Each applicant may submit only one work. Composer's name may not appear on submission. Pseudonyms required. Students must not be enrolled in any

undergraduate program at the time of application. There are two age categories, 13-15 and 16-18. Prizes vary in each category. All submissions reviewed by an independent jury. Visit Website or contact via e-mail (yaffe@mail.hartford.edu) for additional information.

Amount of award:	$250-$1,000
Number of awards:	5
Application deadline:	April 19
Notification begins:	June 15

Contact:
Michael Yaffe, Director The Hartt School Community Division
University of Hartford
200 Bloomfield Avenue
West Hartford, CT 06117
Phone: 860-768-4451
Web: www.natguild.org

National Institute for Labor Relations Research

Future Teacher Scholarship

Type of award: Scholarship.
Intended use: For undergraduate or graduate study at accredited postsecondary institution in United States.
Basis for selection: Major/career interest in education. Applicant must demonstrate financial need and high academic achievement.
Application requirements: Essay, transcript. Applicant must also include financial aid information with application materials.
Additional information: Must be majoring in education. Applicants must demonstrate potential for completion of degree program and obtainment of teaching license. Must also demonstrate understanding of principals of voluntary unionism and problems of compulsory unionism in relation to education. Only first 150 applications will be considered.

Amount of award:	$1,000
Number of awards:	2
Number of applicants:	150
Application deadline:	March 31
Notification begins:	July 15
Total amount awarded:	$2,000

Contact:
National Institute for Labor Relations Research
Attn: Program Director
5211 Port Royal Road, Suite 510
Springfield, VA 22151
Phone: 703-321-9606
Fax: 703-321-7342
Web: www.nilrr.org

William B. Ruggles Right to Work Scholarship

Type of award: Scholarship.
Intended use: For undergraduate or graduate study at accredited 2-year or 4-year institution.
Basis for selection: Major/career interest in journalism. Applicant must demonstrate financial need, high academic achievement, depth of character and seriousness of purpose.
Application requirements: Essay, transcript. Applicant must also include financial aid information with application materials.

Additional information: Applicants must demonstrate potential for completion of degree program and obtainment of teaching license. Must also demonstrate understanding of principals of voluntary unionism and economic and social problems of compulsory unionism. Only first 150 applications will be considered.

Amount of award:	$2,000
Number of awards:	1
Number of applicants:	150
Application deadline:	March 31
Total amount awarded:	$2,000

Contact:
National Institute for Labor Relations Research
Attn: Program Director
5211 Port Royal Road, Suite 510
Springfield, VA 22151
Phone: 703-321-9606
Fax: 703-321-7342
Web: www.nilrr.org

National Institutes of Health

National Institutes of Health Undergraduate Scholarship Program

Type of award: Scholarship.
Intended use: For full-time undergraduate study at accredited 4-year institution in United States.
Eligibility: Applicant must be U.S. citizen or permanent resident.
Basis for selection: Major/career interest in biology; chemistry; medical specialties/research or life sciences. Applicant must demonstrate financial need and high academic achievement.
Application requirements: Recommendations, transcript, proof of eligibility. Must show commitment to pursuing career in biomedical research at NIH. Applicant must be from disadvantaged background.
Additional information: Up tp 15 awards given. Minimum 3.5 GPA or be within top 5% of class. Student must work ten consecutive weeks (in summer) during scholarship year and 12 months as full-time employee at NIH laboratories after graduation for each year that scholarship is awarded. Award covers tuition/fees for up to $20,000.

Amount of award:	$20,000
Application deadline:	March 31

Contact:
NIH Office of Loan Repayment and Scholarships
2 Center Drive
MSC 0230
Bethesda, MD 20892-0230
Web: www.ugsp.info.nih.gov

National Italian American Foundation

Agnes E. Vaghi-Cornaro Scholarship

Type of award: Scholarship.

Intended use: For undergraduate study at 2-year or 4-year institution in United States.
Eligibility: Applicant must be female. Applicant must be Italian. Applicant must be U.S. citizen or permanent resident.
Basis for selection: Applicant must demonstrate financial need and high academic achievement.
Application requirements: $10 application fee. Essay, transcript. Photograph, College Scholarship Service Financial Aid Profile, three-page essay on a famous Italian-American woman.
Additional information: Must have completed 13 hours of community service within the Italian-American community. Send business-size SASE for application.

Amount of award:	$2,000
Number of awards:	1
Application deadline:	May 31

Contact:
National Italian American Foundation
Dr. Maria Lombardo
1860 19 Street NW
Washington, DC 20009
Phone: 202-387-0600
Web: www.niaf.org

Alex and Henry Recine Scholarship

Type of award: Scholarship.
Intended use: For undergraduate study at 2-year or 4-year institution in United States.
Eligibility: Applicant must be Italian. Applicant must be U.S. citizen or permanent resident residing in New York.
Basis for selection: Applicant must demonstrate financial need and high academic achievement.
Application requirements: $10 application fee. Essay, transcript, proof of eligibility. Photograph, College Scholarship Service Financial Aid Profile.
Additional information: Must have completed 13 hours of community service in Italian-American community. Send business-size SASE to receive application.

Amount of award:	$2,500
Number of awards:	1
Application deadline:	May 31

Contact:
National Italian American Foundation
Dr. Maria Lombardo
1860 19 Street NW
Washington, DC 20009
Phone: 202-387-0600
Web: www.niaf.org

Alyce M. Cafaro Scholarship

Type of award: Scholarship.
Intended use: For undergraduate study at 2-year or 4-year institution in United States.
Eligibility: Applicant must be Italian. Applicant must be U.S. citizen or permanent resident residing in Ohio.
Basis for selection: Applicant must demonstrate financial need and high academic achievement.
Application requirements: $10 application fee. Essay, transcript, proof of eligibility. Photograph, College Scholarship Service Financial Aid Profile.
Additional information: Must have completed 13 hours of community service within the Italian-American community. Send business-size SASE for application.

Amount of award:	$5,000
Number of awards:	1
Application deadline:	May 31

Contact:
National Italian American Foundation
Dr. Maria Lombardo
1860 19 Street NW
Washington, DC 20009
Phone: 202-387-0600
Web: www.niaf.org

Angela Scholarship

Type of award: Scholarship.
Intended use: For freshman study at 2-year or 4-year institution in United States.
Eligibility: Applicant must be high school senior. Applicant must be Italian. Applicant must be U.S. citizen or permanent resident.
Basis for selection: Applicant must demonstrate financial need, high academic achievement and service orientation.
Application requirements: $10 application fee. Essay, transcript. Photograph, College Scholarship Service Financial Aid Profile.
Additional information: Must have completed 13 hours of community service in Italian-American community. Strong demonstration of social responsibility during the high school years. Send business-size SASE to receive application.

Amount of award:	$2,500
Number of awards:	1
Application deadline:	May 31

Contact:
National Italian American Foundation
Dr. Maria Lombardo
1860 19 Street NW
Washington, DC 20009
Phone: 202-387-0600
Web: www.niaf.org

Antonio and Felicia Marinelli Scholarships

Type of award: Scholarship.
Intended use: For undergraduate study in Italy. Designated institutions: American University of Rome.
Eligibility: Applicant must be Italian. Applicant must be U.S. citizen or permanent resident.
Basis for selection: Competition/talent/interest in study abroad. Applicant must demonstrate financial need and high academic achievement.
Application requirements: $10 application fee. Essay, transcript, proof of eligibility. Photograph, College Scholarship Service Financial Aid Profile.
Additional information: Must have completed 13 hours of community service within the Italian-American community. Student must have been accepted at American University of Rome. Interested candidates call 202-331-8327.

Amount of award:	$2,000
Number of awards:	1
Application deadline:	May 31

Contact:
National Italian American Foundation
Dr. Maria Lombardo
1860 19th Street, NW
Washington, DC 20009
Phone: 202-387-0600
Web: www.niaf.org

Scholarships

Antonio F. Marinelli Founders Scholarship

Type of award: Scholarship.
Intended use: For undergraduate study at 2-year or 4-year institution in United States. Designated institutions: Washington, D.C. area institutions.
Eligibility: Applicant or parent must be member/participant of National Utility Contractors Association. Applicant must be Italian. Applicant must be U.S. citizen.
Basis for selection: Applicant must demonstrate high academic achievement.
Application requirements: $10 application fee. Essay, transcript, proof of eligibility. Photograph, College Scholarship Service Financial Aid Profile.
Additional information: Applicant's parent must belong to National Utility Contractors Association or be employee of member. Must have completed 13 hours of community service within Italian-American community. Award based on merit, not need. Send business-size SASE for application.

Amount of award:	$2,500
Application deadline:	May 31

Contact:
National Italian American Foundation
Dr. Maria Lombardo
1890 19th Street, NW
Washington, DC 20009
Phone: 202-387-0600
Web: www.niaf.org

Assunta Lucchetti Martino Scholarship for International Studies

Type of award: Scholarship.
Intended use: For undergraduate study at 2-year or 4-year institution.
Eligibility: Applicant must be Italian. Applicant must be U.S. citizen or permanent resident.
Basis for selection: Major/career interest in international relations. Applicant must demonstrate financial need and high academic achievement.
Application requirements: $10 application fee. Essay, transcript. Photograph, College Scholarship Service Financial Aid Profile.
Additional information: Must have completed 13 hours of communty service in Italian-American community. Send business-size SASE for application.

Amount of award:	$2,000
Number of awards:	1
Application deadline:	May 31

Contact:
National Italian American Foundation
Dr. Maria Lombardo
1860 19th Street, NW
Washington, DC 20009
Phone: 202-387-0600
Web: www.niaf.org

Bolla Wines Scholarship

Type of award: Scholarship.
Intended use: For undergraduate or graduate study at 2-year, 4-year or graduate institution in United States.
Eligibility: Applicant must be at least 21. Applicant must be Italian. Applicant must be U.S. citizen or permanent resident.

Basis for selection: Major/career interest in business, international or international relations. Applicant must demonstrate financial need and high academic achievement.
Application requirements: $10 application fee. Essay, transcript. Applicants must submit three-page double-spaced essay on "The Importance of Italy In Today's Business World."
Additional information: Designated for students in international studies with emphasis on Italian business or Italian-American history. Minimum 3.0 GPA required. Must have completed 13 hours of community service in Italian-American community. Send business-size SASE for application.

Amount of award:	$5,000
Number of awards:	1
Application deadline:	May 31

Contact:
National Italian American Foundation Scholarships
Dr. Maria Lombardo
1860 19th Street, NW
Washington, DC 20009
Phone: 202-387-0600
Web: www.niaf.org

Capital Area Regional Scholarship

Type of award: Scholarship.
Intended use: For undergraduate study at 2-year or 4-year institution.
Eligibility: Applicant must be Italian. Applicant must be U.S. citizen or permanent resident residing in Virginia, District of Columbia, Maryland or West Virginia.
Basis for selection: Applicant must demonstrate financial need and high academic achievement.
Application requirements: $10 application fee. Essay, transcript. Photograph, College Scholarship Service Financial Aid Profile.
Additional information: Must have completed 13 hours of community service within the Italian-American community. Send business size SASE to receive application form.

Amount of award:	$5,000
Number of awards:	2
Application deadline:	May 31
Total amount awarded:	$10,000

Contact:
National Italian American Foundation
Dr. Maria Lombardo
1860 19 Street NW
Washington, DC 20009
Phone: 202-387-0600
Web: www.niaf.org

Communications Scholarship

Type of award: Scholarship.
Intended use: For undergraduate study at postsecondary institution in United States.
Eligibility: Applicant must be Italian. Applicant must be U.S. citizen or permanent resident.
Basis for selection: Major/career interest in communications or journalism.
Application requirements: $10 application fee. Essay, transcript, proof of eligibility. Example of best work, photograph, College Scholarship Service Financial Aid Profile.
Additional information: Must have completed 13 hours of community service within the Italian-American community. Send business-size SASE to receive application form.

Amount of award:	$5,000
Number of awards:	1
Application deadline:	May 31
Total amount awarded:	$5,000

Contact:
National Italian American Foundation
Dr. Maria Lombardo
1860 19 Street NW
Washington, DC 20009
Phone: 202-387-0600
Web: www.niaf.org

Congressman Alfred E. Santangelo and Betty Santangelo Scholarship

Type of award: Scholarship.
Intended use: For undergraduate study at 2-year or 4-year institution in United States.
Eligibility: Applicant must be Italian. Applicant must be U.S. citizen or permanent resident.
Basis for selection: Major/career interest in Italian or political science/government. Applicant must demonstrate financial need and high academic achievement.
Application requirements: $10 application fee. Essay, transcript. Photograph, College Scholarship Service Financial Aid Profile.
Additional information: Must have completed 13 hours of community service with the Italian-American community. Send business-size SASE to receive application form.

Amount of award:	$2,000
Number of awards:	1
Application deadline:	May 31

Contact:
National Italian American Foundation
Dr. Maria Lombardo
1860 19 Street NW
Washington, DC 20009
Phone: 202-387-0600
Web: www.niaf.org

Daniel Stella Scholarship

Type of award: Scholarship.
Intended use: For undergraduate or graduate study at 2-year, 4-year or graduate institution in United States.
Eligibility: Applicant must be Italian. Applicant must be U.S. citizen or permanent resident.
Basis for selection: Applicant must demonstrate financial need and high academic achievement.
Application requirements: $10 application fee. Essay, transcript, proof of eligibility. Photograph, College Scholarship Service Financial Aid Profile.
Additional information: For students with Cooley's Anemia disease. Must have completed 13 hours of community service within the Italian-American community. Send business-size SASE for application.

Amount of award:	$5,000
Number of awards:	1
Application deadline:	May 31

Contact:
National Italian American Foundation
Dr. Maria Lombardo
1860 19 Street NW
Washington, DC 20009
Phone: 202-387-0600
Web: www.niaf.org

Dr. William L. Amoroso Jr. Scholarship

Type of award: Scholarship.
Intended use: For undergraduate study outside United States. Designated institutions: American University of Rome.
Eligibility: Applicant must be Italian. Applicant must be U.S. citizen or permanent resident.
Basis for selection: Applicant must demonstrate financial need and high academic achievement.
Application requirements: $10 application fee. Essay, transcript, proof of eligibility. Photograph, College Scholarship Service Financial Aid Profile.
Additional information: Must have completed 13 hours of community service within the Italian-American community. For students accepted into the American University of Rome. Interested candidates call 202-331-8327.

Amount of award:	$2,000
Number of awards:	1
Application deadline:	May 31

Contact:
National Italian American Foundation
Dr. Maria Lombardo
1860 19th Street, NW
Washington, DC 20009
Phone: 202-387-0600
Web: www.niaf.org

F.D. Stella Scholarship

Type of award: Scholarship.
Intended use: For undergraduate or graduate study at postsecondary institution in United States.
Eligibility: Applicant must be Italian. Applicant must be U.S. citizen or permanent resident.
Basis for selection: Major/career interest in business. Applicant must demonstrate financial need and high academic achievement.
Application requirements: $10 application fee. Essay, transcript, proof of eligibility. Photograph, College Scholarship Service Financial Aid Profile.
Additional information: Must have completed 13 hours of community service in Italian-American community. Send business-size SASE to receive application form.

Amount of award:	$5,000
Number of awards:	1
Application deadline:	May 31

Contact:
National Italian American Foundation
Dr. Maria Lombardo
1860 19 Street NW
Washington, DC 20009
Phone: 202-387-0600
Web: www.niaf.org

Frank J. Corsaro Scholarship

Type of award: Scholarship.
Intended use: For undergraduate study at 2-year or 4-year institution in United States.
Eligibility: Applicant must be Italian. Applicant must be U.S. citizen or permanent resident.
Basis for selection: Major/career interest in law; medicine or political science/government. Applicant must demonstrate financial need and high academic achievement.

Application requirements: $10 application fee. Essay, transcript. Photograph, College Scholarship Service Financial Aid Profile.

Additional information: Must have completed 13 hours of community service in Italian-American community. Send business-size SASE for application.

Amount of award:	$2,000
Number of awards:	1
Application deadline:	May 31

Contact:
National Italian American foundation
Dr. Maria Lombardo
1860 19 Street NW
Washington, DC 20009
Phone: 202-387-0600
Web: www.niaf.org

Gianni Versace Scholarship in Fashion Design

Type of award: Scholarship.

Intended use: For undergraduate study at 2-year or 4-year institution in United States.

Eligibility: Applicant must be Italian. Applicant must be U.S. citizen or permanent resident.

Basis for selection: Major/career interest in fashion design. Applicant must demonstrate financial need and high academic achievement.

Application requirements: $10 application fee. Essay, transcript. Photograph, College Scholarship Service Financial Aid Profile.

Additional information: Must be majoring in fashion design. Must have completed 13 hours of community service in Italian-American community. Send business-size SASE for application.

Amount of award:	$2,000
Number of awards:	1
Application deadline:	May 31

Contact:
National Italian American Foundation
Dr. Maria Lombardo
1860 19th Street, NW
Washington, DC 20009
Phone: 202-387-0600
Web: www.niaf.org

Greater New York Regional Scholarship

Type of award: Scholarship.

Intended use: For undergraduate study at 2-year or 4-year institution in United States.

Eligibility: Applicant must be Italian. Applicant must be U.S. citizen or permanent resident residing in New Jersey or New York.

Basis for selection: Applicant must demonstrate financial need and high academic achievement.

Application requirements: $10 application fee. Essay, transcript, proof of eligibility. Photograph, College Scholarship Service Financial Aid Profile.

Additional information: Residents of New Jersey must live north of Trenton. Must have completed 13 hours of community service within the Italian-American community. Send business-size SASE to receive application form.

Amount of award:	$5,000
Number of awards:	2
Application deadline:	May 31
Total amount awarded:	$10,000

Contact:
National Italian American Foundation
Dr. Maria Lombardo
1860 19 Street NW
Washington, DC 20009
Phone: 202-387-0600
Web: www.niaf.org

Italian Cultural Society and NIAF Matching Scholarship

Type of award: Scholarship.

Intended use: For undergraduate study at 2-year or 4-year institution in United States.

Eligibility: Applicant must be Italian. Applicant must be U.S. citizen or permanent resident residing in Virginia, District of Columbia or Maryland.

Basis for selection: Major/career interest in science, general or humanities/liberal arts. Applicant must demonstrate financial need and high academic achievement.

Application requirements: $10 application fee. Essay, transcript, proof of eligibility. Photograph, College Scholarship Service Financial Aid Profile.

Additional information: Must have completed 13 hours of community service in Italian-American community. Send business-size SASE for application.

Amount of award:	$5,000
Number of awards:	2
Application deadline:	May 31

Contact:
National Italian American Foundation
Dr. Maria Lombardo
1860 19th Street, NW
Washington, DC 20009
Phone: 202-387-0600
Web: www.niaf.org

Italian Regional Scholarship

Type of award: Scholarship.

Intended use: For undergraduate study in Italy.

Eligibility: Applicant must be Italian.

Basis for selection: Competition/talent/interest in study abroad. Applicant must demonstrate financial need and high academic achievement.

Application requirements: $10 application fee. Essay, transcript. Photograph, College Scholarship Service Financial Aid Profile.

Additional information: Must have completed 13 hours of community service in Italian-American community. Send business-size SASE to receive application form.

Amount of award:	$5,000
Number of awards:	2
Application deadline:	May 31
Total amount awarded:	$10,000

Contact:
National Italian American Foundation
Dr. Maria Lombardo
1860 19 Street NW
Washington, DC 20009
Phone: 202-387-0600
Web: www.niaf.org

John A. Volpe Scholarship

Type of award: Scholarship.

Intended use: For undergraduate study at 2-year or 4-year institution in United States.
Eligibility: Applicant must be Italian. Applicant must be U.S. citizen or permanent resident residing in Connecticut, Massachusetts, Maine, New Hampshire, Rhode Island or Vermont.
Basis for selection: Applicant must demonstrate financial need and high academic achievement.
Application requirements: Essay, transcript, proof of eligibility. Photograph, College Scholarship Service Financial Aid Profile.
Additional information: Must have completed 13 hours of community service in Italian-American community. Send business-size SASE for application.

Amount of award:	$5,000
Number of awards:	1
Application deadline:	May 31

Contact:
National Italian American Foundation
Dr. Maria Lombardo
1860 19 Street NW
Washington, DC 20009
Phone: 202-387-0600
Web: ww.niaf.org

Louis A. Caputo, Jr. Scholarship

Type of award: Scholarship.
Intended use: For undergraduate study at 2-year or 4-year institution in United States.
Eligibility: Applicant must be Italian.
Basis for selection: Major/career interest in music.
Application requirements: $10 application fee. Essay, transcript. Photograph, College Scholarship Service Financial Aid Profile.
Additional information: Must have completed 13 hours of community service within the Italian-American community. Send business-size SASE to receive application form.

Amount of award:	$2,500
Number of awards:	1
Application deadline:	May 31

Contact:
National Italian American Foundation
1860 19 Street NW
Washington, DC 20009
Phone: 202-387-0600
Web: www.niaf.org

Lower Mid-Atlantic Regional Scholarship

Type of award: Scholarship.
Intended use: For undergraduate study at 2-year or 4-year institution in United States.
Eligibility: Applicant must be Italian. Applicant must be U.S. citizen or permanent resident residing in Delaware, New Jersey or Pennsylvania.
Basis for selection: Applicant must demonstrate financial need and high academic achievement.
Application requirements: $10 application fee. Essay, transcript, proof of eligibility. Photograph, College Scholarship Service Financial Aid Profile.
Additional information: Residents of New Jersey must live south of Trenton. Must have completed 13 hours of community service within the Italian-American community. Send business-size SASE to receive application form.

Amount of award:	$5,000
Number of awards:	2
Application deadline:	May 31
Total amount awarded:	$10,000

Contact:
National Italian American Foundation
Dr. Maria Lombardo
1860 19 Street NW
Washington, DC 20009
Phone: 202-387-0600
Web: www.niaf.org

Merrill Lynch Scholarship

Type of award: Scholarship.
Intended use: For undergraduate study at 2-year or 4-year institution in United States.
Eligibility: Applicant must be Italian. Applicant must be U.S. citizen or permanent resident residing in New York.
Basis for selection: Major/career interest in business. Applicant must demonstrate financial need and high academic achievement.
Application requirements: $10 application fee. Essay, transcript, proof of eligibility. Photograph, College Scholarship Service Financial Aid Profile.
Additional information: Must have completed 13 hours of communty service in Italian-American community. Send business-size SASE for application.

Amount of award:	$2,000
Number of awards:	1
Application deadline:	May 31

Contact:
National Italian American Foundation
Dr. Maria Lombardo
1860 19th Street, NW
Washington, DC 20009
Phone: 202-387-0600
Web: www.niaf.org

Mid-America Regional Scholarship

Type of award: Scholarship.
Intended use: For undergraduate study at 2-year or 4-year institution in United States.
Eligibility: Applicant must be Italian. Applicant must be U.S. citizen or permanent resident residing in Missouri, Oklahoma, Nebraska, Iowa, Kansas, Colorado or Arkansas.
Basis for selection: Applicant must demonstrate financial need and high academic achievement.
Application requirements: $10 application fee. Essay, transcript, proof of eligibility. Photograph, College Scholarship Service Financial Aid Profile.
Additional information: Must have completed 13 hours of community service within the Italian-American community. Send business-size SASE to receive application form.

Amount of award:	$5,000
Number of awards:	2
Application deadline:	May 31
Total amount awarded:	$10,000

Contact:
National Italian American Foundation
Dr. Maria Lombardo
1860 19 Street NW
Washington, DC 20009
Phone: 202-387-0600
Web: www.naif.org

Mid-Pacific Regional Scholarship

Type of award: Scholarship.
Intended use: For undergraduate study at 2-year or 4-year institution in United States.
Eligibility: Applicant must be Italian. Applicant must be U.S. citizen or permanent resident residing in Nevada, Utah, California or Hawaii.
Basis for selection: Applicant must demonstrate financial need and high academic achievement.
Application requirements: $10 application fee. Essay, transcript, proof of eligibility. Photograph, College Scholarship Service Financial Aid Profile.
Additional information: Residents of California and Nevada must be from northern regions (e.g., Reno). Residents of Guam are also eligible. Must have completed 13 hours of community service within the Italian-American community. Send business-size SASE to receive application form.

Amount of award:	$5,000
Number of awards:	2
Application deadline:	May 31
Total amount awarded:	$10,000

Contact:
National Italian American Foundation
Dr. Maria Lombardo
1860 19 Street NW
Washington, DC 20009
Phone: 202-387-0600
Web: www.niaf.org

Nerone/NIAF Matching Art Scholarship

Type of award: Scholarship.
Intended use: For undergraduate or graduate study at 2-year, 4-year or graduate institution in United States.
Eligibility: Applicant must be Italian. Applicant must be U.S. citizen or permanent resident.
Basis for selection: Major/career interest in art/art history; arts management or arts, general. Applicant must demonstrate financial need and high academic achievement.
Application requirements: $10 application fee. Essay, transcript. Photograph, College Scholarship Service Financial Aid Profile.
Additional information: Must have completed 13 hours of community service in Italian-American community. Send business-size SASE for application.

Amount of award:	$2,000
Number of awards:	1
Application deadline:	May 31

Contact:
National Italian American Foundation
Dr. Maria Lombardo
1860 19th Street, NW
Washington, DC 20009
Phone: 202-387-0600
Web: www.niaf.org

New England Regional Scholarship

Type of award: Scholarship.
Intended use: For undergraduate study at 2-year or 4-year institution in United States.
Eligibility: Applicant must be Italian. Applicant must be U.S. citizen or permanent resident residing in Connecticut, Massachusetts, Maine, New Hampshire, Rhode Island or Vermont.

Basis for selection: Applicant must demonstrate financial need and high academic achievement.
Application requirements: $10 application fee. Essay, transcript, proof of eligibility. Photograph, College Scholarship Service Financial Aid Profile.
Additional information: Must have completed 13 hours of community service within the Italian-American community. Send business-size SASE to receive application form.

Amount of award:	$5,000
Number of awards:	2
Application deadline:	May 31
Total amount awarded:	$10,000

Contact:
National Italian American Foundation
Dr. Maria Lombardo
1860 19 Street NW
Washington, DC 20009
Phone: 202-387-0600
Web: www.niaf.org

NIAF Pavarotti Scholarship

Type of award: Scholarship.
Intended use: For undergraduate or graduate study at 2-year, 4-year or graduate institution in United States.
Eligibility: Applicant must be Italian. Applicant must be U.S. citizen or permanent resident residing in California.
Basis for selection: Major/career interest in music. Applicant must demonstrate financial need and high academic achievement.
Application requirements: $10 application fee. Essay, transcript, proof of eligibility. Cassette tape of voice in performance. Photograph, College Scholarship Service Financial Aid Profile.
Additional information: Must be resident of Southern California. Must have completed 13 hours of community service within Italian-American community. Send business-size SASE to receive application.

Amount of award:	$5,000
Number of awards:	1
Application deadline:	May 31

Contact:
National Italian American Foundation
Dr. Maria Lombardo
1860 19 Street NW
Washington, DC 20009
Phone: 202-387-0600
Web: www.niaf.org

NIAF/NOIAW Cornaro Scholarship

Type of award: Scholarship.
Intended use: For undergraduate or graduate study at 2-year, 4-year or graduate institution in United States.
Eligibility: Applicant must be female. Applicant must be Italian. Applicant must be U.S. citizen or permanent resident.
Basis for selection: Applicant must demonstrate financial need and high academic achievement.
Application requirements: $10 application fee. Essay, transcript, proof of eligibility. Photograph, College Scholarship Service Financial Aid Profile, three-page double-spaced essay on current issue of concern to Italian-American women or on famous Italian-American woman.
Additional information: Must have completed 13 hours of community service in Italian-American community. Send business-size SASE to receive application form.

Amount of award:	$5,000
Number of awards:	2
Application deadline:	May 31
Total amount awarded:	$5,000

Contact:
National Italian American Foundation
Dr. Maria Lombardo
1860 19 Street NW
Washington, DC 20009
Phone: 202-387-0600
Web: www.niaf.org

Nina Santavicca Scholarship

Type of award: Scholarship.
Intended use: For undergraduate or graduate study at accredited 2-year, 4-year or graduate institution in United States.
Eligibility: Applicant must be Italian. Applicant must be U.S. citizen or permanent resident.
Basis for selection: Major/career interest in music. Applicant must demonstrate financial need and high academic achievement.
Application requirements: $10 application fee. Essay, transcript, proof of eligibility. Photograph, College Scholarship Service Financial Aid Profile.
Additional information: Pianist preferred. Must have completed 13 hours of community service within Italian-American community. Send business-size SASE to receive application.

Amount of award:	$2,000
Number of awards:	1
Application deadline:	May 31

Contact:
National Italian American Foundation
Dr. Maria Lombardo
1860 19 Street NW
Washington, DC 20009
Phone: 202-387-0600
Web: www.niaf.org

North Central Regional Scholarship

Type of award: Scholarship.
Intended use: For undergraduate study at 2-year or 4-year institution in United States.
Eligibility: Applicant must be Italian. Applicant must be U.S. citizen or permanent resident residing in North Dakota, Illinois, Ohio, Kentucky, Indiana, South Dakota, Wisconsin, Michigan or Minnesota.
Basis for selection: Applicant must demonstrate financial need and high academic achievement.
Application requirements: $10 application fee. Essay, transcript. Photograph, College Scholarship Service Financial . Aid Profile.
Additional information: Must have completed 13 hours of community service within the Italian-American community. Send business-size SASE for application.

Amount of award:	$5,000
Number of awards:	2
Application deadline:	May 31
Total amount awarded:	$10,000

Contact:
National Italian American Foundation
Dr. Maria Lombardo
1860 19th Street, NW
Washington, DC 20009
Phone: 202-387-0600
Web: www.niaf.org

Northwest Regional Scholarship

Type of award: Scholarship.
Intended use: For undergraduate study at 2-year or 4-year institution in United States.
Eligibility: Applicant must be Italian. Applicant must be U.S. citizen or permanent resident residing in Idaho, Montana, Alaska, Oregon, Washington or Wyoming.
Basis for selection: Applicant must demonstrate financial need and high academic achievement.
Application requirements: $10 application fee. Essay, transcript. Photograph, College Scholarship Service Financial Aid Profile.
Additional information: Must have completed 13 hours of community service within the Italian-American community. Send business-size SASE for application.

Amount of award:	$5,000
Number of awards:	2
Application deadline:	May 31

Contact:
National Italian American Foundation
Dr. Maria Lombardo
1860 19th Street, NW
Washington, DC 20009
Phone: 202-387-0600
Web: www.niaf.org

Paragano Scholarship

Type of award: Scholarship.
Intended use: For undergraduate study at 2-year or 4-year institution in United States.
Eligibility: Applicant must be Italian. Applicant must be U.S. citizen or permanent resident residing in New Jersey.
Basis for selection: Major/career interest in Italian or Italian-american studies. Applicant must demonstrate financial need and high academic achievement.
Application requirements: $10 application fee. Essay, transcript, proof of eligibility. Photograph, College Scholarship Service Financial Aid Profile.
Additional information: Must have completed 13 hours of community service in Italian-American community. Send business-size SASE to receive application form.

Amount of award:	$5,000
Number of awards:	1
Application deadline:	May 31

Contact:
National Italian American Foundation
Dr. Maria Lombardo
1860 19 Street NW
Washington, DC 20009
Phone: 202-387-0600
Web: www.niaf.org

Piancone Family Agriculture Scholarship

Type of award: Scholarship.

Intended use: For undergraduate or graduate study at 2-year, 4-year or graduate institution in United States.
Eligibility: Applicant must be Italian. Applicant must be U.S. citizen or permanent resident residing in Delaware, Virginia, District of Columbia, Maryland, Massachusetts, New Jersey, New York or Pennsylvania.
Basis for selection: Major/career interest in agriculture. Applicant must demonstrate financial need and high academic achievement.
Application requirements: $10 application fee. Essay, transcript, proof of eligibility. Photograph, College Scholarship Service Financial Aid Profile.
Additional information: Must have completed 13 hours of community service in Italian-American community. Send business-size SASE to receive application form.

Amount of award:	$2,000
Number of awards:	1
Application deadline:	May 31

Contact:
National Italian American Foundation
Dr. Maria Lombardo
1860 19 Street NW
Washington, DC 20009
Phone: 202-387-0600
Web: www.niaf.org

Richard Perrone Scholarship

Type of award: Scholarship.
Intended use: For undergraduate or graduate study at 2-year, 4-year or graduate institution in United States. Designated institutions: Connecticut postsecondary institutions.
Eligibility: Applicant must be Italian. Applicant must be U.S. citizen or permanent resident.
Basis for selection: Major/career interest in communications; radio/television/film or electronics. Applicant must demonstrate financial need and high academic achievement.
Application requirements: $10 application fee. Essay, transcript. Photograph, College Scholarship Service Financial Aid Profile.
Additional information: Major in telecommunications. Must have completed 13 hours of community service in the Italian-American community. Send business-size SASE to receive application.

Amount of award:	$2,000
Number of awards:	1
Application deadline:	May 31

Contact:
National Italian American Foundation
Dr. Maria Lombardo
1860 19 Street NW
Washington, DC 20009
Phone: 202-387-0600
Web: www.niaf.org

Robert J. Di Pietro Scholarship

Type of award: Scholarship.
Intended use: For undergraduate or graduate study at 2-year, 4-year or graduate institution in United States.
Eligibility: Applicant must be no older than 25. Applicant must be Italian. Applicant must be U.S. citizen or permanent resident.
Basis for selection: Applicant must demonstrate high academic achievement.
Application requirements: $10 application fee. Essay, transcript, proof of eligibility. Photograph.

Additional information: Applicant must write essay of 400-600 words on how applicant intends to use his/her ethnicity throughout his/her chosen field of education to preserve and support his/her ethnicity throughout life. Must have completed 13 hours of community service in Italian-American communty. Send business-size SASE to receive application.

Amount of award:	$2,000
Number of awards:	1
Application deadline:	May 31

Contact:
National Italian American Foundation
Dr. Maria Lombardo
1860 19 Street NW
Washington, DC 20009
Phone: 202-387-0600
Web: www.niaf.org

Rose Basile Green Scholarship for Literature

Type of award: Scholarship.
Intended use: For undergraduate study at 2-year or 4-year institution in United States.
Eligibility: Applicant must be Italian. Applicant must be U.S. citizen or permanent resident.
Basis for selection: Major/career interest in Italian-american studies. Applicant must demonstrate financial need and high academic achievement.
Application requirements: $10 application fee. Essay, transcript, proof of eligibility. Photograph, College Scholarship Service Financial Aid Profile.
Additional information: Must have completed 13 hours of community service within the Italian-American community. Send business-size SASE to receive application.

Amount of award:	$2,000
Number of awards:	1
Application deadline:	May 31

Contact:
National Italian American Foundation
Dr. Maria Lombardo
1860 19 Street NW
Washington, DC 20009
Phone: 202-387-0600
Web: www.niaf.org

Sergio Franchi Music Scholarship for Voice Performance

Type of award: Scholarship.
Intended use: For undergraduate or graduate study at 2-year, 4-year or graduate institution in United States.
Eligibility: Applicant must be Italian. Applicant must be U.S. citizen or permanent resident.
Basis for selection: Major/career interest in music.
Application requirements: $10 application fee. Audition, essay, transcript. Cassette tape of voice in performance, photograph, College Scholarship Service Financial Aid Profile.
Additional information: Available to students of voice only (sopranos and tenors). Must have completed 13 hours of community service in Italian-American community. Send business-size SASE to receive application form.

Amount of award:	$1,000
Number of awards:	15
Application deadline:	May 31

Contact:
National Italian American Foundation
Dr. Maria Lombardo
1860 19 Street NW
Washington, DC 20009
Phone: 202-387-0600
Web: www.niaf.org

South Central Regional Scholarship

Type of award: Scholarship.
Intended use: For full-time undergraduate study at 2-year or 4-year institution in United States.
Eligibility: Applicant must be Italian. Applicant must be U.S. citizen or permanent resident residing in Tennessee, Alabama, Texas, Louisiana or Mississippi.
Basis for selection: Applicant must demonstrate financial need and high academic achievement.
Application requirements: $10 application fee. Essay, transcript, proof of eligibility. Photograph, College Scholarship Service Financial Aid Profile.
Additional information: Must have completed 13 hours of community service within the Italian-American community. Send business-size SASE to receive application.

Amount of award:	$5,000
Number of awards:	2
Application deadline:	May 31
Total amount awarded:	$10,000

Contact:
National Italian American Foundation
Dr. Maria Lombardo
1860 19 Street NW
Washington, DC 20009
Phone: 202-387-0600
Web: www.niaf.org

Southeast Regional Scholarship

Type of award: Scholarship.
Intended use: For undergraduate study at 2-year or 4-year institution in United States.
Eligibility: Applicant must be Italian. Applicant must be U.S. citizen or permanent resident residing in Florida, Georgia, North Carolina or South Carolina.
Basis for selection: Applicant must demonstrate financial need and high academic achievement.
Application requirements: $10 application fee. Essay, transcript, proof of eligibility. Photograph, College Scholarship Service Financial Aid Profile.
Additional information: Must have completed 13 hours of community service within the Italian-American community. Send business-size SASE to receive application form.

Amount of award:	$5,000
Number of awards:	2
Application deadline:	May 31
Total amount awarded:	$10,000

Contact:
National Italian American Foundation
Dr. Maria Lombardo
1860 19 Street NW
Washington, DC 20009
Phone: 202-387-0600
Web: www.niaf.org

Southwest Regional Scholarship

Type of award: Scholarship.

Intended use: For undergraduate study at 2-year or 4-year institution in United States.
Eligibility: Applicant must be Italian. Applicant must be U.S. citizen or permanent resident residing in New Mexico, Nevada, Arizona or California.
Basis for selection: Applicant must demonstrate financial need and high academic achievement.
Application requirements: $10 application fee. Essay, transcript, proof of eligibility. Photograph, College Scholarship Service Financial Aid Profile.
Additional information: California and Nevada residents must be from southern areas (e.g., Las Vegas). Must have completed 13 hours of community service within the Italian-American community. Send business-size SASE to receive application form.

Amount of award:	$5,000
Number of awards:	2
Application deadline:	May 31
Total amount awarded:	$10,000

Contact:
National Italian American Foundation
Dr. Maria Lombardo
1860 19 Street NW
Washington, DC 20009
Phone: 202-387-0600
Web: www.niaf.org

Study Abroad Scholarship

Type of award: Scholarship.
Intended use: For undergraduate or graduate study at accredited 4-year or graduate institution in Italy.
Eligibility: Applicant must be Italian. Applicant must be U.S. citizen or permanent resident.
Basis for selection: Competition/talent/interest in study abroad. Applicant must demonstrate financial need and high academic achievement.
Application requirements: $10 application fee. Essay, transcript, proof of eligibility. Photograph, College Scholarship Service Financial Aid Profile, letter of acceptance from accredited school.
Additional information: Must have completed 13 hours of community service in Italian-American community. Send business-size SASE for application.

Amount of award:	$2,000
Number of awards:	5
Application deadline:	May 31
Total amount awarded:	$10,000

Contact:
National Italian American Foundation
Dr. Maria Lombardo
1860 19 Street NW
Washington, DC 20009
Phone: 202-387-0600
Web: www.niaf.org

Thomas Joseph "Willie" Ambrosole Scholarship

Type of award: Scholarship.
Intended use: For undergraduate study at 2-year or 4-year institution in United States.
Eligibility: Applicant must be Italian. Applicant must be U.S. citizen or permanent resident residing in New Jersey or New York.

Basis for selection: Major/career interest in arts, general or humanities/liberal arts. Applicant must demonstrate financial need and high academic achievement.
Application requirements: $10 application fee. Recommendations, essay. Photograph, College Scholarship Service Financial Aid Profile.
Additional information: Must have completed 13 hours of community service in Italian-American community. Send business-size SASE for application.

Amount of award:	$2,000
Number of awards:	1
Application deadline:	May 31

Contact:
National Italian American Foundation
Dr. Maria Lombardo
1860 19th Street, NW
Washington, DC 20009
Phone: 202-387-0600
Web: www.niaf.org

Vincent Zecchino, M.D. Scholarship

Type of award: Scholarship.
Intended use: For undergraduate study at 2-year or 4-year institution in United States.
Eligibility: Applicant must be U.S. citizen or permanent resident.
Basis for selection: Applicant must demonstrate financial need and high academic achievement.
Application requirements: $10 application fee. Essay, transcript. Photograph, College Scholarship Service Financial Aid Profile.
Additional information: Need not be Italian-American. Must have completed 13 hours of community service within the Italian-American community. Send a business-size SASE to receive application.

Amount of award:	$5,000
Number of awards:	1
Application deadline:	May 31

Contact:
National Italian American Foundation
Dr. Maria Lombardo
1860 19 Street NW
Washington, DC 20009
Phone: 202-387-0600
Web: www.niaf.org

Vincente Minelli Scholarship

Type of award: Scholarship.
Intended use: For undergraduate study at postsecondary institution in United States.
Eligibility: Applicant must be Italian. Applicant must be U.S. citizen or permanent resident residing in California.
Basis for selection: Major/career interest in performing arts or theater arts. Applicant must demonstrate financial need and high academic achievement.
Application requirements: $10 application fee. Essay, transcript, proof of eligibility. Photograph, College Scholarship Service Financial Aid Profile.
Additional information: Must have completed 13 hours of community service within the Italian-American community. Send business-size SASE to receive application form.

Amount of award:	$2,000
Number of awards:	1
Application deadline:	May 31

Contact:
National Italian American Foundation
Dr. Maria Lombardo
1860 19 Street NW
Washington, DC 20009
Phone: 202-387-0600
Web: www.niaf.org

West Virginia Italian Heritage Festival Scholarship

Type of award: Scholarship.
Intended use: For undergraduate study at 2-year or 4-year institution in United States.
Eligibility: Applicant must be Italian. Applicant must be U.S. citizen or permanent resident residing in West Virginia.
Basis for selection: Applicant must demonstrate financial need and high academic achievement.
Application requirements: $10 application fee. Essay, transcript, proof of eligibility. Photograph, College Scholarship Service Financial Aid Profile.
Additional information: Must have completed 13 hours of community service in Italian-American community. Send business-size SASE to receive application.

Amount of award:	$6,000
Number of awards:	1
Application deadline:	May 31

Contact:
National Italian American Foundation
Dr. Maria Lombardo
1860 19 Street NW
Washington, DC 20009
Phone: 202-387-0600
Web: www.niaf.org

National Jewish Committee on Scouting, Boy Scouts of America

Frank L. Weil Memorial Eagle Scout Scholarship

Type of award: Scholarship.
Intended use: For full-time undergraduate study at accredited 2-year or 4-year institution.
Eligibility: Applicant or parent must be member/participant of Boy Scouts of America, Eagle Scouts. Applicant must be male, high school senior. Applicant must be Jewish. Applicant must be U.S. citizen or permanent resident.
Application requirements: Recommendations.
Additional information: Recipient of scholarship receives $1,000. Two $500 second-place scholarship awards also given. Applicant must be active member of synagogue. Applicants must submit at least four letters of recommendation and testimony with nominating application. One letter required from leaders of each of the following groups: religious institution, school, community, and Scouting unit. Open to Eagle Scouts who have earned their Ner Tamid emblem. To request application form, contact National Jewish Committee on Scouting. Visit Website for more information.

Amount of award:	$500-$1,000
Number of awards:	3
Application deadline:	December 31

Contact:
National Jewish Committee on Scouting, BSA
1325 West Walnut Hill Lane
P.O. Box 152079
Irving, TX 75015-2079
Phone: 972-580-2032
Fax: 972-580-2502
Web: www.jewishscouting.org

National League of American Pen Women

American Pen Women Award: Arts

Type of award: Scholarship.
Intended use: For non-degree study.
Eligibility: Applicant must be female, at least 35. Applicant must be U.S. citizen.
Basis for selection: Competition/talent/interest in visual arts, based on quality, originality, workmanship, creativity, and/or performance. Major/career interest in arts, general.
Application requirements: $8 application fee. Portfolio, proof of eligibility. Proof of age and U.S. citizenship: birth certificate, copy of passport page, or voter's registration with driver's license.
Additional information: Awards offered in even-numbered years. Portfolio must include three four-by-six color prints (no slides) in any media. Photographic entries should submit three four-by-six color or black and white photographs. Submission may not have previously won an award. Awards to be used to further artistic purpose. Include business-size SASE with all information requests. In order to have pictures returned and receive list of winners, applicant should include SASE. Application deadline is October 1 of odd-numbered years. In addition to grant, recipients receive a two-year paid Honorary Associate membership in the NLAPW.

Amount of award:	$1,000
Number of awards:	1
Application deadline:	October 1
Notification begins:	March 1
Total amount awarded:	$1,000

Contact:
(Must send SASE or no reply will be sent.)
National League of American Pen Women
1300 Seventeenth Street, N.W.
Washington, DC 20036-1973
Phone: 410-522-2557

American Pen Women Award: Letters

Type of award: Scholarship.
Intended use: For non-degree study.
Eligibility: Applicant must be female, at least 35. Applicant must be U.S. citizen.
Basis for selection: Competition/talent/interest in writing/journalism, based on quality, originality, workmanship, creativity, and/or performance.
Application requirements: $8 application fee. Portfolio, proof of eligibility. Proof of age and U.S. citizenship: birth

certificate, copy of passport page, or voter's registration and driver's license.
Additional information: Awards offered in even-numbered years. Application deadline is October 1 of odd-numbered years. Applicant may submit essay or short story not exceeding 4,000 words, three poems, television script or play, first chapter of a novel with outline, or an editorial. Submission may not have previously won an award. Awards to be used to further artistic purpose. Include business-size SASE with all information requests. Will return manuscripts if sufficient postage and mailer are sent. Will send list of winners if SASE is sent. In addition to the grant, recipients receive two-year paid Honorary Associate membership in the NLAPW.

Amount of award:	$1,000
Number of awards:	1
Application deadline:	October 1
Notification begins:	March 1
Total amount awarded:	$1,000

Contact:
(Must send SASE or no reply will be sent.)
National League of American Pen Women
1300 Seventeenth Street, N.W.
Washington, DC 20036-1973
Phone: 410-522-2557

American Pen Women Award: Music

Type of award: Scholarship.
Intended use: For non-degree study.
Eligibility: Applicant must be female, at least 35. Applicant must be U.S. citizen.
Basis for selection: Competition/talent/interest in music performance/composition, based on quality, originality, workmanship, creativity, and/or performance. Major/career interest in music.
Application requirements: $8 application fee. Portfolio, proof of eligibility. Proof of U.S. citizenship and age: birth certificate, copy of passport page, or voter's registration with driver's license.
Additional information: Awards offered in even-numbered years. Application deadline is October 1 of odd-numbered years. Applicants must submit two scores of at least 10 minutes and at most 25 minutes. Must not have received previous award for work. One score must have been written within past five years. Awards to be used to further creative purpose. Include business-size SASE with information requests. To have score returned and receive list of winners, include appropriate SASE. In addition to grant, recipient will receive a two-year paid Honorary Associate membership in the NLAPW.

Amount of award:	$1,000
Number of awards:	1
Number of applicants:	7
Application deadline:	October 1
Notification begins:	March 1
Total amount awarded:	$1,000

Contact:
(Must send SASE or no reply will be sent.)
National League of American Pen Women
1300 Seventeenth Avenue, N.W.
Washington, DC 20036-1973
Phone: 410-522-2557

National Merit Scholarship Corporation

Achievement Scholarship Awards

Type of award: Scholarship.
Intended use: For full-time undergraduate study in United States.
Eligibility: Applicant must be African American. Applicant must be U.S. citizen or permanent resident.
Basis for selection: Applicant must demonstrate high academic achievement and leadership.
Application requirements: Recommendations, essay.
Additional information: Selection based on academic ability, school and community activities, test scores, and school recommendations. Students must take PSAT/NMSQT in the proper year of high school (usually junior year). Requirements are published each year in PSAT/NMSQT Student Bulletin which is sent to high schools for distribution to students in advance of October test administration. Some 1,500 of highest scoring participants are named Semifinalists; scholarship applications are sent to these students through their high schools. Approximately 700 Achievement Scholarship awards are offered for full-time undergraduate study. There are 450 $2,500 single-payment awards for which all Finalists compete. Majority of remaining Achievement Scholarship awards are renewable for four years of undergraduate study and offered to Finalists who have qualifications that particularly interest corporate or college sponsors of scholarships. Corporate-sponsored scholarships may be designated for Finalists who are children of company's employees, residents of sponsor organization's service areas, or Finalists planning particular college major. The names Achievement Scholarship and Achievement Scholar are service marks of National Merit Scholarship Corporation.

Number of awards:	700
Number of applicants:	110,000
Notification begins:	February 16
Total amount awarded:	$2,500,000

Contact:
National Achievement Scholarship Program
1560 Sherman Avenue
Suite 200
Evanston, IL 60201-4897
Web: www.nationalmerit.org

Merit Scholarship Program Awards

Type of award: Scholarship.
Intended use: For full-time undergraduate study in United States.
Eligibility: Applicant must be high school junior. Applicant must be U.S. citizen or permanent resident.
Basis for selection: Applicant must demonstrate high academic achievement and leadership.
Application requirements: Recommendations, essay.
Additional information: Competition is open to all U.S. high school students who take PSAT/NMSQT in proper year in high school and meet other participation requirements. Requirements are published each year in PSAT/NMSQT Student Bulletin, which is sent to high schools for distribution to students in advance of October test administration. Some 16,000 of highest scoring participants are designated Semifinalists, on state representational basis. Applications will be sent to these students through their schools. Finalists are considered for Merit Scholarship awards based on academic and other requirements, and winners are chosen on basis of abilities, skills, and accomplishments. About 7,900 Merit Scholarship awards of three types are offered annually. 2,500 single-payment $2,500 scholarships are awarded for which all Finalists compete. More than 4,000 four-year Merit Scholarship awards are financed by colleges and universities for Finalists who must attend sponsor institution. About 1,200 Merit Scholarship awards are sponsored by corporations and other business organizations for Finalists who meet sponsor's preferential criteria. In addition, approximately 1,700 Special Scholarships for high performers are awarded. Permanent residents eligible if in the process of becoming U.S. citizen. The names Merit Scholarship, Merit Scholar and National Merit are service marks of National Merit Scholarship Corporation.

Number of awards:	9,600
Notification begins:	March 9
Total amount awarded:	$45,000,000

Contact:
National Merit Scholarship Program
1560 Sherman Avenue
Suite 200
Evanston, IL 60201-4897
Web: www.nationalmerit.org

National Press Photographers Foundation, Inc.

Bob East Scholarship Fund

Type of award: Scholarship.
Intended use: For undergraduate or graduate study in United States.
Eligibility: Applicant must be U.S. citizen or permanent resident residing in Florida.
Basis for selection: Major/career interest in journalism.
Additional information: Open to students studying Newspaper Photojournalism. Preference given to Florida Residents.

Application deadline:	February 1
Total amount awarded:	$1,500

Contact:
National press Photographers Foundation,Inc.
3200 Croasdaile Dr. # 306
Durham, NC 27705
Phone: 919-383-7246

National Restaurant Association Educational Foundation

Undergraduate Academic Scholarship for College Students

Type of award: Scholarship.

Intended use: For sophomore, junior, senior or post-bachelor's certificate study at accredited vocational, 2-year or 4-year institution in United States.
Eligibility: Applicant must be U.S. citizen or permanent resident.
Basis for selection: Major/career interest in food production/management/services; culinary arts; hotel/restaurant management; hospitality administration/management or food science/technology. Applicant must demonstrate financial need and high academic achievement.
Application requirements: Recommendations, transcript, proof of eligibility.
Additional information: Applicant must have completed at least one term of two- or four-year degree program. Must have performed minimum 750 hours food service/hospitality-related work experience. Minimum 2.75 GPA. For more information on program requirements and to apply electronically, visit www.fastweb.com.

Application deadline:	November 30, May 4
Notification begins:	December 22, June 29
Total amount awarded:	$2,000

Contact:
National Restaurant Assn. Educational Foundation
Scholarships Program Coordinator
250 S. Wacker Drive, Suite 1400
Chicago, Il 60606-5834
Phone: 800-765-2122 ext. 733
Web: www.edfound.org

Undergraduate Academic Scholarships for High School Students

Type of award: Scholarship.
Intended use: For undergraduate study at accredited postsecondary institution in United States.
Eligibility: Applicant must be high school senior. Applicant must be U.S. citizen or permanent resident.
Basis for selection: Major/career interest in food production/management/services; culinary arts; hotel/restaurant management; hospitality administration/management or food science/technology. Applicant must demonstrate seriousness of purpose.
Application requirements: Recommendations, transcript, proof of eligibility.
Additional information: Applicant must be accepted to foodservice-related postsecondary program. Must have performed minimum 250 hours food service/hospitality-related work experience. Minimum 2.75 GPA. For more information on program requirements and to apply electronically, visit www.fastweb.com.

Amount of award:	$2,000
Application deadline:	April 16
Notification begins:	May 28

Contact:
Scholarships Program Coordinator
250 South Wacker Drive
Suite 1400
Chicago, IL 60606-5834
Phone: 800-765-2122 ext. 733
Web: www.cdfound.org

Undergraduate Merit Scholarship for High School Seniors

Type of award: Scholarship.

Intended use: For full-time undergraduate study at vocational, 2-year or 4-year institution. Designated institutions: Foodservice-related postsecondary programs.
Eligibility: Applicant must be high school senior.
Basis for selection: Major/career interest in food science/technology; hotel/restaurant management; food science/technology; communications or marketing.
Application requirements: Recommendations, transcript. Must have performed minimum 250 hours of restaurant/foodservice related work. Must be accepted into accredited restaurant/food service related postsecondary program and plan to enroll in minimum of two terms for following school year.
Additional information: Minimum 2.75 high school GPA required. Applicants with majors/career interest in Environmental Health and Facilities Design also eligible. An equal opportunity scholarship program. To apply online, visit www.fastweb.com.

Amount of award:	$2,000
Application deadline:	April 16
Notification begins:	May 28

Contact:
National Restaurant Association Educational Foundation
Scholarships Program Coordinator
250 S. Wacker Drive, Suite 1400
Chicago, IL 60606-5834
Phone: 800-765-2122 ext. 733
Fax: 312-715-1362
Web: www.edfound.org

National Rifle Association

Jeanne E. Bray Law Enforcement Dependents Scholarship

Type of award: Scholarship.
Intended use: For undergraduate or graduate study at accredited 2-year, 4-year or graduate institution in United States.
Eligibility: Applicant or parent must be member/participant of National Rifle Association. Applicant must be U.S. citizen.
Application requirements: Recommendations, essay, transcript, proof of eligibility. SAT I combined score of 950 or ACT score of 25.
Additional information: Number of awards varies. Parent must be active, disabled, deceased, discharged, or retired law enforcement officer and member of National Rifle Association. Applicant must also be NRA member. Minimum 2.5 GPA. Award given for up to four years or until applicable monetary cap is reached, as long as student maintains eligibility.

Amount of award:	$500-$2,000
Application deadline:	November 15
Notification begins:	February 15

Contact:
National Rifle Association, Attn: Sandy S. Elkin
Jeanne E. Bray Memorial Scholarship
11250 Waples Mill Road
Fairfax, VA 22030
Web: www.nra.org

National Roofing Foundation

Roofing Industry Scholarship

Type of award: Scholarship, renewable.
Intended use: For full-time undergraduate study at vocational, 2-year or 4-year institution.
Eligibility: Applicant or parent must be member/participant of National Roofing Contractors Association.
Basis for selection: Applicant must demonstrate high academic achievement, depth of character and seriousness of purpose.
Application requirements: Recommendations, essay.
Additional information: Number of awards given varies from five to ten each year. Applicant must be employee, immediate family member of employee or immediate family member of contractor-member of the National Roofing Contractors Association.

Amount of award:	$1,000
Number of applicants:	100
Application deadline:	January 31
Notification begins:	May 1

Contact:
National Roofing Foundation
10255 West Higgins Road
Suite 600
Rosemont, IL 60018
Phone: 847-299-9070
Fax: 847-299-1183

National Science Teachers Association

Toshiba ExploraVision Award

Type of award: Scholarship.
Intended use: For undergraduate or non-degree study in United States or Canada.
Eligibility: Applicant must be enrolled in high school.
Basis for selection: Competition/talent/interest in science project, based on scientific accuracy, creativity, communication and feasibility of vision. Major/career interest in science, general.
Application requirements: Essay. Description paper, five graphics simulating web pages. Applicant must be enrolled in K-12 School in U.S. or Canada. Applications must be full-time students, no older than 21 years of age.
Additional information: Technology study project. Each student member of first place team receives $10,000 savings bond, each student member of second-place team receives $5,000 savings bond, and regional winners receive Toshiba digital camera. Contact sponsor for entry kit. Alternate phone no.: 800-EXPLOR-9. E-mail: exploravision@nsta.org. Visit Website to download application.

Amount of award:	$5,000-$10,000
Application deadline:	February 1
Notification begins:	March 1
Total amount awarded:	$340,000

Contact:
Toshiba/NSTA ExploraVision Awards
1840 Wilson Boulevard
Arlington, VA 22201-3000
Phone: 703-243-7100
Web: www.toshiba.com/tai/exploravision

National Sculpture Society

Sculpture Society Scholarship

Type of award: Scholarship, renewable.
Intended use: For undergraduate, master's or doctoral study at postsecondary institution in United States.
Eligibility: Applicant must be U.S. citizen or permanent resident.
Basis for selection: Competition/talent/interest in Visual arts, based on slides or photos of figurative or representational sculpture created by the applicant. Major/career interest in arts, general. Applicant must demonstrate financial need.
Application requirements: Portfolio, recommendations, essay, proof of eligibility. 8x10-inch photographs of sculpture, proof of financial need, letter of background and interest in sculpture.
Additional information: Must be studying figurative sculpture. Number of awards varies. Please include SASE.

Amount of award:	$1,000
Number of awards:	6
Number of applicants:	40
Application deadline:	May 31
Notification begins:	June 15
Total amount awarded:	$6,000

Contact:
Send SASE to: National Sculpture Society
237 Park Avenue, Ground Floor
New York, NY 10017
Phone: 212-764-5645
Web: www.NationalSculpture.org

National Security Agency

National Security Agency Undergraduate Training Program

Type of award: Scholarship, renewable.
Intended use: For full-time undergraduate study at accredited 4-year institution in United States.
Eligibility: Applicant must be high school senior. Applicant must be U.S. citizen.
Basis for selection: Major/career interest in computer/information sciences; mathematics; engineering, computer; engineering, electrical/electronic; engineering or foreign languages. Applicant must demonstrate high academic achievement, depth of character, leadership, patriotism, seriousness of purpose and service orientation.
Application requirements: Interview, recommendations, transcript, proof of eligibility. Must have at least 1100 on SAT or 25 on ACT. Must undergo polygraph and security screening.
Additional information: Must have 3.0 GPA. Current applications available after September 1 of each year.

Amount of award:	Full tuition
Number of awards:	20
Number of applicants:	600
Application deadline:	November 30
Notification begins:	April 1

Contact:
National Security Agency Undergraduate Training Program
9800 Savage Road
MB3-UTP, Suite 6779
Fort Meade, MD 20755-6779
Phone: 800-669-0703
Fax: 410-854-4593

National Semiconductor Corporation

Charles E. Sporck Scholarship Program

Type of award: Scholarship, renewable.
Intended use: For freshman study at 2-year or 4-year institution.
Eligibility: Applicant or parent must be employed by National Semiconductor Corporation. Applicant must be high school senior.
Additional information: For further information or an application, contact National Semiconductor Corporation directly.

Amount of award:	$2,000

National Society of Accountants

National Society of Accountants Scholarship

Type of award: Scholarship.
Intended use: For undergraduate study at accredited vocational, 2-year or 4-year institution in United States.
Eligibility: Applicant must be U.S. citizen, international student or Canadian citizen.
Basis for selection: Major/career interest in accounting. Applicant must demonstrate financial need, high academic achievement and leadership.
Application requirements: Transcript. Application, appraisal form. Students applying in college freshman year must submit high school transcript.
Additional information: Minimum 3.0 GPA. Competition's most outstanding student receives additional stipend. Applications available on Website in October, or call or write sponsor.

Amount of award:	$500-$1,000
Number of awards:	40
Number of applicants:	1,400
Application deadline:	March 10
Total amount awarded:	$40,000

Contact:
National Society of Accountants
Scholarship Foundation
1010 North Fairfax Street
Alexandria, VA 22314-1574
Phone: 800-966-6679
Fax: 703-549-2984
Web: www.nsacct.org.

National Society of Black Engineers

Fulfilling the Legacy Scholarship

Type of award: Scholarship, renewable.
Intended use: For undergraduate or graduate study at accredited postsecondary institution.
Eligibility: Applicant or parent must be member/participant of National Society of Black Engineers. Applicant must be African American. Applicant must be U.S. citizen.
Basis for selection: Major/career interest in engineering. Applicant must demonstrate high academic achievement, depth of character, leadership, seriousness of purpose and service orientation.
Application requirements: Portfolio, recommendations, essay, transcript, proof of eligibility.
Additional information: Number of awards and amount depends on the total contributions made by members and others.

Application deadline:	December 3

Contact:
National Society of Black Engineers
1425 Duke St.
Alexandria, VA 22314
Phone: 703-549-2207
Fax: 703-683-5312
Web: www.nsbe.org

The IBM Student Research Scholarship

Type of award: Scholarship.
Intended use: For sophomore or junior study at accredited postsecondary institution.
Eligibility: Applicant or parent must be member/participant of National Society of Black Engineers. Applicant must be African American. Applicant must be U.S. citizen.
Basis for selection: Major/career interest in chemistry; physics; engineering; mathematics; materials science or computer/information sciences. Applicant must demonstrate high academic achievement and seriousness of purpose.
Application requirements: Recommendations, essay, transcript, proof of eligibility. Essay must describe research interests and how opportunity will serve applicant's career goals and IBM.
Additional information: Award is $2,500 for two years. Must be able to accept paid summer internship at IBM's Almaden Research Center in San Jose, CA.

Amount of award:	$2,500
Application deadline:	November 30

Scholarships

Contact:
National Society of Black Engineers
IBM Research Scholarship Program
1454 Duke Street
Alexandria, VA 22314
Phone: 703-549-2207
Fax: 703-683-5312
Web: www.nsbe.org

National Society of Black Engineers/GE African American Forum Scholarship

Type of award: Scholarship, renewable.
Intended use: For sophomore, junior or senior study at postsecondary institution.
Eligibility: Applicant or parent must be member/participant of National Society of Black Engineers. Applicant must be African American. Applicant must be U.S. citizen.
Basis for selection: Major/career interest in business or engineering. Applicant must demonstrate high academic achievement.
Application requirements: Transcript, proof of eligibility.
Additional information: Minimum 3.2 GPA required. Applicant must have completed at least 12 hours of credit in major or concentration by spring of sophomore year. Funded by General Electric employees and Foundation.

Application deadline:	December 1
Total amount awarded:	$1,500

Contact:
National Society of Black Engineers
1454 Duke Street
Alexandria, VA 22314
Phone: 703-549-2207
Fax: 703-683-5312
Web: www.nsbe.org

NSBE Fellows Scholarship

Type of award: Scholarship, renewable.
Intended use: For full-time undergraduate or graduate study at accredited 4-year or graduate institution in United States.
Eligibility: Applicant or parent must be member/participant of National Society of Black Engineers. Applicant must be African American. Applicant must be U.S. citizen.
Basis for selection: Major/career interest in engineering. Applicant must demonstrate high academic achievement, depth of character, leadership, seriousness of purpose and service orientation.
Application requirements: Recommendations, essay, transcript, proof of eligibility.
Additional information: Inteded for those applicants who have dedicated time to the Society's cause and other community organizations, and show promise in their studies and professional pursuits.

Amount of award:	$1,500-$2,500
Number of awards:	75
Application deadline:	December 3

Contact:
National Society of Black Engineers
1454 Duke St.
Alexandria, VA 22314
Phone: 703-549-2207
Fax: 703-683-5312
Web: www.nsbe.org

National Society of Professional Engineers

National Society of Professional Engineers Auxiliary National Scholarship

Type of award: Scholarship, renewable.
Intended use: For undergraduate study at 4-year institution in United States. Designated institutions: ABET-accredited institutions.
Eligibility: Applicant must be high school senior. Applicant must be U.S. citizen or permanent resident.
Basis for selection: Major/career interest in engineering. Applicant must demonstrate high academic achievement.
Additional information: Application available at Website. Award is $1,000 per year for four years. Contact respective state society to determine program participation. Not all states accept standard Website application.

Amount of award:	$4,000
Number of awards:	1
Application deadline:	December 1
Total amount awarded:	$4,000

Contact:
National Society of Professional Engineers
Education Services Department
1420 King Street
Alexandria, VA 22314-2794
Web: www.nspe.org/students

National Society of the Sons of the American Revolution

Sons of the American Revolution Eagle Scout Scholarship

Type of award: Scholarship.
Intended use: For undergraduate study.
Eligibility: Applicant or parent must be member/participant of Boy Scouts of America, Eagle Scouts. Applicant must be male, no older than 18.
Basis for selection: Applicant must demonstrate depth of character, leadership and patriotism.
Application requirements: Essay, proof of eligibility. Application form and four generation ancestor chart.
Additional information: Open to all Eagle Scouts currently registered in active unit who have not reached their 19th birthday during the year of application. Applicant must research and prepare four generation ancestor chart. Competition conducted in three phases: Chapter (local), Society (state), and National. Applicants need only apply at Chapter level. Winners at local level entered into state competition; state winners used in National contest. Number of awards varies. State awards may also be available. For more information contact State Eagle Scout Chairman. Visit Website for more information and to download application.

Amount of award:	$2,000-$8,000
Number of awards:	3
Application deadline:	December 31
Total amount awarded:	$14,000

Contact:
Web: www.sar.org

National Space Society

National Space Society Research Scholarship Program

Type of award: Research grant.
Intended use: For undergraduate or graduate study at 4-year or graduate institution.
Basis for selection: Major/career interest in geology/earth sciences; geophysics or astronomy. Applicant must demonstrate seriousness of purpose.
Application requirements: Recommendations, transcript, research proposal. Resume.
Additional information: Student must be working specifically on data analysis related to identification and retrieval of lunar resources. Work to be performed during 6-week summer scholarship period. Applicants must have support of a research advisor. Unpaid internships at NSS are also available.

Amount of award:	$2,000
Number of awards:	3

Contact:
National Space Society
Internship/Scholarship Coordinator
600 Pennsylvania Avenue, Suite 201
Washington, DC 20003
Phone: 202-543-1900
Fax: 202-546-4189
Web: www.nss.org

National Speakers Association

National Speakers Association Scholarship

Type of award: Scholarship.
Intended use: For full-time junior, senior or graduate study.
Basis for selection: Major/career interest in communications; public relations or radio/television/film. Applicant must demonstrate high academic achievement, leadership and seriousness of purpose.
Application requirements: Recommendations, essay, transcript.
Additional information: Applicant must have an above-average academic record and major or minor in speech. Complete application can be found on Website under "About NSA."

Amount of award:	$4,000
Number of awards:	4
Application deadline:	June 1
Notification begins:	September 1
Total amount awarded:	$16,000

Contact:
National Speakers Association
1500 South Priest Drive
Tempe, AZ 85281
Phone: 480-968-2552
Fax: 480-968-0911
Web: www.nsaspeaker.org

National Stone, Sand & Gravel Association

Quarry Engineering Scholarship

Type of award: Scholarship.
Intended use: For full-time junior, senior or graduate study.
Eligibility: Applicant must be U.S. citizen or permanent resident.
Basis for selection: Major/career interest in engineering, mining; engineering, structural; engineering, civil; engineering, mechanical or engineering, electrical/electronic. Applicant must demonstrate high academic achievement, depth of character, leadership, seriousness of purpose and service orientation.
Application requirements: Recommendations, essay. Recommendations must come from faculty advisor. Essay should be 300-500 words on applicant's plans for a career in aggregate industry.
Additional information: Visit Website for application.

Amount of award:	$2,500
Number of awards:	8
Application deadline:	May 30
Total amount awarded:	$20,000

Contact:
National Stone, Sand & Gravel Association
Attn: Scholarship Administator
2101 Wilson Blvd., Ste. 100
Arlington, VA 22201
Phone: 703-525-8788 or 1-800-342-1415
Web: www.nssga.org

National Tourism Foundation

Bill Carpenter Memorial Certificate School Scholarship

Type of award: Scholarship.
Intended use: For full-time undergraduate certificate study at accredited vocational institution.
Basis for selection: Major/career interest in tourism/travel or culinary arts. Applicant must demonstrate high academic achievement.
Application requirements: Recommendations, essay, transcript, proof of eligibility. Resume, application, as well as travel curriculum in which applicant is involved and proof of enrollment. Minimum 3.0 GPA.
Additional information: This award does not apply for students attending a two-year or technical institution. This award is for use in certificate schools in the travel and tourism profession only.

Amount of award: $500
Application deadline: April 16
Contact:
National Tourism Foundation
546 East Main Street
Lexington, KY 40508
Phone: 800-682-8886
Web: www.ntfonline.org

Dr. Tom Anderson Memorial Scholarship

Type of award: Scholarship.
Intended use: For full-time junior or senior study at 4-year institution.
Eligibility: Applicant must be U.S. citizen, permanent resident, international student or Canadian citizen.
Basis for selection: Major/career interest in tourism/travel or culinary arts. Applicant must demonstrate high academic achievement.
Application requirements: Recommendations, essay, transcript. Resume and application. Minimum 3.0 GPA.
Amount of award: $2,000
Application deadline: April 16
Contact:
National Tourism Foundation
546 East Main Street
Lexington, KY 40508
Phone: 800-682-8886
Web: www.ntfonline.org

Eric and Bette Friedhiem Scholarship

Type of award: Scholarship.
Intended use: For full-time junior or senior study at 4-year institution.
Eligibility: Applicant must be U.S. citizen, permanent resident, international student or Canadian citizen.
Basis for selection: Major/career interest in tourism/travel or culinary arts. Applicant must demonstrate high academic achievement.
Application requirements: Recommendations, essay, transcript. Resume and application. Minimum 3.0 GPA.
Amount of award: $500
Application deadline: April 16
Contact:
National Tourism Foundation
546 East Main Street
Lexington, KY 40508
Phone: 800-682-8886
Web: www.ntfonline.org

H. Neil Mecaskey Scholarship

Type of award: Scholarship.
Intended use: For full-time junior or senior study at 4-year institution.
Eligibility: Applicant must be U.S. citizen, permanent resident, international student or Canadian citizen.
Basis for selection: Major/career interest in tourism/travel or culinary arts. Applicant must demonstrate high academic achievement.
Application requirements: Recommendations, essay, transcript. Resume and application. Minimum 3.0 GPA.
Additional information: Must be enrolled in a four-year institution at time of application.

Amount of award: $500
Application deadline: April 16
Contact:
National Tourism Foundation
546 East Main Street
Lexington, KY 40508
Phone: 800-682-8886
Web: www.ntfonline.org

Louise Dessureault Memorial Scholarship

Type of award: Scholarship.
Intended use: For full-time junior or senior study at 4-year institution in or outside United States.
Eligibility: Applicant must be international student or resident of Canada.
Basis for selection: Major/career interest in tourism/travel or culinary arts. Applicant must demonstrate high academic achievement.
Application requirements: Recommendations, essay, transcript. Resume and application. Minimum 3.0 GPA.
Amount of award: $500
Application deadline: April 16
Contact:
National Tourism Foundation
546 East Main Street
Lexington, KY 40508
Phone: 800-682-8886
Web: www.ntfonline.org

Tourism Foundation Alabama-Birmingham Legacy

Type of award: Scholarship.
Intended use: For full-time junior or senior study at 2-year or 4-year institution in United States.
Eligibility: Applicant must be residing in Alabama.
Basis for selection: Major/career interest in tourism/travel; hotel/restaurant management or culinary arts. Applicant must demonstrate high academic achievement.
Application requirements: Recommendations, essay, transcript, proof of eligibility. Resume and application. Minimum 3.0 GPA.
Amount of award: $1,000
Application deadline: April 16
Contact:
National Tourism Foundation
546 East Main Street
Lexington, KY 40508
Phone: 800-682-8886
Web: www.ntfonline.org

Tourism Foundation Cleveland Legacy 1 Scholarship

Type of award: Scholarship.
Intended use: For full-time junior or senior study at 4-year institution in United States.
Eligibility: Applicant must be U.S. citizen residing in Ohio.
Basis for selection: Major/career interest in tourism/travel; hotel/restaurant management or culinary arts. Applicant must demonstrate high academic achievement.
Application requirements: Recommendations, essay, transcript. Resume and application. Minimum 3.0 GPA.

Scholarships

Amount of award:	$500
Application deadline:	April 16

Contact:
National Tourism Foundation
546 East Main Street
Lexington, KY 40508
Phone: 800-682-8886
Web: www.ntfonline.org

Tourism Foundation Cleveland Legacy 2 Scholarship

Type of award: Scholarship.
Intended use: For full-time junior or senior study at 2-year institution in United States.
Eligibility: Applicant must be U.S. citizen residing in Ohio.
Basis for selection: Major/career interest in tourism/travel; hotel/restaurant management or culinary arts. Applicant must demonstrate high academic achievement.
Application requirements: Recommendations, essay, transcript. Resume and application. Minimum 3.0 GPA.
Additional information: Must be enrolled in a two-year college at time of application.

Amount of award:	$500
Application deadline:	April 16

Contact:
National Tourism Foundation
546 East Main Street
Lexington, KY 40508
Phone: 800-682-8886
Web: www.ntfonline.org

Tourism Foundation Connecticut Scholarship

Type of award: Scholarship.
Intended use: For full-time junior or senior study at 4-year institution in United States.
Eligibility: Applicant must be residing in Connecticut.
Basis for selection: Major/career interest in tourism/travel; hotel/restaurant management or culinary arts. Applicant must demonstrate high academic achievement.
Application requirements: Recommendations, essay, transcript. Minimum 3.0 GPA.
Additional information: Must be enrolled in a four-year institution at time of application.

Amount of award:	$1,000
Application deadline:	April 16

Contact:
National Tourism Foundation
546 East Main Street
Lexington, KY 40508
Phone: 800-682-8886
Web: www.ntfonline.org

Tourism Foundation Florida Scholarship

Type of award: Scholarship.
Intended use: For full-time junior or senior study at 4-year institution in United States.
Eligibility: Applicant must be residing in Florida.
Basis for selection: Major/career interest in tourism/travel; hotel/restaurant management or culinary arts. Applicant must demonstrate high academic achievement.

Application requirements: Recommendations, essay, transcript. Minimun 3.0 GPA.
Additional information: Must be enrolled in a four-year institution at time of application.

Amount of award:	$500
Application deadline:	April 16

Contact:
National Tourism Foundation
546 East Main Street
Lexington, KY 40508
Phone: 800-682-8886
Web: www.ntfonline.org

Tourism Foundation Michigan Scholarship

Type of award: Scholarship.
Intended use: For full-time junior or senior study at 4-year institution. Designated institutions: Michigan.
Eligibility: Applicant must be residing in Michigan.
Basis for selection: Major/career interest in tourism/travel; hotel/restaurant management or culinary arts. Applicant must demonstrate high academic achievement.
Application requirements: Recommendations, essay, transcript. Resume and application. Minimum 3.0 GPA.
Additional information: Must be permanent resident of or attending school in Michigan.

Amount of award:	$1,000
Application deadline:	April 16

Contact:
National Tourism Foundation
546 East Main Street
Lexington, KY 40508
Phone: 800-682-8886
Web: www.ntfonline.org

Tourism Foundation Montana Scholarship

Type of award: Scholarship.
Intended use: For full-time junior or senior study at 2-year or 4-year institution in or outside United States. Designated institutions: North America.
Eligibility: Applicant must be residing in Montana.
Basis for selection: Major/career interest in tourism/travel; hotel/restaurant management or culinary arts. Applicant must demonstrate high academic achievement.
Application requirements: Recommendations, essay, transcript. Resume and application. Minimun 3.0 GPA.

Amount of award:	$500
Application deadline:	April 16

Contact:
National Tourism Foundation
546 East Main Street
Lexington, KY 40508
Phone: 800-682-8886
Web: www.ntfonline.org

Tourism Foundation Nebraska-Lois Johnson Scholarship

Type of award: Scholarship.
Intended use: For full-time junior or senior study at 2-year or 4-year institution in or outside United States.
Eligibility: Applicant must be residing in Nebraska.

Basis for selection: Major/career interest in tourism/travel; hotel/restaurant management or culinary arts. Applicant must demonstrate high academic achievement.

Application requirements: Recommendations, essay, transcript. Resume and application. Minimum 3.0 GPA.

 Amount of award: $500
 Application deadline: April 16
Contact:
National Tourism Foundation
546 East Main Street
Lexington, KY 40508
Phone: 800-682-8886
Web: www.ntfonline.org

Tourism Foundation New Jersey 1 Scholarship

Type of award: Scholarship.
Intended use: For full-time junior or senior study at 4-year institution in or outside United States.
Eligibility: Applicant must be residing in New Jersey.
Basis for selection: Major/career interest in tourism/travel; hotel/restaurant management or culinary arts. Applicant must demonstrate high academic achievement.
Application requirements: Recommendations, essay, transcript. Resume and application. Minimum 3.0 GPA.
Additional information: Applicant must be enrolled in a four-year college.

 Amount of award: $1,000
 Application deadline: April 16
Contact:
National Tourism Foundation
546 East Main Street
Lexington, KY 40508
Phone: 800-682-8886
Web: www.ntfonline.org

Tourism Foundation New Jersey 2 Scholarship

Type of award: Scholarship.
Intended use: For full-time junior or senior study at 2-year institution in or outside United States.
Eligibility: Applicant must be residing in New Jersey.
Basis for selection: Major/career interest in tourism/travel; hotel/restaurant management or culinary arts. Applicant must demonstrate high academic achievement.
Application requirements: Recommendations, essay, transcript. Resume and application. Minimum 3.0 GPA.

 Amount of award: $500
 Application deadline: April 16
Contact:
National Tourism Foundation
546 East Main Street
Lexington, KY 40508
Phone: 800-682-8886
Web: www.ntfonline.org

Tourism Foundation New York Scholarship

Type of award: Scholarship.
Intended use: For full-time junior or senior study at 4-year institution in United States. Designated institutions: New York schools.
Eligibility: Applicant must be residing in New York.

Basis for selection: Major/career interest in tourism/travel; hotel/restaurant management or culinary arts. Applicant must demonstrate high academic achievement.

Application requirements: Recommendations, essay, transcript. Resume and application. Minimum 3.0 GPA.

Additional information: Must be enrolled in four-year institution at time of application. Must have essay signed by school's Tour and Travel Department Head. Must be a resident of New York and/or full time student in New York.

 Amount of award: $500
 Application deadline: April 16
Contact:
National Tourism Foundation
546 East Main Street
Lexington, KY 40508
Phone: 800-682-8886
Web: www.ntfonline.org

Tourism Foundation North Carolina Scholarship

Type of award: Scholarship.
Intended use: For full-time junior or senior study at 4-year institution in or outside United States.
Eligibility: Applicant must be residing in North Carolina.
Basis for selection: Major/career interest in tourism/travel; hotel/restaurant management or culinary arts. Applicant must demonstrate high academic achievement.
Application requirements: Recommendations, essay, transcript. Resume and application. Minimum 3.0 GPA.

 Amount of award: $500
 Application deadline: April 16
Contact:
National Tourism Foundation
546 East Main Street
Lexington, KY 40508
Phone: 800-682-8886
Web: www.ntfonline.org

Tourism Foundation Ohio Scholarship

Type of award: Scholarship.
Intended use: For full-time junior or senior study at 2-year or 4-year institution in or outside United States.
Eligibility: Applicant must be residing in Ohio.
Basis for selection: Major/career interest in tourism/travel; hotel/restaurant management or culinary arts. Applicant must demonstrate high academic achievement.
Application requirements: Recommendations, essay, transcript. Resume and application. Minimum 3.0 GPA.

 Amount of award: $1,000
 Application deadline: April 16
Contact:
National Tourism Foundation
546 East Main Street
Lexington, KY 40508
Phone: 800-682-8886
Web: www.ntfonline.org

Tourism Foundation Quebec Scholarship

Type of award: Scholarship.
Intended use: For full-time junior, senior, master's or doctoral study at 4-year or graduate institution in Quebec, Canada.

Eligibility: Applicant must be international student, Residents of Canada; Quebec.
Basis for selection: Competition/talent/interest in study abroad. Major/career interest in tourism/travel; hotel/restaurant management or culinary arts. Applicant must demonstrate high academic achievement.
Application requirements: Recommendations, essay, transcript. Resume and application. Minimum 3.0 GPA.
Additional information: For persons residing or studying in Quebec only.

Amount of award:	$500
Application deadline:	April 16

Contact:
National Tourism Foundation
546 East Main Street
Lexington, KY 40508
Phone: 800-682-8886
Fax: 859-226-4437
Web: www.ntfonline.org

Tourism Foundation Tulsa Scholarship

Type of award: Scholarship.
Intended use: For full-time junior or senior study at 4-year institution in or outside United States. Designated institutions: Institutions in Oklahoma only.
Eligibility: Applicant must be U.S. citizen or permanent resident residing in Oklahoma.
Basis for selection: Major/career interest in tourism/travel; hotel/restaurant management or culinary arts. Applicant must demonstrate high academic achievement.
Application requirements: Recommendations, essay, transcript. Resume and application. Minimum 3.0 GPA.
Additional information: Must be resident of or studying in Oklahoma and be enrolled in a four-year institution at time of application.

Amount of award:	$500
Application deadline:	April 16

Contact:
National Tourism Foundation
546 East Main Street
Lexington, KY 40508
Phone: 800-682-8886
Fax: 859-226-4437
Web: www.ntfonline.org

Tourism Foundation Wyoming Scholarship

Type of award: Scholarship.
Intended use: For full-time junior or senior study at 2-year or 4-year institution.
Eligibility: Applicant must be U.S. citizen or permanent resident residing in Wyoming.
Basis for selection: Major/career interest in tourism/travel or culinary arts. Applicant must demonstrate high academic achievement.
Application requirements: Recommendations, essay, transcript. Resume and application.

Amount of award:	$1,000
Application deadline:	April 16

Contact:
National Tourism Foundation
546 East Main Street
Lexington, KY 40508
Phone: 800-682-8886
Web: www.ntfonline.org

Tourism Foundation Yellow Ribbon Scholarship

Type of award: Scholarship.
Intended use: For full-time undergraduate study at postsecondary institution in or outside United States. Designated institutions: Any in North America.
Eligibility: Applicant must be visually impaired, hearing impaired or physically challenged. Applicant must be high school senior. Applicant must be U.S. citizen, permanent resident, international student or Canadian citizen.
Basis for selection: Major/career interest in tourism/travel or culinary arts. Applicant must demonstrate high academic achievement.
Application requirements: Recommendations, essay, transcript. Resume and application. Minimum 3.0 GPA.

Amount of award:	$5,000
Application deadline:	April 16

Contact:
National Tourism Foundation
546 East Main Street
Lexington, KY 40508
Phone: 800-682-8886
Web: www.ntfonline.org

Treadway Inns, Hotels, and Resorts Scholarship

Type of award: Scholarship.
Intended use: For full-time junior or senior study at 4-year institution in or outside United States. Designated institutions: Any in North America.
Eligibility: Applicant must be U.S. citizen, permanent resident, international student or Canadian citizen.
Basis for selection: Major/career interest in tourism/travel or culinary arts. Applicant must demonstrate high academic achievement.
Application requirements: Recommendations, essay, transcript. Resume and application. Minimum 3.0 GPA.
Additional information: Must be attending a four-year institution at time of application.

Amount of award:	$500
Application deadline:	April 16

Contact:
National Tourism Foundation
546 East Main Street
Lexington, KY 40508
Phone: 800-682-8886
Fax: 859-226-4437
Web: www.ntfonline.org

Weeta F. Colebank Scholarship

Type of award: Scholarship.
Intended use: For full-time junior or senior study at 4-year institution in United States. Designated institutions: Mississippi schools only.
Eligibility: Applicant must be U.S. citizen or permanent resident residing in Mississippi.

Basis for selection: Major/career interest in tourism/travel or culinary arts. Applicant must demonstrate high academic achievement.
Application requirements: Recommendations, essay, transcript. Resume and application. Minimum 3.0 GPA.
Additional information: Must be a resident of and studying in Mississippi and be enrolled in a four-year institution at time of application.

Amount of award:	$1,000
Application deadline:	April 16

Contact:
National Tourism Foundation
546 East Main Street
Lexington, KY 40508
Phone: 800-682-8886
Web: www.ntfonline.org

National Urban League

American Chemical Society Minority Scholars Program

Type of award: Scholarship.
Intended use: For full-time undergraduate study at accredited 2-year or 4-year institution in United States.
Eligibility: Applicant must be African American, Mexican American, Hispanic American or Puerto Rican. Applicant must be U.S. citizen or permanent resident.
Basis for selection: Major/career interest in chemistry; biochemistry or engineering, chemical. Applicant must demonstrate financial need, high academic achievement and seriousness of purpose.
Application requirements: Recommendations, transcript.
Additional information: Open to students planning to pursue full-time study in chemicals-related field, including two-year chemical technology programs.

Amount of award:	$2,500
Number of awards:	75
Application deadline:	February 15

Contact:
National Urban League Scholarship Programs
120 Wall Street
New York, NY 10005
Phone: 888-839-0467
Web: www.nul.org

Freddie Mac Scholarships

Type of award: Scholarship, renewable.
Intended use: For freshman or sophomore study at accredited 2-year or 4-year institution in United States.
Eligibility: Applicant must be African American. Applicant must be high school senior. Applicant must be U.S. citizen or permanent resident.
Basis for selection: Applicant must demonstrate financial need, depth of character and seriousness of purpose.
Additional information: Scholarships awarded to students from low- and moderate-income families in urban communities. Students must demonstrate potential for success in competitive academic environment. Initial funding $5,000 per year for first two years of college study.

Amount of award:	$5,000
Number of awards:	15
Application deadline:	January 15

Contact:
National Urban League Scholarship Programs
120 Wall St.
New York, NY 10005
Phone: 888-839-0467
Web: www.nul.org

Gillette/National Urban League Minority Intern Scholarship

Type of award: Scholarship.
Intended use: For full-time junior study at accredited 4-year institution.
Eligibility: Applicant must be Alaskan native, Asian American, African American, Mexican American, Hispanic American, Puerto Rican or American Indian.
Basis for selection: Major/career interest in engineering; marketing; business; finance/banking; business/management/administration; manufacturing or human resources. Applicant must demonstrate financial need, high academic achievement, leadership and service orientation.
Application requirements: Interview, nomination by Urban League affiliates and Gillette staff. Resume; work experience in related fields; extracurricular activities; applicant must be in top 25% of class.
Additional information: Scholarship awarded in two $5,000 yearly increments. Scholarship recipients receive paid summer internship with Gillette company between junior and senior year.

Amount of award:	$10,000
Number of awards:	15
Number of applicants:	400
Application deadline:	January 15
Notification begins:	June 30
Total amount awarded:	$150,000

Contact:
National Urban League
Director of Education & Youth Development
120 Wall Street, 8th Floor
New York, NY 10005
Phone: 212-558-5300
Fax: 212-344-5332
Web: www.nul.org

Jerry Bartow Scholarships

Type of award: Scholarship.
Intended use: For full-time sophomore, junior or senior study at 4-year institution. Designated institutions: Historically Black College/University participating in Black Executive Exchange Program (BEEP).
Eligibility: Applicant must be Asian American. Applicant must be U.S. citizen or permanent resident.
Basis for selection: Major/career interest in business/management/administration; computer/information sciences or education.
Additional information: Awardees notified by BEEP office and should be available to receive award at BEEP's Annual Conference; travel and hotel arrangements provided.

Amount of award:	$1,500
Number of awards:	2
Application deadline:	January 15

Contact:

National Urban League Scholarship Programs
120 Wall St.
New York, NY 10005
Phone: 888-839-0467
Web: www.nul.org

National Achievers Society Scholars Award

Type of award: Scholarship.
Intended use: For full-time undergraduate study at accredited 4-year institution in United States.
Eligibility: Applicant or parent must be member/participant of National Achievers Society. Applicant must be African American. Applicant must be high school senior. Applicant must be U.S. citizen or permanent resident.
Basis for selection: Applicant must demonstrate financial need and high academic achievement.
Application requirements: Transcript, proof of eligibility.
Additional information: Award given over course of four years.

Amount of award:	$10,000
Number of awards:	100
Application deadline:	January 15

Contact:

National Urban League Scholarship Programs
120 Wall St.
New York, NY 10005
Phone: 888-839-0467
Web: www.nul.org

NUL/CNBC Scholars Award

Type of award: Scholarship.
Intended use: For full-time undergraduate study at accredited 4-year institution in United States.
Eligibility: Applicant must be African American. Applicant must be high school senior. Applicant must be U.S. citizen or permanent resident.
Basis for selection: Applicant must demonstrate high academic achievement, depth of character, leadership, seriousness of purpose and service orientation.
Application requirements: Transcript.
Additional information: Award given over course of four years. Special consideration given to candidates affiliated with any of more than 20 Campaign for African-American Achievement partner organizations and with Urban League affiliates.

Amount of award:	$10,000
Number of awards:	100
Application deadline:	January 15

Contact:

National Urban League Scholarship Programs
120 Wall St.
New York, NY 10005
Phone: 888-839-0467
Web: www.nul.org

Reginald K. Brack, Jr. NULITES Scholarship

Type of award: Scholarship.
Intended use: For undergraduate study in United States.
Eligibility: Applicant must be African American. Applicant must be high school senior. Applicant must be U.S. citizen or permanent resident.

Basis for selection: Major/career interest in communications; radio/television/film; public relations; publishing or journalism. Applicant must demonstrate financial need, high academic achievement, depth of character, seriousness of purpose and service orientation.
Additional information: Awarded to current or former National Urban League Incentives To Excel & Succeed (NULITES) program participants. Award given anually for four years.

Amount of award:	$2,500
Application deadline:	January 15

Contact:

National Urban League Scholarship Programs
120 Wall St.
New York, NY 10005
Phone: 888-839-0467
Web: www.nul.org

Native Daughters of the Golden West

Native Daughters of the Golden West Scholarship

Type of award: Scholarship, renewable.
Intended use: For full-time undergraduate or graduate study at accredited postsecondary institution in United States.
Eligibility: Applicant or parent must be member/participant of Native Daughters of the Golden West. Applicant must be U.S. citizen residing in California. Applicant must be in military service or veteran; or dependent of active service person or veteran.
Basis for selection: Major/career interest in business; education; social work or nursing. Applicant must demonstrate financial need, high academic achievement, depth of character, leadership, patriotism, seriousness of purpose and service orientation.
Application requirements: Recommendations, essay, transcript, nomination by local club or parlor.
Additional information: High school seniors may also apply.

Amount of award:	$100-$1,500
Application deadline:	April 15
Notification begins:	May 15

Contact:

Native Daughters of the Golden West
543 Baker Street
San Francisco, CA 94117-1405

Navy League of the United States

Samuel Eliot Morison Essay Contest

Type of award: Scholarship.
Intended use: For undergraduate study at postsecondary institution.
Eligibility: Applicant must be U.S. citizen.
Basis for selection: Competition/talent/interest in writing/journalism.

Application requirements: Essay. 1,500 to 2,000 words. Topic changes annually.

Additional information: 19 contest award winners selected as regional contest award winners. National champion selected from regional winners. Regional winners receive $400 savings bond. National winner receives $4,000 grand prize. National winner's school receives $500. Essay information, application available on Website.

Amount of award:	$400-$4,000
Number of awards:	20
Number of applicants:	100
Application deadline:	April 1
Total amount awarded:	$15,600

Contact:
The Navy League of the United States
Attn. Essay Coordinator
2300 Wilson Blvd.
Arlington, VA 22201-3308
Web: www.navyleague.org

Navy Supply Corps Foundation

Navy Supply Corps Foundation Scholarship

Type of award: Scholarship.
Intended use: For full-time undergraduate study at vocational, 2-year or 4-year institution.
Eligibility: Applicant must be single. Applicant must be U.S. citizen. Applicant must be dependent of active service person or veteran in the Navy. Must be dependent of Active Duty, Reserve, Retired Supply Corps Officer or of a prior service Supply Corps officer along with the associated enlisted ratings (MS, DK, SK, AK, LI, PC,and SH).
Basis for selection: Applicant must demonstrate financial need, high academic achievement, depth of character, leadership and service orientation.
Application requirements: Transcript, proof of eligibility.
Additional information: Minimum 3.0 GPA required. Up to 90 awards given. Only applications downloaded from Website accepted.

Amount of award:	$1,000-$10,000
Application deadline:	April 10
Notification begins:	April 30

Contact:
Navy Supply Corps Foundation
Navy Supply Corps School
1425 Prince Avenue
Athens, GA 30606-2205
Web: www.usnscf.com

Navy-Marine Corps Relief Society

Vice Admiral E.P. Travers Scholarship

Type of award: Scholarship, renewable.
Intended use: For full-time undergraduate study.
Eligibility: Applicant must be U.S. citizen. Applicant must be in military service; or dependent of active service person or veteran; or spouse of active service person or veteran in the Marines or Navy.
Basis for selection: Applicant must demonstrate financial need.
Application requirements: Proof of eligibility. Current military ID required for dependent and servicemember.
Additional information: Minimum 2.0 GPA.

Amount of award:	$2,000
Application deadline:	March 1

Contact:
Navy-Marine Corps Relief Society
801 North Randolph Street
Suite 1228
Arlington, VA 22203-1978

NBC News and Tom Brokaw

Tom Brokaw Scholarship Program

Type of award: Scholarship.
Intended use: For undergraduate or graduate study at vocational, 2-year, 4-year or graduate institution.
Eligibility: Applicant or parent must be employed by NBC News and Tom Brokaw. Applicant must be high school senior.
Additional information: For further information or application, contact NBC News and Tom Brokaw directly.

Amount of award:	$5,000

Contact:
Director of Communications, NBC News Press Office

Nebraska Coordinating Commission for Postsecondary Education

Nebraska Postsecondary Education Award

Type of award: Scholarship, renewable.
Intended use: For undergraduate study at accredited 4-year institution. Designated institutions: Private, not-for-profit institutions in Nebraska.
Eligibility: Applicant must be residing in Nebraska.
Basis for selection: Applicant must demonstrate financial need.
Application requirements: Transcript.

Additional information: Applicant must be Pell Grant recipient and Nebraska resident. Dollar amount of award, application deadlines and application requirements all determined by individual institution.

> **Amount of award:** Full tuition
> **Total amount awarded:** $2,434,050

Contact:
Contact potential institution for more information.
Phone: 402-471-0030
Fax: 402-471-2886
Web: www.ccpe.state.ne.us

Nebraska Scholarship Assistance Program

Type of award: Scholarship, renewable.
Intended use: For undergraduate study at accredited vocational, 2-year or 4-year institution. Designated institutions: Nebraska schools.
Eligibility: Applicant must be residing in Nebraska.
Basis for selection: Applicant must demonstrate financial need.
Application requirements: Transcript.
Additional information: Applicant must be Pell Grant recipient and Nebraska resident. Dollar amount of award, application deadlines and application requirements all determined by individual institution.

> **Total amount awarded:** $1,619,988

Contact:
Contact potential institution for more information.
Phone: 402-471-0030
Fax: 402-471-2886
Web: www.ccpe.state.ne.us

Nebraska State Scholarship Award

Type of award: Scholarship, renewable.
Intended use: For undergraduate study at accredited vocational, 2-year or 4-year institution. Designated institutions: Nebraska schools.
Eligibility: Applicant must be residing in Nebraska.
Basis for selection: Applicant must demonstrate financial need.
Application requirements: Transcript.
Additional information: Applicant must be Pell Grant recipient. Dollar amount of award, application deadlines and application requirements all determined by individual institution.

> **Total amount awarded:** $1,921,090

Contact:
Contact potential institution for more information.
Phone: 402-471-0030
Fax: 402-471-2886
Web: www.ccpe.state.ne.us

Nebraska State Department of Education

Nebraska Robert C. Byrd Honors Scholarship

Type of award: Scholarship, renewable.

Intended use: For full-time freshman study at accredited postsecondary institution in United States.
Eligibility: Applicant must be high school senior. Applicant must be U.S. citizen or permanent resident residing in Nebraska.
Basis for selection: Applicant must demonstrate high academic achievement.
Application requirements: Transcript. SAT/ACT scores.
Additional information: Renewable up to four years with good academic standing.

> **Amount of award:** $1,500
> **Application deadline:** March 15
> **Total amount awarded:** $258,000

Contact:
Nebraska State Department of Education
Robert C. Byrd Scholarship
P.O. Box 94987
Lincoln, NE 68509-4987

NECA-IBEW Electrical Training Trust

NECA-IBEW Electrical Training Scholarship

Type of award: Scholarship.
Intended use: For freshman study at 2-year or 4-year institution.
Eligibility: Applicant must be high school senior. Applicant must be U.S. citizen residing in Oregon or Washington.
Basis for selection: Applicant must demonstrate high academic achievement.
Application requirements: Essay, transcript, proof of eligibility.
Additional information: Minimum 2.5 GPA. Available to children of NECA-IBEW employers including those participating in National Electrical Contractors Association-International Brotherhood of Electrical Workers Electrical Training Trust agreement. Program administered by Oregon Student Assistance Commission. Contact human resources office of NECA-IBEW employer or Commission (send business-sized SASE).

> **Application deadline:** March 1

Contact:
Oregon Student Assistance Commission
Grant Department
1500 Valley River Drive, Suite 100
Eugene, OR 97401
Phone: 541-687-7375
Web: www.osac.state.or.us

Nevada Department of Education

Nevada Robert C. Byrd Honors Scholarship

Type of award: Scholarship, renewable.

Intended use: For undergraduate study at postsecondary institution.
Eligibility: Applicant must be high school senior. Applicant must be U.S. citizen or permanent resident residing in Nevada.
Basis for selection: Applicant must demonstrate high academic achievement, depth of character and seriousness of purpose.
Additional information: Applicant must be Nevada High School Scholar. Minimum 3.5 GPA and SAT I score of 1100 or ACT score of 25 required.

Amount of award:	$1,500
Number of awards:	40
Number of applicants:	850

Contact:
Contact high school guidance counselor.

Nevada Student Incentive Grant

Type of award: Scholarship.
Intended use: For undergraduate or graduate study at vocational, 2-year, 4-year or graduate institution. Designated institutions: Nevada institutions.
Eligibility: Applicant must be U.S. citizen or permanent resident residing in Nevada.
Basis for selection: Applicant must demonstrate financial need.

Amount of award:	$5,000
Number of awards:	613
Total amount awarded:	$374,000

Contact:
Contact financial aid office of institution or
Phone: 775-687-9228

New England Association of Independent Tire Dealers

New England Tire and Service Association

Type of award: Scholarship.
Intended use: For undergraduate study at accredited vocational, 2-year or 4-year institution.
Eligibility: Applicant or parent must be member/participant of New England Tire and Service Association.
Basis for selection: Applicant must demonstrate financial need.
Additional information: For further information or an application, contact New England Tire and Service Association directly.

Amount of award:	$500

New England Board of Higher Education

New England Board of Higher Education's Regional Student Program

Type of award: Scholarship.

Intended use: For undergraduate or graduate study in United States. Designated institutions: 78 New England public colleges and universities.
Eligibility: Applicant must be permanent resident residing in Connecticut, Massachusetts, Maine, New Hampshire, Rhode Island or Vermont.
Additional information: Regional Student Program provides New England residents with a tuition break when they study approved majors not offered at public institutions in their own state at out-of-state public colleges in New England. Savings on tuition up to 75 percent. Approved majors listed in annual catalog.
Contact:
New England Board of Higher Education
45 Temple Place
Boston, MA 2111
Phone: 617-357-9620
Web: www.nebhe.org

New Hampshire Postsecondary Education Commission

New Hampshire Incentive Program

Type of award: Scholarship, renewable.
Intended use: For freshman, sophomore, junior or senior study at accredited vocational, 2-year or 4-year institution.
Eligibility: Applicant must be U.S. citizen or permanent resident residing in New Hampshire.
Basis for selection: Applicant must demonstrate financial need.
Application requirements: Proof of eligibility. Completed FAFSA form.

Amount of award:	$450-$1,000
Number of awards:	2,858
Application deadline:	May 1
Total amount awarded:	$1,496,894

Contact:
New Hampshire Postsecondary Education Commission
2 Industrial Park Drive
Concord, NH 03301-8512
Web: www.state.nh.us/postsecondary

New Hampshire Scholarship for Orphans of Veterans

Type of award: Scholarship, renewable.
Intended use: For full-time undergraduate or graduate study at vocational, 2-year or 4-year institution.
Eligibility: Applicant must be at least 16, no older than 25. Applicant must be U.S. citizen residing in New Hampshire. Applicant must be dependent of disabled veteran or deceased veteran during Korean War, WW I, WW II or Vietnam.
Application requirements: Proof of eligibility.
Additional information: Parent must have been legal resident of New Hampshire at time of service-related death.

Amount of award:	$1,000
Number of awards:	9
Number of applicants:	10
Total amount awarded:	$9,000

Contact:
New Hampshire Postsecondary Education Commission
2 Industrial Park Drive
Concord, NH 03301-8512
Web: www.state.nh.us/postsecondary

New Jersey Commission on Higher Education

New Jersey Educational Opportunity Fund Grant

Type of award: Scholarship, renewable.
Intended use: For full-time freshman, sophomore, junior, senior or graduate study at accredited 2-year, 4-year or graduate institution. Designated institutions: 41 participating New Jersey community colleges and four-year colleges and universities.
Eligibility: Applicant must be U.S. citizen or permanent resident residing in New Jersey.
Basis for selection: Applicant must demonstrate financial need.
Application requirements: Send FAFSA.
Additional information: For students from educationally disadvantaged backgrounds with demonstrated financial need. Must be New Jersey resident for at least 12 consecutive months prior to receiving grant. Students are admitted into EOF program by the college. Program includes summer sessions, tutoring, and counseling. Contact financial aid office at institution.

Amount of award:	$200-$2,300
Application deadline:	October 1

Contact:
New Jersey Commission on Higher Education
P.O. Box 542
Trenton, NJ 08625-0542
Phone: 609-984-2709
Web: www.state.nj.us/highereducation

New Jersey Department of Military and Veterans Affairs

New Jersey POW/MIA Program

Type of award: Scholarship, renewable.
Intended use: For full-time freshman, sophomore, junior or senior study at accredited 4-year institution in United States. Designated institutions: New Jersey schools.
Eligibility: Applicant must be residing in New Jersey. Applicant must be dependent of active service person or POW/MIA. Parent must have been officially declared Prisoner of War or Missing in Action after January 1, 1960.
Application requirements: Proof of eligibility.
Additional information: Award is full tuition waiver (no room, board, or expenses) at eligible institution.

Amount of award:	Full tuition
Number of awards:	1
Application deadline:	October 1, March 1
Total amount awarded:	$4,762

Contact:
New Jersey Department of Military and Veterans Affairs
DCVA-FO
P.O. Box 340
Trenton, NJ 08625-0340
Phone: 609-530-6961

New Jersey Veteran Tuition Credit Program

Type of award: Scholarship, renewable.
Intended use: For undergraduate or graduate study at postsecondary institution in United States.
Eligibility: Applicant must be residing in New Jersey. Applicant must be veteran who served in the Army, Air Force, Marines, Navy, Coast Guard or Reserves/National Guard during Vietnam. Must have served in Armed Forces between December 31, 1960 and May 7, 1975. Must have been New Jersey resident at time of induction or discharge, or for at least a year prior to application, excluding active duty time.
Application requirements: Proof of eligibility.
Additional information: Must be New Jersey resident for at least one year prior to application.

Amount of award:	$200-$400
Number of awards:	59
Application deadline:	October 1, March 1
Total amount awarded:	$17,200

Contact:
New Jersey Department of Military and Veterans Affairs
DCVA-FO
P.O. Box 340
Trenton, NJ 08625-0340
Phone: 609-530-6961

New Jersey Higher Education Student Assistance Authority

New Jersey Edward J. Bloustein Distinguished Scholars

Type of award: Scholarship, renewable.
Intended use: For full-time freshman, sophomore, junior or senior study at accredited 2-year or 4-year institution. Designated institutions: New Jersey colleges.
Eligibility: Applicant must be high school senior. Applicant must be U.S. citizen or permanent resident residing in New Jersey.
Basis for selection: Applicant must demonstrate high academic achievement.
Application requirements: Transcript, nomination by high school. Standardized test scores.
Additional information: Academic criteria: Open to students with high SAT scores and minimum 3.5 GPA. Must be New Jersey resident for at least 12 consecutive months prior to receiving award. Students demonstrating financial need may receive additional $1,000 per year. Candidates nominated by high schools at the end of junior year for consideration; notification given by fall of senior year. Students may not apply directly to this program. Candidates will be selected for consideration by their secondary schools based upon standard academic criteria. See guidance counselor for more information.

Amount of award: $1,000
Application deadline: October 1
Contact:
New Jersey Higher Education Student Assistance Authority
4 Quakerbridge Plaza, P.O. Box 540
Trenton, NJ 08625-0540
Phone: 800-792-8670
Web: www.hesaa.org

New Jersey Survivor Tuition Benefits Program

Type of award: Scholarship, renewable.
Intended use: For freshman, sophomore, junior or senior study at accredited 2-year or 4-year institution. Designated institutions: Must attend a New Jersey postsecondary institution.
Eligibility: Applicant must be U.S. citizen residing in New Jersey. Applicant's parent must have been killed or disabled in work-related accident as fire fighter, police officer or public safety officer.
Application requirements: Proof of eligibility.
Additional information: Parent or spouse must have been New Jersey law enforcement or emergency service personnel killed in line of duty. Applications available by calling state of New Jersey Office of Student Assistance toll-free financial aid hotline. Grants pay cost of tuition up to highest tuition charged at a New Jersey public postsecondary school. Volunteer service record preferred.
Amount of award: Full tuition
Application deadline: October 1, March 1
Contact:
New Jersey Higher Education Student Assistance Authority
4 Quakerbridge Plaza, PO Box 540
Trenton, NJ 08625-0540
Phone: 800-792-8670
Web: www.hesaa.org

New Jersey Tuition Aid Grants

Type of award: Scholarship, renewable.
Intended use: For full-time freshman, sophomore, junior or senior study at accredited 2-year or 4-year institution in United States. Designated institutions: Approved New Jersey colleges, universities and degree-granting proprietary institutions.
Eligibility: Applicant must be U.S. citizen or permanent resident residing in New Jersey.
Basis for selection: Applicant must demonstrate financial need.
Application requirements: Proof of eligibility. Send FAFSA.
Additional information: Must have lived in New Jersey at least 12 consecutive months before receiving grant. Must maintain 2.0 GPA for renewals. Deadline for Fall and Spring awards June first for renewal students, and October first for new applicants who did not receive a TAG in the prior academic year.
Amount of award: $866-$7,074
Application deadline: June 1, October 1
Contact:
New Jersey Higher Education Student Assistance Authority
4 Quakerbridge Plaza, P.O. Box 540
Trenton, NJ 08625-0540
Phone: 800-792-8670
Web: www.hesaa.org

New Jersey Urban Scholars

Type of award: Scholarship, renewable.

Intended use: For undergraduate study at accredited 2-year or 4-year institution in United States. Designated institutions: Must attend approved New Jersey postsecondary institution.
Eligibility: Applicant must be high school senior. Applicant must be U.S. citizen or permanent resident residing in New Jersey.
Basis for selection: Applicant must demonstrate high academic achievement.
Application requirements: Nomination by high school.
Additional information: Academic criteria: Open to students in top 10 percent of their high school class, with minimum 3.0 GPA or equivalent, attending high schools in New Jersey's urban and economically distressed areas. Candidates nominated for consideration by high schools at end of junior year. Notification by fall of senior year. Students may not apply directly for award.
Amount of award: $1,000
Contact:
New Jersey Higher Education Student Assistance Authority
4 Quakerbridge Plaza
P.O. Box 540
Trenton, NJ 08625-0540
Phone: 800-792-8670
Fax: 609-588-2228
Web: www.hesaa.org

New Jersey Society of Architects

New Jersey Society of Architects Scholarship

Type of award: Scholarship.
Intended use: For full-time sophomore, junior, senior or master's study at accredited 4-year or graduate institution in United States.
Eligibility: Applicant must be residing in New Jersey.
Basis for selection: Major/career interest in architecture. Applicant must demonstrate financial need and high academic achievement.
Application requirements: $5 application fee. Portfolio, recommendations, essay, transcript. Photos of projects and FAFSA.
Additional information: Number of awards varies. Total amount awarded $5,000-$10,000.
Amount of award: $1,000-$2,000
Application deadline: April 30
Notification begins: June 30
Contact:
New Jersey Society of Architects
AIA New Jersey Schol. Fndn
212 White Avenue
Old Tappan, NJ 07675
Phone: 201-767-5541

New Jersey State Policemen's Benevolent Association, Inc.

New Jersey State Policemen's Benevolent Association Scholarship

Type of award: Scholarship.
Intended use: For full-time freshman study at accredited vocational, 2-year or 4-year institution in United States.
Eligibility: Applicant or parent must be member/participant of Policemen's Benevolent Association. Applicant must be high school senior. Applicant must be U.S. citizen.
Basis for selection: Applicant must demonstrate financial need and high academic achievement.
Application requirements: Recommendations, transcript.
Additional information: Application available from parent member's PBA Local. Parent must belong to PBA.

Amount of award:	$700
Number of awards:	35
Application deadline:	February 1
Total amount awarded:	$24,500

Contact:
New Jersey State Policemen's Benevolent Association, Inc.
158 Main Street
Woodbridge, NJ 07095
Phone: 732-636-8860

New Mexico Commission on Higher Education

New Mexico Athlete Scholarship

Type of award: Scholarship, renewable.
Intended use: For undergraduate study at accredited 2-year or 4-year institution. Designated institutions: Selected New Mexico public institutions.
Eligibility: Applicant must be U.S. citizen or permanent resident residing in New Mexico.
Additional information: Awards vary, but are applied toward tuititon and fees. For more information and application/deadlines, contact Athletic Department or financial aid office of any New Mexico public post-secondary institution. Non-resident eligible if attending eligible New Mexico institution.
Contact:
New Mexico Commission on Higher Education
Financial Aid and Student Services
1068 Cerrillos Road
Santa Fe, NM 87501
Phone: 800-279-9777
Web: www.nmche.org/

New Mexico Legislative Endowment Program

Type of award: Scholarship, renewable.
Intended use: For undergraduate study at accredited postsecondary institution. Designated institutions: Public postsecondary New Mexico institutions.

Eligibility: Applicant must be U.S. citizen or permanent resident residing in New Mexico.
Basis for selection: Applicant must demonstrate financial need.
Application requirements: FAFSA.
Additional information: Contact financial aid office of any public postsecondary institution in New Mexico. Four-year public institutions may award up to $2,500 per student per academic year. Two-year public institutions may award up to $1,000 per student per year. Part-time students eligible for pro-rated awards. Deadlines set by each institution.

Amount of award:	$1,000-$2,500

Contact:
New Mexico Commission on Higher Education
Financial Aid and Student Services
1068 Cerrillos Road
Santa Fe, NM 87501
Phone: 800-279-9777
Web: www.nmche.org

New Mexico Scholars Program

Type of award: Scholarship, renewable.
Intended use: For undergraduate study at accredited 2-year or 4-year institution. Designated institutions: Public or private nonprofit institutions in New Mexico.
Eligibility: Applicant must be at least 16, no older than 21. Applicant must be U.S. citizen or permanent resident residing in New Mexico.
Basis for selection: Applicant must demonstrate financial need and high academic achievement.
Application requirements: ACT or SAT score, FAFSA.
Additional information: Tuition waiver (tuition, books and required fees). Number of awards based on availability of funds. Must be graduate of New Mexico high school. Must score at least 1020 on SAT, 25 on ACT or rank in top five percent of high school graduating class and have family income no greater than $30,000 per year. Contact financial aid office of New Mexico postsecondary institution of choice for information and application. Application deadlines set by each institution.

Amount of award:	Full tuition

Contact:
New Mexico Commission on Higher Education
Financial Aid and Student Services
1068 Cerrillos Rod
Santa Fe, NM 87501
Phone: 800-279-9777
Web: www.nmche.org/

New Mexico Student Choice Program

Type of award: Scholarship, renewable.
Intended use: For undergraduate study at postsecondary institution. Designated institutions: St. John's College, College of Southwest, College of Santa Fe.
Eligibility: Applicant must be U.S. citizen or permanent resident residing in New Mexico.
Basis for selection: Applicant must demonstrate financial need.
Application requirements: FAFSA.
Additional information: Award varies, with maximum based on highest tuition at state of New Mexico public university. Apply to financial aid office at one of three private non-profit colleges where award may be used. Must be enrolled in eligible institution as undergraduate. Part-time students eligible for pro-rated awards.

Contact:
New Mexico Commission on Higher Education
Financial Aid and Student Services
1068 Cerrillos Road
Santa Fe, NM 87501
Phone: 800-279-9777
Web: www.nmche.org/

New Mexico Student Incentive Grant

Type of award: Scholarship, renewable.
Intended use: For undergraduate study at accredited postsecondary institution. Designated institutions: Public and selected private nonprofit New Mexico postsecondary institutions.
Eligibility: Applicant must be U.S. citizen or permanent resident residing in New Mexico.
Basis for selection: Applicant must demonstrate financial need.
Application requirements: FAFSA.
Additional information: Must demonstrate exceptional financial need. Contact financial aid office of any New Mexico public postsecondary institution or eligible private nonprofit for information, application and deadline. Part-time students eligible for pro-rated awards.
   Amount of award: $200-$2,500
Contact:
New Mexico Commission on Higher Education
Financial Aid and Student Services
1068 Cerrillos Road
Santa Fe, NM 87501
Phone: 800-279-9777
Web: www.nmche.org/

New Mexico Three Percent Scholarship

Type of award: Scholarship, renewable.
Intended use: For undergraduate or graduate study at accredited postsecondary institution. Designated institutions: Public New Mexico postsecondary institutions.
Eligibility: Applicant must be U.S. citizen or permanent resident residing in New Mexico.
Basis for selection: Applicant must demonstrate depth of character and leadership.
Application requirements: Transcript.
Additional information: Maximum award covers tuition and required fees. One-third of scholarships awarded on basis of financial need. Contact school's financial aid office for details. Each postsecondary institution establishes its own eligibility requirements and application deadlines.
   Amount of award: Full tuition
Contact:
New Mexico Commission on Higher Education
1068 Cerrillos Road
Santa Fe, NM 85701
Phone: 800-279-9777
Web: www.nmche.org/

New Mexico Vietnam Veteran's Scholarship

Type of award: Scholarship, renewable.
Intended use: For undergraduate or master's study at postsecondary institution. Designated institutions: Public and selected private non-profit postsecondary institutions in New Mexico.
Eligibility: Applicant must be U.S. citizen residing in New Mexico. Applicant must be veteran during Vietnam.
Application requirements: Proof of eligibility. Coursework must be certified by New Mexico Veterans' Service Commission (call 505-827-6300).
Additional information: Maximum award provides tuition/fees and book allowance on first come, first served basis. Eligibility must be certified by New Mexico Veterans Service Commission. Contact financial aid office of any New Mexico public postsecondary institution for information, deadline and application.
   Amount of award: Full tuition
Contact:
New Mexico Veteran's Service Commission
P.O. Box 2324
Santa Fe, NM 87503
Phone: 505-827-6300
Web: www.nmche.org/

New United Motor Manufacturing Scholarship Foundation

New United Motor Manufacturing, Inc. Scholarship Program

Type of award: Scholarship, renewable.
Intended use: For undergraduate study at vocational, 2-year or 4-year institution in United States.
Eligibility: Applicant or parent must be employed by New United Motor Manufacturing, Inc. Applicant must be high school senior.
Additional information: For further information or application, contact New United Motor Manufacturing, Scholarship Foundation directly.
   Amount of award: $1,500
Contact:
New United Motor Manufacturing, Inc.

New York Association of Black Journalists

Stephen H. Gayle Essay Contest

Type of award: Scholarship.
Intended use: For undergraduate study in United States. Designated institutions: Must be located in New York City, Westchester County or Long Island.
Eligibility: Applicant must be enrolled in high school. Applicant must be U.S. citizen residing in New York.
Basis for selection: Competition/talent/interest in writing/journalism, based on essay on a current affairs topic. Major/career interest in journalism. Applicant must demonstrate seriousness of purpose.
Application requirements: Essay, transcript. Proof of enrollment, writing sample, cover letter and resume.

Additional information: Applicants can be in middle school, high school or any year of undergraduate study and must attend school in New York City, Westchester County or Long Island. Recipients will be honored at the NYABJ Awards dinner in December. Graduate scholarships also available. Contact NYABJ or see Website for essay topic and additional details. Essay criteria includes originality, creativity, style, accuracy, and thoroughness of reporting.

Amount of award:	$250-$3,000
Application deadline:	November 17

Contact:
New York Association of Black Journalists
P.O. Box 2446
Rockefeller Center
New York, NY 10185
Phone: 212-522-6969
Web: www.nyabj.org

New York Lottery

Leaders of Tomorrow Scholarship

Type of award: Scholarship.
Intended use: For full-time undergraduate study at accredited vocational, 2-year or 4-year institution in United States. Designated institutions: Eligible New York state postsecondary institutions.
Eligibility: Applicant must be high school senior. Applicant must be permanent resident residing in New York.
Basis for selection: Applicant must demonstrate high academic achievement, leadership and service orientation.
Application requirements: Transcript, proof of eligibility. Documentation of extracurricular, community activities. Must complete studies within 5-year period from high school graduation date.
Additional information: $4,000 scholarship paid over four years, at $1,000/yr. Every public and private high school in New York State awarded one scholarship. Applicant should have at least B average based on seven semesters of high school. Student must plan to attend New York State-accredited college, university, trade school or community college.

Amount of award:	$1,000
Number of awards:	1,200
Number of applicants:	2,010
Application deadline:	March 19
Notification begins:	May 31
Total amount awarded:	$1,033,000

Contact:
CASDA (Capital Area School Development Association)
One University Place - A 409
East Campus
Rensselaer, NY 12144-3456
Phone: 518-525-2788 or 2789
Web: www.nylottery.org/education/programs.php3

New York State Education Department

New York State Higher Education Opportunity Program

Type of award: Scholarship.
Intended use: For undergraduate study at 2-year or 4-year institution. Designated institutions: Private New York state institutions.
Eligibility: Applicant must be residing in New York.
Basis for selection: Applicant must demonstrate financial need.
Additional information: For use at private New York State institutions only. Must be both academically and economically disadvantaged. Apply at time of admission. Support services include pre-session summer program and tutoring, counseling, and special course work during academic year. Contact institution for application and additional information. Award amounts vary; contact sponsor for information.
Contact:
New York State Education Department
Bureau of HEOP/VTEA/Scholarship
Room 1076 EBA
Albany, NY 12234
Phone: 518-486-1319
Fax: 518-486-5346

New York State Readers Aid Program

Type of award: Scholarship, renewable.
Intended use: For undergraduate, master's or doctoral study at 2-year, 4-year or graduate institution.
Eligibility: Applicant must be visually impaired or hearing impaired. Applicant must be residing in New York.
Application requirements: Proof of eligibility.
Additional information: Number of awards varies. Applications available at degree-granting institutions. For deaf or blind students, award provides funds for notetakers, readers, or interpreters.

Total amount awarded:	$300,000

Contact:
Office of Vocational and Ed. Services for People with Disabilities
Readers Aid Program
Education Building, Room 1601
Albany, NY 12234
Phone: 518-474-5652
Web: www.nysed.gov

New York State Robert C. Byrd Federal Honors Scholarship

Type of award: Scholarship, renewable.
Intended use: For full-time undergraduate study at accredited 2-year or 4-year institution in United States.
Eligibility: Applicant must be high school senior. Applicant must be U.S. citizen or permanent resident residing in New York.
Basis for selection: Applicant must demonstrate high academic achievement.
Application requirements: Applications available in early Fall at student's high school.

Additional information: Must have 1250 combined SAT score and 3.5 GPA.

Amount of award:	$1,500

Contact:
New York State Education Department
Scholarship Processing Unit
Room 1078 EBA
Albany, NY 12234
Phone: 518-486-1319

New York State Grange

Grange Denise Scholarship

Type of award: Scholarship, renewable.
Intended use: For full-time undergraduate study at 2-year or 4-year institution.
Eligibility: Applicant must be residing in New York.
Basis for selection: Major/career interest in agriculture; agribusiness; agricultural education; agricultural economics or natural resources/conservation. Applicant must demonstrate financial need.
Application requirements: Recommendations, transcript.
Additional information: Send SASE for application.

Amount of award:	$1,000
Number of awards:	6
Number of applicants:	20
Application deadline:	April 15
Notification begins:	June 15
Total amount awarded:	$6,000

Contact:
New York State Grange
100 Grange Place
Cortland, NY 13045
Phone: 607-756-7553

Grange Susan W. Freestone Education Award

Type of award: Scholarship, renewable.
Intended use: For full-time undergraduate or graduate study at 2-year or 4-year institution in United States.
Eligibility: Applicant or parent must be member/participant of New York State Grange. Applicant must be residing in New York.
Basis for selection: Applicant must demonstrate financial need, depth of character and service orientation.
Additional information: Applicant must be current Grange member in New York state to qualify for grant. Send SASE for application. Award granted by scholarship committee, based on many factors.

Amount of award:	$1,000
Number of awards:	2
Number of applicants:	5
Application deadline:	April 15
Notification begins:	June 15
Total amount awarded:	$2,000

Contact:
New York State Grange
100 Grange Place
Cortland, NY 13045
Phone: 607-756-7553

New York State Higher Education Services Corporation

City University Seek/College Discovery Program

Type of award: Scholarship.
Intended use: For undergraduate study at 2-year or 4-year institution. Designated institutions: City University of New York campuses only.
Eligibility: Applicant must be U.S. citizen or permanent resident residing in New York.
Basis for selection: Applicant must demonstrate financial need.
Application requirements: Proof of eligibility. FAFSA.
Additional information: Applicant must be both academically and economically disadvantaged. Apply to financial aid office of CUNY. Available at City University of New York and community college campuses. For SEEK, student must have resided New York State for at least a year; for College Discovery, student must have resided in New York City for at least a year.
Contact:
City University of New York
Office of Admission Services
101 West 31 Street
New York, NY 10001-3503
Phone: 212-947-4800
Web: www.cuny.edu

New York State Aid for part-time Study Program

Type of award: Scholarship, renewable.
Intended use: For half-time undergraduate study at accredited postsecondary institution. Designated institutions: Postsecondary institutions in New York.
Eligibility: Applicant must be U.S. citizen or permanent resident residing in New York.
Basis for selection: Applicant must demonstrate financial need.
Application requirements: Proof of eligibility.
Additional information: Must fall within income limits. Campus-based program; recipients selected and award amount determined by school. Apply to financial aid office of institution. Maximum award is $2,000. Must not have used up TAP eligibility or be in default on Federal Family Education Loan. Visit Website for additional information.
Contact:
New York State Higher Education Services Corporation
Scholarships and Grants Unit
99 Washington Avenue
Albany, NY 12255
Phone: 888-NYS-HESC
Web: www.hesc.com

New York State Memorial Scholarship for Families of Deceased Police/Firefighters/Peace Officers

Type of award: Scholarship, renewable.
Intended use: For full-time undergraduate study at 2-year or 4-year institution. Designated institutions: New York institutions.
Eligibility: Applicant must be U.S. citizen or permanent resident residing in New York. Applicant's parent must have been killed or disabled in work-related accident as fire fighter or police officer.
Application requirements: Proof of eligibility. Must submit Memorial Scholarship Supplement, FAFSA and TAP application.
Additional information: Spouse and/or children of police officer/firefighter/peace officer who died as result of injuries sustained in the line of duty are eligible. Award will equal the applicant's actual tuition cost or the SUNY undergraduate tuition cost, whichever is less. Also provides funds to meet non-tuition costs, such as room and board, books, supplies and transportation. Visit Website for additional information.

    Application deadline: May 1
Contact:
New York State Higher Education Services Corporation
Grants and Scholarships
99 Washington Avenue
Albany, NY 12255
Phone: 888-NYS-HESC
Web: www.hesc.com

New York State Scholarships for Academic Excellence

Type of award: Scholarship, renewable.
Intended use: For full-time undergraduate study at accredited postsecondary institution in United States. Designated institutions: New York State postsecondary institution.
Eligibility: Applicant must be enrolled in high school. Applicant must be U.S. citizen or permanent resident residing in New York.
Basis for selection: Competition/talent/interest in Academics. Applicant must demonstrate high academic achievement.
Application requirements: Nomination by high school.
Additional information: Awards are based on student grades in certain Regents exams. See your high school guidance counselor to apply. State Education Department will notify students who have been nominated by their high school. Must be used within seven years commencing with first academic year for which scholarship was awarded, for up to four years of full-time study (or five years if enrolled in approved program normally requiring five years). Visit Website for additional information.

    Amount of award: $500-$1,500
    Number of awards: 8,000
    Application deadline: May 1
Contact:
High School guidance counselor or
New York State Higher Education Services Corp
99 Washington Avenue
Albany, NY 12255
Phone: 888-NYS-HESC
Web: www.hesc.com

New York State Tuition Assistance Program

Type of award: Scholarship, renewable.
Intended use: For full-time undergraduate or graduate study at accredited postsecondary institution in United States. Designated institutions: TAP-eligible postsecondary schools in New York.
Eligibility: Applicant must be U.S. citizen or permanent resident residing in New York.
Basis for selection: Applicant must demonstrate financial need.
Application requirements: Proof of eligibility.
Additional information: Must fall within income limits. Submit FAFSA and receive prefilled Express TAP Application (ETA) to review, sign and return. Institution must be approved by New York State Education Department to offer TAP eligible programs of study. Award subject to budget appropriations. Check Website for additional information, current dollar range and to download TAP Change Form.

    Amount of award: $75-$5,000
    Application deadline: May 1
Contact:
New York State Higher Education Services Corporation
Grants and Scholarships
99 Washington Avenue
Albany, NY 12255
Phone: 888-NYS-HESC
Web: www.hesc.com

New York State Vietnam Veteran Tuition Award/Persian Gulf Veteran Tuition Award

Type of award: Scholarship, renewable.
Intended use: For undergraduate or graduate study at accredited vocational, 2-year or 4-year institution. Designated institutions: Postsecondary schools in New York.
Eligibility: Applicant must be returning adult student. Applicant must be U.S. citizen or permanent resident residing in New York. Applicant must be veteran during Persian Gulf War or Vietnam. Must have served in armed forces in Indochina between December 1961 and May 1975 for VVTA. Must have served in hostilities beginning August 2, 1990 for Persian Gulf. Must have other than dishonorable discharge for either.
Application requirements: Proof of eligibility. Documentation of Indochina service.
Additional information: Maximum award is $2,000 annually for full-time students; $1,000 annually for part-time students. Students must have also applied for TAP and Federal Pell Grant awards. Visit Website for additional information.

    Amount of award: $2,000
    Application deadline: May 1
Contact:
New York State Higher Education Services Corporation
Grants and Scholarships
99 Washington Avenue
Albany, NY 12255
Phone: 888-NYS-HESC
Web: www.hesc.com

Regents Award for Child of Veteran

Type of award: Scholarship.

Intended use: For full-time undergraduate or non-degree study at 2-year or 4-year institution. Designated institutions: Postsecondary institutions in New York.
Eligibility: Applicant must be residing in New York. Applicant must be dependent of veteran, disabled veteran or deceased veteran during Persian Gulf War, WW I, WW II or Vietnam.
Application requirements: Proof of eligibility. FAFSA.
Additional information: Student's parents must have been disabled or deceased veteran, prisoner of war or classified as Missing In Action. Students whose parent(s) have been a recipient of the Armed Forces, Navy or the Marine Corps expeditionary medal for participation in operations in Lebanon, Grenada and Panama also eligible. Visit Website for additional information.

Amount of award:	$450
Application deadline:	May 1

Contact:
New York State Higher Education Services Corporation
Grants and Scholarships
99 Washington Avenue
Albany, NY 12255
Phone: 888-NYS-HESC
Web: www.hesc.com

New York State Native American Education Unit

New York State Native American Student Aid Program

Type of award: Scholarship, renewable.
Intended use: For undergraduate study at accredited vocational, 2-year or 4-year institution. Designated institutions: New York institutions.
Eligibility: Applicant must be American Indian. Must be on official tribal roll of New York State tribe, or be a child of enrolled member. Applicant must be U.S. citizen residing in New York.
Application requirements: Proof of eligibility. Tribal certification form, documentation of high school graduation and college acceptance letter.
Additional information: Minimum 2.0 semester GPA required. Summer application deadline May 20.

Amount of award:	$1,750
Application deadline:	July 15, December 31

Contact:
New York State Native American Education Unit
New York State Education Department
Room 374, Education Building Annex
Albany, NY 12234
Phone: 518-474-0537
Fax: 518-474-3666

Nexen Petroleum USA, Inc.

Nexen Scholarship Program

Type of award: Scholarship, renewable.
Intended use: For freshman study at accredited vocational, 2-year or 4-year institution.

Eligibility: Applicant or parent must be employed by Nexen Petroleum USA, Inc.
Additional information: For further information or an application, contact Nexen Petroleum USA, Inc. directly.

Amount of award:	$500-$2,000

NFPA Scholarship Chair

Benjamin Eaton Scholarship

Type of award: Scholarship.
Intended use: For undergraduate or non-degree study at postsecondary institution.
Eligibility: Applicant or parent must be member/participant of National Foster Parent Association. Applicant must be high school senior.
Basis for selection: Applicant must demonstrate financial need.
Application requirements: Recommendations, essay, transcript. Photograph, extracurricular activities.
Additional information: For postsecondary education in both degree and non-degree granting institutions. Consideration to applicants with physical disability, handicap or other special needs. Foster children, adoptive and birth children of licensed, approved foster parents who are members of NFPA are eligible.

Amount of award:	$1,000
Number of awards:	5
Number of applicants:	50
Application deadline:	March 31
Notification begins:	May 31
Total amount awarded:	$5,000

Contact:
NFPA Scolarship Chair
P.O. Box 81
Alpha, OH 45301
Phone: 800-557-5238

NIKE, Inc.

Nike Scholarship Fund

Type of award: Scholarship.
Intended use: For undergraduate study at accredited postsecondary institution.
Eligibility: Applicant or parent must be employed by Nike, Inc. Applicant must be high school senior.
Basis for selection: Applicant must demonstrate financial need.
Additional information: For further information or an application, contact Nike, Inc., directly.

Amount of award:	$500-$3,000

Non-Commissioned Officers Association

Non-Commissioned Officers Association Scholarship for Children of Members

Type of award: Scholarship, renewable.
Intended use: For full-time undergraduate study at accredited vocational, 2-year or 4-year institution in United States.
Eligibility: Applicant or parent must be member/participant of Non-Commissioned Officers Association. Applicant must be no older than 25. Applicant must be U.S. citizen or permanent resident. Applicant must be dependent of active service person, veteran or disabled veteran who serves or served in the Army, Air Force, Marines, Navy, Coast Guard or Reserves/National Guard.
Application requirements: Recommendations, essay, transcript. Include two letters of recommendation from school, 1 personal letter of recommendation from an adult who is not a relative, autobiography, ACT or SAT scores (for academic applications only), and a 200-word or more composition on Americanism.
Additional information: Applicant must be dependent of member of Non-Commissioned Officers Association. Applicant can apply for either academic or vocational grant.

Amount of award:	$900-$1,000
Number of awards:	25
Number of applicants:	300
Application deadline:	March 31
Total amount awarded:	$23,750

Contact:
Non-Commissioned Officers Association
P.O. Box 33610
San Antonio, TX 78265
Phone: 210-653-6161

Non-Commissioned Officers Association Scholarship for Spouses

Type of award: Scholarship, renewable.
Intended use: For full-time undergraduate study at vocational, 2-year or 4-year institution in United States.
Eligibility: Applicant or parent must be member/participant of Non-Commissioned Officers Association. Applicant must be no older than 25. Applicant must be U.S. citizen. Applicant must be spouse of active service person, veteran or disabled veteran. Must be spouse of non-commissioned officer or petty officer.
Application requirements: Transcript. Send copy of high school diploma or GED, brief biographical background, certificates of completion for any other courses of training, letter of intent describing degree course of study, plans for completion of a degree program, and a closing paragraph on "What a College Degree Means to Me."
Additional information: Must be spouse of member of Non-Commissioned Officers Association. Recipient must apply for auxiliary membership in Non-Commissioned Officers Association.

Amount of award:	$900
Number of awards:	10
Number of applicants:	100
Application deadline:	March 31

Contact:
Non-Commissioned Officers Association
P.O. Box 33610
San Antonio, TX 78265
Phone: 210-653-6161

North American Limousin Foundation

Limouselle Scholarship

Type of award: Scholarship.
Intended use: For undergraduate study at 2-year or 4-year institution.
Eligibility: Applicant or parent must be member/participant of North American Limousin Junior Association.
Basis for selection: Major/career interest in agriculture; agribusiness; agricultural economics or agricultural education. Applicant must demonstrate financial need, high academic achievement, depth of character, leadership, patriotism, seriousness of purpose and service orientation.
Application requirements: Transcript, proof of eligibility.
Additional information: Must rank in top third of class.

Amount of award:	$500
Number of awards:	3
Application deadline:	May 15
Notification begins:	July 25

Contact:
North American Limousin Foundation
7383 South Alton Way
Englewood, CO 80112

Limousin Award of Excellence

Type of award: Scholarship.
Intended use: For undergraduate study at 2-year or 4-year institution.
Eligibility: Applicant or parent must be member/participant of North American Limousin Junior Association. Applicant must be at least 19, no older than 21.
Basis for selection: Major/career interest in agriculture. Applicant must demonstrate high academic achievement, depth of character, leadership, patriotism, seriousness of purpose and service orientation.
Application requirements: Interview, recommendations, proof of eligibility.
Additional information: Up to three awards given. Experience with Limousin cattle preferred.

Amount of award:	$750
Application deadline:	May 15
Notification begins:	July 25

Contact:
North American Limousin Foundation
7383 South Alton Way
Englewood, CO 80112

North Carolina Association of Educators

Mary Morrow-Edna Richards Scholarship

Type of award: Scholarship.
Intended use: For full-time senior study in United States.
Eligibility: Applicant must be residing in North Carolina.
Basis for selection: Major/career interest in education or education, teacher. Applicant must demonstrate financial need, high academic achievement, depth of character, leadership and service orientation.
Application requirements: Recommendations, essay, transcript.
Additional information: Must agree to teach in North Carolina for two years after graduation. Application should be made through college or university with department of education head during junior year. Other eligible students may request application forms from NCAE office. Preference may be given to Student NCAE members or children of NCAE members. Number of awards varies annually according to funding, minimum four per year.

Amount of award:	$1,000
Number of awards:	17
Number of applicants:	54
Application deadline:	January 10
Notification begins:	February 15
Total amount awarded:	$17,000

Contact:
North Carolina Association of Educators
P.O. Box 27347
Raleigh, NC 27611
Phone: 800-662-7924 ext. 214
Web: www.ncae.org

North Carolina Bar Association

North Carolina Law Enforcement Dependents Scholarship

Type of award: Scholarship, renewable.
Intended use: For full-time undergraduate, master's, doctoral or first professional study at accredited postsecondary institution.
Eligibility: Applicant must be no older than 26. Applicant's parent must have been killed or disabled in work-related accident as police officer or public safety officer.
Basis for selection: Applicant must demonstrate financial need.
Application requirements: Essay, transcript. Applicant's parent must have been working as North Carolina law enforcement officer at time of death or disablement.
Additional information: Must apply before 27th birthday. Award maximum is $2,000 per year; up to $8,000 total.

Amount of award:	$2,000
Number of awards:	17
Number of applicants:	17
Application deadline:	April 1
Notification begins:	May 31

Contact:
North Carolina Bar Association
Young Lawyers Division Scholarship Committee
P. O. Box 3688
Cary, NC 27519
Phone: 919-677-0561
Web: www.ncbar.org

North Carolina Department of Community Colleges

North Carolina Community Colleges Bell South Telephone/ Telegraph Scholarship

Type of award: Scholarship, renewable.
Intended use: For freshman, sophomore or non-degree study. Designated institutions: North Carolina schools.
Eligibility: Applicant must be returning adult student. Applicant must be residing in North Carolina.
Basis for selection: Applicant must demonstrate financial need.
Additional information: Must enroll in degree or diploma program at one of eight eligible community colleges located in Bell South service area. Must apply through financial aid office at institution. Employees displaced because of obsolete job skills also eligible. Criteria subject to change.

Amount of award:	$500
Number of awards:	48
Total amount awarded:	$23,000

Contact:
Must apply through financial aid office at institution.

North Carolina Community Colleges Petroleum Marketers Association Scholarship

Type of award: Scholarship.
Intended use: For freshman or sophomore study at 2-year institution. Designated institutions: North Carolina community colleges.
Eligibility: Applicant or parent must be employed by North Carolina Petroleum Marketers Association. Applicant must be residing in North Carolina.
Additional information: For employees and their children. Applications available at financial aid office at institution or offices of North Carolina Petroleum Marketers Association members.

Amount of award:	$500
Number of awards:	10
Number of applicants:	25
Application deadline:	July 30
Total amount awarded:	$5,000

Contact:
North Carolina Department of Community Colleges
200 West Jones Street
Raleigh, NC 27603-1379

North Carolina Community Colleges Sprint College Transfer Scholarship

Type of award: Scholarship.
Intended use: For full-time freshman or sophomore study at 2-year institution.
Eligibility: Applicant must be residing in North Carolina.
Additional information: Must be enrolled in transfer program at community college in service area of Carolina Telephone and Telegraph Company. Apply through financial aid office of institution where enrolled. Priority given to African-American students.

Amount of award:	$500
Number of awards:	20
Total amount awarded:	$10,000

Contact:
North Carolina Department of Community Colleges
200 West Jones Street
Raleigh, NC 27603-1379

North Carolina Community Colleges Sprint Scholarship

Type of award: Scholarship.
Intended use: For full-time freshman, sophomore or non-degree study at 2-year institution. Designated institutions: North Carolina community colleges in Sprint service area.
Eligibility: Applicant must be residing in North Carolina.
Basis for selection: Applicant must demonstrate financial need.
Additional information: Priority given to minorities and "displaced workers." Must graduate from institution where initially enrolled. Must attend 1-day seminar. Apply through financial aid office of college.

Amount of award:	$550
Number of awards:	70

Contact:
North Carolina Department of Community Colleges
200 West Jones Street
Raleigh, NC 27603-1379

North Carolina Community Colleges Wachovia Technical Scholarship

Type of award: Scholarship.
Intended use: For full-time sophomore study at vocational or 2-year institution.
Eligibility: Applicant must be residing in North Carolina.
Basis for selection: Applicant must demonstrate financial need and high academic achievement.
Additional information: Must be enrolled in second year of two-year technical program. Apply through financial aid office of institution where enrolled.

Amount of award:	$500
Number of awards:	113
Total amount awarded:	$56,500

Contact:
North Carolina Department of Community Colleges
200 West Jones Street
Raleigh, NC 27603-1379

North Carolina Division of Veterans Affairs

North Carolina Scholarships for Children of War Veterans

Type of award: Scholarship.
Intended use: For undergraduate or graduate study at accredited postsecondary institution. Designated institutions: North Carolina schools.
Eligibility: Applicant must be dependent of disabled veteran, deceased veteran or POW/MIA who served in the Army, Air Force, Marines, Navy, Coast Guard or Reserves/National Guard. Parent must have served during a period of war.
Basis for selection: Applicant must demonstrate financial need and high academic achievement.
Application requirements: Interview, transcript, proof of eligibility. Birth certificate.
Additional information: Award is tuition waiver plus minimum room and board expenses, for up to four years. Parent must have been North Carolina resident at time of enlistment or child must have been born in and resided permanently in North Carolina. Parent must have served during period of war.

Amount of award:	Full tuition
Number of awards:	312
Number of applicants:	590
Application deadline:	May 31
Notification begins:	July 15
Total amount awarded:	$5,000,000

Contact:
North Carolina Division of Veterans Affairs
325 North Salisbury Street, Suite 1065
Raleigh, NC 27603

North Carolina Division of Vocational Rehabilitation Services

North Carolina Vocational Rehabilitation Award

Type of award: Scholarship, renewable.
Intended use: For full-time undergraduate study at vocational, 2-year or 4-year institution. Designated institutions: North Carolina institutions.
Eligibility: Applicant must be physically challenged or learning disabled. Applicant must be residing in North Carolina.
Application requirements: Interview, proof of eligibility.
Additional information: Applicant must have physical or mental disability.

Number of awards:	9,618
Total amount awarded:	$10,667,661

Contact:
North Carolina Division of Vocational Rehabilitation Services
2801 Mail Service Center
Raleigh, NC 27699-2801
Phone: 919-733-3364
Fax: 919-733-7968

Scholarships

North Carolina State Education Assistance Authority

Governor James G. Martin Scholarships

Type of award: Scholarship, renewable.
Intended use: For full-time freshman study at accredited 4-year institution in United States. Designated institutions: 51 North Carolina colleges.
Eligibility: Applicant must be high school senior. Applicant must be U.S. citizen residing in North Carolina.
Basis for selection: Applicant must demonstrate high academic achievement, leadership and service orientation.
Application requirements: Nomination by one of 51 eligible institutions in North Carolina.
Additional information: Renewable for up to five years of undergraduate study, provided student continues to be enrolled full time, maintains at least C average, and otherwise remains in good standing at eligible school. Applications available in financial aid offices of eligible institutions in North Carolina.

Amount of award:	$1,000
Number of awards:	5
Application deadline:	March 16
Notification begins:	April 1

Contact:
North Carolina State Education Assistance Authority
PO Box 13663
Research Triangle Park, NC 27709-3663
Web: www.cfnc.org/html/merit.asp

Incentive Scholarship and Grant Program for Native Americans

Type of award: Scholarship, renewable.
Intended use: For full-time undergraduate or doctoral study. Designated institutions: University of North Carolina constituent institutions. Grants also available for doctoral students at North Carolina State University, UNC at Chapel Hill, and UNC at Greensboro.
Eligibility: Applicant must be American Indian. Must be member of Native American tribe recognized by State of North Carolina or federal government. Applicant must be U.S. citizen or permanent resident residing in North Carolina.
Basis for selection: Applicant must demonstrate high academic achievement and service orientation.
Application requirements: FAFSA. Must be in top half of high school graduating class. If transferring from North Carolina community college, must have earned degree or certificate. Applicant must agree to perform required public service and apply for financial aid.
Additional information: Initially restricted to new freshmen and new transfer students at University of North Carolina's 16 constituent institutions. Eligible students must carry minimum 15 credit hours per term. Renewal contingent upon completion of required public service hours and maintenance of GPA standards. Contact graduate program office at eligible institution for doctoral grant information. See Website for other details.
Contact:
Apply at financial aid office of eligible institution.
Web: www.cfnc.org/html/other.asp

Incentive Scholarship Program

Type of award: Scholarship, renewable.
Intended use: For undergraduate study at accredited 4-year institution. Designated institutions: Elizabeth City State University, Fayetteville State University, North Carolina Agricultural and Technical State University, North Carolina Central University, University of North Carolina at Pembroke, and Winston-Salem State University.
Eligibility: Applicant must be U.S. citizen or permanent resident residing in North Carolina.
Basis for selection: Applicant must demonstrate financial need, high academic achievement, depth of character, leadership and service orientation.
Application requirements: FAFSA.
Additional information: Grants available to eligible students taking at least three hours of degree-credit coursework per semester at University of NC constituent institution. Applicants must apply for financial aid and meet certain admission standards including specified GPA. Public service required. Amount of award depends on financial need and availability of funds.

Amount of award:	$3,000

Contact:
Apply at financial aid office of eligible institution.
Web: www.cfnc.org/html/merit.asp Click link for this program.

North Carolina Legislative Tuition Grant

Type of award: Scholarship, renewable.
Intended use: For full-time undergraduate study at accredited 2-year or 4-year institution. Designated institutions: North Carolina private institutions.
Eligibility: Applicant must be U.S. citizen or permanent resident residing in North Carolina.
Application requirements: Complete application at North Carolina private institution.
Additional information: Award is not applicable for theology, divinity, or religious education programs. Applicants should contact North Carolina private institution he/she attends or North Carolina State Education Assistance Authority. Student must maintain full-time status.

Amount of award:	$1,800
Number of awards:	24,078
Application deadline:	October 1
Total amount awarded:	$43,911,790

Contact:
North Carolina State Education Assistance Authority
P.O. Box 13663
Research Triangle Park, NC 27709-3663
Web: www.cfnc.org/html/other.asp

North Carolina Minority Presence Grant Program I

Type of award: Scholarship, renewable.
Intended use: For undergraduate or graduate study. Designated institutions: University of North Carolina's 16 constituent institutions.
Eligibility: Applicant must be African American. Applicants must attend predominantly white UNC system campuses. White students considered if attending predominantly African-American UNC campuses. Applicant must be U.S. citizen or permanent resident residing in North Carolina.

Basis for selection: Applicant must demonstrate financial need.

Application requirements: FAFSA, generally. Required forms determined by each campus.

Additional information: Grants available to students taking at least three hours of degree-credit course work per semester at a University of North Carolina (UNC) constituent institution where their race is in the minority. Amount of award depends on financial need and availability of funds. Grants renewable as funding permits, but priority given to entering students.

Contact:
Apply at financial aid office of eligible institution.
Web: www.cfnc.org/html/need.asp

North Carolina Minority Presence Grant Program II

Type of award: Scholarship, renewable.

Intended use: For undergraduate or graduate study. Designated institutions: University of North Carolina's 16 constituent institutions.

Eligibility: Applicant must be Alaskan native, Asian American, Mexican American, Hispanic American, Puerto Rican or American Indian. Applicant must be U.S. citizen or permanent resident residing in North Carolina.

Basis for selection: Applicant must demonstrate financial need.

Application requirements: FAFSA, generally. Required forms determined by each campus.

Additional information: Grants available to students taking at least three hours of degree-credit course work per semester at a University of North Carolina (UNC) constituent institution. Amount of award depends on financial need and availability of funds. Grants renewable as funding permits, but priority given to entering students.

Contact:
Apply at financial aid office of eligible institution.
Phone: 919-248-4686
Fax: 919-248-4687
Web: www.cfnc.org/html/need.asp

State Contractual Scholarship Fund

Type of award: Scholarship, renewable.

Intended use: For undergraduate study at accredited 2-year or 4-year institution. Designated institutions: Private institutions in North Carolina.

Eligibility: Applicant must be U.S. citizen or permanent resident residing in North Carolina.

Basis for selection: Applicant must demonstrate financial need.

Application requirements: Proof of eligibility.

Additional information: Theology/divinity students not eligible. Contact NC private instutution student attends or address below.

Total amount awarded: $31,763,002

Contact:
NCSEAA
P.O. Box 13663
Research Triangle Park, NC 27709-3663
Web: www.cfnc.org/html/need.asp

North Dakota University System

North Dakota Indian Scholarship Program

Type of award: Scholarship, renewable.

Intended use: For full-time undergraduate or graduate study.

Eligibility: Applicant must be American Indian. Must be enrolled member of an Indian tribe. Applicant must be U.S. citizen residing in North Dakota.

Basis for selection: Applicant must demonstrate financial need and high academic achievement.

Application requirements: Proof of eligibility.

Amount of award:	$700-$2,000
Number of awards:	150
Number of applicants:	600
Application deadline:	July 15

Contact:
North Dakota University System
Indian Scholarship Program
600 East Boulevard - Dept. 215
Bismarck, ND 58505-0230
Phone: 701-328-2166
Web: www.ndus.nodak.edu

North Dakota Scholars Program

Type of award: Scholarship, renewable.

Intended use: For full-time undergraduate study at 2-year or 4-year institution.

Eligibility: Applicant must be high school senior. Applicant must be residing in North Dakota.

Basis for selection: Applicant must demonstrate high academic achievement.

Application requirements: Proof of eligibility.

Additional information: Must score in at least 95th percentile on ACT, rank in top fifth of class. Must maintain 3.5 GPA for renewal. Deadline for applications will be October test date of ACT. Contact sponsor for more information.

Amount of award:	$1,700-$2,600
Number of awards:	50
Number of applicants:	400

Contact:
North Dakota University System
600 East Boulevard
Dept. 215
Bismarck, ND 58505-0230
Phone: 701-328-4114
Web: www.ndus.nodak.edu

North Dakota State Grant

Type of award: Scholarship, renewable.

Intended use: For full-time undergraduate study at vocational, 2-year or 4-year institution. Designated institutions: North Dakota schools.

Eligibility: Applicant must be U.S. citizen or permanent resident residing in North Dakota.

Basis for selection: Applicant must demonstrate financial need.

Application requirements: Proof of eligibility. Submit FAFSA.

Additional information: Application automatic with FAFSA.

Amount of award:	$600
Number of awards:	3,700
Number of applicants:	28,000
Application deadline:	April 15
Total amount awarded:	$2,220,000

Contact:
North Dakota University System
Student Financial Assistance Program
600 East Boulevard - Dept. 215
Bismarck, ND 58505-0230
Phone: 701-328-4114
Web: www.ndus.nodak.edu

North Pacific Lumber Company

NOR PAC Scholarship Program

Type of award: Scholarship, renewable.
Intended use: For freshman, sophomore, junior or senior study at accredited vocational, 2-year or 4-year institution.
Eligibility: Applicant or parent must be employed by North Pacific Lumber Co.
Basis for selection: Applicant must demonstrate financial need.
Additional information: For further information and an application, contact North Pacific Lumber Company directly.

Amount of award:	$1,000

Northeastern Loggers' Association

Northeastern Loggers' Association Contest

Type of award: Scholarship.
Intended use: For undergraduate study at vocational, 2-year or 4-year institution in United States.
Eligibility: Applicant or parent must be member/participant of Northeastern Loggers' Association.
Basis for selection: Competition/talent/interest in writing/journalism, based on 1,000 word essay.
Application requirements: Essay, transcript. Application form.
Additional information: Applicant must be an immediate family member of an individual associate or employee of the Northeastern Loggers' Assoc. or member company. Decision based largely on quality of 1,000-word essay on "What It Means to Grow Up in the Forest Industry." Awards are given to high school seniors and students in four-year and two-year colleges.

Amount of award:	$500
Number of awards:	3
Number of applicants:	18
Application deadline:	March 31
Notification begins:	May 1
Total amount awarded:	$1,500

Contact:
Northeastern Loggers' Association
P.O. Box 69
Old Forge, NY 13420
Phone: 315-369-3078
Fax: 315-369-3736

Northern Cheyenne Tribal Education Department

Northern Cheyenne Higher Education Program

Type of award: Scholarship, renewable.
Intended use: For undergraduate study at postsecondary institution.
Eligibility: Applicant must be American Indian. Must be enrolled with the Northern Cheyenne Tribe. Applicant must be U.S. citizen.
Basis for selection: Applicant must demonstrate financial need.
Application requirements: Recommendations, essay, transcript, proof of eligibility. Northern Cheyenne Tribal Application and FAFSA.

Amount of award:	$100-$6,000
Number of awards:	70
Number of applicants:	137
Application deadline:	March 1, October 1
Notification begins:	August 1, November 1
Total amount awarded:	$278,762

Contact:
Northern Cheyenne Tribal Education Department
Attn: Norma Bixby
Box 307
Lame Deer, MT 59043
Phone: 406-477-6602

Northland Aluminum Products, Inc.

The Dalquist Scholarship

Type of award: Scholarship.
Intended use: For undergraduate or graduate study at accredited vocational, 2-year, 4-year or graduate institution.
Eligibility: Applicant or parent must be employed by Northland Aluminium Products, Inc.
Additional information: For further information or an application, contact Northland Aluminum Products, Inc. directly.

Amount of award:	$1,000

Northwest Danish Foundation

Danish Foundation Scholarship

Type of award: Scholarship, renewable.
Intended use: For undergraduate or graduate study at postsecondary institution in or outside United States. Designated institutions: May be used at institutions in Denmark.
Eligibility: Applicant must be Danish. Applicant must be U.S. citizen or permanent resident residing in Oregon or Washington.
Basis for selection: Applicant must demonstrate depth of character and service orientation.
Application requirements: Recommendations, essay, transcript. Three recommendations, personal essay on educational goals, and Danish heritage or commitment to the Danish community required.
Additional information: Spouses of persons of Danish descent eligible as well as applicants of non-Danish descent . Must have interest in Danish culture and community. One recommendation must be from non-family member of Danish community, explaining applicant's involvement in Danish activities/community.

Amount of award:	$250-$1,000
Number of awards:	20
Number of applicants:	40
Application deadline:	March 15
Notification begins:	May 1
Total amount awarded:	$15,000

Contact:
Northwest Danish Foundation
1833 North 105th Street
Suite 203
Seattle, WA 98133-8973
Phone: 206-523-2363 or 800-564-7736

Northwestern Mutual Foundation

Northwestern Mutual Scholars Program

Type of award: Scholarship, renewable.
Intended use: For undergraduate study at accredited postsecondary institution.
Eligibility: Applicant or parent must be employed by Northwestern Mutual Foundation, Inc. Applicant must be high school senior.
Basis for selection: Applicant must demonstrate financial need.
Additional information: For Further information or an application, contact Northwestern Mutual Foundation, Inc. directly.

Amount of award:	$2,000-$5,000

Contact:
Northwestern Mutual Foundation, Inc.

Oak Ridge Institute for Science and Education

ORISE Energy Research Undergraduate Laboratory Fellowship

Type of award: Scholarship.
Intended use: For full-time undergraduate study at 4-year institution in United States. Designated institutions: Argonne National Laboratory (Argonne, Ill.); Brookhaven National Laboratory (Upton, N.Y.); Ernest Orlando Lawrence Berkeley National Laboratory (Berkeley, Calif.); Fermi National Accelerator Laboratory (Batavia, Ill.); Idaho National Environmental and Engineering Laboratory (Idaho Falls, Idaho); National Renewable Energy Laboratory (Golden, Colo.); Oak Ridge National Laboratory (Oak Ridge, Tenn.); Pacific Northwest National Laboratory (Richland, Wash.); Princeton Plasma Physics Laboratory (Princeton, N.J.); Stanford Linear Accelerator Center (Stanford, Calif.); Thomas Jefferson National Accelerator Laboratory (Newport News, Va.).
Eligibility: Applicant must be U.S. citizen or permanent resident.
Basis for selection: Major/career interest in computer/ information sciences; engineering; environmental science; mathematics; science, general or health sciences.
Application requirements: Recommendations, transcript.
Additional information: Provides opportunities to participate in research relating to energy production, use, conservation, and societal implications. Weekly stipend of $350 for ten-week summer or 16-week semester appointment. Call contact for deadlines. Number of awards varies.

Amount of award:	$3,500-$5,600

Contact:
Oak Ridge Institute for Science and Technology
P.O. Box 117
Oak Ridge, TN 37831-0117
Phone: 865-576-3192
Web: www.orau.org

ORISE Office of Civilian Radioactive Waste Management Scholarship

Type of award: Scholarship.
Intended use: For junior or senior study at accredited 4-year institution in United States. Designated institutions: Historically Black Colleges and Universities.
Eligibility: Applicant must be African American. Applicant must be U.S. citizen or permanent resident.
Basis for selection: Major/career interest in science, general; mathematics; social/behavioral sciences or engineering.
Additional information: Provides scholarships and practical experience for students from historically black colleges and universities pursuing degrees in areas related to the Office of Civilian Radioactive Waste Management. Tuition and fees paid to maximum $8,000. Monthly stipend of $600.

Amount of award:	Full tuition
Number of awards:	10

Contact:
Oak Ridge Institute for Science and Education
P.O. Box 117
Oak Ridge, TN 37831-0117
Phone: 865-576-9272
Web: www.orau.org

ORISE Student Research at U.S. Army Garrison, Directorate of Safety, Health and Environment

Type of award: Research grant, renewable.
Intended use: For undergraduate or graduate study at postsecondary institution. Designated institutions: U.S. Army Garrison, Aberdeen Proving Ground, MD, Directorate of Safety, Health and Environment.
Eligibility: Applicant must be U.S. citizen.
Basis for selection: Major/career interest in environmental science; science, general; physical sciences; health sciences or engineering.
Additional information: Provides opportunities to participate in research on issues related to safety, health, and the environment. Three months to one year; full-time or part-time appointments. Stipend based on research area(s) and academic classification. Applications accepted on year-round basis.
Contact:
Oak Ridge Institute for Science and Education
P.O. Box 117
Oak Ridge, TN 37831-0117
Phone: 410-671-1598
Web: www.orau.org

Ocean Spray Cranberries, Inc.

Hal Thorkilsen Scholarship Fund

Type of award: Scholarship.
Intended use: For undergraduate study at accredited vocational, 2-year or 4-year institution.
Eligibility: Applicant or parent must be employed by Ocean Spray Cranberries, Inc.
Basis for selection: Applicant must demonstrate financial need.
Additional information: For further information or an application, contact Ocean Spray Cranberries, Inc. directly.

Amount of award:	$500-$3,000

Contact:
Ocean Spray Cranberries, Inc.
Phone: 800-662-3263 (9 A.M. to 4 P.M.)

Ohio Board of Regents

Ohio Academic Scholarship

Type of award: Scholarship, renewable.
Intended use: For full-time freshman, sophomore, junior or senior study at accredited 2-year or 4-year institution. Designated institutions: Ohio schools.

Eligibility: Applicant must be high school senior. Applicant must be U.S. citizen or permanent resident residing in Ohio.
Basis for selection: Applicant must demonstrate high academic achievement.
Application requirements: ACT scores.
Additional information: Applications may be obtained from high school guidance counselors after December.

Amount of award:	$2,000
Number of awards:	1,000
Number of applicants:	4,500
Application deadline:	February 23
Notification begins:	May 1
Total amount awarded:	$7,000,000

Contact:
Sue Minturn, Program Administrator
Ohio Board of Regents
P.O. Box 182452
Columbus, OH 43218-2452

Ohio Instructional Grant

Type of award: Scholarship.
Intended use: For full-time undergraduate study at accredited 2-year or 4-year institution. Designated institutions: Ohio schools and some select Pennsylvania schools.
Eligibility: Applicant must be U.S. citizen or permanent resident residing in Ohio.
Basis for selection: Applicant must demonstrate financial need.
Additional information: By completing the FAFSA form, you automatically apply for this scholarship. Number of awards given varies.

Amount of award:	$252-$3,750
Application deadline:	October 1
Notification begins:	March 1
Total amount awarded:	$93,600,000

Contact:
Ohio Board of Regents
P.O. Box 182452
Columbus, OH 43218-2452

Ohio Part-Time Student Instructional Grant Program

Type of award: Scholarship, renewable.
Intended use: For half-time freshman, sophomore, junior or senior study at accredited 2-year or 4-year institution.
Eligibility: Applicant must be U.S. citizen residing in Ohio.
Basis for selection: Applicant must demonstrate financial need.
Additional information: For application, contact college financial aid office.

Number of awards:	30,000
Total amount awarded:	$10,000,000

Contact:
Barbara Metheney, Program Administrator
Ohio Board of Regents
P.O. Box 182452
Columbus, OH 43218-2452

Ohio Robert C. Byrd Honors Scholarship

Type of award: Scholarship, renewable.
Intended use: For full-time freshman study at accredited 2-year or 4-year institution in United States.
Eligibility: Applicant must be residing in Ohio.

Basis for selection: Applicant must demonstrate high academic achievement and leadership.

Application requirements: GPA, SAT/ACT scores.

Amount of award:	$1,100
Number of awards:	200
Number of applicants:	872
Application deadline:	March 10
Total amount awarded:	$415,000

Contact:
Contact your undergraduate institution for application information.

Ohio Safety Officers College Memorial Fund

Type of award: Scholarship, renewable.

Intended use: For freshman, sophomore, junior or senior study at vocational, 2-year or 4-year institution. Designated institutions: Ohio schools.

Eligibility: Applicant must be U.S. citizen or permanent resident residing in Ohio.

Application requirements: Proof of eligibility.

Additional information: Parent or spouse must have been firefighter or police officer killed in line of duty. Apply at college financial aid office.

Amount of award:	Full tuition
Number of awards:	46
Number of applicants:	46
Total amount awarded:	$121,068

Contact:
Barbara Metheney, Program Administrator
Ohio Board of Regents
P.O. Box 182452
Columbus, OH 43218-2452

Ohio Student Choice Grant

Type of award: Scholarship, renewable.

Intended use: For full-time freshman, sophomore, junior or senior study at 4-year institution. Designated institutions: Award must be used at private nonprofit Ohio colleges or universities.

Eligibility: Applicant must be U.S. citizen or permanent resident residing in Ohio.

Additional information: Apply at college financial aid office.

Number of awards:	45,000
Total amount awarded:	$24,200,000

Contact:
Barbara Metheney, Program Administrator
Ohio Board of Regents
P.O. Box 182452
Columbus, OH 43218-2452

Ohio War Orphans Scholarship

Type of award: Scholarship, renewable.

Intended use: For full-time freshman, sophomore, junior or senior study at accredited 2-year or 4-year institution. Designated institutions: Ohio schools.

Eligibility: Applicant must be at least 16, no older than 21. Applicant must be U.S. citizen or permanent resident residing in Ohio. Applicant must be dependent of veteran, disabled veteran, deceased veteran or POW/MIA. Child of wartime veteran or POW/MIA in Asian war eligible.

Application requirements: Proof of eligibility.

Amount of award:	Full tuition
Number of applicants:	341
Application deadline:	July 1
Notification begins:	August 1
Total amount awarded:	$3,600,000

Contact:
Sue Minturn, Program Administrator
Ohio Board of Regents
P.O. Box 182452
Columbus, OH 43218-2452

Ohio National Guard

Ohio National Guard Scholarship Program

Type of award: Scholarship, renewable.

Intended use: For freshman, sophomore, junior or senior study at accredited postsecondary institution. Designated institutions: Degree-granting institution in Ohio, approved by Ohio Board of Regents.

Eligibility: Applicant or parent must be member/participant of Ohio National Guard. Applicant must be in military service in the Reserves/National Guard. Must enlist, reenlist, or extend current enlistment to equal 6 years with Ohio National Guard. Must remain in good standing.

Application requirements: Proof of eligibility. Must be member of Ohio National Guard. Must not already possess Baccalaureate degree.

Additional information: Must be member of Ohio National Guard and approved by Ohio Board of Regents. Minimum of 6 credit hours. Award covers 100% instructional & general fee for state assisted institutions; average of state-assisted universities for proprietary institutions. Application deadlines: fall-July 1, winter-November 1, spring-February 1, summer-April 1.

Amount of award:	Full tuition
Number of awards:	5,000

Contact:
Adjutant General's Department
Ohio National Guard Scholars
2825 West Dublin Granville Road
Columbus, OH 43235
Phone: 888-400-6484

Ohio Newspapers Foundation

Harold K. Douthit Scholarship

Type of award: Scholarship.

Intended use: For freshman study at 2-year or 4-year institution in United States. Designated institutions: In Ohio counties; Cuyahoga, Loraine, Huron, Erie, Wood, Sandusky, Ottawa, Geauga, or Lucas.

Eligibility: Applicant must be high school senior. Applicant must be U.S. citizen residing in Ohio.

Basis for selection: Major/career interest in journalism. Applicant must demonstrate financial need and high academic achievement.

Application requirements: Recommendations, essay, transcript. Samples of published work.
Additional information: 3.0 GPA required.
Amount of award:	$1,000
Number of awards:	1
Number of applicants:	14
Application deadline:	March 31
Total amount awarded:	$1,000

Contact:
Ohio Newspapers Foundation
1335 Dublin Road
Suite 216-B
Columbus, OH 43215
Phone: 614-486-6677

Ohio Newspapers Minority Scholarship

Type of award: Scholarship.
Intended use: For full-time freshman study in United States. Designated institutions: Ohio postsecondary institutions.
Eligibility: Applicant must be Alaskan native, Asian American, African American, Mexican American, Hispanic American, Puerto Rican or American Indian. Applicant must be residing in Ohio.
Basis for selection: Major/career interest in journalism. Applicant must demonstrate high academic achievement.
Application requirements: Recommendations, essay, transcript, proof of eligibility. Students may include writing samples or articles that have been published.
Additional information: Minimum GPA of 2.5.
Amount of award:	$1,000
Number of awards:	3
Number of applicants:	8
Application deadline:	March 31
Notification begins:	May 15
Total amount awarded:	$3,000

Contact:
Ohio Newspapers Foundation
1335 Dublin Road
Suite 216-B
Columbus, OH 43215
Phone: 614-486-6677

Oklahoma Engineering Foundation

Oklahoma Engineering Foundation Scholarship

Type of award: Scholarship.
Intended use: For freshman study at accredited 4-year institution in United States. Designated institutions: Engineering institution in Oklahoma.
Eligibility: Applicant must be high school senior. Applicant must be U.S. citizen residing in Oklahoma.
Basis for selection: Major/career interest in engineering. Applicant must demonstrate depth of character, leadership and service orientation.
Application requirements: Interview, essay, transcript. Minimum 3.0 GPA. ACT composite score not to exceed maximum of 32.

Additional information: Must be used at specific institutions in Oklahoma, Iowa or Kansas. Contact office for more information.
Amount of award:	$500-$1,000
Application deadline:	November 15
Notification begins:	April 30

Contact:
Executive Director
201 Northeast 27th Street
Room 125
Oklahoma City, OK 73105

Oklahoma State Regents for Higher Education

Oklahoma Academic Scholars Program

Type of award: Scholarship, renewable.
Intended use: For full-time freshman or sophomore study at 2-year, 4-year or graduate institution. Designated institutions: Oklahoma institutions.
Eligibility: Applicant must be U.S. citizen.
Basis for selection: Applicant must demonstrate high academic achievement.
Application requirements: Proof of eligibility.
Additional information: Must be graduating high school senior, first-time freshman or transfer student entering within 27 months of high school graduation. Oklahoma resident must score in at least 99.5th percentile on SAT or ACT or meet National Merit Scholarship finalist criteria. Out-of-state students eligible if National Merit Scholar, Presidential Scholar, or National Merit Finalist.
Amount of award:	$3,500-$5,500

Contact:
Oklahoma State Regents for Higher Education
Academic Scholars Program
500 Education Building
Oklahoma City, OK 73105-4500
Phone: 405-524-9131
Fax: 405-524-9230

Oklahoma Future Teachers Scholarship

Type of award: Scholarship, renewable.
Intended use: For undergraduate, master's or doctoral study at accredited 2-year, 4-year or graduate institution.
Eligibility: Applicant must be U.S. citizen or permanent resident residing in Oklahoma.
Basis for selection: Major/career interest in education, teacher or education. Applicant must demonstrate high academic achievement.
Application requirements: Proof of eligibility.
Additional information: Requires ranking in top 15 percent of class or admission to professional education program. Applications reviewed first by institutions, then sent to Regents Scholarship Committee with recommendations. Must pursue certification and plan to teach in critical teacher shortage area.

Amount of award:	$500-$1,500
Number of awards:	140
Number of applicants:	140
Application deadline:	May 1
Notification begins:	July 1
Total amount awarded:	$100,000

Contact:
Oklahoma State Regents For Higher Education
State Capitol Complex
500 Education Building
Oklahoma City, OK 73105-4500
Phone: 405-524-9131
Fax: 405-524-9230

Oklahoma Tuition Aid Grant

Type of award: Scholarship, renewable.
Intended use: For undergraduate or graduate study at accredited vocational, 2-year, 4-year or graduate institution. Designated institutions: Oklahoma postsecondary institutions and nonprofit public technology institutions only.
Eligibility: Applicant must be U.S. citizen or permanent resident residing in Oklahoma.
Basis for selection: Applicant must demonstrate financial need.
Application requirements: Proof of eligibility.
Additional information: Apply early as funding is limited: for best consideration, apply by April 30. Final deadline June 30. Must meet minimum standards of academic progress for financial aid recipients. Must be enrolled in program leading to degree or certificate.

Amount of award:	$200-$1,000
Number of applicants:	300
Application deadline:	June 30

Contact:
Oklahoma State Regents For Higher Education
P.O. Box 3020
Oklahoma City, OK 73101-3020
Phone: 405-858-4356
Fax: 405-858-4392

Olympic Steel, Inc.

Olympic Steel, Inc. Scholarship Program

Type of award: Scholarship, renewable.
Intended use: For undergraduate study at accredited vocational, 2-year or 4-year institution.
Eligibility: Applicant or parent must be employed by Olympic Steel, Inc.
Additional information: For further information or an application, contact Olympic Steel, Inc. directly.

Amount of award:	$1,250

OMNE/Nursing Leaders of Maine

OMNE/Nursing Leaders of Maine Scholarship

Type of award: Scholarship.
Intended use: For undergraduate study.
Eligibility: Applicant must be U.S. citizen residing in Maine.
Basis for selection: Major/career interest in nursing. Applicant must demonstrate seriousness of purpose and service orientation.
Application requirements: Recommendations, transcript, proof of eligibility. Enrollment in baccalaureate program.
Additional information: Must be a nursing school student. Applicant must attend college in Maine.

Amount of award:	$500
Number of awards:	2
Number of applicants:	12
Application deadline:	May 1
Total amount awarded:	$500

Contact:
Sherry Rogers, RN, MS
Redington Fairview General Hospital
P.O. Box 468
Skowhegan, ME 04976

ONS Foundation

Ethnic Minority Bachelor's Scholarships

Type of award: Scholarship.
Intended use: For undergraduate study in United States. Designated institutions: Schools accredited by the National League for Nursing.
Eligibility: Applicant must be Alaskan native, Asian American, African American, Mexican American, Hispanic American, Puerto Rican or American Indian.
Basis for selection: Major/career interest in nursing or oncology. Applicant must demonstrate high academic achievement, depth of character, leadership and service orientation.
Application requirements: $5 application fee. Essay, transcript, proof of eligibility.
Additional information: Must be licensed registered nurse and currently enrolled in or applying to an oncology degree nursing program at school accredited by National League for Nursing.

Amount of award:	$2,000
Number of awards:	3
Application deadline:	February 1
Notification begins:	March 15
Total amount awarded:	$6,000

Contact:
ONS Foundation
Bonny Revo
501 Holiday Drive
Pittsburgh, PA 15220
Phone: 412-921-7373
Fax: 412-921-1762
Web: www.ons.org

Oncology Nursing Certification Corporation Bachelor's Scholarships

Type of award: Scholarship.
Intended use: For undergraduate study in United States. Designated institutions: Schools accredited by National League for Nursing.
Basis for selection: Major/career interest in nursing or oncology. Applicant must demonstrate high academic achievement, depth of character, leadership and service orientation.
Application requirements: $5 application fee. Essay, transcript, proof of eligibility.
Additional information: Must be licensed registered nurse and currently enrolled in or applying to oncology nursing degree program at school accredited by National League for Nursing.

Amount of award:	$2,000
Number of awards:	10
Application deadline:	February 1
Notification begins:	March 15
Total amount awarded:	$20,000

Contact:
ONS Foundation
Bonny Revo
501 Holiday Drive
Pittsburgh, PA 15220
Phone: 412-921-7373 ext. 231
Fax: 412-921-1762
Web: www.ons.org

Roberta Pierce Scofield Bachelor's Scholarships

Type of award: Scholarship.
Intended use: For undergraduate study. Designated institutions: Schools accredited by the National League for Nursing.
Basis for selection: Major/career interest in nursing or oncology. Applicant must demonstrate high academic achievement, depth of character, leadership and service orientation.
Application requirements: $5 application fee. Essay, transcript, proof of eligibility.
Additional information: Must be licensed registered nurse and currently enrolled in or applying to an oncology degree nursing program at school accredited by National League for Nursing.

Amount of award:	$2,000
Number of awards:	3
Application deadline:	February 1
Notification begins:	March 15
Total amount awarded:	$6,000

Contact:
ONS Foundation
Bonny Revo
501 Holiday Drive
Pittsburgh, PA 15220
Phone: 412-921-7373
Fax: 412-921-1762
Web: www.ons.org

Order of AHEPA

AHEPA Scholarship

Type of award: Scholarship, renewable.
Intended use: For full-time undergraduate or graduate study at postsecondary institution.
Eligibility: Applicant or parent must be member/participant of American Hellenic Educational Progressive Association. Applicant must be Greek.
Basis for selection: Applicant must demonstrate financial need, high academic achievement, depth of character, leadership, patriotism, seriousness of purpose and service orientation.
Application requirements: Recommendations, essay, transcript, proof of eligibility.
Additional information: Applicant must be member in good standing of AHEPA family including Daughters of Penelope, Sons of Pericles, and Maids of Athena or son or daughter of same. High school seniors welcome to apply. Information and application available online.

Amount of award:	$500-$1,000
Number of awards:	8
Application deadline:	March 31
Notification begins:	September 1
Total amount awarded:	$10,000

Contact:
AHEPA Educational Foundation--Scholarships
1909 Q Street, NW
Suite 500
Washington, DC 20009-1007
Web: www.ahepa.org

Oregon Student Assistance Commission

Alpha Delta Kappa/Harriet Simmons Scholarship

Type of award: Scholarship, renewable.
Intended use: For full-time senior, post-bachelor's certificate or master's study at accredited postsecondary institution in United States.
Eligibility: Applicant must be U.S. citizen or permanent resident residing in Oregon.
Basis for selection: Major/career interest in education or education, teacher. Applicant must demonstrate financial need and high academic achievement.
Application requirements: Transcript. Include FAFSA and two essays.

Additional information: Applicants must be elementary or secondary education majors. For those with disabilities: TYY 541-687-7395 (voice), 800-452-8807 ext. 7395. Visit Website for additional information and to apply.

> **Application deadline:** March 1
> **Notification begins:** March 15

Contact:
Oregon Student Assistance Commission
Attn: Grant Division
1500 Valley River Drive, Suite 100
Eugene, OR 97401-2146
Phone: 541- 687-7400
Web: www.osac.state.or.us

American Ex-Prisoner of War, Peter Connacher Memorial Scholarship

Type of award: Scholarship, renewable.
Intended use: For full-time undergraduate or graduate study at postsecondary institution in United States.
Eligibility: Applicant must be U.S. citizen or permanent resident residing in Oregon. Applicant must be veteran or descendant of veteran; or dependent of veteran or POW/MIA. Must be American former prisoner of war or descendant.
Basis for selection: Applicant must demonstrate financial need and high academic achievement.
Application requirements: Transcript, proof of eligibility. Include FAFSA and two essays. Must submit copy of U.S. Armed Forces discharge papers, proof of P.O.W. status and relationship to P.O.W.
Additional information: Intended for American former prisoners of war and their descendents. Contact high school guidance office, undergraduate financial aid office, or OSAC (send SASE). For those with disabilities: TYY 542-687-7395 (voice), 800-452-8807 ext. 7395. Visit Website for additional information and to apply.

> **Application deadline:** March 1
> **Notification begins:** March 15

Contact:
Oregon Student Assistance Commission
Attn: Grant Division
1500 Valley River Drive, Suite 100
Eugene, OR 97401-2146
Phone: 541-687-7400
Web: www.osac.state.or.us

Ben Selling Scholarship

Type of award: Scholarship, renewable.
Intended use: For full-time sophomore, junior or senior study at postsecondary institution in United States.
Eligibility: Applicant must be U.S. citizen or permanent resident residing in Oregon.
Basis for selection: Applicant must demonstrate high academic achievement.
Application requirements: Transcript. Two essays, FAFSA. Minimum 3.5 GPA.
Additional information: Wells Fargo employees, children, or near relatives must provide complete disclosure of employment status. For those with disabilities: TYY 542-687-7395 (voice), 800-452-8807 ext. 7395. Visit Website for additional information and to apply.

> **Application deadline:** March 1
> **Notification begins:** March 15

Contact:
Oregon Student Assistance Commission
Attn: Grant Division
1500 Valley River Drive, Suite 100
Eugene, OR 97401-2146
Phone: 541-687-7400
Web: www.osac.state.or.us

Bertha P. Singer Scholarship

Type of award: Scholarship, renewable.
Intended use: For full-time undergraduate or graduate study at accredited postsecondary institution. Designated institutions: Oregon postsecondary schools with nursing programs.
Eligibility: Applicant must be U.S. citizen or permanent resident residing in Oregon.
Basis for selection: Major/career interest in nursing.
Application requirements: Transcript, proof of eligibility. FAFSA, two essays. Minimum 3.0 GPA. Must provide documentation of enrollment in third year of four-year nursing degree program or second year of two-year associate degree nursing program.
Additional information: Employees of U.S. Bancorp., their children or near relatives are not eligible. For those with disabilities: TYY 542-687-7395 (voice), 800-452-8807 ext. 7395. Visit Website for additional information and to apply.

> **Application deadline:** March 1
> **Notification begins:** March 15

Contact:
Oregon Student Assistance Commission
Attn: Grant Division
1500 Valley River Drive, Suite 100
Eugene, OR 97401-2146
Phone: 541-687-7400
Web: www.osac.state.or.us

David Family Scholarship

Type of award: Scholarship, renewable.
Intended use: For undergraduate or graduate study at postsecondary institution in United States.
Eligibility: Applicant must be U.S. citizen or permanent resident residing in Oregon.
Basis for selection: Applicant must demonstrate financial need and high academic achievement.
Application requirements: Transcript. Include FAFSA and two essays. Minimum 2.50 GPA.
Additional information: Intended for residents of Clackamas, Lane, Linn, Marion, Multnomah, Washington and Yamhill counties. Preference: 1) applicants enrolling at least half-time in upper-division or graduate programs at four-year colleges, 2) graduating high school seniors from West Linn-Wilsonville, Lake Oswego, Portland, Tigard-Tualatin or Beaverton school districts. For those with disabilities: TYY 542-687-7395 (voice), 800-452-8807 ext. 7395. Visit Website for additional information and to apply.

> **Application deadline:** March 1
> **Notification begins:** March 15

Contact:
Oregon Student Assistance Commission
Attn: Grant Division
1500 Valley River Drive, Suite 100
Eugene, OR 97401-2146
Phone: 541-687-7400
Web: www.osac.state.or.us

Dorothy Campbell Memorial Scholarship

Type of award: Scholarship, renewable.
Intended use: For full-time undergraduate study at accredited 4-year institution. Designated institutions: Four-year colleges in Oregon.
Eligibility: Applicant must be female. Applicant must be U.S. citizen or permanent resident residing in Oregon.
Basis for selection: Applicant must demonstrate financial need and high academic achievement.
Application requirements: Transcript. FAFSA, two essays required by OSAC. Minimum cumulative GPA of 2.75. Additional essay: one page describing strong and continuing interest in golf and contribution that golf has made to applicant's development.
Additional information: Intended for female graduates of Oregon high schools. For those with disabilities: TYY 541-687-7395 (voice), 800-452-8807 ext. 7395. Visit Website for additional information and to apply.

    Application deadline: March 1
    Notification begins: March 15

Contact:
Oregon Student Assistance Commission
Attn: Grant Division
1500 Valley River Drive, Suite l00
Eugene, OR 97401-2146
Phone: 541-687-7400
Web: www.osac.state.or.us

Ford Opportunity Program

Type of award: Scholarship, renewable.
Intended use: For full-time undergraduate study at accredited 4-year institution. Designated institutions: Oregon colleges or community colleges.
Eligibility: Applicant must be U.S. citizen or permanent resident residing in Oregon.
Basis for selection: Applicant must demonstrate financial need and high academic achievement.
Application requirements: Transcript. FAFSA, two essays. Minimum 3.0 GPA or 260 GED score, unless application is accompanied by Special Recommendation Form from counselor or OSAC.
Additional information: Must be single head of household with custody of dependent children. Apply to this program or Ford Scholars Program, not both. For those with disabilities: TYY 541-687-7395 (voice), 800-452-8807 ext. 7395. Visit Website for additional information and to apply. Attention counselors: If you wish to intervene on behalf of applicant who does not meet minimum requirements, please check in your Financial Aid Handbook for recommendation form. College counselors: call 800-452-8807 ext. 7388 for recommendation form.

    Number of awards: 30
    Application deadline: March 1
    Notification begins: March 15

Contact:
Oregon Student Assistance Commission
Attn: Grant Division
1500 Valley River Drive, Suite l00
Eugene, OR 97401-2146
Phone: 541-687-7400
Web: www.osac.state.or.us

Ford Scholars Program

Type of award: Scholarship, renewable.
Intended use: For full-time undergraduate study at accredited 4-year institution. Designated institutions: Oregon colleges or community colleges.
Eligibility: Applicant must be U.S. citizen or permanent resident residing in Oregon.
Basis for selection: Applicant must demonstrate financial need, high academic achievement, depth of character and seriousness of purpose.
Application requirements: Transcript. FAFSA, two essays. Minimum 3.0 GPA or 260 GED score, unless application is accompanied by Special Recommendation Form from counselor or OSAC.
Additional information: Intended for high school seniors/graduates who have not yet been full-time undergraduates, or for individuals who have completed two years at Oregon community college and are entering junior year at Oregon four-year college. Apply to this program or Ford Opportunity Program, not both. For those with disabilities: TYY 541-687-7395 (voice), 800-452-8807 ext. 7395. Visit Website for additional information and to apply. Attention counselors: If you wish to intervene on behalf of applicant who does not meet minimum requirements, please check your Financial Aid Handbook for recommendation form. College counselors: call 800-452-8807 ext. 7388 for recommendation form.

    Number of awards: 100
    Application deadline: March 1
    Notification begins: March 15

Contact:
Oregon Student Assistance Commission
Attn: Grant Division
1500 Valley River Drive, Suite l00
Eugene, OR 97401-2146
Phone: 541-687-7400
Web: www.osac.state.or.us

Friends of Oregon Students Scholarship

Type of award: Scholarship, renewable.
Intended use: For undergraduate or graduate study at 4-year or graduate institution in United States.
Eligibility: Applicant must be returning adult student. Applicant must be U.S. citizen or permanent resident residing in Oregon.
Basis for selection: Major/career interest in health education; social work; public health; education; nursing; physical therapy; environmental science; mental health/therapy; education, teacher or education, special. Applicant must demonstrate service orientation.
Application requirements: Transcript. FAFSA, two essays. Preferences: 1) volunteer or work experience relevant to chosen profession; 2) graduate of public alternative Oregon high school or GED recipient or transferring from Oregon community college to 4-year college; 3) GPA of 2.5 over last three quarters of solid course work.
Additional information: For non-traditional students (e.g., older, returning, single parent) who are working and will continue to work at least 20 hours weekly while attending college at least 3/4 time. Must be pursuing career in the helping professions. For those with disabilities: TYY 541-687-7395 (voice), 800-452-8807 ext. 7395. Visit Website for additional information and to apply. Additional information and requirements will be sent to applicants from donor upon receipt of application.

Application deadline: March 1
Notification begins: March 15
Contact:
Oregon Student Assistance Commission
Grant Division/Friends of Oregon Students
1500 Valley River Drive, Suite 100
Eugene, OR 97401-2146
Phone: 541-687-7400
Web: www.osac.state.or.us

Glenn Jackson Scholars

Type of award: Scholarship, renewable.
Intended use: For full-time undergraduate study at postsecondary institution in United States.
Eligibility: Applicant or parent must be employed by Oregon Department of Transportation/Parks and Recreation Dept. Applicant must be high school senior. Applicant must be U.S. citizen or permanent resident residing in Oregon.
Application requirements: Transcript. FAFSA, two essays required by OSAC. Additional essays: two one-page essays: (1) "How do you plan to finance your college education?" and (2) "If you could have a personal meeting with the Governor of Oregon, what would you talk about and why?"
Additional information: Intended for dependents of employees or retirees of Oregon Department of Transportation or Parks and Recreation Department. Employees must have been employed by their departments at least three years. For those with disabilities: TYY 541-687-7395 (voice), 800-452-8807 ext. 7395. Visit Website for additional information and to apply.

Application deadline: March 1
Notification begins: March 15
Contact:
Oregon Student Assistance Commission
Attn: Grant Division
1500 Valley River Drive, Suite 100
Eugene, OR 97401-2146
Phone: 541-687-7400
Web: www.osac.state.or.us

Howard Vollum American Indian Scholarship

Type of award: Scholarship, renewable.
Intended use: For undergraduate study at postsecondary institution in United States.
Eligibility: Applicant must be American Indian. For American Indian residents of Clackamas, Multnomah, or Washington County in Oregon, or Clark County, Washington. Applicant must be U.S. citizen residing in Oregon or Washington.
Basis for selection: Major/career interest in science, general; computer/information sciences; mathematics; engineering or engineering, computer. Applicant must demonstrate service orientation.
Application requirements: Transcript, proof of eligibility. FAFSA, two essays. Additional essay topic: "How do you view your cultural heritage and its importance to you?" Submit certification of tribal enrollment or American Indian ancestry: photocopy of (1) tribal enrollment card that includes enrollment number and/or blood quantum, (2) Johnson O'Malley student cligibility form or (3) letter from tribe stating blood quantum and/or enrollment number of parent or grandparent.
Additional information: Applicants with demonstrated commitment to the American Indian community preferred. For those with disabilities: TYY 542-687-7395 (voice), 800-452-

8807 ext. 7395. Visit Website for additional information and to apply.
Application deadline: March 1
Notification begins: March 15
Contact:
Oregon Student Assistance Commission
Attn: Grant Division
1500 Valley River Drive, Suite 100
Eugene, OR 97401-2146
Phone: 541-687-7400
Web: www.osac.state.or.us

Ida M. Crawford Scholarship

Type of award: Scholarship, renewable.
Intended use: For full-time undergraduate study at accredited postsecondary institution in United States.
Eligibility: Applicant must be U.S. citizen residing in Oregon.
Basis for selection: Applicant must demonstrate financial need and high academic achievement.
Application requirements: Transcript, proof of eligibility. FAFSA, two essays. Minimum 3.5 GPA.
Additional information: Intended for graduates of accredited Oregon high schools. Not available to those majoring in law, medicine, music, theology, or teaching. U.S. Bancorp employees, their children and near relatives not eligible. Award amounts vary. For those with disabilities: TYY 541-687-7395 (voice), 800-452-8807 ext. 7395. Visit Website for additional information and to apply.
Application deadline: March 1
Notification begins: March 15
Contact:
Oregon Student Assistance Commission
Attn: Grant Division
1500 Valley River Drive, Suite l00
Eugene, OR 97401-2146
Phone: 541-687-7400
Web: www.osac.state.or.us

James Carlson Memorial Scholarship

Type of award: Scholarship, renewable.
Intended use: For full-time senior or post-bachelor's certificate study at accredited 4-year or graduate institution in United States.
Eligibility: Applicant must be U.S. citizen or permanent resident residing in Oregon.
Basis for selection: Major/career interest in education; education, teacher; education, special or education, early childhood. Applicant must demonstrate financial need and high academic achievement.
Application requirements: Transcript. FAFSA, two essays. Preference: 1) African-American, Asian, Hispanic, and Native American ethnic groups; 2) dependents of Oregon Education Association members; 3) others committed to teaching autistic children.
Additional information: Intended for elementary, secondary education majors entering senior or fifth-year OR graduate students in fifth year for elementary or secondary certificate. Award amounts vary. For those with disabilities: TYY 541-687-7395 (voice), 800-452-8807 ext. 7395. Visit Website for additional information and to apply.
Application deadline: March 1
Notification begins: March 15

Contact:
Oregon Student Assistance Commission
Attn: Grant Division
1500 Valley River Drive, Suite 100
Eugene, OR 97401-2146
Phone: 541-687-7400
Web: www.osac.state.or.us

Jerome B. Steinbach Scholarship

Type of award: Scholarship, renewable.
Intended use: For full-time sophomore, junior or senior study at accredited postsecondary institution in United States.
Eligibility: Applicant must be U.S. citizen residing in Oregon.
Basis for selection: Applicant must demonstrate financial need and high academic achievement.
Application requirements: Transcript. FAFSA, two essays. Minimum 3.5 GPA required. Must submit proof of U.S. birth.
Additional information: U.S. Bancorp employees, their children and near relatives not eligible. For those with disabilities: TYY 542-687-7395 (voice), 800-452-8807 ext. 7395. Visit Website for additional information and to apply.

Application deadline:	March 1
Notification begins:	July 31

Contact:
Oregon Student Assistance Commission
Attn: Grant Division
1500 Valley River Drive, Suite 100
Eugene, OR 97401-2146
Phone: 541-687-7400
Web: www.osac.state.or.us

Jose D. Garcia Migrant Education Scholarship

Type of award: Scholarship.
Intended use: For freshman study at postsecondary institution in United States. Designated institutions: Oregon postsecondary schools.
Eligibility: Applicant must be U.S. citizen or permanent resident residing in Oregon.
Application requirements: Transcript. FAFSA, two essays. Must be high school graduate or GED recipient. Must enter parents' names in Item 16 of Application.
Additional information: Applicant must be participant in Oregon Migrant Education Program. For those with disabilities: TYY 541-687-7395 (voice), 800-452-8807 ext. 7395. Visit Website for additional information and to apply.

Application deadline:	March 1
Notification begins:	March 15

Contact:
Oregon Student Assistance Commission
Attn: Grant Division
1500 Valley River Drive, Suite 100
Eugene, OR 97401-2146
Phone: 541-687-7400
Web: www.osac.state.or.us

Kaiser-Permanente Dental Assistant Scholarship

Type of award: Scholarship.
Intended use: For full-time undergraduate certificate study at accredited vocational or 2-year institution. Designated institutions: Blue Mountain Community College, Chemeketa Community College, Concorde Career Institute, Lane Community College, Linn-Benton Community College and Portland Community College.
Eligibility: Applicant must be U.S. citizen or permanent resident residing in Oregon.
Basis for selection: Major/career interest in dental assistant. Applicant must demonstrate financial need.
Application requirements: Transcript. FAFSA, two essays.
Additional information: For those with disabilities, TYY 541-687-7395 (voice), 800-452-8807 ext. 7395. Visit Website for additional information and to apply.

Application deadline:	March 1
Notification begins:	July 31

Contact:
Oregon Student Assistance Commission
Attn: Grant Division
1500 Valley River Drive, Suite 100
Eugene, OR 97401-2146
Phone: 541-687-7400
Web: www.osac.state.or.us

Lawrence R. Foster Memorial Scholarship

Type of award: Scholarship, renewable.
Intended use: For junior, senior or graduate study at accredited 4-year or graduate institution in United States.
Eligibility: Applicant must be U.S. citizen or permanent resident residing in Oregon.
Basis for selection: Major/career interest in nursing; medical specialties/research; physician assistant; public health; medical assistant; health-related professions; bioengineering; engineering, biomedical or nurse practitioner. Applicant must demonstrate service orientation.
Application requirements: Transcript. FAFSA, two essays. Provide three names/phone numbers of references and additional one-page essay describing interest, experience (if any) in public health career, migrant clinics, or community primary care clinics. Preference: 1) persons working, or graduates majoring, in public health; 2) undergraduates entering junior/senior-year health programs.
Additional information: Applicant must be seeking career in public health, not private practice. For those with disabilities: TYY 541-687-7395 (voice), 800-452-8807 ext. 7395. Visit Website for additional information and to apply.

Application deadline:	March 1
Notification begins:	March 15

Contact:
Oregon Student Assistance Commission
Attn: Grant Division
1500 Valley River Drive, Suite 100
Eugene, OR 97401-2146
Phone: 541-687-7400
Web: www.osac.state.or.us

Maria Jackson-General George White Scholarship

Type of award: Scholarship, renewable.
Intended use: For full-time undergraduate or graduate study at accredited postsecondary institution. Designated institutions: Oregon postsecondary institutions.
Eligibility: Applicant must be U.S. citizen or permanent resident residing in Oregon. Applicant must be veteran; or dependent of active service person, veteran, disabled veteran, deceased veteran or POW/MIA who serves or served in the Army, Air Force, Marines, Navy, Coast Guard or Reserves/

National Guard. Enlisted individual must have resided in Oregon at time of enlistment.
Basis for selection: Applicant must demonstrate financial need and high academic achievement.
Application requirements: Transcript, proof of eligibility. FAFSA, two essays. Minimum 3.75 GPA. Provide documentation (DD93, DD214, discharge papers).
Additional information: U.S. Bancorp employees, their children or near relatives not eligible. For those with disabilities: TYY 541-687-7395 (voice), 800-452-8807 ext. 7395. Visit Website for additional information and to apply.

Application deadline:	March 1
Notification begins:	July 31

Contact:
Oregon Student Assistance Commission
Attn: Grant Division
1500 Valley River Drive, Suite 100
Eugene, OR 97401-2146
Phone: 541-687-7400
Web: www.osac.state.or.us

Mark Hass Journalism Scholarship

Type of award: Scholarship.
Intended use: For full-time undergraduate study at accredited postsecondary institution in United States.
Eligibility: Applicant must be U.S. citizen or permanent resident residing in Oregon.
Basis for selection: Major/career interest in journalism. Applicant must demonstrate financial need.
Application requirements: Transcript. FAFSA, two essays.
Additional information: For those with disabilities: TYY 541-687-7395 (voice), 800-452-8807 ext. 7395. Visit Website for additional information and to apply.

Application deadline:	March 1
Notification begins:	March 15

Contact:
Oregon Student Assistance Commission
Attn: Grant Division
1500 Valley River Drive, Suite 100
Eugene, OR 97401-2146
Phone: 541-687-7400
Web: www.osac.state.or.us

Mentor Graphics Scholarship

Type of award: Scholarship, renewable.
Intended use: For full-time junior or senior study at accredited 4-year institution in United States.
Eligibility: Applicant must be U.S. citizen or permanent resident residing in Oregon.
Basis for selection: Major/career interest in computer/ information sciences; engineering, electrical/electronic or engineering, computer. Applicant must demonstrate financial need.
Application requirements: Transcript. FAFSA, two essays. Preference: one award to female, Hispanic or African American applicant.
Additional information: For those with disabilities: TYY 541-687-7395 (voice), 800-452-8807 ext. 7395. Visit Website for additional information and to apply.

Application deadline:	March 1
Notification begins:	July 31

Contact:
Oregon Student Assistance Commission
Attn: Grant Division
1500 Valley River Drive, Suite 100
Eugene, OR 97401-2146
Phone: 541-687-7400
Web: www.osac.state.or.us

Oregon AFL-CIO Scholarship

Type of award: Scholarship.
Intended use: For full-time undergraduate or graduate study at postsecondary institution in United States.
Eligibility: Applicant must be high school senior. Applicant must be U.S. citizen or permanent resident residing in Oregon.
Application requirements: Essay, transcript. FAFSA. two essays required by OSAC; additional 500-word essay required by AFL-CIO on one of following topics: "Explain why you think that unions must maintain a strong political voice or why not" or "Explain how the labor movement can attract people of your generation who may be about to enter the labor force." Be detailed and descriptive.
Additional information: Preference may be given to applicants from union families. For more about essay topic, call Oregon AFL-CIO at 503-585-6320. For those with disabilities: TYY 541-687-7395 (voice), 800-452-8807 ext. 7395. Visit Website for additional information and to apply.

Application deadline:	March 8
Notification begins:	March 15

Contact:
Oregon Student Assistance Commission
Attn: Grant Division
1500 Valley River Drive, Suite 100
Eugene, OR 97401-2146
Phone: 541-687-7400
Web: www.osac.state.or.us

Oregon Collectors Association Bob Hasson Memorial Scholarship Fund Essay

Type of award: Scholarship.
Intended use: For full-time freshman study at postsecondary institution. Designated institutions: Oregon colleges and vocational schools.
Eligibility: Applicant must be high school senior. Applicant must be U.S. citizen or permanent resident residing in Oregon.
Basis for selection: Competition/talent/interest in Writing/ journalism, based on three- to-four page essay: "The Proper Use of Credit in the 21st Century" Applicant must demonstrate financial need.
Application requirements: Essay, transcript. Include FAFSA and two essays required by OSAC. Applicant's name, address and social security number should appear on each page of competitive essay, "The Proper Use of Credit."
Additional information: Applicant must be enrolling in Oregon college within 12 months of high school graduation. Children and grandchildren of owners and officers of collection agencies in Oregon not eligible. Finalists read their essays at Association annual Spring meeting. Essays may be printed/ published at discretion of Oregon Collectors Association. For those with disabilities: TYY 541-687-7395 (voice), 800-452-8807 ext. 7395. Visit Website for additional information and to apply.

Amount of award:	$1,500-$3,000
Application deadline:	March 1
Notification begins:	July 31

Contact:
Oregon Student Assistance Commission
Attn: Grant Division
1500 Valley River Drive, Suite 100
Eugene, OR 97401-2146
Phone: 541-687-7400
Web: www.osac.state.or.us

Oregon Disabled Peace Officer Grant Program

Type of award: Scholarship.
Intended use: For full-time undergraduate study at accredited 2-year or 4-year institution. Designated institutions: Oregon public college or university or independent, private, non-profit college or university.
Eligibility: Applicant must be U.S. citizen or permanent resident residing in Oregon. Applicant's parent must have been killed or disabled in work-related accident as fire fighter, police officer or public safety officer.
Basis for selection: Applicant must demonstrate financial need.
Application requirements: Transcript, proof of eligibility. Certification of Eligibility for Disabled Peace Officer Scholarship from Oregon Student Assistance Commission Commission (OSAC). FAFSA.
Additional information: Send SASE. Must be natural or adopted child or stepchild of eligible Oregon public safety officers including firefighters, State Fire Marshall, chief deputy fire marshal, deputy state fire marshals, police chiefs and police officers, sheriffs and deputy sheriffs, county adult parole and probation officers, correction officers, and investigators of Criminal Justice Division of Department of Justice. Public safety officer must have been killed or disabled in line of duty. At eligible Oregon private college, award amount equals sum of tuition and fees charged to students attending University of Oregon. Deadline variable.

  Amount of award: Full tuition
Contact:
Disabled Public Safety Officer Program
Oregan State Scholarship Commission
1500 Valley River Drive, Suite 100
Eugene, OR 97401
Phone: 541-687-7400
Web: www.osac.state.or.us

Oregon Dungeness Crab Commission

Type of award: Scholarship.
Intended use: For full-time undergraduate study at postsecondary institution in United States.
Eligibility: Applicant or parent must be employed by Oregon Dungeness Crab Fishermen. Applicant must be high school senior. Applicant must be residing in Oregon.
Application requirements: Transcript. FAFSA, two essays. Identify vessel in place of "work site" on item 16 of Application.
Additional information: For dependents of licensed Oregon Dungeness Crab fishermen or crew. For those with disabilities: TYY 541-687-7395 (voice), 800-452-8807 ext. 7395. Visit Website for additional information and to apply.

  Application deadline: March 1
  Notification begins: March 15

Contact:
Oregon Student Assistance Commission
Attn: Grant Division
1500 Valley River Drive, Suite 100
Eugene, OR 97401-2146
Phone: 541-687-7400
Web: www.osac.state.or.us

Oregon Metro Federal Credit Union Scholarship

Type of award: Scholarship, renewable.
Intended use: For full-time freshman study at postsecondary institution in United States. Designated institutions: Oregon postsecondary institutions given preference.
Eligibility: Applicant or parent must be member/participant of Oregon Metro Federal Credit Union. Applicant must be U.S. citizen or permanent resident residing in Oregon.
Basis for selection: Applicant must demonstrate financial need and high academic achievement.
Application requirements: Transcript. FAFSA, two essays.
Additional information: Intended for graduates of Oregon high schools who are Oregon Metro Federal Credit Union Members. Preference given to graduating high school seniors attending Oregon colleges. For those with disabilities: TYY 541-687-7395 (voice), 800-452-8807 ext. 7395. Visit Website for additional information and to apply.

  Application deadline: March 1
  Notification begins: March 15

Contact:
Oregon Student Assistance Commission
Attn: Grant Division
1500 Valley River Drive, Suite 100
Eugene, OR 97401-2146
Phone: 541-687-7400
Web: www.osac.state.or.us

Oregon National Guard Tuition Assistance

Type of award: Scholarship, renewable.
Intended use: For undergraduate study at accredited postsecondary institution. Designated institutions: Oregon postsecondary institutions.
Eligibility: Applicant must be U.S. citizen residing in Oregon. Applicant must be in military service; or dependent of active service person; or spouse of active service person in the Reserves/National Guard. Must be serving in Oregon Army or Air National Guard, or Oregon National Guard Association (Life Members).
Basis for selection: Applicant must demonstrate high academic achievement, leadership and seriousness of purpose.
Application requirements: Proof of eligibility. FAFSA.
Additional information: Maximum 12 undergraduate quarters or equivalent. Applicant must have demonstrated traits and qualities of leadership by having participated in school and civic activities and demonstrated a strong motivation for continued education.

  Number of awards: 1

Contact:
Oregon Student Assistance Commission
Private Awards
1500 Valley River Drive, Suite 100
Eugene, OR 97401-2146
Phone: 541-687-7400
Fax: 541-687-7419
Web: www.ossc.state.or.us

Oregon Occupational Safety and Health Division Workers Memorial Scholarship

Type of award: Scholarship, renewable.
Intended use: For full-time undergraduate or graduate study at postsecondary institution in United States.
Eligibility: Applicant must be U.S. citizen or permanent resident residing in Oregon. Applicant's parent must have been killed or disabled in work-related accident as public safety officer.
Basis for selection: Applicant must demonstrate high academic achievement.
Application requirements: Transcript, proof of eligibility. FAFSA, two essays required by OSAC. Additional 500-word essay: "How has the injury or death of your parent or spouse affected or influenced your decision to further your education?" Must provide name, social security number and workers compensation claim number of worker permanently disabled or fatally injured; location of incident; exact relationship to disabled or fatally injured worker.
Additional information: Intended for high school graduates or GED recipients who are dependents or spouses of Oregon worker permanently disabled on job or are receiving fatality benefits as dependent or spouse of worker fatally injured in Oregon. Contact Oregon Occupational Safety and Health Division or school guidance office or financial aid office of Commission. Send SASE. For those with disabilities: TYY 541-687-7395 (voice), 800-452-8807 ext. 7395. Visit Website for additional information and to apply.

Application deadline:	March 1
Notification begins:	March 15

Contact:
Oregon Student Assistance Commission
Attn: Grant Division
1500 Valley River Drive, Suite l00
Eugene, OR 97401-2146
Phone: 541-687-7400
Web: www.osac.state.or.us

Oregon Opportunity Grant

Type of award: Scholarship, renewable.
Intended use: For full-time undergraduate study at accredited 2-year or 4-year institution. Designated institutions: Public or non-profit private colleges or universities in Oregon.
Eligibility: Applicant must be U.S. citizen or permanent resident residing in Oregon.
Basis for selection: Applicant must demonstrate financial need.
Application requirements: Proof of eligibility. FAFSA.
Additional information: Students pursuing theology, divinity, or religious education degree not eligible. Contact high school guidance office, undergraduate financial aid office, or Commission (send SASE). Submit FAFSA as soon as possible after January 1. Opportunity Grants are awarded solely on the basis of financial need. Amount of award depends on cost of education. Qualifying applicants will be notified by school they plan to attend. Grant may be received for twelve terms or eight semesters if student maintains satisfactory academic progress and files a new FAFSA each year to demonstrate continued financial need.

Contact:
Oregon Student Assistance Commission
Grant Department
1500 Valley River Drive, Suite 100
Eugene, OR 97401
Phone: 541-687-7400
Web: www.osac.state.or.us

Oregon Public Employees Union (OPEU) Scholarship

Type of award: Scholarship, renewable.
Intended use: For undergraduate or graduate study at postsecondary institution in United States.
Eligibility: Applicant or parent must be member/participant of Oregon Public Employees Union (OPEU). Applicant must be U.S. citizen or permanent resident residing in Oregon.
Application requirements: Transcript. FAFSA, two essays.
Additional information: Priority: 1) OPEU members; 2) children, grandchildren, spouses or active or retired members in good standing; 3) dependents of deceased members who were active OPEU members at time of death; 4) laid-off members. Qualifying members must have been active OPEU members for at least one year. Children, grandchildren of qualifying members must be under age 25 at time of application and will be considered only for undergraduate program. Part-time enrollment or graduate program enrollment considered only for OPEU active members, spouses or laid-off members. For those with disabilities: TYY 541-687-7395 (voice), 800-452-8807 ext. 7395. Visit Website for additional information and to apply.

Application deadline:	March 1

Contact:
Oregon Student Assistance Commission
Attn: Grant Division
1500 Valley River Drive, Suite 100
Eugene, OR 97401-2146
Phone: 541-687-7400
Web: www.osac.state.or.us

Oregon Robert C. Byrd Honors Scholarship

Type of award: Scholarship, renewable.
Intended use: For full-time undergraduate study at accredited postsecondary institution in United States.
Eligibility: Applicant must be high school senior. Applicant must be U.S. citizen or permanent resident residing in Oregon.
Basis for selection: Applicant must demonstrate high academic achievement.
Application requirements: Transcript. FAFSA, two essays. Minimum 3.85 cumulative GPA or Oregon GED 325. Minimum 1300 combined SAT or 29 composite ACT.
Additional information: Intended for graduating seniors of any Oregon high school. 15 recipients per federal congressional district. For those with disabilities: TYY 542-687-7395 (voice), 800-452-8807 ext. 7395. Visit Website for additional information and to apply.

Amount of award:	$1,500
Number of awards:	75
Application deadline:	March 1
Notification begins:	March 15

Contact:
Oregon Student Assistance Commission
Attn: Grant Division
1500 Valley River Drive, Suite l00
Eugene, OR 97401-2146
Phone: 541-687-7400
Web: www.osac.state.or.us

Oregon State Personnel Management Association Scholarship

Type of award: Scholarship, renewable.
Intended use: For undergraduate or graduate study at postsecondary institution in United States.
Eligibility: Applicant or parent must be member/participant of Oregon State Personnel Management Association (OSPMA). Applicant must be U.S. citizen or permanent resident residing in Oregon.
Basis for selection: Major/career interest in business/management/administration; public administration/service; human resources; computer/information sciences; engineering, computer; engineering, materials; engineering, structural; information systems; communications or public relations.
Application requirements: Transcript. FAFSA, two essays.
Additional information: For members of Oregon State Personnel Management Association studying at least part-time college toward academic degree or professional certificate in personnel management, personnel administration, human resources management, safety management, labor relations, industrial relations, industrial engineering, business administration or closely related field. Certificate program applicants must apply directly to OSPMA. For those with disabilities: TYY 541-687-7395 (voice), 800-452-8807 ext. 7395. Visit Website for additional information and to apply.
  Application deadline: March 1
  Notification begins: March 15
Contact:
Oregon Student Assistance Commission
Attn: Grant Division
1500 Valley River Drive, Suite 100
Eugene, OR 97401-2146
Phone: 541-687-7400
Web: www.osac.state.or.us

Oregon Trucking Association

Type of award: Scholarship.
Intended use: For full-time undergraduate study at postsecondary institution in United States.
Eligibility: Applicant or parent must be member/participant of Oregon Trucking Association (OTA). Applicant must be high school senior. Applicant must be U.S. citizen or permanent resident residing in Oregon.
Application requirements: Transcript. FAFSA, two essays.
Additional information: Intended for graduating seniors of any Oregon high school who are children of Oregon Trucking Association (OTA) members or children of employees (for at least one year) of OTA members. For those with disabilities: TYY 541-687-7395 (voice), 800-452-8807 ext. 7395. Visit Website for additional information and to apply.
  Application deadline: March 1
  Notification begins: March 15

Contact:
Oregon Student Assistance Commission
Attn: Grant Division
1500 Valley River Drive, Suite 100
Eugene, OR 97401-2146
Phone: 541-687-7400
Web: www.osac.state.or.us

Pendleton Postal Workers (APWU Local 110) Scholarship

Type of award: Scholarship.
Intended use: For full-time freshman study at postsecondary institution in United States.
Eligibility: Applicant or parent must be member/participant of Pendleton Postal Workers (APWU Local 110). Applicant must be high school senior. Applicant must be U.S. citizen or permanent resident residing in Oregon.
Application requirements: Transcript. FAFSA, two essays required by OSAC. Additional essay topic: "What has the labor movement accomplished historically for working people?"
Additional information: For graduating high school seniors and dependents/descendants of active, retired or deceased members of Pendleton APWU #110 who have been members for at least one year preceding application deadline. For those with disabilities: TYY 541-687-7395 (voice), 800-452-8807 ext. 7395. Visit Website for additional information and to apply.
  Application deadline: March 1
  Notification begins: March 15
Contact:
Oregon Student Assistance Commission
Attn: Grant Division
1500 Valley River Drive, Suite 100
Eugene, OR 97401-2146
Phone: 541-687-7400
Web: www.osac.state.or.us

Professional Land Surveyors of Oregon Scholarship

Type of award: Scholarship, renewable.
Intended use: For full-time junior or senior study at postsecondary institution. Designated institutions: Oregon postsecondary institutions.
Eligibility: Applicant must be U.S. citizen or permanent resident residing in Oregon.
Basis for selection: Major/career interest in surveying/mapping.
Application requirements: Transcript. FAFSA, two essays. Additional essay: brief statement of education-career goals relating to land surveying.
Additional information: Students must be enrolled in curricula leading to land-surveying career. Community college applicants must intend to transfer to eligible four-year schools. Four-year applicants must intend to take Fundamentals of Land Surveying (FLS) exam. For those with disabilities: TYY 541-687-7395 (voice), 800-452-8807 ext. 7395. Visit Website for additional information and to apply.
  Application deadline: March 1
  Notification begins: March 15

Contact:
Oregon Student Assistance Commission
Attn: Grant Division
1500 Valley River Drive, Suite 100
Eugene, OR 97401-2146
Phone: 541-687-7400
Web: www.osac.state.or.us

Richard F. Brentano Memorial Scholarship

Type of award: Scholarship, renewable.
Intended use: For full-time undergraduate study at postsecondary institution in United States.
Eligibility: Applicant or parent must be employed by Waste Control Systems, Inc. Applicant must be no older than 26. Applicant must be U.S. citizen or permanent resident residing in Oregon.
Application requirements: Transcript. FAFSA, two essays.
Additional information: Intended for children or IRS-legal dependents (24 years of age and under) of employees of Waste Control Systems, Inc., and subsidiaries. Exception: age extended to maximum age 26 for children or IRS-legal dependents entering U.S. armed forces directly from high school. Employees must have been employed by Waste Control Systems one year minimum as of application deadline. For those with disabilities: TYY 541-687-7395 (voice), 800-452-8807 ext. 7395. Visit Website for additional information and to apply.

Application deadline:	March 1
Notification begins:	March 15

Contact:
Oregon State Scholarship Commission
Attn: Grant Division
1500 Valley Drive, Suite 100
Eugene, OR 97401-2146
Phone: 541-687-7400
Web: www.osac.state.or.us

Roger W. Emmons Memorial Scholarship

Type of award: Scholarship, renewable.
Intended use: For full-time undergraduate study at accredited postsecondary institution in United States.
Eligibility: Applicant or parent must be employed by Oregon Refuse & Recycling Association. Applicant must be high school senior. Applicant must be U.S. citizen or permanent resident residing in Oregon.
Application requirements: Transcript, proof of eligibility. FAFSA, two essays.
Additional information: Intended for graduating seniors of any Oregon high school. Parent(s) or grandparent(s) must have been solid waste company member(s) or employees (for at least three years) of members of Oregon Refuse & Recycling Association. For those with disabilities: TYY 542-687-7395 (voice), 800-452-8807 ext. 7395. Visit Website for additional information and to apply.

Application deadline:	March 1
Notification begins:	March 15

Contact:
Oregon Student Assistance Commission
Attn: Grant Division
1500 Valley River Drive, Suite 100
Eugene, OR 97401-2146
Phone: 541-687-7400
Web: www.osac.state.or.us

Teamsters Council #37 Federal Credit Union Scholarship

Type of award: Scholarship.
Intended use: For undergraduate or graduate study at postsecondary institution in United States.
Eligibility: Applicant or parent must be member/participant of International Brotherhood of Teamsters. Applicant must be U.S. citizen or permanent resident residing in Oregon.
Application requirements: Transcript. FAFSA, two essays required by OSAC. Additional essay topic: "The Importance of Preserving the Right to Strike in a Free Enterprise System." Applicant must have cumulative GPA between 2.0 and 3.0 and be enrolled at least half-time in college.
Additional information: For members (or dependents) of Council #37 credit union who are active, retired, disabled, or deceased members of Joint Council of Teamsters #37. Members must have been active in local affiliated with the Joint Council of Teamsters #37 at least one year. For those with disabilities: TYY 542-687-7395 (voice), 800-452-8807 ext. 7395. Visit Website for additional information and to apply.

Application deadline:	March 1
Notification begins:	March 15

Contact:
Oregon Student Assistance Commission
Attn: Grant Division
1500 Valley River Drive, Suite 100
Eugene, OR 97401-2146
Phone: 541-687-7400
Web: www.osac.state.or.us

Teamsters Local 305 Scholarship

Type of award: Scholarship, renewable.
Intended use: For full-time undergraduate study at postsecondary institution in United States.
Eligibility: Applicant or parent must be member/participant of International Brotherhood of Teamsters. Applicant must be high school senior. Applicant must be U.S. citizen or permanent resident residing in Oregon.
Application requirements: Transcript. FAFSA, two essays.
Additional information: For children or dependent stepchildren of active, retired, disabled, or deceased members of Local 305 of the Joint Council of Teamsters Number 37. Members must have been active at least one year. For those with disabilities: TYY 542-687-7395 (voice), 800-452-8807 ext. 7395. Visit Website for additional information and to apply.

Application deadline:	March 1
Notification begins:	March 15

Contact:
Oregon Student Assistance Commission
Attn: Grant Division
1500 Valley River Drive, Suite 100
Eugene, OR 97401-2146
Phone: 541-687-7400
Web: www.osac.state.or.us

Teamsters/Clyde C. Crosby/Joseph M. Edgar Memorial Scholarship

Type of award: Scholarship, renewable.
Intended use: For full-time undergraduate study at postsecondary institution in United States.
Eligibility: Applicant or parent must be member/participant of International Brotherhood of Teamsters. Applicant must be high school senior. Applicant must be U.S. citizen or permanent resident residing in Oregon.
Basis for selection: Applicant must demonstrate high academic achievement.
Application requirements: Transcript. FAFSA, two essays. Minimum 3.0 cumulative GPA.
Additional information: Graduating high school seniors who are children or dependent stepchildren of active, retired, disabled or deceased members of local unions affiliated with Joint Council of Teamsters #37. Qualifying members must have been active at least one year. For those with disabilities: TYY 542-687-7395 (voice), 800-452-8807 ext. 7395. Visit Website for additional information and to apply.
> **Application deadline:** March 1
> **Notification begins:** March 15
Contact:
Oregon Student Assistance Commission
Attn: Grant Division
1500 Valley River Drive, Suite 100
Eugene, OR 97401-2146
Phone: 541-687-7400
Web: www.osac.state.or.us

Troutman's Emporium Scholarship

Type of award: Scholarship.
Intended use: For undergraduate study at postsecondary institution in United States. Designated institutions: Postsecondary institutions in Oregon, Washington, Idaho and California preferred.
Eligibility: Applicant or parent must be employed by Emporium Corporation. Applicant must be U.S. citizen or permanent resident residing in Oregon.
Application requirements: Transcript. FAFSA, two essays.
Additional information: For employees of Emporium Corp. employed full- or part-time (1,000 hours within the past year) who have worked there at least one year and IRS-legal dependents. Preference given to students attending college in Oregon, Washington, Idaho, and California. For those with disabilities: TYY 542-687-7395 (voice), 800-452-8807 ext. 7395. Visit Website for additional information and to apply.
> **Application deadline:** March 1
> **Notification begins:** March 15
Contact:
Oregon Student Assistance Commission
Attn: Grant Division
1500 Valley River Drive, Suite 100
Eugene, OR 97401-2146
Phone: 541-687-7400
Web: www.osac.state.or.us

Vietnam-Era Veterans' Children Scholarship

Type of award: Scholarship.
Intended use: For full-time undergraduate or graduate study at accredited 2-year, 4-year or graduate institution in United States. Designated institutions: Oregon postsecondary institutions.
Eligibility: Applicant must be U.S. citizen or permanent resident residing in Oregon. Applicant must be dependent of veteran, disabled veteran, deceased veteran or POW/MIA during Vietnam. Must be veteran who served between February 28, 1961 and May 7, 1975.
Basis for selection: Applicant must demonstrate financial need.
Application requirements: Transcript, proof of eligibility. FAFSA, two essays and proof of parent's active duty (certificate of discharge or DD form 214).
Additional information: For Oregon residents who are children of U.S. veterans who served any portion of their military service between February 1961 and May 1975. For those with disabilities: TYY 542-687-7395 (voice), 800-452-8807 ext. 7395. Visit Website for additional information and to apply.
> **Application deadline:** March 1
> **Notification begins:** July 31
Contact:
Oregon Student Assistance Commission
Attn: Grant Division
1500 Valley River Drive, Suite l00
Eugene, OR 97401-2146
Phone: 541-687-7400
Web: www.osac.state.or.us

Walter and Marie Schmidt Scholarship

Type of award: Scholarship, renewable.
Intended use: For undergraduate study at accredited postsecondary institution in United States.
Eligibility: Applicant must be U.S. citizen or permanent resident residing in Oregon.
Basis for selection: Major/career interest in nursing or gerontology.
Application requirements: Transcript. FAFSA, two essays required by OSAC. Additional essay describing desire to pursue career in geriatric health care.
Additional information: Priority given to students from Lane County. U.S. Bancorp employees, their children or near relatives not eligible. For those with disabilities: TYY 542-687-7395 (voice), 800-452-8807 ext. 7395. Visit Website for additional information and to apply.
> **Application deadline:** March 1
> **Notification begins:** July 31
Contact:
Oregon Student Assistance Commission
Attn: Grant Division
1500 Valley River Drive, Suite 100
Eugene, OR 97401-2146
Phone: 541-687-7400
Web: www.osac.state.or.us

Osage Tribal Education Committee

Osage Tribal Education Scholarship

Type of award: Scholarship, renewable.

Intended use: For undergraduate or graduate study at accredited postsecondary institution in United States.
Eligibility: Applicant must be American Indian. Must be a member of the Osage Nation of Oklahoma. Applicant must be U.S. citizen.
Application requirements: Must provide proof of Osage Indian blood and may be enrolled in any post-secondary institution.
Additional information: Must maintain 2.0 GPA. Deadline for summer funding is May 1. Deadlines strictly followed. July 1 deadline is for fall semester; December 31 is for spring deadline. Application must be received by Committee by deadline.

Number of awards:	220
Number of applicants:	250
Application deadline:	July 1, December 31

Contact:
Osage Tribal Education Committee
Oklahoma Area Education Office
4149 Highline Boulevard, Suite 380
Oklahoma City, OK 73108
Phone: 405-605-6051 ext. 303
Fax: 405-605-6057

OSI Industries, Inc.

OSI Group Scholarship Program

Type of award: Scholarship.
Intended use: For undergraduate study at vocational, 2-year or 4-year institution.
Eligibility: Applicant or parent must be employed by OSI Industries, Inc. Applicant must be high school senior.
Additional information: For further information or an application, contact OSI Industries Incorporated directly.

Amount of award:	$1,500

Otter Tail Power Company

Otter Tail Power Company Scholarship

Type of award: Scholarship.
Intended use: For undergraduate study at accredited vocational, 2-year or 4-year institution.
Eligibility: Applicant or parent must be employed by Otter Tail Power Company.
Basis for selection: Applicant must demonstrate financial need.
Additional information: For further information or an application, contact Otter Tail Power Company directly.

Amount of award:	$500-$1,000

PACE International Union

PACE International Union Scholarship

Type of award: Scholarship.
Intended use: For full-time freshman study at 4-year institution in United States.
Eligibility: Applicant must be high school senior. Applicant must be U.S. citizen or permanent resident.
Basis for selection: Applicant must demonstrate financial need, high academic achievement, depth of character, leadership, patriotism, seriousness of purpose and service orientation.
Application requirements: Transcript.
Additional information: Scholarship recipients required to take one course in labor relations. Applicant or parent must be a member of PACE International Union.

Amount of award:	$1,000
Number of awards:	22
Number of applicants:	1,500
Application deadline:	March 15
Notification begins:	June 15

Contact:
Scholarship Coordinator
PACE International Union
P.O. Box 1475
Nashville, TN 37202
Phone: 615-834-8590
Web: www.paceunion.org

Pacific Life Insurance Company

Pacific Life Scholarship Program for Children of Employees

Type of award: Scholarship, renewable.
Intended use: For undergraduate study at accredited 4-year institution.
Eligibility: Applicant or parent must be employed by Pacific Life Insurance Company. Applicant must be U.S. citizen.
Basis for selection: Applicant must demonstrate financial need.
Additional information: For further information or application, contact Pacific Life Insurance Company directly.

Amount of award:	$1,000-$2,000

Pacific Printing and Imaging Association

Pacific Printing and Imaging Scholarship

Type of award: Scholarship, renewable.
Intended use: For full-time undergraduate study at accredited vocational, 2-year or 4-year institution.

Eligibility: Applicant must be residing in Idaho, Montana, Alaska, Oregon, Washington or Hawaii.
Basis for selection: Major/career interest in printing. Applicant must demonstrate high academic achievement and seriousness of purpose.
Application requirements: Recommendations, essay, transcript, proof of eligibility.
Additional information: For technical majors in printing and imaging. Not for fine arts, graphic design, or graphic illustration. Applicants must be accepted to school they plan to attend.

Amount of award:	$1,250-$3,500
Number of awards:	10
Number of applicants:	25
Application deadline:	April 1
Notification begins:	May 15

Contact:
Pacific Printing and Imaging Association
Scholarship Department
5319 SW Westgate Drive, Suite 117
Portland, OR 97221-2488
Phone: 503-297-3328
Fax: 503-297-3320

Patient Advocate Foundation

Scholarships for Survivors

Type of award: Scholarship.
Intended use: For undergraduate study.
Eligibility: Applicant must be U.S. citizen.
Basis for selection: Applicant must demonstrate depth of character and leadership.
Application requirements: Recommendations, essay, transcript, proof of eligibility.
Additional information: The primary criterion for eligibility is that the recipients pursue a course of study that renders them immediately employable after graduation. Student must be a survivor of a life threading, chronic or debilitating disease. Must maintain an overall 3.0 GPA. Must complete 20 hours of community service for the year the scholarship will be dispensed; must write an essay on why they have chosen that particular field, how some illness in their family may have affected their decision and how they feel they can help others by earning this degree.

Amount of award:	$5,000
Number of awards:	8
Total amount awarded:	$400,000

Contact:
Patient Advocate Foundation
753 Thimble Shoals Blvd., Suite B
Newport News, VA 23606

Payless Cashways, Inc.

Payless Cashways, Inc. Scholarship Program

Type of award: Scholarship.

Intended use: For undergraduate study at accredited 2-year or 4-year institution.
Eligibility: Applicant or parent must be employed by Payless Cashways, Inc.
Basis for selection: Applicant must demonstrate financial need.
Additional information: For further information or an application, contact Payless Cashways, Inc. directly.

Amount of award:	$1,000-$2,500

PDE

PDE Scholarship Program

Type of award: Scholarship.
Intended use: For freshman study at 2-year or 4-year institution.
Eligibility: Applicant or parent must be employed by Philadelphia Drug Exchange. Applicant must be high school senior.
Additional information: For further information or an application, contact Philadelphia Drug Exchange directly.

Amount of award:	$2,500

Pearson Education

Pearson Education Scholarship Program

Type of award: Scholarship, renewable.
Intended use: For undergraduate study at 4-year institution.
Eligibility: Applicant or parent must be employed by Addison-Wesley Publishing Company.
Basis for selection: Applicant must demonstrate financial need.
Additional information: For further information or an application, contact Addison Wesley Longman directly.

Amount of award:	$500-$2,000

Pebble Beach Company Foundation

Pebble Beach Company Scholarship Program for Employees' Children

Type of award: Scholarship, renewable.
Intended use: For undergraduate study at accredited vocational, 2-year or 4-year institution.
Eligibility: Applicant or parent must be employed by Pebble Beach Company Foundation. Applicant must be high school senior.
Additional information: For further information or application, contact Pebble Beach Company Foundation directly.

Amount of award:	$1,500

Contact:
Pebble Beach Company Foundation

Penguin Putnam Inc.

Signet Classic Scholarship Essay Contest

Type of award: Scholarship.
Intended use: For undergraduate study.
Eligibility: Applicant must be high school junior or senior. Applicant must be U.S. citizen or permanent resident.
Basis for selection: Competition/talent/interest in writing/journalism, based on style, content, grammar and originality; clear, concise writing that is articulate, logically organized and well-supported. Major/career interest in English or literature.
Application requirements: Essay, proof of eligibility, nomination by high school English teacher. Cover letter on high school letterhead.
Additional information: Entrant must read designated book and answer one of several book-related questions in 2-3 page essay. Winning essays must demonstrate comprehensive understanding of themes and issues in book. Applications and further information available on Website or from high school English department. School library of winning entrants receive Signet Classic Library ($1,700 value). For more information, send e-mail to academic@penguinputnam.com.

Amount of award:	$1,000
Number of awards:	5
Application deadline:	April 15
Notification begins:	June 15
Total amount awarded:	$5,000

Contact:
Penguin Putnam Inc. Signet Classic Scholarship Essay Contest
375 Hudson Street
New York, NY 10014
Phone: 212-366-2377
Web: www.penguinputnam.com

Pennsylvania Department of Environmental Protection

Environmental Journalism Contest

Type of award: Scholarship.
Intended use: For freshman study at 2-year or 4-year institution.
Eligibility: Applicant must be high school senior. Applicant must be U.S. citizen or permanent resident residing in Pennsylvania.
Basis for selection: Competition/talent/interest in writing/journalism. Major/career interest in environmental science or journalism.
Application requirements: Proof of eligibility.
Additional information: Must submit individual entry: reporting on recycling and waste minimization, or portfolio of cartoons or news photographs on same. Group entries do not qualify for scholarship awards. Visit Website for application and additional information.

Amount of award:	$2,000
Number of awards:	3
Application deadline:	March 29
Total amount awarded:	$6,000

Contact:
Pennsylvania Department of Environmental Protection
Rachel Carson
400 Market Street
Harrisburg, PA 17105
Phone: 717-233-4781
Web: www.dep.state.pa.us

Pennsylvania Higher Education Assistance Agency

Pennsylvania Grant Program

Type of award: Scholarship, renewable.
Intended use: For undergraduate study at accredited vocational, 2-year or 4-year institution in United States. Designated institutions: Pennsylvania postsecondary institutions.
Eligibility: Applicant must be residing in Pennsylvania.
Basis for selection: Applicant must demonstrate financial need.
Application requirements: Proof of eligibility. FAFSA.
Additional information: Grants are portable to approved institutions in other states. Number of awards and total amount awarded varies.

Amount of award:	$300-$3,200
Application deadline:	May 1

Contact:
Pennsylvania Higher Education Assistance Agency
State Grant and Special Programs Divisions
1200 North Seventh Street
Harrisburg, PA 17102-1444
Phone: 717-720-2550
Web: www.pheaa.org

Pennsylvania Robert C. Byrd Honors Scholarship

Type of award: Scholarship, renewable.
Intended use: For full-time freshman study at accredited 2-year or 4-year institution in United States.
Eligibility: Applicant must be high school senior. Applicant must be U.S. citizen or permanent resident residing in Pennsylvania.
Basis for selection: Applicant must demonstrate high academic achievement.
Application requirements: Transcript. SAT, ACT or GED scores.
Additional information: Applicant must rank in top five percent of class, have 3.5 GPA, 1150 combined score on SAT (25 on ACT), or 289 on GED, and must enroll following graduation. Information available from high school guidance office.

Amount of award:	$1,500
Application deadline:	May 1

Contact:
Pennsylvania Higher Education Assistance Agency
Robert C. Byrd Scholarship
P.O. Box 8114
Harrisburg, PA 17105-8114
Phone: 717-720-2550
Web: www.pheaa.org

Pennzoil-Quaker State Company

Pennzoil-Quaker State Scholars Scholars Program

Type of award: Scholarship, renewable.
Intended use: For freshman study at accredited 2-year or 4-year institution.
Eligibility: Applicant or parent must be employed by Pennzoil Company.
Additional information: For further information or an application, contact Pennzoil Company directly.
  Amount of award: $2,500

Pentair, Inc.

Pentair Scholarship Fund

Type of award: Scholarship, renewable.
Intended use: For undergraduate study at vocational, 2-year or 4-year institution.
Eligibility: Applicant or parent must be employed by Pentair, Inc. Applicant must be high school senior.
Additional information: For further information or an application, contact Pentair Incorporated directly.
  Amount of award: $2,000-$5,000

Phi Delta Kappa International

Phi Delta Kappa Scholarship for Prospective Educators

Type of award: Scholarship.
Intended use: For full-time freshman study at accredited postsecondary institution outside United States.
Eligibility: Applicant must be high school senior.
Basis for selection: Major/career interest in education. Applicant must demonstrate high academic achievement, leadership, seriousness of purpose and service orientation.
Application requirements: Recommendations, essay, transcript.
Additional information: Minimum four awards to racial minorities and two to dependents of PDK members. Minimum 3.5 GPA required, 3.7 recommended. Two of the scholarships are renewable. Make application to local chapter.
  Amount of award: $1,000-$5,000
  Number of awards: 30
  Number of applicants: 800
  Application deadline: January 31
  Notification begins: June 1
  Total amount awarded: $30,000

Contact:
Phi Delta Kappa Headquarters
Scholarship Program
Box 789, 408 N. Union Street
Bloomington, IN 47402-0789
Phone: 812-339-1156
Web: www.pdkintl.org

PHICO Insurance Company

PHICOScholarship

Type of award: Scholarship.
Intended use: For undergraduate study at accredited vocational, 2-year or 4-year institution.
Eligibility: Applicant or parent must be employed by PHICO Insurance Company.
Additional information: For further information or an application, contact PHICO Insurance Company directly.
  Amount of award: $1,500

Philips Electronics North America

Philips Electronics Scholarship Program

Type of award: Scholarship, renewable.
Intended use: For full-time senior study at accredited 4-year institution.
Eligibility: Applicant or parent must be employed by North American Philips. Applicant must be U.S. citizen or permanent resident.
Basis for selection: Applicant must demonstrate financial need, high academic achievement, depth of character, leadership and seriousness of purpose.
Application requirements: Recommendations, essay, transcript.
Additional information: Scholarships are available to children of regular, full-time employees, retirees, or deceased employees of Philips, its divisions and subsidiaries. Applicant must be a high school senior who will graduate during the current school year. Student must register and take either the SAT or ACT no later than December. Applicants will receive a Biographical Questionnaire and Secondary School Report Form. Applicants are automatically considered for other funding as well.
  Amount of award: $500-$3,500
  Number of applicants: 200
  Application deadline: December 31, March 1
  Notification begins: May 1
  Total amount awarded: $300,000
Contact:
Coleman Associates Henry S. Coleman, Director
Philips Electronics Scholarship Program
P.O. Box 1686
New Canaan, CT 06840
Phone: 203-966-7517

Phillips Petroleum Company

Phillips Petroleum Dependent Scholarship Program

Type of award: Scholarship, renewable.
Intended use: For full-time freshman study at accredited postsecondary institution.
Eligibility: Applicant or parent must be employed by Phillips Petroleum Company. Applicant must be high school senior. Applicant must be U.S. citizen.
Basis for selection: Applicant must demonstrate financial need, high academic achievement, leadership and seriousness of purpose.
Application requirements: Transcript, proof of eligibility.
Additional information: No more than 25% of applicants are awarded.

Amount of award:	$8,000
Number of applicants:	293
Application deadline:	March 1
Notification begins:	May 1

Contact:
Phillips Petroleum Company
1650 Phillips Building
Bartlesville, OK 74004

Playtex Products, Inc.

Playtex Scholarship

Type of award: Scholarship, renewable.
Intended use: For full-time freshman study at accredited 4-year institution in United States or Canada.
Eligibility: Applicant or parent must be employed by Playtex Products, Inc. and subsidiaries. Applicant must be high school senior.
Basis for selection: Applicant must demonstrate high academic achievement, depth of character, leadership, seriousness of purpose and service orientation.
Application requirements: Recommendations, essay, transcript, proof of eligibility. SAT I scores.
Additional information: Parent or guardian must have completed one year of continuous service with Playtex by time of application. Canadian citizens also qualify. Two scholarships were given in most recent year, six were renewed.

Amount of award:	$2,000
Number of awards:	8
Number of applicants:	9
Application deadline:	November 7
Notification begins:	May 1
Total amount awarded:	$16,000

Contact:
Playtex Products Inc. Scholarship Program
300 Nyala Farms Road
Westport, CT 06880
Web: playtexproducts.com

Plumbing-Heating-Cooling Contractors - National Assoc. Educational Foundation

Delta Faucet Company Scholarship

Type of award: Scholarship.
Intended use: For full-time undergraduate study at accredited 4-year institution in United States.
Basis for selection: Major/career interest in air conditioning/heating/refrigeration technology; architecture; business; engineering, construction or construction management.
Application requirements: Recommendations, essay, transcript. Submit SAT or ACT scores.
Additional information: High school seniors and college students are eligible to apply. Applicants must pursue studies in a major related to the plumbing-heating-cooling industry and must be sponsored by an active member of PHCC--National Association. Funds provided by Delta Faucet Company and administered by PHCC Educational Foundation.

Amount of award:	$2,500
Number of awards:	6
Number of applicants:	45
Application deadline:	June 1
Total amount awarded:	$15,000

Contact:
PHCC - National Assoc. Educational Foundation Scholarship Coordinator
P.O. Box 6808
180 S. Washington St.
Falls Church, VA 22046
Phone: 703-237-8100
Fax: 703-237-7442
Web: www.naphcc.org/education

Plumbing-Heating-Cooling Contractors - National Association Educational Foundation Scholarship

Type of award: Scholarship, renewable.
Intended use: For full-time undergraduate study in United States.
Basis for selection: Major/career interest in air conditioning/heating/refrigeration technology; architecture; business; engineering, construction or construction management. Applicant must demonstrate high academic achievement.
Application requirements: Interview, recommendations, transcript. Completed application.
Additional information: High school seniors and college students are eligible to apply. Applicants must pursue studies in a major related to the plumbing-heating-cooling industry and must be sponsored by an active member of PHCC--National Association. Award is per year, for up to four years ($12,000). Recipients must continue study in a p-h-c-related major and maintain "C" average or better throughout period for which scholarship is awarded.

Amount of award:	$3,000
Number of awards:	4
Number of applicants:	30
Application deadline:	May 1
Notification begins:	August 1
Total amount awarded:	$48,000

Contact:
PHCC Educational Foundation
180 S. Washington St.
P.O. Box 6808
Falls Church, VA 22046
Phone: 800-533-7694
Fax: 703-237-7442
Web: www.naphcc.org

Polaris Industries, Inc.

Polaris Industries Inc. Scholarship Program

Type of award: Scholarship.
Intended use: For undergraduate study at accredited vocational, 2-year or 4-year institution.
Eligibility: Applicant or parent must be employed by Polaris Industries.
Basis for selection: Applicant must demonstrate financial need.
Additional information: For further information or an application, contact Polaris Industries directly.
   Amount of award: $1,000

Police and Fire Fighters' Association

Police and Fire Fighters' Association Scholarship

Type of award: Scholarship, renewable.
Intended use: For undergraduate study at accredited 2-year or 4-year institution.
Eligibility: Applicant or parent must be member/participant of Police & Fire Fighters' Association.
Additional information: For further information or an application, contact Police and Fire Fighters' Association directly.
   Amount of award: $1,000

Portuguese Continental Union

Portuguese Continental Union Scholarship

Type of award: Scholarship.
Intended use: For undergraduate study at accredited vocational, 2-year or 4-year institution.
Eligibility: Applicant or parent must be member/participant of Portuguese Continental Union.
Basis for selection: Applicant must demonstrate financial need, high academic achievement, depth of character, leadership and seriousness of purpose.

Application requirements: Recommendations, essay, transcript, proof of eligibility, nomination. SAT scores, report from secondary school or college attended by student.
Additional information: Applicant must have been PCU member with at least one year in good standing. If not currently enrolled in college or university, must plan to enroll in the current academic year. Award amounts based on individual financial needs.
   Number of awards: 8
   Number of applicants: 8
   Application deadline: February 15
   Notification begins: April 30
   Total amount awarded: $5,000
Contact:
Portuguese Continental Union
Scholarship Committee
30 Cummings Park
Woburn, MA 01801
Phone: 781-376-0271
Fax: 781-376-2033
Web: members.aol.com/upceua

Precision Castparts Corp.

Precision Castparts Scholarship

Type of award: Scholarship, renewable.
Intended use: For undergraduate study at accredited vocational, 2-year or 4-year institution.
Eligibility: Applicant or parent must be employed by Precision Castparts Corp.
Basis for selection: Applicant must demonstrate financial need.
Additional information: For further information or application, contact Precision Castparts Corp. directly.
   Amount of award: $2,000

Premcor Refining Group

Educate Our Children Scholarship

Type of award: Scholarship.
Intended use: For undergraduate study at accredited postsecondary institution.
Eligibility: Applicant or parent must be employed by Premcor Refining Group. Applicant must be high school senior.
Additional information: For further information or an application, contact Premcor Refining Group directly.
   Amount of award: $1,000

Presbyterian Church (USA)

Ira Page Wallace Bible Scholarship

Type of award: Scholarship.
Intended use: For undergraduate study in United States. Designated institutions: Barber-Scotia College, Johnson C. Smith University, Knoxville College, Mary Holmes College, Stillman College.

Eligibility: Applicant must be African American. Applicant must be Presbyterian. Applicant must be U.S. citizen.
Basis for selection: Major/career interest in religion/theology. Applicant must demonstrate financial need and high academic achievement.
Additional information: Must demonstrate superior academic progress in Bible studies. Contact chairperson of Department of Religion at your school for application information.

Amount of award:	$3,089
Number of awards:	6
Number of applicants:	6
Total amount awarded:	$18,535

Contact:
Presbyterian Church (USA)
Financial Aid for Studies
100 Witherspoon Street, M042
Louisville, KY 40202-1396
Phone: 888-728-7228 ext. 5646
Web: www.pcusa.org/highered

National Presbyterian Scholarship

Type of award: Scholarship, renewable.
Intended use: For full-time undergraduate study in United States. Designated institutions: Presbyterian-related institutions.
Eligibility: Applicant must be high school senior. Applicant must be Presbyterian. Applicant must be U.S. citizen or permanent resident.
Basis for selection: Applicant must demonstrate financial need and high academic achievement.
Additional information: SAT I/ACT must be taken no later than December 15 of senior year of high school. Must be preparing to enter one of the participating colleges related to the Presbyterian Church (USA). Applications and additional requirements available after December 1.

Amount of award:	$500-$1,400
Number of awards:	440
Application deadline:	December 1
Notification begins:	March 1

Contact:
Presbyterian Church (USA)
Financial Aid for Studies
100 Witherspoon Street, M042
Louisville, KY 40202-1396
Phone: 888-728-7228 -8235
Fax: 502-569-8766
Web: www.pcusa.org/highered

Presbyterian Appalachian Scholarship

Type of award: Scholarship, renewable.
Intended use: For full-time undergraduate study at postsecondary institution in United States.
Eligibility: Applicant must be Presbyterian. Applicant must be U.S. citizen or permanent resident.
Basis for selection: Applicant must demonstrate financial need and high academic achievement.
Application requirements: Transcript, proof of eligibility.
Additional information: Must be member of Presbyterian Church (USA) and full-time resident of Appalachia. Nontraditional-age students with no previous college experience encouraged to apply. Must be high school graduate or GED recipient. Previous recipients must reapply.

Amount of award:	$100-$1,000
Number of awards:	148
Application deadline:	July 1
Notification begins:	August 7

Contact:
Presbyterian Church (USA)
Financial Aid for Studies
100 Witherspoon Street, M042
Louisville, KY 40202-1396
Phone: 888-728-7228 -5738
Fax: 502-569-8766
Web: www.pcusa.org/highered

Presbyterian Student Opportunity Scholarship

Type of award: Scholarship.
Intended use: For full-time undergraduate study at accredited 2-year or 4-year institution in United States.
Eligibility: Applicant must be Alaskan native, Asian American, African American, Mexican American, Hispanic American, Puerto Rican or American Indian. Applicant must be high school senior. Applicant must be Presbyterian. Applicant must be U.S. citizen or permanent resident.
Basis for selection: Applicant must demonstrate financial need.
Application requirements: Proof of eligibility.
Additional information: Applications available after February 1. Possibility of renewal; award recipients must reapply yearly.

Amount of award:	$100-$1,400
Number of awards:	144
Number of applicants:	365
Application deadline:	April 1
Notification begins:	May 7
Total amount awarded:	$202,000

Contact:
Presbyterian Church (USA)
Financial Aid for Studies
100 Witherspoon Street, M042
Louisville, KY 40202-1396
Phone: 888-728-7228 -5760
Fax: 502-569-8766
Web: www.pcusa.org/highered

Samuel Robinson Award

Type of award: Scholarship.
Intended use: For full-time junior or senior study at 4-year institution. Designated institutions: One of 69 colleges related to Presbyterian Church (USA).
Eligibility: Applicant must be Presbyterian. Applicant must be U.S. citizen or permanent resident.
Application requirements: Essay.
Additional information: One time award. Applicant must successfully recite answers of the Westminster Shorter Catechism and write a 2,000-word essay on assigned topic related to the Catechism.

Amount of award:	$1,000
Application deadline:	April 1
Notification begins:	May 15

Contact:
Presbyterian Church (USA)
Financial Aid for Studies
100 Witherspoon Street, M042
Louisville, KY 40202-1396
Phone: 888-728-7228 -5745
Fax: 502-569-8766
Web: www.pcusa.org/highered

President's Committee on Employment of People with Disabilities

"Ability Counts" Journalism Scholarship Program About Disabled People

Type of award: Scholarship.
Intended use: For undergraduate study in United States.
Eligibility: Applicant must be enrolled in high school.
Applicant must be U.S. citizen.
Basis for selection: Applicant must demonstrate depth of character, leadership, seriousness of purpose and service orientation.
Application requirements: Essay.
Additional information: Scholarships range from $1,000 to $3,000 to high school students between sixteen and nineteen who are interested in journalism. Students must conduct surveys, take field trips, and seek out information, insights, and firsthand observations and then write an essay on their findings. Essay themes vary from year to year. Based on content, research, originality, language sensitivity, impact, organization, clarity, and neatness. Write to above address to find out if your state sponsors this program. Deadline early fall.
  Amount of award: $1,000-$3,000
Contact:
President's Committee on Employment of People with Disabilities
1111 20th Street, N.W., Suite 636
Washington, DC 20036

Press Club of Houston Educational Foundation

Press Club of Houston Scholarship

Type of award: Scholarship.
Intended use: For full-time junior or senior study at accredited 4-year institution in United States.
Eligibility: Applicant must be U.S. citizen.
Basis for selection: Major/career interest in journalism; radio/television/film or communications. Applicant must demonstrate financial need and high academic achievement.
Application requirements: Interview, recommendations, transcript. Writing samples, statement from college financial aid office of current financial aid package, statement of parents' annual income.

Additional information: Applicant must be student at college in Greater Houston Area (Harris, Brazoria, Chambers, Fort Bend, Galveston, Liberty, Montgomery, and Waller Counties) or resident of Greater Houston Area attending college anywhere. Applications available after January 1; write to sponsor to request application materials. Total amount available for awards depends on proceeds from annual Gridiron Show.
  Amount of award: $500-$3,000
  Number of awards: 18
  Application deadline: March 1
  Total amount awarded: $25,000
Contact:
Press Club of Houston Educational Foundation
Scholarship Chairman
P.O. Box 541038
Houston, TX 77254-1038
Phone: 713-866-8844
Web: www.houstonpressclub.org

Princess Grace Foundation-USA

Princess Grace Award

Type of award: Scholarship.
Intended use: For full-time senior or graduate study in United States.
Eligibility: Applicant must be U.S. citizen or permanent resident.
Basis for selection: Major/career interest in film/video; theater arts; performing arts or playwriting/screen writing.
Application requirements: Portfolio, recommendations, essay, nomination by Dean or Department Chair. Include work samples as well as completed application.
Additional information: Up to 21 scholarships awarded. Major/career interest in theater, dance, playwriting. Deadlines as follows: Theater and playwriting: March 31, Dance: April 30, Film: June 1.
  Amount of award: $2,500-$25,000
  Number of awards: 21
  Number of applicants: 300
  Application deadline: March 31, April 30
  Notification begins: July 30
  Total amount awarded: $280,000
Contact:
Princess Grace Foundation-USA
150 East 58 St., 21st floor
New York, NY 10155
Phone: 212-317-1470
Web: www.pgfusa.com

Print and Graphics Scholarship Foundation

PGSF Annual Scholarship Competition

Type of award: Scholarship, renewable.
Intended use: For full-time undergraduate study at 2-year or 4-year institution.

Eligibility: Applicant must be U.S. citizen.
Basis for selection: Major/career interest in graphic arts/ design; printing or publishing. Applicant must demonstrate high academic achievement.
Application requirements: Recommendations, transcript. Biographical information including extracurricular activities and academic honors.
Additional information: To renew, recipients must maintain 3.0 GPA and continue as a graphic arts or printing technology major. Application deadlines are March 1 for high school seniors and high school graduates not currently attending college, and April 1 for current undergraduate students. Application requirements and criteria may vary by trust fund member institution. Contact sponsor for application or obtain from Website.

Amount of award:	$500-$3,500
Number of awards:	320
Number of applicants:	1,500
Application deadline:	March 1, April 1
Notification begins:	June 30

Contact:
Print and Graphics Scholarship Foundation
200 Deer Run Road
Sewickley, PA 15154
Web: www.gatf.org

Pro2Net, John Wiley & Sons, and KPMG

Account for Your Future Scholarship

Type of award: Scholarship.
Intended use: For full-time sophomore, junior, senior or graduate study at accredited postsecondary institution.
Eligibility: Applicant must be U.S. citizen, permanent resident, international student or non-US citizen pursuing degree in accounting.
Basis for selection: Major/career interest in accounting; information systems or computer/information sciences. Applicant must demonstrate high academic achievement and seriousness of purpose.
Additional information: Offered twice annually. Applicants must have completed minimum of 24 semester hours or 45 quarter hours with declared major in accounting. Applicants should have interest in accounting-technology relationship and understanding of importance of technology to future of accounting industry. Applications accepted exclusively online. Visit Website to apply online.

Amount of award:	$1,000
Number of awards:	10
Number of applicants:	2,000
Application deadline:	December 1, June 1
Total amount awarded:	$10,000

Contact:
Phone: 888-522-PRO2
Web: www.accountingstudents.com

Procter and Gamble Fund

Procter and Gamble Scholarship Competition

Type of award: Scholarship.
Intended use: For full-time undergraduate study at 2-year or 4-year institution in United States.
Eligibility: Applicant or parent must be employed by Procter and Gamble.
Basis for selection: Applicant must demonstrate high academic achievement, depth of character and leadership.
Application requirements: Recommendations, transcript, proof of eligibility. Submit SRP Profile.
Additional information: Parent must be Procter & Gamble employee. Parent may obtain application for their child(ren) through their office. 25% of applicants, up to 250, are awarded scholarships.

Amount of award:	$2,500
Number of awards:	250
Number of applicants:	505
Application deadline:	January 15
Notification begins:	April 15
Total amount awarded:	$1,024,200

Contact:
Procter and Gamble Scholarship Fund
P.O. Box 599
Cincinnati, OH 45201-0599
Phone: 513-945-8450
Fax: 513-945-8979

Professional Association of Georgia Educators Foundation, Inc.

PAGE Scholarships

Type of award: Scholarship.
Intended use: For junior, senior or post-bachelor's certificate study at accredited postsecondary institution in United States.
Eligibility: Applicant or parent must be member/participant of Professional Association of GA Educators /Student Professional Association of GA Educators. Applicant must be U.S. citizen or permanent resident residing in Georgia.
Basis for selection: Major/career interest in education; education, teacher; education, early childhood or education, special. Applicant must demonstrate high academic achievement and service orientation.
Application requirements: Recommendations, essay, transcript. Application. Minimum 3.0 GPA.
Additional information: Must be PAGE, SPAGE member. Intended for future teachers and certified teachers seeking advanced degrees. Must agree to teach in Georgia for three years. Several scholarships offered. Applications available from September to December, due in January and awarded in April. Visit Website for additional information, deadlines and application procedures.

Amount of award:	$1,000
Number of awards:	15
Number of applicants:	100
Total amount awarded:	$15,000

Contact:
PAGE
P.O. Box 942270
Atlanta, GA 31141-2270
Phone: 800-334-6861
Fax: 770-216-8589
Web: www.pageinc.org/foundation

Professional Grounds Management Society

Anne Seaman Memorial Scholarship

Type of award: Scholarship.
Intended use: For undergraduate or graduate study at postsecondary institution.
Basis for selection: Major/career interest in horticulture.
Application requirements: Recommendations, transcript, proof of eligibility. Cover letter, resume, and application.
Additional information: Additional fields of study: Plant nursery, arboriculture, turf care and grounds management. Applications accepted April through June. Applicants must be sponsored by PGMS members or not eligible to apply.

Amount of award:	$500-$1,500
Number of awards:	3
Number of applicants:	100
Application deadline:	July 1
Notification begins:	October 1
Total amount awarded:	$3,000

Contact:
Professional Grounds Management Society
720 Light Street
Baltimore, MD 21230
Phone: 410-223-2861
Fax: 410-752-8295
Web: www.pgms.org

Progress Energy Foundation Inc.

Progress Energy Merit Awards Program

Type of award: Scholarship, renewable.
Intended use: For freshman study at 4-year institution.
Eligibility: Applicant or parent must be employed by Progress Energy. Applicant must be high school senior.
Additional information: For further information or an application, contact Progress Energy Foundation Inc. directly.

Amount of award:	$1,500

Prudential Foundation

Prudential Foundation Scholarship

Type of award: Scholarship, renewable.
Intended use: For freshman study at accredited 4-year institution.
Eligibility: Applicant or parent must be employed by Prudential Foundation.
Basis for selection: Applicant must demonstrate financial need.
Additional information: For further information or an application, contact Prudential Foundation directly.

Amount of award:	$300-$3,000

Prudential Insurance Company of America

The Prudential Spirit of Community Awards

Type of award: Scholarship.
Intended use: For freshman study.
Eligibility: Applicant must be enrolled in high school.
Basis for selection: Applicant must demonstrate service orientation.
Application requirements: Nomination by principal.
Additional information: Recognizes students from middle level and high schools who have demonstrated exemplary community service. Two honorees named from each state and receive $1,000 each. Ten national honorees each receive $5,000, gold medallion, and trophy.

Amount of award:	$1,000-$5,000
Number of awards:	104
Application deadline:	October 30
Notification begins:	February 4

Contact:
National Association of Secondary School Principals
Department of Student Activities
1904 Association Drive
Reston, VA 20191
Phone: 800-253-7746

Puerto Rico Department of Education

Puerto Rico Robert C. Byrd Honors Scholarship

Type of award: Scholarship, renewable.
Intended use: For full-time undergraduate study in United States.
Eligibility: Applicant must be high school senior. Applicant must be U.S. citizen residing in Puerto Rico.
Basis for selection: Applicant must demonstrate high academic achievement and leadership.
Application requirements: Recommendations, essay, transcript, proof of eligibility.

Additional information: Minimum 3.5 GPA and evidence of leadership. Candidates selected by local committee from local Puerto Rican school districts; interview required. Scholarship offered to students studying in the Puerto Rican school system. Contact high school guidance office for information and application materials.

Amount of award:	$1,500
Number of awards:	449
Total amount awarded:	$673,500

Contact:
Max Pacheco Department of Education
Educational Development Office
P.O. Box 190759, Suite 1106
San Juan, PR 00919-0759
Phone: 787-759-2000 ext. 2657, 2755

Quadion Corporation

Quadion Corporation Scholarship

Type of award: Scholarship.
Intended use: For undergraduate study at accredited vocational, 2-year or 4-year institution.
Eligibility: Applicant or parent must be employed by Quadion.
Additional information: For further information or an application, contact Quadion Corporation directly.
Amount of award: $1,500

Quill and Scroll Foundation

Edward J. Nell Memorial Scholarship

Type of award: Scholarship.
Intended use: For full-time freshman study at accredited 2-year or 4-year institution in United States.
Eligibility: Applicant must be enrolled in high school. Applicant must be U.S. citizen.
Basis for selection: Major/career interest in journalism. Applicant must demonstrate seriousness of purpose.
Application requirements: Essay. Statement of intent to major in journalism.
Additional information: Open only to winners of Quill and Scroll Annual National Yearbook Excellence or Writing/Photo Contests at any time during high school career. Yearbook Excellence deadline is November 1. Writing/Photo deadline is February 5.

Amount of award:	$500-$1,000
Number of awards:	10
Number of applicants:	120
Total amount awarded:	$5,500

Contact:
Quill and Scroll Foundation
School of Journalism
312 West Seashore Hall
Iowa City, IA 52242-1528
Web: www.uiowa.edu/~quill-sc

R. Brouilette Agency, Inc.

Robert B. Brouillette Memorial Tuition Assistance Program

Type of award: Scholarship.
Intended use: For undergraduate study at vocational, 2-year or 4-year institution.
Eligibility: Applicant or parent must be employed by R. Brouilette Agency, Inc. Applicant must be high school senior.
Additional information: For further information or an application, contact R. Brouilette Agency Incorporated directly.
Amount of award: $500-$5,000

Radio and Television News Directors Foundation, Inc.

Radio and Television News Directors Foundation Scholarship

Type of award: Scholarship.
Intended use: For sophomore, junior or senior study at postsecondary institution in United States.
Eligibility: Applicant must be U.S. citizen or permanent resident.
Basis for selection: Major/career interest in journalism.
Additional information: You must be in good standing in order to be eligible for this award. The award is for students majoring in Broadcast and Electronic Journalism.

Amount of award:	$1,000
Number of awards:	9
Application deadline:	May 4
Total amount awarded:	$9,000

Contact:
Radio and Television News Directors Foundation, Inc.
100 Connecticut Ave., NW
Siute 615
Washington, DC 20036-5302
Phone: 202-659-6510
Fax: 202-223-4007
Web: www.rtnda.org

Radio-Television News Directors Association and Foundation

The George Forman Tribute to Lyndon B. Johnson Scholarship

Type of award: Scholarship.
Intended use: For sophomore, junior or senior study at 4-year institution in United States.
Eligibility: Applicant must be U.S. citizen or permanent resident residing in Texas.
Basis for selection: Major/career interest in journalism.
Additional information: This award was developed by George Foreman, television commentator and former

heavyweight champion, for a broadcast journalism student at the University of Texas-Austin. For more information and application requirements visit Website.

Number of awards: 1
Application deadline: May 4
Total amount awarded: $6,000
Contact:
Radio-Television News Directors Association & Foundation
1000 Connecticut Ave., NW Suite 615
Washington, DC 20036-5302
Phone: 202-659-6510
Fax: 202-223-4007
Web: www.rtnda.org

Radio-Television News Directors Foundation

Carole Simpson Scholarship

Type of award: Scholarship.
Intended use: For full-time sophomore, junior, senior or graduate study at 4-year or graduate institution.
Eligibility: Preference given to undergraduate minority students.
Basis for selection: Major/career interest in journalism; radio/television/film or communications. Applicant must demonstrate depth of character and seriousness of purpose.
Application requirements: Recommendations, essay, transcript, proof of eligibility. Audio- or videotape of one to three work samples, maximum 15 minutes, with accompanying scripts. Statement explaining reasons for seeking career in broadcast or cable journalism, and specific career preferences of radio or television, reporting, producing, or news management. Dean or faculty sponsor letter of reference certifying eligibilty.
Additional information: Must have at least one full year of school remaining. Previous Radio and Television News Directors Foundation scholarship or internship winners not eligible.

Amount of award: $2,000
Number of awards: 1
Number of applicants: 300
Application deadline: May 3
Total amount awarded: $2,000
Contact:
Radio-Television News Directors Foundation
Suite 615
1000 Connecticut Avenue, NW
Washington, DC 20036
Phone: 202-467-5218
Web: www.rtndf.org

Ed Bradley Scholarship

Type of award: Scholarship.
Intended use: For full-time sophomore, junior, senior or graduate study at 4-year or graduate institution.
Eligibility: Priority given to minority undergraduate students.
Basis for selection: Major/career interest in journalism; radio/television/film or communications. Applicant must demonstrate seriousness of purpose.
Application requirements: Recommendations, essay, transcript, proof of eligibility. Audio or video tape of one to three work samples, maximum length 15 minutes total, with accompanying scripts. Essay explaining reasons for seeking a

career in broadcast or cable journalism, and specific career preferences of radio or television, reporting, producing, or news management. Dean or faculty sponsor endorsement letter certifying eligibility.
Additional information: Must have at least one full year of school remaining. Previous Radio-Television News Directors Foundation scholarship or internship winners not eligible. Preference given to minority undergraduates.

Amount of award: $5,000
Number of awards: 1
Application deadline: May 3
Total amount awarded: $10,000
Contact:
Radio-Television News Directors Foundation
Suite 615
1000 Connecticut Avenue, NW
Washington, DC 20036
Phone: 202-467-5218
Web: www.rtndf.org

Len Allen Award of Merit

Type of award: Scholarship.
Intended use: For full-time sophomore, junior, senior or graduate study at accredited 4-year or graduate institution.
Basis for selection: Major/career interest in journalism; radio/television/film or communications.
Application requirements: Recommendations, essay, transcript, proof of eligibility. Essay explaining reasons for seeking career in radio news management. Dean or faculty sponsor recommendation letter certifying eligibility.
Additional information: Must have at least one full year of school remaining and have career objective of radio news management. Previous Radio-Television News Directors Foundation scholarship or internship winners not eligible.

Amount of award: $2,000
Number of awards: 1
Application deadline: May 3
Total amount awarded: $2,000
Contact:
Radio-Television News Directors Foundation
Suite 615
1000 Connecticut Avenue, NW
Washington, DC 20036
Phone: 202-467-5218
Web: www.rtndf.org

RTNDA President's $2,000 Award for Television Newsroom Management

Type of award: Scholarship.
Intended use: For full-time sophomore, junior, senior or graduate study at 4-year or graduate institution.
Basis for selection: Major/career interest in journalism; communications or radio/television/film. Applicant must demonstrate high academic achievement and seriousness of purpose.
Application requirements: Recommendations, essay, transcript. Statement of professional intent. Resume. One to three examples of journalistic work on audio or video cassette. Letter of recommendation from dean or faculty sponsor.
Additional information: Any major is acceptable so long as applicant's career intent is television or radio news. Must have at least one full year of college remaining. Contact Foundation for list of specific scholarships available.

Number of awards:	15
Number of applicants:	300
Application deadline:	May 1
Total amount awarded:	$2,000

Contact:
Radio-Television News Directors Foundation
RTNDF Scholarships
1000 Connecticut Avenue, NW Suite 615
Washington, DC 20036
Web: www.rtndf.org

Undergraduate Scholarships

Type of award: Scholarship.
Intended use: For full-time sophomore, junior or senior study at 2-year or 4-year institution.
Basis for selection: Major/career interest in journalism; communications or radio/television/film. Applicant must demonstrate high academic achievement and seriousness of purpose.
Application requirements: Recommendations, essay. One to three samples showing reporting or producing skills on audio or video tape, accompanied by scripts. Letter of endorsement from Dean or Faculty Advisor certifying proof of eligibility.
Additional information: Previous winners not eligible. Must have at least one full year of school remaining. Applicant may be enrolled in any major so long as career intent is television or radio news.

Amount of award:	$1,000
Number of awards:	9
Number of applicants:	300
Application deadline:	May 3

Contact:
Radio-Television News Directors Foundation
RTNDF Scholarships
1000 Connecticut Avenue, NW Suite 615
Washington, DC 20036
Phone: 202-467-5218
Web: www.rtndf.org

Rainbow Unity Foundation

Rainbow Unity Memorial Scholarship

Type of award: Scholarship, renewable.
Intended use: For undergraduate study at postsecondary institution.
Eligibility: Aplicant must self-identify as Gay, Lesbian, Bisexual or Transgendered. Applicant must be no older than 29. Applicant must be U.S. citizen residing in Iowa.
Basis for selection: Applicant must demonstrate financial need and high academic achievement.
Application requirements: Recommendations, essay, transcript, proof of eligibility.
Additional information: Applicant must have graduated or be planning to graduate from an Iowa high school; GED acceptable. Minimum 3.0 GPA. Recipient must attend Imperial Court of Iowa Coronation held during the month of September every year at a Des Moines hotel announced yearly. Failure to attend results in forfeiture of scholarship. One ticket provided at no cost; two additional tickets available at discount price for guests of recipient. Visit Website to download application form.

Amount of award:	$1,000
Application deadline:	August 1

Contact:
Rainbow Unity Foundation
Rainbow Unity Memorial Scholarship
P.O. Box 8126
Des Moines, IA 50301
Phone: 800-823-2363
Web: www.rainbowunity.org

Raytheon Company

Raytheon Scholars Program

Type of award: Scholarship, renewable.
Intended use: For freshman study at vocational, 2-year or 4-year institution.
Eligibility: Applicant or parent must be employed by Raytheon Company. Applicant must be high school senior.
Additional information: For further information or an application, contact Raytheon Company directly.

Amount of award:	$500-$3,000

Real Estate Educators Association

Harwood Memorial Scholarship

Type of award: Scholarship, renewable.
Intended use: For full-time undergraduate study in United States.
Eligibility: Applicant must be U.S. citizen.
Basis for selection: Major/career interest in real estate.
Application requirements: Recommendations, transcript.
Additional information: Number of awards varies. Minimum 3.2 GPA. Recommendations must come from REEA member. Must have completed two semesters of college work and be currently enrolled in undergraduate program specializing in real estate. Must have professor on campus who is member of Real Estate Educators Association.

Amount of award:	$250-$500
Application deadline:	December 30

Contact:
Real Estate Educators Association
320 W. Sabal Palm Pl. #150
Longwood, FL 32779

Recording for the Blind and Dyslexic

Marion Huber Learning Through Listening Award

Type of award: Scholarship.
Intended use: For full-time undergraduate study at vocational, 2-year or 4-year institution in United States.

Eligibility: Applicant or parent must be member/participant of Recording for the Blind & Dyslexic. Applicant must be learning disabled. Applicant must be high school senior.
Basis for selection: Applicant must demonstrate high academic achievement, leadership and service orientation.
Application requirements: Essay, transcript. Must obtain two teacher/school administrator referrals. Applicant must be enterprising.
Additional information: Must have 3.0 GPA or better in grades 10-12. Must be a registered member of Recording for the Blind & Dyslexic for at least one year prior to the application deadline.

Amount of award:	$2,000-$6,000
Number of awards:	6
Number of applicants:	200
Application deadline:	February 21
Total amount awarded:	$24,000

Contact:
Recording for the Blind & Dyslexic
c/o Public Affairs Office
20 Roszel Road
Princeton, NJ 08540
Phone: 609-520-8044
Web: www.rfbd.org

Mary P. Oenslager Scholastic Achievement Award

Type of award: Scholarship.
Intended use: For undergraduate study.
Eligibility: Applicant or parent must be member/participant of Recording for the Blind & Dyslexic. Applicant must be visually impaired.
Basis for selection: Applicant must demonstrate high academic achievement, leadership, or service orientation. Applicant must demonstrate high academic achievement, leadership and service orientation.
Application requirements: Essay, transcript. Two professors/college administrators report forms must be completed.
Additional information: Applicants must receive a Bachelor's degree from an accredited four-year college or university in the U.S. or its territories during the current year. Must have 3.0 GPA or more on a 4.0 scale (or the equivalent if based on a different grading system). Must be a registered member of RFB&D for at least one year prior to the application deadline. Continuing education beyond a bachelor's degree is not required.

Amount of award:	$1,000-$6,000
Number of awards:	9
Number of applicants:	50
Application deadline:	February 21
Notification begins:	May 31
Total amount awarded:	$30,000

Contact:
Recording for the Blind & Dyslexic
c/o Public Affairs Office
20 Roszel Road
Princeton, NJ 08540
Phone: 609-520-8044
Web: www.rfbd.org

Red River Valley Fighter Pilots Association

Red River Valley Fighter Pilots Scholarship Program

Type of award: Scholarship, renewable.
Intended use: For undergraduate or graduate study at accredited 2-year, 4-year or graduate institution in United States.
Eligibility: Applicant must be U.S. citizen. Applicant must be dependent of deceased veteran or POW/MIA; or spouse of deceased veteran or POW/MIA who served in the Army, Air Force, Marines, Navy, Coast Guard or Reserves/National Guard. Must be the spouse or child of a member of any branch of the U.S. armed forces who is listed as KIA or MIA since August 1964. In addition, the immediate dependants of military aircrew members killed in non-combat missions, as well as dependants of current or deceased "River Rats" can qualify.
Basis for selection: Applicant must demonstrate financial need, depth of character, leadership, patriotism, seriousness of purpose and service orientation.
Application requirements: Transcript, proof of eligibility.

Application deadline:	May 15

Contact:
Executive Director
Red River Valley Fighter Pilots Association
P.O. Box 1551
North Fork, CA 93643
Phone: 209-877-5000
Fax: 209-877-5001

Regions Financial Corporation

Regions Right Way Scholarship

Type of award: Scholarship.
Intended use: For freshman study at accredited 4-year institution.
Eligibility: Applicant or parent must be employed by First Alabama Bancshares, Inc.
Additional information: For further information or an application, contact Regions Financial Corporation directly.

Amount of award:	$2,000

ReliaStar Foundation

ReliaStar Financial Corporation Scholarship Program

Type of award: Scholarship, renewable.
Intended use: For undergraduate study at accredited vocational, 2-year or 4-year institution.
Eligibility: Applicant or parent must be employed by Northwestern National Life.
Basis for selection: Applicant must demonstrate financial need.

Additional information: For further information or an application, contact ReliaStar Foundation directly.
  Amount of award: $600-$2,400

Reserve Officers Association

Henry J. Reilly Memorial College Scholarship

Type of award: Scholarship, renewable.
Intended use: For full-time undergraduate study at accredited 4-year institution in United States.
Eligibility: Applicant or parent must be member/participant of Reserve Officers Association or ROAL. Applicant must be U.S. citizen.
Basis for selection: Applicant must demonstrate high academic achievement, depth of character, leadership and seriousness of purpose.
Application requirements: Essay, transcript, proof of eligibility. Must have registered for the draft, if elgible.
Additional information: Applicant, parent, or grandparent must be member of either Reserve Officers Association or ROAL. Designated for study at regionally accredited institution. Require 1250 SAT I or ACT combined English/math score of 55 if taken April 1995 or later. If taken from October 1989 to March 1995, then 1200 SAT or ACT score of 62 is required. Minimum GPA of 3.0. For more information, visit Website.
  Amount of award: $500
  Number of awards: 75
  Application deadline: April 10
  Notification begins: June 15
  Total amount awarded: $25,000
Contact:
Reserve Officers Association
Ms. Mickey Hagen
One Constitution Avenue, NE
Washington, DC 20002-5655
Phone: 800-809-9448; 202-479-2200
Fax: 202-646-7762
Web: www.roa.org Click on "Members"

Henry J. Reilly Memorial Scholarship

Type of award: Scholarship, renewable.
Intended use: For full-time freshman or sophomore study at accredited 4-year institution in United States.
Eligibility: Applicant or parent must be member/participant of Reserve Officers Association or ROAL. Applicant must be U.S. citizen.
Basis for selection: Applicant must demonstrate high academic achievement, depth of character, leadership and seriousness of purpose.
Application requirements: Essay, transcript, proof of eligibility. Must have registered for the draft, if eligible.
Additional information: Applicant, parent, or grandparent must be either member of Reserve Officers Association or ROAL. Designated for study at regionally accredited institution. Require 1250 SAT I or ACT combined English/math score of 55 if taken April 1995 or later. If taken from October 1989 to March 1995, then a 1200 SAT or an ACT score of 62 is required; 57 for tests taken before 1989. Open to high school seniors as well as college freshmen. . Minimum GPA is 3.3 for high school seniors and college freshmen.

  Amount of award: $500
  Number of awards: 50
  Application deadline: April 10
  Notification begins: June 15
  Total amount awarded: $25,000
Contact:
Reserve Officers Association
Ms. Mickey Hagen
One Constitution Avenue NE
Washington, DC 20002-5655
Phone: 800-809-9448; 202-479-2200
Fax: 202-479-0416
Web: www.roa.org

Rex Lumber Company

Paul Forester, Jr., Scholarship

Type of award: Scholarship, renewable.
Intended use: For freshman study at accredited vocational, 2-year or 4-year institution.
Eligibility: Applicant or parent must be employed by Rex Lumber Company.
Additional information: For further information or an application, contact Rex Lumber Company directly.
  Amount of award: $1,000

Reynolds and Reynolds Company Foundation

Reynolds and Reynolds Company Foundation Scholarship

Type of award: Scholarship, renewable.
Intended use: For undergraduate study at accredited vocational, 2-year or 4-year institution.
Eligibility: Applicant or parent must be employed by Reynolds and Reynolds Company.
Additional information: For further information or an application, contact Reynolds and Reynolds Company Foundation directly.
  Amount of award: $2,500

Rhode Island Higher Education Assistance Authority

Rhode Island State Grant

Type of award: Scholarship, renewable.
Intended use: For undergraduate study at accredited vocational, 2-year or 4-year institution. Designated institutions: North American institutions.
Eligibility: Applicant must be U.S. citizen or permanent resident residing in Rhode Island.

Scholarships

Basis for selection: Applicant must demonstrate financial need.
Application requirements: Proof of eligibility.

Amount of award:	$250-$750
Number of awards:	10,088
Number of applicants:	37,000
Application deadline:	March 1
Total amount awarded:	$6,098,118

Contact:
Rhode Island Higher Education Assistance Authority
560 Jefferson Boulevard
Warwick, RI 02886
Phone: 401-736-1100
Fax: 401-732-3541

Richard F. Walsh/Alfred W. Di Tolla Foundation

Richard F. Walsh/Alfred W. Di Tolla Scholarship

Type of award: Scholarship, renewable.
Intended use: For full-time undergraduate study at accredited 4-year institution.
Eligibility: Applicant or parent must be employed by International Alliance of Theatrical Stage Employees. Applicant must be high school senior.
Basis for selection: Applicant must demonstrate high academic achievement.
Application requirements: Recommendations, transcript. SAT, College Entrance Examination, or equivalent examination results.
Additional information: Must be son or daughter of a member in good standing of the International Alliance of Theatrical Stage Employes. Renewable throughout undergraduate studies.

Amount of award:	$1,750
Number of awards:	2
Number of applicants:	54
Application deadline:	December 31
Notification begins:	May 1
Total amount awarded:	$3,500

Contact:
Richard F. Walsh/Alfred W. Di Tolla Foundation
1515 Broadway
Suite 601
New York, NY 10036
Phone: 212-730-1770

Ricoh Corporation

Ricoh Scholarship

Type of award: Scholarship.
Intended use: For undergraduate study at accredited vocational, 2-year or 4-year institution.
Eligibility: Applicant or parent must be employed by RICOH Corporation. Applicant must be high school senior.
Basis for selection: Applicant must demonstrate financial need.

Additional information: Must be child of employee of RICOH Corporation. For further information or application, contact RICOH Corporation directly.

Amount of award:	$1,000-$3,000

Robert W. Geyer

Geyer Educational Award Program

Type of award: Scholarship.
Intended use: For undergraduate study at vocational, 2-year or 4-year institution.
Eligibility: Applicant or parent must be employed by Robert W. Geyer. Applicant must be high school senior.
Additional information: For further information or an application, contact Robert W. Geyer directly.

Amount of award:	$500-$1,000

Roche Brothers Supermarkets, Inc.

Roche Brothers Supermarkets Scholarship

Type of award: Scholarship.
Intended use: For undergraduate study at accredited vocational, 2-year or 4-year institution.
Eligibility: Applicant or parent must be employed by Roche Bros. Supermarkets, Inc.
Basis for selection: Applicant must demonstrate financial need.
Additional information: For further information or an application, contact Roche Brothers Supermarkets, Inc. directly.

Amount of award:	$1,000

Rocky Mountain Coal Mining Institute

Rocky Mountain Coal Mining Scholarship

Type of award: Scholarship, renewable.
Intended use: For full-time junior or senior study at 4-year institution in United States. Designated institutions: Mining schools approved by Rocky Mountain Coal Mining Institute.
Eligibility: Applicant must be U.S. citizen residing in New Mexico, Montana, Texas, North Dakota, Arizona, Utah, Colorado or Wyoming.
Basis for selection: Major/career interest in engineering; engineering, mining or geology/earth sciences. Applicant must demonstrate high academic achievement.
Application requirements: Interview, recommendations.
Additional information: Applicant must apply during sophomore year. Must have interest in western coal mining as possible career. Recommended GPA of 3.0 or above. One new award made per Rocky Mountain Coal Mining Institute member

state per year. Can be renewed as senior. Money paid directly to school as tuition reimbursement. Applications available after November first.

Amount of award:	$2,000
Number of awards:	16
Number of applicants:	30
Application deadline:	February 1
Notification begins:	March 1
Total amount awarded:	$32,000

Contact:
Rocky Mountain Coal Mining Institute
8057 S. Yukon Way
Littletown, CO 80128-5510
Phone: 303-948-3300
Fax: 303-948-1132

Rocky Mountain NASA Space Grant Consortium

Undergraduate Scholarship

Type of award: Scholarship, renewable.
Intended use: For full-time undergraduate study in United States. Designated institutions: Utah State University, University of Utah, Brigham Young University, University of Denver, Weber State University, Snow College and Southern Utah University.
Eligibility: Applicant must be U.S. citizen.
Basis for selection: Major/career interest in science, general; aerospace or engineering. Applicant must demonstrate high academic achievement.
Application requirements: Recommendations, transcript, research proposal. Resume.
Additional information: Award varies from year to year. Contact sponsor for deadline information. Must be used at a Rocky Mountain Space Grant Consortium member institution.

Amount of award:	$200-$1,000
Number of awards:	40
Number of applicants:	120

Contact:
Rocky Mountain NASA Space Grant Consortium
Utah State University
EL Building, Room 302
Logan, UT 84332-4140
Phone: 435-797-3666
Fax: 435-797-3382
Web: www.rmc.sdl.usu.edu

Rodale, Inc.

Rodale Scholarship Program

Type of award: Scholarship, renewable.
Intended use: For undergraduate study at accredited vocational, 2-year or 4-year institution.
Eligibility: Applicant or parent must be employed by Rodale Press.
Basis for selection: Applicant must demonstrate financial need.
Additional information: For further information or an application, contact Rodale, Inc. directly.

Amount of award:	$500-$2,000

Roger Von Amelunxen Foundation

Roger Von Amelunxen Scholarship

Type of award: Scholarship, renewable.
Intended use: For full-time undergraduate study.
Eligibility: Applicant or parent must be employed by U.S. Customs.
Basis for selection: Applicant must demonstrate high academic achievement, depth of character, leadership, seriousness of purpose and service orientation.
Application requirements: Recommendations, transcript.
Additional information: Number and amount of awards varies. Scholarship available only to children of U.S. Customs employees.

Amount of award:	$1,000-$4,000
Application deadline:	August 1
Notification begins:	August 31

Contact:
Roger Von Amelunxen Foundation
8321 Edgerton Boulevard
Jamaica, NY 11432
Phone: 718-641-4800

RoNetco Supermarkets, Inc.

RoNetco Supermarkets Scholarship Program

Type of award: Scholarship, renewable.
Intended use: For undergraduate study at vocational, 2-year or 4-year institution.
Eligibility: Applicant or parent must be employed by RoNetco Supermarkets, Inc. Applicant must be high school senior.
Additional information: For further information or an application, contact RoNetco Supermarkets Scholarship Program directly.

Amount of award:	$500-$1,000

Rosemount Inc.

Vernon Heath Scholarship Program

Type of award: Scholarship, renewable.
Intended use: For freshman study at 2-year or 4-year institution.
Eligibility: Applicant or parent must be employed by Rosemount Inc. Applicant must be high school senior.
Additional information: For further information or an application, contact Rosemount Incorporated directly.

Amount of award:	$1,250

Rotary Foundation of Rotary International

Academic-Year Ambassadorial Scholarship

Type of award: Scholarship.
Intended use: For junior, senior or graduate study at postsecondary institution in countries having Rotary Clubs.
Basis for selection: Competition/talent/interest in study abroad. Applicant must demonstrate high academic achievement, leadership, seriousness of purpose and service orientation.
Application requirements: Interview, recommendations, essay, transcript, proof of eligibility. Language certification.
Additional information: Deadlines will be between March and July, one year in advance, as set by the local Rotary clubs. Provides funding for nine months of study in another country, specifically for tuition, room and board, round-trip transportation, and one month of language training if necessary (funding not to exceed $25,000). Must have completed two years of postsecondary work or have appropriate professional experience, and be proficient in the language of the proposed host country. Must be citizen of country that has Rotary clubs. Spouses or descendants of Rotarians ineligible. Check with local Rotary Club for further information and scholarship availability.

Number of awards:	1,000
Notification begins:	December 15

Contact:
Local Rotary Club
Web: www.rotary.org

Cultural Ambassadorial Scholarship

Type of award: Scholarship.
Intended use: For junior, senior, graduate or non-degree study in countries having Rotary Clubs.
Basis for selection: Competition/talent/interest in study abroad. Major/career interest in foreign languages. Applicant must demonstrate leadership, seriousness of purpose and service orientation.
Application requirements: Interview, recommendations, essay, transcript, proof of eligibility. Language certification.
Additional information: Deadlines will be between March and July, one year in advance, as set by the local Rotary clubs. Scholarship for three or six months of intensive language study in foreign country at designated language institute. Must have completed at least one year of college-level course work of the language one is planning to study. Spouses or descendants of Rotarians ineligible. Funding covers tuition, round-trip transportation, and homestay expenses (not to exceed $12,000 for three months study, $19,000 for six months study). Applications will be considered for those interested in studying English, French, German, Hebrew, Japanese, Italian, Mandarin Chinese, Polish, Russian, Portuguese, Spanish, Swahili and Swedish. Check with local Rotary Club for further information and scholarship availability.

Amount of award:	Full tuition
Number of awards:	150

Contact:
Local Rotary Club or website.
Phone: 847-866-3000
Web: www.rotary.org

Multi-Year Ambassadorial Scholarship

Type of award: Scholarship, renewable.
Intended use: For junior, senior, master's or doctoral study at postsecondary institution in countries having Rotary Clubs.
Basis for selection: Competition/talent/interest in study abroad. Major/career interest in foreign languages. Applicant must demonstrate leadership, seriousness of purpose and service orientation.
Application requirements: Interview, recommendations, essay, transcript, proof of eligibility. Language certification.
Additional information: Deadlines will be between March and July, one year in advance, as set by local Rotary Clubs. Provides partial funding for two or three years of degree-oriented study abroad. Must have completed two years of postsecondary work or have appropriate professional experience and be proficient in the language of the proposed host country. Spouse or descendant of Rotarians ineligible. Check with local Rotary Club for further information and scholarship availability.

Amount of award:	$12,000
Number of awards:	100
Notification begins:	December 15

Contact:
Local Rotary Club
Phone: 847-866-3000
Web: www.rotary.org

ROTC/Air Force

ROTC/Air Force Four-Year Scholarship (Types 1, 2 and Targeted)

Type of award: Scholarship.
Intended use: For freshman study at accredited 4-year institution in United States.
Eligibility: Applicant must be at least 17, no older than 25, high school senior. Applicant must be U.S. citizen.
Basis for selection: Major/career interest in engineering; mathematics; physics; computer/information sciences; meteorology or architecture. Applicant must demonstrate high academic achievement.
Application requirements: Interview, recommendations, transcript.
Additional information: Minimum GPA 2.5 and be in top 40% of class. Minimum test scores: ACT Composite 24, Math 21, English 21. SAT Total 1100, Math 520, Verbal 530. Opportunities now available in any major. Applicants must not have been enrolled in college full-time prior to application. Type One provides full tuition, fees and textbook allowance, without restriction. $150 per month stipend during academic year. Type Two provides tuition, fees up to $15,000 per year. $150 per month stipend during academic year. Targeted scholarships provide tuition and fees at a "low cost" school (mostly state institutions). $150 per month stipend during academic year. Tuition cap, $9,000. Scholarship board decides which type of scholarship is offered. Scholarship recipients agree to serve four years active duty.

Amount of award:	Full tuition
Application deadline:	December 1

Contact:
Contact local ROTC recruiter.
Phone: 800-USA-ROTC

ROTC/Air Force Three-Year Scholarship (Types 2 and Targeted)

Type of award: Scholarship.
Intended use: For sophomore study at accredited 4-year institution in United States.
Eligibility: Applicant must be at least 17, no older than 25. Applicant must be U.S. citizen.
Basis for selection: Major/career interest in engineering; mathematics; physics; computer/information sciences or architecture. Applicant must demonstrate high academic achievement.
Application requirements: Interview, recommendations, transcript.
Additional information: Minimum GPA 2.5 and be in top 40 percent of class. Minimum test scores: ACT Composite 24, Math 21, English 21. SAT Total 1100, Math 520, Verbal 530. Opportunities now available in any major. Type two provides tuition, fees allowance up to $15,000 per year. $150 per month stipend during academic year. Targeted scholarships provide full tuition and fees at a "low cost" school (mostly state institutions). $150 per month stipend during academic year. ROTC scholarship board decides which type of scholarship is offered. Tuition cap of $9,000 per year. Scholarship recipients agree to serve four years active duty.

    Amount of award: Full tuition
    Application deadline: December 1
Contact:
Contact local ROTC recruiter.

ROTC/United States Army

ROTC/United States Army Four-Year Historically Black College/University Scholarship

Type of award: Scholarship.
Intended use: For freshman study at accredited 4-year institution in United States. Designated institutions: AL A&M, Tuskegee, U of AK-Pine Bluff, Howard, FL A&M, Fort Valley St., Grambling St., Southern U, A&M Coll, Bowie St., Morgan St., Alcorn St., Jackson St., Lincoln U, Elizabeth City St., NC A&T St., St. Augustine's, Central St. (OH), SC St., Prairie View A&M U, Hampton U, Norfolk St., WV St.
Eligibility: Applicant must be at least 17, no older than 25, high school senior. Applicant must be U.S. citizen.
Basis for selection: Applicant must demonstrate high academic achievement and depth of character.
Application requirements: Interview, transcript. Class rank. SAT or ACT score.
Additional information: Minimum SAT score of 920 points (composite of Verbal and Math) or an ACT composite score of 19. Scholarships are offered at different levels up to $16,000 annually, providing college tuition and educational fees. Same requirements as Army ROTC four-year Scholarship. Limited number of scholarships for attendance at Historically Black College or University. Designated book allowance. Tax-free subsistence allowance of $150 a month for up to 10 months each year the scholarship is in effect. Scholarships do not pay

flight fees. To apply, complete item 11 on the first page of the application. You will still be considered for the national four-year scholarship program. Your first school choice must be one of the schools identified in the list of HBCUs. If your first school choice is not one of these schools, your application will not be considered for these dedicated HBCU scholarships. Contact your local ROTC recruiter for further information.
Contact:
Army ROTC Scholarship
Fort Monroe
VA 23651-5238
Phone: 800-USA-ROTC

United States Army Four-Year Nursing Scholarship

Type of award: Scholarship.
Intended use: For freshman study at accredited 4-year institution in United States.
Eligibility: Applicant must be at least 17, no older than 25. Applicant must be U.S. citizen.
Basis for selection: Major/career interest in military science or nursing. Applicant must demonstrate high academic achievement and depth of character.
Application requirements: Interview, transcript.
Additional information: Minimum SAT score of 920 points (composite of Verbal and Math) or an ACT composite score of 19. Scholarships are offered at different levels up to $16,000 annually, providing college tuition and educational fees. All applicants are considered for each level. Designated book allowance. Tax-free subsistence allowance of $150 a month for up to ten months each year scholarship is in effect. Scholarships do not pay flight fees. Limited numbers of three- and two-year scholarships are available once a student is on campus. Applicants should check with the Professor of Military Science once they are attending classes. Contact your local Army ROTC recruiter. Individuals applying for nurse program scholarships must indicate "JXX" as choice of major in item four of page eight of the four-year scholarship application; item three should include approved institution applicant wishes to attend.
Contact:
Army ROTC Scholarship
Fort Monroe
VA 23651-5238
Phone: 800-USA-ROTC

United States Army Four-Year Scholarship

Type of award: Scholarship.
Intended use: For freshman study at accredited 4-year institution in United States.
Eligibility: Applicant must be at least 17, no older than 25. Applicant must be U.S. citizen.
Basis for selection: Major/career interest in military science. Applicant must demonstrate high academic achievement and depth of character.
Application requirements: Interview, recommendations, transcript. SAT score or ACT. High school class rank.
Additional information: Tuition waiver up to $16,000 per year, plus $150/month subsistence allowance; also book allowance. Minimum SAT score of 920 points (composite of Verbal and Math) or an ACT composite score of 19. Scholarships do not pay flight fees. Limited numbers of three- and two-year scholarships are available once a student is on campus. Applicants should check with the Professor of Military Science once they are attending classes. Contact your local

Scholarships

Army ROTC recruiter. Must enlist in Army Reserve or Army National Guard for minimum eight years.
Contact:
Army ROTC Scholarship
Fort Monroe
VA 23651-5238
Phone: 800-USA-ROTC

Ruud Lighting, Inc.

Ruud Lighting Scholarship

Type of award: Scholarship.
Intended use: For undergraduate study at accredited postsecondary institution.
Eligibility: Applicant or parent must be employed by Ruud Lighting, Inc. Applicant must be high school senior.
Additional information: For further information or an application, contact Ruud Lighting, Inc. directly.
    Amount of award: $1,500

S.C. Holman Foundation

S.C. Holman Scholarship

Type of award: Scholarship, renewable.
Intended use: For undergraduate study at accredited vocational, 2-year or 4-year institution.
Eligibility: Applicant or parent must be employed by S. C. Holman.
Basis for selection: Applicant must demonstrate financial need.
Additional information: For further information or an application, contact S.C. Holman Foundation directly.
    Amount of award: $250-$5,000

S.J. Electro Systems Foundation

S.J. Electro Systems Foundation Scholarship Program

Type of award: Scholarship.
Intended use: For undergraduate or graduate study at vocational, 2-year, 4-year or graduate institution.
Eligibility: Applicant or parent must be employed by S.J. Electro Systems Foundation. Applicant must be high school senior.
Additional information: For further information or an application, contact S.J. Electro Systems Foundation directly.
    Amount of award: $500-$1,000

Sachs Foundation

Sachs Scholarship

Type of award: Scholarship, renewable.
Intended use: For full-time undergraduate study at accredited 2-year or 4-year institution.
Eligibility: Applicant must be African American. Applicant must be high school senior. Applicant must be U.S. citizen or permanent resident residing in Colorado.
Basis for selection: Applicant must demonstrate financial need, high academic achievement, depth of character and leadership.
Application requirements: Interview, recommendations, transcript, proof of eligibility. Financial statement.
Additional information: Must be resident of Colorado for more than five years. Must have minimum high school GPA of 3.6 and maintain high academic achievement throughout college for renewal consideration.

Amount of award:	$4,000
Number of applicants:	300
Application deadline:	March 1
Notification begins:	April 15
Total amount awarded:	$1,000,000

Contact:
Sachs Foundation
90 South Cascade Avenue
Suite 1410
Colorado Springs, CO 80903
Phone: 719-633-2353

Saint David's Society

Saint David's Society Scholarship

Type of award: Scholarship, renewable.
Intended use: For undergraduate, graduate or non-degree study.
Eligibility: Applicant must be Welsh.
Basis for selection: Applicant must demonstrate high academic achievement, depth of character and seriousness of purpose.
Application requirements: Recommendations, transcript.
Additional information: Recepients that are Welsh can use this award for any topic of study. Recepients that are not Welsh must use the award for Welsh-related study.

Amount of award:	$250-$1,500
Number of awards:	12
Number of applicants:	700
Application deadline:	May 30
Notification begins:	July 15
Total amount awarded:	$12,000

Contact:
Saint David's Society
3 West 51 Street
New York, NY 10019
Phone: 212-989-5159

St. Patrick Hospital

St. Patrick Hospital Sons and Daughters Scholarship Program

Type of award: Scholarship.
Intended use: For undergraduate study at vocational, 2-year or 4-year institution.
Eligibility: Applicant or parent must be employed by St. Patrick Hospital. Applicant must be high school senior.
Additional information: For further information or an application, contact St. Patrick Hospital directly.

Amount of award: $500

Santee Cooper

Santee Cooper Employees' Children Scholarship

Type of award: Scholarship, renewable.
Intended use: For undergraduate study at accredited postsecondary institution.
Eligibility: Applicant or parent must be employed by Santee Cooper. Applicant must be high school senior.
Basis for selection: Applicant must demonstrate financial need.
Additional information: For further information or an application, contact Santee Cooper directly.

Amount of award: $1,000-$2,000

Sargent and Lundy

Sargent and Lundy Centennial Scholarship

Type of award: Scholarship.
Intended use: For undergraduate study at accredited vocational, 2-year or 4-year institution.
Eligibility: Applicant or parent must be employed by Sargent & Lundy.
Additional information: For further information or an application, contact Sargent and Lundy directly.

Amount of award: $500-$2,000

SAS Institute Inc.

SAS Institute Scholar Award Program

Type of award: Scholarship, renewable.
Intended use: For freshman study at 4-year institution.
Eligibility: Applicant or parent must be employed by SAS Institute Inc. Applicant must be high school senior.
Additional information: For further information or an application, contact SAS Institute Incorporated directly.

Amount of award: $2,000

SBC Foundation

SBC Foundation Scholarship Program

Type of award: Scholarship, renewable.
Intended use: For undergraduate study at accredited 4-year institution.
Eligibility: Applicant or parent must be employed by Southwestern Bell.
Additional information: For further information and an application, contact SBC directly.

Amount of award: $3,500

Schering-Key Pharmaceuticals

"Will to Win" Asthma Athlete Scholarship

Type of award: Scholarship.
Intended use: For full-time freshman study in United States.
Eligibility: Applicant must be high school senior. Applicant must be U.S. citizen.
Basis for selection: Applicant must demonstrate high academic achievement, depth of character, leadership, seriousness of purpose and service orientation.
Application requirements: Recommendations, essay, transcript, proof of eligibility. Application.
Additional information: Applicants must be outstanding athletes who also suffer from asthma. Applications become available in Fall. Awards given are: five: $1,000; four: $5,000; one: $10,000.

Amount of award: $1,000-$10,000
Number of awards: 10
Number of applicants: 4,000
Application deadline: April 30
Notification begins: June 15

Contact:
Request applications from Schering-Key by phone.
Phone: 800-558-7305
Web: www.SchoolAsthmaAllergy.com

Scholastic, Inc.

New York Times James B. Reston Writing Portfolio Award

Type of award: Scholarship.
Intended use: For freshman study at postsecondary institution.
Eligibility: Applicant must be high school senior.
Basis for selection: Competition/talent/interest in writing/journalism, based on originality, technical competence, emergence of personal voice and style. Major/career interest in journalism. Applicant must demonstrate seriousness of purpose.
Application requirements: $5 application fee. Portfolio. Portfolios must contain three to eight pieces but cannot exceed

50 pages. Application must be signed by student's teacher, guidance counselor or principal.

Additional information: Application deadlines vary. Submission must be collection of nonfiction works intended to instruct, inform, explain, persuade, or entertain, such as essays, journalistic articles or editorials. Applications available between September and December. Include SASE with all application requests. Award includes participation in national readings, publishing opportunity. Runners-up may be eligible for participation in readings, publishing opportunities.

Amount of award:	$5,000
Number of awards:	1
Notification begins:	May 1
Total amount awarded:	$5,000

Contact:
The Scholastic Art and Writing Awards
555 Broadway
New York, NY 10012
Web: www.scholastic.com

Scholastic Art Portfolio Gold Award

Type of award: Scholarship.
Intended use: For freshman study at postsecondary institution.
Eligibility: Applicant must be high school senior.
Basis for selection: Competition/talent/interest in visual arts, based on originality and quality of portfolio. Major/career interest in arts, general. Applicant must demonstrate seriousness of purpose.
Application requirements: Portfolio, essay, transcript. Eight-piece portfolio with at least three drawings. Application form signed by student's art teacher.
Additional information: Application deadlines vary. Applications available between September and December. Include SASE with all application requests. Award includes participation in national exhibitions and publishing oportunities.

Amount of award:	$5,000
Number of awards:	4
Notification begins:	May 1
Total amount awarded:	$20,000

Contact:
The Scholastic Art and Writing Awards
555 Broadway
New York, NY 10012
Web: www.scholastic.com

Scholastic Art Portfolio Silver Award

Type of award: Scholarship.
Intended use: For freshman study at postsecondary institution.
Eligibility: Applicant must be high school senior.
Basis for selection: Competition/talent/interest in visual arts, based on originality and quality of portfolio. Major/career interest in arts, general. Applicant must demonstrate seriousness of purpose.
Application requirements: Portfolio, recommendations, essay, transcript. Eight-piece art portfolio with at least 3 drawings. Application must be signed by student's art teacher.
Additional information: Application deadlines vary. Award consists of nomination to postsecondary institution for scholarship, participation in national exhibitions, publishing opportunity. Applications available between September and December. Include SASE with all application requests.

Number of awards:	100
Notification begins:	May 1

Contact:
The Scholastic Art and Writing Awards
555 Broadway
New York, NY 10012
Web: www.scholastic.com

Scholastic Photography Portfolio Gold Award

Type of award: Scholarship.
Intended use: For freshman study at postsecondary institution.
Eligibility: Applicant must be high school senior.
Basis for selection: Competition/talent/interest in photography, based on originality and quality of portfolio. Major/career interest in arts, general. Applicant must demonstrate seriousness of purpose.
Application requirements: Portfolio, recommendations, essay, transcript. Eight-piece photography portfolio in prints, slides or transparencies. Application must be signed by student's art teacher.
Additional information: Applications available between September and December. Deadlines vary. Include SASE with all application requests. Award includes participation in national exhibitions and publishing opportunity.

Amount of award:	$5,000
Number of awards:	1
Notification begins:	May 1
Total amount awarded:	$5,000

Contact:
The Scholastic Art and Writing Awards
555 Broadway
New York, NY 10012
Web: www.scholastic.com

Scholastic Photography Portfolio Silver Award

Type of award: Scholarship.
Intended use: For freshman study at postsecondary institution.
Eligibility: Applicant must be high school senior.
Basis for selection: Competition/talent/interest in photography, based on originality and quality of portfolio. Major/career interest in arts, general. Applicant must demonstrate seriousness of purpose.
Application requirements: Portfolio, recommendations, essay, transcript. Eight-piece photography portfolio in prints, slides or transparencies. Application must be signed by student's art teacher.
Additional information: Applications available between September and December. Deadlines vary. Include SASE with all application requests. Award includes nomination to postsecondary institution for scholarship, participation in national exhibitions, publishing opportunity.

Number of awards:	50

Contact:
The Scholastic Art and Writing Awards
555 Broadway
New York, NY 10012
Web: www.scholastic.com

Scholastic Writing Portfolio Gold Award

Type of award: Scholarship.
Intended use: For freshman study at postsecondary institution.
Eligibility: Applicant must be high school senior.

Basis for selection: Competition/talent/interest in writing/ journalism, based on originality, technical competence, emergence of personal voice and style. Major/career interest in English; journalism; literature or theater arts. Applicant must demonstrate seriousness of purpose.

Application requirements: $5 application fee. Portfolio. Portfolio of three to eight pieces, not to exceed 50 pages of narratives, individual poems and/or dramatic scripts demonstrating diversity and talent. Excerpts from longer works encouraged. Application signed by student's teacher, counselor principal, parent or guardian.

Additional information: Applications available between September and December. Deadlines vary. Include SASE with all application requests. Award includes participation in national readings and opportunity to have work published.

Amount of award:	$5,000
Number of awards:	4
Notification begins:	May 1
Total amount awarded:	$20,000

Contact:
The Scholastic Art and Writing Awards
555 Broadway
New York, NY 10012
Web: www.scholastic.com

Scholastic Writing Portfolio Silver Award

Type of award: Scholarship.
Intended use: For freshman study at postsecondary institution.
Eligibility: Applicant must be high school senior.
Basis for selection: Competition/talent/interest in writing/ journalism, based on orginality, technical competence, emergence of personal voice and style. Major/career interest in English; journalism; literature or theater arts. Applicant must demonstrate seriousness of purpose.

Application requirements: $5 application fee. Portfolio. Portfolio of three to eight pieces, not to exceed 50 pages in length. Application must be signed by student's teacher, counselor or principal.

Additional information: Applications available between September and December. Deadlines vary. Awards available in each of the following categories: short story, short-short story, essay/nonfiction/opinion writing, dramatic script, poetry, humor, science fiction/fantasy. Include SASE with all application requests. Award consists of participation in national readings, publishing opportunity.

Notification begins:	May 1

Contact:
The Scholastic Art and Writing Awards
555 Broadway
New York, NY 10012
Web: www.scholastic.com

Schweitzer-Mauduit International Inc.

Schweitzer-Mauduit Tomorrow's Leaders Scholarship Program

Type of award: Scholarship, renewable.
Intended use: For freshman study at 2-year or 4-year institution.

Eligibility: Applicant or parent must be employed by Schweitzer-Mauduit International Inc. Applicant must be high school senior.

Additional information: For further information or an application, contact Schweitzer-Mauduit International Incorporated directly.

Amount of award:	$2,500

Screen Actors Guild Foundation

John L. Dales Scholarship

Type of award: Scholarship.
Intended use: For full-time undergraduate or graduate study at accredited 2-year, 4-year or graduate institution in United States.
Eligibility: Applicant or parent must be member/participant of Screen Actor's Guild.
Basis for selection: Applicant must demonstrate financial need.
Application requirements: Recommendations, essay, transcript, proof of eligibility. Most recent federal income tax return and additional financial information. SAT scores.
Additional information: Must be member of Guild for five years or child of eight-year Guild member. Guild employees, scholarship committee members, Foundation trustees and their relatives are not eligible.

Amount of award:	$3,000-$5,000
Number of awards:	20
Number of applicants:	75
Application deadline:	April 1
Notification begins:	July 1
Total amount awarded:	$150,000

Contact:
Screen Actors Guild Foundation
John L. Dales Scholarship Fund
5757 Wilshire Boulevard
Hollywood, CA 90036
Phone: 323-549-6708

John L. Dales Transitional Scholarship

Type of award: Scholarship.
Intended use: For full-time undergraduate or graduate study at accredited postsecondary institution in United States.
Eligibility: Applicant or parent must be member/participant of Screen Actor's Guild.
Basis for selection: Applicant must demonstrate financial need.
Application requirements: Recommendations, essay, transcript, proof of eligibility. Most recent federal income tax return and additional financial information. SAT or ACT scores.
Additional information: Must be Guild member for at least ten years. Guild employees, scholarship committee members, Foundation board members, their families, relatives or employees not eligible. Not to be used for a theater or related study degree. For those reentering school to make a transition to another field of study. Award based on financial need.

Amount of award:	$3,000-$5,000
Number of awards:	22
Number of applicants:	150
Application deadline:	April 15

Contact:
Screen Actors Guild Foundation
John L. Dales Scholarship Fund
5757 Wilshire Boulevard
Los Angeles, CA 90036
Phone: 323-549-6773

Seabee Memorial Scholarship Association, Inc.

Seabee Memorial Scholarship

Type of award: Scholarship, renewable.
Intended use: For full-time undergraduate study at accredited 4-year institution in United States.
Eligibility: Applicant must be U.S. citizen. Applicant must be descendant of veteran who served in the Navy. Applicant must be a child or grandchild of a Seabee or member of Naval Civil Engineer Corps - deceased, retired, reserve, active or honorably discharged.
Basis for selection: Applicant must demonstrate financial need, depth of character, leadership, patriotism, seriousness of purpose and service orientation.
Application requirements: Essay, transcript, proof of eligibility. Submit completed application form.
Additional information: Application may be downloaded from Website or requested by e-mail: smsa@erols.com.

Amount of award:	$2,200-$5,000
Number of awards:	86
Number of applicants:	350
Application deadline:	April 15
Notification begins:	June 15
Total amount awarded:	$192,000

Contact:
Scholarship Committee
P.O. Box 6574
Silver Spring, MD 20916
Phone: 301-570-2850
Web: www.seabee.org

Sealed Air Corporation

Sealed Air Corporation Scholarship

Type of award: Scholarship, renewable.
Intended use: For undergraduate study at accredited vocational, 2-year or 4-year institution.
Eligibility: Applicant or parent must be employed by Sealed Air Corporation.
Basis for selection: Applicant must demonstrate financial need.
Additional information: For further information or an application, contact Sealed Air Corporation directly.

Amount of award:	$500-$2,000

Seattle Jaycees

Seattle Jaycees Scholarship

Type of award: Scholarship, renewable.
Intended use: For undergraduate or graduate study at accredited postsecondary institution. Designated institutions: Postsecondary institutions in Washington state.
Basis for selection: Applicant must demonstrate depth of character and service orientation.
Application requirements: $5 application fee. Transcript. Resume and proof of community service.
Additional information: Send SASE to receive application; application fee not necessary until completed application is returned. Scholarships granted for exemplary civic involvement, volunteerism and community service.

Amount of award:	$1,000
Number of awards:	20
Number of applicants:	480
Application deadline:	April 1

Contact:
Seattle Jaycees
Scholarship Committee
109 West Mercer Street
Seattle, WA 98119
Phone: 206-286-2014

Second Marine Division Association Memorial Scholarship Fund

Second Marine Division Scholarship

Type of award: Scholarship, renewable.
Intended use: For full-time undergraduate study at accredited vocational, 2-year or 4-year institution.
Eligibility: Applicant must be single. Applicant must be descendant of veteran; or dependent of active service person, veteran, disabled veteran or deceased veteran who serves or served in the Marines. Must be child or grandchild of person who served or is serving in Second Marine Division, U.S. Marine Corps or a unit attached to the Division.
Basis for selection: Applicant must demonstrate financial need, high academic achievement, depth of character, leadership, patriotism, seriousness of purpose and service orientation.
Application requirements: Recommendations, essay, transcript, proof of eligibility. Must include SASE when requesting applications.
Additional information: Must be dependent or grandchild of individual currently serving or having previously served in Second Marine Division, United States Marine Corps, or unit attached thereto; annual family income $42,000 or less. Minimum 2.5 GPA. Must reapply for renewal.

Amount of award:	$1,000
Number of awards:	32
Number of applicants:	32
Application deadline:	April 1
Notification begins:	September 30
Total amount awarded:	$32,000

Contact:
Second Marine Division Association Memorial Scholarship
Fund
P.O. Box 8180
Camp Lejeune, NC 28547

Securities Operations Division

Securities Operations Division Scholarship Program

Type of award: Scholarship, renewable.
Intended use: For freshman study at accredited vocational,
2-year or 4-year institution.
Eligibility: Applicant or parent must be member/participant of
Securities Operations Division.
Additional information: For further information or an
application, contact Securities Operations Division directly.

Amount of award:	$1,000

SEG Foundation

SEG Foundation Scholarship

Type of award: Scholarship, renewable.
Intended use: For full-time undergraduate or graduate study.
Eligibility: Applicant must be high school senior. Applicant
must be U.S. citizen.
Basis for selection: Major/career interest in physics;
mathematics or geology/earth sciences. Applicant must
demonstrate depth of character and leadership.
Application requirements: Recommendations, essay,
transcript, proof of eligibility. An applicant in need of financial
assistance will also be considered. However, the competence of
the student as indicated by the application is given first
consideration. Results of aptitude tests, college entrance exams,
National Merit Scholarship competition, etc., are not required
but should be furnished if taken.
Additional information: The Number of scholarships
available depends chiefly upon the number of sponsors and the
amounts they contribute. Last year, 12 companies, nine
individuals, and nine SEG Sections sponsored scholarships
available to students meeting certain specific criteria.

Amount of award:	$500-$12,000
Number of awards:	104
Total amount awarded:	$180,000

Contact:
SEG FOUNDATION
P.O. Box 702740
Tulsa, OK 74170-2740
Phone: 918-497-5500
Fax: 918-497-5557
Web: www.seg.org

Sempra Energy

Sempra Energy Scholarship Program for Employees' Children

Type of award: Scholarship, renewable.
Intended use: For undergraduate study at vocational, 2-year or
4-year institution.
Eligibility: Applicant or parent must be employed by Pacific
Enterprises. Applicant must be high school senior.
Additional information: For further information or an
application, contact Pacific Enterprises directly.

Amount of award:	$1,500-$4,000

Senator George J. Mitchell Scholarship Research Institute

Senator George J. Mitchell Scholarship Fund

Type of award: Scholarship, renewable.
Intended use: For full-time undergraduate study at accredited
4-year institution in United States. Designated institutions:
Accredited four-year college or university in Maine.
Eligibility: Applicant must be U.S. citizen residing in Maine.
Basis for selection: Applicant must demonstrate financial
need, high academic achievement and service orientation.
Application requirements: Transcript, proof of eligibility.
Application form, letter from guidance counselor, SAR, copy of
financial aid award from college student plans to attend.
Additional information: One award made to graduating
senior from every public high school in Maine. Total
scholarship award is $4,000 with students receiving $1,000 in
each of their four years of college. Maine residents entering
their first year at Maine college or university are eligible.
Nontraditional students, home-schooled students, parochial and
private school students, and students who earned high school
diploma through GED or Job Corps Programs also eligible; 30
additional awards reserved for these students.

Amount of award:	$4,000
Number of awards:	160
Number of applicants:	470
Application deadline:	April 5
Total amount awarded:	$311,000

Contact:
Senator George J. Mitchell Scholarship Research Institute
22 Monument Way
Suite 200
Portland, ME 04101
Phone: 207-773-7700
Web: www.mitchellinstitute.org

Seneca Nation of Indians

Seneca Nation Higher Education Program

Type of award: Scholarship, renewable.
Intended use: For undergraduate or graduate study at accredited 2-year, 4-year or graduate institution.
Eligibility: Applicant must be American Indian. Must be an enrolled member of Seneca Nation of Indians. Applicant must be U.S. citizen.
Basis for selection: Applicant must demonstrate financial need.
Application requirements: Essay, transcript, proof of eligibility. Tribal enrollment proof, letter of reference from person not a relative.
Additional information: Amount and number of awards vary. There are three levels regarding residency requirements. Level 1: Must be a permanent resident on the reservation. Level 2: Must be a permanent resident within New York State. Level 3: Must be permanent resident outside of New York Sate. Applicants of any age can apply.

    Application deadline: July 1, December 1
Contact:
Seneca Nation of Indians
Higher Education Program
P.O. Box 231
Salamanca, NY 14779
Phone: 716-945-1790 ext.3013
Fax: 716-945-7170

Sertoma International

Serteen Scholarships

Type of award: Scholarship.
Intended use: For undergraduate study at vocational, 2-year or 4-year institution in United States.
Eligibility: Applicant or parent must be member/participant of Serteen Club. Applicant must be high school senior. Applicant must be U.S. citizen, permanent resident, international student or Canadian or Mexican citizen.
Basis for selection: Applicant must demonstrate high academic achievement and service orientation.
Application requirements: Transcript, proof of eligibility. Application form. Minimum 3.0 GPA during high school sophomore, junior and senior years.
Additional information: Visit Website or contact via e-mail (cneely@sertoma.org) for application and additional information.

Amount of award:	$1,000
Number of awards:	4
Application deadline:	April 1
Total amount awarded:	$4,000

Contact:
Sertoma International
Scholarships
1912 East Meyer Boulevard
Kansas City, MO 64132-1174
Web: www.sertoma.org

Sertoma Collegiate Scholarships

Type of award: Scholarship, renewable.
Intended use: For undergraduate or graduate study at postsecondary institution in United States.
Eligibility: Applicant or parent must be member/participant of Sertoma Collegiate Club. Must be Canadian or Mexican citizen. Applicant must be U.S. citizen or permanent resident.
Basis for selection: Competition/talent/interest in Academics. Applicant must demonstrate high academic achievement and service orientation.
Application requirements: Recommendations, transcript. Application form, statement of purpose, letters of acceptance from college or university. Minimum 3.0 cumulative GPA.
Additional information: Recipients may reapply. Recipients are notified in June. Visit Website or contact via e-mail (cneely@sertoma.org) for application and additional information.

Amount of award:	$1,000
Number of awards:	4
Application deadline:	April 1
Total amount awarded:	$4,000

Contact:
Sertoma International
Scholarships
1912 East Meyer Boulevard
Kansas City, MO 64132-1174
Web: www.sertoma.org

Sertoma Communicative Disorders Scholarships

Type of award: Scholarship, renewable.
Intended use: For full-time senior or graduate study at accredited 4-year or graduate institution in United States or Canada. Designated institutions: Institution with program accredited by ASHA (in U.S.), institution with audiology or speech pathology program (in Canada) or University of the Americas in Mexico City, Mexico.
Eligibility: Applicant or parent must be member/participant of Sertoma Collegiate Club. Applicant must be U.S. citizen, permanent resident, international student or Canadian or Mexican citizen.
Basis for selection: Major/career interest in speech pathology/ audiology or deafness studies. Applicant must demonstrate high academic achievement and service orientation.
Application requirements: Recommendations, transcript, proof of eligibility. Application form, statement of purpose, letters of acceptance. Minimum 3.2 cumulative GPA.
Additional information: Recipients may reapply but may only receive award twice. Recipients are notified in June. Visit Website or contact via e-mail (cneely@sertoma.org) for application and additional information.

Amount of award:	$2,500
Number of awards:	30
Application deadline:	March 31
Total amount awarded:	$75,000

Contact:
Sertoma International
Scholarships
1912 East Meyer Boulevard
Kansas City, MO 64132-1174
Web: www.sertoma.org

Sertoma Scholarships for Hearing-Impaired Students

Type of award: Scholarship, renewable.
Intended use: For full-time undergraduate study at 4-year institution in United States or Canada.
Eligibility: Applicant or parent must be member/participant of Sertoma Collegiate Club. Applicant must be hearing impaired. Applicant must be U.S. citizen, permanent resident, international student or Canadian citizen.
Basis for selection: Applicant must demonstrate high academic achievement, depth of character and seriousness of purpose.
Application requirements: Recommendations, transcript, proof of eligibility. Application form, statement of purpose, letter(s) of acceptance from college or university, documentation of hearing impairment in form of recent audiogram or signed statement by hearing health professional, minimum 3.2 GPA.
Additional information: Applicant must be deaf or hearing impaired. May reapply for up to four years. Funding provided by Knowles Electronics, Belton Generation Club, Atel Securities Corp. and other contributors. Recipients notified in June. Visit Website or contact via e-mail (cneely@sertoma.org) for application and additional information.

Amount of award:	$1,000
Number of awards:	25
Application deadline:	May 1
Total amount awarded:	$25,000

Contact:
Sertoma International
Scholarships
1912 East Meyer Boulevard
Kansas City, MO 64132-1174
Web: www.sertoma.org

Service Employees International Union

Charles Hardy Memorial Scholarship

Type of award: Scholarship.
Intended use: For full-time freshman study at accredited 4-year institution in United States.
Eligibility: Applicant or parent must be member/participant of Service Employees International Union. Applicant must be high school senior. Applicant must be residing in California.
Basis for selection: Applicant must demonstrate financial need and high academic achievement.
Application requirements: Recommendations, essay, transcript. Download application and take online, open-book test on Website.
Additional information: Parent must be a member of the Service Employees International Union. Visit Website for application and online test.

Amount of award:	$1,000
Number of awards:	1
Application deadline:	March 15
Total amount awarded:	$1,000

Contact:
Service Employees International Union
1007 7th Street
4th Floor
Sacramento, CA 95814
Phone: 916-442-3838
Fax: 916-442-0976
Web: www.seiu.org

Sharp Electronics Corporation

Sharp Scholarship Program

Type of award: Scholarship, renewable.
Intended use: For freshman study at accredited vocational, 2-year or 4-year institution.
Eligibility: Applicant or parent must be employed by Sharp Electronics Corporation.
Basis for selection: Applicant must demonstrate financial need.
Additional information: For further information or an application, contact Sharp Electronics Corporation directly.

Amount of award:	$2,500

Shoshone Tribe

Shoshone Tribal Scholarship

Type of award: Scholarship, renewable.
Intended use: For undergraduate study at accredited vocational, 2-year or 4-year institution in United States.
Eligibility: Applicant must be American Indian. Must be enrolled member of Eastern Shoshone Tribe.
Basis for selection: Applicant must demonstrate financial need.
Application requirements: Transcript, proof of eligibility.
Additional information: Must first apply for Pell Grant and appropriate campus-based aid. Minimum 2.5 GPA required. Application deadline for summer is April 15.

Amount of award:	$50-$5,000
Number of awards:	90
Number of applicants:	100
Application deadline:	June 1, November 15
Total amount awarded:	$300,000

Contact:
Shoshone Education Program
P.O. Box 628
Fort Washakie, WY 82514
Phone: 307-332-3538 ext. 15

Sid Richardson Memorial Fund

Sid Richardson Scholarship

Type of award: Scholarship, renewable.

Intended use: For full-time undergraduate or graduate study at accredited postsecondary institution.
Eligibility: Applicant or parent must be employed by Sid Richardson/Bass Companies. Applicant must be high school senior.
Basis for selection: Applicant must demonstrate financial need and high academic achievement.
Application requirements: Essay, transcript, proof of eligibility. Submit SAT or ACT scores.
Additional information: Must be direct descendant of person retired from or employed with three years' full time service for Sid Richardson companies. Employees themselves are not eligible. Sid Richardson companies include: Sid Richardson Carbon Co., Sid Richardson Gasoline Co., Richardson Products II Co., SRCG Aviation, Inc., Leapartners, L.P., Bass Enterprises Production Company, Bass Brothers Enterprises, Inc., Richardson Oils, Inc., Perry R. Bass, Inc., Sid W. Richardson Foundation, San Jose Cattle Company, City Center Development Company and Richardson Aviation. Award amount varies. Minimum 2.0 GPA required. Award is renewable if GPA and financial need remains consistent. Grandchildren of employees also eligible. Applications available in January.

Amount of award:	$500-$5,000
Number of awards:	52
Number of applicants:	101
Application deadline:	March 31
Total amount awarded:	$158,250

Contact:
Sid Richardson Memorial Fund
309 Main Street
Fort Worth, TX 76102
Phone: 817-336-0494
Fax: 817-332-2176

Siemens Foundation

Siemens Awards for Advanced Placement

Type of award: Scholarship.
Intended use: For full-time freshman study at accredited 4-year institution.
Eligibility: Applicant must be high school freshman, sophomore or junior. Applicant must be U.S. citizen or permanent resident.
Basis for selection: Competition/talent/interest in Academics, based on the highest AP grades of five across seven subjects: Caculus BC, Computer Science AB, Statistics, Chemistry, Biology, Environmental Science and Physics C (Physics C: Mechanics and Physics C: Electricity and Magnetism each count as 1/2). Major/career interest in science, general; engineering; computer/information sciences; mathematics; physics; chemistry or biology. Applicant must demonstrate high academic achievement.
Application requirements: Proof of eligibility. Must take AP exams.
Additional information: The two highest-ranking male and two highest-ranking female students are chosen from each of the six College Board Regions. Thus, four students are chosen from each of the six regions for a total of twenty-four awards.

Amount of award:	$3,000-$8,000
Number of awards:	24
Number of applicants:	600,000
Application deadline:	October 2
Notification begins:	October 19
Total amount awarded:	$82,000

Contact:
Siemens Foundation Program Coordinator, National Recognition Programs
1233 20th Street, NW
Suite 600
Washington, DC 20036-2304
Phone: 202-822-5900 ext.114
Fax: 202-822-5920
Web: www.siemens-foundation.org

Siemens Westinghouse Science & Technology Competition

Type of award: Scholarship.
Intended use: For full-time undergraduate or graduate study at accredited 4-year or graduate institution in or outside United States.
Eligibility: Applicant must be enrolled in high school. Applicant must be U.S. citizen or permanent resident.
Basis for selection: Competition/talent/interest in science project, based on competition of science research project displaying originality, creativity, academic rigor, and clarity of communication. Major/career interest in biology; chemistry; engineering; environmental science; materials science; mathematics or physics. Applicant must demonstrate high academic achievement, leadership and seriousness of purpose.
Application requirements: Transcript, proof of eligibility, research proposal. A 20-page (maximum) research project. Candidate Data Sheet signed by school Principal. Completed Project Advisor or Mentor Comments Form. Applicant must be a high school senior or high school student as part of a two or three member team with a senior leader.
Additional information: The competition is to encourage students to do research. It gives young scientists the opportunity to present their research to leading scientists in their field. If the student is selected as a Regional Finalist, he/she will be awarded an expense paid trip to compete at one of six regional competitions. At a regional event, after presenting a poster, giving an oral presentation, and participating in a question and answer session, the student or team of students will qualify for either a $1,000 or $3,000 scholarship. If the student advances to National Finalist, then the student or team of students will qualify for a $10,000 to $100,000 scholarship. Download application from Website.

Amount of award:	$1,000-$103,000
Number of awards:	60
Number of applicants:	455
Application deadline:	October 2
Notification begins:	October 19
Total amount awarded:	$584,000

Contact:
Siemens Foundation Manager, National Recognition Programs
1233 20th Street, NW
Suite 600
Washington, DC 20036-2304
Phone: 202-822-5900 ext.114
Fax: 202-822-5920
Web: www.siemens-foundation.org

Sigma Alpha Epsilon Foundation

Sigma Alpha Epsilon Scholarships

Type of award: Scholarship.
Intended use: For full-time junior, senior or graduate study at accredited 4-year or graduate institution.
Eligibility: Applicant or parent must be member/participant of Sigma Alpha Epsilon. Applicant must be male.
Basis for selection: Applicant must demonstrate high academic achievement, depth of character, leadership and service orientation.
Application requirements: Recommendations, essay, transcript, proof of eligibility, nomination by chapter of fraternity.
Additional information: Applicant must be a Sigma Alpha Epsilon brother in good standing with fraternity office. Applicant must be involved in fraternity and community. Awards based on merit.

Amount of award:	$500-$5,000
Number of awards:	34
Number of applicants:	100
Application deadline:	April 26
Notification begins:	July 1
Total amount awarded:	$41,500

Contact:
Sigma Alpha Epsilon Foundation
1856 Sheridan Road
Evanston, IL 60204-1856
Web: www.sae.net

Sigma Xi The Scientific Research Society

Scientific Research Grant-In-Aid

Type of award: Research grant, renewable.
Intended use: For undergraduate, master's or doctoral study at accredited 4-year or graduate institution.
Basis for selection: Major/career interest in science, general; astronomy; optometry/ophthalmology or engineering. Applicant must demonstrate high academic achievement.
Application requirements: Recommendations, proof of eligibility.
Additional information: Online application preferred. Student researchers in astronomy or eye or vision research may apply for up to $2,500. Award renewable only once.

Amount of award:	$100-$1,000
Number of awards:	577
Number of applicants:	2,000
Application deadline:	October 15, March 21
Total amount awarded:	$368,000

Contact:
Sigma Xi, The Scientific Research Society Committee on Grants-in-Aid
99 Alexander Drive
P.O. Box 13975
Research Triangle Park, NC 27709
Phone: 919-549-4691
Web: www.sigmaxi.org

Simpson Manufacturing Co., Inc.

Simpson Scholarship Program

Type of award: Scholarship, renewable.
Intended use: For undergraduate or graduate study at vocational, 2-year, 4-year or graduate institution.
Eligibility: Applicant or parent must be employed by Simpson Manufacturing Co., Inc. Applicant must be high school senior.
Additional information: Further information or an application, contact Simpson Manufacturing Co., Inc. directly.

Amount of award:	$2,500

Sippican, Inc.

W. Van Alan Clark Jr. and Burgess Dempster Memorial Scholarship

Type of award: Scholarship, renewable.
Intended use: For undergraduate study at accredited vocational, 2-year or 4-year institution.
Eligibility: Applicant or parent must be employed by Sippican, Inc.
Basis for selection: Applicant must demonstrate financial need.
Additional information: For further information or an application, contact Sippican, Inc. directly.

Amount of award:	$3,000

Sisters of Mercy Health System - St. Louis

Charles E. Thoele Scholarship

Type of award: Scholarship.
Intended use: For undergraduate study at accredited postsecondary institution.
Eligibility: Applicant or parent must be employed by Sisters of Mercy Health System. Applicant must be high school senior.
Additional information: For further information or an application, contact Sisters of Mercy Health System - St. Louis directly.

Amount of award:	$1,000

Slovak Gymnastic Union Sokol, USA

USA Milan Getting Scholarship

Type of award: Scholarship, renewable.
Intended use: For full-time undergraduate study at accredited 4-year institution.

Eligibility: Applicant or parent must be member/participant of Slovak Gymnastic Union Sokol, USA. Applicant must be high school junior or senior. Applicant must be U.S. citizen.
Basis for selection: Applicant must demonstrate high academic achievement, depth of character, leadership, patriotism and seriousness of purpose.
Application requirements: Recommendations, transcript. Write sponsor for application form.
Additional information: Applicant must be a member of Slovak Gymnastic Union Sokol, USA, in good standing for four years. Recipient must attend a four-year college or university. A minimum scholastic average of C+ or equivalent is required. Recipients are chosen on the basis of scholastic merit, leadership, and character. Award renewable for four years.

Amount of award:	$500
Number of awards:	9
Number of applicants:	11
Application deadline:	April 1
Total amount awarded:	$4,500

Contact:
Slovak Gymnastic Union Sokol, USA
P.O. Box 189
East Orange, NJ 07019
Phone: 973-676-0280

Slovene National Benefit Society

Slovene Scholarship

Type of award: Scholarship, renewable.
Intended use: For undergraduate or graduate study at accredited postsecondary institution in United States.
Eligibility: Applicant or parent must be member/participant of Slovene National Benefit Society.
Basis for selection: Applicant must demonstrate financial need.
Application requirements: Transcript, proof of eligibility. Financial information, tax forms and proof of involvement with the SNPJ.
Additional information: Any qualified member of the Slovene National Benefit Society is eligible for scholarship, provided they are enrolled as a full- or part-time student in an accredited college, university or trade school. Applicant must have a minimum of $2,000 permanent SNJP insurance at the date of application and be a member of the Society for at least two years. Contact local lodge for application.

Number of applicants:	250

Contact:
Slovene National Benefit Society
Joseph C. Evanish, National President
247 West Allegheny Road
Imperial, PA 15126
Web: www.snpj.com/scholar.htm

Slovenian Women's Union of America

Slovenian Women's Union Scholarship

Type of award: Scholarship.
Intended use: For full-time freshman study at vocational, 2-year or 4-year institution in United States.
Eligibility: Applicant or parent must be member/participant of Slovenian Women's Union of America. Applicant must be high school senior.
Basis for selection: Applicant must demonstrate financial need, high academic achievement, depth of character, leadership and service orientation.
Application requirements: Recommendations, essay, transcript. Submit 200-word essay on "Importance of My Heritage and Culture."
Additional information: Must be a Slovenian Women's Union member for at least three years. Open to women and men.

Amount of award:	$1,000
Number of awards:	4
Number of applicants:	8
Application deadline:	March 10
Notification begins:	April 20
Total amount awarded:	$4,000

Contact:
Slovenian Women's Union of America
Scholarship Director
52 Oakridge Drive
Marguette, MI 49855
Phone: 906-249-4288

Slovenian Women's Union Scholarship Program

Type of award: Scholarship.
Intended use: For undergraduate study at accredited vocational, 2-year or 4-year institution in United States.
Eligibility: Applicant or parent must be member/participant of Slovenian Women's Union of America. Applicant must be returning adult student.
Basis for selection: Applicant must demonstrate financial need, high academic achievement, depth of character, leadership and service orientation.
Application requirements: Recommendations, essay, proof of eligibility.
Additional information: Must be Slovenian Women's Union member or active participant of this organization for the past three years. Open to men and women with interest in promoting Slovene culture. Scholarships consist of two general awards and two awards for teachers to update skills.

Amount of award:	$500
Number of awards:	4
Application deadline:	March 10
Total amount awarded:	$2,000

Contact:
Slovenian Women's Union of America
Scholarship Director
52 Oakridge Dr.
Marquette, MI 49855
Phone: 906-249-4288

Smith's Food and Drug Centers Inc.

Personal Best Scholarship

Type of award: Scholarship.
Intended use: For freshman study at postsecondary institution.
Eligibility: Applicant must be high school senior. Applicant must be residing in New Mexico.
Basis for selection: Applicant must demonstrate financial need and seriousness of purpose.
Application requirements: Recommendations, essay, nomination by person who knows applicant well, but is not family member. Applicant must be New Mexico resident.
Additional information: Applicants must have overcome an adversity. Must demonstrate strong motivation to continue education, but have need for financial incentive.

Amount of award:	$1,000
Number of awards:	5
Number of applicants:	120
Application deadline:	March 1
Notification begins:	May 15
Total amount awarded:	$5,000

Contact:
Smith's Food and Drug Centers Inc.
P.O. Box 27020
Albuquerque, NM 87125-7020
Phone: 505-345-3371 ext. 279

Sociedad Honoraria Hispanica

Joseph S. Adams Scholarship

Type of award: Scholarship.
Intended use: For full-time freshman study in United States.
Eligibility: Applicant or parent must be member/participant of Sociedad Honoraria Hispanica. Applicant must be high school senior.
Basis for selection: Major/career interest in Latin american studies or foreign languages. Applicant must demonstrate high academic achievement, depth of character, leadership, patriotism, seriousness of purpose and service orientation.
Application requirements: Recommendations, essay, transcript, proof of eligibility, nomination by local high school chapter sponsor. Must be presently enrolled in high school Spanish or Portuguese class.
Additional information: Applicant must be active senior member of the honor society. All majors eligible; strong interest in Latin American Studies, Spanish, Portugese preferred. Contact Sociedad Honoraria Hispanica sponsor for official application before December 31. One member per chapter may apply.

Amount of award:	$1,000-$2,000
Number of awards:	44
Number of applicants:	200
Application deadline:	February 15
Notification begins:	April 15
Total amount awarded:	$52,000

Contact:
American Association of Teachers of Spanish and Portuguese
Ms. Bertie Green, SHH National Director
P.O. Box 10
Turbeville, SC 29162-0010
Web: www.aatsp.org

Society for Human Resource Management

SHRM Management Sons and Daughters Scholarship

Type of award: Scholarship.
Intended use: For undergraduate study at accredited 4-year institution.
Eligibility: Applicant or parent must be member/participant of Society for Human Resource Management.
Additional information: For further information or an application, contact Society for Human Resource Management directly.

Amount of award:	$1,500

Society for Technical Communication

Society For Technical Communication Scholarship Program

Type of award: Scholarship.
Intended use: For full-time undergraduate or graduate study at accredited 2-year, 4-year or graduate institution.
Basis for selection: Major/career interest in graphic arts/design or communications. Applicant must demonstrate high academic achievement, depth of character, leadership and seriousness of purpose.
Application requirements: Recommendations, essay, transcript. Must have at least one year of postsecondary education to be eligible.
Additional information: Seven awards for undergraduates, seven for graduate students. Applicants must be full-time students, have completed at least one year of post-secondary education, and have major/career interest in technical communications. Additional contact: Society for Technical Communication. 901 North Stuart Street, Suite 904. Arlington, VA, 22203-1822. Phone: 703-522-4114.

Amount of award:	$2,500
Number of awards:	14
Application deadline:	February 15
Notification begins:	April 15
Total amount awarded:	$35,000

Contact:
Ms. Lenore S. Ridgway
19 Johnston Avenue
Kingston, NY 12401-5211
Phone: 914-339-4927
Web: www.stc-va.org

Scholarships

Society of Actuaries/ Casualty Actuarial Society

Joint CAS/SOA Minority Scholarships for Actuarial Students

Type of award: Scholarship.
Intended use: For full-time undergraduate or graduate study at accredited 4-year or graduate institution.
Eligibility: Applicant must be African American, Mexican American, Hispanic American, Puerto Rican or American Indian. Applicant must be U.S. citizen or permanent resident.
Basis for selection: Major/career interest in insurance/actuarial science or mathematics. Applicant must demonstrate financial need and high academic achievement.
Application requirements: Recommendations, transcript, proof of eligibility, nomination by faculty members or actuarial supervisors. SAT or ACT scores. CSS PROFILE application required.
Additional information: Number of awards granted varies. Also awards advanced calculators to recipients. Open to minority groups which are underrepresented in the actuarial profession.

Amount of award:	$500-$3,000
Number of awards:	20
Application deadline:	May 1
Notification begins:	July 15
Total amount awarded:	$48,000

Contact:
Society of Actuaries/Casualty Actuarial Society
Minority Scholarship Coordinator
475 North Martingale Road, Suite 800
Schaumburg, IL 60173-2226
Phone: 847-706-3509

Society of Automotive Engineers

Society of Automotive Engineers (SAE) Engineering Scholarships

Type of award: Scholarship.
Intended use: For full-time freshman study at accredited 4-year institution in United States. Designated institutions: Must have ABET accredited program.
Eligibility: Applicant must be high school senior. Applicant must be U.S. citizen.
Basis for selection: Major/career interest in engineering. Applicant must demonstrate high academic achievement, depth of character and leadership.
Application requirements: $5 application fee. Essay, transcript.
Additional information: Awards vary from $500 to full tuition. Some awards may have additional criteria. Must have 3.25 GPA and rank in 90th percentile on ACT/SAT I.

Amount of award:	Full tuition
Number of awards:	53
Number of applicants:	3,400
Application deadline:	December 1
Notification begins:	June 1
Total amount awarded:	$278,000

Contact:
Society of Automotive Engineers
SAE Educational Relations
400 Commonwealth Drive
Warrendale, PA 15096-0001
Phone: 724-772-4047
Web: www.sae.org/students/engschlr.htm

Society of Automotive Engineers (SAE) Longterm Member Sponsored Scholarship

Type of award: Scholarship.
Intended use: For full-time senior study at 4-year institution.
Eligibility: Applicant or parent must be member/participant of Society of Automotive Engineers.
Basis for selection: Support of SAE activities and programs. Applicant must demonstrate leadership.
Application requirements: Proof of eligibility, nomination by SAE Faculty Advisor, SAE Section Chair or Vice Chair for Student Activities. SAE student member.
Additional information: Applicant must be an SAE student member.

Amount of award:	$1,000
Number of awards:	2
Application deadline:	April 1
Notification begins:	June 1
Total amount awarded:	$2,000

Contact:
Society of Automotive Engineers
Educational Relations Divison
400 Commonwealth Drive
Warrendale, PA 15096-0001
Phone: 724-722-4047
Web: www.sae.org/students/schlrshp.htm

Society of Automotive Engineers (SAE) Yanmar Scholarship

Type of award: Scholarship, renewable.
Intended use: For full-time senior study at 4-year institution.
Eligibility: Applicant must be U.S. citizen, international student or Canadian or Mexican citizen.
Basis for selection: Major/career interest in engineering. Applicant must demonstrate leadership.
Application requirements: Essay, transcript, proof of eligibility.
Additional information: Must pursue course of study or research related to conservation of energy in transportation, agriculture, construction, or power generation. Emphasis is placed on research or study related to internal combustion engine.

Amount of award:	$2,000
Number of awards:	1
Number of applicants:	55
Application deadline:	April 1
Notification begins:	June 1
Total amount awarded:	$2,000

Contact:
Society of Automotive Engineers
Educational Relations Division
400 Commonwealth Drive
Warrendale, PA 15096-0001
Phone: 724-772-4047
Web: www.sae.org/students/yanmar.htm

Society of Daughters of the United States Army

Society of Daughters of United States Army Scholarship Program

Type of award: Scholarship, renewable.
Intended use: For full-time undergraduate study at accredited postsecondary institution.
Eligibility: Applicant must be female. Applicant must be descendant of veteran; or dependent of active service person, veteran, disabled veteran or deceased veteran who serves or served in the Army. Must be daughter or granddaughter (incl. step or adopted) of U.S. Army veteran career warrant officer (Warrant Officer 1-5) or U.S. Army veteran career commissioned officer [2nd & 1st Lieutenant (LT), Captain (CPT), Major (MAJ), Lieutenant Colonel (LTC), Colonel (COL), and Brigadier General (BG), Major General (MG), (Lieutenant General (LTG) or full General (GEN)] of U.S. Army who: 1) is currently on active duty, 2) retired after at least 20 years active service, 3) was medically retired before 20 years active service or; 4) died while on active duty or; 5) died after retiring from active duty with 20 or more years of service. U.S. Army must have been officer's primary occupation.
Basis for selection: Applicant must demonstrate high academic achievement, depth of character, leadership, patriotism and seriousness of purpose.
Application requirements: Recommendations, essay, transcript. Include resume. Minimum 3.0 GPA required for at least three years. Applicant must provide name, rank, component (Active, Regular, Reserve), social security number and inclusive dates of active duty of her qualifying family member. Include SASE.
Additional information: Scholarships are awarded for undergraduate study only. Amount of awards varies annually. Send business sized SASE and one letter of request only. Do not use registered/certified mail. All application submissions become the property of DUSA.

Amount of award:	$1,000
Number of applicants:	400
Application deadline:	March 1
Notification begins:	May 15

Contact:
Society of Daughters of the United States Army
Janet B. Otto, Chairman
7717 Rockledge Court
Springfield, VA 22152-3854

Society of Exploration Geophysicists

Society of Exploration Geophysicists Scholarship

Type of award: Scholarship, renewable.
Intended use: For full-time freshman, sophomore, junior, senior or graduate study at 4-year or graduate institution in or outside United States.
Basis for selection: Major/career interest in geophysics; geology/earth sciences or physics. Applicant must demonstrate high academic achievement.

Application requirements: Recommendations, transcript, proof of eligibility.
Additional information: Minimum 3.0 GPA. Must intend to pursue career in exploration geophysics (graduate students in operations, teaching, or research). In addition, one special award per year offered at $10,000 and one special award per year offered at $12,000.

Amount of award:	$500-$12,000
Number of awards:	106
Number of applicants:	300
Application deadline:	March 1
Notification begins:	June 1
Total amount awarded:	$183,500

Contact:
SEG Foundation
P.O. Box 702740
Tulsa, OK 74137-2740

Society of Hispanic Professional Engineers Foundation

Hispanic Professional Engineers Educational Grant

Type of award: Scholarship, renewable.
Intended use: For full-time undergraduate or graduate study at 2-year, 4-year or graduate institution.
Basis for selection: Major/career interest in engineering or science, general. Applicant must demonstrate financial need and high academic achievement.
Application requirements: Recommendations, essay. Submit completed application.
Additional information: All sciences except medical eligible. Include SASE with application requests, or download application from Website. Applications available beginning of September.

Amount of award:	$500-$7,000
Number of awards:	313
Number of applicants:	990
Application deadline:	April 15
Notification begins:	June 15
Total amount awarded:	$250,000

Contact:
Society of Hispanic Professional Engineers Foundation
5400 East Olympic Boulevard
Suite 210
Los Angeles, CA 90022
Web: www.shpefoundation.org

Society of Manufacturing Engineers Education Foundation

Albert E. Wischmeyer Memorial Scholarship Award

Type of award: Scholarship, renewable.

Intended use: For undergraduate study at accredited 4-year institution. Designated institutions: New York schools with manufacturing engineering, manufacturing engineering technology, or mechanical technology degree program.
Eligibility: Applicant must be high school senior. Applicant must be U.S. citizen or permanent resident residing in New York.
Basis for selection: Major/career interest in manufacturing or engineering. Applicant must demonstrate high academic achievement.
Application requirements: Recommendations, essay, transcript.
Additional information: Applicants must reside in Western New York State (West of Interstate 81). Applicants must be enrolled in manufacturing engineering, manufacturing engineering technology or mechanical technology degree program. Minimum GPA 3.0. Applicants must reapply for renewal. Financial need a consideration only between two otherwise equal applicants. Award amount may increase depending on endowment funds. Application available on Website.

Amount of award:	$1,900
Number of awards:	2
Application deadline:	February 1
Total amount awarded:	$3,800

Contact:
Society of Manufacturing Engineers
Scholarship Review Committee
One SME Drive, P.O. Box 930
Dearborn, MI 48121
Phone: 313-271-1500
Web: www.sme.org/foundation

Arthur and Gladys Cervenka Scholarship

Type of award: Scholarship, renewable.
Intended use: For full-time sophomore, junior or senior study at accredited 4-year institution in United States or Canada. Designated institutions: Schools with manufacturing engineering or technology degree program.
Basis for selection: Major/career interest in manufacturing or engineering. Applicant must demonstrate high academic achievement.
Application requirements: Recommendations, essay, transcript. Supply foundation with name of intended college or university.
Additional information: Preference given, but not limited, to students attending colleges or universities in state of Florida. Applicants must be enrolled in manufacturing engineering or technology degree program and must have completed a minimum of 30 college credit hours. Minimum GPA 3.0. Applicants must reapply for renewal. Financial need a consideration only between two otherwise equal applicants. Application available on Website.

Amount of award:	$1,250
Number of awards:	1
Application deadline:	February 1
Total amount awarded:	$1,250

Contact:
Society of Manufacturing Engineers
Scholarship Review Committee
One SME Drive, P.O. Box 930
Dearborn, MI 48121
Phone: 313-271-1500
Web: www.sme.org/foundation

Caterpillar Scholars Award

Type of award: Scholarship, renewable.
Intended use: For full-time freshman, sophomore, junior or senior study at accredited 4-year institution in United States or Canada. Designated institutions: Schools with manufacturing engineering degree program.
Basis for selection: Major/career interest in manufacturing or engineering. Applicant must demonstrate high academic achievement.
Application requirements: Recommendations, essay, transcript. Supply Foundation with name of intended college or university; freshmen must supply SAT scores.
Additional information: Applicants must be enrolled in manufacturing engineering degree program and must have completed a minimum of 30 college credit hours. Minority applicants may apply as incoming freshmen. Minimum 3.0 GPA. Applicants must reapply for renewal. Summer internships may be offered to select Caterpillar scholars. Financial need a consideration only between two otherwise equal applicants. Application available on Website.

Amount of award:	$2,000
Number of awards:	5
Application deadline:	February 1
Total amount awarded:	$10,000

Contact:
Society of Manufacturing Engineers
Scholarship Review Committee
One SME Drive, P.O. Box 930
Dearborn, MI 48121
Phone: 313-271-1500
Web: www.sme.org/foundation

Chapter 4 Lawrence A. Wacker Memorial Scholarship

Type of award: Scholarship, renewable.
Intended use: For undergraduate study at accredited 4-year institution. Designated institutions: Wisconsin schools with manufacturing engineering, mechanical engineering, or industrial engineering degree program.
Eligibility: Applicant must be high school senior. Applicant must be U.S. citizen or permanent resident.
Basis for selection: Major/career interest in manufacturing; engineering or engineering, mechanical. Applicant must demonstrate high academic achievement.
Application requirements: Recommendations, essay, transcript.
Additional information: Applicants must be seeking a bachelor's degree in manufacturing, mechanical or industrial engineering. Minimum GPA 3.0. One scholarship granted to graduating high school senior, the other granted to current undergraduate. First preference given to SME Chapter 4 members or spouses, children, or grandchildren of members. Second preference given to residents of Milwaukee, Ozaukee, Washington and Waukesha counties. Third preference given to Wisconsin residents. Applicants must reapply for renewal. Financial need a consideration only between two otherwise equal applicants. Application available on Website.

Amount of award:	$1,500
Number of awards:	2
Application deadline:	February 1
Total amount awarded:	$3,000

Scholarships

Contact:
Society of Manufacturing Engineers
Scholarship Review Committee
One SME Drive, P.O. Box 930
Dearborn, MI 48121
Phone: 313-271-1500
Web: www.sme.org/foundation

Clinton J. Helton Manufacturing Scholarship Award

Type of award: Scholarship.
Intended use: For full-time sophomore, junior or senior study at accredited 4-year institution. Designated institutions: Colorado State University, all University of Colorado campuses.
Basis for selection: Major/career interest in manufacturing or engineering. Applicant must demonstrate high academic achievement.
Application requirements: Recommendations, essay, transcript. Supply Foundation with name of intended college or university.
Additional information: Applicants must be enrolled in manufacturing engineering or technology degree program and must have completed at least 30 credit hours. Minimum 3.3 GPA. Applicants must reapply for renewal. Financial need a consideration only between two otherwise equal applicants. Application available on Website.

Amount of award:	$3,500
Number of awards:	1
Application deadline:	February 1
Total amount awarded:	$3,500

Contact:
Society of Manufacturing Engineers Education Foundation
Scholarship Review Committee
One SME Drive, P.O. Box 930
Dearborn, MI 48121
Phone: 313-271-1500
Web: www.sme.org/foundation

Community College Scholarship

Type of award: Scholarship, renewable.
Intended use: For full-time freshman or sophomore study at accredited vocational or 2-year institution in United States or Canada. Designated institutions: Community colleges, trade schools, or other two-year-degree-granting institutions with manufacturing or related degree program.
Basis for selection: Major/career interest in manufacturing. Applicant must demonstrate high academic achievement.
Application requirements: Recommendations, essay, transcript. Supply Foundation with name of intended college or university.
Additional information: Applicants must be enrolled in manufacturing engineering or closely related degree program and must have completed less than 60 college credit hours. Minimum GPA 3.5. Applicants must reapply for renewal. Financial need a consideration only between two otherwise equal applicants. Application available on Website.

Amount of award:	$1,000
Number of awards:	3
Application deadline:	February 1
Total amount awarded:	$3,000

Contact:
Society of Manufacturing Engineers
Scholarship Review Committee
One SME Drive, P.O. Box 930
Dearborn, MI 48121
Phone: 313-271-1500
Web: www.sme.org/foundation

Connie and Robert T. Gunter Scholarship

Type of award: Scholarship.
Intended use: For full-time sophomore, junior or senior study at accredited 4-year institution. Designated institutions: Georgia Institute of Technology, Georgia Southern University, Southern Polytechnic State University.
Basis for selection: Major/career interest in manufacturing or engineering. Applicant must demonstrate high academic achievement.
Application requirements: Supply Foundation with name of intended college or university.
Additional information: Applicants must be enrolled in manufacturing engineering or technology degree program and must have completed at least 30 credit hours. Minimum 3.5 GPA. Applicants must reapply for renewal. Financial need a consideration only between two otherwise equal applicants. Application available on Website.

Amount of award:	$1,000
Number of awards:	1
Total amount awarded:	$1,000

Contact:
Society of Manufacturing Engineers Education Foundation
Scholarship Review Committee
One SME Drive, P.O. Box 930
Dearborn, MI 48121
Phone: 313-271-1500
Web: www.sme.org/foundation

Detroit Chapter One - Founding Chapter Scholarship Award

Type of award: Scholarship, renewable.
Intended use: For full-time undergraduate or graduate study at accredited 2-year, 4-year or graduate institution. Designated institutions: Wayne State University, Lawrence Technical University, University of Detroit Mercy, Focus: HOPE Center for Advanced Technologies, Henry Ford Community College.
Eligibility: Applicant or parent must be member/participant of Society of Manufacturing Engineers.
Basis for selection: Major/career interest in manufacturing or engineering. Applicant must demonstrate high academic achievement, depth of character and leadership.
Application requirements: Recommendations, essay, transcript. Supply Foundation with name of intended college or university.
Additional information: Awarded to one student each at associate, baccalaureate, and graduate levels. Applicants must be enrolled in manufacturing engineering, manufacturing engineering technology or closely related degree or certificate program. Minimum 3.0 GPA. Applicants must reapply for renewal. Financial need a consideration only between two otherwise equal applicants. Application available on Website.

Amount of award:	$1,000
Number of awards:	3
Application deadline:	February 1
Total amount awarded:	$3,000

Contact:
Society of Manufacturing Engineers Education Foundation
Scholarship Review Committee
One SME Drive, P.O. Box 930
Dearborn, MI 48121
Phone: 313-271-1500
Web: www.sme.org/foundation

Directors Scholarship

Type of award: Scholarship, renewable.
Intended use: For full-time sophomore, junior or senior study at accredited 4-year institution in United States or Canada.
Basis for selection: Major/career interest in manufacturing. Applicant must demonstrate high academic achievement and leadership.
Application requirements: Recommendations, essay, transcript. Supply Foundation with name of intended college or university.
Additional information: Applicants must have completed a minimum of 30 college credit hours. Minimum GPA 3.5. Applicants must reapply for renewal. Financial need a consideration only between two otherwise equal applicants. Application available on Website.

Amount of award:	$5,000
Number of awards:	1
Application deadline:	February 1
Total amount awarded:	$5,000

Contact:
Society of Manufacturing Engineers
Scholarship Review Committee
One SME Drive, P.O. Box 930
Dearborn, MI 48121
Phone: 313-271-1500
Web: www.sme.org/foundation

Edward S. Roth Manufacturing Engineering

Type of award: Scholarship.
Intended use: For full-time undergraduate or graduate study at accredited 4-year or graduate institution. Designated institutions: California Polytechnic State University, California State Polytechnic University, University of Miami, Bradley University, Central State University, Miami University, Boston University, Worcester Polytechnic Institute, University of Massachusetts, St. Cloud State University, The University of Texas - Pan American, Brigham Young University, Utah State University.
Basis for selection: Major/career interest in manufacturing or engineering. Applicant must demonstrate high academic achievement.
Application requirements: Recommendations, essay, transcript. Supply Foundation with name of intended college or university.
Additional information: Applicants must be enrolled in manufacturing engineering degree program. Minimum 3.0 GPA. Preference given to students demonstrating financial need, minority students and students participating in Co-Op program. Applicants must reapply for renewal. Application available on Website.

Amount of award:	$2,500
Number of awards:	1
Application deadline:	February 1
Total amount awarded:	$2,500

Contact:
Society of Manufacturing Engineers Education Foundation
Scholarship Review Committee
One SME Drive, P.O. Box 930
Dearborn, MI 48121
Phone: 313-271-1500
Web: www.sme.org/foundation

Guiliano Mazzetti Scholarship

Type of award: Scholarship, renewable.
Intended use: For full-time sophomore, junior or senior study at accredited 4-year institution in United States or Canada. Designated institutions: Schools with manufacturing engineering or technology degree program.
Basis for selection: Major/career interest in manufacturing or engineering. Applicant must demonstrate high academic achievement.
Application requirements: Recommendations, essay, transcript. Supply Foundation with name of intended college or university.
Additional information: Applicants must be enrolled in manufacturing engineering or technology degree program and must have completed a minimum of 30 college credit hours. Minimum GPA 3.0. Applicants must reapply for renewal. Financial need a consideration only between two otherwise equal applicants. Application available on Website.

Amount of award:	$1,500
Number of awards:	2
Application deadline:	February 1
Total amount awarded:	$3,000

Contact:
Society of Manufacturing Engineers
Scholarship Review Committee
One SME Drive, P.O. Box 930
Dearborn, MI 48121
Phone: 313-271-1500
Web: www.sme.org/foundation

Kalamazoo Chapter 116 - Roscoe Douglas Scholarship Award

Type of award: Scholarship.
Intended use: For full-time sophomore, junior or senior study at accredited 2-year or 4-year institution. Designated institutions: Glen Oaks Community College, Jackson Community College, Kalamazoo Valley Community College, Kellogg Community College, Southwestern Michigan College, Western Michigan University.
Basis for selection: Major/career interest in manufacturing or engineering. Applicant must demonstrate high academic achievement.
Application requirements: Recommendations, essay, transcript. Supply Foundation with name of intended college or university.
Additional information: Applicants must be enrolled in manufacturing engineering or manufacturing engineering technology degree program and must have completed at least 30 credit hours. Minimum 3.0 GPA. Applicants must reapply for renewal. Financial need a consideration only between two otherwise equal applicants. Application available on Website.

Amount of award:	$1,500
Number of awards:	1
Application deadline:	February 1
Total amount awarded:	$1,500

Scholarships

Contact:
Society of Manufacturing Engineers Education Foundation
Scholarship Review Committee
One SME Drive, P.O. Box 930
Dearborn, MI 48121
Phone: 313-271-1500
Web: www.sme.org/foundation

Lucile B. Kaufman Women's Scholarship

Type of award: Scholarship, renewable.
Intended use: For full-time sophomore, junior or senior study at 4-year institution in United States or Canada. Designated institutions: Schools with manufacturing engineering or technology degree program.
Eligibility: Applicant must be female.
Basis for selection: Major/career interest in manufacturing or engineering. Applicant must demonstrate high academic achievement.
Application requirements: Recommendations, essay, transcript. Supply Foundation with name of intended college or university.
Additional information: Applicants must be enrolled in manufacturing engineering or manufacturing engineering technology degree program and must have completed minimum of 30 credits. Minimum GPA 3.5. Applicants must reapply for renewal. Financial need a consideration only between two otherwise equal applicants. Application available on Website, and visit Society of Women Engineers Website at www.swe.org for additional award opportunities.

Amount of award:	$1,000
Number of awards:	1
Application deadline:	February 1
Total amount awarded:	$1,000

Contact:
Society of Manufacturing Engineers
Scholarship Review Committee
One SME Drive, P.O. Box 930
Dearborn, MI 48121
Phone: 313-271-1500
Web: www.sme.org/foundation

Myrtle and Earl Walker Scholarship

Type of award: Scholarship, renewable.
Intended use: For full-time freshman, sophomore, junior or senior study at accredited 4-year institution in United States or Canada. Designated institutions: Schools with manufacturing engineering or technology degree program.
Basis for selection: Major/career interest in manufacturing or engineering. Applicant must demonstrate high academic achievement.
Application requirements: Recommendations, essay, transcript. Supply Foundation with name of intended college or university.
Additional information: Applicants must be enrolled in manufacturing engineering or technology degree program and must have completed minimum 15 credits. Minimum GPA 3.5. Applicants must reapply for renewal. Financial need a consideration only between two otherwise equal applicants. Application available on Website.

Amount of award:	$1,000
Number of awards:	25
Application deadline:	February 1
Total amount awarded:	$25,000

S-B Power Tool Scholarship Award

Type of award: Scholarship, renewable.
Intended use: For full-time sophomore, junior or senior study at accredited 4-year institution in United States. Designated institutions: Arkansas, Illinois, and North Carolina schools with manufacturing engineering or technology degree program.
Eligibility: Applicant must be U.S. citizen or permanent resident.
Basis for selection: Major/career interest in manufacturing or engineering. Applicant must demonstrate high academic achievement.
Application requirements: Recommendations, essay, transcript. Supply Foundation with name of intended college or university.
Additional information: Applicants must be enrolled in manufacturing engineering or technology degree program and must have completed a minimum of 30 college credit hours. Minimum GPA 3.5. Applicants must reapply for renewal. Financial need a consideration only between two otherwise equal applicants. Application available on Website. Sponsored by S-B Power Tool Company through the SME Education Foundation.

Amount of award:	$1,500
Number of awards:	1
Application deadline:	February 1
Total amount awarded:	$1,500

Contact:
Society of Manufacturing Engineers
Scholarship Review Committee
One SME Drive, P.O. Box 930
Dearborn, MI 48121
Phone: 313-271-1500
Web: www.sme.org/foundation

St. Louis Chapter 17 Scholarship

Type of award: Scholarship.
Intended use: For full-time freshman, sophomore or junior study at accredited 2-year or 4-year institution. Designated institutions: Jefferson College, Mineral Area College, St. Louis Community College at Florissant Valley, University of Missouri, Southeast Missouri State University, Southern Illinois University.
Eligibility: Applicant or parent must be member/participant of Society of Manufacturing Engineers.
Basis for selection: Major/career interest in manufacturing or engineering. Applicant must demonstrate high academic achievement.
Application requirements: Recommendations, essay, transcript. Supply Foundation with name of intended college or university.
Additional information: Applicants must be enrolled in manufacturing engineering, industrial technology or related degree program and be member of SME Chapter 17 student chapter. Sophomores at two-year institutions must be accepted to eligible four-year institution to receive award. Minimum 3.5 GPA at application; 3.0 GPA must be maintained. Applicants must reapply for renewal. Financial need a consideration only

between two otherwise equal applicants. Application available on Website.

Amount of award:	$1,000
Number of awards:	2
Application deadline:	February 1
Total amount awarded:	$2,000

Contact:
Society of Manufacturing Engineers Education Foundation
Scholarship Review Committee
One SME Drive, P.O. Box 930
Dearborn, MI 48121
Phone: 313-271-1500
Web: www.sme.org/foundation

Walt Bartram Memorial Education Award (Region 12)

Type of award: Scholarship.
Intended use: For full-time undergraduate study at accredited 2-year or 4-year institution. Designated institutions: Schools with manufacturing engineering program within Desert Pacific Region 12 (Arizona, New Mexico, Southern California).
Eligibility: Applicant must be residing in New Mexico, Arizona or California.
Basis for selection: Major/career interest in manufacturing or engineering. Applicant must demonstrate high academic achievement.
Application requirements: Recommendations, essay, transcript. Supply Foundation with name of intended college or university.
Additional information: Applicants must reside within Desert Pacific Region 12, and, unless high school senior, must be member of SME. Applicants must be enrolled in manufacturing engineering or closely related degree program. Minimum GPA 3.5. Financial need a consideration only between two otherwise equal applicants. Application available on Website.

Amount of award:	$500-$1,200
Application deadline:	February 1

Contact:
Society of Manufacturing Engineers Education Foundation
Scholarship Review Committee
One SME Drive, P.O. Box 930
Dearborn, MI 48121
Phone: 313-271-1500
Web: www.sme.org/foundation

Wayne Kay Co-op Scholarship

Type of award: Scholarship, renewable.
Intended use: For full-time sophomore, junior or senior study in United States or Canada.
Basis for selection: Major/career interest in manufacturing or engineering. Applicant must demonstrate high academic achievement.
Application requirements: Essay, transcript, proof of eligibility. Supply Foundation with name of intended college or university. Two letters of recommendation from employer(s) and letter of support from faculty member at college or university.
Additional information: Applicants must be enrolled in manufacturing engineering or technology degree program and working through co-op program in a manufacturing-related environment. Applicants must have completed a minimum of 30 college credit hours. Minimum GPA 3.5. Applicants must reapply for renewal. Financial need a consideration only between two otherwise equal applicants. Application available on Website.

Amount of award:	$2,500
Number of awards:	2
Application deadline:	February 1
Total amount awarded:	$5,000

Contact:
Society of Manufacturing Engineers
Scholarship Review Committee
One SME Drive, P.O. Box 930
Dearborn, MI 48121
Phone: 313-271-1500
Web: www.sme.org/foundation

Wayne Kay High School Scholarship

Type of award: Scholarship, renewable.
Intended use: For full-time freshman study at accredited 4-year institution in United States or Canada. Designated institutions: Schools with manufacturing engineering or technology degree program.
Eligibility: Applicant must be high school senior.
Basis for selection: Major/career interest in manufacturing or engineering. Applicant must demonstrate high academic achievement.
Application requirements: Recommendations, essay, transcript. Supply foundation with name of intended college or university.
Additional information: Applicants must commit to enroll in manufacturing engineering or technology degree program. Minimum GPA 3.5 for high school senior year. Award is $1,000 for first year, renewable for $1,500 for second year based on recipient's academic excellence and career path. Financial need a consideration only between two otherwise equal applicants. Application available on Website.

Amount of award:	$1,000-$2,500
Number of awards:	2
Application deadline:	February 1
Total amount awarded:	$5,000

Contact:
Society of Manufacturing Engineers
Scholarship Review Committee
One SME Drive, P.O. Box 930
Dearborn, MI 48121
Phone: 313-271-1500
Web: www.sme.org/foundation

Wayne Kay Scholarship

Type of award: Scholarship, renewable.
Intended use: For full-time sophomore, junior or senior study at accredited 4-year institution in United States or Canada. Designated institutions: Schools with manufacturing engineering or technology degree program.
Basis for selection: Major/career interest in manufacturing or engineering. Applicant must demonstrate high academic achievement.
Application requirements: Recommendations, essay, transcript. Supply Foundation with name of intended college or university.
Additional information: Applicants must be enrolled in manufacturing engineering or technology degree program and must have completed 30 credit hours. Minimum 3.5 GPA. Applicants must reapply for renewal. Financial need a consideration only between two otherwise equal applicants. Application available on Website.

Amount of award:	$2,500
Number of awards:	10
Application deadline:	February 1
Total amount awarded:	$25,000

Contact:
Society of Manufacturing Engineers
Scholarship Review Committee
One SME Drive, P.O. Box 930
Dearborn, MI 48121
Phone: 313-271-1500 ext. 1709
Web: www.sme.org/foundation

William E. Weisel Scholarship

Type of award: Scholarship, renewable.
Intended use: For full-time sophomore, junior or senior study at accredited 4-year institution in United States or Canada. Designated institutions: Schools with manufacturing engineering or technology degree programs.
Basis for selection: Major/career interest in manufacturing; engineering or robotics. Applicant must demonstrate high academic achievement.
Application requirements: Recommendations, essay, transcript. Supply Foundation with name of intended college or university.
Additional information: Applicant must be U.S. or Canadian citizen. Applicants must be enrolled in manufacturing engineering or technology degree program and must have completed minimum of 30 credits. Must be seeking a career in robotics or automated systems used in manufacturing, or robotics used in medical field. Minimum GPA 3.5. Applicants must reapply for renewal. Financial need a consideration only between two otherwise equal applicants. Application available on Website.

Amount of award:	$1,000
Number of awards:	1
Application deadline:	February 1
Total amount awarded:	$1,000

Contact:
Society of Manufacturing Engineers
Scholarship Review Committee
One SME Drive, P.O. Box 930
Dearborn, MI 48121
Phone: 313-271-1500
Web: www.sme.org/foundation

Society of Physics Students

Society of Physics Students Scholarship

Type of award: Scholarship.
Intended use: For full-time junior or senior study at 4-year institution.
Eligibility: Applicant or parent must be member/participant of Society of Physics Students.
Basis for selection: Major/career interest in physics. Applicant must demonstrate high academic achievement and seriousness of purpose.
Application requirements: Recommendations, transcript. Application. Letters from at least two full-time members of the faculty must be filed in support of your application.
Additional information: Applicants also considered for potential for future academic achievement in physics. Must be active participant in Society of Physics Students. Awards payable in equal installments at the beginning of each semester or quarter of full-time study in the final year of study leading to a baccalaureate degree. Number of awards varies. Application forms can be obtained from SPS Chapter Advisors. Visit Website for further information.

Amount of award:	$1,000-$4,000
Application deadline:	February 15
Notification begins:	April 15

Contact:
Society of Physics Students Scholarship Committee
1 Physics Ellipse
College Park, MD 20740
Phone: 301-209-3007
Web: www.aip.org

Society of Professional Journalists (Sigma Delta Chi) Los Angeles Chapter

Bill Farr Scholarship

Type of award: Scholarship.
Intended use: For full-time undergraduate study in United States.
Eligibility: Applicant must be U.S. citizen.
Basis for selection: Major/career interest in journalism or English.
Application requirements: Must be attending a Los Angeles Educational Institution or be a Los Angeles Resident.

Amount of award:	$1,000

Contact:
Society of Professional Journalists
Daily Breeze
5215 Torrance Blvd.
Torrance, Ca 90509
Phone: 818-345-5044

Society of Range Management

Masonic Range Science Scholarship

Type of award: Scholarship.
Intended use: For full-time freshman or sophomore study.
Basis for selection: Major/career interest in agriculture; environmental science or range science. Applicant must demonstrate high academic achievement and leadership.
Application requirements: Recommendations, essay, transcript, nomination by SRM, NACD or SWCS member.
Additional information: Award amount may vary.

Amount of award:	$1,000-$4,000
Number of awards:	1
Number of applicants:	145
Application deadline:	January 15

Contact:
Society of Range Management
445 Union Boulevard, Suite 230
Lakewood, CO 80228-1259
Phone: 303-986-3309
Web: www.srm.org

Society of Women Engineers

Admiral Grace Murray Hopper Scholarship

Type of award: Scholarship.
Intended use: For full-time freshman study at accredited 4-year institution in United States.
Eligibility: Applicant must be female, high school senior. Applicant must be U.S. citizen or permanent resident.
Basis for selection: Major/career interest in engineering. Applicant must demonstrate high academic achievement.
Application requirements: Recommendations, essay, transcript, proof of eligibility.
Additional information: Applicants must be enrolled or plan to be enrolled in an ABET- or CSAB-accredited program or SWE approved school. Minimum 3.5 GPA. Application forms available through the Deans of Engineering at eligible schools, through SWE sections, SWE student sections and from SWE Headquarters. Include SASE with requests for hard copy from SWE Headquarters. Application form also available on Website. Applicants considered for all scholarships for which they are eligible and need submit only one application package.

Amount of award:	$1,000
Number of awards:	5
Application deadline:	May 15
Notification begins:	September 15
Total amount awarded:	$5,000

Contact:
Society of Women Engineers
World Headquarters
230 E. Ohio Street, Suite 400
Chicago, IL 60611-3265
Phone: 312-644-0828
Fax: 312-644-8557
Web: www.swe.org

Adobe Systems Computer Science Scholarships

Type of award: Scholarship.
Intended use: For full-time junior or senior study at accredited 4-year institution in United States.
Eligibility: Applicant must be female. Applicant must be U.S. citizen or permanent resident.
Basis for selection: Major/career interest in computer/information sciences. Applicant must demonstrate high academic achievement.
Application requirements: Recommendations, essay, transcript, proof of eligibility.
Additional information: Preference given to students attending selected San Fransico Bay area schools. Applicants must be enrolled or plan to be enrolled in an ABET- or CSAB-accredited program or SWE approved school. Minimum 3.0 GPA. Application forms available through the Deans of

Engineering at eligible schools, through SWE sections, SWE student sections and from SWE Headquarters. Include SASE with requests for hard copy from SWE Headquarters. Application form also available on Website. Applicants considered for all scholarships for which they are eligible and need submit only one application package.

Amount of award:	$1,500-$2,000
Number of awards:	2
Application deadline:	February 1
Notification begins:	May 15
Total amount awarded:	$3,500

Contact:
Society of Women Engineers
World Headquarters
230 E. Ohio Street, Suite 400
Chicago, IL 60611-3265
Phone: 312-644-0828
Fax: 312-644-8557
Web: www.swe.org

Anne Maureen Whitney Barrow Memorial Scholarship

Type of award: Scholarship, renewable.
Intended use: For full-time freshman study at accredited 4-year institution in United States.
Eligibility: Applicant must be female, high school senior. Applicant must be U.S. citizen or permanent resident.
Basis for selection: Major/career interest in engineering. Applicant must demonstrate high academic achievement.
Application requirements: Recommendations, essay, transcript, proof of eligibility.
Additional information: Renewable for three additional years, given continued academic achievement. Applicants must be enrolled or plan to be enrolled in an ABET- or CSAB-accredited program or SWE approved school. Minimum 3.5 GPA. Application forms available through the Deans of Engineering at eligible schools, through SWE sections, SWE student sections and from SWE Headquarters. Include SASE with requests for hard copy from SWE Headquarters. Application form also available on Website. Applicants considered for all scholarships for which they are eligible and need submit only one application package.

Amount of award:	$5,000
Number of awards:	1
Application deadline:	May 15
Notification begins:	September 15
Total amount awarded:	$5,000

Contact:
Society of Women Engineers
World Headquarters
230 E. Ohio Street, Suite 400
Chicago, IL 60611-3265
Phone: 312-644-0828
Fax: 312-644-8557
Web: www.swe.org

B. J. Harrod Scholarships

Type of award: Scholarship.
Intended use: For full-time freshman study at accredited 4-year institution in United States.
Eligibility: Applicant must be female, high school senior. Applicant must be U.S. citizen or permanent resident.
Basis for selection: Major/career interest in engineering. Applicant must demonstrate high academic achievement.

Application requirements: Recommendations, essay, transcript, proof of eligibility. Two letters of reference: one from a high school teacher, one from a person who knows the applicant, but not a family member.

Additional information: Applicants must be enrolled or plan to be enrolled in an ABET- or CSAB-accredited program or SWE approved school. Minimum 3.5 GPA. Application forms available through the Deans of Engineering at eligible schools, through SWE sections, SWE student sections and from SWE Headquarters. Include SASE with requests for hard copy from SWE Headquarters. Application form also available on Website. Applicants considered for all scholarships for which they are eligible and need submit only one application package.

Amount of award:	$1,000
Number of awards:	2
Application deadline:	May 15
Notification begins:	September 15
Total amount awarded:	$2,000

Contact:
Society of Women Engineers
World Headquarters
230 E. Ohio Street, Suite 400
Chicago, IL 60611-3265
Phone: 312-644-0828
Fax: 312-644-8557
Web: www.swe.org

B. K. Krenzer Reentry Scholarship

Type of award: Scholarship.
Intended use: For undergraduate or graduate study at accredited 4-year or graduate institution in United States.
Eligibility: Applicant must be female, returning adult student. Applicant must be U.S. citizen or permanent resident.
Basis for selection: Major/career interest in engineering; engineering, electrical/electronic; engineering, structural or engineering, mechanical. Applicant must demonstrate high academic achievement.
Application requirements: Recommendations, essay, transcript, proof of eligibility.
Additional information: Eligibility restricted to women who have been out of school for at least two years prior to reentry. Also open to women who have been out of engineering workforce and school at least two years. Preference given to degreed engineers. Applicants must be enrolled or plan to be enrolled in an ABET- or CSAB-accredited program or SWE approved school. Minimum 3.0 GPA after first year of reentry. Application forms available through the Deans of Engineering at eligible schools, through SWE sections, SWE student sections and from SWE Headquarters. Include SASE with requests for hard copy from SWE Headquarters. Application form also available on Website. Applicants considered for all scholarships for which they are eligible and need submit only one application package.

Amount of award:	$2,000
Number of awards:	1
Application deadline:	May 15
Notification begins:	September 15
Total amount awarded:	$2,000

Contact:
Society of Women Engineers
World Headquarters
230 E. Ohio Street, Suite 400
Chicago, IL 60611-3265
Phone: 312-644-0828
Fax: 312-644-8557
Web: www.swe.org

Bechtel Corporation Scholarship

Type of award: Scholarship.
Intended use: For full-time sophomore, junior or senior study at accredited 4-year institution in United States.
Eligibility: Applicant or parent must be member/participant of Society of Women Engineers. Applicant must be female. Applicant must be U.S. citizen or permanent resident.
Basis for selection: Major/career interest in engineering, chemical; engineering, electrical/electronic; engineering, environmental; engineering, mechanical; engineering or architecture. Applicant must demonstrate high academic achievement.
Application requirements: Recommendations, essay, transcript, proof of eligibility.
Additional information: Architectural engineering majors also eligible to apply. Applicants must be enrolled or plan to be enrolled in an ABET- or CSAB-accredited program or SWE approved school. Minimum 3.0 GPA. Application forms available through the Deans of Engineering at eligible schools, through SWE sections, SWE student sections and from SWE Headquarters. Include SASE with requests for hard copy from SWE Headquarters. Application form also available on Website. Applicants considered for all scholarships for which they are eligible and need submit only one application package.

Amount of award:	$3,050
Number of awards:	1
Application deadline:	February 1
Notification begins:	May 15
Total amount awarded:	$3,050

Contact:
Society of Women Engineers
World Headquarters
230 E. Ohio Street, Suite 400
Chicago, IL 60611-3265
Phone: 312-644-0828
Fax: 312-644-8557
Web: www.swe.org

Chevron Corporation Scholarships

Type of award: Scholarship.
Intended use: For full-time sophomore or junior study at accredited 4-year institution in United States.
Eligibility: Applicant or parent must be member/participant of Society of Women Engineers. Applicant must be female. Applicant must be U.S. citizen or permanent resident.
Basis for selection: Major/career interest in engineering, civil; engineering, chemical; engineering, petroleum or engineering, mechanical. Applicant must demonstrate high academic achievement.
Application requirements: Recommendations, essay, transcript, proof of eligibility. Must be an active SWE Student Member.
Additional information: One award each for sophomore and junior engineering student. Applicants must be enrolled or plan to be enrolled in an ABET- or CSAB-accredited program or SWE approved school. Minimum 3.5 GPA. Application forms available through the Deans of Engineering at eligible schools, through SWE sections, SWE student sections and from SWE Headquarters. Include SASE with requests for hard copy from SWE Headquarters. Application form also available on Website. Applicants considered for all scholarships for which they are eligible and need submit only one application package.

Amount of award: $2,000
Number of awards: 2
Application deadline: February 1
Notification begins: May 1
Total amount awarded: $4,000
Contact:
Society of Women Engineers
World Headquarters
230 E. Ohio Street, Suite 400
Chicago, IL 60611-3265
Phone: 312-644-0828
Fax: 312-644-8557
Web: www.swe.org

DaimlerChrysler Corporation Fund Scholarships

Type of award: Scholarship, renewable.
Intended use: For full-time sophomore study at accredited 4-year institution in United States.
Eligibility: Applicant or parent must be member/participant of Society of Women Engineers. Applicant must be female. Applicant must be U.S. citizen or permanent resident.
Basis for selection: Major/career interest in engineering, electrical/electronic or engineering, mechanical. Applicant must demonstrate high academic achievement.
Application requirements: Recommendations, essay, transcript, proof of eligibility.
Additional information: Applicants must be enrolled or plan to be enrolled in an ABET- or CSAB-accredited program or SWE approved school. Minimum 3.0 GPA. Application forms available through the Deans of Engineering at eligible schools, through SWE sections, SWE student sections and from SWE Headquarters. Include SASE with requests for hard copy from SWE Headquarters. Application form also available on Website. Applicants considered for all scholarships for which they are eligible and need submit only one application package.
Amount of award: $2,000
Number of awards: 1
Application deadline: February 1
Notification begins: May 15
Contact:
Society of Women Engineers
World Headquarters
230 E. Ohio Street, Suite 400
Chicago, IL 60611-3265
Phone: 312-644-0828
Fax: 312-644-8557
Web: www.swe.org

David Sarnoff Reseach Center Scholarship

Type of award: Scholarship.
Intended use: For full-time junior study at accredited 4-year institution.
Eligibility: Applicant must be female. Applicant must be U.S. citizen or permanent resident.
Basis for selection: Major/career interest in engineering or computer/information sciences. Applicant must demonstrate high academic achievement.
Application requirements: Recommendations, essay, transcript, proof of eligibility.
Additional information: Applicants must be enrolled or plan to be enrolled in an ABET- or CSAB-accredited program or SWE approved school. Minimum 3.5 GPA. Application forms available through the Deans of Engineering at eligible schools,

through SWE sections, SWE student sections and from SWE Headquarters. Include SASE with requests for hard copy from SWE Headquarters. Application form also available on Website. Applicants considered for all scholarships for which they are eligible and need submit only one application package.
Amount of award: $1,500
Number of awards: 1
Application deadline: February 1
Notification begins: May 15
Total amount awarded: $1,500
Contact:
Society of Women Engineers
World Headquarters
230 E. Ohio Street, Suite 400
Chicago, IL 60611-3265
Phone: 312-644-0828
Fax: 312-644-8557
Web: www.swe.org

Dorothy Lemke Howarth Scholarships

Type of award: Scholarship.
Intended use: For full-time sophomore study at accredited 4-year institution.
Eligibility: Applicant must be female. Applicant must be U.S. citizen.
Basis for selection: Major/career interest in engineering. Applicant must demonstrate high academic achievement.
Application requirements: Recommendations, essay, transcript, proof of eligibility.
Additional information: Applicants must be enrolled or plan to be enrolled in an ABET- or CSAB-accredited program or SWE approved school. Minimum 3.0 GPA. Application forms available through the Deans of Engineering at eligible schools, through SWE sections, SWE student sections and from SWE Headquarters. Include SASE with requests for hard copy from SWE Headquarters. Application form also available on Website. Applicants considered for all scholarships for which they are eligible and need submit only one application package.
Amount of award: $2,000
Number of awards: 5
Application deadline: February 1
Notification begins: May 15
Total amount awarded: $10,000
Contact:
Society of Women Engineers
World Headquarters
230 E. Ohio Street, Suite 400
Chicago, IL 60611-3265
Phone: 312-644-0828
Fax: 312-644-8557
Web: www.swe.org

Dorothy M. & Earl S. Hoffman Scholarships

Type of award: Scholarship, renewable.
Intended use: For full-time freshman study at accredited 4-year institution in United States.
Eligibility: Applicant must be female, high school senior. Applicant must be U.S. citizen or permanent resident.
Basis for selection: Major/career interest in engineering. Applicant must demonstrate high academic achievement.
Application requirements: Recommendations, essay, transcript, proof of eligibility.

Additional information: Applicants must be enrolled or plan to be enrolled in an ABET- or CSAB-accredited program or SWE approved school. Preference given to students attending Bucknell University and Rensselaer Polytechnic University. Minimum 3.5 GPA. Application forms available through the Deans of Engineering at eligible schools, through SWE sections, SWE student sections and from SWE Headquarters. Include SASE with requests for hard copy from SWE Headquarters. Application form also available on Website. Applicants considered for all scholarships for which they are eligible, therefore need only submit one application package.

Amount of award:	$3,000
Number of awards:	3
Application deadline:	May 15
Notification begins:	September 15
Total amount awarded:	$9,000

Contact:
Society of Women Engineers
World Headquarters
230 E. Ohio Street, Suite 400
Chicago, IL 60611-3265
Phone: 312-644-0828
Fax: 312-644-8557
Web: www.swe.org

DuPont Scholarships

Type of award: Scholarship.
Intended use: For full-time freshman, sophomore, junior or senior study at accredited 4-year institution in United States. Designated institutions: Insitutions in states east of and including Minnesota, Iowa, Missouri, Arkansas and Mississippi.
Eligibility: Applicant must be female. Applicant must be U.S. citizen or permanent resident.
Basis for selection: Major/career interest in engineering, chemical or engineering, mechanical. Applicant must demonstrate high academic achievement.
Application requirements: Recommendations, essay, transcript, proof of eligibility.
Additional information: Two awards for incoming freshmen; two for sophomores, juniors, seniors. Applicants must be enrolled or plan to be enrolled in an ABET- or CSAB-accredited program or SWE approved school. Minimum 3.5 GPA for freshmen, 3.0 for others. Application forms available through the Deans of Engineering at eligible schools, through SWE sections, SWE student sections and from SWE Headquarters. Include SASE with requests for hard copy from SWE Headquarters. Application form also available on Website. Applicants considered for all scholarships for which they are eligible and need submit only one application package. Early deadline is for sophomores, juniors, seniors.

Amount of award:	$2,000
Number of awards:	4
Application deadline:	February 1, May 15
Notification begins:	May 15, September 15
Total amount awarded:	$8,000

Contact:
Society of Women Engineers
World Headquarters
230 E. Ohio Street, Suite 400
Chicago, IL 60611-3265
Phone: 312-644-0828
Fax: 312-644-8557
Web: www.swe.org

General Electric Fund Scholarships

Type of award: Scholarship, renewable.

Intended use: For full-time freshman study at accredited 4-year institution.
Eligibility: Applicant must be female, high school senior. Applicant must be U.S. citizen.
Basis for selection: Major/career interest in engineering. Applicant must demonstrate high academic achievement.
Application requirements: Recommendations, essay, transcript, proof of eligibility.
Additional information: Fund includes $500 travel grant to attend the SWE National Conference. Applicants must be enrolled or plan to be enrolled in an ABET- or CSAB-accredited program or SWE approved school. Minimum 3.5 GPA. Application forms available through the Deans of Engineering at eligible schools, through SWE sections, SWE student sections and from SWE Headquarters. Include SASE with requests for hard copy from SWE Headquarters. Application form also available on Website. Applicants considered for all scholarships for which they are eligible and need submit only one application package.

Amount of award:	$1,000
Number of awards:	3
Application deadline:	May 15
Notification begins:	September 15
Total amount awarded:	$3,000

Contact:
Society of Women Engineers
World Headquarters
230 E. Ohio Street, Suite 400
Chicago, IL 60611-3265
Phone: 312-644-0828
Fax: 312-644-8557
Web: www.swe.org

General Motors Foundation Scholarships

Type of award: Scholarship, renewable.
Intended use: For full-time junior study at accredited 4-year institution in United States.
Eligibility: Applicant must be female. Applicant must be U.S. citizen or permanent resident.
Basis for selection: Major/career interest in engineering; automotive technology; engineering, electrical/electronic; engineering, mechanical; engineering, chemical or engineering, materials. Applicant must demonstrate financial need, high academic achievement and leadership.
Application requirements: Recommendations, essay, transcript, proof of eligibility.
Additional information: Industrial engineering and manufacturing engineering majors also eligible to apply. Applicants must be enrolled or plan to be enrolled in an ABET- or CSAB-accredited program or SWE approved school. Applicants should have career interest in automotive industry or manufacturing. Foundation provides $500 travel grant to attend the SWE National Convention and Student Conference. Minimum 3.5 GPA. Application forms available through the Deans of Engineering at eligible schools, through SWE sections, SWE student sections and from SWE Headquarters. Include SASE with requests for hard copy from SWE Headquarters. Application form also available on Website. Applicants considered for all scholarships for which they are eligible and need submit only one application package.

Amount of award:	$1,000
Number of awards:	2
Application deadline:	February 1
Notification begins:	May 15
Total amount awarded:	$2,000

Contact:
Society of Women Engineers
World Headquarters
230 E. Ohio Street, Suite 400
Chicago, IL 60611-3265
Phone: 312-644-0828
Fax: 312-644-8557
Web: www.swe.org

GTE Foundation Scholarships

Type of award: Scholarship.
Intended use: For full-time sophomore or junior study at accredited 4-year institution in United States.
Eligibility: Applicant must be female. Applicant must be U.S. citizen or permanent resident.
Basis for selection: Major/career interest in engineering, electrical/electronic; engineering, computer or computer/information sciences. Applicant must demonstrate high academic achievement.
Application requirements: Recommendations, essay, transcript, proof of eligibility.
Additional information: Applicants must be enrolled or plan to be enrolled in an ABET- or CSAB-accredited program or SWE approved school. Minimum 3.5 GPA. Application forms available through the Deans of Engineering at eligible schools, through SWE sections, SWE student sections and from SWE Headquarters. Include SASE with requests for hard copy from SWE Headquarters. Application form also available on Website. Applicants considered for all scholarships for which they are eligible and need submit only one application package.

Amount of award:	$1,000
Number of awards:	9
Application deadline:	February 1
Notification begins:	May 15
Total amount awarded:	$9,000

Contact:
Society of Women Engineers
World Headquarters
230 E. Ohio Street, Suite 400
Chicago, IL 60611-3265
Phone: 312-644-0828
Fax: 312-644-8557
Web: www.swe.org

Ivy Parker Memorial Scholarship

Type of award: Scholarship.
Intended use: For full-time junior or senior study at accredited 4-year institution in United States.
Eligibility: Applicant must be female. Applicant must be U.S. citizen or permanent resident.
Basis for selection: Major/career interest in engineering. Applicant must demonstrate financial need and high academic achievement.
Application requirements: Recommendations, essay, transcript, proof of eligibility.
Additional information: Applicants must be enrolled or plan to be enrolled in an ABET- or CSAB-accredited program or SWE approved school. Minimum 3.0 GPA. Application forms available through the Deans of Engineering at eligible schools, through SWE sections, SWE student sections and from SWE Headquarters. Include SASE with requests for hard copy from SWE Headquarters. Application form also available on Website. Applicants considered for all scholarships for which they are eligible and need submit only one application package.

Amount of award:	$2,500
Number of awards:	1
Application deadline:	February 1
Notification begins:	May 15
Total amount awarded:	$2,500

Contact:
Society of Women Engineers
World Headquarters
230 E. Ohio Street, Suite 400
Chicago, IL 60611-3265
Phone: 312-644-0828
Fax: 312-644-8557
Web: www.swe.org

Judith Resnik Memorial Scholarship

Type of award: Scholarship.
Intended use: For full-time sophomore, junior or senior study at accredited 4-year institution.
Eligibility: Applicant or parent must be member/participant of Society of Women Engineers. Applicant must be female. Applicant must be U.S. citizen or permanent resident.
Basis for selection: Major/career interest in engineering or aerospace. Applicant must demonstrate high academic achievement.
Application requirements: Recommendations, essay, transcript, proof of eligibility.
Additional information: Aeronautical/aerospace engineering and astronautical engineering majors also eligible to apply. Applicants must be enrolled or plan to be enrolled in an ABET- or CSAB-accredited program or SWE approved school. Minimum 3.0 GPA. Application forms available through the Deans of Engineering at eligible schools, through SWE sections, SWE student sections and from SWE Headquarters. Include SASE with requests for hard copy from SWE Headquarters. Application form also available on Website. Applicants considered for all scholarships for which they are eligible and need submit only one application package.

Amount of award:	$2,500
Number of awards:	1
Application deadline:	February 1
Notification begins:	May 15
Total amount awarded:	$2,500

Contact:
Society of Women Engineers
World Headquarters
230 E. Ohio Street, Suite 400
Chicago, IL 60611-3265
Phone: 312-644-0828
Fax: 312-644-8557
Web: www.swe.org

Lillian Moller Gilbreth Scholarship

Type of award: Scholarship.
Intended use: For full-time junior or senior study at accredited 4-year institution in United States.
Eligibility: Applicant must be female. Applicant must be U.S. citizen or permanent resident.
Basis for selection: Major/career interest in engineering. Applicant must demonstrate high academic achievement.
Application requirements: Recommendations, essay, transcript, proof of eligibility.
Additional information: Applicants must be enrolled or plan to be enrolled in an ABET- or CSAB-accredited program or SWE approved school. Minimum 3.0 GPA. Application forms

Scholarships

available through the Deans of Engineering at eligible schools, through SWE sections, SWE student sections and from SWE Headquarters. Include SASE with requests for hard copy from SWE Headquarters. Application form also available on Website. Applicants considered for all scholarships for which they are eligible and need submit only one application package.

Amount of award:	$6,000
Number of awards:	1
Application deadline:	February 1
Notification begins:	May 15
Total amount awarded:	$6,000

Contact:
Society of Women Engineers
World Headquarters
230 E. Ohio Street, Suite 400
Chicago, IL 60611-3265
Phone: 312-644-0828
Fax: 312-644-8557
Web: www.swe.org

Lockheed Aeronautics Company Scholarships

Type of award: Scholarship.
Intended use: For full-time junior study at accredited 4-year institution in United States.
Eligibility: Applicant must be female. Applicant must be U.S. citizen or permanent resident.
Basis for selection: Major/career interest in engineering, electrical/electronic or engineering, mechanical. Applicant must demonstrate high academic achievement.
Application requirements: Recommendations, essay, transcript, proof of eligibility. 3.5/4.0 Minimum GPA.
Additional information: Awards given to one student in each of above majors. Applicants must be enrolled or plan to be enrolled in an ABET- or CSAB-accredited program or SWE approved school. Minimum 3.5 GPA. Application forms available through the Deans of Engineering at eligible schools, through SWE sections, SWE student sections and from SWE Headquarters. Include SASE with requests for hard copy from SWE Headquarters. Application form also available on Website. Applicants considered for all scholarships for which they are eligible and need submit only one application package.

Amount of award:	$1,000
Number of awards:	2
Application deadline:	February 1
Notification begins:	May 15
Total amount awarded:	$2,000

Contact:
Society of Women Engineers
World Headquarters
230 E. Ohio Street, Suite 400
Chicago, IL 60611-3265
Phone: 312-644-0828
Fax: 312-644-8557
Web: www.swe.org

Lockheed Martin Corporation Scholarships

Type of award: Scholarship.
Intended use: For full-time freshman study at accredited 4-year institution in United States.
Eligibility: Applicant must be female, high school senior. Applicant must be U.S. citizen or permanent resident.
Basis for selection: Major/career interest in engineering. Applicant must demonstrate high academic achievement.

Application requirements: Recommendations, essay, transcript, proof of eligibility.
Additional information: Applicants must be enrolled or plan to be enrolled in an ABET- or CSAB-accredited program or SWE approved school. Minimum 3.5 GPA. Application forms available through the Deans of Engineering at eligible schools, through SWE sections, SWE student sections and from SWE Headquarters. Include SASE with requests for hard copy from SWE Headquarters. Application form also available on Website. Applicants considered for all scholarships for which they are eligible therefore need only submit one application package.

Amount of award:	$3,000
Number of awards:	2
Application deadline:	May 15
Notification begins:	September 15
Total amount awarded:	$6,000

Contact:
Society of Women Engineers
World Headquarters
230 E. Ohio Street, Suite 400
Chicago, IL 60611-3265
Phone: 312-644-0828
Fax: 312-644-8557
Web: www.swe.org

MASWE Scholarships

Type of award: Scholarship.
Intended use: For full-time sophomore, junior or senior study at accredited 4-year institution in United States.
Eligibility: Applicant must be female. Applicant must be U.S. citizen or permanent resident.
Basis for selection: Major/career interest in engineering. Applicant must demonstrate financial need and high academic achievement.
Application requirements: Recommendations, essay, transcript, proof of eligibility.
Additional information: Applicants must be enrolled or plan to be enrolled in an ABET- or CSAB-accredited program or SWE approved school. Minimum 3.0 GPA. Application forms available through the Deans of Engineering at eligible schools, through SWE sections, SWE student sections and from SWE Headquarters. Include SASE with requests for hard copy from SWE Headquarters. Application form also available on Website. Applicants considered for all scholarships for which they are eligible and need submit only one application package.

Amount of award:	$2,000
Number of awards:	4
Application deadline:	February 1
Notification begins:	May 15
Total amount awarded:	$8,000

Contact:
Society of Women Engineers
World Headquarters
230 E. Ohio Street, Suite 400
Chicago, IL 60611-3265
Phone: 312-644-0828
Fax: 312-644-8557
Web: www.swe.org

Meridith Thoms Memorial Scholarships

Type of award: Scholarship.
Intended use: For full-time undergraduate study at accredited 4-year institution in United States.

Eligibility: Applicant must be female. Applicant must be U.S. citizen or permanent resident.

Basis for selection: Major/career interest in engineering. Applicant must demonstrate high academic achievement.

Application requirements: Recommendations, essay, transcript, proof of eligibility. 3.0/4.0 Minimum GPA.

Additional information: Applicants must be enrolled or plan to be enrolled in an ABET- or CSAB-accredited program or SWE approved school. Minimum 3.5 GPA for freshmen, 3.0 for others. Application forms available through the Deans of Engineering at eligible schools, through SWE sections, SWE student sections and from SWE Headquarters. Include SASE with requests for hard copy from SWE Headquarters. Application form also available on Website. Applicants considered for all scholarships for which they are eligible and need submit only one application package.

Amount of award:	$2,000
Number of awards:	2
Application deadline:	February 1, May 15
Notification begins:	May 15, September 15
Total amount awarded:	$4,000

Contact:
Society of Women Engineers
World Headquarters
230 E. Ohio Street, Suite 400
Chicago, IL 60611-3265
Phone: 312-644-0828
Fax: 312-644-8557
Web: www.swe.org

Microsoft Corporation Scholarships

Type of award: Scholarship.

Intended use: For full-time sophomore, junior, senior or master's study at accredited 4-year institution in United States.

Eligibility: Applicant must be female. Applicant must be U.S. citizen or permanent resident.

Basis for selection: Major/career interest in engineering, computer or computer/information sciences. Applicant must demonstrate high academic achievement.

Application requirements: Recommendations, essay, transcript, proof of eligibility.

Additional information: Graduate students eligible only in first year of master's study. Applicants must be enrolled or plan to be enrolled in an ABET- or CSAB-accredited program or SWE approved school. Minimum 3.5 GPA. Application forms available through the Deans of Engineering at eligible schools, through SWE sections, SWE student sections and from SWE Headquarters. Include SASE with requests for hard copy from SWE Headquarters. Application form also available on Website. Applicants considered for all scholarships for which they are eligible and need submit only one application package.

Amount of award:	$1,000
Number of awards:	9
Application deadline:	February 1
Notification begins:	May 15
Total amount awarded:	$9,000

Contact:
Society of Women Engineers
World Headquarters
230 E. Ohio Street, Suite 400
Chicago, IL 60611-3265
Phone: 312-644-0828
Fax: 312-644-8557
Web: www.swe.org

New Jersey Scholarship

Type of award: Scholarship.

Intended use: For full-time freshman study at accredited 4-year institution in United States.

Eligibility: Applicant must be female, high school senior. Applicant must be U.S. citizen or permanent resident residing in New Jersey.

Basis for selection: Major/career interest in engineering. Applicant must demonstrate high academic achievement.

Application requirements: Recommendations, essay, transcript, proof of eligibility.

Additional information: Applicants must be enrolled or plan to be enrolled in an ABET- or CSAB-accredited program or SWE approved school. Minimum 3.5 GPA. Application forms available through the Deans of Engineering at eligible schools, through SWE sections, SWE student sections and from SWE Headquarters. Include SASE with requests for hard copy from SWE Headquarters. Application form also available on Website. Applicants considered for all scholarships for which they are eligible and need submit only one application package.

Amount of award:	$1,000
Number of awards:	1
Application deadline:	May 15
Notification begins:	September 15
Total amount awarded:	$1,000

Contact:
Society of Women Engineers
World Headquarters
230 E. Ohio Street, Suite 400
Chicago, IL 60611-3265
Phone: 312-644-0828
Fax: 312-644-8557
Web: www.swe.org

Olive Lynn Salembier Reentry Scholarship

Type of award: Scholarship.

Intended use: For undergraduate or doctoral study at accredited 4-year or graduate institution in United States.

Eligibility: Applicant must be female. Applicant must be U.S. citizen or permanent resident.

Basis for selection: Major/career interest in engineering.

Application requirements: Recommendations, essay, transcript, proof of eligibility.

Additional information: Eligibility restricted to women who have been out of school for at least two years prior to reentry. Also open to women who have been out of engineering workforce and school at least two years. Applicants must be enrolled or plan to be enrolled in an ABET- or CSAB-accredited program or SWE approved school. Minimum 3.0 GPA after first year of reentry. Application forms available through the Deans of Engineering at eligible schools, through SWE sections, SWE student sections and from SWE Headquarters. Include SASE with requests for hard copy from SWE Headquarters. Application form also available on Website. Applicants considered for all scholarships for which they are eligible and need submit only one application package.

Amount of award:	$2,000
Number of awards:	1
Application deadline:	May 15
Notification begins:	September 15
Total amount awarded:	$2,000

Contact:
Society of Women Engineers
World Headquarters
230 E. Ohio Street, Suite 400
Chicago, IL 60611-3265
Phone: 312-644-0828
Fax: 312-644-8557
Web: www.swe.org

Past Presidents Scholarships

Type of award: Scholarship.
Intended use: For full-time undergraduate or graduate study at accredited 4-year or graduate institution in United States.
Eligibility: Applicant must be female. Applicant must be U.S. citizen.
Basis for selection: Major/career interest in engineering. Applicant must demonstrate high academic achievement.
Application requirements: Recommendations, essay, transcript, proof of eligibility. 3.0/4.0 Minimum GPA.
Additional information: Applicants must be enrolled or plan to be enrolled in an ABET- or CSAB-accredited program or SWE approved school. Minimum 3.5 GPA for freshmen, 3.0 for all others. Application forms available through the Deans of Engineering at eligible schools, through SWE sections, SWE student sections and from SWE Headquarters. Include SASE with requests for hard copy from SWE Headquarters. Application form also available on Website. Applicants considered for all scholarships for which they are eligible therefore need only submit one application package. Early deadline for sophomores, juniors, seniors, and graduate students.

Amount of award:	$1,500
Number of awards:	2
Application deadline:	February 1, May 15
Notification begins:	May 15, September 15
Total amount awarded:	$3,000

Contact:
Society of Women Engineers
World Headquarters
230 E. Ohio Street, Suite 400
Chicago, IL 60611-3265
Phone: 312-644-0828
Fax: 312-644-8557
Web: www.swe.org

Rockwell Corporation Scholarships

Type of award: Scholarship.
Intended use: For full-time junior study at accredited 4-year institution in United States.
Eligibility: Applicant must be Alaskan native, Asian American, African American, Mexican American, Hispanic American, Puerto Rican or American Indian. Applicant must be female. Applicant must be U.S. citizen or permanent resident.
Basis for selection: Major/career interest in engineering. Applicant must demonstrate financial need, high academic achievement and leadership.
Application requirements: Recommendations, essay, transcript, proof of eligibility.
Additional information: Preference given to members of groups underrepresented in engineering. Applicants must be enrolled or plan to be enrolled in an ABET- or CSAB-accredited program or SWE approved school. Minimum 3.5 GPA. Application forms available through the Deans of Engineering at eligible schools, through SWE sections, SWE student sections and from SWE Headquarters. Include SASE with requests for hard copy from SWE Headquarters.

Application form also available on Website. Applicants considered for all scholarships for which they are eligible and need submit only one application package.

Amount of award:	$3,000
Number of awards:	2
Application deadline:	February 1
Notification begins:	May 15
Total amount awarded:	$6,000

Contact:
Society of Women Engineers
World Headquarters
230 E. Ohio Street, Suite 400
Chicago, IL 60611-3265
Phone: 312-644-0828
Fax: 312-644-8557
Web: www.swe.org

Symbol Technologies Scholarship

Type of award: Scholarship.
Intended use: For full-time junior study at accredited 4-year institution in United States.
Eligibility: Applicant must be female. Applicant must be U.S. citizen or permanent resident.
Basis for selection: Major/career interest in engineering, electrical/electronic; engineering, mechanical or computer/information sciences. Applicant must demonstrate high academic achievement.
Application requirements: Recommendations, essay, transcript, proof of eligibility.
Additional information: Applicants must be enrolled or plan to be enrolled in an ABET- or CSAB-accredited program or SWE approved school. Minimum 3.2 GPA. Application forms available through the Deans of Engineering at eligible schools, through SWE sections, SWE student sections and from SWE Headquarters. Include SASE with requests for hard copy from SWE Headquarters. Application form also available on Website. Applicants considered for all scholarships for which they are eligible therefore need only submit one application package.

Amount of award:	$2,500
Number of awards:	1
Application deadline:	February 1
Notification begins:	May 15
Total amount awarded:	$2,500

Contact:
Society of Women Engineers
World Headquarters
230 E. Ohio Street, Suite 400
Chicago, IL 60611-3265
Phone: 312-644-0828
Fax: 312-644-8557
Web: www.swe.org

Texaco Scholarship

Type of award: Scholarship.
Intended use: For full-time junior study at accredited 4-year institution in United States.
Eligibility: Applicant must be female. Applicant must be U.S. citizen.
Basis for selection: Major/career interest in engineering, electrical/electronic; engineering, mechanical; engineering, civil; engineering, computer; engineering, chemical or engineering, petroleum. Applicant must demonstrate high academic achievement.
Application requirements: Recommendations, essay, transcript, proof of eligibility.

Additional information: Applicants must be enrolled or plan to be enrolled in an ABET- or CSAB-accredited program or SWE approved school. Minimum 3.0 GPA. Application forms available through the Deans of Engineering at eligible schools, through SWE sections, SWE student sections and from SWE Headquarters. Include SASE with requests for hard copy from SWE Headquarters. Application form also available on Website. Applicants considered for all scholarships for which they are eligible and need submit only one application package.

Amount of award:	$2,000
Number of awards:	6
Application deadline:	February 1
Notification begins:	May 15
Total amount awarded:	$12,000

Contact:
Society of Women Engineers
World Headquarters
230 E. Ohio Street, Suite 400
Chicago, IL 60611-3265
Phone: 312-644-0828
Fax: 312-644-8557
Web: www.swe.org

Soil and Water Conservation Society

Donald A. Williams Soil Conservation Scholarship

Type of award: Scholarship.
Intended use: For undergraduate study.
Eligibility: Applicant or parent must be member/participant of Soil and Water Conservation Society.
Basis for selection: Major/career interest in natural resources/conservation. Applicant must demonstrate financial need, depth of character and seriousness of purpose.
Application requirements: Must have been member of SWCS for more than one year. Send SASE for application or download from Website.
Additional information: Must have been member of SWCS for more than one year. Must demonstrate integrity, ability, and competence in line of work. Must have completed at least one year of full-time employment and be currently employed in a natural resource conservation endeavor.

Amount of award:	$1,500
Number of awards:	3
Application deadline:	February 12
Total amount awarded:	$4,500

Contact:
Soil and Water Conservation Society
7515 Northeast Ankeny Road
Ankeny, IA 50021-9764
Phone: 515-289-2331
Web: www.swcs.org

Melville H. Cohee Student Leader Conservation Scholarship

Type of award: Scholarship.
Intended use: For senior or master's study at accredited 4-year or graduate institution.
Eligibility: Applicant or parent must be member/participant of Soil and Water Conservation Society.

Basis for selection: Major/career interest in natural resources/conservation; agricultural economics; forestry; engineering, agricultural; hydrology or wildlife/fisheries. Applicant must demonstrate high academic achievement and leadership.
Application requirements: Minimum 3.0 GPA. Must have been member of and held office in student chapter of SWCS for more than one year. Send SASE for application or download from Website.
Additional information: Must have been member of and held office in student chapter of SWCS for more than one year; chapter must have had at least fifteen members. Those studying soils, planned land use management, wildlife biology, rural sociology, agronomy or water management also eligible. May not be combined with other SWCS scholarships. Financial need not a factor in selection. Visit Website for additional information.

Amount of award:	$1,000
Number of awards:	2
Application deadline:	February 12
Total amount awarded:	$2,000

Contact:
Soil and Water Conservation Society
7515 Northeast Ankeny Road
Ankeny, IA 50021-9764
Web: www.swcs.org

Sons of Italy Foundation

Henry Salvatori Scholarship

Type of award: Scholarship.
Intended use: For full-time undergraduate study.
Eligibility: Applicant must be high school senior. Applicant must be Italian. Applicant must be U.S. citizen.
Basis for selection: Applicant must demonstrate high academic achievement, depth of character, leadership, patriotism, seriousness of purpose and service orientation.
Application requirements: $25 application fee. Recommendations, essay, transcript, proof of eligibility. SAT I/ACT scores and two letters of recommendation from public figures who have demonstrated the ideals of liberty, freedom, and equality in their work.
Additional information: Application deadline in late January. Contact sponsor for exact date and application materials after beginning of October.

Amount of award:	$5,000
Number of awards:	1
Total amount awarded:	$5,000

Contact:
Order of Sons of Italy in America
219 E Street NE
Washington, DC 20002
Phone: 202-547-5106
Web: www.osia.org

Sons of Italy National Leadership Grant

Type of award: Scholarship.
Intended use: For full-time undergraduate, master's, doctoral or first professional study at accredited 4-year or graduate institution in United States.
Eligibility: Applicant must be Italian. Applicant must be U.S. citizen.

Basis for selection: Applicant must demonstrate high academic achievement, depth of character, leadership, seriousness of purpose and service orientation.

Application requirements: $25 application fee. Recommendations, essay, transcript, proof of eligibility. SAT I/ACT scores; activities list; two recommendations; application fee.

Additional information: Deadline in late January; contact sponsor for exact date. Call for further information on deadlines, availability of awards, and application fee after the beginning of October.

Amount of award:	$4,000-$10,000
Number of awards:	12

Contact:
Order of Sons of Italy in America
219 E Street NE
Washington, DC 20002
Phone: 202-547-5106
Web: www.osia.org

Sons of Norway Foundation

Astrid G. Cates Scholarship Fund and Myrtle Beinhauer Scholarship

Type of award: Scholarship.

Intended use: For undergraduate study at postsecondary institution.

Eligibility: Applicant or parent must be member/participant of Sons of Norway. Applicant must be U.S. citizen.

Basis for selection: Applicant must demonstrate financial need, high academic achievement, depth of character and service orientation.

Application requirements: Recommendations, transcript, proof of eligibility.

Additional information: Applicant, parent, or grandparent must be a current member of Sons of Norway. Student must include the following information with application: GPA, what type of study is intended and at which institution, and when. Related fees must be specified as well as long-term career goals, involvement in The Sons of Norway, and extracurricular activities, and financial need. The Astrid G. Cates Scholarship ranges from $500 to $750; the Myrtle Beinhauer Scholarship is $3,000 and is awarded to the most qualified of all candidates. A student can be awarded a maximum of two scholarships within a five-year period.

Amount of award:	$500-$3,000
Number of awards:	6
Number of applicants:	99
Application deadline:	March 1
Notification begins:	May 1

Contact:
Sons of Norway Foundation
c/o Sons of Norway
1455 West Lake Street
Minneapolis, MN 55408
Phone: 612-827-3611

King Olav V Norwegian-American Heritage Fund

Type of award: Scholarship.

Intended use: For full-time undergraduate or graduate study at accredited postsecondary institution.

Eligibility: Applicant must be international student or Norwegian or American.

Basis for selection: Major/career interest in Scandinavian studies/research. Applicant must demonstrate financial need, high academic achievement, depth of character, leadership and service orientation.

Application requirements: Recommendations, essay, transcript, proof of eligibility.

Additional information: Any American who has demonstrated keen and sincere interest in Norwegian heritage and/or any Norwegian who has demonstrated interest in American heritage, and who now desires to further study their heritages at recognized educational institution (arts, crafts, literature, history, music, folklore, etc.) is eligible to apply.

Amount of award:	$500-$2,000
Number of awards:	9
Number of applicants:	100
Application deadline:	March 1
Notification begins:	May 1
Total amount awarded:	$10,000

Contact:
Sons of Norway Foundation
1455 West Lake Street
Minneapolis, MN 55408
Phone: 612-827-3611

Nancy Lorraine Jensen Memorial Scholarship

Type of award: Scholarship, renewable.

Intended use: For full-time freshman, sophomore, junior or senior study.

Eligibility: Applicant or parent must be member/participant of Sons of Norway. Applicant must be female, at least 17, no older than 35. Applicant must be U.S. citizen.

Basis for selection: Major/career interest in chemistry; physics; engineering, electrical/electronic or engineering, mechanical. Applicant must demonstrate high academic achievement, depth of character and seriousness of purpose.

Application requirements: Recommendations, essay, transcript, proof of eligibility.

Additional information: Employees of NASA Goddard Space Flight Center, Greenbelt, Maryland for at least three years also eligible. Minimum SAT score of 1200 or ACT score of 26. Must apply each year.

Amount of award:	Full tuition
Number of awards:	1
Application deadline:	March 1

Contact:
Sons of Norway Foundation
1455 West Lake Street
Minneapolis, MN 55408
Phone: 612-827-3611

Sony Music Entertainment, Inc.

Sony Music Scholarship Program

Type of award: Scholarship, renewable.

Intended use: For undergraduate study at accredited vocational, 2-year or 4-year institution.

Eligibility: Applicant or parent must be employed by Sony Music Entertainment Inc.
Basis for selection: Applicant must demonstrate financial need.
Additional information: For further information or an application, contact Sony Music Entertainment Inc. directly.
> Amount of award: $500-$2,000

Soo Line Credit Union

SLCU Y.E.S. Scholarship Program

Type of award: Scholarship.
Intended use: For undergraduate study at vocational, 2-year or 4-year institution.
Eligibility: Applicant or parent must be employed by Soo Line Credit Union. Applicant must be high school senior.
Additional information: For further information or an application, contact Soo Line Credit Union directly.
> Amount of award: $500

South Carolina Commission on Higher Education

LIFE Scholarship

Type of award: Scholarship, renewable.
Intended use: For full-time undergraduate study at 2-year or 4-year institution. Designated institutions: Eligible public and private institutions in South Carolina.
Eligibility: Applicant must be U.S. citizen or permanent resident residing in South Carolina.
Basis for selection: Applicant must demonstrate high academic achievement.
Application requirements: Transcript, proof of eligibility. Applicant must be a resident of South Carolina.
Additional information: Applicant must be a full-time enrolled degree-seeking undergraduate. Must have scored 1050 on SAT or 22 on ACT, and have graduated with a 3.0 GPA. SAT or ACT not required for students attending 2-year or technical colleges.

Amount of award:	$1,000-$3,000
Number of awards:	17,028
Total amount awarded:	$30,381

Contact:
South Carolina Commission on Higher Education
1333 Main Street, Suite 200
Columbia, SC 29201
Phone: 803-737-2260
Web: www.che400.state.sc.us

Palmetto Fellows Scholarship Program

Type of award: Scholarship, renewable.
Intended use: For full-time undergraduate study at 4-year institution. Designated institutions: Eligible South Carolina public and private institutions.

Eligibility: Applicant must be high school senior. Applicant must be U.S. citizen or permanent resident residing in South Carolina.
Basis for selection: Applicant must demonstrate high academic achievement.
Application requirements: Transcript, proof of eligibility. Applicant must be a South Carolina resident.
Additional information: Must score 1200 on SAT or 27 on ACT, earn 3.5 GPA on 4.0 scale, and rank in top 5 percent of sophomore or junior class. High school graduate or completed a home school program as prescribed by law is eligible. Scholarship must be used towards the cost-of-attendance at a four year baccalaureate degree-granting institution. For additional information, student should contact guidance counselor or the S.C. Commission on Higher Education.

Amount of award:	$5,000
Number of awards:	2,263
Total amount awarded:	$11,315,000

Contact:
South Carolina Commission on Higher Education
1333 Main Street, Suite 200
Columbia, SC 29201
Phone: 803-737-2260
Web: www.che400.state.sc.us

South Carolina Need-Based Grants Program

Type of award: Scholarship.
Intended use: For undergraduate study at vocational, 2-year or 4-year institution outside United States. Designated institutions: South Carolina public and independent vocational, technical, two- and four-year institutions.
Eligibility: Applicant must be U.S. citizen or permanent resident residing in South Carolina.
Basis for selection: Applicant must demonstrate financial need and depth of character.
Application requirements: FAFSA.
Additional information: Students eligible to receive award for a maximum of eight full-time equivalent terms or until baccalaureate degree is earned, whichever is less. Must earn and maintain at least 2.0 GPA and earn at least twelve credit hours per semester if full-time or six credit hours per semester if part-time. For more information, contact Sherry Hubbard at 803-737-2262, shubbard@che400.state.sc.us or Bichevia Green at 803-737-2280, bgreen@che400.state.sc.us or use contact information below.

Amount of award:	$1,250-$2,500
Number of awards:	20,567
Total amount awarded:	$16,331,120

Contact:
Financial aid office at public college or university or
S.C. Higher Ed. Tuition Grants Commission
101 Business Park Boulevard, Suite 2100
Columbia, SC 29203-9498
Phone: 803-734-1200 or 877-349-7183
Web: www.che400.state.sc.us

South Carolina Higher Education Tuition Grants Commission

South Carolina Tuition Grants

Type of award: Scholarship, renewable.
Intended use: For full-time undergraduate study at accredited 2-year or 4-year institution in United States. Designated institutions: SACS-accredited South Carolina private, nonprofit institutions.
Eligibility: Applicant must be U.S. citizen residing in South Carolina.
Basis for selection: Applicant must demonstrate financial need and high academic achievement.
Application requirements: FAFSA.
Additional information: Recipient may reapply for up to four years of grant assistance. Incoming freshmen must score 900 on SAT or graduate in upper 3/4 of high school class. Upperclassmen must complete 24 semester hours and meet college's satisfactory progress requirements. Application is automatic with FAFSA; submit to federal processor and list eligible college in college choice section. All eligible applicants funded if deadline is met. Contact campus financial aid office for details. Average award, $2,350, renewable three times.

Amount of award:	$100-$3,730
Number of awards:	10,013
Number of applicants:	21,200
Application deadline:	June 30
Total amount awarded:	$23,895,000

Contact:
South Carolina Higher Education Tuition Grants Commission
101 Business Park Blvd., Suite 2100
Columbia, SC 29203-9498
Phone: 803-734-1200
Fax: 803-734-1426
Web: www.state.sc.us/tuitiongrants

South Carolina Space Grant Consortium

South Carolina Space Grant Research Fellowship

Type of award: Research grant, renewable.
Intended use: For full-time junior or senior study at accredited 4-year institution in United States. Designated institutions: Benedict College, The Citadel, Clemson University, Coastal Carolina University, Furman University, South Carolina State University, University of Charleston, University of South Carolina, Medical University of South Carolina, University of the Virgin Islands, and Wofford College.
Eligibility: Applicant must be U.S. citizen residing in South Carolina.
Basis for selection: Major/career interest in aerospace; arts, general; astronomy; education; engineering; environmental science; geology/earth sciences; geophysics; journalism or science, general.

Application requirements: Recommendations, essay, transcript, research proposal, nomination by and sponsorship from faculty advisor.
Additional information: Applicants must attend a South Carolina Space Grant Consortium member institution. Fellowships available for academic year or summer research. The Consortium actively encourages women, minority, and disabled students to apply.

Amount of award:	$3,000
Number of applicants:	25
Application deadline:	February 1

Contact:
NASA Space Grant South Carolina Space Grant Consortium
College of Charleston
Department of Geology
Charleston, SC 29424
Phone: 843-953-5463
Fax: 843-953-5446
Web: www.cofc.edu/~scsgrant/

South Dakota Board of Regents

South Dakota Annis I. Fowler/Kaden Scholarship

Type of award: Scholarship.
Intended use: For freshman study. Designated institutions: University of South Dakota, Black Hills State University, Dakota State University or Northern State University.
Eligibility: Applicant must be U.S. citizen residing in South Dakota.
Basis for selection: Major/career interest in education. Applicant must demonstrate financial need, high academic achievement, depth of character, leadership, seriousness of purpose and service orientation.
Application requirements: Recommendations, essay, transcript, proof of eligibility. Transcript must include class rank, cumulative grade point average and a list of courses to be taken during the senior year. Complete Fowler/Kaden application form.
Additional information: Open to high school seniors who have a cumulative GPA of 3.0 after three years. Applicants must select elementary education as major field. Special consideration given to applicants with demonstrated motivation, a disability, or who are self-supporting.

Amount of award:	$1,000
Number of awards:	2
Total amount awarded:	$1,000

Contact:
South Dakota Board of Regents
Scholarship Committee
306 E. Capitol Avenue, Suite 200
Pierre, SD 57501-3159
Phone: 605-773-3455

South Dakota Ardell Bjugstad Scholarship

Type of award: Scholarship.
Intended use: For freshman study at postsecondary institution in United States.

Eligibility: Applicant must be American Indian. Member of federally recognized Indian tribe whose reservation is in North Dakota or South Dakota. Applicant must be high school senior. Applicant must be U.S. citizen residing in North Dakota or South Dakota.

Basis for selection: Major/career interest in agribusiness; agriculture; natural resources/conservation or environmental science. Applicant must demonstrate depth of character, leadership and seriousness of purpose.

Application requirements: Recommendations, transcript, proof of eligibility. Transcript must include class rank and culumlative average. Completed Bjugstad Scholarship application form.

Additional information: Verification of tribal enrollment required.

Amount of award:	$500
Number of awards:	1
Application deadline:	February 23

Contact:
South Dakota Board of Regents
Scholarship Committee
306 E. Capitol Avenue, Suite 200
Pierre, SD 57502-3159
Phone: 605-773-3455

South Dakota Haines Memorial Scholarship

Type of award: Scholarship.

Intended use: For full-time sophomore, junior or senior study at accredited 4-year institution in United States. Designated institutions: South Dakota public universities including: BHSU, DSU, NSU, SDSU, USD.

Eligibility: Applicant must be residing in South Dakota.

Basis for selection: Major/career interest in education. Applicant must demonstrate depth of character, leadership, seriousness of purpose and service orientation.

Application requirements: Essay, transcript, proof of eligibility. Resume. Two-page essay describing personal philosophy and two-page essay describing your philosophy of education. Haines Memorial Scholarship application form.

Additional information: Minimum 2.5 GPA and typed resume of extracurricular activities, services, and memberships.

Amount of award:	$2,150
Number of awards:	1
Application deadline:	February 23
Notification begins:	March 24

Contact:
South Dakota Board of Regents Scholarship Committee
306 E. Capitol, Suite 200
Pierre, SD 57501-3159
Phone: 605-773-3455

South Dakota Marlin R. Scarborough Memorial Scholarship

Type of award: Scholarship.

Intended use: For full-time junior study at accredited 4-year institution in United States. Designated institutions: South Dakota public universities.

Eligibility: Applicant must be residing in South Dakota.

Basis for selection: Applicant must demonstrate high academic achievement, depth of character, leadership, seriousness of purpose and service orientation.

Application requirements: Essay, transcript, proof of eligibility, nomination by a participating South Dakota public university. Scarborough Scholarship application form.

Additional information: For junior year study. Minimum 3.5 GPA and have completed three full semesters at same university. Call or e-mail sponsor for deadlines and application; e-mail address: info@ris.sdbor.edu. For junior study only; must be sophomore at time of application.

Amount of award:	$1,500
Number of awards:	1

Contact:
South Dakota Board of Regents Scholarship Committee
306 East Capitol, Suite 200
Pierre, SD 57501-3159
Phone: 605-773-3455

South Dakota Department of Education and Cultural Affairs

South Dakota National Guard Tuition Assistance

Type of award: Scholarship, renewable.

Intended use: For undergraduate study at vocational or 4-year institution.

Eligibility: Applicant or parent must be member/participant of South Dakota National Guard. Applicant must be residing in South Dakota. Applicant or parent must be currently serving in South Dakota National Guard.

Application requirements: Proof of eligibility.

Additional information: Provides tuition/fee waiver of 50 percent.

Amount of award:	Full tuition
Number of awards:	500
Number of applicants:	500
Total amount awarded:	$110,000

Contact:
SDNG Unit or South Dakota Department of Military and Veterans Affairs
Soldiers and Sailors Building
500 East Capitol Avenue
Pierre, SD 57501-5070
Phone: 605-773-3269

South Dakota Robert C. Byrd Honors Scholarship

Type of award: Scholarship, renewable.

Intended use: For full-time undergraduate study in United States.

Eligibility: Applicant must be high school senior. Applicant must be U.S. citizen or permanent resident residing in South Dakota.

Basis for selection: Applicant must demonstrate high academic achievement.

Application requirements: Transcript. Must have ACT score of 24 or above.

Additional information: Minimum 3.5 GPA.

Amount of award:	$1,500
Number of awards:	80
Number of applicants:	200
Application deadline:	May 1
Notification begins:	April 30
Total amount awarded:	$121,000

Contact:
South Dakota Department of Education and Cultural Affairs
700 Governors Drive
Pierre, SD 57501-2291
Phone: 605-773-5669

Southeastern Claim Executives Association

Southeastern Claim Executives Association Scholarship

Type of award: Scholarship.
Intended use: For undergraduate study at accredited 2-year or 4-year institution.
Eligibility: Applicant or parent must be member/participant of Southeastern Claim Executives Association.
Additional information: For further information or an application, contact Southeastern Claim Executives Association directly.

Amount of award:	$1,500

Southwest Research Institute

Martin Goland Scholarship Program

Type of award: Scholarship, renewable.
Intended use: For undergraduate study at 2-year or 4-year institution.
Eligibility: Applicant or parent must be employed by Southwest Research Institute. Applicant must be high school senior.
Additional information: For further information or an application, contact Southwest Research Institute directly.

Amount of award:	$5,000

Spear, Leeds and Kellogg Foundation

Spear, Leeds and Kellogg Scholarship Award

Type of award: Scholarship, renewable.
Intended use: For undergraduate study at accredited vocational, 2-year or 4-year institution.
Eligibility: Applicant or parent must be employed by Spear, Leeds, and Kellogg.
Basis for selection: Applicant must demonstrate financial need.
Additional information: For further information or an application, contact Spear, Leeds and Kellogg directly.

Amount of award:	$500-$12,000

SPIE - The International Society for Optical Engineering

SPIE Educational Scholarships and Grants in Optical Engineering

Type of award: Scholarship.
Intended use: For undergraduate, graduate or non-degree study at accredited postsecondary institution in United States.
Basis for selection: Major/career interest in engineering.
Application requirements: Recommendations. Application.
Additional information: Applicant should have interest/major in optical engineering including any of its many applications. Application available online.

Amount of award:	$1,000-$10,000
Number of awards:	77
Number of applicants:	354
Application deadline:	February 3
Notification begins:	September 1
Total amount awarded:	$220,000

Contact:
SPIE/Scholarship Committee
PO Box 10
Bellingham, WA 98227-0010
Phone: 360-676-3290 ext. 659
Web: www.spie.org/info/scholarships

Spina Bifida Association of America

Spina Bifida Association of America Scholarship Fund

Type of award: Scholarship.
Intended use: For undergraduate or graduate study at postsecondary institution in United States.
Basis for selection: Applicant must demonstrate financial need and high academic achievement.
Application requirements: Recommendations, essay, transcript, proof of eligibility. Statement verifying disability from physician. Letter verifying acceptance at school/college. Financial aid forms.
Additional information: Open to all persons with spina bifida. May be used for any postsecondary study, vocational or specialized training. Applicant must be high school graduate or GED recipient. Awards in $500 and $1,000 increments.

Amount of award:	$500-$1,000
Number of awards:	2
Application deadline:	April 1
Notification begins:	June 1
Total amount awarded:	$10,000

Contact:
Scholarship Committee
4590 MacArthur Boulevard, NW
Suite 250
Washington, DC 20007
Phone: 202-944-3285
Fax: 202-944-3295
Web: www.sbaa.org

Spinsters Ink

Young Feminist Scholarship Program

Type of award: Scholarship.
Intended use: For freshman study.
Eligibility: Applicant must be female, high school senior. Applicant must be U.S. citizen.
Basis for selection: Competition/talent/interest in writing/journalism, based on best essay on feminism. Major/career interest in women's studies; journalism or English.
Application requirements: Essay. Essays must be no longer than three pages, typed, and double-spaced. Do not send your entry via email. Applications and essays submitted electronically will not be considered.
Additional information: Winners may have their prize-winning essay published in national women's magazine. Scholarship can be used for the college of her choice and winner will also be invited to attend Norcroft: A Writing Retreat for Women for one week. Visit Website for additional information.

Amount of award:	$1,000
Number of awards:	1
Application deadline:	December 31
Notification begins:	March 8

Contact:
Young Feminist Scholarship
Spinsters Ink
P.O. Box 22005
Denver, CO 80222
Phone: 218-727-3222
Web: www.spinsters-ink.com

Stanadyne Automotive Corporation

Stanadyne Automotive Corporation Scholarship Program

Type of award: Scholarship.
Intended use: For freshman study at accredited 4-year institution.
Eligibility: Applicant or parent must be employed by Stanadyne Automotive Corp.
Additional information: For further information or an application, contact Stanadyne Automotive Corporation directly.

Amount of award:	$2,500

Stanley Works

Stanley Sons and Daughters Scholarship Program

Type of award: Scholarship.
Intended use: For undergraduate study at accredited postsecondary institution.

Eligibility: Applicant or parent must be employed by Stanley Works. Applicant must be high school senior.
Basis for selection: Applicant must demonstrate financial need.
Additional information: For further information or application, contact Stanley Works directly.

Amount of award:	$500-$2,500

State Council of Higher Education for Virginia

Eastern Shore Tuition Assistance Program

Type of award: Scholarship, renewable.
Intended use: For junior or senior study in United States. Designated institutions: University of Maryland-Eastern Shore or Salisbury State University.
Eligibility: Applicant must be U.S. citizen or permanent resident residing in Virginia.
Application requirements: Completed application. Applicant cannot hold any prior baccalaureate or higher degree.
Additional information: No more than two years of full-time awards or equivalent. Theology or divinity majors not eligible.

Application deadline:	July 31

Contact:
Eastern Shore Tuition Assistance Program
State Council of Higher Education for VA
James Monroe Building, 101 N. Fourteenth St.
Richmond, VA 23219
Phone: 804-225-2632
Fax: 804-225-2604
Web: www.schev.edu

Virginia Academic Common Market

Type of award: Scholarship.
Intended use: For full-time undergraduate or graduate study at 4-year or graduate institution.
Eligibility: Applicant must be permanent resident residing in Virginia.
Application requirements: Application (available online). Applicant must be enrolled full-time at eligible institution.
Additional information: Awards Virginia residents in-state tuition at non-Virginia institutions in 13 states in the South. Institution must offer programs unavailable in Virginia public institutions.

Contact:
Virginia Academic Common Market/SCHEV
James Monroe Building
101 North Fourteenth Street
Richmond, VA 23219
Phone: 804-225-2632
Fax: 804-225-2638
Web: www.schev.edu

Virginia Regional Contract Program

Type of award: Scholarship.
Intended use: For undergraduate or graduate study at accredited 2-year or 4-year institution. Designated institutions: For library science: Univeristy of North Carolina, Chapel Hill, and North Carolina Central University; for optometry:

Stephen T. Marchello Scholarship Foundation: Stephen T. Marchello Scholarship for Survivors of Childhood Cancer

Pennsylvania College of Optometry, Southern College of Optometry and University of Alabama, Birmingham; for forensic science: George Washington University; for paper, pulp and technology: North Carolina State University.
Eligibility: Applicant must be U.S. citizen or permanent resident residing in Virginia.
Basis for selection: Major/career interest in library science; forensics or optometry/ophthalmology.
Additional information: Provides assistance to Virginia residents studying specific fields at designated out-of-state institutions. Paper, pulp and technology students must be junior or senior status. Recipients are selected by institution. Fact sheet and application available online.

Number of awards:	60
Total amount awarded:	$300,000

Contact:
Virginia Council of Higher Education/Financial Aid Programs
James Monroe Building
101 North Fourteenth Street
Richmond, VA 23219
Web: www.schev.edu

Virginia Tuition Assistance Grant

Type of award: Scholarship, renewable.
Intended use: For full-time undergraduate, master's, doctoral or first professional study at accredited postsecondary institution. Designated institutions: Private, nonprofit institutions in Virginia.
Eligibility: Applicant must be permanent resident residing in Virginia.
Application requirements: Proof of eligibility. Applicant must not be enrolled in program leading to second bachelor, graduate or professional degree.
Additional information: Non-need based award. Applicant must be in eligible degree program. Theology and divinity majors not eligible. If funding insufficient, priority given first to renewals, then to new applicants who apply prior to July 31.

Amount of award:	$3,000
Number of awards:	15,500
Application deadline:	July 31
Total amount awarded:	$42,000,000

Contact:
Financial aid office of qualifying postsecondary institution.
Web: www.schev.edu

State Farm Companies Foundation

State Farm Companies Exceptional Student Fellowship

Type of award: Scholarship.
Intended use: For senior or graduate study at accredited 4-year institution in United States.
Eligibility: Applicant must be U.S. citizen.
Basis for selection: Major/career interest in business; computer/information sciences; mathematics; accounting; finance/banking; insurance/actuarial science or economics. Applicant must demonstrate depth of character and leadership.
Application requirements: Recommendations, transcript.
Additional information: Minimum 3.6 GPA. Application comes with nomination/recommendation form which must be completed by professor or faculty member. Applications without these forms are not considered. Notifications mailed in March.

Amount of award:	$3,000
Number of awards:	50
Number of applicants:	523
Application deadline:	February 15
Total amount awarded:	$150,000

Contact:
State Farm Companies Foundation
One State Farm Plaza, B-4
Bloomington, IL 61710-0001
Phone: 309-766-2039
Web: www.statefarm.com

State of Maine-Department of Agriculture, Food and Rural Resources

Maine Rural Rehabilitation Fund Scholarship

Type of award: Scholarship.
Intended use: For undergraduate study at accredited vocational, 2-year or 4-year institution in United States.
Eligibility: Applicant must be U.S. citizen or permanent resident residing in Maine.
Basis for selection: Major/career interest in agriculture; forestry; environmental science or agricultural education. Applicant must demonstrate financial need, high academic achievement and seriousness of purpose.
Application requirements: Transcript, proof of eligibility. Application form, financial aid forms, letter confirming school acceptance for first-time applicant.
Additional information: Cumulative GPA of at least 2.7 or current GPA of at least 3.0. Applicants must meet one or more qualifications: At least 50 percent of applicant's family gross income for past year has been derived from farm and/or woodswork occupation; and/or applicant is child of deceased or physically impaired person who has operated farm or has been employed in qualifying woodswork occupation; and/or applicant is FAA member in good standing who plans to pursue career in agriculture or woodswork. Contact sponsor for application.

Application deadline:	June 15

Contact:
Maine Rural Rehabilitation Fund Scholarship Committee
Dept. of Agriculture, Food and Rural Resource
28 State House Station
Augusta, ME 04333
Phone: 207-287-7628

Stephen T. Marchello Scholarship Foundation

Stephen T. Marchello Scholarship for Survivors of Childhood Cancer

Type of award: Scholarship, renewable.

449

Intended use: For undergraduate study at accredited vocational, 2-year or 4-year institution in United States.
Eligibility: Applicant must be survivor of childhood cancer. Applicant must be high school senior. Applicant must be U.S. citizen residing in Arizona, California or Colorado.
Application requirements: Interview, recommendations, essay, transcript, proof of eligibility. Submit SAT/ACT scores when available. Send SASE.
Additional information: Award is per semester for up to four years. Visit Website for more information and to submit application or send SASE to address below.

Amount of award:	$1,250
Number of awards:	2
Number of applicants:	16
Application deadline:	March 15
Total amount awarded:	$10,000

Contact:
Stephen T. Marchello Scholarship Foundation
1170 E. Long Place
Littleton, CO 80122
Phone: 303-798-0406
Web: www.stmfoundation.org

Sto Corporation

Sto Corporation Scholarship Fund

Type of award: Scholarship.
Intended use: For undergraduate study at vocational, 2-year or 4-year institution.
Eligibility: Applicant or parent must be employed by Sto Corp. Applicant must be high school senior.
Additional information: For further information or an application, contact Sto Corp. directly.

Amount of award:	$1,500

Stratus Computer (DE), Inc.

Daniel M. Clemson Scholarship for Young Engineers

Type of award: Scholarship.
Intended use: For undergraduate or graduate study at accredited postsecondary institution.
Eligibility: Applicant or parent must be employed by Stratus Computer (DE), Inc.
Additional information: For further information and to receive application, contact Stratus Computers (DE), Inc. directly.

Amount of award:	$5,000

Stratus Scholarship Program

Type of award: Scholarship.
Intended use: For undergraduate study at accredited vocational, 2-year or 4-year institution.
Eligibility: Applicant or parent must be employed by Stratus Computer (DE), Inc.
Basis for selection: Applicant must demonstrate financial need.

Additional information: For further information or an application, contact Stratus Computers (DE), Inc. directly.

Amount of award:	$1,000

Student Pilot Network

"SPN Flight Dreams" Scholarship Program

Type of award: Scholarship.
Intended use: For undergraduate or non-degree study at vocational or 2-year institution. Designated institutions: Student Pilot Network participating institutions.
Basis for selection: Major/career interest in aviation.
Application requirements: Essay. School-endorsed application certificate.
Additional information: Applicant must register to become SPN member. Visit Website to search for SPN participating schools using SPN's Flight School Search Engine.

Amount of award:	$250-$1,000
Application deadline:	November 30
Notification begins:	January 15

Contact:
Student Pilot Network
PO Box 1156
Wheeling, IL 60090-1156
Phone: 847-229-1694
Web: www.ufly.com

Sub-Zero Freezer Company, Inc.

Walter Wiest Scholarship Program

Type of award: Scholarship, renewable.
Intended use: For freshman study at vocational, 2-year or 4-year institution.
Eligibility: Applicant or parent must be employed by Sub-Zero Freezer Company, Inc. Applicant must be high school senior.
Additional information: For further information or an application, contact Sub-Zero Freezer Company Incorporated directly.

Amount of award:	$1,000

Suddath Companies

Richard H. Suddath Scholarship Foundation

Type of award: Scholarship, renewable.
Intended use: For freshman study at 2-year or 4-year institution.
Eligibility: Applicant or parent must be employed by The Suddath Companies. Applicant must be high school senior.
Additional information: For further information or an application, contact Suddath Companies directly.

Sunkist Growers

A.W. Bodine Sunkist Memorial Scholarship

Type of award: Scholarship, renewable.
Intended use: For full-time undergraduate study at accredited 2-year or 4-year institution.
Eligibility: Applicant must be residing in Arizona or California.
Basis for selection: Applicant must demonstrate financial need, high academic achievement, depth of character, leadership, seriousness of purpose and service orientation.
Application requirements: Recommendations, essay, transcript, proof of eligibility. Tax return or parents' tax return for applicants younger than 21. SAT scores.
Additional information: Must have a 3.0 GPA. Applicant or someone in immediate family must have derived the majority of his/her income from California or Arizona-based agriculture. All majors eligible. Award renewable up to four years based on annual review. Must maintain 2.7 GPA and carry 12 credits per semester to qualify for renewal.

Amount of award:	$2,000
Number of awards:	20
Number of applicants:	300
Application deadline:	April 30
Notification begins:	August 30

Contact:
A.W. Bodine Sunkist Memorial Scholarship
Sunkist Growers
PO Box 7888
Van Nuys, CA 91409-7888
Phone: 818-986-4800

Supreme Guardian Council, International Order of Job's Daughters

Supreme Guardian Council, International Order of Job's Daughters Scholarship

Type of award: Scholarship.
Intended use: For undergraduate study at vocational, 2-year or 4-year institution.
Eligibility: Applicant or parent must be member/participant of International Order of Job's Daughters. Applicant must be single, female, no older than 30.
Basis for selection: Applicant must demonstrate financial need, high academic achievement, depth of character, leadership, seriousness of purpose and service orientation.
Application requirements: Recommendations, transcript, proof of eligibility. Photograph.
Additional information: High school seniors eligible to apply.

Amount of award:	$750
Number of awards:	17
Number of applicants:	80
Application deadline:	April 30
Notification begins:	August 1
Total amount awarded:	$12,750

Contact:
Supreme Guardian Council
International Order of Job's Daughters
233 West 6 Street
Papillion, NE 68046
Phone: 402-592-7987
Fax: 402-592-2177
Web: www.iojd.org

Swiss Benevolent Society of New York

Sonia Streuli Maguire Outstanding Scholastic Achievement Award

Type of award: Scholarship.
Intended use: For full-time senior, post-bachelor's certificate, master's, doctoral or first professional study at accredited 4-year or graduate institution in United States.
Eligibility: Applicant must be Swiss. Applicant must be permanent resident residing in Delaware, Connecticut, New Jersey, New York or Pennsylvania.
Basis for selection: Applicant must demonstrate high academic achievement.
Application requirements: Recommendations, transcript, proof of eligibility.
Additional information: Applicant or one parent must be Swiss citizen. Must have a minimum 3.8 GPA.

Amount of award:	$2,500-$5,000
Number of awards:	2
Application deadline:	March 31
Notification begins:	June 1
Total amount awarded:	$5,000

Contact:
Swiss Benevolent Society
608 Fifth Avenue
Room 309
New York, NY 10020

Swiss Benevolent Society Medicus Student Exchange

Type of award: Scholarship.
Intended use: For full-time junior, senior, post-bachelor's certificate, master's, doctoral or first professional study at accredited 4-year or graduate institution in Universities and Polytechnic institutes in Switzerland.
Eligibility: Applicant must be Swiss. Applicant must be permanent resident, international student or Swiss citizen.
Basis for selection: Competition/talent/interest in study abroad. Applicant must demonstrate high academic achievement.
Application requirements: Recommendations, transcript, proof of eligibility. Fluency in language of instruction.
Additional information: For U.S. students one parent must be a Swiss national. Minimum 3.7 GPA.

Application deadline: March 31
Notification begins: June 1
Contact:
Swiss Benevolent Society
608 Fifth Avenue
Room 309
New York, NY 10020

Swiss Benevolent Society Pellegrini Scholarship

Type of award: Scholarship, renewable.
Intended use: For undergraduate, graduate or non-degree study at accredited postsecondary institution in United States.
Eligibility: Applicant must be Swiss. Applicant must be permanent resident residing in Delaware, Connecticut, New Jersey, New York or Pennsylvania.
Basis for selection: Applicant must demonstrate financial need and high academic achievement.
Application requirements: Recommendations, transcript, proof of eligibility. Proof of Swiss parentage and tax return.
Additional information: Applicant or one parent must be Swiss. Minimum 3.0 GPA required.
Amount of award: $500-$4,000
Number of awards: 55
Number of applicants: 61
Application deadline: March 31
Notification begins: June 1
Total amount awarded: $95,550
Contact:
Scholarship Fund of the Swiss Benevolent Society
608 Fifth Avenue
Room 309
New York, NY 10020

Sykes Enterprises, Incorporated

Sykes Student Scholarships

Type of award: Scholarship, renewable.
Intended use: For undergraduate study at 2-year or 4-year institution.
Eligibility: Applicant or parent must be employed by Sykes Enterprises, Incorporated. Applicant must be high school senior.
Additional information: For further information or an application, contact Sykes Enterprises, Incorporated directly.
Amount of award: $2,000

SYSCO Corporation

John F. Eula Mae Baugh SYSCO Scholarship Program

Type of award: Scholarship, renewable.
Intended use: For undergraduate study at 4-year institution.
Eligibility: Applicant or parent must be employed by SYSCO Corporation. Applicant must be high school senior.
Additional information: For further information or an application, contact SYSCO Corporation directly.

Amount of award: $1,000-$12,000

T.D. Williamson, Inc.

T.D. Williamson, Jr., Scholarship

Type of award: Scholarship.
Intended use: For undergraduate study at accredited vocational, 2-year or 4-year institution.
Eligibility: Applicant or parent must be employed by T. D. Williamson, Inc.
Additional information: For further information or an application, contact T.D. Williamson, Inc. directly.
Amount of award: $2,000

T.J. Hale Company

T.J. Hale Company Scholarship

Type of award: Scholarship.
Intended use: For undergraduate study at accredited postsecondary institution.
Eligibility: Applicant or parent must be employed by T.J. Hale Company. Applicant must be high school senior.
Additional information: For further information or an application, contact T.J. Hale Company directly.
Amount of award: $1,500
Contact:
T.J. Hale Company

Talbots

Talbots Scholarship Fund

Type of award: Scholarship.
Intended use: For undergraduate study at accredited vocational, 2-year or 4-year institution.
Eligibility: Applicant or parent must be employed by Talbots.
Basis for selection: Applicant must demonstrate financial need.
Additional information: For further information or an application, contact Talbots directly.
Amount of award: $2,000

Target

Target All -Around Scholarship

Type of award: Scholarship.
Intended use: For undergraduate study at accredited vocational, 2-year or 4-year institution.
Eligibility: Applicant must be high school senior.
Additional information: Information and application available at Target stores.
Amount of award: $1,000-$10,000

Target Team Member Scholarship

Type of award: Scholarship.
Intended use: For freshman study at vocational, 2-year or 4-year institution.
Eligibility: Applicant or parent must be employed by Target. Applicant must be high school senior.
Additional information: For further information or an application, contact Target directly.
  Amount of award: $1,000

Taylor Packing Co., Inc.

Taylor Packing Co., Inc. Scholarship Program

Type of award: Scholarship, renewable.
Intended use: For undergraduate study at vocational, 2-year or 4-year institution.
Eligibility: Applicant or parent must be employed by Taylor Packing Co., Inc. Applicant must be high school senior.
Additional information: For further information or an application, contact Taylor Packing Company, Inc. directly.
  Amount of award: $1,000

TCF BANK

TCF Scholarship Program

Type of award: Scholarship.
Intended use: For undergraduate study at vocational, 2-year or 4-year institution.
Eligibility: Applicant or parent must be employed by TCF Foundation. Applicant must be high school senior.
Additional information: For further information or an application, contact TCF Foundation directly.
  Amount of award: $500-$2,500

TDS Telecom and TDS Corporate

TDS Scholarship Program

Type of award: Scholarship.
Intended use: For undergraduate study at accredited vocational, 2-year or 4-year institution.
Eligibility: Applicant or parent must be employed by TDS Inc. Applicant must be high school senior.
Additional information: For further information or application, contact TDS Telecom and TDS Corporate directly.
  Amount of award: $2,000
Contact:
Pioneers Scholarship Program
Scholarship Management Services, CSFA
1505 Riverview Rd, P.O. Box 297
St. Peter, MN 56082

Techneglas

Techneglas Scholarship Program

Type of award: Scholarship, renewable.
Intended use: For freshman study at vocational, 2-year or 4-year institution.
Eligibility: Applicant or parent must be employed by Techneglas. Applicant must be high school senior.
Additional information: For further information or an application, contact Techneglas directly.
  Amount of award: $1,000

Technology Association of Georgia

Web Challenge Contest

Type of award: Scholarship.
Intended use: For full-time undergraduate study. Designated institutions: Georgia college or university.
Eligibility: Applicant must be enrolled in high school. Applicant must be U.S. citizen or permanent resident residing in Georgia.
Basis for selection: Competition/talent/interest in Web-site design, based on originality, creativity and sophistication in Website design. Major/career interest in computer/information sciences or computer graphics.
Application requirements: Proof of eligibility.
Additional information: Visit current site on web for 2001 contest information and theme. Must submit registration form online. Open to all Georgia high school students. Applicants must assemble team of at least two participants to design and build Website, and be sponsored by one faculty advisor. Applications due in fall, scholarships awarded in March. Total amount awarded varies, but expected to be at least $25,000.
Contact:
Phone: 404-817-3333
Web: www.webchallenge.org

Telephone and Data Systems, Inc.

TDS Corporate Scholarship Program

Type of award: Scholarship.
Intended use: For undergraduate study at vocational, 2-year or 4-year institution.
Eligibility: Applicant or parent must be employed by Telephone and Data Systems, Inc. Applicant must be high school senior.
Additional information: For further information or an application, contact Telephone and Data Systems Incorporated directly.
  Amount of award: $2,500

TENNANT

TENNANT Scholarship

Type of award: Scholarship, renewable.
Intended use: For undergraduate study at accredited vocational, 2-year or 4-year institution.
Eligibility: Applicant or parent must be employed by Tennant.
Additional information: For further information or an application, contact TENNANT directly.

    Amount of award: $1,250

Tennessee Space Grant Consortium

NASA Space Grant Tennessee Undergraduate Scholarship

Type of award: Scholarship, renewable.
Intended use: For full-time undergraduate study in United States. Designated institutions: Awardees must attend Tennessee Space Grant Consortium member institution. Consortium members include: Vanderbilt University, University of Tennessee-Knoxville, Fisk University, Tennessee State University, Rhodes College, Austin Peay State University, Columbia State Community College. Awards are not given to incoming students. While it is not required that the awardee be a resident of Tennessee, they must attend one of the aforementioned schools.
Eligibility: Applicant must be U.S. citizen.
Basis for selection: Major/career interest in science, general; mathematics or engineering. Applicant must demonstrate high academic achievement and seriousness of purpose.
Additional information: Topics related to space exploration in any field of study may qualify. Application deadlines, criteria, and award amounts vary by member institutions. Contact Consortium office for more specific information. Most awards are for upper level students and do not cover tuition costs. Application requirements vary by school.
Contact:
NASA Space Grant Tennessee Space Grant Consortium
Vanderbilt University
Box 1592, Station B
Nashville, TN 37235
Phone: 615-343-1148
Fax: 515-343-6687
Web: www.vuse.vanderbilt.edu/~tnsg/homepage.html

Tennessee Student Assistance C orporation

Tennessee Christa McAuliffe Scholarship

Type of award: Scholarship.
Intended use: For junior or senior study.
Basis for selection: Major/career interest in education, teacher; education; education, early childhood or education,

special. Applicant must demonstrate high academic achievement, depth of character, leadership, seriousness of purpose and service orientation.
Application requirements: Transcript. Written statement of intent to teach in a Tennessee elementary or secondary school.
Additional information: To be eligible, applicant must be enrolled full-time in a teacher education program in accredited Tennessee postsecondary institution. Applicant must have completed at least the first semester of the junior year with cumulative grade point average of at least 3.5 and ACT or SAT score that meets or exceeds the national norm.

    Amount of award: $500
    Number of awards: 1
    Application deadline: April 1
    Total amount awarded: $500
Contact:
Tennessee Student Assistance Corporation
Parkway Towers, Suite 1950
404 James Robertson Parkway
Nashville, TN 37243-1346
Phone: 615-741-1346
Web: www.state.tn.us/tsac

Tennessee Student Assistance Corporation

Tennessee Dependent Children Scholarship

Type of award: Scholarship, renewable.
Intended use: For full-time undergraduate study at accredited postsecondary institution.
Eligibility: Applicant must be single. Applicant must be U.S. citizen residing in Tennessee. Applicant's parent must have been killed or disabled in work-related accident as fire fighter or police officer.
Basis for selection: Applicant must demonstrate financial need.
Application requirements: Proof of eligibility. FAFSA.
Additional information: Applicant must be enrolled full time in a degree-granting program. Applicant's parent must have been killed or disabled in work-related accident as: law enforcement office, fireman, or an emergency medical technician in Tennessee.

    Amount of award: Full tuition
    Number of awards: 5
    Number of applicants: 5
    Application deadline: July 15
    Total amount awarded: $16,000
Contact:
Tennessee Student Assistance Corporation
Parkway Towers, Suite 1950
404 James Robertson Parkway
Nashville, TN 37243-0820
Phone: 615-741-1346
Fax: 615-741-6101
Web: www.state.tn.us/tsac

Tennessee Minority Teaching Fellows Program

Type of award: Scholarship, renewable.

Intended use: For full-time freshman, sophomore, junior or senior study at accredited 2-year or 4-year institution. Designated institutions: In Tennessee.

Eligibility: Applicant must be Alaskan native, Asian American, African American, Mexican American, Hispanic American, Puerto Rican or American Indian. Applicant must be U.S. citizen residing in Tennessee.

Basis for selection: Major/career interest in education, teacher; education; education, special or education, early childhood. Applicant must demonstrate seriousness of purpose and service orientation.

Application requirements: Recommendations, essay, transcript, proof of eligibility.

Additional information: Entering freshmen applicants have priority and must have a minimum 2.75 GPA, rank in top 25 percent of class, or score at least 18 on ACT (780 SAT). Undergraduate applicatants must have a minimum of 2.50 college GPA. Must make commitment to teaching. Loan forgiveness given by teaching in Tennessee public K-12 schools.

Amount of award:	$5,000
Number of awards:	29
Number of applicants:	200
Application deadline:	April 15
Total amount awarded:	$145,000

Contact:
Tennessee Student Assistance Corporation
Parkway Towers, Suite 1950
404 James Robertson Parkway
Nashville, TN 37243-0820
Phone: 615-741-1346
Web: www.state.tn.us/tsac

Tennessee Ned McWherter Scholarship

Type of award: Scholarship, renewable.

Intended use: For full-time freshman study at accredited 2-year or 4-year institution. Designated institutions: In Tennessee.

Eligibility: Applicant must be high school senior. Applicant must be U.S. citizen residing in Tennessee.

Basis for selection: Applicant must demonstrate leadership.

Application requirements: Transcript, proof of eligibility. Applicant must score at 95th percentile on ACT/SAT, minimum 3.5 GPA through seven semesters. Difficulty level of high school courses considered.

Amount of award:	$6,000
Number of awards:	50
Number of applicants:	902
Application deadline:	February 15
Total amount awarded:	$300,000

Contact:
Tennessee Student Assistance Corporation
Parkway Towers, Suite 1950
404 James Robertson Parkway
Nashville, TN 37243-1820
Phone: 615-741-1346
Web: www.state.tn.us/tsac

Tennessee Robert C. Byrd Honors Scholarship

Type of award: Scholarship, renewable.

Intended use: For full-time freshman study at accredited vocational, 2-year or 4-year institution in United States.

Eligibility: Applicant must be high school senior. Applicant must be U.S. citizen or permanent resident residing in Tennessee.

Application requirements: Transcript, proof of eligibility.

Additional information: Minimum 3.5 GPA or 3.0 GPA, and either 24 ACT(1090 SAT) or score of 57 or above on GED. Random selection from eligible applicants.

Amount of award:	$1,500
Number of awards:	122
Number of applicants:	3,500
Application deadline:	March 1
Total amount awarded:	$183,000

Contact:
Tennessee Student Assistance Corporation
Parkway Towers, Suite 1950
404 James Robertson Parkway
Nashville, TN 37243-0820
Phone: 615-741-1346
Fax: 615-741-6101
Web: www.state.tn.us/tsac

Tennessee Student Assistance Award

Type of award: Scholarship, renewable.

Intended use: For undergraduate study. Designated institutions: Eligible Tennessee postsecondary institutions.

Eligibility: Applicant must be U.S. citizen or permanent resident residing in Tennessee.

Basis for selection: Applicant must demonstrate financial need.

Application requirements: FAFSA must be processed by May 1. Expected family contribution range: $0-1900.

Amount of award:	$4,530
Number of awards:	22,000
Number of applicants:	140,000
Application deadline:	May 1
Total amount awarded:	$30,000,000

Contact:
Tennessee Student Assistance Corporation
Parkway Towers, Suite 1950
404 James Robertson Parkway
Nashville, TN 37243-0820
Phone: 615-741-1346
Web: www.state.tn.us/tsac

Tennessee Teaching Scholarship

Type of award: Scholarship, renewable.

Intended use: For junior, senior, post-bachelor's certificate or master's study at accredited 4-year or graduate institution. Designated institutions: In Tennessee.

Eligibility: Applicant must be U.S. citizen residing in Tennessee.

Basis for selection: Major/career interest in education; education, teacher; education, special or education, early childhood. Applicant must demonstrate high academic achievement.

Application requirements: Recommendations, transcript, proof of eligibility. Must provide verification of standardized test score and be accepted into Teacher Licensure Program.

Additional information: Loan forgiveness for teaching in Tennessee public schools, K-12. Minimum 2.75 cumulative GPA and a standardized test score adequate for admission to the Teacher Education Program in Tennessee schools.

Amount of award:	$3,900
Number of awards:	195
Number of applicants:	301
Application deadline:	April 15
Total amount awarded:	$500,000

Contact:
Tennessee Student Assistance Corporation
Parkway Towers, Suite 1950
404 James Robertson Parkway
Nashville, TN 37243-0820
Phone: 615-741-1346
Web: www.state.tn.us/tsac

Tescom Corporation

Tescom Scholarship

Type of award: Scholarship, renewable.
Intended use: For undergraduate study at accredited vocational, 2-year or 4-year institution.
Eligibility: Applicant or parent must be employed by Tescom Corporation.
Additional information: For further information or an application, contact Tescom Corporation directly.

    Amount of award: $1,500

Tesoro Petroleum Corporation

Tesoro Petroleum Corporation Scholarship Program

Type of award: Scholarship, renewable.
Intended use: For undergraduate study at accredited vocational, 2-year or 4-year institution.
Eligibility: Applicant or parent must be employed by Tesoro Petroleum Companies, Inc.
Basis for selection: Applicant must demonstrate financial need.
Additional information: For further information or an application, contact Tesoro Petroleum Companies, Inc. directly.

    Amount of award: $500-$1,250

Texas Higher Education Coordinating Board

Certified Educational Aide Exemption

Type of award: Scholarship.
Intended use: For undergraduate or graduate study. Designated institutions: Public postsecondary institutions in Texas.
Eligibility: Applicant must be U.S. citizen or permanent resident residing in Texas.
Application requirements: Must be certified by Texas Board of Teacher Certification as a Certified Aide.

Additional information: Assists educational aides by exempting them from payment of tuition and fees. Applicant must have applied for financial aid through college of attendance, including filing FAFSA or qualifying based on income. Applicant must have worked with students in classroom for at least two years (includes library aides, computer lab aides, and P.E. aides). Applicant must also be working as Certified Aide in a Texas public school during semester for which exemption is appied and must be enrolled in classes toward teacher certification. Maintenance of good academic standing required. Applicants should contact their college/university financial aid office for other information on applying for this program.

    Number of awards: 2,912

Contact:
Texas Higher Education Coordinating Board
Student Services Division
P. O. Box 12788
Austin, TX 78711-2788
Phone: 800-242-3062
Fax: 512-427-6420
Web: www.collegefortexans.com

Firefighter Exemption

Type of award: Scholarship.
Intended use: For undergraduate study at 2-year or 4-year institution. Designated institutions: Public postsecondary institutions in Texas.
Eligibility: Applicant must be U.S. citizen or permanent resident residing in Texas.
Basis for selection: Major/career interest in fire science/ technology.
Additional information: Assists firefighters enrolled in fire science courses as part of fire science curriculum. Courses must have tax support cover some of their costs. Maximum award is exemption from one year's tuition and laboratory fees. Applicants must provide registrar with proof of employment as firefighter by a political subdivision of the State of Texas. Applicants should contact their college/university financial aid office for other information on applying for this program.

    Number of awards: 1,132

Contact:
Texas Higher Education Coordinating Board
Student Services Division
P. O. Box 12788
Austin, TX 78711-2788
Phone: 800-242-3062
Fax: 512-427-6420
Web: www.collegefortexans.com

Senior Citizen, 65 or Older, Free Tuition for 6 Credit Hours

Type of award: Scholarship.
Intended use: For half-time undergraduate or graduate study at 2-year or 4-year institution. Designated institutions: Texas public colleges or universities honoring this program.
Eligibility: Applicant must be at least 65, returning adult student. Applicant must be residing in Texas.
Application requirements: Proof of eligibility.
Additional information: Program open to Texas residents, nonresidents, and foreign students. Pays tuition up to six semester credit hours per semester or summer term. Average award last year: $146. To qualify for program, applicants must enroll in courses at college or university offering program. Texas institutions not required to offer program; applicants

should check with registrar. Classes must not already be filled with students paying at full price and must use tax support for some of their cost.

Number of awards: 3,472

Contact:
Texas Higher Education Coordinating Board
Student Services Division
P. O. Box 12788
Austin, TX 78711-2788
Phone: 800-242-3062
Fax: 512-427-6420
Web: www.collegefortexans.com

Texas Aid to Families with Dependent Children or Temporary Assistance for Needy Families Students Exemption

Type of award: Scholarship.
Intended use: For undergraduate certificate or freshman study at accredited 2-year or 4-year institution in United States. Designated institutions: Texas public institutions.
Eligibility: Applicant must be U.S. citizen or permanent resident residing in Texas.
Basis for selection: Applicant must demonstrate financial need.
Application requirements: Proof of eligibility.
Additional information: Average award $915. Must have graduated from Texas public high school. Must have received financial assistance under Chapter 31 Human Resources Code (AFDC) for not less than six months during senior year in high school. Must enroll within one year of high school graduation.

Number of awards: 112
Total amount awarded: $102,480

Contact:
Contact the college/university financial aid office to apply.
Phone: 800-242-3062
Fax: 512-427-6420
Web: www.collegefortexans.com

Texas Early High School Graduation Scholarship

Type of award: Scholarship, renewable.
Intended use: For undergraduate study in United States. Designated institutions: Public postsecondary institutions in Texas.
Eligibility: Applicant must be high school senior. Applicant must be U.S. citizen or permanent resident residing in Texas.
Application requirements: Proof of eligibility.
Additional information: Average award $509. Must have completed graduation requirements from a Texas public high school in less than 36 consecutive months. Applicants should contact the Board for copy of letter submitted by their high school counselor. Contact the college/university financial aid office for information on applying for this scholarship.

Amount of award: $1,000
Number of awards: 2,739
Total amount awarded: $850,843

Contact:
Contact the college/university financial aid office to apply.
Phone: 800-242-3062
Fax: 512-427-6420
Web: www.collegefortexans.com

Texas Fifth-Year Accountancy Scholarship Program

Type of award: Scholarship.
Intended use: For senior, post-bachelor's certificate or master's study in United States. Designated institutions: Public non-profit or independent institutions in Texas.
Basis for selection: Major/career interest in accounting. Applicant must demonstrate financial need.
Application requirements: Proof of eligibility. Signed statement of intent to take CPA exam in Texas.
Additional information: Average award $3,000. Must be enrolled as fifth-year accounting student who has completed at least 120 credit hours.

Amount of award: $3,000
Number of awards: 375
Total amount awarded: $578,490

Contact:
Contact college financial aid office for application
Phone: 800-242-3062
Web: www.collegefor texans.com

Texas Foster Care Students Exemption

Type of award: Scholarship, renewable.
Intended use: For undergraduate or graduate study at accredited vocational, 2-year or 4-year institution in United States. Designated institutions: Public institutions in Texas.
Eligibility: Applicant must be U.S. citizen or permanent resident residing in Texas.
Application requirements: Proof of eligibility.
Additional information: Average award $806. Must have been in foster or other residential care before 18th birthday. Must enroll in college before third anniversary of discharge from foster care. Contact college's financial aid office for application.

Amount of award: Full tuition
Number of awards: 325
Total amount awarded: $261,950

Contact:
Contact the college/university financial aid office to apply.
Phone: 800-242-3062
Fax: 512-427-6420
Web: www.collegefortexans.com

Texas General Scholarship for Nursing Students

Type of award: Scholarship.
Intended use: For undergraduate or graduate study at accredited 2-year, 4-year or graduate institution. Designated institutions: Public institutions in Texas.
Eligibility: Applicant must be U.S. citizen or permanent resident residing in Texas.
Basis for selection: Major/career interest in nursing or health-related professions. Applicant must demonstrate financial need.
Application requirements: Proof of eligibility. Must be enrolled in program leading to license as a Licensed Vocational Nurse or a degree in professional nursing.
Additional information: Degree students must not be licensed as a Licensed Vocational Nurse. Students with associate and bachelors degrees in nursing must not be licensed to practice as a Registered Nurse. For the 1999-2000 academic year, 44 awards were granted to students at public universities at $1,974 per award; 181 awards were granted to students at

public Community Colleges at $1,012 per award; and 31 awards were granted to students at private, non-profit colleges aat $1,996 per award.

Amount of award: $3,000
Number of awards: 256
Total amount awarded: $331,904
Contact:
Contact the college/university financial aid office to apply.
Phone: 800-242-3062
Fax: 512-427-6420
Web: www.collegefortexans.com

Texas Good Neighbor Scholarship

Type of award: Scholarship.
Intended use: For undergraduate or graduate study at accredited 2-year, 4-year or graduate institution in United States. Designated institutions: Public institutions in Texas.
Eligibility: Applicant must be international student or native-born citizen of any Western Hemisphere country other than Cuba residing in Texas. Applicant must be residing in Texas.
Application requirements: Proof of eligibility.
Additional information: Award is exemption from tuition for citizens of another country of the Americas. Must reside in Texas.
Contact:
Contact college/university financial aid office/int'l student office.
Phone: 800-242-3062
Fax: 512-427-6420
Web: www.collegefortexans.com

TEXAS Grant (Toward EXcellence, Access, and Success)

Type of award: Scholarship, renewable.
Intended use: For undergraduate study at vocational, 2-year or 4-year institution. Designated institutions: Public and private non-profit Texas colleges and universities.
Eligibility: Applicant must be U.S. citizen or permanent resident residing in Texas.
Basis for selection: Applicant must demonstrate financial need and high academic achievement.
Application requirements: Selective Service registration or exemption from requirement.
Additional information: GED and home school students not eligible. Applicants must have graduated from a Texas public or accredited private high school in Fall 1998 or later. Applicant must have completed the Recommended or Advanced High School Curriculum. Applicant must enroll in college on at least a 3/4-time basis (unless granted hardship waiver). Applicant must receive first award within 16 months of high school graduation. Applicant must not have been convicted of felony or crime involving controlled substance. No awards given for more than student's need or public institution tuition and fees; maximum for private institution attendees is $2,650. Applicants should contact the financial aid office at the college/university they plan to attend for other information on applying for this program.
Number of awards: 10,855
Contact:
Texas Higher Education Coordinating Board
Student Services Division
P. O. Box 12788
Austin, TX 78711-2788
Phone: 800-242-3062
Fax: 512-427-6420
Web: www.collegefortexans.com

Texas Hazlewood Act Tuition Exemption: Veterans and Dependents

Type of award: Scholarship, renewable.
Intended use: For undergraduate or graduate study at accredited 2-year, 4-year or graduate institution. Designated institutions: Public institutions in Texas.
Eligibility: Applicant must be residing in Texas. Applicant must be veteran; or dependent of veteran or deceased veteran.
Application requirements: Proof of eligibility.
Additional information: Average award $855. Must have tuition and fee charges that exceed all federal education benefits. Applicant or parent must have been resident of Texas prior to enlistment.
Number of awards: 8,398
Total amount awarded: $7,180,290
Contact:
Contact the college/university financial aid office to apply.
Phone: 800-242-3062
Fax: 512-427-6420
Web: www.collegefortexans.com

Texas Highest Ranking High School Graduate Tuition Exemption

Type of award: Scholarship.
Intended use: For freshman study at accredited 2-year or 4-year institution. Designated institutions: Public postsecondary Texas institutions.
Eligibility: Applicant must be U.S. citizen or permanent resident residing in Texas.
Basis for selection: Applicant must demonstrate high academic achievement.
Application requirements: Proof of eligibility.
Additional information: Average award $1,451. Must be valedictorian of accredited high school. Recipient is exempt from certain charges for first two semesters. Deadline varies.
Amount of award: Full tuition
Number of awards: 935
Total amount awarded: $1,356,685
Contact:
Contact college/university financial aid office to apply.
Phone: 800-242-3062
Web: www.collegefortexans.com

Texas Public Educational Grant/ LEAP

Type of award: Scholarship.
Intended use: For undergraduate or graduate study at accredited 2-year, 4-year or graduate institution. Designated institutions: Public institutions in Texas.
Eligibility: Applicant must be residing in Texas.
Basis for selection: Applicant must demonstrate financial need.
Additional information: For the 1998-99 academic year, 53,688 awards were granted to students from public universities at an average of $1,016 per award. Additionally, 27,254 awards were granted to public Community Colleges at an average of $432 per award.
Number of awards: 80,942
Total amount awarded: $66,320,736

Scholarships

Contact:
Apply through school's financial aid office.
Phone: 800-242-3062
Web: www.collegefortexans.com

Texas Robert C. Byrd Honors Scholarship

Type of award: Scholarship, renewable.
Intended use: For undergraduate study at vocational, 2-year or 4-year institution. Designated institutions: Public postsecondary institutions in Texas.
Eligibility: Applicant must be high school senior. Applicant must be U.S. citizen residing in Texas.
Basis for selection: Applicant must demonstrate high academic achievement.
Application requirements: Transcript, nomination by high school guidance counselor or GED center director.
Additional information: Average award $1,487. Must be high school senior or person completing GED to receive initial award. Must rank in top 10% of class and have minimum 3.75 GPA. High school guidance officer or GED center director will submit applications of top candidates to Texas Higher Education Coordinating Board.

Number of awards:	1,987
Application deadline:	March 15
Total amount awarded:	$2,980,500

Contact:
High school guidance office or GED center director
Phone: 800-242-3062
Fax: 512-427-6420
Web: www.collegefortexans.com

Texas Student Leveraging Educational Assistance Partnership Program (SSIG-LEAP)

Type of award: Scholarship.
Intended use: For undergraduate or graduate study at accredited vocational, 2-year, 4-year or graduate institution. Designated institutions: Eligible postsecondary institutions in Texas.
Eligibility: Applicant must be U.S. citizen or permanent resident residing in Texas.
Basis for selection: Applicant must demonstrate financial need.
Application requirements: Proof of eligibility. Applicant must register for selective service or be exempt.
Additional information: Average award $828. No individual award may be for more than the student's financial need or $1,250. Deadlines vary. Visit Website for additional information.

Number of awards:	2,697
Total amount awarded:	$1,384,956

Contact:
College/university financial aid office for information on applying
for this grant/scholarship.
Phone: 800-242-3062 or 877-782-7322
Web: www.collegefortexans.com

Texas Tuition Exemption for Blind or Deaf Students

Type of award: Scholarship, renewable.

Intended use: For undergraduate or graduate study at accredited 2-year, 4-year or graduate institution in United States. Designated institutions: Public postsecondary institutions in Texas.
Eligibility: Applicant must be visually impaired or hearing impaired. Applicant must be U.S. citizen or permanent resident residing in Texas.
Basis for selection: Applicant must demonstrate depth of character.
Application requirements: Proof of eligibility. Certification of disability.
Additional information: Average award $951. Must be certified by relevant state vocational rehabilitation agency and have high school diploma or equivalent. Deadlines vary.

Amount of award:	$976
Number of awards:	2,478
Total amount awarded:	$2,423,484

Contact:
Apply to financial aid office at institution.
Phone: 800-242-3062
Fax: 512-427-6420
Web: www.collegefortexans.com

Tuition Equalization Grant (TEG)

Type of award: Scholarship.
Intended use: For undergraduate or graduate study at accredited 2-year, 4-year or graduate institution in United States. Designated institutions: Private, non-profit colleges or universities in Texas.
Eligibility: Applicant must be U.S. citizen or permanent resident residing in Texas.
Basis for selection: Applicant must demonstrate financial need.
Application requirements: Proof of eligibility. Selective Service registration or exemption from requirement.
Additional information: Religion, theology majors or athletic scholarship recipients not eligible. National Merit finalists who are not Texas residents are eligible. Award covers difference between applicant's tuition at private institution and what applicant would pay at public institution. Applicants should contact the financial aid office at the Texas private college/ university they plan to attend for other information on applying for this program.

Number of awards:	23,935

Contact:
Texas Higher Education Coordinating Board
Student Services Division
P. O. Box 12788
Austin, TX 78711-2788
Phone: 800-242-3062
Web: www.collegefortexans.com

Tuition Exemption for Children of Disabled or Deceased Firefighters, Peace Officers, Game Wardens, and Employees of Correctional Institutions

Type of award: Scholarship, renewable.
Intended use: For undergraduate or graduate study at 2-year or 4-year institution in United States. Designated institutions: Public postsecondary institutions in Texas.
Eligibility: Applicant must be no older than 21. Applicant must be residing in Texas. Applicant's parent must have been

killed or disabled in work-related accident as fire fighter, police officer or public safety officer.

Application requirements: Proof of eligibility. Completed Texas Higher Education Coordinating Board form.

Additional information: Applicants must be child of paid or volunteer firefighter; paid municipal, county, or state peace officer; custodial employee of Department of Corrections; or game warden disabled or killed in the line of duty. Applicant must apply before 21st birthday. Applicant must enroll in courses that use tax support to cover some of their cost. Maximum award is one year's tuition and fees. Applicant must obtain form letter from Texas Higher Education Coordinating Board, have parent's former employer complete form, and submit form back to Texas Higher Education Coordinating Board. The Board will notify applicant's institution of eligibility.

   Number of awards: 74

Contact:
Texas Higher Education Coordinating Board
Student Services Division
P O. Box 12788
Austin, TX 78711-2788
Phone: 800-242-3062
Web: www.collegefortexans.com

Tuition Exemption for Children of U.S. Military POW/MIAs

Type of award: Scholarship, renewable.
Intended use: For undergraduate study at accredited 2-year or 4-year institution. Designated institutions: Public postsecondary institutions in Texas.
Eligibility: Applicant must be no older than 25. Applicant must be U.S. citizen or permanent resident residing in Texas. Applicant must be dependent of POW/MIA.
Application requirements: Proof of eligibility. Documentation from Department of Defense that a parent, classified as Texas resident, is missing in action or a prisoner of war.
Additional information: Applicants 22 to 25 years of age must receive most of their support from a parent. Applicant must enroll in courses that use tax support to cover some of their cost. Maximum award is tuition and fees. Average award last year: $857. Applicants should contact the financial aid office at the college/university they plan to attend for other information on applying for this program.

   Number of awards: 3
   Number of applicants: 3

Contact:
Apply through financial aid office of institution.
Phone: 800-242-3062
Web: www.collegefortexans.com

Textilease Corporation

Oscar Stempler Scholarship

Type of award: Scholarship, renewable.
Intended use: For undergraduate study at accredited vocational, 2-year or 4-year institution.
Eligibility: Applicant or parent must be employed by Textilease Corporation.
Basis for selection: Applicant must demonstrate financial need.

Additional information: For further information or an application, contact Textilease Corporation directly.
   Amount of award: $600-$2,000

Theodore R. and Vivian M. Johnson Scholarship Foundation

The Theodore R. and Vivian M. Johnson Scholarship

Type of award: Scholarship, renewable.
Intended use: For undergraduate study at accredited 2-year or 4-year institution.
Eligibility: Applicant or parent must be employed by United Parcel Service--Florida.
Basis for selection: Applicant must demonstrate financial need.
Additional information: For further information or an application, contact UPS-Florida directly or write to Citizens' Scholarship Foundation of America.
   Amount of award: $500-$5,000

Contact:
Citizens' Scholarship Foundation of America
Theodore R. and Vivian M. Johnson Scholarship
P.O. Box 297
St. Peter, MN 56082

ThinkQuest

ThinkQuest Internet Challenge

Type of award: Scholarship, renewable.
Intended use: For undergraduate study.
Eligibility: Applicant must be at least 12, no older than 19.
Basis for selection: Competition/talent/interest in Web-site design.
Additional information: Website design contest. Students work in teams of two or three to build Websites used as learning tools by other students. Categories include arts & literature, science & mathematics, social sciences, sports & health and interdisciplinary. Must register with ThinkQuest (no fee). First deadline for proposal (submit on Website); second deadline for entry. Visit Website for rules and details.

   Amount of award: $100-$5,000
   Number of awards: 100
   Number of applicants: 10,000
   Application deadline: May 31, September 5
   Notification begins: October 15

Contact:
ThinkQuest
200 Business Park Drive
Armonk, NY 10504
Phone: 800-618-4465
Web: www.thinkquest.org

Third Marine Division Association

Third Marine Division Memorial Scholarship Fund

Type of award: Scholarship, renewable.
Intended use: For undergraduate study at accredited vocational, 2-year or 4-year institution in United States.
Eligibility: Applicant or parent must be member/participant of Third Marine Division Association. Applicant must be U.S. citizen. Applicant must be dependent of active service person in the Marines. Must be dependent child of active duty Marines or Navy Corpsmen now serving or who have served in 3rd Marine division.
Basis for selection: Applicant must demonstrate financial need.
Application requirements: Proof of eligibility. Financial aid form.
Additional information: Number of awards varies. Parent must be a member of Third Marine Division Association for at least two years. Eligible dependent children automatically receive renewal application forms upon submission of copies of grade reports.

Amount of award:	$500-$1,500
Application deadline:	April 15

Contact:
Third Marine Division Association
3111 Sundial Drive
Dallas, TX 75229-3757

Third Wave Foundation

Scholarship Program for Young Women

Type of award: Scholarship.
Intended use: For undergraduate or graduate study at accredited vocational, 2-year, 4-year or graduate institution in United States.
Eligibility: Applicant must be female, no older than 29.
Basis for selection: Applicant must demonstrate financial need and service orientation.
Application requirements: Recommendations, essay, transcript, proof of eligibility.
Additional information: Applicant should also be involved as activist, artist, or cultural worker working on issues such as racism, homophobia, sexism, or other forms of inequality. Visit Website for additional details and application.

Amount of award:	$500-$5,000
Number of awards:	10
Number of applicants:	180
Application deadline:	April 1, October 1

Contact:
Third Wave Foundation
116 E 16th Street, 7th Floor
New York, NY 10003
Phone: 212-388-1898
Fax: 212-982-3321
Web: www.thirdwavefoundation.org

Thurgood Marshall Scholarship Fund

Thurgood Marshall Scholarship Award

Type of award: Scholarship, renewable.
Intended use: For full-time undergraduate study at 4-year institution. Designated institutions: One of 44 designated historically black public universities.
Eligibility: Applicant must be U.S. citizen.
Basis for selection: Applicant must demonstrate high academic achievement and service orientation.
Application requirements: Recommendations, essay, transcript. Minimum 3.0 GPA. Must have 1100 combined SAT scores and 25 ACT score.
Additional information: Must be admitted to one of 44 historically black colleges and universities before applying. Download list of institutions from Website. Must have a high school GPA of not less than 3.0 and maintain 3.0 GPA throughout duration of the scholarship. Awards are made directly to applicant's university. Contact university's Thurgood Marshall Scholarship Fund campus coordinator directly for more information.

Amount of award:	$4,400
Number of awards:	2,000
Number of applicants:	3,000
Total amount awarded:	$1,700,000

Contact:
Thurgood Marshall Scholarship Fund
100 Park Avenue
10th Floor
New York, NY 10017
Phone: 877-690-TMSF
Web: www.thurgoodmarshallfund.org

Time Warner Inc.

Time Warner Academic Award

Type of award: Scholarship, renewable.
Intended use: For undergraduate study at accredited vocational, 2-year or 4-year institution.
Eligibility: Applicant or parent must be employed by Time Warner Inc.
Basis for selection: Applicant must demonstrate financial need.
Additional information: For further information or an application, contact Time Warner Inc. directly.

Amount of award:	$2,000-$5,000

TJX Companies, Inc.

TJX Companies, Inc. Scholarship Program

Type of award: Scholarship.
Intended use: For undergraduate study at vocational, 2-year or 4-year institution.

Eligibility: Applicant or parent must be employed by The TJX Companies, Inc. Applicant must be high school senior.
Additional information: For further information or an application, contact TJX Companies Incorporated directly.
    Amount of award: $1,000

TMI Companies

Larry R. Strand Memorial Scholarship Program

Type of award: Scholarship.
Intended use: For undergraduate study at vocational, 2-year or 4-year institution.
Eligibility: Applicant or parent must be employed by TMI Companies. Applicant must be high school senior.
Additional information: For further information or an application, contact TMI Companies directly.
    Amount of award: $750

Transportation Clubs International

Charlotte Woods Memorial Scholarship

Type of award: Scholarship.
Intended use: For sophomore, junior, senior or graduate study.
Basis for selection: Major/career interest in transportation. Applicant must demonstrate financial need, high academic achievement and depth of character.
Application requirements: Recommendations, essay, transcript.
Additional information: Student must be a member or a dependent of a member of the Transportation Clubs International.
    Amount of award: $1,000
    Number of awards: 1
    Application deadline: April 30
    Total amount awarded: $1,000
Contact:
Transportation Clubs International
P.O. Box 52
Arabi, LA 70032

Denny Lydic Scholarship

Type of award: Scholarship.
Intended use: For sophomore, junior, senior or graduate study.
Basis for selection: Major/career interest in transportation. Applicant must demonstrate financial need, high academic achievement and depth of character.
Application requirements: Recommendations, essay, transcript.
    Amount of award: $500
    Number of awards: 1
    Application deadline: April 30
    Total amount awarded: $500

Contact:
Transportation Clubs International
P.O. Box 52
Arabi, LA 70032

Ginger and Fred Deines Canada Scholarship

Type of award: Scholarship.
Intended use: For sophomore, junior, senior or graduate study in United States or Canada.
Eligibility: Applicant must be international student or Canadian citizen.
Basis for selection: Major/career interest in transportation. Applicant must demonstrate financial need, high academic achievement and depth of character.
Application requirements: Recommendations, essay, transcript.
Additional information: For a student of Canadian nationality enrolled in a Canadian or U.S. institution.
    Amount of award: $1,500
    Number of awards: 1
    Application deadline: April 30
    Total amount awarded: $1,500
Contact:
Transportation Clubs International
P.O. Box 52
Arabi, LA 70032

Ginger and Fred Deines Mexico Scholarship

Type of award: Scholarship.
Intended use: For sophomore, junior, senior or graduate study. Designated institutions: Institutions in United States or Mexico.
Eligibility: Applicant must be international student or Mexican citizen.
Basis for selection: Major/career interest in transportation. Applicant must demonstrate financial need, high academic achievement and depth of character.
Application requirements: Recommendations, essay, transcript.
Additional information: For a student of Mexican nationality enrolled in a Mexican or U.S. institution.
    Amount of award: $1,500
    Number of awards: 1
    Application deadline: April 30
    Total amount awarded: $1,500
Contact:
Transportation Clubs International
P.O. Box 52
Arabi, LA 70032

Hooper Memorial Scholarship

Type of award: Scholarship.
Intended use: For sophomore, junior, senior or graduate study.
Basis for selection: Major/career interest in transportation. Applicant must demonstrate financial need, high academic achievement and depth of character.
Application requirements: Recommendations, essay, transcript.
    Amount of award: $1,500
    Number of awards: 1
    Application deadline: April 30
    Total amount awarded: $1,500

Contact:
Transportation Clubs International
P.O. Box 52
Arabi, LA 70032

Texas Transportation Scholarship

Type of award: Scholarship.
Intended use: For sophomore, junior, senior or graduate study.
Basis for selection: Major/career interest in transportation. Applicant must demonstrate financial need, high academic achievement and depth of character.
Application requirements: Recommendations, essay, transcript.
Additional information: Applicant must have been enrolled in a Texas school for some phase of education (elementary through high school).

Amount of award:	$1,500
Number of awards:	1
Application deadline:	April 30
Total amount awarded:	$1,000

Contact:
Transportation Clubs International
P.O. Box 52
Arabi, LA 70032

Travel and Tourism Research Association

J. Desmond Slattery Award: Student

Type of award: Scholarship.
Intended use: For undergraduate study at postsecondary institution.
Basis for selection: Competition/talent/interest in research paper, based on originality, clarity, overall marketing excellence. Major/career interest in tourism/travel.
Application requirements: Application (available online after November 1).
Additional information: Must submit original research paper of any length and abstract of 500-1,000 words. Paper will be judged on quality of research, originality, creativity, relation to tourism and travel, applicability and quality of presentation. Only undergraduates enrolled in degree-granting program qualify. Winner also receives plaque, one-year student TTRA membership, $300 travel allowance and complementary registration at TTRA annual conference. Award presented at annual conference in June.

Amount of award:	$700
Application deadline:	March 1

Contact:
Travel and Tourism Research Association
P.O. Box 2133
Boise, ID 83701
Phone: 208-429-9511
Fax: 208-429-9512
Web: www.ttra.com

Travel Research Grant

Type of award: Research grant.
Intended use: For undergraduate, graduate or non-degree study.
Basis for selection: Major/career interest in tourism/travel.

Application requirements: Research proposal.
Additional information: Applicant must propose to develop technique or methodology which improves measurement, decreases costs, demonstrates reliability and improves information for better application and understanding by management. Project must show significant benefits to travel and tourism industry. Grant recipient has three years to complete project. Material must be submitted in English. Winner also receives plaque, travel expenses to and complimentary registration at TTRA annual conference.

Amount of award:	$2,000
Number of awards:	1
Application deadline:	March 1

Contact:
Travel and Tourism Research Association
P.O. Box 2133
Boise, ID 83701
Phone: 208-429-9511
Fax: 208-429-9512
Web: www.ttra.com

Treacy Company

Treacy Company Scholarship

Type of award: Scholarship, renewable.
Intended use: For full-time freshman or sophomore study at postsecondary institution.
Eligibility: Applicant must be residing in Idaho, Montana, North Dakota or South Dakota.
Basis for selection: Applicant must demonstrate financial need, depth of character, leadership, seriousness of purpose and service orientation.
Application requirements: Transcript. Completed application; letter stating reason for applying, including personal information.
Additional information: Student must be resident of North Dakota, South Dakota, Idaho, or Montana; student's school need not be in those states. Must write for application; applications available from January to end of May.

Amount of award:	$400
Number of awards:	70
Number of applicants:	350
Application deadline:	June 15
Notification begins:	July 31
Total amount awarded:	$28,000

Contact:
Treacy Company
P. O. Box 1479
Helena, MT 59624

Tri-Gas Inc.

Matheson Tri-Gas Scholarship Program

Type of award: Scholarship, renewable.
Intended use: For undergraduate study at vocational, 2-year or 4-year institution.
Eligibility: Applicant or parent must be employed by Matheson Tri-Gas Inc. Applicant must be high school senior.

Additional information: For further information or an application, contact Matheson Tri-Gas Incorporated directly.

    Amount of award: $2,000

Trinity Episcopal Church

Shannon Scholarship

Type of award: Scholarship, renewable.
Intended use: For undergraduate study.
Eligibility: Applicant must be female. Applicant must be Episcopal. Applicant must be residing in Pennsylvania.
Basis for selection: Applicant must demonstrate financial need.
Application requirements: Proof of eligibility. Application (available April 15).
Additional information: Only open to daughters of Episcopal clergy in state of Pennsylvania. Must apply for state and federal financial assistance first. Previous recipients may reapply.

Amount of award:	$500-$4,000
Number of awards:	14
Number of applicants:	14
Application deadline:	May 30
Total amount awarded:	$34,000

Contact:
Trinity Episcopal Church
200 South Second Street
Pottsville, PA 17901

True Value

True Value Scholarship

Type of award: Scholarship.
Intended use: For freshman study at accredited 2-year or 4-year institution.
Eligibility: Applicant or parent must be employed by ServiStar/Coast to Coast Corp.
Additional information: Parent must be a Coast to Coast store owner. For further information or an application, contact ServiStar/Coast to Coast Corporation directly or write to Citizens' Scholarship Foundation of America.

    Amount of award: $1,000

Contact:
Citizens' Scholarship Foundation of America
Servistar/Coast to Coast Melamed Scholarship
P.O. Box 297
St. Peter, MN 56082

Trustmark Foundation

Trustmark's Ralph J. Echert Foundation College Scholarship Program

Type of award: Scholarship, renewable.
Intended use: For undergraduate study at accredited vocational, 2-year or 4-year institution.

Eligibility: Applicant or parent must be employed by Trustmark Foundation.
Additional information: For further information or an application, contact Trustmark Foundation directly.

    Amount of award: $1,000

Tuttle-Click Automotive Group

Tuttle-Click Automotive Group Education Assistance Program

Type of award: Scholarship, renewable.
Intended use: For undergraduate study at accredited vocational, 2-year or 4-year institution.
Eligibility: Applicant or parent must be employed by Tuttle-Click Automotive Group. Applicant must be high school senior.
Additional information: For further information or application, contact Tuttle-Click Automotive Group directly.

    Amount of award: $3,000

Twin City Fan Companies, Ltd.

Twin City Fan Scholarship Program

Type of award: Scholarship.
Intended use: For undergraduate study at accredited vocational, 2-year or 4-year institution.
Eligibility: Applicant or parent must be employed by Twin City Fan Companies, Ltd.
Additional information: For further information or an application, contact Twin City Fan Companies, Ltd. directly.

    Amount of award: $500-$1,000

Two/Ten International Footwear Foundation

Two/Ten International Footwear Foundation Scholarship

Type of award: Scholarship, renewable.
Intended use: For full-time undergraduate study at accredited vocational, 2-year or 4-year institution.
Eligibility: Applicant or parent must be employed by Footwear/Leather Industry. Applicant must be U.S. citizen.
Basis for selection: Applicant must demonstrate financial need, high academic achievement, depth of character, leadership and seriousness of purpose.
Application requirements: Recommendations, essay, transcript, proof of eligibility.
Additional information: Must have worked 500 hours in footwear or leather industries or have parent currently employed in this field for minimum of one year.

Amount of award:	$200-$3,000
Number of awards:	514
Application deadline:	December 15
Notification begins:	June 15
Total amount awarded:	$627,000

Contact:
Two/Ten International Footwear Foundation
Attn: Scholarship Department
1466 Main Street
Waltham, MA 02451-1623
Phone: 800-346-3210

U.S. Army Recruiting Command

Montgomery GI Bill (MGIB)

Type of award: Scholarship.
Intended use: For undergraduate or graduate study at accredited postsecondary institution in United States.
Eligibility: Applicant must be at least 18, no older than 34. Applicant must be U.S. citizen. Applicant must be in military service in the Army.
Basis for selection: Applicant must demonstrate depth of character, leadership, patriotism, seriousness of purpose and service orientation.
Application requirements: Interview. Armed Services Vocational Aptitude Battery required.
Additional information: Enlistment in U.S. active Army for two to four years required.

Amount of award:	$19,008-$23,400
Number of awards:	68,255

Contact:
U.S. Army Recruiting Command
P.O. Box 3219
Warminster, PA 18974-9844
Phone: 800-USA-ARMY

Montgomery GI Bill Plus Army College Fund

Type of award: Scholarship.
Intended use: For undergraduate or graduate study at accredited postsecondary institution.
Eligibility: Applicant must be at least 18, no older than 34, returning adult student. Applicant must be U.S. citizen. Applicant must be in military service in the Army.
Basis for selection: Applicant must demonstrate depth of character, leadership, patriotism, seriousness of purpose and service orientation.
Application requirements: Interview. Armed Services Vocational Aptitude Battery required.
Additional information: Enlistment in active Army for two to four years required. Enrollment in colleges outside United States must be approved by Veterans Administration.

Amount of award:	$26,500-$50,000
Number of awards:	15,550

Contact:
U.S. Army Recruiting Command
P.O. Box 3219
Warminster, PA 18974-9844
Phone: 800-USA-ARMY

Selected Reserve Montgomery GI Bill

Type of award: Scholarship.
Intended use: For undergraduate or graduate study at accredited postsecondary institution.
Eligibility: Applicant must be at least 17, no older than 34. Applicant must be U.S. citizen. Applicant must be veteran who served in the Army or Reserves/National Guard.
Basis for selection: Applicant must demonstrate depth of character, leadership, patriotism, seriousness of purpose and service orientation.
Application requirements: Interview. Armed Services Vocational Aptitude Battery required.
Additional information: Enlistment in U.S. Army Reserve for minimum of six years required.

Amount of award:	$9,468
Number of awards:	39,560

Contact:
U.S. Army
P.O. Box 3219
Warminster, PA 18974-9844
Phone: 800-USA-ARMY

U.S. Bancorp

U.S. Bancorp Educational Awards Program

Type of award: Scholarship, renewable.
Intended use: For undergraduate study at 4-year institution in United States.
Eligibility: Applicant or parent must be employed by U.S. Bancorp. Applicant must be U.S. citizen or permanent resident.
Basis for selection: Applicant must demonstrate financial need and high academic achievement.
Additional information: Applicant's parent must be employed by U.S. Bancorp.

Amount of award:	$1,000

Contact:
Contact U.S. Bancorp for application and further details.

U.S. Bank Student Banking Division

U.S. Bank Internet Scholarship Program

Type of award: Scholarship.
Intended use: For full-time undergraduate study at 2-year or 4-year institution in United States. Designated institutions: Eligible schools must participate in Federal Family Education Loan Program (FFELP).
Eligibility: Applicant must be high school senior. Applicant must be U.S. citizen or permanent resident.
Basis for selection: Applicant must demonstrate depth of character.

Application requirements: Essay, transcript, proof of eligibility. Must provide GPA. Must provide transcript if merit award; must provide signed letter from counselor on goals.
Additional information: Selection based on merit-based awards and statement of goals, involvement awards. Application available exclusively online. Visit Website for complete information.

Amount of award:	$1,000
Number of awards:	25
Application deadline:	February 28
Notification begins:	April 1
Total amount awarded:	$25,000

Contact:
See Website for application and complete information.
Phone: 800-242-1200
Web: www.usbank.com/studentloans

U.S. Cellular

The U.S. Cellular Scholarship Program

Type of award: Scholarship.
Intended use: For undergraduate study at vocational, 2-year or 4-year institution.
Eligibility: Applicant or parent must be employed by U.S. Cellular. Applicant must be high school senior.
Additional information: For further information or an application, contact U.S. Cellular directly.

Amount of award:	$2,500

U.S. Department of Agriculture

USDA 1890 National Scholars Program

Type of award: Scholarship.
Intended use: For full-time undergraduate study at 4-year institution in United States. Designated institutions: Must be used at one of 17 designated Historically Black 1890 Institutions.
Eligibility: Applicant must be high school senior.
Basis for selection: Major/career interest in agriculture; agribusiness; agricultural education; agricultural economics; food science/technology; computer/information sciences; veterinary medicine; biology or chemistry. Applicant must demonstrate high academic achievement.
Application requirements: Recommendations, transcript. Must have minimum 1000 SAT, 21 ACT and 3.0 GPA. Transcript with official school seal and signature.
Additional information: Scholarship covers full tuition and fees for four years. Number of awards varies depending on funding.

Amount of award:	$60,000
Number of applicants:	800
Application deadline:	January 15

Contact:
U.S. Department of Agriculture
USDA 1890 National Scholars Program Manager
STOP 5474, 5601 Sunnyside Avenue
Beltsville, MD 20705
Phone: 301-504-2229
Fax: 301-504-2248
Web: http://1890scholars.program.usda.gov

U.S. Department of Education

Federal Pell Grant Program

Type of award: Scholarship, renewable.
Intended use: For undergraduate study at 2-year or 4-year institution.
Eligibility: Applicant must be U.S. citizen or permanent resident.
Basis for selection: Applicant must demonstrate financial need.
Application requirements: Proof of eligibility. Send FAFSA.
Additional information: $3,125 represents maximum yearly award through June 30, 2001. Grant based on financial need. Pell grants often provide foundation of financial aid to which other aid may be added. Additional need analysis form may be required. Must not have defaulted on federal grant or educational loan. Must not have previously earned baccalaureate or professional degree.

Amount of award:	$3,125
Application deadline:	June 30
Notification begins:	August 29

Contact:
Federal Student Aid Information Center
PO Box 84
Washington, DC 20044-0084
Phone: 800-4-FED-AID or 800-730-8913
Web: www.ed.gov

Federal Supplemental Educational Opportunity Grant Program

Type of award: Scholarship, renewable.
Intended use: For undergraduate study at accredited vocational, 2-year or 4-year institution in United States.
Eligibility: Applicant must be U.S. citizen or permanent resident.
Basis for selection: Applicant must demonstrate financial need.
Application requirements: Proof of eligibility. Send FAFSA.
Additional information: Priority given to Federal Pell Grant recipients with exceptional financial need. Must not have defaulted on federal grant or educational loan. Awards not generally made to students enrolled less than half-time. Unlike Pell Grants, availability FSEOG awards not federally guaranteed, but depends on availability of funds at student's institution.

Amount of award:	$100-$4,000
Application deadline:	July 2

Contact:
Federal Student Aid Information Center
PO Box 84
Washington, DC 20044-0084
Phone: 800-4-FED-AID
Web: www.ed.gov

Robert C. Byrd Honors Scholarship Program

Type of award: Scholarship, renewable.
Intended use: For undergraduate study at postsecondary institution in United States.
Eligibility: Applicant must be high school senior. Applicant must be U.S. citizen or permanent resident.
Basis for selection: Applicant must demonstrate high academic achievement.
Application requirements: Proof of eligibility.
Additional information: Merit-based. Renewable up to three years. Funds very limited. Selections by state agencies supervising public elementary/secondary schools. Awards made in all 50 states, District of Columbia, Puerto Rico and Insular Areas. Contact your high school guidance counselor for details. Total dollars and number of awards are national totals. Number of awards represents first-time awards.

Amount of award:	$1,500
Number of awards:	6,928
Total amount awarded:	$41,001,000

Contact:
Higher Education Program
U.S. Department of Education
1990 K Street NW, 6th Floor
Washington, DC 20006-8511
Phone: 202-502-7777
Web: www.ed.gov

U.S. Department of Educational Rehabilitation Services Administration

Vocational Rehabilitation Scholarship

Type of award: Scholarship, renewable.
Intended use: For undergraduate or graduate study at postsecondary institution in United States.
Eligibility: Applicant must be physically challenged.
Application requirements: Proof of eligibility.
Additional information: The VR program provides a wide range of services and job training to people with disabilities who want to work. Must have medically verifiable disability that constitutes substantial impediment to employment. Award may be used for programs of study leading to development of employment skills. Number of scholarships awarded varies; amounts vary depending on state vocational rehabilitation agency. See Website for more info.

Number of awards:	1,500
Total amount awarded:	$233,897,700

Contact:
Rehabilitation Services Administration
330 C Street, S.W.
Room 3028
Washington, DC 20203
Web: www.ed.gov/offices/OSERS/

U.S. Department of Health and Human Services

National Health Services Corps Scholarship

Type of award: Scholarship.
Intended use: For full-time undergraduate, post-bachelor's certificate or postgraduate study at accredited 4-year or graduate institution in United States.
Eligibility: Applicant must be U.S. citizen.
Basis for selection: Major/career interest in midwifery; nursing; nurse practitioner; physician assistant or osteopathic medicine. Applicant must demonstrate depth of character, seriousness of purpose and service orientation.
Application requirements: Interview, proof of eligibility. The scholarship is specifically for students pursuing allopathic (MD) and osteopathic (DO) medecine; nurse midwifery; family nurse practitioner and physician assistant education. Doctorate nurse training ineligable, pre-medical students ineligable. Submission of required documentation; personal interview.
Additional information: Awardees commit to providing health care service in underserved communities anywhere in the U.S. A one year service owed for every year of scholarship support: minimum service commitment is two years; maximum is four years. Entire scholarship award is taxable. Federal taxes only withheld from monthly stipend payment. Must be in training program.

Amount of award:	Full tuition
Number of awards:	284
Number of applicants:	1,838
Application deadline:	March 30

Contact:
United States Department of Health and Human Services
National Health Service Corps
4350 East West Highway, 10th Floor
Bethesda, MD 20814
Phone: 800-638-0824

U.S. Department of Interior-Bureau of Indian Affairs

Indians Higher Education Grant Program

Type of award: Scholarship.
Intended use: For full-time undergraduate study at accredited 2-year or 4-year institution.
Eligibility: Applicant must be Alaskan native or American Indian. Member of tribal group served by bureau. Applicant must be U.S. citizen.

Basis for selection: Applicant must demonstrate financial need.
Application requirements: Proof of eligibility. Application.
Additional information: Deadlines vary. Contact tribe or bureau agency serving tribe for application. Check Website for tribal eligibility and for tribal directory contact information. Only write Department of the Interior/Bureau of Indian Affairs for information.
Contact:
U.S. Department of Interior-Bureau of Indian Affairs
Office of Education Programs MS 3512- MIB
1849 C Street, NW
Washington, DC 20240
Web: www.doi.gov/bureau-indian-affairs.html

U.S. Dept. of Justice, Office of the Police Corps and Law Enforcement Education

Police Corps Scholarship

Type of award: Scholarship, renewable.
Intended use: For full-time undergraduate or graduate study at accredited 4-year or graduate institution.
Eligibility: Applicant must be U.S. citizen or permanent resident.
Basis for selection: Major/career interest in criminal justice/law enforcement. Applicant must demonstrate high academic achievement, leadership and service orientation.
Application requirements: Interview, recommendations, essay, proof of eligibility. Each state has its own application form and requirements.
Additional information: Must be interested in law enforcement but may major in any subject. Program is active in 30 states. May be resident of one state and study in another. Applicants must commit to serving as law enforcement officers after graduation for at least four years. Must undergo 16-24 weeks of training prior to police service. Must be chosen based on mental, physical and emotional criteria. Tuition reimbursement available for upperclassmen; transfer students from community colleges to 4-year schools are eligible for scholarship/tuition reimbursement. Total of up to $30,000 may be awarded toward individual's degree. Visit Website for list of participating states, eligibility requirements and application information.

Amount of award:	$7,500-$30,000
Number of awards:	600
Total amount awarded:	$3,000,000

Contact:
Office of the Police Corps and Law Enforcement Education
U.S. Department of Justice
810 Seventh Street, NW
Washington, DC 20503
Phone: 800-421-6770 or 888-942-6777
Fax: 202-353-0598
Web: www.ojp.usdoj.gov/opclee

Police Corps Scholarships for Children of Officers Killed in the Line of Duty

Type of award: Scholarship.
Intended use: For undergraduate or graduate study.
Eligibility: Applicant's parent must have been killed or disabled in work-related accident as police officer.
Basis for selection: Applicant must demonstrate high academic achievement.
Application requirements: Proof of eligibility. To be considered "dependent," at time of parent's death student must be under 21 or be receiving more than half of financial support from parents. Each state has own application form.
Additional information: For dependent children of local, state or Federal law enforcement officers killed in the line of duty. Program is active in 30 states. Program must have been in existence in officer's state at time of death. A total of up to $30,000 may be awarded toward an individual's degree. Visit Website for list of participating states, eligibility requirements and application information.

Amount of award:	$7,500-$30,000

Contact:
Office of the Police Corps and Law Enforcement Education
U.S. Department of Justice
810 Seventh Street, NW
New York, NY 20513
Phone: 800-421-6770 or 888-942-6777
Fax: 202-353-0598
Web: www.ojp.usdoj.gov/opclee

U.S. Environmental Protection Agency

EPA National Network for Environmental Management Studies Fellowship

Type of award: Research grant.
Intended use: For undergraduate or graduate study.
Eligibility: Applicant must be U.S. citizen or permanent resident.
Basis for selection: Major/career interest in environmental science; public relations; communications; computer/information sciences or law.
Application requirements: Recommendations, transcript. One-page work plan proposal. Must submit one letter of reference from faculty member or department head very familiar with student's work/ qualifications; letter must state how research project will benefit student's academic studies. Undergraduate students must: 1) enroll in academic program directly related to pollution abatement/control; 2) have cumulative 3.0 GPA; 3) have already completed four courses related to environmental field. Seniors who graduate prior to completion of advertised NNEMS fellowship period ineligible unless admitted to graduate school with submittable verification.
Additional information: NNEMS Program provides undergraduate/graduate students with research opportunities/ experience at EPA locations nationwide. NNEMS develops/ distributes annual catalog listing all available research opportunities for coming year. Selected students receive stipend for performing research project. Projects available in additional

areas: environmental management/administration, environmental policy, regulation and law.

Amount of award:	$5,400-$9,160
Number of awards:	80

Contact:
US Environmental Protection Agency NNEMS Fellowship Program
Office of Environmental Education
1200 Pennsylvania Avenue, NW (1704A)
Washington, DC 20460
Web: www.epa.gov/enviroed/students.html

Minority Academic Institutions Undergraduate Student Fellowships

Type of award: Scholarship.
Intended use: For full-time junior or senior study at accredited 2-year or 4-year institution in United States. Designated institutions: .
Eligibility: Applicant must be African American, Mexican American, Hispanic American, Puerto Rican or American Indian. Applicant must be U.S. citizen or permanent resident.
Basis for selection: Major/career interest in environmental science; biology; atmospheric sciences/meteorology; oceanography/marine studies; cartography or zoology. Applicant must demonstrate financial need, high academic achievement and seriousness of purpose.
Application requirements: Recommendations, essay, transcript, proof of eligibility.
Additional information: Full tuition waiver (with expenses, travel) up to $15,200/yr. for two years. Must complete summer internship at EPA facility between funded junior and senior years. Must be enrolled in environmental program at eligible institution. Minority Academic Institutions are defined as Historically Black Colleges or Universities (HBCU's), Hispanic Serving Institutions (HIS's), and Tribal Colleges (TC's). Visit Website for more information and to request "pre-application".

Number of awards:	25
Application deadline:	November 20

Contact:
U.S. Environmental Protection Agency
Peer Review Division (8703R)
401 M Street NW
Washington, DC 20460
Phone: 800-490-9194
Web: http://es.epa.gov/ncerqa/rfa/ungradmaifell01.html

U.S. Navy

NROTC Scholarship Program Immediate Selection Decision (ISD)

Type of award: Scholarship.
Intended use: For full-time undergraduate study at 4-year institution.
Eligibility: Applicant must be at least 17, no older than 22. Applicant must be U.S. citizen.
Basis for selection: Major/career interest in engineering, nuclear; automotive technology; aviation repair or engineering, electrical/electronic. Applicant must demonstrate high academic achievement, depth of character, leadership, patriotism, seriousness of purpose and service orientation.

Application requirements: Interview, recommendations, transcript. Must achieve competitive SAT or ACT scores and be ranked in the top 20% of their high school class.
Additional information: Highly competitive and based on individual merit, the program targets students who plan on taking technical majors. Immediate Selection Decision scholarships can only be used at schools hosting the NROTC program or cross-enrolled with a host school. SAT scores required. ISD scholarships pay for tuition, fees, book allowance, uniforms and a $250 monthy allowance. They do not pay for room and board. Scholarship nominees must be medically qualified for the NROTC Scholarship Program.

Amount of award:	Full tuition
Number of awards:	55
Number of applicants:	58
Application deadline:	December 1

Contact:
U.S. Navy-Marine Corps
Contact Local Recruiter
Phone: 800-USA-NAVY (800-872-6289)

U.S. Navy-Marine Corps

NROTC Scholarship Program

Type of award: Scholarship.
Intended use: For full-time undergraduate study at 2-year or 4-year institution.
Eligibility: Applicant must be at least 17, no older than 22. Applicant must be U.S. citizen.
Basis for selection: Major/career interest in military science. Applicant must demonstrate high academic achievement, depth of character, leadership, patriotism, seriousness of purpose and service orientation.
Application requirements: Interview, recommendations, transcript. Must achieve competitive SAT or ACT scores.
Additional information: Applicants with previous active duty service may be eligible for age waivers. NROTC scholarships must be used at schools hosting the NROTC Program or schools cross-enrolled with host school. SAT scores must me submitted by December 31. NROTC scholarships pay for college tuition, fees, book allowance, uniforms and a $250 monthly allowance. They do not pay for room and board. Scholarship nominees must be medically qualified for the NROTC Scholarship Program.

Amount of award:	Full tuition
Number of awards:	2,524
Number of applicants:	4,536
Application deadline:	December 31, January 31

Contact:
Contact local Navy Recruiter
Phone: 800-872-6289

U.S. Navy/Marine NROTC College Scholarship Program

ROTC/Navy Marine Two-Year Scholarship Program

Type of award: Scholarship.
Intended use: For full-time junior or senior study at accredited 4-year institution in United States. Designated institutions: At a college or university hosting the NROTC Program.
Eligibility: Applicant must be at least 17, no older than 22. Applicant must be U.S. citizen.
Basis for selection: Applicant must demonstrate high academic achievement.
Application requirements: Interview, transcript. Supply SAT scores.
Additional information: NROTC scholarships must be used at a college or university hosting the NROTC Program or cross-enrolled with a host school. NROTC scholarships pay for college tuition, fees, book allowance, uniforms and a $250 monthly allowance. They do not pay for room and board. Scholarship nominees must be medically qualified for the NROTC Scholarship Program. To have SAT score report sent, use code 0656.

  Amount of award: Full tuition
  Application deadline: December 31, January 31
Contact:
Recruitment Officer
801 North Randolph
Arlington, VA 22203-9933
Phone: 800-USA-NAVY
Web: www.nrotc.navy.mil

ROTC/Navy Nurse Corps Scholarship Program

Type of award: Scholarship.
Intended use: For full-time undergraduate study at accredited 4-year institution in United States.
Eligibility: Applicant must be at least 17, no older than 25, high school senior. Applicant must be U.S. citizen.
Basis for selection: Major/career interest in nursing. Applicant must demonstrate high academic achievement.
Application requirements: Interview, transcript.
Additional information: Four-year NROTC scholarships are available to students interested in pursuing bachelor of science degree in nursing (BSN). Must be enrolled in nursing degree program leading to BSN. Upon graduation, Nurse NROTC Scholarship Program midshipmen will be commissioned as reserve officers in the Navy Nurse Corps. Nurse NROTC eligibility and selection processes are the same as the regular four year NROTC Scholarship Program requirements. Academic, physical and military requirements differ slightly from regular NROTC. Does not cover room and board. To have SAT scores sent, use codes 0656. Contact your local recruiter for further details.

  Amount of award: Full tuition
Contact:
Recruitment Officer
801 North Randolph
Arlington, VA 22203-9933
Phone: 800-NAV-ROTC ext.325
Web: www.cnet.navy.mil

ROTC/Navy/Marine Four-Year Scholarship

Type of award: Scholarship.
Intended use: For full-time freshman study at accredited 4-year institution in United States. Designated institutions: At a college or university hosting the NROTC Program.
Eligibility: Applicant must be at least 17, no older than 25, high school senior. Applicant must be U.S. citizen.
Application requirements: Interview, transcript. Supply SAT scores.
Additional information: Scholarships are highly competitive and based on individual merit. ROTC scholarships must be used at a college or university hosting the ROTC Program or cross-enrolled with a host school. Provides full tuition, fees and $250 monthy allowance. They do not pay for room and board. Scholarship nominees must be mecically qualified for the ROTC Scholarship Program. To have SAT scores sent, use codes 0656.

  Amount of award: Full tuition
  Application deadline: July 1, December 1
Contact:
United States Navy/Marine NROTC College Scholarship Program
801 North Randolph
Arlington, VA 22203-9933
Phone: 800-NAV-ROTC
Web: www.cnet.navy.mil

Ukrainian Fraternal Association

Eugene and Elinor Kotur Scholarship

Type of award: Scholarship, renewable.
Intended use: For full-time sophomore, junior or senior study at accredited 4-year institution. Designated institutions: Contact sponsor for list of eligible institutions.
Eligibility: Applicant must be Ukrainian.
Basis for selection: Applicant must demonstrate financial need, high academic achievement and depth of character.
Application requirements: Essay, transcript, proof of eligibility. Autobiographical statement containing information regarding Ukrainian roots. Small photograph.
Additional information: Must have completed first year of undergraduate studies. Membership in the Ukrainian Fraternal Association is encouraged but not required for this scholarship.
  Amount of award: $1,000-$3,000
  Application deadline: May 1
Contact:
Ukranian Fraternal Association Scholarship Coordinator
440 Wyoming Avenue
Scranton, PA 18503

Ukrainian Fraternal Association Scholarship

Type of award: Scholarship, renewable.
Intended use: For full-time sophomore, junior or senior study.
Eligibility: Applicant or parent must be member/participant of Ukrainian Fraternal Association. Applicant must be Ukrainian.

Basis for selection: Applicant must demonstrate financial need and high academic achievement.
Application requirements: Essay, transcript.
Additional information: Applicant must be member of Ukrainian Fraternal Association, and must have completed first year of undergraduate study.

Amount of award:	$200-$1,000
Number of awards:	50
Number of applicants:	50
Application deadline:	June 15
Total amount awarded:	$10,000

Contact:
Ukrainian Fraternal Association Scholarship Coordinator
440 Wyoming Avenue
Scranton, PA 18503

ULLICO Inc. Family of Companies

ULLICO Scholarship

Type of award: Scholarship.
Intended use: For undergraduate study at accredited vocational, 2-year or 4-year institution.
Eligibility: Applicant or parent must be employed by ULLICO, Inc.
Basis for selection: Applicant must demonstrate financial need.
Additional information: Aplicant must be dependent of ULLICO employee. For further information or application, contact ULLICO directly.

Amount of award:	$500-$1,000

Ultramar Diamond Shamrock Corporation

Ultramar Diamond Shamrock Scholarship Program

Type of award: Scholarship.
Intended use: For undergraduate study at accredited vocational, 2-year or 4-year institution.
Eligibility: Applicant or parent must be employed by Ultramar Diamond Shamrock Corp. Applicant must be high school junior.
Basis for selection: Applicant must demonstrate high academic achievement.
Application requirements: Must take PSAT in fall of junior year of high school.
Additional information: Financial circumstances taken into account. Administered by National Merit Scholarship Corporation. Applicant need not be National Merit Scholarship winner. For further information and application, contact Ultramar Diamond Shamrock Corporation directly.

Amount of award:	$500-$2,000
Number of awards:	8
Number of applicants:	50

Contact:
Ultramar Diamond Shamrock Corporation
Attn. Scholarship Program
P.O. Box 696000
San Antonio, TX 7869-6000
Web: www.udscorp.com

Unico Foundation, Inc.

Alphonse A. Miele Scholarship

Type of award: Scholarship.
Intended use: For undergraduate study.
Eligibility: Applicant must be high school senior.
Basis for selection: Applicant must demonstrate financial need, high academic achievement, depth of character and leadership.
Application requirements: Recommendations, essay, transcript, proof of eligibility.
Additional information: Student must reside in the corporate limits of a city wherein an active chapter of Unico National is located. Award is for $1,500 per year for four years. Student does not have to be Italian.

Amount of award:	$6,000
Application deadline:	April 15

Contact:
Unico Foundation, Inc.
72 Burroughs Place
Bloomfield, NJ 07003
Phone: 973-748-9144

Major Don S. Gentile Scholarship

Type of award: Scholarship.
Intended use: For undergraduate study.
Eligibility: Applicant must be high school senior. Applicant must be Italian.
Basis for selection: Applicant must demonstrate financial need, high academic achievement, depth of character and leadership.
Application requirements: Recommendations, essay, transcript, proof of eligibility.
Additional information: Students must reside in corporate limits of a city wherein an active chapter of Unico National is located. Award is distributed in four annual installments of $1,500.

Amount of award:	$6,000
Application deadline:	April 15

Contact:
Unico Foundation, Inc.
72 Burroughs Place
Bloomfield, NJ 07003
Phone: 973-748-9144

Theodore Mazza Scholarship

Type of award: Scholarship.
Intended use: For undergraduate study.
Eligibility: Applicant must be high school senior.
Basis for selection: Major/career interest in architecture; art/art history, music or arts, general. Applicant must demonstrate financial need, high academic achievement, depth of character and leadership.
Application requirements: Recommendations, essay, transcript, proof of eligibility.

Additional information: Student must reside in the corporate limits of a city wherein an active chapter of Unico National is located. Award is distributed in four annual installments of $1,500.

Amount of award:	$6,000
Application deadline:	April 15

Contact:
Unico Foundation, Inc.
72 Burroughs Place
Bloomfield, NJ 07003

William C. Davini Scholarship

Type of award: Scholarship.
Intended use: For undergraduate study.
Eligibility: Applicant must be high school senior. Applicant must be Italian.
Basis for selection: Applicant must demonstrate financial need, high academic achievement, depth of character and leadership.
Application requirements: Recommendations, essay, transcript, proof of eligibility.
Additional information: Students must reside in the corporate limits of a city wherein an active chapter of Unico National is located. Award is distributed in four annual installments of $1,500.

Amount of award:	$6,000
Application deadline:	April 15

Contact:
Unico Foundation, Inc.
72 Burroughs Place
Bloomfield, NJ 07003

Union Pacific Corporation

Union Pacific Scholarship

Type of award: Scholarship, renewable.
Intended use: For full-time undergraduate study at 2-year or 4-year institution.
Eligibility: Applicant or parent must be employed by Union Pacific Corporation. Applicant must be high school junior.
Basis for selection: Applicant must demonstrate high academic achievement.
Application requirements: PSAT score taken in October.
Additional information: Award is given $1,000 per year for five years. Program not open to dependents of elected railroad officers. Applicant must be son or daughter of a full-time, retired, or deceased employee of Union Pacific.

Amount of award:	$5,000
Number of awards:	37
Number of applicants:	540
Application deadline:	January 1
Notification begins:	April 1

Contact:
Scholarship Administrator, Union Pacific Corporation
1700 Farnam Street
10th Floor North
Omaha, NE 68102
Phone: 402-271-3233

Unique Industries, Inc.

Unique Industries Inc. Scholarship Program

Type of award: Scholarship.
Intended use: For undergraduate study at accredited postsecondary institution.
Eligibility: Applicant or parent must be employed by Unique Industries, Inc. Applicant must be high school senior.
Basis for selection: Applicant must demonstrate financial need.
Additional information: For further information or an application, contact Unique Industries, Inc. directly.

Amount of award:	$2,000-$10,000

Unitarian Universalist Association

Stanfield and D'Orlando Art Scholarship

Type of award: Scholarship.
Intended use: For full-time undergraduate or first professional study in United States.
Eligibility: Applicant must be at least 16, returning adult student, high school senior. Applicant must be Unitarian Universalist.
Basis for selection: Major/career interest in arts, general. Applicant must demonstrate financial need, high academic achievement, depth of character and service orientation.
Application requirements: Portfolio, recommendations, essay, transcript, proof of eligibility.
Additional information: Total number of awards varies. Supporting materials due on or before March 1.

Application deadline:	February 15, March 1
Notification begins:	May 15

Contact:
Unitarian Universalist Association
25 Beacon Street
Boston, MA 02108-2824
Phone: 617-742-2100
Fax: 617-742-7025
Web: www.uua.org/info/scholarships.html

Unitarian Universalist Stanfield Art Scholarship

Type of award: Scholarship, renewable.
Intended use: For full-time undergraduate or graduate study at postsecondary institution.
Eligibility: Applicant must be Unitarian Universalist.
Basis for selection: Major/career interest in art/art history. Applicant must demonstrate financial need, high academic achievement, depth of character and service orientation.
Application requirements: Portfolio, recommendations, transcript, proof of eligibility.
Additional information: Must be preparing for career in fine arts: painting, drawing, or sculpture. Renewable with reapplication. Amount and number of awards vary.

Number of applicants: 10
Application deadline: February 15
Notification begins: May 15
Contact:
Unitarian Universalist Association
25 Beacon Street
Boston, MA 02108-2824
Phone: 617-742-2100

Unite

Unite National Scholarship

Type of award: Scholarship.
Intended use: For full-time freshman study at accredited 2-year or 4-year institution.
Eligibility: Applicant or parent must be member/participant of Unite.
Application requirements: Proof of eligibility. Proof of college acceptance.
Additional information: Parent must be Unite union member in good standing for at least two years. Children or grandchildren of officers or employees of Unite not eligible. Applicant must be entering college for first time. Award given over period of four years in $325 installments. Number of awards varies.

Amount of award: $1,300
Application deadline: June 15
Contact:
Unite
Scholarship Program/Education Department
1710 Broadway
New York, NY 10019

United Food and Commercial Workers Union

United Food and Commercial Workers Union Scholarship Program

Type of award: Scholarship.
Intended use: For full-time undergraduate study at accredited 4-year institution.
Eligibility: Applicant or parent must be member/participant of United Food and Commerical Workers. Applicant must be high school senior.
Application requirements: Transcript. Complete biographical questionaire. All applicants must submit SAT or ACT scores (except Canadian applicant).
Additional information: Applicant or applicant's parent must be member of United Food and Commercial Workers Union for one year prior to application.

Amount of award: $4,000
Number of awards: 7
Number of applicants: 4,000
Application deadline: December 31, March 15
Total amount awarded: $28,000

Contact:
United Food and Commercial Workers Union
1775 K Street, N.W.
Washington, DC 20006
Phone: 202-223-3111
Web: www.ufcw.org

United Methodist Church

United Methodist Bass Scholarship

Type of award: Scholarship, renewable.
Intended use: For full-time undergraduate study at postsecondary institution in United States.
Eligibility: Applicant must be United Methodist. Applicant must be U.S. citizen or permanent resident.
Basis for selection: Major/career interest in religion/theology. Applicant must demonstrate seriousness of purpose.
Additional information: Preference given to applicants preparing for ministry or other full-time religious work. Must be active member of United Methodist Church one year prior to application.

Application deadline: June 1
Contact:
United Methodist Church/Board of Higher Education and Ministry
Office of Loans and Scholarships
P.O. Box 340007
Nashville, TN 37203-0007

United Methodist Church Conference Merit Award

Type of award: Scholarship, renewable.
Intended use: For undergraduate study at 2-year or 4-year institution. Designated institutions: Must be used at United Methodist affiliated college or university.
Eligibility: Applicant must be United Methodist. Applicant must be U.S. citizen or permanent resident.
Basis for selection: Applicant must demonstrate leadership.
Additional information: Must reside and participate in United Methodist Church Annual Conference. Must be full, active member of United Methodist Church one year prior to application. Amount of award and deadline vary. Application and additional information available at Annual Conference office where local church is member.
Contact:
United Methodist Church/Board of Higher Education and Ministry
Office of Loans and Scholarships
PO Box 340007
Nashville, TN 37203-0007

United Methodist Ethnic Scholarship

Type of award: Scholarship, renewable.
Intended use: For full-time undergraduate study in United States.
Eligibility: Applicant must be Asian American, African American, Mexican American, Hispanic American, Puerto Rican or American Indian. Applicant must be United Methodist.
Basis for selection: Applicant must demonstrate financial need.

473

Application requirements: Recommendations, nomination by applicant's pastor.
Additional information: Must be active member of United Methodist Church for one year prior to application. Persons of Pacific Islander parentage also eligible. Applicant must have minimum 2.5 GPA. If not U.S. citizen or permanent resident, must be recommended by president of United Methodist college/university where enrolled.

Application deadline: May 1
Contact:
United Methodist Church/Board of Higher Education and Ministry
Office of Loans and Scholarships
P.O. Box 340007
Nashville, TN 37203-0007

United Methodist Hana Scholarship

Type of award: Scholarship, renewable.
Intended use: For full-time junior, senior, master's, doctoral or first professional study at 4-year or graduate institution in United States.
Eligibility: Applicant must be Asian American, Mexican American, Hispanic American, Puerto Rican or American Indian. At least one parent of applicant must be 100 percent minority. Applicant must be United Methodist. Applicant must be U.S. citizen or permanent resident.
Basis for selection: Applicant must demonstrate financial need, high academic achievement, leadership and service orientation.
Application requirements: Recommendations, transcript.
Additional information: Persons of Pacific Islander parentage also eligible. Must be active member of United Methodist Church for one year prior to application. Above average scholarship expected.

Application deadline: April 1
Contact:
United Methodist Church/Board of Higher Education and Ministry
Office of Loans and Scholarships
P.O. Box 340007
Nashville, TN 37203-0007

United Methodist J.A. Knowles Memorial Scholarship

Type of award: Scholarship, renewable.
Intended use: For undergraduate or graduate study. Designated institutions: One of the eight United Methodist affiliated institutions in Texas.
Eligibility: Applicant must be United Methodist. Applicant must be U.S. citizen or permanent resident residing in Texas.
Basis for selection: Applicant must demonstrate financial need.
Additional information: Must be active member of United Methodist Church one year prior to application. Recipients must attend one of eight United Methodist affiliated institutions in Texas.

Application deadline: June 1
Contact:
United Methodist Church/Board of Higher Education and Ministry
Office of Loans and Scholarships
P.O. Box 340007
Nashville, TN 37203-0007

United Methodist Priscilla R. Morton Scholarship

Type of award: Scholarship, renewable.
Intended use: For full-time sophomore, junior or senior study at accredited 4-year institution in United States.
Eligibility: Applicant must be United Methodist. Applicant must be U.S. citizen or permanent resident.
Basis for selection: Applicant must demonstrate high academic achievement.
Additional information: Highly competitive academic scholarship. Must be active member of United Methodist Church one year prior to application. Minimum 3.5 college GPA required. Not open to high school seniors entering college. Must have completed at least one semester of college.

Application deadline: June 1
Contact:
United Methodist Church/Board of Higher Education and Ministry
Office of Loans and Scholarships
P.O. Box 340007
Nashville, TN 37203-0007

United Methodist Scholarship

Type of award: Scholarship, renewable.
Intended use: For full-time freshman, sophomore, junior or senior study at 2-year or 4-year institution in United States. Designated institutions: United Methodist affiliated institutions.
Eligibility: Applicant must be United Methodist.
Basis for selection: Applicant must demonstrate financial need and high academic achievement.
Application requirements: Transcript.
Additional information: Available to undergraduate students attending United Methodist affiliated institutions who have been active members of United Methodist Church for one year prior to application. Must have minimum 3.0 GPA. Information and application available through financial aid director at United Methodist institution student plans to attend.
Contact:
United Methodist Church/Board of Higher Education and Ministry
Office of Loans and Scholarships
PO Box 340007
Nashville, TN 37203-0007

United Methodist Communications

Leonard M. Perryman Communications Scholarship for Ethnic Minority Students

Type of award: Scholarship.
Intended use: For full-time junior or senior study at accredited 4-year institution in United States.
Eligibility: Applicant must be Alaskan native, Asian American, African American, Mexican American, Hispanic American, Puerto Rican or American Indian. Applicant must be Christian.
Basis for selection: Major/career interest in journalism; communications; radio/television/film or religion/theology. Applicant must demonstrate seriousness of purpose.

Application requirements: Portfolio, recommendations, essay, transcript. Three examples of journalistic work in any media; statement of interest in religious journalism and planned course of study; photograph (appropriate for publicity purposes).

Additional information: Must plan to pursue career in religious journalism or religious communication. Application forms available October 1 and may be downloaded from Website. One of two scholarships will be awarded to a United Methodist.

Amount of award:	$2,500
Number of awards:	2
Number of applicants:	6
Application deadline:	March 15
Total amount awarded:	$5,000

Contact:
United Methodist Communications
Scholarship Committee
PO Box 320
Nashville, TN 37202
Phone: 800-476-7766
Web: www.umcom.org/scholarships/

United Negro College Fund

Alfred R. Chisholm Memorial Scholarship

Type of award: Scholarship, renewable.
Intended use: For full-time undergraduate study at accredited 4-year institution in United States. Designated institutions: One of 39 UNCF member institutions.
Eligibility: Applicant must be African American. Applicant must be U.S. citizen or permanent resident residing in Texas, Illinois, Ohio, Louisiana, New Jersey, North Carolina, Michigan or South Carolina.
Basis for selection: Major/career interest in accounting; biology; chemistry; mathematics; engineering or law. Applicant must demonstrate high academic achievement and service orientation.
Application requirements: Recommendations, essay, transcript, proof of eligibility, nomination by Financial aid office of designated institution. FAF, photographs.
Additional information: Minimum GPA 3.0. Must be enrolled at UNCF member institution. Computer Science majors also eligible. New Jersey residents favored.

Amount of award:	$2,500
Number of awards:	325,000
Application deadline:	November 12

Contact:
United Negro College Fund
8260 Willow Oaks Corporate Drive
Box 10444
Fairfax, VA 22031-4511
Phone: 800-331-2244
Web: www.uncf.org

Alton R. Higgins, MD and Dorothy Higgins Scholarship

Type of award: Scholarship, renewable.
Intended use: For full-time junior, senior or first professional study at accredited 4-year or graduate institution in United States. Designated institutions: Dillard University, Fisk University, Morehouse College, Oakwood College, Spelman College, Talladega College, Tuskegee University, Xavier University.
Eligibility: Applicant must be African American. Applicant must be U.S. citizen or permanent resident.
Basis for selection: Major/career interest in medicine. Applicant must demonstrate financial need and high academic achievement.
Application requirements: Recommendations, essay, transcript, proof of eligibility, nomination by Financial aid office of designated institution. FAF, photographs.
Additional information: Minimum GPA 2.5. Must be enrolled at UNCF member institution. Undergraduates eligible for $5,000 award, renewable in senior year. Graduate medical students must attend Morehouse. Graduate award is $10,000.

Amount of award:	$5,000-$10,000
Number of applicants:	13

Contact:
United Negro College Fund
8260 Willow Oaks Corporate Drive
P. O. Box 10444
Fairfax, VA 22031-4511
Web: www.uncf.org/noflash/scholarship/

American Home Products Wyeth Ayerst Scholars Program

Type of award: Scholarship, renewable.
Intended use: For full-time undergraduate study in United States. Designated institutions: One of 39 UNCF member institutions.
Eligibility: Applicant must be U.S. citizen or permanent resident.
Basis for selection: Major/career interest in business/management/administration; health-related professions or agricultural economics. Applicant must demonstrate financial need, high academic achievement and leadership.
Application requirements: Portfolio, recommendations, essay, transcript, proof of eligibility, nomination by Financial aid office of designated institution. Photographs, FAF.
Additional information: Minimum GPA 2.5. Must be enrolled at UNCF member institution.

Amount of award:	$5,000
Number of awards:	4
Application deadline:	November 26
Total amount awarded:	$20,000

Contact:
United Negro College Fund
8260 Willow Oaks Corporate Drive
P. O. Box 10444
Fairfax, VA 22031-4511
Phone: 800-331-2244
Web: www.uncf.org

Amway/Ebony Business Leadership Scholarship Program

Type of award: Scholarship, renewable.
Intended use: For full-time undergraduate study at accredited 4-year institution in United States. Designated institutions: One of 39 UNCF member institutions.
Eligibility: Applicant must be Alaskan native, Asian American, African American, Mexican American, Hispanic American, Puerto Rican or American Indian. Applicant must be U.S. citizen or permanent resident.

Basis for selection: Major/career interest in business/management/administration. Applicant must demonstrate financial need and high academic achievement.
Application requirements: Recommendations, essay, transcript, proof of eligibility, nomination by Financial aid office of institution. FAF or FFS (Family Financial Statement) and photographs.

    Total amount awarded: $50,000
Contact:
United Negro College Fund
8260 Willow Oaks Corporate Drive
P. O. Box 10444
Fairfax, VA 22031-4511
Phone: 800-331-2244
Web: www.uncf.org

Bryant Gumbel/Walt Disney World Tournament Scholarships

Type of award: Scholarship, renewable.
Intended use: For full-time junior or senior study at accredited 4-year institution in United States. Designated institutions: One of 39 UNCF institutions.
Eligibility: Applicant must be Alaskan native, Asian American, African American, Mexican American, Hispanic American, Puerto Rican or American Indian.
Basis for selection: Applicant must demonstrate financial need and high academic achievement.
Application requirements: Recommendations, essay, transcript, proof of eligibility, nomination by Financial aid office of designated institution. FAF, photographs.
Additional information: Minimum GPA 3.0. Must be enrolled at UNCF member institution. Application and list of colleges available online. Applicant must major in Liberal Arts. Funded with proceeds from the golf tournament.

    Number of awards: 80
    Application deadline: October 29
Contact:
United Negro College Fund
8260 Willow Oaks Corporate Drive
P. O Box 10444
Fairfax, VA 22031-4511
Phone: 800-331-2244
Web: www.uncf.org

CBS Career Horizons Internships/Scholarship Program

Type of award: Scholarship, renewable.
Intended use: For full-time sophomore, junior or graduate study at accredited 4-year institution in United States. Designated institutions: 39 UNCF institutions and Florida A&M.
Eligibility: Applicant must be Alaskan native, Asian American, African American, Mexican American, Hispanic American, Puerto Rican or American Indian. Applicant must be U.S. citizen or permanent resident.
Basis for selection: Major/career interest in accounting; business; finance/banking; marketing; journalism or communications. Applicant must demonstrate financial need and high academic achievement.
Application requirements: Recommendations, essay, transcript, proof of eligibility, nomination by Financial aid office of desginated institution. FAF, resume and photographs.
Additional information: Minimum GPA 3.0. Applicant must be enrolled in UNCF member institution. Application and list of colleges available online. Program awards summer internship at

CBS with stipend o $5,000 plus $8,000 scholarship. Also open to MBA students at Florida A&M.

    Amount of award: $13,000
    Number of awards: 10
    Application deadline: January 10
    Notification begins: March 1
    Total amount awarded: $130,000
Contact:
United Negro College Fund
8260 Willow Oaks Corporate Drive
P O. Box 10444
Fairfax, VA 22031-4511
Phone: 800-331-2244
Web: www.uncf.org

CSX Scholars Program

Type of award: Scholarship, renewable.
Intended use: For full-time undergraduate study at accredited 2-year or 4-year institution. Designated institutions: Barber-Scotia College, Benedict College, Bennett College, Bethune-Cookman College, Claflin College, Clark Atlanta University, Dillard University, Edward Waters College, Fisk University, Florida Memorial College, Huston-Tillotson College, Interdenominational Theological Center, Jarvis Christian College, Johnson C. Smith University, Lane College, LeMoyne-Owen College, Livingstone College, Miles College, Morehouse College, Morris Brown College, Morris College, Oakwood College, Paine College, Paul Quinn College, Philander Smith College, Rust College, Saint Augustine's College, Saint Paul's College, Shaw University, Spelman College, Stillman College, Talladega College, Tougaloo College, Tuskegee University, Virginia Union University, Voorhees College, Wilberforce University, Wiley College, Xavier University. Exceptions may be made for students at non-qualifying institutions, but such exceptions are very rare.
Eligibility: Applicant must be Alaskan native, Asian American, African American, Mexican American, Hispanic American, Puerto Rican or American Indian.
Basis for selection: Major/career interest in biology; atmospheric sciences/meteorology; environmental science; natural resources/conservation or oceanography/marine studies. Applicant must demonstrate financial need and high academic achievement.
Application requirements: Recommendations, essay, transcript, proof of eligibility, nomination by financial aid officer of eligible institution. Application, photograph, FAFSA.
Additional information: Award is full tuition waiver of up to $13,000 for each of two years. Renewal only if eligibility requirements met and funds available. Award also includes two summer internships at National Audubon Society and CSX Corporation. Contact sponsor for application or visit Website.

    Amount of award: $13,000
    Application deadline: January 27
Contact:
United Negro College Fund Program Services
8260 Willow Oaks Corporate Drive
P.O. Box 10444
Fairfax, VA 22031-4511
Phone: 800-331-2244
Web: www.uncf.org

Gates Millennium Scholars Program

Type of award: Scholarship, renewable.
Intended use: For full-time undergraduate or graduate study at accredited 4-year or graduate institution.

Eligibility: Applicant must be Alaskan native, Asian American, African American, Mexican American, Hispanic American, Puerto Rican or American Indian.

Basis for selection: Major/career interest in mathematics; science, general; education; library science; engineering or humanities/liberal arts. Applicant must demonstrate financial need, high academic achievement, leadership and service orientation.

Application requirements: Recommendations, nomination by high school principal, teacher or counselor; or college president, professor or dean.

Additional information: Must participate in community service, volunteer work or extracurricular activities, including athletics. Provides tuition, room, materials and board costs over and above existing financial aid. Eliminates loans, work-study and outside jobs for scholarship recipients. Minimum 3.3 GPA required. All majors accepted for undergraduate scholarships. Graduate students must be enrolled in degree program in engineering, mathematics, science, education or library science. Funded by Bill and Melinda Gates Foundation.

Number of awards:	4,000
Application deadline:	March 15
Notification begins:	May 1
Total amount awarded:	$50,000,000

Contact:
United Negro College Fund Program Services
8260 Willow Oaks Corporate Drive
P. O. Box 10444
Fairfax, VA 22031-4511
Phone: 800-331-2244 or 877-690-4677
Web: www.uncf.org or www.gmsp.org

Hewlett Packard Scholarship Program

Type of award: Scholarship, renewable.
Intended use: For full-time undergraduate study at accredited 4-year institution in United States. Designated institutions: Barber-Scotia College, Benedict College, Bennett College, Bethune-Cookman College, Claflin College, Clark Atlanta University, Dillard University, Edward Waters College, Fisk University, Florida Memorial College, Huston-Tillotson College, Interdenominational Theological Center, Jarvis Christian College, Johnson C. Smith University, Lane College, LeMoyne-Owen College, Livingstone College, Miles College, Morehouse College, Morris Brown College, Morris College, Oakwood College, Paine College, Paul Quinn College, Philander Smith College, Rust College, Saint Augustine's College, Saint Paul's College, Shaw University, Spelman College, Stillman College, Talladega College, Tougaloo College, Tuskegee University, Virginia Union University, Voorhees College, Wilberforce University, Wiley College, Xavier University. Exceptions may be made for students at non-qualifying institutions, but such exceptions are very rare.
Eligibility: Applicant must be Alaskan native, Asian American, African American, Mexican American, Hispanic American, Puerto Rican or American Indian. Applicant must be U.S. citizen or permanent resident residing in California.
Basis for selection: Applicant must demonstrate financial need and high academic achievement.
Application requirements: Recommendations, essay, transcript, proof of eligibility, nomination by financial aid office of designated institution. FAFSA and photograph.
Additional information: Minimum GPA 2.5. Visit Website for additional information. Contact financial aid office of member institution for application, deadlines, award amount and details.

Total amount awarded:	$25,000

Contact:
United Negro College Fund
8260 Willow Oaks Corporate Drive
P. O. Box 10444
Fairfax, VA 22031-4511
Phone: 800-331-2244
Web: www.uncf.org

Janet Jackson Rhythm Nation Scholarships

Type of award: Scholarship, renewable.
Intended use: For full-time undergraduate study at accredited 4-year institution in United States. Designated institutions: Barber-Scotia College, Benedict College, Bennett College, Bethune-Cookman College, Claflin College, Clark Atlanta University, Dillard University, Edward Waters College, Fisk University, Florida Memorial College, Huston-Tillotson College, Interdenominational Theological Center, Jarvis Christian College, Johnson C. Smith University, Lane College, LeMoyne-Owen College, Livingstone College, Miles College, Morehouse College, Morris Brown College, Morris College, Oakwood College, Paine College, Paul Quinn College, Philander Smith College, Rust College, Saint Augustine's College, Saint Paul's College, Shaw University, Spelman College, Stillman College, Talladega College, Tougaloo College, Tuskegee University, Virginia Union University, Voorhees College, Wilberforce University, Wiley College, Xavier University. Exceptions may be made for students at non-qualifying institutions, but such exceptions are very rare.
Eligibility: Applicant must be Alaskan native, Asian American, African American, Mexican American, Hispanic American, Puerto Rican or American Indian.
Basis for selection: Major/career interest in communications; performing arts; English or music.
Application requirements: Recommendations, essay, proof of eligibility, nomination by financial aid office of designated institution. FAFSA, resume and photograph.
Additional information: Minimum GPA 3.0. Fine arts majors also eligible. Awards funded by $395,000 endowment. Applications available online.

Application deadline:	November 26

Contact:
United Negro College Fund
8260 Willow Oaks Corporate Deive
P. O. Box 10444
Fairfax, VA 22031-4511
Phone: 800-331-2244
Web: www.uncf.org

John Lennon Scholarship Fund

Type of award: Scholarship, renewable.
Intended use: For full-time undergraduate study at accredited 4-year institution in United States. Designated institutions: Barber-Scotia College, Benedict College, Bennett College, Bethune-Cookman College, Claflin College, Clark Atlanta University, Dillard University, Edward Waters College, Fisk University, Florida Memorial College, Huston-Tillotson College, Interdenominational Theological Center, Jarvis Christian College, Johnson C. Smith University, Lane College, LeMoyne-Owen College, Livingstone College, Miles College, Morehouse College, Morris Brown College, Morris College, Oakwood College, Paine College, Paul Quinn College, Philander Smith College, Rust College, Saint Augustine's College, Saint Paul's College, Shaw University, Spelman College, Stillman College,

Talladega College, Tougaloo College, Tuskegee University, Virginia Union University, Voorhees College, Wilberforce University, Wiley College, Xavier University. Exceptions may be made for students at non-qualifying institutions, but such exceptions are very rare.

Eligibility: Applicant must be Alaskan native, Asian American, African American, Mexican American, Hispanic American, Puerto Rican or American Indian.

Basis for selection: Major/career interest in performing arts or communications. Applicant must demonstrate financial need and high academic achievement.

Application requirements: Recommendations, essay, transcript, proof of eligibility, nomination by financial aid office of designated institution. FAFSA and photograph.

Additional information: Minimum GPA 2.5. $800,000 endowed scholarship fund created by Yoko Ono. Visit Website for additional information. Contact financial aid office of member institution for application, deadlines, award amount and details.

Contact:
United Negro College Fund
8260 Willow Oaks Corporate Drive
P. O. Box 10444
Fairfax, VA 22031-4451
Phone: 800-331-2244
Web: www.uncf.org

Leo Burnett Scholarship Program

Type of award: Scholarship, renewable.
Intended use: For full-time undergraduate study at accredited 4-year institution in United States. Designated institutions: Barber-Scotia College, Benedict College, Bennett College, Bethune-Cookman College, Claflin College, Clark Atlanta University, Dillard University, Edward Waters College, Fisk University, Florida Memorial College, Huston-Tillotson College, Interdenominational Theological Center, Jarvis Christian College, Johnson C. Smith University, Lane College, LeMoyne-Owen College, Livingstone College, Miles College, Morehouse College, Morris Brown College, Morris College, Oakwood College, Paine College, Paul Quinn College, Philander Smith College, Rust College, Saint Augustine's College, Saint Paul's College, Shaw University, Spelman College, Stillman College, Talladega College, Tougaloo College, Tuskegee University, Virginia Union University, Voorhees College, Wilberforce University, Wiley College, Xavier University. Exceptions may be made for students at non-qualifying institutions, but such exceptions are very rare.
Eligibility: Applicant must be Alaskan native, Asian American, African American, Mexican American, Hispanic American, Puerto Rican or American Indian. Applicant must be U.S. citizen or permanent resident residing in Illinois.
Basis for selection: Major/career interest in business; English or marketing. Applicant must demonstrate financial need and high academic achievement.
Application requirements: Transcript, proof of eligibility, nomination by financial aid office of designated institution. Photograph, FAFSA and resume.
Additional information: Minimum GPA 2.5. Preference to Chicago area resident. Applicants with liberal arts and creative design majors/career interest also eligible. Must participate in summer internship at Leo Burnett Company and mentoring program. Application available online.

Amount of award:	$5,000
Application deadline:	November 26

Contact:
United Negro College Fund
8260 Willow Oaks Corporate Drive
P. O. Box 10444
Fairfax, VA 22031-4511
Phone: 800-331-2244
Web: www.uncf.org

Malcolm X Scholarship for Exceptional Courage

Type of award: Scholarship, renewable.
Intended use: For full-time junior study at accredited 4-year institution in United States. Designated institutions: 39 UNCF member institutions.
Eligibility: Applicant must be Alaskan native, Asian American, African American, Mexican American, Hispanic American, Puerto Rican or American Indian.
Basis for selection: Applicant must demonstrate financial need, high academic achievement, leadership and seriousness of purpose.
Application requirements: Recommendations, essay, transcript, proof of eligibility, nomination by Academic Dean or Vice President for Academic Affairs of UNCF member institution. Photographs.
Additional information: Minimum GPA 2.5. Application and list of colleges available online. Renewable each year until graduation. Scholarship designed to reward students who have overcome tremendous odds, hardships and special circumstances.

Amount of award:	$4,000
Number of awards:	1
Application deadline:	October 22
Total amount awarded:	$16,000

Contact:
United Negro College Fund
8260 Willow Oaks Corporate Drive
P. O. Box 10444
Fairfax, VA 22031-4511
Phone: 800-331-2244
Web: www.uncf.org

Michael Jackson Scholarships

Type of award: Scholarship, renewable.
Intended use: For undergraduate study at accredited 4-year institution in United States. Designated institutions: One of 39 UNCF member institutions.
Eligibility: Applicant must be Alaskan native, Asian American, African American, Mexican American, Hispanic American, Puerto Rican or American Indian.
Basis for selection: Major/career interest in performing arts or communications. Applicant must demonstrate financial need and high academic achievement.
Application requirements: Recommendations, essay, transcript, proof of eligibility, nomination by Financial aid office of institution. FAF, photographs.
Additional information: Awards funded by $1.5 million endowment. Minimum GPA 3.0. Must be enrolled at UNCF member school. Application and list of colleges available online. Renewal each year.

Amount of award:	$4,000
Application deadline:	October 22

Contact:
United Negro College Fund
8260 Willow Oaks Corporate Drive
P. O. Box 10444
Fairfax, VA 22031-4511
Phone: 800-331-2244
Web: www.uncf.org

Paine Webber Scholarships

Type of award: Scholarship, renewable.
Intended use: For full-time undergraduate study at accredited 4-year institution. Designated institutions: Barber-Scotia College, Benedict College, Bennett College, Bethune-Cookman College, Claflin College, Clark Atlanta University, Dillard University, Edward Waters College, Fisk University, Florida Memorial College, Huston-Tillotson College, Interdenominational Theological Center, Jarvis Christian College, Johnson C. Smith University, Lane College, LeMoyne-Owen College, Livingstone College, Miles College, Morehouse College, Morris Brown College, Morris College, Oakwood College, Paine College, Paul Quinn College, Philander Smith College, Rust College, Saint Augustine's College, Saint Paul's College, Shaw University, Spelman College, Stillman College, Talladega College, Tougaloo College, Tuskegee University, Virginia Union University, Voorhees College, Wilberforce University, Wiley College, Xavier University. Exceptions may be made for students at non-qualifying institutions, but such exceptions are very rare.
Eligibility: Applicant must be Alaskan native, Asian American, African American, Mexican American, Hispanic American, Puerto Rican or American Indian.
Basis for selection: Major/career interest in business; economics; business/management/administration or finance/banking.
Application requirements: Recommendations, essay, transcript, proof of eligibility, nomination by financial aid office of institution. FAFSA and photograph.
Additional information: Minimum GPA 3.0. Applicant with career interest in sales also eligible. Visit Website for additional information. Contact financial aid office of member institution for application, deadlines, award amount and details.
Contact:
United Negro College Fund
8260 Willow Oaks Corporate Drive
P. O. Box 10444
Fairfax, VA 22031-4511
Web: www.uncf.org

Reader's Digest Foundation Scholarship Program

Type of award: Scholarship, renewable.
Intended use: For full-time junior or senior study at accredited 4-year institution in United States. Designated institutions: Barber-Scotia College, Benedict College, Bennett College, Bethune-Cookman College, Claflin College, Clark Atlanta University, Dillard University, Edward Waters College, Fisk University, Florida Memorial College, Huston-Tillotson College, Interdenominational Theological Center, Jarvis Christian College, Johnson C. Smith University, Lane College, LeMoyne-Owen College, Livingstone College, Miles College, Morehouse College, Morris Brown College, Morris College, Oakwood College, Paine College, Paul Quinn College, Philander Smith College, Rust College, Saint Augustine's College, Saint Paul's College, Shaw University, Spelman College, Stillman College, Talladega College, Tougaloo College, Tuskegee University,

Virginia Union University, Voorhees College, Wilberforce University, Wiley College, Xavier University. Exceptions may be made for students at non-qualifying institutions, but such exceptions are very rare.
Eligibility: Applicant must be Alaskan native, Asian American, African American, Mexican American, Hispanic American, Puerto Rican or American Indian.
Basis for selection: Major/career interest in journalism; communications or English. Applicant must demonstrate financial need and high academic achievement.
Application requirements: Recommendations, essay, transcript, proof of eligibility, nomination by financial aid director at eligible institution. Application, published writing sample, photograph, FAFSA.
Additional information: Minimum 2.5 GPA. Renewal only if eligibility requirements met and funds available. Contact sponsor for application or visit Website.

Amount of award:	$5,000
Number of awards:	6
Application deadline:	November 4
Total amount awarded:	$30,000

Contact:
United Negro College Fund Program Services
8260 Willow Oaks Corparate Drive
P.O. Box 10444
Fairfax, VA 22031-4511
Phone: 800-331-2244
Web: www.uncf.org

Reader's Digest Scholarship

Type of award: Scholarship, renewable.
Intended use: For full-time undergraduate study in United States. Designated institutions: Barber-Scotia College, Benedict College, Bennett College, Bethune-Cookman College, Claflin College, Clark Atlanta University, Dillard University, Edward Waters College, Fisk University, Florida Memorial College, Huston-Tillotson College, Interdenominational Theological Center, Jarvis Christian College, Johnson C. Smith University, Lane College, LeMoyne-Owen College, Livingstone College, Miles College, Morehouse College, Morris Brown College, Morris College, Oakwood College, Paine College, Paul Quinn College, Philander Smith College, Rust College, Saint Augustine's College, Saint Paul's College, Shaw University, Spelman College, Stillman College, Talladega College, Tougaloo College, Tuskegee University, Virginia Union University, Voorhees College, Wilberforce University, Wiley College, Xavier University. Exceptions may be made for students at non-qualifying institutions, but such exceptions are very rare.
Eligibility: Applicant must be Alaskan native, Asian American, African American, Mexican American, Hispanic American, Puerto Rican or American Indian.
Basis for selection: Major/career interest in journalism or English. Applicant must demonstrate financial need and high academic achievement.
Application requirements: Recommendations, essay, transcript, proof of eligibility, nomination by financial aid office of designated institution. FAFSA and photograph.
Additional information: Minimum GPA 2.5. Visit Website for additional information. Contact financial aid office of member institution for application, deadlines, award amount and details.

Total amount awarded:	$30,000

Contact:
United Negro College Fund
8260 Willow Oaks Corporate Drive
P. O. Box 10444
Fairfax, VA 22031-4511
Phone: 800-331-2244
Web: www.uncf.org

UNCF/GTE Summer Science Program

Type of award: Scholarship, renewable.
Intended use: For full-time sophomore or junior study at accredited 4-year institution in United States. Designated institutions: One of 39 UNCF member institutions.
Eligibility: Applicant must be Alaskan native, Asian American, African American, Mexican American, Hispanic American, Puerto Rican or American Indian. Applicant must be U.S. citizen or permanent resident.
Basis for selection: Major/career interest in engineering; mathematics; physics or education. Applicant must demonstrate financial need and high academic achievement.
Application requirements: Recommendations, essay, transcript, proof of eligibility, nomination by Financial aid office of designated institution. FAF, resume and photographs.
Additional information: Award: $3,500 summer internship at GTE Laboratories (Boston) plus $3,500 scholarship. Minimum GPA 3.2. Must have completed introductory course in mathematics, computer science, physical science or engineering. Computer science majors also eligible. Application and list of colleges available online.

Amount of award:	$7,000
Number of awards:	20
Application deadline:	February 11
Notification begins:	March 10
Total amount awarded:	$130,000

Contact:
United Negro College Fund
8260 Willow Oaks Corporate Drive
P. O. Box 10444
Fairfax, VA 22031-4511
Phone: 800-331-2244
Web: www.uncf.org

UNCF/Revlon Women's Scholarship Program

Type of award: Scholarship, renewable.
Intended use: For full-time junior or senior study at accredited 4-year institution in United States. Designated institutions: One of 39 UNCF member institutions.
Eligibility: Applicant must be Alaskan native, Asian American, African American, Mexican American, Hispanic American, Puerto Rican or American Indian.
Basis for selection: Major/career interest in medicine; nursing or psychology. Applicant must demonstrate financial need, high academic achievement, leadership and service orientation.
Application requirements: Recommendations, essay, transcript, proof of eligibility, nomination by Financial aid office of institution. Must submit SAT and ACT scores, FAF and photographs.
Additional information: Number of awards varies. Minimum GPA 3.0 required. Must be enrolled at UNCF member school. Applicants with pre-medicine and healthcare majors also eligible. Application and list of colleges available online. Must demonstrate financial need, community service related to women's healthcare issues, interpersonal skills.

Amount of award:	$10,000
Application deadline:	November 16

Contact:
United Negro College Fund
8260 Willow Oaks Corporate Drive
P. O. Box 10444
Fairfax, VA 22031-4511
Phone: 800-331-2244
Web: www.uncf.org

United Negro College Fund Scholarships

Type of award: Scholarship.
Intended use: For undergraduate study in United States. Designated institutions: Barber-Scotia College, Benedict College, Bennett College, Bethune-Cookman College, Claflin College, Clark Atlanta University, Dillard University, Edward Waters College, Fisk University, Florida Memorial College, Huston-Tillotson College, Interdenominational Theological Center, Jarvis Christian College, Johnson C. Smith University, Lane College, LeMoyne-Owen College, Livingstone College, Miles College, Morehouse College, Morris Brown College, Morris College, Oakwood College, Paine College, Paul Quinn College, Philander Smith College, Rust College, Saint Augustine's College, Saint Paul's College, Shaw University, Spelman College, Stillman College, Talladega College, Tougaloo College, Tuskegee University, Virginia Union University, Voorhees College, Wilberforce University, Wiley College, Xavier University. Exceptions may be made for students at non-qualifying institutions, but such exceptions are very rare.
Eligibility: Applicant must be African American.
Basis for selection: Applicant must demonstrate financial need.
Application requirements: Nomination by financial aid director at eligible college. Application, FAFSA, photograph.
Additional information: Must have minimum 2.5 GPA. Renewal only if eligibility requirements met and funds available. Contact sponsor for application or visit Website.

Amount of award:	$500-$10,000

Contact:
United Negro College Fund Program Services
8260 Willow Oaks Corporate Drive
P.O. Box 10444
Fairfax, VA 22031-4511
Phone: 800-331-2244
Web: www.uncf.org

Virginia Health and Human Services Fund

Type of award: Scholarship.
Intended use: For undergraduate study in United States. Designated institutions: Barber-Scotia College, Benedict College, Bennett College, Bethune-Cookman College, Claflin College, Clark Atlanta University, Dillard University, Edward Waters College, Fisk University, Florida Memorial College, Huston-Tillotson College, Interdenominational Theological Center, Jarvis Christian College, Johnson C. Smith University, Lane College, LeMoyne-Owen College, Livingstone College, Miles College, Morehouse College, Morris Brown College, Morris College, Oakwood College, Paine College, Paul Quinn College, Philander Smith College, Rust College, Saint Augustine's College, Saint Paul's College, Shaw University, Spelman College, Stillman College, Talladega College, Tougaloo College, Tuskegee University, Virginia Union

University, Voorhees College, Wilberforce University, Wiley College, Xavier University. Exceptions may be made for students at non-qualifying institutions, but such exceptions are very rare.
Eligibility: Applicant must be Alaskan native, Asian American, African American, Mexican American, Hispanic American, Puerto Rican or American Indian. Applicant must be U.S. citizen or permanent resident residing in Virginia.
Basis for selection: Applicant must demonstrate financial need and high academic achievement.
Application requirements: Recommendations, essay, transcript, proof of eligibility, nomination by financial aid office of designated institution. FAFSA and photograph.
Additional information: Annual award offsets living expenses for students from Virginia. Minimum GPA 2.5. Visit Website for additional information. Contact financial aid office of member institution for application, deadlines, award amount and details. Funds provided by Richmond, VA United Way.
   Total amount awarded: $100,000
Contact:
United Negro College Fund
8260 Willow Oaks Corporate Drive
P. O. Box 10444
Fairfax, VA 22031-4511
Phone: 800-331-2244
Web: www.uncf.org

United Parcel Service

UPS Earn and Learn Program Grant

Type of award: Scholarship, renewable.
Intended use: For half-time undergraduate study at accredited vocational, 2-year or 4-year institution in United States.
Eligibility: Applicant or parent must be employed by United Parcel Service (UPS).
Application requirements: Proof of eligibility. Must be UPS employee at participating location.
Additional information: Visit Website for current list of participating locations and additional information (or visit www.upsjobs.com to apply at job Website). Employees attending college part-time qualify for up to $15,000 in lifetime tuition assistance as benefit.
Contact:
United Parcel Service
55 Glenlake Parkway N.E.
Atlanta, GA 30328
Phone: 404-828-6374
Web: www.community.ups.com

United States Association for Blind Athletes

Arthur E. Copeland Scholarship for Males

Type of award: Scholarship.
Intended use: For full-time freshman study at postsecondary institution.

Eligibility: Applicant or parent must be member/participant of United States Association of Blind Athletes. Applicant must be visually impaired. Applicant must be male, high school senior. Applicant must be U.S. citizen.
Application requirements: Transcript, proof of eligibility. Autobiographical sketch outlining USABA involvement and academic goals. References.
Additional information: Applicants who are legally blind, have participated in USABA activities for at least two years, and are current USABA members are eligible. Applications must be postmarked no later than June 15. Open to all majors.
   Amount of award: $500
   Number of awards: 1
   Application deadline: June 15
   Notification begins: August 1
Contact:
Scholarship Director
33 North Institute St.
Brown Hall, Suite 015
Colorado springs, CO 80903
Web: www.usaba.org

United States Golf Association

USGA Education Assistance Program

Type of award: Scholarship, renewable.
Intended use: For undergraduate or graduate study at vocational, 2-year, 4-year or graduate institution.
Eligibility: Applicant or parent must be employed by United States Golf Association. Applicant must be high school senior.
Additional information: For further information or an application, contact United States Golf Association directly.
   Amount of award: $2,000-$30,000

United Transportation Union Insurance Association

United Transportation Union Insurance Association Scholarship

Type of award: Scholarship, renewable.
Intended use: For full-time undergraduate study at accredited vocational, 2-year or 4-year institution in or outside United States.
Eligibility: Applicant or parent must be member/participant of United Transportation Union. Applicant must be no older than 25, high school senior. Applicant must be permanent resident.
Application requirements: Proof of eligibility.
Additional information: Members and direct descendants of living or deceased members eligible. Scholarships awarded by lottery. Notification takes place prior to fall enrollment.

Amount of award:	$500
Number of awards:	50
Number of applicants:	2,400
Application deadline:	March 31

Contact:
United Transportation Union Insurance Association
14600 Detroit Ave.
Cleveland, OH 44107-4250

University Film and Video Association

Carole Fielding Video Grant

Type of award: Scholarship.
Intended use: For undergraduate or graduate study at accredited 2-year, 4-year or graduate institution.
Basis for selection: Major/career interest in film/video.
Application requirements: Application form. Research/ production proposal.
Additional information: Project categories include narrative, documentary, experimental, multi-media/installation, animation, and research. Applicant must submit one-page resume and summary proposal. Applicant must be sponsored by faculty member who is active member of University Film and Video Association. Number of awards varies. Send five collated and stapled copies of completed application.

Amount of award:	$1,000-$4,000
Number of applicants:	86
Application deadline:	January 1
Notification begins:	March 31
Total amount awarded:	$5,000

Contact:
Professor Robert Johnson Jr., Grants Chair
Framingham State College, Commun. Arts Dept.
100 State Street
Framingham, MA 01701
Phone: 508-626-4684
Web: www.ufva.org

Univest Corporation

Univest Corporation Scholarship Program

Type of award: Scholarship.
Intended use: For undergraduate study at vocational, 2-year or 4-year institution.
Eligibility: Applicant or parent must be employed by Univest Corporation. Applicant must be high school senior.
Additional information: For further information or an application, contact Univest Corporation directly.

Amount of award:	$1,000-$2,000

Unocal Foundation

Unocal Foundation Scholarship

Type of award: Scholarship, renewable.
Intended use: For freshman study at accredited 2-year or 4-year institution.
Eligibility: Applicant or parent must be employed by Unocal Corporation.
Basis for selection: Applicant must demonstrate financial need.
Additional information: Available to children of employees only. For further information or an application, contact Unocal Foundation directly.

Amount of award:	$500-$3,000

UnumProvident Corporation Foundation

UnumProvident Foundation Scholarship

Type of award: Scholarship, renewable.
Intended use: For undergraduate study at accredited 2-year or 4-year institution.
Eligibility: Applicant or parent must be employed by UNUM.
Basis for selection: Applicant must demonstrate financial need.
Additional information: For further information or an application, contact UnumProvident Foundation directly.

Amount of award:	$1,000-$5,000

UPS Foundation

George D. Smith Scholarship Program

Type of award: Scholarship, renewable.
Intended use: For freshman study at accredited vocational or 2-year institution.
Eligibility: Applicant or parent must be employed by United Parcel Service--Florida.
Basis for selection: Applicant must demonstrate financial need.
Additional information: For further information or an application, contact UPS Foundation directly.

Amount of award:	$500-$2,000

James E. Casey Scholarship

Type of award: Scholarship, renewable.
Intended use: For freshman study at accredited 4-year institution.
Eligibility: Applicant or parent must be employed by United Parcel Service-Canada.
Basis for selection: Applicant must demonstrate financial need.
Additional information: For further information or an application, contact UPS Foundation directly.

Amount of award: $2,000-$6,000

USA Education Inc. - Sallie Mae

USA Funds Scholarship

Type of award: Scholarship, renewable.
Intended use: For full-time undergraduate study at accredited vocational, 2-year or 4-year institution.
Eligibility: Applicant must be U.S. citizen, permanent resident, international student or eligible non-U.S. citizens.
Application requirements: Transcript, proof of eligibility. Copy of applicant's or parent's 1040 tax return. Copy of INS papers for non-citizens.
Additional information: Applicant must have adjusted gross family income of $35,000 or less. Up to 50 percent of awards targeted to physically disabled and ethnic minority applicants. Special consideration given to residents of Alaska, Arizona, Hawaii and the Pacific Islands, Indiana, Kansas, Maryland, Mississippi, Nevada, and Wyoming.
  Number of awards: 1,000
  Application deadline: April 16
Contact:
Web: www.wiredscholar.com/usafunds

USAA Educational Foundation

USAA Employee Dependent Scholarship Program

Type of award: Scholarship, renewable.
Intended use: For freshman study at accredited 4-year institution.
Eligibility: Applicant or parent must be employed by USAA Educational Foundation.
Basis for selection: Applicant must demonstrate financial need.
Additional information: For further information or an application, contact USAA Educational Foundation directly.
  Amount of award: $2,000

UST

UST Sons and Daughters Scholarship

Type of award: Scholarship, renewable.
Intended use: For undergraduate study at accredited vocational, 2-year or 4-year institution.
Eligibility: Applicant or parent must be employed by UST.
Basis for selection: Applicant must demonstrate financial need.
Additional information: For further information or an application, contact UST directly.

Amount of award: $500-$4,000

USX Foundation Inc.

U.S. Steel Scholarship

Type of award: Scholarship, renewable.
Intended use: For undergraduate study at accredited vocational, 2-year or 4-year institution.
Eligibility: Applicant or parent must be employed by USX Foundation, Inc. Applicant must be high school senior.
Basis for selection: Applicant must demonstrate financial need.
Additional information: Must be child of employee of USX Foundation, Inc or U.S. Steel. For further information or application, contact the foundation directly.
  Amount of award: $2,500
  Number of awards: 15
  Total amount awarded: $150,000
Contact:
USX Foundation, Inc.

Utah Higher Education Assistance Authority

Utah State Student Incentive Grant

Type of award: Scholarship, renewable.
Intended use: For undergraduate study at vocational, 2-year or 4-year institution. Designated institutions: Utah postsecondary schools.
Eligibility: Applicant must be residing in Utah.
Basis for selection: Applicant must demonstrate financial need.
  Amount of award: $300-$5,000
  Number of awards: 1,874
  Total amount awarded: $1,112,622
Contact:
Contact campus financial aid office.

Utah State Office of Education

Utah Robert C. Byrd Honors Scholarship

Type of award: Scholarship, renewable.
Intended use: For undergraduate study.
Eligibility: Applicant must be high school senior. Applicant must be permanent resident residing in Utah.
Basis for selection: Applicant must demonstrate high academic achievement.
Application requirements: Transcript. Should have high ACT scores.
Additional information: Contact high school counselor or financial aid adviser for application after January 15.

Amount of award: $1,500
Number of awards: 62
Number of applicants: 500
Application deadline: March 31
Notification begins: May 15
Total amount awarded: $385,500
Contact:
High school counselor or financial aid advisor for application.

Vectren

Vectren Scholarship Program

Type of award: Scholarship.
Intended use: For freshman study at vocational, 2-year or 4-year institution.
Eligibility: Applicant or parent must be employed by Vectren. Applicant must be high school senior.
Additional information: For further information or an application, contact Vectren directly.
Amount of award: $1,000

Veeder-Root Company

Wilbur C. Stauble Trust Scholarship

Type of award: Scholarship.
Intended use: For freshman study at accredited 4-year institution.
Eligibility: Applicant or parent must be employed by Veeder-Root Company.
Additional information: For further information or an application, contact Veeder-Root Company directly.
Amount of award: $500-$5,000

Venture Clubs of the Americas

Venture Clubs of America Student Aid Award

Type of award: Scholarship.
Intended use: For full-time undergraduate, graduate or non-degree study at accredited vocational, 2-year, 4-year or graduate institution in United States.
Eligibility: Applicant must be physically challenged. Applicant must be at least 15, no older than 40. Applicant must be U.S. citizen.
Basis for selection: Applicant must demonstrate financial need.
Application requirements: Recommendations, essay.
Additional information: This award program exists at club, region, and federation levels. Each club and region determines amount of its own award. Successful applicants on seven regional levels are submitted to federation level. Federation then gives two awards: one first-place ($5,000) and one second-place ($2,500). This award does not specify any particular level of study; however, applicants must demonstrate both financial

need and the capacity to profit from further education. Applicants living outside territorial limits of a Venture Club should apply to nearest club. Applications obtained by sending SASE with request to contact address. The Venture Student Aid Award is available to applicants who reside within the territorial limits of the Venture organization only. This territory currently includes the United States, Japan, Korea, Mexico, and the Philippines.
Amount of award: $2,500-$5,000
Number of awards: 2
Number of applicants: 300
Application deadline: December 31
Total amount awarded: $7,500
Contact:
Venture Clubs of the Americas
C/O Soroptimist International of the Americas
Two Penn Center Plaza, Ste. 1000
Philadelphia, PA 19102-1883

Vermont Golf Association Scholarship Fund, Inc.

Vermont Golf Association Scholarship

Type of award: Scholarship, renewable.
Intended use: For full-time undergraduate study at 2-year or 4-year institution.
Eligibility: Applicant must be high school senior. Applicant must be permanent resident residing in Vermont.
Application requirements: Interview, recommendations, transcript. FAFSA Student Aid Report. Applicant must be interested in some aspect of golf.
Additional information: Must be graduate of Vermont high school and in top 40% of class. Personal involvement with golf required. Can renew scholarship up to four years.
Amount of award: $800
Number of awards: 40
Number of applicants: 40
Application deadline: April 20
Total amount awarded: $32,000
Contact:
Vermont Golf Association Scholarship Fund, Inc
c/o Keyser Crowley
29 South Main St
Rutland, VT 05701
Web: www.vtga.org

Vermont Space Grant Consortium

Vermont Space Grant Consortium Undergraduate Scholarships

Type of award: Scholarship, renewable.
Intended use: For full-time undergraduate study in United States. Designated institutions: Vermont colleges and universities.

Eligibility: Applicant must be high school senior. Applicant must be U.S. citizen residing in Vermont.
Basis for selection: Major/career interest in science, general; engineering; mathematics; aerospace or physics.
Application requirements: Recommendations, essay, transcript.
Additional information: Open to high school seniors who intend to be enrolled full time in the following year. Applicant must be enrolled in program relevant to NASA's goals at a Vermont institution. Minimum 3.0 GPA. Out-of-state recipients qualify for in-state tuition. Three awards designated for Native American applicants. Can be used at any accredited Vermont institution of higher education.

Amount of award:	$1,500
Number of awards:	10
Number of applicants:	30
Application deadline:	March 1
Notification begins:	March 15

Contact:
NASA Space Grant Vermont Space Grant Consortium
Votey Bldg, College of Engineering and Math
University of Vermont
Burlington, VT 05405-0156
Phone: 802-656-1429
Web: www.emba.uvm.edu/VSGC

Vermont Student Assistance Corporation

Vermont Incentive Grant

Type of award: Scholarship.
Intended use: For full-time undergraduate study at vocational, 2-year or 4-year institution in United States. Designated institutions: Any undergraduate institution or University of Vermont College of Medicine or veterinary school.
Eligibility: Applicant must be U.S. citizen or permanent resident residing in Vermont.
Basis for selection: Based on residency in Vermont, must be enrolled full-time at an approved postsecondary institution, and must meet needs test. Applicant must demonstrate financial need.
Application requirements: Proof of eligibility.
Additional information: Available to all undergraduate students who meet criteria. Available to graduate students enrolled at the University of Vermont Medical School or to graduate students enrolled at an approved school of veterinary medicine who meet the criteria.

Amount of award:	$500-$7,550
Number of awards:	9,078
Number of applicants:	16,260
Total amount awarded:	$12,379,526

Contact:
Grant Department
Vermont Student Assistance Corporation
P.O. Box 2000
Winooski, VT 05404-2601
Phone: 802-655-9602; in state 800-642-3177
Fax: 802-654-3765
Web: www.vsac.org

Vermont Non-Degree Program

Type of award: Scholarship.

Intended use: For non-degree study at postsecondary institution in United States.
Eligibility: Applicant must be permanent resident residing in Vermont.
Basis for selection: Applicant must demonstrate financial need.
Application requirements: Proof of eligibility. Available to Vermont residents enrolled in a non-degree course that will improve employability or encourage further study. Must meet needs test.
Additional information: Must be a Vermont resident. Maximum amount for this award is $625 for one course per semester. Available to all Vermont residents enrolled in a non-degree course that will improve employability or encourage further study.

Amount of award:	$625
Number of awards:	936
Number of applicants:	1,679
Total amount awarded:	$412,143

Contact:
Grant Department
Vermont Student Assistance Coirporation
P.O. Box 2000
Winooski, VT 05404-2601
Phone: 802-655-9602; in state 800-642-3765
Fax: 802-654-3765
Web: www.vsac.org

Vermont Part-Time Grant

Type of award: Scholarship.
Intended use: For half-time undergraduate study at vocational, 2-year or 4-year institution in or outside United States.
Eligibility: Applicant must be permanent resident residing in Vermont.
Basis for selection: Applicant must demonstrate financial need.
Application requirements: Proof of eligibility.
Additional information: Must be taking fewer than 12 credits and have not received bachelor's degree. Award amounts vary according to the number of credits the student is taking. Must be a Vermont resident.

Amount of award:	$250-$5,660
Number of awards:	2,364
Number of applicants:	4,593
Total amount awarded:	$958,392

Contact:
Grant Department
Vermont Student Assistance Corporation
P.O. Box 2000
Winooski, VT 05404-2601
Phone: 802-655-9602
Fax: 802-654-3765
Web: www.vsac.org

Veterans of Foreign Wars

Voice of Democracy Scholarship

Type of award: Scholarship.
Intended use: For undergraduate study at postsecondary institution in United States.
Eligibility: Applicant must be no older than 19, high school freshman, sophomore, junior or senior.

Basis for selection: Competition/talent/interest in writing/ journalism, based on interpretation of assigned patriotic theme, content and presentation of recorded 3-5 minute audio-essay.
Application requirements: Essay. Audio cassette tape of essay. Participants are judged by cassette tape, not written essay script.
Additional information: Must apply through high school or local Veterans of Foreign Wars Post. Any entry submitted to VFW National Headquarters will be returned to sender. Visit Website for additional information. This is a one time award; it is non-renewable.

Amount of award:	$1,000-$25,000
Number of awards:	56
Number of applicants:	100,000
Application deadline:	November 1
Total amount awarded:	$139,500

Contact:
Veterans of Foreign Wars National Headquarters
Voice of Democracy Program
406 West 34 Street
Kansas City, MO 64111
Phone: 816-968-1117
Fax: 816-968-1149
Web: www.vfw.org/vod

VF Corporation

VF Corporation Scholarship for Children of Employees

Type of award: Scholarship, renewable.
Intended use: For undergraduate study at accredited 2-year or 4-year institution.
Eligibility: Applicant or parent must be employed by VF Corporation.
Additional information: For further information or an application, contact VF Corporation directly.

Amount of award:	$1,000-$2,000

VF Knitwear, Inc.

Barry E. Pruett Scholarship

Type of award: Scholarship, renewable.
Intended use: For undergraduate study at accredited vocational, 2-year or 4-year institution.
Eligibility: Applicant or parent must be employed by Bassett-Walker, Inc.
Basis for selection: Applicant must demonstrate financial need.
Additional information: For further information or an application, contact Bassett-Walker, Inc. directly.

Amount of award:	$500

Virgin Islands Board of Education

Virgin Islands Leveraging Educational Assistance Partnership Program

Type of award: Scholarship, renewable.
Intended use: For full-time undergraduate or graduate study at postsecondary institution.
Eligibility: Applicant must be U.S. citizen or permanent resident residing in Virgin Islands.
Basis for selection: Applicant must demonstrate financial need and high academic achievement.
Application requirements: Transcript. Application, acceptance letter from institution for first-time applicants or transfer students. Must fill out profile (CSS code 0396).
Additional information: Minimum 2.0 GPA required.

Amount of award:	$500-$3,000
Number of awards:	5
Number of applicants:	50

Contact:
Virgin Islands Board of Education-Financial Aid Office
P.O. Box 11900
St. Thomas, VI 801
Phone: 340-774-4546

Virgin Islands Music Scholarship

Type of award: Scholarship, renewable.
Intended use: For full-time undergraduate study at accredited 2-year or 4-year institution in United States.
Eligibility: Applicant must be high school senior. Applicant must be U.S. citizen or permanent resident residing in Virgin Islands.
Basis for selection: Major/career interest in music. Applicant must demonstrate financial need and high academic achievement.
Application requirements: Transcript. Application.
Additional information: Contact sponsor for application, deadlines. Must be graduating from or graduate of Virgin Islands high school. Minimum GPA 2.0. Number of awards varies.

Amount of award:	$2,000

Contact:
Virgin Islands Board of Education - Financial Aid Office
P.O. Box 11900
St. Thomas, VI 00801
Phone: 340-774-4546

Virginia Department of Education

Virginia Lee-Jackson Scholarship

Type of award: Scholarship.
Intended use: For full-time freshman study at accredited 2-year or 4-year institution in United States.
Eligibility: Applicant must be high school junior or senior. Applicant must be residing in Virginia.

Basis for selection: Competition/talent/interest in writing/journalism, based on essay demonstrating appreciation for virtues exemplified by General Robert E. Lee or General Thomas J. Stonewall Jackson.

Application requirements: Essay, transcript.

Additional information: Awards $1,000 for best three essays from eight Virginia regions. Additional awards for exceptional essays.

Amount of award:	$1,000-$10,000
Number of awards:	24

Contact:
High school guidance counselor.
Web: www.schev.edu

Virginia Robert C. Byrd Honor Scholarship

Type of award: Scholarship, renewable.

Intended use: For full-time undergraduate study at accredited 4-year institution.

Eligibility: Applicant must be high school senior. Applicant must be U.S. citizen or permanent resident residing in Virginia.

Basis for selection: Applicant must demonstrate high academic achievement and service orientation.

Application requirements: Recommendations, transcript by high school principal. SAT/ACT scores, application.

Additional information: Application and information sent to all high school principals (public and private) in February.

Contact:
Local high school principal's office.
Web: www.schev.edu

Virginia Department of Health

Mary Marshall Nursing Scholarship

Type of award: Scholarship.

Intended use: For full-time undergraduate or graduate study at accredited 4-year or graduate institution. Designated institutions: Any nursing school in state of Virginia.

Eligibility: Applicant must be U.S. citizen or permanent resident residing in Virginia.

Basis for selection: Major/career interest in nursing. Applicant must demonstrate financial need.

Application requirements: Transcript. Application; financial aid forms (FAF, FFS, or FAFSA).

Additional information: Minimum 3.0 GPA in required courses, not electives. Provides awards to students who agree to work in nursing profession in Virginia at rate of one month for every $100 of aid received. Must reside in Virginia at least one year prior to application. Recipient may reapply for succeeding years. Applications and guidelines available from Dean/Director or Financial Aid Office at applicant's nursing school or from below address. Applications not accepted prior to April 30.

Amount of award:	$2,000
Application deadline:	June 30

Contact:
Center for Primary Care and Rural Health, Virginia Dept. of Health
1500 E. Main Street, Suite 227
P.O. Box 2448 (23218)
Richmond, VA 23219
Phone: 804-371-4090

Virginia Museum of Fine Arts

Virginia Museum of Fine Arts Fellowship

Type of award: Scholarship, renewable.

Intended use: For full-time undergraduate or graduate study at accredited 4-year or graduate institution.

Eligibility: Applicant must be high school senior. Applicant must be U.S. citizen residing in Virginia.

Basis for selection: Major/career interest in arts, general; film/video or art/art history. Applicant must demonstrate financial need and high academic achievement.

Application requirements: Portfolio, recommendations, transcript.

Additional information: May apply in one of the following categories: crafts, drawing, sculpture, filmmaking, painting, photography, printmaking, video, on the graduate or undergraduate levels. Candidates in art history may apply on the graduate level only. Must submit either ten 35mm slides representing recent work or three of the following: 16mm or video format films, videos, research papers, or published articles. Visit Website for guidelines and application.

Amount of award:	$4,000-$6,000
Number of awards:	14
Number of applicants:	600
Application deadline:	March 1
Notification begins:	May 15
Total amount awarded:	$77,000

Contact:
Virginia Museum of Fine Arts Fellowships
Education and Outreach Division
2800 Grove Avenue
Richmond, VA 23221-2466
Phone: 804-204-2661
Web: www.vmfa.state.va.us

Virginia Space Grant Consortium

Aerospace Undergraduate Research Scholarship Program

Type of award: Scholarship.

Intended use: For full-time junior or senior study at accredited 4-year institution in United States. Designated institutions: College of William and Mary, Hampton University, Old Dominion University, The University of Virginia, Virginia Tech.

Eligibility: Applicant must be U.S. citizen residing in Virginia.

Basis for selection: Major/career interest in aerospace; astronomy; biology; chemistry; computer/information sciences; education; engineering; geology/earth sciences; mathematics or physics. Applicant must demonstrate high academic achievement.

Application requirements: Recommendations, essay, transcript, research proposal.

Additional information: Applicants must provide a resume, and show a GPA of 3.0 or greater. Awards can include $3,000 stipend plus $1,000 travel/research during the academic year, and $3,500 stipend plus $1,000 travel/research during the summer (ten weeks). Awardees must attend a Virginia Space Grant Consortium member institution. The Consortium actively encourages women, minorities, and students with disabilities to apply.

Amount of award:	$3,000-$8,500
Number of awards:	12
Number of applicants:	30
Application deadline:	February 5
Notification begins:	April 15

Contact:
Virginia Space Grant Consortium
Old Dominion University Peninsula Center
2713-D Magruder Blvd.
Hampton, VA 23666
Phone: 757-865-0726
Fax: 757-865-7965
Web: www.vsgc.odu.edu

NASA Space Grant Teacher Education Scholarship

Type of award: Scholarship.
Intended use: For full-time undergraduate study in United States. Designated institutions: College of William and Mary, Hampton University, Old Dominion University, University of Virginia, Virginia Tech.
Eligibility: Applicant must be high school senior. Applicant must be U.S. citizen.
Basis for selection: Major/career interest in education; computer/information sciences; mathematics or science, general.
Application requirements: Recommendations, essay, transcript.
Additional information: Applicants must be enrolled in course of study leading to pre-college teacher certification. Priority given to technology, education, mathematics, and earth/space/environmental science majors. The Consortium actively encourages women, minorities, and students with disabilities to apply.

Amount of award:	$1,000
Number of awards:	10
Number of applicants:	20
Application deadline:	February 8
Notification begins:	April 1
Total amount awarded:	$10,000

Contact:
Virginia Space Grant Consortium
Old Dominion University Peninsula Center
2713-D Magruder Blvd.
Hampton, VA 23666
Phone: 757-865-0726
Fax: 757-865-7965
Web: www.vsgc.odu.edu

NASA Space Grant Virginia Community College Scholarship

Type of award: Scholarship.
Intended use: For sophomore study in United States. Designated institutions: Community colleges in Virginia.
Eligibility: Applicant must be U.S. citizen residing in Virginia.
Basis for selection: Major/career interest in aerospace; computer/information sciences; electronics; engineering; mathematics or science, general.
Application requirements: Recommendations, essay, transcript.
Additional information: Awards are generally to full-time students (12 semester hours), but part-time students (6-9 hours) demonstrating academic achievements are also eligible. Applicants must provide resume, photograph, and biographical information, and show GPA of 3.0 or greater. Scholarship is open to students at all community colleges in Virginia. Application deadline may vary. Consortium actively encourages women, minorities, and students with disabilities to apply.

Amount of award:	$1,500
Number of awards:	10
Number of applicants:	20
Application deadline:	February 8
Notification begins:	April 1

Contact:
Virginia Space Grant Consortium
Old Dominion University Peninsula Center
2713-D Magruder Blvd.
Hampton, VA 23666
Phone: 757-865-0726
Fax: 757-865-7965
Web: www.vsgc.odu.edu

Voith Paper Inc.

Voith Paper Inc. Scholarship

Type of award: Scholarship.
Intended use: For undergraduate study at accredited vocational, 2-year or 4-year institution.
Eligibility: Applicant or parent must be employed by Voith Paper Inc.
Additional information: For further information or an application, contact Voith Paper Inc. directly.

Amount of award:	$1,000

Voith Siemens Hydro Power Generation, Inc.

Voith Siemens Hydro Power Generation, Inc.

Type of award: Scholarship.
Intended use: For undergraduate study at accredited vocational, 2-year or 4-year institution.
Eligibility: Applicant or parent must be employed by Siemens Hydro Power Generation, Inc.
Basis for selection: Applicant must demonstrate financial need.

Additional information: Must be child of employee of Voith Siemens. For further information or an application, contact Voith Siemens Hydro Power Generation, Inc. directly.

    Amount of award: $2,000-$2,500

Vollrath Company, L.L.C.

Vollrath Company Scholarship Program

Type of award: Scholarship, renewable.
Intended use: For freshman study at accredited vocational, 2-year or 4-year institution.
Eligibility: Applicant or parent must be employed by Vollrath Company, Inc.
Additional information: For further information or an application, contact Vollrath Company, L.L.C. directly.

    Amount of award: $2,000-$3,000

Volvo Cars of North America, Inc.

Volvo Scholars Program

Type of award: Scholarship, renewable.
Intended use: For undergraduate study at accredited postsecondary institution.
Eligibility: Applicant or parent must be employed by Volvo Cars of North America, Inc. Applicant must be high school senior.
Additional information: For further information or an application, contact Volvo Cars of North America, Inc. directly.

    Amount of award: $2,000
Contact:
Volvo Cars of North America, Inc.

VPI Foundation Inc.

VPI Foundation Scholarship for Sons and Daughters

Type of award: Scholarship, renewable.
Intended use: For undergraduate study at vocational, 2-year or 4-year institution.
Eligibility: Applicant or parent must be employed by VPI Foundation, Inc. Applicant must be high school senior.
Additional information: For further information or an application, contact VPI Foundation directly.

    Amount of award: $1,000-$2,000

W.E. Lahr Co.

William E. Lahr Scholarship Program

Type of award: Scholarship.
Intended use: For undergraduate study at vocational, 2-year or 4-year institution.
Eligibility: Applicant or parent must be employed by W.E. Lahr Co. Applicant must be high school senior.
Additional information: For further information or an application, contact W.E. Lahr Company directly.

    Amount of award: $500-$3,000

Wakefern Food Corporation

Wakefern/Shoprite Scholarship Program

Type of award: Scholarship, renewable.
Intended use: For undergraduate study at accredited vocational, 2-year or 4-year institution.
Eligibility: Applicant or parent must be employed by Wakefern Food Corporation.
Additional information: For further information or an application, contact Wakefern Food Corporation directly.

    Amount of award: $1,000-$3,000

Wal-Mart Foundation

Sam Walton Community Scholarship

Type of award: Scholarship.
Intended use: For full-time undergraduate study at accredited 2-year or 4-year institution.
Eligibility: Applicant must be high school senior.
Basis for selection: Applicant must demonstrate financial need, high academic achievement, leadership and service orientation.
Application requirements: Recommendations, transcript. SAT/ACT scores.
Additional information: Formally known as the Community Scholarship, award is given to one college-bound senior in a community where a Wal-Mart store or Sam's Club is operating. Wal-Mart associates and their children not eligible. Local store contacts area high schools and make available application packets in January. Applications not available year-round. If unable to obtain one, call local store personnel manager. Applications not available through Foundation or at corporate level. Winners announced by mid-March.

    Amount of award: $1,000
    Number of awards: 2,400
    Total amount awarded: $2,400,000
Contact:
Contact your high school guidance counselor for application.
Phone: 800-530-9925
Web: www.walmartfoundation.org

Walton Foundation Scholarship

Type of award: Scholarship.
Intended use: For full-time undergraduate study at accredited 2-year or 4-year institution.
Eligibility: Applicant or parent must be employed by Wal-Mart Stores, Inc. Applicant must be high school senior.
Basis for selection: Applicant must demonstrate financial need and high academic achievement.
Application requirements: Recommendations, transcript, proof of eligibility. SAT/ACT scores.
Additional information: $6,000 scholarship payable over four years. Applicant's parent or guardian must have been employed with Wal-Mart full-time (28 hrs/wk) at least one year as of March 1. Applicant must demonstrate both financial need and high academic achievement. Applications available in January from personnel office.

Amount of award:	$6,000
Number of awards:	100
Number of applicants:	1,500
Application deadline:	March 1
Total amount awarded:	$600,000

Contact:
Wal-Mart Foundation
702 SW 8 Street
Bentonville, AR 72716-8071
Phone: 800-530-9925
Web: www.walmartfoundation.org

Walker Forge, Inc.

Walker Forge, Inc. Scholarship Program

Type of award: Scholarship, renewable.
Intended use: For undergraduate study at accredited vocational, 2-year or 4-year institution.
Eligibility: Applicant or parent must be employed by Walker Forge, Inc.
Basis for selection: Applicant must demonstrate financial need.
Additional information: For further information or an application, contact Walker Forge, Inc. directly.

Amount of award:	$500-$3,000

Walter O. Wells Foundation

Walter O. Wells Foundation Scholarship Program

Type of award: Scholarship.
Intended use: For undergraduate study at vocational, 2-year or 4-year institution.
Eligibility: Applicant or parent must be employed by Walter O. Wells Foundation. Applicant must be high school senior.
Additional information: For further information or an application, contact Walter O. Wells Foundation directly.

Amount of award:	$500-$2,000

Washington Crossing Foundation

Washington Crossing Foundation Scholarship

Type of award: Scholarship, renewable.
Intended use: For full-time freshman study at accredited 4-year institution.
Eligibility: Applicant must be high school senior. Applicant must be U.S. citizen.
Basis for selection: Major/career interest in political science/government or public administration/service. Applicant must demonstrate high academic achievement, depth of character, leadership, patriotism, seriousness of purpose and service orientation.
Application requirements: Interview, recommendations, essay, transcript, proof of eligibility. SAT or ACT scores.
Additional information: Applicants must write essay on why they plan a career in government service, including any inspiration to be derived from Washington's famous crossing of the Delaware. One award is reserved for Pennsylvania's five southeastern counties.

Amount of award:	$1,000-$20,000
Number of awards:	9
Number of applicants:	1,300
Application deadline:	January 15
Notification begins:	April 15
Total amount awarded:	$57,000

Contact:
Attn: Vice Chairman-Washington Crossing Foundation
P.O. Box 503
Levitton, PA 19058
Phone: 215-949-8841
Web: www.gwcf.org

Washington Gas

Washington Gas Scholarships

Type of award: Scholarship.
Intended use: For full-time freshman study at accredited postsecondary institution in United States.
Eligibility: Applicant must be high school senior. Applicant must be residing in District of Columbia.
Basis for selection: Major/career interest in business; science, general; mathematics; computer/information sciences; accounting; marketing or engineering. Applicant must demonstrate high academic achievement, depth of character, leadership, patriotism, seriousness of purpose and service orientation.
Application requirements: Recommendations, transcript. PSAT or SAT; resume; brief description of what student wishes to accomplish at school and after graduation; list of community work that student has done.
Additional information: Minimum GPA of 3.0. Program may change; contact sponsor for updated information.

Amount of award:	$1,000
Number of awards:	16
Application deadline:	March 20
Notification begins:	May 15

Contact:
Washington Gas DC Public Affairs
Attn. Scholarship Coordinator
1100 H Street, NW
Washington, DC 20080
Phone: 202-624-6697
Fax: 202-624-6221

Washington NASA Space Grant Consortium

Community College Transfer Scholarship

Type of award: Scholarship, renewable.
Intended use: For full-time undergraduate study at accredited 4-year institution in United States. Designated institutions: Washington community colleges.
Eligibility: Applicant must be U.S. citizen residing in Washington.
Basis for selection: Major/career interest in engineering; mathematics or science, general. Applicant must demonstrate high academic achievement.
Application requirements: Recommendations, essay, transcript.
Additional information: The Washington Space Grant Consortium Community College Transfer Scholarships are for community college students planning to transfer to University of Washington to continue their studies in math, engineering or science. Award for full or partial tuition. The Consortium actively encourages women, minority and disabled students to apply. Recipients may reapply for two years depending on availability of funding and providing that they maintain program requirements.

Number of awards:	5
Number of applicants:	35
Application deadline:	March 31
Notification begins:	May 15

Contact:
NASA Space Grant Washington Space Grant Consortium
401A Johnson Hall
Box 351650
Seattle, WA 98195-1650
Phone: 206-543-1943 or 800-659-1943
Fax: 206-543-0179
Web: www.waspacegrant.org

Washington Space Grant Consortium

Undergraduate Scholarship Program

Type of award: Scholarship, renewable.
Intended use: For full-time undergraduate study at 4-year institution. Designated institutions: University of Washington.
Eligibility: Applicant must be high school senior. Applicant must be U.S. citizen residing in Washington.
Basis for selection: Major/career interest in mathematics; science, general or engineering. Applicant must demonstrate high academic achievement.

Application requirements: Interview, recommendations, essay, transcript. State applicant must attend high school in the state of Washington.
Additional information: Consortium actively encourages women, minority, and disabled students to apply. Visit Website for additional details.

Amount of award:	$1,500-$3,000
Number of awards:	25
Number of applicants:	210

Contact:
Washington Space Grant Consortium
401A Johnson Hall
Box 351650
Seattle, WA 98195-1650
Phone: 206-543-1943 or 800-659-1943
Fax: 206-543-0179
Web: www.waspacegrant.org

Washington State Higher Education Coordinating Board

Washington Promise Scholarship

Type of award: Scholarship, renewable.
Intended use: For freshman or sophomore study at accredited vocational, 2-year or 4-year institution.
Eligibility: Applicant must be high school senior. Applicant must be permanent resident residing in Washington.
Basis for selection: Applicant must demonstrate financial need and high academic achievement.
Application requirements: Nomination by high school. Applicant must be in top 15% of WA high school senior class. Must meet certain income cutoffs.
Additional information: Eligible students must be nominated by high school.

Amount of award:	$1,650
Number of awards:	5,500
Number of applicants:	6,000
Total amount awarded:	$8,350,000

Contact:
Washington State Higher Education Coordinating Board
917 Lakeridge Way SW
P.O. Box 43430
Olympia, WA 98504-3430
Phone: 888-535-0747
Fax: 360-753-7808
Web: www.hecb.wa.gov

Washington State American Indian Endowed Scholarship

Type of award: Scholarship.
Intended use: For full-time undergraduate study at accredited vocational, 2-year, 4-year or graduate institution. Designated institutions: Postsecondary schools in the state of Washington.
Eligibility: Must have close social and cultural ties to American Indian community within Washington state. Applicant must be U.S. citizen residing in Washington.
Basis for selection: Applicant must demonstrate financial need, high academic achievement and service orientation.
Application requirements: Proof of eligibility. Application form.

Scholarships

Additional information: Applicant must have strong commitment to return service to state's American Indian community.

- **Amount of award:** $1,000-$2,000
- **Number of awards:** 20
- **Application deadline:** June 1

Contact:
Washington State Higher Education Coordinating Board
917 Lakeridge Way SW
P.O. Box 43430
Olympia, WA 98504-3430
Phone: 360-753-7800
Web: www.hecb.wa.gov

Washington State Educational Opportunity Grant

Type of award: Scholarship, renewable.
Intended use: For full-time junior or senior study at accredited 4-year institution. Designated institutions: Eligible postsecondary institutions in Washington.
Eligibility: Applicant must be U.S. citizen or permanent resident residing in Washington.
Basis for selection: Applicant must demonstrate financial need.
Application requirements: Essay, proof of eligibility. Application (available online).
Additional information: Must reside in specific counties and be transferring into college (public or private) with existing unused capacity. Must be "place-bound." Must be transfer students at junior or senior level. Application deadlines vary. Contact financial aid office of institution for details.

- **Amount of award:** $2,500
- **Number of awards:** 400
- **Total amount awarded:** $1,500,000

Contact:
Washington State Higher Education Coordinating Board
917 Lakeridge Way SW
P.O. Box 43430
Olympia, WA 98504-3430
Phone: 360-753-7800
Web: www.hecb.wa.gov

Washington State Need Grant

Type of award: Scholarship, renewable.
Intended use: For undergraduate study at accredited vocational, 2-year or 4-year institution. Designated institutions: Eligible postsecondary insitutions in Washington and some designated institutions in Oregon and Idaho.
Eligibility: Applicant must be U.S. citizen or permanent resident residing in Washington.
Basis for selection: Applicant must demonstrate financial need.
Application requirements: Proof of eligibility. FAFSA.
Additional information: Theology/religion majors not eligible. Contact institution financial aid office for additional requirements and deadlines. Grants are only given to students from low income families. Average grant in most recent year was $1,500. Must meet qualifications every year for renewal, up to five years.

- **Number of awards:** 53,000
- **Total amount awarded:** $86,000,000

Contact:
Washington State Higher Education Coordinating Board
917 Lakeridge Way SW
P.O. Box 43430
Olympia, WA 98504-3430
Phone: 360-753-7800
Web: www.hecb.wa.gov

Washington State Scholars Program

Type of award: Scholarship.
Intended use: For undergraduate study at accredited vocational, 2-year or 4-year institution. Designated institutions: Postsecondary institutions in Washington.
Eligibility: Applicant must be high school senior. Applicant must be U.S. citizen or permanent resident residing in Washington.
Basis for selection: Applicant must demonstrate high academic achievement, depth of character, leadership, seriousness of purpose and service orientation.
Application requirements: Transcript, proof of eligibility, nomination by high school principal or guidance counselor. SAT/ACT scores.
Additional information: Four-year award of $3,646/yr. Must rank in top one percent of class. May not defer enrollment. Students must be nominated by high school principal or guidance counselor to be eligible. Eligible high school seniors should contact their high school counselors for more information.

- **Number of awards:** 400
- **Total amount awarded:** $1,600,000

Contact:
Washington State Higher Education Coordinating Board
917 Lakeridge Way SW
P.O. Box 43430
Olympia, WA 98504-3430
Phone: 360-753-7800
Web: www.hecb.wa.gov

Washington State PTA Scholarship Foundation

Washington State PTA Scholarship

Type of award: Scholarship.
Intended use: For full-time freshman study at accredited vocational, 2-year or 4-year institution.
Eligibility: Applicant must be U.S. citizen or permanent resident residing in Washington.
Basis for selection: Applicant must demonstrate financial need, depth of character, leadership, seriousness of purpose and service orientation.
Application requirements: Recommendations, essay, transcript, proof of eligibility.
Additional information: Applicant must be graduate of Washington state public high school. Grant administered according to college's determination. Not transferable to another institution if already enrolled in classes. Applications available after December 1. Visit Website for additional information and to download application.

Amount of award:	$500-$1,000
Number of awards:	60
Number of applicants:	2,000
Application deadline:	March 1
Notification begins:	May 1
Total amount awarded:	$55,000

Contact:
Washington State PTA Scholarship Foundation
2003 65 Avenue West
Tacoma, WA 98466-6215
Phone: 253-565-2153 or 800-562-3804
Fax: 253-565-7753
Web: www.wastatepta.org

Waters Corporation

Waters Scholarship Program

Type of award: Scholarship, renewable.
Intended use: For freshman study at 4-year institution.
Eligibility: Applicant or parent must be employed by Waters Corporation. Applicant must be high school senior.
Additional information: For further information or an application, contact Waters Corporation directly.

Amount of award:	$5,000

Watlow Electric Manufacturing Co.

Watlow Employee Children Scholarship Fund

Type of award: Scholarship.
Intended use: For undergraduate study at vocational, 2-year or 4-year institution.
Eligibility: Applicant or parent must be employed by Watlow Electric Manufacturing Co.
Additional information: For further information or an application, contact Watlow Electric Manufacturing directly.

Amount of award:	$1,500

Wells Fargo

CollegeSTEPS Program

Type of award: Scholarship.
Intended use: For freshman study at 2-year or 4-year institution.
Eligibility: Applicant must be high school senior. Applicant must be U.S. citizen or permanent resident.
Additional information: Scholarships and educational postcards on college-preparatory topics offered. Call between 6am and 10pm, Central time, Monday to Friday or visit Website to apply. High school freshmen, sophomores, and juniors can also sign up to receive postcards. Employees of Wells Fargo and immediate family members not eligible for scholarship.

Amount of award:	$1,000
Number of awards:	250
Total amount awarded:	$250,000

Contact:
Education Financial Services
Wells Fargo
P.O. Box 5185
Sioux Falls, SD 57117-5185
Phone: 800-658-3567
Web: www.wellsfargo.com/per/accounts/student/finaid/collegesteps

Wells Fargo Foundation

Wells Fargo Team Members' Dependent Children Scholarship

Type of award: Scholarship, renewable.
Intended use: For undergraduate study at accredited vocational, 2-year or 4-year institution.
Eligibility: Applicant or parent must be employed by Wells Fargo Foundation.
Additional information: For further information or application, contact Wells Fargo Foundation directly.

Amount of award:	$1,000

Welsh Society of Philadelphia

Welsh Heritage Scholarship

Type of award: Scholarship, renewable.
Intended use: For full-time undergraduate study at accredited postsecondary institution. Designated institutions: Must be located within 150 miles of Philadelphia, if applicant not resident of same area.
Eligibility: Applicant must be Welsh.
Basis for selection: Applicant must demonstrate high academic achievement and seriousness of purpose.
Application requirements: Recommendations, essay, transcript. Statement of purpose. College Board test scores.
Additional information: Applicant must be a resident of, or attending college within 150 miles of Philadelphia. Participation in Welsh organizations or events preferred.

Amount of award:	$1,000
Number of awards:	5
Number of applicants:	50
Application deadline:	March 1
Notification begins:	May 1
Total amount awarded:	$5,000

Contact:
Welsh Society of Philadelphia
Scholarship Committee Chairman
P.O. Box 7287
St. David's, PA 19087-7287
Phone: 610-527-1832

Wendell J. Kelley

Evelyn K. Kelley Scholarship

Type of award: Scholarship, renewable.
Intended use: For full-time undergraduate study at accredited 2-year or 4-year institution in United States.
Eligibility: Applicant must be Alaskan native, Asian American, African American, Mexican American, Hispanic American, Puerto Rican or American Indian.
Basis for selection: Based on activities, awards, honors, and work experience. Applicant must demonstrate high academic achievement, depth of character, leadership, seriousness of purpose and service orientation.
Application requirements: Transcript. Minimum 3.0 GPA required.
Additional information: Highly competitive. Minorities receive one-third of awards. Applications must be postmarked by June 1 for consideration. For further information or an application, contact Wendell J. Kelley Scholarship directly.

Amount of award:	$1,000

Contact:
Citizens' Scholarship Foundation of America
Evelyn K. Kelley Scholarship
P.O. Box 297
St. Peter, MN 56082

West Group

West Group Scholarship Program

Type of award: Scholarship, renewable.
Intended use: For undergraduate study at accredited vocational, 2-year or 4-year institution.
Eligibility: Applicant or parent must be employed by West Publishing Company.
Additional information: For further information or an application, contact West Group directly.

Amount of award:	$2,500

West Pharmaceutical Services, Inc.

Herman O. West Scholarship

Type of award: Scholarship, renewable.
Intended use: For full-time undergraduate study at accredited 2-year or 4-year institution.
Eligibility: Applicant or parent must be employed by West Pharmaceutical Services, Inc. Applicant must be high school senior. Applicant must be U.S. citizen.
Basis for selection: Applicant must demonstrate high academic achievement.
Application requirements: Proof of eligibility.
Additional information: Parent must be employee of West Pharmaceutical Services, Inc. Award is renewable annually for a maximum of four years.

Amount of award:	$2,500
Application deadline:	February 28
Notification begins:	May 1
Total amount awarded:	$50,000

Contact:
H.O. West Foundation
101 Gordon Drive
Lionville, PA 19341-0645

West Virginia Division of Veterans Affairs

West Virginia War Orphans Educational Assistance

Type of award: Scholarship, renewable.
Intended use: For undergraduate, graduate or non-degree study in United States. Designated institutions: West Viriginia supported colleges or universities.
Eligibility: Applicant must be at least 16, no older than 23. Applicant must be U.S. citizen residing in West Virginia. Applicant must be dependent of deceased veteran who served in the Army, Air Force, Marines, Navy, Coast Guard or Reserves/ National Guard. Applicant's parent must be veteran killed while on active duty during war-time or died of injury or illness resulting from war -time service.
Application requirements: Proof of eligibility.
Additional information: Award is waiver of tuition and registration fees. Toll-free number for in-state calls: 888-838-2332.

Amount of award:	Full tuition
Number of awards:	35
Number of applicants:	35
Application deadline:	July 1, December 1
Notification begins:	July 15, December 15

Contact:
West Virginia Division of Veterans Affairs
1321 Plaza East-Suite 101
Charleston,, WV 25301-1400
Phone: 304-558-3661
Fax: 304-558-3662

West Virginia Higher Education Policy Commission

West Virginia Engineering, Science and Technology Scholarship

Type of award: Scholarship, renewable.
Intended use: For full-time undergraduate study at postsecondary institution in United States. Designated institutions: Eligible institutions of higher learning in West Virginia.
Eligibility: Applicant must be U.S. citizen or permanent resident.
Basis for selection: Major/career interest in science, general; engineering; engineering, civil; engineering, computer;

engineering, electrical/electronic; engineering, mechanical; computer/information sciences; life sciences; physical sciences or natural sciences. Applicant must demonstrate high academic achievement and seriousness of purpose.

Application requirements: Completed application. High school GPA of 3.0 or equivalent or cumulative GPA of 3.0 after two years at postsecondary institution. Interested high school students should apply through HS counselor, currently enrolled college/university students should apply through their institution.

Additional information: The objective of this scholarship is for recipient to obtain a degree/certificate in engineering, science or technology and to commit to pursuit a career in West Virginia. Recipient must agree that within one year after ceasing to be full-time student to begin working full-time in engineering, science or technology field in West Virginia or begin a program of community service relating to these fields in West Virginia, for a duration of one year for each year scholarship was received. If work requirement fails to be met, recipient is responsible for repayment of scholarship plus interest and any required collection fees.

Amount of award:	$3,000
Number of awards:	184
Number of applicants:	400
Application deadline:	April 1
Total amount awarded:	$554,000

Contact:
West Virginia Higher Education Policy Commission
Engineering, Science and Technology Program
1018 Kanawha Boulevard East, Suite 700
Charleston, WV 25301-2827
Phone: 888-825-5707
Web: www.hepc.wvnet.edu

West Virginia Higher Education Adult Part-time Student (HEAPS) Grant Program

Type of award: Scholarship, renewable.
Intended use: For half-time undergraduate study at postsecondary institution. Designated institutions: Community colleges, technical colleges, adult technical preparatory educ. program/training, state colleges/universities, independent colleges/universities, or any approved distance education, including world wide web based courses. Approved distance educ. classes must be authorized by institution with course credits transferred back to that institution. Institution must be eligible to participate in Federal Pell Grant Program.
Eligibility: Applicant must be returning adult student. Applicant must be U.S. citizen or permanent resident residing in West Virginia.
Basis for selection: Applicant must demonstrate financial need.
Application requirements: FAFSA and any supplemental materials required by individual institutions. Applicant must not have been enrolled in high school diploma program (other than GED) for at least two years, must be making satisfactory progress at time of application, must either be enrolled with cumulative GPA of 2.0 (for renewal applicants) or be accepted for enrollment by intended institution (for first time applicants), must have complied with Military Selective Service Act, must qualify as independent student according to federal financial aid criteria, must not be in default on higher education loan, and must not be incarcerated in correctional facility.
Additional information: Students may receive 3-11 hours of college coursework or its equivalent. At public colleges/

universities, award is actual amount of tuition and fees. At independent colleges/universities/vocational or technical schools, award is based upon average per credit/term hours tuition and fee charges assessed by all public undergraduate institutions. Applicant must meet deadline of institution to be attended. Contact Financial Aid Officer at institution student plans to attend or address listed below, or visit Website for additional information.

Amount of award:	Full tuition
Number of awards:	1,329
Number of applicants:	2,135
Total amount awarded:	$728,314

Contact:
West Virginia Higher Education Policy Commission
Daniel Crockett or Betty MacQueen
1018 Kanawha Boulevard, Fourth Floor
Charleston, WV 25301
Phone: 304-558-4618
Web: www.hepc.wvnet.edu

West Virginia Higher Education Grant

Type of award: Scholarship, renewable.
Intended use: For full-time undergraduate study at accredited 2-year or 4-year institution. Designated institutions: Public or private non-profit degree-granting colleges and universities in West Virginia or Pennsylvania.
Eligibility: Applicant must be U.S. citizen residing in West Virginia.
Basis for selection: Based on certain academic standards. Applicant must demonstrate financial need and high academic achievement.
Application requirements: Transcript. FAFSA. ACT/SAT I test scores must be submitted.
Additional information: Applicants must be resident of West Virginia for one year preceding date of application, but may attend school in public or private non-profit institutions in West Virginia or Pennsylvania. Award restricted for payment of tuition at non-profit institutions or hospital schools of nursing.

Amount of award:	$350-$2,570
Number of awards:	10,200
Number of applicants:	55,824
Application deadline:	March 1
Notification begins:	June 15
Total amount awarded:	$17,407,779

Contact:
West Virginia Higher Education Policy Commission
West Virginia Higher Education Grant Program
1018 Kanawha Boulevard East, Suite 700
Charleston, WV 25301-2827
Phone: 888-825-5707 or 304-558-4614
Web: www.hepc.wvnet.edu

West Virginia Robert C. Byrd Honors Scholarship

Type of award: Scholarship, renewable.
Intended use: For full-time freshman study at vocational, 2-year or 4-year institution in United States.
Eligibility: Applicant must be high school senior. Applicant must be U.S. citizen residing in West Virginia.
Basis for selection: Applicant must demonstrate high academic achievement.
Application requirements: Transcript, proof of eligibility, nomination by high school.
Additional information: SAT I or ACT required.

Amount of award:	$1,500
Number of awards:	39
Number of applicants:	165
Application deadline:	March 15
Notification begins:	April 1
Total amount awarded:	$247,500

Contact:
West Virginia Higher Education Policy Commission
Robert C. Byrd Honors Scholarship Program
1018 Kanawha Boulevard East, Suite 700
Charleston, WV 25301-2827
Phone: 304-558-4618
Web: www.hepc.wvnet.edu

West Virginia Space Grant Consortium

Undergraduate Scholarship

Type of award: Scholarship, renewable.
Intended use: For full-time undergraduate study at accredited 4-year institution in United States. Designated institutions: West Virginia University, Bethany College, Fairmont State College, Marshall University, Salem International University, Shepherd College, West Virginia University Institute of Technology, West Virginia State College, Wheeling-Jesuit University, West Liberty State College, and West Virginia Wesleyan College.
Eligibility: Applicant must be U.S. citizen residing in West Virginia.
Basis for selection: Major/career interest in aerospace; science, general or engineering. Applicant must demonstrate high academic achievement and seriousness of purpose.
Application requirements: Research proposal.
Additional information: Consortium makes it possible for undergraduate scholars to work with faculty members in their major department on research project to supplement classwork. Alternatively, some undergraduate scholars participate in the Consortium Challenge Program, working with elementary students on their science projects. Application deadline usually falls in mid- to late-September.

Amount of award:	$1,000-$2,000
Number of applicants:	16

Contact:
West Virginia Space Grant Consortium
College of Engineering and Mineral Resources
P.O. Box 6070, G60 ESB
Morgantown, WV 26506-6070
Phone: 304-293-4099
Fax: 304-293-4970
Web: www.cemr.wvu.edu/~wwwnasa/

Western Beef

Western Beef Scholarship Program

Type of award: Scholarship.
Intended use: For undergraduate study at 4-year institution.
Eligibility: Applicant or parent must be employed by Western Beef. Applicant must be high school senior.
Additional information: For further information or an application, contact Western Beef directly.

Amount of award:	$1,000

Western Golf Association / Evans Scholars Foundation

Chick Evans Caddie Scholarship

Type of award: Scholarship, renewable.
Intended use: For full-time undergraduate study at accredited 4-year institution in United States. Designated institutions: State institutions.
Eligibility: Applicant must be high school senior.
Basis for selection: Competition/talent/interest in Athletics/sports, based on a consistent caddie record. Applicant must demonstrate financial need, high academic achievement, depth of character and leadership.
Application requirements: Interview, recommendations, transcript, proof of eligibility. Tax returns and SAT or ACT test scores required. Financial aid profile.
Additional information: Scholarship for full tuition plus housing. Must have caddied minimum two years at Western Golf Association affiliated club and rank in top 25 percent of class. Most recipients attend one of the 14 universities where Evans Scholars Foundation owns and operates chapter house. Approximately 225 new Evans Scholarships awarded each year.

Amount of award:	Full tuition
Number of awards:	825
Application deadline:	September 30

Contact:
Scholarship Committee
Western Golf Assoc./Evans Scholars Foundation
1 Briar Road
Golf, IL 60029
Phone: 847-724-4600

Westlake Scholarship Foundation

Westlake Scholarship

Type of award: Scholarship, renewable.
Intended use: For full-time freshman study at accredited 2-year or 4-year institution in United States.
Eligibility: Applicant must be U.S. citizen or permanent resident residing in Missouri.
Basis for selection: Based on ambition to succeed. Applicant must demonstrate financial need, high academic achievement, depth of character, leadership and seriousness of purpose.
Application requirements: Recommendations, essay, transcript, proof of eligibility. Must submit ACT or SAT. Must submit FAFSA/SAR that indicates an EFC of $10,000 or less.
Additional information: Award covers tuition, fees, books, supplies, college housing and food plans.

Number of applicants:	800
Application deadline:	March 15
Notification begins:	June 1
Total amount awarded:	$1,049,000

Contact:
Westlake Scholarship Foundation
c/o Mercantile Trust Co.
Box 387
St. Louis, MO 63166
Phone: 314-725-6410

WestPlains Energy

WestPlains Energy Scholarship

Type of award: Scholarship, renewable.
Intended use: For undergraduate study at accredited vocational, 2-year or 4-year institution.
Eligibility: Applicant or parent must be employed by WestPlains Energy.
Additional information: For further information or an application, contact WestPlains Energy directly.
    Amount of award: $500-$1,500

Weyerhaeuser Company Foundation

Weyerhaeuser Company Foundation Community Education Scholarship Program

Type of award: Scholarship, renewable.
Intended use: For freshman study at accredited vocational or 2-year institution.
Eligibility: Applicant or parent must be employed by Weyerhaeuser Company.
Basis for selection: Applicant must demonstrate financial need.
Additional information: For further information or an application, contact Weyerhaeuser Company Foundation directly.
    Amount of award: $1,000

Wheaton Franciscan Services, Inc.

Sister Rose Mary Pint Scholarship Program

Type of award: Scholarship.
Intended use: For undergraduate study at vocational, 2-year or 4-year institution.
Eligibility: Applicant or parent must be employed by Wheaton Franciscan Services, Inc. Applicant must be high school senior.
Additional information: For further information or an application, contact Wheaton Franciscan Services Incorporated directly.
    Amount of award: $3,000

William Beaumont Hospital

William Beaumont Hospital Scholarship Program

Type of award: Scholarship, renewable.
Intended use: For undergraduate study at vocational, 2-year or 4-year institution.
Eligibility: Applicant or parent must be employed by William Beaumont Hospital. Applicant must be high school senior.
Additional information: For further information or an application, contact William Beumont Hospital directly.
    Amount of award: $1,000

William Randolph Hearst Foundation

Hearst Journalism Award

Type of award: Scholarship.
Intended use: For freshman, sophomore, junior or senior study at accredited 4-year institution. Designated institutions: Institution must be accredited by Accrediting Council on Education in Journalism and Mass Communication.
Basis for selection: Competition/talent/interest in writing/journalism, based on newsworthiness, research, excellence of journalistic writing, photojournalism, or broadcast news. Major/career interest in journalism; radio/television/film or communications.
Application requirements: Entries must be submitted by journalism department. Student must be journalism major actively involved in campus media.
Additional information: Field of study may also include photojournalism. Applicants must submit work that has been published or aired to be considered. Competition consists of eleven monthly contests and one championship. Scholarships are awarded to student winners with matching grants awarded to their departments of journalism. For additional information, applicants should contact journalism department chair or Hearst Foundation.
    Amount of award: $500-$5,000
    Number of awards: 130
Contact:
Hearst Journalism Awards Program
90 New Montgomery Street
Suite 1212
San Francisco, CA 94105-4504
Phone: 415-543-6033
Fax: 415-243-0760

United States Senate Youth Program

Type of award: Scholarship.
Intended use: For freshman, sophomore, junior or senior study at accredited 2-year or 4-year institution in United States.
Eligibility: Applicant must be high school junior or senior. Applicant must be U.S. citizen or permanent resident.
Basis for selection: Applicant must demonstrate leadership and service orientation.
Application requirements: Nomination by high school principal based on merit and community service. Application

available from high school principal or visit Website for state-level Selection Administrator information.

Additional information: Must be currently serving in elected capacity as student body officer, class officer, student council representative, or student representative to district, regional, or state-level civic or educational organization. Selection process managed by state-level department of education of each applicant. Scholarship includes all-expenses-paid week in Washington. Application deadline is in early Fall for most states. Actual deadline dates vary by state. Visit Website for more information.

Amount of award:	$2,000
Number of awards:	104
Total amount awarded:	$208,000

Contact:
Rita Almon, Program Director William Randolph Hearst Foundation
Suite 1212
90 New Montgomery Street
San Francisco, CA 94105-4504
Phone: 800-841-7048
Fax: 415-243-0760
Web: www.ussenateyouth.org

William S. Davila Scholarship Fund Endowment

William S. Davila Scholarship Fund

Type of award: Scholarship.
Intended use: For freshman study at accredited 4-year institution.
Eligibility: Applicant or parent must be employed by Food Industry. Applicant must be residing in Nevada or California.
Additional information: Must work in the food industry or be son or daughter of person working in the food industry, including retail supermarket companies, manufacturers, brokers and distributors of food products sold in retail stores. Must attend public high school in one of the following Southern California counties: Los Angeles, Orange, San Diego, Fresno, Kearns, Tulare, San Luis Obispo, Santa Barbara. Students in Clark County, Nevada also eligible. Further information and application available from high school guidance office.

Amount of award:	$1,000-$2,500

Williams Steel and Hardware

Williams Steel and Hardware Scholarship

Type of award: Scholarship, renewable.
Intended use: For undergraduate study at accredited vocational, 2-year or 4-year institution.
Eligibility: Applicant or parent must be employed by Williams Steel & Hardware.
Basis for selection: Applicant must demonstrate financial need.

Additional information: For further information or an application, contact Williams Steel and Hardware directly.

Amount of award:	$300-$1,200

Wilson Ornithological Society

George A Hall/Harold F. Mayfield Award

Type of award: Research grant.
Intended use: For non-degree study.
Basis for selection: Major/career interest in ornithology.
Application requirements: Recommendations, research proposal. Application (available online), budget. Research proposal must be no longer than three pages.
Additional information: Research grant for studies of birds. Award restricted to amateur researchers, including high school students, without access to funds and facilities of academic institutions or governmental agencies. Willingness to report research results as oral or poster paper is condition of award. Applicants whose first language is not English may submit proposal in their first language. Contact sponsor for more information.

Amount of award:	$1,000
Number of awards:	1
Number of applicants:	3
Application deadline:	January 15
Notification begins:	April 15
Total amount awarded:	$1,000

Contact:
Wilson Ornithological Society c/o Dr. Richard B. Stiehl
USGS-BRD/Mid-continent Ecol. Science Center
4512 McMurray Ave
Ft. Collins, CO 80525-3400
Phone: 970-226-9421
Web: http://www.ummz.lsa.umich.edu/birds/wosawards.html

Paul A. Stewart Award

Type of award: Research grant.
Intended use: For undergraduate, master's, doctoral, postgraduate or non-degree study at graduate institution.
Basis for selection: Major/career interest in ornithology.
Application requirements: Recommendations, research proposal. Application (available online), budget.
Additional information: Research grant for studies of birds. Preference given to proposals studying bird movements based on banding, analysis of recoveries and returns of banded birds, with an emphasis on economic ornithology. Willingness to report research results as oral or poster paper is condition of award. Multiple awards given annually. Applicant's whose first language is not English may submit proposal in their first language. Contact sponsor for details.

Amount of award:	$500
Number of awards:	4
Number of applicants:	21
Application deadline:	January 15
Notification begins:	April 15
Total amount awarded:	$2,000

Scholarships

Contact:
Wilson Ornithological Society c/o Dr. Richard B. Stiehl
USGS-BRD/Mid-continent Ecol. Science Center
4512 McMurray Ave.
Ft. Collins, CO 80525-3400
Phone: 970-226-9466
Web: www.ummz.lsa.umich.edu/birds/wosawards.html

Winegard Company

Winegard Company Scholarship

Type of award: Scholarship.
Intended use: For undergraduate or graduate study at accredited postsecondary institution.
Eligibility: Applicant or parent must be employed by Winegard Company. Applicant must be high school senior.
Additional information: Must be child of employee of Winegard Company. For further information or application, contact Winegard Company directly.
> **Amount of award:** $2,000

Contact:
Winegard Company

Wisconsin Central Systems

Wisconsin Central Systems & Algoma Central Railway Inc. Scholarship

Type of award: Scholarship.
Intended use: For undergraduate study at accredited vocational, 2-year or 4-year institution.
Eligibility: Applicant or parent must be employed by Wisconsin Central Systems.
Additional information: For further information or an application, contact Wisconsin Central Systems directly.
> **Amount of award:** $1,000

Wisconsin Dental Foundation

Wisconsin Dental Foundation Scholarship

Type of award: Scholarship.
Intended use: For sophomore study at accredited postsecondary institution. Designated institutions: Marquette University and other technical schools in Wisconsin.
Eligibility: Applicant must be residing in Wisconsin.
Basis for selection: Major/career interest in dental hygiene or dentistry. Applicant must demonstrate financial need, high academic achievement, depth of character, leadership, seriousness of purpose and service orientation.
Application requirements: Recommendations, nomination by committees at each campus.

Additional information: Applicant must be attending participating school in Wisconsin.
> **Amount of award:** $500-$1,000
> **Number of awards:** 20
> **Total amount awarded:** $11,000

Contact:
Participating Wisconsin postsecondary institutions.
Phone: 414-276-4520
Fax: 414-276-8431

Wisconsin Department of Veterans Affairs

Wisconsin Veterans Affairs Part-Time Study Grant

Type of award: Scholarship.
Intended use: For half-time undergraduate study at accredited vocational, 2-year or 4-year institution. Designated institutions: Approved Wisconsin postsecondary schools.
Eligibility: Applicant must be residing in Wisconsin. Applicant must be veteran; or dependent of deceased veteran; or spouse of deceased veteran. Must have served two years of active duty during peacetime or 90 days of active duty during specified wartime period.
Basis for selection: Applicant must demonstrate financial need.
Application requirements: Proof of eligibility.
Additional information: Veterans may be reimbursed for up to 65 percent of tuition and fees (not to exceed cost at UW-Madison for the same number of undergraduate credits) after successfully completing part-time classroom or correspondence courses at most Wisconsin schools. Veterans with service-connected disability rated by VA as 30 percent or higher may be reimbursed for up to 100% of their tuition and fees at qualifying schools (not to exceed cost at UW-Madison for same number of undergraduate credits). Alternate phone: 800-947-8387. Statutory combined income limit of $47,500. Limit increases by $500 for each dependent child in excess of two. Application deadline is 60 days after completion of semester/quarter.

Contact:
Wisconsin Department of Veterans Affairs
P.O. Box 7843
30 West Mifflin Street
Madison, WI 53703-7843
Phone: 800-947-8387
Web: www.dva.state.wi.us

Wisconsin Veterans Affairs Retraining Grant

Type of award: Scholarship.
Intended use: For undergraduate study at accredited vocational institution. Designated institutions: Wisconsin vocational institutions.
Eligibility: Applicant must be residing in Wisconsin. Applicant must be veteran. Must have served two years of continuous active duty during peacetime or 90 days of active duty during designated wartime period.
Basis for selection: Applicant must demonstrate financial need.

Application requirements: Must have either have been a resident of Wisconsin on entry into military service or a continuous resident of Wisconsin for at least five years after separation from military service.

Additional information: Applicant must be recently unemployed or underemployed veteran and registered for or enrolled in education program that will lead to reemployment and be completed within two years. Must have been employed for six consecutive months with same employer or in the same or similar occupation. Certification and counseling is provided only at accredited Wisconsin schools. Training at other schools does not qualify. Apply year-round at local county Veterans' Service Office to establish eligibility.

   Amount of award: $3,000

Contact:
Wisconsin Department of Veterans Affairs
P.O. Box 7843
30 West Mifflin Street
Madison, WI 53703-7843
Phone: 800-947-8387
Web: www.dva.state.wi.us

Wisconsin Veterans Affairs Tuition and Fee Reimbursement Grant

Type of award: Scholarship, renewable.
Intended use: For undergraduate study at postsecondary institution. Designated institutions: Approved Wisconsin post-secondary schools.
Eligibility: Applicant must be residing in Wisconsin. Applicant must be veteran.
Basis for selection: Applicant must demonstrate financial need.
Application requirements: Proof of eligibility. Federal tax return or proof of annual income.
Additional information: Family income limit of $47,500. Limit increases by $500 for each dependent child. Veterans may receive up to 65% reimbursement of cost of tuition and fees. May receive reimbursement for up to 120 credits of part-time study or eight semesters of full-time study. Courses must be taken within 10 years of separation from active military service.
Contact:
Wisconsin Department of Veterans Affairs
PO Box 7843
30 West Mifflin Street
Madison, WI 53703-7843
Phone: 800-947-8387
Web: www.dva.state.wi.us

Wisconsin Energy Corporation Foundation, Inc.

Wisconsin Energy Corporation Daughters & Sons Scholarship

Type of award: Scholarship, renewable.
Intended use: For undergraduate study at vocational, 2-year or 4-year institution.
Eligibility: Applicant or parent must be employed by Wisconsin Energy Corporation Foundation, Inc. Applicant must be high school senior.

Additional information: For further information or an application, contact Wisconsin Energy Corporation directly.
   Amount of award: $500-$5,000

Wisconsin Higher Educational Aids Board

Wisconsin Academic Excellence Scholarship

Type of award: Scholarship, renewable.
Intended use: For full-time undergraduate study at vocational, 2-year or 4-year institution.
Eligibility: Applicant must be high school senior. Applicant must be residing in Wisconsin.
Basis for selection: Applicant must demonstrate high academic achievement.
Application requirements: Nomination by high school guidance counselor by February 15.
Additional information: 3.0 GPA must be maintained for renewal. Awards range from $2,250 to full tuition and fees. Private school students eligible.
   Amount of award: $2,250
   Number of awards: 2,721
   Application deadline: February 15
   Total amount awarded: $2,846,799
Contact:
Higher Education Aids Board
Attn: Alice Winters
131 West Wilson
Madison, WI 53707
Phone: 608-267-2213

Wisconsin Handicapped Student Grant

Type of award: Scholarship, renewable.
Intended use: For undergraduate study.
Eligibility: Applicant must be visually impaired or hearing impaired. Applicant must be residing in Wisconsin.
Basis for selection: Applicant must demonstrate financial need.
Application requirements: Proof of eligibility.
Additional information: May study at eligible out-of-state institutions.
   Amount of award: $250-$1,800
   Number of awards: 71
   Total amount awarded: $110,803
Contact:
Higher Educational Aids Board
Attn: Sandy Thomas
P.O. Box 7885, 131 West Wilson
Madison, WI 53707-7885
Phone: 608-266-0888

Wisconsin Higher Education Grant

Type of award: Scholarship, renewable.
Intended use: For undergraduate study at vocational or 4-year institution. Designated institutions: University of Wisconsin and Wisconsin technical institutions.
Eligibility: Applicant must be residing in Wisconsin.

Basis for selection: Applicant must demonstrate financial need.
Application requirements: Proof of eligibility.
Additional information: Apply with FAFSA through high school guidance counselor or financial aid office of institution.

Amount of award:	$250-$1,800
Number of awards:	32,141
Total amount awarded:	$28,583,574

Contact:
Higher Educational Aids Board
Attn: Sandra Thomas
131 West Wilson
Madison, WI 53707
Phone: 608-267-0888

Wisconsin Indian Student Assistance Grant

Type of award: Scholarship, renewable.
Intended use: For undergraduate or graduate study.
Eligibility: Applicant must be American Indian. Must be at least one-quarter Native American. Applicant must be residing in Wisconsin.
Basis for selection: Major/career interest in humanities/liberal arts. Applicant must demonstrate financial need.
Application requirements: Proof of eligibility. FAFSA, Indian Student Assistance Grant Application.

Amount of award:	$250-$1,100
Number of awards:	825
Total amount awarded:	$755,205

Contact:
Higher Educational Aids Board
Attn: Sandra Thomas
Madison, WI 53707
Phone: 608-267-2206

Wisconsin Minority Retention Grant

Type of award: Scholarship, renewable.
Intended use: For sophomore, junior or senior study at vocational, 2-year or 4-year institution. Designated institutions: Private and non-profit schools in Wisconsin.
Eligibility: Applicant must be Asian American, African American, Mexican American, Hispanic American, Puerto Rican or American Indian. Asian American applicants must be former citizens or children of former citizens of Laos, Vietnam, or Cambodia admitted to United States after 12/31/75. Applicant must be residing in Wisconsin.
Basis for selection: Applicant must demonstrate financial need.

Amount of award:	$250-$2,500
Number of awards:	638
Total amount awarded:	$690,574

Contact:
Higher Educational Aids Board
Attn: May Lou Kuzdas
131 West Wilson
Wisconsin, WI 53707
Phone: 608-267-2212

Wisconsin Talent Incentive Program Grant

Type of award: Scholarship, renewable.

Intended use: For freshman, sophomore, junior or senior study. Designated institutions: University of Wisconsin, Wisconsin Technical College or independent institutions in the state.
Eligibility: Applicant must be residing in Wisconsin.
Basis for selection: Major/career interest in humanities/liberal arts. Applicant must demonstrate financial need.
Application requirements: Nomination by Student Financial Aid Department or WEOP. FAFSA.

Amount of award:	$250-$1,800
Number of awards:	4,133
Total amount awarded:	$4,468,058

Contact:
Higher Educational Aids Board
Attn: John Whitt
131 West Wilson
Madison, WI 53707
Phone: 608-266-1665

Wisconsin Tuition Grant

Type of award: Scholarship, renewable.
Intended use: For undergraduate or post-bachelor's certificate study. Designated institutions: Independent, nonprofit institutions in Wisconsin.
Eligibility: Applicant must be residing in Wisconsin.
Basis for selection: Applicant must demonstrate financial need.
Additional information: Applicant must be Wisconsin resident who will be attending a university of Wisconsin, Wisconsin technical college, or independent institution in the state of Wisconsin. Must be enrolled at least half time.

Amount of award:	$250-$2,300
Number of awards:	9,306
Total amount awarded:	$17,412,235

Contact:
Higher Educational Aids Board
Attn: Mary Lou Kuzdas
131 West Wilson
Madison, WI 53707
Phone: 608-267-2212

Wisconsin Space Grant Consortium

NASA Academy Wisconsin Awards

Type of award: Scholarship.
Intended use: For full-time junior, senior or graduate study at accredited 4-year or graduate institution in United States. Designated institutions: NASA Field Centers.
Eligibility: Applicant must be U.S. citizen residing in Wisconsin.
Basis for selection: Major/career interest in aerospace; engineering; science, general; robotics or geology/earth sciences. Applicant must demonstrate high academic achievement, depth of character, leadership and seriousness of purpose.
Application requirements: Recommendations, transcript. Good SAT/ACT scores. Minimum 3.0 GPA. Two-page statement of intent, interest, and experience in space, aerospace, or space-related studies.
Additional information: Awards include competitive scholarships and fellowships for research programs at NASA

Field Centers such as Goddard Space Flight Center and Ames Research Center. Deadline varies based on Field Center. Applications sent directly to Academy not accepted. See Website for requirements and details or contact Sharon Brandt at address below.

Contact:
Program Manager, Wisconsin Space Grant Consortium
Dept. of Natural and Applied Sciences, UW-GB
2420 Nicolet Drive
Green Bay, WI 54311-7001
Phone: 920-465-2941
Fax: 920-465-2376
Web: www.uwgb.edu/WSGC

NASA Wisconsin Space Grant Consortium Undergraduate Scholarship

Type of award: Scholarship, renewable.
Intended use: For full-time undergraduate study at accredited 4-year institution in United States. Designated institutions: Alverno College; Carroll College; College of the Menominee Nation: Lawrence University: Marquette University: Medical College of Wisconsin; Milwaukee School of Engineering; Ripon College; the University of Wisconsin at Green Bay, La Crosse, Madison, Milwaukee, Oshkosh, Parkside and Whitewater.
Eligibility: Applicant must be U.S. citizen residing in Wisconsin.
Basis for selection: Major/career interest in aerospace; astronomy; engineering; physics; science, general; architecture; law; business or medicine. Applicant must demonstrate high academic achievement.
Application requirements: Recommendations, essay, transcript. SAT/ACT scores.
Additional information: Applicant must attend Wisconsin Space Grant Consortium member institution and reside in Wisconsin during school year. Minimum 3.0 GPA. Qualified students may also apply for summer session Undergraduate Research Award. Consortium actively encourages women, minority, and/or disabled students to apply. See Website for application and details.

Amount of award:	$1,000
Application deadline:	March 30
Notification begins:	April 24

Contact:
Program Office, Wisconsin Space Grant Consortium
University of Wisconsin - Green Bay
2420 Nicolet Drive
Green Bay, WI 54311-7001
Phone: 920-465-2941
Fax: 920-465-2376
Web: www.uwgb.edu/WSGC/

Undergraduate Research Award

Type of award: Research grant.
Intended use: For full-time undergraduate study at 2-year or 4-year institution. Designated institutions: Alverno College; Carroll College; College of the Menominee Nation: Lawrence University: Marquette University: Medical College of Wisconsin; Milwaukee School of Engineering; Ripon College; the University of Wisconsin at Green Bay, La Crosse, Madison, Milwaukee, Oshkosh, Parkside and Whitewater.
Eligibility: Applicant must be U.S. citizen.
Basis for selection: Major/career interest in aerospace; astronomy; engineering; science, general; architecture; law;

business or medicine. Applicant must demonstrate high academic achievement and seriousness of purpose.
Application requirements: Recommendations, transcript, research proposal. Agreement by faculty or research staff member on their campus to act as advisor for project. Project proposal with budget. Good SAT/ACT scores required.
Additional information: Funding for qualified students to create and implement a small research study of their own related to aerospace, space science, or other interdisciplinary space-related studies. For academic year or summer term use. Award up to $3,500; additional $500 may be awarded for exceptional expenses. Consortium especially encourages applications from members of minority groups, women, and persons with disabilities. To obtain additional information, contact WSGC Office of Research Infrastructure.

Amount of award:	$4,000
Application deadline:	March 30

Contact:
Wisconsin Space Grant Consortium
Space Science and Engineering Center
1225 W. Dayton Street, Room 251
Madison, WI 53706-1280
Phone: 608-263-4206
Fax: 608-263-5974
Web: www.uwgb.edu/WSGC

Women Grocers of America

Mary Macey Scholarship

Type of award: Scholarship, renewable.
Intended use: For sophomore, junior, senior or graduate study at accredited 2-year, 4-year or graduate institution in United States.
Basis for selection: Major/career interest in food production/management/services.
Application requirements: Recommendations, essay, transcript.
Additional information: Must plan on a career in any facet of the Grocery industry (retail, wholesale, or manufacturing). Majors in public health and hotel management are not eligible. Must have GPA of 2.0. Minimum of two awards each year.

Amount of award:	$1,000-$1,500
Number of awards:	9
Number of applicants:	16
Application deadline:	June 1
Notification begins:	July 1
Total amount awarded:	$9,000

Contact:
Women Grocers of America
1825 Samuel Morse Drive
Reston, VA 20190-5317
Phone: 703-437-5300

Women of the Evangelical Lutheran Church in America

Lutheran Laywomen Scholarships

Type of award: Scholarship.
Intended use: For undergraduate or graduate study.
Eligibility: Applicant must be female, at least 21, returning adult student. Applicant must be Lutheran. Applicant must be U.S. citizen.
Basis for selection: Applicant must demonstrate financial need, high academic achievement and service orientation.
Application requirements: Essay, transcript, proof of eligibility. Academic and personal references. Reference from pastor or, if pastor is a relative, from chairperson or vice-chairperson of congregation.
Additional information: Must be member of Evangelical Lutheran Church in America. Must have interrupted education since high school for at least two years. Must show clear educational goals. Cannot be studying for ordination, diaconate, or church-certified professions. Must be laywoman. Applicants may reapply and receive assistance for maximum of two years. Visit Website or write to address below for more information and to request application.

Amount of award:	$2,000
Number of applicants:	100
Application deadline:	February 15
Notification begins:	May 25

Contact:
Women of the ELCA Scholarship Program
8765 W. Higgins Rd
Chicago, IL 60631-4189
Phone: 773-380-2736 or 800-638-3522 ext. 2747
Fax: 773-380-2419
Web: www.elca.org/wo/scholpro.html

Women's Sports Foundation

AQHA National Female Equestrian Award

Type of award: Scholarship.
Intended use: For undergraduate or graduate study at vocational institution in United States.
Eligibility: Applicant must be female. Applicant must be U.S. citizen or permanent resident.
Basis for selection: Applicant must demonstrate financial need and leadership.
Application requirements: Recommendations, essay, proof of eligibility.
Additional information: Must be accomplished equestrian of caliber to compete in American Quarter Horse Association (AQHA) sanctioned events. Award funded by AQHA. Award must be used to further recipient's equestrian career.

Amount of award:	$2,000
Number of awards:	1
Application deadline:	June 30
Total amount awarded:	$2,000

Contact:
Women's Sports Foundation
Eisenhower Park
Nassau County, NY 11554
Phone: 800-227-3988
Web: www.womenssportsfoundation.org

Linda Riddle Sporting Goods Scholarship

Type of award: Scholarship.
Intended use: For full-time freshman study at accredited 4-year institution in United States.
Eligibility: Applicant must be high school senior.
Basis for selection: Applicant must demonstrate financial need, high academic achievement, depth of character and leadership.
Application requirements: Recommendations, transcript. Must participate in high school sports and have a 3.5 GPA.
Additional information: GPA requirement: 3.5.

Amount of award:	$1,500
Number of awards:	10
Application deadline:	December 1
Total amount awarded:	$15,000

Contact:
Women's Sports Foundation
Eisenhower Park
East Meadow, NY 11554
Phone: 800-227-3988
Fax: 516-542-4716
Web: www.womenssportsfoundation.org

Linda Riddle/SGMA Endowed Scholarship

Type of award: Scholarship.
Intended use: For full-time freshman study at accredited 2-year or 4-year institution.
Eligibility: Applicant must be female, high school senior. Applicant must be U.S. citizen or permanent resident.
Basis for selection: Major/career interest in athletic training or sports/sports administration. Applicant must demonstrate financial need, high academic achievement and leadership.
Application requirements: Recommendations, transcript.
Additional information: Must be enrolled as full-time freshman in Sept. 2001. Goal is to provide young women athletes opportunity to continue to pursue their sport in addition to their college studies. Download application form from Website. Must be student athlete to apply.

Amount of award:	$250-$10,000
Number of awards:	466
Number of applicants:	466
Application deadline:	December 8
Total amount awarded:	$530,000

Contact:
Women Sports Foundation
Eisenhower Park
Nassau County, NY 11554
Phone: 800-227-3988
Fax: 516-542-4716
Web: www.womenssportsfoundation.org

Mervyn's California College Scholarship

Type of award: Scholarship.

Intended use: For full-time senior study at accredited 4-year institution in United States.
Eligibility: Applicant must be female, high school senior. Applicant must be U.S. citizen or permanent resident.
Basis for selection: Applicant must demonstrate financial need, high academic achievement and depth of character.
Application requirements: Recommendations, transcript. Must participate in high school sports and have a minimum 3.5 GPA.

Amount of award:	$1,500
Number of awards:	10
Application deadline:	December 1
Total amount awarded:	$15,000

Contact:
Women's Sports Foundation
Eisenhower Park
East Meadow, NY 11554
Phone: 800-227-3988
Fax: 516-542-4716
Web: www.womenssportsfoundation.org

Women's Western Golf Foundation

Women's Western Golf Foundation Scholarship

Type of award: Scholarship, renewable.
Intended use: For full-time freshman study at accredited 4-year institution in United States.
Eligibility: Applicant must be female, high school senior. Applicant must be U.S. citizen.
Basis for selection: Competition/talent/interest in athletics/sports. Applicant must demonstrate financial need, high academic achievement, depth of character, leadership and seriousness of purpose.
Application requirements: Essay, transcript, proof of eligibility. SAT/ACT scores, FAFSA. Personal recommendation required from high school teacher or counselor. List of high school activities.
Additional information: Must be in top 15 percent of class. 3.5 GPA is recommended. Must demonstrate involvement in sport of golf, but skill not criterion. Deadline to request application is March 1; SASE required. Must file FAFSA with U.S. government and provide copy with application. Awards renew for each of four years, assuming scholarship terms are fulfilled (financial need, GPA above 3.0). Nineteen or 20 new awards each year, plus 50 renewals.

Amount of award:	$2,000
Number of awards:	70
Number of applicants:	500
Application deadline:	April 5
Notification begins:	May 15
Total amount awarded:	$150,000

Contact:
Director of Scholarship
Women's Western Golf Foundation
393 Ramsay Road
Deerfield, IL 60015

Woodrow Wilson National Fellowship Foundation

U.S. Department of Agriculture/ Woodrow Wilson Fellowship Program

Type of award: Scholarship.
Intended use: For junior, senior, master's or doctoral study at 4-year or graduate institution. Designated institutions: Alabama A & M University; Alcorn State University; University of Arkansas, Pine Bluff; Delaware State College; Florida A & M University; Fort Valley State College; Kentucky State University; Lincoln University; Langston University; University of Maryland, Eastern Shore; North Carolina A & T University; Prairie View A & M University; South Carolina State College; Southern University; Tennessee State University; Tuskegee University; and Virginia State University.
Eligibility: Applicant must be U.S. citizen.
Basis for selection: Major/career interest in agriculture; food science/technology; forestry; natural resources/conservation; range science or wildlife/fisheries. Applicant must demonstrate high academic achievement, leadership and service orientation.
Application requirements: Nomination by U.S. Department of Agriculture and the Presidents of the 1890 Land Grant Schools from pool of 1890 National Scholars Program participants.
Additional information: Nominee must be a U.S. Department of Agriculture/1890 National Scholar in sophomore year at an Historically Black 1890 Land Grant School listed above. Minimum 3.0 GPA. Graduate Fellows must pay for own room and board. Awardees must sign written agreement to accept appointment in U.S. Department of Agriculture upon completion of studies, one year of service for each year of fellowship support.

Amount of award:	Full tuition
Number of awards:	9

Contact:
The Woodrow Wilson National Fellowship Foundation
CN 5281
Princeton, NJ 08543-5281
Phone: 609-452-7007
Fax: 609-452-0066
Web: www.woodrow.org

U.S. Department of Commerce/Ron Brown Commercial Service Fellowship

Type of award: Scholarship.
Intended use: For full-time junior, senior or graduate study at 4-year or graduate institution in United States. Designated institutions: Graduate portion of the fellowship must be used at participating institution of international business or commerce.
Eligibility: Applicant must be U.S. citizen.
Basis for selection: Major/career interest in business. Applicant must demonstrate high academic achievement, depth of character, leadership and seriousness of purpose.
Application requirements: Recommendations, essay, transcript, proof of eligibility. Application.
Additional information: For students planning careers in international business and/or commerce. Apply in sophomore year. 3.0 GPA required. Covers junior and senior years and first

year of graduate school. Attendance required between junior and senior years at junior year summer institute. After graduation from undergraduate program, student works for Department of Commerce in preparation for graduate school. Award incurs four-and-a-half year service commitment to Commercial Service. Selection takes place in alternate years.

Amount of award:	Full tuition
Application deadline:	February 18

Contact:
USDC Ronald H. Brown Commercial Fellowship
CN 5281
Princeton, NJ 08543-5281
Fax: 609-452-7007
Web: www.woodrow.org

U.S. Department of State Foreign Affairs Fellowship

Type of award: Scholarship.
Intended use: For full-time sophomore or graduate study at accredited 4-year or graduate institution in United States. Designated institutions: Graduate portion of fellowship must be used at institutions affiliated with Association of Professional Schools of International Affairs.
Eligibility: Applicant must be U.S. citizen.
Basis for selection: Major/career interest in international relations. Applicant must demonstrate financial need, high academic achievement, depth of character, leadership, seriousness of purpose and service orientation.
Application requirements: Interview, recommendations, essay, transcript, proof of eligibility.
Additional information: Number of fellowships determined by available funding. Finalists will attend interview session in Princeton, N.J. or Washington, D.C.; transportation to interview site paid. Inductees will attend orientation in Washington, D.C. Medical and security clearances required for program participation. Applicants must have minimum 3.2 cumulative GPA at time of application and maintain GPA throughout fellowship. Women and members of minority groups historically underrepresented in the Foreign Service encouraged to apply.

Amount of award:	Full tuition
Application deadline:	February 16

Contact:
Dr. Richard Hope, Director Foreign Affairs Fellowship Program
Woodrow Wilson National Fellowship Foundation
P.O. Box 2437
Princeton, NJ 08543-2437
Phone: 609-452-7007
Web: www.woodrow.org

Worcester County Horticultural Society

Worcester County Horticultural Society

Type of award: Scholarship, renewable.
Intended use: For full-time junior, senior or graduate study at 4-year or graduate institution in United States. Designated institutions: Must be a resident of New England or attending a New England college or university.

Eligibility: Applicant must be residing in Connecticut, Massachusetts, Maine, New Hampshire, Rhode Island or Vermont.
Basis for selection: Major/career interest in horticulture or landscape architecture. Applicant must demonstrate financial need, high academic achievement and seriousness of purpose.
Application requirements: Recommendations, essay, transcript. Completed application form.
Additional information: Number of scholarships awarded varies.

Amount of award:	$500-$2,000
Number of applicants:	60
Application deadline:	May 1
Notification begins:	June 15

Contact:
Scholarship Committee of the Worcester County Horticultural Society
Tower Hill Botanic Garden
11 French Drive, P.O. Box 598
Boylston, MA 01505-0598
Phone: 508-869-6111
Fax: 508-869-0314

World Federalist Association

"Builders of a Better World" Scholarship Program

Type of award: Scholarship, renewable.
Intended use: For undergraduate study at accredited 2-year or 4-year institution in or outside United States.
Eligibility: Applicant must be at least 16, no older than 28.
Basis for selection: Applicant must demonstrate depth of character, leadership, seriousness of purpose and service orientation.
Application requirements: Recommendations, essay, transcript, proof of eligibility. The applicant must be a member of the World Federalist Association.
Additional information: Applicant must be a member in order to apply. Student membership dues are $10 and must be received by February 1.

Amount of award:	$500-$1,500
Number of awards:	3
Number of applicants:	11
Application deadline:	April 15
Notification begins:	August 30
Total amount awarded:	$3,500

Contact:
World Federalist Association
418 7th St., SE
Washington, DC 20003-2796

World Studio Foundation

Indigenous Peoples Award

Type of award: Scholarship.
Intended use: For undergraduate study at postsecondary institution in United States.

Eligibility: Applicant must be Alaskan native or American Indian. Applicant must be U.S. citizen or permanent resident.
Basis for selection: Major/career interest in art/art history; arts, general or design. Applicant must demonstrate financial need, high academic achievement and seriousness of purpose.
Application requirements: Essay.
Additional information: A special scholarship awarded to artists of Native American, Alaska Native/Inuit, or other indigenous tribes of the Americas. With an emphasis on artists, designers or craftspeople seeking to maintain traditional forms. Visit Website for more information.

Amount of award:	$100-$5,000
Application deadline:	April 27

Contact:
Worldstudio Foundation
225 Varick Street, Ninth Floor
New York, NY 10014
Phone: 212-366-1317
Fax: 212-807-0024
Web: www.worldstudio.org

World Studio Foundation Scholarship

Type of award: Scholarship.
Intended use: For undergraduate study at postsecondary institution in United States.
Eligibility: Applicant must be Alaskan native, Asian American, African American, Mexican American, Hispanic American, Puerto Rican or American Indian. Applicant must be U.S. citizen.
Basis for selection: Demonstrated commitment to giving back to the larger community through artwork. Major/career interest in arts, general; architecture; advertising; film/video; design or urban planning. Applicant must demonstrate seriousness of purpose and service orientation.
Application requirements: Portfolio, recommendations, transcript. Portfolio must be in slide format. A short autobiography and a statement of purpose are also needed.
Additional information: The Foundation's primary aim is to increase diversity in the creative professions and to foster social and environmental responsibility in the artists, designers, and studios of tomorrow. Awards are paid directly to college or university to be applied towards students tuition. Students studying photography, Interior, Furniture, Product, Fashion, and Textile Design, and Illustration encouraged to apply. To download guidelines and an application, visit Website or send a self-addressed stamped envelope to receive an application via mail.

Amount of award:	$100-$5,000
Application deadline:	April 27

Contact:
Worldstudio Foundation
225 Varick Street, Ninth Floor
New York, NY 10014
Phone: 212-366-1317
Fax: 212-807-0024
Web: www.worldstudio.org

Xcel Energy

Xcel Energy Scholarship for Children of Employees

Type of award: Scholarship.
Intended use: For undergraduate study at accredited vocational, 2-year or 4-year institution.
Eligibility: Applicant or parent must be employed by Xcel Energy of Colorado.
Basis for selection: Applicant must demonstrate financial need.
Additional information: For further information or an application, contact Xcel Energy of Colorado directly.

Amount of award:	$1,000

Yakama Nation Office of Higher Education Program

Yakama Nation Tribal Scholarship

Type of award: Scholarship.
Intended use: For freshman, sophomore, junior, senior, master's or doctoral study at accredited 2-year, 4-year or graduate institution.
Eligibility: Applicant must be American Indian. Must be enrolled member of Yakama Indian Nation.
Application requirements: Transcript. Tribal ID number.
Additional information: There is a priority list for selection.

Amount of award:	$2,000
Number of awards:	280
Number of applicants:	300
Application deadline:	July 1
Notification begins:	August 1
Total amount awarded:	$384,000

Contact:
Yakama Nation Office of Higher Education Program
P.O. Box 151
Toppenish, WA 98948
Phone: 509-865-5121

Yankee Gas Services Company

Yankee Gas Scholarship Program

Type of award: Scholarship, renewable.
Intended use: For undergraduate study at accredited postsecondary institution.
Eligibility: Applicant or parent must be employed by Yankee Gas Services Company. Applicant must be high school senior.
Basis for selection: Applicant must demonstrate financial need.
Additional information: For further information or an application, contact Yankee Gas Services Company directly.

Amount of award:	$1,000

Contact:
Yankee Gas Services Company

YKK Corporation of America

YKK Dependent Children Scholarship Program

Type of award: Scholarship, renewable.
Intended use: For undergraduate study at accredited vocational, 2-year or 4-year institution.
Eligibility: Applicant or parent must be employed by YKK Corporation of America. Applicant must be high school senior.
Additional information: For further information or application, contact YKK Corporation of America directly.
   Amount of award: $750-$1,500
Contact:
YKK Corporation of America

Zee Medical, Inc.

The Zee Medical Memorial Scholarship Program

Type of award: Scholarship.
Intended use: For undergraduate study at accredited vocational, 2-year or 4-year institution.
Eligibility: Applicant or parent must be employed by Zee Service, Inc.
Additional information: For further information or an application, contact Zee Medical Inc. and its distributors directly.
   Amount of award: $1,000

Internships

3Com Corporation

3Com Undergraduate Internships

Type of award: Internship, renewable.
Intended use: For undergraduate study at accredited 4-year institution.
Basis for selection: Major/career interest in computer/information sciences.
Application requirements: Resume. Cover letter.
Additional information: Summer internship program and paid internships as available through the year. Visit Website for current openings and application information. Computer programming, technology and artificial intelligence majors also eligible.
Contact:
3Com Corporation
College Relations
5400 Bayfront
Santa Clara, CA 95052
Phone: 508-323-5000
Fax: 408-326-5959
Web: www.3com.com/inside/college

3M

3M Internship

Type of award: Internship.
Intended use: For undergraduate or graduate study.
Eligibility: Applicant must be U.S. citizen or permanent resident.
Basis for selection: Major/career interest in engineering; finance/banking; marketing or business. Applicant must demonstrate high academic achievement, depth of character and seriousness of purpose.
Application requirements: All recruiting is done on campus at specific colleges/universities for specific disciplines based on current business need.
Additional information: For further information, applicant should contact his/her campus career office for recruiting schedule and/or visit Website.
Contact:
Your campus placement/career services office.
Phone: 800-328-1343
Fax: 651-575-1591
Web: www.3m.com

Aeromet, Inc.

Atmospheric Science Internship

Type of award: Internship.
Intended use: For senior or graduate study at 4-year or graduate institution in United States.
Eligibility: Applicant must be single. Applicant must be U.S. citizen.
Basis for selection: Major/career interest in atmospheric sciences/meteorology. Applicant must demonstrate high academic achievement.
Application requirements: Transcript. Resume, three references.
Additional information: Should have completed two years physics, two years calculus, four courses in atmospheric science or meteorology. Position from May 15 to September 1. Salary $9 to $11/hour, depending on experience. Visit Website or contact via e-mail (recruiting@aeronet.com) for additional information.

Number of awards:	2
Application deadline:	May 1

Contact:
Aeromet, Inc.
P.O. Box 701767
Tulsa, OK 74170-1767
Phone: 918-299-2621
Fax: 918-299-8211
Web: www.aeromet.com

Allstate, Inc.

Allstate Internships

Type of award: Internship, renewable.
Intended use: For full-time undergraduate study at accredited 4-year institution.
Eligibility: Applicant must be residing in Illinois.
Basis for selection: Major/career interest in insurance/actuarial science; accounting; marketing; business; business/management/administration; computer/information sciences or finance/banking. Applicant must demonstrate high academic achievement.
Application requirements: Resume, cover letter.
Additional information: In addition to salary and amenities of Illinois headquarters, eligible interns receive daily transportation and subsidized housing. Send resume by fax or e-mail (as RTF file to careers@allstate.com) to attn: HOPI or mail to address below. Applications accepted on rolling deadline basis.
Contact:
Allstate Insurance Company
Attn: HOPI
2775 Sanders Rd., Suite A-1
Northbrook, IL 60062
Fax: 800-526-4831
Web: www.allstatecareers.com

American Association of Advertising Agencies

Multicultural Advertising Intern Program

Type of award: Internship, renewable.
Intended use: For full-time junior, senior or graduate study at accredited 4-year or graduate institution.
Eligibility: Applicant must be Asian American, African American, Mexican American, Hispanic American, Puerto Rican or American Indian. Applicant must be U.S. citizen or permanent resident.
Basis for selection: Major/career interest in advertising; communications; marketing or humanities/liberal arts.
Application requirements: Interview. Semi-finalists are interviewed by agency professionals before selection. Submission of Multicultural Advertising Intern Program application, also available under "Initiatives" section of Website.
Additional information: Must have completed junior year of college and have strong interest in advertising. Minimum 3.0 GPA required. Applicants with lesser GPA (2.7-2.9) must complete an essay question on application. Students are placed in member agency offices for ten weeks during the summer. Salary minimum $350 per week. 60 percent of housing and travel costs (if applicable) are provided. Can apply for following departments: account management, creative, interactive technologies, media, production, traffic, or strategic planning.

Number of awards:	101
Number of applicants:	280
Application deadline:	January 25

Contact:
American Association of Advertising Agencies
Manager of Diversity Programs
405 Lexington Avenue, 18th Floor
New York, NY 10174-1801
Phone: 800-676-9333
Fax: 212-573-8968
Web: www.aaaa.org

American Bar Foundation

Law and Social Sciences Summer Research Fellowship for Minority Undergraduates

Type of award: Internship.
Intended use: For sophomore or junior study.
Eligibility: Applicant must be U.S. citizen or permanent resident.
Basis for selection: Major/career interest in law; social/behavioral sciences; criminal justice/law enforcement or public administration/service. Applicant must demonstrate high academic achievement.
Application requirements: Recommendations, essay, transcript. Minimum 3.0 GPA.
Additional information: Interns work ten 35-hour weeks as research assistants at American Bar Foundation in Chicago and receive $3,600 stipend. Fellowships are intended for, but not limited to, persons who are African American, Mexican, Native American or Puerto Rican.

Amount of award:	$3,600
Number of awards:	4
Application deadline:	March 1
Notification begins:	April 17

Contact:
American Bar Foundation
750 North Lake Shore Drive, Fourth Floor
Chicago, IL 60611
Phone: 312-988-6580
Web: www.abf-sociolegal.org

American Conservatory Theater

American Conservatory Theater Production Internships

Type of award: Internship.
Intended use: For undergraduate or graduate study.
Eligibility: Applicant must be U.S. citizen.
Basis for selection: Major/career interest in performing arts; theater arts or theater/production/technical. Applicant must demonstrate high academic achievement.
Application requirements: $15 application fee. Interview, portfolio, recommendations, essay. Work permit. Internships intended for college students and graduates who intend professional career in theater.
Additional information: Provides intern with practical experience in many areas of theater production. Departments include costume rentals, costume shop, lighting design, properties, sound design, stage management, technical design, wig construction/makeup, producation. Weekly stipend for full-time, seasonal internships. Must have valid work permit. Visit Website for more information.

Number of awards:	10
Number of applicants:	70
Application deadline:	April 15
Notification begins:	June 1

Contact:
American Conservatory Theater
Susan West - Intern Coordinator
30 Grant Avenue, 6th Floor
San Francisco, CA 94108
Phone: 415-834-3200
Fax: 415-433-2711
Web: www.act-sfbay.org

Artistic and Administrative Internships

Type of award: Internship.
Intended use: For undergraduate or graduate study at 2-year, 4-year or graduate institution.
Eligibility: Applicant must be U.S. citizen.
Basis for selection: Major/career interest in theater arts; theater/production/technical; arts management; arts, general; public relations; marketing; English; English literature; literature or performing arts. Applicant must demonstrate high academic achievement.
Application requirements: $15 application fee. Interview, portfolio, recommendations, essay. Work permit.

Additional information: Provides intern with opportunity to work in artistic, literary/publications, management, development and markekting/public relations departments. Some internships require writing and art samples. There is no stipend. If intern needs paying employment, ACT will adjust hours. Different departments have available positions at different times of year. Application deadlines are rolling. Visit Website for more information.

Number of awards:	6
Number of applicants:	75

Contact:
American Conservatory Theater
Susan West - Intern Coordinator
30 Grant Avenue, 6th Floor
San Francisco, CA 94108
Phone: 415-834-3200
Fax: 415-433-2711
Web: www.act-sfbay.org

American Electric Power, Inc. (AEP)

AEP College Programs

Type of award: Internship, renewable.
Intended use: For undergraduate or graduate study.
Basis for selection: Major/career interest in information systems; computer/information sciences; engineering or business/management/administration. Applicant must demonstrate high academic achievement and leadership.
Application requirements: Resume which includes GPA, expected graduation date, term(s) available for co-op/internship, core courses taken to date, extracurricular activities relating to major.
Additional information: For undergraduate majors in information technology and graduates studying business administration. Co-ops preferred; internships possible. Programs consist of paid year-round co-ops and summer internships for course credit. Interns must be juniors or seniors. Co-ops must be sophomores and generally serve two terms. Applicants with 3.0 or above GPA preferred. U.S. citizens or permanent residents preferred but other applicants considered. Number of awards varies. Location of award positions could include Columbus, OH; Tulsa, OK; and Roanoke,VA.

Contact:
AEP
College Relations
1 Riverside Plaza
Columbus, OH 43215
Fax: 614-223-1864
Web: www.aep.com/college

American Museum of Natural History

Research Experience for Undergraduates

Type of award: Internship.

Intended use: For undergraduate study at accredited 4-year institution in United States.
Eligibility: Applicant must be U.S. citizen.
Basis for selection: Major/career interest in science, general; biology or microbiology. Applicant must demonstrate high academic achievement and seriousness of purpose.
Application requirements: Recommendations, essay, research proposal. Scientific proposal.
Additional information: Internship in evolutionary biology at Museum. Applicant must have a very strong scientific background, including but not limited to polymerase chain reactions, systematics and biodiversity and conservation interests. Travel and research expenses reimbursed. Application deadline is the third Friday in April. No applications will be accepted before January 1.

Amount of award:	$3,500
Number of awards:	10
Number of applicants:	70
Notification begins:	May 1
Total amount awarded:	$35,000

Contact:
American Museum of Natural History
Office of Grants and Fellowships
Central Park West at 79th Street
New York, NY 10024-5192
Web: www.amnh.org

American Nuclear Society

Washington Internships for Students of Engineering

Type of award: Internship.
Intended use: For full-time senior study at accredited 4-year institution in United States.
Eligibility: Applicant must be U.S. citizen or permanent resident.
Basis for selection: Major/career interest in engineering, nuclear or nuclear science. Applicant must demonstrate high academic achievement, depth of character, leadership, seriousness of purpose and service orientation.
Application requirements: Recommendations, transcript, proof of eligibility. Applicant must be in junior year of study.
Additional information: Up to fifteen outstanding third-year students selected for ten-week summer intern positions located in Washington, D.C. Internship is geared toward understanding how government officials/engineers work together in making legislative/regulatory policy decisions. Round-trip airfare and lodging covered. ANS is guaranteed support for two students.

Amount of award:	$1,800
Number of awards:	15
Application deadline:	February 1

Contact:
American Nuclear Society
555 North Kensington Avenue
La Grange Park, IL 60526
Phone: 708-352-6611
Fax: 708-352-0499
Web: www.ans.org

American Society of Magazine Editors

American Society of Magazine Editors Internship

Type of award: Internship.
Intended use: For junior study.
Basis for selection: Major/career interest in journalism. Applicant must demonstrate seriousness of purpose.
Application requirements: Recommendations, essay, nomination by dean, department head or professor from school of journalism. Must submit writing and editing samples.
Additional information: 10-week summer internship. Emphasis on consumer magazine and business publication editing. Most assignments in New York City. Interns receive $325 weekly stipend. Dormitory housing is available at cost of $1,900 for ten-week summer. Obtain application from dean, department head or professor.

Number of applicants:	180
Application deadline:	December 15
Notification begins:	March 1

Contact:
American Society of Magazine Editors
919 Third Avenue
New York, NY 10022
Phone: 212-872-3700
Fax: 212-906-0128
Web: www.asme.magazine.org

Applied Materials

Applied Materials Internships and Co-ops

Type of award: Internship.
Intended use: For full-time undergraduate study.
Eligibility: Applicant must be residing in Texas or California.
Basis for selection: Major/career interest in electronics; computer/information sciences; materials science or information systems. Applicant must demonstrate high academic achievement.
Application requirements: Resume.
Additional information: Paid internships and co-op programs based in Texas and California. Course credit available. Summer and year-round positions. Resumes can be sent via mail to the attention of Co-op/Intern Coordinator. Visit Website for additional addresses, to submit resume, and to find out when internship interviews wiil be held at college campuses. Resumes sent from Hotmail e-mail addresses not accepted.

Number of awards:	400

Contact:
Applied Materials -- Attn: Co-op/Intern Coordinator
3195 Kifer Road
M/S 2963
Santa Clara, CA 95051
Web: www.appliedmaterials.com

Baxter International Inc.

Baxter International Summer Internships

Type of award: Internship.
Intended use: For undergraduate or graduate study at 2-year or 4-year institution.
Eligibility: Applicant must be U.S. citizen or permanent resident.
Basis for selection: Major/career interest in finance/banking; engineering; biochemistry; information systems; accounting; chemistry; human resources or marketing. Applicant must demonstrate high academic achievement.
Additional information: Paid internships. Number of awards varies. Apply Jan. 1 to March 1 for summer internships. Send resume via e-mail to internships@baxter.com. Visit Website for additional information.

Application deadline:	March 1
Notification begins:	April 28

Contact:
Baxter International Inc.
Manager: College Relations; DF5-2E
One Baxter Parkway
Deerfield, IL 60015
Fax: 847-948-4494
Web: www.baxter.com

Bechtel Corporation

Bechtel Cooperative Education Program

Type of award: Internship.
Intended use: For sophomore, junior or senior study at postsecondary institution.
Basis for selection: Major/career interest in engineering; accounting; business; computer/information sciences or finance/banking.
Additional information: Students enrolled in college's co-op program can work at Bechtel to fulfill part of requirements. All co-op positions are paid and last six months. Bechtel hires only from local colleges and universities near the hiring office. Visit Website for list of recruitment offices, available positions and additional information.
Contact:
Bechtel Corporation
Bechtel College Relations Department
P.O. Box 193965
San Francisco, CA 94119-6359
Web: www.bechtel.com

Bechtel Corporation Summer-Hire (Intern) Program

Type of award: Internship.
Intended use: For full-time sophomore, junior or senior study at 4-year institution.
Eligibility: Applicant must be U.S. citizen.
Basis for selection: Major/career interest in engineering; architecture; accounting; business; computer/information sciences or finance/banking.

Additional information: All internships paid and last three months, June-August. Provides opportunity for intern to gain experience, while working for global company. Priority given to students within one year of graduation. Bechtel hires only from local colleges and universities near the hiring office. Visit Website for list of recruitment offices, available positions and additional information.

Contact:
Bechtel Corporation
Bechtel College Relations Department
P.O. Box 193965
San Francisco, CA 94119-6359
Web: www.bechtel.com

Bernstein-Rein

Advertising Internship (Summer Only)

Type of award: Internship.
Intended use: For junior or senior study.
Basis for selection: Major/career interest in advertising; journalism; marketing or communications.
Application requirements: Interview, recommendations, essay, proof of eligibility. Resume, cover letter, completed application, 3 reference names (essay is 1-page writing sample).
Additional information: In order to qualify, applicant must be second semester junior or first semester senior (will graduate in 1-2 semesters after summer). Pay is $8/hour.

Number of awards:	9
Number of applicants:	150
Application deadline:	February 1
Total amount awarded:	$27,000

Contact:
Human Resources
Bernstein-Rein
4600 Madison, Suite 1500
Kansas City, MO 64112

Bethesda Lutheran Homes and Services, Inc.

Bethesda Lutheran Homes and Services Cooperative Program Internship

Type of award: Internship.
Intended use: For full-time junior or senior study at accredited postsecondary institution.
Eligibility: Applicant must be Lutheran.
Basis for selection: Major/career interest in social work; psychology; nursing or education. Applicant must demonstrate high academic achievement, depth of character, seriousness of purpose and service orientation.
Application requirements: Interview, recommendations.
Additional information: Must have 3.0 GPA. Housing is provided during 12-week summer internship in the form of wage of $7.50/hour for 40 hours a week. Applicants may also study public relations or chaplaincy.

Amount of award:	$3,451
Number of awards:	12
Application deadline:	March 1
Total amount awarded:	$41,414

Contact:
Bethesda Lutheran Homes and Services, Inc.
Coordinator, Outreach Programs
700 Hoffmann Drive
Watertown, WI 53094
Phone: 800-369-4636 ext. 416
Fax: 920-262-6513
Web: www.blhs.org

Black & Veatch

Black & Veatch Internships, Co-op, and Summer Employment

Type of award: Internship.
Intended use: For freshman, sophomore, junior or senior study.
Basis for selection: Major/career interest in engineering; construction or architecture.
Application requirements: Transcript. Send e-mail with cover letter and resume in body of message, not as attachment, to e-mail address indicated in position listing on Website, or send hard copy to address below.
Additional information: Internship compensation varies on discipline and major. Majority of positions located in Kansas City area.

Contact:
Black & Veatch Job Code: CB00
College Relations Coordinator (PGA-1)
P.O. Box 8405
Kansas City, MO 64114-9859
Web: www.bv.com/bv/careers/college

BMI Foundation, Inc.

Pete Carpenter Fellowship

Type of award: Internship.
Intended use: For undergraduate, graduate or non-degree study at postsecondary institution.
Eligibility: Applicant must be no older than 34.
Basis for selection: Based on original one- to three-minute composition or selection from score appropriate for theme to theatrical or television film or series. Major/career interest in music or radio/television/film.
Application requirements: Application form and cassette tape of composition.
Additional information: Applicant must be under age of 35 at deadline. Winner of competition will work for one month in Los Angeles on day-to-day basis with distinguished television and theatrical film composers. Up to $2,000 for travel and living expenses included. For an application, visit Website, send e-mail to foundation@bmi.com, or write to foundation.

Amount of award:	$2,000
Number of awards:	1
Application deadline:	December 6

513

Contact:
BMI Foundation, Inc.
320 W. 57th Street
New York, NY 10019
Web: www.bmi.com/bmifoundation/index.asp

Board of Governors of the Federal Reserve System

Federal Reserve Cooperative Education Program

Type of award: Internship, renewable.
Intended use: For undergraduate or graduate study.
Basis for selection: Major/career interest in law; accounting; economics; information systems or finance/banking. Applicant must demonstrate high academic achievement.
Application requirements: Recommendations, transcript. Resume and cover letter.
Additional information: For local applicants, work is during the school year so students can obtain credit.
Contact:
Board of Governors of the Federal Reserve System
Cooperative Education Program, Mail Stop 129
Management Division, Human Resources
Washington, DC 20551
Phone: 202-452-3880
Web: www.federalreserve.gov

Boeing Corporation

Boeing Internship Program

Type of award: Internship.
Intended use: For undergraduate or graduate study in United States. Designated institutions: Boeing sites in Seattle, WA; Arizona; Florida; Southern California; St. Louis, MO; Texas and Wichita, KS.
Eligibility: Applicant must be U.S. citizen.
Basis for selection: Major/career interest in aerospace; computer/information sciences; finance/banking; human resources; manufacturing; marketing; public relations or engineering.
Application requirements: Recommendations, transcript, proof of eligibility. Resume.
Additional information: See Website for detailed information on available positions and to submit resume. Deadlines, eligibility requirements and compensation vary from location to location; contact sponsor for more information.
Contact:
Internship Coordinator
PO Box 516
Mailcode S2761740
St. Louis, MO 63166-0516
Phone: 314-232-0232
Web: www.boeing.com

Bok Tower Gardens

Bok Tower Gardens Internship

Type of award: Internship.
Intended use: For full-time undergraduate or graduate study at 4-year or graduate institution. Designated institutions: Bok Tower Gardens.
Basis for selection: Major/career interest in horticulture; landscape architecture or botany.
Application requirements: Interview, recommendations, transcript. Letter outlining interests, resume.
Additional information: Major/interest in plant science also eligible. Preference given to students who will receive college credit for internship. Program offers on-the-job training in horticulture and conservation. Two ten-week programs, one six-month program. Intern receives $240 for 40-hour work week. Housing provided. Other application deadlines: Summer, April 1; Winter, October 1. Write or call for application packet.
    Application deadline: January 1, July 1
Contact:
Selection Committee
Horticulture Intern Coordination
1151 Tower Boulevard
Lake Wales, FL 33853-3412
Phone: 863-676-1408

Boston Globe

Boston Globe One-Year Development Program

Type of award: Internship.
Intended use: For non-degree study.
Eligibility: Members of minority groups and candidates with unusual cultural backgrounds are strongly encouraged to apply.
Basis for selection: Major/career interest in journalism.
Application requirements: Resume, writing samples.
Additional information: Award provides one-year full-time employment at $751.53/week. Applicants must have six months newspaper experience.
    Amount of award: $36,560
    Number of awards: 1
Contact:
The Boston Globe
P.O. Box 2378
Boston, MA 02107-2378
Phone: 617-929-3120

Boston Globe Summer Internship

Type of award: Internship.
Intended use: For freshman, sophomore or junior study at 4-year institution.
Basis for selection: Major/career interest in journalism.
Application requirements: Interview, recommendations. Writing samples and clips.
Additional information: Award is for 12 weeks full-time summer employment at $575/week.
    Amount of award: $6,900
    Number of awards: 15
    Application deadline: November 5
    Notification begins: January 30

Internships

Contact:
The Boston Globe
P.O. Box 2378
Boston, MA 02107-2378
Phone: 617-929-3120

Bucks County Courier Times

Bucks County Courier Times Minority Internship

Type of award: Internship, renewable.
Intended use: For junior, senior or graduate study.
Eligibility: Applicant must be Alaskan native, Asian American, African American, Mexican American, Hispanic American, Puerto Rican or American Indian. Applicant must be U.S. citizen.
Basis for selection: Major/career interest in journalism; publishing; public relations; English or graphic arts/design.
Application requirements: Resume, clips, driver's license, and vehicle.
Additional information: Internship duration is 12 weeks. Applicant must have basic journalism skills. Interns work as news reporters, bureau reporters, copy desk assistants, photographers, graphic artists, sports writers, and feature writers.

Amount of award:	$4,380
Number of awards:	5
Number of applicants:	100
Application deadline:	February 1

Contact:
Bucks County Courier Times
8400 Route 13
Levittown, PA 19057

California Student Aid Commission

California State Work-Study Program

Type of award: Internship, renewable.
Intended use: For undergraduate or graduate study. Designated institutions: Participating California postsecondary institutions.
Eligibility: Applicant must be residing in California.
Basis for selection: Applicant must demonstrate financial need.
Application requirements: Applicants must apply through financial aid office at their school.
Additional information: Colleges identify jobs that relate to student's course of study, career goals, or exploration of careers. Contact financial aid office at participating postsecondary institutions.

Total amount awarded:	$5,200,000

Contact:
California Student Aid Commission
Specialized Programs
P.O. Box 419026
Rancho Cordova, CA 95741-9026
Phone: 916-526-7590 or 888-224-7268
Web: www.csac.ca.gov

Center for Defense Information

Center for Defense Information Internship

Type of award: Internship.
Intended use: For undergraduate or graduate study.
Basis for selection: Major/career interest in political science/government; military science; international relations; communications or computer/information sciences. Applicant must demonstrate high academic achievement, depth of character, leadership, seriousness of purpose and service orientation.
Application requirements: Recommendations, essay, transcript. Send a resume and cover letter stating interests and reasons for wanting to work at CDI.
Additional information: Students must work full time for the duration of the internship (three to five months) to receive the monthly stipend of $1,000. Deadline for summer application is March 15. Internships divided into three sections: research, television, and computers. Deadlines are for the fall and spring semesters, respectively.

Amount of award:	$3,000-$5,000
Number of awards:	12
Application deadline:	July 1, October 15
Notification begins:	July 22, November 7

Contact:
Center for Defense Information
1779 Massachusetts Avenue
Washington, DC 20036
Phone: 202-332-0600
Web: www.cdi.org

Chevron

Chevron Accounting Internship Program

Type of award: Internship.
Intended use: For full-time junior or senior study.
Eligibility: Applicant must be U.S. citizen, permanent resident, international student or non-U.S. citizen qualified to work in the U.S. Applicant must be residing in California.
Basis for selection: Major/career interest in business; accounting or finance/banking.
Application requirements: Interview, transcript, proof of eligibility. Resume. Applicant must have already completed accounting and finance courses through the intermediate level. Must have maintained a 3.0 grade point average overall.
Additional information: Paid full-time internships, terms vary. Minumum 3.0 GPA. Must be BA or BS candidate

finishing junior year to apply. Must have senior status by semester following internship. Excellent analytical ability, strong communication and interpersonal skills are essential. Positions are in San Francisco headquarters. Visit Website for details. Meet us on campus at one of our recruiting events or at a special event.

Contact:
Chevron Professional Recruiting Staff
575 Market Street
15th Floor
San Francisco, CA 94105-2856
Phone: 415-894-7700
Web: www.chevron.com

City & Suburban Styles Magazine

CSS Editorial Internships

Type of award: Internship.
Intended use: For junior or senior study at accredited 2-year or 4-year institution in United States. Designated institutions: Colleges and universities in White Plains.
Eligibility: Applicant must be African American. Applicant must be U.S. citizen or permanent resident.
Basis for selection: Major/career interest in English or publishing. Applicant must demonstrate seriousness of purpose.
Application requirements: Interview, portfolio. Send sample writing clips from school newspaper or periodicals.
Additional information: 6-12 week internships. Interns receive weekly stipend for travel expenses. African-American students residing and attending school in White Plains welcomed. Interns assist editors and advertising executives in all aspects of their work.

    Number of awards: 4
    Application deadline: April 15, January 15
Contact:
City & Suburban Styles Magazine
31 Mamaroneck Avenue 5th. floor
White Plains
New York, NY 10601
Phone: 914-997-6440

Congressional Hispanic Caucus Institute

CHCI Summer Internship Program

Type of award: Internship.
Intended use: For full-time sophomore, junior or senior study at accredited 2-year or 4-year institution.
Eligibility: Applicant must be Mexican American, Hispanic American or Puerto Rican. Applicant must be U.S. citizen or permanent resident residing in District of Columbia.
Basis for selection: Applicant must demonstrate high academic achievement, depth of character, leadership, seriousness of purpose and service orientation.
Application requirements: Recommendations, essay, transcript. Application, resume, GMAT and LSAT scores.

Additional information: Eight-week internship in Washington, D.C. Transportation, housing, and $2,000 stipend provided. Must have excellent writing and communications skills and active interest in community affairs. Interns assigned to congressional offices regardless of political affiliation. Work experience is complemented by leadership development curriculum. Minimum 3.0 GPA. Application available on Website.

    Number of awards: 30
    Number of applicants: 30
    Application deadline: January 31
Contact:
Congressional Hispanic Caucus Institute Program Coordinator
504 C Street, NE
Washington, DC 20002
Phone: 202-543-1771
Fax: 202-546-2143
Web: www.chci.org

Congressional Institute

Congressional Institute Internships

Type of award: Internship.
Intended use: For undergraduate study at accredited 2-year or 4-year institution in United States.
Eligibility: Applicant must be U.S. citizen or permanent resident residing in District of Columbia.
Basis for selection: Major/career interest in political science/ government; public administration/service; law or communications. Applicant must demonstrate high academic achievement.
Application requirements: Recommendations. Resume and writing samples.
Additional information: Paid internships available throughout the year on flexible terms. Must be undergraduate student with interest in public policy or legislative policy issues. For application and additional information visit internet site.
Contact:
Congressional Institute, Inc.
316 Pennsylvania Avenue, SE
Suite 403
Washington, DC 20003-1172
Phone: 202-547-4600
Fax: 202-547-3556
Web: www.conginst.org

Congressman Bob Schaffer

Congressional Internship

Type of award: Internship, renewable.
Intended use: For undergraduate study at accredited 4-year institution in United States.
Eligibility: Applicant must be U.S. citizen or permanent resident residing in District of Columbia or Colorado.
Basis for selection: Major/career interest in political science/ government; law; communications or public relations. Applicant must demonstrate high academic achievement.
Application requirements: Recommendations, proof of eligibility.

Additional information: Course credit arranged. Internships available at four Fourth Congressional District offices in Colorado and in Washington, DC. Contact district offices or visit internet site for more information.

Contact:
Congressman Bob Schaffer
212 Cannon House Office Building
Washington, DC 20515
Phone: 202-225-4676
Web: www.house.gov/schaffer/congressional_internship.htm

CORPORATEinterns, Inc.

CORPORATEinterns.com Student Placement

Type of award: Internship.
Intended use: For full-time undergraduate or graduate study at accredited 4-year institution.
Eligibility: Applicant must be U.S. citizen or permanent resident.
Basis for selection: Major/career interest in accounting; business/management/administration; finance/banking; computer/information sciences; communications or marketing. Applicant must demonstrate high academic achievement.
Application requirements: Visit Website to register.
Additional information: CORPORATEinterns, Inc. is a free-to-students (employer-paid) intern placement service. Positions available appropriate to most major fields of study. Wages are competitive. Most placements in Minnesota.
Contact:
CORPORATEinterns, Inc.
449 East Seventh Street
Suite 200
St. Paul, MN 55101
Phone: 888-875-3565
Fax: 651-224-6003
Web: www.corporateinterns.com

Creede Repertory Theatre

Creede Repertory Theatre Summer Internship

Type of award: Internship.
Intended use: For undergraduate, graduate or non-degree study at postsecondary institution.
Basis for selection: Major/career interest in business; design; humanities/liberal arts; performing arts; theater arts or theater/production/technical.
Application requirements: Audition, recommendations. Resume or application. Interview preferred, but not required.
Additional information: Mainly for students interested in theatre and business-related fields, but open to all majors. Offers internships in costumes, set building, box office, business management. High school seniors may apply, but must graduate by summer. Also hire actors, designers (set, costume, lights, etc.) and stage managers. Applicants awarded positions on basis of qualifications for particular jobs. Actors must audition. All others fill out internship application and/or send resume. We

will consider any age/sex/race applicant. Housing is free, interns receive $175 a week.
    Application deadline: March 1
Contact:
Creede Repertory Theatre
Summer Internships
P.O. Box 269
Creede, CO 81130

Cushman School

Cushman School Internship

Type of award: Internship, renewable.
Intended use: For undergraduate or graduate study. Designated institutions: Cushman school campus.
Basis for selection: Major/career interest in education. Applicant must demonstrate depth of character.
Application requirements: Resume, cover letter.
Additional information: 17-week internships for fall and spring. Award is only for internships on the Cushman School campus.
    Amount of award: $2,000-$3,000
    Number of awards: 4
    Application deadline: April 1
Contact:
Cushman School
592 Northeast 60th St.
Miami, FL 33137

Davis and Company

Employee Communication Internship

Type of award: Internship.
Intended use: For undergraduate or graduate study.
Eligibility: Applicant must be U.S. citizen or permanent resident.
Basis for selection: Major/career interest in graphic arts/design; communications; journalism; marketing or English. Applicant must demonstrate depth of character.
Application requirements: Interview. Resume.
Additional information: 6-12 week internship. Interns receive $7/hour for a 40-hour work week. Interns assist account executives in all aspects of their work.
Contact:
Davis and Company
80 Grand Ave.
River Edge, NJ 07661
Web: www.davisandco.com

Deloitte and Touche

SELECT Internship Program

Type of award: Internship.

Intended use: For full-time sophomore, junior or senior study at accredited 4-year institution.
Eligibility: Applicant must be U.S. citizen, permanent resident, international student or students eligible to work in the United States.
Basis for selection: Major/career interest in accounting; business/management/administration; engineering or finance/banking. Applicant must demonstrate high academic achievement.
Application requirements: Resume, cover letter.
Additional information: Majors in risk management, industrial management also eligible. Many other majors accepted. Internships in more than 40 Deloitte and Touche offices nationwide. Classes available for interns. Interns also attend annual conference. Visit Website to submit resume online directly to office of applicant's choice.

   Number of awards: 900
Contact:
Deloitte and Touche
SELECT Internship Program
1633 Broadway
New York, NY 10019-6754
Phone: 212-398-1600
Fax: 212-492-4154
Web: www.dttus.com/us/career/intern.htm

Denver Rescue Mission

Denver Rescue Mission Interns

Type of award: Internship.
Intended use: For undergraduate study in United States.
Basis for selection: Major/career interest in social work or religion/theology. Applicant must demonstrate service orientation.
Additional information: Work in full-service ministry to the needy in Colorado Front Range area, including work with homeless families and children. Check with sponsor for pay, college credit opportunity, current openings, and job qualifications.
Contact:
Denver Rescue Mission
P.O. Box 5206
Denver, CO 80217
Phone: 303-297-1815
Web: www.denverrescuemission.org

Dow Jones Newspaper Fund

Business Reporting Intern Program

Type of award: Internship.
Intended use: For full-time sophomore or junior study at 2-year or 4-year institution.
Eligibility: Applicant must be Alaskan native, Asian American, African American, Mexican American, Hispanic American, Puerto Rican or American Indian. Applicant must be U.S. citizen.

Basis for selection: Major/career interest in journalism or business. Applicant must demonstrate high academic achievement and seriousness of purpose.
Application requirements: Essay, transcript, proof of eligibility. Must also take a reporting test.
Additional information: Applications available June 15 to November 1. Finalists notified mid-January. All applicants notified by January 31. Reporting test administered by designated professor on applicant's campus. Telephone interview required for finalists. Paid summer internships as editors at daily newspapers last ten to twelve weeks. Interns returning to school receive scholarship at end of summer to apply toward following year. All interns attend pre-internship training that lasts one week.

   Amount of award: $1,000
   Number of awards: 12
   Application deadline: November 15
   Total amount awarded: $12,000
Contact:
Dow Jones Newspaper Fund
Business Reporting Intern Program
P.O. Box 300
Princeton, NJ 08543-0300
Web: www.dowjones.com/newsfund

Newspaper Editing Intern Fund

Type of award: Internship.
Intended use: For full-time junior, senior or graduate study at 4-year or graduate institution in United States.
Eligibility: Applicant must be U.S. citizen.
Basis for selection: Major/career interest in journalism. Applicant must demonstrate high academic achievement and seriousness of purpose.
Application requirements: Essay, transcript, proof of eligibility. Must also take editing test.
Additional information: Applications available June 15 to November 1. Finalists notified mid-December. All applicants notified by December 31. Editing test administered by designated professor on applicant's campus. Telephone interview required for finalists. Paid summer internships, as editors at daily newspapers, online newspapers, or real-time financial news services last ten to twelve weeks. Interns returning to school receive scholarship at end of summer to apply toward following year. All interns attend pre-internship training that lasts one to two weeks.

   Amount of award: $1,000
   Number of awards: 116
   Number of applicants: 500
   Application deadline: November 15
   Total amount awarded: $65,000
Contact:
Dow Jones Newspaper Fund
Newspaper Editing Intern Fund
P.O. Box 300
Princeton, NJ 08543-0300
Web: www.dowjones.com/newsfund

E. I. du Pont de Nemours and Company

DuPont Cooperative Education Program

Type of award: Internship.
Intended use: For full-time sophomore, junior or senior study at accredited 4-year institution in United States. Designated institutions: DuPont company sites throughout the U.S.
Eligibility: Applicant must be U.S. citizen or permanent resident.
Basis for selection: Major/career interest in engineering, chemical; engineering, mechanical; engineering, electrical/electronic; science, general; biology; chemistry; information systems; business; accounting or materials science.
Application requirements: Resume and cover letter.
Additional information: Participants alternate work assignments and academic terms. Applicants can start no earlier than after completion of freshman year and work a minimum of three industrial work periods. Must have minimum 3.0 GPA. Non-U.S. citizens must have green card; temporary work authorization does not meet eligibility requirements. Contact school co-op office or visit Website for further information and to submit resume.
   Application deadline: January 15
Contact:
DuPont Resume Processing Center
P.O. Box 540117
Waltham, MA 02453-0177
Fax: 1-800-978-9774
Web: www.dupont.com/careers

DuPont Internships

Type of award: Internship.
Intended use: For full-time junior or senior study at accredited 4-year institution in United States. Designated institutions: DuPont company sites throughout the U.S.
Eligibility: Applicant must be U.S. citizen or permanent resident.
Basis for selection: Major/career interest in engineering, chemical; engineering, mechanical; engineering, electrical/electronic; science, general; biology; chemistry; information systems; business; accounting or computer/information sciences.
Application requirements: Resume and cover letter.
Additional information: Position normally awarded for summer between junior and senior year; other periods may be available. Can apply for extended internship (summer and fall semester). Must have minimum 2.8 GPA. Non-U.S. citizens must have green card; temporary work authorization does not meet eligibility requirements. Number and amount of awards vary. Contact school co-op office or visit Website for further information and to submit resume.
   Application deadline: January 15
Contact:
DuPont Resume Processing Center
P.O. Box 540117
Waltham, MA 02453-0177
Fax: 800-978-9774
Web: www.dupont.com/careers

Eastman Kodak Company

Eastman Kodak Cooperative Internship Programs

Type of award: Internship.
Intended use: For full-time sophomore, junior, senior or graduate study.
Eligibility: Applicant must be U.S. citizen or permanent resident.
Basis for selection: Major/career interest in computer/information sciences; engineering; science, general; physics; accounting; mathematics; manufacturing; chemistry or business.
Application requirements: Resume and cover letter.
Additional information: Internship must be minimum of 10 consecutive weeks anytime during the year (not limited to summer). Most positions are technical in nature. Internship includes competitive salary based upon discipline and education level, travel expenses, paid holidays, and vacation. Assistance in locating housing, health benefits and life insurance available. Applicant must be drug screened as a condition of employment. Minimum GPA 2.8. E-mail resume and cover letter to: staffing@kodak.com (ASCII text only).
   Application deadline: February 1
Contact:
Eastman Kodak Company
Staffing, Dept. HCIP
343 State Street
Rochester, NY 14650-1139
Web: www.kodak.com

Eaton Corporation

Eaton Internships

Type of award: Internship.
Intended use: For full-time sophomore, junior or senior study at accredited 4-year institution in United States. Designated institutions: Targeted core institutions.
Eligibility: Applicant must be U.S. citizen or permanent resident.
Basis for selection: Major/career interest in engineering; computer/information sciences; information systems; finance/banking or accounting. Applicant must demonstrate high academic achievement.
Application requirements: Apply on Website: www.eatonjobs.com.
Additional information: Paid internships available in many departments/locations. Visit Website for list of target schools and recruitment events. Terms vary, summer or year-round. Rolling application deadline.
Contact:
Web: www.eatonjobs.com

EDS Recruiting

Student Internship Program

Type of award: Internship.

Intended use: For sophomore, junior or senior study at accredited 2-year or 4-year institution.
Eligibility: Applicant must be U.S. citizen or permanent resident.
Basis for selection: Major/career interest in computer/ information sciences; engineering; business/management/ administration; communications; finance/banking; accounting or marketing. Applicant must demonstrate leadership.
Application requirements: Cover letter, resume, transcript, interview. Applicants should have strong communication skills.
Additional information: Internships are paid, with possibility of course credit. To be considered, mail resume and cover letter to sponsor.
Contact:
EDS Recruiting
Student Programs
700 Tower Drive, 5th Floor
Troy, MI 49098
Phone: 248-265-4500
Fax: 800-562-6241
Web: www.eds.com

Eli Lilly and Company

Eli Lilly and Co. Summer Internships

Type of award: Internship, renewable.
Intended use: For full-time undergraduate or graduate study at accredited 4-year institution.
Eligibility: Applicant must be single. Applicant must be U.S. citizen or permanent resident.
Basis for selection: Major/career interest in marketing; finance/banking; information systems; engineering; medical specialties/research; human resources or science, general. Applicant must demonstrate high academic achievement, depth of character, leadership, patriotism, seriousness of purpose and service orientation.
Application requirements: Interview. Send resume, academic history and work history.
Additional information: Paid summer internships with housing assistance. Rolling application deadline. Lilly visits selected campuses on a regular basis throughout the academic year. Check Website for details, to submit an application and resume, or send letter of inquiry. Must major in marketing, finance, information tehcnology, engineering, sciences, human resources, medical science or statistics.
Contact:
Eli Lilly and Company Corporate Center
Intern Coordinator DC 1811
Indianapolis, IN 46285
Phone: 317-276-2000
Web: www.lilly.com/careers

Elizabeth Dow Ltd.

Elizabeth Dow Internship Program

Type of award: Internship.
Intended use: For undergraduate, graduate or non-degree study.

Eligibility: Applicant must be returning adult student. Applicant must be U.S. citizen or permanent resident.
Basis for selection: Major/career interest in interior design; arts, general; design or marketing. Applicant must demonstrate seriousness of purpose.
Application requirements: Interview, recommendations. Resume and cover letter.
Additional information: Duration of this internship is flexible. Position available as unpaid or at $5.15 per hour minimum. Candidates should have ability to work independently, ability to work with others, oral communication skills, personal interest in the field, and self motivation. Application deadline is continuous, but apply as early as possible for summer. Current high school students also eligible to apply. Visit Website for more information.

Number of awards:	45
Number of applicants:	450

Contact:
Elizabeth Dow Ltd.
155 6th Avenue, 4th Floor
New York, NY 10013
Web: www.elizabethdow.com/internships.html

Elizabeth Glaser Pediatric AIDS Foundation

Elizabeth Glaser Pediatric AIDS Foundation Student Intern Award

Type of award: Internship.
Intended use: For undergraduate or graduate study.
Basis for selection: Major/career interest in medical specialties/research. Applicant must demonstrate seriousness of purpose.
Application requirements: Nomination by research sponsor. Sponsor (M.D., Ph.D., C.C.S.W.) must have pediatric HIV/ AIDS research experience. Applicant must demonstrate seriousness of purpose in pediatric research.
Additional information: This program is to encourage students to choose career in pediatric HIV/AIDS research. Provides $2,000 for 320 hours of work. Must work minimum of four hours per week. High school seniors, undergraduates, graduates and medical students are eligible. Applications available in January. Applications available online.

Amount of award:	$2,000
Number of awards:	50
Number of applicants:	91
Application deadline:	March 28
Total amount awarded:	$100,000

Contact:
Elizabeth Glaser Pediatric AIDS Foundation
2950 31st Street
Suite 125
Santa Monica, CA 90405
Phone: 310-314-1459
Fax: 310-314-1469
Web: www.pedaids.org

Internships

EMC

EMC Summer Internship Program and Co-ops

Type of award: Internship.
Intended use: For full-time undergraduate study at accredited 4-year institution.
Eligibility: Applicant must be U.S. citizen or permanent resident residing in Massachusetts.
Basis for selection: Major/career interest in accounting; engineering; finance/banking; human resources; manufacturing; marketing; computer/information sciences; computer/information sciences or engineering, computer. Applicant must demonstrate high academic achievement.
Application requirements: Send resume. Must be committed to the duration of the assignment. GPA 3.0 minimum.
Additional information: EMC, which builds information storage infrastructures, software and networks is ranked as one of the "100 Best Companies to Work For in America". Offering both co-op and summer internship positions, the program is designed to provide a challenging learning experience. Fax or e-mail resume. E-mail address: university_emc@emc.com. Visit Website for further information.
Contact:
EMC University Recruiting
5 Technology Road
Millford, MA 01757
Fax: 508-497-7121
Web: www.emc.com

Entergy

Entergy Co-ops and Internships

Type of award: Internship, renewable.
Intended use: For full-time undergraduate or graduate study at accredited 4-year or graduate institution in United States. Designated institutions: Selected schools in Southern US, from Texas to Florida.
Eligibility: Applicant must be U.S. citizen or permanent resident residing in Florida, Texas, Louisiana, Mississippi or Arkansas.
Basis for selection: Major/career interest in engineering or business. Applicant must demonstrate high academic achievement.
Additional information: Visit Website for list of targeted campuses in the South, recruiting schedule, current openings and to apply online. Undergraduate and graduate, co-ops and internships available. Rolling application deadline.
Contact:
Entergy Co-ops and Internships
PO Box 61000
New Orleans, LA 70113
Phone: 800-368-3749
Web: www.entergy.com

Entertainment Weekly

Entertainment Weekly Internship

Type of award: Internship.
Intended use: For junior, senior or graduate study at postsecondary institution.
Basis for selection: Major/career interest in journalism or publishing. Applicant must demonstrate seriousness of purpose.
Application requirements: Resume, cover letter and five writing samples.
Additional information: Opportunities to work in such departments as Editorial, Photo and Design. Internship lasts 12-18 weeks and pays $8/hour. Overtime available. Summer deadline is February 15. Fall, spring internships are for graduate students only. Summer internships are open to seniors and graduates.

Number of awards:	5
Number of applicants:	400
Application deadline:	June 1, October 15

Contact:
Entertainment Weekly Internship Coordinator
1675 Broadway
New York, NY 10019
Phone: 212-522-5600
Fax: 212-522-6104

ESPN Inc.

ESPN Internship

Type of award: Internship.
Intended use: For full-time junior or senior study.
Eligibility: Applicant must be U.S. citizen.
Basis for selection: Major/career interest in journalism; communications; radio/television/film; graphic arts/design; marketing or accounting. Applicant must demonstrate high academic achievement.
Application requirements: A resume, cover letter and a sports knowledge/interest.
Additional information: Sports knowledge/interest/participation highly desirable. ESPN will assist interns in finding housing. Interns will receive an hourly wage of $7. Applicants should submit a resume.

Number of awards:	30
Number of applicants:	1,000
Application deadline:	March 1

Contact:
ESPN Inc. Internship Coordinator
935 Middle St.
Bristol, CT 06010
Phone: 860-766-2000

Essence Magazine

Essence Internship

Type of award: Internship, renewable.
Intended use: For undergraduate study at 2-year or 4-year institution in United States.

Eligibility: Applicant must be Alaskan native, Asian American, African American, Mexican American, Hispanic American, Puerto Rican or American Indian. Applicant must be U.S. citizen.
Basis for selection: Applicant must demonstrate depth of character.
Application requirements: Interview.
Additional information: This six week summer internship is open to students of all majors.

Amount of award:	$1,800
Number of awards:	10
Application deadline:	December 28
Total amount awarded:	$18,000

Contact:
Essence Magazine
1500 Broadway, Suite 600
New York, NY 10036
Web: www.essence.com

Federal Bureau of Investigation

Honors Internship Program

Type of award: Internship, renewable.
Intended use: For full-time junior, senior or graduate study at accredited 4-year or graduate institution in United States.
Eligibility: Applicant must be U.S. citizen.
Basis for selection: Major/career interest in criminal justice/law enforcement. Applicant must demonstrate high academic achievement, leadership and seriousness of purpose.
Application requirements: Interview, recommendations, essay, transcript, proof of eligibility. Extensive background screening with drug test.
Additional information: Graduate-level students must currently be attending school. All students must be returning to their respective schools for at least one semester immediately following internship. Positions available in Washington, D.C., Virginia and Maryland. Deadline for application submission is November 1, but application process must start in July or August to complete necessary vetting. Individuals selected based on how their specific skills and educational background meets current FBI needs. Must have minumum 3.0 GPA. Must be able to pass extensive background check. Visit internet site for application materials and contact information.

Application deadline:	November 1

Contact:
Federal Bureau of Investigation
J. Edgar Hoover Building
935 Pennsylvania Avenue, N.W.
Washington, DC 20535-0001
Phone: 202-324-3000
Web: www.fbi.gov

Federal Reserve Bank of New York

Federal Reserve Summer Internship

Type of award: Internship.
Intended use: For full-time junior, senior or graduate study.
Eligibility: Applicant must be U.S. citizen, permanent resident, international student or legally authorized to work in the U.S. on a multi-year basis.
Basis for selection: Major/career interest in finance/banking or economics. Applicant must demonstrate high academic achievement and leadership.
Application requirements: Interview, transcript. Cover letter, resume, and writing sample.
Additional information: Paid internships beginning in May/June. Bachelor's level applicants should have completed junior year of college before beginning internship. Master's level applicants should have completed first year of graduate program. Housing not provided.

Application deadline:	January 31

Contact:
Federal Reserve Bank of New York
Summer Internship Coordinator
33 Maiden Lane, 26th Floor
New York, NY 10038-4502
Phone: 212-720-6922
Web: www.ny.frb.org

Federated Department Stores, Inc.

Federated Department Stores Internships

Type of award: Internship, renewable.
Intended use: For full-time undergraduate study at accredited 2-year institution.
Basis for selection: Major/career interest in marketing; business or retailing/merchandising. Applicant must demonstrate high academic achievement.
Application requirements: Interview.
Additional information: Nine-to-12-week paid summer internships; some fall and spring positions available. May apply online. Visit Website for additional information and campus recruiting schedule.
Contact:
Federated Department Stores, Inc.
7 West Seventh Street
Cincinnatti, OH 45202
Phone: 212-695-4400
Web: www.retailology.com/internships

Feminist Majority Foundation

National Internship Program in Feminism and Public Policy

Type of award: Internship.
Intended use: For full-time undergraduate study at accredited 4-year institution.
Basis for selection: Major/career interest in law; public relations; social/behavioral sciences; women's studies or political science/government. Applicant must demonstrate leadership.
Application requirements: Proof of eligibility. Resume, cover letter, writing sample (3-5 pages), 2 recommendations.
Additional information: Internships available in Washington, D.C., area or Los Angeles. For Los Angeles, contact Diana Garcia, Feminist Majority, 8105 West Third Street, Suite 1, Los Angeles, CA 90048. Internships pay $80/wk for September-May; unpaid in summer, although interns may be paid for clerical work as needed. Female or male feminist undergraduates encouraged to apply. Preference to applicants with experience working on feminist issues. People of color and math/science majors given special consideration due to diversity goal of sponsor.
Contact:
Feminist Majority
Shonali Shome
1600 Wilson Boulevard, Suite 801
Arlington, VA 22209
Phone: 703-522-2214
Fax: 703-522-2219
Web: www.feminist.org

Filoli Center

Filoli Center Garden Internship

Type of award: Internship.
Intended use: For undergraduate, graduate or non-degree study. Designated institutions: Filoli Center.
Basis for selection: Major/career interest in horticulture; landscape architecture or botany. Applicant must demonstrate depth of character, leadership and seriousness of purpose.
Application requirements: Interview, recommendations, transcript. Cover letter outlining interests.
Additional information: Internships designed for students pursuing career in horticulture, public garden management, landscape maintenance or landscape architecture. Techniques of planting, watering, hedging, fertilizing, mowing and pruning; operation of power equipment; and use of hand tools taught. Interns required to learn garden and greenhouse plants, weeds and native plants. Students paid $8.00 per hour and may earn college credits for ten-week program. Applicants must have at least fifteen units of horticulture classes, 3.0 GPA. Ability to work well with public and work teams essential. Application deadline for summer internship is March 30.

Amount of award:	$3,200
Number of awards:	15
Application deadline:	July 16, January 14
Total amount awarded:	$48,000

Contact:
Filoli Center
Filoli Garden Internships
86 Cañada Road
Woodside, CA 94062
Phone: 650-364-8300 ext. 214
Web: www.filoli.org

First Union

Finance Undergraduate Internships

Type of award: Internship.
Intended use: For full-time undergraduate study at accredited 4-year institution.
Eligibility: Applicant must be U.S. citizen or permanent resident.
Basis for selection: Major/career interest in finance/banking; accounting or business/management/administration.
Application requirements: Resume, cover letter.
Additional information: Undergraduate paid internships in Corporate Accounting, Cost Development, Value-Based Planning, Financial Planning and Analysis. Offers interaction with CFO Groups for Consumer Bank, Capital Markets, Automation & Operations and Wholesale Bank. Number of awards varies. Visit Website for application and to apply online. Graduate program also offered.
Contact:
First Union Corporation
ATTN: Resume Scanning
1525 West W. T. Harris Blvd.
Charlotte, NC 28288-0970
Phone: 800-ASK-FUNB
Web: www.firstunion.com/employment/college

Florida Department of Education

Florida Work Experience Program

Type of award: Internship, renewable.
Intended use: For undergraduate study at 2-year or 4-year institution. Designated institutions: Eligible Florida postsecondary institutions.
Eligibility: Applicant must be U.S. citizen or permanent resident residing in Florida.
Basis for selection: Applicant must demonstrate financial need.
Application requirements: Proof of eligibility. Submit FAFSA. Minimum 2.0 GPA.
Additional information: Provides students with opportunity to be employed off-campus in jobs related to their academic major or area of career interest. Applications available from participating universities financial aid offices. Amount of award determined by institution's financial aid office, and may not exceed student's financial need.

Number of awards:	517

Contact:
Florida Department of Education
Bureau of Student Financial Assistance
1940 North Monroe Street, Suite 70
Tallahassee, FL 32303-4759
Phone: 888-827-2004
Web: www.firn.edu/doe

Florida Power & Light Company

Florida Power & Light Co-op Program

Type of award: Internship, renewable.
Intended use: For full-time undergraduate or graduate study at accredited 4-year or graduate institution in United States. Designated institutions: Cornell University, Florida A&M University, Florida Atlantic University, Florida International University, Florida State University, Georgia Tech, Tuskegee University, University of Central Florida, University of Florida, University of Miami, University of South Florida, University of Miami, Florida Institute of Technology.
Eligibility: Applicant must be U.S. citizen or permanent resident.
Basis for selection: Major/career interest in engineering. Applicant must demonstrate high academic achievement.
Application requirements: Proof of eligibility. Resume.
Additional information: For more information contact designated institution's Cooperative Education Coordinator or write Florida Power & Light's Co-op Coordinator at sponsor address.
Contact:
Florida Power & Light Company
College Coordinator
P. O. Box 14000, HRR/JB
Juno Beach, FL 33408-0420
Phone: 561-694-4000
Fax: 305-552-3641
Web: www.fpl.com

Forbes Magazine

Forbes Internship

Type of award: Internship.
Intended use: For undergraduate or graduate study.
Eligibility: Applicant must be U.S. citizen.
Basis for selection: Major/career interest in business or journalism. Applicant must demonstrate depth of character.
Application requirements: Interview. Resume and cover letter.
Additional information: Interns work in editorial department, doing research and writing for Forbes 400 Magazine. Undergraduate interns paid $8-10/hr for 35-hr work week during summer. Prefer applicants living in New York metro area. Contact sponsor for further information.

Number of awards:	6
Application deadline:	February 1

Contact:
Internship Coordinator
Forbes Magazine
60 Fifth Ave.
New York, NY 10011

Franklin D. Roosevelt Library

Franklin D. Roosevelt Library/ Roosevelt Summer Internship

Type of award: Internship.
Intended use: For undergraduate or graduate study.
Basis for selection: Major/career interest in library science; computer/information sciences; museum studies; history or political science/government.
Application requirements: Transcript. Application and resume required. Some familiarity with FDR presidency helpful.
Additional information: Applicants must be undergraduates or graduate students. Interns work at FDR library with other interns and staff organizing archival materials, making indices, finding aids and databases, digitizing documents and photographs, and assisting with other projects. Internship can last six or seven weeks and must take place during summer break (mid-May through end of August). FDR Library is in Hyde Park, NY, 80 miles north of NYC. Housing not provided. Work Monday through Friday, nine to five. Stipend of $250/ week for summer interns, academic credit for fall and spring. Number of awards depends on funding.

Application deadline:	April 1

Contact:
Franklin D. Roosevelt Library
4079 Albany Post Rd.
Hyde Park, NY 12538
Phone: 845-229-8114
Fax: 845-229-0872

Friends of the National Zoo

Zoo Research Traineeships

Type of award: Internship.
Intended use: For undergraduate or graduate study.
Basis for selection: Major/career interest in animal sciences; zoology; landscape architecture; veterinary medicine; science, general or biology.
Application requirements: Recommendations, essay, transcript. Social Security number, two references, 500 to 1000 word statement, academic status and curriculum.
Additional information: Paid 12-week traineeships at the National Zoological Park in Washington, D.C. Positions available in Animal Behaviour, Reproductive Physiology, Nutrition, Genetics, Husbandry/Exhibit, Interpretation, Zoo Animal Medicine and Veterinary Pathology. Notification within two months of application deadline. See Website for details. Women and minority students encouraged to apply.

Amount of award:	$2,400-$3,000
Application deadline:	December 31

Contact:
Friends of the National Zoological Park
Traineeship Program
National Zoological Park
Washington, DC 20008
Phone: 202-673-4640
Web: www.fonz.org

Genentech, Inc.

Genentech Internship Program

Type of award: Internship, renewable.
Intended use: For full-time junior or senior study at accredited 4-year institution.
Eligibility: Applicant must be U.S. citizen, permanent resident, international student or appropriate visa or green card.
Basis for selection: Major/career interest in biology; chemistry; engineering, chemical; computer/information sciences or business. Applicant must demonstrate high academic achievement.
Application requirements: Resume and cover letter.
Additional information: Internships paid by competitive monthly stipend and membership at health club. Students majoring in biochemical engineering also eligible. Resumes in plain text-only format may be sent in body of e-mail message to sponsor. E-mail address genetechjobpost@webhirepc.com. If you are selected for an internship, you will be contacted during April or May. Internships may also be available during school year.
Contact:
Genetech tech, Inc.
Attn: Summer Internship Program
P. O. Box 1950
South San Francisco, CA 94083-1950
Phone: 650-225-1695
Web: www.gene.com

General Mills

General Mills Summer Internship

Type of award: Internship, renewable.
Intended use: For sophomore, junior or senior study.
Eligibility: Applicant must be U.S. citizen.
Basis for selection: Major/career interest in marketing; advertising; food science/technology or engineering.
Additional information: Ten to 14-week internship. Manufacturing and engineering interns will be placed in plants. All others will intern at company headquarters. General Mills recruits at over 40 campuses nationwide. Visit Website for more information and to submit resume.
Contact:
Internship Coordinator
P.O. Box 1113
Minneapolis, MN 55440
Phone: 763-764-2505
Web: www.generalmills.com

General Motors North America

General Motors Corporation Talent Acquisition Internship

Type of award: Internship, renewable.
Intended use: For full-time undergraduate or graduate study at 4-year or graduate institution.
Basis for selection: Major/career interest in engineering; accounting; science, general or automotive technology. Applicant must demonstrate leadership.
Application requirements: Interview, transcript. Resume.
Additional information: Co-ops and paid internships available. Salary varies with job, skills and degree/program of study. Temporary, full-time positions during semester break, three months in summer. Visit Website for details or to submit resume. For Saturn Corp. and other GM divisions, see Website or contact sponsor. In most cases, applicant must have completed freshman year of study to be eligible.
Contact:
General Motors North America
Student Programs
P.O. Box 69
Nutting Lake, MA 01865-0069
Web: www.gm.com/careers

Georgia-Pacific Corporation

Georgia-Pacific Internships and Co-ops

Type of award: Internship, renewable.
Intended use: For undergraduate study in United States.
Eligibility: Applicant must be U.S. citizen or permanent resident.
Basis for selection: Major/career interest in accounting; computer/information sciences; communications; engineering; forestry; human resources or marketing. Applicant must demonstrate high academic achievement.
Application requirements: Transcript, proof of eligibility.
Additional information: Must have minimum 2.5 GPA, or minimum 3.0 GPA for accounting majors. Internships and co-ops are paid, and number awarded varies. Co-ops must be able to commit 3-5 quarters or 3 semesters as a co-op. Submit resume by fax, e-mail (to coop@gapac.com or intern@gapac.com) or surface mail to apply.
Contact:
Georgia Pacific Corporation
Attn: College Relations
P.O. Box 105605
Atlanta, GA 30248-5605
Phone: 404-652-5463
Fax: 404-584-1481
Web: www.gp.com/center/career

Internships

525

Goodyear Tire & Rubber Company

Goodyear Internships and Co-ops

Type of award: Internship, renewable.
Intended use: For undergraduate study.
Eligibility: Applicant must be residing in Ohio.
Basis for selection: Major/career interest in accounting; computer/information sciences; engineering; finance/banking or chemistry.
Application requirements: Resume.
Additional information: Must major in engineering, finance, accounting, or computer science. Must be legally authorized to work in the U.S. Check with campus placement officer to interview with Goodyear representative during scheduled recruiting event. If Goodyear does not recruit on your campus, visit Website to submit resume. Co-ops alternate between work assignments in Akron, Ohio and on-campus classroom education. Visit Website for detailed work assignment descriptions. Housing assistance provided. Amount of payment or course credit awarded varies.
Contact:
Goodyear Tire & Rubber Co.
Goodyear Internships and Co-ops
1144 East Market Street
Akron, OH 44316
Phone: 800-321-2136
Web: www.goodyear.com

Hallmark Cards

Hallmark Internship Program

Type of award: Internship.
Intended use: For full-time senior or master's study.
Eligibility: Applicant must be U.S. citizen.
Basis for selection: Applicant must demonstrate high academic achievement,leadership experience and excellent interpersonal and communication skills. Applicant must demonstrate high academic achievement, depth of character and leadership.
Application requirements: Interview, recommendations, transcript. Resume and cover letter.
Additional information: Internships open to students entering final year of graduate or undergraduate program. Applicants must have experience and excellent interpersonal and communications skills. Open to all majors. Program seeks to create pool of qualified candidates to be considered for full-time employment.

Number of awards:	17
Application deadline:	January 15

Contact:
Internship Coordinator
Mail Drop #112
P.O. Box 419580
Kansas City, MO 64141

Hannaford Brothers Company

Hannaford Internships

Type of award: Internship.
Intended use: For undergraduate study. Designated institutions: Albany College of Pharmacy, University of Connecticut, University of Rhode Island, Massachusetts College of Pharmacy, Northeastern University, Virginia College of Medicine, University of No. Carolina, Campbell University, Hampton University.
Eligibility: Applicant must be U.S. citizen, permanent resident, international student or legally authorized to work in the U.S.
Basis for selection: Major/career interest in pharmacy/pharmaceutics/pharmacology.
Application requirements: Resume.
Additional information: Interns at Hannaford are exposed to a multi-cultural organization with support systems and training opportunities. Internships available at Hannaford's corporate offices, retail locations and distribution facilities. Enquire at campus placement office to schedule recruiting interview or e-mail sponsor (working@hannaford.com) for additional information. Must be legally authorized to work in the U.S. Amount of payment or course credit awarded varies. Visit Website for additional information.
Contact:
Hannaford Brothers Company
P.O. Box 1000
Portland, ME 04104
Phone: 800-213-9000
Web: www.hannaford.com

Hartford Life

The Hartford Life Internship and Co-op Opportunities

Type of award: Internship.
Intended use: For full-time junior or senior study at accredited 4-year institution.
Basis for selection: Major/career interest in accounting; business; information systems; computer/information sciences; insurance/actuarial science or finance/banking. Applicant must demonstrate seriousness of purpose.
Application requirements: Interview. Include resume and cover letter.
Additional information: Must have completed sophomore year, be enrolled in school's formal co-op or intern program, possess a 3.0 GPA. Paid, course credit. Co-op positions offered twice yearly in six-month assignments: January through June (recruiting starts in mid-October) and June throught December (recruiting starts in mid-April). Summer internships run from late May through late August. Visit Website for schedules and to submit resume.
Contact:
Hartford Life
200 Hopmeadow Street
Simsbury, CT 06089
Phone: 860-843-8594
Web: www.thehartford.com

Hispanic Association of Colleges and Universities

HACU National Internship Program

Type of award: Internship.
Intended use: For junior, senior or graduate study at 4-year or graduate institution. Designated institutions: Institutions with significant numbers of Hispanic students.
Eligibility: Applicant must be U.S. citizen or permanent resident.
Basis for selection: Applicant must demonstrate high academic achievement and service orientation.
Application requirements: Recommendations, essay, transcript, proof of eligibility. Resume, letter from registrar stating class status. Minimum 3.0 GPA.
Additional information: Paid internships provide students from institutions with significant numbers of Hispanic students the opportunity to explore potential careers with Federal agencies and private corporations. Weekly pay varies according to class level: sophomores and juniors--$420, seniors--$450, graduates--$520. Must be active in college and community service. Fall and spring internships 15 weeks, summer internships 10 weeks. Deadlines as follows: summer--March 2, spring--November 17, fall--June 15. Contact HACU for list of assignments. Visit Website to download application.
  Application deadline: November 17, March 2
Contact:
Hispanic Association of Colleges and Universities
One Dupont Circle, NW
Suite 605
Washington, DC 20036
Phone: 202-467-0893
Fax: 202-496-9177
Web: www.hacu.net

Hoffman-La Roche Inc.

Hoffman-La Roche Inc. Student Internship

Type of award: Internship.
Intended use: For full-time freshman, sophomore, junior or graduate study. Designated institutions: Carnegie Mellon, Fuqua, Johnson School, Rutgers, Yale.
Basis for selection: Major/career interest in pharmacy/pharmaceutics/pharmacology; engineering; computer/information sciences; science, general; business or business/management/administration.
Application requirements: Interview.
Additional information: Applicant must be authorized to work in the U.S. Internship fields and topics vary. Inexpensive housing arranged through a local College dormitory. Applicant must be attending one of Roche's eight target schools.
Contact:
University Relations Department
340 Kingsland St.
Nutley, NJ 07110-1199
Phone: 973-235-5000
Web: www.rocheusa.com

Houghton Mifflin Company

School Division Internship

Type of award: Internship.
Intended use: For undergraduate or graduate study.
Basis for selection: Major/career interest in publishing.
Application requirements: Must submit resume and cover letter.
Additional information: Full-time, 12-week summer internships pay minimum of $8/hour and up. Interns will be assigned to work in one of the School Division's editorial, design or business departments.
  Application deadline: May 15
Contact:
Houghton Mifflin Company School Division
Intern Coordinator
222 Berkeley St.
Boston, MA 02116
Web: www.hmco.com

IBM

IBM Internship and Co-op Program

Type of award: Internship.
Intended use: For undergraduate study at accredited 4-year or graduate institution in United States.
Basis for selection: Major/career interest in computer/information sciences; engineering, computer; engineering, electrical/electronic; information systems; accounting or finance/banking. Applicant must demonstrate high academic achievement and leadership.
Application requirements: Resume.
Additional information: Applicant must submit resume via mail or Website. Salary based upon number of credits completed toward degree. Application deadlines are rolling. Positions available at all large IBM locations as well as numerous cities throughout the U.S.
  Number of awards: 1,000
  Number of applicants: 10,000
Contact:
IBM Staffing Services Dept. 1DPA Source Code IBMNICSMR
3808 Six Forks Road
Raleigh,, NC 27609
Web: www.ibm.com

IBP, Inc.

IBP Intern Program

Type of award: Internship.
Intended use: For full-time undergraduate study at accredited vocational, 2-year or 4-year institution.
Basis for selection: Major/career interest in computer/information sciences; food science/technology or engineering, agricultural. Applicant must demonstrate high academic achievement.
Application requirements: Proof of eligibility. Resume, cover letter.

Internships

Additional information: Paid summer internships in computer programming, industrial engineering, livestock (pork) procurement, quality control. Program locations in South Dakota, Iowa and elsewhere. Must be eligible to work in the U.S. Visit Website for job descriptions, list of campus recruiting events, or to submit resume and cover letter.

Application deadline:	November 15

Contact:
College Relations Representative
IBP, Inc. World Headquarters
800 Stevens Port Drive-Suite 818
Dakota Dunes, SD 57049
Phone: 605-235-2061
Fax: 605-235-2025
Web: www.ibpinc.com

The Indianapolis Star, a Gannett Newspaper

Pulliam Journalism Fellowship

Type of award: Internship.
Intended use: For undergraduate or postgraduate study.
Basis for selection: Competition/talent/interest in writing/ journalism, based on quality of editorial written for competition, required essays, and previously published writing clips. Past internships, academic record, and commitment to newspaper journalism as career also considered. Major/career interest in humanities/liberal arts or journalism. Applicant must demonstrate high academic achievement, depth of character, leadership and seriousness of purpose.
Application requirements: Portfolio, recommendations, essay, transcript, proof of eligibility.
Additional information: Fellowship lasts ten weeks during summer. Ten recipients work for The Indianapolis Star, ten for The Arizona Republic in Phoenix. Applicants must be college students or already possess degree. November deadline is early deadline; March deadline is final postmark deadline.

Amount of award:	$6,000
Number of awards:	20
Number of applicants:	140
Application deadline:	November 15, March 1
Notification begins:	April 1

Contact:
Russell B. Pulliam, Director
The Pulliam Fellowship
P.O. Box 145
Indianapolis, IN 46206-0145
Phone: 317-444-6001
Web: www.starnews.com/pjf

INROADS, Inc.

INROADS Internship

Type of award: Internship, renewable.
Intended use: For full-time freshman or sophomore study.
Eligibility: Applicant must be Alaskan native, Asian American, African American, Mexican American, Hispanic American, Puerto Rican or American Indian.

Basis for selection: Major/career interest in engineering; business; computer/information sciences; communications; science, general; information systems or engineering, computer. Applicant must demonstrate high academic achievement and leadership.
Application requirements: Interview, essay, transcript. Minimum H.S. 2.8 GPA or College 3.0 GPA, Minimum 900 SAT or 20 ACT, and resume required.
Additional information: Internship duration and compensation varies; contact sponsor for specific information. Visit Website for additional information.

Number of awards:	300
Number of applicants:	700
Application deadline:	December 1

Contact:
INROADS, Inc.
10 S. Broadway
Suite 700
St. Louis, MO 63102
Phone: 314-241-7488
Web: www.inroads.org

Interns for Peace

Interns for Peace Internship

Type of award: Internship, renewable.
Intended use: For non-degree study in Israel.
Eligibility: Applicant must be Arab or Jewish.
Basis for selection: Competition/talent/interest in study abroad. Applicant must demonstrate depth of character, seriousness of purpose and service orientation.
Application requirements: Interview, recommendations, essay, proof of eligibility.
Additional information: Open to persons of either Arab or Jewish descent. Two-year internship on ethnic conflict resolution in assigned community in Israel for Jews, Israeli Arabs, and Arabs. Must have knowledge of and commitment to furthering Jewish-Arab relations. Must have B.A., M.A., or equivalent; prior residence in Israel for six months; proficiency in advanced level Hebrew or Arabic; some previous work experience. Salary approximately $500 per month plus housing and health benefits. Internship begins in fall; applications accepted year-round. Travel expenses are the responsibility of intern.

Number of awards:	2
Number of applicants:	180

Contact:
Interns for Peace
475 Riverside Drive, Room 240
New York, NY 10115

Iowa College Student Aid Commission

Iowa Work Study

Type of award: Internship, renewable.
Intended use: For undergraduate study at accredited vocational, 2-year or 4-year institution. Designated institutions: Iowa schools.

Internships

Eligibility: Applicant must be U.S. citizen or permanent resident residing in Iowa.
Basis for selection: Applicant must demonstrate financial need.
Application requirements: Proof of eligibility.

Number of awards:	4,594
Application deadline:	July 1
Total amount awarded:	$3,172,983

Contact:
Iowa College Student Aid Commission
200 Tenth Street, Fourth Floor
Des Moines, IA 50309-3609
Phone: 515-242-3344
Fax: 515-242-3388
Web: www.state.ia.us/collegeaid/

J. Paul Getty Trust

Getty Multicultural Undergraduate Internships

Type of award: Internship.
Intended use: For full-time undergraduate study at 4-year institution.
Eligibility: Applicant must be Asian American, African American, Mexican American, Hispanic American, Puerto Rican or American Indian.
Basis for selection: Major/career interest in arts management; communications; humanities/liberal arts; architecture; museum studies/administration or art/art history.
Application requirements: Interview, recommendations, transcript. Include application form, which is available online or from Grant Program office.
Additional information: Ten-week internship in specific departments of Getty Museum and other programs located at the Getty Center in Los Angeles. Priority given to students attending school or residing in L.A. Intended for outstanding students who are members of groups currently underrepresented in museum professions and fields related to visual arts and humanities. Applicants must have completed at least one semester of college by June and not be graduating before December. Housing and transportation not included. Applicants notified of acceptance in early May.

Amount of award:	$3,000
Number of awards:	16
Number of applicants:	124
Application deadline:	March 1

Contact:
The Getty Grant Program
Multicultural Undergraduate Internships
1200 Getty Center, Suite 800
Los Angeles, CA 90049-1685
Phone: 310-440-6545
Web: www.getty.edu/grants

Getty Multicultural Undergraduate Internships at Los Angeles Area Museums and Visual Arts Organizations

Type of award: Internship.
Intended use: For full-time undergraduate study at 4-year institution.

Eligibility: Applicant must be Asian American, African American, Mexican American, Hispanic American, Puerto Rican or American Indian.
Basis for selection: Major/career interest in art/art history; arts management; museum studies/administration; humanities/liberal arts; architecture; communications or parks/recreation.
Application requirements: Interview, recommendations, transcript. Apply directly to participating organizations for available positions. A list of these organizations will be available online beginning April 2001.
Additional information: Ten week internship at Los Angeles area museums and visual arts organizations. Applicant must be currently enrolled undergraduate who either resides in or attends college in Los Angeles County. Organizations will be seeking eligible interns for summer during April and May. Intended specifically for outstanding students who are members of groups currently underrepresented in museum professions and fields related to visual arts and humanities. Pacific Islanders also eligible. Applicants must have completed at least one semester of college by June and not be graduating before December. Housing and transportation not included. Finalists contacted in mid-April for in-person or telephone interviews. All applicants notified of Grant Program's decision in early May.

Amount of award:	$3,000

Contact:
The Getty Grant Program
1200 Getty Center Drive
Suite 800
Los Angeles, CA 90049-1685
Phone: 310-440-6545
Web: www.getty.edu/grant/internships

Jeppesen Dataplan

Jeppesen Meteorology Internship

Type of award: Internship.
Intended use: For non-degree study.
Basis for selection: Major/career interest in atmospheric sciences/meteorology.
Application requirements: Resume.
Additional information: Meteorology internship available all year. Salary $8-10/hr. Must be enrolled in accredited meteorology degree program. Ideally, applicant is a junior.

Number of awards:	1

Contact:
Jeppesen Dataplan
Attn: Judy Graun, Human Resources
121 Albright Way
Los Gatos, CA 95032
Phone: 408-866-7611
Web: judy_graun@jepplg.com

John Deere

John Deere Student Programs

Type of award: Internship, renewable.
Intended use: For undergraduate or graduate study at accredited 2-year, 4-year or graduate institution.

Eligibility: Applicant must be U.S. citizen or permanent resident.

Basis for selection: Major/career interest in accounting; finance/banking; human resources; health services administration; engineering; information systems or marketing. Applicant must demonstrate high academic achievement.

Application requirements: Transcript. Send resume.

Additional information: Deere and Company offers paid internships, course credit and academic scholarships through Student Training Program. Applicants may also be interested/majoring in supply management, and credit. Open to all levels of undergraduates; graduate students may also be eligible. Applicants for co-ops must be enrolled undergraduates and meet academic requirement. Co-ops work one term, study on campus one term. Number and amount of awards vary.

Contact:
Manager, Recruiting
Deere and Company
One John Deere Place
Moline, IL 61265
Phone: 309-765-4126
Fax: 309-749-0041
Web: www.deere.com Click on "Career / Job Seekers" tab

The John F. Kennedy Center for the Performing Arts

Vilar Institute for Arts Management Internship

Type of award: Internship.

Intended use: For junior, senior or post-bachelor's certificate study at accredited 4-year or graduate institution.

Basis for selection: Major/career interest in arts management.

Application requirements: Recommendations, transcript. Cover letter stating career goals, computer skills, three internship interests, current resume and a writing sample.

Additional information: Internship stipend $650 a month. Internships are for students with an interst in arts management and/or arts education management. Visit Website for more information.

Number of awards:	60
Number of applicants:	800
Application deadline:	June 23, November 1

Contact:
The John F. Kennedy Center for the Performing Arts
2700 F Street N.W
Washington, DC 20566
Phone: 202-416-8821
Fax: 202-416-8853
Web: www.kennedy-center.org/internships

John F. Kennedy Library Foundation

Kennedy Library Archival Internship

Type of award: Internship.

Intended use: For undergraduate or graduate study at 4-year or graduate institution.

Basis for selection: Major/career interest in history; political science/government; library science; English; journalism; communications or museum studies. Applicant must demonstrate high academic achievement.

Application requirements: Interview, recommendations, transcript. Must be studying in U.S.

Additional information: Minimum 12 hrs/week, $9/hr. Provides intern with opportunity to work with projects such as preservation of papers of Kennedy and his administration. Interns given career-relevant archival experience. Limited number of additional internships may open up during fall, winter, and spring. Library considers proposals for unpaid internships, independent study, work-study and internships undertaken for academic credit. See Website for latest information.

Application deadline:	February 15
Notification begins:	April 1

Contact:
John F. Kennedy Library Foundation
Columbia Point
Boston, MA 02125-3313
Phone: 617-929-4533
Fax: 617-929-4538
Web: www.cs.umb.edu/jfklibrary/index.htm

Johnson Controls

Johnson Controls Co-op and Internship Programs

Type of award: Internship, renewable.

Intended use: For full-time undergraduate or graduate study at accredited 4-year institution in United States.

Basis for selection: Major/career interest in engineering; law; business/management/administration; manufacturing or automotive technology. Applicant must demonstrate high academic achievement.

Application requirements: Proof of eligibility. Resume, cover letter.

Additional information: Johnson Controls offers several co-op and Internship programs in locations throughout the U.S. and abroad. The Engineering Co-op Program develops and trains students in all aspects of the Automotive Systems Group at Johnson Controls. Over a period of two-to-five years, Mechanical and Design Engineering students from colleges and universities alternate between work terms at Johnson Controls and school terms at college until graduation. Paid summer internships and positions in most other company divisions also. Visit Website for complete program descriptions.

Contact:
Johnson Controls Human Resources
PO Box 591
Milwaukee, WI 53201
Web: www.johnsoncontrols.com/hr/jobs/coops.htm

Kentucky Higher Education Assistance Authority (KHEAA)

Kentucky Work-Study Program

Type of award: Internship, renewable.
Intended use: For undergraduate, master's, doctoral, first professional or postgraduate study at vocational, 2-year, 4-year or graduate institution. Designated institutions: Postsecondary institutions in Kentucky.
Eligibility: Applicant must be U.S. citizen residing in Kentucky.
Application requirements: Interview, proof of eligibility.
Additional information: Job must be related to major course of study. Work-study wage is at least federal minimum wage. May also be enrolled in technical schools. Cannot be enrolled in religion, theology, or divinity program. Visit Website for additional information.

Number of awards:	1,120
Total amount awarded:	$862,000

Contact:
Kentucky Higher Education Assistance Authority (KHEAA)
KHEAA Work-Study Program
1050 U.S. 127 South
Frankfort, KY 40601-4323
Phone: 800-928-8926
Fax: 502-695-7345
Web: www.kheaa.com

KIMT

KIMT Weather/News Internships

Type of award: Internship.
Intended use: For undergraduate study.
Basis for selection: Major/career interest in atmospheric sciences/meteorology; journalism; radio/television/film or sports/sports administration.
Application requirements: Interview. Resume.
Additional information: Ideally, student should have completed junior year, have valid driver's license, good driving record, computer experience, and ability to shoot video. All internships are for college credit only. Student must arrange to receive college credit. Contact Doug Merbach directly, by phone or by e-mail (dmerbach@kimt). Internships available year-round. Hours are flexible.

Number of awards:	6

Contact:
KIMT Weather/News Internships
112 North Pennsylvania
Attn: Doug Merbach
Mason City, IA 50401
Phone: 641-423-2540

Landscape Architecture Foundation

CLASS Internship Program

Type of award: Internship.
Intended use: For full-time undergraduate study. Designated institutions: Cal Poly Pomona, Cal Poly San Luis Obispo, University of California at Davis.
Eligibility: Applicant must be residing in California.
Basis for selection: Major/career interest in landscape architecture or construction. Applicant must demonstrate financial need.
Application requirements: Recommendations, essay, transcript. Academic, community and professional involvement background. 300-word statement on the profession. 100-word statement on intended use of funds. Two faculty recommendation letters. One confidential department head recommendation.
Additional information: Award given for internship in selected field within the green industry. $2,000 stipend for internship. Firm/office sponsoring internship provides participant with an additional $6 per hour.

Amount of award:	$2,000
Number of awards:	2
Application deadline:	March 31
Total amount awarded:	$4,000

Contact:
Landscape Architecture Foundation
636 Eye Street NW
Washington, DC 20001
Phone: 201-898-2444
Web: www.asla.org

Liberty Mutual Group

Liberty Mutual Internships

Type of award: Internship.
Intended use: For full-time undergraduate study at accredited 4-year institution.
Basis for selection: Major/career interest in finance/banking; insurance/actuarial science or business/management/administration. Applicant must demonstrate high academic achievement.
Application requirements: Resume, cover letter.
Additional information: Paid summer internships. Submit resume online, by fax, or surface mail.
Contact:
Liberty Mutual Group, College Recruiting, Dept. CRGEN
175 Berkeley Street
Boston, MA 02117
Phone: 617-357-9500 ext. 44556
Fax: 603-422-9670
Web: www.libertymutual.com

Library of Congress

Library of Congress Anvario Hispano Hispanic Division Fellowship

Type of award: Internship.
Intended use: For junior, senior or graduate study.
Basis for selection: Major/career interest in library science; Latin american studies; political science/government; foreign languages; ethnic/cultural studies or international studies.
Application requirements: Interview, recommendations, transcript. Include cover letter indicating subject area of interest along with resume. Spanish language fluency.
Additional information: 8-week summer internship. Stipend is $300 per week. Room, board, and transportation not covered. Knowledge of Spanish or Portuguese required. All majors that can be related to Hispanic studies acceptable. Applications by women, minorities, and people with disabilities encouraged. E-mail: akur@loc.gov for more information. Funded by the Hispanic Yearbook.

Amount of award:	$2,400
Number of awards:	1
Number of applicants:	55
Application deadline:	April 14
Notification begins:	May 11

Contact:
Library of Congress
Hispanic Division
Washington, DC 20540-4580
Phone: 202-707-5400

Library of Congress Junior Fellows Internship

Type of award: Internship.
Intended use: For junior, senior or graduate study. Designated institutions: Library of Congress.
Eligibility: Applicant must be U.S. citizen or permanent resident.
Basis for selection: Major/career interest in library science. Applicant must demonstrate seriousness of purpose.
Application requirements: Interview, recommendations, transcript. Cover letter indicating subject areas applicant is interested in, as well as any language abilities. Application for federal employment (SF 171) or resume.
Additional information: One paid position at $300 per week for 14 weeks. Variable number of unpaid positions available. Applications from women, minorities, and people with disabilities encouraged. Deadline vary each year; contact program coordinator for details. Applicants usually notified by May.

Number of awards:	12
Number of applicants:	500

Contact:
Library of Congress
LS / PSC
Washington, DC 20540-4850
Phone: 202-707-5330

Los Angeles Times

Los Angeles Times Editorial Internship

Type of award: Internship.
Intended use: For junior, senior, master's or doctoral study at postsecondary institution.
Basis for selection: Major/career interest in journalism.
Application requirements: Interview, portfolio. Samples of published work, resume.
Additional information: Paid part-time internships available in spring and fall. Intern applicants should have experience on campus daily and/or professional daily newspaper, preferably one with circulation of at least 100,000.

Application deadline:	June 1, December 1

Contact:
Los Angeles Times Internship Coordinator
Times Mirror Square
Los Angeles, CA 90053
Phone: 800-LATIMES

Maine Space Grant Consortium

Undergraduate Internship Program

Type of award: Internship.
Intended use: For sophomore, junior or senior study at accredited 2-year or 4-year institution. Designated institutions: Maine two- and four-year colleges and universities.
Eligibility: Applicant must be U.S. citizen.
Basis for selection: Major/career interest in geology/earth sciences; astronomy; aerospace; engineering; biology or medicine.
Application requirements: Determined by Maine Educational Research Internships for Teachers and Students (MERITS); see Website (www.mstf.org/merits) for details.
Additional information: Space-related summer internships conducted at Maine-based businesses and research institution. For details call toll-free information number. The Maine Space Grant Consortium actively encourages applications from women and minority students.
Contact:
Maine Space Grant Consortium
87 Winthrop Street, Suite 200
Augusta, ME 04330
Phone: 877-397-7223
Web: www.msgc.org

Makovsky & Company Inc.

Public Relations Internship

Type of award: Internship.
Intended use: For junior or senior study at vocational institution in United States or Canada.
Eligibility: Applicant must be U.S. citizen.

Basis for selection: Applicant must demonstrate high academic achievement.

Application requirements: Interview. Resume, cover letter. One writing sample.

Additional information: Two to three full-time or part-time positions offered in both the spring and summer. $1,000/month stipend (full-time); $8/hr. (part-time). Applicant must be responsible, diligent, and energetic. Provides opportunity to receive hands-on experience in conducting all facets of public relations under the direction of the forums staff. Summer deadline--March 15; fall deadline--August 15; spring deadline--December 15. Submit resume at Website.

Amount of award:	$2,200
Number of awards:	3
Number of applicants:	150
Application deadline:	August 15, December 15

Contact:
Makovsky & Company, Inc. Internship Coordinator
575 Lexington Ave.
15th floor
New York, NY 10022
Phone: 212-508-9600
Fax: 212-751-9710
Web: www.makovsky.com

Maria Mitchell Observatory

Maria Mitchell Internships for Astronomical Research

Type of award: Internship.

Intended use: For undergraduate study at 4-year institution. Designated institutions: Maria Mitchell Observatory, Nantucket.

Eligibility: Applicant must be U.S. citizen or permanent resident.

Basis for selection: Major/career interest in astronomy or physics. Applicant must demonstrate high academic achievement.

Application requirements: Recommendations, transcript. Application (available on the Website).

Additional information: Positions provide opportunity for students to conduct independent research and opportunity to participate in common project. Students expected to develop their ability to communicate with the public. Furnished housing is available at no cost. Partial travel funds available. Program starts June 1st and continues through August 31st, with $1,100. monthly stipend.

Amount of award:	$2,200-$3,300
Number of awards:	6
Number of applicants:	100
Application deadline:	February 15
Notification begins:	March 15
Total amount awarded:	$19,800

Contact:
Maria Mitchell Observatory
3 Vestal St.
Nantucket, MA 02554
Web: www.mmo.org

Mashantucket Pequot Tribal Nation

Mashantucket Pequot Public Policy Internship Program

Type of award: Internship.

Intended use: For junior, senior or graduate study.

Eligibility: Applicant must be Alaskan native or American Indian. Native Hawaiians also eligible. Applicant must be U.S. citizen.

Basis for selection: Major/career interest in law; public administration/service; governmental public relations; Native American studies or political science/government. Applicant must demonstrate leadership.

Application requirements: Recommendations, essay, transcript.

Additional information: Twelve-week internship. Minimum GPA 2.5. Must be computer literate. Deadlines for application are: Winter term-November 1, Spring term-February 1, Summer term-April 1, and Fall term-July 1. Interns aid with congressional votes analysis, tribal political action forums, political fundraising, issues tracking, and legislative analysis. Credit may be arranged with institution. $500 per month stipend available.

Amount of award:	$1,500-$6,000
Number of awards:	3
Number of applicants:	30
Total amount awarded:	$18,000

Contact:
Mashantucket Pequot Tribal Nation
Internship Coordinatior
1299 Pennsylvania Ave., NW, Suite 1250 East
Washington, DC 20004
Phone: 202-942-9000
Fax: 202-942-7035

Massachusetts Democratic Party

Paid Summer Internship: JFK Scholars Award

Type of award: Internship, renewable.

Intended use: For junior or senior study at accredited 4-year institution.

Eligibility: Applicant must be U.S. citizen or permanent resident residing in Massachusetts.

Basis for selection: Major/career interest in political science/government or public administration/service. Applicant must demonstrate financial need, high academic achievement and seriousness of purpose.

Additional information: One male and one female intern chosen annually. Preference given to registered Democrats and students with a 3.0 GPA or higher. Visit Website for additional program information or e-mail sponsor (mwalsh@massdems.org) for application.

Amount of award:	$1,500
Number of awards:	2
Application deadline:	April 14
Total amount awarded:	$3,000

Internships

533

Contact:
Massachusetts Democratic Party
129 Portland Street
Boston, MA 02114
Phone: 617-742-6770
Fax: 617-742-6598
Web: www.massdems.org

MCC Theater

MCC Theater Internships

Type of award: Internship.
Intended use: For undergraduate study at vocational institution.
Eligibility: Applicant must be residing in New York.
Basis for selection: Major/career interest in theater arts; theater/production/technical; performing arts; design; business/management/administration or arts management.
Application requirements: Resume.
Additional information: Stipend, rolling application deadlines, negotiable schedule. Internships available in general management/theater administration, development, box office and arts education.
Contact:
MCC Theater
120 West 28th Street, 2nd Floor
New York, NY 10001
Phone: 212-727-7722
Fax: 212-727-7780
Web: www.mcctheater.org/jobs

Metropolitan Museum of Art

The Cloisters Summer Internship Program

Type of award: Internship.
Intended use: For undergraduate study. Designated institutions: Metropolitan Museum of Art: The Cloisters.
Basis for selection: Major/career interest in art/art history or history.
Application requirements: Recommendations, essay, transcript. Include resume and list of art history related courses taken.
Additional information: Students with interest in medieval studies especially encouraged to apply. Nine-week, full-time internship from June to August. Five-day, 40-hour work week.

Amount of award:	$2,500
Number of awards:	8
Number of applicants:	300
Application deadline:	February 2
Notification begins:	April 15

Contact:
The Cloisters
College Internship Program
Fort Tryon Park
New York, NY 10040
Phone: 212-650-2280
Web: www.metmuseum.org/education/er_internship.asp

Summer Internship for College Students

Type of award: Internship.
Intended use: For junior, senior, graduate or non-degree study at postsecondary institution.
Eligibility: Applicant must be U.S. citizen, international student or non-U.S. citizens with permission to work in U.S.
Basis for selection: Major/career interest in art/art history; arts management or museum studies/administration. Applicant must demonstrate seriousness of purpose.
Application requirements: No application form. Typed application should indicate internships for which applicant would like to be considered and include applicant's name, home and school addresses and phone numbers, full resume of education and employment, two academic recommendations, official transcripts, separate list of art-history or relevant courses taken and knowledge of foreign languages, and 500-word (maximum) essay describing career goals and reason for applying.
Additional information: Ten-week program for college students and recent graduates not yet entered in graduate school. Interns work full-time, 35-hour weeks in the following Museum departments: curatorial, education, conservation, administration, or library. Applicants should have broad background in art history. Program begins in June with two-week orientation, ends in August, and includes $3,000 honorarium. Graduate students and other students showing special interest in museum careers considered for Roswell L. Gilpatrick Internship but need not apply separately. Later deadline for graduate students.

Application deadline:	January 15, January 22
Notification begins:	April 15

Contact:
Attn: Internship Programs
Metropolitan Museum of Art
1000 Fifth Avenue
New York, NY 10028-0198
Phone: 212-570-3710
Web: www.metmuseum.org/education/er_internship.asp

Michigan Higher Education Assistance Authority

Michigan Work-Study Program

Type of award: Internship, renewable.
Intended use: For undergraduate or graduate study at 2-year, 4-year or graduate institution. Designated institutions: Eligible colleges and universities in Michigan.
Eligibility: Applicant must be U.S. citizen or permanent resident residing in Michigan.
Basis for selection: Applicant must demonstrate financial need.
Application requirements: Proof of eligibility.

Additional information: Program pays students with financial need to work in school-related jobs while enrolled.

Number of awards:	6,433
Number of applicants:	89,909
Total amount awarded:	$7,072,810

Contact:
College financial aid office.
P.O. Box 30462
Lansing, MI 48909-7966
Phone: 517-241-3537
Fax: 517-335-5984

Minnesota Higher Education Services Office

Minnesota Work-Study Program

Type of award: Internship.
Intended use: For undergraduate or graduate study at accredited vocational, 2-year, 4-year or graduate institution. Designated institutions: Minnesota institutions only.
Eligibility: Applicant must be U.S. citizen or permanent resident residing in Minnesota.
Basis for selection: Applicant must demonstrate financial need.
Application requirements: Interview.
Additional information: Work placement must be approved by school or non-profit agency. Apply to financial aid office. Must be used at Minnesota college or for internship with non-profit or private sector employer located in Minnesota.

Number of awards:	11,481
Total amount awarded:	$12,543,134

Contact:
Financial Aid Office or
MHESO
1450 Energy Park Drive, Suite 350
St. Paul, MN 55108-5227
Phone: 651-642-0576 or 800-657-3866
Web: www.mheso.state.mn.us

Mississippi Office of State Student Financial Aid

Mississippi Psychology Apprenticeship Program

Type of award: Internship.
Intended use: For freshman, sophomore, junior, senior, master's or doctoral study.
Eligibility: Applicant must be U.S. citizen or permanent resident residing in Mississippi.
Basis for selection: Major/career interest in psychology; health sciences; mental health/therapy; social/behavioral sciences; neuroscience or neurology.
Application requirements: Recommendations, proof of eligibility.
Additional information: Summer training program in conjunction with Biloxi Veterans Affairs Medical Center.

Amount of award:	$500-$3,000
Application deadline:	March 31
Notification begins:	August 1
Total amount awarded:	$4,500

Contact:
Mississippi Office of State Student Financial Aid
3825 Ridgewood Road
Jackson, MS 39211-6453
Phone: 601-432-6997

Missouri NASA Space Grant Consortium

Missouri State NASA Space Grant Undergraduate Scholarship

Type of award: Internship, renewable.
Intended use: For full-time undergraduate study at accredited 4-year institution in United States. Designated institutions: Southwest Missouri State University, University of Missouri - Columbia, University of Missouri - Rolla, University of Missouri - St. Louis, and Washington University in St. Louis.
Eligibility: Applicant must be residing in Missouri.
Basis for selection: Major/career interest in aerospace; astronomy; engineering; geology/earth sciences or physics.
Application requirements: Recommendations, essay, transcript.
Additional information: Program encourages applications from eligible space science students. Awardees must attend Missouri Space Grant Consortium member institution. Women, minority, and physically challenged students are actively encouraged to apply.

Amount of award:	$2,000-$3,000
Number of awards:	30
Application deadline:	March 7
Total amount awarded:	$75,000

Contact:
Missouri NASA Space Grant Consortium
University of Missouri - Rolla
101 Mechanical. Eng. Bldg.
Rolla, MO 65401-0249
Phone: 573-341-4887
Fax: 573-341-6899
Web: www.umr.edu/~spaceg/

Mobility International USA

Mobility Internship Program

Type of award: Internship.
Intended use: For full-time junior, senior or graduate study at accredited 4-year institution in United States.
Eligibility: People with disabilities encouraged to apply.
Basis for selection: Major/career interest in international relations; public relations; communications; governmental public relations or tourism/travel. Applicant must demonstrate depth of character, leadership and service orientation.
Application requirements: Interview, recommendations, essay, proof of eligibility. Questionnaire completion, resume.

Internships

535

Additional information: Interest in disability issues recommended. Rolling deadline. Reimbursement stipends provided for full-time, 6-month internships, based on receipts from living expenses ($750). Internships can begin at any time of year and last 3-6 months. Part-time internships available. One to four internships offered per year. Housing not provided. Internships located in Eugene, Oregon.

Contact:
Intern Coordinator
P.O. Box 10767
Eugene, OR 97440
Web: www.miusa.org

Morris Arboretum of the University of Pennsylvania

Morris Arboretum Arboriculture Internship

Type of award: Internship.
Intended use: For undergraduate study.
Basis for selection: Major/career interest in landscape architecture; horticulture or forestry.
Application requirements: Recommendations, transcript. Letter of intent, resume.
Additional information: Interest in arboriculture. Interns work 40 hrs/week at hourly rate for one full year. This intern works with the Chief Arborist in all aspects of tree care, including tree assessment, pruning, cabling, and removal. Safety-conscious techniques are emphasized, and recent innovations in climbing and rigging are demonstrated and put into practice. Other opportunities include participation in the management of the Arboretum's woodland and assisting with outreach activities including workshops and off-site consulting. Benefits include health insurance and dental plan. Must have solid academic background in arboriculture and horticulture. Tree climbing ability helpful. Drivers license required. Both semesters of program receive academic credit from U. Penn.

Application deadline: February 15
Contact:
Morris Arboretum of the University of Pennsylvania
Internship Coordinator
9414 Meadowbrook Avenue
Philadelphia, PA 19118
Phone: 215-247-5777
Web: www.upenn.edu/morris/

Morris Arboretum Education Internship

Type of award: Internship.
Intended use: For undergraduate study.
Basis for selection: Major/career interest in education; botany; horticulture; forestry; ecology or education, teacher.
Application requirements: Recommendations, transcript. Letter of intent, resume.
Additional information: Interns work 40 hours/week at hourly wage for one full year. Interns develop workshops for experienced guides, training sessions for new guides, lead tours. This intern develops workshops for experienced guides and training sessions to recruit new guides. Other responsibilities include: supervising the school tour program, running special programs for school children and for the public, helping to prepare the adult education course brochure, and writing promotional copy including a newsletter for volunteer guides. Benefits include insurance and dental plan. Academic background or experience in education or educational programming preferred. Knowledge of plant-related subjects helpful. Strong writing and interpersonal skills essential. Both semesters of program receive academic credit from U. Penn.

Application deadline: February 15
Contact:
Morris Arboretum of the University of Pennsylvania
Internship Coordinator
9414 Meadowbrook Avenue
Philadelphia, PA 19118
Phone: 215-247-5777
Web: www.upenn.edu/morris/

Morris Arboretum Horticulture Internship

Type of award: Internship.
Intended use: For undergraduate study.
Basis for selection: Major/career interest in horticulture; botany or forestry.
Application requirements: Recommendations, transcript. Letter of intent, resume.
Additional information: Assists in all phases of garden development and care of collections. The horticulture intern assists in all phases of garden development and care of the collections. Specific emphasis is placed on refining practical horticultural skills. Supervisory skills are developed by directing and activities of volunteers and part-time staff. Other activities include developing integrated pest management (IPM) skills, arboricultural techniques, and the operation and maintenance of garden machinery. Special projects will be assigned to develop individual skills in garden planning and management. Must have strong academic background in horticulture or closely related field. Interns work 40 hours/week at hourly wage for one full-year. Benefits include health insurance and dental plan. Some internships require travel. Drivers license is required. Both semesters of program receive academic credit from U. Penn.

Application deadline: February 15
Contact:
Morris Arboretum of the University of Pennsylvania
Internship Coordinator
9414 Meadowbrook Avenue
Philadelphia, PA 19118
Phone: 215-247-5777
Web: www.upenn.edu/morris/

Morris Arboretum Plant Propagation Internship

Type of award: Internship.
Intended use: For undergraduate study.
Basis for selection: Major/career interest in botany or horticulture.
Application requirements: Recommendations, transcript. Letter of intent, resume.
Additional information: Strong background in woody landscape plants, plant propagation, nursery management and plant physiology required. Interns work 40 hours/week at hourly rate for one full year. Benefits include health insurance and dental plan. Both semesters of program receive academic credit from U. Penn. Intern assists the Propagator in the development of plant propagation and production schemes for the Arboretum. Emphasis is placed on the refinement of skills

Internships

in traditional methods of plant propagation, nursery production and greenhouse management. Opportunities exist to explore the use of tissue culture as a propagation technique. Other duties include coordinating the Arboretum's autumn seed collection activities, management of the field nursery, and data collection for ongoing research projects.

Application deadline: February 15
Contact:
Morris Arboretum of the University of Pennsylvania
Internship Coordinator
9414 Meadowbrook Avenue
Philadelphia, PA 19118
Phone: 215-247-5777
Web: www.upenn.edu/morris/

Morris Arboretum Plant Protection Internship

Type of award: Internship.
Intended use: For undergraduate study.
Basis for selection: Major/career interest in horticulture; entomology or botany.
Application requirements: Recommendations, transcript. Letter of intent, resume.
Additional information: Interns work 40 hours/week at hourly wage for one full year. Course work in entomology, mycology or plant pathology required. This intern assists the Arboretum's plant pathologist with the Integrated Pest management (IPM) program which includes regular monitoring of the living collection and communicating information on pests and diseases to staff members. Related projects include establishing threshold levels for specific plant pests and evaluating the effectiveness of control measures. Modern laboratory facilities are available for identifying plant pests and pathogens. The intern also participates in the daily operation of the Plan Clinic, providing diagnostic services to the public about horticultural problems. Provides opportunity to assist Arboretum's plant pathologist with the Integrated Pest Management (IPM) program which includes monitoring living collection and communicating information on pests and diseases to staff. Benefits include health insurance and dental plan. Strong writing skills essential. Both semesters of program receive academic credit from U. Penn.

Application deadline: February 15
Contact:
Morris Arboretum of the University of Pennsylvania
Internship Coordinator
9414 Meadowbrook Avenue
Philadelphia, PA 19118
Phone: 215-247-5777
Web: www.upenn.edu/morris

Morris Arboretum Urban and Community Forestry Internship

Type of award: Internship.
Intended use: For undergraduate study.
Basis for selection: Major/career interest in forestry; horticulture; landscape architecture or ecology.
Application requirements: Recommendations, transcript. Letter of intent, resume.
Additional information: Program combines government, botanic garden and community experience in administration, education and outreach. Interns work with USDA Forest Service and Morris Arboretum staff. Jointly sponsored by the Center for Urban Forestry at the Morris Arboretum and the USDA Forest Service, this program combines government,

botanic garden, and community experience in administration, education, and outreach. Interns work on projects both with Forest Service and with Morris Arboretum Staff. Interns work 40 hours/week at hourly wage for one full year. Benefits include health insurance and dental plan. Academic background in forestry, horticulture, landscape design, or a related field. Communication skills essential. Car required; mileage reimbursed. Both semesters of program receive academic credit from U. Penn.

Application deadline: February 15
Contact:
Morris Arboretum of the University of Pennsylvania
Internship Coordinator
9414 Meadowbrook Avenue
Philadelphia, PA 19118
Phone: 215-247-5777
Web: www.upenn.edu/morris/

Mother Jones

Mother Jones Magazine Editorial Internship

Type of award: Internship.
Intended use: For junior, senior, graduate or non-degree study.
Basis for selection: Major/career interest in political science/ government; communications; journalism or publishing. Applicant must demonstrate high academic achievement.
Application requirements: Interview, recommendations. Resume and cover letter. Writing samples.
Additional information: Deadlines are rolling. Internships run four months with $100/month stipend. After four months, interns are reviewed for fellowship program which also lasts four months with $1,000/month stipend. Hours vary according to magazine production schedule, can be as little as 24/week or 40+/week during production cycle. No course credit offered. Reporting, writing and researching skills preferred.
Contact:
Mother Jones
731 Market St., Suite 600
San Francisco, CA 94103
Web: www.motherjones.com

Mother Jones MoJo Wire Internship

Type of award: Internship.
Intended use: For junior, senior, graduate or non-degree study.
Basis for selection: Major/career interest in journalism; publishing; graphic arts/design or computer/information sciences. Applicant must demonstrate high academic achievement.
Application requirements: Interview, recommendations. Writing samples.
Additional information: Deadlines are rolling. Internships run four months at 35 hr./week, with $100/month stipend. After four months, interns are reviewed for fellowship program which lasts eight months, with $1,000/month stipend. Reporting and writing skills preferred. No course credit offered.
Contact:
Mother Jones
731 Market St., Suite 600
San Francisco, CA 94103
Web: www.motherjones.com

Museum of Modern Art

Museum of Modern Art Internship

Type of award: Internship.
Intended use: For junior, senior or graduate study.
Eligibility: Applicant must be U.S. citizen, permanent resident, international student or officially registered in accredited undergraduate or graduate program.
Basis for selection: Major/career interest in arts management; museum studies/administration; arts, general; art/art history; architecture; communications; education; film/video; graphic arts/design or marketing.
Application requirements: Interview, recommendations, essay, transcript. Resume, application form.
Additional information: Course credit available. Fall, Spring, Summer and 12-month internships. Summer internship may pay $2,000 depending on available funds. 12-month internships are for recent college graduates, paid, and are full-time. Applicant must be legal resident or citizen for 12-month program. Fall deadline: July 2; Spring deadline: Nov. 16; Summer deadline: January 25; 12-month deadline: June 3. Fields of study encompass broad spectrum of topics. Contact coordinator for specific information. Visit Website for specifications and for application.

Number of awards:	90
Number of applicants:	550
Application deadline:	July 2, November 16
Notification begins:	August 5, January 18

Contact:
The Museum of Modern Art
Internship Coordinator, Dept. of Education
11 W. 53rd St.
New York, NY 10019
Phone: 212-708-9893
Web: www.moma.org

NASA Space Grant Arizona Space Grant Consortium

NASA Space Grant Arizona Undergraduate Research Internship

Type of award: Internship, renewable.
Intended use: For full-time sophomore, junior or senior study at accredited 2-year or 4-year institution in United States. Designated institutions: Arizona State University, Dine College, Eastern Arizona College, Eastern Arizona University, Embry-Riddle, Northern Arizona University, Pima Community College and University of Arizona.
Eligibility: Applicant must be U.S. citizen residing in Arizona.
Basis for selection: Major/career interest in aerospace; astronomy; engineering; physics; geology/earth sciences; science, general; journalism or education.
Additional information: Approximately 130 full-time undergraduate students will be employed for 10-20 hours per week, for the academic year in research programs, working alongside upper-level graduate students and practicing scientists. Awardees must attend an Arizona Space Grant Consortium member institution. Availability of internships varies. Current announcements/application posted on Website.

Amount of award:	$500-$27,000
Number of awards:	130
Number of applicants:	350
Total amount awarded:	$469,752

Contact:
NASA Space Grant Arizona Space Grant Consortium
Lunar and Planetary Laboratory, Room 345
U of Arizona, 1629 E. University Blvd.
Tucson, AZ 85721-0092
Phone: 520-621-8556
Web: spacegrant.arizona.edu

NASA Space Grant Hawaii Space Grant Consortium

NASA Space Grant Hawaii Undergraduate Traineeship

Type of award: Internship.
Intended use: For freshman or sophomore study. Designated institutions: Must attend a Consortium member school in Hawaii.
Eligibility: Applicant must be U.S. citizen residing in Hawaii.
Basis for selection: Major/career interest in science, general; astronomy; geology/earth sciences; oceanography/marine studies or physics.
Additional information: Award covers one semester, plus up to $250 for travel and supplies. Deadlines, number of positions. Application criteria vary; contact sponsor for more information. Women, under-represented minorities (specifically Native Hawaiians, Filipinos, other Pacific Islanders, Native Americans, Blacks, Hispanics), physically challenged students who have interest in space-related fields are particularly encouraged to apply.

Amount of award:	$1,000

Contact:
Hawaii Space Grant College
2525 Correa Rd.
Honolulu, HI 96822
Phone: 808-956-3138
Web: www.soest.hawaii.edu/SPACEGRANT

NASA Space Grant Massachusetts Space Grant Consortium

NASA Space Grant Massachusetts Summer Jobs for Students

Type of award: Internship, renewable.
Intended use: For undergraduate or graduate study in United States. Designated institutions: Massachusetts Space Grant Consortium members: Boston University, Harvard University, Massachusetts Institute of Technology, Tufts University, University of Massachusetts, Wellesley College, Worcester Polytechnic Institute, Charles Stark Draper Laboratory, and The Marine Biological Laboratory, The Five College Astronomy Department, The Boston Museum of Science.

Eligibility: Applicant must be U.S. citizen or permanent resident residing in Massachusetts.
Basis for selection: Major/career interest in aerospace; astronomy; engineering or physics.
Application requirements: Interview, recommendations.
Additional information: The Space Grant Summer Jobs program is designed to give college students a practical learning experience in industry. Each summer 20-30 students are placed in space-related technical positions. Must attend Massachusetts Space Grant Consortium member institution. Deadline in mid-February; call coordinator for exact date.

Number of awards:	30
Application deadline:	December 10

Contact:
NASA Space Grant Massachusetts Space Grant Consortium
MIT, Aeronautics & Astronautics
77 Massachusetts Ave., Bldg. 33, Rm. 208
Cambridge, MA 02139
Phone: 617-258-5546
Web: www.mit.edu

NASA Space Grant Pennsylvania Space Grant Consortium

NASA Academy Internship

Type of award: Internship.
Intended use: For full-time junior, senior or graduate study at accredited 4-year or graduate institution in United States. Designated institutions: Pennsylvania colleges and universities.
Eligibility: Applicant must be U.S. citizen or permanent resident residing in Pennsylvania.
Basis for selection: Major/career interest in engineering; science, general or mathematics. Applicant must demonstrate high academic achievement.
Application requirements: Recommendations, essay, transcript.
Additional information: Awards are for ten-week internships at NASA Academy: Goddard Space Flight Center, Ames Research Center. Stipend, plus room and board. Applicants should be juniors, seniors, or first year graduate students. Awardees must attend Pennsylvania institution or be a full-time resident. Consortium actively encourages women, minority, and physically challenged students to apply. Visit the NASA Academy Website to download application.

Amount of award:	$3,000-$4,000
Number of awards:	1
Number of applicants:	14
Application deadline:	January 31

Contact:
NASA Space Grant Pennsylvania Space Grant Consortium
Penn State, University Park
101 S. Frear Laboratory
University Park, PA 16802
Phone: 814-863-5957
Web: www.nasa-academy.nasa.gov

National Association of Latino Elected and Appointed (NALEO)

Ford Motor Company Fellows Program

Type of award: Internship.
Intended use: For senior or graduate study at accredited 4-year or graduate institution in United States.
Eligibility: Applicant must be Mexican American, Hispanic American or Puerto Rican. Must possess sense of commitment to Latino community. Applicant must be at least 21. Applicant must be U.S. citizen or permanent resident residing in Puerto Rico, Florida, Texas, Illinois, California or Michigan.
Basis for selection: Major/career interest in social work; public administration/service; political science/government; sociology; psychology; public relations; urban planning or Latin american studies. Applicant must demonstrate high academic achievement, leadership and service orientation.
Application requirements: Recommendations, transcript. Personal statement. Applicant must be of Latino background.
Additional information: Applicant must include a personal statement. $1,200 stipend, plus airfare and housing. Two participants are selected from Northeast and Southwest regions, as well as two additional participants from national pool of applicants. Visit Website for additional information.

Number of awards:	10
Number of applicants:	10
Application deadline:	March 22

Contact:
National Association of Latino Elected and Appointed Officials (NALEO)
Educational Fund
5800 S. Eastern Avenue, Suite 365
Los Angeles, Ca 90040
Phone: 323-720-1932
Fax: 323-720-9519
Web: www.naleo.org

National Association of Latino Elected and Appointed Officials (NALEO)

Shell Legislative Internship Program (SLIP)

Type of award: Internship.
Intended use: For junior or senior study at accredited 4-year institution.
Eligibility: Applicant must be Mexican American, Hispanic American or Puerto Rican. Must possess sense of commitment to Latino community. Applicant must be U.S. citizen or permanent resident residing in New Mexico, Florida, Illinois, Texas, Arizona, California, Colorado or New York.
Basis for selection: Major/career interest in public administration/service; political science/government; urban

planning or Latin american studies. Applicant must demonstrate depth of character, leadership and service orientation.
Application requirements: Recommendations, transcript. Personal statement. Applicant must be of Latino background.
Additional information: Additional field of study includes public policy. Up to two applicants are chosen from each qualifying state. Applicant can be of any Latino descent. Notification begins late April. Visit Website for additional information.

Amount of award:	$1,500
Number of awards:	14
Number of applicants:	145
Application deadline:	March 26
Total amount awarded:	$21,000

Contact:
National Association of Latino Elected and Appointed Officials (NALEO)
Educational Fund
5800 S. Eastern Avenue, Suite 365
Los Angeles, CA 90040
Phone: 323-720-1932
Fax: 323-720-9519
Web: www.naleo.org

National Basketball Association

NBA Internship Program

Type of award: Internship.
Intended use: For undergraduate study.
Basis for selection: Major/career interest in sports/sports administration; marketing; theater/production/technical; public relations; finance/banking or computer/information sciences.
Application requirements: Resume and cover letter.
Additional information: Career interest in sports, entertainment and e-commerce also encouraged. Interns work 10-12 weeks in summer sessions. A few less structured internships offered in spring and fall, with deadlines varying for those programs. Stipend of $350/week. Provides opportunity to work in varied fields in New York City and Secaucus, New Jersey offices.

Amount of award:	$3,500-$4,000
Application deadline:	December 15

Contact:
National Basketball Association
Internship Coordinator
645 Fifth Ave.
New York, NY 10022

National Collegiate Athletic Association

NCAA Ethnic Minority Internship

Type of award: Internship.
Intended use: For non-degree study.
Eligibility: Applicant must be Alaskan native, Asian American, African American, Mexican American, Hispanic American, Puerto Rican or American Indian.

Basis for selection: Major/career interest in athletic training or sports/sports administration. Applicant must demonstrate high academic achievement.
Application requirements: Interview, recommendations, essay, transcript, proof of eligibility. Applicant must submit a resume.
Additional information: For applicants seeking careers in athletic administration. Must have at least completed undergraduate degree. Awarded monthly stipend of $1,400.

Number of applicants:	100
Application deadline:	February 1
Notification begins:	June 8
Total amount awarded:	$19,000

Contact:
National Collegiate Athletic Association
John Williams
P.O. Box 6222
Indianapolis, IN 46206-6222
Phone: 317-917-6222
Web: www.ncaa.org

National Credit Union Administration

National Credit Union Administration Student Intern Program

Type of award: Internship.
Intended use: For full-time junior, senior or graduate study at accredited 4-year institution in United States.
Eligibility: Applicant must be U.S. citizen.
Basis for selection: Major/career interest in accounting; finance/banking; business; marketing; human resources; law or business/management/administration. Applicant must demonstrate depth of character, leadership, seriousness of purpose and service orientation.
Application requirements: Interview, recommendations, essay, transcript, proof of eligibility.
Additional information: Paid and non-paid internships offered to students year-round. February 16 deadline is for summer.

Application deadline:	February 16

Contact:
National Credit Union Administration Attn: Recruitment Coordinator
Human Resources
1775 Duke Street
Alexandria, VA 22314
Phone: 703-518-6510
Fax: 703-518-6539
Web: www.ncua.gov

National Geographic Society

Geography Students Internship

Type of award: Internship.

Intended use: For junior, senior or master's study in United States.
Basis for selection: Major/career interest in geography or cartography.
Application requirements: Recommendations, essay, transcript. Resume. Applicant must have a Geography or Cartography major.
Additional information: Spring, summer, and fall internships for 14 to 16 weeks in Washington, D.C. at $325/week. Emphasis on editorial and cartographic research. Students should contact their school's geography department chair or call internship hotline for more information.

Number of awards:	25
Number of applicants:	100

Contact:
Web: www.nationalgeographic.com

National Institutes of Health

NIH Summer Internship Program in Biomedical Research

Type of award: Internship, renewable.
Intended use: For undergraduate or graduate study. Designated institutions: Main campus in Bethesda, Maryland and off-campus facilities in Frederick and Baltimore, Maryland; Hamilton, Montana; Phoenix, Arizona; and Research Triangle Park, North Carolina.
Eligibility: Applicant must be at least 16. Applicant must be U.S. citizen or permanent resident.
Basis for selection: Major/career interest in science, general; medicine or medical specialties/research. Applicant must demonstrate high academic achievement.
Application requirements: Recommendations, transcript, proof of eligibility. Cover letter, resume. Applicant must be enrolled at least half-time in accredited U.S. high school, college or university.
Additional information: Offers opportunity for students to research procedures in environment devoted to biomedical research and training. Program also includes Summer Lecture Series for Students featuring lectures by NIH investigators and Summer Research Program Poster Day which gives students opportunity to present their work before the NIH community. Internships last from eight to ten weeks, beginning in late May and ending in mid-to-late August. Applicants are notified as early as beginning of April and as late as May. Visit Website for additional information and to apply.

Number of awards:	1,000
Number of applicants:	3,000
Application deadline:	March 1

Contact:
National Institutes of Health, Office of Education
Building 2, Room 2E10
2 Center Drive MSC 0240
Bethesda, MD 20892-0240
Phone: 301-402-1915
Web: www.training.nih.gov

National Instruments

Engineering Leadership Program

Type of award: Internship, renewable.
Intended use: For full-time junior or senior study at accredited 4-year institution.
Eligibility: Applicant must be residing in Texas.
Basis for selection: Major/career interest in computer/information sciences; engineering or physics.
Application requirements: Interview. Resume and cover letter.
Additional information: Course credit arranged. Reimbursement for college credit fees. $1,000 for relocation expenses for out-of-state interns, $750 for those in the Austin metro area. If later employed by National Instruments, intern time counts toward 401K benefits, seniority and vacation accrual. E-mail resume, cover letter to sponsor to request application/interview. E-mail address: info@ni.com. Visit internet site for additional information.
Contact:
National Instruments
HR Coordinator
11500 N. Mopac Expressway
Austin, TX 78759-3504
Phone: 512-794-0100
Fax: 512-683-8745
Web: www.ni.com/employ/interns.htm

National Italian American Foundation

Silvio Conte Internship

Type of award: Internship.
Intended use: For undergraduate or graduate study.
Eligibility: Applicant must be Italian. Applicant must be U.S. citizen or permanent resident.
Basis for selection: Applicant must demonstrate financial need and high academic achievement.
Application requirements: $10 application fee. Essay, transcript, proof of eligibility. Photograph, College Scholarship Service Financial Aid Profile.
Additional information: One-semester internship on Capitol Hill. Must submit paper (2-3 pages double-spaced typed) on importance of this experience to career. Must include letter of acceptance from congressional office with application and have completed 13 hours of community service in Italian-American community. Send business-size SASE to receive application.

Amount of award:	$2,000
Number of awards:	1
Application deadline:	May 31

Contact:
National Italian American Foundation
Dr. Maria Lombardo
1860 19 Street NW
Washington, DC 20009
Phone: 202-387-0600
Web: www.niaf.org

National Journal

National Journal Editorial Internship

Type of award: Internship.
Intended use: For full-time senior or graduate study at 4-year or graduate institution.
Basis for selection: Major/career interest in political science/government; journalism or economics.
Application requirements: Samples of writing, resume.
Additional information: Pays approximately $275/wk. Summer application deadline is March 15, Spring deadline November 15 (begins in January). Good writing skills and strong interest in government and politics required. Recent grads may apply.

Number of awards:	4
Application deadline:	March 15, November 15

Contact:
National Journal
1501 M St., NW
Washington, DC 20036

National Museum of the American Indian

National Museum of the American Indian Internship

Type of award: Internship.
Intended use: For undergraduate, graduate or non-degree study.
Application requirements: Recommendations, transcript. Resume.
Additional information: Intended to provide educational work/research experience for students in area of museum practice and related programming using resources of National Museum of the American Indian and other Smithsonian offices. Internships available at NMAI in Washington, DC (Suitland, MD) and New York City. Applicants must have minimum 3.0 GPA. Deadlines as follows: February 2 for summer; October 13 for winter; July 13 for fall; and December 1 for spring positions. Limited number of stipends targeted primarily at American Indian, Native Hawaiian and Alaskan Native students. Students receiving stipends must work full-time; non-stipendiary students must work at least 20 hours/week. Visit Website or contact via e-mail (interns@nmai.si.edu) for additional information.

Number of awards:	20
Number of applicants:	40

Contact:
Internship Program, National Museum of the American Indian
Community Services, Cultural Resource Center
4220 Silver Hill Road
Suitland, MD 20746-2863
Phone: 301-238-6624 exts. 6300, 6239, or 6235
Fax: 301-238-3200
Web: www.si.edu/nmai

National Museum of Women in the Arts

Clara Hoffberger Lebovitz Internship

Type of award: Internship.
Intended use: For undergraduate, graduate or non-degree study at postsecondary institution in United States. Designated institutions: National Museum of Women in the Arts.
Basis for selection: Major/career interest in women's studies; art/art history; business/management/administration; education; arts management; museum studies; library science; public relations or publishing. Applicant must demonstrate high academic achievement and seriousness of purpose.
Application requirements: Recommendations, essay, transcript. One personal and one academic recommendation. Resume, cover letter and writing sample.
Additional information: 12-week full-time summer internship. Open to applicants who have not yet entered graduate school. Must have 3.25 GPA.

Amount of award:	$1,500
Number of awards:	1
Number of applicants:	35
Application deadline:	March 15
Total amount awarded:	$1,500

Contact:
National Museum of Women in the Arts
Edcuation Dept./ Volunteer Coordinator
1250 New York Ave.
Washington, DC 20005-3920
Phone: 800-222-7270
Web: www.nmwa.org

Museum Coca-Cola Internship

Type of award: Internship.
Intended use: For junior, senior, graduate or non-degree study in United States. Designated institutions: National Museum of Women in the Arts.
Basis for selection: Major/career interest in public relations; advertising; library science; publishing; museum studies; art/art history or museum studies/administration. Applicant must demonstrate high academic achievement and seriousness of purpose.
Application requirements: Recommendations, transcript. One personal and one academic recommendation. Resume, cover letter and writing sample of 1-2 pages in length.
Additional information: Internship lasts 12 weeks. Available to students interested in pursuing museum careers. Minimum 3.25 GPA. Application deadline for winter is October 30; summer is March 15; fall is June 15.

Amount of award:	$1,500
Number of awards:	1
Number of applicants:	50
Total amount awarded:	$1,500

Contact:
National Museum of Women in the Arts
Education Dept./Volunteer Coordinator
1250 New York Ave. NW
Washington, DC 20005-3920
Phone: 800-222-7270
Web: www.nmwa.org

National Museum of Women in the Arts Internships

Type of award: Internship.
Intended use: For junior, senior, graduate or non-degree study. Designated institutions: National Museum of Women in the Arts.
Basis for selection: Major/career interest in museum studies/administration; education; library science; publishing; women's studies; art/art history; accounting or public relations. Applicant must demonstrate high academic achievement and seriousness of purpose.
Application requirements: Recommendations, transcript. Resume, letter of purpose, writing sample (required for internship in publications, optional for others).
Additional information: Full-time or part-time internships last 12 weeks and are unpaid. Minimum 3.0 GPA. Application deadline for winter is October 30; summer is March 15; fall is June 15.
Contact:
National Museum of Women in the Arts
Education Dept./ Volunteer Coordinator
1250 New York Ave. NW
Washington, DC 20005-3920
Phone: 800-222-7270
Web: www.nmwa.org

National Tourism Foundation

Patrick Murphy Internship

Type of award: Internship.
Intended use: For junior or senior study.
Basis for selection: Major/career interest in tourism/travel or political science/government. Applicant must demonstrate high academic achievement.
Application requirements: Resume and application. Minimum 3.0 GPA.
Additional information: Two to three month internship. $1,000 stipend. Minimum 3.0 GPA. Must have excellent written, oral and interpersonal skills.

Amount of award:	$1,000
Application deadline:	April 16

Contact:
National Tourism Foundation
546 East Main Street
Lexington, KY 40508
Phone: 800-682-8886
Web: www.ntfonline.org

Tourism Foundation Internship

Type of award: Internship.
Intended use: For full-time junior or senior study.
Basis for selection: Major/career interest in tourism/travel. Applicant must demonstrate high academic achievement and service orientation.
Application requirements: Resume and application. Minimum 3.0 GPA.
Additional information: Must have at least 3.0 GPA and excellent written, oral and interpersonal skills. Interns receive $3,000 stipend to offset travel and lodging expenses while in Lexington, Kentucky. Interns also travel to NTA Annual Convention, all expenses paid.

Amount of award:	$3,000
Application deadline:	April 16

Contact:
National Tourism Foundation
546 East Main Street
Lexington, KY 40508
Phone: 800-682-8886
Web: www.ntfonline.org

NCR Corporation

NCR Summer Internships

Type of award: Internship.
Intended use: For full-time undergraduate or graduate study at accredited 4-year institution.
Eligibility: Applicant must be residing in District of Columbia, Georgia, California or South Carolina.
Basis for selection: Major/career interest in computer/information sciences; engineering, computer; engineering, electrical/electronic; information systems; finance/banking; accounting or human resources.
Application requirements: Proof of eligibility. Apply via NCR Career Website; NCR no longer accepts resumes vie e-mail or in hard copy.
Additional information: Applicants must complete personal profile, including resume, on Website prior to applying for internship positions. Students can use profile stored in NCR system to apply for individual internship opportunities posted on Website. Applicants encouraged to check Website frequently during spring to review newly-added offerings.
Contact:
Visit Website for further information.
Web: www.ncr.com/Careers

New Dramatists

New Dramatists Internship

Type of award: Internship.
Intended use: For undergraduate or graduate study.
Basis for selection: Major/career interest in public relations; literature; theater arts or performing arts.
Application requirements: Interview.
Additional information: Major/career interest in playwriting. 20-wk internship, $25/wk stipend, 40 hrs/wk. Unpaid part-time internships available. College credit may be available. Computer and writing skills essential.
Contact:
New Dramatists
Internship Coordinator
424 West 44th Street
New York, NY 10036
Web: www.newdramatists.org

Internships

New Jersey Space Grant Consortium

Undergraduate Summer Fellowships in Engineering and Science

Type of award: Internship, renewable.
Intended use: For junior or senior study at accredited 4-year institution in United States. Designated institutions: New Jersey Institute of Technology, Princeton University, Rutgers University, Stevens Institute of Technology, University of Medicine and Dentistry of N.J.
Eligibility: Applicant must be U.S. citizen.
Basis for selection: Major/career interest in aerospace; biology; computer/information sciences; engineering, computer; engineering, chemical; engineering, electrical/electronic; engineering, mechanical; materials science; natural sciences or physical sciences.
Application requirements: Recommendations, essay. Biographical sketch, statement of career goals, plans for the immediate future, and reference letter from faculty advisor.
Additional information: Applicants must have completed at least two, but preferable three, years of college. Award for ten week at $500 per week with an additional $500 per student for laboratory supplies. Applicants must submit C.V. Consortium actively encourages women, minority, and physically challenged students to apply. Awardees must attend New Jersey Space Grant Consortium member insititution. Visit Website for more details.

Amount of award:	$5,000-$5,500
Number of awards:	12
Number of applicants:	30
Application deadline:	March 11
Notification begins:	April 20
Total amount awarded:	$54,000

Contact:
Program Director
The New Jersey Space Grant Consortium
Stevens Institute of Technology
Hoboken, NJ 07030-5991
Phone: 201-216-8964
Fax: 201-216-8929
Web: attila.stevens-tech.edu/njsgc

New Mexico Commission on Higher Education

New Mexico Work-Study Program

Type of award: Internship, renewable.
Intended use: For undergraduate or graduate study at postsecondary institution. Designated institutions: Public or approved private non-profit postsecondary institutions in New Mexico.
Eligibility: Applicant must be U.S. citizen or permanent resident residing in New Mexico.
Basis for selection: Applicant must demonstrate financial need.
Application requirements: FAFSA.
Additional information: Awards vary. Limit of 20 hrs/wk, on-campus or off-campus in federal, state or local public agency. New Mexico residents receive state portion of funding. Contact financial aid office of any New Mexico public postsecondary institution for information, deadlines and application.
Contact:
New Mexico Commission on Higher Education
Financial Aid and Student Services
1068 Cerrillos Road
Santa Fe, NM 87501
Phone: 800-279-9777
Web: www.nmche.org/

New Republic

New Republic Internship

Type of award: Internship.
Intended use: For undergraduate, graduate or non-degree study.
Eligibility: Applicant must be U.S. citizen.
Basis for selection: Major/career interest in journalism. Applicant must demonstrate depth of character and seriousness of purpose.
Application requirements: Recommendations. Two recommendations required. Must submit resume, cover letter, and 3-5 writing samples.
Additional information: Paid internships are offered in the summer (June-August) and during the academic year (September-May). Provides intern with the opportunity to gain editorial experience at a leading opinion magazine. Must have strong writing, administrative and editorial abilities and be willing to work long hours.
Contact:
New Republic
1220 19th Street, NW, Suite 600
Washington, DC 20036
Fax: 202-331-0275
Web: www.tnr.com

New Stage Theatre

New Stage Theatre Internship

Type of award: Internship.
Intended use: For undergraduate or graduate study.
Basis for selection: Major/career interest in performing arts; theater/production/technical or theater arts. Applicant must demonstrate seriousness of purpose.
Application requirements: Interview, audition, portfolio, recommendations, essay, proof of eligibility.
Additional information: Nine month internships starting in August. $155 per week. Travel extensively in Mississippi.

Amount of award:	$6,200
Application deadline:	May 1

Contact:
New Stage Theatre
1100 Carlisle Street
Jackson, MS 39202-4792

Internships

New York State Assembly

New York State Assembly Session Internship Program

Type of award: Internship, renewable.
Intended use: For full-time sophomore, junior, senior or graduate study at accredited vocational, 2-year, 4-year or graduate institution.
Eligibility: Applicant must be residing in New York.
Basis for selection: Applicant must demonstrate high academic achievement.
Application requirements: Recommendations, essay, transcript, proof of eligibility. Application, letter from college endorsing candidate and outlining course credit arrangements.
Additional information: Must be New York resident or attending college in New York. All majors eligible. Interns assigned to work with assembly members or assembly staff. Visit Website for more information.

Amount of award:	$3,500
Number of awards:	150

Contact:
New York State Assembly
Assembly Intern Committee
Legislative Office Building, Room 104A
Albany, NY 12248
Phone: 518-455-4704
Fax: 518-455-4705
Web: www.assembly.state.ny.us

New York State Bar Association, Department of Media Services and Public Affairs

New York State Bar Association Summer Public Relations Internship

Type of award: Internship.
Intended use: For senior study at 4-year institution.
Eligibility: Applicant must be U.S. citizen.
Basis for selection: Major/career interest in public relations.
Application requirements: Interview, portfolio.
Additional information: For study in the field of public relations only. There is a two hour writing test. There is no application per se. Interested students should send a letter detailing their interest and providing specific examples of work-related experience. Three writing samples required.

Amount of award:	$2,800
Application deadline:	April 1

Contact:
New York State Bar Association
One Elk Street
Albany, NY 12207
Phone: 518-463-3200
Fax: 518-463-4276
Web: www.nysba.org

New York Times

New York Times Summer Internship Program

Type of award: Internship.
Intended use: For junior, senior, graduate or non-degree study.
Basis for selection: Major/career interest in journalism. Applicant must demonstrate seriousness of purpose and service orientation.
Application requirements: Portfolio, proof of eligibility. Resume; eight to ten writing samples or portfolio.
Additional information: Program open to all applicants, regardless of race or ethnicity. Stipend $700 per week plus housing allowance. Applicants must have journalism experience. All queries by mail or e-mail (rulesh@nytimes.com).
Contact:
The New York Times
Sheila Rule, Senior Mgr. Reporter Recruiting
229 West 43rd Street
New York, NY 10036
Phone: 212-556-1234

Norfolk Chamber Music Festival

Norfolk Chamber Music Festival Summer Internship Program

Type of award: Internship, renewable.
Intended use: For undergraduate, master's, doctoral, first professional, postgraduate or non-degree study. Designated institutions: Yale Summer School of Music.
Basis for selection: Major/career interest in music or arts management.
Application requirements: Recommendations. Resume.
Additional information: Summer internships provide opportunity to gain experience in arts administration. Contact office for stipend information. No phone calls please.

Amount of award:	$2,500
Number of awards:	8
Number of applicants:	200
Application deadline:	March 1
Total amount awarded:	$7,500

Contact:
Norfolk Chamber Music Festival
P.O. Box 208246
New Haven, CT 06520

North Carolina Arts Council

North Carolina Arts Council Community Arts Administration Internship

Type of award: Internship.
Intended use: For non-degree study.

Basis for selection: Major/career interest in business/management/administration or arts management.
Application requirements: Interview, recommendations, essay.
Additional information: Applicant must possess four-year college degree, have strong administrative and/or business capability, preferably demonstrated by work experience, and have close familiarity with the arts. Interns assigned to sponsoring North Carolina community arts council or cultural center for three months between September 1 and June 30. Out-of-state applicants eligible to apply. Preference given to North Carolina residents.

Amount of award:	$4,000
Number of awards:	3
Number of applicants:	35
Application deadline:	May 1
Total amount awarded:	$12,000

Contact:
North Carolina Arts Council
Department of Cultural Resources
Mail Service Center #4632
Raleigh, NC 27699-4632
Web: www.ncarts.org

North Carolina Botanical Garden

North Carolina Botanical Garden Internship Program

Type of award: Internship.
Intended use: For undergraduate, graduate or non-degree study.
Basis for selection: Major/career interest in horticulture; botany; natural resources/conservation; forestry; environmental science; education or ecology.
Application requirements: Interview, essay. Interview may be by phone or in person.
Additional information: Full-time internship lasts three to seven months from April 1 to October 30. Stipend of $8.00 an hour. Provides opportunity to gain experience in maintenance and interpretation of Southeastern U.S. plants and rare and exotic species. All internships include horticultural maintenance and development and interpretation of garden collections; focus areas are native habitat displays and plant records, tour guide programming and training, horticulture therapy and herb gardening, and native plant propagation and wildflower displays. Applications accepted year-round.

Amount of award:	$3,600-$8,400
Number of awards:	4
Number of applicants:	35
Total amount awarded:	$30,000

Contact:
Internship Program
North Carolina Botanical Garden
CB#3375 Totten Center, UNC-CH
Chapel Hill, NC 27599-3375
Phone: 919-962-0522
Fax: 919-962-3531

Three- to Eight-Month Gardener Internship

Type of award: Internship.
Intended use: For undergraduate, graduate or non-degree study.
Basis for selection: Major/career interest in horticulture; botany; forestry; natural resources/conservation; environmental science; education or ecology. Applicant must demonstrate depth of character, leadership, seriousness of purpose and service orientation.
Application requirements: Essay. Resume, application form, letter outlining interests/career goals.
Additional information: Up to four awards given. Internship provides experience in maintenance, conservation, and interpretation of horticultural plants. Position pays $8.00/hour and interns work 40 hours/week. Duration of internship flexible: three to eight months. Must be enrolled in or recent graduate of plant-related program or have substantial gardening experience. Encouraged to arrange for academic credit.

Application deadline:	February 14
Notification begins:	March 21

Contact:
North Carolina Botanical Garden James L. Ward, Curator
CB #3375 Totten Center
University of North Carolina at Chapel Hill
Chapel Hill, NC 27599-3375
Phone: 919-962-0522

Oak Ridge Institute for Science and Education

Office of Biological and Environmental Research Minority Institutions Student Research Participation

Type of award: Internship.
Intended use: For undergraduate or graduate study at accredited 4-year or graduate institution in United States. Designated institutions: Ames Lab; Argonne National Lab; Brookhaven National Lab; Ernest Orlando Lawrence Berkeley National Lab; Lawrence Livermore National Lab; Los Alamos National Lab; Oak Ridge National Lab; Pacific NW National Lab; Savannah River Site; Oak Ridge Institute for Science and Education; and Savannah River Ecology Lab.
Eligibility: Must attend historically black college or university. Applicant must be U.S. citizen or permanent resident.
Basis for selection: Major/career interest in biology; environmental science; science, general; biochemistry or medical specialties/research.
Application requirements: Nomination.
Additional information: Ten-week summer internship open to undergraduate and graduate students from historically black colleges and universities. Provides opportunities to participate in research relating to health and the environment. Stipend of $300 per week for undergraduate students, $1,800 per month stipend for graduate students. Limited travel reimbursement (round-trip transportation expenses between facility and home or campus). Participants must contact researcher as part of the application process.

Amount of award: $3,000-$3,600
Application deadline: January 16
Contact:
ORISE Office of Biol. and Env. Rsrch.
P.O. Box 117
MS 44
Oak Ridge, TN 37831-0117
Phone: 865-576-4813
Web: www.orau.org

Office of Nuclear Energy Minority Institutions Nuclear Energy Training Program

Type of award: Internship, renewable.
Intended use: For full-time junior, senior, master's or doctoral study at 4-year institution in or outside United States. Designated institutions: Historically black, Hispanic, and Native American colleges and universities.
Eligibility: Applicant must be U.S. citizen or permanent resident.
Basis for selection: Major/career interest in nuclear science; engineering, electrical/electronic; engineering, mechanical; physics; chemistry; engineering or science, general.
Additional information: Provides competitive scholarships for study and research careers in nuclear energy-related technologies, including an off-campus research opportunity at a DOE-designated laboratory and a training institute at ORISE. Paid tuition and fees, $9,600-$14,400 per year in stipends. Dislocation allowance during summer research appointment; off-campus study.
Amount of award: $9,600-$14,400
Application deadline: January 16
Contact:
Office of Nuclear Energy Minority Institutions Training Program
P.O. Box 117
Oak Ridge, TN 37831-0117
Phone: 865-576-3000
Web: www.orau.org

ORISE Energy Research Undergraduate Laboratory Fellowships (DOE)

Type of award: Internship.
Intended use: For full-time undergraduate study at accredited 4-year institution in United States. Designated institutions: Argonne National Laboratory (Argonne, IL); Brookhaven National Laboratory (Upton, NY); Ernest Orlando Lawrence Berkeley National Laboratory (Berkeley, CA); Fermi National Accelerator Laboratory (Batavia, IL); Idaho National Environmental and Engineering Laboratory (Idaho Falls, ID); National Renewable Energy Laboratory (Golden, CO); Oak Ridge National Laboratory (Oak Ridge, TN); Pacific Northwest National Laboratory (Richland, WA); Princeton Plasma Physics Laboratory (Princeton, NJ); Stanford Linear Accelerator Center (Stanford, CA); Thomas Jefferson National Accelerator Laboratory (Newport News, VA).
Eligibility: Applicant must be U.S. citizen or permanent resident.
Basis for selection: Major/career interest in engineering; life sciences; mathematics; physical sciences or computer/ information sciences.
Additional information: Provides opportunities to participate in research relating to energy production, use, conservation, and

societal implications. Limited number of non-research appointments at Department of Energy Headquarters. Ten-week or 16-week semester appointments. Weekly stipend of $350; limited travel reimbursement (round-trip transportation expenses between facility and home or campus). Call program contact for deadlines.
Contact:
Oak Ridge Institute for Science and Technology
P.O. Box 117
Oak Ridge, TN 37831-0117
Phone: 865-576-3192
Web: www.orau.org

ORISE Fossil Energy Technology Internship

Type of award: Internship.
Intended use: For freshman or sophomore study at accredited 2-year institution in United States. Designated institutions: Federal Energy Technology Center (Pittsburgh, PA., and Morgantown, WV).
Eligibility: Applicant must be U.S. citizen.
Basis for selection: Major/career interest in chemistry; computer/information sciences; engineering; mathematics; physics; geology/earth sciences or environmental science.
Additional information: Provides opportunities for associate's degree students to participate in fossil energy-related research. Three to 18 months; full-time or part-time appointments. Weekly stipend of $275 to $300; limited travel reimbursement (round-trip transportation expenses between facility and home or campus); off-campus tuition and fees if required by home institution. Applications accepted on year-round basis.
Amount of award: $23,400
Number of awards: 5
Contact:
Fossil Energy Technology Internship
MS 36, Education Training Division
P.O. Box 117
Oak Ridge, TN 37831-0117
Phone: 865-576-3426
Web: www.orau.org

ORISE National Oceanic and Atmospheric Administration Student Research Participation

Type of award: Internship.
Intended use: For undergraduate or graduate study at 2-year, 4-year or graduate institution in United States. Designated institutions: NOAA Headquarters and field centers.
Eligibility: Applicant must be U.S. citizen or permanent resident.
Basis for selection: Major/career interest in computer/ information sciences; health sciences; engineering; physical sciences; business or life sciences.
Additional information: Provides opportunities to participate in research and development relating to science, math, and engineering. Ten-week summer internship. Weekly stipend of $400 to $500, depending on academic classification; limited travel reimbursement (round-trip transportation expenses between facility and home or campus). Applications accepted on year-round basis. Number of internships varies.

Contact:
Oak Ridge Institute for Science and Education
P.O. Box 117
Oak Ridge, TN 37831-0117
Phone: 865-576-8158
Web: www.orau.org

ORISE Professional Internship at Oak Ridge National Laboratory

Type of award: Internship.
Intended use: For undergraduate or graduate study at postsecondary institution in United States. Designated institutions: Oak Ridge National Laboratory (Oak Ridge, Tenn.) and sites of the Hazardous Waste Remedial Actions Program.
Eligibility: Applicant must be U.S. citizen or permanent resident.
Basis for selection: Major/career interest in chemistry; environmental science; geology/earth sciences; hydrology; engineering, chemical; engineering, civil; engineering, environmental; engineering, mechanical; computer/information sciences or science, general.
Additional information: Provides opportunities for students to participate in energy-related research. Three to 18 consecutive months, full-time or part-time appointments. Weekly stipend of $250 to $400. Limited travel reimbursement (round-trip transportation expenses between facility and home or campus). Off-campus tuition and fees if required by the home institution. Additional deadline. Number of awards varies.
   Application deadline: October 1, February 15
Contact:
Oak Ridge Institute for Science and Education
MS 36, Education Training Division
P.O. Box 117
Oak Ridge, TN 37831-0117
Phone: 865-576-3426
Web: www.orau.org

ORISE Professional Internship at Savannah River Site

Type of award: Internship.
Intended use: For undergraduate or graduate study at postsecondary institution in United States. Designated institutions: Savannah River Site (Aiken, SC).
Eligibility: Applicant must be U.S. citizen or permanent resident.
Basis for selection: Major/career interest in environmental science; chemistry; engineering; geology/earth sciences; physics; science, general or computer/information sciences.
Additional information: Provides opportunities to participate in energy-related and environmental research. Three to 18 consecutive months; full-time or part-time appointments. Weekly stipend of $338 to $871; limited travel reimbursement (round-trip transportation expenses between facility and home or campus). Additional deadline June 1. Funded by Westinghouse Savannah River Company.
   Application deadline: October 1, February 1
Contact:
Professional Internship Program at the Savannah River Site
MS 36, Education Training Division
P.O. Box 117
Oak Ridge, TN 37831-0117
Phone: 865-576-3426
Web: www.orau.org

ORISE Professional Internship Program at Federal Energy Technology Center

Type of award: Internship, renewable.
Intended use: For undergraduate or graduate study at accredited postsecondary institution in United States. Designated institutions: Federal Energy Technology Center (Pittsburgh, Pa., and Morgantown, W.Va.)
Eligibility: Applicant must be U.S. citizen.
Basis for selection: Major/career interest in chemistry; computer/information sciences; engineering; environmental science; geology/earth sciences; mathematics or physics.
Additional information: Provides opportunities to participate in fossil energy-related research. Three to eighteen consecutive months, full-time or part-time appointments. Weekly stipend of $260 to $375. Limited travel reimbursement (round-trip transportation expenses between facility and home or campus). Off-campus tuition and fees if required by the home institution. Additional deadline June 1. Number of awards varies.
   Application deadline: October 1, February 15
Contact:
Oak Ridge Institute for Science and Education
Professional Internship at FETC
P.O. Box 117
Oak Ridge, TN 37831-0117
Phone: 865-576-3426
Web: www.orau.org

ORISE Student Environmental Management Participation at the U.S. Army Environmental Center

Type of award: Internship, renewable.
Intended use: For undergraduate or graduate study at postsecondary institution. Designated institutions: U.S. Army Environmental Center (Aberdeen Proving Ground, Md.) and other approved locations.
Eligibility: Applicant must be U.S. citizen.
Basis for selection: Major/career interest in anthropology; archaeology; biology; chemistry; computer/information sciences; zoology; ecology; engineering; entomology or environmental science.
Additional information: Provides opportunities to participate in research in environmental programs involving cultural and natural resources, restoration, compliance, conservation, pollution prevention, validation, demonstration, transfer, quality assurance and quality control, training, information management and reporting, and related programs. Three months to one year; full-time or part-time appointments. Stipend based on research area(s) and academic classification. Applications accepted year-round. Number of awards varies.
Contact:
Oak Ridge Institute for Science and Education
MS 36, Education Training Division
P.O. Box 117
Oak Ridge, TN 37831-0117
Phone: 865-671-1598
Web: www.orau.org

Internships

ORISE Student Internship at the U.S. Army Center for Health Promotion and Preventative Medicine

Type of award: Internship, renewable.
Intended use: For undergraduate or graduate study at accredited postsecondary institution in United States. Designated institutions: U.S. Army Center for Health Promotion and Preventive Medicine (Aberdeen Proving Ground, Md.) and other approved locations.
Eligibility: Applicant must be U.S. citizen.
Basis for selection: Major/career interest in biology; chemistry; computer/information sciences; engineering; environmental science; physical sciences; science, general or health sciences.
Additional information: Provides opportunities to participate in applied research and development in the areas of occupational and environmental health engineering programs, health promotion projects, and activities. Three months to one year; full-time or part-time appointments. Stipend based on research area(s) and academic classification. Number of awards varies. Applications accepted year-round.
Contact:
Oak Ridge Institute for Science and Education
MS 36, Education Training Division
P.O. Box 117
Oak Ridge, TN 37831-0117
Phone: 410-671-1598
Web: www.orau.org

ORISE Student Research - National Center for Toxicological Research

Type of award: Internship, renewable.
Intended use: For undergraduate or graduate study at accredited 2-year, 4-year or graduate institution in United States. Designated institutions: National Center for Toxicological Research (Jefferson, AK.)
Eligibility: Applicant must be U.S. citizen or permanent resident.
Basis for selection: Major/career interest in biology; chemistry; computer/information sciences; mathematics; pharmacy/pharmaceutics/pharmacology; science, general or medicine.
Additional information: Provides opportunities to participate in research on biological effects of potentially toxic chemicals and solutions to toxicology problems that have a major impact on human health and the environment. Three months to one year; full-time or part-time appointments. Stipend based on research area(s) and academic classification. Summer deadline is March 1; applications accepted year-round for academic year appointments. Number of awards varies.
Application deadline: March 1
Contact:
Student Research Participation
National Center for Toxological Research
Education Training -P.O. Box 117, MS 44
Oak Ridge, TN 07831-0117
Phone: 865-576-1089
Web: www.orau.org

ORISE Student Research at the Agency for Toxic Substances and Disease Registry

Type of award: Internship.
Intended use: For undergraduate or graduate study at accredited postsecondary institution in United States. Designated institutions: Agency for Toxic Substances and Disease Registry (Atlanta, GA).
Basis for selection: Major/career interest in biology; environmental science; public health; epidemiology; medicine; pharmacy/pharmaceutics/pharmacology; physical sciences or science, general.
Additional information: Provides opportunities to participate in research relating to exposure and disease registries, health investigations, public health assessments, toxicological profiles, emergency response and health education. Ten weeks to one year; full-time or part-time appointments. Stipend based on research area(s) and academic classification. Number of internships vary.
Application deadline: February 1
Contact:
Oak Ridge Institute for Science and Education
MS 36, Education Training Division
P.O. Box 117
Oak Ridge, TN 37831-0117
Phone: 865-576-9361
Web: www.orau.org

ORISE Student Research at the Centers for Disease Control and Prevention

Type of award: Internship.
Intended use: For undergraduate or graduate study at accredited 2-year, 4-year or graduate institution in United States. Designated institutions: Centers for Disease Control and Prevention: Division of AIDS, Sexually Transmitted Diseases, and Tuberculosis Laboratory Research (Atlanta, GA); Division of Environmental Health Laboratory Sciences (Atlanta, GA); Division of Mycotic and Bacterial Diseases (Atlanta, GA); Division of Prevention Research and Analytic Methods (Atlanta, GA); Division of Public Health Surveillance and Infomatics (Atlanta, GA); Division of Sexually Transmitted Diseases Prevention (Atlanta, GA); Division of Viral and Rickettsial Diseases (Atlanta, GA); National Immunization Program (Atlanta, GA); National Institute for Occupational Safety and Health (Atlanta, GA; Cincinnati, OH; Morgantown, WV; Washington, DC); and Office of Health Communication (Atlanta, GA).
Eligibility: Applicant must be U.S. citizen or permanent resident.
Basis for selection: Major/career interest in epidemiology; health sciences; environmental science; communications; economics; science, general; life sciences; medicine or physical sciences.
Additional information: Provides opportunities to participate in research on infectious diseases, environmental health, epidemiology, or occupational safety and health. One month to one year; full-time or part time appointments. Stipend based on research area(s) and academic classification. Applications accepted year-round except at Division of Prevention Research and Analytic Methods; call for deadline.

Contact:
Oak Ridge Institute for Science and Education
MS 36, Education Training Division
P.O. Box 117
Oak Ridge, TN 37831-0117
Phone: 865-576-1089
Web: www.orau.org

ORISE Student Research at the U.S. Army Environmental Policy Institute

Type of award: Internship.
Intended use: For undergraduate or graduate study at accredited 4-year or graduate institution in United States. Designated institutions: U.S. Army Environmental Policy Institute (Atlanta, GA) and other approved locations.
Eligibility: Applicant must be U.S. citizen.
Basis for selection: Major/career interest in law; social/behavioral sciences; science, general or engineering.
Additional information: Provides opportunities to participate in research in developing policies and strategies to address environmental issues that may have an impact on the Army and assist the Army in its overall strategy for compliance, restoration, prevention, and conservation. Three months to one year; full-time or part-time appointments. Stipend based on research area(s) and academic classification. Applications accepted on year-round basis. Number of awards varies.
Contact:
Oak Ridge Institute for Science and Education
MS 36, Education Training Division
P.O. Box 117
Oak Ridge, TN 37831-0117
Phone: 865-241-2875
Web: www.orau.org

ORISE Technology Internship Program at Oak Ridge National Laboratory

Type of award: Internship.
Intended use: For freshman or sophomore study at accredited 2-year institution in United States. Designated institutions: Oak Ridge National Laboratory (Oak Ridge, Tenn.) and sites of the Hazardous Waste Remedial Actions Program.
Eligibility: Applicant must be U.S. citizen or permanent resident.
Basis for selection: Major/career interest in engineering, chemical; engineering, electrical/electronic; health sciences or engineering, mechanical.
Additional information: Provides opportunities to participate in energy-related research. Three to 18 months; full-time or part-time appointments. Weekly stipend of $300. Associate Degree students only.

  Number of awards: 10
Contact:
Oak Ridge Institute for Science and Education
MS 36, Education Training Division
P.O. Box 117
Oak Ridge, TN 37831-0117
Phone: 865-576-3426
Web: www.orau.org

ORISE University Coal Research Internship

Type of award: Internship.

Intended use: For senior study at accredited 4-year institution in United States. Designated institutions: Appointment will be served at a host university under the guidance of a principal investigator who has an active university coal research grant from the U.S. Department of Energy's Federal Energy Technology Center at Pittsburgh, Pa.
Eligibility: Applicant must be U.S. citizen or permanent resident.
Basis for selection: Major/career interest in chemistry; biology; environmental science; geology/earth sciences; engineering; physics or science, general.
Additional information: Provides opportunities to participate in coal-related research in an on-campus, graduate-level research environment. Ten weeks during the summer. Weekly stipend of $225. Limited travel reimbursement (round-trip transportation expenses between facility and home or campus). Housing. Must be college senior at time of application, enrolled at a university that does not have a graduate program in the applicant's major.

  Amount of award: $2,250
  Number of awards: 10
  Application deadline: February 11
Contact:
Oak Ridge Institute for Science and Education
MS 36, Education Training Division
P.O. Box 117
Oak Ridge, TN 37831-0117
Phone: 865-576-3426
Web: www.orau.org

Owens Corning

Owens Corning Internships

Type of award: Internship.
Intended use: For full-time junior or senior study at accredited 4-year institution.
Eligibility: Applicant must be U.S. citizen, permanent resident, international student or foreign student eligible to work in U.S. on full-time basis.
Basis for selection: Major/career interest in engineering; finance/banking; human resources; information systems; marketing or materials science. Applicant must demonstrate high academic achievement.
Application requirements: Proof of eligibility.
Additional information: Summer internship with housing assistance, competitive salary, access to credit union and fitness center. Most majors considered. Other intern opportunities year-round. Most positions in Toledo, Ohio. Owens Corning also supports scholarships awarded through certain targeted universities.
Contact:
Owens Corning
One Owens Corning Parkway
Toledo, OH 43659
Phone: 800-GET-PINK
Web: www.owenscorning.com/career

Pacific Gas and Electric Company

Pacific Gas and Electric Internships

Type of award: Internship.
Intended use: For full-time junior or senior study in United States.
Eligibility: Applicant must be U.S. citizen or permanent resident.
Basis for selection: Major/career interest in accounting; business; communications; computer/information sciences; economics; engineering, mechanical; engineering, civil; engineering, electrical/electronic or mathematics. Applicant must demonstrate high academic achievement.
Application requirements: Send resume, cover letter.
Additional information: Students with major/career interest in statistics also preferred. Apply for summer internships starting in January. No deadline, but early applications encouraged. Resume may be submitted online or via e-mail (to employment@pge.com); format specifications available online. Visit Website or call sponsor for available openings, campus recruitment dates. Must be eligible to work in the United States. Number and amount of awards vary.
Contact:
Pacific Gas and Electric Company
College Relations/CHP
P.O. Box 770000, N14 G
San Francisco, CA 94177
Phone: 415-973-2798
Web: www.pge.com/jobs

Pennsylvania Higher Education Assistance Agency

Pennsylvania Work-Study Program

Type of award: Internship, renewable.
Intended use: For full-time undergraduate, master's, doctoral or first professional study at accredited postsecondary institution. Designated institutions: PHEAA-approved institutions.
Eligibility: Applicant must be U.S. citizen or permanent resident residing in Pennsylvania.
Basis for selection: Applicant must demonstrate financial need.
Application requirements: Interview, proof of eligibility. State grant or subsidized Stafford loan.
Additional information: Student must demonstrate ability to benefit from career-related high-tech or community service work experience. Funds earned must be used to pay school costs at PHEAA-approved postsecondary institution. Amount and number of awards varies. Deadlines: Fall and entire year - Oct. 1, Spring January 1, Summer - May 15.

Number of applicants:	3,400
Application deadline:	October 1, January 1

Contact:
Pennsylvania Higher Education Assistance Agency
State Grant and Special Programs Division
1200 North Seventh Street
Harrisburg, PA 17102
Phone: 717-720-2550
Web: www.pheaa.org

PGA Tour

PGA Minority Internship Program

Type of award: Internship.
Intended use: For junior, senior or master's study.
Eligibility: Applicant must be Alaskan native, Asian American, African American, Mexican American, Hispanic American, Puerto Rican or American Indian. Applicant must be U.S. citizen.
Basis for selection: Major/career interest in marketing; business/management/administration; communications; information systems; human resources; journalism; radio/television/film; sports/sports administration; law or public relations. Applicant must demonstrate high academic achievement, depth of character, leadership, seriousness of purpose and service orientation.
Application requirements: Interview, recommendations, essay, transcript.
Additional information: Internship lasts nine weeks at $360/week with $120/month deducted for housing. Site locations include California, Connecticut, Florida, Georgia, Illinois, New York, Kansas, Michigan, and Texas. E-mail mip@mail.pgatour.com for additional information.

Amount of award:	$2,940
Number of awards:	35
Number of applicants:	150
Application deadline:	March 15
Notification begins:	April 26
Total amount awarded:	$102,900

Contact:
PGA Minority Internship Program
Attn:Mike Cooney
112 TPC Boulevard
Ponte Vedra Beach, FL 32082

Phillips Academy

Phillips Academy Summer Teaching Assistant Program

Type of award: Internship.
Intended use: For senior or graduate study.
Basis for selection: Applicant must demonstrate high academic achievement and seriousness of purpose.
Application requirements: Recommendations, essay, transcript. Application, resume and cover letter, or curriculum vitae. Teaching assistant finalists must have on-campus interview.
Additional information: Applicants must have baccalaureate by June 2002. Position includes room and board. Candidates notified of acceptance by April or May. Summer-session only, late June to early August six-week program. Interns receive

$2,400 plus room and board for six weeks. Visit Website for additional information.

Number of awards:	20
Number of applicants:	100
Application deadline:	February 15

Contact:
Phillips Academy
Summer Session Teaching Assistant Program
Andover, MA 01810-4166
Web: www.andover.edu/summersession

Phipps Garden Center

Jane Demaree Internship

Type of award: Internship, renewable.

Intended use: For full-time junior, senior or graduate study at accredited 2-year, 4-year or graduate institution.

Eligibility: Applicant must be U.S. citizen residing in Pennsylvania.

Basis for selection: Major/career interest in horticulture; landscape architecture; environmental science or botany. Applicant must demonstrate high academic achievement, depth of character, leadership, seriousness of purpose and service orientation.

Application requirements: Recommendations, transcript.

Additional information: Interns paid $6.50/hr. Must reapply to renew.

Amount of award:	$500-$2,000
Number of awards:	5
Number of applicants:	15
Application deadline:	January 31
Total amount awarded:	$10,000

Contact:
Education Director
Phipps Garden Center
1059 Shady Avenue
Pittsburgh, PA 15232
Phone: 412-441-4442

Playhouse on the Square

Playhouse on the Square Internship

Type of award: Internship.

Intended use: For undergraduate, graduate or non-degree study.

Basis for selection: Major/career interest in performing arts; theater arts or theater/production/technical. Applicant must demonstrate depth of character, leadership, seriousness of purpose and service orientation.

Application requirements: Interview, audition, portfolio, recommendations, proof of eligibility.

Additional information: $100 per week, free housing. Internships are located in Memphis, TN and last a full year, beginning in August. Write or visit Website for an application.

Amount of award:	$5,200
Number of awards:	10

Contact:
Playhouse on the Square
51 South Cooper
Memphis, TN 38014
Web: www.playhouseonthesquare.org

Population Institute

Population Institute Internship

Type of award: Internship.

Intended use: For junior, senior or graduate study.

Eligibility: Applicant must be no older than 25.

Basis for selection: Major/career interest in social/behavioral sciences. Applicant must demonstrate depth of character, leadership, seriousness of purpose and service orientation.

Application requirements: Interview, recommendations, essay, transcript, proof of eligibility. Three letters of recommendation required, two of which must be academic. Resume and cover letter also required.

Additional information: Internship pays $2,000 per month, 6 months long. Full medical and dental benefits start immediately.

Amount of award:	$12,000
Number of awards:	12
Application deadline:	April 15, September 15

Contact:
The Population Institute
Internship Coordinator
107 2nd Street, NE
Washington, DC 20002

Princeton Plasma Physics Laboratory

Plasma Physics National Undergraduate Fellowship Program

Type of award: Internship.

Intended use: For junior study.

Eligibility: Applicant must be U.S. citizen or permanent resident.

Basis for selection: Major/career interest in engineering; physics; mathematics or computer/information sciences. Applicant must demonstrate high academic achievement, depth of character, leadership, seriousness of purpose and service orientation.

Application requirements: Recommendations, essay, transcript.

Additional information: Student must be a U.S. citizen or PRA, and have a 3.5 GPA. Internship is ten weeks in the summer.

Amount of award:	$4,800
Number of awards:	25
Number of applicants:	100
Application deadline:	February 1
Notification begins:	March 15

Internships

Contact:
Princeton Plasma Physics Laboratory
P.O. Box 451
Princeton, NJ 08543
Phone: 609-243-3049
Web: www.pppl.gov

Pro-Found Software

Pro-Found Software Internship

Type of award: Internship.
Intended use: For junior, senior or graduate study.
Basis for selection: Major/career interest in computer/information sciences; engineering, computer or information systems. Applicant must demonstrate high academic achievement, depth of character, leadership, seriousness of purpose and service orientation.
Application requirements: Recommendations, transcript, proof of eligibility. Cover letter and resume.
Additional information: Must be studying in technical fields and be proficient in JAVA or C/C++. UNIX and Windows desirable. International students eligible. Year-round positions, $550-$800 per week, located in Teaneck, NJ. Interns work full life-cycle on real world software development with professionals. Focus on component-based distributed systems, JAVA, Internet/Intranet. Relocation assistance and other benefits. Minutes from NYC.

   Number of awards: 5
Contact:
Pro-Found Software
Glenpointe Centre West
500 Frank W. Burr Blvd.
Teaneck, NJ 07666
Phone: 201-928-0400
Web: www.pro-found.com

Random House

Random House Internship

Type of award: Internship.
Intended use: For senior study at 4-year institution.
Basis for selection: Major/career interest in publishing; communications; history or literature.
Application requirements: Resume, cover letter. Apply in junior year.
Additional information: All majors encouraged to apply. $300 per week stipend. Application accepted beginning January 1. If invited, applicant must travel to New York City at own expense for an interview. E-mail or surface mail resume and cover letter. e-mail address: internship@randomhouse.com.

   Amount of award: $3,000
   Number of awards: 7
   Application deadline: March 31
Contact:
Random House Internship Coordinator
Human Resources, 22nd floor
1540 Broadway
New York, NY 10036
Web: www.randomhouse.com

Rhode Island State Government

Rhode Island Government Intern Program

Type of award: Internship, renewable.
Intended use: For junior, senior or graduate study in United States.
Eligibility: Applicant must be residing in Rhode Island.
Basis for selection: Major/career interest in public administration/service or governmental public relations.
Application requirements: Interview, recommendations. Cover letter.
Additional information: Interns are placed in various state offices. Students from other states may work for academic credit in unpaid internships.

   Amount of award: $100-$800
   Number of awards: 180
   Application deadline: May 15
Contact:
Rhode Island Government Intern Program
Room 8AA, State House
Providence, RI 02903
Phone: 401-222-6782

Rhode Island State Government Internship Program

Type of award: Internship.
Intended use: For undergraduate or postgraduate study.
Eligibility: Applicant must be residing in Rhode Island.
Basis for selection: Major/career interest in governmental public relations or public administration/service. Applicant must demonstrate high academic achievement, depth of character, leadership, seriousness of purpose and service orientation.
Application requirements: Interview, recommendations, essay, transcript, proof of eligibility.
Additional information: Minimum GPA 2.5, freshman and sophomores must be in participating RI schools. Eight weeks in spring, summer and fall. Fall application deadline is rolling. Compensation for summer interns only, $100 per week. Spring and fall participants earn academic credit. All located in Rhode Island.

   Application deadline: May 15, November 15
Contact:
Rhode Island State Government
State Capitol, Rm. 8AA
Providence, RI 02903
Phone: 401-222-6782

San Francisco Chronicle

San Francisco Chronicle Internship Program

Type of award: Internship.
Intended use: For freshman, sophomore, junior, senior or graduate study.
Basis for selection: Major/career interest in journalism or publishing.

Application requirements: Recommendations. Cover letter (which should also state desired position), resume, at least one letter of recommendation, the names of three references, and samples of work.

Additional information: Summer internship program offers newsroom experience to current college students and new college graduates. New college graduates are those who have been out of school no longer than one year prior to the start of the internship. 12-week program begins in mid-June and will pay approximately $535 a week. Two-year internship program offers newsroom experience to new college graduates. Interns paid approximately $35,000 the first year and $40,000 the second year. Two-year interns eligible for comprehensive health benefits after three months. Program begins in mid-June 2001. Visit Website for more information.

Number of applicants:	800
Application deadline:	November 15

Contact:
Summer/Two-Year Internship Program San Francisco Chronicle
Attn: Leslie Guevarra
901 Mission Street
San Francisco, CA 94103-2988
Web: www.sfgate.com/chronicle/internships

Seventeen Magazine

Seventeen Magazine Journalism Internship

Type of award: Internship.
Intended use: For undergraduate or graduate study at postsecondary institution.
Basis for selection: Major/career interest in journalism.
Application requirements: Interview, portfolio, recommendations. Resume, cover letter, writing samples.
Additional information: Eight week program, $250/week. Course credit available. Applicants notified approximately one month following application submission. Summer deadline is March 1.

Number of awards:	25
Number of applicants:	1,000
Application deadline:	March 1, July 15

Contact:
Seventeen Magazine
Internship Coordinator
850 Third Ave., 8th Floor
New York, NY 10022

SGI (Silicon Graphics)

SGI (Silicon Graphics) Internship/ Co-op Program

Type of award: Internship.
Intended use: For undergraduate or graduate study.
Basis for selection: Major/career interest in computer/ information sciences; engineering, computer; engineering, electrical/electronic; mathematics; information systems; human resources; business or marketing.
Application requirements: Resume and cover letter.

Additional information: Positions, locations and awards vary. Deadlines vary. Visit Website to view internship descriptions and submit resume. Undergraduate and postgraduate students in Computer Science/Computer Engineering, Electrical Engineering, Math, MIS, Human Resources and Business (analysis, marketing, development) preferred.

Contact:
SGI (Silicon Graphics)
Internship Program
1600 Amphiteatre Parkway
Mountain View, CA 94043
Fax: 650-933-4666
Web: www.sgi.com

Sigma Alpha Epsilon Foundation

Sigma Alpha Epsilon Resident Educational Advisor

Type of award: Internship, renewable.
Intended use: For full-time undergraduate or graduate study at accredited graduate institution.
Eligibility: Applicant or parent must be member/participant of Sigma Alpha Epsilon. Applicant must be male.
Basis for selection: Applicant must demonstrate high academic achievement, depth of character, leadership and service orientation.
Application requirements: Recommendations, essay, transcript, proof of eligibility.
Additional information: Highly qualified undergraduates are accepted, but graduate students are preferred. Members of Sigma Alpha Epsilon preferred but not required. Applicants must reside in a fraternity house and coordinate educational and academic programs at least 15 hours per week. A $2,000 salary is provided, with a $1,000 bonus when all requirements have been met at the end of the academic year. Room and board provided. Expenses paid weekend training seminar before the start of the academic year required.

Amount of award:	$2,000-$3,000
Number of awards:	20
Number of applicants:	50
Application deadline:	April 15
Notification begins:	May 30
Total amount awarded:	$60,000

Contact:
Residential Advisor Program Director
Sigma Alpha Epsilon Foundation
1856 Sheridan Road
Evanston, IL 60204-1856
Web: www.sae.net

Smithsonian Environmental Research Center

Smithsonian Environmental Research Center Work/Learn Program

Type of award: Internship, renewable.
Intended use: For undergraduate or graduate study. Designated institutions: Smithsonian Environmental Research Center in Edgewater, Maryland.
Basis for selection: Major/career interest in biology; chemistry; environmental science; engineering, environmental or ecology. Applicant must demonstrate seriousness of purpose.
Application requirements: Recommendations, essay, transcript.
Additional information: Stipends are $300 per week. Available during spring and summer months. Projects are 40 hours per week, lasting from 12 weeks to four months. Dorm space is available for $60 per week on a limited basis. Applications accepted on an ongoing basis; deadlines posted indicate priority consideration.

Number of awards:	25
Number of applicants:	250
Application deadline:	March 1, November 1
Notification begins:	April 15, December 15
Total amount awarded:	$60,000

Contact:
Smithsonian Environmental Research Center
Work/Learn Program
P.O. Box 28
Edgewater, MD 21037
Phone: 443-428-2217
Fax: 443-428-2380
Web: www.serc.si.edu

Smithsonian Institution

Smithsonian Minority Internship

Type of award: Internship.
Intended use: For undergraduate or graduate study. Designated institutions: Smithsonian Institution.
Application requirements: Applicants must have major/career interest in any research or museum-related activity pursued by the Smithsonian Institution. Contact Office of Fellowships and Grants for application procedures.
Additional information: Research internships at Smithsonian Institution in anthropology/archaeology, astrophysics, earth sciences/paleontology, ecology/environmental, behavioral (tropical animals), evolutionary and systematic biology, history of science and technology, history of art (including American contemporary, African, Asian), 20th century American crafts, social and cultural history and folk life of America. Stipend of $300 a week for ten weeks. February 1 deadline applies to Summer and Fall. October 15 deadline applies to Spring. Minority students encouraged to apply.

Amount of award:	$3,000
Application deadline:	February 1, October 15

Contact:
Smithsonian Institution
Office of Fellowships and Grants
750 9th Street, NW, Suite 9300 MRC 902
Washington, DC 20560-0902
Phone: 202-275-0655
Web: www.si.edu/research+study

Smithsonian Native American Internship

Type of award: Internship.
Intended use: For undergraduate or graduate study. Designated institutions: Smithsonian Institution.
Basis for selection: Major/career interest in Native American studies.
Application requirements: Contact Office of Fellowships and Grants for application procedures.
Additional information: Internship at Smithsonian Institution in research or museum activities related to Native American studies. Stipend of $300 a week for ten weeks. Deadline for Summer is February 1; Fall is June 1; Spring is October 1. American Indian students encouraged to apply.

Amount of award:	$3,000
Application deadline:	June 1, October 1

Contact:
Smithsonian Institution
Office of Fellowships and Grants
750 9th Street, NW, Suite 9300 MRC902
Washington, DC 20560-0902
Phone: 202-275-0655
Web: www.si.edu/research+study

Solomon R. Guggenheim Museum

Guggenheim Museum Internship

Type of award: Internship.
Intended use: For junior, senior or graduate study.
Eligibility: Applicant must be U.S. citizen, permanent resident, international student or International student with J-1 visa.
Basis for selection: Major/career interest in arts management; art/art history; arts, general; film/video; museum studies or museum studies/administration. Applicant must demonstrate high academic achievement.
Application requirements: Interview, recommendations, essay, transcript. Cover letter, resume. Separate list of relevant coursework and foreign languages. All official academic transcripts with official seal of universities. 500-word typed, double-spaced essay indicating interest in program, museum work, reason for applying.
Additional information: Summer application deadline is February 5. Must have taken at least one course in modern art. Spring and Fall internships are full- or part-time, minimum commitment of 15 hours/week for three months. Summer internships are full-time. See Website for list of individual programs and departments. Related Museum Internship Program gives preference to minority students who are residents of New York.

Number of applicants:	300
Application deadline:	May 1, November 1

Contact:
Solomon R. Guggenheim Museum Education Program
Coordinator
Internship Program
1071 Fifth Avenue
New York, NY 10128
Phone: 212-423-3526
Web: www.guggenheim.org

Peggy Guggenheim Internship

Type of award: Internship.
Intended use: For undergraduate or graduate study.
Basis for selection: Successful applicants tend to be in their mid-twenties. Major/career interest in arts, general; art/art history or museum studies. Applicant must demonstrate high academic achievement, depth of character, leadership and seriousness of purpose.
Application requirements: Recommendations, essay. Photograph.
Additional information: One-to-three month internship at Peggy Guggenheim Collection in Venice, Italy. Must be fluent in English with knowledge of spoken Italian. Interns receive a monthly stipend. Request futher information and application forms from the Peggy Guggenheim Collection. Visit Website for details.

Number of awards:	139
Number of applicants:	800

Contact:
Peggy Guggenheim Collection Internship Coodinator
Palazzo Venier dei Leoni
701 Dorsoduro, 30123 VENEZIA, Italy
Phone: 39-041-2405-411
Web: www.guggenheim.org

Sony Corporation of America

Sony Summer Internship

Type of award: Internship.
Intended use: For full-time junior, senior or graduate study at postsecondary institution.
Basis for selection: Major/career interest in engineering; marketing; accounting; computer/information sciences; communications; business/management/administration; public relations or information systems. Applicant must demonstrate high academic achievement.
Application requirements: Resume, cover letter.
Additional information: Paid internships in variety of projects at Sony Electronics. Apply during sophomore or junior year. Associate degree candidates considered on case-by-case basis. Compensation on hourly basis: $10-20/hr. for undergraduates, $15-25/hr. for graduate students.

Application deadline:	April 1

Contact:
Internship Coordinator, Sony Corporation of America
1 Sony Drive
Park Ridge, NJ 07656-8003
Fax: 201-930-6065

Sony Music Entertainment

Sony Credited Internship

Type of award: Internship.
Intended use: For undergraduate or graduate study at accredited postsecondary institution.
Basis for selection: Major/career interest in business; accounting; finance/banking; computer/information sciences; law or music.
Application requirements: Interview, transcript, proof of eligibility. Resume and cover letter.
Additional information: Non-paid internship; must be available to work at least two full days a week. Deadlines for Spring and Fall are rolling. Summer session deadline is March 31. Must be enrolled at an accredited university and provide verification of course credit. Interns are placed in various departments throughout company. Send resume and cover letter via mail in envelope clearly marked Sony Credited Internship.
Contact:
Sony Music Entertainment, Inc.
Credited Internship Program
550 Madison Avenue, Sky Lobby
New York, NY 10022-3211
Phone: 212-833-7980
Web: www.sony.com

Sony Minority Internship

Type of award: Internship.
Intended use: For full-time undergraduate or master's study at postsecondary institution in United States.
Eligibility: Applicant must be Asian American, African American, Mexican American, Hispanic American, Puerto Rican or American Indian.
Application requirements: Interview. Resume and cover letter. Minimum GPA 3.0. Applicant must be returning to school in the fall.
Additional information: Ten-week paid internship. Undergraduates must submit resume and cover letter by March 31;graduates by January 15. Graduate applicants must be first-year law or MBA student. Applicants who wish to be placed at regional sales and distribution offices outside New York must have application materials postmarked by January 31. The majority of interns are placed in New York offices and one will be placed in each of Sony's regional offices in: Illinois, Massachusetts, Ohio, Georgia, California, Texas, Marilyn, and Jerico, NY. In coverletter and outside of envelope, indicate preferred geographic location.

Application deadline:	March 31, December 31

Contact:
Sony Music Entertainment
Minority Internship Program
550 Madison Avenue, 13th Floor
New York, NY 10022-3211
Phone: 212-833-7980
Web: www.sony.com

Southern Progress Corporation

Southern Progress Corporation Internship Program

Type of award: Internship.
Intended use: For undergraduate or graduate study.
Basis for selection: Major/career interest in journalism; graphic arts/design; marketing; advertising; accounting; computer/information sciences; human resources; public relations or culinary arts.
Application requirements: Recommendations. Cover letter, resume and writing samples.
Additional information: Summer application deadline February 15; Fall deadline June 15; Spring deadline September 15. Pays $10/hr. Writing samples required. Three-to-five month internships in editorial, graphic design, market research, advertising and accounting departments.

Amount of award:	$3,720-$6,200
Number of awards:	30
Number of applicants:	500
Application deadline:	June 15, September 15

Contact:
Internship Coordinator
P.O. Box 2581
Birmingham, AL 35202
Web: southernprogress.com

Southface Energy Institute

Southface Internship

Type of award: Internship.
Intended use: For undergraduate or graduate study at accredited 2-year, 4-year or graduate institution in United States.
Eligibility: Applicant must be U.S. citizen or permanent resident.
Basis for selection: Major/career interest in landscape architecture; economics; business/management/administration; environmental science; horticulture or engineering, environmental. Applicant must demonstrate high academic achievement.
Application requirements: Interview, recommendations, essay.
Additional information: Provides intern with opportunity to work in alternative energy field. Interest in sustainable building construction, environmental and economic energy issues, organic gardening and xeriscaping, non-profit management and program development. Three to six-month internship, 40 hrs/wk. $335 a month for the first 3 months; $50 per month increase thereafter to $485. Accommodations provided for non-Atlanta residents. Limited number of part-time internships available. Application deadlines are rolling.
Contact:
Southface Energy Institute
P.O. Box 5506
Atlanta, GA 30307
Web: www.southface.org/home/events/intern.html

Spoleto Festival USA

Spoleto Festival Apprenticeship Program

Type of award: Internship, renewable.
Intended use: For undergraduate, graduate or non-degree study in United States. Designated institutions: Spoleto Festival U.S.A.
Basis for selection: Major/career interest in arts management; arts, general; music; public relations or theater/production/technical. Applicant must demonstrate seriousness of purpose.
Application requirements: Recommendations. Application, resume, and two letters of recommendation. Media relations applicants submit two writing samples.
Additional information: Interested students should contact sponsor in fall to get on mailing list. Six week apprenticeship with arts professionals producing and operating international arts festival. Posts available in media relations, development, finance, box office, production, housing, general administration, merchandising, orchestra management, chamber music assistant, and rehearsal assistant. Weekly stipend of $225 and housing included.

Amount of award:	$200-$1,200
Number of awards:	45
Application deadline:	February 1

Contact:
Spoleto Festival USA
PO Box 157, Apprentice Program
Charleston, SC 29402-0157
Web: www.spoletousa.org

Spoleto Festival Production Internship

Type of award: Internship, renewable.
Intended use: For full-time undergraduate, graduate or non-degree study in United States. Designated institutions: Spoleto Festival U.S.A.
Eligibility: Applicant must be U.S. citizen.
Basis for selection: Major/career interest in performing arts; electronics; construction; cosmetology/hairdressing or theater/production/technical. Applicant must demonstrate seriousness of purpose.
Application requirements: Recommendations. Application, resume, two letters of recommendation.
Additional information: Interested students should contact sponsor in fall to get on mailing list. Six week apprenticeship with arts professionals producing and operating international arts festival. Posts available for stage carpenters, stage electricians, sound, properties, wardrobe, wigs and makeup, and production administrators. Must have related experience in technical theater. Weekly stipend of $225 and housing included.

Amount of award:	$1,300
Number of awards:	30
Application deadline:	February 1

Contact:
Spoleto Festival USA
P.O. Box 157, Apprentice Program
Charleston, SC 29402-0157
Web: www.spoletousa.org

Student Conservation Association

SCA Conservation Internships

Type of award: Internship, renewable.
Intended use: For undergraduate or graduate study at accredited postsecondary institution in United States.
Eligibility: Applicant must be at least 18. Applicant must be U.S. citizen or permanent resident.
Basis for selection: Major/career interest in archaeology; ecology; forestry; natural resources/conservation; history; education; wildlife/fisheries; biology or communications.
Application requirements: $10 application fee. Interview, recommendations, transcript. Application fee $10. Interview by telephone.
Additional information: Internships themselves are expenses-paid: food allowance, travel, housing, and insurance. Various locations in the U.S. Successful completion earns an Americorps Education Award. Five deadlines yearly: January 15, March 1, June 1, September 15, November 15. Major/career interest in environmental education, interpretation, marine biology, wilderness preservation also eligible.

Amount of award:	$1,180-$4,725
Number of awards:	1,500
Number of applicants:	5,000
Total amount awarded:	$1,500,000

Contact:
Recruiting Department Student Conservation Association
P.O. Box 550
Charlestown, NH 03603
Phone: 603-543-1700
Fax: 603-543-1828
Web: www.sca-inc.org

Sun Microsystems

Sun Microsystems Student Intern and Co-op Program

Type of award: Internship.
Intended use: For full-time sophomore, junior, senior or graduate study at accredited 4-year or graduate institution in United States.
Eligibility: Applicant must be U.S. citizen, permanent resident, international student or foreign student with unrestricted permission to work in U.S.
Basis for selection: Major/career interest in computer/ information sciences; engineering, electrical/electronic; engineering, computer; engineering, mechanical; information systems; marketing; finance/banking; human resources or business/management/administration. Applicant must demonstrate high academic achievement.
Additional information: Students enrolled in industrial engineering degree program also eligible to apply. Must maintain 3.0 GPA or higher. Visit Website to submit resume and sign up to search for current openings. Best-qualified students contacted within two weeks. Most internships located in northen California, Massachusetts, Colorado, but occasional positions elsewhere in U.S.

Contact:
Sun Microsystems
University Relations
901 San Antonio Road M/S UPAL01-471
Palo Alto, CA 94303
Phone: 650-960-1300
Web: www.zoneinonsun.com

Texas Higher Education Coordinating Board

Texas College Work-Study Program

Type of award: Internship.
Intended use: For undergraduate, graduate or non-degree study at accredited 2-year, 4-year or graduate institution. Designated institutions: Public postsecondary institutions in Texas.
Eligibility: Applicant must be U.S. citizen or permanent resident residing in Texas.
Basis for selection: Applicant must demonstrate financial need.
Additional information: Average award $841. Not available at proprietary schools. Number of hours of part-time work based on need. May reapply.

Number of awards:	3,232
Total amount awarded:	$2,718,112

Contact:
Contact the college/university financial aid office to apply.
Phone: 800-242-3062
Fax: 512-427-6420
Web: www.collegefortexans.com

Twentieth Century Fox

Twentieth Century Fox Internship

Type of award: Internship.
Intended use: For undergraduate or master's study.
Basis for selection: Major/career interest in accounting; law; public relations; marketing or computer/information sciences.
Application requirements: Resume, cover letter that includes areas of interest.
Additional information: Ten-week paid summer internships in many divisions of Fox Filmed Entertainment. Compensation is up to $400/week for undergraduates, $700/week for MBA students amd includes college credit. Most internships are in Los Angeles area. Some publications and Websites list Fox having Scholarship Program but this is not currently accurate. Due to large volume of resumes received, receipt of resume can not be verified. Students interested in production and publicity also encouraged to apply.

Number of awards:	75

Contact:
Twentieth Century Fox
c/o Resume Processing Center
P.O. Box 705
Orinda, CA 94563-3032
Web: www.fox.com

Internships

U.S. Department of Agriculture

USDA Summer Intern Program

Type of award: Internship.
Intended use: For undergraduate or graduate study.
Eligibility: Applicant must be U.S. citizen.
Basis for selection: Major/career interest in public administration/service; political science/government; science, general or business/management/administration.
Application requirements: Recommendations, transcript. Resume, cover letter, US government forms.
Additional information: Internships last approximately four months. Stipend amounts are based on level of education, prior experience and position. Open to undergraduates and high school graduates entering college. Applications available in January. All majors encouraged to apply.

Application deadline:	March 1
Notification begins:	May 31

Contact:
United States Department of Agriculture
Summer Intern Program Manager
14th & Independence Ave., SW
Washington, DC 20250-9600
Phone: 202-720-6905
Web: www.usda.gov/da/employ/intern.htm

U.S. Department of Education

Federal Work-Study Program

Type of award: Internship.
Intended use: For undergraduate or graduate study at accredited postsecondary institution in United States.
Eligibility: Applicant must be U.S. citizen or permanent resident.
Basis for selection: Applicant must demonstrate financial need.
Application requirements: Proof of eligibility. FAFSA.
Additional information: On-campus and off-campus employment assignments based on health, class schedule, and academic progress. Students earn at least minimum wage. Alternate phone number: 800-730-8913. Must not have defaulted on federal grant/loan. Compensation may not exceed amount of award.

Application deadline:	July 2

Contact:
Federal Student Aid Information Center
PO Box 84
Washington, DC 20044-0084
Phone: 800-4-FED-AID
Web: www.ed.gov

U.S. Department of Energy

ORISE U.S. Nuclear Regulatory Commission Historically Black Colleges and Universities Student Research Participation

Type of award: Internship.
Intended use: For undergraduate or graduate study at accredited postsecondary institution in United States. Designated institutions: Laboratories where NRC research is being conducted; some appointments on HBCU campuses; some appointments at host universities under the guidance of principal investigators who have NRC research grant.
Eligibility: Applicant must attend historically black college or university. Applicant must be U.S. citizen or permanent resident.
Basis for selection: Major/career interest in computer/information sciences; engineering; geology/earth sciences; mathematics; geophysics; physics; materials science or physical sciences.
Additional information: Provides opportunities for students from historically black colleges to participate in research relating to science and engineering. Ten to 12 weeks during the summer. Weekly stipend of $400 to $500. Limited travel reimbursement (round-trip transportation expenses between facility and home or campus). Funded by U.S. Nuclear Regulatory Commission through cooperative agreement with U.S. Department of Energy.

Application deadline:	January 16

Contact:
ORISE-NRC HBCU Student Research Participation
Oak Ridge Institute for Science and Education
P.O. Box 117
Oak Ridge, TN 37831-0117
Phone: 865-576-9975
Web: www.orau.gov/orise/educ.htm#how

Student Research at the U.S. Army Edgewood Chemical Biological Center

Type of award: Internship, renewable.
Intended use: For undergraduate or graduate study at accredited 4-year or graduate institution in United States. Designated institutions: U.S. Army Edgewood Chemical Biological Center (Aberdeen Proving Ground, MD) and other approved locations.
Eligibility: Applicant must be U.S. citizen.
Basis for selection: Major/career interest in biology; computer/information sciences; engineering; environmental science; physical sciences or science, general.
Additional information: Provides opportunities to participate in research and development in support of military missions. Three months to one year; full-time or part-time appointments. Stipend based on research area(s) and academic classification. Applications accepted on year-round basis. Funded by U.S. Army Edgewood Chemical Biological Center through interagency agreement with U.S. Department of Energy.
Contact:
Kim Haskins or Diane Lewis
Phone: 410-436-7258 or 410-436-5461
Web: www.orau.org

Internships

559

U.S. Department of State

U.S. Department of State Internship

Type of award: Internship.
Intended use: For junior, senior or graduate study at 4-year or graduate institution.
Eligibility: Applicant must be U.S. citizen.
Basis for selection: Major/career interest in political science/ government; foreign languages; governmental public relations; business; public administration/service; social work; economics; information systems; journalism or science, general. Applicant must demonstrate high academic achievement.
Application requirements: Essay, transcript. Applcation form, statement of interest, SAR, successful completion of security clearance.
Additional information: Applicant must be a continuing student. Provides opportunities working in varied administrative branches of the Department of State, both abroad and in Washington D.C. Internships are generally unpaid, but many institutions provide academic credit and/or financial assistance for overseas assignments. Paid internships primarily granted to students in financial need. Must be able to work a minimum of 10 weeks. Additional application deadline for summer is November 1. Contact intern coordinator or visit Website for further details.

   Application deadline: March 1, July 1
Contact:
U.S. Department of State Intern Coordinator HR/REE
SA-1 2401
E Street, NW, 5th Floor
Washington, DC 20522
Web: www.state.gov

U.S. House of Representatives

House Member Internships

Type of award: Internship, renewable.
Intended use: For full-time undergraduate study.
Eligibility: Applicant must be U.S. citizen or permanent resident.
Basis for selection: Major/career interest in political science/ government; public administration/service; public relations or communications. Applicant must demonstrate high academic achievement.
Additional information: Members of the United Stated House of Representatives use undergraduate interns for a variety of jobs including constituent contact, research and correspondence. Positions are based in Congressional District Offices and in Washington, DC. Internships generally facilitate course credit, but offer no stipend. Some paid internships are funded through private nonprofit organizations. Information about the individual House member intern programs can usually be found online. A complete set of links to House Member Office sites is available at www.house.gov. In general, applicants residing in the member's home district and enrolled in the same political party are favored. Typically, many Washington, D.C.-based internships are filled by students from outside the member district. Applicants may also be interested in working for congressperson serving on committee (i.e. Agriculture, Financial Services) relevant to their major.

Contact:
U.S. House of Representatives
Washington, DC 20515
Phone: 202-224-3121
Web: www.house.gov/house/MemberWWW.html

U.S. National Arboretum

U.S. National Arboretum Internship

Type of award: Internship.
Intended use: For sophomore, junior, senior or graduate study at postsecondary institution.
Eligibility: Applicant must be U.S. citizen or permanent resident.
Basis for selection: Major/career interest in horticulture; botany; agriculture or forestry.
Application requirements: Recommendations, transcript. Resume and cover letter.
Additional information: Internships are full or part time, last from three months to one year and pay stipend of $8.47/hr. Provides opportunity to gain experience in plant research in premier horticultural collection. Applicants should have completed six months of general horticulture experience or one year of related post-high school coursework. Basic gardening or laboratory skills, interest in plants, strong communication skills and ability to work independently preferred. Course credit may be arranged.

   Number of awards: 17
   Number of applicants: 50
   Application deadline: February 20
Contact:
Internship Coordinator
U.S. National Arboretum
3501 New York Ave., NE
Washington, DC 20002
Web: www.ars-grin.gov/na

United States Holocaust Memorial Museum

United States Holocaust Memorial Museum Internship

Type of award: Internship, renewable.
Intended use: For undergraduate or graduate study.
Eligibility: Applicant must be U.S. citizen, permanent resident, international student or qualified to work in the U.S.
Basis for selection: Major/career interest in museum studies/ administration or Jewish studies.
Application requirements: Interview, recommendations, transcript. Resume, brief personal statement, cover letter.
Additional information: Semester-long internships available during summer, fall, and spring in Holocaust Research and Museum Studies. Not all positions paid. Applicants with disabilities may also apply for Estelle Schickler Internship by indicating interest in letter of intent. Applications available online.

Contact:
Internship Coordinator, Office of Volunteer and Intern Services
United States Holocaust Memorial Museum
100 Raoul Wallenburg Place, SW
Washington, DC 20024-2150
Phone: 202-479-9738
Web: www.ushmm.org

United States Senate

United States Senate Member Internships

Type of award: Internship.
Intended use: For full-time undergraduate study at accredited 4-year institution.
Eligibility: Applicant must be U.S. citizen or permanent resident.
Basis for selection: Major/career interest in political science/government; law; communications; public relations; public administration/service or economics. Applicant must demonstrate high academic achievement.
Application requirements: Generally resume, cover letter, writing sample.
Additional information: Senate member interns generally reside or attend college in senator's state. Positions available in Washington, D.C., or member's state. Internships may be unpaid or (less frequently) paid, but generally offer assistance obtaining college credit. Term of service, eligibility vary. Some internships restricted to upper-level undergraduates. Contact individual senator's office directly. Visit Website for complete links to member sites, e-mail addresses and telephone contact numbers.
  Number of awards: 500
Contact:
Office of (Name of Senator)
United States Senate
Washington, DC 20510
Web: www.senate.gov

University of Georgia Marine Institute

UGA Marine Institute Student Intern Program

Type of award: Internship.
Intended use: For full-time junior, senior or graduate study at accredited 4-year or graduate institution.
Eligibility: Applicant must be residing in Georgia.
Basis for selection: Major/career interest in oceanography/marine studies or engineering.
Application requirements: Recommendations, transcript. Cover letter explaining interests and goals.
Additional information: Visit Website for application and program information. Internships available year-round, but usually conducted in summer. Requires three-month stay on Sapelo Island, Georgia. Juniors, seniors and graduates with less than two years post-graduate education may apply. Visit Website for additional and updated information.

  Amount of award: $2,400
  Application deadline: February 4
Contact:
Dr. Steven C. Pennings, Coordinator
UGAMI Intern Program
UGA Marine Institute
Sapelo Island, GA 31327
Phone: 912-485-2293
Web: www.uga.edu/ugami

Wall Street Journal

Wall Street Journal Internship

Type of award: Internship.
Intended use: For undergraduate or graduate study.
Basis for selection: Major/career interest in journalism.
Application requirements: Cover letter, resume, two newspaper clips.
Additional information: 10-week full-time summer internship. Previous journalism and/or college newspaper experience required. Interns paid $600 a week. All majors encouraged to apply.
  Number of awards: 18
  Application deadline: November 1
Contact:
The Wall Street Journal
Internships
200 Liberty St.
New York, NY 10281

Walt Disney World

Walt Disney World College Program

Type of award: Internship.
Intended use: For full-time undergraduate study.
Eligibility: Applicant must be U.S. citizen or permanent resident.
Application requirements: Interview, recommendations. Submit employment application and attend Walt Disney World College Program presentation.
Additional information: Applicant must have completed one semester at college or university.
Contact:
Walt Disney World
P.O. Box 10090
Lake Buena Vista, FL
Web: www.careermosaic.com

Walt Disney World Horticulture Summer Internship

Type of award: Internship.
Intended use: For junior or senior study in United States. Designated institutions: Walt Disney World.
Basis for selection: Major/career interest in landscape architecture; horticulture or entomology. Applicant must demonstrate high academic achievement, seriousness of purpose and service orientation.
Application requirements: Interview, transcript, Resume.

Internships

Additional information: Students paid $8.75 per hour. Please visit Website for more information and application deadline.

   Number of awards: 50

Contact:
Walt Disney World
Horticulture Creative Services
P.O. Box 10000
Lake Buena Vista, FL 32830-1000
Web: www.wdwcollegeprogram.com

Warwick, Baker, O'Neill

Warwick, Baker, O'Neill Internship Program

Type of award: Internship.
Intended use: For junior or senior study.
Eligibility: Applicant must be U.S. citizen.
Basis for selection: Major/career interest in advertising. Applicant must demonstrate seriousness of purpose.
Application requirements: Resume with cover letter.
Additional information: Due to high volume of applicants, receipt of resumes cannot be verified. Only applicants under consideration for the internship will be contacted. Internships pay $300/week.

   Number of awards: 2
   Application deadline: May 15

Contact:
Warwick, Baker, O'Neill Internship Coordinator
100 Avenue of the Americas
New York, NY 10013
Phone: 212-941-4200
Web: www.warwick.com

Washington Internships for Students of Engineering

Washington Internships for Students of Engineering

Type of award: Internship.
Intended use: For senior study.
Eligibility: Applicant must be U.S. citizen.
Basis for selection: Major/career interest in engineering.
Application requirements: Recommendations, transcript. Application form and reference forms.
Additional information: Ten-week summer internship available to students who have completed three years of study. Interns write required research paper as part of process. Round trip travel expenses to Washington D.C. covered. Lodging expenses covered. If seeking sponsorship by ANS, ASCE, ASME, IEEE, or AIChE, student must be member. ASHRAE, NSPE and SAE will consider non-members.

   Amount of award: $1,800
   Number of awards: 15
   Application deadline: December 1

Contact:
Washington Internships for Students of Engineering
Attn: Anne Hickox
400 Commonwealth Dr.
Warrendale, PA 15096-0001
Phone: 724-776-4841 ext. 7476
Web: www.wise-intern.org

The Weather Channel

The Weather Channel Meteorology Minority Summer Internship

Type of award: Internship.
Intended use: For senior study at accredited 4-year institution.
Eligibility: Applicant must be Alaskan native, Asian American, African American, Mexican American, Hispanic American, Puerto Rican or American Indian.
Basis for selection: Major/career interest in atmospheric sciences/meteorology.
Application requirements: Recommendations, transcript. Include cover letter and resume. Applicant can be from any minority group.
Additional information: Meteorologist intern. Preference given to those who have taken several atmospheric science/ meteorology courses, be highly computer literate and have interest in operational forecast career. Salary approximately $12 per hour, 40 hr/ wk. Intern trained and incorporated into daily behind-the-scenes forecast, graphical and production work (not on-camera).

   Number of awards: 1
   Application deadline: March 31

Contact:
The Weather Channel
Attn: Kathy Strebe, Meteorology Manager
300 Interstate North Parkway
Atlanta, GA 30339

The Weather Channel Meteorology Summer Internship

Type of award: Internship.
Intended use: For senior study.
Basis for selection: Major/career interest in atmospheric sciences/meteorology.
Application requirements: Recommendations, transcript. Include cover letter and resume.
Additional information: Meteorologist intern. Preference given to those who have taken several atmospheric science/ meteorology courses, be highly computer literate and have interest in operational forecast career. Salary approximately $12 per hour, 40 hr/wk. Intern trained and incorporated into daily behind-the-scenes forecast, graphical and production work (not on-camera).

   Number of awards: 1
   Application deadline: March 31

Contact:
The Weather Channel
Attn: Kathy Strebe, Meteorology Manager
300 Interstate North Parkway
Atlanta, GA 30339

Wilhelmina Models

Wilhelmina Models Internship

Type of award: Internship.
Intended use: For undergraduate or graduate study.
Eligibility: Applicant must be U.S. citizen or permanent resident.
Basis for selection: Applicant must demonstrate seriousness of purpose and service orientation.
Application requirements: Recommendations. Resume.
Additional information: Internships available in New York City. Stipend of $35 a day to cover lunch and travel expenses. High school graduates, undergraduates, recent college graduates and graduate students eligible. High school graduates and college graduates of any age are also eligible to work at New York City office only. Interns assist booking agents in men's, women's, children's, and marketing divisions.

Number of awards:	8
Number of applicants:	1,000
Application deadline:	April 3

Contact:
Internship Coordinator
Cassi Caesar
300 Park Ave. S.
New York, NY 10010
Web: www.wilhelmina.com

Wolf Trap Foundation for the Performing Arts

Wolf Trap Foundation for the Performing Arts Internship

Type of award: Internship.
Intended use: For undergraduate or graduate study in United States.
Eligibility: Applicant must be U.S. citizen, permanent resident, international student or able to meet INS I-9 requirement.
Basis for selection: Major/career interest in arts management. Applicant must demonstrate seriousness of purpose.
Application requirements: Cover letter outlining personal statement, career goals and specification of desired departments, resume, two letters of recommendation, two contrasting writing samples.
Additional information: March 1 deadline for full-time summer internships; July 1 deadline for part-time fall internships; November 1 deadline for part-time spring internships. Stipend: up to $210 per week in summer and $126 per week in fall and spring. College credit available. Applicants may also indicate interest in the Josie A. Bass Career Development Program for African American Students. Must have own transportation. Internships available in the following areas: Opera (Directing, Administrative, Stage Management, Technical); Education; Development; Special Projects; Communications and Marketing (Advertising/Marketing, Graphic Design, Publications, Media Relations, Photography); Human Resources; Accounting; Special Events; Food & Beverage Events Catering. Notification of awardees begins approximately one month following application deadline.

Amount of award:	$1,500-$2,500
Number of awards:	30
Number of applicants:	250
Application deadline:	July 1, November 1
Notification begins:	August 1, December 1

Contact:
Wolf Trap Foundation for the Performing Arts
Internship Program
1624 Trap Road
Vienna, VA 22182
Phone: 703-255-1933
Fax: 703-255-1924
Web: www.wolftrap.org

Women's Sports Foundation

Jackie Joyner Kersee/Minority Internship

Type of award: Internship, renewable.
Intended use: For full-time undergraduate or graduate study in United States.
Eligibility: Applicant must be Alaskan native, Asian American, African American, Mexican American, Hispanic American, Puerto Rican or American Indian. Applicant must be female. Applicant must be U.S. citizen or permanent resident.
Basis for selection: Major/career interest in athletic training; sports/sports administration; law or marketing. Applicant must demonstrate financial need and high academic achievement.
Application requirements: Recommendations, essay, proof of eligibility.
Additional information: Open to students or women in career change. Applicants with equestrian interests also eligible. Stipend is $1,000/month, with a minimum three-month term. Other internships available with base $450/month stipend. Download application form from Website. Internships available throughout the year.

Amount of award:	$3,000-$6,000
Number of awards:	6
Number of applicants:	50
Total amount awarded:	$6,000

Contact:
Women's Sports Foundation
Eisenhower Park
East Meadow, NY 11554
Phone: 800-227-3988
Web: www.womenssportsfoundation.org

Y.E.S. To Jobs

Youth Entertainment Summer

Type of award: Internship.
Intended use: For undergraduate study.
Eligibility: Applicant must be at least 16, no older than 18, enrolled in high school. Applicant must be U.S. citizen residing in Tennessee, District of Columbia, Florida, Georgia, Illinois, Texas, California, New York or Michigan.
Basis for selection: Major/career interest in film/video; law; business or computer/information sciences.

563

Application requirements: Interview, recommendations, essay, transcript. Resume.

Additional information: Provides summer employment in various aspects of entertainment industry. Must be resident of Los Angeles, San Francisco Bay area, Dallas, Nashville, Chicago, Detroit, New York, Washington, D.C., Miami, or Atlanta.

Number of awards:	250
Number of applicants:	1,300
Application deadline:	April 1

Contact:
Program Coordinator, Y.E.S. To Jobs
P.O. Box 3390
Los Angeles, CA 90078-3390
Web: www.yestojobs.org

Yosemite National Park

Yosemite National Park Internships

Type of award: Internship.

Intended use: For junior or senior study.

Basis for selection: Major/career interest in environmental science; history; education or physical sciences.

Additional information: Full-time assignment; minimum of 12 weeks. Internships available during summer (mid-June through Labor Day). Two Internships available in spring (one in education; one in wilderness) from March to June. $10 per day (or $50 per 40-hour week) to defray expenses. Free housing and up to $300 for travel to/from the park. One seminar. Each intern receives $1,000 scholarship at end of 12-week commitment. Opportunities in archaeology, search and rescue, resource management/research, wilderness management, and interpretation. Application available online; look for updated information in autumn of each year.

Number of awards:	30
Number of applicants:	125
Application deadline:	February 1

Contact:
Internship Coordinator
Wawona Ranger Office
PO Box 2027
Wawona, CA 95389
Web: www.nps.gov/yose/intern.htm

Internships

Loans

Alaska Commission on Postsecondary Education

Alaska Family Education Loan

Type of award: Loan, renewable.
Intended use: For full-time undergraduate or graduate study at postsecondary institution. Designated institutions: Must be approved by U.S. Department of Education or Alaska Commission on Postsecondary Education.
Eligibility: Applicant must be U.S. citizen or permanent resident residing in Alaska.
Basis for selection: Applicant must demonstrate financial need.
Application requirements: Proof of eligibility. Must be a U.S. citizen and a permanent resident of Alaska.
Additional information: Low interest loan for family member of student, to assist with student's educational costs. Must reapply each year. Recipients not eligible for Alaska Student Loan. Amount of awards: $9,500 graduates, $8,500 undergraduates.

Amount of award:	$8,500-$9,500

Contact:
Alaska Commission on Postsecondary Education
Alaska Student Loan
3030 Vintage Boulevard
Juneau, AK 99801-7100
Phone: 800-441-2962

Alaska Teacher Scholarship Loan

Type of award: Loan, renewable.
Intended use: For full-time undergraduate or post-bachelor's certificate study at 4-year institution. Designated institutions: Must be approved by U.S. Department of Education or Alaska Commission on Postsecondary Education.
Eligibility: Applicant must be U.S. citizen or permanent resident residing in Alaska.
Basis for selection: Major/career interest in education, teacher; education, early childhood or education, special.
Application requirements: Recommendations, proof of eligibility, nomination by rural school districts (pop. under 5,500 and not on road or rail route to Fairbanks or Anchorage or pop. under 1,500 and on road or rail route). Must be a U.S. citizen and permanent resident of Alaska.
Additional information: Must be graduate of Alaskan high school and have sponsorship of rural Alaskan school district. Loan forgiveness possible for teaching in rural Alaskan school district. May not borrow more than $37,500 in total. Must reapply each year. Minimum GPA of 2.0 required.

Amount of award:	$7,500
Number of awards:	181
Application deadline:	July 1
Notification begins:	June 1

Contact:
Alaska Commission on Postsecondary Education
Alaska Teacher Scholarship Loan
3030 Vintage Boulevard
Juneau, AK 99801-7100
Phone: 800-441-2962

Alaska Winn Brindle Memorial Scholarship Loan Program

Type of award: Loan, renewable.
Intended use: For full-time undergraduate or graduate study at postsecondary institution. Designated institutions: Must be approved by U.S. Department of Education or Alaska Commission on Postsecondary Education.
Eligibility: Applicant must be U.S. citizen or permanent resident residing in Alaska.
Basis for selection: Major/career interest in wildlife/fisheries or food science/technology.
Application requirements: Proof of eligibility. Must be a U.S. citizen and a permanent resident of Alaska.
Additional information: Applicants with recommendation from an Alaskan fisheries business may be given priority. Minimum GPA of 2.0 required. Amounts of loans are based on budget. Contact office for more information.

Number of awards:	49
Number of applicants:	49
Application deadline:	May 15
Notification begins:	June 30
Total amount awarded:	$510,391

Contact:
Alaska Commission on Postsecondary Education
Winn Brindle Memorial Scholarship Loan
3030 Vintage Boulevard
Juneau, AK 99801-7100
Phone: 800-441-2962

American Legion Kentucky Auxiliary

Mary Barrett Marshall Student Loan Fund

Type of award: Loan, renewable.
Intended use: For undergraduate study at vocational, 2-year or 4-year institution. Designated institutions: Eligible postsecondary institutions in Kentucky.
Eligibility: Applicant must be female. Applicant must be residing in Kentucky. Applicant must be descendant of veteran; or dependent of veteran; or spouse of veteran or deceased veteran.
Basis for selection: Applicant must demonstrate financial need.
Additional information: Maximum $800 per year, payable monthly, without interest after graduation or upon securing

employment; 6% interest after five years. Sisters of veterans also eligible.

Amount of award: $800
Contact:
American Legion Auxiliary, Department of Kentucky
Chairman: Velma Greenleaf
1448 Leafdale Rd.
Hodgenville, KY 42748
Phone: 606-987-6864

American Legion South Dakota

American Legion South Dakota Educational Loan

Type of award: Loan, renewable.
Intended use: For undergraduate study at vocational, 2-year or 4-year institution. Designated institutions: College or vocational school in South Dakota.
Eligibility: Applicant must be residing in South Dakota. Applicant must be dependent of veteran.
Additional information: Loan amount varies; up to $1,000 per year, $2,000 maximum.

Amount of award: $2,000
Contact:
American Legion South Dakota
Department Adjutant
P.O. Box 67
Watertown, SD 57201-0067
Phone: 605-886-3604
Fax: 605-886-2870

American Legion Wisconsin Auxiliary

M. Louise Wilson Educational Loan

Type of award: Loan.
Intended use: For undergraduate study.
Eligibility: Applicant must be female. Applicant must be residing in Wisconsin. Applicant must be veteran; or dependent of veteran; or spouse of veteran during Grenada conflict, Korean War, Lebanon conflict, Panama conflict, Persian Gulf War, WW I, WW II or Vietnam.
Basis for selection: Applicant must demonstrate financial need and high academic achievement.
Additional information: $400 annually up to five years, but must reapply each year if grades are acceptable. No interest. Repayments begin three months after graduation at a minimum of $35 per month. Minimum GPA 3.2.

Amount of award: $400-$2,000
Application deadline: March 15
Contact:
American Legion Wisconsin Auxiliary
Department Headquarters
812 East State Street, Second Floor
Milwaukee, WI 53202-3493
Phone: 414-271-0124
Fax: 414-271-9355

American Society of Mechanical Engineers

ASME Student Loan Program

Type of award: Loan, renewable.
Intended use: For full-time undergraduate or graduate study in United States or Canada.
Eligibility: Applicant or parent must be member/participant of American Society of Mechanical Engineers.
Basis for selection: Major/career interest in engineering, mechanical. Applicant must demonstrate financial need, depth of character and leadership.
Application requirements: Recommendations.
Additional information: Applicant must be member of ASME in the U.S., Canada, or Mexico, and enrolled in either mechanical engineering or mechanical engineering technology. $3,000 per year, $9,000 maximum for a particular degree.

Amount of award: $3,000
Application deadline: October 15, April 15
Contact:
American Society of Mechanical Engineers
Three Park Avenue
New York, NY 10016-5990
Phone: 212-591-8131
Fax: 212-591-7143
Web: www.asme.org/educate/aid

Arkansas Department of Higher Education

Arkansas Emergency Secondary Education Loan

Type of award: Loan, renewable.
Intended use: For full-time sophomore, junior, senior or master's study at accredited 2-year, 4-year or graduate institution.
Eligibility: Applicant must be U.S. citizen or permanent resident residing in Arkansas.
Basis for selection: Major/career interest in education, teacher; education, special; foreign languages; science, general; mathematics; biology; chemistry; education; natural sciences or physical sciences. Applicant must demonstrate high academic achievement.
Application requirements: Transcript, proof of eligibility.
Additional information: Must teach mathematics, the sciences, foreign languages or special education at the secondary level. Must be Arkansas resident for at least six months. Loan forgiveness for teaching at secondary level in Arkansas designated teacher shortage area: 20 percent of amount borrowed forgiven for each year of teaching.

Amount of award: $2,500
Number of awards: 60
Number of applicants: 100
Application deadline: April 1
Notification begins: June 1
Total amount awarded: $139,471

Contact:
Arkansas Department of Higher Education
114 East Capitol Street
Little Rock, AR 72201-3818
Phone: 800-547-8839
Web: www.arkansashighered.com

Arkansas Minority Teachers Loan

Type of award: Loan, renewable.
Intended use: For full-time junior or senior study at accredited 4-year institution. Designated institutions: Arkansas institutions.
Eligibility: Applicant must be Asian American, African American, Mexican American, Hispanic American, Puerto Rican or American Indian. Applicant must be U.S. citizen or permanent resident residing in Arkansas.
Basis for selection: Major/career interest in education, teacher.
Application requirements: Transcript.
Additional information: Applicant must be pursuing course of study for teacher education and have completed at least 60 credit hours. Loan forgiveness for teaching five years in Arkansas public schools or three years in Arkansas teacher shortage area.

Amount of award:	$5,000
Number of awards:	110
Application deadline:	June 1
Total amount awarded:	$500,000

Contact:
Arkansas Department of Higher Education
114 East Capitol Street
Little Rock, AR 72201-3818
Phone: 800-547-8839
Web: www.arkansashighered.com

California Student Aid Commission

California Assumption Program Loans for Education

Type of award: Loan, renewable.
Intended use: For junior, senior or post-bachelor's certificate study at accredited postsecondary institution. Designated institutions: Any California post-secondary institution with Commision on Teacher Credentialing approved program.
Eligibility: Applicant must be U.S. citizen residing in California.
Basis for selection: Major/career interest in education, teacher. Applicant must demonstrate financial need and high academic achievement.
Application requirements: Interview, recommendations, transcript, proof of eligibility, nomination by each participating institution. Loan indebtedness; must not hold an initial teaching credential. Applicants must be pursuing teaching credentials to teach K-12.
Additional information: Current educational loans must be in good status. Participants receive awards after providing eligible teaching service in a designated shortage area. Loans assumed for up to four years: up to $2,000 for first year and up to $3,000 for second, third and fourth years of consecutive eligible teaching service. Bonus amounts for teaching in the areas of mathematics, science, special education, and at low-performing schools.

Amount of award:	$19,000
Number of awards:	6,500
Application deadline:	July 15
Notification begins:	September 1

Contact:
California Student Aid Commission
Specialized Programs
P.O. Box 419029
Rancho Cordova, CA 95741-9029
Phone: 888-224-7268
Fax: 916-526-7998
Web: www.csac.ca.gov

Connecticut Higher Education Supplemental Loan Authority

Connecticut Family Education Loan Program (CT FELP)

Type of award: Loan, renewable.
Intended use: For undergraduate or first professional study in United States. Designated institutions: Connecticut residents may attend any non-profit institution in the United States. Non-residents must attend non-profit Connecticut institution to be eligible.
Eligibility: Applicant must be U.S. citizen or permanent resident residing in Connecticut.
Application requirements: Non-citizens must have alien registration receipt card (I-151 or I-551).

Amount of award:	$2,000-$125,000
Number of awards:	1,363
Total amount awarded:	$14,775,977

Contact:
Connecticut Higher Education Supplemental Loan Authority (CHESLA)
342 North Main Street
Suite 202
West Hartford, CT 06117
Phone: 800-252-FELP (in state) 860-2361400 (out of state)
Web: www.chesla.org

Delaware Higher Education Commission

Delaware Christa McAuliffe Scholarship Loan

Type of award: Loan, renewable.
Intended use: For full-time freshman, sophomore, junior or senior study at accredited 4-year institution. Designated institutions: Delaware schools.
Eligibility: Applicant must be permanent resident residing in Delaware.
Basis for selection: Major/career interest in education, teacher. Applicant must demonstrate high academic achievement.
Application requirements: Recommendations, essay, transcript, proof of eligibility. Must be Delaware resident.

567

Additional information: Minimum award is $1,000. Loan forgiveness for teaching in Delaware public schools.

Number of awards:	80
Application deadline:	March 31
Notification begins:	May 1
Total amount awarded:	$170,000

Contact:
Delaware Higher Education Commission
820 North French Street
Wilmington, DE 19801
Phone: 302-577-3240
Fax: 302-577-6765

Delaware Nursing Incentive Program

Type of award: Loan, renewable.
Intended use: For full-time undergraduate or non-degree study at vocational, 2-year or 4-year institution in United States.
Eligibility: Applicant must be permanent resident residing in Delaware.
Basis for selection: Major/career interest in nursing. Applicant must demonstrate high academic achievement.
Application requirements: Recommendations, essay, transcript, proof of eligibility. Must be Delaware resident.
Additional information: Minimum 2.5 GPA required. Loan forgiveness for practicing nursing at state-owned hospital: one year for each year of financial assistance.

Amount of award:	$3,000
Number of awards:	10
Number of applicants:	20
Application deadline:	March 31
Notification begins:	May 1
Total amount awarded:	$150,000

Contact:
Delaware Higher Education Commission
820 North French Street
Wilmington, DE 19801
Phone: 302-577-3240
Fax: 302-577-6765

Delta Gamma Foundation

Delta Gamma Student Loan

Type of award: Loan.
Intended use: For undergraduate or graduate study in or outside United States.
Eligibility: Applicant or parent must be member/participant of Delta Gamma.
Basis for selection: Applicant must demonstrate financial need.
Application requirements: Recommendations, transcript.
Additional information: Applicant must be an initiated member of Delta Gamma, child or sister of Delta Gamma.

Amount of award:	$1,000-$2,000

Contact:
Delta Gamma Foundation
3250 Riverside Drive
P.O. Box 21397
Columbus, OH 43221-0397
Phone: 614-481-8169

Florida Department of Education

Critical Occupational Therapist or Physical Therapist Shortage Loan Forgiveness Program

Type of award: Loan, renewable.
Intended use: For undergraduate or graduate study.
Eligibility: Applicant must be residing in Florida.
Basis for selection: Major/career interest in occupational therapy or physical therapy.
Application requirements: Must be licensed or have valid temporary permit as therapist from Florida Department of Business and Professional Regulation; have been employed as therapist in Florida public schools for at least half school year, and declare intent to be employed for minimum of 3 years.
Additional information: Up to $2,500/year for undergraduate loans and $5,000/year for graduate loans for maximum of four years or $10,000, whichever comes first. These awards are for licensed therapists with valid temporary permit who have worked full-time in Florida public schools for one year and who intend to be employed in Florida public schools for minimum of three years. Priority given to renewal applicants.

Amount of award:	$2,500-$10,000
Application deadline:	July 15

Contact:
Florida Department of Education
Bureau of Student Financial Assistance
1940 North Monroe Street, Suite 70
Tallahassee, FL 32303-4759
Phone: 888-827-2004
Web: www.firn.edu/doe

Critical Occupational/Physical Therapist Scholarship Loan Program

Type of award: Loan, renewable.
Intended use: For full-time undergraduate or graduate study at graduate institution. Designated institutions: Florida institutions.
Eligibility: Applicant must be residing in Florida.
Basis for selection: Major/career interest in physical therapy or occupational therapy.
Additional information: Applicant must be enrolled in therapist assistant program, or upper division or graduate level therapist program. Must declare intent to be employed for a minimum of three years as a licensed therapist in public schools, and must do so upon graduation or else loan will have to be repaid. Must have minimum 2.0 GPA for undergraduates and 3.0 GPA for graduates who are renewing.

Amount of award:	$4,000
Application deadline:	April 15

Contact:
Florida Department of Education
Bureau of Instructional Support/Com. Services
601 Turlington Bldg.- 325 West Gaines Street
Tallahassee, FL 32399-0400
Phone: 850-488-1106

Critical Teacher Shortage Student Loan Forgiveness Program

Type of award: Loan, renewable.

Intended use: For undergraduate certificate or post-bachelor's certificate study at 4-year or graduate institution in United States.
Eligibility: Applicant must be U.S. citizen or permanent resident residing in Florida.
Basis for selection: Major/career interest in education, teacher; education, special or education.
Application requirements: Must be full-time teacher in critical teacher shortage subject area in Florida public or developmental research school.
Additional information: Must have graduated from undergraduate or graduate teacher preparation program and have been certified in critical teacher shortage subject area. Applicants must apply within 12 months of certification and teach full-time in critical subject area for at least 90 days. Loan must be repaid by teaching in Florida public school or in cash. Applications may be obtained from Critical Teacher Shortage contact person at public school district where applicant is employed, or Florida Department of Education, Bureau of Student Financial Assistance.

Amount of award:	$2,500-$10,000
Number of awards:	360
Application deadline:	July 15

Contact:
Florida Department of Education
Bureau of Student Financial Assistance
1940 North Monroe Street, Suite 70
Tallahassee, FL 32303-4759
Phone: 888-827-2004
Web: www.firn.edu/doe

Florida Teacher Scholarship and Forgivable Loan (Juniors/Seniors)

Type of award: Loan, renewable.
Intended use: For freshman, sophomore, junior, senior or graduate study at accredited vocational, 2-year, 4-year or graduate institution in United States. Designated institutions: Florida institutions.
Eligibility: Applicant must be Mexican American, Hispanic American or Puerto Rican. Applicant must be U.S. citizen or permanent resident residing in Florida.
Basis for selection: Major/career interest in education, teacher or education. Applicant must demonstrate high academic achievement.
Application requirements: Proof of eligibility. Submit SAT or ACT scores. Principal or Dean must review application for before signing and submitting application to Office of Student Financial Assistance by April 1.
Additional information: Applicants must have 2.5 cumulative GPA, be in 40th percentile of ACT or SAT, and pursue teaching in Florida Teaching Shortage Area. Loan forgiveness one year for each year of award for teaching anywhere in Florida and two years for teaching in teacher shortage area. Loans must be paid back in cash if student decides not to teach in designated areas. Loan limit for graduate students is $8,000 each year for maximum two years. 15 percent of scholarship awards given to minority students.

Amount of award:	$4,000
Number of awards:	360
Application deadline:	March 15

Contact:
Florida Department of Education
Bureau of Student Financial Assistance
1940 North Monroe Street, Suite 70
Tallahassee, FL 32303-4759
Phone: 888-827-2004
Web: www.firn.edu/doe

Nursing Student Loan Forgiveness Program

Type of award: Loan, renewable.
Intended use: For undergraduate or non-degree study at accredited postsecondary institution. Designated institutions: Institution with accredited/approved nursing program.
Eligibility: Applicant must be residing in Florida.
Basis for selection: Major/career interest in nursing or nurse practitioner.
Application requirements: Proof of eligibility. Nurses must be employed full-time in eligible designated site. Contact program for complete list of qualifying sites.
Additional information: 25% of outstanding loan, per year, for maximum of four years. Must be licensed in Florida as Licensed Practical Nurse (LPN), Registered Nurse (RN), or Advanced Registered Nurse Practitioner (ARNP). Applications accepted continuously, with deadlines 30 days prior to quarterly awards (December 1, March 1, June 1, and September 1). Renewal applicants receive priority for awards.

Amount of award:	$4,000
Number of awards:	250
Application deadline:	September 1, December 1

Contact:
Florida Department of Education, Bureau of Student Finan. Assistance
Nursing Loan Forgiveness Program
1940 North Monroe Street, Suite 70
Tallahassee, FL 32303-4759
Phone: 888-827-2004
Web: www.firn.edu/doe

Franklin Lindsay Student Aid Fund

Franklin Lindsay Student Aid Loan

Type of award: Loan, renewable.
Intended use: For full-time sophomore, junior, senior or graduate study at accredited postsecondary institution. Designated institutions: Must be used at institutions approved by Southern Association of Accredited Schools in state of Texas.
Eligibility: Applicant must be U.S. citizen residing in Texas.
Basis for selection: Applicant must demonstrate financial need, depth of character, seriousness of purpose and service orientation.
Application requirements: Interview. Loan package must be completed and must have a co-signer other than spouse.
Additional information: Must have a GPA of 2.0 for undergraduates and 3.0 for graduates. Full-time study requires 12 credit hours undergraduate, nine credit hours graduate. Must have completed 24 credits before applying. Upon graduation or termination from school, loan goes to repayment structure at six percent.

Loans

Amount of award: $5,000
Number of awards: 441
Application deadline: May 1
Notification begins: June 1
Total amount awarded: $1,249,407
Contact:
Franklin Lindsay Student Aid Fund
P.O. Box 550
Austin, TX 78789
Phone: 512-479-2634
Web: www.franklinlindsay.org

Georgia Student Finance Commission

Georgia Promise Teacher Scholarship

Type of award: Loan, renewable.
Intended use: For junior or senior study at accredited 4-year institution. Designated institutions: Any public or private colleges and universities in Georgia currently offering teacher education programs approved by Georgia Professional Standards Commission.
Eligibility: Applicant must be U.S. citizen or permanent resident residing in Georgia.
Basis for selection: Major/career interest in education, teacher or education. Applicant must demonstrate high academic achievement and seriousness of purpose.
Application requirements: Transcript, proof of eligibility.
Additional information: Provides cancelable loans ($6,000 maximum). Must commit to teach one year in Georgia public school for each $1,500 awarded. Teaching must be at preschool, elementary, middle or secondary level. Out-of-state residents attending accredited Georgia teacher-education program also eligible. Must have 3.2 GPA at end of sophomore year; be academically classified as junior; have declared education as major and/or be accepted for enrollment into teacher education program leading to initial certification. Must obtain signatures from institution's Department of Education teacher certification official and financial aid office.
Amount of award: $1,500-$6,000
Number of awards: 305
Total amount awarded: $833,700
Contact:
Scholarship Committee
2082 East Exchange Place
Suite 100
Tucker, GA 30084
Phone: 800-776-6878
Fax: 770-724-9031

Georgia Regents Scholarship

Type of award: Loan.
Intended use: For full-time undergraduate study at accredited postsecondary institution in United States. Designated institutions: .
Eligibility: Applicant must be U.S. citizen or permanent resident residing in Georgia.
Basis for selection: Applicant must demonstrate financial need and high academic achievement.

Additional information: Must be ranked in upper 25 percent of class. Must repay by working full time in Georgia one year for each $1,000 received, or by making cash repayment with 3 percent interest per annum.
Amount of award: $750
Contact:
Contact school's financial aid office for application
Phone: 800-776-6878
Fax: 770-724-9031

Georgia Scholarship for Engineering Education

Type of award: Loan, renewable.
Intended use: For full-time undergraduate study at accredited postsecondary institution in United States. Designated institutions: GSFA-approved postsecondary private schools offering programs of study accredited by the Engineering Accreditation Commission.
Eligibility: Applicant must be U.S. citizen or permanent resident residing in Georgia.
Basis for selection: Major/career interest in engineering; engineering, civil or engineering, construction.
Application requirements: Transcript. Include signed promissory note.
Additional information: Sophomores, juniors and seniors must maintain 2.5 GPA. Must work in Georgia in an engineering field one year for each $3,000 received or repay within six years.
Amount of award: $3,000
Number of awards: 182
Total amount awarded: $510,500
Contact:
Georgia Student Finance Commission
2082 East Exchange Place
Suite 100
Tucker, GA 30084
Phone: 800-776-6878
Fax: 770-724-9052

Grand Encampment of Knights Templar of the USA

Knights Templar Educational Foundation Loan

Type of award: Loan, renewable.
Intended use: For junior, senior, master's, doctoral, first professional or postgraduate study at vocational, 4-year or graduate institution.
Eligibility: Applicant must be U.S. citizen.
Basis for selection: Major/career interest in history or religion/theology. Applicant must demonstrate high academic achievement and depth of character.
Application requirements: Recommendations.
Additional information: Student should request application from Grand Encampment of Knights Templar of U.S.A. in state of residence. Personal dependability important. Send SASE for application.

Amount of award: $6,000
Number of awards: 700
Total amount awarded: $645,943
Contact:
Grand Encampment of Knights Templar of the USA
5097 North Elston Avenue
Suite 101
Chicago, IL 60630-2460
Phone: 773-777-3300

Hattie M. Strong Foundation

Strong Foundation Interest-Free Student Loan

Type of award: Loan, renewable.
Intended use: For full-time senior, master's or doctoral study at accredited 4-year or graduate institution.
Eligibility: Applicant must be U.S. citizen or permanent resident residing in District of Columbia.
Basis for selection: Applicant must demonstrate financial need, high academic achievement, depth of character, leadership, seriousness of purpose and service orientation.
Application requirements: Recommendations, essay, proof of eligibility. SASE.
Additional information: Must be entering final year of undergraduate or graduate degree program. Terms of repayment are based upon monthly income after graduation. Students should write between January 1 and March 31, giving brief personal history and identification of educational institution attended, the subject studied, date expected to complete studies and amount of funds needed. Enclose SASE with application.

Amount of award: $1,000-$5,000
Number of awards: 179
Number of applicants: 325
Application deadline: March 31
Notification begins: July 1
Total amount awarded: $486,000
Contact:
Hattie M. Strong Foundation
1620 Eye Street, NW
Suite 700
Washington, DC 20006-4005
Phone: 202-331-1619
Fax: 202-466-2894
Web: www.dml.georgetown.edu/scholarship/strong.html

Idaho State Board of Education

Idaho Education Incentive Loan Forgiveness Program

Type of award: Loan, renewable.
Intended use: For full-time undergraduate study. Designated institutions: Idaho postsecondary schools.
Eligibility: Applicant must be residing in Idaho.

Basis for selection: Major/career interest in education, teacher or nursing.
Application requirements: Must have graduated from Idaho secondary school within last two years.
Additional information: Loan forgiveness for teaching or nursing service in Idaho. Contact financial aid office of postsecondary Idaho public institutions for application materials and information.
Contact:
Financial aid office at designated institution

Kansas Board of Regents

Kansas Nursing Scholarship

Type of award: Loan, renewable.
Intended use: For full-time undergraduate, master's or non-degree study at postsecondary institution. Designated institutions: Kansas postsecondary schools with approved nursing programs.
Eligibility: Applicant must be U.S. citizen or permanent resident residing in Kansas.
Basis for selection: Major/career interest in nursing.
Application requirements: $10 application fee. Proof of eligibility. Complete State of Kansas Student Aid Application, FAFSA.
Additional information: Must obtain sponsorship from hospital or long-term care facility. Loan forgiveness for nursing service with sponsoring facility: one year for each year of financial assistance. One time $10 processing fee for any or all programs listed on application form.

Amount of award: $2,500-$3,500
Number of awards: 125
Application deadline: May 15
Notification begins: June 15
Total amount awarded: $412,000
Contact:
Kansas Board of Regents
700 SW Harrison
Suite 1410
Topeka, KS 66603-3760
Phone: 785-296-3517
Web: www.kansasregents.com

Kentucky Higher Education Assistance Authority (KHEAA)

Kentucky Teacher Scholarship

Type of award: Loan, renewable.
Intended use: For full-time undergraduate or graduate study at 2-year, 4-year or graduate institution. Designated institutions: Postsecondary institutions in Kentucky.
Eligibility: Applicant must be U.S. citizen residing in Kentucky.
Basis for selection: Major/career interest in education, teacher; education, early childhood or education, special. Applicant must demonstrate financial need.

Application requirements: Proof of eligibility. FAFSA, separate application.

Additional information: Must enroll in course of study leading to Kentucky teacher certification. Loan forgiveness for teaching in Kentucky schools: one semester for each semester of financial assistance, two semesters if service is in teacher shortage area. Cannot be enrolled in a program that leads to degree, diploma or certificate in religion, divinity or theology. Visit Website for additional information.

Amount of award:	$100-$5,000
Number of awards:	510
Number of applicants:	920
Application deadline:	May 1
Notification begins:	May 30
Total amount awarded:	$1,503,100

Contact:
Kentucky Higher Education Assistance Authority (KHEAA)
Teacher Scholarship Program
1050 U.S. 127 South
Frankfort, KY 40601-4323
Phone: 800-928-8926
Fax: 502-695-7345
Web: www.kheaa.com

Knights of Columbus

Knights of Columbus Student Loan

Type of award: Loan, renewable.
Intended use: For undergraduate or master's study at 2-year or 4-year institution. Designated institutions: Schools recognized by U.S. government under Federal Stafford Loan program.
Eligibility: Applicant or parent must be member/participant of Knights of Columbus. Applicant must be Roman Catholic. Applicant must be U.S. citizen or permanent resident.
Basis for selection: Applicant must demonstrate financial need.
Application requirements: Proof of eligibility.
Additional information: Available to Knights of Columbus members, wives and children of active and deceased members, and Columbian Squires members. Nonmember priests, brothers, nuns, seminarians and postulants at college, seminary, and postgraduate levels also eligible. Contact sponsor for loan amounts and interest rates.

Contact:
Knights of Columbus
Student Loan Committee
P.O. Box 1670
New Haven, CT 06507
Phone: 203-772-2130 ext. 224

Maine Education Services

Maine Loan

Type of award: Loan.
Intended use: For undergraduate or graduate study at accredited vocational, 2-year, 4-year or graduate institution in United States or Canada.
Eligibility: Applicant must be residing in Maine.

Application requirements: Proof of eligibility. Income information/credit analysis.
Additional information: Loans available to Maine residents for school of their choice. Out-of-state students attending Maine schools also eligible. May borrow full cost of education minus other financial aid. Loans are not forgiveable. Amount of loan varies.

Amount of award:	$2,000
Number of awards:	771
Number of applicants:	1,308
Total amount awarded:	$6,160,000

Contact:
Maine Education Services
One City Center, 11th Floor
Portland, ME 04101
Phone: 800-922-6352
Web: www.mesfoundation.com

Maryland Higher Education Commission State Scholarship Administration

Maryland Distinguished Scholar: Teacher Education Program

Type of award: Loan, renewable.
Intended use: For full-time freshman, sophomore, junior or senior study at accredited 2-year or 4-year institution. Designated institutions: Eligible institutions in Maryland.
Eligibility: Applicant must be high school senior. Applicant must be U.S. citizen or permanent resident residing in Maryland.
Basis for selection: Major/career interest in education, teacher; education, early childhood or education, special.
Additional information: Must enroll in course of study leading to teacher certification. Awardees agree to work as teacher in Maryland. Must work one year for each year, or portion thereof, award held. Must be recipient of Distinguished Scholar Award. Award automatically renewed if 3.0 GPA maintained.

Amount of award:	$3,000
Number of awards:	80
Application deadline:	July 1
Notification begins:	August 31
Total amount awarded:	$241,500

Contact:
Maryland Higher Education Commission State Scholarship Administration
Distinguished Scholar Teacher Ed. Program
16 Francis Street
Annapolis, MD 21401-1781
Phone: 410-260-4565
Web: www.mhec.state.md.us

Maryland HOPE Scholarship Program Community College Transfer Student Hope Scholarship

Type of award: Loan, renewable.
Intended use: For full-time undergraduate study. Designated institutions: Maryland institutions.

Eligibility: Applicant must be U.S. citizen or permanent resident residing in Maryland.
Application requirements: Transcript, proof of eligibility. FAFSA and completed HOPE Scholarship Program application form.
Additional information: Applicant must have earned associate's degree or be community college student with at least 60 credits and be accepted into degree program at four-year institution. Minimum 3.0 GPA. Applicant must have combined annual family income of $80,000 or less. Awardees agree to work full-time in Maryland one year for every year award held.

Amount of award:	$3,000
Application deadline:	March 1

Contact:
Maryland Higher Education Commission State Scholarship Administration
16 Francis Street
Annapolis, MD 24101-1781
Phone: 410-260-4565
Web: www.mhec.state.md.us

Maryland Loan Assistance Repayment Program

Type of award: Loan, renewable.
Intended use: For undergraduate study. Designated institutions: Maryland schools.
Eligibility: Applicant must be residing in Maryland.
Basis for selection: Applicant must demonstrate financial need.
Additional information: Loan repayment program for graduates who received degree from Maryland institution and are working for state or local government or nonprofit sector in Maryland. Priority given to current critical shortage fields. Applications available June through September.

Amount of award:	$200-$7,500
Number of awards:	270
Application deadline:	September 30
Notification begins:	October 31
Total amount awarded:	$788,706

Contact:
Maryland Higher Education Commission State Scholarship Administration
Loan Assistance Repayment Program
16 Francis Street
Annapolis, MD 21401-1781
Phone: 410-260-4565
Web: www.mhec.state.md.us

Massachusetts Board of Higher Education

Massachusetts No Interest Loan

Type of award: Loan.
Intended use: For full-time undergraduate study at accredited vocational, 2-year or 4-year institution. Designated institutions: Massachusetts institutions.
Eligibility: Applicant must be U.S. citizen or permanent resident residing in Massachusetts.
Basis for selection: Applicant must demonstrate financial need.
Application requirements: Submit FAFSA.

Amount of award:	$1,000-$4,000
Number of applicants:	5,000
Application deadline:	March 16
Total amount awarded:	$9,200,000

Contact:
Office of Student Financial Assistance
Massachusetts Board of Higher Education
454 Broadway, Suite 200
Revere, MA 02151
Phone: 617-727-9420

Michigan Higher Education Student Loan Authority

Michigan Alternative Student Loan (MI-LOAN)

Type of award: Loan.
Intended use: For undergraduate or graduate study. Designated institutions: Degree granting colleges & universities located in Michigan.
Eligibility: Applicant must be at least 18. Applicant must be U.S. citizen or permanent resident.
Basis for selection: Applicant must demonstrate financial need.
Application requirements: Proof of eligibility.
Additional information: MI-LOAN consists of two programs: Creditworthy Loan Program and Credit Ready Loan Program. Creditworthy program applicants must not be in default on any educational loans and must meet all credit standards. Credit Ready program applicants must attend certain eligible schools, but income, expenses and employment history not reviewed. Students or parents/guardians eligible to apply; student may be emancipated minor. Students can be attending less than half-time.

Amount of award:	$500-$125,000
Number of applicants:	12,500
Total amount awarded:	$75,000,000

Contact:
Michigan Higher Education Student Loan Authority
MI-LOAN Program
P.O. Box 30051
Lansing, MI 48909
Phone: 888-964-2890
Web: www.MI-StudentAid.org

Minnesota Higher Education Services Office

Minnesota Student Educational Loan Fund (SELF)

Type of award: Loan.
Intended use: For undergraduate or graduate study at vocational, 2-year, 4-year or graduate institution.
Eligibility: Applicant must be U.S. citizen or permanent resident residing in Minnesota.
Additional information: May be Minnesota resident attending eligible out-of-state institution or student attending

Loans

eligible Minnesota institution. Must seek aid from all other sources before applying, except Federal unsubsidized & subsidized Stafford loans, National Direct Student loans, HEAL loans, other private loans. Institution must approve application. Maximum eligibility for freshmen and sophomores $4,500; juniors, seniors and fifth year students $6,000; graduate students $9,000.

Amount of award:	$500-$9,000
Number of awards:	22,840
Total amount awarded:	$81,101,654

Contact:
MHESO
1450 Energy Park Drive, Suite 350
St. Paul, MN 55108-5227
Phone: 651-642-0567 or 800-657-3866
Web: www.mheso.state.mn.us

Mississippi Office of Student Financial Aid

Mississippi Health Care Professional Loan/Scholarship

Type of award: Loan, renewable.
Intended use: For full-time junior, senior or graduate study at accredited postsecondary institution. Designated institutions: Mississippi public institutions.
Eligibility: Applicant must be residing in Mississippi.
Basis for selection: Major/career interest in occupational therapy; speech pathology/audiology or psychology. Applicant must demonstrate high academic achievement.
Application requirements: Proof of eligibility.
Additional information: Must be enrolled in accredited training program of critical need in Mississippi public institution. Loan forgiveness for service in Mississippi health care institution: one year for each year of financial assistance, with a maximum of two years. Eligible junior and senior year.

Amount of award:	$1,500
Application deadline:	March 31
Notification begins:	August 1
Total amount awarded:	$30,000

Contact:
Mississippi Office of Student Financial Aid
3825 Ridgewood Road
Jackson, MS 39211-6453
Phone: 601-432-6997

Mississippi Nursing Education Loan/Scholarship

Type of award: Loan, renewable.
Intended use: For undergraduate, master's or doctoral study at accredited 4-year or graduate institution. Designated institutions: Mississippi public or pivate schools.
Eligibility: Applicant must be U.S. citizen residing in Mississippi.
Basis for selection: Major/career interest in nursing; nurse practitioner; pediatric nurse practitioner; health education or health-related professions. Applicant must demonstrate high academic achievement.
Application requirements: Proof of eligibility.
Additional information: Loan forgiveness for nursing service in Mississippi, one year for each year of financial assistance,

for a maximum of two years. Undergraduate awards for RN to BSN and BSN study.

Amount of award:	$1,500-$5,000
Application deadline:	March 31
Notification begins:	August 1
Total amount awarded:	$620,859

Contact:
Mississippi Office of Student Financial Aid
3825 Ridgewood Road
Jackson, MS 39211-6453
Phone: 601-432-6997

Mississippi William Winter Teacher Scholar Loan Program

Type of award: Loan, renewable.
Intended use: For full-time undergraduate study at postsecondary institution. Designated institutions: Mississippi schools.
Eligibility: Applicant must be U.S. citizen residing in Mississippi.
Basis for selection: Major/career interest in education, teacher. Applicant must demonstrate high academic achievement.
Application requirements: Proof of eligibility.
Additional information: Entering freshmen must have 3.0 GPA and ACT score of at least 21. Undergraduate applicants must have 2.5 college GPA. Loan forgiveness for teaching service in Mississippi public school or public school district: one year for each year of financial assistance, for a maximum of four years. Early decision deadline April 1, regular deadline April 30.

Amount of award:	$1,000-$3,000
Application deadline:	March 31
Notification begins:	August 1
Total amount awarded:	$3,416,831

Contact:
Miss. Office of Student Financial Aid
3825 Ridgewood Road
Jackson, MS 39211-6453
Phone: 601-432-6997

Missouri Coordinating Board for Higher Education

Advantage Missouri Program

Type of award: Loan, renewable.
Intended use: For full-time undergraduate study at postsecondary institution. Designated institutions: Participating post secondary Missouri institutions.
Eligibility: Applicant must be U.S. citizen or permanent resident residing in Missouri.
Basis for selection: Applicant must demonstrate financial need.
Application requirements: Must be Missouri resident. Must file FAFSA by April 1st before the upcoming year.
Additional information: This is a loan forgiveness program. The student must pursue an occupation in a designated area of high demand in Missouri. The student has one year after graduation to obtain employment in the designated high-demand occupation. One year of loans will be forgiven for each full year of employment. For information about the designated high demand occupational fields and related academic programs,

Loans

contact your school's financial aid office or MOSTARS 573-751-3940.

Amount of award:	$200-$2,500
Number of awards:	1,322
Application deadline:	April 1
Total amount awarded:	$2,876,836

Contact:
Missouri Coordinating Board for Higher Education
3515 Amazonas Drive
Jeffserson City, MO 65109
Phone: 800-473-6757
Web: www.cbhe.state.mo.us

Navy-Marine Corps Relief Society

Vice Admiral E.P. Travers Loan

Type of award: Loan, renewable.
Intended use: For full-time undergraduate study.
Eligibility: Applicant must be U.S. citizen. Applicant must be dependent of active service person or veteran; or spouse of active service person or veteran in the Marines or Navy.
Basis for selection: Applicant must demonstrate financial need.
Application requirements: Proof of eligibility. Current military I.D. required for both applicant and servicemember.
Additional information: Loan must be repaid in allotments over 24-month period (minimum monthly repayment is $50) and are not forgiveable. Must reapply to renew. Minimum 2.0 GPA.

Amount of award:	$500-$3,000
Application deadline:	March 1

Contact:
Navy-Marine Corps Relief Society
801 North Randolph Street
Room 1228
Arlington, VA 22203

New Hampshire Higher Education Loan Corporation

TREE, The Resource for Education Expenses

Type of award: Loan, renewable.
Intended use: For undergraduate or graduate study.
Eligibility: Applicant must be residing in New Hampshire.
Additional information: Must be New Hampshire resident enrolled in institution anywhere in U.S. or non-resident enrolled in New Hampshire institution. Fee of six to eight percent of principal borrowed charged upon disbursement.

Amount of award:	$500-$15,000

Contact:
New Hampshire Higher Education Assistance Foundation (NHHEAF)
P.O. Box 877
Concord, NH 03302
Phone: 800-525-2577
Web: www.nhheaf.org

New Hampshire Postsecondary Education Commission

Career Incentive Program

Type of award: Loan, renewable.
Intended use: For full-time undergraduate or graduate study at accredited 2-year, 4-year or graduate institution. Designated institutions: New Hampshire institutions.
Eligibility: Applicant must be U.S. citizen or permanent resident residing in New Hampshire.
Basis for selection: Major/career interest in education, special; foreign languages; nursing or nurse practitioner. Applicant must demonstrate financial need.
Application requirements: Must be NH resident for 12 months prior to applying.
Additional information: Loan amount is up to maximum of $1,500/semester.

Application deadline:	June 1, December 15

Contact:
New Hampshire Postsecondary Education Commission
2 Industrial Park Drive
Concord, NH 03301-8512
Phone: 603-271-2555
Fax: 603-271-2696
Web: www.state.nh.us/postsecondary

New Jersey Higher Education Student Assistance Authority

New Jersey Class Loan Program

Type of award: Loan, renewable.
Intended use: For undergraduate or graduate study at accredited vocational, 2-year, 4-year or graduate institution in United States. Designated institutions: Approved institutions.
Eligibility: Applicant must be U.S. citizen or permanent resident residing in New Jersey.
Application requirements: Proof of eligibility.
Additional information: Must demonstrate credit-worthiness or provide co-signer. Parent or other eligible family member may borrow on behalf of student, or student may borrow. Must have filed all financial information required by the school to determine eligibility for a Federal Stafford Loan or a W.D. Ford Federal Direct Loan. Maximum loan amount varies, may not exceed education cost (less all other financial aid). Minimum loan amount $500. No interest subsidy. Call sponsor toll-free hotline/visit Website to obtain current fixed rates. Variable interest rate loans available for graduate students. Apply year-round. Three and a half percent administrative fee deducted from gross loan amount. Out-of-state students who attend an approved New Jersey School are also eligible.
Contact:
New Jersey Higher Education Student Assistance Authority
4 Quakerbridge Plaza, P.O. Box 540
Trenton, NJ 08625-0540
Phone: 800-792-8670
Web: www.hesaa.org

New Mexico Commission on Higher Education

New Mexico Allied Health Student Loan-for-Service Program

Type of award: Loan, renewable.
Intended use: For undergraduate or graduate study at accredited postsecondary institution. Designated institutions: Public New Mexico postsecondary institutions.
Eligibility: Applicant must be U.S. citizen or permanent resident residing in New Mexico.
Basis for selection: Major/career interest in health-related professions; occupational therapy; mental health/therapy; physical therapy; pharmacy/pharmaceutics/pharmacology or dietetics/nutrition. Applicant must demonstrate financial need.
Application requirements: FAFSA.
Additional information: Loan forgiveness offered to those who practice in medically underserved areas in New Mexico. Must be accepted by or enrolled in following allied health programs at accredited New Mexico public postsecondary institution: physical therapy, occupational therapy, speech-language pathology, audiology, pharmacy, nutrition, respiratory care, laboratory technology, radiologic technology, mental health services, emergency medical services, or licensed or certified health profession as defined by Commission. Call sponsor number or visit Website for application.
>   **Amount of award:** $12,000
>   **Application deadline:** July 1

Contact:
New Mexico Commission on Higher Education
Financial Aid and Student Services
1068 Cerrillos Road
Santa Fe, NM 87501
Phone: 800-279-9777
Web: www.nmche.org/

New Mexico Medical Student Loan-for-Service

Type of award: Loan, renewable.
Intended use: For undergraduate or first professional study in United States. Designated institutions: Accredited public schools of medicine.
Eligibility: Applicant must be U.S. citizen or permanent resident residing in New Mexico.
Basis for selection: Major/career interest in medicine or physician assistant. Applicant must demonstrate financial need.
Application requirements: FAFSA.
Additional information: Loan forgiveness for New Mexico residents to practice in medically underserved areas in New Mexico. Part-time students eligible for pro-rated awards. Preference given to students accepted for enrollment at the UNM School of Medicine. Number of awards and total dollar amount cover (cumulatively) New Mexico's higher education loan programs.
>   **Amount of award:** $12,000
>   **Application deadline:** July 1

Contact:
New Mexico Commission on Higher Education
Financial Aid and Student Services
1068 Cerrillos Road
Santa Fe, NM 87501
Phone: 800-279-9777
Web: www.nmche.org/

New Mexico Nursing Student Loan-for-Service

Type of award: Loan, renewable.
Intended use: For undergraduate or graduate study at accredited 2-year or 4-year institution. Designated institutions: New Mexico postsecondary institutions.
Eligibility: Applicant must be U.S. citizen or permanent resident residing in New Mexico.
Basis for selection: Major/career interest in nursing. Applicant must demonstrate financial need.
Application requirements: FAFSA.
Additional information: Loan forgiveness to New Mexico resident for practice in medically underserved areas in New Mexico. Number of awards and total dollar amount cover (cumulatively) New Mexico's higher education loan programs.
>   **Amount of award:** $12,000
>   **Application deadline:** July 1

Contact:
New Mexico Commission on Higher Education
Financial Aid and Student Services
1068 Cerrillos Road
Santa Fe, NM 87501
Phone: 800-279-9777
Web: www.nmche.org/

Southeastern New Mexico Teacher's Loan-for-Service

Type of award: Loan.
Intended use: For undergraduate or post-bachelor's certificate study at accredited postsecondary institution. Designated institutions: Public New Mexico postsecondary institutions.
Eligibility: Applicant must be U.S. citizen or permanent resident residing in New Mexico.
Basis for selection: Major/career interest in education, teacher. Applicant must demonstrate financial need.
Application requirements: FAFSA.
Additional information: Must be current or former resident of Lea, Chaves, Roosevelt, Otero or Eddy counties. Loan forgiveness for qualified students who, after graduation, become teachers in any designated eligible county. Part-time students are eligible for pro-rated awards. Preference given to ethnic minorities and those with physical disabilities.
>   **Amount of award:** $4,000
>   **Application deadline:** July 1

Contact:
New Mexico Commission on Higher Education
Financial Aid and Student Services
1068 Cerrillos Road
Santa Fe, NM 87501
Phone: 800-279-9777
Web: www.nmche.org/

New York State Grange

Grange Student Loan Fund

Type of award: Loan, renewable.
Intended use: For full-time undergraduate or graduate study at postsecondary institution.
Eligibility: Applicant or parent must be member/participant of New York State Grange. Applicant must be residing in New York.
Basis for selection: Applicant must demonstrate financial need.
Additional information: Must send SASE for application.

Amount of award:	$2,000
Number of awards:	11
Number of applicants:	11
Application deadline:	April 15
Notification begins:	June 15
Total amount awarded:	$22,000

Contact:
New York State Grange
100 Grange Place
Cortland, NY 13045
Phone: 607-756-7553

North Carolina State Education Assistance Authority

North Carolina Nurse Education Scholarship Loan

Type of award: Loan.
Intended use: For undergraduate study at accredited 2-year or 4-year institution. Designated institutions: Designated North Carolina institutions.
Eligibility: Applicant must be U.S. citizen residing in North Carolina.
Basis for selection: Major/career interest in nursing. Applicant must demonstrate financial need and service orientation.
Application requirements: Proof of eligibility.
Additional information: Must attend specific participating North Carolina institutions. Applicant must be a resident of North Carolina for tuition purposes. Recipient agrees to work for one year as a full-time nurse in North Carolina for each year of NESLP funding. Nontraditional students, including older individuals, ethnic minorities, males and individuals with previous careers and/or degree encouraged to apply.

Amount of award:	$400-$5,000
Number of awards:	973
Total amount awarded:	$1,055,000

Contact:
Scholarship Loan Program
P.O. Box 14223
Research Triangle Park, NC 27709-4223
Phone: 1800-700-1775 ext. 624
Web: www.ncseaa.edu

North Carolina Nurse Scholars Program

Type of award: Loan, renewable.
Intended use: For full-time undergraduate study at accredited postsecondary institution. Designated institutions: North Carolina schools.
Eligibility: Applicant must be U.S. citizen residing in North Carolina.
Basis for selection: Major/career interest in nursing. Applicant must demonstrate high academic achievement, leadership and service orientation.
Application requirements: Recommendations, essay, transcript, proof of eligibility.
Additional information: Applicant must be a resident of North Carolina for tuition purposes. Minimum 3.0 GPA required for undergraduate applicants. Loan forgiveness for nursing service in North Carolina.

Amount of award:	$3,000-$5,000
Number of awards:	890
Number of applicants:	1,600
Application deadline:	February 15, May 3
Total amount awarded:	$4,000,000

Contact:
North Carolina Nurse Scholars Program
P.O. Box 14223
Research Triangle Park, NC 27709-4223
Phone: 1800-700-1775-624
Web: www.cfnc.org cfnc.org

North Carolina Student Loans for Health/Science/Mathematics

Type of award: Loan, renewable.
Intended use: For full-time undergraduate, master's or first professional study at accredited postsecondary institution in United States. Designated institutions: North Carolina institutions.
Eligibility: Applicant must be residing in North Carolina.
Basis for selection: Major/career interest in health-related professions; mathematics or science, general. Applicant must demonstrate financial need.
Application requirements: Transcript, proof of eligibility. FAFSA, Surety Statement.
Additional information: Must express commitment to practice health professions or teach underserved populations in North Carolina. Loan forgiveness for service in North Carolina is one year for each year of financial assistance.

Amount of award:	$500-$8,500
Number of awards:	421
Number of applicants:	1,400
Application deadline:	June 1
Notification begins:	July 1
Total amount awarded:	$2,765,267

Contact:
North Carolina Student Loan Program
Health, Science and Mathematics
P.O. Box 14223
Research Triangle Park, NC 27709-4223
Phone: 1800-700-1775-624
Web: www.cfnc.org

Loans

Ohio Board of Regents

Ohio Nurse Education Assistance Loan Program

Type of award: Loan, renewable.
Intended use: For freshman, sophomore, junior, senior, post-bachelor's certificate or master's study in United States. Designated institutions: Ohio Hospital School of Nursing, public supported college or university, private nonprofit college or university, or vocational school with an approved nursing education program.
Eligibility: Applicant must be U.S. citizen or permanent resident residing in Ohio.
Basis for selection: Major/career interest in nursing. Applicant must demonstrate financial need.
Additional information: Must be accepted to or enrolled in approved pre- or post-licensure licensed practical nurse or registered nurse nursing education program. Debt cancellation at rate of 20 percent per year (for maximum of four years) if borrower is employed in clinical practice of nursing in Ohio after graduation. Applications available January.

Amount of award:	$2,800
Number of awards:	98
Number of applicants:	446
Application deadline:	June 1
Notification begins:	July 15
Total amount awarded:	$271,103

Contact:
Contact college financial aid office for an application

Pickett and Hatcher Educational Fund, Inc.

Pickett and Hatcher Educational Loan

Type of award: Loan, renewable.
Intended use: For full-time freshman, sophomore, junior or senior study at 4-year institution. Designated institutions: Four-year institutions in Alabama, Florida, Georgia, Kentucky, Mississippi, North Carolina, South Carolina, Tennessee, and Virginia.
Eligibility: Applicant must be high school senior. Applicant must be U.S. citizen residing in Tennessee, Alabama, Virginia, Florida, Georgia, Kentucky, Mississippi, North Carolina or South Carolina.
Basis for selection: Applicant must demonstrate financial need and high academic achievement.
Application requirements: First-time applicant must be entering freshman.
Additional information: First-time applicants must be entering freshmen. Not available to law, medicine, or ministry students. Loans renewed up to $22,000.

Amount of award:	$1,000-$5,500
Number of awards:	510
Number of applicants:	1,400
Total amount awarded:	$2,480,374

Contact:
Pickett and Hatcher Educational Fund, Inc.
Loan Program
P.O. Box 8169
Columbus, GA 31908-8169
Phone: 706-327-6586
Fax: 706-324-6788

Presbyterian Church (USA)

Presbyterian Service Program for Undergraduates

Type of award: Loan.
Intended use: For full-time junior or senior study at accredited 4-year institution in United States.
Eligibility: Applicant must be Presbyterian. Applicant must be U.S. citizen or permanent resident.
Basis for selection: Applicant must demonstrate financial need and high academic achievement.
Application requirements: Recommendations, transcript.
Additional information: This service project is a one-time award. Recommendation must be from campus pastor or chaplain's office of institution. Difficulty of course work considered. In lieu of repayment may perform 250 hours volunteer service in Mission PC (USA), complete a campus or church-related project, or work with a community organization.

Amount of award:	$1,500
Number of applicants:	25
Application deadline:	April 1
Notification begins:	May 1
Total amount awarded:	$22,500

Contact:
Financial Aid for Studies
Presbyterian Church (USA)
100 Witherspoon Street, M011
Louisville, KY 40202-1396
Phone: 888-728-7228 ext. 5735
Fax: 502-569-8766

Presbyterian Undergraduate and Graduate Loan

Type of award: Loan, renewable.
Intended use: For full-time undergraduate or graduate study at accredited 2-year, 4-year or graduate institution in United States.
Eligibility: Applicant must be Presbyterian. Applicant must be U.S. citizen or permanent resident.
Basis for selection: Applicant must demonstrate financial need and high academic achievement.
Additional information: Must establish and maintain minimum 2.0 GPA. Contact office for current interest rates and deferment policies. Must give evidence of financial reliability. Undergraduates and graduates can apply for up to $7,000 spread out over three years. If student is in the last year of study and has not yet applied for these loans, undergraduates can apply for the full amount.

Amount of award:	$200-$7,000
Number of awards:	183
Application deadline:	April 1

Loans

Contact:
Presbyterian Church (USA)
Financial Aid for Studies
100 Witherspoon Street, M011
Louisville, KY 40202-1396
Phone: 888-728-7228 -5738
Fax: 502-569-8766
Web: www.pcusa.org/highered

Retired Officers Association

TROA Scholarship Fund

Type of award: Loan, renewable.
Intended use: For full-time undergraduate study at accredited 2-year or 4-year institution in United States.
Eligibility: Applicant must be no older than 24. Applicant must be U.S. citizen. Applicant must be dependent of disabled veteran, deceased veteran or POW/MIA.
Basis for selection: Applicant must demonstrate financial need, high academic achievement, depth of character, leadership, patriotism, seriousness of purpose and service orientation.
Application requirements: Transcript, proof of eligibility. Resume, SAT/ACT scores, and first page of most recent federal income tax form from student and parent, only if semifinalists.
Additional information: Loan is interest-free. Applicant must be under 24 and children of TROA members, active and retired enlisted personnel. If such a child served in Uniformed Service before completing college, maximum age for eligibility increased by number of years served--up to five years. Applications are only available through Website.

Amount of award:	$3,000
Number of applicants:	2,000
Application deadline:	March 1
Notification begins:	June 1
Total amount awarded:	$3,000

Contact:
Loan Committee
Attn.: EAP
201 North Washington Street
Alexandria, VA 22314-2529
Phone: 800-245-8762
Fax: 703-838-5819
Web: www.troa.org/education

South Carolina Student Loan Corporation

South Carolina Teacher Loans

Type of award: Loan, renewable.
Intended use: For freshman, sophomore, junior, senior or graduate study at accredited 2-year, 4-year or graduate institution. Designated institutions: South Carolina institutions.
Eligibility: Applicant must be U.S. citizen residing in South Carolina.
Basis for selection: Major/career interest in education, teacher; education; education, early childhood or education, special. Applicant must demonstrate financial need and high academic achievement.

Application requirements: FAFSA.
Additional information: Master's or graduate study eligible only if required for initial teacher certification. Entering freshman must have minimum SAT I score of 838 (ACT 19.1); rank in top 40 percent of high school class. First-time undergraduate and entering graduate applicants must have 2.75 GPA and have passed Education Entrance Examination. Graduate applicant must have 3.5 GPA. Loan forgiveness for service in teacher shortage area in South Carolina public schools: 20 percent for each year of service, 33 percent if service in geographic and subject shortage area. $1,250 part-time maximum, $2,500 full-time maximum.

Amount of award:	$2,500
Number of awards:	13
Application deadline:	June 1
Notification begins:	July 15
Total amount awarded:	$12,500,000

Contact:
South Carolina Student Loan Corporation
P.O. Box 21487
Columbia, SC 29221
Phone: 803-737-2260
Web: www.slc.sc.edu/

Student Aid Foundation

Student Aid Foundation Undergraduate Loan

Type of award: Loan, renewable.
Intended use: For full-time undergraduate, master's, doctoral or first professional study at accredited vocational, 2-year, 4-year or graduate institution in United States.
Eligibility: Applicant must be female. Applicant must be U.S. citizen residing in Georgia.
Basis for selection: Applicant must demonstrate financial need, high academic achievement and seriousness of purpose.
Application requirements: Recommendations, essay, transcript.
Additional information: Non-Georgia residents attending Georgia institutions can qualify. Loan not forgivable. Must have financially responsible endorser. Minimum GPA of 3.0. Send SASE with request for application.

Amount of award:	$3,000-$4,000
Number of awards:	100
Application deadline:	April 15
Notification begins:	June 1

Contact:
Student Aid Foundation
2520 East Piedmont Road
Suite F180
Marietta, GA 30062
Phone: 770-973-7077

Texas Higher Education Coordinating Board

Hinson-Hazlewood College Access Loan (CAL)

Type of award: Loan.
Intended use: For undergraduate or graduate study at 2-year, 4-year or graduate institution. Designated institutions: Public and private non-profit postsecondary institutions in Texas.
Eligibility: Applicant must be U.S. citizen or permanent resident residing in Texas.
Application requirements: Cosigner required.
Additional information: Texas colleges and universities have a limited number of CAL loans. Applicants need not show financial need. The loan may be used to cover the family's expected contribution (EFC). Cosigners must have good credit and meet other program criteria. Total amount available for loan is $7,500 per academic year or lifetime total of $30,000. Applicants should contact their college/university financial aid office for other information and application packet.

Number of awards:	21,299
Total amount awarded:	$53,821,592

Contact:
Texas Higher Education Coordinating Board
Student Services Division
P. O. Box 12788
Austin, TX 12788-2788
Phone: 800-242-3062
Fax: 512-427-6420
Web: www.collegefortexans.com

Hinson-Hazlewood College Student Loan Program-Health Education Loan Program

Type of award: Loan, renewable.
Intended use: For undergraduate or graduate study at 2-year, 4-year or graduate institution. Designated institutions: Public postsecondary institutions institutions in Texas.
Eligibility: Applicant must be permanent resident residing in Texas.
Basis for selection: Major/career interest in health education; health sciences or medicine. Applicant must demonstrate financial need.
Application requirements: Proof of eligibility.
Additional information: Average award varies. Renewable loans for applicants enrolled full-time. Renewable up to four years. Provides loans when overall state demand exceeds federal funding.

Number of awards:	3,263
Total amount awarded:	$14,663,816

Contact:
Contact the college/university financial aid office to apply.
Phone: 800-242-3062
Web: www.collegefortexans,com

Teach for Texas Conditional Grant Program

Type of award: Loan.

Intended use: For junior or senior study at 4-year institution. Designated institutions: Colleges and universities offering degree programs leading to teacher certification.
Eligibility: Applicant must be residing in Texas.
Additional information: Student loan with cancellation provisions for teaching. Available only to upper division students. Must be enrolled in a teaching field designated as having a critical shortage of teachers or agree to teach in Texas community with certified critical shortage of teachers.
Contact:
Texas Higher Education Coordinating Board
Student Services Division
P. O. Box 12788
Austin, TX 78711-2788
Phone: 800-242-3062
Fax: 512-427-6420
Web: www.thecb.state.tx.us

U.S. Department of Education

Federal Direct Stafford Loans

Type of award: Loan, renewable.
Intended use: For undergraduate or graduate study at postsecondary institution.
Eligibility: Applicant must be U.S. citizen or permanent resident.
Basis for selection: Applicant must demonstrate financial need.
Application requirements: Proof of eligibility. Send FAFSA, loan application and promissory note.
Additional information: Must not have defaulted on federal grant or educational loan. Maximum interest rate 8.25 percent. Some loans subsidized, based on need eligibilty. Telecommunications Device for the Deaf at 800-730-8913. FAFSA available online. Student financial aid guide available online at www.ed.gov/StudentGuide.

Amount of award:	$2,500-$15,000
Application deadline:	June 30
Notification begins:	August 29

Contact:
Federal Student Aid Information Center
PO Box 84
Washington, DC 20044-0084
Phone: 800-4-FED-AID
Web: www.ed.gov

Federal Family Education Loan Program

Type of award: Loan, renewable.
Intended use: For undergraduate or graduate study at accredited postsecondary institution in or outside United States or Canada. Designated institutions: Schools approved by the U.S. Department of Education.
Eligibility: Applicant must be U.S. citizen or permanent resident.
Basis for selection: Applicant must demonstrate financial need.
Application requirements: Proof of eligibility. Send FAFSA.
Additional information: Subsidized and unsubsidized loans. Maximum combined loan total $23,000 (dependent

undergraduates), $46,000 (independent undergraduates), and $138,500 (graduate or professional). Repayment period 5-10 years. Alternate phone number: 800-730-8913. Must not have defaulted on federal grant or educational loan.

Application deadline: July 2
Contact:
Federal Student Aid Information Center
PO Box 84
Washington, DC 20044-0084
Phone: 800-4-FED-AID
Web: www.ed.gov

Federal Perkins Loan

Type of award: Loan, renewable.
Intended use: For undergraduate or graduate study at accredited postsecondary institution in United States.
Eligibility: Applicant must be U.S. citizen or permanent resident.
Basis for selection: Applicant must demonstrate financial need.
Application requirements: Proof of eligibility. Send FAFSA.
Additional information: Loan limits: $15,000 for undergraduate study ($3,000 per year), $30,000 for graduate study--including undergraduate loan ($5,000 per year). Repayment begins nine months after course load drops below one-half time. Interest 5 percent. Alternate phone number: 800-730-8913. Must demonstrate exceptional financial need. Must not have defaulted on federal grant or educational loan.

Application deadline: July 2
Contact:
Federal Student Aid Information Center
PO Box 84
Washington, DC 20044-0084
Phone: 800-4-FED AID
Web: www.ed.gov

Federal Plus Loan

Type of award: Loan.
Intended use: For undergraduate or graduate study at accredited postsecondary institution in or outside United States or Canada. Designated institutions: Schools approved by the U.S. Department of Education.
Eligibility: Applicant must be U.S. citizen or permanent resident.
Basis for selection: Applicant must demonstrate financial need.
Application requirements: Must pass credit check. Must file PLUS loan application and sign promissory note.
Additional information: Loans for parents of student. First payment within 60 days. Term up to ten years. Alternate phone number: 800-730-8913. Must not have defaulted on federal grant or educational loan. FAFSA available online. Yearly loan limit equal to student's cost of attendance minus any other financial aid received. Interest rate is flexible, but capped at 9 percent annually.

Application deadline: June 30
Notification begins: August 29
Contact:
Federal Student Aid Information Center
PO Box 84
Washington, DC 20044-0084
Phone: 800-4-FED-AID
Web: www.ed.gov

United Methodist Church

United Methodist Loan Program

Type of award: Loan, renewable.
Intended use: For undergraduate or graduate study at accredited postsecondary institution in United States.
Eligibility: Applicant must be United Methodist. Applicant must be U.S. citizen or permanent resident.
Additional information: Must be active member of United Methodist Church one year prior to application. Must maintain "C" average. May reapply for loan to maximum of $15,000. Interest rate 6%; cosigner required. Ten years permitted to repay loan after graduation or withdrawal from school.
Amount of award: $2,400
Contact:
United Methodist Church/ Board of Higher Education and Ministry
Office of Loans and Scholarships
P.O. Box 340007
Nashville, TN 37203-0007

United Parcel Service

United Parcel Service Earn & Learn Program Loans

Type of award: Loan.
Intended use: For half-time undergraduate study at accredited vocational, 2-year or 4-year institution in United States.
Eligibility: Applicant or parent must be employed by United Parcel Service (UPS).
Application requirements: Proof of eligibility. Must be UPS employee at participating location.
Additional information: Award is $2,000 per year in forgivable student loans. UPS pays back loan as long as student remains employed by UPS. Visit Website for specifics.
Contact:
United Parcel Service
55 Glenlake Parkway N.E.
Atlanta, GA 30328
Web: www.upsjobs.com

Utah State Office of Education

Utah Career Teaching Scholarship/ T.H. Bell Teaching Incentive Loan

Type of award: Loan, renewable.
Intended use: For full-time undergraduate study at accredited postsecondary institution. Designated institutions: Utah-based schools.
Eligibility: Applicant must be high school senior. Applicant must be U.S. citizen residing in Utah.
Basis for selection: Major/career interest in education, teacher; education; education, early childhood or education, special.

Additional information: Provides tuition waiver with additional awards to limited number of qualified recipients. Loan forgiveness for teaching in Utah public schools. Application available after Jan. 15.

Amount of award:	Full tuition
Number of awards:	50
Number of applicants:	320
Application deadline:	March 31
Notification begins:	May 15

Contact:
High school counselor or financial aid officer

Vermont Student Assistance Corporation

Vermont Extra Classic Loan

Type of award: Loan.
Intended use: For undergraduate or graduate study at vocational, 2-year, 4-year or graduate institution in United States.
Eligibility: Applicant must be U.S. citizen residing in Vermont.
Basis for selection: Applicant must demonstrate financial need.
Additional information: Applicant must be enrolled in degree program. Student's school must be eligible for Title 4 loans. Loan eligibility based on credit and income requirements. Most borrowers need co-signer to meet income qualifications. Co-signer must be creditworthy and agree to be equally responsible for debt. Students must be Vermont residents or enrolled in Vermont postsecondary institution. Students must first borrow maximum allowed under Federal (Stafford) loans through VSAC or Vermont direct-lending institution. Maximum loan equals cost of admission minus other financial aid. If parents eligible for PLUS loan, student cannot use this program.
Contact:
Vermont Student Assistance Corporation
Education Loan Finance Department
P.O. Box 900
Winooski, VT 05404

Virgin Islands Board of Education

Virgin Islands Territorial Grants/ Loans Program

Type of award: Loan, renewable.
Intended use: For full-time undergraduate or graduate study at accredited postsecondary institution.
Eligibility: Applicant must be U.S. citizen or permanent resident residing in Virgin Islands.
Basis for selection: Applicant must demonstrate financial need and high academic achievement.
Application requirements: Transcript. Application, acceptance letter from institution for first-time applicants or transfer students.
Additional information: Combined loan and grant program to assist Virgin Islands residents. For off-island study, maximum award is $2,500. Minimum required GPA 2.0. Must agree to

accept employment in Virgin Islands government one year for every year of award upon completion of studies. Number of awards and amounts vary.

Amount of award:	$500-$1,500
Application deadline:	May 1

Contact:
Scholarship Committee
Virgin Islands Board of Education
P.O. Box 11900
St. Thomas, VI 801
Phone: 340-774-4546

West Virginia Higher Education Policy Commission

West Virginia Underwood-Smith Teacher Scholarship

Type of award: Loan, renewable.
Intended use: For full-time junior, senior or graduate study at 2-year, 4-year or graduate institution. Designated institutions: West Virginia institutions.
Eligibility: Applicant must be U.S. citizen or permanent resident residing in West Virginia.
Basis for selection: Major/career interest in education, teacher. Applicant must demonstrate high academic achievement.
Application requirements: Essay, proof of eligibility.
Additional information: Must rank in top 10 percent of class. Must be permanent resident of West Virginia. Undergraduate applicants must be juniors or seniors already majoring in education. Number of applicants varies.

Amount of award:	$5,000
Number of awards:	51
Application deadline:	April 15
Notification begins:	July 1
Total amount awarded:	$227,646

Contact:
West Virginia Higher Education Policy Commission
Underwood-Smith Teacher Scholarship Program
1018 Kanawha Boulevard East, Suite 700
Charleston, WV 25301-2827
Phone: 304-558-4618
Web: www.hepc.wvnet.edu

Wisconsin Department of Veterans Affairs

Wisconsin Veterans Affairs Personal Loan Program

Type of award: Loan.
Intended use: For undergraduate or graduate study at postsecondary institution in United States.
Eligibility: Applicant must be residing in Wisconsin. Applicant must be veteran; or dependent of veteran or deceased veteran; or spouse of veteran or deceased veteran. Must meet WDVA

Loans

Service requirements. Must have 90 days of active duty during wartime and/or two years of continuous active duty.

Application requirements: Applicant must either have been a resident of Wisconsin on entry into military service or a continuous resident of Wisconsin for at least five years immediately preceding the application date. Must be a current Wisconsin resident.

Additional information: Loan amount up to $10,000 annually. May be used for veteran's education and for education of veteran's children or spouse. Subsidized annual interest rate varies and has a ten-year term. Apply to local county Veterans' Service Officer to establish eligibility.

Contact:
Wisconsin Department of Veterans Affairs
PO Box 7843
30 West Mifflin Street
Madison, WI 53703-7843
Phone: 800-947-8387
Web: www.dva.state.wi.us

Wisconsin Higher Educational Aids Board

Wisconsin Minority Teacher Loan Program

Type of award: Loan, renewable.
Intended use: For full-time junior or senior study at accredited 4-year institution.
Eligibility: Applicant must be Asian American, African American, Mexican American, Hispanic American, Puerto Rican or American Indian. Asian American applicants must be either former citizens or descendants of former citizens of Laos, Vietnam, or Cambodia. Applicant must be residing in Wisconsin.
Basis for selection: Major/career interest in education; education, special or education, teacher. Applicant must demonstrate financial need.
Application requirements: Nomination by Student Financial Aid Department. FAFSA.
Additional information: Recipient must agree to teach in Wisconsin school district where minority students constitute at least 29% of enrollment. For each year student teaches in eligible district, 25% of loan is forgiven; otherwise loan must be repaid at interest rate of 5%.

Amount of award:	$250-$2,500
Number of awards:	117
Total amount awarded:	$236,978

Contact:
Higher Educational Aids Board
Attn: Mary Lou Kuzdas
131 West Wilson
Madison, WI 53707
Phone: 608-267-2212

Sponsor Index

Program Index

Kansas State Scholarship, 276
Kansas Teacher Scholarship, 276
Kansas Vocational Scholarship, 277
Kaplan/Newsweek "My Turn" Essay
   Contest, 277
Kappa Kappa Gamma
   Scholarship, 277
Karl F. Hoenecke Memorial
   Scholarship, 219
Karla Scherer Foundation
   Scholarship, 277
Katharine M. Grosscup
   Scholarship, 230
Katherine F. Gruber Scholarship
   Program, 171
Kathleen S. Anderson Award, 293
Kathryn D. Sullivan Science and
   Engineering Undergraduate
   Fellowship, 317
Kawasaki-McGaha Scholarship
   Fund, 245
Keane Educational Scholarship, 278
Kemper Scholars Grant Program, 272
Kennedy Library Archival
   Internship, 530
Kenneth Andrew Roe Mechanical
   Engineering Scholarship, 146
Kenneth F. Merrill Scholarship, 303
Kenneth Jernigan Memorial
   Scholarship, 335
Kentucky College Access Program
   Grant (KCAPG), 278
Kentucky Educational Excellence
   Scholarship (KEES), 278
Kentucky Teacher Scholarship, 571
Kentucky Tuition Grant, 278
Kentucky Work-Study Program, 531
KIMT Weather/News Internships, 531
King Olav V Norwegian-American
   Heritage Fund, 443
The Klumb Family Scholarship
   Program, 154
K.M. Hatano Scholarship, 244
Knights of Columbus Student
   Loan, 572
Knights Templar Educational
   Foundation Loan, 570
Kohler Co. College Scholarship
   Program, 279
Koloa Scholarship, 245
Kosciuszko Foundation Tuition
   Scholarships, 279
Kosciuszko Foundation Year Abroad
   Program, 280
Kottis Family Award, 206
Kucher-Killian Memorial
   Scholarship, 335
L. Gordon Bittle Memorial
   Scholarship for Student CTA, 186
L. Phil Wicker Scholarship, 138
Laidlaw Scholarship, 280
Lance Stafford Larson Student
   Scholarship, 256
Larry R. Strand Memorial Scholarship
   Program, 462
LaSPACE Undergraduate Research
   Assistantship, 289

Latin American Educational
   Scholarship, 283
Latin Honor Society Scholarship, 73
Laura Blackburn Memorial
   Scholarship, 99
Laura N. Dowsett Fund, 245
Law and Social Sciences Summer
   Research Fellowship for Minority
   Undergraduates, 510
Lawrence R. Foster Memorial
   Scholarship, 388
Leaders of Tomorrow
   Scholarship, 369
Lee Dubin Scholarship, 194
Lee Tarbox Memorial Scholarship, 63
Leggett & Platt Scholarship Program
   for Children of Employees, 285
Legion Oratorical Contest, 99
Lele Cassin Scholarship, 265
Len Allen Award of Merit, 406
Leo Burnett Scholarship Program, 478
Leon Harris/Les Nichols Memorial to
   Spartan School of Aeronautics, 63
Leonard M. Perryman
   Communications Scholarship for
   Ethnic Minority Students, 474
Leroy E. Dettman Foundation
   Scholarship, 285
Lesbian Leadership Scholarship, 152
Lester F. Kuzmick Memorial
   Scholarship, 202
Leveraging Educational Assistance
   Partnership Program, 313
Leveraging Educational Assistance
   Partnership Program (LEAP), 310
Leveraging Educational Assistance
   State Partnership Program
   (LEAP), 255
Levi Strauss Foundation
   Scholarship, 285
Lew Wasserman College
   Scholarship, 285
Liberty Mutual Internships, 531
Library of Congress Anvario Hispano
   Hispanic Division Fellowship, 532
Library of Congress Junior Fellows
   Internship, 532
LIFE Scholarship, 444
LifeScan Scholarship Program/Dana
   Pettengill Scholarship Fund, 285
Lighthouse College-Bound Incentive
   Award, 286
Lighthouse Undergraduate Incentive
   Award I, 286
Lighthouse Undergraduate Incentive
   Award II, 286
Lillian Moller Gilbreth
   Scholarship, 438
Limited Access Competitive
   Grant, 224
Limouselle Scholarship, 373
Limousin Award of Excellence, 373
Linda Riddle Sporting Goods
   Scholarship, 503
Linda Riddle/SGMA Endowed
   Scholarship, 503
Lindbergh Foundation Grant, 190

Link-Belt Scholarship, 286
Literary Achievement Awards, 235
Lockheed Aeronautics Company
   Scholarships, 439
Lockheed Martin Corporation
   Scholarships, 439
Lora E. Dunetz Scholarship, 335
Los Angeles Times Editorial
   Internship, 532
Louis A. Caputo, Jr. Scholarship, 343
Louise Dessureault Memorial
   Scholarship, 356
Louisiana Leveraging Educational
   Assistance Partnership, 287
Louisiana Rockefeller Wildlife
   Scholarship, 287
Louisiana Social Services
   Rehabilitation/Vocational Aid For
   Disabled Persons, 287
Louisiana Tuition Opportunity
   Program for Students Honors
   Award, 288
Louisiana Tuition Opportunity
   Program for Students Opportunity
   Award, 288
Louisiana Tuition Opportunity
   Program for Students Performance
   Award, 288
Louisiana Tuition Opportunity
   Program for Students Tech
   Award, 289
Louisiana Veterans Affairs
   Educational Assistance for
   Dependent Children, 287
Louisiana Veterans Affairs
   Educational Assistance for
   Surviving Spouse, 287
Lowell Gaylor Memorial
   Scholarship, 64
Lower Mid-Atlantic Regional
   Scholarship, 343
The Loy McCandless Marks
   Scholarship, 230
Lucent Global Science Scholars
   Program, 327
Lucile B. Kaufman Women's
   Scholarship, 431
Luck Stone Corporation
   Scholarship, 289
Lutheran Campus Scholarship
   Program, 59
Lutheran Laywomen
   Scholarships, 503
Lynden Memorial Scholarship
   Program, 289
Lynn Marie Vogel Scholarship, 213
M. Louise Wilson Educational
   Loan, 566
MacDermid Graphic Arts, Inc.
   Scholarship Program, 290
Macerich Scholarship, 260
MagneTek Scholarship Plan, 290
Maine Innkeepers Association
   Scholarship, 290
Maine Lesbian/Gay Political Alliance
   Scholarship, 290
Maine Loan, 572

Program Index

605

Michigan Adult Part-Time Grant, 304
Michigan Alternative Student Loan (MI-LOAN), 573
Michigan Competitive Scholarship, 304
Michigan Educational Opportunity Grant, 304
Michigan Petroleum Association/Michigan Association of Convenience Stores Scholarship, 305
Michigan Robert C. Byrd Honors Scholarship, 305
Michigan Society of Professional Engineers Scholarships, 305
Michigan Tuition Grant, 305
Michigan Work-Study Program, 534
Microfibres Scholarship Program, 306
Microscopy Presidential Student Award, 306
Microscopy Society of America Undergraduate Research Scholarship, 306
Microsoft Corporation Scholarships, 440
Mid-America Regional Scholarship, 343
Mid-Continent Instrument Scholarship, 64
Mid-Pacific Regional Scholarship, 344
Midwest Student Exchange Program, 307
Mike Harper Leadership Scholars Program, 196
Mildred R. Knoles Opportunity Scholarship, 95
Mildred Towle Trust Fund Scholarship, 246
Military Order of the Purple Heart Scholarship, 307
Miller Electric Manufacturing Company Ivic Scholarship, 152
Millipore Foundation Scholarship Program, 308
Minnesota Educational Assistance for Veterans, 308
Minnesota Educational Assistance for War Orphans, 308
Minnesota Mutual Life Presidents' Scholarship Fund, 309
Minnesota Post-Secondary Child Care Grant, 308
Minnesota Safety Officers Survivors Program, 308
Minnesota Service Scholarship Matching Grant, 309
Minnesota State Grant Program, 309
Minnesota Student Educational Loan Fund (SELF), 573
Minnesota Work-Study Program, 535
Minolta Five-Plus Club Scholarship, 309
Minorities Scholarship Program, 134
Minority Academic Institutions Undergraduate Student Fellowships, 469

Minority Dental Student Scholarship, 56
Miss America Competition Awards, 309
Mississippi Eminent Scholars Grant, 310
Mississippi Health Care Professional Loan/Scholarship, 574
Mississippi Higher Education Legislative Plan for Needy Students, 310
Mississippi Law Enforcement Officers/Firemen Scholarship, 311
Mississippi Nursing Education Loan/Scholarship, 574
Mississippi Psychology Apprenticeship Program, 535
Mississippi Resident Tuition Assistance Grant, 311
The Mississippi Scholarship, 138
Mississippi Southeast Asia POW/MIA Scholarship, 311
Mississippi William Winter Teacher Scholar Loan Program, 574
Missouri Higher Education Academic Scholarship, 311
Missouri Minority Teaching Scholarship, 312
Missouri Nursing Scholarship, 313
Missouri Public Service Survivor Grant, 312
Missouri Robert C. Byrd Honors Scholarship, 312
Missouri State NASA Space Grant Undergraduate Scholarship, 535
Missouri Teacher Education Scholarship, 312
Mitsui USA's Sons' & Daughters' Scholarship Program, 313
Mobility Internship Program, 535
Montana Tuition Fee Waiver for Dependents of POW/MIA, 313
Montana Tuition Fee Waiver for Veterans, 314
Montana University System Community College Honor Scholarship, 314
Montana University System High School Honor Scholarship, 314
Monte R. Mitchell Global Scholarship, 64
Montgomery GI Bill (MGIB), 465
Montgomery GI Bill Plus Army College Fund, 465
Moonves Scholarship, 86
Mooty Scholarship, 201
Morris Arboretum Arboriculture Internship, 536
Morris Arboretum Education Internship, 536
Morris Arboretum Horticulture Internship, 536
Morris Arboretum Plant Propagation Internship, 536
Morris Arboretum Plant Protection Internship, 537

Morris Arboretum Urban and Community Forestry Internship, 537
Mortuary Education Grant, 250
Mother Jones Magazine Editorial Internship, 537
Mother Jones MoJo Wire Internship, 537
Moyer Packing Company Sons and Daughters Scholarship Program, 314
Multicultural Advertising Intern Program, 510
Multi-Year Ambassadorial Scholarship, 412
Museum Coca-Cola Internship, 542
Museum of Modern Art Internship, 538
M.V. O'Donnell Memorial Teacher Training Award, 73
Myasthenia Gravis Foundation Nursing Research Fellowship, 315
Myrtle and Earl Walker Scholarship, 431
NAACP/NASA Louis Stokes Science & Technology Award, 316
NABJ Non-Sustaining Scholarship, 329
Nancy Goodhue Lynch Scholarship, 204
Nancy Lorraine Jensen Memorial Scholarship, 443
NASA Academy Internship, 539
NASA Academy Wisconsin Awards, 501
NASA District of Columbia Undergraduate Scholarship, 317
NASA Idaho Space Grant Undergraduate Scholarship, 319
NASA North Carolina Space Grant Consortium Undergraduate Scholarship, 323
NASA Pennsylvania Space Grant Undergraduate Scholarship, 324
NASA Space Grant Alabama Undergraduate Scholarship, 318
NASA Space Grant Arizona Undergraduate Research Internship, 538
NASA Space Grant Arkansas Undergraduate Scholarship, 318
NASA Space Grant Connecticut Undergraduate Fellowship, 319
NASA Space Grant Florida Summer Undergraduate Scholarships, 226
NASA Space Grant Georgia Fellowship Program, 231
NASA Space Grant Hawaii Undergraduate Fellowship, 319
NASA Space Grant Hawaii Undergraduate Traineeship, 538
NASA Space Grant Illinois Undergraduate Scholarship, 320
NASA Space Grant Indiana Undergraduate Scholarship, 320
NASA Space Grant Kansas Undergraduate Scholarship, 320

Here is your *Real Stuff* CD-ROM

Real SAT prep—see how you'll do

Real advice—ten tips to think about

Real facts—online college and scholarship searches

System Requirements:
- Pentium processor
- Windows® 95 or later
- 64 MB RAM or higher
- 12X CD-ROM drive or faster
- 800 x 600 screen resolution or higher
- 16 bit color or better
- Sound card
- Internet browser

To Install:
1. Insert disk in drive D (CD-ROM) drive.
2. Choose Run from Start menu.
3. Type d:\setup.exe, then click OK.
4. Follow on-screen instructions